KU-687-742

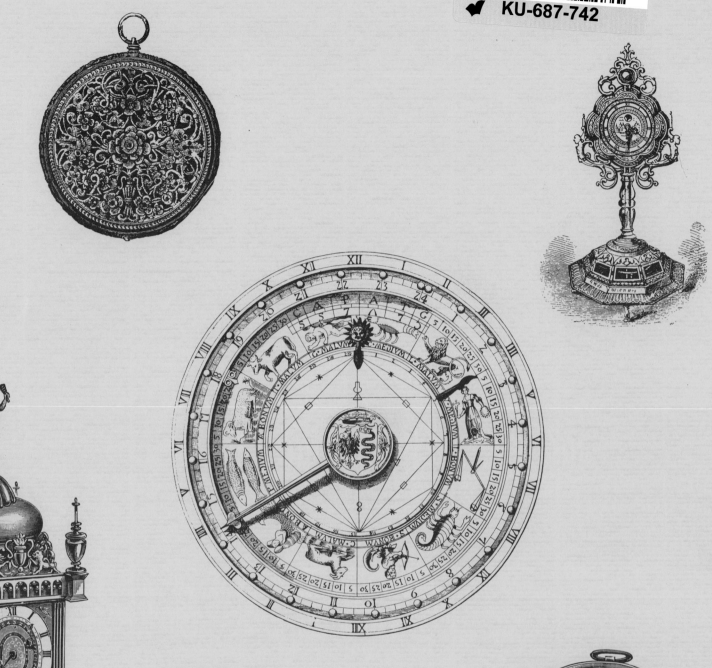

The Antique Collectors' Club edition of

OLD CLOCKS AND WATCHES & THEIR MAKERS

Being an Historical and Descriptive Account
of the different Styles of Clocks and Watches
of the past, in England and Abroad

TO WHICH IS ADDED

A LIST OF ELEVEN THOUSAND MAKERS

BY

F. J. BRITTEN

AUTHOR OF "THE WATCH AND CLOCKMAKERS'
HANDBOOK, DICTIONARY, AND GUIDE," "WATCH
SPRING AND ADJUSTING," &c.

A revision of the Third Edition
with another 250 illustrations
added to the original 800, together with
an introduction and additional comments.

ANTIQUE COLLECTORS' CLUB

© 1977 Antique Collectors' Club
World copyright reserved
Reprinted 1983
Reprinted 1988

ISBN 0 902028 69 3

All rights reserved. No part of this publication may be reproduced,
stored in a retrieval system, or transmitted in any form or by any means
electronic, mechanical, photocopying, recording or otherwise, except
for the quotation of brief passages in criticism.

British Library CIP Data
Britten, F.J.
  The Antique Collectors' Club edition of old clocks and watches and their
  makers. — 3rd ed. [rev.]/with an introduction and additional comments
  1. Clocks and watches — Collectors and collecting
  I. Title II. Antique Collectors' Club
  739.3   NK7484

Published for the Antique Collectors' Club
by the Antique Collectors' Club Ltd.

Printed in England by
Antique Collectors' Club, Church Street, Woodbridge, Suffolk.

Introduction

Britten's *Old Clocks and Watches and their Makers* is a classic of horology. It will so remain. Despite the fact that it is now largely out of date it retains value as a repository of illustrations of interesting pieces (some of which have now been destroyed or altered), and it is also useful as a summary of knowledge in the history of horology during the early part of this century. More interesting however is the book's historical importance. For the general reader Britten's was a highly significant book. At the date of its first appearance (1899), there were few writings which treated of clocks and watches in a general and non-technical way, and fewer lists of makers and retailers such as Britten supplied from which names could be identified and roughly dated. The only real rival to Britten in scope and popular appeal perhaps was E.J. Wood's compilation and augmentation of newspaper articles by William J. Pinks, *Curiosities of Clocks and Watches* (1866), but probably somewhat scarce by 1899. Of other rivals James W. Benson's *Time and Time-tellers* (1875) was a small far less well illustrated book, while J.F. Kendal's *History of Watches* (1892) was more restricted in range.

Britten's book was indeed ripe for the time. It met a growing demand. By the 1890s general interest in horology and its history was increasing. Great collections were being formed, and the artistic qualities of early watches and clocks were beginning to be appreciated. A demand for information began to be felt, and Britten, as secretary of the British Horological Institute felt the pressure more strongly than most. As he remarked in the preface to *Former Clock and Watch Makers and their Work* (1894) he received so many queries "that I am induced to collate for publication, facts and information relating to the subject which I have been enabled to gather". The statement is exact. For not only had Britten already published numerous bits of the information which makes up *Old Clocks and Watches* ... anonymously in the *Horological Journal* of which he was editor, but it suggests that he was aware of the rag bag nature of his book. As a history of the subject it is poor being ill-organised, badly arranged, and totally miscellaneous. Anything Britten found out he included. Any old clock he came upon was described, but he made no effort to relate the various facts in a significant way, and as edition succeeded edition with more and more additions, the confusion only grew worse. Innocent of any sort of plan, the book nonetheless brought together a mass of information (and misinformation) of exactly the kind required. Its influence in inspiring, widening, or merely reinforcing interest in the subject is incalculable. The worst excesses in the book moreover were perpetrated after Britten's death. In the final, sixth edition, the book had not only become of a quite uncomfortable bulk and weight but, as Sir Ambrose Heal pointed out (see checklist), had become almost unuseable. The list of makers had been printed from the same typesetting as the fifth edition, which meant that the additions could not be intercalated but had to be added in a supplementary list, while a two page errata list was needed to convert all the now inaccurate page references to the body of the text from the list of makers. That a seventh edition should have been so long delayed was not to be expected. That it should have been completely rewritten was wise. That it should have retained Britten's name in its title was entirely just since without him there might not have been an audience for so serious a work as the book had now become.

Britten, though a familiar name, is nonetheless an unfamiliar figure. Who was he? A native of Bath, Frederick James Britten was born in 1843 and died at Westcliff-on-Sea, Southend, on 11 April, 1913. By profession he was a draughtsman but in 1872 for reasons unknown he was appointed as the first paid secretary of the British Horological Institute then still struggling to establish itself and unlucky in its recent honorary secretaries. Britten was a success and retained the post until 1905, combining with it in the early years directorship of the institute's drawing class, and from 1874 until his resignation, the editorship of the *Horological Journal*. He, it is clear, was in large measure responsible for the revitalisation of the Institute which took place in the following years. Exhibitions were mounted, visits for members to places of relevant interest such as Woolwich Arsenal, the Royal Observatory, Westminster Clock and the Royal Mint were arranged, and soon the Institute was acquiring buildings in Northampton Square and a whole range of educational activities in association with the City & Guilds. Britten had the energy for all these undertakings. "He was" says Henry Bickley in his obituary notice *(Horological Journal* LV, 1913 pp.133-137), "of a mercurial disposition, one of those exciteable, restless spirits, that must always be doing something."

"Of medium height, spare build, and refined appearance, Mr Britten's personality was in itself attractive, but it must be owned that his temperament was variable and uncertain . . . . If his mind was made up to a certain course, argument would not avail; if met beforehand he was open to reason, but not always to conviction. He was strong in his likes and dislikes, and easily offended. He would take up a cause with enthusiasm, but his adherence was not always constant or lasting. He resented control, but if given a free hand would work with energy and clearness of vision. His temperament there can be no doubt, was governed to a great extent by his health, which was never robust; in fact during the time that I knew him he was always more or less an invalid, and how he achieved so much is little short of a marvel. Sparing of words and not always articulate, his meaning was often expressed as much by gesture as speech."

On his death Britten was buried in the family grave (16 April, 1913) in Highgate cemetery. He was survived by a wife and four children of whom one, Annie, had been his assistant as secretary to the Institute, continuing in the post after his retirement in 1905.

October 1977

A Summary List of the Writings of F. J. Britten

In the following list (which does not claim to be complete) no attempt has been made to list pieces published anonymously in the *Horological Journal* which are possibly or even certainly by Britten. Signed articles only are listed. The signed annual reports of the Horological Institute have also been ignored.

Books

1. Tables for Watch and Clock Trains based on those of W. Breeze.
   This publication is mentioned by Bickley as Britten's first, and was a sixteen page pamphlet? *c.*1875/76. It has now however been seen and details are therefore uncertain. Evidently it was this work that was the source of the *Watchmakers' Handbook.*

2. Escapement drawings.
   According to Bickley "simultaneously with his first book of trains he [Britten] issued coloured drawings of the verge, horizontal [i.e. cylinder], duplex, lever, and chronometer escapements on one large sheet; an artistic as well as useful production, at an absurdly low price."

3. *The Watch and Clockmakers' Handbook containing simple Rules for calculating Conversions, lever trains, &c,* 1st edition [1878], 2nd edition [1879], 3rd edition [1880], 4th edition 1881.
   The Watch and Clockmakers' Handbook, Dictionary and Guide, remodelled and with change of title, but 5th edition [1884], 6th edition [1886], 7th edition [1889], 8th edition 1892, 9th edition [1897], 10th edition [1902], 11th edition 1907 (see *Horological Journal* L, 1907/8, pp.41-42 for an exchange of letters concerning aspects of this edition), reprinted 1915, reprinted 1946 and reprinted 1976 by the Antique Collectors' Club, 12th edition 1920, 13th edition edited by Annie M. Britten 1922, 14th edition revised by J.W. Player 1938, 15th edition revised by J.W. Player 1955, 16th edition revised by R. Good 1977.

4. *On the Springing and Adjusting of Watches,* 1892.

5. *Former Clock & Watchmakers and their Work, including an Account of the development of Horological Instruments from the earliest Mechanism, with Portraits of Masters of the Art; A Directory of over Five Thousand Names and some examples of Modern Construction,* 1894.
   Many of the engraved illustrations were taken from the *Horological Journal* where they had been used to illustrate anonymous articles by Britten on the same subjects. They survived unchanged into the sixth edition of the work.

6. *Old Clocks and Watches & their Makers, being an Historical and Descriptive Account of the different Styles of Clocks and Watches of the Past in England and Abroad, to which is added a list of eight thousand Makers*, first edition, 1899, 2nd edition 1904, 3rd edition 1911.

   Old Clocks and their Makers. An Historical and Descriptive Account of the different Styles of Clocks of the Past in England and Abroad, 4th edition, [1919-20].

   This edition comprised the chapters on clocks only from *Old Clocks and Watches* . . . It was in preparation at the time of Britten's death, the editorial work being completed by his daughter Annie. The watch chapters were omitted because of the increase of production costs after the war. It was however intended to produce a companion volume *Old Watches and their Makers*.

   5th edition [1922], edited by Annie M. Britten, the work was returned to the old form in response to repeated requests.

   6th edition [1932], with a preface by F.W. Britten who presumably carried out the editing. Although much larger than previous editions it was more difficult to use. The reasons for this are described by Sir Ambrose Heal, 'A List of Clock & Watch Makers supplementary to that given by Britten', *The Connoisseur*, 1943-44, pp.110-111, 1944-45, pp.38-39, 110-111, 120.

   Britten's Old Clocks and Watches and their Makers . . ., revised by G.H. Baillie, Cecil Clutton, & C.A. Ilbert, seventh edition 1956.

   Seventh edition, new impression with corrections, 1969. 8th edition, 1973. Antique Collectors' Club edition, 1977 — Text of the third edition, with additional illustrations, captions and an introduction.

7. *Old English Clocks: The Wetherfield Collection*, 1907.

Articles

8. Watches and Clocks in G. Phillips Bevan (ed) *British Manufacturing Industries* (vol 10). London, 1876 (2nd edition 1878). One of a series of 13 popular volumes on different groups of industries. (Review *Horological Journal*, xix, 1876, p.54.

9. 'Drawing and Mechanics' (Introductory address at the re-assembling of pupils for the B.H.I. drawing class of which Britten was Director). *Horological Journal*, xvii, 1874, pp.33-37.

10. 'Watch Manufacturing', *Horological Journal*, xlix, 1906-7, pp.106-107.

11. 'Charles Dunn' (obituary), *Horological Journal*, xlix, 1906-7, p.145.

12. 'The Manufacture of Watches', *Horological Journal*, xlix, 1906-7, pp.170-171.

13. 'Letter', *Horological Journal*, L. 1907-8, p.41.

14. 'Early Easter — Reformation of the Calendar', *Horological Journal*, lvi, 1914, pp.118-119.

15. Obituary:
    Henry Bickley, 'The Late Mr Frederick James Britten and the Early Secretaries of the Horological Institute', *Horological Journal*, LV, 1913, pp.133-137.

16. Patent. 'A Winding Mechanism for Marine Chronometers' No. 12898, 23 September 1887.

Preface to the Third Edition

THIS edition is not merely a revision. There is much additional matter and one hundred new engravings. To utilise the particulars placed at my disposal by many owners of old timekeepers, without making the book of undue bulk, special paper of fine texture, lighter and thinner than that formerly used, has been obtained.

From the Wetherfield collection of English clocks, which comprises over two hundred examples, and affords, as nearly as possible, a perfect historical review, fifty representative pieces have been reproduced.

Over a thousand fresh names of makers have been obtained from inspection of old timekeepers and information furnished by the proprietors of them. In addition to these, Mr John H. Buck, Mr Evan Roberts, and Mr S. H. Hamer have favoured me with lists of makers; for information respecting Lancaster freemen I am indebted to a list by the Town-Clerk which appeared in *Notes and Queries,* and for particulars of some York makers to the research of Mr T. P. Cooper.

The Czar of Russia has a collection of about fifty very finely decorated English watches deposited in the Winter Palace, St Petersburg. They are mostly productions of the eighteenth century, and, in many instances, are attached to splendidly wrought chatelaines adorned with precious stones. Mr E. Alfred Jones has examined and photographed these treasures, and for notes respecting some of them I am indebted to an article by him in *"The Connoisseur."*

The kind assistance of Mr Albert Schloss and Mr C. F. Bell was acknowledged in the Second Edition. I regret to say that Mr Schloss, who was a collector of acute discrimination and world-wide knowledge, is now no more. Mr F. Hilton Price must also be reckoned with the departed. The Hilton Price collection of watches and the greater part of the Marfels collection have been acquired by Mr J. Pierpont Morgan, and may be seen at the Victoria and Albert Museum.

F.J.B.

1 SILVERDALE AVENUE, SOUTHEND, ESSEX.
April 1911.

Preface to the First Edition

SINCE the publication, in 1894, of "Former Clock and Watchmakers and their Work," so many suggestions have reached me from lovers of old clocks and watches that I have been induced to recast the volume. Much additional information of a general character has been embodied in the present book, and details relating to modern construction which appeared before are now omitted.

Technical terms are, I am told, particularly exasperating to people unacquainted with horological phrases, and I have therefore avoided them as much as possible. "The Watch and Clockmakers' Handbook, Dictionary, and Guide" may be consulted by those especially interested in the mechanism of clocks and watches, and who desire more explicit details than I have given here.

Few places can boast of a finer display of eighteenth-century clocks than Windsor Castle. The principal representative specimens I have been enabled to illustrate and describe by special permission of the Queen.

Additions have been made to the list of old makers and some inaccuracies corrected. Several items of information in connection with this list I have obtained from the collection of tradesmen's cards owned by the Hon. Gerald Ponsonby, who allowed me free access to this most interesting record. A perusal of the Banks collection of tradesmen's cards at the British Museum has also elicited particulars not to be met with in ordinary channels. Mr J. E. Hodgkin, F.S.A., furnished me with a list of the clock and watchmakers in his collection, which proved a useful check in several instances. Mr C. H. Read, of the British Museum, has given me every possible help in going over the unsurpassed display of timekeepers in his charge, for the purpose of revising the references thereto. A similar favour in respect of the collection at South Kensington Museum has been accorded by Mr A. B. Skinner.

I have to acknowledge the kindness of many owners of old timekeepers who permitted me to inspect their treasures. In particular I should mention Mr Albert Schloss, who has choice examples of every period; he placed the whole of them in my hands for examination, and of these between sixty and seventy have been selected for illustration.

April 1899.

THE ANTIQUE COLLECTORS' CLUB

The Antique Collectors' Club was formed in 1966 and now has a five figure membership spread throughout the world. It publishes the only independently run monthly antiques magazine *Antique Collecting* which caters for those collectors who are interested in widening their knowledge of antiques, both by greater awareness of quality and by discussion of the factors which influence the price that is likely to be asked. The Antique Collectors' Club pioneered the provision of information on prices for collectors and the magazine still leads in the provision of detailed articles on a variety of subjects.

It was in response to the enormous demand for information on ''what to pay'' that the price guide series was introduced in 1968 with the first edition of *The Price Guide to Antique Furniture* (completely revised, 1978), a book which broke new ground by illustrating the more common types of antique furniture, the sort that collectors could buy in shops and at auctions rather than the rare museum pieces which had previously been used (and still to a large extent are used) to make up the limited amount of illustrations in books published by commercial publishers. Many other price guides have followed, all copiously illustrated, and greatly appreciated by collectors for the valuable information they contain, quite apart from prices. The Antique Collectors' Club also publishes other books on antiques, including horology and art reference works, and a full book list is available.

Club membership, which is open to all collectors, costs £15.95 per annum. Members receive free of charge *Antique Collecting,* the Club's magazine (published every month except August), which contains well-illustrated articles dealing with the practical aspects of collecting not normally dealt with by magazines. Prices, features of value, investment potential, fakes and forgeries are all given prominence in the magazine.

Among other facilities available to members are private buying and selling facilities, the longest list of ''For Sales'' of any antiques magazine, an annual ceramics conference and the opportunity to meet other collectors at their local antique collectors' clubs. There are over eighty in Britain and more than a dozen overseas. Members may also buy the Club's publications at special pre-publication prices.

As its motto implies, the Club is an amateur organisation designed to help collectors get the most out of their hobby: it is informal and friendly and gives enormous enjoyment to all concerned.

For Collectors — By Collectors — About Collecting

The Antique Collectors' Club, 5 Church Street, Woodbridge, Suffolk

Contents

Frederick James Britten, a photographic portrait which was also used in the fifth edition of Old Clocks and Watches and their Makers, *1932, where it also served as the frontispiece.*

Editor's Note on the Use of the Book

The new illustrations are not numbered and their captions are in italics so that there should be no confusion with Britten's text and figures — all of which are numbered.

Britten's text has been reproduced as exactly as possible, allowing of course for alterations to page numbers. All his remarks as to ownership of the watches he illustrates, or their whereabouts, are as of 1911. The South Kensington Museum is now the Victoria and Albert Museum.

Chapter I

Time, and early Recorders

AS DEFINED BY the title, our subject may be said to begin with the introduction of clocks; and, although primitive methods of timekeeping should not, perhaps, be passed over without notice, it will be unnecessary to make more than a brief reference to them. It may be convenient and useful to begin with some explanation of the various time standards.

SOLAR TIME A solar day is the period which elapses between two successive returns of the sun to the meridian. The instant the sun is seen at its greatest height above the horizon it is true midday, which sometimes takes place 16 min. 18 sec. sooner, and at others 14 min. 28 sec. later, than twelve o'clock mean time. The diurnal rotation of the earth on its axis might naturally be supposed to bring each place to the meridian at regular intervals; this would

Horizontal sundial signed 'Johan^s Lenns Dublini Fecit Latt 53^d 20^m año 1684'. An attractive dial decorated with rosettes, a sun emblem and an hour glass; the gnomon is pierced and engraved. The hour scale is divided to five minutes and there is a subsidiary hour scale at the centre. An unusual feature is the 16 point windrose, with 32 compass directions indicated by their initials set at the south point of the gnomon and read in conjunction with the scale of degrees engraved between the hour and minute scales. Christie, Manson & Wood Ltd.

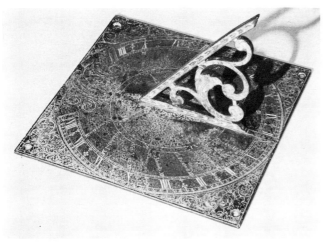

Above:
A rectangular English horizontal sundial signed 'I. Rowley fecit', not dated but c.1700. A particularly good example of the common garden sundial unusual only in that various place names are engraved against the hour scale to show the time in these other parts of the world when it is noon in Britain. The circular scale reads to minutes and the corners are filled with foliate decoration. Museum of the History of Science, Oxford.

Right:
An unusually large and well made ring dial of gilt brass signed 'M.F. Popell fecit Passauij Ao 1696'. On any such dial the time is found by the position of a spot of sunlight shining through a hole in one part of the ring on to an hour scale engraved on the inside. Since the position of the sun varies throughout the year, the hole is usually cut in a central collar which may be slid around the ring and set against a zodiac calendar. Occasionally however, as in the present example, two holes are provided, one for use in the winter, the other in summer. See p.25. National Maritime Museum.

be nearly the case if the earth had no other movement; but it advances at the same time in its orbit, and as the meridians are not perpendicular to the ecliptic, the days are not of equal duration. This may be easily perceived by placing a mark at every 15° of the equator and ecliptic on a terrestrial globe, as, by turning it to the westward, the marks on the ecliptic, from Aries to Cancer, will come to the brazen meridian sooner than the corresponding ones on the equator, those from Cancer to Libra later, from Libra to Capricornus sooner, and from Capricornus to Aries later; the marks on the ecliptic and equator only coming to the meridian together at Aries, Cancer, Libra, and Capricornus. True and mean time do not agree though on the days in which the sun enters these signs, in March, June, September, and December, for the earth moves with greater rapidity in December, when it is nearer the sun, than it does in July, when it is farther from it. The regularity of the earth's motion is also further disturbed by the attraction of the moon, Venus, and Jupiter. True and mean agree about the 25th December, 15th April, 14th June, and 31st August; these coincidences vary slightly in different years, because the earth takes about a quarter of a day more than a year to complete a revolution in its orbit, and this error accumulates from leap year till the fourth year, when the extra day is taken in.

Sun-dials mark apparent time, while clocks measure equal or mean time; if, therefore, a timekeeper, perfectly regular in its motion, were set to apparent solar time, it would be found to agree with it only on four days in the year.

Right:

An ivory Gunter quadrant signed 'I. Rowley fecit', c.1700, mounted on a stand with three levelling screws. Devised c.1618 by Edmund Gunter (1581-1626), the instrument consists of a stereographic projection of the equator, the tropics, and the horizon on to the equinoctial plane. It is in fact a quarter of an astrolabe and when star positions are marked (there are five on this example), it could be used to solve the same kind of astronomical problems as the astrolabe itself. It was most popular however for time-finding by day or by night and many examples survive in boxwood or in brass. An individual stand is however a most unusual feature. Museum of the History of Science, Oxford.

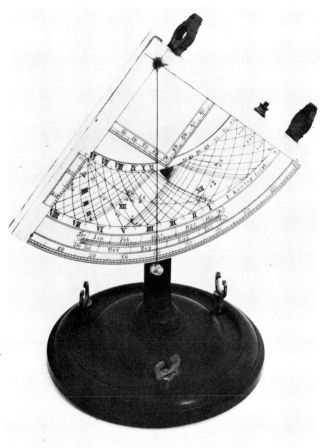

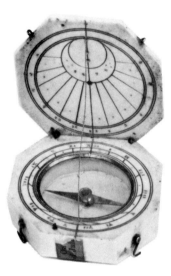

Left:

An octagonal diptych dial with compass inset in the base for orientation. On the inside of the lid is a vertical dial, around the edge of the compass box a horizontal dial. The string gnomon, which may be adjusted for three different latitudes, serves for both the dials. German, c.1600. Christie, Manson & Wood Ltd.

CYCLE OF THE SUN

A cycle of the sun is a period of twenty-eight years, after which the days of the week again fall on the same days of the month as during the first year of the former cycle. The cycle of the sun has no relation to the sun's course, but was invented for the purpose of finding the Dominical Letter which points out the days of the month on which the Sundays fall during each year of the cycle.

SIDEREAL TIME

Sidereal time, the standard used by astronomers, is measured by the diurnal rotation of the earth, which turns on its axis in 23 hours 56 min. 4.1 sec. The sidereal day is therefore 3 min. 56 sec. less than the mean solar day, and a clock to show sidereal time must have its pendulum a trifle shorter than a mean-time clock with the same train.

Mean-time clocks can be regulated by the stars with greater facility than by the sun, for the motion of the earth with regard to the fixed stars is uniform, and a star will always appear at the meridian 3 min. 56 sec. sooner than it did on the preceding day. In the absence of a transit instrument and a table giving the right ascension of particular stars, choose a window having a southern aspect, from which the steeple of a church, a chimney, or any other fixed point may be seen. To the side of the window attach a thin plate of brass having a small hole in it, in such a manner that by looking through the hole towards the edge of the elevated object, some of the fixed stars may be seen; the progress of one of these being watched, the instant it vanishes behind the fixed point a signal is made to a person observing the clock, who then notes the exact time at which the star disappeared, and on the following night the same star will vanish behind the same object 3 min. 56 sec. sooner. If a clock mark ten hours when the observation is made, when the star vanishes the following night it should indicate 3 min. 56 sec. less than ten hours. If cloudy nights intervene and render it impossible to compare the clock with the star, it will be necessary to multiply 3 min. 56 sec. by the number of days that have elapsed since the previous observation. The same star can only be observed during a few weeks. Care must be taken that a planet is not observed instead of a star. The planets may, however, be distinguished, for being comparatively near the earth, they appear larger than the stars; their light also is steady because reflected, while the fixed stars scintillate and have a twinkling light.

DURATION OF A YEAR

The sidereal year starts with the spring equinox, when the sun enters the sign Aries, that is, when the sun crosses from the south to the north of the equator. The earth in its revolution round the sun makes rather over 366 rotations or 366 sidereal days, which are equal to 365 solar days. The sidereal year is equal to 365 days 6 hours 9 min. 11 sec., nearly, of mean solar time. The earth, on the completion of its revolution, returns to the same place among the stars, but not exactly at the spring equinox, owing to the precession of the equinoxes, so in order that the year may accord with the seasons the sidereal year is disregarded in favour of the equinoctial, tropical or solar year, taken as 365 days 5 hours 48 min. 48 sec. Among the Romans no regular account was taken of the difference between the year and 365 days till B.C. 45. Then the surplus was reckoned as six hours, making one day in four years; and one day was accordingly added to every fourth year. There still remained the apparently trifling difference of 11 min. 11 sec. between the civil and the tropical year; this, however, produced an error of about seven days in 900 years. In 1582, Pope Gregory XII struck out ten days, which represented the accumulated error, from the calendar, and it was decided that three leap years should be omitted every 400 years; thus, as 1600 was leap year, the years 1700, 1800, and 1900 were not, but 2000 will be leap year. This rectification was not adopted in England till 1752, when eleven days were omitted from the calendar. As our year still exceeds the true year, although by an extremely small fraction, another leap year in addition to those should be omitted once in 4,000 years.

A typical example of the equinoctial dials produced in large quantities in the Augsburg region of Germany in the late 17th and early 19th centuries. These dials are very rarely dated. They were made in brass, gilt or silvered brass, and, although rarely, silver. In use the dial is oriented using the inset compass. The circular ring which has an hour scale engraved on its inside, is set to the appropriate latitude against the scale engraved on the arm, and the crosspiece which carries the gnomon flicked upright. The example shown is signed 'Johann Martin in Augspurg', one of the more prolific makers of these dials. Sotheby Parke Bernet & Co.

An octagonal silver Butterfield dial, signed 'Butterfield à Paris'. An entirely typical example of a type of pocket horizontal dial invented by Michael Butterfield, an English instrument maker who lived and worked in Paris. The dial consists of an ordinary horizontal dial but with the gnomon adjustable over a range of latitudes (40°-60° in this example). The beak of the bird supporting the gnomon acts as an index to this scale. Four separate sets of hour scales are provided, each appropriate to a different latitude, and there is an inset compass for orientation. Sotheby Parke Bernet & Co.

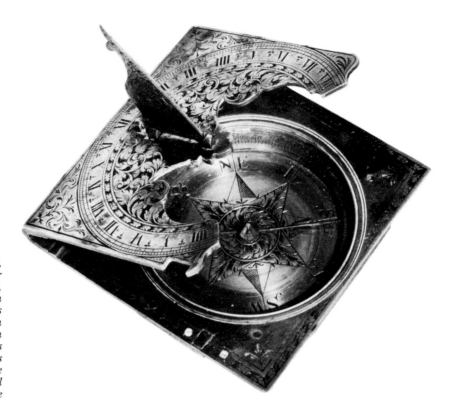

An inclining dial signed 'B. Scott fecit', c.1725. Dials of this kind are a further variant of the horizontal dial adapted, like the Butterfield dial, so that they can be used in more than one place. In this case the whole plate carrying the gnomon and the hour scale can be inclined at an angle to the horizontal base plate, thus compensating for changes in latitude as the user moves north or south. The whole instrument folds flat to fit into a small box when it is not in use. Sotheby Parke Bernet & Co.

There is a distinction to be noticed between the sign Aries and the constellation of that name. The first point of the sign Aries or the equinoctial point ♈ is the zero from which the right ascension, or longitude, of celestial bodies is measured, just as Greenwich is an initial meridian for measuring the longitude of terrestrial places. Ancient astronomers called it the first point of Aries because in their time the phrase correctly described its position, but the vernal equinox retrogrades 50¼ seconds of a degree each year, and so the first point of Aries is now really in the constellation Pisces. The moment the point ♈ passes the meridian it is sidereal noon, and sidereal time would then be 0 hour 0 min. 0 sec.

The civil year began on 25th March before 1752, when the present reckoning for the year to commence on 1st January was adopted.

THE GOLDEN NUMBER   Meton, an Athenian astronomer, B.C. 432, discovered that after a period of nineteen years the new and full moons returned on the same days of the month as they had done before; this period is called the cycle of the moon. The Greeks thought so highly of this calculation, that they had it written in letters of gold, hence the name Golden Number; and at the Council of Nice, A.D. 325, it was determined that Meton's cycle should be used to regulate the movable feasts of the Church.

THE EPACT   The Epact serves to find the moon's age by showing the number of days which must be added to each lunar year, in order to complete a solar year. A lunar month is composed of 29 days 12 hours 44 min. 3 sec., or rather more than 29.5 days; 12 lunar months are, therefore, nearly 11 days short of the solar year — thus, the new moons in one year will fall 11 days earlier than they did in the preceding year, so that were it new moon on 1st January, it would be nearly 11 days old on the 1st of January of the ensuing year, and 22 days on the third year; on the fourth year it would be 33; but 30 days are taken off as an intercalary month (the moon having made a revolution in that time), and the 3 remaining would be the Epact; the Epact thus continues to vary, until, at the expiration of 19 years, the new moons again return in the same order as before.

THE NUMBER OF DIRECTION The Council of Nice decided that Easter Day is always the first Sunday after the full moon which happens upon or next after the 21st of March. In 463 it was decreed that instead of the actual full moon the fourteenth day of the moon should be considered the paschal moon. Easter Day cannot take place earlier than the 22nd of March or later than the 25th of April. The Number of Direction is that day of the thirty-five on which Easter Sunday falls.

THE ROMAN INDICATION The Roman Indiction was a period of fifteen years, appointed A.D. 312 by the Emperor Constantine for the payment of certain taxes.

THE JULIAN PERIOD The Julian Period of 7,980 years is the product obtained by multiplying together 29, 19, and 15, which numbers represent the cycles of the sun, the moon, and the Roman Indiction. The beginning of the Julian Period is reckoned from 709 before the creation of the world, so that its completion will occur A.D. 3267, until which time there cannot be two years having the same numbers for three cycles.

TIMEKEEPERS Timekeepers are more immediately concerned with the sub-divisions of a day. The Persians divided the day into twenty-four hours, starting from sunrise; the Athenians began the day at sunset; the present civil day begins at midnight, and is divided into two equal periods of twelve hours each, but astronomers reckon from noon and count the hours continuously from 1 to 24.

An equinoctial ring dial (late 17th century) of the type devised by William Oughtred c.1620 and produced in great numbers by English instrument makers until the middle of the 19th century. German examples of this type, mainly 18th century, are also to be found. The dial's popularity presumably stemmed from the ease with which it could be used. The suspension piece was slid on its collar round the outer ring to the appropriate latitude position, and the cursor in the central bridge was set to the requisite date. The dial was then held up and the bridge turned until a spot of sunlight passed through the cursor on to the edge of the hour ring thus indicating the time. Sotheby Parke Bernet & Co.

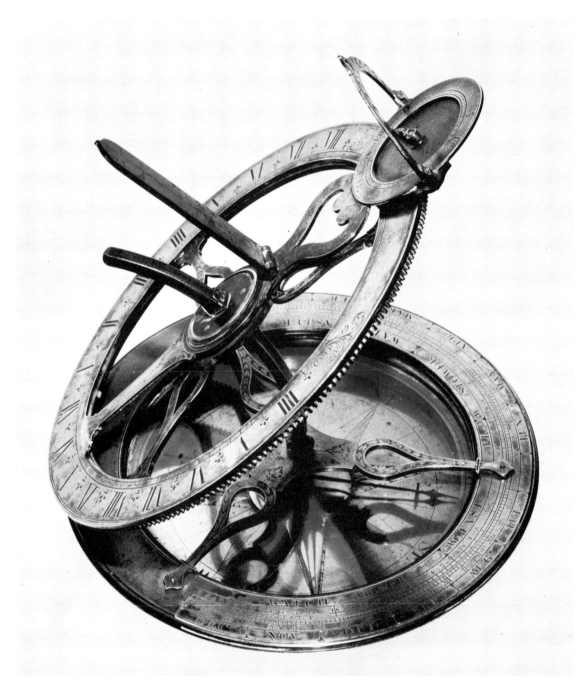

A mechanical equinoctial ring dial with the equation of time, c.1730. Mechanical equinoctial dials first appeared towards the end of the 17th century and were much used for checking the setting of clocks and watches. The dial was first oriented correctly using the compass in the base, and the upper ring lifted up the central arc to the requisite latitude. If the subsidiary dial is then moved round until a spot of light passing through the hole at the top of the arc above the subsidiary ring falls exactly in the centre of the sight facing it, the hour may be read off from the main dial, and the minutes from the position of the index on the subsidiary dial. Engraved on the base of the instrument is an equation of time scale, so that the correction between apparent solar time and clock mean time can be calculated before a clock or watch is adjusted. Sotheby Parke Bernet & Co.

SUN DIALS

The simplest form of sun-dial, and a useful one for setting a timekeeper when no standard is available for comparison, is one for showing when the sun is on the meridian. With a timekeeper showing mean time and an equation table, a meridian line may, of course, be at once traced for future reference. In the absence of these, the following, which are practically Ferguson's instructions, may be followed: "Make four or five concentric circles, a quarter of an inch from one another, on a flat stone, and let the outmost circle be but little less than the stone will contain. Fix a pin perpendicularly in the centre, and of such a length that its whole shadow may fall within the innermost circle for at least four hours in the middle of the day. The stone being set exactly level, in a place where the sun shines, suppose from eight in the morning till four in the afternoon, about which hours the end of the shadow should fall without all the circles; watch the times in the forenoon when the extremity of the shortening shadow just touches the several circles, and there make marks. Then, in the afternoon of the same day, watch the lengthening shadow, and where its end touches the several circles, in going over them, make marks also. With a pair of compasses, find exactly the middle points between the two marks on any circle, and draw a straight line from the centre to that point, which line will be covered at noon by the shadow of the pin."

By observation the hours of the morning and afternoon may also be marked on the meridian dial, and it will be noticed that, although the position of the hour immediately preceding corresponds with the one immediately after noon, these divisions will not answer for any of the remaining hours.

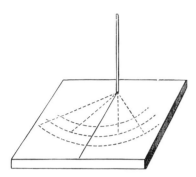

Fig. 1. — Meridian Dial.

CURIOUS MERIDIAN DIAL

The very ingeniously contrived meridian dial shown below and reproduced from "L'Horlogerie" by Joseph Rambal, formed part of St. Peter's Cathedral, Geneva, from 1760 till the renovation of the building in 1894, and has since been restored on the initiative of the Society of Arts. The white spot in the centre of the disc's shadow not only indicates accurately solar noon when it is bisected by the central vertical line, but also approximately mean solar noon when it is centrally over a line of the figure-of-8 loop which allows for the equation of time on each particular day. The full line of the loop serves from June to December, and the dotted

Fig. 2. — Curious Meridian Dial.

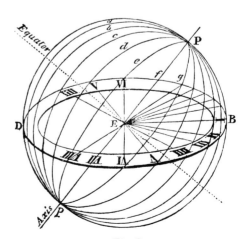

Fig. 3.

A polyhedral sun dial signed 'E.C. Stockhert', 18th century. On each of the outer five faces of the cube is a separate sundial. Basically, these are drawn for latitude 48° North, but as the dial is mounted on an adjustable joint, it may be set for a range of latitudes from 23° to 77°. There are a compass and a plumb line to facilitate setting. When the dial is correctly set up, the five dials will all indicate the same hour. Cubical dials made of wood overlaid with printed and attractively coloured paper scales, as is this example, were very popular in 18th century Germany. More complicated forms of polyhedral dials, with eight, ten, fifteen or more faces, were fashionable in the Renaissance throughout Europe. National Maritime Museum, Greenwich.

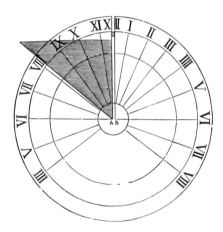

Fig. 4. — Horizontal Sun-dial.

line during the complement of the year. As the year is not made up of a complete number of days, and a day is interpolated every fourth year, the exact equation in each year of the four is different; still the approximate equation would be practically sufficient for all but scientific purposes.

The art of dialling is somewhat complex. A glance at Fig. 3 will show why, except for places on the equator, the hour spaces are not all equal. A sun-dial may be regarded as a circle round the earth, or as the edge of a disc which passes through the centre of the earth from the spot where the dial is fixed. *a, b, c, d, e, f, g, &c.,* are longitudinal circles, representing the hours, B the spot where the dial is situated, D the corresponding latitude, PP the poles, and E the centre of the earth.

A dial prepared for any particular place is useless for another place in a different latitude, with the exception that a *horizontal* dial for a certain latitude will be a vertical dial for a latitude which is the complement of the first, or what it wants of 90°. That is, a horizontal dial for our latitude of 51½°, would have to be placed in a vertical position facing the south in latitude 38½°.

HORIZONTAL DIAL

To set out a horizontal dial, first draw two lines parallel to each other, at a distance equal to the thickness of the gnomon which is to cast the shadow. Next, draw a line at right angles to these, the extremities of which will indicate respectively the hours of six in the morning and six in the evening. Then, with A and B as centres (see Fig. 4), draw quadrants of circles, and divide each into 90°. Now, assuming the dial to be for the latitude of London, lay a rule over B, and draw the first line through 11⅔°, the second through $24\frac{1}{4}°$, third $38\frac{1}{12}°$, fourth $53\frac{1}{2}°$, and fifth $71\frac{1}{15}°$. Proceed the same with the other side. Extend the afternoon hour lines of four and five across the dial, and these will form the morning hours, while eight and seven of the morning hours prolonged will give the same evening hours. To form the style or gnomon, draw a radial line through that degree of the quadrant which corresponds to the latitude = $51\frac{1}{2}°$. This will show the elevation of the style, which is here represented as if lying on the surface of the dial. The thickness of the style must be equal to the distance between A and B. Place the style truly upright on the dial, and it is finished.

Fig. 5. — Dials at Whitehall, 1669.

A dial, or rather a series of dials of every conceivable description, forming a structure, as shown in Fig. 5, was erected at Whitehall in 1669, by order of Charles II. It was the invention of Francis Hall, *alias* Line, a Jesuit and professor of mathematics at Liege. Vertical dials, inclining dials, and dials for showing time as computed by various nations at different periods were all included.

Of these, the bowls or brackets appear to be the most attractive. One, on the first platform, to show the hour by fire, consisted of a little glass bowl filled with clear water. This bowl was about 3 ins. diameter, placed in the middle of another sphere, about 6 ins. diameter, consisting of several iron rings or circles, representing the hour circles in the heavens. The hour was known by applying the hand to these circles when the sun shone, and that circle where you felt the hand burnt by the sunbeams passing through the bowl filled with water showed the true hour.

This curious erection had no covering; exposure to the elements and other destroying influences led to its speedy decay and subsequent demolition. The engraving is taken from the *Mirror,* vol. xiv.

The commonest form of portable dial is shown in Fig. 6. When held to the sun, by means of the small ring at top, a ray of light passed through a tiny hole and impinged on the inner surface of the opposite side of the rim, which was engraved with numerals corresponding to the hours of daylight. The hole was formed in a slide which covered a slit in the rim. The slide could be moved higher or lower, and signs of the zodiac were engraved on the rim as a guide to its position in different months of the year. Dials of this sort were in general use during the sixteenth and seventeenth centuries. A small horizontal dial like Fig. 4, but with a hinged style and a compass attached, formed a more costly pocket "horologium."

Fig. 6. — Pocket Sun-dial.

CLEPSYDRAE, OR WATER CLOCKS

These indicate intervals of time by the passage of water, and may be divided into two classes: the ancient recorders for hours of varying length, and the more simple instruments used during and after the seventeenth century, when equal hours were measured.

Clepsydrae are of remote antiquity. They were known by the Egyptians, in Judea, Babylon, Chaldea, and Phoenicia, but these contrivances for measuring time were of the simplest description. They appear to have consisted each of a basin filled with water and exposed in some niche or corner of a public place. At the extreme end of the vessel was a spout or tap, from which trickled the liquid, drop by drop, into a receiver having on its inside marks for indicating the hours of the day and night.

In parts of Southern India was used a thin copper bowl about 5 ins. in diameter, and rather deeper than a half sphere, having a very small hole in the bottom. The bowl, placed in a vessel containing water and floating thereon, gradually filled. At the expiration of an arranged interval it sank, and a boy or other watcher then struck a gong, and thus announced the time. The Brahmins divided the day into 60 hours and 24 minutes each, and, I am told, used a timekeeper of this sort which sank in twenty-four minutes. One of the bowls which is among the collection of the Horological Institute sinks after the lapse of forty-five minutes with tolerable accuracy, but the time is varied somewhat with the temperature of the water.

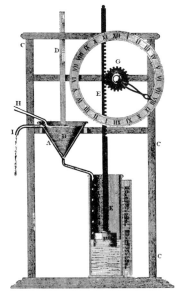

Fig. 7.

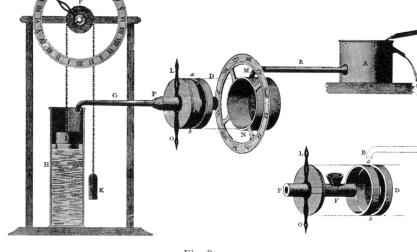

Fig. 8.

A form of clepsydra, said to have been in use in Egypt about 300 B.C., is shown in Fig. 7, for which I am indebted to Dr Pearson's article in Rees' "Cyclopaedia." A supply of water ran through the pipe H into the cone A, and from there dropped into the cylinder E. A conical stopper B regulated the flow, and the superfluous water escaped by the waste pipe I. The Egyptians divided the period between sunrise and sunset into twelve equal hours, so that the conical stopper had to be adjusted each day, and marks for every day in the year, and for the particular latitude of the place, were cut on the stalk D as a guide to the position of the stopper. A floating piston terminating in a rack served to actuate a pinion, to the arbor of which an hour hand was fixed.

In Fig. 8 is shown an improved clepsydra, constructed so that its aperture is adjusted as the year advances by the putting of an index to the sun's place in an ecliptic circle. It consists, first, of a reservoir A, to the top of which is attached a waste pipe to carry off the superfluous water, and thus keep it at the same level. A pipe B projects from this vessel into the rim of a drum M N, on the front of which is a circle with the signs of the ecliptic engraved thereon. A smaller drum O F L passes within the large one, having attached to it an index. This drum has a groove or slot *a b* cut through it, tapering in breadth both ways to a point. When in its place, this tapering groove comes just under the orifice of the pipe leading from the reservoir. This inner drum turns on a pipe or tube F, which is continued within and has a funnel at the end (not seen) for receiving the water as it drops through the groove in the

26

Three German diptych dials: left not signed, c.1600; centre signed 'Lienhart Miller 1626'; right signed 'Linhart Mieler 1625'. Among the most attractive of all dials and offering considerable variety both in decoration and in the scales engraved upon them, dials of this kind were produced in Germany throughout the 16th and 17th centuries. Similar, although stylistically distinct, dials were made also in France and Spain. Only very occasionally were such dials executed in metal. Sotheby Parke Bernet & Co.

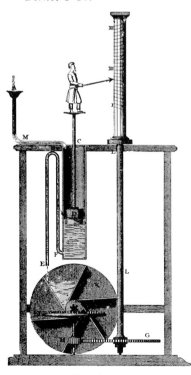

Fig. 9.

drum. The index is double, L for day and O for night, and it will be evident that, as it is turned, the capacity of the orifice is altered, and the water passes more or less rapidly through the pipe. The ecliptic being properly divided, the hand was set to the proper sign in which the sun then was, and was altered as he shifted round the ecliptic. The water, thus regulated, dropped into a cylindrical vessel H, within which was a float I, connected by a chain passing over a pulley on an arbor P, and having a counterpoise K at its other end. This pulley carried an index which pointed out the hours on a circle.

The next is ascribed to Ctesibius, about 200 B.C. It was a self-adjusting machine, and is shown in Fig. 9. The water dropped into a funnel A, from the eyes of a figure placed over it, and connected with a full reservoir, thus ensuring a constant pressure. The tube conveyed the water into an open cylinder with a float and a light pillar C attached. On the top of this pillar a human figure is placed, which points to the divisions on a large column. As the water rises in the cylinder, it also rises in the small tube or short leg of a syphon F B E, till it reaches the top, when it flows over the bent part, and quickly empties the cylinder, bringing down the float, and with it the index to the starting-point. So far it would have measured hours of equal length; but the Egyptian method required some further contrivance to

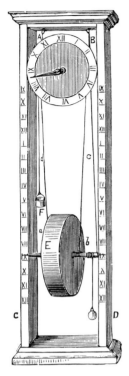

Fig. 10.

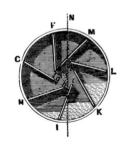

Fig. 11. — Section of Drum.

accommodate it to hours of varying length. This was done by drawing the divisions around the large column out of a horiztonal line, so as to vary in their distance on different sides. The water as it came from the syphon fell into a chambered drum K, which turned with the weight as each compartment became filled. On the axis of this drum was placed a pinion gearing with a contrate wheel I, which, by another pinion H, turned a wheel G, to the axis L of which the column was fixed. The lines were drawn slanting round the column to suit the hours of varying length throughout the year. The clepsydra was introduced into Greece by Plato. The introduction of the clepsydra into Rome took place about 157 B.C., by Scipio Nasica. Pliny tells us that Pompey brought a valuable one among the spoils from the Eastern nations, which he made use of for limiting the speeches of the Roman orators. Julius Caesar met with an instrument of the kind in England, by the help of which he observed that the summer nights of this country are shorter than they are in Italy.

With the decadence of Rome, when orators had certain periods of time allotted to them in the law courts for accusation or defence, the clepsydra was often, it is said, tampered with in the interest of particular suitors by adding to or subtracting from the wax used in the lawful regulation of the flow of water, or by using the fluid in an impure condition.

In 807 a water clock of bronze inlaid with gold was presented by the King of Persia to Charlemagne. Gifford in his history of France says: "The dial was composed of twelve small doors, which represented the hours; each door opened at the hour it was intended to represent, and out of it came the same number of little balls, which fell one by one, at equal intervals of time, on a brass drum. It might be told by the eye what hour it was by the number of doors that were open, and by the ear by the number of balls that fell. When it was twelve o'clock twelve horsemen in miniature issued forth at the same time and shut all the doors."

Hamburger, in Beckmann's "History of Inventions," dates the revival of clepsydrae to some time between 1643 and 1646; and Dr Hutton asserts that in 1693 the first water clock was brought to Paris from Burgundy.

Fig. 10 represents a clepsydra of the seventeenth century, consisting of an oblong frame of wood, A B C D, to the upper part of which two cords are fixed, their lower ends being wound round the axis of the drum E. The drum is shown in section at Fig. 11. It has seven water-tight metallic partitions, F f, G g, H h, I i, K k, L l, and M m. If the cord be wound around the axis until the drum rises to the top of the frame, and the drum be left to obey the force of gravity, it will tend to fall, and the cord resisting this tendency will cause it to rotate rapidly as it descends. But if water is introduced into the vessel, it will be retained in certain parts by these partitions, and, one side being heavier than the other, the tendency to rotate will be counteracted, and the drum will remain stationary. If now a small hole is pierced near the bottom of each cell, the water will slowly ooze from one cell into another, thus reducing the opposing weight of water, and causing the drum slowly to rotate. The rate of motion being properly regulated by altering the size of the apertures, the axis will point out the hours on the side of the frame; or a cord c d, with a weight F, may be made to pass over a pulley attached to an arbor bearing an index or hand to point out the hours on an engraved or painted ring. A night clock, with transparent dial, on this principle by Arnold Finchett of Cheapside, is in the British Museum, the date assigned to it being 1735.

The sealed water drum with partitions was utilised in another way which was described in *Engineering* some years ago, and will be understood on reference to the front and side views (Figs. 12 and 13). The drum A is suspended from two cords *e e*. An index placed loosely on the end of the arbor *a* is weighted at its lower end *p*. A grooved pulley *b* is fixed to the arbor, and on it hangs the hour ring R which is carried round by its adhesion to the pulley *b*.

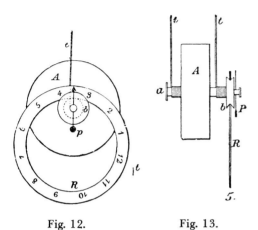

Fig. 12.   Fig. 13.

Above:

Design for an astrolabic clock controlled by a mercury escapement by Isaac b. Sid c.1276/7. From the Libros del saber de astronomia del D. Rey Alfonso X. *The clock consists of an astrolabe dial which is fitted with thirty gear teeth. This is driven by a pinion of six leaves mounted on the horizontal axle attached to a weight driven drum containing a mercury 'escapement'. In the centre of the drum are twelve chambers, six of which are filled with mercury. As the drum revolves, the mercury is supposed to trickle through the small holes in the chamber walls, thus retarding the speed with which the drum can turn.*

Left:

Design for a water clock or clepsydra from Traité des horloges elementaires ou la manière de faire des horloges avec l'eau, la terre, l'air, et le feu, *translated from the Italian of Domenico Martinelli* Horologi Elementari, *1663, and published in* Récréations Mathématiques et Physiques *by Jaques Ozanam (first edition 1694 and several thereafter). Martinelli's book is the classic 17th century work on water clocks which enjoyed something of a revival during this period, possibly because they seemed to offer advantages in terms of smoothness and silence of performance, constant force and perhaps cheapness of manufacture. Figs. 1 and 2 of this illustration show sections through the control barrel of the water clock, Fig. 3 a close up of the barrel between the hour scales with its pointers, Fig. 4 the adjustable mounting arrangement and Fig. 5 the whole clock.*

Left:
A 17th century table clepsydra c.1670, consisting of two glass ampoules like those of a sand glass, with a cork seal between them. Through this seal pass four glass syphons which control the movement of water from one ampoule to the other by a drip-feed system. The instrument is similar to, although not identical with, one shown in Martinelli's Horologi Elementari and in Ozanam. For details of the instrument see S.A. Bedini, 'The Seventeenth Century Table Klepsydra', Physis, x, 1968. National Maritime Museum, Greenwich.

Right:
A sinking bowl water clock or inflow clepsydra from Ceylon. This simple device for measuring intervals of time consists of a bowl with a small hole pierced in the base. When the unit of time which the bowl represents was to be measured, it was floated on a larger container of water. Gradually it would fill with water until it sank, a process which creates sufficient noise to attract the attention of the attendant who would strike some kind of gong. If several such time units were to be measured a pebble would be transferred from one pile to another and the process repeated. Bowls of this kind were widely used in Islamic Spain and North Africa for timing water distribution in the irrigation system. Horniman Museum and Library.

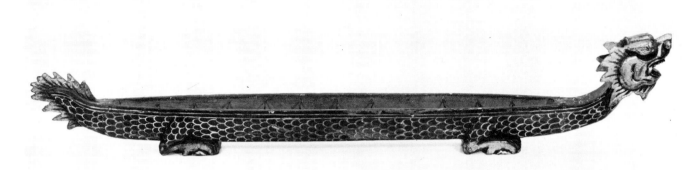

Chinese wick or incense clock in the form of a dragon, 19th century. The wick or some incense sticks were laid along the cross struts with a metal tray beneath. The elapse of time could be estimated by seeing how many sections (measured by the cross struts) had smouldered away. If small metal balls were hung over the wick so that they fell into the bowl when the wick burnt away, an audible time signal could be obtained. A further indication could be given by using differently perfumed sticks of incense. Sotheby Parke Bernet & Co.

The construction of clepsydrae, sand glasses, and weight clocks went on contemporaneously for a long period. With the introduction of the pendulum, clocks were made in which water acted as the motor and a pendulum as the controller. Such a clock was invented by Perrault in 1699. At the Royal Observatory, Greenwich, I remember seeing, a few years ago, a water-driven clock with a revolving pendulum, which was used for driving the equatorial telescope. Water at a pressure escaping from holes in a pair of horizontal arms caused the arms to revolve. One of the earliest steam engines was made on this principle; a similar contrivance, under the name of a sparger, has long been used by brewers to sprinkle water on their malt, and more recently a sprinkler of the same kind has been adapted for watering gardens.

WICK AND LAMP TIMEKEEPERS

Fig. 14.

Among the primitive timekeepers adopted by Chinese and Japanese was a kind of wick about two feet in length, made of material resembling flax or hemp, which underwent some process, so that when ignited it would smoulder without breaking into a flame. Knots were tied at particular distances, and the effluxion of time estimated as the sections between the knots smouldered away. Mons. Planchon, of Paris, has one of these curiosities, which I am assured is a genuine relic.

Asser narrates how King Alfred, who reigned from 872 to 900, contrived a timekeeper consisting of wax candles twelve inches long with marks an inch apart. Each candle burnt for four hours. The king, finding the time varied owing to the guttering of the candle, then devised a lantern of white horn scraped thin so as to be transparent. This is an unsatisfactory story. Having to provide and light a fresh candle every four hours was a clumsy device, costly to maintain and not so accurate in action as the clepsydra, which was certainly known in England at the time.

In "Le Passe Temps" of Jehan Lhermite, who was born at Antwerp in 1560, and died at Madrid in 1622, having served as Gentleman of the Chamber to Philippe II. of Spain, mention is made of a lamp timekeeper to show the hours at night as among the contents of his royal master's room. Fig. 14 is a drawing of what appears to be a similar instrument in the Schloss collection. On a stand of pewter is a glass reservoir, fastened with longitudinal slips of pewter, on one of which are cast the hour numerals from IIII at the top downwards to XII and then from I to VIII, thus covering

31

the period of darkness during winter. From the base of the reservoir extends a nose to receive the wick, which, when alight, illuminates the hour hand and the reservoir.

Lamp timekeepers of this kind were, I am told, to be met with occasionally in German and Dutch outlying country dwellings till a comparatively recent date.

SAND GLASSES

Fig. 15.

These, consisting of two glass bulbs joined by an intervening neck, measure a prearranged period by the falling of fine sand from the upper into the lower bulb. The invention of clepsammia, as they are called by several writers, is ascribed to Luitprand, a monk of Chartres, who at the end of the eighth century resuscitated the art of blowing glass. As already related, Charlemagne in 807 received from Persia a magnificent clepsydra. He then ordered to be made an immense sablier, or sand glass, with the horal divisions marked on the outside and which required to be turned once only in twelve hours. Sand glasses perform with a remarkable approach to accuracy and from this time became popular, especially in France. In Fig. 15 is shown a handsome sand glass of the sixteenth century. Great care seems to have been taken in the preparation of the sand. According to a prescription in "Le Menagier de Paris," "pour faire sablon à mettre ès orloges," ground black marble dust was to be boiled in wine, and, after being thoroughly dried, to be ground again, the process to be repeated about nine times.

To this day a sand glass is used in the House of Commons to measure certain intervals, and in comparatively recent times it was not uncommon to see a preacher, as he began his discourse, turn a sand glass attached to the pulpit.

Sand glass set in 'cloth of gold' from the Beeson Collection. Late 16th century with 17th century case. The set consists of four glasses running for ¼, ½, ¾ and one hour. Ten pillar frame covered in silk with laid and couch work, i.e. gold thread (gilt-silver wire wound round silk) laid on the surface of the cloth and secured by transverse couching stitches. Incorporated in the design are pearls and other stones including garnets. Outer case of ebony inlaid with ivory stringing; glazed sides and silver gilt finials. See Antiquarian Horology V, 11, 1968 pp. 417-8. Museum of the History of Science, Oxford.

Right:
An extremely good fake sand glass which purports to be the work of one Brother Benedict of the Order of Templars. If it were genuine, it would be the earliest sandglass known, but its faulty lettering and unlikely construction make clear that it is a relatively recent forgery. It was not however detected for many years. No sandglass earlier than the 16th century is at present known to survive. National Maritime Museum.

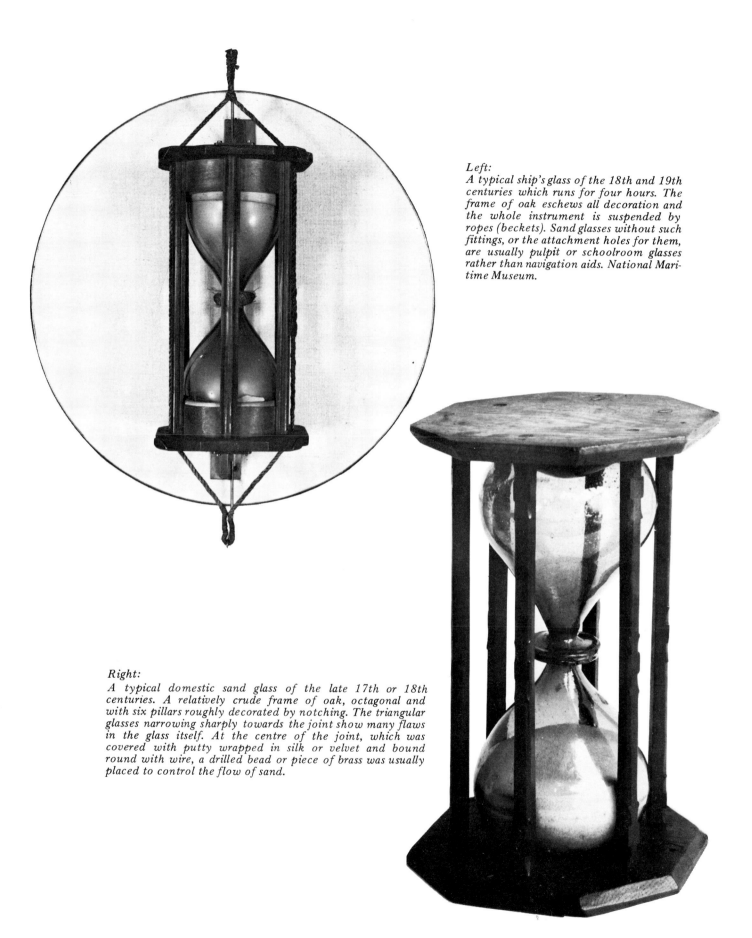

Left:
A typical ship's glass of the 18th and 19th centuries which runs for four hours. The frame of oak eschews all decoration and the whole instrument is suspended by ropes (beckets). Sand glasses without such fittings, or the attachment holes for them, are usually pulpit or schoolroom glasses rather than navigation aids. National Maritime Museum.

Right:
A typical domestic sand glass of the late 17th or 18th centuries. A relatively crude frame of oak, octagonal and with six pillars roughly decorated by notching. The triangular glasses narrowing sharply towards the joint show many flaws in the glass itself. At the centre of the joint, which was covered with putty wrapped in silk or velvet and bound round with wire, a drilled bead or piece of brass was usually placed to control the flow of sand.

Chapter II

Weight Clocks

SO MANY VAGUE and contradictory records exist as to the invention of clocks composed of an assemblage of wheels actuated by a weight, that any attempt to fix the exact date of their introduction would be mere guesswork.

According to the "Anthologia" quoted by E.M. Antoniadi, the Byzantine Emperor, Justin II., and his wife Sophia, in the sixth century offered to the building called the Basilica of Constantinople a horologium in which "the ingeniously devised brass was beating the hours from one to twelve." In the tenth century the Byzantine Emperor, Constantine VII., mentions "a small silver horologium which must stand in the chamber, and another one of brass which must stand where the chamberlains are residing."

It is claimed that Pacificus, Archdeacon of Verona, who died in the middle of the ninth century, devised a clock which Bailly, in his "History of Modern Astronomy," considers was furnished with an escapement; but this is not substantiated, and other authorities decide that it was a water clock. Charlemagne's clepsydra which sounded the hours is also sometimes erroneously referred to as a weight clock.

In Stow's "Chronicles," under date 606, it is stated: "This year dyed St Gregory; he commanded clocks and dials to be set up in churches to distinguish the houres of the day." These were probably sun-dials, and Stow's introduction of the word clocks is therefore unwarranted. The Latin "horologium" or the Italian "orologio" was used indiscriminately for sun-dials, clepsydrae, and other timekeepers. Clocks other than sun-dials were also designated nocturnal dials to distinguish them from those which showed the hour by the solar shadow only.

Havard says there is hardly a word in the French language that underwent so many transformations as the word *horloge*. It is assumed in turn *reologe*, *oroloige*, *orloge*, *oreloge*, *ologe*, and even *auloge*, before arriving at *horloge*. In an inventory of Charles V. made in 1380, a reference is found of "ung grand orloge de mer," consisting of "deux grans fiolles (flasks) plains de sablon." In other words, an hour glass.

The French equivalent for dial has been for several centuries *cadran*. But at one time, *heurier*, from *heure*, the hour, appears to have served. Richard, Archbishop of Reims, at the Chateau de Porte Mars, in 1389, refers to "ung petit orloge à ung heurier de cuivre peint en vert, prix IIII. livres p.," that is, a small clock with a dial of copper painted in green colour, price 4 livres parisis.

Gerbert, a monk, afterwards Pope Sylvester II., placed a clock in Magdeburg Cathedral at the end of the tenth century; but Dithmar declares it was only a kind of sun-dial; other writers consider Gerbert to be the originator of the escapement. Whatever may be inferred, there is no absolute proof that an escapement was constructed for more than two centuries after Gerbert's time, though it is pretty certain that clocks of some sort existed in cathedrals and monasteries during the twelfth and thirteenth centuries.

The word "clock" whether derived from the Saxon *clugga*, the Teutonic *glocke*, the Latin *glocio*, or the French *cloche*, signified "a bell," and there is reason to suppose that many of the early efforts consisted merely of a bell sounded at regular intervals by hand, the instant of ringing being determined by a sun-dial or sand glass.

In monasteries prayers were recited at certain fixed hours of the night as well as of the day, and as the monks were not always unfettered by sleep at the needful moment, this horologe or alarm was probably invented to rouse the drowsy *religieux* to a due sense of his duties. In the "Rule" of the monks of Citeaux, drawn up about 1120, and quoted by Calmet, the duty is prescribed to the sacristan of so adjusting the abbey clock that it may strike and wake the monks for matins. Durandus, in the thirteenth century, alludes to the clock as one of the essential features of a church. Dante, who was

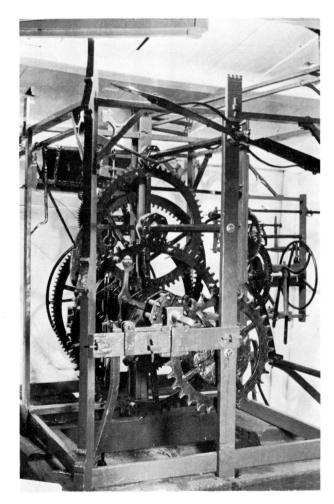

The movement of the church clock at Rye (see Fig.18) which was originally built by Lewis Billiard and installed in 1561-62. That the clock was presented by Elizabeth I, as is often asserted, is highly unlikely. Billiard's movement which replaced an earlier clock of 1514-16 is of the four-post 'bedstead' or 'birdcage' type with trains end to end, a central count wheel without a hoop wheel, and a separately hinged locking piece. The clock thus belongs to type 6b of C.F.C. Beeson's classification of turret clocks set out in his English Church Clocks 1280-1850 *(Antiquarian Horological Society monograph no 5), London and Chichester, 1971, pp.36-37. Although originally with a verge and foliot escapement the movement, which has been extensively rebuilt, was converted to a 2¼ seconds pendulum of eighteen feet long in 1810. The possibility of an earlier conversion cannot however be ruled out. The present quarter striking mechanism and jacks were installed in 1761-62 replacing earlier ones, and the 18th century jacks shown in Fig.18 were themselves replaced in 1969-70 with fibre-glass copies. The illustration shows the movement in situ. The movement has since been electrified by* THWAITES & REED, *who have added a "bicycle chain" connection for the external motors. For the detailed history of the clock see E.J. Tyler 'Rye Church Clock',* Antiquarian Horology, *X, 1, 1976 pp.41-54.*

born in 1265 and died in 1321, mentions an "orologia" which struck the hours; and Chaucer, who was born in 1328 and died in 1400, speaks of the cock crowing as regularly as clock or abbey horloge.

Berthoud considered it likely that a revolving fly was used as a controller prior to the invention of an escapement.

Captain Smyth, R.N. (*Archaeologia*, vol. xxxiii), suggests that John Megestein of Cologne, who is spoken of as having improved clocks in the fourteenth century, was possibly the inventor of the escapement. Still it is only surmise.

An early clock often referred to is the one which was presented by Saladin of Egypt to the Emperor Frederick II. of Germany, in the year 1232. It is described as resembling internally a celestial globe, in which figures of the sun, moon, and other planets, formed with the greatest skill, moved, being impelled by weights and wheels. There were also the twelve signs of the zodiac, with appropriate characters, which moved with the firmament.

In 1359 John II. of France, then a prisoner in London, desirous of measuring the time, addressed himself to "the King of the Minstrels" to whom was delegated the task of entertaining this royal personage, and in the "Journal de la depense du roy Jean" the following occurred: "Dymench XII. jour de Janvier le roy des menestereulx, sur la façon de l'auloge qui'il fait pour le roy, VII. nobles valent CXIII. sols X. deniers et a promis que parmi cette somme et XX. sols, qui paravant li ont ésté baillier le VI. de Janvier, il rendra l'auloge parfait," the translation of which is that on the 12th January, Sunday, the king of the minstrels was paid for making a clock for the King seven "nobles" worth 113 sous and 10 derniers, and promised, having already been lent on the 6th January the sum of 29 sous, to deliver the clock in perfect condition.

JACKS   Mechanical figures for striking the hour on bells seem to have been in use before the introduction of dials, and they proved to be a lasting attraction. There was, prior to 1298, a clock at St Paul's Cathedral with such figures; and Decker, in his "Gull's Hornbook," calls them "Paul's Jacks." In the accounts of the cathedral for the year 1286, allowances to Bartholomo Orologiario the clock-keeper are entered, namely, of bread at the rate of a loaf daily. In 1344 the dean and chapter entered into a contract with Walter the Orgoner of Southwark to supply and fix a dial, from which it may be inferred that the clock previously had no dial. In Dugdale's history of the old cathedral the dial is referred to as follows: "Somewhat above the stonework of the steeple was a fine dial, for which there was order taken in the 18th of Edward III., that it should be made with all splendour imaginable, which was accordingly done; having the image of an angel pointing to hours both of the day and night." The dial was placed below the "Jacks," which were not ousted from office, but continued to strike the hour with their accustomed regularity. Decker says "the time of St. Paul's goes truer by five notes than St Sepulchre's chimes."

Other writers confirm the supposition that dials were absent from most of the early clocks. M. Viollet-le-Duc ("Dictionnaire Raisonné de l'Architecture Française") observes that from the twelfth to the fourteenth century no space was arranged in the towers of churches for dials which could be seen at a distance. The earliest dials, he says, were covered by small projecting roofs and made either of wood or lead and decorated in colours.

The jacks from York Minster which strike the quarters, and date from c.1480. They consist of two plate-armour clad men who strike with their halberds on tubular gongs. The inscription on the dial above them may be translated as 'Praise the Lord's name alleluia, from the rising to the setting of the sun'. The earliest record of a clock at York dates from 1371. Nicholas Servian FIIP, Woodmansterne Ltd.

Fig. 16. — Jacquemarts at Dijon.

Froissart, who had an affection for clocks, speaks of one which existed at Courtray prior to 1370 as the largest which had then been made. It was brought from thence with other spoils of war in 1382, by Philip, Duke of Burgundy, who presented it to the people of Dijon. The clock was surmounted with his crest, and set up at Dijon in a tower of the Church of Notre Dame. In a turret over it were a bell and the figures of a man and woman, one on each side, which struck the hours, as shown in Fig. 16. To the present day these automata are locally called *Jacquemarts*, and G. Peignot, author of a dissertation on them, contended that they received their name from Jacquemart, a clock and lock maker of Lille, who was employed by the Duke of Burgundy in the year 1442. The appellation, however, seems to be merely a corruption of *Jaccomarchiadus, i.e.*, a man in a suit of armour. During the Middle Ages it was the custom to place as sentries on the belfries on tops of towers mailed men to watch over the safety of castles and towers, and their office was to give alarm at the approach of an enemy, a fire, or other disturbing event. And at many castles in Europe till quite late in the seventeenth century a trumpeter was posted on a tower to announce by a blast on his instrument the time of day for meals to be served.

In Fig. 17 is shown a "Jack" which, though not on active service, is still in Southwold Church. It is an oak figure, 3 ft. 6 ins. in height, of a man clad in armour, and is said to date from early in the fifteenth century. Locally it is known as "Jack the Smiter." The engraving is from a photograph by Mr. J. Martyn, Southwold. At the Parish Church, Rye, Sussex, is a clock said to have been the gift of Queen Elizabeth. This may be so, but the hands are certainly of much later date, and the movement has undergone reconstruction, for it is now fitted with a pendulum which beats but once in two seconds and a half, and projects below the clock into the church. Fig. 18, from a photograph by Mr. W. L. F. Wastell, shows the dial surmounted

Fig. 17. — "Jack The Smiter," Southwold Church.

Fig. 19. — Portable Clock, with Striking Jack.

by a canopy, under which stand two Jacks, which strike the quarters on small bells. Between these two figures, within an ornamental border, is a label thus inscribed: *"For our time is a very shadow that passeth away. Wisdom i. 5."* An excellent representative of striking Jacks exists at the Church of St. Mary Steps, Exeter; there is a pair at York Cathedral, and a pair, from Glastonbury, at Wells; a pair, formerly on the eastern wall of St. Martin's Church, Oxford, has lately been restored and placed upon the tower of the church; the quarters are struck by Jacks at All Saint's Church, Leicester, where the clock, which is said to date from the time of James I., was restored in 1899; in the tower of Holy Trinity Church, Bristol, which was demolished in 1787, was a pair; and in a recess of the south aisle of Norwich Cathedral were two small Jacks which, actuated by wires from the clock, struck the quarters on adjacent bells. Of the Exeter Jacks, and two at the Church of St. Dunstan's, Fleet Street, which were dear to Londoners of the last century, I shall be able to give engravings.

Fig. 18. — Jacks at Rye.

The peculiar clock shown in Fig. 19 appears to be a sixteenth century production. There are three trains of wheels, all arranged to face the sides of the clock. The clock is 12 ins. wide, 11 ins. high, 9 ins. from front to back, and 2 ft. 2½ ins. from the bottom of the clock to the top of the figure. By means of wires at the back, which extend to levers actuated by the striking and quarter trains, the figure on top of the clock strikes the hours on the large bell with the large hammer in his hands, and at the quarters kicks the two small bells with his heels.

In the early part of the fourteenth century, a large stone tower was built in Palace Yard, opposite to Westminster Hall, and a clock placed therein which struck every hour upon a great bell. There is a tradition that in the sixteenth year of the reign of Edward I. (1298) the Lord Chief Justice Randulphus de Hengham, having made an alteration in a record, was fined 800 marks by the king's order, and the money was applied to defray the cost of erecting a public clock opposite the entrance to Westminster Hall. The first official mention of Hengham's punishment extant appears to be in a

Year Book of the time of Richard III., where it is stated that on an occasion when the king closeted the judges in the Inner Star Chamber to consider various points submitted to them, one of the judges cited the case of Hengham, and said the offence consisted of altering a record so that a poor defendant might have to pay but 6s. 8d. instead of 13s. 4d., but nothing is said respecting the building of a clock. Stow, who was born in 1525 and died in 1605, in his "Account of Westminster" (vol. ii., p. 55) states that the clock was provided from Hengham's fine; and the Hon. Daines Barrington, in an interesting letter to Mr Justice Blackstone in 1778 (*Archaeologia*, vol. v.), accepts the tradition, which is very possibly well founded, although it must be confessed that the evidence on the point is not conclusive. In an Issue Roll of the forty-fourth year of the reign of Edward III. is recorded the payment of two pounds to John Nicole, keeper of the great clock of the king within the Palace of Westminster, being his wages for eighty days at the rate of sixpence a day. In subsequent reigns further references are made to the keeper of this clock. In the first year of Henry V. was granted a patent to "Henricus Berton Valectus camerae Regis custos horologii Regis infra Palatium Westm. pro vita. cum feod. VI dem per diem." Henry VI. entrusted its custody to William Warby, Dean of St. Stephen's, together with sixpence a day remuneration. The tower was standing in the time of Elizabeth, for Judge Southcote mentions the tradition, stating that the clock still remained

The movement of the Wells cathedral clock which dates from c.1300 and was built specifically for Wells. It was not transferred from Glastonbury and was not built by a monk called Peter Lightfoot who appears to be a purely legendary figure. See p. 41 and p. 44. It is however virtually certain that the Wells clock and the slightly earlier Salisbury clock are by the same maker or makers. The clock consists of going and quarter striking trains set end to end, and an hour train at right angles to them, all contained in a bird cage frame with external count wheel and hoop wheel (Beeson classification 5b). The locking piece is lifted by a sliding vertical rod moved at its lower end by a lever pivoted in its middle and depressed by a rotating lever on the end of the arbor of the main wheel in the going train. The method according to Beeson is unique. Winding was originally effected by a capstan but has since been converted to gear wheel and pinion. This movement was removed from the clock in 1838 and was transferred to the Science Museum in 1883. For a view of the dial and automata see p.54. Lent to the Science Museum, London, by the Dean and Chapter of Wells Cathedral.

which had been made out of the Chief Justice's fine. The engraving which I am enabled to give of this interesting erection is from the *Mirror*, vol. xi., which was published in 1825. The sketch is copied from an engraving by Hollar, who was born in 1607 and died in 1677. It doubtless represents the locality as it existed about the middle of the seventeenth century, shortly after which time the tower was pulled down, but the exact date of its destruction is unknown.

On the old Houses of Parliament, which were destroyed by fire in 1834, a dial on the second pediment of the buildings in Palace Yard marked the site, the remarkable motto on which, "Discite Justitiam Moniti," may be taken to relate to its origin. The clock tower of the present home of our Legislature is, it is conjectured, but a few paces from the situation of the original clock. The great bell, "Tom of Westminster," was broken up and recast for the St. Paul's Cathedral clock, of which more particulars will be given later on.

There was a large clock in Canterbury Cathedral at the end of the thirteenth century, which, according to Dart's history of the sacred edifice, was put up at a cost of £30 in 1292, and one at Exeter at the beginning of the fourteenth century.

An "orologium" of some kind was under construction at Norwich Cathedral in 1323. From that date numerous entries relating to it occur in the Sacrist's Rolls. There were twenty-four small images, which it may be conjectured represented the hours of the day and night; thirty images, probably corresponding to the days of the month, and also painted and gilded plates portraying the sun and moon.

A print of the original 17th century jacks, replaced in the mid-19th century by accurate copies, which struck the quarters at St. Martin's Church, Oxford.

Fig. 20. — Clock Tower in Palace Yard, Westminster.

The jacks of St. Dunstan in the West, Fleet Street, London, as they are now, mounted on the 19th century building which replaced the earlier medieval church demolished in 1830 and whence the jacks were removed. The picture may be compared with Fig. 449. The clock has always held particular significance for Londoners and in 1893 supplied the title and leit motif *for E. Ward's novel about the great fire,* St. Dunstan's Clock.

About 1326 Richard Wallingford, Abbot of Saint Albans, placed a "horologe" in his monastery, and the account which he gave of his machine is still preserved in the Bodleian Library at Oxford. From this, Wallingford's conception really appears to have been more of a planetarium for showing the course of the heavenly bodies than a timekeeper, for his description contains no mention of any escapement or regulator for ensuring equable motion.

The earliest clock worthy of our modern definition, of which we have any authentic details, is the one which is said to have been made about the year 1335, by Peter Lightfoot, an ingenious monk of Glastonbury Abbey, for and at the expense of his superior, Adam de Lodbury, who was promoted to the Abbacy of Glastonbury in 1322 and died in 1335. The fourteenth century was distinguished by the introduction of the peculiar class of clocks which, besides indicating the flight of time, were furnished with mechanism for other purposes. One of the earliest of this kind was described by Viollet-le-Duc as having been given about the year 1340 to the monastery of Cluny by the Abbot Pierre de Chastelux. In addition to its indication of the phases of the moon, the movements of the sun, &c., this clock had a quantity of little figures which acted various scenes, as "The Mystery of the Resurrection," "Death," &c. The hours were announced by a cock, which fluttered its wings and crowed twice. At the same time an angel opened a door and saluted the Virgin Mary, the Holy Ghost descended on her head in the form of a dove, God the Father gave her His benediction, a musical carillon chimed, animals shook their wings and moved their eyes; at last the clock struck, and all retreated within it.

41

الجانب بالنبؤ وهؤلاء صورة ماؤ وصفتة واضحة

The construction of water-driven time-measuring mechanisms adorned with a variety of automata was transmitted to Islam from ancient Greece. The clock shown here, known as the Castle Water clock, is described in one of the most detailed Arabic treatises on mechanical devices the Kitāb fī maᶜrifat al-hiyal al-handasīya *by Ibn al-Razzaz al-Jazarī which was completed in c.1206 A.D. The illustration comes from a leaf now in the Museum of Fine Arts, Boston, detached from a manuscript dated 1355-56 now in the Top Kapu Saray, Istanbul.*

At the top of the clock is a disc which revolves to show the sign of the zodiac and the position of the sun and moon in it. Beneath this arc two rows of doors, of which one pair opens each hour. One pair only is shown open in the illustration. Each hour also the birds lean forward and drop a brass ball into the copper bowl in front of them. Every four hours the trumpeters trumpet, the drummers beat their drums and the cymbalist clashes his cymbal.

From a horological point of view such marionette exhibitions may be puerile and contemptible; still they caught and held the popular fancy, their producers being as a rule more honoured than those who merely strove after exactness of timekeeping.

Horological construction of this kind was not confined to the western part of Europe. Anent the wonders in the Palace of Abu Hammou, Sultan of Tlemcen, the Abbé Barges, a French scholar and Orientalist, speaks of a clock in the king's palace, ornamented by figures wrought in solid silver. Above the case containing the works was a scene representing a thicket in which was a bird spreading its wings over its young. A serpent stealthily crawled out of its hiding place towards the birds, endeavouring to surprise and devour them. Ten doors introduced in the forepart of the clock represented the ten hours of the night. At the end of each hour one of these doors creaked and shook. Two wider and higher doors occupied the lateral extremity of the case. Above these doors and near the cornice, a sphere of the moon moved in the direction of the equatorial line and indicated the course of this heavenly body. At the commencement of each hour, when one of the smaller doors rattled, an eagle swooped out of each of the two bigger doors and settled on a copper vase or basin, dropping into it a piece of metal — also copper — which they had carried in their beaks. These weights, which glided into a cavity introduced at the bottom of the vase, dropped into the interior of the clock, subsequently rising again when required. Then the serpent, which by that time had wound itself up to the top of the thicket, emitted a sharp hiss, pounced upon and bit one of the young birds, its mother meanwhile squeaking and endeavouring to defend it. At this moment the door which marked the time opened by itself, a young female slave appeared, and in her right hand presented an open book whereon the name of the hour could be read in verses. She held her left hand up to her lips as if to salute a khalifa. This clock was named in Arabic "Menganah," and was first seen in 1358.

The first of the celebrated Strasburg Cathedral clocks was begun about 1350, under the direction of John, Bishop of Lichtenberg. Henry Wieck, of Wurtemberg, constructed a clock for Charles V. of France, surnamed the Wise, and it was erected at Paris in the Royal Palace (now the Palais de Justice). Henry Wieck, or, as he was afterwards known, Henry de Vick, began his task in 1370 and completed it eight years after. He was lodged in the tower and received six sous parisis per day during the time he was employed. Somewhat similar clocks were, probably about the same time, erected at Caen and Montargis, though some French writers assert that the Caen clock was made by one Beaumont in 1314. In Rymer's "Federa" there is printed a protection given by King Edward III. of England to three Dutchmen named John Lietuyt, John Uneman, and William Uneman, who were "orologiers," invited from Delft to England in 1368. The title of this protection is, "De Horlogiorum Artificio exercendo." There were probably also English artificers practising their craft at the same time as that of the issue of the decree which gave the Dutch men protection, for that document enacted that the English artificers should not be molested. The "horologium" of John Dondi, constructed at Padua in 1344 by order of Hubert, Prince of Carrara, seems also to have been a true clock. It is described as being placed on the top of a turret on the steeple, and designating the twenty-four hours of the day and night. De Maizières, a contemporary writer, says it was visited by all the scientific men of the day, and from thenceforward the family of Dondi took the name of "Dondi d'Orologia." He also speaks of Joseph Dondi, apparently a son of John, as one who excelled in clockmaking, and after sixteen year's labour constructed a sphere or clock governed by a single balance, and which correctly showed the motion of the celestial bodies. John Visconti, Archbishop of Milan, set up a clock at Genoa in 1353; in 1356 one was fixed at Bologna.

Froissart has left a descriptive eulogium of a clock, written in 1370 in the form of a fragmentary poem, entitled "l'Horloge Amoureuse." In this the controlling medium is referred to as a "foliot," which was doubtless the straight armed balance with weights such as appears in the drawing of De Vick's clock presently to be described. In 1389 a splendid clock, made by Jehan de Féalins, was erected at Rouen, which with some modern alterations to the movements is still a reliable timekeeper, showing the hours and also the days of the week and the phases of the moon. The handsome dial shown in Fig. 21 is about 6 ft. square. At Spires, in Bavaria, there was a clock in the year 1395. Dr Helein describes a complicated clock which at the end of the fourteenth century was erected at Lund, in Sweden. When the hours were struck, two knights came forward, and gave each other as many blows as the number of the hour; a door then opened and showed the Virgin Mary, seated on a throne with the infant Jesus in her arms. The Magi then presented their offerings, during which trumpets sounded, and the figures disappeared. From the beginning of the fifteenth century mathematicians, astronomers, and mechanicians throughout Europe vied with each other in contriving timekeepers with various supplementary actions. In 1401 a large clock with bells was placed in the Cathedral of Seville, and in 1404 a similar one for

Fig. 21. — Clock at Rouen. "Dictionnaire de l'Ameublement."

Moscow was constructed by Lazare, a Servian. The clock of Lubeck was made in 1405 and one at Pavia by G. Visconti a little later. In 1442 Nuremberg had a clock with figures to represent soldiers which went through evolutions periodically. The Auxerre clock was finished in 1483, and shortly after an astronomical clock was erected at Prague; the clock at Munich dates from the same period. The first monumental timekeeper in the Square of St Mark's, Venice, was put up in 1495. Among clocks of the sixteenth century may be cited one at Brussels, one at Berne, the latter constructed in 1557 by Gaspard Brunner, having performing soldiers something in the style of the Nuremberg one; "Hans of Jena," in which a pilgrim offered an apple to an immense open-mouthed grotesque head as the hours struck; the clock at Coblentz, where, in the belfry of the Kaufhaus, was fixed a large helmeted head, the mouth of which opened and shut as the hours were sounded; an astronomical clock at Beauvais Cathedral, of 36 ft. in height and having fifty dials; the second great Strasburg clock, which was begun in 1570; a clock with numerous mechanical figures set up at Niort, in Poitou, the same year; a clock at Calais, with two figures which attacked each other as in the Lund clock; and the celebrated Lyons clock which dates from 1598. These are but some of the more notable clocks erected up to the close of the sixteenth century, by which time nearly every town in Europe had at least one public timekeeper of some pretensions. Of several typical ones among those enumerated I am enabled to give fuller particulars.

The Glastonbury ancient and complicated piece of machinery was, according to William of Worcester, originally in the south transept of the abbey church; but it was removed with all its appendages from thence to Wells Cathedral at the time of the dissolution of the monastery in the reign of Henry VIII., where, in an old chapel in the north transept, it still remains. The face of the clock as it now appears is shown in Fig. 22. The dial is 6ft. 6ins. in diameter, and contained in a square frame, the spandrels of which are filled with angels, holding in their hands each the head of a man. The outer band is painted blue, with gilt stars scattered over it, and is divided into twenty-four parts, corresponding with the twenty-four hours of the day and night, in two, divisions of twelve hours each. The horary numbers are painted in old English characters, on circular tablets, and mark the hours from twelve at noon to midnight, and from thence to twelve at midday again. The hour-index, a large gilt star, is attached to the machinery behind a second circle, which conceals all except the index. On this second circle are marked the minutes, indicated by a smaller star. A third and lesser circle contains numbers for indicating the age of the moon, which is marked by a point attached to a small circular opening in the plate, through which the phases of the moon are shown. Around this aperture is an inscription, not very intelligible, which one author reads as "Ab hinc monstrat micro . . . ericus archery pung," meaning, probably, that in this microcosm were displayed all the wonders of the vast sidereal hemisphere. Corresponding to the moon aperture on the opposite side of the centre is a circle, in which is a female figure, with the motto "Semper peragrat Phoebe." An arched pediment surmounts the whole, with an octangular projection from its base line, forming a cornice to the face of the clock. A panelled turret is fixed in the centre, around which four equestrian knights, equipped for a tournament and mounted on two pieces of carved wood, used to revolve in opposite

Fig. 22. — Dial of Glastonbury Clock.

Two views of a modern reconstruction of the astrarium of Giovanni de' Dondi (p.43), made by P.N. Haward and engraved by F.N. Fryer. The original instrument was constructed by de' Dondi between 1348 and 1364. It is only incidentally a clock, being primarily developed to represent the motions of the planets as predicted by Ptolemaic planetary theory. To this end the seven main dials on the hectagonal frame show the positions of the sun, the moon, and the five planets, the hour dial being placed below on a subsidiary frame together with dials for the fixed and moveable church festivals, and one for the nodes, i.e. the moments when the orbits of sun and moon intersect. The wings on either side of the hour dial give the times of sunrise and sunset at Padua throughout the year. In the view of the exterior the dial of the sun is seen at left, that of Venus centrally and that of Mercury, the most complicated (with the moon), at the right. The whole instrument is driven by a single weight and regulated by a verge escapement with balance wheel. It was constructed by de' Dondi entirely in brass or bronze, and copper. The Science Museum, London.

directions, two on each side as if running at the ring in a tilt, when set in motion by a connection with the clock. A "Jack" seated at one angle of the transept, within the church, is connected by rods with the clock, and he is made to strike the quarters with his feet on two little bells, and the hours on another bell before him with a battle-axe in his hands. If the date of the construction of the clock be correct, the figures at present moved by its machinery cannot, according to J. R. Planché, be the original ones, or they have undergone strange alteration. Those that circulated in a sort of tilting match are very clumsily carved, and have suffered some injury from time; but two of them appear to be intended for jousters; one wears a hood with ears to it; the third is a nondescript; the fourth is painted in the civil costume of the reign of James or Charles I., with falling collar, striped doublet, and the peaked beard and moustache of that period. Outside the transept is another dial surmounted by two figures of knights clad in armour of the fifteenth century. They strike the quarters on bells with their battle-axes.

The old interior works of this clock were of iron, not differing materially in principle from the mechanism of much later date clocks, except that the appliances for the variety of the movements of the dial-plate were necessarily complicated. They exhibited a rare and interesting specimen of the art of clockmaking at so early a period, in which the monks particularly excelled. After going for nearly five centuries, the works were found to be so completely worn out that, about the year 1835, they were replaced by a new train. The old movement, now controlled by a pendulum, may be seen in action at South Kensington Museum. Except for the quarter striking part and the lunation work, the movement is identical with that of De Vick's clock, presently to be described.

Another clock attributed to Lightfoot was erected at Wimborne in Dorsetshire. The dial as it at present appears is represented in Fig. 23, and an examination will show many features in common with these two fourteenth century clocks.

Figs. 24, 25 and 26 represent De Vick's clock in front and in profile. There was but one hand, and that in its revolution round a dial-plate indicated the hours. A heavy wieght tied to a rope, which was wound round a cylinder or barrel, served as the power to cause the hand to revolve; but the hand, instead of being fixed to the axis of the barrel, had its motion communicated through a wheel and pinion, so that the weight did not need to be wound up so frequently as would otherwise be the case. If the weight were freely subjected to

Fig. 23. — Dial of Wimborne Clock.

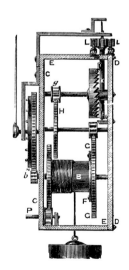

Left: Fig. 24. — Side view of going part.

B, barrel; C, D, E, plates; F, ratchet and click; G, great wheel; P, O, winding pinion and wheel; H, second wheel; g, escape pinion.

Right: Fig. 25. — Front view of De Vick's clock.

K, verge; L, bar-balance; m, shifting weights for adjusting the clock to time; b, pinion driving hour wheel; N, hour wheel, the arbor of which carries the hand.

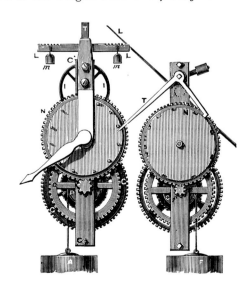

Fig. 26. — Side view of striking part.

F, weight; A, B, plates; C, barrel; *c*, pins for raising the hammer tail; L, fly; *f*, pinion for driving count wheel; N, count wheel or locking-plate; T, lever for letting off striking work.

Fig. 26a. — Verge Escapement with Cross-bar or "Foliot" Balance.

influence of gravity, its motion would have been accelerated, and so an escapement and controller had to be devised in order that all the spaces traversed by the hand should be passed through in the same time as each other. The device adopted to check the progress of the weight was as follows: Connected with the arbor carrying the hand is a spindle carrying a wheel with ratchet-shaped teeth, as will be seen from Fig. 24. This wheel, called the "escape wheel," has an odd number of teeth, and on a vertical rod or "verge" are two beds or "pallets," of a distance from each other equal to the diameter of the wheel. The acting faces of these pallets form nearly a right angle, and the verge is planted close to the teeth of the wheel, so that one of the projecting pallets is always intercepting the path of the wheel teeth. In this way an alternating rotary motion is imparted to the verge, the escape wheel slipping by a space equal to half the distance between two teeth at every alternation. The action of the teeth of the wheel on the pallets will perhaps be better understood by a reference to Fig. 26A, which is drawn to an enlarged scale. A tooth of the escape wheel is pressing on the upper pallet; as it drops off the under tooth will reach the root of the lower pallet, but the motion of the verge will not be at once reversed. The escape wheel will recoil until the impetus of the cross-bar and weights mounted on the verge is exhausted. The teeth of the wheel are undercut to free the face of the pallet during the recoil. The inertia of the cross-bar and weights, by opposing the rotary motion, forms the regulator, and as the centre of gyration may be altered by shifting the weights along the bar, the time occupied by each vibration can be increased or lessened, as may be required. The verge was usually suspended by a cord to lessen the friction and wear at the pivot or "toe" on which it rested. This controller, the foliot of Froissart, admirable as it was, did not give anything like the exact result now attained by means of a superior escapement and pendulum, for its constancy was seriously affected through variations in the motive force, such as would be caused by deterioration and thickening of the lubricant used to the pivots and bearing surfaces. It is, however, curious to note that the balance of a modern chronometer or watch, which vibrates with such marvellous accuracy, is analogous in its action to that of the early cross-bar regulator.

To understand the way the weight was raised after the rope was uncoiled from the barrel, it may be necessary to explain that, though the great wheel is tight on its arbor, the barrel on the same arbor is loosely fitted, the connection between the two being established by means of a ratchet-wheel and click. To lessen the labour of winding, a wheel is attached to the barrel, into which a pinion gears, and on the squared extremity of the pinion arbor the winding handle is placed. The different parts are shown and lettered in Fig. 24.

The manner of striking the hours in regular order will be apparent from Figs. 25 and 26, with a little explanation. The striking part of the clock is distinct from the going part, and is actuated by a separate weight. It occupies the right in Fig. 25. The wheel to which the hand is attached turns once in twelve hours, and it will be observed that, projecting from its face, are twelve pins, equidistant from each other. Although continually solicited by the weight, the striking train of wheels cannot turn except once at each hour, because it is locked by a tooth at one extremity of a "bell-crank" lever T, engaging with one of a series of notches in the locking-plate N. At the completion of each hour this tooth is lifted out by one of the twelve pins depressing the other end of the lever, and the striking train then rotates till the tooth of the lever falls into the next notch of the locking-plate. The tail of the hammer which strikes the bell intersects the path of the lifting pins c, which are arranged around the great wheel of the striking train. The notches around the edge of the locking-plate are placed at such distances that at one o'clock the tooth enters a notch directly one blow has been struck on the bell. At the next hour there is a longer space before a notch is reached, and so two blows are struck before the train is again locked; at the succeeding

Above: the verge and foliot escapement of the clock from Salisbury Cathedral. Right: a general view of the clock.
The clock was built c.1386 on the instruction of Bishop Erghum of Salisbury. That this clock and that at Wells were made by the same craftsmen is, from the stylistic similarities of the two, virtually certain. The bird cage type frame is held together by wedges and tenons. The clock was restored in 1956 by John Smith & Sons, Derby, to its original verge and foliot form from the anchor and pendulum which it had been given at a later date. There are two end to end trains, and an external locking plate (Beeson type 5a,b). Only the hours are sounded, unlike Wells which also has a quarter train. Although the time keeping qualities of such clocks were low, some degree of regulation was possible both by altering the size of the driving weight, and by adjusting the positions of the small weights carried at each end of the foliot bar.

Striking Parts		Going Parts	
C	Count wheel	D1	Winding drum
D2	Winding drum	E	Escape wheel
F	Fly	G	Great wheel
H	Hoop wheel	P	Operating pin
S	Striking studs	V	Verge with foliat cross arm

hour the space permits of three blows and so on, till at twelve o'clock the plate has made a complete rotation, and the action of the preceding twelve hours recurs. The striking train would run down with increasing velocity but for the fan *L*, which keeps the periods between the strokes of the bell practically uniform. This is the principle of the striking work still used in most turret clocks, and till recently in nearly all small clocks of French make. The chief objection to it is that the hours are struck in regular progression without reference to the position of the hands; so that if the striking part happens to run down before the going part, the striking will be all wrong when it is started again, unless the precaution has been taken to set it going at the same hour as that at which it stopped.

Fig. 27 shows the dial of De Vick's clock and its splendid surroundings, adjoining the side of the Palais de Justice, which faces the Quai aux Fleurs. Though the clock appears to have been erected in the round tower of the palace in 1370, the present architectural environment was not completed till 1585. The engraving is from "Les Merveilles de l'Horlogerie."

Fig. 27. — Clock of the Palais de Justice, Paris.

The figures of Piety and Justice flanking the dial, and the angels supporting the coat of arms which crowns the pediment, are by Germaine Pilon. On the upper tablet is the inscription, "Qui dedit ante duas triplicem dabit ille coronam." The panel below the dial perpetuates the quotation from Passerat:-
"Machina que bis sex tam juste dividit horas,
Justitiam servare monet legesque tueri."

This celebated clock has experienced several long intervals of neglect, and been many times repaired. In 1852, after thorough examination, its defects were made good, and it was in some measure reconstructed. The bell on which the hours are struck was cast by John Jouvance, and it is said that upon this bell was repeated the signal from St Germain l'Auxerrois for the massacre of St Bartholomew in 1572. The bell for the Montargis clock was also made by Jouvance.

A turret clock which was erected at Dover Castle in the fourteenth century is still in action at South Kensington Museum. In construction it is somewhat similar to those of Lightfoot and De Vick. On the wrought-iron frame are the letters R.L. arranged as a monogram. The train, however, consists of only one wheel, which drives the escape-pinion so fast that there must have been either a very long driving-cord, or the clock must have been wound at frequent intervals. The winding is accomplished by means of handles or spokes projecting radially from one end of the barrel, which runs freely on the arbor of the wheel. On the face of the barrel which is nearest the wheel is a spring click, catching into the arms of the wheel, the arms thus serving the purpose of a ratchet. This click and ratchet arrangement was long favoured by some makers, and is often found in lantern clocks of the seventeenth century. The wheels of these early clocks were of wrought iron, the arms being riveted into the rim. A clock very similar to the Dover one was erected at Peterborough about the same date.

Few places probably can show more interesting relics of primitive horology than Exeter. "From the Patent Rolls of Edward II.," the late Mr Britton observes, in his description of Exeter Cathedral, "it is evident there was a clock in this church in 1317. Other entries relating to the clock appear in the Rolls. In 1376-77, the sum of 119s. 9d. is set down for expenses *'circa cameram in boreali turre pro Horlogio quod vocatur de novo construendam.'* The whole charge in the roll *nova camera pro horlogio'* is £10. 6s. 5½d. In 1424-25, two men were sent off on horseback to fetch Roger, clockmaker, from Barnstaple."

Whatever its construction, no trace of the original horologe can be found, but Bishop Courtenay is credited with having presented a clock in 1480. It is said that this clock was made by Peter Lightfoot, but if the date of its construction (1480) is correct, this cannot be true, for Lightfoot had then been dead some years. The dial which still does duty bears a resemblance to the one of Lightfoot's at Glastonbury, from which it was possibly copied, though Mr J. J. Hall suggests that it formed part of the clock mentioned as existing in 1317. It shows the hour of the day, and the age of the moon; upon the face or dial, which is about 7 ft. in diameter, are two circles, one marked from one to thirty for the moon's age, the other figured from I. to XII. twice over, for the hours. In the centre is a semi-globe, representing the earth, round which a smaller ball, the moon painted half white and half black, revolves every month, and in turning upon its axis shows the varying

Fig. 28. — Exeter Cathedral Clock.

EXETER CLOCKS

50

phases of the luminary which it represents; between the two circles is a third ball, representing the sun with a *fleur-de-lis,* which points to the hours as the sun, according to the ancient theory, daily revolved round the earth. Underneath it is the inscription, "Pereunt et imputantur" (they [the hours] pass and are placed to our account). In 1760 the clock was thoroughly repaired by William Howard, when an additional dial to show the minutes was provided and placed on the top of the case as shown in Fig. 28. The movement was replaced by a modern one in 1885.

The hours are still struck on "Great Peter," a fine-toned bell in the north tower. This bell was the gift of Bishop Courtenay, and was brought from Llandaff (1478-86). According to Worth's excellent Guide to Exeter Cathedral, it was recast in 1676 by Thomas Perdue. Its weight, as computed by the Rev. H. T. Ellacombe, is 14,000 lbs., its diameter at the mouth 76 in., and its height 56 in.

In the tower of the Church of St Mary Steps, near by where once stood the old West Gate, is a most curious clock, which is probably a production of the sixteenth century. The corners of the dial are embellished with basso-relievos representing the four seasons, and in an alcove over the dial are three automatic figures, as shown in Fig. 29. The centre one is a statue of Henry VIII. in a sitting posture, which, on the clock striking the hour, inclines the head at every stroke. On each side is a soldier in military attire, holding a javelin in one hand and a hammer with a long handle in the other. These soldiers strike the quarters by alternate blows on two bells beneath their feet.

The three figures are termed by many Exonians "Matthew the Miller and his two sons," from the fact that "Matthew the Miller," who resided in a place known as Cricklepit Lane, was remarkable for his integrity and regular course of life. His punctuality of going at one hour for and returning with his grist led his neighbours to judge with tolerable exactness the time of day from his passing. By this the statue received its vulgar name. The following distich used to be current in Exeter:—

> Matthew the Miller's alive,
> Matthew the Miller is dead,
> For every hour in Westgate Tower
> Matthew nods his head.

A clock placed in the tower of the Church of St Mary Ottery about 1340, by John de Grandison, Bishop of Exeter, has been recently restored by Mr J. J. Hall. In the tower of St Petrock's Church, in the High Street, was till recently a clock believed to date from 1470. In the tower also is a peal of six bells, the oldest of which bears the arms of Henry V. or VI., not later than 1425.

There was a clock at St Mary's Church, Oxford, in the fifteenth century, and one of the ancient Latin statutes of the University is devoted to the duties of its custodian. Other references are made to it in the proctor's accounts. Under date 1469 is "Pro custodia horilogij vjs. viijd," and a somewhat similar entry occurs in 1473. In 1523 a new clock was erected from fines imposed on negligent students. In the vice-chancellor's accounts from 1550 to 1554 is an item, "Paid to Thos. Masey for mendinge St Maryes clocke, 25 Junii, travellinge (travailing) by the space of two weekes thereon, and was moreover paid the sum of tenpence for a clock for the said

Fig. 29. — St. Mary Steps, Exeter.

ST MARY'S CHURCH.
OXFORD

Oriental Calendar clock (p.59) showing the 28 'Mansions of the moon'. The dots around the edge of the dial represent different constellations of stars. Metropolitan Museum of Art, New York. Bequest of Thomas Egleston, 1900.

52

machine." On some parchment rolls in the tower of the schools, among the proctor's accounts, appears, "1469, Pro custodia Horilogii, iijs.," and "1472, Pro reparatione horilogij, vjs. viijd."

Although details are in most instances wanting, there are sufficient references among the ecclesiastical records of the country to show that church clocks were pretty general throughout England in the fifteenth century. According to the churchwardens' accounts for Walberswick, in Suffolk, 11d. was paid to the clockmaker in 1451, and 12s. 8d. in the following year. In 1495, John Payn, the smith, of Southwold, received 6s. 8d. for a new clock, and in 1499, Nicholas Schrebbys was paid four sums — £1. 13s. 4d., 6s. 8d., £1. 2s., and 13s. 4d. — for the clock.

John Baret, of Bury St Edmunds, by his will dated 1463, bequeathed 8s. yearly to the sexton of St Mary's Church, "To keep the clokke, take hede to the chymes, wynde vp the peys and the plummeys as ofte as nede is."

The records of Dunstable mention a clock over the pulpit in 1483, and the churchwardens' accounts of Wigtoft, Lincolnshire, refer to several sums paid

Fig. 30. — The Second Strasburg Clock.

to Richard Angel for keeping the clock from 1484 onward.

An old clock at York Cathedral, which was fixed to the wall near the south door and covered with a large Gothic case, was removed in 1752, when the present clock, made by John Hindley, was erected.

STRASBURG CLOCKS   The first clock set up in the interior of the cathedral at Strasburg was begun in 1352, and completed two year's after, under John, Bishop of Lichtenberg. It consisted of a calendar, representing in a painting some indications relative to the principal movable feasts. In the middle part there was an astrolabe, whose pointers showed the movements of the sun and moon, the hours, and their subdivisions. There was placed at the same elevation the prime mover, and the other wheel work which caused the clock to go. The upper compartment was adorned with a statuette of the Virgin, before which, at noon, the three Magi (wise men of the East) bowed themselves. An automaton cock, placed upon the crown of the case, crowed at the same moment, moving its beak and flapping its wings. A small set of chimes, composed of several cymbals, formed a part of this work.

THE SECOND CLOCK   The Second Clock, of which an exterior view is given in Fig. 30, was certainly a triumph of ingenuity. It was projected in 1547; but though the designs appear to have been then ready, the execution went no further than the building of the chamber and the preparation of some of the heavier ironwork, till 1570, when Conrad Dasypodius, a mathematician of Strasburg, and David Wolkstein, of Augsburg, undertook to supervise the completion of the horologium. The mechanical works were confided to Isaac and Josiah Habrecht, mechanicians of Schaffhausen, in Switzerland, while Tobias Stimmer (or Sturmer), of the same place, was employed to do the paintings and the sculpture which were to serve as decorations of the achievement. Josiah Habrecht being summoned to Cologne for other work, the construction of the clock was left in the hands of Isaac alone.

Before, and at the foot of the clock, there was a celestial globe supported on four columns of wood richly carved. It performed a revolution on its axis, showing the stars known in the time of Ptolemy, about A.D. 140. These stars, to the number of 1,020, were grouped in forty-eight constellations, represented by as many figures. Two circles, one carrying the sun and the other the moon, turned round the globe, the first in twenty-four hours, the second in the space of about twenty-five hours.

Immediately behind the celestial globe there was a large wooden disc, in which was painted a calendar for the space of a century, the months, the days, the Dominical letter, the names of the saints, and the dates of the principal movable feasts. The calendar made an entire revolution every year. The statues of Apollo and Diana, placed on two sides of the disc, pointed out, with their sceptres, the one the day of the year, the other the corresponding day at the end of six months. The central part of the calendar was immovable; on it were represented the countries of Germany situated along the Rhine, and the topographical plan of the city of Strasburg.

The compartments on each side of the calendar were occupied by large panels upon which were painted the principal eclipses of the sun and moon visible in the northern hemisphere, and answering to the interval of thirty-two years from 1573 to 1605.

Above the calendar there were seen in the clouds the seven pagan divinities that have given their names to planets, and afterwards to the days of the week. These allegorical figures, seated in cars, each one drawn by the animals which mythology assigns to that particular divinity, showed themselves successively on the days which were sacred to them. On Sunday, Apollo was seen, this day being dedicated to the sun. The ancients name it *Dies solis* (the day of the sun), and the Christians the Lord's day *(Dies Dominica)*, whence is derived the French word, *Dimanche*, for Sunday. A representation of Diana was shown on the second day, which was called *Dies luna* (day of the moon) — *Lundi* — Monday. Mars, the god of war, appeared on *(Mardi)* Tuesday, the English word being derived from *Tuesco*, the Saxon name of the god of war. The fourth day was represented by Mercury, the messenger of Olympus; French, *Mercredi;* English, Wednesday (the latter being derived from *Wodin*, the Saxon name of the same deity). The following day *Dies Jovis*, Jupiter's day; French, *Jeudi;* English, Thursday (derived from *Thor*, the Saxon name of Jupiter). Venus succeeded on Friday (which in English is derived from *Friga*, the saxon name of the goddess Venus). Saturn, the god of Time, came on Saturday, to close the Olympian procession.

Immediately above the divinities of the week was erected a gallery, in the middle of which a small dial plate indicated the quarter-hours and the minutes, the hours being represented upon the astrolabe; at the sides of the dial plate were seated two genii, of which the one placed on the right raised a sceptre each time the hour was to strike, and of which the other at the same moment turned upside down an hour glass which he held in one hand, turning it always in the same direction. An astrolabe, constructed according to Ptolemy's system, occupied the greater part of the middle story, in the interior of which was contained the wheel work of the clock. Six pointers, bearing the same number of planets, indicated, upon twenty-four divisions of the astronomical day, the movements of these heavenly bodies; one pointer, larger than the others and terminated by a sun, finished in twenty-four hours an entire revolution round a small map of the world placed in the central part of a large dial plate, which was ornamented at the same time by the circles of a horoscope and by the twelve signs of the zodiac. The upper part of the astrolabe was crowned with the phases of the moon. There was visible a small dial plate cut in its lower part by two semicircles, behind which the moon, represented by a golden disc, disappeared at the time of the new moon, and came out from day to day to show successively a quarter part of its orb, till it presented to view its entire disc, at the time of full moon.

At the third story of the clock there was a platform, upon which were fixed four small statues representing the four periods of life — infancy, youth, manhood, and old age; these figures struck the quarter-hours upon cymbals.

Above this platform was suspended the bell intended for sounding the hours. Two figures stood beside this bell; the one was Death under the form of a skeleton, the other represented Christ, having in one hand the cross and the palm branch. At the instant the hour ought to strike, the Saviour came forward, and the skeleton drew back; but hardly had this movement taken place when Christ retreated precipitately, and Death advanced in the same way, to strike on the bell the number of strokes required. This movement was repeated as many times as there were strokes in the hour.

The turret, placed on the left of the principal edifice, contained the weights of the clock, as well as the machinery intended for the cock which was perched on the summit of this turret. This cock (the only piece which was preserved from the first clock, called the clock of the three kings) crowed at first daily, at noon, flapping its wings and opening its beak; but having been struck with lightning in 1640, it was made to crow only on Sundays and feast days. It ceased crowing entirely in 1789, at the time when overwhelming attention bestowed upon the great events that were taking place caused it to be completely forgotten.

THIRD STRASBURG CLOCK

At length it was evident that some reconstruction was necessary. After considerable debate, the necessary work was entrusted to Jean Baptiste Schwilgue, who entered on his task in 1838, and completed it about the middle of 1842. On the 2nd of October of that year the life of the resuscitated marvel was solemnly inaugurated. Some of the former actions were altered or omitted, and fresh ones added, the greater part of the movement being entirely new, for only in some few cases was a restoration of the former mechanism practicable.

The structure of the second clock was retained to encase the mechanism with but slight alteration. It is over 20 ft. in height, and is surmounted by a remarkably handsome dome, as shown in Fig. 30. On the right is a spiral staircase, by means of which the various galleries are reached.

The motions now are briefly as follows:— On the floor level is a celestial globe, indicating sidereal time. In its motion round its axis the globe carries with it the circles that surround it — namely, the equator, the ecliptic, the solstitial and equinoctial colures, while the meridian and horizon circles remain motionless, so that there are shown the rising and setting, as well as the passage over the meridian of Strasburg, of all stars that are visible to the naked eye, and which appear above the horizon. Behind the celestial globe is the calendar; on a metallic band, 9 in. wide and 30 ft. in circumference, are the months, the days of the month, Dominical letters, fixed and movable feast days. The band is shifted at midnight, and a statue of Apollo points out the day of the month and the name of the saint corresponding to that day. The internal part of the annular band indicates true solar time; the rising and setting of the sun; the diurnal motion of the moon round the earth, and its passage over the meridian; the phases of the moon, and the eclipses of the sun and moon. Adjacent compartments are devoted to a perpetual calendar, solar and lunar cycles, and other periodic recurrences, solar and lunar equations, &c. Above the calendar appear allegorical figures, seated in chariots, and representing the days of the week. These chariots, drawn by such animals as are assigned as attributes of the divinities, run on a circular iron railway and appear each in order.

The dial for showing mean solar time is in the gallery above, called the Gallery of Lions. A genius stands on each side of the dial. The one on the left strikes the first note of each quarter-hour with a sceptre he holds in his hand, the second note being struck by one of the four ages in a still higher gallery, as will be described presently. At the completion of each sixty minutes the genius on the right of the dial reverses an hour glass filled with red sand.

The story above is occupied by a planetarium, in which the revolutions of the planets are represented upon a large dial plate.

An iron framed 'Gothic' clock, presumably 16th century, with architectural buttress type corner standards, and open leaf tracery for the sides of the case, horizontal verge escapement, two trains, superior bell struck by a hammer, mounted outside the case.

Although clocks of this type are not too uncommon, it is not yet clear that they are all genuine. Most probably clocks, like architecture and other art forms, were produced during the 18th and 19th centuries in medieval form in order to satisfy the taste for Gothic revival. There is however little evidence available and until the subject is investigated more fully, little definite can be said. Christie, Manson and Woods Ltd.

Above the planetarium, and upon a star-decked sky, is a globe devoted to showing the phases of the moon.

Next come movable figures representing the four ages, one of which in turn appears and gives upon a bell the second stroke of each quarter of an hour. At the first quarter a child strikes the bell with a rattle; a youth in the form of a hunter strikes it with an arrow at the half-hour; at the third quarter the blows are given by a warrior with his sword; at the fourth quarter an old man produces the notes with his crutch. When he has retired a figure of Death appears and strikes the hour with a bone.

In the upper apartment is a figure of Christ; and when Death strikes the hour of noon the twelve Apostles pass before the feet of their Master, bowing as they do so. Then Christ makes the sign of the cross. During the procession of the Apostles, the cock perched at the top of the weight-turret flaps his wings, ruffles his neck, and crows three times.

In addition to the mean time dial in the gallery, there is one, 17 ft. in diameter, above the principal entrance to the cathedral.

A clock with performing automata and calendar register was in 1405 erected in the church of St Mary at Lübeck. Doubtless it has been much altered since that time; but in 1820, from the description of Downes, it was in going order, as it is still, I am told. Downes also described another extraordinary clock of much later date which is in the Dome Church at Lübeck. The full account just given of the Strasburg clocks will suffice as an example of ingenuity displayed in this direction.

A short time ago in the *Jewelers' Circular-Weekly* there appeared a masterly analysis of ancient Oriental methods of recording the progression of days and seasons, by Mr Daniel Arthur, of New York. Under the title of "The Calendar Concept and its Evolution" this has been issued in book form, and by permission of Mr Arthur I reproduce in Fig. 31 an engraving of a remarkably interesting example showing the early Oriental conception of using the heavenly motions as day counters, and how the sidereal month was formed. The moon's path is divided into twenty-eight mansions, or "halting" places. The sun is regarded as a great clock hand making a daily sweep around the sky, its progress being marked off by "Kih" or double-hour discs, twelve in number, each having an animal name. The "Yin" discs or night hours are dark, the sunrise and sunset hours grey, while the sunlit hours of day are white. These "Yang Kih," or bright hours, average longer than the "Yin Kih," or black hours of the night. The central dark hour is "rat" (midnight), while the central bright hour is "horse" (noon). "Dragon" and "snake" constitute the forenoon known as "before-horse," while "sheep" and "monkey" are afternoon hours ("after-horse"). Particulars relating to the arrangement of these hour marks will be given in Chapter VI. under the head of Japanese clocks. The moon hand is shown as going in the opposite direction to its apparent motion. The lower of the two arrows shows normal moon direction, the upper one how it moves in the mansions with a left-hand motion. Each time the sun-hand gets to the evening hours, or near "dog," the moon-hand will be in a new mansion of heaven. Mr Richard S.

ANCIENT ORIENTAL CALENDAR CLOCK

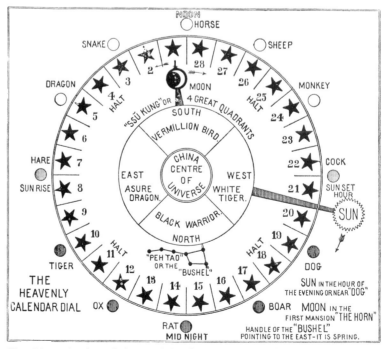

Fig. 31. — Ancient Oriental Calendar Timepiece, of Heavenly Calendar Dial.

Geoghagen, formerly Chinese scholar of Oxford, has pointed out that the 4th, 11th, 18th, and 25th mansions invariably correspond to what are now our western Sundays. At first in these calendar timepieces the days were distinguished by titles instead of numbers, their English equivalents being "the horn" which was the first mansion, representing the frontier gate of heaven; then in order came the Neck, Bottom, the Room, Heart, the Tail, the Sieve, the Bushel, the Ox, Woman, the Void, Danger, the House, the Wall, Astride, Wound, Stomach, Pleiades, the End, Bristling Up, Mixture, the Well, the Ghost, the Willow, the Star, Drawn Bow, the Wing, Crossbar. Of the "Ssu Kung," or four great quadrants, the first is named Azure Dragon, the second Black Warrior, the third White Tiger, and the last Vermilion Bird. The third hand, or season indicator, is the group of stars which we call Ursa Major (Chinese name "Peh Tao"). In Dr Carus' "Chinese Thought" we are told that when the handle of this "big dipper" points to the east at nightfall it is spring throughout the land; when to south it is summer, to the west it is autumn, and when north it is winter.

In the Metropolitan Museum of Art, New York, is an Oriental calendar clock on the dial of which are depicted the twenty-eight groups of stars, "Erhshih-pa Su" is the Chinese name for them (the twenty-eight mansions of heaven). These constellations vary a great deal in degrees of width, and were selected in prehistoric times to guide the eye to single stars of about the proper distances apart.

While this book is in the hands of the printers I learn of the accidental death of Mr Daniel Arthur, an event which may be regarded as a world-wide loss. He advocated uniform months of twenty-eight days, thirteen months, and one *dies-non* in the year. The days would then recur on the same date of each month.

The Hans of Jena clock, already referred to, is shown in Fig. 32, which is reproduced from Dubois' work. The legend is that Hans of Jena, represented by a monstrous head of bronze, is to be tantalised for three centuries by the pilgrim who presents to the open mouth a golden apple as the clock strikes, but quickly withdraws it before the mouth can be closed. The figure of an angel on the right raises its eyes and shakes the bell as each blow of the hour is struck.

Whatever variations were made in the form or size of clocks during the fifteenth century, the principle of the mechanism remained unaltered, and such as were constructed appear to have been mostly for public buildings or persons of exalted position.

The fact that small clocks and portable clocks are mentioned as existing in the fourteenth century, seems to have led to the supposition that the mainspring as a motor was then in use, but such a conclusion is unwarranted. Most of these descriptions, or rather references, though interesting, are of the vaguest character, for instance, among the ancient inventories quoted by M. de Laborde are "A.D. 1380, a clock of silver, entirely without iron"; and "a clock of white silver for placing on a column." In 1381, "l'oreloge" of Charles VI. being out of order, a smith from Senlis, named Robert d'Origny, who repaired it, received sixteen sols parisis. The accounts of the Duke of Burgundy recite that in 1407 a smith (fevre) named "Jehan d'Alemaigne," supplied a movement for a small clock (petite orloge) to be placed in the chamber of "Madame."

Fig. 32. — Hans of Jena.

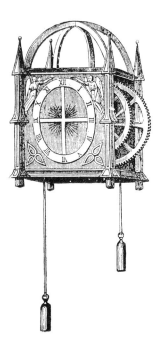

Fig. 33. — Chamber Clock, Fifteenth Century. Bib. Nat. Paris.

ANNE BOLEYN'S CLOCK

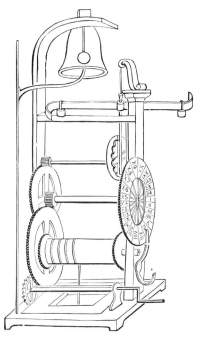

Fig. 34. — Fifteenth Century Clock from Italian tarsia-work.

Sir John Paston, in the course of a letter written in the spring of 1469, says: "I praye you speke wt Harcourt off the Abbeye ffor a lytell clokke whyche I sent him by James Gressham to amend and yt ye woll get it off him an it be redy, and send it me, and as ffor mony for his labour, he hath another clok of myn whiche St Thoms Lyndes, God have hys sowle, gave me. He maye kepe that tyll I paye him. This klok is my Lordys Archebysshopis but late him not wote off it."

The appended Fig. 33, from the Bibliothèque Nationale at Paris, purports to represent the remains of a fifteenth century chamber clock. It is pretty evident there was originally a bell at the top of the case, and perhaps a hand to indicate the hour. It is not, however, certain there was a hand, for some of the early clocks had revolving dials. In the South Kensington Museum there is on a "tarsia," or inlaid wood panel of Italian late fifteenth century production, a representation of a clock with a revolving ring, on which the twenty-four hours are marked, the current hour being indicated by a fixed pointer, as seen in Fig. 34. The whole panel represents an open cupboard, in which there are, besides the clock, a flagon, a chalice, a cross, &c.; so one may infer that the clock was of comparatively small size, and of course of older date than the panel, which careful comparison by the experts of the Museum fixes at *certainly not later than* 1500. The action of the winding work is obscure, but with that exception the construction of the clock is tolerably clear.

In the *Bibliothèque de l'Arsenal* at Paris is a MS. prayer book containing two small pictures of chamber clocks called, from the family name of the person for whom the book was executed, the "Heures de Bossu." It dates from about 1490-1500.

In the corridor at Windsor Castle is a clock which is said to have been presented to Anne Boleyn on her wedding morning by Henry VIII. It is rather over 4 in. square and 10 in. high, exclusive of the bracket on which it is mounted, as shown in Fig. 35. It was purchased on behalf of Queen Victoria for £110. 5s. when Horace Walpole's collection at Strawberry Hill was sold, and was then described as "a clock of silver gilt richly chased, engraved and ornamented with fleurs-de-lys, little heads, &c. On the top sits a lion holding the arms of England, which are also on the sides." This description is not quite correct, for the case is of copper gilt; the weights are of lead cased in copper, gilt and engraved; on the one visible in the engraving are the initial letters of Henry and Anne with true lovers' knots above and below; on the other H.A. alone; at the top of each is "Dieu et mon droit"; at the bottom "the most happye!" The movement at present in the case has brass wheels, a crown wheel escapement and a short pendulum; though not modern it is certainly later than the middle of the sixteenth century. A sight of the clock evoked from Harrison Ainsworth a reflection to which but few will take exception. "This love token of enduring affection remains the same after three centuries, but four years after it was given the object of Henry's eternal love was sacrificed on the scaffold. The clock still goes! It should have stopped for ever when Anne Boleyn died." And whether by accident or design, though the weights are suspended below the supporting bracket, the mechanism, which appears to be in fairly good condition, is now silent, and the hand remains stationary. There is no record as to the maker of this interesting relic, but at this time most of the "orologes" were the production

60

of foreign artists, judging from the names quoted in State Papers of the period.

In the "Privy Purse Expenses of Henry VIII., from 1529 to 1532," edited by Sir Harris Nicolas, it is recorded that in July 1530 £15 was paid to the Frenchman who sold the king "ij clocks at Oking." In the following month was paid to "a Frenchman called Drulardy, for iij dyalls and a clokk for the King's Grace the sum of £15." In December of the same year £19. 6s. 8d. was "paid to Vincent Keney clok maker for xj clokks and dialls." So many payments within a brief period warrant the assumption that clocks were a form of present favoured by his Majesty.

In the "Sixth Report of the Historical Manuscripts Commission" mention is made of an agreement, dated 1599, between one Michael Neuwers, a clockmaker, and Gilbert, Earl of Shrewsbury, for the construction of a clock. "It is agreed that Michael should make a striking clock about the bigness of that which he made for the Earl six years past; it is to be made by the last of December next. The cover or case of it to be of brass, very well gilt, with open breaking through all over, with a small fine hand like an arrow, clenly and strongly made, the . . . or white dial plate to be made of French crown gold, and the figures to show the hour and the rest to be enamelled the fynelyest and daintyest that can be, but no other colour than blew, white, and carnalian; the letters to be somewhat larger than ordinary; the price of the clock must be £15, which makes with the earnest already given £16, but the circle I must pay for, besides the gold which shall make it; the sides of the brass case must not be sharp, but round, and the case very curiously made."

Fig. 35. — Anne Boleyn's Clock.

The Michael Neuwers here referred to was probably Michael Nouwen, a sixteenth century horologist, several specimens of whose work survive. That the Earl of Shrewsbury was somewhat of a connoisseur of time-keepers, as well as an authority on horological matters, is borne out by the following letter, dated 1611, from him to Sir Michael Hickes, which is preserved in the Lansdowne MSS. at the British Museum:—

"I perceived by you to-day that you understood My Lord Treasurer's design was to have a watch, but I conceaved he wysshed a stryknge clock, made lyke a Watch, to stande oppon a Cubbart, & suche a one (though no new one, & yet under a dozen years ould) I have found oute, & send you by this bearer, which I pray you deliver to his Lordship from me, & tell him that I am very well perswaded of the truth of it, or else I should be ashamed to send him so gross & rude a piece as this is, & if I hadd thought his Lordship could have well forborne it but for four or five days longer, I would have bestowed a new case for it, for this is a very bad one. If his Lordship would not have it stryke, either in the dayes or nights, the striker may be forborne to be wounde up, and so the Watch being wounde up it will go alone. It will goe twenty-six houres, but I wysh it may be wounde up every mornyng or nyght about eight or nine o'clock, which will be sufficient until the next day or nyght at the same tyme."

Among the State Papers of the time of James I. there is an original letter, dated 4th August 1609, addressed by Sir Julius Caesar to the clerks of the signet, requesting them to prepare a warrant to pay £300 to Hans Niloe, a Dutchman, for a clock with music and motions. And on the 17th of the same month Sir Julius wrote from the Strand to Salisbury, stating that he

Front and back of the clock from the Hospital Santa Cruz, Barcelona, commissioned from Emanuel Boffill, a carpenter, in 1732. Three trains (going, hours, quarters), set side by side with the going train placed centrally. Bird cage-type posted frame secured by tenon joints but with the uprights fixed by double tenons hooking over and into the cross bars, the whole being secured with dovetail wedges flush to the bar. Original anchor escapement (replaced and repositioned) which can be disengaged from the escape wheel by raising a shutter covering the pivot holes of the anchor arbor, and sliding it away. Quarter striking release by a star wheel and transverse lever, hour strike by internal locking plate. The clock provides an excellent example of the way in which additions and changes are made to existing mechanisms, and has been described in detail by G. Berman, An Essay on Church Clocks, London, 1974.

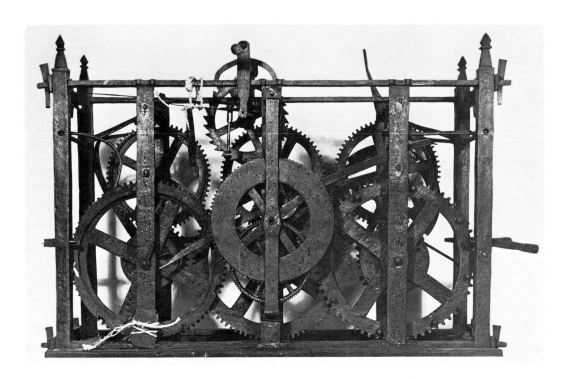

Strap work turret clock, unsigned, c.1765. Steel with brass wheels and bearings, wood barrels. The unusual frame consists of six vertical straps rigidly bolted to the base of two inverted U-pieces joined by three cross pieces. Three further cross pieces link the top. There are two trains, an anchor escapement embracing ten teeth and locking plate strike.

This clock is almost identical with one built for the church of St Mary, East Bergholt, Suffolk, by Nathaniel Hedge the fourth and installed in 1764. See Bernard Mason, Clock and Watch making in Colchester England, *London, 1969, pp.140, 146-7, 342.*

was pressed by Hans Niloe for the £300 for his clock.

In "A true certificat of the names of the Straungers residing and dwellinge within the City of London," &c., taken by direction of the Privy Council, by letters dated 7th September 1618, it is stated that in the ward of Farringdon Within was then living "Barnaby Martinot, clockmaker; *b.* in Paris; a Roman Catholicque." In Portsoken ward was living "John Goddard, clockmaker; lodger and servant with Isack Sunes in Houndsditch; *b.* at Paris, in Fraunce; heer three years; a papist; yet hee hath the oath of allegiance to the king's supremacy, & doth acknowledg the king for his soveraigne dureing his abode in England; & is of the Romish church."

CLOCK AT HAMPTON
COURT PALACE

Derham gives the numbers of the wheels and pinions of a large clock which appears to have been erected at Hampton Court Palace about 1540. This date is assumed from the marks N.O. or N.C. and the figures 1540 which were engraved on a bar of the original wrought-iron framework. If the letters were N.C., they may have referred to Nicholas Cratzer. In 1711 the clock was repaired by Langley Bradley. The original and curious dial of the clock is on the eastern side of the gate-tower in the second quadrangle. It is composed of three separate copper discs of different sizes, with a common centre, but revolving at varying rates. The smallest of these is 3 ft. 3½ in. in diameter, and in the middle of this is a slightly projected globe, painted to represent the earth. The quarters marked on the centre disc by thick lines are numbered with large figures, and round the edge this disc is divided into twenty-four parts, a red arrow painted on the second disc pointing to these figures and showing at once the quarter in which the moon is, and the time of southing. Next to the figure of the earth in this centre disc, a circular hole, 10 in. in diameter, allows a smaller disc travelling behind to show the phases of the moon. On the second disc, 4 ft. 1½ in. in diameter, but of which only the outer rim is seen, are twenty-nine divisions, and a triangular pointer, projecting from behind the central disc, shows the moon's age in days. The largest of the three discs is 7 ft. 10 in. in diameter. There are many circles painted on so much of the rim of this as is seen, the inner, or, following the order above observed and proceeding from the centre, the first circle, giving the names of the months, the second the days of the months (only twenty-eight for February), the third the signs of the zodiac, and on the rim, with 30° for each space filled by a sign, a circle divided into 360 parts. A long pointer with a gilded figure of the sun attached, projecting from behind the second disc, shows on this third or outmost disc of the dial the day of the month and the position of the sun in the ecliptic. This pointer performs another duty, acting like the hour hand of an ordinary clock, and showing the time of day or night as it passes the twenty-four figures — two sets of twelve — painted on the stonework within which the dial revolves. The diameter of this outer immovable circle on the stone is 9 ft. 8 in., and the characters for the hours are Roman numerals, 9 in. in length.

In 1575 a payment appears to have been made to George Gaver, serjeant painter, for painting the great dial at Hampton Court Palace, containing hours of the day and night, the course of the sun and moon, and doubtless

Fig. 37. — Planetary Clock of Oronce Fine.

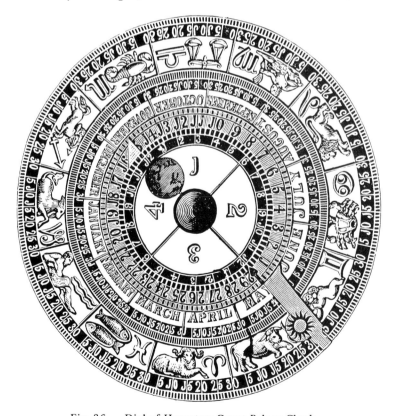

Fig. 36. — Dial of Hampton Court Palace Clock.

64

since that time the same necessary restoration has been often undertaken. In 1835 an extraordinary transposition was made, for the works of the old clock were removed, and have since disappeared. In their place was fixed a movement with the following inscription: "This clock, originally made for the Queen's Palace in St. James's Palace, and for many years in use there, was, A.D. 1835, by command of his Majesty King William IV., altered and adapted to suit Hampton Court Palace by B. L. Vulliamy, clockmaker to the king"; and on another plate on the clock – "Vulliamy, London, No. 352, A.D. 1799." Worse than all, the precious dial was taken down and stowed away in a workshop at the palace, the gap left being filled by a painted board. In 1879, however, a new and sufficient clock movement was provided, the dial found, restored by Mr James Thwaites, and replaced. It now shows the hours, the motions of the sun and moon, &c., with certainly as much regularity as formerly, and as well as N.O. or N.C. could have desired. For the appended sketch of the dial I am indebted to Mr Thwaites.

Oronce Fine, mathematician to Francis I. and Henry II. of France, devised what is often spoken of as a planetary clock, which is shown in Fig. 37. The construction of this machine was begun in 1553, and after seven years, when it was completed, it was presented to the Cardinal de Lorraine. Afterwards it was placed in the library of St Geneviève at Paris. It is in the form of a pentagonal column 17 in. in diameter and 6 ft. high. The movement concealed in the pillar is composed of over one hundred wheels, and actuated by a weight which falls 1 ft. per day, and was calculated to keep the apparatus going for forty-eight hours.

CLOCK BY ISAAC HABRECHT

At the top of the main staircase of the British Museum is a most curious clock, which was bequeathed to the nation by Mr Octavius Morgan. It was constructed in 1587 by Isaac Habrecht, who made the second famous clock mechanism at Strasburg. It is about 4 ft. in height, and the general design is the same as that of the left tower of the Strasburg clock, and on the sides of both are figures of the three Fates, Clotho, Lachesis, and Atropos, and each is surmounted by a figure of the cock of St Peter, which at the stroke of the hour flaps its wings and crows. It had originally a balance as a controller, for which a pendulum was subsequently substituted. The quarters are struck by four figures, representing the ages of man, and the hour by a figure of Death. On a lower balcony is a seated figure of the Virgin and Child, before whom passes a circle of angels, who, as they are set in movement by the striking of the clock, are caused to make an obeisance in front of the Virgin. Below this, the gods of the days of the week perform their circuit, each driving in a chariot, while the dials on the lower stages fulfil the more useful functions of indicating the hour, the phases of the moon, the feasts of the Church, &c. The case is of gilt copper, with well-engraved figures and ornamental designs, perhaps by Tobias Stimmer, who was employed to decorate the original clock at Strasburg. The history of this clever piece of mechanism is somewhat curious, though it rests upon slender foundations. It is stated that Pope Sixtus V. was so pleased with the Strasburg clock that he ordered Habrecht to make one of the same kind. The timekeeper of which a view is given in Fig. 38 was the result, and it remained at the Vatican for two hundred years. Its next appearance was in Holland, where it was in the possession of the king; from Holland it was brought to London and exhibited about 1850.

The movement of the Westminster clock (Big Ben) made by Frederick Dent to designs by E.B. Denison (Lord Grimthorpe), and a specification by Sir George Airy, the Astronomer Royal. The clock was ordered in February 1852, beginning to strike the hours in July 1859 and the quarters in September 1859. The final cost was £4,080, and the frame is 15 ft. 6 in. by 4 ft. 7 in. The escapement is a double three legged gravity escapement, and since it takes 20 minutes to wind the going train, a special maintaining power was devised. A detailed description of the clock, and a lively, if somewhat biased account of its construction, is given by Denison in later editions of his A Rudimentary Treatise on Clocks and Watches and Bells (1st edition London, 1850). Crown Copyright – reproduced with permission of the Controller of Her Majesty's Stationery Office.

Fig. 38. — Clock by Isaac Habrecht.

Fig. 39. — Lyons Clock.

In the royal palace of Rosenborg, Copenhagen, is a similar clock by Isaac Habrecht, and at the Historical Museum, Dresden, is one, also very similar, which was made for the Elector Augustus between 1563 and 1568 by the astronomer-horologist Baldwein, of Marburg, and H. Bucher, under the direct superintendence of the learned Landgraf William IV. of Hesse Cassel.

LYONS CLOCK The cathedral of Lyons contains a remarkable specimen of complicated horological work, which is in the form of a tower 40 ft. high. The original clock was constructed by a mechanician named Nicholas Lippius, of Basle, who completed it in 1598. Guillaume Nourisson in 1660 repaired the structure, and among other alterations introduced a large oval dial. Not only was the outline of the dial oval, but also the graduated and figured band, which was divided into sixty to represent the minutes, and with distinct marks for the quarter-hours. From a description of this curious clock published in 1677 are taken the accompanying engravings, which show how the hand dilated and contracted as it travelled around the dial in order that one tip might always indicate the minute and the other the quarter-hour.

Fig. 40 is the exterior of the hand stretched to its maximum length. As

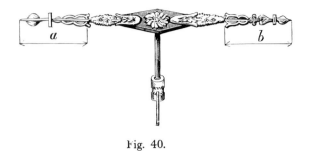

Fig. 40.

Fig. 41.

the hand approaches the narrower part of the oval, the inner socket-like ends of *a* and *b* pass over the extremities of the fixed central portion.

Fig. 41 is a view of the central part with the ornamental covering removed.

Fixed to the centre part is a cannon pinion driven by a bevelled pinion which also drives another pinion, the stalk of which passes through the cannon to the upper part of the hand, and there engages with a double crank attached by means of connecting rods with the solid core of the parts *a* and *b*.

This dial is on one side of the tower. On the front are two dial plates as shown in the engraving in Fig. 39. The lower one is a calendar, and the other an astrolabe. The calendar is divided into 365 divisions, on which are fixed crowns. Each crown represents the day of the month in the calendar, and the name of the saint, when the anniversary of the latter is due. The names of the months are on the circumference. The circle forming the centre is divided into sixty-six years, and moves one division forward on the 31st of every December. The inscriptions about the religious festivals, &c., are in handwriting on parchment. The astrolabe is exceedingly ingenious. Thereon all the zodiacal and other astronomical signs are displayed, the solar and lunar movements, &c. In the upper part of the tower are various automatic pieces. There is a gilt niche in which appear representations of the days of the week. For Sunday the symbol is the Resurrection; Monday, Death; Tuesday and Wednesday, Saints Stephen and John; Thursday, the Sacrament; Friday, the Passion; Saturday, the Virgin. At midnight, the statue that has finished duty cedes the place to that for the coming day. On the left is an angel which turns a sand glass every hour; on the right, another angel beats the measure with head, hand, and foot, as the clock strikes each hour. Above all is a large space, where the Almighty in the scene of the Annunciation bestows His benediction. The cupola terminates the monument and covers the bells, which play several religious chants and the *Ave Maria*. There is the figure of a beadle who appears, and marches round the gallery, to inspect, as it were, the bells.

In 1895, Chateau, of Paris, thoroughly repaired the clock, by direction of the French Government.

VENICE CLOCK The first clock in the Square of St Mark, at Venice, the work of Giovanni P. Rainaldi, of Reggio, and his son Carlo, was completed in 1495. Of its construction but little is known. Its successor, the monumental timekeeper shown in Fig. 42, was erected at the Grand Piazza early in the seventeenth

Fig. 42. — The Original Venice Clock.

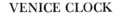

The interior astronomical dial of the Wells Cathedral clock with its associated automata. The dial is arranged according to the Ptolemaic system with a central earth. The age and phase of the moon are shown and a gilt sun indicates the hour on a 24-hour dial. The minute dial is presumably a later addition. Above the dial are four wooden horsemen, two of whom joust at each hour. One of each pair is pivoted through the knees so that, when hit by his adversary, he falls backwards and is carried away by his horse. The clock movement which controls these motions also controls those of three jacks, placed on the outside of the north transept, which date from the fifteenth century. In the Triforium above the clock-face sits a large oak figure in a sentry-box known locally as Jack Blandifer. He strikes the hours on the bell in front of him using the hammer held in his right hand. He also holds a hammer in his left hand and the left elbow is jointed but does not move. With each stroke of the hour-bell he slightly turns his head as if listening to the note. He also strikes bells at the hours and quarters with his heels. The original movement is illustrated on p.39.

Based on information from The Wells Clock by R.P. Howgrave-Graham, edited by L.S. Colchester. Courtesy The Friends of Wells Cathedral.

century. There is a large dial showing the hours, and above is a balcony of gilt lattice surrounding an image of the Blessed Virgin, seated between two doors overlaid with gold. Evelyn, in his "Memoirs," under date 1645, speaks of this "admirable clock, celebrated next to that of Strasburgh for its many movements; amongst which about twelve and six — which are their houres of Ave Maria, when all the towne are on their knees — come forth the 3 kings led by a starr, and passing by ye image of Christ in his Mother's armes do their reverence, and enter into ye clock by another doore." Another writer in 1841 remarked that at a certain period of every year, on the Feast of the Ascension, and fourteen days afterwards, as the hour struck, the door on the right hand opened and an angel with a trumpet issued forth, followed by three Eastern kings, each of whom, as he passed the Virgin, raised his crown, bowed, and then disappeared through the other door. The hours are struck by two bronze giants on a large bell which surmounts the structure.

Alterations to the movements appear to have been made from time to time, the most recent in 1859. The clock as it now exists is shown in Fig. 43, reproduced from a photograph taken by Mr Julian Tripplin. Above the balcony is seated a figure of the Virgin Mary, and the doors on each side are utilised to exhibit by means of jumping figures the hour and minute. On the left facing the structure appear Roman numerals representing the last completed hour, and on the right the number of minutes past, these figures changing automatically every five minutes.

Fig. 43. — Venice Clock as now.

Chapter III

Portable Timekeepers

Fig. 44. — Canister case; covers pressed on back and front (no hinged joints).

Fig. 45. [side view Fig. 44.]

IT WAS NOT until driving weights depending from cords or chains were superseded by a more compact motor, which allowed small timekeepers to be readily transported from place to place, that they became objects of particular interest, the acquisition of which was sought in fashionable circles.

The Hon. Daines Barrington, in vol. v. of the *Archaeologia,* speaks of a watch as belonging to Robert Bruce, who died in 1328. This watch was of small size, with an enamelled case, a piece of transparent horn over the dial, and had engraved on the plate "Robertus Bruce," in Roman characters. Though it passed current for some time at the end of the eighteenth century, and eventually became the property of George III., carefully examination revealed the fact that the inscription was undoubtedly a recent addition, and the watch a production of three centuries later than Bruce. Except that the quotation of Barrington's statement is perennial, it would be hardly worth while to refer to so clumsy an imposition. A watch now in the Schloss collection is, I believe, the one referred to. It will be illustrated in Chapter IV.

It is now generally conceded that the production of a portable timekeeper was accomplished by Peter Henlein or Hele, a clockmaker of Nuremberg, who was born in 1480 and died in 1542. He, shortly after 1500, used a long ribbon of steel tightly coiled round a central spindle to maintain the motion of the mechanism. The invention has been ascribed to Habrecht and others, at a much later date, but Johannes Coccleus, who was born in 1470, in his commentary dated 1511, accurately describes a striking watch and distinctly credits its introduction to Henlein. Although portable timekeepers were not in general use for a long period afterwards, a taste for table clocks and watches was at once apparent among wealthy people, who delighted in the possession of curious novelties.

The earliest watches are scarcely to be distinguished from small table clocks. The case was a cylindrical box, generally of metal, chased and gilt, usually with a hinged lid on one side to enclose the dial, the lid being engraved, and, as a rule, pierced with an aperture over each hour, through which the position of the hand might be seen. Most of the watches were provided with a bell, on which in some cases the hours were sounded in regular progression; in other instances the bell was merely utilised for an alarum. When furnished with a bell the case was, as a rule, worked *à jour* to emit the sound. Cases in which the covers over the dial and back are quite flat, and the edges of which project over the middle of the body, are often

Fig. 46. — Cover closed.

Fig. 47. — Cover open.

Fig. 49.

Left: Fig. 48. — Tambourine case, Jointed Cover.

Right: Fig. 50

Fig. 51.

spoken of as tambourine or drum cases. A canister case is understood to be one in which the covers are not hinged to the body of the case, but simply pressed on in the same way as is the cover of a canister.

Illustrations of dissimilar examples are appended. All are worth examination. In Fig. 49, to form twelve apertures through which the position of the hand might be seen, and to connect the outer part of the cover with the centre, are six pairs of male and female figures joining hands, well carved with very pretty effect. A happier combination of ornament and utility would be difficult to conceive.

At the South Kensington Museum is a circular table clock, about 3 in. in diameter, in an engraved brass case having a perforated dome surmounted by a small horizontal dial. On the inside of the bottom cover is inscribed, "P. H. Nor .. 1505." This led to the supposition that "Nor" stood for Norimbergae, "at Nuremberg," and that the clock was the handiwork of Hele. The plates of the movement are of steel, and the piece appears to be evidently a production of the sixteenth century, but the balance and its accessories are comparatively modern, and it would be unsafe to rely on the inscription as conclusive evidence of authenticity.

A somewhat similar piece, of rather later date, is shown in Fig. 52, which is about two-thirds of the actual size of the clock.

The square table clock of which two views, Figs. 53 and 54, are appended, is, judging from the engraving and general construction, a sixteenth century production. It is furnished with the primitive cross-bar balance. There is no indication of the maker or his place of abode.

On very early productions the maker's name is exceptional; initials were a more usual signature, and occasionally a work stamp is to be found, from which it may be possible to ascertain the locality of manufacture. Some towns had a distinctive trade or work mark, that for Nuremberg being the letter N in a circle, for Augsburg a pineapple, for Berne a bear, and for Mayence a wheel. Sebastian Lehr, clockmaker to the city of Nuremberg, who died in 1556, may be taken to have been an eminent craftsman. Among others of the period of whom mention is made is Hans Gruber, clockmaker and master of the Locksmiths' Guild about the middle of the sixteenth century.

Fig. 52.

Fig. 53.

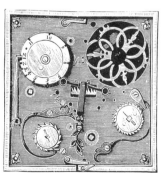

Fig. 54.

Fig. 55.

There are several specimens in the British Museum of a date between 1535 and 1570. Of two by Jeremia Metzger (or Metzker), Augsburg, one is furnished with a bow, and one is without any provision for suspending the watch. The South Kensington collection includes a circular striking and alarum clock, supported by a figure of Atlas on a pedestal of gilt brass, inscribed thus: "Jeremias . Metzger . Vrmacher . 15.60 . in Avgspvrg." A clock with complicated movements by this maker in the Vienna Treasury is dated 1564. In the same repository are two watches in cylindrical brass cases which match each other. The movements bear the letters A.S. arranged as a monogram, but there is no other indication of the maker.

Fig. 55, from the Soltykoff collection, is one of the earliest of the kind. It is unnamed, but doubtless of German make, in a brass gilt case with covers top and bottom. In the open top cover may be seen the twenty-four perforations, through which the position of the hand could be discerned. For this engraving and other illustrations of sixteenth century horology, formerly in the magnificent collection of Prince Pierre Soltykoff, I am indebted to the sumptuous descriptive quarto prepared by Pierre Dubois.

Figs. 56, 57, 58, 59, are four views of a fine mid-sixteenth century alarum watch, in a case of gilt metal, the front, back, and edge of which is perforated. On each of the covers is a bust as shown.

Fig. 56. — Front with Cover closed.

Fig. 57. — Front with Cover removed.

Fig. 58. — Edge.

Fig. 59. — Back.

74

Above: Fig. 60.

Fig. 62.

Fig. 63. — Early oval watch.

Fig. 61.

Fig. 64. — Early oval watch.

Of an early example from the Schloss collection three views are appended (Figs. 60, 61, 62). The movement is especially interesting. It is of the most primitive character, the balance for controlling the motion of the wheels being of the cross-bar type, designated by Froissard *"le foliot"* and by German writers *"waag."* Another feature, the "stackfreed," for equalising the power, will be referred to a little further on.

A large oval case, with geometrical perforations in the lid, was almost contemporaneous with the circular box form, and an oval shape, either small and plain or larger with more or less of decoration, remained in favour for over a century. An early specimen is shown in Figs. 63 and 64. The oval striking and alarum watch reproduced in Figs. 65 and 66 is sixteenth century work by Jacques Duduict, *"maitre orologier en la bonne ville de Blois,"* and is from the Soltykoff collection. It has covers back and front, on each of which is a tableau reproducing a scene in the life of Esther.

The luxury and extravagance in dress which characterised the Elizabethan period required more variety of form and colour than could be found in a

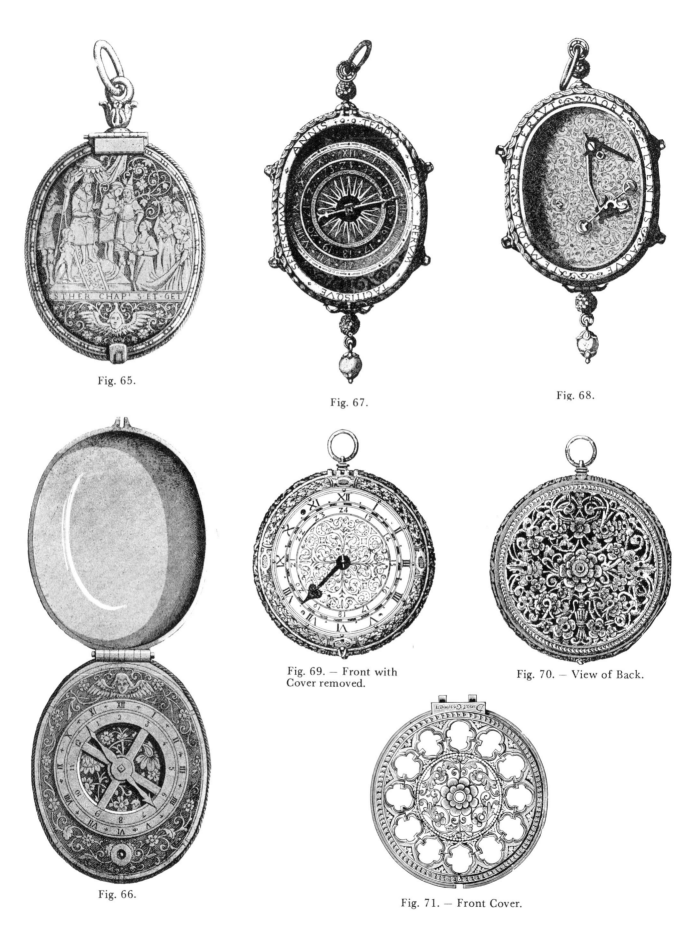

Fig. 65.

Fig. 67.

Fig. 68.

Fig. 69. — Front with
Cover removed.

Fig. 70. — View of Back.

Fig. 66.

Fig. 71. — Front Cover.

plain regular form of gold or silver, so rock crystal and other stones were often converted into cases, which were cut in the form of crosses, stars, shells, and other extraordinary fancies, while the dials and mounts were occasionally enriched with coloured enamels. The most elegant of these costly toys emanated from France, Blois being distinguished as an early seat of manufacture.

Figs. 67 and 68 represent what Dubois declared to be one of the richest productions of the kind which has survived. It is from the Soltykoff collection, oval in form, with square edges, in a case of crystal, with mountings engraved, splendidly enamelled, and further embellished with diamonds and rubies. The ball depending from the bottom of the case is a fine pearl. The dial is of gold, the borders above and below being enriched with enamel of various colours. The back plate is engraved all over with arabesques, giving a delightful effect. In the midst of the engraving may be discerned the letter N, the Nuremberg work mark. It bears no indication of the maker's name, but from the primitive *foliot* balance and other features it may safely be classed as not later than mid-sixteenth century work.

There is at the Horological Institute a print of a very old striking or clock-watch, the case of which is enriched with remarkably fine arabesque work, pierced to emit the sound. Three views of it are appended: Figs. 69, 70, 71. The dial has two hour circles, the divisions of the outer circle being marked with Roman, and those of the inner with Egyptian characters, while between the two is a circle of minute marks. I have had an opportunity of examining the watch, which is in the Schloss collection. It is 1³/₄ in. in thickness, and 3 in. in diameter; the wheels are of iron, but it has neither barrel nor fusee. There are two springs, one the motive power for timekeeping, and the other for striking, which is effected upon a broad bell occupying the whole bottom of the watch. The outer end of the mainspring appears to be attached to a pillar between the plates — an arrangement reintroduced in quite modern times for cheap clocks.

There has been lately added to the British Museum a table watch in a drum-shaped case, dating from about 1550. It is from the Zschille collection, and is shown in Fig. 72. The mechanism is very crude, without screws, and includes a *foliot* balance and "stackfreed." The movement bears, in a shield, the work mark M and a *fleur-de-lis*.

The watch case shown in Fig. 73 is interesting as a specimen of pierced chasing, probably German, dating from about 1560.

A fine striking watch in a circular table case, from the Soltykoff collection, is shown in Fig. 74. It dates from about 1575, and is by Charles Cusin, *"maitre horloger de la ville d'Autun."* The hour band is of silver and the hand of blue steel. It has covers top and bottom, the upper one pierced as shown; the solid centre is the reverse of a mounted cavalier, of which the obverse is visible when the cover is closed; this it is averred represents Henri IV., King of France and of Navarre. The under-cover, similarly pierced, contains in the centre a mounted figure, said to be a counterfeit of the son of Marie de Médicis, afterwards King of France.

The origin of the term "watch" is not very clear. It may have been taken from the Swedish *vacht,* or from the Saxon *waecca,* "to wake"; but whatever its derivation, it had not, when introduced, the signification we now attach to it, because timekeepers were not then worn in the pocket. But "watch,"

Fig. 72.

Fig. 73.

Fig. 74.

Fig. 75. — Mainspring and Barrel.

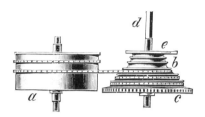

Fig. 76. — Mainspring Barrel and Fusee.
a, mainspring barrel; *b*, fusee; *c*, great wheel; *d*, winding square; *e*, snail-shaped flange.

or "clock," or "orologe," seems to have been used indifferently as a title for timekeepers, and so it is often difficult to decide whether a weight clock of large size or a very minute spring timepiece is meant. Derham, in all the editions of his book, speaks of timekeepers driven by weights as watches, reserving the work clock for parts connected with the striking.

The action of the mainspring, which still retains its place as a motor for portable timekeepers, will be understood with the aid of Fig. 75. Here, as is usually the case, the spring is contained in a circular box or barrel *c,* its inner edge being hooked on to the enlarged part of the arbor *a,* and its outer end attached to the inside of the rim of the barrel. The arbor passes through and fits easily a hole in the bottom of the barrel, and a hole in the barrel cover *e,* The spring is wound by turning the arbor, and then if the spring barrel is attached to the largest wheel of the clock, in place of the cylinder or drum from which the weight was suspended, the spring in its effort to unwind turns the barrel, and with it the wheels composing the clock train. Of course some provision must be made to prevent the spring from at once uncoiling when the arbor is released after winding, and the simplest plan is to have a ratchet wheel fixed on one end of the arbor, with which a click pivoted to the framing of the timekeeper engages. When the barrel is used in conjunction with a fusee, as will be described presently, the spring is wound by turning the barrel instead of the arbor.

But it is evident that just as the spring offered increased resistance to every successive turn of the arbor in winding, so the force transmitted by it when fully wound would be very much greater than the force exerted after the barrel had made a few turns and the spring had partially run down, and this variation of force was the cause of considerable perplexity for some time after the invention of the mainspring, for with the verge escapement variation of force means variation of timekeeping. The first contrivance applied with a view of overcoming or abating the drawback was that known as the "stackfreed." I have tried in vain to trace the derivation of this curious word, but am told it is of Persian origin. The device did not prove to be an enduring one; but it was applied to most portable timekeepers up to about 1540, and occasionally afterwards to the end of the century. It is shown in Fig. 77, which is a watch in a canister case with the back cover removed. The front and edge of the case have already been illustrated. The action of the "stackfreed" may be gathered from an examination of the engraving with the following explanation.

Fixed to the mainspring arbor above the top plate is a pinion having eight leaves. This gears with a wheel having twenty-four teeth, which do not quite fill out the circumference of the wheel, but leave a block of two spaces in width which acts as a stop to the pinion when the mainspring is wound, and after it has run down three whole turns. Fastened to the wheel is a cam, nearly concentric for about seven-eights of its circumference and indented for the remainder. There is a groove in the concentric portion of the edge, into which is pressed a roller which is pivoted at the free end of a strong curved spring. When the mainspring is fully wound the roller rests in the curved depression of the cam, and the effort required to lift the roller up the incline till it is placed upon the concentric contour absorbs so much of the force of the mainspring as to prevent banking. When the mainspring has nearly run down, the roller, in entering the depression by pressing the cam in the direction that it is moving, really aids the mainspring in its effort. Besides the stackfreed and its appurtenances may be noticed in Fig. 77 the cross-bar balance, the very small balance cock, and two hinged bolts which shut into holes in the edge of the case, and so secure the movement in position. The plates, the train wheels, stackfreed, balance-cock, and balance are all of iron or steel, and the various fastenings are made by means of pins or rivets, there being no screws used throughout. This movement is, in fact, an excellent example of the very earliest kind of portable timekeepers.

In Fig. 78, which shows a later stackfreed movement, is a point worthy of note. As a form of regulator are two banking pins of stiff bristle, which the straight arm of the balance knocks against. These are mounted on a lever which is pivoted at one end by means of a screw near the edge of the plate. The pins may be caused to approach or recede from the centre of the balance by moving the free end of the lever, and in this way the vibrations of the balance would be retarded or quickened. An engraved scale on the plate registers the movement of the free end of the lever.

It is not a matter for surprise that a frictional brake like the stackfreed, which must have absorbed an appreciable proportion of the force, failed to give satisfaction for equalising the pull of the mainspring. The fusee invented for the same purpose by, it is said, Jacob Sech, of Prague, about 1525, is of a far different nature, and still survives. It consists of a spirally grooved pulley, which is interposed between the mainspring barrel and the great or driving wheel of a clock or watch, the connection between the barrel and the fusee being made by a cord or chain, one end of which is attached to the barrel and the other to the fusee. When the spring is relaxed there must be at least as many coils of the cord around the outside of the barrel as the barrel is to make turns in winding the spring. To wind the spring, the fusee is rotated by means of a key fitting a square formed at one end of its arbor, whereby the cord is drawn from the barrel on to the fusee, the first coil being on the larger end of the fusee, as shown in Fig. 76.

Fig. 77.   Fig. 78
Watch movements with "Stackfreed."

Then, as the mainspring runs down, the barrel rotates and coils the cord on to its periphery again. But while the mainspring when fully wound turns the fusee by uncoiling the cord from the smallest part of the fusee, it gets the advantage of a larger radius as its energy becomes lessened, and by proportioning the diameter of the fusee to the varying pull of each successive turn of the mainspring an excellent adjustment is obtained, so that the pressure exerted by the great wheel on the centre pinion is constant. The fusee is fixed to its arbor, on which, in the simplest arrangement, the great wheel rides easily, the connection between the fusee and great wheel being made by means of a ratchet wheel and click; this allows of the fusee being rotated to wind the mainspring. To prevent undue strain on the cord when the winding is completed, the cord, as it is being coiled on to the smallest turn of the fusee, pushes an arm which is pivoted to the framing of the timekeeper in the path of a small-shaped flange of the fusee, and this forms a stop. The barrel arbor is always stationary. In the early fusees the cord was of catgut, and this material is still sometimes used for clocks. Chains were introduced in place of catgut for watches in 1664, by one Gruet, a Swiss, and they are still used for marine chronometers, for some clocks, and for the few fusee watches that are made.

Table clocks or watches of the sixteenth century are exceedingly rare. Many specimens put forward as such are found on examination to be of a later date. There is no doubt that the manufacture of portable timepieces extended to Holland and France before the end of the century, but very few examples of that period survive. A genuine specimen would have no covering glass over the dial, and, if a fusee were present, the connection between it and the barrel would be by a piece of catgut, and not a chain. There would be, of course, no controlling spring to the balance at that period, while the balance-cock, instead of being spread over the whole extent of the balance, would be narrow. The workmanship of the movement would be comparatively rough, however lavishly the case might be ornamented.

During the first quarter of the century the frames and wheels were of iron or steel; productions of the second quarter having brass plates and pillars are occasionally to be met with. But brass wheels before the middle of the century were quite exceptional. Screws seem to have been introduced to join pieces of metal in German timekeepers about 1550, so that in early sixteenth century timekeepers these convenient fasteners would be absent, and the various junctions made by riveting or the use of either pins or cotters. Screws are not met with in English work till quite late in the century, and are absent in some early seventeenth century watches. There were rarely any winding holes in the cases of sixteenth century watches; to attach the key to the winding square the case had to be opened and usually the movement to be turned out of the case, a cover at the back being the alternative.

The Society of Antiquaries possess an undoubted example of the handiwork of Jacob Zech, the inventor of the fusee. It is a table timepiece with a circular brass gilt case 9¾ in. in diameter, and 5 in. in height, which was bequeathed to the Society by Mr Henry Peckitt, an apothecary, of Compton Street, Soho, and handed over by his executrix in 1808. It was given to James Ferguson, the astronomer and mechanician, by Mudge, and at the sale of Ferguson's effects it was bought by Mr Peckitt in 1777. Captain W. H. Smyth gives a minute description of this relic in *Archaeologia,* vol. xxxiii., from which the engraving of the dial (Fig. 79) is taken.

From the decoration of the case and dial, it is inferred that the clock was made for Sigismund I., King of Poland, and that he presented it to Bona

Fig. 79. — Dial of Table Clock by Jacob Zech.

Three views of a late 16th century German table clock, stamped with the initials HS and a shield with a cross, probably those of Johann (Hanns) Schönmann of Constance, and stamped on the base with the date 1592. The sides of the case are cast and decorated with strapwork, fruit, and grotesque masks against a punched background. Above the case is a flattened dome covering the bell, and carrying the chapter ring and hand. This dome is of open strapwork with grotesque masks. The centre of the one-handed dial is of silver against a black mastic background.

Left: the movement is of steel and has a verge escapement, fusee in the going train having an early chain with long links. Plain three arm balance with a later balance spring added, and a very simple s-shaped cock. Above: the locking plate from the striking train and the bow shaped mainspring regulator into a ratchet can be seen. Sotheby Parke Bernet & Co.

Sforza, to whom he was married in 1518. There are three shields equidistant round the case, which is altogether nicely decorated. On one shield is an eagle displayed and crowned, representing Poland; the second contains a serpent entwined and wavy pale crowned, a child issuant from its mouth and surmounted by a ducal crown — the coat of the house of Visconti; the third shield bears the arms of Lithuania, a knight armed *cap-à-pie,* and mounted on a horse proper, holding in his dexter hand a drawn sword, and having pendent from his neck a shield charged with the Hungarian cross. The frame is fastened by buttons on dogs. The verge pivots act on iron dovetails. The regulator is a cross-bar balance of the kind used in De Vick's clock, except that instead of loose weights of iron there are leaden weights screwed one on each end of the cross-bar, and the adjustment is made by screwing to or from the centre of motion. Originally these were doubtless fixed weights riveted on and without any provision for adjustment. There are two yielding brass arms to act as a banking and check excessive vibration of the cross-bar. There are eight turns to the fusee, which is of soft metal, and in a circle on the face of the barrel is engraved in Bohemian an inscription which Smyth translates thus: "When we counted 1525 years, then made me Jacob Zech" (or rather Jacob the Bohemian) "at Prague; it is true."

There was originally some additional wheelwork to show the motion of the sun and moon on an engraved ecliptic, and also a contrivance to strike one at every hour. The wheels are of iron and show punch marks of division, proving that they had been cut with a file by hand. A catgut had been used to connect the barrel with the fusee, but the metallic chain was subsequently applied, which destroyed several of the threads. Before this was done it went for forty-eight hours with one winding, and gave about 3,600 beats in the hour.

Fig. 80 shows a primitive table timepiece which formerly belonged to

Fig. 80.

Fig. 81.

Fig. 82.

Baron Pichon and is now in the Schloss collection. The drum-shaped case of brass gilt is engraved in the Renaissance style, and measures 5½ in. across. On the bottom is stamped in a scroll "N. Plantart." A very similar piece is in the South Kensington Museum.

In the British Museum is an excellent specimen of a German early table clock of a square oblong shape. The works are of iron. It has no fusee. It fits into an engraved metal box, having a hinged cover. The date of production is stated to be 1530.

Among the collection of Prince Soltykoff was the square table clock shown in Fig. 81. The sides are of bronze gilt, very finely engraved with allegorical subjects. Representations of St Paul, Matthew, Mark, and Luke are engraved on silver medallions which occupy the centres. Inside the perforated dome is a bell, and surmounting it a horizontal dial enriched with coloured enamels. It was the work of Louis David, and dates from the middle of the sixteenth century.

Nuremberg and Augsburg pursued the manufacture of portable timekeepers with considerable spirit. The plain square brass towers, round and octagonal boxes, gave place to cases of a much more ornate design when expense was no object. A very choice example from Dubois' historical work is shown in Fig. 82; it is of iron, damascened with precious metals, a style of work for which Augsburg was particularly famous.

Several good representative specimens belonging to the King of Saxony are to be seen in Dresden, part of them in the treasury of the palace and part in the Historical Museum. In the green vaulted chambers or treasury of the palace is the so-called Venetian astronomical clock, which is, though, really of German workmanship. A front view of it is given in Fig. 83, but a photograph naturally fails to adequately convey the splendour of the case, which is of gold and silver covered with gorgeous work in enamel, or the

The astronomical table clock made by Jacob the Czech and dated 1525. Side view showing part of the armorial and other decorations with which the case is engraved. As can be seen from the illustration of the dial in Fig. 79, the clock has two 24-hour scales with touch pins on the inner scale, a zodiac scale with the astrological significations of the different signs marked, and in the centre an aspectarium. Apart from the hour, the dial thus supplies information as to the ascendant sign of the zodiac for the hour at day or night, and the position of sun and moon in the ecliptic/zodiac. The Society of Antiquaries, London.

The movement of Jacob's clock showing the fusee. For a long time this was the earliest known example of a fusee existing in a clock. Several earlier examples have now been discovered however, one of which an unsigned specimen dated 1504 is illustrated by H. Alan Lloyd in Old Clocks (4th edition, London, 1970), plates 2a and 2b. The Society of Antiquaries, London.

Fig. 83.

Fig. 84.

extraordinary complexity of the mechanism. The movement bears no maker's name, but of two somewhat similar clocks of the same collection one is signed by Andreas Schelhorn, of Schneeberg, in Saxony, 1570, and the other by Christoph Ullmeyer, of Augsburg.

Of other specimens in the same repository may be mentioned a table clock of very rich appearance which belonged to the queen of Augustus the Strong, and was made, presumably about 1700, by Jakob Streller, of Nuremberg. Another very wonderful clock, the so-called Hunting clock, the movement of which was made about 1700 by J. G. Graupner, is set in a magnificent case with figures of huntsmen at the corners and a group representing the legend of St Hubert on the top, all enamelled in brilliant colours and blazing with diamonds and emeralds, the work of Johann Christoph Köhler. Then there is the famous "Tower of Babel Kugeluhr" (Ball clock), made in 1602 by Hans Schlotheim, of Augsburg. It is in the form of a tower of gilded metal about 4 ft. high, with a gallery in the manner of an inclined plane running round it spiralwise from top to bottom; every minute a little crystal ball comes out of a door at the top of the tower and, running all the way down the spiral gallery, enters a door at the bottom, when a bell rings.

Of the horological treasures in the Historical Museum at Dresden I can give three illustrations, and will begin with the remarkable clock of which a view appears in Fig. 84. It was bought in 1587 for 500 gulden of Sebald Schwerzer, who was alchemist to the Elector Augustus of Saxony

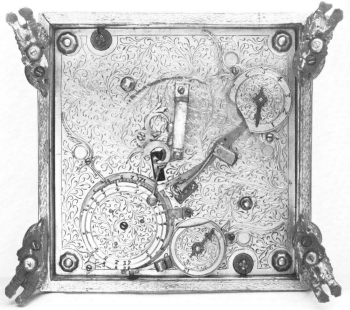

The well-known Orpheus clocks are the only group of Renaissance clocks to have been studied in detail. The remains of ten clocks are known of which nine are discussed in *P.G. Coole & E. Neumann, The Orpheus Clocks, London, 1972;* and of which two are square, the rest being circular. That shown here in two views has been somewhat altered, the whole of the centre of the dial having been replaced. Originally it probably contained lunation work and the two hands were independently geared.

The movement of the clock is of steel with an unusual overlaid brass engraved back-plate. The clock is controlled by a verge and foliot escapement with hog's bristle regulation, six and twelve hour striking, strike release, hammer and bell outside the plates. The eight day duration is extremely uncommon before the late 17th century. Mounted above the clock on four legs is a completely separate but probably original alarum mechanism. The frieze and the case, showing scenes from the Orpheus legend, are of gilt hand-finished repoussé work, and the whole sits on four lion feet. The Trustees of the British Museum.

(1526-1586) and afterwards ennobled by the Emperor Rudolph II., and he is supposed by some to have been the maker of the clock, though the claim has been disputed. The silver work of the case bears the mark of Elias Lenker, of Nuremberg, who died in 1591.

Fig. 85 is a very elaborate clock with eleven dials and automata. The case is decorated with many beautiful plaques of *basse taille* enamel upon silver. It is considered to be the masterpiece of its maker, Paul Schuster, of Nuremberg; it was bought in 1591, and so was presumably completed in that year.

In Fig. 86 is another curious clock of the same type, with moving figures representing an Indian king hunting with elephants. The maker's name is unknown, but the clock was already in the collection of the Elector of Saxony in 1587.

There is as well a curious clock which has upon it the figure of a man leading a dancing bear; when the hours strike, the bear beats a drum, and the man blows a horn. This piece also bears no maker's name, but it has Augsburg marks, and probably dates from the end of the sixteenth century.

The Comte de Lambilly has a clock somewhat resembling Fig. 86, in which, at the striking of the hour, figures of the twelve Apostles move round in the upper gallery. The main front dial shows the hours and the lower one quarters and half quarters.

The examples in Figs. 87 and 88 are from the Schloss collection. Fig. 87, a

Fig. 85.

Fig. 86.

Fig. 87.

Fig. 88.

Fig. 89.

CURIOUS OCTAGONAL TABLE CLOCK

sixteenth century production, is notable as being an early instance of table clock having provision for striking the quarter-hours. There are three bells: a large one, concealed by the base; a smaller one, enclosed by the gallery above the tower; and a third, still smaller, which serves as a canopy over the figure seated above the gallery on a ball. The quarter-hours are struck on the smallest bell, and the last hour then repeated on the bell behind the gallery. On completion of the hour it is sounded on the largest bell. There are two dials, one on the front and one on the back. On the main dial in front are shown the hours, and outside the hour numerals are marked, the quarter-hours, which are indicated by a hand, travelling round in one hour, but moving independently of the hour hand. The movment bears the signature V.M. in a shield. It has a cross-bar balance with shifting weights, and there are no fusees. The chasing of the case is exceedingly good, and the sides of the square part bear evidence of having been beautifully enamelled with birds and flowers.

Fig. 88 is of later date. There are three dials on the front and one on the opposite face. The movement is controlled by a pendulum which swings outside of the case at the back.

In the South Kensington Museum is an Augsburg astronomical striking table clock, in an engraved brass and damascened iron case. On the bottom is a sun-dial and the inscription:—

Jacob . Marqvart . von . Avgspvrg . bin . ih . genant .
mein . Nam . ist . in . VVelslandt . gar . vvol . bekant .
der . hat . das . VVerck . gemacht . firvvar .
im . 1657 . Jar .
ain . svnenvr . ist . das . genant .
avf . Wels . vnd . Deisch . Landt . erkant .

(I am called Jacob Marquart, of Augsburg;
My name is right well known in Foreign Lands,
Who has indeed done the work
In the year 1567;
This is called a sundial,
Available in Foreign Lands and Germany.)

The hexagonal clock in the form of a temple from the collection of Prince Soltykoff and shown in Fig. 89 is also a sixteenth century production. The movement is arranged in stories, the watch part being at the bottom and the striking work above. The six doors or panels between the fluted columns are of steel damascened with arabesques of elegant design. In the arched centre of one of the panels is the dial with a band of blue steel for indicating the hours of the day; various planetary and astronomical motions were shown on the horizontal dial at the top of the structure. The upper part of the case in the style of Henri II. is very handsome; the entablature is supported at the angles by six caryatides, and in the centre of each panel is a medallion with the head of a Roman emperor or warrior sculptured in high relief and surrounded by a gilt border. A clock similar to the engraving, but surmounted by a statuette, is in the British Museum.

Some time ago, by favour of Mr Charles Shapland, I had through my hands a curious sixteenth century striking clock of octagonal form, of which a view is subjoined (Fig. 90). This clock which is now in the British Museum, is probably of Nuremberg or Augsburg manufacture, and has a peculiar method of indicating the rising and setting of the sun daily throughout the

Fig. 90. — Curious Table Clock, Early Sixteenth Century.

year, by means of two thin metal dials within the hour circle. One of these dials is of silver and the other of steel for contrast; each of them forms a segment nineteen twenty-fourths of a circle, divided by radial lines into nineteen parts, which are numbered at the circumference from one onward in Arabic figures, so that each division is one twenty-fourth of the whole circle. A brass disc, divided into twenty-four, is fixed to the steel dial by rivets at Nos. 1 and 3; No. 24, or zero point of the circle, coinciding with what may be called the initial edge of the steel dial. The steel and silver dials are interlaced — that is to say, the concealed portion of the steel dial is underneath the silver one, while the initial edge is above it. At the shortest day in the year the least portion of the silver dial would be visible, and the figure on the silver dial next to the initial edge of the steel dial would represent the number of hours the sun was above the horizon, while the figure on the central brass circle, which happend to be coincident with the initial edge of the silver dial, would represent the number of hours he was below the horizon, and the subdivisions of the hour could be well estimated to within a tenth. The dials are continually rotating in opposite directions, so that as the days lengthened more of the silver and less of the steel dial would be seen. At the close of the longest day the motion of the dials would be

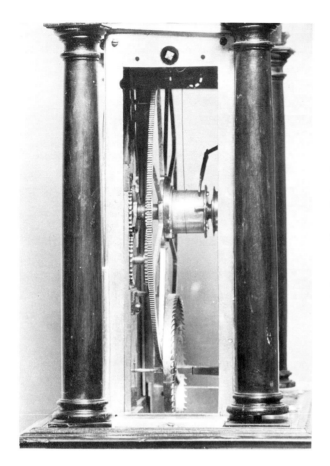

The only important modifications to the escapement, and improvements in timekeeping to be made before the invention of the pendulum, were carried out by the Swiss clockmaker Jobst Burgi (1552-1632), who was clockmaker successively to the Landgraf Wilhelm IV of Hesse and to the Emperor Rudolph II at Prague. Burgi, whose attempts to develop a precise clock were stimulated by the astronomical interests of Wilhelm IV, made three main innovations. First he employed a three month running period, second he invented and used a remontoire in the form of a weight box; thirdly he developed a type of double verge escapement usually referred to as the cross-beat. Virtually all knowledge of this had been lost at the time that Britten wrote his book. In essence it consists of two arms geared together each carrying a pallet, and working with a large and very finely cut escape wheel.

Opposite below right and left and above left: three views of an unsigned cross-beat clock of c.1580 ascribed to Burgi and which because of its plainess has been considered to be an experimental piece. The cross-beat arms can be seen in the circular tray at the bottom of the clock. Astronomisch-Physikalisches Kabinett, Kassel.

Below left and right:
The remains of two further cross-beat clocks recently discovered. Sotheby Parke Bernet & Co.

Fig. 91.

Fig. 92.

reversed, and the visible surface of the silver dial would be diminished each day in the same ratio that it was formerly increased, till the shortest day recurred. It is probable that these dials were arranged to show the beginning of the Hebrew day at sunset, as well as its duration and close at the succeeding sunset.

On removing the dial plate, the way in which the dials are actuated is apparent. Fitting loosely on the centre wheel which carries the hour hand is a pinion of twenty-four leaves. The pipe of this has a cruciform top fitting into the centre of the silver dial. On the pipe of this pinion is another, larger in diameter, but also of twenty-four leaves, and with a similar top to carry the steel dial. A double rack or segment of a wheel, having internal and external teeth, is pivoted close to the edge of the movement, and engages with both of the dial plate pinions, the internal teeth being farthest from the centre of motion, and of such a distance that they reach beyond the centre arbor and engage with the teeth of the larger pinion on the other side of it; the external teeth are so placed that they engage with the teeth of the smaller pinion, but on the side of the centre arbor nearest to the centre of motion of the rack. There is on the plate of the movement, midway between its centre and its edge and driven from the fusee, a wheel which turns once a year. This carries a crank, from which is a connecting rod catching hold of the double rack; so that, as the crank revolves, it gives a to-and-fro motion to the rack. To meet the varying length of the years from leap year to leap year, there are four pins by which the position of the crank could be altered, but, so far as one could see, there is no provision for automatic regulation, so that, if the reading of the seals is to be exact, the dial would have to be removed and the position of the crank altered once a year.

Recessed into the under-side of the clock case is an annual dial engraved with the signs of the zodiac, the titles of the months, and the days. The index for this is fixed to the arbor of the annual wheel already mentioned, and the annual dial is therefore less than half the diameter of the movement.

The case is of brass, engraved and gilt. The hour band is of silver, divided into two periods of twelve hours each, and marked with Roman numerals. Within the hour ring, and separating it from the sun rising and setting discs, is a brass gilt ring engraved with a cable pattern.

All the dial work, the striking train and the going train wheels, up to the fusee, are of iron or steel; the connection between the fusee and barrel is by a catgut, and the balance is very light, of the old cross-bar pattern, but with weights riveted on with no provision for after-adjustment. There is, of course, no balance-spring. The hours are struck on a cap-shaped or cylindrical bell.

In the construction of this timekeeper there is not a single screw used. All fastenings are either pins or wedge-shaped keys or rivets.

The quaint hexagonal striking and alarm table clock shown in Fig. 91 is a mid-sixteenth century production from the Schloss collection. On the six faces of the case are engraved allegorical figures representing the sun, the moon, Mars, Mercury, Jupiter, and Venus, corresponding to the days of the week from Sunday to Friday, and, on the bottom of the case, Saturn for Saturday. A little door seen on the face immediately to the right of the dial permits the inspection of the fusee in order to estimate the period for winding. The movement is arranged in stories, the striking mechanism below

Fig. 93. — (Havard, "Dictionnaire de l'Ameublement.")

EARLY CLOCK WITH MINUTE HAND

and the going part above, the hemispherical bell being supported from the upper plate and covered by a perforated dome. On the upper surface of the plinth is the maker's punch mark, a square shield with M.H.B. arranged as a monogram.

The example engraved in Fig. 92 is from the Soltykoff collection. The case appears to be a reproduction in miniature of a mediaeval hexagonal fortress. It is a striking clock, probably German, dating from about 1560. In the Webb collection at the South Kensington Museum is a somewhat similar clock; the bottom of the case is stamped "AIX * A * P" (perhaps for Aix in Provence).

"Nef," or Ship clocks, were a peculiar fancy of the sixteenth century. There is one in the British Museum, by Hanns Schlott, dating from about 1580, which is supposed to have belonged to Rudolf II., and another in the Vienna Treasury. The clock mechanism included provision for showing various astronomical movements, and was quite subsidiary to the ship and its appurtenances, as will be gathered from the excellent example given in Fig. 93.

In Fig. 94 is shown a German octagonal clock from the Soltykoff collection.

At the South Kensington Museum is a clock, in an elegant case of metal gilt, in the form of a temple, as shown in Fig. 95. Its height is 13½ in. and its width 8 in. It is most elaborately chased and engraved with figures and arabesques. The piered dome covers two bells, and is surmounted by a figure standing on a globe. The base is chased with masks and cartouche ornaments, with winged horses at the angles, and a dial on each of the four sides showing, besides the hours and minutes, motions of various heavenly bodies. This choice and interesting timekeeper, which formed part of the Bernal collection, was produced at Munich, and is dated 1587. Every minute is figured from 1 to 60, as was the custom on early timekeepers with minute hands. Though the pressure of the concentric minute hand on sixteenth

Fig. 94.

Fig. 95.

Fig. 96.

Fig. 97.

century work is exceptional, there is nothing to lead one to suppose that it is in this case an addition to the original construction; and providing the minute hand would certainly present no difficulty to the mind capable of devising such intricate mechanism as is contained in the astronomical motions of this clock.

I recently saw another clock of very similar character, which was inscribed, "ASMUS BIRLN B RYNLR IN AVGVSTA VINDLLICORUM 1577," and the letters A.B. formed into a monogram.

A somewhat similar portable clock (Fig. 96) from the Soltykoff collection is about 15 in. high and 10 in. across the base, which is supported by four heraldic lions. There are five dials, two on the front face and one on each of the others; they mark the hours of the day, the day of the month, the phases of the moon, the signs of the zodiac, and the course of certain planets.

This clock bears no maker's name, but a very similar one, also in the Soltykoff collection, was inscribed, "Andreas Muller, Tristen." It is probably mid-sixteenth century work.

The next example, from the South Kensington Museum, is an elegant form of medallion clock in a rock-crystal case, on a stem as shown in Fig. 97. The plinth is of metal gilt, with crystal plaques, and contains the striking train. The remainder of the movement is in the upper case. The longer of the two hands, which at the first glance seems to be a minute hand, really points to the day of the month marked on a ring outside the hour ring. The age of the moon is shown by a revolving gilt plate behind the dial, which is cut away to make the moon plate visible. The total height is 7¾ in. It is signed "J. Wolf, Wienn," and dated 1609, but the name "J. Wolf" appears on examination to be a recent addition. It was formerly in the Bernal collection.

The table clock represented in Fig. 98 resembles one at South Kensington Museum, which, as already mentioned, was probably made by Peter Hele, except that in the present example the body of the case is square. It is of brass gilt, with bold mouldings as shown, and very nicely engraved. Rising

Fig. 98.

Nef *or ship clock attributed to Hans Schlottheim (1547-1625) and made for the Emperor Rudolph II c.1580 (p.93). Top left shows a general view; bottom right a view of the movement with verge escapement and held between plates. Top right is a view down onto the deck. The clock dial is extremely small but the hours and quarters are struck by the figures in the crowsnests on bells. The ship which is on wheels would, when placed upon a table, run across it with a rolling motion produced by a kidney shaped cam, while an organ below decks played and a cannon in the stern fired. At the same time the figures on the deck, representing the heralds and electors of the Holy Roman Empire, would process round in front of the Emperor seated on his throne, while drummers rolled on their drums and trumpeters trumpeted. The Trustees of the British Museum.*

Fig. 99.

Fig. 100.

**EARLY CLOCK WITH
BALANCE-SPRING**

from this is a hemispherical dome pierced to emit the sound of the bell which it covers, and supporting above it a horizontal dial. The arrangement of placing the bell between the movement and the dial allows a handsome and appropriate design with which no fault can be found, except, perhaps, that in order to keep the dial from over-shadowing the dome it is necessarily rather small. On the exterior of the bottom of the case is engraved the word VALLIN. The Roman numerals I. to XII. are engraved on a silver band, and within are smaller Arabic figures, 13 to 24.

The chief plate of the movement is square and pinned to the upper part of the square box. Running vertically inside the box are two feathers; these pass through notches in the lower plate of the movement; two turn-buckles on the lower plate butt against the ends of the feathers, and so secure the box after it is placed over the movement. The hand is driven from a pinion on the great wheel by means of an arbor, which passes through the post to which the bell is secured. It is probably a late sixteenth century French production. An almost identical specimen is in the library at Welbeck Abbey.

In Fig. 99 is shown a table clock, apparently English, dating from about 1580, in a square brass case, gilded and beautifully engraved. It belongs to Mr J. Hall, and very closely resembles one by Bartholomew Newsam, which is at the British Museum and illustrated in Chapter V.

A good example of early seventeenth century table clocks is shown in Fig. 100. It is in a brass case, with silver hour ring, divided into twelve, and a *fleur-de-lis* midway between each hour. The characteristic features which note the departure from the earliest specimens are the glass panels in the sides of the case and the bronze feet, which give a better effect than is obtained with primitive flat hexagonal and octagonal clocks, besides allowing space for the bell to project below the bottom surface of the case.

The cocks and hammer are very nicely engraved and pierced, and on the plate is the name Johan Scheirer. A balance-spring has been applied subsequently to the manufacture of the piece, and as the original balance-cock is retained, the spring is much cramped. The balance appears to be the original one, and is weighted with pieces of metal to keep the vibration sufficiently slow after the addition of the spring. A notable peculiarity is that the fly pinion has but four leaves.

The handsome striking and alarm clock shown in Fig. 101 is from the Soltykoff collection. It bears no indication of its origin, but the monogram G.O. engraved on it leads to the conjecture that it belonged to Gaston of Orleans, son of Henry IV.

The interesting clock shown in Fig. 102 I saw recently at Messrs Thwaites & Reed's. In the centre of the dial is a plate with the moon's age marked on it and carrying the hour hand; concentric with this a disc with a round hole showing the phases of the moon and age. In front, and also concentric with these, is an alarm dial with hands. This turns once in twenty-four hours. The wheel carrying the hour hand and moon's age has sixty teeth, the one carrying the disc showing the phases and age of the moon sixty-one teeth, and the wheel carrying the alarm dial sixty teeth. The two wheels showing the moon's age and hours are driven by a pinion of twenty, and the alarm wheel by a pinion of ten, both fixed on same arbor, which makes one revolution in four hours.

The clock strikes one blow at the first quarter, two at the second, three at

Fig. 101.

the third and four at the hour, besides the ordinary hours from one to twelve; and then repeats the hours at any interval the clock is set for: that is, one, two, three, or more minutes after the ordinary hours are struck. This part strikes the hours up to twenty-four, and while striking the figure on the top of the clock revolves. There is a separate train for each part, and the chain on the fusee of the going part has the appearance of having been made at the same time as the clock. The other springs are in brass barrels screwed to the frame.

The small dial indicates quarter-hours only, and the hand makes a revolution in one hour. There are two hands on this; the under one is to set the interval between the ordinary striking and the twenty-four hour striking.

The escapement is of course a verge. It has a plain circular balance rather large in diameter. Over the balance is a straight spring, one end of which is fixed to the plate, the free end being embraced by two pins standing up from the rim of the balance, and so acting as a controller.

On the bottom of the clock is engraved:—

A.D. 1634. ADAM KLYZOVICZ KIAKOVIE FECIT POLONYS.

Two views of an exceedingly pretty early seventeenth century alarm table clock of small size from the Schloss collection are given in Figs. 103 and 104. The case is of brass gilt, the exterior of the bottom and the under-side of the movement plate are covered with beautiful engraving, and over the body of the case is a silver ring or jacket with piercing so fine as to appear almost like filigree work. The dome, of silver, similarly pierced, covers a hemispherical bell, and supports the horizontal dial, on which are engraved the horary numerals in Roman characters, the time being indicated by a projecting ornament at the edge of the centre, which rotates and is figured as a guide for setting the alarm hand.

Fig. 102. — Clock with early Balance-Spring.

Left: Fig. 103.
Above: Fig. 104. — Plan, showing Dial.

A small calendar table clock in a gilt metal case with its leather carrying box, dating from the mid-17th century and signed 'Andreas Raeb Hamburg Fecit'. On the face are four one-handed dials, each with their centres engraved with scenes of buildings, for hours, date, day of the week and age of the moon. Incorporated in the latter is a lunar phase volvelle. The movement has a fusee with chain for the going train, a fixed barrel for the striking train, verge escapement, balance with later spring and cock but an early conversion nevertheless since Barrow's straight line balance regulator is employed. This was introduced c.1680 but was superseded by Tompion's form of balance spring regulation soon afterwards. The bell is mounted on the hinged base plate, its hammer being visible in the illustration. Christie, Manson & Wood Ltd.

SEVENTEENTH CENTURY PENDULUM CLOCKS

Fig. 105.

Fig. 105 represents the front of an astronomical clock by Marcus Bohm, Augsburg. It is 21 in. high and 10 in. wide, engraved, chased, and gilded. Under the dome, which is hammered out of one piece of metal, are two bells, the smaller being struck at the quarters, and the larger at the hours and as an alarm. By adjustment at pleasure the clock can be made to sound the hours from one to twelve or from one to twenty-four. The large dial shows the time, the length of days, and a calendar of saints. In front hangs the pendulum, the bob being in the form of a cherub. The back is very similar to the front; the main dial there indicates the annual course of the astral world. Some of the subsidiary dials on the front, back, and sides exhibit other motions, and the remainder are for adjustment and regulation of the mechanism.

At the Ashmolean Museum is a fine German astronomical clock 22½ in. high, belonging to Mr Henry J. Pfungst. The case is of gilt metal with dials on each of the four sides, of which the chief one is seen in Fig. 106. On the opposite side to that shown in the engraving a pendulum is suspended. The dials are of silver, decorated with *basse taille* enamel red, white, blue, and green.

During the latter part of the sixteenth and the first half of the seventeenth century, timepieces with horizontal dials over which a dome containing an alarm could be placed at pleasure were in favour. There are several in the British Museum. An early example is shown in Fig. 107. Fig. 108, from the Schloss collection, is of a rather later date. Three springy legs fixed to the alarm were made to clasp the outside of the dial of the timepiece in such a position that a wire depending from the alarm case was moved by the hand at the hour it was desired the alarm should be discharged.

These timepieces must have been exceedingly useful before the advent of lucifer matches, when recourse had to be made to the tinder box in order to obtain a light; but, apart from these and machines with complicated movements such as were designed by astronomers, regard seems to have been

Fig. 106.

Fig. 107.

Fig. 108.

(Havard, "Dictionnaire de l'Ameublement.")

more generally paid to the effectiveness of the exterior as a whole rather than to its fitness and convenience for showing the hour. Some instances of the more or less grotesque conceptions then in favour are appended, most of them being from the Schloss collection.

Fig. 109 shows a crowned lion of gilt copper holding an orb in its right paw and supporting the dial with its left. By means of two wires standing up from the balance the eyes, which have bright red pupils, move to and fro when the clock is going. As the hours are struck the animal's lower jaw moves up and down. The movement is contained in an ebony box, which forms the plinth.

A dog guarding the dial with its paw, as shown in Fig. 110, is of much the same character.

Fig. 109.

Fig. 110.

Fig. 111.

Fig. 111 shows a splendid example of its kind, in which a boldly modelled figure of Bacchus sitting astride a cask is utilised as an automaton. As the hours are struck it opens its mouth and raises to its lips the bottle held in the right hand. In its left hand is a staff entwined with grape leaves and fruit and surmounted by a pineapple, the Augsburg mark. On a silver dial attached to the front of the cask the hours are indicated, and at the back, between a pineapple in a shield, are the letters C. K., which very possibly stand for Conrad Kreizer, a well-known early seventeenth century maker. Just in front of the cask is a horizontal dial divided into quarter-hours for setting the striking. The eyes of the figure move to and fro continuously while the clock is going; but instead of being connected directly to the balance, as in the preceding examples, they are worked by a separate escapement and ingenious mechanism actuated by the fusee wheel which drives the train. In this way the motion of the eyes is slower, and the timekeeping of the clock is not affected. The plates of the movement are gilded, and the train wheels are of steel. The case is of ebony.

A peculiar early seventeenth century striking clock is shown in Fig. 112. As the hours are sounded the negro's head moves, and the dog at his feet jumps. He indicates the time on a revolving band which bears the hour numerals. Another of these quaint conceptions is in the British Museum.

On similar lines are Figs. 113 and 114. The one with a revolving hollow globe, on which the hours are marked, dates from about 1650; the figure of the Virgin bearing the horary numerals on a revolving crown and holding a sceptre and the infant Christ with an orb is a little later. The movement of this is inscribed "Jereme Pfaff, Augsburg."

Fig. 115 shows a clock which belongs to Mr Robert W. de Forest. It has three horizontal band dials showing respectively the hour, the day of the week, and the day of the month. Below are portrayed Adam and Eve in the Garden of Eden. As the hours are struck Eve turns and presents an apple to Adam, who appears to hesitate, and then retires, refusing the gift. Abundance of foliage and fruit is spread over the three trees or columns supporting the dials, while a huge serpent gazing menacingly at Adam is twined around the central trunk, and indicates the hour with its tail. For the photograph from which the engraving is produced I am indebted to M. Eugène Wehrle, of Brussels.

The flagellation of Jesus Christ forms the subject of the clock with moving figures which is shown in Fig. 116. An hour dial is at the feet of the Captive, whose bound hands are tied to a post, surmounted by a rotating band, on which the quarter-hours are engraved. As the hour strikes the passive Prisoner is belaboured by the soldiers, their weapons rising and falling with each sound of the bell. The movement contained in the ebony case is signed, "Nicolaus Schmidt der Junger."

The crucifix clock represented in Fig. 117 is from the Schloss collection. The drawing is one third of the actual size of the clock, which measures 12 in. in height and 6 in. across the widest part. The base is made of wood and gilt metal, the top being covered with cloth or velvet, now very much

Fig. 112.

Fig. 113.

Fig. 114.

Fig. 115.

Fig. 116.

Fig. 117. — Crucifix Clock.

worn. The cross is of gilt metal, the figures and mounts of silver. The figure on the cross is most beautifully modelled. St John, standing at the left of the cross, holds in his hands a chalice, which he raises when the clock strikes the hours. The ball surmounting the structure revolves once in twelve hours, and on it is a band containing the Roman hour numerals, the time being indicated by the pointer fixed to the cross. No minutes are shown, and subdivisions of an hour would have to be estimated. The escapement is, of course, a verge. The clock goes thirty hours between windings, and strikes on a bell below the plinth. Portions of the movement can be seen through apertures in chased metal gratings fixed in the front and back panels of the plinth. There is no maker's name, but it is probably a French seventeenth century production.

The style and decoration of the late seventeenth century clock, shown in Fig. 118, may be studied with advantage by those who wish to be able to distinguish pieces of different periods. The ornament at the sides of the case is in bold relief; the feet are of bronze, as was the usual practice, and form a contrast to the yellower metal of which the case is composed. The movement of this clock is regulated by a very short balance spring, and bears the signature "Andreas Fehmel."

Fig. 119 shows a diminutive table clock by Hanns Buschman dating from about 1690. There are dials front and back, and a pendulum which swings at the rear outside of the case.

Janvier speaks of the watches made between 1560 and 1590 as being beautifully ornamented and of all sizes, and there is no doubt that by the last named date watchmaking had become in France a flourishing art of considerable magnitude, Blois and Rouen being two of the most important seats of manufacture. But I am unable to trace any reliable evidence of

102

English watches having been made before quite the end of the sixteenth century, although German and French productions were doubtless imported earlier.

Among the collection of Mr T. Whitcombe Greene is an early box-shaped, metal gilt case and dial, probably of German make. Around the projecting bead at the bottom of the case is engraved the following: "Sr. Wm Cooper to Eleanor, daughter of Sr. Michael Stanhope, wife to Thomas Cooper, his son, of Thurgarton, Co. Nots, 1539." A coat of arms is engraved on the cover. The dial is engraved with the figure of the Saviour and emblems of Death, with the mottoes, "Vigilate et orate quia nescitis horam," and "Quaelibet hora ad mortem vestigium" ("Watch and pray, for ye know not the hour," and "Every hour is a step towards death"). If the dedicatory inscription is an authentic record, this relic certainly represents one of the first table watches seen in England. The case has no bow. Derham, in his second and subsequent editions, mentions an eight-day watch which, he was told, belonged to Henry VIII., but the context clearly shows a weight timepiece is referred to. Among the possessions of Edward VI., as quoted by Wood from a Royal Household Book, is "oone larum or watch of iron, the case being likewise of iron gilt, with two plummettes of lead." The first words of this description may seem to indicate a watch with a mainspring, but such an assumption is at once dispelled by the mention of the "plummettes of lead."

QUEEN ELIZABETH That Elizabeth owned a large number of watches is certain, and the following relating to her horological possessions will be of interest. In 1571 the Earl of Leicester gave to his royal mistress "one armlet or shakell of

Fig. 118.

Fig. 119.

A very fine astronomical table clock signed 'Caspar Buschmann' (Caspar Buschmann III, 1536-1613), which is said to have belonged to Casimir V, King of Poland. Of one day duration, the clock has a verge escapement with a weighted balance and a later hairspring. Originally there was a hog's bristle regulator, and there are going, striking (12 or 24 hours), quarter striking, and alarm trains. The fusees are of gilt brass, originally for gut line but later modified to take chains.

On the detachable dial plate of gilt copper are pin gnomon sundials for 42° and 48° latitude (Italian hours), an horizontal dial with a folding gnomon, a central inset compass for orientation and a table of latitudes for 96 European towns. The dial itself has a calendar ring with the name, number, days and date in the year, dominical letters and saint's days, minutes and quarter hours with touch pins for the quarter hours. Originally there were two pointers for the calendar ring, one indicating according to the Julian era, the other according to the Gregorian. The 24-hour chapter ring is divided 1-12 twice and there are two hands one with a sun emblem, the other for the moon with a phase indicator. In the centre is an astrolabe drawn for 48° North.

Additional scales are engraved on the sides of the clock, and include tables of the lunar cycle, a solar calendar, the epacts, dominical letter and the Roman indiction, day of the week and the associated planetary influences, climate zones and the length of daylight hours. National Maritime Museum, Greenwich.

A globe clock by Jaques de la Garde, 1552, designed originally to be suspended, but now mounted on a late 17th or early 18th century stand (not shown). The exterior of the sphere is flattened at one side to provide a dial and the rest is engraved with a map of the world, the tropics and the equator being marked. The movement has two trains for going and striking with finely engraved barrels and a verge escapement. The National Maritime Museum, Greenwich.

golde, all over fairly garnished with rubyes and dyamondes, haveing in the closing thearof a clocke." In the same year two other gifts are mentioned, a "juell, being a chrsolite garnished with rubyes and dyamondes, haveing in the closing thearof a clocke"; and "a juell, being a chrsolite garnished with golde, flagon facyon, th'one side sett with two emeraldes, ... th'other side having in it a clocke." In 1573 Elizabeth received from Margaret, Countess of Derby, "a white beare of gold and mother of perle, holding a ragged staffe, standing upon a toune of golde, whearin is a clocke, the same toune staffe garnished with dyamondes and rubyes." The "clock and all" weighed three ounces. In 1575 Mr Hatton, captain of the guard, gave the queen "a riche juell, being a clocke of golde, garnished with dyamondes, rubyes in the bottome, and a fayre emeralde pendante sett in golde and two mene perles pendaunte, all ix oz. iii qᵃ." In 1578 the Earl of Leicester presented Elizabeth with "a tablet of golde, being a clocke fully furnished with small diamondes and rubyes; abowte the same are six bigger diamondes pointed, and a pendaunte of golde, diamondes, and rubyes very smale. And upon eche side losengye diamonde, and an apple of golde enamuled green and russet." In the same year the Earl of Russell gave to the queen "a ring of golde, called a parmadas, sett with vj small diamonds and garnished round about with small rubies and two sparcks of ophalls, and in the same backeside a dyall." In 1580 the Earl of Leicester gave her "a cheyne of golde made like a payre of beades concayning viii long peeces fully garnished with small diamondes, and fower score and one smaller peeces fullie garnished with like diamondes; and hanging thereat a rounde clocke fullie garnished with dyamonds, and an

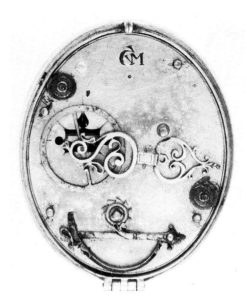

An oval verge watch in a gilt metal case, c.1600 stamped with the initials CvM. On the dial plate are three dials for hours, the date, and the month, and an aperture for the age and phase of the moon. The movement has a three wheel train, fusee with gut line, and bow and arrow into a ratchet set up. There is a flat steel balance. The cock is of delicate open work, pinned at the waist, while the pillars are of an unusual twisted form. The case is plain. Sotheby Parke Bernet & Co.

appendante of diamondes hanging thearat." In the same year was presented to the queen by Lord Russell, "item, a watche sett in mother of pearle with three pendaunts of goulde garnished with sparckes of rubyes, and an ophall in everie of them, and three small pearles pendaunte." In the same year Mr Edward Stafford gave her "a little clocke of goulde with a cristall, garnished with sparckes of emeraldes, and furnished on the back syde with other dyamondes, rubies, and other stones of small value." There were also many humbler contributors to her store. In 1556 her clockmaker, Nicholas Urseau, presented "a faire clocke in a case cover with blake vellat"; and her "clocke keeper, John Demolyn, a cloke with a lambe on it of copper guilt."

The following is from an inventory of the possessions of Queen Elizabeth: — "A watche of golde sett with small rubies, small diamondes, and small emerodes, with a pearle in the toppe called a buckett, watinge two rubies; a clocke of golde conteyning in the border four table diamonds and two very small rocke rubies, havinge on th'one side foure table rubies and size small diamondes; and on th'other side eleven table diamondes, whereof the one is more bigger than the residue. On the one side a man sitting aslepe with a childe before him; a clocke or tablett of golde garnished on th'one side with five faire diamondes and one faier rubie; and on th'other side five faire rubies and one faire emerod garnished with lij little diamonds, and liij little rubies, with a pearle pendent at it; one clocke of golde curiosly wrought and fullie furnished with diamonds, rubies, emerodes, and opalls, havinge in middes thereof a beare and a ragged staffe of sparkes of diamondes and rubies; one clock of gold curiously wrought with flowers and beastes, with a queene on the toppe on th'one side; and on the other side a beare and a ragged staff of sparkes of diamonds, fullie furnished with diamonds and rubies of sundry sortes and bignes; one emerode under it, a faier table diamond with a ragged staff in the foyle thereof and a faier rubie under it squared, and a pearle pendaunt of either side of the clocke; one clocke of golde wrought like deyses and paunseyes, garnished with little sparks of diamonds, rubies, and emerodes, and eight small pearles on the border, and a pendant acorn; one clocke of gold curiously wrought with small sparkes of stones, having on th'one side a horse bearing a globe with a crowne over it; one clocke of gold with a George on both sides garnished with sparkes of diamondes and a pendant of opalls; a litle watche of christall slightly garnished with golde;

A good example of a brass oval watch of the early 17th century. Signed 'Gribelin a Blois 1614', the watch emanates from one of the best known of the Blois ateliers which was, at this period, an important jewellery and watch-making centre. The chapter ring of silver is surrounded by engraved figures and formal foliage containing two rabbits. Inside the chapter ring is a representation of a scene from the story of Abraham and Isaac. The single hand is of steel.

The view of the back plate shows the finely engraved and pierced cock, and clearly displays the early method of fixing it by a pin through the waist. There is a flat steel balance, and a ratchet and click mainspring regulator which may be compared with that shown on page 105. The watch is slightly unusual in being both signed and dated.

Fig. 120. — Clock-Watch about 1580.

one litle clocke of golde th'one side being agate with a mouse on the toppe and heddes round aboute it; one litle watch golde; one litle clocke of golde th'one side being agate with a mouse on the toppe and heddes round aboute it; one litle watch pendand garnished with golde like a flesh flye; one rounde clocke of golde enameled with a man on horseback, and divers colors aboute it; a watch of golde garnished with three small diamondes and eight sparks of rubies, with a very little pearle; one little clocke of golde enameled of the History of Time; a litle watche of golde, th'one side with a frogge on the topp, th'other side garnished with small garnets like a pomegranite; one litle clocke sett in eliotropie and garnished with golde; a litle watche of golde enameled with sundry colors on both sides alike; a litle watche of christall slightlie garnished with golde, with her Ma'ties picture in it; one faier flower of golde fully garnished with rubies and diamonds enameled on the backside with a man and a scripture about him having a watch in it and a pearl pendant; one flower of gold fully garnished with emerodes of sondrie bignes and sparkes of emerods and rubies, with thre antique women and five litle perles with a watch or clocke therein; a watch of agatte made like an egg garnished with golde; one clocke garnished with golde, being round and sett with 6 table diamondes and 6 rubies in the same border, and garnished with xvij diamondes on th'one side, and 8 diamonds and one rubie on th'other side, lacking two pearles."

In Fig. 120 is shown a clock watch from the Pierpont Morgan collection. It is in a polygonal case, which measures nearly 4 in. across. On the top plate of the movement is the mark B x N, and the piece, which dates from about 1580, is very possibly the production of Bartholomew Newsam.

Mr Edward Parr had a watch or table clock dating from about 1581, and probably of English make. It is in a circular case, about 4½ in. in diameter, as shown in Fig. 121. A large hemispherical bell rises from the space inside the dial ring, and the hand is curved down over the bell to read the hour numerals. The head of Queen Elizabeth in high relief, and other chasing,

Fig. 121.

ornament the side of the case. In a ring on the bottom of the case is the inscription:—

POSVI DEVM ADIVTOREM MEVM.
(*I have placed God as my Helper.*)

Against one of the winding holes is the letter W, and against the other the letter S; these stand doubtless for Watch and Striking, and strengthen the conclusion that the clock is an early English production.

Fig. 122.

SKULL WATCHES — MARY, QUEEN OF SCOTS

The skull watch (Fig. 122) is an excellent example of the fantastic forms in which some of the early makers delighted to encase their work. It is from the Soltykoff collection, and is said to have belonged to Henri III. The case

Fig. 123.

is of crystal, the dial of silver bordered with chased brass gilt, the centre being adorned with what is called *champ-levé* engraving to a floral design. The movement is inscribed "Jacques Joly."

Fig. 123 represents one of the ghastly productions of a larger size. The skull is of silver gilt, and on the forehead is the figure of Death with his scythe and sand glass; he stands between a palace on the one hand and a cottage on the other, with his toes applied equally to the door of each; around this is the legend, from Horace:—

"Pallida mors aequo pulsat pede pauperum tabernas regumque turres."
(Pale Death visits with impartial foot the cottages of the poor and the palaces of the rich.)

On the opposite or posterior part of the skull is a representation of Time, with another inscription from Horace:—

"Tempus edax rerum tuque invidiosa vetustas."
(Time, and thou too, envious Old Age, devour all things.)

He has a scythe; and near him is a serpent with his tail in his mouth, being an emblem of Eternity.

The upper part of the skull is divided into two compartments. On one are represented our First Parents in the Garden of Eden, attended by some of the animals, with the motto:—

"Peccando perditionem miseriam aeternam posteris mernere."
(By sin they brought eternal misery and destruction on their posterity.)

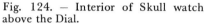

Fig. 124. — Interior of Skull watch above the Dial.

Fig. 125.

Fig. 126.

Fig. 127.

The opposite compartment is filled with the subject of the salvation of lost man by the crucifixion of our Saviour, who is represented as suffering between two thieves, whilst the Marys are in adoration below: the motto to this is:—

"Sic justitiae satis fecit mortem superavit, salutem comparavit."
(Thus was Justice satisfied, Death overcome, and salvation obtained.)

Running below these compartments on both sides there is an open work, of about an inch in width, to permit the sound to come out freely when the watch strikes. This is formed of emblems belonging to the Crucifixion — scourges of various kinds, swords, the flagon and cup of the Eucharist, the cross, pincers, lantern used in the garden, spears of different kinds, one with the sponge on its point, thongs, ladder, the coat without seam, and the dice that were thrown for it, the hammer and nails, and the crown of thorns. Under all these is the motto:—

"Scala coeli ad gloriam via."
(The way to glory is the "ladder" to heaven.)

The watch is opened by reversing the skull and placing the upper part of it in the hollow of the hand, and then lifting the under-jaw, which rises on a hinge. Inside, on the palate, is an excellent engraving of apparently a later date than the rest of the work. It shows the Holy Family in the stable, with the infant Jesus laid in the manger, and angels ministering to Him; in the upper part an angel is seen descending with a scroll, on which is written:—

"Gloria [in] excelsis Deo, et in terra pax hominibus bona voluntatis."
(Glory to God in the highest; on earth peace to men of goodwill.)

In the distance are the shepherds with their flocks. A representation of this cover is given separately.

The works of the watch occupy the position of the brain in the skull itself, the dial plate being on a flat where the roof of the mouth and parts behind it under the base of the brain are to be found in the human subject. The dial is of silver, and fixed with a golden circle richly carved in a scroll pattern; the hours are marked in large Roman letters, and within them is the figure of Saturn devouring his children, with this legend:—

"Sicut meis sic et omnibus idem."

There is no date, but the maker's name and the place of manufacture, "Moyse, Blois," are distinctly engraven on the plate. A silver bell fills the entire hollow of the skull, and receives the works within it when shut; a small hammer, set in motion by a separate train, strikes the hours on it.

The workmanship of the case is admirable, and the engraving really superb. The date of this relic may be taken to be between 1550 and 1600.

It is stated that it belonged to Mary, Queen of Scots, by whom it was given to Mary Seaton, one of her maids of honour, and much circumstantial evidence has been adduced in support thereof. I have recently had an opportunity of examining an almost similar Death's-head watch, which is also said to have been the property of the same royal lady and now belongs to Miss Mary Laura Browne, of Anerley. Except that beside the ring on the top of the skull is a screw for the reception of a cross, the case is an exact *facsimile* of the Mary Seaton one, with the additional inscription around the eyebrows, "EX DONO FRs. R. FR. AD. MARIAS DE SCOTORUM FR. REGINA." The original movement has, however, unfortunately been replaced by a comparatively modern one.

These two skull watches were doubtless intended to occupy stationary positions; the cross on one of them suggests a *prie-dieu* or small altar in a private oratory. At all events, they are too large and heavy to be worn on the person. The engravings represent the natural size of the relics, each of which weighs over three quarters of a pound.

In the British Museum are two Death's-head watches, much smaller and with plain cases. One of these was made by Johann Maurer, and the other by J.C. Vuolf. A similar watch, dating from about 1630, which was in the Dunn Gardner collection, and is now in the possession of Mr J. Pierpont Morgan, bears the signature of Isaac Penard. Another of these extraordinary conceptions, which belonged to Mr Robert Roskell, of Liverpool, and now forms part of the Schloss collection, is shown in Figs. 125 and 126. The skull or case of silver, much darkened by age, is a startlingly excellent counterfeit and a fine example of silver work. The plate bears the name of the maker thus, "Johann Leudl." On the dial of silver is an engraving evidently intended to portray the day of judgment. Inside the lower jaw, which closes on to the dial, is roughly cut the following inscription: "Lor logeur francoient duducq d'aremberque a mons." This specimen dates from about 1625; but the inscription is later, as the first Duke of Aremberg obtained his title in 1644.

A very diminutive Death's-head watch in the form of a seal is shown open in Fig. 127. The movement is furnished with the stack freed, and dates apparently from the first half of the seventeenth century.

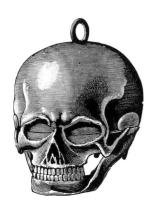

Fig. 128.

Fig. 129.

Of about the same period is the example by David Habrecht, shown in Figs. 128 and 129.

In the Vienna Treasury is a small skull watch of the time of the Emperor Rudolph II. in which the movable lower jaw strikes the number of hours against the upper one.

The late Rev. H. L. Nelthropp, who presented his splendid collection of watches to the Clockmakers' Company for exhibition in the Guildhall, considered the statements as to the ownership of skull watches by Mary, Queen of Scots, to be apocryphal, and said that a careful investigation of the catalogues of the jewels, dresses, furniture, belonging to Queen Mary proved beyond doubt that watches were not among her valuables. I cannot say that Mr Nelthropp's criticism is quite destructive of the original account, for if both of the watches were given away by the Queen, they could hardly be expected to figure in any subsequent inventory of her property. It is certain that watches were made during her lifetime; also that Blois was one of the earliest manufactories of watches, and that the family of Moyse flourished there during the sixteenth century. In face of the fact that Elizabeth had such a large number of watches, it seems almost incredible that the Scottish queen should never have possessed any of the fashionable novelties.

While the probability is that Mary, Queen of Scots, had watches of some kind, it must be confessed that the statements made respecting her ownership of specimens which have survived will not always bear examination. Among others which tradition has assigned to the Scottish queen, Octavius Morgan examined two which he considered to be of the period claimed for them. One was a ghastly *Memento Mori* watch in a case of crystal formed like a coffin, and the other an octagonal watch. The latter, which is now in the British Museum, is said to have been given by Mary to John Knox the reformer. The case of crystal had covers front and back, and the movement was inscribed "N. Forfaict à Paris." A large oval watch made by F. Le Grand, and said to have been found, immediately after the queen's escape from her imprisonment, in Lochleven Castle, was exhibited to the Philosophical Society of Edinburgh in 1850. A small circular watch by Estinne Hubert, of Rouen, presented, it is averred, by the queen the night before her execution to a French attendant named Massey, was a few years ago in the possession of Rev. Mr Torrance, of Glencross. In the Massey-Mainwaring collection was a round rather thin watch by Moysant, of Blois, in a case whereon is splendidly painted, in enamel, a representation of the Adoration of the Magi. This watch was some time ago exhibited at the Bethnal Green Museum with a label stating that it was given by Mary, Queen of Scots, to the Earl of Mar, from whom it passed into the possession of the family of Lord Forbes. But the style of the watch and the enamel painting did not seem to me to be entirely in accord with other productions of the sixteenth century.

In 1575, Parker, Archbishop of Canterbury, bequeathed to his brother Richard, Bishop of Ely, his walking stick of Indian cane having a "horologium" in the top. This is generally quoted as a watch, but is quite likely to have been a portable sundial.

The possession of many watches is ascribed to James I., but such as he did possess do not appear to have been utilised as timekeepers on every occasion, for in Savile's record of a state journey to Theobalds in 1603, it is stated that

Figs. 130-134. — Spherical Watch, about 1535. 1, plan of top; 2, dial and case partly opened; 3, elevation; 4, movement and dial removed from case; 5, movement showing top plate.

the king stopped at the Bell at Edmonton, and, wishing to count the number of vehicles passing in a certain time, he "called for an houreglass."

An early striking watch in a nearly spherical case of brass, chased and gilded, having the dial at the bottom of the sphere and a ring for carrying at the top, is shown in Figs. 130-134. The form and arrangement of the mechanism are exceedingly rare. The movement is in stories, and the dial, which is seen in Fig. 131, is attached to the lowest plate of the movement and not to the case. Between the dial and the plate, besides the wheels for actuating the hand direct from the mainspring and not through the intervention of the train, is the count wheel or locking plate. Above this plate is the striking train; then another plate, between which and the top plate are the going train and escapement. All wheels save the escape wheel are of iron or steel; the pillars are of iron shaped as shown, the plates and balance cock are also of iron: there are no screws nor barrels to contain the main springs; one of the mainsprings broken into many pieces is visible in the engraving (Fig. 133). The case is divided in the centre horizontally and fastened with a hooked catch; it opens on a hinged joint exposing the movement, which occupies the whole of the lower half of the case and extends into the upper part of the sphere. Over the top plate, of which a view is given in Fig. 134, are the primitive stackfreed, the cross bar balance or *foliot* and the hammer for sounding the hours on a silver bell fixed to the crown of the sphere, which is perforated as shown in Fig. 130. Through the case and the bell are holes for obtaining access to the winding squares, and near the bottom of the case is another aperture covered by a shutter; this, apparently, was for the purpose of adjusting the striking of the hours in case it had been allowed to become incorrect. The movement is fitted to the case in a peculiar way. Inside the lower half of the case are projections, and the movement together with the dial having been pressed into position, is twisted round till corresponding slits catch the projections and make it fast. The fixing is in fact what is known as a bayonet joint. This watch, I should judge, dates from about 1535. M. Paul Garnier has, I believe, a somewhat similar one, which was stolen from him a few years ago, and which he recovered by journeying to America and repurchasing it.

A mechanical celestial globe of gilt brass, held in a horizon ring carried by four caryatids, supported on the back of a kneeling figure of Atlas. The mechanism is signed by Isaac Habrecht III of Strasbourg and dated 1646. The dial at the north pole, once surmounted by a figure now missing, has two hands, one showing sunrise and sunset. The other turns once every two hours thus indicating the quarter hours and minutes in a 24-hour day. The sun and moon both move round the track of the ecliptic so showing their position in the zodiac, and the horizon ring is engraved with both the Julian and the Gregorian calendars. The mechanism runs for 28 hours and strikes the hours and quarters. National Maritime Museum, Greenwich.

Fig. 135.

Fig. 136.

Fig. 137.

A French globe clock, not signed or dated but c.1580. The globe of gilt copper is mounted on a gilt brass single column stand with engraved decoration. Marked on the globe which revolves, are 3-hour scales, a 24-hour scale perhaps for Italian hours, and two 12-hour scales. Also marked are the ecliptic with the signs of the zodiac, the equator, the tropics, the Arctic and Antarctic circles. When going the globe revolves and the time is indicated by a fixed pointer. There is a verge escapement with later balance wheel and spring, regulated by an index arm outside and at the bottom of the globe. This index is geared to a regulator on top of the balance cover. The fusee is now with chain but originally with gut as is evident from the flanges on the mainspring barrel. There is a ratchet and click mainspring regulator. The movement is wound through the stand, a winding arbor in the pillar of the stand being geared to the fusee arbor.

Originally the globe was surmounted by a figure, which at a later date has been replaced by a scaphe dial by Ulrich Schniep. Museum of the History of Science, Oxford.

Towards the end of the sixteenth century watches designed for use rather than to excite wonder or admiration were constructed with plain exteriors, as in Figs. 135 and 136, which show an alarm watch formerly in the Dunn Gardner collection at South Kensington. The little hand in the centre of the dial is for setting the alarm, and the hour indicator consists of an ornament attached to a disc around the edge of which are figures from 1 to 12 marked backwards, reversely to the usual direction, as a guide for setting the alarm. The hour numerals are on a silvered band with an unusually prominent pin at each hour so that the time could be more readily estimated by feeling. The case is of brass with plain cover and back; the only attempt at enrichment being the fine perforated work around the edge.

Fig. 137 shows a tambourine or drum-shaped watch from the collection of M. Paul Garnier. The case, brass gilt, is furnished with a bow, and has hinged covers back and front. The front cover is finely engraved and is pierced over each of the hour numerals on the dial. Inside the back cover is a representation of Christ rising from the tomb, well engraved after the design by Albert Dürer. The dial is of silver, finely engraved with rays and flames in the centre, beyond which are the hour marks with Roman numerals from I. to XII. on the outside of the circle, and smaller figures from 13 to 24 within.

Fig. 138.

A striking watch in a curious octagonal case of gilded brass fixed to a stand is shown in Fig. 138. The plates of the movement are of iron; it is fitted with the stackfreed, and its construction altogether shows it to be a mid-sixteenth century production. An interesting feature of this watch is the pierced door at the back, which is shown open in the illustration. Amid the piercing are represented the Man of Sorrows preparatory to the Crucifixion and around Him various items appertaining to His torture — a hammer, pincers, sponge, lamp, ladder, sword, spear or javelin, staves, lanterns, torches, cup, bunch of hyssop, &c. Two views of a pretty pedestal watch furnished with an alarm of about forty years later date are given in Figs. 139 and 140. Mr J. C. Joicey has a somewhat similar piece.

In the British Museum is a splendid watch made by Nicklaus Rugendas, of Augsburg. The case of metal, gilt, with open work very nicely pierced, is of an oval shape measuring 2¾ in. by 2¼ in. and 1¾ in. thick. It is mounted on a plain brass pillar 4 in. high. The hours are shown on a silver dial, and the minutes on a gilt bevelled outer rim which really forms part of the case. This arrangement and the fact that each five minutes space is figures, as is the modern custom, may lead to the assumption that the concentric minute indicator was a later addition; but Octavius Morgan, in whose collection the watch was, expressed his conviction (*Archaeologia*, vol. xxxiii.) that it

Fig. 139.

A continental coach watch made by Gautrin, Paris, in the late 18th or early 19th century. It has an hour and quarter striking mechanism, with alarm, and an unusual cylinder escapement. By courtesy of George Baptiste, Brussels. (First appeared in Carriage Clocks *by Charles Allix.)*

Fig. 140.

formed part of the original construction, and an examination of the hand work which I have been allowed to make quite removed a doubt I previously felt as to the correctness of his judgment. The internal arrangement shows considerable ingenuity, every atom of the space being utilised to the best advantage. There are four mainsprings, but no fusee. Between the dial and the movement is a small bell on which the quarter hours are sounded. The hours are struck from one to six and then over again in conformity with what was formerly an Italian method of computation, the hour bell being oval to suit the shape of th case; at the back is a large bell on which an alarm may be rung. The train wheels are of brass, and the quarter part of steel. Mr Morgan considered this watch to be a production of the second quarter of the sixteenth century, but the general style of the work and the construction of the movement negative such an assumption; 1610 or a little later would be nearer the correct date. Messrs Patek Phillipe & Co. have an octagonal calendar watch by the same maker, which, judging from a photograph of the movement, I should say was produced about 1630.

In the Vienna Treasury is a clock marked "Nicklaus Rugendas junger," dating from the middle of the seventeenth century.

Fig. 141 is an exterior view of a large circular clock watch in the possession of Mr Evan Roberts. It is unnamed, and is most probably of German or Dutch origin; the silver dial and brass open work case are very fine, as may be judged from the drawing. The stackfreed and the wheels are of steel, and the plates of brass. This watch has been pronounced to be a production of the second quarter of the sixteenth century, and the construction in many respects agrees with that period.

Although most, if not all, of the so-called 'sedan watches' appear to have no connection whatever with sedan chairs, the name has unfortunately become established. The example shown here is signed 'Ward London 1784' (this apparent date is more likely to be the serial number). It has a verge escapement plain flat steel balance with balance spring regulation, and is mounted in a mahogany case with brass mounts and inlaid decoration, c.1820.

117

Fig. 141. — Clock-Watch. Type of early German manufacture.

Three views of a splendid oval watch from the Schloss collection are seen in Figs. 142-144. Fig. 143 shows the dial with the front cover raised. Fig. 142 shows the back cover and edge of the case; and Fig. 144 the back cover raised, exhibiting the movement. The case is of brass, gilt and very finely chased. The front cover is pierced to receive a small glass, allowing the centre of the dial to be viewed without opening the cover. This style of glass, and the method of fixing it by means of a loose ring, is perhaps the most primitive; and taking the date on the inside of the back cover (1607) to represent the period the watch was made, it may be assumed to be an early instance of the application. The dial, also of brass, gilt, is very handsome. On looking at the movement (Fig. 144) a lever carrying two pins at one end and pointed at the other may be observed. These two pins are of stiff bristle, and by shifting the lever they may be caused to approach or recede from the arm of the balance, whose path they intercept. In this way the vibration of the balance and the timekeeping of the watch were controlled. The pointed end of the lever traverses a divided arc, and serves to indicate the movement given to the lever. At the top and bottom of the plate are pivoted bolts, which pass into holes in the edge of the case to secure the movement in position.

In the Pierpont Morgan collection is an oval brass watch of extreme beauty signed "Jan Jansen Bockelts van Aacken," dating from about 1640. It is shown in Figs. 145 and 146. Round the sides of the pierced case are a greyhound chasing a hare and a hound chasing a stag amidst floral designs. The back is finely engraved, representing figures of a naked shepherd with his crook and horn, a squirrel, and a monkey. In the centre a river scene, beneath the figure of a warrior in armour with a prancing horse on each side,

Fig. 142.

Fig. 143.

Fig. 144.

Fig. 145. — View of back

Fig. 147. — French Astronomical watch.

Fig. 148.

Fig. 146. — Dial with cover open.

TOY WATCHES

intermixed with scrolls and flowers. The outside of the lid is engraved with allegorical subjects, one represents Abraham offering up Isaac; upon the right hand top corner is a scroll on which is engraved, IAN. IANSEN-BOCKELTZ INV. ET SCVLP. The inside of the lid, which together with the dial plate is brass gilt, contains a compass and a sun dial with a movable gnomon. The dial plate is very fine. There is a small silver dial with alarm dial in the centre, and also a dial for the moon, one for the minutes, one for months — the seasons are engraved with LENTEN HERBST. WINTER.

Adam Thomson mentions an interesting astronomical watch of French make which is shown in Figs. 147 and 148. It has a silver case highly ornamented, with mythological subjects elaborately chased, bearing the following inscription on the inside of the back cover: "From Alethea Covntess of Arvndel, for her deare sone, Sir William Howard, K.B. 1629." It is of an oval form, the extreme size 2½ in., and 1½ in. in thickness. It struck the hours and has an alarm; showed the days of the week, the age and phases of the moon, with the days and months of the year, and the signs of the zodiac. On the inside of the front cover there is a Roman Catholic calendar with the date 1613. The watch movement is inscribed "P. Combret, à Lyons." A watch by Combret with a shell shaped silver case is in the South Kensington Museum.

These were occasionally shaped to imitate books, animals, fruit, flowers, and insects.

Of cases formed to resemble books several examples are known to exist. A very early watch of this kind dating from the first half of the sixteenth century is shown, rather smaller than the actual size, in Figs. 149, 150 and 151. On the back plate of the movement is the maker's punch mark, F.C., and another impression partly obliterated, which appears to be a pineapple.

Figs. 149-151. — Sixteenth Century Book-Watch. Outside with Covers open, inside of front Cover and Dial. View of mechanism inside back Cover.

Fig. 152.

Fig. 153.

There is a stackfreed for regulating the force of the mainspring, and sticking up from the longer end of a bell crank lever is a short stiff bristle, against which the cross bar balance banks. By means of its shorter arm this lever may be moved and its position noted by an index on the plate.

In the British Museum is a book shaped watch dated 1550. The specimen shown in Fig. 152 was in the Bernal collection which was dispersed by auction in 1855, and belonged to Bogislaus XIV., Duke of Pomerania, in the time of Gustavus Adolphus. On the dial side there is an engraved inscription of the duke and his titles, with the date 1627, together with his armorial bearings; on the back there are engraved two male portraits, buildings, &c. The covers are of brass gilt; the clasps and other ornaments are of silver; the dial is of silver, chased in relief; the insides of the covers are chased with birds and foliage. There are apparently two separate movements, and a large bell at the back; over the bell, the metal is ornamentally pierced in a circle with a dragon, &c.; the sides are pierced and engraved in scrolls. The maker's name is "Dionistus Hessichti."

Fig. 153, also from the Bernal collection, is in the form of a padlock. It has a crystal front and ribbed crystal back; gilt metal engraved mounting, dial of gilt metal; the days of the month are noted on a silver circle, with a steel plate apparently for the moon's age. The maker's name is Gio. Batt. Mascarone, and it is probably sixteenth century work.

Fig. 154. — Lion-shaped watch.

Fig. 155

Fig. 156.

Three views of a peculiar watch, dating probably from about 1600, are given in Fig. 154. The case, of silver, is in the form of a lion, the tail being looped, evidently for the attachment of a guard or other suspender. The movement is inscribed, "Jean Baptiste Duboule." A watch by the same maker in a nut shaped case forms part of the Wallace collection at Hertford House.

Of other more quaint and grotesque designs for watch cases favoured by the early makers may be mentioned one in the form of an eagle, which was in the collection of Lady O. Fitzgerald. It illustrated the story of Jupiter and Ganymede, and could either be suspended from a ring in the back of the bird or rested by its claws on a flat surface. In the British Museum is a watch shaped like an acorn, another resembling a dog, and one with silver cases made in imitation of cockle shells. In the South Kensington Museum is a French watch resembling a pelican, and a diminutive timekeeper concealed in one of two enamelled cherries with stalks connected was in the Mainwaring collection.

Memento Mori watches in the form of a Latin cross, and usually with scenes from the life of the Saviour engraved on the dials, were for a long period a favourite pattern, especially with French artists, among whom they were known as *montres d'abbesse*. Dubois says cruciform watches were probably devised by Myrmécides, a watchmaker of Paris, who flourished

121

between 1530 and 1550, and whose name appears on several early specimens. They appear to have been worn, generally, on the breast, and are often spoken of as pectoral cross watches. Of three in the British Museum, one, in a case of rock crystal, very similar to Fig. 155, was made by Jean Rousseau the elder about 1580; another, also a sixteenth century production, is by Tinnelly, Aix; the third dates from the latter part of the seventeenth century, and is cased in emerald glass.

The watch, Fig. 156, which is unnamed, seems to be late sixteenth century work.

In the *Archaeological Journal* is mentioned a Latin cross watch by the celebrated Johannes van Ceulen, which has a cover of crystal and is enamelled in opaque colours; on the front the Man of Sorrows and emblems of the Passion, and on the back the Crucifixion.

Of three cruciform watches in South Kensington Museum, one, dating from about 1590, is signed "Senebier"; another, of slightly later date, bears the initials "N.R."; and the third, which forms part of the Salting collection, has a silver and crystal case, and is by Charles Bobinet, a French seventeenth century maker of repute.

Portable clock with balance, No. 61 by Ferdinand Berthoud, 1795. For reasons unknown this clock now bears the signature 'Breguet No. 11' on the chapter ring. Since however it is clearly described and illustrated by Berthoud in his Histoire de la Mesure du Temps *(1802) there is no question about the attribution. Intended by Berthoud to act as a portable astronomical regulator, and having a regulator-type dial, it is fitted with a form of pivoted detent escapement with a compensated balance, has anti-friction rollers, Harrison's maintaining power fitted to the fusee, and jewelled end pieces set in the cocks. The case is glazed on all four sides and the small button at the lower right of the dials controls stopwork acting directly on the balance. National Maritime Museum, Greenwich.*

A striking and repeating carriage clock in a well-proportioned, gilt-metal case, with corinthian capitals and barley twist pillars. It has a white enamel dial with the hour, minute and seconds dial filling the upper part, together with a lunar phase sector. In the lower half are subsidiary dials for the alarm, day of the week and day of the month. Christie, Manson & Woods Ltd.

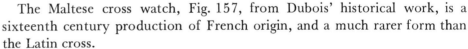

The Maltese cross watch, Fig. 157, from Dubois' historical work, is a sixteenth century production of French origin, and a much rarer form than the Latin cross.

A very early crystal case watch by Thomas Franck, from the Soltykoff collection, is shown in Fig. 158.

In Fig. 159 is shown a clock watch by Conrad Kreizer, from the Soltykoff collection. The case is of crystal, the dial of silver, and the cover of brass gilt. A peculiar feature is the oval raised pierced work of brass, introduced evidently to allow the sound of the bell to be heard more distinctly. The movement is of a primitive character, and the maker is said to have been contemporary with the brothers Habrecht. An octagonal watch in the South Kensington Museum, signed "Conrad Kreizer," is certainly early seventeenth century work.

The crystal case watch in the form of a cockle shell, shown in Fig. 160, also from the Soltykoff collection, is a late sixteenth century production. It has covers back and front; the dial is gilt, with silver hour band and steel hand.

Another specimen from the Soltykoff collection, in a crystal escallop case, shown in Fig. 161, has very primitive mechanism, by *Phélisot, horloger de la ville de Dijon*. The dial, finely engraved, is of silver, with gilt hour band; the hand is in the form of a lizard.

The pear shaped watch shown in Fig. 162 was made by Conrad Kreizer, of Strasbourg, and is also gathered from the Soltykoff treasures. A similar watch is in the British Museum.

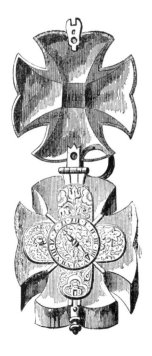

Fig. 157.

Fig. 158.

Fig. 159.

Fig. 160.

Fig. 161.

The circular specimen shown in Fig. 163, selected from the same repository as the preceding, has covers back and front; around the band are figures typical of spring, summer, autumn, and winter. The dial is of silver gilt, with a white band on which the hour numerals are engraved. In the centre of the dial is engraved a representation of Christ and the woman of Samaria; on the upper cover is portrayed the spectacle of Mary Magdalene washing the feet of Jesus, and on the lower cover another Biblical scene. The movement is inscribed, "James Vanbroff," and it dates from about 1605.

Fig. 164, with crystal case in the form of a *bonbonnière*, is from the Soltykoff collection. From the movement, which is inscribed "Denis Bordier," one may judge that it was made about 1640.

Of a little later date is the beautiful specimen by Benjamin Hill, a well known London maker, which is shown in Fig. 165.

Of all the quaint fancies exhibited in the formation of early watch cases, none are, I think, more charming than the various floral designs popular during the sixteenth and seventeenth centuries.

Fig. 162.

Fig. 163.

Fig. 164.

Fig. 165.

124

Five 19th century French carriage clocks showing different styles of decoration, all with platform lever escapements. Top left: the movement is stamped 'C.V.', the clock has grande sonnerie striking on two gongs, while the dial is decorated in champlevé enamel on a plain yellow ground. Top right: a typical plain white enamel example in classic style also with grande sonnerie striking. Bottom left: a larger example stamped on the back plate with the initials 'G.L.' and having the dial and side panels painted with flamingoes around a lake. Bottom centre: an unusual case which imitates bamboo, while the dial and sides are painted with scenes of birds flying and in the trees. Bottom right: an example made for the Chinese market with grande sonnerie sriking, and alarm and repeating work on two gongs. The dial has centre seconds and a subsidiary alarm dial surrounded by floral designs in cloisonné enamel on a puce ground which extends to the corinthian columns and base of the classical case. Christie, Manson & Woods Ltd.

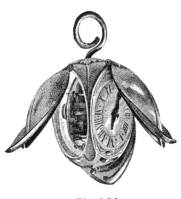

Fig. 166.

Fig. 167

The opening tulip bud, from the Soltykoff collection, which is shown in Fig. 166, must be admitted to be a very pretty artistic conceit. The dial and the covers or leaves are of silver, and so is the twisted stalk that forms a ring for the attachment of a chain or cord. The movement bears the name of Rugend of Auch, and dates from the beginning of the seventeenth century. A very similar specimen by Bayr, who was, I think, a Dutch maker, is to be seen in the British Museum.

A larger counterfeit of the same flower appears in Fig. 167. The body of the case is of gold, and there are three bezels or covers of silver, each comprising a piece of rock crystal formed in the shape of a tulip petal. The hand is of gold, the dial of silver, with a landscape engraved thereon. Through one cover the dial is seen, and through the other two the movement is visible. It has a three armed steel balance and a balance spring. Jean Rousseau the younger, who is said to have died in 1684, was the maker of this watch. The presence of a balance spring would therefore stamp it as one of his later productions.

There is a splendid tulip watch among the Nelthropp collection at the Guildhall Museum, without a balance spring, by F. Sermand, dating from about 1650; another at the South Kensington Museum, and one at the British Museum by Henry Ester.

A very pretty floral watch of an early date, from the Soltykoff collection, is shown in Figs. 168 and 169. The case is gold, adorned with fine floral ornaments in green and Cassius purple enamel on a white ground. The dial is of gold, decorated also in green and purple enamel on a white ground. The plates and train wheels of the movement are of brass. It is provided with a fusee with catgut and a circular balance. The movement is signed "J. Jolly," and dates from about 1600. Fig. 168 shows the dial and edge fairly well, but

Fig. 168.

does not give a good idea of the elegant form of the case, which will be better gathered from Fig. 169, which is a back view with the cover open.

Fig. 170, another diminutive watch of a later date from the same collection, is in the shape of a poppy bud. The case is of amber with mountings of gold, finely engraved and maintained on the amber by means of close gold wire running down the angles to the knob which holds the ring on which the chain is to be fastened. The dial is of silver with enamelled ornaments; it is covered with a piece of rock crystal fitted in a bezel.

Back and front views of a very pretty English watch in the form of a flower bud, which formed part of the Dunn Gardner collection, and was purchased for the South Kensington Museum, where it may be seen, are given in 171 and 172. It dates from about 1610, and is inscribed "Henry Grendon at y Exchange Fecit."

Fig. 169.

Fig. 170.

Fig. 171.

Fig. 172.

An elaborately decorated carriage clock signed 'Caudron Eleve de Breguet Place Beauveau Paris', c.1860, in a gilt case. It has a lever escapement, two going barrels, quarter hour striking on a large gong shaped to fit exactly round the edge of the case. There are three white enamel dials recessed in a chased and gilded brass plate for hours and minutes, day of the month, and the alarm which sounds on a bell. Bobinet Ltd.

126

A strut clock by Thomas Cole, London, No. 1 671 37 (c.1847) the first number being the running number of the clock in Cole's production series, and 37 its number in the oval strut type series. A typical example of Cole's very thin portable desk top clocks with a standard engraved silver guilloche dial and gilt metal case. Geneva bar cylinder movement signed 'aine Geneve'. On the dial is the signature of C.F. Hancock, London, one of the main retailers of Cole's work. For details of Cole's manufactory see J.B. Hawkins, Thomas Cole and Victorian Clockmaking, Antique Collectors' Club, 1975, particularly pp. 66-67 for a description of a closely similar example. Sotheby Parke Bernet & Co.

In the British Museum are three watches in the form of insects or fritillary flowers. One labelled as English work, by Edward Bysse, is in a nielloed silver case. Another, also English, in a silver case, is by Thos. Sande.

The watch case in the form of a basket of flowers (Fig. 173) is of gold, enamelled and studded with diamonds.

A watch set in a finger ring is shown in Fig. 174.

Figs. 175 and 176 represent an olive-shaped watch in the Schloss collection. The case of gold is beautifully enamelled in green and dark blue.

Three views are appended, the exact size of an exceedingly diminutive watch. Its dial and tiny case of gold are beautifully decorated with *champ levé* enamel, and the movement is fitted with the primitive stackfreed for regulating the force of the mainspring (Fig. 177). One might with tolerable confidence say that this is the smallest enamelled watch of the stackfreed period.

A pretty star shaped watch, decorated with enamel and pearls, is shown to two thirds the actual size in Fig. 178.

Fig. 173.

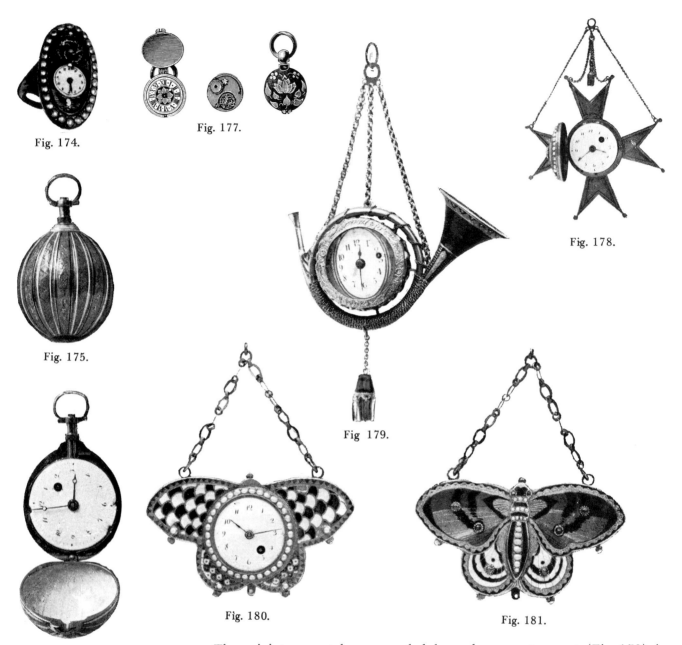

Fig. 174.

Fig. 177.

Fig. 178.

Fig. 175.

Fig 179.

Fig. 176.

Fig. 180.

Fig. 181.

The miniature watch surrounded by a horn or trumpet (Fig. 179) is engraved to the actual size.

Front and back views of a superb specimen in the form of a butterfly are given in Figs. 180 and 181. It is impossible to give more than an idea of the choicely enamelled back by reproduction in black and white.

Most of these "toy" watches are of French or Swiss origin. It is curious to note in eighteenth century advertisements the references to the sellers of them as "toymen."

Irregular shaped octagonal watches are met with among the productions of the latter part of the sixteenth till quite the close of the seventeenth century. Many variations in the size and material of the cases were made by French and afterwards by English artists to suit their own tastes or the desires of their patrons; the cover was often of crystal, lapis lazuli, agate, or other semi precious stone. The crystal case specimen (Fig. 182) is an early

A brass cased mail guard's watch signed *Thwaites & Reed* London *14175, c.1840.* Designed specifically to be carried about, perhaps so that post office officials could carry mean time with them into different parts of the country where local time differed materially from that of London, and also carried on stage coaches, the guard handing his locked time piece to the local post-master at certain points for the time of arrival to be recorded. The watch has a conventional full plate lever movement, without any decoration, and a steel three arm balance. It is mounted in a large and robust outer case. The example shown is slightly unusual in being set from the back.

Fig. 182.

Fig. 183.

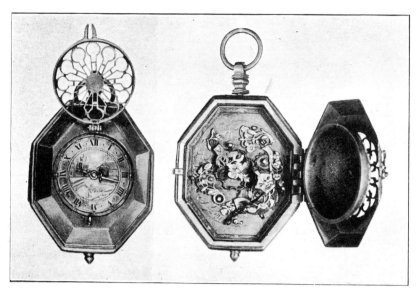

Fig. 184. — Striking or Clock-Watch.

Fig. 185.

Fig. 186. — Watch by Jeremie East, about 1600.

one, apparently of French origin. Another, from the Soltykoff collection, is shown in Fig. 183. The covers are of silver, and by means of a second dial and two small apertures in the dial plate it indicated the sign of the zodiac corresponding to the month, the day of the month, the day of the week, and planetary motions. It also struck the hour and provided an alarm. It is unnamed, but probably late sixteenth century work. Back and front views of a striking or clock watch of nearly the same period are given in Fig. 184. There is a cage like covering over the dial, and the back is similarly perforated. Very nice engraving is to be seen on the head of the hammer as well as on the balance-cock and other fittings connected with the plate of the movement, which is signed "J. Boudon, à S. Flour."

Fig. 185 is probably French early seventeenth century work. It has covers of crystal and side panels of brown topaz. The movement is signed "J. Dubie à Paris."

Fig. 186 represents a watch in a case of crystal, which is in the possession of Messrs Lambert, who allowed me to examine it. On the plate of the movement is inscribed "Jeremie East, fecit," and it is, I should say, a very early example of English work, dating from not later than 1600.

In Fig. 187 is shown a superb watch of large size in an octagonal case of crystal, with a crystal cover and gilt brass mountings. The movement is oval, and bears the signature of "P. Cuper," who was a well-known maker of Blois. The dial plate is beautifully engraved, and near the joint is the date 1634. It indicates the phases of the moon and her age, the days of the week, and days of the month.

An octagonal crystal case watch by Henry Grendon, "of ye Exchange," which dates from about 1660, is shown in Fig. 188. It was formerly an attractive item in the Dunn Gardner collection and now belongs to Mr J. Pierpont Morgan. On the gilt dial plate are engravings of tulips; the hour ring is of silver. There is an outer case of grey fish skin studded with silver pins, rosettes, hinges and clasps, which is shown open in Fig. 189.

Some time ago I saw a small octangular watch movement inscribed "Nicasius, London," dating from about 1605.

In the British Museum is a choice octagonal watch, dated 1620, by the celebrated Edward East. The body, as well as the cover of the case, is of crystal, faceted, and the exterior altogether closely resembles Fig. 186. Another, somewhat similar, but dated 1609, is inscribed, "Michael Nouwen, London." A watch of this shape, said to have belonged to Abbot Whiting, is shown in Fig. 190, which is copied from Warner's 'History of Glaston Abbey." On the inside of the cover will be noticed the inscription, "Richard Whytinge, 1536." Warner seems to have accepted the inscription, but beyond it there is really no evidence except a seal attached to the watch by a string; this is certainly not conclusive, and I confess I do not believe such a watch was made so early as 1536.

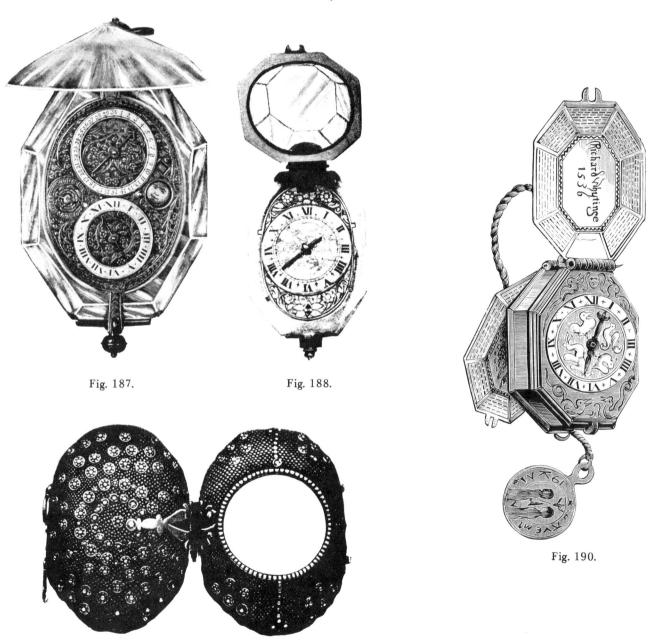

Fig. 187.

Fig. 188.

Fig. 189.

Fig. 190.

One of the marine timekeepers made on the pattern of Thomas Mudge's blue and green timekeepers, to the commission of his son Thomas Mudge Jnr. This example is signed 'Pennington Pendleton and others for the son of the inventor No. 11, 1796', and has a duration of one day. About three dozen of these copies were made fitted with Mudge's escapement, but being both expensive and relatively unsuccessful they were soon discontinued and many were subsequently converted to more conventional forms of escapement. The example shown here now has a standard Earnshaw type spring detent escapement with compensated balance and helical spring. The separate dials for hours and seconds are surrounded by applied silver decoration. The stand is not original. Sotheby Parke Bernet & Co.

A two day marine chronometer by John Arnold & Son, No. 69 c.1794. The machine is fitted with Arnold's type of spring detent escapement and has a large Z-shaped balance with gold and blued steel, detachable bimetallic rims, oversprung with helical blued steel spring. There is a silvered dial with subsidiary seconds dial and the whole instrument is housed in an octagonal mahogany box without gimbals. For an exhaustive account of Arnold's work see Vaudrey Mercer, John Arnold & Son Chronometer Makers 1762-1843, London, 1972. Bobinet Ltd.

Fig. 191.

Fig. 191 is from the collection of M. Paul Garnier. The square case has a ground of bluish steel, overlaid with chased gold ornament, the combination producing a very striking effect. The edges are decorated in the same way. The dial is square, enamelled blue in the centre and white all round, the corners being adorned with *motifs* in red enamel. The movement is signed "Balthazer Martinot," who was horologer to Louis XIII. in 1637. Steel cases with gold filigree work attached were rather popular at the middle of the seventeenth century. Among others in the British Museum is a choice specimen by Benjamin Hill.

Two views of a clock watch in a remarkably well pierced circular case are given in Figs. 192, 193. The dial of brass gilt is finely engraved, and altogether it is a good example of the style in vogue about 1640. The movement is signed "Martinot Au gros Orloge, Rouen."

OVAL WATCHES   From the designation "Nuremberg eggs," which is often applied to watches of a flattened oval form, it may be supposed that they originated in

Fig. 192.

Fig. 193.

Fig. 194.

A typical example of the developed 8-day English marine chronometer, signed 'Jas McCabe No. 319 Royal Exchange London', c.1840. Left: the watch gimballed in its box as it would have been when at sea, although then it would normally have been viewed through the observation window under the top lid, and not with the box open. Below: the movement with split level spotted plates, a temperature compensated balance with Earnshaw's spring detent escapement. There is a helical blued steel balance spring with terminal curves, and a balance guard. Boninet Ltd.

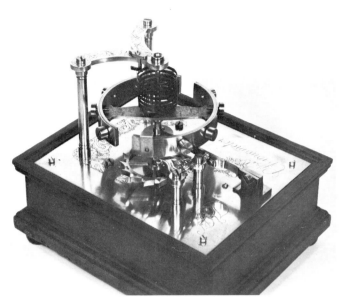

Two extremely well-made and finished models of escapements. Left: the spring detent escapement usually fitted to chronometers. Right: a tourbillon escapement which although relatively rare is found fitted to some expensive and complicated pocket watches. Both models are signed with the initials in a monogram 'ARD'. Christie, Manson & Woods Ltd.

Nuremberg. They appear to have been manufactured here as early as 1600. Figs. 194 and 195 are two specimens from the Schloss collection. That reproduced in Fig. 194 is a striking watch of a very early date. The movement, furnished with the primitive stackfreed, is fitted into a case of brass nicely pierced at the sides as shown. On the joint of the case is the signature "J. Burgis." The outer part of the dial is of brass, the centre, including the hour ring, of silver, and on the cover over it is fixed a circular crystal, an addition doubtless made subsequent to the manufacture of the watch.

Some of these early oval watches had covers back and front — the movement not being hinged to the case but simply pressed into it and supported by tenons which projected from the dial. Fig. 195, an example of this kind, represents a watch the movement of which is signed "R. Delander fecit." It is in a silver case having brass mouldings at the edges; the outsides of the covers are finely engraved with groups typical of the beneficial use of fire and water respectively; and on the inside of the back cover is a sun-dial with a stud for the reception of a movable gnomon. The dial is wholly of silver.

In Fig. 196 is shown an oval watch belonging to Mr Evan Roberts. The dial is of silver, and has mounted thereon a brass hour ring. At each hour, near the exterior edge of the ring, is a slight knob to allow of the time being ascertained by feeling the hand and estimating its position with relation to the knobs. Over the hour ring is the engraved inscription, "Our time doth passe a way." The case is of silver. On the movement plate is engraved, "Thomas Aspinwall fecit." The name of Aspinwall is not unknown among the celebrated early English watchmakers; it is recorded that in 1675 Josiah Aspinwall was admitted as a brother of the Clockmakers' Company. His

Fig. 195.

Fig. 196.

Fig. 197.

Fig. 198.

admission as a "brother" probably signifies that he was free of one of the other City Guilds. In 1863 Lord Torphichen exhibited, at the Archaeological Institute, a clock watch made by Samuel Aspinwall, of a date presumably about 1650 or 1660. But I should be inclined to place this watch as among the productions of a much earlier date. A few years ago I saw a watch very similar to the one here depicted, on which was engraved, "Samuel Aspinall fecit." Bearing in mind the vagaries of seventeenth century orthography, we may assume that this referred to a member of the same family.

Oval or egg-shaped watches were usually worn on chatelaines. They were apparently more popular than any other form from 1610 to 1625, and continued in fashion with the fair sex for a long time. In Hollar's plates of the four seasons, dated 1641, summer is represented by a lady having an egg-shaped watch on her left side depending from her girdle. The British Museum contains several similar specimens, most of which are assigned to the first quarter of the seventeenth century. One, by Nicholas Waller, is dated 1610. Another, almost a counterpart of the one illustrated in Fig. 197, is by John Limpard, and was made about 1610. It is calculated for going sixteen hours between windings. The case is of silver, partially gilt and very elegantly chased; on one side is a figure representing Hope, and on the other a corresponding figure of Faith.

An exterior view of an oval watch by Simon Bartram is given in Fig. 197. The circular patch on the left is a "hit or miss" shutter, which covers the winding hole to prevent the ingress of dirt. This shutter is found on many really seventeenth century watches. It had to be moved round when the watch was wound, and on completion of the operation was replaced. The dial is very similar to that shown in Fig. 196. A drawing of the movement, which is of particular interest, will be given later on.

In the Pierpont Morgan collection is a watch of the same kind by the same maker, another oval one by Edward East, which has an outer capsule case, one by Samuel Linaker, and that shown in Fig. 198, which is by Denis Bordier, Paris. It has a brass gilt dial prettily engraved and a fluted silver case.

The small oval watch in a case of crystal which belongs to Mr Max Rosenheim and is shown in Fig. 199 bears the signature "Jean Nuer, A Saintes."

Fig. 200 represents an oval watch, apparently English, in a silver case and with a silver dial. There are no screws used in the movement, which is signed "William Yate." Mr Edward Parr had a somewhat similar watch in a brass case, the movement of which is signed "Wm. Nash, London."

There is a very small oval watch in the British Museum. It measures but half an inch across by three quarters of an inch long, and has plain silver capsule shaped outer cases. The South Kensington Museum contains a still smaller one.

Early in the seventeenth century plain circular watch cases came into favour, but not to the entire exclusion of more fanciful shapes.

Figures 201 to 206 show examples of some diminutive round watches of the period. Fig. 201, in a case of silver gilt, dates from about 1630, and the movement is signed "Jacob Wibrandt, Leuwarden." A plainer specimen of a slightly later date bearing the name "Chaunes le jeune" is shown in Fig. 202.

Front and back views of a watch bearing the signature, "Arnolts, Hamburg," are given in Figs. 203, 204. The case of silver is handsomely

Fig. 199.

Fig. 200.

Fig. 201.

Fig. 202.

Fig. 204.

Fig. 203.

Fig. 205.

Fig. 206.

chased in *repoussé*, with a remarkably well executed portrait on the back. It is a production of about 1635.

Figs. 205 and 206 represent a watch by Jeremie Gregory, a well-known English maker. The outside of the case is covered with *champ levé* engraving, a style of decoration rather uncommon and very effective if well done, as it is in this instance.

Holbein the painter seems to have taken a remarkable interest in horology. In his famous picture of "The Family of Sir Thomas More," painted 1526-30, is to be seen hanging on the wall a clock much resembling the one of Anne Boleyn which is illustrated in Fig. 35. The bracket on which Anne Boleyn's clock now stands was probably added by Horace Walpole.

HOLBEIN   Holbein was on very intimate terms with Nicholas Cratzer (or Kratzer), horologer to Henry VIII., and painted a superb portrait of him, which is dated 1528, and is at the Louvre, Paris. Cratzer is there represented at work on a sun-dial, with other instruments of the kind near him. Holbein's last dated drawing (1543) now at the British Museum, is a design for the casing of a combination of clock and sun-dial, intended for presentation to Henry VIII. by Sir Anthony Denny. But Holbein's interest in the craft was quite exceptional in England at that period, and it must be confessed that up to nearly the end of the sixteenth century English horologists had but a very small share in the production of portable timekeepers.

SALT CELLAR CLOCKS   In the early part of the seventeenth century it was apparently the custom to have clocks combined with salt cellars on the table at state banquets, to judge by the following curious items from an inventory of the plate in the lower and upper jewel rooms of the Tower, 1649:— "A salt of state with a clocke in it, valued att £12 0 0; a clocke salt with a christall case, supported with 4 pillars, silver-gilt, valued at £4 10 0; an aggatt salt and cover garnisht with gold, enamelled, supported by 3 men, and a shipp on the top of the cover, p. oz. 10½ oz., valued att £33 0 0; two clocke salts standing upon 4 christall balls and 4 christall pillars, each with aggatt salts on the topp, and gold covers, p. oz. 3 lb. 2½ oz., valued att £3 6 8 per oz. = £77 0 0; a christall watch salt garnisht with gold, and supported with 3 faces with several fruitcages hanging about them, p. oz. 30 oz., valued att £30 0 0."

The cnronometer room at the Royal Observatory, Greenwich, c.1890, showing rows of box chronometers on test for the Royal Navy. Besides assessing new chronometers each year in the premium trials, the observatory had also to carry out routine rating tests on chronometers which had been in use and returned for overhaul after extended periods of service. By the end of the 19th century this was a considerable quantity of work. National Maritime Museum, Greenwich.

Left and below:
A watchman's time-check clock by Frank Woodward Maker Derby c.1840. Simple plated movement with anchor escapement. Around the edge of the dial plate are 48 pins free to move through the plate when pressed by the hammer. The pins are restored to their place by a small inclined plane mounted behind the plate. Museum of the History of Science, Oxford.

Chapter IV

Pocket Watches, etc.

POCKETS WERE USED for the reception of timekeepers in Shakespeare's time, for Jaques, in "As You Like It," remarks, "And then he drew a dial from his poke." Portable sun-dials, sometimes with a compass attached, were then made, and the reference was probably to one of these.

Watches were not usually carried in the pocket for more than a century after the mainspring was invented. The larger ones would be kept on a table or cabinet, and the smaller kinds, when worn on the person, were originally held by a chain around the neck, or attached to the dress in other ways, unless incorporated with bracelets and such like ornaments, as many of Queen Elizabeth's seem to have been.

Fig. 207. — Oliver Cromwell's Watch and Fob Chain.

The grotesque and uneven cases applied to most of the early watches clearly rendered them unsuitable for the pocket. Decker in 1609 (Gull's Hornbook), apostrophising the fashionable young bloods idling in the cathedral, says, "Here you may have fit occasion to discover your watch by taking it forth and setting it to the time of St Paul's." This suggests a pocket, but long after this date oval and round watches were made with a pointed projection depending from the bottom of the case, and these were clearly never intended for the pocket, nor fit for it. The fob, from the German *fuppe*, "a small pocket," was very possibly introduced by the Puritans, whose dislike of display may have induced them to conceal their timekeepers from the public gaze. This conjecture is strengthened by the fact that a short "fob" chain attached to a watch of Oliver Cromwell's, in the British Museum, is, in point of date, the first appendance of the kind to be found. The watch is a small oval one, in a silver case, and was made about 1625, by John Midnall, of Fleet Street, who was one of the first members of the court of the Clockmakers' Company, and warden in 1638. On one side of a silver plate at the seal end of the chain are the Cromwell arms, and on the other the crest of the Protector with the letters O. C. as shown in the appended engraving, Fig. 207. The Cromwell crest was a demi-lion holding a ring in its paw, but the Protector substituted for the ring the handle of a tilting spear as here represented.

This watch and chain formed part of the Fellows collection. By the will of Dame Harriet Fellows (relict of Sir Charles Fellows), late of West Cowes, Isle of Wight, who died in 1874, the testatrix bequeathed to the trustees of the British Museum her collection of watches, to be placed and held with Milton's watch, bequeathed to them by her late husband.

Fig. 208. — Clock-Watch of Oliver Cromwell.

WATCH GLASSES

Fig. 209.

Fig. 208 is an illustration from the *Illustrated London News*, February 1850, of a clock watch which is said to have belonged to Oliver Cromwell. It is, I believe, the property of Mr J. H. Fawkes, of Farnley Hall, and bears the name of Jaques Cartier. The outer case of leather is perforated and studded with silver.

In the *Gentleman's Magazine* for December 1808 is shown a small oval watch, similar to the one by East, Fig. 399, which, it is stated, Cromwell at the siege of Clonmel took out of his fob and presented to Colonel Bagwell.

In the South Kensington Museum is a circular clock watch by Johannes Bayes, which probably belonged to Cromwell's secretary. The outer case of tortoiseshell bears the inscription, "John Pyme hes watch, A.D. 1628.

A very handsome watch by Henry Harpur is shown in Fig. 209. It has a silver dial with day of the month ring and beautifully pierced centre; the inner case is of silver, having on the back the arms of Cromwell, to whose daughter Bridget the ownership of the watch is assigned; the outer case of fish skin is *piqué* with silver pins.

Watch glasses seem to have been introduced about 1610. At first they were flat, rather thick, and fitted into split bezels, as the containing rings are called, the opening in the bezel being at the middle of the joint, so that the corresponding knuckles of the case would keep the slit tightly closed on to the glass. Glasses of this kind are found on oval watches, and also on circular ones with dials much smaller than the cases, which were a fashion at the beginning of the seventeenth century. Then followed the high, rounded glasses, which were cut from spheres. Afterwards came the bull's eyes, with a circular flat centre; these, which were of German origin, gave place to the flatter "lunettes" from France, such as to-day divide popular favour with the thick "crystal" glasses.

Glasses were apparently used for table clocks some years before they were applied to watches. German and French table clocks, dating from the latter part of the sixteenth century, are occasionally to be met with having glasses over the dials, and some octagonal ones with glass panels in the sides. But the innovation did not at once prevail, as table clocks, either without any covering over the dial, or with metal covers, were made long after the first examples with glasses, and watches with metal covers continued in fashion till the middle of the seventeenth century.

In the British museum is an oval watch by Guy Mellin, Blackfriars, the dial of which is covered with a glass in a split bezel; also a circular watch by John Duke, Fleet Street, with a dial one-half the size of the case, and a glass of a corresponding size fitted into a split bezel. Mellin's watch is considered by the authorities to have been made about 1600, but I should be inclined to put the date of its production a few years later. Several other watches, whose manufacture is ascribed to the beginning of the seventeenth century, may be noticed with glasses; but these adjuncts in some instances have been subsequent applications. The split bezel is perhaps a tolerable criterion of originality, but it does not absolutely follow that such a bezel was originally fitted with a glass, for the frames of early watches and clocks were occasionally furnished with crystal.

Another method of fixing the glass prior to the introduction of the present practice of springing or snapping it into the bezel consisted of forming three or four thin metal ears on the bezel and bending them over the

Three watches with their original chatelaines, c.1780-90. At top left is a verge watch by Vezit à Paris with a white enamel dial and an outer case of blue and white enamel decoration, surrounding a scene of two putti engaged in building which is perhaps of masonic significance. The matching chatelaine with four hooks has enamelled scenes of putti and doves. Centre is a small quarter repeating verge watch by André, Paris No. 1075. The engine turned case has gold foil stars on a transparent blue enamel surrounded by a circle of alternating leaves and pearls in enamel on the bezel. The chatelaine is of gold and enamel, the oval miniatures being in coloured gold in a frame of split pearls. At the right is a verge watch by William Hughes, London, No. 3644 the case and chatelaine being decorated by miniatures in the style of Moser on a chocolate ground in a green and white enamel frame surrounded by blue enamel. Attached to the chatelaine also is the gold key for the watch. Sotheby Parke Bernet & Co.

glass when it had been placed into a suitable rebate. I saw this in a watch by Benjamin Hill. It was, however, but a survival of the mode in which crystal was held in octagonal and other fancy cases, and must be regarded as an inferior arrangement which does not seem to have been at all general, whereas the split bezel was used preferentially by some makers long after the custom of snapping the glass in was introduced. The watch shown in Fig. 450, and made about 1700 by the celebrated Langley Bradley, has a split bezel.

CHATELAINES

Fig. 210.

The convenience of the "fob" to those who carried watches for use rather than for ornament was soon apparent, and its adoption speedily became general with men, though ladies continued to wear their watches suspended from chatelaines till the latter part of the eighteenth century. Some of the chatelaines were exceedingly handsome, as may be judged by an example from the Schloss collection which is shown in Fig. 210. The plaques are painted in enamel in the style of Huaud; the mounting and painting are French. In 1749 Benjamin Cartwright patented a secret spring to secure a watch hanging by a lady's side. In the Winter Palace, St Petersburg, is a splendid array of chatelaines. They are attached to English watches, and probably of English make. Many of them are set with gems of the most costly description.

Like many other fancies, the one of wearing two watches is but a revival *pace* the *Universal Magazine* for 1777, where the description of a "modern fop" includes —

"A lofty cane, a sword with silver hilt,
A ring, two watches and a snuff-box gilt."

Fig. 211. — Front, with Cover closed.

Fig. 212. — Dial and inside of clock.

WATCH CASES

It will be observed from the preceding examples that a great number of dissimilar materials were used to enclose portable timekeepers: wood of various kinds, precious and semi-precious stones, amber, metal and leather were all utilised for this purpose. With few exceptions the earliest watches had but a single case. Metal was the predominating material, the plainest

A physician's pulse watch, signed 'Jno Tolputt Portsea No. 19177', c.1770. Silver pair case watch with enamel dial on which the seconds, indicated by a centre hand, are written in large Arabic numerals around the circumference of the dial for ease of reading and counting. The hours and minutes are shown on the small subsidiary dial in the upper centre. The watch has a verge escapement, fusee with chain, a plain steel balance and stopwork. It was intended for use by physicians when counting pulse beats, a technique first described by Sir John Floyer in The Physicians Pulse Watch (1707-10). Despite this specialist use however the movement of the watch is in no way unusual.

Fig. 213.

cases being usually of brass, or of polished steel; silver also was favoured both for smooth and engraved cases; for the most costly coverings gold was of course selected, either by itself or in combination with precious stones, and occasionally the two precious metals would be used together with pleasing effect.

Sometimes the watch movement, instead of being fastened to the case, was simply placed in, four tenons which projected from the edge of the dial fitting into corresponding mortices in the middle band of the case. The case then had two hinged covers, one over the dial and one over the back, the movement being rendered secure by the closing of the front cover; the back cover had to be opened to wind the watch. The oval watch by R. Delander, which is illustrated in Fig. 195; the one by David Bouquet formerly in the Mainwaring collection, and another by David Ramsay in the South Kensington Museum, are examples of this method. But more often the movement was joined to the case by means of a hinge near the pendant and a spring bolt at the opposite point of the dial, four projecting tenons on the dial resting in notches cut from the middle of the case. This mode of construction is clearly shown in the engraving of the oval watch by Thomas Aspinwall in Fig. 196. Till about 1720 the spring bolt generally projected through the dial; after that the nib for unbolting was more often arranged outside the circle of the dial and below the surface of it.

ENAMEL   Decoration in enamel is sometimes to be found on watch dials and cases produced during the early part of the seventeenth century. An exceptionally good specimen is shown in Figs. 211 and 212. The outside of the cover and the back are embellished with enamel, the ground being of turquoise blue

Fig. 214.

Fig. 215.

with white arabesques moulded thereon in relief and studded with fine garnets of large size. Though "jewelled watches" are referred to as belonging to Queen Elizabeth, and in other records of the period, it is very rarely that so early a combination of enamel and gems is now to be met with. The inside of the case and of the cover are also painted in enamel, and so is the dial. There is no glass over the dial. The hand is well shaped. The plate of the watch is inscribed "Pierre Soret."

Front and back views of a watch covered with the same kind of enamel, but of later date, are given in Figs. 213 and 214. The centre of the dial is blue, and a portrait on an enamelled plaque occupies the centre of the back. A very thin name-plate is engraved "James Coupé, London," and underneath the name-plate appears the signature "Marc Grangier."

In Fig. 215, by permission of Mr Charles Shapland, I am enabled to give a representation of a specimen in a different style, dating from about 1630. On the top plate of the movement is the inscription "Georgius Merkell, Dantzig." The case is of gold, and is wholly incrusted with enamel both inside and outside; flowers of various colours and kinds, as well as winged insects, are charmingly represented.

Of other kinds of enamelling to be met with but rarely on early seventeenth century watches may be mentioned *champ levé*. This somewhat resembles the well-known *cloisonné*, but, instead of the various sections being divided by the insertion of metal strips, the partitions are solid with the base, and the intervening spaces cut out to receive the enamel. A watch, signed "Du Hamel à Paris," dating from about 1635, in a gold case very effectively decorated in this way with cream-coloured enamel, which is at South Kensington Museum, is shown in Fig. 216. Another example is given in Fig. 217, which is the back of a watch with a peculiar notoriety, referred to in Chapter III.: the dial bears the inscription "Robertus Bruce Rex Scottorum," as shown in Fig. 217*A*, while the watch is a production of about 1645, the movement of it being signed "Johann Kreitt Mayr." The diminutive watch in Fig. 177 is also decorated with *champ levé* enamel.

Occasionally translucent enamel was employed, and effects of light and shade obtained by varying the depth of a cavity which was cut to the required design in a metal base.

Watches with enamel painting before about 1640 are exceedingly rare, and there is a marked difference in the character of such decorative work executed at the beginning, compared with that done during the later years of

Fig. 216.

Fig. 217.

Fig. 217A.

Figs. 218-220. — Watch by Salomon Plairas, Blois, with Enamel Painting, about 1625. 1, outside of cover; 2, back of case; 3, inside of cover and dial.

Fig. 221.

Fig. 222.

Fig. 223.

Fig. 224.

Front and back views of Watch. The movement signed "Barthelmy Mace a Blois"

146

Fig. 225.

Fig. 226.

Fig. 227.

the seventeenth century. As examples of the earlier style, which presented a comparatively lustreless surface and subdued tints, may be taken the watches shown in Figs. 218 to 224. During the first quarter of the century the Holy Family appears to have afforded the theme for decoration in nearly every instance. Afterwards, though sacred subjects were not ignored, mythological incidents were sometimes selected by artists for reproduction, and occasionally original conceptions and portraits of contemporary personages were applied to watches intended most probably for presentation.

In Figs. 218 to 220 are three views of an early and very fine sixteenth century enamelled watch from the Schloss collection. The movement is signed "Salomon Plairas, horlogeur, A Blois."

Fig. 221, from the collection at the South Kensington Museum, shows the front of a watch dating from about 1630, on which is a painting of the Holy Family, after Rubens.

Fig. 222 represents the back of a watch of the same period at the British Museum, for which the artist has apparently taken the romance of Theseus and Hippolyta as the subject of his painting. The movement is signed "B. Foucher, Blois."

Front and back views of a watch, the movement of which is signed "Barthelmy Mace a Blois," are given in Figs. 223 and 224. Nearly all artists who painted watch cases up to the end of the eighteenth century seem to have included the "Roman Piety" in their selections; the representation on the back of this watch could, I think, hardly be excelled.

Fig. 225, from the British Museum, shows the back of a watch by Jean Hebrat, of Brussels, of a slightly later date than Fig. 224; the painting is bordered with turquoises.

Back and front views of a very beautiful watch, the enamel painting of which is probably English as well as the movement, are given in Figs. 226-227. On the back of the case, within a charming floral border, is a well-painted portrait, said to be that of Henrietta Maria, daughter of Henry IV. of France and wife of Charles I. of England. The dial is finely painted to a floral design and covered by a glass kept into a recess in a primitive way by six pins bent over from the bezel. The hand is of brass, pierced and chased. On the plate of the movement is engraved "Simon Hackett, Londini." He was elected a member of the Clockmakers' Company on its formation in 1632, and served as master in 1646.

An improved method of painting in opaque enamel, which appears to have been discovered about 1635, is generally credited to Jean Petitot, who was born in Geneva in 1607, and attained much success as a miniature painter in France and in England. The new process consisted of applying to thin gold plates thick colours of different tints which would, after being subjected to fire, retain their brilliance and lustre. Petitot exercised his art on snuff-boxes, but I have never met with enamel decoration on a watch which bore his signature. The invention of this particular kind of enamel painting is also claimed for Jean Toutin, a goldsmith of Château Surr, who was previously distinguished for painting in enamels, and who certainly seems to have been one of the first to apply it to watches. Other French and Swiss artists quickly devoted themselves to the new kind of enamel painting. Among those who excelled in it may be mentioned Henry Toutin, brother of Jean, a goldsmith and enameller at Blois; Dubie, a court goldsmith who worked at

147

An unusual verge watch signed 'Francois Dominice a Geneve', c.1700, perhaps made to special order as a lover's token to his lady. The Roman hour numerals are formed from silver covered copper wire on a heart shaped green ground each covered by an individual glass. The hand is supplied by a figure of Cupid who indicates the time with his bow and arrow. On the back the balance cock has been replaced by a miniature of a lady (perhaps the beloved) seated at a table. The balance is also unusual, being made in the shape of an anchor, the vertical member of which returns above the cock carrying a jewel which oscillates like a pendulum (or perhaps the lover's beating heart) over the cock. Museum of the History of Science, Oxford.

Fig. 228. — Front of Case.

Fig. 229. — Back of Case.

Watch about 1640.
Movement signed
"Barbaret à Paris".

Fig. 230. — Movement and inside
of Case.

Fig. 231. — Dial and inside of
Cover.

the Louvre; Paul Viet, of Blois; Morlière, a native of Orleans, who worked at
Blois; Robert Vauquer, of Blois, a pupil of Morlière, of pre-eminent ability,
whose enamel painting has never been excelled either for colour or design,
though specimens of his art are rarely to be met with on watch cases; Pierre
Chartière, of Blois, who was noted for his painting of flowers; and the
brothers Jean Pierre and Ami Huaud (Huaut, also spelt Hualt), of whom
"Huaud le puisne," as he usually signed himself, was particularly celebrated
for figure-painting. Several examples are to be found in the British, South
Kensington, and Guildhall Museums.

Four views of a splendid watch in the Schloss collection, dating from
about 1640, appear in Figs. 228, 229, 230, and 231. The movement is signed
"Jacque Barbaret à Paris."

Fig. 232.

Fig. 233.

Front and back of a smaller watch from the same collection, signed "Romieu, Rouen, Fecit," are given in Figs. 232 and 233.

The representation of the toilet of Venus on the back of a watch by Robert Lochard, which is shown in Fig. 234, is an extremely beautiful example.

The admirable painting of figures and landscape shown in Fig. 235 is signed by "Huaud le puisne," and is on the back of a watch by Steven Tracy, Rotterdam, which is at the British Museum. Among other examples there may be cited a representation of some nymphs bathing, excellently executed in enamel by Jean Toutin; an enamelled case, very finely painted by Henry Toutin, illustrating the story of Tancred and Clorinda in "Orlando Furioso"; another by the same artist which treats of the "Rape of the Sabines"; a watch by David Bouquet, a well-known London maker, the case being ornamented with flowers, in relief, and enriched with diamonds; a very finely enamelled watch case, illustrating the early life of Christ; a very thick rounded watch by Tompion, with case splendidly painted in enamel by Camille André.

Fig. 236 shows the case of a watch by Jean de Choudens, dating from about 1680, which is painted in a really charming manner and bears the inscription "Les deux freres Huaut pintre de son A. E. Berlin." It is at the South Kensington Museum.

Of slightly later date is a watch by "F^dr· De Miere Amsterdam," with a painting on the back of the Roman Piety, as shown in Fig. 237. This is signed "Huaud le puisne fecit," and is also to be seen at South Kensington. A similar painting covering a watch by "Pieter Paulus Amsterdam," which is in the Schloss collection, bears the signature "P. Huaud, P. Genius, F. Geneva."

There were two examples in the Dunn Gardner collection which was dispersed by auction in 1902: a choice piece of figure painting covering a watch by Lucas, Amsterdam, the enamelled case being signed "Huaud l'aisné pinxit a Geneue," and a watch by Julien Le Roy, with enamelled case, bearing the signature of G. Bouvier.

Figs. 238 to 243 are signed specimens of the Huauds' work. The first consists of front and back views of a watch by "Goullons à Marseille,"

Fig. 234.

Fig. 235.

Fig. 236.

Fig. 237.

Fig. 238.

Fig. 239.

Fig. 240.

Fig. 241.

Fig. 242.

Fig. 243.

dating from about 1670, which is signed "Huaud le puisne." On the front are Mars and Venus with Cupid, and on the back "The Hours."

The next two bear the same signature, and are a little later. A pair of lovers is painted on each; the first Apollo and Diana, the second possibly Mars and Venus. The former covers a watch by "Ofard a Gex", and the latter one by "Johannes Van Ceulin, Hague."

"Venus and Adonis" is signed "Le deux frere Huaut, p. d. V. A. Fct, a Berlin," and is on the back of a watch by "Vanenhove, Amsterdam."

Fig. 244.

Fig. 245.

Fig. 246.

Fig. 247.

Fig. 248.

Fig. 249.

The group "Susanna and the Elders," most beautifully painted, is signed "Les deux freres Huaud les jeunes," and is on a watch named "Jan Bern^s Vrythoff, Hague."

Pigments of different composition yielding colours not so superlatively rich and warm as characterises the work of what I will venture to call the Huaud school seem to have been introduced towards the middle of the eighteenth century. Prevost (or Prevaux), who is described as "Peintre du cabinet de S. M." (Louis XV.), may be taken as one of the best exponents of the new method. He painted a portrait of Madam Pompadour, by command of the king, for which he was paid 1,000 livres. A really beautiful piece of his enamel painting, signed "I. Prevaux, pin. 1749," on the back of a watch by

Fig. 250.

Fig. 251.

Pascal Hubert le Jeune, Rouen, from the Schloss collection, is shown in Fig. 244 together with others decorated in a somewhat similar style. The watch in Fig. 245, with a pair of lovers and a landscape on the back, is by Julien Le Roy. Vulcan, Venus, and Cupid are on a repeating watch by the same maker. The sylvan scene with a flute player and a lady holding the music adorns a watch signed "Raphard, London," and the remaining two are watches by Julien Le Roy. Naomi and Ruth are represented in Figure 248, and the tableau in Figure 249 is founded, I believe, on a tragic incident in the romance of Orestes and Hermione.

Painted groups, bordered with translucent enamel over a wavy or engraved metal ground, were favoured during the last half of the eighteenth century, and in many instances the surface of the painting was covered with a transparent flux, which gave it a glassy appearance.

During the first half of the nineteenth century portraits and views in small panels attached to the backs of watch cases were popular and of very uneven merit. Most of them were, I think, of Swiss origin.

In the Vienna Treasury is a watch case finely enamelled inside and out by the brothers Huaud.

Other representative examples of French, Swiss, and English enamel are appended.

Fig. 250 shows the back of a watch by Henry Harper, London, of a style corresponding to 1670. The painting is probably Dutch, and of a later date.

The beautiful painting set in an engraved gold border shown in Fig. 251 encloses a watch signed "Honoré Lieutand, Marseille."

Two views of a half-quarter repeater by Rd. Gregg, London, from the Pierpont Morgan collection, are given in Figs. 252-253. The centre of the outer case is enamelled with figures of cupids in a landscape, and small vignettes are painted around the edge; the dial bears the arms of Herbert, second Viscount Windsor; this title became extinct in 1758. The painting is signed with the initials "A.C."

An unusual verge watch in a silver case hallmarked 1804, by John Holman of Lewes. The white enamel dial is cut away to provide an aperture for the age and phase of the moon, the hours 6-12-6 being indicated around the edge of his aperture. Although watches of this type had been long abandoned by makers in London and the other large manufacturing centres, they are sometimes encountered in late provincial work. Sotheby Parke Bernet & Co.

153

Fig. 252.

Fig. 253.

An excellent specimen of floral decoration in enamel bordered by engraving appears in Fig. 254, which represents the gold back of a watch signed "Jn. Lˢ· Argand, Paris," and dating from about 1770. A back view of a contemporary watch by Romilly, Paris, with pretty flower painting on a brown enamelled ground, is given in Fig. 255.

A choicer piece of flower painting on enamel than is shown in Fig. 256 it has never been my good fortune to see. This watch belongs to the Hon. Gerald Ponsonby, by whose permission it is illustrated. It is a *sourdine* repeater by Julien Le Roy; the hands, bow, push piece at pendant, thumb piece and *sourdine* toucher are all set with diamonds.

As an example of English enamelling dating from about the middle of the eighteenth century, is shown, in Fig. 259, the exterior of a watch by Arl. Dobson, London, which is in the British Museum. I wish I could say the painting is better than contemporary specimens of foreign artists.

Notwithstanding the taste for Chinese art which was so apparent in France during the eighteenth century, it is very seldom a watch is met with having a back of porcelain enamel with a Chinese subject moulded thereon. An example covering a watch by Julien Le Roy may, therefore, be of especial interest, though it makes but a poor picture. The figures are in bright colours, and the ground a dark brown.

Figs. 261 to 266 show some fine examples of varying periods. "The Nativity" is a beautiful piece of painting in the incomparable Huaud style on the back of a watch by Gribelin, Paris, dating from about 1680. Fig. 262

Fig. 254.

Fig. 256.

Fig. 257. — Back of Watch by G. Achard et Fils, Geneva. Enamel painting studded with diamonds.

Fig. 258. — Back of French Watch. Enamel painting studded with diamonds; surmounted by a bust of Louis XVI.

Fig. 255.

Fig. 259.

Fig. 260.

Fig. 261.

Fig. 262.

Fig. 263.

Fig. 264.

Fig. 265.

Fig. 266.

shows a watch the movement of which is signed "Abraham Le Schegs, Amsterdam." The painting is doubtless also by one of the Huauds. Figure 263 shows the back of a watch by the younger Caron. Any appearance of vulgarity in the subject of the painting is quite atoned for by the adjoining view of the inside of the case, where are represented the young mother and her babe. The representation of the mother of Achilles dipping him in the Styx is on the back of a watch by Julien Le Roy. Diana and her attendant nymph, which adorns the last watch on the page, dates from about 1780.

Fig. 268.

Fig. 269.

Fig. 270.

Fig. 267.

Fig. 271. — Watch by J.B. Baillon à Paris, about 1765.

Fig. 272. — Watch by Gregson, Horloger du Roy, Paris, about 1785.

Fig. 273. — Watch by Alexander Patry à Geneva, about 1790, miniature bordered with pearls and coloured stones.

Fig. 267 shows a watch by J. Leroux, Charing Cross, which is said to have belonged to Viscount Windsor, whose title became extinct in 1758. The case is enamelled blue and white on a gold ground.

In Fig. 268 is shown a repeating watch by Lepine; on the gold case in an oval medallion are finely carved figures of gold and silver on a ground of green enamel, outside of which is a wreath carved in silver. This decoration is exceedingly effective. The push piece, thumb piece, and bow are studded with diamonds.

Fig. 269 is a late eighteenth century French painting representing Cymon and Iphigenia.

In Fig. 270 is shown the back of what is called a "Mongolfier" watch, from the Pierpont Morgan collection, on which is painted a representation of a balloon undergoing inflation, intended, I suppose, to commemorate the success of Montgolfier's aerostatic machine in 1782. The movement is signed "Vauchez, Paris."

Fig. 275 shows the back of a thin watch by "Gregson, Paris, Horloger du Roy." The case is enamelled on gold, the outer part rayed and covered with royal blue translucent enamel; on a medallion of opaque enamel in the centre is a well-painted group with Cupid and a dog, denoting love and faith. It is characteristic of the Louis XVI. period, when this style of enamelling was in fashion. Fig. 276 shows an English watch, with the London hall mark corresponding to 1787. The margin is of translucent royal blue as in the preceding example.

Two French watches of slightly later date, finely painted in enamel, are shown in Figs. 277 and 278.

Battersea enamel dates from about 1750, when Sir Theodore Janssen, who was Lord Mayor of London in 1754, established a manufactory at York House, Battersea. Horace Walpole described his collection as "stamped with copper plates." Transfer printing may have been employed for flat surfaces, but certainly not for watch cases, the painting on some of which was by

Fig. 274. — Watch by Lepaute, Paris, about 1790, enamelled portrait bordered with diamonds.

Fig. 275. — Enamelled Watch by Gregson.

Fig. 276. — English Enamelled Watch.

Fig. 277.

Fig. 278.

Fig. 279. — Enamel bordered with Pearls.

Fig. 280. — Enamel Painting on back of Watch by Breguet.

Fig. 281.

artists of note. A very good example is shown in Fig. 281. Back and front views of a very choice little watch by Hughes, London, of a slightly later period, are given in Figs. 282 and 283.

Watch dials of enamel, with pictures painted in bright colours inside of the hour ring, and occasionally outside of it, proved very attractive between 1760 and 1800. They were inexpensive, and as a rule of but little artistic merit, the most favoured designs being those in which shipping and seaports were introduced. Many thousands of these were produced for the Dutch market by English watchmakers.

The miniature of Marat, *"l'ami du peuple,"* on the back of a watch from the Schloss collection, which is shown in Fig. 284, is an admirable piece of work.

Fig. 282.

Fig. 283.

Fig. 284. — Marat.

Fig. 285. — Napoleon.

An interesting silver cased, oval calendar watch of the late 17th century, made at least partly in Turkey, and signed in Arabic script by Dhūnā at Ghalata. The gilt face has two dials for hours and for the age and phase of the moon, and two volvelles for the day of the week and the month of the year. Verge escapement, brass and steel balance, and a back-plate entirely covered in delicate arabesque decoration.

Watch-making was established at Ghalata in Turkey towards the end of the 17th century by a small group of Swiss craftsmen chiefly from Geneva. It survived well into the 18th century by which time a few native makers had been trained. For a general discussion see Otto Kurz, European Clocks and Watches in the Near East, *London & Leiden, 1976. British Museum, London.*

A fine miniature of Napoleon Buonaparte on the back of a musical half-quarter repeater of French make, which is shown in Fig. 285, is in the Pierpont Morgan collection. This watch is said to have been given by Napoleon to Murat on the fête day after the battle of Marengo, 1800. No cost seems to have been spared either with the mechanism or the embellishment. A tune is played at the completion of each hour; the miniature and dial are bordered with pearls; the bow also is studded with them.

A French novelty watch, sometimes referred to as a bras-en-l'air, unsigned, c.1800. Full plate movement, verge escapement, fusee with chain, ratchet and click mainspring regulator, wound and set through the dial. On the white enamel dial are vertical sectors for the hours and minutes and an applied gilt oriental figure whose head turns from side to side with the going of the watch. When the pendant is pressed the figures arms rise to indicate the time on the sectors of hours and minutes beside it. In a plain gold case as is normal for these watches. The watch may be compared with the 'fencing soldiers' watch on pp.185-7. Sotheby Parke Bernet & Co.

Fig. 286.

A pretty little watch, which in many respects is a credit to English mechanical and artistic work of the first quarter of the nineteenth century, is shown in Fig. 286. It bears the hall mark for 1813, and is engraved "Markwick Markham, Borrell, London," a form of signature induced doubtless by the regulations applied to watches imported into Turkey, for the dial is marked with Turkish numerals. It may be assumed that Borrell was the manufacturer. The movement is of admirable finish, has a verge escapement and fancy pillars, but the particular attraction is the beautiful gold cases, of which there are three. The outer one, instead of having a flat surface where the halves meet, is scalloped all round, but still forming a well-fitting junction by no means easy to attain. This case is enamelled, with a glass in the back, through which a very choice bit of floral enamel painting is to be seen. The backs of the two cases are so well fitted together that it requires minute scrutiny to detect that the enamelled centre is not part of the outer case. The innermost case is a plain one, but exceedingly well made.

Fig. 287.

During the eighteenth century the cock or bridge covering the balance of the watch, and concealed until the movement was turned out of the case, was occasionally decorated with painting in enamel. Fig. 287, given as an illustration, is a watch signed "Flamant à Paris." It has a gilt metal case, and dates from about 1710; over the balance is a gold enamelled plaque with a finely painted representation of Cleopatra.

A complex watch by Thomas Mudge, No. 574, 1764, with a perpetual calendar showing the date, day of the week, month, age and phase of the moon through volvelles in the white enamelled dial. Around the edge of the dial is a revolving calendar scale. The watch is controlled by a cylinder escapement and has plain gold pair cases, the outer of which contains a trade paper of Mudge carrying scales for the equation of time. Sotheby Parke Bernet & Co.

A silver cased, verge calendar watch signed 'Courvoisier & Frères', c.1810. The escapement is inverted so that the balance may be seen through a hole cut in the dial. White enamel dial painted with a scene of two distressed girls in a garden. Subsidiary dials for hours and minutes, date and day of the week. Surrounding the dial is a calendar scale half being marked with the month name and length, the other half with the signs of the zodiac, thus allowing the month and its corresponding zodiacal sign to be read off from either end of the central calendar hand. Sotheby Parke Bernet & Co.

PAIR CASES

Fig. 288. — Flat Chasing on Single Case Watch by Daniel Le Count, about 1680.

To protect the surface of the decoration watches with exterior ornament of enamel were generally provided with an additional cover, and from about 1640 the practice of adding a loose outer case to watches, forming what are called "pair cases," continued to the early part of the nineteenth century.

Loose cases of gold and silver, with designs chased in *repoussé*, were at this period an important art in connection with watchmaking. Chasing as distinguished from engraving and carving is the formation of ornament in relief by punching or pressing, rather than by cutting away the material. It is a very ancient art, and chased ornament is to be found on some of the earliest of watch cases. Much of the work on old clocks, which at first sight appears to be engraving, proves on examination to be chasing. All the small numerals on Habrecht's clock at the British Museum are stamped.

The silver chased work applied to the edges of English oval cases at the beginning of the seventeenth century is said to have been imported in strips from France.

An excellent piece of flat chasing, including the head of Charles II., with the Royal Crown and supporters, on the case of a watch by Daniel Le Count, dating from about 1680, is shown in Fig. 288. The case is a single one, and on the right is a little catch, by pressing which a disc on the left springs on one side, exposes a round hole in the case, and thus allows access to the winding square. The dial of this watch is shown in Fig. 330 and the movement in Chapter VIII.

The same style of decoration of a later date on the outer case of a watch, by William Scafe, may be seen in Fig. 289.

In *repoussé* chasing the material is punched or pressed up from the back, whereby the design is obtained in higher relief than is the case with the ordinary method of punching from the face. Some very choice specimens of *repoussé* work, marked "H. Manley" in very small characters, are in the British Museum. An outer case at the South Kensington Museum is

161

Fig. 289. — Flat Chasing on Outer Case of Watch by William Scafe.

signed "H. Manly fec.," and a watch by Ellicott, bearing the hall mark for 1767, in a fine *repoussé* case, which appears to be signed "Manby," is in the Guildhall Museum. Among the signatures on other good examples may be mentioned Parbury, Cochin, and Moser, but as a rule decorative work of this kind bears no indication of the producer.

Occasionally cases decorated in *repoussé à jour* are to be met with, some of the best of them being the work of Dutch artists, but this form of ornament is hardly suitable for watch cases, as it affords no protection against the ingress of dirt, unless a separate lining is employed. For striking watches, apertures of course serve a useful purpose.

A large verge watch by William Story, London, c.1790 in gilt metal cases. The outer case is decorated with an oval miniature of a shepherdess in an idealised landscape with sheep, surrounded by red and green translucent enamel on an engine turned ground. The edge of the case is engraved with foliate decoration and imitation jewels. Well balanced white enamel dial with three subsidiary dials for seconds, day of the week, and age and phase of the moon. A stop lever can be seen at the left hand side. Sotheby Parke Bernet & Co.

Fig. 290. — Pair Case Repeating Watch by Paul Dupin, about 1700, showing *repoussé* outer cover. The chasing is of exceptional fineness.

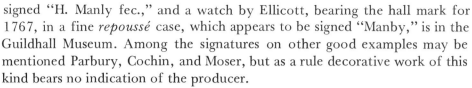

Fig. 291. — Repeating Watch by Paul Dupin, showing pierced work of inner case.

Sometimes, and particularly with *à jour* cases, the ornament is in high relief, and to obtain the best possible effect the metal constituting the case is not only worked in *repoussé*, but the figures, or parts of some of the figures standing up farthest from the ground, are soldered on, considerable skill and judgment being displayed. Illustrations of *repoussé* chasing are given in Figs. 292-303, but bright gold cases embellished in this way do not, it must be

Fig. 292. — Silver *repoussé* signed D. Cochin.

Fig. 293. — *Repoussé* Chasing on Gold Out-case.

Fig. 294. — Gold *repoussé* Chasing.

Fig. 295. — Gold *repoussé* Chasing.

Fig. 296.

Fig. 297.

Fig. 298.

Fig. 299.

Fig. 300.

Fig. 301.

Left: Fig. 302. — Half-quarter English Repeater with Silver Out-case.

Fig. 303. — Silver Out-case of Watch by J. Murray, hall mark 1810.

confessed, lend themselves kindly to reproduction by photography. Incidents from English history were occasionally portrayed, but mythological and Biblical subjects appear to have been more favoured. Among the examples may be recognised "King John signing Magna Charta," "Alexander and Roxana," "The Conversion of Saul," "The Judgment of Paris," "Rebecca at the Well," "Aeneas and Dido," &c.

Fig. 303 is an exceptionally late and fine specimen, covering a watch by James Murray, London. It has an oval pendant, and the date mark corresponding to 1810. On the outside of the inner case is engraved "Francisco Joseph, 1811."

A combination of chasing and engraving was also effectively employed in the embellishment of gold cases; some of the choicest specimens of early eighteenth century work which survive being the work of George Michael Moser, R.A.

What is called *champ levé* engraving, in which the ground is cut away, leaving the design in relief, was often adopted for decorating English dials and inner cases from about 1640 to 1680. The watch by Jeremie Gregory (Fig. 206) is an instance of this work. Many French watches and clocks of an earlier date were so treated.

In the Nelthropp collection is a watch by Thomas Windmills, the cases of which are engraved in an exceptional style, corresponding to the Italian niello work, where the effect of light and shade is produced by rubbing in a preparation of lead and sulphur. On the outer case is a view representing the yard of an inn with the sign of a pitcher. In the yard is being played the

Three examples of the 18th century taste for watches made to look like something else. Such pieces are usually known as form watches. Normally highly decorated with enamel, engraving, or precious stones, they are more interesting as jewellery than as watches usually having totally standard movements. Sotheby Parke Bernet & Co.

A large verge watch with musical mechanism and repeating the quarter hours, by Joseph Martineau Senior, London, number 1849, mid-18th century. The dial is of champlevé silver with Turkish numerals. The musical train plays two tunes by twelve hammers on seven bells and there is a selector for the tune. The inner case of the watch shows an extremely detailed landscape scene in gold repoussé within a symmetrical frame, with classical ruins on the right foreground and a small town in the distance in front of hills. The scene is signed with the initials C.H. The outer case is of leather with four pierced and engraved panels and with a symmetrical floral decoration silver piqué at the centre. Sotheby Parke Bernet & Co.

Fig. 304. — Watch by "Flower, London," with Out-case of Steel.

game of Pale Maille, popular in the time of Charles II., and from which the thoroughfare of Pall Mall takes its name. Under the title of Croquet a pastime bearing some resemblance to it was introduced in recent years.

The watch shown in Fig. 349 has an outer case of steel, damascened, and Fig. 304 represents a steel out-case of a watch by "Flower, London," decorated with engraving; such cases are, however, quite exceptional. The dial of this watch is also of steel, blued and having gilt figures. A watch by Vulliamy, having a steel pendant and steel out-case pierced, is shown in Fig. 305. The monogram (C. A. R., Charles Albert Rex) refers to the King of Sardinia, for whom the watch is said to have been made. He was father of Victor Emmanuel, first King of United Italy.

Occasionally, during the latter part of the seventeenth century and early in the eighteenth century, outer cases were made of gold filigree work. An example is shown in Fig. 307.

As a curiosity may be mentioned an outer case of carnelian which is to be seen in the British Museum. It belongs to a watch made by Strigner for

Fig. 305.

Fig. 306. — Out-case of Fish Skin *piqué* with Gold Pins, about 1690.

Fig. 307. — Gold Filigree Out-case.

Fig. 308.

Fig. 309. — Watch by Cabrier, with Outer Case of Carnelian and Mother-or-Pearl set in Gold.

James II., and by him given to his daughter, Catherine, Countess of Anglesey and Duchess of Buckingham, about 1687. In the Hawkins collection was a magnificently clothed repeater by John Ferron, London, dating from about 1710. The watch now belongs to Mr James W. Usher, of Lincoln. It has a pierced and engraved inner case of gold; the second case, also of gold, is chased with flowers and arabesques, inlaid with plaques of moss agate, and set with numerous brilliants and coloured stones. A view of this is given in Fig. 308. There is also a shark-skin outer case. Fig. 309 shows a watch by Cabrier which is furnished with an outer case of gold, carnelian, and mother-of-pearl, and Fig. 310 another, by the same maker, with an out-case of gold, studded with large garnets. Mr George Carr Glyn, at the Guelph Exhibition, showed a watch by Jas. Hubert, which had an agate case studded with diamonds.

In Fig. 315 appears a water scene and landscape very finely carved in ivory and applied under a glass to the back of a watch case, which is coated with royal blue enamel. The carving is enclosed in an oval frame of pearls, outside of which is a floral design also executed in pearls. Around the edge of the case at both back and front is a leaf border enamelled green, and within it a ring composed of pearls and garnets alternately. This watch dates from about 1790, and though the case is Swiss, the movement bears the signature "Jaquet Droz, London." The mechanism is marked by one or two interesting features. The mainspring is wound by pushing in and withdrawing a shaft passing through the pendant, a device known as "pumping keyless," of which this is an early example. Jaquet Droz was a well-known Swiss mechanician, and he may possibly have at one time resided in London. The cap, balance-cock, and other pieces are quite in the English style. The dial is furnished with a centre seconds hand, which is placed between the hour and minute indicators. At this period such an adjunct was not at all common.

Outer cases of horn and of tortoiseshell, either plain or *piqué*, were not uncommon, and the semi-transparency of these materials was sometimes utilised for a superior kind of decoration. A thin disc of tortoiseshell having been moulded to the metal foundation, a landscape or other design was either etched or painted on the under side and a row of pins inserted around the edge of the tortoiseshell to secure it to the metal. The picture could be

Fig. 310. — Watch by Cabrier about 1750. Out-case *repoussé* and studded with large Garnets.

A lever watch by Houriet Père et fils, Locle, in a highly decorated case. The movement of steel and blued steel has a lever escapement, a bimetallic compensated balance and a winding barrel with damascene decoration. White enamel dial with blued steel moon hands. The bezel, pendant and bow are decoratively cast and the back of the case shows a cornucopia with peacocks set in a landscape with mountains, executed in coloured enamels surrounded by a formal gold frame itself surrounded with further floral decorations in enamel. Sotheby Parke Bernet & Co.

Fig. 311. — Out-case of Watch by Tompion, about 1695. Tortoiseshell with Silver inlaid as shown.

Fig. 312. — Tortoiseshell Outcase, decorated with Silver in the Chinese style; about 1730.

clearly seen through the tortoiseshell and appeared to be covered with a kind of glaze. Strong and inexpensive outer cases of metal, covered with some kind of skin, were also made. Among these coverings shagreen was perhaps the most popular. The true shagreen is a remarkably tough kind of leather, made chiefly at Astrachan from the strong skin that covers the crupper of the ass or horse. In its preparation a peculiar roughness is produced by treading into the skin hard round seeds, which are shaken out when the skin has been dried; it is then stained green with copper filings and sal-ammoniac, and the grains or warts are then rubbed down to a level with the rest of the surface, which thus presents the appearance of white dots on a green ground.

The skin of the shark and of various other fishes, when properly prepared, formed an excellent covering, being thin and durable. This if dyed green was also known as shagreen. It was left with a slightly matted face, whereas the true shagreen bore a high polish.

The *piqué* surface on outer cases of leather or shagreen obtained by pins, usually of silver, passing through the covering and the inner metal case, had a good effect and afforded considerable scope for the skill of the producer, see Figs. 306, 313, 314. Besides an ornamental border there was usually a central design which in some instances embodied the crest or initials of the owner. These outer cases had of course to be removed when the watches were wound, and many of them left in coaches and other places, were advertised for in the *London Gazette* during the latter part of the seventeenth and beginning of the eighteenth centuries. Where considerable cost had been lavished on the decoration of the removable case, covering the box or watch case proper, a third case would be provided to protect the second one.

In some instances two second cases would be fitted to the "box," or inner case. A leather or tortoiseshell one for everyday use, and a more elaborate and costly one to be worn on gala days or other special occasions, when the watch, hanging from a chatelaine, could be displayed on the person.

Fig. 313. — Leather covered Outcase studded with Silver Pins.

Fig. 314. — Leather, *piqué* with Gold Pins, back of Watch by I. Mornand, Paris.

Fig. 315. — Watch by Jaquet Droz.

167

Fig. 316. — Tortoiseshell with Silver Overlay. Fig. 317. — Tortoiseshell with Silver Overlay.

Fig. 318. — Clock Watch by Abraham Beckner, Pope's Head Alley, with finely pierced Inner Case, about 1670.

As both the box and the loose case of striking watches and repeaters were pierced to emit the sound something further was required to prevent the ingress of dirt or other obstructive matter, and a thin metal cap to cover the movement was invented almost contemporaneously with repeating watches. These caps were sometimes of silver but more generally of brass; they performed their office of keeping dust and dirt from the movement very efficiently, and have remained a feature of the English full plate watch to this day.

"Bull's eye," also known as "Ram's eye," cases, introduced about 1780, were the last variety of pair cased watches; they derived their titles from the form of the bezel of the outer metal case, which from the groove to the outer edge followed the curve of the glass. In many of the later "Bull's eyes" the usual round form of pendant was abandoned in favour of a broad flattened-oval shape which was much stronger. A good example on a case decorated with Prince of Wales' plumes, &c., in gold of various colours, is given in Fig. 320, which represents a watch made by James M'Cabe and bearing the hall mark of 1811.

Fig. 319. — Pierced Case of Clock-Watch. "Louis Arthaud à Lyon."

A 19th century watch with a portrait on the front cover. This straight forward lever watch by Patek & Cie, Geneva, number 8512, with a white enamel dial with subsidiary seconds, becomes interesting because of the equestrian portrait inscribed 'Ponia-towski' executed in taille douce. *The portrait is probably that of Prince Joseph Poniatowski, equerry to Napoleon III. Sotheby Parke Bernet & Co.*

Fig. 320. — Back of Watch by Jas. M'Cabe, decorated with Gold of various tints.

Fig. 321.

Fig. 322.

After the introduction of pair cases it gradually became the custom to insert in the outer case a thin pad consisting of a circular piece of velvet, muslin, or other material, adorned with fancy needlework, a favourite form being a piece of white cambric having the initials of the owner as well as a fancy border worked in gold thread, or hair; in the latter case hair from the head of the fair artist would presumably be used for the purpose. The following lines were very neatly executed in needlework on a silk pad in a watch dating from 1780:—

"Take this token which I give thee,
It is one from friendship's shrine,
Place it where thou'lt think upon me,
When it meets those eyes of thine —
FORGET ME NOT."

"Watch papers" formed an alternative pad. Some of these were cut to geometrical designs more or less intricate and covering the whole surface or leaving the central space either circular or oval on which a miniature or sketch could be painted. Papers of this kind had a backing of bright coloured silk or satin to give the best effect to the perforations. Some time ago I saw in a watch by Isaac Alexander, Nottingham, a paper, in the centre of which was an excellent coloured portrait of Charles Stuart and the following rhyme arranged in a circle round it:—

"O'er this loved form
Let every British breast,
With conscious joy
Its gratitude attest,
And hail ye Prince
In whom ye nation's blest."

In very tiny characters was the signature "J. June," and the date 1745. The paper had probably been transferred, for the watch dated from about 1760. Papers having printed thereon a likeness of the Duke of Cumberland were issued in 1746, and in 1821 a superior pad of white and pink satin, bearing a portrait of Queen Caroline, was produced and speedily became popular among admirers of the Royal Lady. Two examples from the Ponsonby collection giving really fair portraits of Queen Charlotte and Queen Victoria, the latter when she ascended the throne, are illustrated in Figs. 321 and 323.

An extremely fine example of a filigree outer watch case of the 17th century. Such cases were popular for a relatively short time and were often, as here, re-used at a later period. The inner case is of plain gold and contains an 18th century verge watch by William Allam, London, No. 1367, with a white enamel dial. Sotheby Parke Bernet & Co.

The 18th and early 19th centuries saw thousands of watches produced in England, Switzerland and Germany for sale in Turkey. These, which are readily identifiable by the Turkish numerals used on the dial, were produced in very large quantities, three examples being illustrated, see right and pp.171 and 173. The example here is a relatively scarcer example made by the Danish manufacturer Frederich Jurgensen of Copenhagen. The watch is an ordinary cylinder movement (No. 4112) but has two plain inner cases of gold and a third outer case of gilt metal and tortoise-shell with piqué decoration on the bezel. Sotheby Parke Bernet & Co.

Papers printed on the frozen Thames during the prolonged frost of 1814 were a cheap novelty which commanded a ready sale. Most commonly watch papers contained an advertisement of the watchmaker, and sometimes an equation or time table for comparing the watch with the sun-dial, as in Fig. 322; and occasionally admonitory or sentimental verses in addition.

" *Memento Mori*" formed the text of many rhymes; the following, often met with, may be taken as examples:—

Fig. 323.

> "Onward perpetually moving,
> These faithful hands are ever proving
> How quick the hours fly by;
> This monitory, pulse-like beating,
> Is oftentimes, methinks, repeating,
> 'Swift! swift! the moments fly.'
> Reader, by ready, for perhaps before
> These hands have made one revolution more
> Life's spring is snapped — you die!"

The next example was printed around the edge of a paper by John Herron, Cowpen Quay, Blyth:—

> "Behold, O mortal man,
> How swift thy moments fly,
> Thy Life is but a Span,
> Prepare, Prepare to die."

Another from the Ponsonby collection is as follows:—

> "Time is, thou hast, employ the portion small.
> Time past is gone, thou can'st not it recall.
> Time future is not, and may never be.
> Time present is the only time for thee."

An English watch for the Turkish market by James Cox & Son, London, No. 6852. Full plate movement with cylinder escapement striking the hour by two hammers on a bell. Three silver cases, the inner is plain and has a pierced and engraved band. The second has pierced bezels and fine cross-hatching beneath a formal decoration, while the outer case is of tortoise-shell mounted in silver with decoration in the form of roundels and pin-work. There is a hallmark for 1809 on the second case. The watch is entirely typical of its kind, the only unusual feature being the stand of ebonised wood inlaid with tortoise-shell and with ivory mounts. Sotheby Parke Bernet & Co.

Another admonitory verse equally popular runs:—

> "Time is — the present moment well employ;
> Time was — is past — thou can'st not it enjoy;
> Time future — is not and may never be;
> Time present — is the only time for thee."

The next I take from a watch paper by T. Humphreys, Barnard Castle:—

> "Could but our tempers move like this machine,
> Not urged by passion nor delayed by spleen.
> And true to Nature's regulating power,
> By virtuous acts distinguish every hour.
> Then health and joy would follow as they ought
> The laws of motion and the laws of thought.
> Sweet health to pass the present moments o'er,
> And everlasting joy when time shall be no more."

These lines appear on papers of many other makers. They are from the pen of "Dr" J. Byrom, and appeared in the *Scots Magazine* for October 1747.

An apposite but more uncommon inscription for timekeepers is *Tempus metitur omnia sed metior ipsum;* "Time measures all things, but I measure it."

Fig. 324. — Early Engine-turned Case.

DIALS

Fig. 325.

Loose outer cases are troublesome, and, after being endured for two centuries or so, they gave place gradually to the more compact modern styles, with ornament of a different character.

A series of wavy curves cut into the material and known as "Engine turning," which is said to have been introduced as a decoration for watch cases about 1770 by Francis Guerint of Geneva, was long in fashion. It has a good effect, does not readily show scratches, and will doubtless again return to favour. The earliest specimens were cut very deep into the metal, leaving coarse "barleys," as the projections are called, and could only be applied to a considerable thickness of metal. Finer divisions with shallower cutting, applicable to lighter cases, speedily became the rule, and an early specimen of coarse-cut engine turning is now rarely to be met with. The example shown in Fig. 324 is on a repeating watch by Terroux l'Aine, Geneva, and is very little later than 1770.

Shortly after the middle of the eighteenth century a very beautiful art was utilised to enhance the effect of chasing and engraving as applied to watch cases and dials. A subject having been selected and drawn upon the gold or other metal ground, pieces of gold of various colours were formed to represent the parts in relief and soldered to the ground. A good artist was then able to produce a fine effect with the chasing tool and graver. As a specimen is shown in Fig. 325 a watch signed Gudin à Paris, dating from about 1760. Here the chased decoration with gold of green, yellow, copper, and silvery tints is very effective, but its whole charm cannot, of course, be justly conveyed in a black and white engraving. Lepine seems to have been fond of this coloured gold decoration, for it appears on the cases of many of his watches. Whatever the number of tints employed, this style of decoration is generally spoken of as *à quatre couleurs*.

With few exceptions the earliest clocks and watches had the hours marked with Roman numerals placed radially with the bottom of each numeral towards the centre of the dial, so that the V., VI., and VII. appear to be upside down. Another peculiarity is that the fourth hour was denoted in a very primitive way, thus: IIII., instead of by IV., which was then the more orthodox manner. And it is somewhat remarkable that these features have been continued to the present day almost unnoticed, as may be proved by asking anyone to sketch the figuring of his watch without looking at the timekeeper, for in most instances such a sketch would be incorrect. But the fact is, we do not read the figures when looking at a watch or clock, but judge the time from the position of the hands. Lord Grimthorpe was instrumental in having the hours of the turret clock at the dining-hall of Lincoln's Inn marked each by a short thick radial stroke instead of figures, and it is rarely that passers-by notice anything unusual, except that the dial seems particularly clear.

Some of the very earliest portable timekeepers had incised figures cut in the dial plate, but more often the numerals were engraved on a separate belt, which was generally of silver, the inner ground of the dial being of brass gilt (or gold) and matted or engraved. In addition to the numeral, many early watches were furnished with a knob at each hour, for the convenience of estimating the position of the hand by feeling. The first noticeable departure from this construction took place about 1600, when watch dials wholly of one metal were introduced, with landscapes and other views engraved on the

A pocket chronometer made for the Turkish market by August Courvoisier & Co., number 51394. The gilt and barred movement has a pivoted detent escapement with compensated balance. The gold dial has a floral decoration in the centre, and Turkish numbers surrounded by two colour gold decoration and a band of engine turned decoration. The inner case of gold has engraved bezels, and blue and green champlevé enamel decoration on the pendant and bow. On the back is an enamelled scene of sunset over a Turkish harbour with boats, contained within a blue, green and red enamel border with a white frame. On the outer case is a miniature portrait in enamels of Sultan Abdul Hamid of Turkey. There is also a gold chain and key with matching enamel decoration. Sotheby Parke Bernet & Co.

Fig. 326. – Watch by Nathaniel Barrow.

Fig. 327. – Watch by V. Costontin.

centre. These dials were usually of silver and recessed into what is now called a "brass edge," that is, a ring independent of the plate of the movement, and to which the dial was attached. The dial was rather smaller than the movement, and a narrow margin of the brass edge, which appeared outside of the dial, was engraved, the contrast of the silver and brass having a good effect. A fine example by Nathaniel Barrow is shown in Fig. 326. The watch by Edward East, said to have been given by Charles I. to Mr Herbert, and engraved in Fig. 399, had a very similar dial. Instead of a landscape a floral design sometimes occupied the centre, while occasionally it was engraved to a geometrical pattern and filled in with coloured enamel or wax, as in a watch by Vincent Costontin, Dieppe, which is shown in Fig. 327.

Illustrations have already been given of the painted dials on the coastly enamelled watches in vogue during the seventeenth century. The single hand of the earliest of these was usually of brass, and, except for watches with cases and dials painted in enamel, gold and silver dials with long figures in relief came into general use in England shortly after the middle of the seventeenth century. On a watch by Henry Harper, shown in Fig. 328, the outer part of the dial is of metal, the centre being filled by an enamelled painting, which is, however, of a later date than the movement. A still more exceptional and somewhat grotesque treatment of the dial is shown in Fig. 329, representing a watch made about 1665, by Richard Jarrett, who was master of the Clockmakers' Company in 1685. The centre of the dial is of brass matted, and the ring, on the inner edge of which is engraved quarter-hour spaces, of silver, finely matted, with polished plaques for the hour numerals.

With the introduction of the minute hand, the minute circle and figures to indicate each five minutes appeared outside the hour numerals. These additions, with the long hour numerals, allowed of but a very short hour indicator, and this occupied a slightly recessed centre, as shown in Fig. 330, which represents a watch by Daniel Le Count, dating from about 1680. Shortly afterwards the hour numerals were shortened and the hour hand lifted out of the recess and lengthened, as in the watch by P. Dupin,

Fig. 328.

Fig. 329.

Fig. 330. – Daniel Le Count, about 1680.

Fig. 331. — P. Dupin, about 1700.

Fig. 332. — Pink and White Enamel Dial on Tompion Watch.

represented in Fig. 331. In this the outlines of the hour numerals are polished, and the bodies filled in with black wax, the small ornament between the numerals being polished and the minute figures engraved on polished plaques. Except that the inner circle, marked with subdivisions of an hour, was discontinued, dials of this kind, with slight variations, remained in favour for many years. The central disc was a separate piece recessed into the brass edge, and was as a rule nicely chased and engraved. It usually bore two tablets for the name of the maker and the place of origin of the watch. An excellent example is the watch by Langley Bradley, shown in Fig. 450. Sometimes the lower label was omitted and a day-of-the-month aperture substituted therefor. Dials of this description had a very handsome appearance, and must have been costly, for cutting out the groundwork to leave the plaques for the minute figures, the outline for the hour numerals, and the ornament between the numerals in relief involved considerable labour. In 1729, engravers petitioned the Clockmakers' Company to debar one Griliat from proceeding with a project he had for producing dial plates by stamping. Nevertheless, many later ones were embossed in this way.

Painted enamel dials of the Huaud period had often an outer ring of white enamel for the reception of the numerals, and towards the end of the seventeenth century dials with a gold centre and outer ring of enamel were favoured by some French makers. Plain white enamel dials seem to have been introduced in France and Switzerland about 1690, but were not used in England for at least ten years afterwards.

A pink and white enamel dial, with angels in the centre, on a watch by Tompion, from the Pierpont Morgan collection, and dating from about 1700, is shown in Fig.332.

Though English watches of the seventeenth century are occasionally to be met with having dials of white enamel, it will generally be found that they

A very unusual example of a Japanese verge watch with a continental movement having a bridge cock. The dial has Japanese hour indications with movable plaques at a single hand. The plain case is covered in painted paper. Sotheby Parke Bernet & Co.

A verge watch by 'Suarts London' contained in an elaborate repoussé *case studded with glass imitation jewels. Bobinet Ltd.*

175

An attractive watch key of gold and chalcedony carved with a scene of a reclining artist sketching on a tablet behind which is a pillar and leaves. The scene is executed in a style with oriental overtones. Sotheby Parke Bernet & Co.

A watch key held on a padlock ornamented with a miniature of a shepherdess leaning against a tree, with a sheep behind and a bird flying in the distance. 18th century. Sotheby Parke Bernet & Co.

are subsequent applications, the original dials having probably been discarded owing to the superior legibility of the white enamelled discs.

So far as my observation goes, the earliest plain enamelled dials on English watches are those of a bluish tinge, the enamel of which is generally spoken of as Venetian. They date from about 1705, and have the nib for unlocking the movement projecting through a slit at the VI. numeral, as in some of the older and contemporary metal dials. The visible margin of the brass edge was usually either engraved or knurled, and the hands were of steel. An example, given in Fig.333, has hands of the "beetle" pattern, a kind very popular then and onwards to the middle of the century. Dials with the minute band formed in a series of wavy curves were made here during the eighteenth century chiefly for the Dutch market. They usually had hands of gold or of brass, nicely pierced, as in Fig.334.

Fig. 333.

The bold minute figures which occupied so much room outside the hour circle were gradually discarded. On a watch by Cabrier, dating from about 1740, and shown in Fig.335, there are small minute figures at the quarter hours only, and a little later came into favour dials with small and stumpy hour numerals, as in Fig.336, the minute figures being entirely omitted. The hands of the Cabrier watch are of gold. Owing to the character and arrangement of the figures, the hour indicator, which is beautifully pierced, appears to be rather short. If it were a solitary example one might suppose the hands or the dial to be not original, but I incline to the belief that a certain proportionate length of hand was as a matter of course selected for a certain size of dial. The French and, I think, the Swiss, adhered longer to the large minute figures than did English manufacturers.

Fig. 334.

Fig.337 shows a French watch dating from about 1770, which is a good example of the period, with a hole for winding cut through the dial, a plan much favoured in France for fifty years or so from that date, but not so popular in England. Lepine, who reconstructed the movements of watches, was, I believe, responsible for the systematic adoption of this feature, though winding at the dial was occasionally resorted to for watches having painted enamel cases a century before his time and for the thick French watches with porcelain enamel hour figures, in some of which the unsightly holes in the dial were avoided by planting the winding square at the centre.

Fig. 335.

Many French and Swiss watches made towards the end of the seventeenth and at the beginning of the eighteenth centuries had the hour numerals on enamelled plaques, though they do not seem to have been favoured here. A dial of this sort is on the alarm watch shown in Fig.338, made about 1680 by Dumont Frères, Besançon. The body of the dial is of brass gilt. Another

Fig. 336.

Fig. 337.

Fig. 338.

specimen of about ten years later, by I. Mornand, Paris, is shown in Fig.339. Watches of this class were very thick, and had cases of brass gilt and engraved to a fine pattern.

Watches made for the Dutch market were often fitted with silver dials having raised numerals filled with wax, and ornamental centres of various designs engraved and pierced. Occasionally a figure of Time was introduced, the Destroyer being represented with a flag in his hand, on which the name of the maker was engraved. A watch with a silver dial by John Van Ceulen, of the Hague, having the wavy minute circle already mentioned, and dating from about 1700, is shown in Fig.340.

Dials of metal, with polished hour numerals of a different tint soldered on, introduced during the latter part of the eighteenth century, were for some time popular; a specimen of this style, on a watch by James M'Cabe, is shown in Fig.341. But though considerable skill has been expended in the enrichment of metal dials by chasing and engraving as well as by variations of colour, enamel has practically ousted all other materials, except for scientific purposes, where extreme accuracy of division is desired.

In modern dials the hour numerals are too long, the position of the hands being more easily discerned with the stumpy figures used in the earliest timekeepers. The fact is, the dialmaker has been allowed to regard his work without reference to the hands, and he has adopted a rule to make the "chapters" in length equal to two and a half minutes of the circle, because they are more obtrusive than the shorter ones previously used. The most effective hands were those seen in clocks and watches of the eighteenth century. The chief fault of most varieties now used is that the spade or heart or other enlargement of the hour hand is too close to and overlaps the numerals. It should be of good size and nearer the root of the hand, the tip of which, though closely approaching, should in its sweep just clear the numerals.

People who are used to reading a dial with but one indicator can estimate the time with astonishing closeness, and it is pretty certain the two hands did not meet with general favour for a long period. Although we are, from long

Fig. 339.

Fig. 340.

A good example of a contemporary Dutch fake of an 18th century English watch. Produced in an effort to obtain the higher prices commanded by English watches such watch products were not infrequently imported by English makers and sometimes appear in extremely fine repoussé *cases. The watches themselves however, are indifferent. This example is signed 'Wilter London' and is somewhat crudely executed. Its true origins are betrayed by the continual bridge-type cock heavily pierced and engraved and the typically Dutch wavy line between the hour and minute numerals of the white enamel dial. The Trustees of the British Museum.*

practice, able to instantly note the minute and hour from the position of the two indicators, it is an acquirement. Children and other tyros seem to go through a slower process by separating the functions of the two and deciding upon the position of each singly. In fact, there can be no doubt that it is at first difficult to decipher the double indication together. Many devices were tried during the latter part of the seventeenth century to give the accuracy of the separate minute circle without the confusion of two similar hands. Of these may be mentioned dials with revolving centres, having a finger to point to the hours. In another plan representations of the sun and moon were utilised for the purpose. Sometimes figures corresponding to the current hour were shown through an aperture in the dial, and warriors with swords as pointers are among the most familiar of other varieties.

Fig. 342 represents a watch by Tompion, from the Schloss collection. It is in an enamelled case, and dates from about 1705. Though the concentric minute hand was introduced certainly thirty years before this date, the specimen here shown has only one hand; but the chief peculiarity in connection with the dial is its division into six hours. This may have been for use in Italy, where in some parts the day was divided into four periods of six

Fig. 341. — Watch by Jas. M'Cabe.

Fig. 342. — Curious Tompion Watch.

A typical example of a late 18th century verge watch in a plain pair silver case, hallmarked 1772, and with casemakers initials 'I.R.' The dial is of white enamel with steel hands, movement of brass, steel, and blued steel signed 'Jnº' Le Roux London 124'. Pierced and engraved symetrical cock with mask, verge escapement, fusee with chain, squared architectural pillars. An excellent example of the standard product of the English trade in its best period. The Trustees of the British Museum.

Fig. 343.

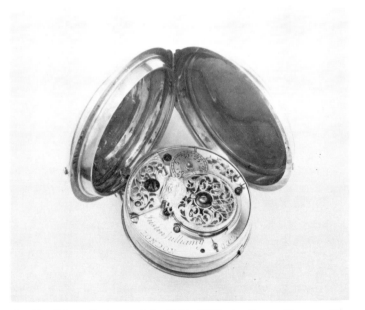

An English cylinder watch, HM 1769, in the gold case. The watch is signed 'Justin Vulliamy London OXZ' and has a symetrical pierced and engraved cock with grotesque mask and diamond endstone, silver regulator disc and a silver band to the movement. Enamel dial in the style of those used by Graham unusual at this date. This is an interesting example of an early English attempt to produce a thinner watch. It was not entirely successful as the winding arbor stands proud of the dial, the hour hand being looped to pass over it. The Trustees of the British Museum.

179

hours each. Or the idea may have been to give with one hand a longer space than usual for more nearly estimating small fractions of an hour. Quare adopted the same method, as will be seen from the following advertisement, quoted from the *London Gazette* for March 25-29, 1686: "Lost, on 2nd inst., a Silver Pendulum Watch, the name Daniel Quare, London; it had but six hours upon the dial plate, with six small cipher figures within every hour, the hand going round every six hours, which shows also the minutes between every hour. Whoever gives notice of it to Daniel Quare, at the King's Arms, in Exchange Alley, London, shall have a guinea reward."

Fig.343 shows the front and Fig.344 the movement of a watch dating from about 1665, which is a particularly interesting specimen, and affords evidence that the maker of it was far in advance of his time. It shows hours, minutes, and seconds, and has a long train containing the same number of wheels and pinions as modern watches, the minute hand being attached to the centre pinion. The dial is of silver, and the middle portion of it, driven by a pinion on the great wheel arbor, revolves once in twelve hours, a figure of Time engraved thereon pointing to the hour; the seconds dial is a silver plate on the back of the movement, the seconds hand being carried by the contrate wheel, which rotates once in a minute. On the plate is engraved "John Fitter, Battersea." There is no balance spring. It has a nicely pierced and engraved silver balance cock and arched top harp pillars. The potence is peculiar, being carried by a pivot into the top plate; the side view of it is very wide, nicely pierced, and engraved to a floral design. On the back of the inner case is engraved a kind of calendar remembrance shown overleaf. It appears to be a key for finding at a glance the days of the month upon which any particular day of the week will fall. The outer case, covered with leather *piqué* with silver pins, is snapped together without a bolt — a most unusual construction. This watch was formerly in the Roskell collection.

Mr. Charles Shapland has an early minute-hand watch by Robert Whitwell, which is shown in Fig. 345. It indicates also the day of the month by a rotating ring.

On a watch by David Lestourgeon, shown in Fig. 346, there are two narrow rotating rings between the centre of the dial and the hour numerals; one of these carries a very short and the other a longer pointer, the former for indicating the hour and the latter for the minutes.

The handsome key for this watch is shown in Fig.347. For winding or setting the hands it is used as a crank; the squared extremity at the bottom is for altering the regulator, which may be done without opening the inner case, an aperture being made in the back of the case for the purpose.

Perhaps the very best method of indicating the hour and minutes with one hand only is that shown in Fig.348, which represents a watch by Peter Garon, illustrated by favour of Mr Henry Levy, to whom it belongs. The central disc on which the hour numerals are engraved rotates, but its speed of progression is one-twelfth less than that of the minute hand. Starting together on the completion of any particular hour, the minute hand would stand exactly over the numeral corresponding to that hour: by the time half an hour had elapsed the minute hand would stand midway between the aforesaid numeral and the next succeeding one, and at any other point the relation of the hand to the hour numerals would correspond to the fraction of the hour, while the tip of the hand would indicate the minutes. In the

EARLY MINUTE-HAND WATCHES

Mar	Nov	1	8	15	22	29
	Augus	2	9	16	23	30
May	Jan	3	10	17	24	31
	Octob	4	11	18	25	+
Apr	Jul	5	12	19	26	+
Sep	Dec	6	13	20	27	+
Jun	Feb	7	14	21	28	+

Fig. 344.

Fig. 345. — Early Minute-hand Watch.

Fig. 346.

Fig. 347

sketch the indication is twenty-five minutes past seven. Both parts of the dial are of silver, the annular space between the hours and minutes being engraved as shown. Though but little is known of PETER Garon, he was elected to the freedom of the Clockmakers' Company in 1694, and appears to have been a maker of repute at the end of the seventeenth century and until 1706, when his bankruptcy was noted in the *London Gazette*.

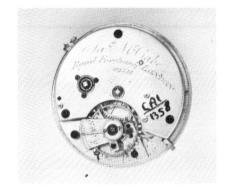

Movement and dial of a watch with duplex escapement signed 'Ja^s. McCabe Royal Exchange London 02513'. Late 18th century. Three quarter plate movement, free sprung, with a bimetallic compensated balance, with quarter screws and a diamond endstone. The dial is enamel and has gold hands, subsidiary seconds hand. A fine straight forward example which may be compared with the encapsulation of the duplex in a cheap watch. The Trustees of the British Museum.

WATCHES WITH SECOND HANDS

The watch by Fitter dating from about 1665, which, as shown in Fig. 344, has a seconds dial on the back of the movement, seems to have been quite an exceptional application of a seconds indicator for watches. Sir John Floyer, a physician, in 1707 speaks of the "Physician's Pulse Watch." which he had invented to take the place of the "common sea minute glass" with which and "common watches" he had been in the habit of trying pulses. The pulse watch which he caused to be made ran, he said, for sixty seconds. Harrison's timekeeper with a centre seconds hand was tested in 1760, and seconds hands were not usually applied to watches till after that date.

SUN AND MOON HOUR INDICATORS

Two examples of a peculiar method of indicating the hour which obtained some popularity at the end of the seventeenth century are shown in Figs. 349 and 350. A semi circular piece is removed from the upper part of the dial, and through it is seen one half of a disc which rotates underneath once in twenty four hours. On one half of the disc is engraved the sun, which points to the hour from 6 A.M. to 6 P.M., and on the other the moon, which performs the same office from 6 P.M. to 6 A.M. The minutes are indicated in the usual way by a hand travelling round the dial in an hour.

Fig. 349 is an early specimen. On the lower portion of the dial is an engraving, possibly representing Venus in a car drawn by Cupid. The movement is furnished with tulip pillars, and on the plate is engraved "Jo Holoway, Newbery." The balance-cock is of floral design with a narrow waist and foot of irregular outline following the curve of the plate. The outer case is of steel damascened with silver.

Fig. 350, of a slightly later date, is inscribed "Harns Smit, Amsterdam."

Fig. 348.

Fig. 349.

Fig. 350.

CHANGING HOUR FIGURES

In this ingenious arrangement, which was probably designed by Cratzer, and applied by Fromanteel, Knibb, and others to clocks, hands are dispensed with altogether, and numerals corresponding to the last completed hour caused to appear through a hole in the dial, a principle favoured in recent years by several inventors, who have devised various means of accomplishing this end. As an example of the contrivance is shown a watch by M. Lögg, of

A watch with a virgule escapement signed 'Lepine invenit et Fecit', late 18th century. Enamelled dial, engine turned gold case with champlevé *enamel and a concealed hinge and catch. Movement without backplate as is typical in Lepine's calibre watches, suspended going barrel and dumb repeating work. Museum of the History of Science, Oxford.*

An open faced keyless pocket chronometer signed 'Parkinson & Frodsham Change Alley London 6416', silver case hallmarked 1882. Three quarter plate movement with Earnshaw's spring detent escapement, bimetallic compensation balance free sprung with an helical blued steel spring. White enamel dial with blued steel hands, subsidiary seconds dial and up and down sector. A typical example of its type by one of the more prestigious makers of the period. Sotheby Parke Bernet & Co.

Fig. 351.

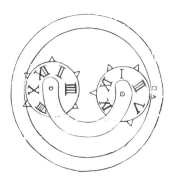

Fig. 352.

Vienna, which was in the Marfels collection. It has an upper silver dial on which is chased a group, representing Saturn dragging the car of Helios. As may be seen by the illustration, Fig. 351, there is above the group on the silver dial a semicircular slit, through which is visible a second dial lying under it. This second dial is gilt, for contrast. Above the opening of the silver dial are engraved the minutes from 1 to 60, and underneath it the quarter-hours I. to IV. The lower dial is movable, revolving once in two hours, and has two circular openings exactly opposite each other, through which the hour chapters appear upon a silver disc. A pin is fixed upon and near the edge of the front plate, over which the dial revolves. The dial passes freely by it, while the projecting teeth of the two numeral wheels in turn meet the pin, and are each time advanced one hour (see Fig. 352). Suppose, in the opening under which is located the disc with the even figures, we see the number II., as in Fig. 351. This number has entered from the left into the semi-circular slit of the silver dial, through which it slowly passes in one hour, while the other numeral wheel (which is during the same time under the Saturn group and therefore invisible), with the odd figures, passes by the stationary pin, and is by it turned one tooth, or from I. to III. When the number II. has passed its course through the semicircle it disappears to the right under the Saturn group, and the number III. enters from the left into the semicircle, in order to pass through its course in the same manner. The disc with the hour II. meanwhile keeps on its way invisibly, passes the stationary pin, and is also turned one tooth further on, so that at the next hour it enters again with the number IV. from the left into the semicircle of

An example of a relatively modern, unsigned, keyless wound, minute repeating watch with a perpetual calendar. The dial enables the hour, minute, and second to be read in the conventional manner, and has a centre seconds hand. The subsidiary dials are for day of the week, age of the moon, moon's phase, month of the year shown on a dial representing four years. The watch is held in a silver case and has a lever escapement. Bobinet Ltd.

Fig. 353.

Fig. 354.

the silver dial. This procedure is repeated with all the succeeding numerals. The number of minutes which have elapsed since the last completed hour is indicated by the position of the revolving hour chapter with relation to the figures which are engraved on the fixed dial plate.

Fig. 353 shows another watch of this character, taken from the catalogue of the Geneva Exhibition, 1896. It is by Paul Lullin, and most probably French. In the lower portion of the fixed dial is an enamelled medallion, with portrait, said to be that of Louis XIV. when a youth.

Mr Henry Levy has one of these curiosities by Fromanteel, which may be either English or Dutch. On the lower part of the fixed dial is a late seventeenth century design, with birds, &c. A peculiarity of this watch is that the fusee may be turned either way to wind it, a device advertised by Thomas Moore, of Ipswich, in 1729, and illustrated by Thiout in 1741.

In Fig. 354 the arrangement is varied, and the whole of the actuating mechanism is visible. On a carriage which revolves once in three hours are three crosses, each carrying four hour numerals on enamelled discs. These in turn pass over an enamelled arc on which every minute is marked.

Cheap watches from the factories of America and Switzerland flooded the market from c.1880 onwards, and brought a personal timepiece within the reach of nearly everyone. The main types are illustrated above and on pp.186, 188, 190, 191. Above: the 'Westclox Pocket Ben' in a case of chromed steel. This was patented 9 October 1907 and has a pin pallet lever escapement with a brass balance. The movement runs for thirty hours. Like the Ansonia watch, the Westclox was produced by a factory normally concerned only with the production of clocks.

"FENCING SOLDIERS' " WATCH

Figs. 355 and 356 show a watch of very peculiar construction, formerly in the Marfels collection, dating probably from about 1760. The metal dial plate has a blue enamelled ground, with thin white lines, and upon it are fastened two quadrants. The hours from I. to XII. are marked upon one, and upon the other the minutes from 1 to 60. It also bears two chased figures of soldiers in a fencing attitude, one on each side of the quadrants. By pressing upon the pendant, the soldiers draw their swords, the one to the left pointing with his sword to the hour, while the one to the right points to the minute upon their respective quadrants. The construction is shown in Fig. 356, which is the movement without the dial. Upon the arbor of the wheel, which is usually in the centre, is the cannon *a*, upon which is fixed the snail used for determining the minutes. The cannon drives in the ordinary manner a minute wheel, the pinion of which depths in a wheel located to one side, which it rotates once in twelve hours. Upon the latter wheel is fastened a snail for determining the hour. When the pendant is pressed down, the two levers *b b* are first unlocked, which unlocking actuates the four racks *c c* and *e e,* each two of which depth together into pinions *f f*. Upon the arbors of the two pinions *f f* are placed the arms of the soldiers. By the unlocking of the levers *b b*, the racks *e e* (situated above the centre of the plate), freed from the arm *d d*, are then moved upward by springs operating on them. The pinions *f f*, into which the racks depth, turn an appropriate distance, and with them the arms of the soldiers, which are located on the pinions, and thereby carry with them downward at the same time the lower stationary racks *c c*. These racks *c c* are provided with projections, which in their downward motion finally strike upon the snails, the one to the left lying upon the hour rack, and that to the right upon the minute rack. When the pressure upon the pendant is removed, all the parts of the motion work, and with them also the arms of the soldiers are by a spring brought back into a position of rest. The cannon pinion *a*, fitting with gentle friction upon the centre wheel arbor, is provided with a setting square passing through the dial, for the purpose of setting the motion work mechanism.

A Waterbury short wind watch (series L) in a chased silver case, c.1889, with an enamel dial. Three quarter plate movement with duplex escapement, keyless winding and hand setting. The appearance of these watches is considerably superior to other cheap watches, and their performance was reliable. Originally selling in its standard form in England c.1880 for 17s. 6d., by 1900 the price had been reduced to 5s.

PENDULUM WATCHES

A curious fancy which obtained some popularity at the end of the seventeenth and beginning of the eighteenth centuries is shown in Fig. 357. The balance was placed under the dial and its arms weighted. A semicircular slit in the dial allowed one weight of the balance to be seen, and this as it vibrated somewhat resembled a pendulum in motion. It was, however, an inconvenient arrangement, by reason of the difficulty of getting at the balance for regulation, and it appears to have been abandoned in favour of a pendulum balance at the back of the watch. The watch here illustrated is by "Mitzell, London," and dates from about 1700.

Fig. 355.

Fig. 356.

Fig. 357. — Pendulum Watch.

Fig. 358. — Musical Watch with Moving Figures.

MUSICAL WATCHES

Musical watches of large size with moving figures were a favourite conceit among French and Swiss makers during the latter part of the eighteenth century. The appended example (Fig. 358) is from the collection of Mr James W. Usher. It is mounted on both sides with fine pearls and chased gold. The back is enamelled with a landscape in colours; in the foreground is a pavilion (supposed to represent a place at Versailles) and figures, in gold of different colours; inside are small figures (couples of lady and gentleman) in

Fig. 359.

Fig. 360.

Fig. 361.

the dress of the Louis Seize period, which dance when the movement is wound. The lady seated outside the pavilion plays the harp, and the gentleman seated opposite beats time with his *bâton*. Inside the pavilion are walls of burnished steel, which reflect and multiply the dancing figures in a remarkable manner. The escapement is a cylinder one with brass scape wheel. The going part is driven direct from the barrel. The musical box and figures are driven by one mainspring, the train passing beneath the pavilion and revolving the centre of the floor upon which the dancers stand; smaller wheels being employed to revolve each pair of dancers three times for every one dance round the room; the conductor and harpist being worked by pins and levers between the plate and the dial.

A musical watch with moving figures of a man playing a violoncello and a lady a dulcimer is shown in Fig.359.

Fig. 360 is a repeating watch of French make. The hours and quarters are really struck on gongs curled around the inside of the case in the usual way, but, when the pendant is pushed in to repeat, the hammermen in the recess at the upper part of the dial appear to strike on the bells shown there, and the woman below works a spinning-wheel.

In Fig. 361 the arrangement is a little different. Here the upper rectangular space is vacant till the pendant is pushed in for repeating. Then the figure on the right bearing a huge gong advances, and the one on the left comes forward and appears to strike the hour on the gong. The quarters are repeated by the figures below, and during that operation the figures above slowly retire out of sight.

The projected invasion of England by Napoleon Buonaparte is treated as an accomplished fact on the dial of a watch from the Schloss collection which is shown in Fig.362. A large moving ship in full sail just appearing above the horizon occupies the centre, in the foreground many vessels are

An expensive version of a cheap watch signed 'Messaggero Echappement Roskopf', having a white enamel dial with a 24-hour dial, the numbers 1-12 being set under glass on a blue ground, and the numbers 13-24 set in a concentric outer ring in red. The hands are of gilt brass as is the case which is decorated with a picture of a retriever. As usual there is a lever escapement and a going barrel beneath the three quarter train movement.

Fig. 362.

portrayed, and armed men are marching up the shore undeterred by the firing of some apparently very primitive cannon. Above is the inscription, "Descente en Angleterre."

Another arrangement of moving figures is shown in Fig. 363. Here the sails of the windmill are constantly moving while the watch is going, and seen through the round aperture is part of a rotating disc with figures of horses and men painted thereon.

Many of the metal watch dials of the seventeenth century which were devoted to other purposes than the indication of the hour or other subdivisions of a day well repay examination. Here are some representative specimens from the Schloss collection. Fig. 364 represents a silver single-cased watch which doubtless dates from about 1640. On the back of the case is the characteristic circular shutter over the winding hole and the owner's name engraved thus, "Richard Baille, at the Abbay." The maker's name is Henry Arlaud. There is a spring to control the balance, but there are unmistakable indications that this was an addition made subsequent to the manufacture of the watch. The dial is prettily arranged, gives a calendar, the age and phases of the moon, the signs of the zodiac, &c. A similar watch by "Jean Rousseau" is to be seen at the South Kensington Museum.

A double-cased watch by N. Bouquet, of which a front view is given in Fig. 365, is of about half a century later date; though attractive and of broadly the same character as the preceding example, the execution is comparatively coarse.

In pendulum watches, such as the one shown in Fig. 366, where the balance was planted immediately under the dial, there was often at the back of the watch, in place of the balance, an enamelled plaque, occasionally exhibiting painting of artistic merit. This fashion seems to have been introduced by some of the Dutch makers, but it was decidedly an inconvenient arrangement, which necessitated an inferior method of regulation from the front, besides crowding the hour division into a smaller circle. The name on this watch is Hilderr.

Fig. 363.

Fig. 364.

Fig. 365.

Fig. 366.

An example of an English attempt to rival the American cheap watch, The John Bull watch from the Lancashire Watch Company, 1905, has an enamel dial, keyless winding and handsetting, lever escapement, visible mainspring and a gilt finished brass case. The fact that it is rather better made and more robust than its rivals probably contributed to its failure to displace them.

Fig. 367.

At first sight the large astronomical watch, dating from about 1690, which is represented in Fig. 367, appears to be of English make, for it bears the name-plate of "Willing, London"; but on removing the name-plate the signature "Ferdinandus Zehng, Hamburg," is revealed. The dial is really excellent; the engraving shows it was prepared for use in Germany. Such a watch at that period would doubtless be made to order for presentation to some person of distinction.

One of the finest calendar watches of late eighteenth century production it has been my privilege to examine is shown in Figs. 368, 369, and 370. It is by Samuel Ruel, Rotterdam, and stamps him as a horologist of the first rank. Besides the age and phases of the moon and the title of the month, it shows through apertures over the XI. and I. the day of the month according to the old style and the new style. The cases bear the English hall mark of 1788 with the duty head; on the back of the inner case is "A.S." arranged as a monogram. The outer case has a diamond thumb piece. There is a rim cap (as seen in Fig. 369) of silver, having perforations covered with horn. The cock, as seen in Fig. 370, is a fine piece of chased work.

Fig. 368.

Fig. 369.

Fig. 370.

PEARL ORNAMENT

There appears to have been quite a rage for pearl ornament at the beginning of the nineteenth century, particularly among French and Swiss watchmakers. Mr Willard H. Wheeler has a heart-shaped repeating and musical watch, ascribed to Froissard, of Geneva, with covers over the front and back. The latter, shown in Fig. 371, conceals a landscape with moving figures of a windmill, and a boy and girl playing on musical instruments. Altogether there are 1,700 pearls used in the decoration. The Napoleon watch in Fig. 285 and the musical watch in Fig. 358 afford other examples of pearl enrichment. In the Marfels collection was a watch by Albery, London, with a very pretty design in pearls over the back.

A souvenir watch, such as is shown in Fig. 372, was deserving of more popularity than it seemed to have attained. The surface enclosed by the large circle was reserved for inscriptions, monograms, or other personal references. Underneath is the mechanism of the watch, whose motion is conveyed to the hands by means of a small rod concealed in the connecting neck. On the movement is engraved, "Inventio Johannis Holtmann in Wienns No. 25." It dates from about 1780.

LARGE TRAVELLING WATCHES

Large travelling watches introduced at the end of the seventeenth century continued in favour till the advent of railways. They were thick and heavy, with dials ranging from 3 in. to nearly 7 in. in diameter, and seem to have been manufactured more in France and Germany than in England. As a rule they struck the hour on a bell inside the case, many of the earlier ones being in addition furnished with an alarm. Afterwards, a repeating motion took the place of an alarm, so that by pulling a string which passed through a pipe at the edge of the cover the number of blows last struck would be again

Fig. 371. — Musical Watch with Pearl Decoration.

Fig. 372.

An Ingersoll cheap watch with a paper dial and a nickel case c.1892. This model was patented 6 May, 1890, and 13 January, 1891. There is a lever escapement and handsetting from the back. Despite the apparent winding knob in the pendant, the watch is wound from the back by the winding key here shown detached.

Figs. 373 and 374.

sounded on the bell. They had generally two cases, an outer one covered with leather or fish skin and an inner one of silver, which latter material was also used for the dial. The pendant was sometimes in two pieces connected by a loose thimble, an arrangement which allowed of sufficient movement to enable the watch to adjust itself to an adjacent surface when it was hung from the bow. Front and edge views of an excellent example in a remarkably well pierced and carved silver case dating from about 1680 are given in Figs. 373 and 374. The central portion of the dial rotates, indicating the age of the moon and exhibiting her phases. Through slits near the outer edge are shown the day of the week, the day of the month, and the title of the month in French. The movement is signed "Samuel Michelin à Langres." This or a very similar instrument was illustrated in Dubois' historical work. Another example by Tompion is illustrated in Chapter V. In Figs. 375, 376, and 377 are shown a rather smaller clock and alarm watch, which strikes the hours and half-hours. The inner and outer cases as well as the dial are of silver. On the movement is the inscription, "Philip Graet, Lintz." It is of slightly later date than the preceding one.

Fig. 378 is a back view of another fine specimen by "Anthony Bradl, Augsburg," which dates from about 1710: the inner case is of silver splendidly pierced and chased, with representations of hunting scenes, flowers, and birds, as shown; there is an outer case of fish skin. The number of blows last struck may be repeated at pleasure by pulling a string depending from the case as already described.

Back and edge of a beautifully pierced and engraved specimen signed, "David Buschmann, Augusta," and dating from about 1680, are given in Fig. 379.

Fig. 375.

Fig. 376. — Side View of Inner Case.

SEDAN CHAIR WATCHES   During the eighteenth century watch movements having plain silver dials from 3 in. to 4 in. in diameter were fixed in circular frames of wood, polished and with a moulded edge. They were called "Sedan Chair Watches," though I cannot aver that they were as a rule carried in those useful but obsolete conveyances. Occasionally one may yet be seen hung on the wall beside a chimney-piece or at the head of a bedstead. I have heard timekeepers of this sort spoken of as "Post Chaise Watches."

Fig. 377. — Back of Outer Cover.

Fig. 378.

Fig. 379.

WATCH KEYS

Before the advent of the most common variety of watch key which had a circular ring to afford the necessary purchase in winding, and a smaller swivelled bow for attachment to the guard or chain, there must have been a considerable number of keys used by our grandmothers and grandfathers and by their progenitors, on the design and construction of which much consideration and labour had been bestowed. M. Paul Garnier, M. Planchon, and Mr Arthur F. Hill are among the few collectors of such interesting adjuncts, of which a few examples are given in Figs. 380-388. Several of them, it will be noticed, are formed to give a crank action for winding the watch, and a separate straight pipe, at right angles to the first, for the purpose of setting the hands. Keys of this kind appear to have been very generally used from the middle of the seventeenth to the end of the eighteenth century. The first of the lowest row seems to have been intended as a winder for a table clock, while the remaining two, with swivelled bows, recall the days of chatelaines and fob chains. Indications are not wanting that hanging chains, as guards or accessories of timekeepers worn on the person, have in part returned to popular favour, even though watch keys may not be numbered among their appendages. Sir James M. Moody has a cranked watch key ornamented with military emblems, and bearing the name "Jno. Cook, London." A watchmaker of this name carried on business at 22 Cheapside in 1760, and afterwards in Wood Street. This is an early instance of impressing a name on the key, a practice adopted in later years by many watchmakers in a large way of business.

In 1761 George Sanderson, of Exeter, patented a lunar and calendar watch key, which, when daily pressed on to the winding square of a watch, caused the mechanism in the key to advance one day. Etienne Tavernier, a Paris watchmaker who devoted particular attention to keys at the end of the eighteenth century, made some of this plan. Eardley Norton, a well-known London maker of musical clocks, obtained in 1771 a patent for a striking arrangement, which he said could be conveniently contained in a key, seal, or trinket.

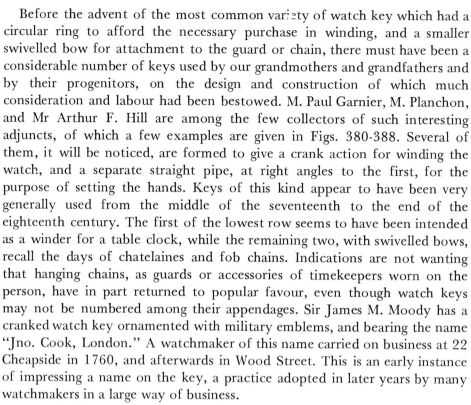

Figs. 380-388. — Watch Keys.

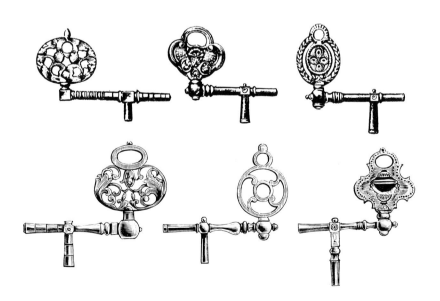

Chapter V

Records
of early Makers, etc.

NICHOLAS CRATZER (or Kratzer), "deviser of the King's horologies and astronomer" to Henry VIII., was a Bavarian, born in 1487, who, it is said, resided for thirty years in this country without being able to speak English. In the second part of the facsimiles of the National Manuscripts, photographed by Colonel Sir Henry James, there is a letter from Cuthbert Tunstal, Master of the Rolls, who was then in Germany, to Cardinal Wolsey. It is dated 12th October 1520, and contains the following: "Please it your Grace to understand that here, in these parts, I met with a servant of the King's, called Nicholas Craczer, a German, deviser of the King's horologes (who showed me how the King had licensed him to be absent for a season, and that he was ready to return into England), whom I desired to tarry until I might write to the King's Highness, to know his pleasure whether he would suffer him to be in company with me for a season, until the assembling of the electors were past." In a Book of Payments by the Treasurer of the Household from Candlemas-day, 29 Henry VIII., to Midsummer, 33 Henry VIII., in the Arundel Manuscripts (No. 97), among the discharges of the former year (1538) is the entry, "Nicholas Cratzer, Astronomer, received five pounds as his quarter's wages."

Cratzer's connection with Holbein was mentioned on p.137, and there is no doubt that Holbein assisted Cratzer by designing cases and decoration for clocks and sun-dials. Horace Walpole purchased at Mons. Mariette's sale a complicated piece of horology which embodied the conceptions of the two masters. On the summit was a clock driven by wheel work, below were fore and afternoon dials showing the time by shadows, and beneath these a clepsydra indicating the quarters of an hour on an exceedingly ingenious plan, the invention of which has been claimed for many subsequent horologists. It is mentioned by Bettinus, and in Plot's "Oxfordshire," 1676, Christopher Wren is credited with having made for Sir Anthony Cope at Hanwell a clepsydra on the same principle which is thus described: "moves by water and shows the hours by a new gilded sun for every hour, moving in a small hemisphere of wood, each carrying in their centres the number of some hour depicted black; as suppose of one a clock, which ascending half

*A good mid-19th century steel
engraving of Holbein's portrait of
Nicholas Kratzer (1487-?1550)
painted in 1528. Kratzer was a
German mathematician who passed
several years at Oxford where he
designed a sundial for Corpus
Christi College. Sundials were a
speciality of Kratzer's and he left
two manuscript volumes of notes
concerning them. A friend of
Erasmus and a member of the circle
of scholars around Sir Thomas
More, he is shown here in a
contrived pose holding a polygonal
sundial and surrounded by various
instruments.*

way to the zenith of the arch, shows it a quarter past one, at the zenith half
hour; whence descending half way towards the horizon, three quarters past
one; and at the last absconding under it, then presently arises another gilded
sun above the horizon at the other side of the arch, carrying in its centre the
figure two; and so of the rest." Fuller particulars of the action will be found
in Chapter IV. The clepsydra for driving appears to have been in the form of
a drum with divisions as shown in Figs. 9 to 13.

BARTHOLOMEW NEWSAM

BARTHOLOMEW NEWSAM was one of the earliest English makers of
portable clocks whose work survives. It is conjectured he was a
Yorkshireman, but he must have attained some position in London before
1568, for in that year he secured a thirty years' crown lease of premises in
the Strand, near Somerset House, where he resided till his death. In the
British Museum is a very fine example of his skill, which proves Newsam to
have been a master of the craft. This is a striking clock, in a case of brass,
gilded and engraved, about 2½ in. square and 4 in. high, exclusive of an

Fig. 389. — Clock by Bartholomew Newsam

ornamental domed and perforated top, which brings the total height to 6½ in. The centre of the dial as far as the hour ring is below the surface of the case, so that on removing the base the movement, together with the centre of the dial and hand, may be drawn out. The hours are engraved on a broad bevelled ring, which extends from the sunk part of the dial to beyond the front of the case. An exterior view of Newsam's clock is appended (Fig. 389). The movement is arranged in stories, there being three plates held in position by four corner posts. Above the top plate is a semi-circular bell; between the upper and middle plates is the going train, and between the middle and lower plates the striking train, the locking-plate occupying a position below the lowest plate. The arbors are placed vertically, and the winding holes are at the bottom of the case. The wheels are of steel or iron, the fusees very long, and with but little curve in their contour; they are connected with the barrels by means of cat-gut. The plates, posts, and barrels are of brass, the barrel covers of iron held in by a number of tenons around the edge. The hand is driven from the great wheel of the going part by a contrate wheel. The escapement is, of course, the verge. The workmanship, unusually fine for the period, is remarkably free from subsequent interference. There is a very small hinged door on each side of the case, giving, when open, a view of the fusees to estimate the period for winding. No screws are used in the construction of the movement, which is inscribed "Bartilmewe Newsum." An equally well-made table clock by Newsam in a case similar to Fig. 98 forms part of the Pierpont Morgan collection. It is in a leather case for travelling with a small hinged cover which may be opened to disclose the dial. The bottom plate bears the signature "Bartholomew Newsam."

A large clock-watch very possibly by him is illustrated in Chapter III. In vol. iv. of *Archaeologia* is illustrated a fine casket by Bartholomew Newsam.

In the "Calendar of State Papers" of the time of Queen Elizabeth is a record of a grant in 1572 to B.N. (who no doubt was Bartholomew Newsam) of the office of clockmaker to the queen in reversion after the death or surrender of N. U. (probably Nicholas Urseau). In the same Calendar is a letter dated 5th August 1583, from Bartilmew Newsham to Sir Francis Walsyngham. This letter probably refers to a renewal of Newsam's lease, and it desires Sir Francis to favour the writer's petition to Her Majesty for the augmenting a certain term of years, wherein he had moved Sir Philip Sidney to speak for him. He was clock-keeper to the queen prior to 1582, and on 4th June 1583, under Privy Seal was paid 32s. 8d. for "mending of clocks during the past year." Under date 1590 is a grant to Bartholomew Newsham of the office of clockmaker to the queen, in place of Nicholas Urseau, deceased. Newsam appears then to have combined the offices of clock-keeper and clockmaker, which had previously been kept distinct.

His tenure of the double appointment was a brief one, for he died in 1593. By his will, dated in 1586, he bequeathed to his apprentice his "seconde clock"; to John Newsam, clockmaker of York, his "best vice save one, a beckhorne to stand upon borde, a great fore hammer, and to (two) hand hammers, a grete longe beckhorne in my backe shoppe; and all the rest of my tools I give unto Edward Newsom, my sonne, with condicion that he become a clockmaker as I am, yf not I will the foresaid tooles to be sold by my executors." He gave to a friend "a sonne dyall of copper gylte"; to

The table clock by Bartholomew Newsam
(p.197). An attractive dome-cased clock with a
silver dial, it shows considerable French influence in its design and layout. The Metropolitan Museum of Art, New York, Gift of
J. Pierpont Morgan, 1917.

another, "one cristall jewell with a watche in it, garnished with goulde"; to another, "one watch clocke, in a silken purse, and a sonne dyall to stande upon a post in his garden"; and to another, "a chamber clocke of fyve markes price."

John Newsam continued at York for some years. In 1593 he repaired the clock on Ousebridge in that city.

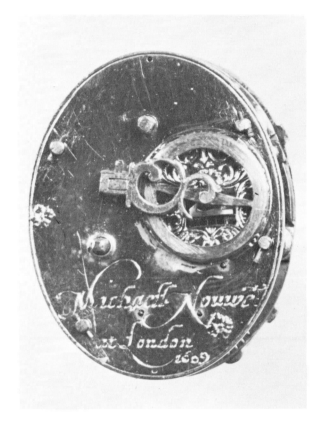

The rock crystal cased watch by 'Michaell Nouwen at London' which Britten thought was 'perhaps slightly later' than 'about 1590' (p. 200), is a fact dated 1609. It has an enamel dial with a single steel hand, brass movement with a tall fusee and gut line, steel balance and brass escape wheel. The enamel plate on the movement mentioned by Britten is a later addition. The watch is held in a rock crystal case of long octagon form which, pace *Britten, is not irregular. The Trustees of the British Museum.*

BULL Rainulph or Randulph Bull appears to have been an English horologist of some note. In the British Museum is a rather large oval watch by him, dated 1590. It has a shield the arms of the owner and his name, "W. Rowley." Bull was also keeper of the Westminster great clock. In Devon's *Issues of the Exchequer* there is an entry under date 1617, 1st of April: "By Order, dated 29th March 1617. To Ranulph Bull, keeper of his Majesty's great clock, in his Majesty's palace at Westminster, the sum of £56. 13s. 4d., in full satisfaction and discharge of and for divers sums by him disbursed for mending the said clock, in taking the same and other quarter clocks all in pieces, and repairing the same in the wheels, pulleys, hammers, weights, and in all other parts, and in new hanging, wiring, and cordings of the same clock, and other necessary reparations thereunto belonging, the charge whereof, with his own workmanship and travail therein, doth amount to the sum aforesaid, appearing by a note of the particular demands, delivered upon his oath, taken before one of the Barons of his Majesty's Exchequer, without account or imprest to be made thereof. By writ dated 27th March 1617, £56. 13s. 4d."

In an account of the household expenses of Prince Henry, in 1610, "Emanuel" Bull, the "clocke-keeper," is mentioned.

199

At the South Kensington Museum are two watches inscribed "Edmund Bull in Fleet Street fecit"; one is in an oval case of brass and silver, and the other in an octagonal case; both are early seventeenth century productions; a watch, similarly inscribed, in a small oval pair of cases of silver, is in the Guildhall Museum, and another watch by the same maker is in the Fitzwilliam Museum, Cambridge.

NOUWEN The watch shown in Fig. 390 is by Michael Nouwen, who was referred to on p.61. It is from the Schloss collection, and dates from about 1590. The very handsome dial is of brass, as is also the case, finely pierced as shown. The movement is furnished with the stackfreed and a straight bar balance. There are no screws used in the construction of the watch. Inside of the case is a bell on which the hours are sounded.

Of perhaps slightly later date is a watch by him in the British Museum, which has an irregular octagonal-shaped case of crystal; the plates of the movement are enamelled. In the Ashmolean Museum at Oxford is an oval watch with a gilt metal case. The dial is engraved with a figure subject, and at each of the hour numerals a pin projects. The movement is signed "Michael Nouwen fecit, 1613."

Fig. 390.

GARRET Among other watches which Octavius Morgan exhibited to the Archaeological Society in 1840 was an early English one in the form of a Tudor rose. The dial he described as elegantly engraved and gilt, with an hour circle of silver. There was no ornament on the balance-cock and the movement was imperfect. The watch was made about 1600 by Ferdinando Garret. In the British Museum is an oval watch by the same maker in a case of metal gilt, of the same period. Another watch by him is mentioned in the *London Gazette* for March 29—April 1, 1680, as follows: "A small eight square Watch, the edges Brass, and the Cover and Bottom silver, made by Ferdinando Garet."

GRINKIN

Appended is a view of an oval watch by Robert Grinkin, London, which dates from about 1605. The case is of silver. In the British Museum is a still smaller oval watch of the same period by him, with outer case of leather *piqué*. In the Pierpont Morgan collection is an oval watch of his make dating from about 1640. Grinkin was admitted to the freedom of the Clockmakers' Company in 1632 and served as master in 1648. He died in 1660.

HENCHE

In Devon's *Issues of the Exchequer*, under date 1605, 10th of October, occurs the entry, "By Order the last of September, 1605, to Uldrich Henche, clockmaker, or to his assignee, the sum of 100*l.* for a clock in manner of a branch made by him and set up in his Highness's at Whitehall." And under date 1607, 5th of July, another entry runs:—

Fig. 391.

Gilt metal oval watch by Ferdinando Garret (p.200). Silver chapter ring with a single steel hand and touch pins, applied on a fully engraved plate showing a view of a town within the chapter ring, and arabesque decoration with rabbits and a cherub outside. Verge escapement, steel balance wheel, blued steel set up work. The case is of gilt brass with a silver band and mandorlks on the inner covers. Within are crudely engraved the initials 'MRB. and SRP'. The Trustees of the British Museum.

FLOOD

"To Humphrey Flood, goldsmith, or his assigns, the sum of £120, in full satisfaction and payment for a clock covered with gold, and set with diamonds and rubies, and by him delivered to his Majesty's use, at the price of £220, whereof received £100."

NORTH

As an example of oval astronomical watches of English make, such as were popular in the early part of the seventeenth century, may be taken one in the British Museum, inscribed "William North, Londini," and of which an exterior view is given in the subjoined engraving (Fig. 392). It shows the hours on the lower and day of the month on the upper circular band. There are, in addition, four apertures in the dial. Through the largest of these, on the left, are shown the days of the week, with the corresponding allegorical figures: Apollo for Sunday, Diana for Monday, Mars for Tuesday, Mercury for Wednesday, Jupiter for Thursday, Venus for Friday, and Saturn for Saturday. Through the three openings on the right are seen the phases of the moon, the quarters of the moon, and its age in days. These three subjects are all engraved on one circular plate below. Symbols representing six planets appear in rotation below the small square on the right, just outside and lower than the centre of the hour ring. It may with tolerable certainty be affirmed that the movement of this watch was made about 1615, although the case is probably of a later date. William North was admitted as a brother of the Clockmakers' Company in 1639, and the fact of his being noted as a brother would indicate that he had then been established for some time, and was free of another Company.

Fig. 392. — Watch by William North, London, about 1615.

Fig. 393.

Fig. 394.

CRAYLE

In the South Kensington Museum is a particularly diminutive watch in a plain oval case, which measures outside but $1/2$ in. in length and $3/8$ in. across, by Richard Crayle, London, and said to have belonged to Lord Hussey, who was beheaded in 1537. I am not aware what evidence exists to warrant this statement, but 1537 is rather an early date for a watch of this character to be in existence, and I should be inclined to think it was the production of the Richard Crayle who was a member of the Blacksmiths' Company before the existence of the Clockmakers' Company, and who signed the petition for its incorporation.

Two views of a large oval alarm watch signed "Richard Crayle Londini fecit," and not later than 1610, are given in Figs. 393 and 394. The first shows the front cover closed, and the second exposes the whole of the dial. On the back plate are two small rotating dials of silver, one engraved with the days of the week, with a mythological figure corresponding to each, while the other, divided into months, contains also the signs of the zodiac.

In the British Museum is a round watch movement inscribed "William Crayle, in Fleete Street, London," a production of about 1620. William Crayle, who in 1676 carried on business in Fleet Street, and afterwards at the Black Boy in the Strand, near the Savoy, was probably a descendant of Richard.

ALCOCK

In the Pierpont Morgan collection is a very fine circular calendar watch by Thomas Alcock, as shown in Fig. 395. The dial is really superb; it indicates the age and phases of the moon by means of the central rotating disc, and the day of the month by a rotating ring outside the hour circle. The movement is very well made and in good order; it dates from about 1635. The case is of brass, curiously engraved, and though old, of later date than the movement. Thomas Alcock was one of the petitioners for the incorporation of the Clockmakers' Company in 1630. In *Kingdom's Intelligencer*, 4th February 1661, was advertised as lost "a round high watch of a reasonable size showing the day of the month, age of the moon, and tides; upon the upper plate Thomas Alcock fecit."

DAVID RAMSAY

One of the earliest British watchmakers of particular renown was David Ramsay.

Among the Salting collection at South Kensington Museum is a very early watch by him in a small irregular octagonal case of gold and silver. It has hinged covers over the front and the back, and is decorated with engravings of the Annunciation and the Nativity.

In the British Museum is an oval watch of his make, with a gold case in the French style. The period assigned to this watch is 1600 to 1610. It is inscribed "David Ramsay, *Scotus*, me fecit."

There is an entry in the account of money expended by Sir David Murray, Kt., keeper of the privy purse to Henry, Prince of Wales, who died in 1612. "Watches three bought of Mr Ramsay the Clockmaker lxj li" (£61). In the same account, among the list of "Guyftes and Rewards," is the item, "Mr Ramsay the clockmaker xjs" (11s.).

Fig. 395.

An oval calendar watch, showing the age of the moon, which is supposed to have belonged to James I., is described in the *Archaeological Journal*, vol. vi., p. 415. It had a plain outer case of silver, the inner one being beautifully engraved; on one side was represented Christ healing a cripple, also the motto used by James, "Beati pacifici," and on the other side the Good Samaritan with the inscription, "S. Lucas *c.* 10." Inside the cover was a well-executed engraving of James, with his style and titles. Under a small shield which concealed the hole for winding was the name of the engraver, "Gerhart de Heck." Around the edge of the case were the Rose, Harp, and Thistle, and the initials J. R. On the plate of the watch was engraved, as before, "David Ramsay, *Scotus*, me fecit," and these inscriptions, together with the fact that he had a grant of denisation in 1619, prove that he was a native of Scotland.

Mr J. Sancroft Holmes had another watch by Ramsay, which was found seventy or eighty years ago behind the tapestry which then covered the wall of the dining-room of Gawdy Hall. With the watch were two apostle spoons and papers relating to the troublous times of Cromwell. The case of the watch is of silver and shaped like a star or heraldic mullet of six points.

The engravings appended show a splendid clock-watch with alarm by him, from the collection of Mr Evan Roberts, dating from about 1615. It has the three wheel train usual in early watches, and Mr Crewe, in describing the movement, remarks that the fusee is cut for twelve turns, and the end of the great wheel arbor, which goes through the pillar plate, is fashioned into six pegs or leaves, identical with a lantern pinion in its action. These leaves work in a wheel pivoted into the centre of the pillar plate, having sixty teeth, and carrying the single hand of the watch. Thus ten turns of the fusee are equivalent to an entire circuit of the hand on the dial and so the watch would require to be wound twice a day. The ratchet wheel, which sets up the mainspring, is on the top plate, and the stop work is identical in principle with that in modern fusee watches. The stop for the alarm part is effected by a wheel and pinion, the wheel having a portion the size of two teeth left uncut, and which serves as a block to the pinion after it has been wound three turns. The wheels and pinions have a wonderfully smooth action, though they appear to be cut by hand rather roughly. The count or locking wheel of the striking portion is made of silver, and the notches have been certainly made with a file. The alarm part has a verge escapement with counter and crown wheels. Attached to its verge is a V-shaped piece of brass with an arm, and this pressed by a spring drops into a notch made in the edge of a brass disc on the hand or hour wheel, and so liberates the verge and lets off the alarm. Between this disc and the hour wheel, and working concentrically with them, is a star wheel having twelve teeth, which by lifting up a brass arm connected with the count wheel causes it to strike. The potence is a rather slender piece of square brass, and is riveted to the top plate, and the banking is made by steps cut in it. These riveted potences are found in nearly all watches made before 1700. The balance-cock is a slender piece of work, and is pierced throughout, and the neck very narrow, so different from specimens of Tompion and other later masters. The case is very elegant in design, and is pierced in the back and band, the bezel being engraved, and in every respect it will compare favourably with any work of the kind. Curiously enough, the band is silver, and bezel and back of bronze, and the whole case gilt. On the margin of the top plate, in tiny characters, as if almost to escape observation, is engraved, "David Ramsay inv^t Fecit," the *et* having been obliterated.

In the Pierpont Morgan collection is an oval calendar watch by Ramsay in a Limoges enamel case. It dates from about 1610. Besides the hour of the day are given the days of the week in order thus — Sondai, Mondai, Tvesdai, Wensdai, Thordai, Fridai, Saturdai, with a symbol for each day. Days of the month and phases of the moon are also shown. The cock over the balance is of silver and pinned on. A balance-spring and the letter A. and R., for regulation, were doubtless added at a later date in France.

R. B. P., in the "Dictionary of National Biography," says David Ramsay belonged to the Ramsays of Dalhousie, and quotes Ramsay's son William to the effect that "when James I. succeeded to the crown of England he sent into France for my father, who was there, and made him page of the bedchamber and keeper of his Majesty's clocks and watches." In 1613, James gave David Ramsay a pension of £200 per annum, and in the same

Fig. 396. — Front View.

Fig. 397. — View of Edge and Back.

Clock-Watch and Alarm by David Ramsay.

Oval watch signed 'Ro. Grinkin fecit' (p. 201). Plain gilt brass covers, silver chapter ring surrounding a scene of houses beside the sea with ships, the sun, moon and stars in the sky above. Single hand of steel, engraved silver band to case. Back plate with engraved friezes, and pierced and engraved cock pinned through the bridge. Brass balance wheel, fusee for gut line and a verge escapement. A well made and typical watch of its period. The Trustees of the British Museum.

year a further pension of £50 per annum. In the grant he is styled "Clockmaker Extraordinary." In 1616 a warrant was signed to pay him £234. 10s. for the purchase and repair of clocks and watches for the king. On 26th November 1618 he was appointed to the office of "Chief Clockmaker" to his Majesty, with fees and allowances for workmanship. On 30th September 1622 he received £232. 15s. for repairing clocks at Theobalds, Oatlands, and Westminster, and for making a chime of bells adjoining the clock at Theobalds.

In 1625 James I., his patron, died, but Ramsay appears to have retained his appointments, for on 25th January 1626 a warrant to pay to David Ramsay £150 for coins to be given by the king, Charles I., on the day of his coronation, was signed. Again, "17th March 1627, is a warrant to David Ramsay, Page of the Bedchamber and Clockmaker, £441. 3s. 4d. for work done for his late Majesty, and £358. 16s. 8d. in lieu of diet and bouche of Court." In 1628, 13th July, a warrant was signed to pay him £415 for clocks and other necessaries delivered for the king's service.

Among the State Papers, *Dom.*, 1653, are two receipts taken from the Jewel House at Whitehall soon after the death of Charles I. The first is as follows: "18 die Feb. 1649. Recd. one clocke with divers mocons, two globes, one case for a clocke, and a glassee, one Bullet Clocke, one clocke with five bells, and one other clocke, all which were lying at Whitehall late in the charge of David Ramsay." The second is merely a subsidiary receipt of the same date for "one other clocke in a Bow received from Ramsay."

The early 17th century oval astronomical watch by William North, London (p. 202). The Movement is of brass and of conventional layout except that a balance spring and regulator have been added at a later date and the balance weighted. The Trustees of the British Museum.

Sir Walter Scott introduces Ramsay in "The Fortunes of Nigel," as the keeper of a shop a few yards to the eastward of Temple Bar, and in a note to that novel he is described as "Constructor of Horologes to His most Sacred Majesty James I."

That Ramsay was the most celebrated watchmaker of the day may be inferred from the fact that when the clockmakers obtained their charter of incorporation, he was therein appointed to the office of master. He does not appear to have taken a very active part in the management of the company. During his absence in the country, Mr Henry Archer was appointed deputy master. William Ramsay dedicated "Vox Stellarum" to his father in 1652, and in a postscript dated 1653 remarks, "from my study in my father's house in Holborn, within two doors of the 'Wounded Hart,' near the King's Gate," and there David Ramsay probably died. The exact date of his death is uncertain, but it occurred about 1654, and though his age is not stated, he was then certainly very much past the meridian.

He is known to have been an inventor or schemer from the beginning of the century, and between 1618 and 1638 he took out no less than eight patents, none of which, however, seemed to be connected with horology; they related to raising water, draining mines, making saltpetre, separating gold and silver from the base metals, smelting iron, constructing furnaces of various kinds, dyeing fabrics, &c. He was a friend of James Lilly the astrologer, who, in his autobiography, relates that he accompanied Ramsay to Westminster at night to make some experiments with a view to discover treasure by means of the divining rod.

WILLIAM PARTRIDGE

In the "Calendar of State Papers" (Domestic Series), under date May 1660, there appears the following petition to the king from Captain William Partridge, setting out "that hee was sworne servant to yor Royall father of blessed memory, and to yor Matie in the yeare 1645, to attend ye in the qualitie of a Clockmaker, and did officiate in that place, all the time of his Maties being at Oxford, And did likewise serve his Matie a yeare and a halfe in his life Guard of foote; And afeterwards did raise a Company att his owne charge; And hath bene a great sufferer by Plundring, Imprisonm^{ts}, and expulcons. Hee most humbly prayeth that yor Matie will vouchsafe unto him the like grace and favo^r as to others of yor servants is extended, That hee may bee restored unto his said place of Clockmaker to yor Matie w^{ith} all such priviledges and Impunities as belong unto it according to his warrant."

On the same page there is also a petition from Sarah his wife, begging that

The gilt brass, oval watch signed 'David Remsay Scotus Me Fecit' (p.203), c.1630. The watch has two trains, one for going, with a verge escapement, and ratchet and click mainspring set up. The second train is for an alarm which has a pierced standing barrel. The case is engraved as is the dial plate which has an applied silver chapter ring within which is the alarm setting ring. The Trustees of the British Museum.

her husband's place may not be filled up until he has been heard for himself; that he was bred under Mr Este (? East), spent much time in improving himself in his trade in France and Flanders, and only discontinued it when in arms or in prison for His Majesty. At the foot of the petition is the note, "To succeede Da. Ramsay." But nothing further is known of Partridge, and he may be passed over. The king's clockmaker, after Ramsay, really seems to have been Edward East, of whom more will be said hereafter.

THE CLOCKMAKERS' COMPANY

In 1627 a proposal to grant letters patent authorising French clockmakers to carry on their trade within the city appears to have occasioned an agitation among the London craftsmen in favour of incorporation as a trade guild. Prior to that date, individual freemen had been associated with one or other of the existing companies, that of the Blacksmiths having been most favoured. In 1630 a committee of clockmakers was formed, funds were

Three views of the star-shaped watch signed 'David Ramsay, Scotus me fecit' (p.203-4) not dated but c.1625, discovered at Gawdy Hall, Harleston, Norfolk. The six point case is in the form of a star of David and is engraved all over the outside and on the inner covers with religious scenes. On each of the six points of the star are angels. That immediately above the 12 of the silver dial holds a shield which carries the name of the engraver 'de Heck Sculp', probably Gerard de Heck of Blois (fl.1608-1629). This signature of the engraver is very unusual. The watch has a verge escapement, pierced and engraved cock pinned through the bridge, and a bow and ratchet mainspring regulator. Worshipful Company of Clockmakers.

raised to defray expenses, and petitions were addressed to the king, with the result that a charter was obtained from Charles I. on the 22nd of August 1631.

In this document, "the Master, Wardens, and Fellowship of the Arts or Mystery of Clockmaking of the City of London" had very comprehensive powers for ruling and protecting the rights of the craft. They were entitled to make by-laws for the government of all persons using the trade in London, or within ten miles thereof, and for the regulation of the manner in which the trade should be carried on throughout the realm. And in order to prevent the public from being injured by persons "making, buying, selling, transporting, and importing any bad, deceitful, or insufficient clocks, watches, larums, sun-dials, boxes, or cases for the said trade," powers were given to the company "to enter with a constable or other officer any ships, vessels, warehouses, shops, or other places where they should suspect such bad and deceitful works to be made or kept, for the purpose of searching for them"; and, if entrance should be denied, they might effect it by force. Any such works as were faulty or deceitfully wrought they had power to seize and destroy, or cause them to be amended. Every member of the fellowship paid fourpence a quarter to meet the necessary expense of these searches. In 1708 this quarterage produced over £28.

By the charter, David Ramsay was appointed to be the first master; Henry Archer, John Willowe, and Sampson Shelton were the first wardens; and James Vantrollier (or Vautrollier), John Smith, Francis Foreman, John Harris, Richard Morgan, Samuel Linnaker, John Charlton, John Midnall, Simon Bartram, and Edward East, assistants of the said fellowship of the said art or mystery.

The charter also declared that future masters and wardens must be, or have been, professed clockmakers, an important regulation, which certainly appears to have been contravened in late years. The right of search was exercised regularly till 1735, when it was abandoned.

On the incorporation of the company, stringent by-laws were made regarding apprentices. No person was to take an apprentice without leave of the master, and then to have but one, until he shall be called to bear the office of master, warden, or assistant, and after that, not to exceed the number of two apprentices at any time whatsoever. But when his first apprentice had served five years, any member of the fellowship might take another, but not sooner, under a penalty of £10. And in the early history of the company several of its members were brought to account and fined for disobeying this regulation. Among them were several eminent members of the craft, including Thomas Loomes and Ahasuerus Fromanteel.

Then it was ordained that after an apprentice had served his time he should serve his master or some other member of the fellowship for two years as journeyman, and produce his "masterpiece" of work before he was allowed to be a workmaster. This period of probation might, if the company saw fit, be commuted to one year on payment of a fine.

Those craftsmen who had joined the Blacksmiths' and other Companies prior to the incorporation of the Clockmakers', were from time to time admitted as "brothers" of the Clockmakers' Company.

As provided by the charter, the "court" or directorate consists of the master, three wardens, and ten or more assistants. The assistants are chosen

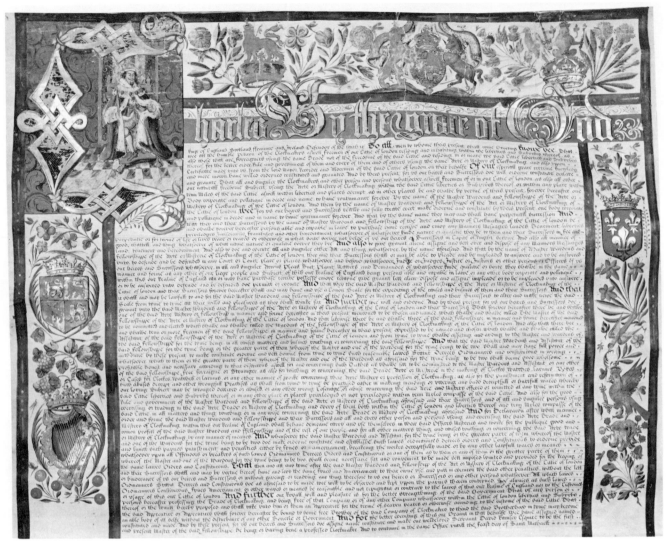

The charter of the Worshipful Company of Clockmakers of the City of London, granted by Charles I, 22 August 1631. Worshipful Company of Clockmakers.

for life from among the freemen, and the usual, but not invariable, course is that the assistants fill the higher offices in succession, according to seniority; each one being elected first as junior warden, the next year as renter, the next year as senior warden, and the following year as master. After his retirement as master, he resumes his seat as an ordinary member of the court.

Occasionally members were transferred from and to other companies. In 1636 Mr Richard Masters was transferred from the Clothiers' at a cost to the Clockmakers' Company of £10. 9s. 6d. A lesser sum sufficed for the transference, in the same year, of Mr Dawson and Mr Durant from the Imbroderers'. In 1724 Mr John Shirley gave a bond to pay the Clockmakers' Company £20 for being transferred to the Vintners'. On Mr James Masters applying in 1811 to be transferred to the Goldsmiths', a little haggling appears to have ensued. The Clockmakers' Company at first demanded £50 for consenting; Masters offered £30 in 1812, and this amount was accepted. George Russell, in 1844, had to pay the Clockmakers' Company £30 for permission to be transferred to the Salters', and an additional £5 for a special meeting of the court to attend the Court of Aldermen with the Salters' Company.

In 1656 Ahasuerus Fromanteel and thirty-one other members complained to the court that, in spite of members having to pay xii$^{d\cdot}$ a quarter, the meetings were held in taverns. They also objected to the presence of Frenchmen among the ruling body, and recounted other grievances. A counter-petition traversed the allegations, and asserted the confidence of the signatories in the management of the company.

In 1671 the company obtained the right to bear arms, and in that year letters patent were granted for this distinction. They recounted "that whereof at present Nicholas Coxeter is Master, Samuel Horne and Jeffery Bailey are Wardens, as also Edward East, the only persons now living of those mentioned in the said Letters Patents of Incorporation, John Nicasius, John Pennock, Edmond Gilpin, Jeremie Gregory, Thomas Taylor, Thomas Clayton, John Freeman, Evan Jones, Isaac Daniell, John Browne, Nicholas Payne, Richard Ames, and Benjamin Bell, are Assistants, and to the rest of the Fellowship and Company thereof, and to their successors for ever: the Armes, Crest, Supporters and Motto hereafter mentioned, viz$^{t\cdot}$ Sable, A Clock y^e 4 Pillars therefore erected on four lyons, and on each capitall a globe with a Crosse, and in the middest an Imperial Crowne all Or, and for Their Crest upon an helmet Proper Mantled Gules Doubled Argent and Wreath of their Colours a Spheare Or, The Armes Supported by the Figures of a Naked Old man holding a Scithe and an Hour Glasse representing Time, and an Emporour in Roabes Crowned holding a Scepter, Their Motto —

Fig. 398.

TEMPVS RERVM IMPERATOR

As in the margent they are all more lively Depicted."

In 1677 Mr George Deane, engraver, a member of the company, "having by the hands of Henry Jones presented to this court the company's coat of arms engraved on a copper-plate fit to be used for tickets and divers other occasions of the company which was very well liked, this court did kindly accept it, and returned him thanks."

During the latter part of the seventeenth century the suitability of watchmaking as a profession for women was recognised, and in 1715 the company sanctioned the taking of female apprentices. The names of several will be found in the list at the end of this book, where also is recorded the admission of a few female members of the company. The employment of female labour in watch work does not, however, seem to have made much progress in England till watch factories were established in quite recent years.

In 1781 it was decided to elect leading members of the trade as honorary freemen. This course, politic as it probably was, seems to indicate that at this period the prestige of the company in the horological world was insufficient to induce distinguished craftsmen to take up the freedom in the ordinary way.

The company has never risen to the importance and comfort of possessing a hall of its own for meetings and other business. For brief periods during its history it had the use of a hall belonging to a more favoured guild, but most of its meetings were held in taverns, more than forty of these establishments having been so favoured. Its last meeting before the Great Fire of London

The clock-watch by East with a tortoise-shell and piqué *case (p.215). Although the case of this watch is now thought to be later, the movement is an excellent example of East's work with a plain silver* champlevé *dial and date aperture beneath the hinge at 12 o'clock. The movement is of brass and steel with silver regulator, and locking plates. The balance wheel has been weighted to accompany a balance-spring since removed, and the stopwork which the watch originally had has been removed. The silver inner case is engraved on the bezel and the back is pierced and engraved in the forms of various intertwining flowers. The Trustees of the British Museum.*

Fig. 399.

was held on 20th August, at the Castle Tavern, in Fleet Street; and the first meeting after, on 8th October 1666, at the Crown Tavern, in Smithfield. Later still, the Devil Tavern, near Temple Bar, was patronised.

Only a certain number of freemen from certain of the companies is permitted to take up the livery or freedom of the City, the whole matter being in the discretion of the Court of Aldermen. The claims of the Clockmakers' Company were not recognised in this respect till 1766, when it was allowed to select sixty of its members for the privilege; this number was upon petition increased to 120 in 1786, a still further increase to 200 was sanctioned in 1810, and in 1826 the present limit of 250 was reached.

No. 2 of the by-laws provided "that every person of the said Fellowship chosen in the said Livery shall accept and take upon him to be of the said Livery, and shall within fourteen days after notice of such election take such oaths as by these ordinances shall be appointed for him."

The honour of election to the livery does not seem to have been always appreciated, for in 1813 "William Mansell, of Rosoman St., Clerkenwell, Watch casemaker, who was summoned to take the Livery on the 19th August 1812, again on 7th September 1812, and repeated on the 11th October last, was peremptorily summoned to be at this court, and being now in attendance for the first time, refused to take the Clothing, and the penalty of Fifteen Pounds being awarded against him for such refusal, he paid the sum in Court, and his Election to the Livery was thereupon discharged."

"William Welborne, of Leather Lane, Holborn, has been summoned to take the Livery in November 1811, and also in January, February, and July 1812, but having failed so to do, was again summoned for that purpose to the last Quarter Court, when he attended and requested until this day,

212

A bracket clock in a walnut veneered case by Henry Jones, London, c.1675. The case is moulded with a basket top and has pierced side frets. The carrying handle, somewhat impractical, is scrolled and of brass as are the bun-and-claw feet. Square dial with a fine matte centre, calendar aperture, silvered chapter ring, cherub spandrels, and pierced blued steel hands. There is a three train plated movement with eight ringed pillars, hour and quarter striking on two bells, and later anchor escapement. Christie, Manson & Woods Ltd.

Fig. 401.

Fig. 402.

Fig. 400.

Fig. 403.

Fig. 404.

promising either to take the clothing or pay the penalty for refusal. He being now present and declining to take the same, the penalty of £15 was ordered to be enforced, which being paid in Court, his election to the Livery was likewise thereupon discharged."

The fine on taking up the livery was then fixed at £21.

In 1820 it was resolved to allow the quarterly payments or quarterage from members in support of the company to be commuted by an immediate payment; the amount to be paid being dependent on the age of the member availing himself of the arrangement. The fee to be paid on taking up the freedom of the company by purchase was in 1876 increased to £20.

As already stated, the company does not possess a hall of its own. Its business is transacted at the Guildhall, where, by permission of the Corporation, its library is kept and its remarkably fine museum of timekeepers displayed for public inspection.

Edward East, watchmaker to Charles I., was a true horologist and a worthy successor to David Ramsay. He at one time resided in Pall Mall, near the tennis court, and attended the king when tennis and other games were being played in the Mall, his Majesty often providing one of East's watches as a prize. Edward East seems to have removed to Fleet Street, for it is related that at a later period the king's attendant, Mr Herbert, failing in the punctual discharge of his duties in the morning, his Majesty provided him with a gold alarm watch, which was fetched from the king's watchmaker, Mr East, in Fleet Street. He was in Fleet Street in 1635, for a correspondent of *Notes and Queries* had in 1900 a MS. Return of Strangers within the ward of Farringdon Without wherein East is referred to as of Fleet Street, in the parish of St Dunstan's in the West, and as the employer of one Elias Dupree, a Dutchman. Lady Fanshawe in her "Memoirs," stated that when she came from France in the autumn of 1646 she lodged in Fleet Street at Mr East's the watchmaker. The locality of a presumably still later residence is indicated by a reference to "Mr East at the Sun, outside Temple Bar," in the *London Gazette*, January 22-26, 1690. A very large silver alarm clock-watch by Edward East, which was kept at the bedside of Charles I., was presented by the king on his way to execution at Whitehall, on 30th January 1649, to his faithful and attached servant, Mr, afterwards Sir, Thomas Herbert. It was illustrated in "Sussex Archaeological Collections," 1850, and in the *Archoeological Journal,* vol. vii., from which Figs. 400 and 401, two-thirds the size of the watch, are reproduced. I presume its history is well authenticated. The owner of it, Mr William Townley Mitford, was quoted as saying, "It came into possession of my family by intermarriage with the Herberts about a century ago, and since that time has remained with us," and the Society of Antiquaries seemed to be quite satisfied with their examination. Still, from the engravings, it is rather a perplexing watch. The dial and pierced back are of Charles I. period, and though a minute hand at that date would be very unusual, it would not be an impossible adjunct; presumably there was also an hour hand, but I can see no alarm disc or indicator; the centre of the dial may, of course, have been turned to set the alarm, but there is no sign of its having been so utilised. Amongst the collection of autographs and manuscripts in the possession of Mr Alfred Morrison, of Fonthill House, Wilts., is a warrant, dated 23rd June 1649, from the Committee of Public Revenue to Thomas Fauconbridge, Esq.,

Left: Fig. 406. — Night Clock.

Right: Fig. 407. — Dial of Night Clock.

Fig. 405.

Receiver-General, authorising him to pay "vnto Mr Edward East, Watchmaker, the so'me of fortie pounds for a Watch and a Larum of gould by him made for the late King Charles by directions of the Earle of Pembrooke, by order of the Committee, and deliuered for the late King's use the xviith of January last." In the Fellows collection at the British Museum is a splendid octangular crystal-cased watch, a recumbent female figure holding an hour-glass being engraved on the dial; 1620 is mentioned as the probable date of this specimen of East's work. Of about the same period is the small oval watch by him shown in Fig. 399. Another example of his work is the pretty little watch of slightly later date having an outer case and with a faceted crystal over the dial which is represented in Fig. 402. Two views of a clock-watch by East in a finely pierced and engraved case and also with a crystal covering for the dial are given in Figs. 403 and 404. These three watches are from the Schloss collection.

In the Pierpont Morgan collection is the little watch by East which is represented in Fig. 405. The dial of silver has a view engraved on it, and the case, of the same metal, is fluted; the channels which broaden radially from the centre of the back extend over the edge and are finely engraved.

Wood refers to another watch by him with a silver case in the form of a cross, the dial being engraved with the Crucifixion and angels. In the Ashmolean Museum at Oxford is a watch by East with gold case in the form of a melon, studded all over with turquoises, the pendant being enamelled blue to match. Two other undoubted specimens of this master's work are in the Guildhall Museum. One, a watch movement, inscribed, "Eduardus East, Londini," was thus described by E.J. Thompson: "The fusee of ten turns is cut for gut. There are great second and contrate wheels, and a left-handed cut balance-wheel, the verge being of course left-handed. The end of the verge is driven into the balance, which has one straight bar or arm. The cock is secured on a stud by a pin. There is no provision for a balance-spring, and the regulating must have depended upon the setting up or down of the mainspring by the endless screw. It had one hand only. The fusee is hollow, having the cap and winding square solid; it is fitted on to an arbor riveted on the great wheel. The great wheel has fifty-five, the second forty-five, the contrate forty, and the balance-wheel fifteen teeth; the second, contrate, and balance pinions being all of five leaves."

The second example is a watch in a silver oval case with hunting cover, having a crystal centre, which E. J. Thompson described as finely worked in to suit its shape. The dial is of silver, and is traversed by an hour hand only. The movement is inscribed, as in the first instance, "Eduardus East, Londini." There is a twelve-turn fusee cut for catgut. The mainspring is white and no doubt original.

In the British Museum is a watch by East with a tortoiseshell case, dating from about 1640. At the South Kensington Museum are two or three watches by him, one, a clock-watch in a pierced and engraved case of silver, has on the back dates of Church Festivals and Law Terms.

In Fig. 406 is shown a night clock 17 in. high by East, belonging to Mr T. W. Bourne. The case is of ebony on oak, and the top lifts off to allow the insertion of a lamp. Showing through a curved slit in the upper part of the dial is a disc with perforated hour numerals so that the time can be seen at night. The light would also shine through a keyhole-shaped aperture above which serves as a pointer. Fig. 407 shows the dial to an enlarged scale. This clock answers to the description of one belonging to Catherine of Braganza, Queen of Charles II., which Pepys refers to under date 24th June 1664 as follows: "After dinner to White Hall; and there met with Mr Pierce, and he showed me the Queene's bed-chamber and her closett, where she had nothing but some pretty pious pictures, and books of devotion; and her holy water at her head as she sleeps, with her clock by her bedside, wherein a lamp burns that tells her the time of the night at any time."

Among the Wetherfield collection are several long-case and bracket clocks by East. Illustrations of some of these will be given in Chapter VII.

Edward East was one of the ten original assistants named in the charter of incorporation of the Clockmakers' Company, and at once took a leading part in its proceedings, and after serving in the subordinate capacities was elected master in 1645, a post he again occupied in 1652. He was the only treasurer ever appointed, and the creation of the office came about in a curious way. In 1647 the renter warden, Mr Helden, refused to give the usual security for the stock of the company, and in this dilemma the office of treasurer was created, Mr East and Mr Hackett being nominated thereto, and the former chosen. On the death of Mr East the office was allowed to lapse.

Edward East lived to a good age. There is no record of his death, but it probably occurred not long after 1693. In 1692 his quondam apprentice and friend, Henry Jones, who was then Master of the Clockmakers' Company, acquainted the court that Mr East desired during his lifetime to make a gift of £100 to the company for the benefit of the poor. Mr Jones added that he would also contribute a like sum for a similar purpose. In the following year Mr East gave the £100, and it was ordered "that the master and wardens do go to Mr East and give him hearty thanks for his charity."

Taking into account that Edward East at the time of the incorporation of the Clockmakers' Company in 1631 must have been a man of considerable standing in the trade, it seems probable that during the seventeenth century there were two of the name, one succeeding the other. In the "Calendar of State Papers (Domestic)" is an entry of a grant in 1662 to Edward East of the office of "chief clockmaker and keeper of the Privy clocks, fee 12d. per

Fig. 408.

day and £3. 6s. 8d. livery."

Under date 4th April 1662 is an entry of a warrant for an order to swear in *James* East, the king's servant, as clockmaker to the queen.

HENRY JONES

Henry Jones, already referred to, was apprenticed to Edward East on 22nd August 1654. He was made free of the Clockmakers' Company in 1663, and served as master in 1691-92. He resided near the Inner Temple Gate, and attained a considerable reputation, which was quite justified judging from what remains of his work. Charles II., according to tradition gave to Mrs Jane Lane a clock, in memory of her services after the battle of Worcester. On the clock was engraved, "Henricus Jones, Londini." In Overall's "History of the Clockmakers' Company" is a record which just possibly refers to this clock. It states that, on 19th January 1673, "Mr Henry Jones, clockmaker, acquainted the Court of the Company that he had made for the King (Charles II.) a clock of the value of £150, whereon was engraven 'Henricus Jones, Londini,' and which stood in His Majesty's closet for about seven years, but being by His Majesty given unto a lady it came into the hands of Robert Seignor, clockmaker, of Exchange Alley, to be repaired, and he caused Edward Staunton, clockmaker, or some other person, to take out the maker's name and insert his own."

In North's "Life" it is stated that barometers were first made and sold by one Jones, a noted clockmaker in the Inner Temple Gate, at the instance of Lord Keeper Guildford; and very probably Jones was the first *Englishman* who constructed a Torricellian tube, as the barometer was originally called, after its inventor, Evangelista Torricelli, who propounded its theory about 1650.

Fig. 409.

In the *London Gazette* for October 21-24, 1689, was the following advertisement: "Lost on the 21st Instant, between the Hay Market near Charing Cross and the Rummer in Queen St. near Cheapside, a round Gold Pendulum Watch of an indifferent small size, showing the hours and minutes, the Pendulum went with a strait Spring, it was made by Henry Jones, Watchmaker in the Temple, the Out-Case had a Cypher pin'd on it, and the Shagreen much worn. If it comes to your hands, you are desired to bring it to the said Mr Jones or Mr Snag, a goldsmith in Lumbard Street, and you shall have two Guineas Reward."

In the Guildhall Museum is one of Henry Jones's watches, which Mr E. J. Thompson speaks of as having very fine pillars. Another watch by the same maker is in the collection of Mr Evan Roberts.

Fig. 408 shows an early bracket clock by Jones, which belongs to Mr A. Riley. The case of oak, veneered with fine pollard oak, is about 15 in. high and 11 in. broad, has the usual glass door in front and back, and glass panels at the sides. At the top is a narrow band or frieze of rosewood fretwork. The signature, "Henry Jones in the Temple", is engraved on the bottom of the dial just under the circle, but concealed when the door is closed.

The bracket clock with basket top "squat" case shown in Fig. 409 was sketched from an example by Henry Jones, by favour of Mr Percy Webster. The chased open basket-work and corner ornaments are particularly choice.

Mr Holden, of Yeadon, has an eight-day long inlaid case-clock with a brass dial, inscribed "Henry Jones in ye Temple", which is a later production than any of those already quoted.

Henry Jones, who was the son of William Jones, vicar of Boulder,

Southampton, died in November 1695 aged sixty-three years, and was buried within the precincts of the old church of St Dunstan's in the West, Fleet Street, where a monument was erected to his memory by his widow.

EDWARD BARLOW (BOOTH)

This talented man was born near Warrington in 1636. He was ordained in the English church at Lisbon, and took the name of Barlow from his godfather, Ambrose Barlow, a Benedictine, who suffered at Lancaster for his religion. Edward Booth devoted considerable attention to horological instruments. He was undoubtedly the inventor of the rack repeating striking work for clocks, which was applied by Tompion about 1676. He also devised a repeating watch on the same principle, and made application to patent it in 1686. His claim was successfully opposed by Daniel Quare, who was backed by the Clockmakers' Company. The king, James II., tried both watches, and gave his preference to Quare's, which repeated the hours and quarters with one push from a pin near the pendant, whereas Barlow's watch was furnished with a pin on each side of the pendant and required two distinct operations to attain the same end.

Booth invented the cylinder escapement, and patented it in conjunction with William Houghton and Thomas Tompion in 1695 (No. 344). The invention is described as a "ballance wheele either flatt or hollow, to worke within and crosse the centre of the verge, one to be circular, concave, and convex." He died in 1716.

BETTS

Fig. 410. — Watch by Samuel Betts, about 1640.

Fig. 410 shows a watch by Samuel Betts remarkable for its particularly handsome dial of silver and brass. The central leaf ornament of silver polished is partly filled in with crimson enamel or hard wax, the pretty effect of which is enhanced by a dull matted surface between it and the hour band, which is also of silver. On a nicely chased revolving brass ring outside the hours is a *fleur-de-lys* to indicate the day of the month on a fixed silver band, divided into thirty-one and figured as shown. An outer chased margin of brass completes the arrangement. At the end of the short months the day of the month ring has to be moved by hand. The boss of the hour indicator is oval, and although but one limb now exists, there was probably a trident tail, as may be seen on other specimens of the period. The case is of silver with a hit-and-miss shutter over the winding hole; the glass is nearly one-third of a sphere and exceedingly thick. Betts carried on business at the back of the Royal Exchange, and appears to have died prior to 1673, when "Mr Marquet" (Markwick?) advertises himself in the *London Gazette* as the successor of "Mr Samuel Betts, deceased." In 1656 Betts attested the genuineness of Jas. Lello's masterpiece to the Clockmakers' Company. The watch here shown dates from about 1645.

TOMPION AND GRAHAM

Thomas Tompion, "the father of English watchmaking," was born at Northhill, Bedfordshire, in 1638. It is said that his father was a farrier, and that he was brought up to the same trade; but the first reliable record shows him to have been in business as a clockmaker at Water Lane, Blackfriars, when quite a young man.

Water Lane was a long, tortuous thoroughfare, the western portion of which is now Whitefriars Street, and Tompion's shop, known by the sign of the Dial and Three Crowns, was at the Fleet Street corner where the offices of the *Daily News* are. His advent marks a distinct epoch in the history of the horological art. Throughout his career he was closely associated with some of the leading mathematicians and philosophers of his time. The

A late 17th century long case clock with walnut veneered case with floral inlay. Signed 'Henry Jones in ye Temple' the clock has a six pillar movement, exterior locking plate and an anchor escapement. The bolt and shutter maintaining power originally fitted has been removed at a later date. Silvered chapter ring with cherub spandrels and acanthus engraving, subsidiary seconds with calendar aperture. The winding holes are ringed. Christie, Manson & Woods Ltd.

Fig. 411. — THOMAS TOMPION, 1638-1713.

theories of Dr Hooke and the Rev Edward Barlow would probably have remained in abeyance but for Tompion's skilful materialisation of them. He soon became the leading watchmaker at the court of Charles II., and was everywhere welcomed as an artist of commanding ability. When he entered the arena the performance of timekeepers was very indifferent. The principles on which they were constructed were defective, and the mechanism was not well proportioned. The movements were as a rule regarded as quite subsidiary to the exterior cases, and English specimens of the art had no distinctive individuality. By adopting the inventions of Hooke and Barlow, and by skilful proportion of parts, he left English watches and clocks the finest in the world and the admiration of his brother artists. Of course he did not reach finality; improvements continued under his immediate successors. Indeed, some of the most remarkable and progressive horological conceptions emanated from the mind of his favourite pupil, Graham, whom he inspired, and who continued the work which Tompion began. Of the few horologists of Tompion's time who can be admitted as his peers, Daniel Quare was perhaps the most notable example. As a clockmaker Joseph Knibb may perhaps be admitted to rank with these.

Among others above mediocrity who made watches before and after the introduction of the balance-spring, Nathaniel Barrow is worthy of mention.

Tompion was primarily a clockmaker; in the records of the Clockmakers' Company he is referred to as a "great clockmaker" when he was associated as a brother in 1671; and it is doubtful if he made watches in the early part of his career. I have never met with a specimen not furnished with a balance-spring, and those with but an hour hand are exceedingly rare.

The portrait in Fig. 411 is from mezzotint produced in 1697 after a

Fig. 412.

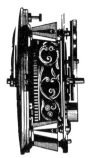

Fig. 415.

Fig. 416.

Fig. 417.

Fig. 413. — Watch by Tompion in Gold Cases.

Fig. 414. — Tompion Watch in Silver Inner Case; Out-Case, Tortoiseshell.

painting by Sir Godfrey Kneller.

One of Tompion's earlier clocks, which belongs to Mr Norman Shaw, is shown in Fig. 412. It has a light pendulum 6 in. in length fixed to the verge; the escapement for the alarm is behind the going train, and when the alarm is let off the hammer strikes the bell which forms the domical top of the clock. In the British Museum is another chamber clock by Tompion, as well as a very thick watch by the master in a case superbly painted in enamel by Camille André. In the same repository is a curious universal pocket sun-dial with compass, all of gold, also by Tompion.

In 1675, he made for Charles II. a watch with two balances and balance-springs as devised by Hooke. Derham says, "This watch was wonderfully approved of by the King; and so the invention grew into reputation and was much talked of at home and abroad. Particularly its fame flew into France, from whence the Dauphin sent for two, which that eminent artist Mr Tompion made for him."

The introduction of the balance-spring involved a reconstruction of the watch movement. The disc or dial for indicating the adjustment of the mainspring was discarded as no longer necessary, and a somewhat similar one introduced for showing the movement of the curb pins round the balance-spring. This disc was placed upon a pinion with a squared extremity for the reception of a watch key to actuate the curb pins, which were carried by a toothed segment or circular rack gearing with the pinion. The tangent wheel and screw for mainspring adjustment were placed beneath the plates. The balance was considerably enlarged and covered with a circular cock. In Tompion's early watches there is a kind of bevelled fringe around the edge of the cock for the more effectual protection of the balance, as in Fig. 416, but after 1688 or 1690 he adopted the now well-known form with a broad base curved to suit the edge of the plate, a circular table the same size as the balance, and just where the table narrows to join the base a cherub's head or a grotesque mask engraved between projecting ears or streamers.

His watch movements were deep, top plates exceedingly thin, and near the edge was usually engraved, "Tho. Tompion, London."

Fig. 418. — One-Year Clock by Tompion.

He was, I believe, the first manufacturer to number his watch movements consecutively in plain figures for the purpose of identification. His early ones were not so marked, and I should judge he commenced the practice about 1685.

Fig. 413 shows a watch by him in plain gold cases, bearing the hall mark corresponding to 1685; the dial is of gold with raised numerals. The hands are very fine, the hour indicator being of the tulip pattern. A watch with silver dial, about ten years later, from the Pierpont Morgan collection, is shown in Fig. 414.

As an example of the versatility of Tompion's genius two views of a watch from the collection of Mr Willard H. Wheeler are given in Figs. 415 and 416. The distinctive feature of this watch is that, although a verge escapement is used, the fusee has been discarded; the mainspring being surrounded by a handsomely pierced guard which is fixed to the plate; and to this the outer end of the mainspring is attached. In order that the watch might have a coil of mainspring of the largest possible dimensions, what is usually the *centre* wheel is planted out of the centre; the cannon pinion rides loose on a stud planted in the centre of the frame; and to get the proper motion for the minute-hand without the introduction of an intermediate wheel in the motion work, the train rotates reversely to the usual direction. The movement is not numbered; this fact, together with the style of the engraving and the form of the balance-cock, enables one to fix the date of its production at about 1680.

Fig. 419. — Travelling Striking and Alarm Watch by Tompion. Fig. 420. — Travelling Striking and Alarm Watch by Tompion.

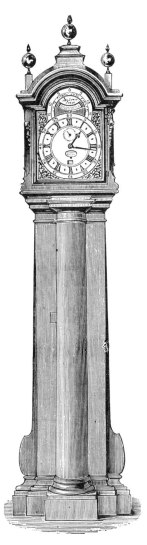

Fig. 421. — Clock by Tompion at the Pump-room, Bath.

Before September 1695, Tompion produced a watch in which the teeth of the horizontal escape wheel dropped on to the cylindrical body of the verge, as shown in the appended drawing (Fig. 417), thus avoiding the recoil incidental to the usual verge construction; and in September 1695 he, in conjunction with Booth and Houghton, patented the cylinder escapement. In the account of Barlow the wording of the description is given.

One of the boldest of Tompion's conceptions was a small clock to strike the hours and quarters, driven by mainsprings and yet requiring to be wound but once a year. The successful embodiment of this is shown in Fig. 418. The clock was made for William III. at a cost of £1,500, and was in his bedroom at Kensington Palace when he died. It was left by him to the Earl of Leicester, and now belongs to Lord Mostyn, in whose family it has been for over 150 years. It is still in going order, and Lord Mostyn has the name of nearly every one who has wound it during the last 100 years.

The total height to the top of the spear is 30 in.; the body or plinth below the dial is 10 in. in width, 7 in. in height, and 6 in. from front to back.

The case, of ebony with silver mounts, is a fine piece of work in one piece, forming really a hood or cover, for it slides down over the movement and rests on the metal feet.

The movement is in three portions; the lower part below the dial is attached to the heavy scroll feet, and contains the two mainspring barrels, the two fusees, and the larger driving wheels. The middle portion behind the dial contains the smaller wheels and pinions; while the verge escapement above is held separately, so that it may be easily detached. The pendulum, 6 in. long, is in front of the movement just behind the dial, and its action may be seen through the glazed door below the dial, which is removed when winding or regulation is needed. Regulation is effected by raising or lowering the chops which embrace the pendulum spring, very much in the way adopted for modern clocks; the sliding chops are actuated by a tangent wheel and screw, and there is on the front plate a micrometer index for noting the amount of adjustment made.

The hours are struck on a bell attached to the front plate, the ting-tang quarters being sounded on this and on a smaller bell, which surmounts the movement. On each side of the case is a pull-repeating arrangement.

The splendid travelling clock-watch, of which two views are given in Figs. 419 and 420, is in the Pierpont Morgan collection, and dates from about 1695. The case and dial are of silver.

During the building of St Paul's, it was frequently reported that Tompion was to construct a wonderful clock for the cathedral; and in "The Affairs of the World," published in October 1700, the following announcement appeared: "Mr Tompion, the famous watchmaker in Fleet Street, is making a clock for St Paul's Cathedral, which it is said will go one hundred years without winding up; will cost £3,000 or £4,000, and be far finer than the clock at Strasburg." Though this statement seems to have been unwarranted, it is quite possible he would have been entrusted with the construction of a timekeeper of some kind, but, after unremitting application to his profession for more than thirty years, he was at this time, it may be assumed, just beginning to indulge in well-earned leisure; during the last years of his life he allowed himself considerable relaxation, and was absent from London for extended periods. In the course of his migrations he visited Bath, possibly to derive benefit from the healing properties of the hot mineral water which wells up in the Queen of the West, as the chief Somersetshire city is called. In the Grand Pump-room there is a splendid example of Tompion's later work, which he presented to the city, as is thus recorded on a tablet adjacent to the timekeeper: "The Watch and Sun-dial was given by Mr Thos. Tompion, of London, Clockmaker. Anno Dom. 1709." In Fig. 421, which is taken from a photograph by Mr Ernest Lambert, I am enabled to give an engraving of this stately timekeeper. Mr Olds has kindly furnished some description of the movement. The dial is of brass, with ornamental corner pieces and silvered rings, the minute circle being 15 in. in diameter; the day of the month is shown through an aperture. On a high arch above is an equation index and scale, 0 being in the centre, and the variation to a maximum of fifteen minutes shown on each side; on the right, "Sun faster," and to the left, "Sun slower." The months and days are engraved on a silvered 10 in. circle, of which an arc is shown through an opening. The date is indicated by a small point in the centre of the opening. The number of minutes shown by the index gives the difference between sun time and mean time; this 10 in. circle has over 2,000 finely cut teeth, and makes its annual circuit by means of an endless screw and pinion, worked from the dial wheel, which makes one revolution per hour. The index is kept in position by a small counterpoise with a pulley fitted to its arbor; the pulley is attached by a fine chain to a cranked arm, which rises and falls with the indentations and protuberances of a properly shaped plate or cam attached securely to the 10 in. circle.

Fig. 422.

The train and frame of the timepiece are in remarkably good order, considering its age. The driving power is a lead weight of 32 lbs. hung on a 3-in. pulley, having a fall of 6 ft. It is wound monthly on a $2\frac{1}{2}$-in. barrel; the great wheel of 94 teeth, and $4\frac{3}{4}$ in. in diameter, drives a pinion of sixteen leaves; thereon is a 3-in. wheel of 80 teeth, and this drives the centre pinion of 10 teeth; the centre wheel is $2\frac{7}{8}$ in. of 72 teeth, driving the third pinion of 9 teeth; on this is a $2\frac{5}{8}$-in. wheel of 60 teeth, driving the escape pinion of 8 teeth; on this is a 2-in. escape wheel of 30 teeth, shaped as in a recoiling escapement. The pallet staff is $2\frac{3}{4}$ in. above the escape arbor, and carries pallets of the anchor pattern, having inclined planes to allow recoil. The one-second pendulum rod is of steel, of a flattened oval section, with 6-in. bob of lenticular form. The amount of oscillation, being only $2\frac{3}{4}°$, causes the recoil of the escapement to be barely apparent.

The day of the month circle is moved by an extra wheel from the hour wheel. Maintaining power while winding is given by a spring-propelled click through a steel arm on an arbor between the plates, acting on the teeth of the centre wheel, which is put into action by lifting the sliding cover of the winder hole in the dial.

The case is of solid unpolished oak, 9 ft. high to the top of the arched head which is surmounted by brass ball ornaments. The body of the case is 17 in. wide and about 6 in. narrower than the head and base, with a semicircular door 8 in. across and 5 ft. in length. As will be seen from the drawing, the case has much the appearance of a pillar rising from a substantial base.

The clock is in a recess at the eastern end of the room, and it occupied a similar position in the old Pump-room, the erection of which was finished in

1706. As the spot is particularly suited for the reception of a clock, it may be conjectured that Tompion was in Bath when the old Pump-room was being built, and that the ever-vigilant "Beau" Nash obtained from him a promise to present a timepiece when the building was completed.

At first sight the phrase "watch and sun-dial" on the tablet recording the gift seems to include a gnomon of some sort for regulating the timekeeper from observations of the sun. There would be nothing far-fetched in this surmise, because sun-dials to check the going of public timekeepers were not at all an unusual adjunct. But I am inclined to think that in this instance sun-dial meant the equation dial over the ordinary one.

Fig. 422 shows another example of Tompion's work, which is almost a facsimile of the Bath clock. It belongs to Mr Philip T. Godsal, of Iscoyd Park, Whitchurch, Shropshire.

A long-case chiming clock by Tompion to go a month between windings which is at Windsor Castle is shown in Chapter VII., and at Buckingham Palace is a very similar one. At the Guildhall Museum is a Tompion clock with a square dial, one hand, and in a long black case, which may be accepted as an indubitable example of his early work. In the same collection is a more modern specimen which goes four months between windings, has an arch dial, and maintaining work similar to that in the Bath Pump-room clock. It is inscribed "Thomas Tompion, London," a form of signature rather unusual. In the Wetherfield collection are no fewer than eighteen Tompion clocks. Some of these and others I propose to illustrate in Chapter VII.

Mr T. W. Bourne owns a good example dating from about 1695. It has a $10\frac{1}{2}$-in. dial, shown in Fig. 645, and is in a long case of burr walnut on oak. According to Reid the Earl of Moray has a clock by Tompion at the house of Donibristle in which the hours are struck on two bells in accordance with the plan explained on p. 245.

A twelve-month long-case clock by Tompion fetched 125 guineas at the sale of the late Duke of Cambridge's effects at Christie's in 1904. The dial and upper part of the case resemble the one-year clock illustrated in Fig. 418. It was presumably made for William III. whose monogram is carved thereon. Underneath the hood are trusses similar to Fig. 669, and like Quare's year clock at Hampton Court the height of the structure is increased by a plinth below the case.

The Royal Society possesses a paper in Hooke's handwriting, imperfect and undated, showing that Tompion and Hooke were in communication on the subject of the barometer, which is of interest as evidence of the estimation in which Tompion was held by Hooke. It occurs about the middle of a parchment-bound volume lettered "20 Hooke's Papers," and is headed

The 9ft. high longcase equation clock which Thomas Tompion presented to the City of Bath in 1709. The clock which has an unusual Doric column case of wainscot oak with carving on the hood, is one of four known equation clocks by Tompion and the only one of month duration the others running for a year. It has a plated movement, recoil escapement and maintaining power. The chapter rings are silvered, there are gilt brass spandrels, and blued steel hands with subsidiary seconds. The signature above the date aperture on a plate is not, according to Symonds, in Tompion's normal style. A second plate records the circumstances of Tompion's gift, and there is a calendar volvelle. In the arch to the dial (which is an early example) is an equation index with its own hand.

Tompion paid several visits to Bath and in 1707 was elected a freeman of the city. In connection with the clock one of his employees was paid £5 7s. 6d. in 1709-10, perhaps his expenses for travelling to Bath to do the setting up. Bath City Council.

"Aerostatick Instruments." In it Hooke states that a form of his barometer, in which the height of the mercury was indicated by a column of water, "was tryed at Mr Thomas Tompion's, a person deservedly famous for his excellent skill in making watches and clocks, and not less curious and dexterous in constructing and handworking of other nice mechanical instruments." A barometer by Tompion is at Hampton Court Palace.

The extent of Tompion's business may be judged from the fact that in the advertisements for the recovery of lost watches during the period he was in business, timekeepers of his make largely preponderate. Trivial though some of them may be, I venture to submit a selection from these announcements, as the quaint descriptions in the words of the owners are interesting, and convey a very good idea of the various styles in favour at the time:—

"Lost on Wednesday 20th of this Instant September at night in or about St. James's, a Gold Pendulum watch of Mr Tompion's making, having three motions, a shagreen case, a cipher on the Back Side, and marked within the Box 277, with a Gold Chain and three seals, viz. one Figure and two Heads. Whoever give notice thereof to Mr Nott, a Bookseller in Pall Mall, or to Mr Loman at the Lord Cavendish's House in St James's Square, shall have 15 Guineas Reward" (*London Gazette*, September 22, 1682).

"Lost on Monday the 25th Instant in the Fields betwixt Islington Church and Newington Green, a gold watch with a Shagreen Case, with a cipher studded in gold on the Bottom. Made by Thos. Tompion, London. Whoever brings the said watch to Mr Robert Halstead, Goldsmith at the Crown in Fleet St. shall have three Guineas Reward" (*London Gazette*, January 25, 1685-6).

"Lost out of a gentleman's Pocket, the 19th past, betwixt Lyme St. end in Fenchurch St. and the end of the Minories, an indifferent small size gold pendulum watch, going without string or chain, showing the hours of the day, and day of the month, the name Tompion, in a shagreen case, pinned with a Cypher in the bottom of the case, wound up on the dial plate, at the hour of 12, a straight key with a Steel Nose. Whoever brings it to Mr Tompion, Clockmaker, at Water Lane, and in Fleet St., shall have one guinea reward, or, if bought, their money again with reasonable profit" (*London Gazette*, November 10-13, 1690).

"Lost, the 3rd inst., between the Sun-Dial, in St James Park, and Man's Coffee House, a silver Minute Pendulum watch, made by Tho. Tompion, in a Shagreen studded case, on the bottom of the inner case the number 458; with a gold Ring hanging upon the silver chain, with the Effigies of their Present Majesties" (*London Gazette*, March 3-7, 1691).

"Lost on the 24th instant, about Kingston-on-Thames, a Gold Minute and Second Chain Pendulum watch, with a Stop, the hours seen through a hole in the Dial plate, and in a plain Shagreen Out-Case, the name Tho. Tompion, London, a number in the bottom of the Box, 0201. Whoever gives notice of it to Mr Tho. Tompion, Clockmaker, at the corner of Water Lane, in Fleet St., shall have 3 guineas reward; or if bought already, your money again with reasonable profit" (*London Gazette*, June 25-29, 1691).

"Lost on the 23rd instant a Gold Pendulum Watch made by Thos. Tompion, Fleet Street, in a Shagreen Studded Case with a Steel Seal set in gold tied to it, bearing a Coat quartered with the arms of the Crown battoned; the Box numbered 422 and the maker's mark [II]" (*London Gazette*, July 23-27, 1691).

"Lost on the 21st instant from the Duke of Richmond's in St James's Square, a gold striking watch with a Shagreen case studded round, with little holes between, having 3 links of plain gold chain, made by Thos. Tompion, in Fleet Street. Whoever brings it to Mr Compton, Goldsmith, in Duke St., near Lincoln's Inn Fields, shall have 6 Guineas" (*London Gazette*, February 21-23, 1694).

"Lost, some time in November last, at Oxon, a Gold Minute Pendulum watch in a plain gold case; the names on the upper peak, Tho. Tompion, Edwd. Banger, London; and on the Dial Plate, Tompion, Banger, London, with this number, 3428, on the bottom of the Box within side, and likewise upon the upper plate. Whoever give notice of it (so as it may be had again) to the Reverend Dr King, of Christ Church College, at Oxon, or to Tho. Tompion, Clockmaker, at the Dial and Three Crowns, at the Corner of Water Lane, Fleet St., London, shall have three guineas reward; or if bought or pawned, your money again with reasonable profit" (*London Gazette*, December 4-7, 1704).

The sundial which Tompion presented to the city of Bath together with the equation clock (p.224) in 1709 so that it could be used to check the performance of the equation work. The dial is octagonal, is signed 'Tho. Tompion London', and is an ordinary horizontal dial with a central sixteen point compass rose. The hour scale is divided to read minutes. Bath City Council.

Prospectus intra cameram stellatam, *a view inside the star room (the main room now known as the Octagon Room) of the Royal Observatory c.1676-77. Two observers are shown, one using an 8½ft. square section telescope, the other a 3ft. radius quadrant. This instrument was chiefly used for equal-altitude observations for checking the going of the three clocks shown behind the assistant seated at the table. The two clocks together to the left of the door were made by Tompion and both survived though in a modified state (one is illustrated on p.231). The third clock however, which was probably not by Tompion, has disappeared.* National Maritime Museum, Greenwich.

Tompion was associated as a brother of the Clockmakers' Company in 1671; admitted as a freeman by redemption in 1674; chosen as assistant in 1691, as warden in 1700, and master in 1704. He died on the 20th November 1713, and was buried in Westminster Abbey. In the same grave were interred the remains of Graham, and particulars of their tomb had therefore better be left till after the brief notice of Graham which follows.

Little is known of Tompion's domestic life, but he appears to have been unmarried. His will, executed on the 21st October 1713, was proved on the 27th November, in the same year, by George Graham, who was one of the executors. By this document he bequeathed to his nephew Thomas Tompion, son of his brother James, his land and property at Northhill, Bedfordshire, and the interest on £100. To his niece Margaret Banger, wife of Edward Banger, clockmaker, and daughter of his late sister, Margaret Kent, he gave a life interest in £500, which at her death was to revert to Elizabeth Graham, wife of George Graham, daughter of his said brother James. Another daughter of his sister Elizabeth Kent is mentioned, and a cousin, Thomas Finch. George Graham and his wife were residuary legatees. Tho. Tompion, junr., was apprenticed to Charles Kemp in 1694 and admitted as a member to the Clockmakers' Company in 1702, presumably when he had completed his apprenticeship. A "Mr Tompion, watchmaker," attended the funeral of Daniel Quare, in 1724. Watches by Tho. Tompion, junr., are to be met with occasionally, and I have examined two or three inscribed "Tho. Tompion, Edw. Banger, London." Edward Banger was apprenticed to *the* Tompion in 1695, and it may therefore be fairly assumed that he was in partnership with Tompion junr. At Buckingham Palace is a one-year clock inscribed "T. Tompion, Edwd. Banger, London." In the Wetherfield collection is a long-case clock, with an oval label just below the centre of the dial, on which is engraved "Tho. Tompion and Edw. Banger, London." I saw a watch for sale but a few months ago inscribed "Tompion, London," the hall mark in the case of which corresponded to the year 1745. But Tompion bequeathed his business to Graham, who, it is pretty certain, secured the best of the trade on the demise of his patron and friend.

GEORGE GRAHAM

Fig. 423.

Fig. 424. – Back of Outer Cover.

George Graham, "Honest George Graham," who was born at Kirklinton, or Rigg, Cumberland, in 1673, tramped to London at an early age, and in 1688 became apprenticed for seven years to Henry Aske. He was admitted a freeman of the Clockmakers' Company on completing his indentures in 1695, and immediately entered the service of Thomas Tompion, thus beginning a life-long friendship, severed only by the death of Tompion in 1713. The following announcement appeared in the *London Gazette* for 28th November to 1st December 1713: "George Graham, Nephew of the late Mr Thomas Tompion, who lived with him upwards of seventeen years, and managed his trade for several years past, whose name was joined with Mr Tompion's for some time before his death, and to whom he left all his stock and work, finished and unfinished, continues to carry on the said trade at the late Dwelling House of the said Mr Tompion, at the sign of the Dial and Three Crowns, at the corner of Water Lane, in Fleet Street, London, where all persons may be accommodated as formerly." In Uphill Castle is a long-case clock with the signature "Tompion Graham."

In 1720 Graham relinquished Tompion's old premises, as will be seen by the appended official notification from the *London Gazette* of March 22-26, 1720: "George Graham, watchmaker, is removed from the corner of Water Lane, in Fleet Street, to the Dial and One Crown on the other side of the way, a little nearer Fleet Bridge, a new house next door to the Globe and Duke of Marlborough's Head Tavern." Here in the rooms over the shop Graham resided till his decease. The quaint little shop had two plain bow windows, with the doorway between them, and with but little alteration in appearance remained as a watchmaker's for many years, being occupied first by Mudge, who succeeded Graham, then by Mudge & Dutton, and afterwards by the younger Duttons. It is No. 148, and now the offices of the *Sporting Life*. Graham was elected as a member of the Royal Society in 1720, and chosen as a member of the council of that body in 1722. He contributed twenty-one papers on various subjects to the "Philosophical Transactions."

After the expiration of Booth, Houghton, and Tompion's patent, Graham devoted some thought to the cylinder escapement, which in 1725 he modified to practically its present form, and introduced into some of his watches. Securing to himself the monopoly of any of his discoveries was foreign to his disposition. The reputation which English horology acquired

Fig. 425. — GEORGE GRAHAM, 1673-1751.

Fig. 426.

on the Continent during the eighteenth century was due in no small measure to Graham's candid treatment of his brethren in the art in other countries. In answer to inquiries, Julien Le Roy received from Graham one of his cylinder escapement watches in 1728, and the French horologist's generous avowal of its superiority is worthy of his acknowledged greatness. But it must be admitted, after examination of surviving specimens, that Graham's cylinder escapements were wanting in the necessary closeness of construction afterwards attained by Ellicott and others; and as Graham continued to use the verge escapement till his death, it may be assumed that he was not oblivious of the constructional difficulties presented by the cylinder. In his younger days he would undoubtedly have pursued the matter with his usual acumen and patience, till nothing was left for later artists to improve; but now his mind was taken up with astronomy and astronomical instruments, and the production of a perfect clock as an aid to the astronomer absorbed him, as I venture to suggest, almost to the exclusion of horological instruments for the pocket.

In all Graham's work his first consideration was to make every part most suitable for its purpose. Judicious embellishment in its proper place was not wanting, but it was quite subsidiary to usefulness. This trait is apparent in many little details of a splendid repeating watch shown in Figs. 423 and 424 made by him in 1714, when he was in the zenith of his power as a watchmaker, which belongs to Mr Paul E. Schweder. Thus the pillars are of a plain cylindrical form with turned bases and caps, whereas other horologists were lavish in shaping, decorating, and piercing these passive items, whose characteristic of strength and holding power was certainly not less apparent by Graham's more simple treatment. A little addition I have not noticed in the watches of any other maker is a light spring jumper or click on the underside of the cap, for securely locking the cap spring. It has a fine enamelled dial and jewelled balance-cock. The piercing of both the gold cases and the *repoussé* chasing of the outer one are perfect. On the movement and on both cases is the number 445. On the back of the inner case are the letters M. P. arranged as a monogram. The lock spring is beyond the edge of the dial.

Attached to this repeater is also a useful little adjunct which appears to have been invented by Graham, and, though not much seen in English work, became very popular with French makers. Projecting from the case is a small nib, or "pulse piece," called by the French *sourdine,* or "deaf piece", which upon being pressed keeps the hammer off the bell and receives each blow. It not only enables those who have defective hearing or sight to ascertain the time by touch, but persons whose organs are perfect, who may desire to know the hour at night without disturbing an adjacent sleeper, can do so by pressing the pulse piece and counting the beats.

Graham used stout proportionate-looking bows for his watch cases in place of the thin wiry rings previously in vogue, but by a curious obliquity Ellicott seems to have reverted to the former style. The difference in the two "handles" is very marked in specimens of the two makers I have before me. Another watch by Graham is in the possession of Mr A Ruskin Severn.

With the introduction of the pendulum, and more exact workmanship and consequent improvement in the performance of timekeepers, the errors arising from expansion and contraction of metals in varying temperatures

Fig. 427.

HERE LIES THE BODY
OF M^R THO TOMPION
WHO DEPARTED THIS
LIFE THE 20TH OF
NOVEMBER 1713 IN THE
75TH YEAR OF HIS AGE

ALSO THE BODY OF
GEORGE GRAHAM OF LONDON
WATCHMAKER AND F.R.S.
WHOSE CURIOUS INVENTIONS
DO HONOUR TO Y^E BRITISH GENIUS
WHOSE ACCURATE PERFORMANCES
ARE Y^E STANDARD OF MECHANIC SKILL
HE DIED Y^E XVI OF NOVEMBER MDCCLI
IN THE LXXVIII YEAR OF HIS AGE

Fig. 428.

became manifest. Graham therefore turned his attention to the best means of preventing irregularity in the going of clocks when exposed to thermal changes, and invented the mercurial pendulum. His paper, communicated to the Royal Society in 1726, on "A Contrivance to avoid Irregularities in a Clock's Motion by the Action of Heat and Cold upon the Pendulum," demonstrated the suitability of mercury as a compensating medium after observations extending over a lengthened period.

The form of Graham's mercurial pendulum is shown in the sketch, Fig. 426. a is the rod, b the stirrup containing the glass jar of mercury o. For regulating the time, Graham employed a sliding weight d upon the rod.

Another of Graham's inventions applicable to clocks of precision, and which is still unsurpassed in the opinion of many leading horologists, is the dead-beat escapement.

In the Wetherfield collection are two of his bracket clocks dating from about 1715, and also a month regulator timepiece which has a dead-beat escapement with jewelled pallets, a gridiron pendulum, bolt and shutter maintaining power; this is in a mahogany case and shows solar as well as mean solar time.

An elegant bracket clock by him, dating from about 1740, is in the possession of Mr J. Rutherford, Jardington, Dumfries, to whom I am

Fig. 429.

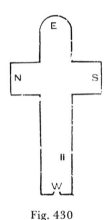

Fig. 430

DANIEL QUARE

indebted for the representation of it which is given in Fig. 427. The case of oak measures 15½ in. in height, and the dial 8¼ in. by 4⅞ in. On the back plate is engraved a Cupid surrounded by scroll work. The regulator hand on the right of the dial raises or lowers the pendulum through the intervention of a snail-shaped cam.

Graham's mode of living was distinguished by its simplicity. As already stated, his later years were chiefly occupied with astronomical work, which he carried on as the valued coadjutor of Halley and Bradley till his death, which occurred in November 1751. By his will, executed in 1747, he left to his wife one-half of his personal estate. He also bequeathed £20 to the Clockmakers' Company, of which he was elected an assistant in 1717, and after filling the subordinate offices served as master in 1722-3. The grave of Tompion, in Westminster Abbey, was opened to receive his pupil, and the exceptional honour of their interment in that place is the best testimony that can be adduced as to the estimation in which these eminent horologists were held. Fig. 428 is a reduced facsimile of the stone placed to mark their resting-place by an appreciative nation.

In 1838 this slab was removed, and small lozenge-shaped stones, with the name and date, as in the sketch in Fig. 429, were substituted. In a little work, "Time and Timekeepers," published in 1842, Adam Thomson, a Bond Street watchmaker, wrote: "Who would suppose that a small lozenge-shaped bit of marble is all that is left to indicate where lie the bodies of the 'Father of Clockmakers,' Thomas Tompion, and honest George Graham, greater benefactors to mankind than thousands whose sculptured urns impudently emblazon merits that never existed?" To this outspoken, indignant protest, and the good feeling of the late Dean Stanley, is due the reinstatement of the original memorial, for which English horologists will be ever grateful. "The passage was pointed out to me by a friend," said the Dean, "in consequence of the strong irritation expressed on the subject by an obscure watchmaker in a provincial town. The gravestone had not been destroyed, and was restored in 1866". Let us hope future generations of clock and watchmakers will jealously guard this tribute to the work of their fellow-craftsmen against any further attempt at desecration.

The position of the tomb is marked by the two parallel lines on the accompanying plan of the Abbey Church (Fig. 430). E is the altar floor; W the nave and western entrance; N, north transept; S, south transept and Poets' Corner.

Two of Graham's clocks were sold by auction in 1765 at the dispersal of the library of the Earl of Macclesfield, "a month clock, that shows equal and sidereal time, with the day of the month perpetual, with a compound pendulum," realised £42. 10s., and was bought by Lord C. Cavendish; "a month clock, that shows equal and apparent time, with a quicksilver pendulum," fell to Lord Morton for £34. 2s. 6d.; "a wheel barometer by Graham" was not sold.

This worthy contemporary of Tompion was born in 1648. Mr Robert Meldrum has a lantern clock, dating from about 1670, inscribed "Daniel Quare Londini fecit." I had a clock-watch by him, inscribed "Daniel Quare, St Martin's le Grand, London." From its construction, one could with tolerable certainty decide that it was made about 1676, and I am therefore inclined to think St Martin's le Grand was his first business address. It is said

Fig. 431.

Above: a modern reconstruction of the dial of the movement of one of Tompion's dead-beat year going clocks installed in the Royal Observatory in 1676 as the gift of Sir Jonas Moore. National Maritime Museum, Greenwich.

he afterwards carried on business at the "Plow and Harrow," in Cornhill, but all the authentic records I have been able to consult refer to him from 1680 to the time of his death as of the "King's Arms," Exchange Alley.

About 1680 he produced repeating watches of his own design, and when the Rev. Edward Barlow, in 1686, sought to patent a repeating device, Quare, backed by the Clockmakers' Company, opposed the monopoly. The case was considered by the Privy Council on 2nd March 1687, and Barlow's application for a patent refused. In Quare's arrangement a single push on a pin projecting from the case near the pendant sufficed to sound the hour and the quarters, while Barlow's required a distinct action for each. The king, after a trial of both repeating watches, gave the preference to that of Quare, which fact was notified in the *Gazette*. This watch was, in 1823, in the possession of Mr John Stanton, of Benwell, near Newcastle-upon-Tyne, from whose description of it in the *Morning Chronicle* the following is taken: "The outer case, of 22-carat gold, is embossed with the king's head in a medallion. The dial is of gold, with black Roman numerals for the hours and figures for the minutes. In the centre is a piece of pierced work in gold upon blue steel, representing the letters J.R. R.J. combined so as to appear like an ornamental scroll, above which is the royal crown. The box is pierced with scroll-work intermixed with birds and flowers. About the joint is engraved a landscape. The watch is considerably thicker than, but otherwise not much above, the common size."

Quare afterwards made another and more highly finished repeating watch for William III.; it appears probable that in this, as in all subsequent repeaters by Quare, the pendant was thrust in to set the mechanism in action, instead of having a separate pin in the edge of the case for the purpose. Repeating watches seem to have taken the public fancy at once. Some of the early records refer to them as "squeezing watches."

Fig. 432.

Fig. 433.

There is in the British Museum a small lantern alarm clock of Quare's make, which has, above the bell, a perforated dome surmounted by a handle for carrying. In the wardens' room at Drapers' Hall stands a long-case clock by Quare. Mr T. W. Bourne owns a repeating bracket clock by him. It is 15 in. high with basket top and has two bells, and is shown in Fig. 431. A fine bracket clock by him in Windsor Castle is shown in Fig. 432; and a little clock, 6 in. in height, illustrated in Fig. 433, is said to have been the favourite timekeeper of William III., and was brought to England by him. This also is at Windsor Castle. A bracket clock similar to 432 is in the possession of the Rev. Walter Scott. There are seven of Quare's clocks in the Wetherfield collection; some of these I shall be able to illustrate in Chapter VII.

As splendid specimens of horological work of this period may be mentioned one-year clocks, of which at least three or four bear Quare's name. One of the most celebrated of these is at Hampton Court Palace. The case is of oak veneered with burr walnut or some similar wood, and, including a stand of gilt brass work, is 10 ft. high, the plinth being 22 in., the waist 48 in., the hood 24; the dome, $10^{1}/_{2}$ in. high, is surmounted by a gilt brass figure 12 in. high. Four other well-modelled gilt figures occupy the corners of the hood, as shown in Fig. 434, which is from a photograph lent to me by Messrs Gaydon, of Kingston. The dial plate is 16 by 14 in., and along the bottom of it are three subsidiary dials; one shows the rising and setting of the sun, the middle one has an index and a scale for latitude; the index for the third is removed, but it was evidently for the purpose of disconnecting certain equation work, the circle being engraved on one side *"Tempus apparens"* and on the opposite *"Tempus aequale."* In 1836 Vulliamy substituted a dead beat escapement and a new pendulum for the original ones, but until 1898 the clock had not been going for some years. In the *Philosophical Transactions* for November and December 1719, is a paper by Joseph Williamson, claiming the invention of equation mechanism for clocks, and in it he mentions having made for Mr Quare, among other twelve-month clocks, the one at Hampton Court, which, by means of a cam moving in a slit in a piece of brass at the top of the pendulum spring, raised or lowered the pendulum as required in order to show apparent time. As this claim appears to have remained unchallenged it may be accepted. Doubtless the reputation of many manufacturers then, as in later years, was acquired in great measure through the ingenuity and excellent workmanship displayed by the chamber masters and other assistants whom they employed. Still, it would be idle to attempt, now, to apportion the merit; the worldwide reputation of Quare remains as evidence of his individuality. He is mentioned in a comedy by Carlo Goldoni as the foremost of English horologists, then considered the first in the world.

Thirty years ago one of Quare's twelve-month clocks was in the possession of Mr J. H. Arkwright, of Hampton Court, near Leominster, where it probably is still. Many stories have been told of the structure of this remarkable production, and in 1873 I obtained the following very precise details concerning it from Mr Palmer, a clockmaker of Leominster. The hour hand, beautifully pierced, fits tight on to the hour socket with a square; the minute hand is pinned on to a square with a collet as usual; it has a counterpoise, and is not so elaborately pierced as the hour hand. The dial is

14 in. square, the centre being matted and gilt; the spandrels are also gilt, but left plain to show up the silver fretwork corner pieces. The hour circle is of brass, silvered; it is divided into minutes on the outside, and into quarters of hours on the inside. The name "Dan Quare" is engraved between the hour figures 7 and 6, and "London" is engraved between the 6 and the 5. On the dial plate just below the figure 6 the name is again inscribed in full, "Daniel Quare, London." The numbers of the teeth of the wheels in the train is as follows:—

	Teeth.		Leaves.
Great wheel	96		
First ,,	96	pinion	12
Second ,,	90	,,	10
Centre ,,	60	,,	10
Third ,,	56	,,	8
Swing ,,	30	,,	7

The minute wheels have each thirty-six teeth, well shaped and very regular; the minute pinion has six leaves; the hour wheel has seventy-two teeth, and it is keyed on to the hour socket. The centre, third, and swing wheels are very small and light, the diameter of the last-named is 7/8 in.; the pivots also are very small. These three pinion arbors are an inch shorter than the other arbors of the train, and are pivoted into a small false plate which is pinned by four small pillars on to the inside of the large pillar plate. The collets on which these three wheels are mounted are either brazed or driven on to the pinion arbors. The third and swing wheel pinions are thickest at the collet, and taper off with a gentle curve to the head of the pinion. The frame plates are 7 in. by 5 in. There are six pillars; they are riveted into the back plate, and the front plate is kept on by pins. The pallets are of the original anchor form. The seconds pendulum has a lenticular bob, and altogether weighs 2 lbs. 1½ oz. It is suspended from the same cock that carries the back pivot of the verge. The suspension spring is 2½ in. long, narrow, and very thin. There is no degree plate, but a brass finger projecting from the base of the case is filed to an edge just below the pendulum, and serves to estimate the vibration (which is about 1° on each side of zero), and also to set the clock in beat when fixing it. The case is of oak, handsomely veneered with walnut.

Fig. 434. — Quare's twelve-month clock at Hampton Court.

Fig. 435. — Dial of Clock by Daniel Quare, about 1705.

Fig. 436.

Fig. 437.

Fig. 438.

The barrel has fourteen grooves. The clock weight and pulley weight 81 lbs.; the fall is 4 ft. 6 in.; the length of the weight and pulley is 1 ft. 6 in., which, added to the fall, makes 6 ft., which is the distance from the bottom of the clock case up to the seat board; the weight is hung by a double line. The clock is still an excellent timekeeper. On casting up the numbers of the train it will be found to go 403 days, 4 hours, and 24 minutes.

Now, I cannot help thinking this is a very extraordinary achievement, for 81 lbs. x 4 ft. 6in. to drive the clock for more than thirteen months seems almost incredible; still, I believe the facts are as I have stated them. There is no doubt that everything was done that was possible to economise the force. The very small and light swing wheel, the balanced minute hand, and the small shortened arbors with extra fine pivots, all conduce to the end in view.

Fig. 439. — Barometer by Quare.

A twelve-month timepiece by Quare with an equation movement, very similar to the Hampton Court one, and in its original condition, forms one of the gems of the Wetherfield collection. Of this I shall be able to give an illustration in Chapter VII.

At Marston House is a month-clock by Quare, belonging to the Earl of Cork. Mr C. F. Bell has another, and in the Wetherfield collection are several calculated for the same period. Quare's dials were particularly good, as may be judged from the specimen shown in Fig. 435, for which I am indebted to Mr H. Cook, of Newark.

Fig. 436 shows a little bracket clock by Quare, which belongs to Mr J. W. Abbott. The extreme height of the clock is 12 in., and the depth of the bracket 5½ in. The clock case is covered with tortoiseshell, and is 6½ in. wide. The handle, the feet, and the bezel of the door are of silver.

By several writers Quare is credited with the invention of the concentric minute hand, but such indicators were in use long before his time, the hour hand being driven from the great wheel, and the minute hand from the centre arbor. Quare's improvement consisted in devising mechanism so that the hour and minute hands should be actuated together. The earliest form of this device is applied to the clock-watch, which has been already referred to. At first sight there appears to be motion work of the kind now in general use, but an important variation is apparent on examination. Both of the hands are driven direct from the great wheel. A wheel and pinion corresponding to the minute wheel and nut fit on to a squared arbor projecting from the great wheel. The canon pinion runs loose on a stud in the centre of the watch, and on it is placed the hour wheel in the usual way. The wheel and pinion attached to the great wheel are of brass, and to allow the hands to be set they fit friction tight on to a steel boss which has a square hole to correspond with the end of the great wheel arbor. Attached to the bottom face of the canon pinion is a snail for releasing the striking work every hour. Under the arrangement in vogue before Quare's time, by which each hand was driven independently of the other, if the minute hand was set forward or backward, the hour hand would cease to correspond with it. As the canon pinion was mounted on a stud, there was no necessity of having the second wheel of the train in the centre of the movement, and so the going train was continued to one side of the centre, leaving the other side for the striking work. The one advantage of the present arrangement of motion work over Quare's is that the minute hand now follows the motion of the centre pinion without shake, but in Quare's plan the position of the minute hand was not so absolute on account of the backlash of the motion wheels.

A watch by him with silver dial and outer case of red tortoiseshell *piqué* dating from about 1690, which is in the Pierpont Morgan collection, is shown in Figs. 437 and 438. A quarter repeating watch of later date, with pierced and engraved silver cases, is in the South Kensington Museum.

In 1695 Quare obtained a patent for a portable weather glass, and six or seven instruments made by him according to his specification are known to exist. One of them is in the United Service Institution; another, belonging to Mr C. F. Bell, is by his favour shown in Fig. 439. The case is of walnut; three urns surmount the head, and two of them when rotated move the pointers on the scale, which is of gilt metal richly engraved. But the contrivance for which the patent was granted consists of a pad to cover the bottom of the tube. The cistern is of ivory, and attached to the bottom of it is a brass nut, through which a threaded rod passes; on the lower extremity of the rod is a knob, and the upper carries the pad. If the barometer is turned upside down until the tube is full of quicksilver and the screwed rod turned for the pad to block the tube, the instrument may be carried about in any position.

Quare was admitted as a brother of the Clockmakers' Company in 1671, and served as master in 1708. During the latter part of his career, he took into partnership Edward Horseman, who had been apprenticed to him, and the business was carried on at the same address under the title of Quare and Horseman.

Reproduction of a selection from the inquiries respecting Quare's timekeepers may not be out of place. On p.180 is one which refers to an attempt to indicate minutes with the hour hand by dividing the circle into but six hours in order to obtain room for the minute marks:—

"Lost, between Firle and Shoram Ferry, in Sussex, a gold watch, made by D. Quare, in a black Shagreen Case with a Cypher J. C. Whoever brings it to Mr Shelley, Goldsmith, in Panton Street, near the Haymarket, shall have 2 guineas reward" (*London Gazette*, 16th May 1691).

"Lost, April 25, a Gold Minute Pendulum Clock, the name on upper plate D. Quare, London, 726 engraven on it, and a Shagrine case. Whoever gives notice of it to Daniel Quare, Clockmaker, at the King's Arms in Exchange Alley, shall have 3 guineas reward; or if already bought, their money returned again with content" (*London Gazette*, 26th May 1692).

"Lost, on the road between Hungerford and Marlborough, a Gold Repeating Watch, made by Quare and Horseman, with an old Gold Chain, and several seals hanging to it. Whosoever will bring them to Mr Horseman, at Mr Quare's, in Exchange Alley, shall have 20 guineas reward and no questions asked" (*London Gazette*, 9th August 1718).

"Lost, on the road between Newark and Tuxford, about 22 of June last, a Gold Watch, made by Quare in London, No. 4448, double cased and winds up on the dyal Plate. Whoever shall secure the watch if offered for sale, or send it or notice of it to Mr Andrew Drummond, Goldsmith, by Charing Cross, shall receive 5 guineas reward" (*London Gazette*, 8th July 1732).

The books of the Society of Friends show that Daniel Quare was a trusted man among the Quakers, and that he at first refused the office of Clockmaker to George I. because he objected to take the oath of allegiance; the difficulty respecting the taking of an oath was, however, overcome, and freedom to enter the palace by the back stairs accorded to him. "The Yeoman of the Guard," he said, "lets me frequently go up without calling anybody for leave, as otherwise he would tho' persons of quality." He had one son, Jeremiah, who does not seem to have followed the craft, and three daughters. At the marriage of his daughter Elizabeth with Silvanus Bevan in 1715, among witnesses who signed the deed of settlement was the Duchess of Marlborough. Daniel Quare died at Croydon in 1724, and was buried in the Quakers' ground at Bunhill Fields, Finsbury.

FROMANTEEL

Fromanteel, also spelt "Fromantel," "Fromantil," and "Fromenteele." Ahasuerus Fromanteel *primus*, of Dutch extraction, was a maker of steeple clocks at East Smithfield. In 1630 he was warned by the Blacksmiths' Company to bring in his certificate of seven years' service as apprentice. With this he complied, and was forthwith elected free of the company. On the incorporation of the clockmakers, he joined them. In 1656 he became restive under the somewhat inquisitorial proceedings of the court relating to his apprentices and the antecedents of his workmen, and for a long period in

Fig. 440.

the history of the guild his account for infraction of its rules, some of which, it must be confessed, could not fail to be exasperating to a man with an extensive business, as Fromanteel appears to have had.

A second Ahasuerus Fromanteel apppears on the list as free of the Clockmakers' Company in 1655.

A third Ahasuerus Fromanteel was, in 1663, on completion of his apprenticeship with Simon Bartram, admitted as a member of the Clockmakers' Company.

In 1663 also, John Fromenteel, who had been apprenticed to Thomas Loomes, was admitted to the freedom.

Then Abraham, son of Ahasuerus Fromanteel, was elected in 1680.

In 1658 proceedings were taken against Ahasuerus Fromanteel and his son Louis for keeping more apprentices than the regulations of the company allowed, so that there was a fairly large family of the Fromenteels in the clock trade at that period, and most of them seem to have been connected in business.

Beyond their squabbles with the Clockmakers' Company, there is a celebrity attaching to them as being the first to introduce the pendulum into England, the assumption being that one of the family had seen or heard of Huygens' clock in Holland, and brought particulars of it over to his relatives. Their claim has been challenged on behalf of Richard Harris; and it has also been asserted that Dr Hooke investigated the properties of the pendulum as a controller for timekeepers before Huygens applied it. However, there is evidence that the claim of the Fromanteels to its introduction from Holland, if not unanimously allowed, was accepted pretty generally at the time.

Under date 1st November 1660, Evelyn, in his Diary, writes: "I went with some of my relations to Court to show them his Maj^{ties} cabinet and closet of rarities. . . Here I saw. . . amongst the clocks one that showed the rising and setting of the sun in Y^e Zodig, the sunn represented by a face and raies of gold upon an azure skie, observing Y^e diurnal and annual motion rising and setting behind, and landscape of hills, the work of our famous Fromantel."

Again, under date 1st April 1661, Evelyn records that he "dined with that great mathematician and virtuoso, Mr Zulichem (Huygens), inventor of the pendule clock"; and on 8th May, "I returned by Fromantel's, the famous clockmaker, to see some pendules, Mr Zulichem being with us."

The clock by John Fromatell which is shown in Fig. 440 belongs to Mr H. A. Bleichert and has a curious history. In the last edition of this book it appeared with a small dial and the signs of the zodiac showing in the curved recess above, but Messrs A. & H. Rowley found the movement had been turned hinder part before, probably for the convenience of winding in front, and that originally the hour was indicated by revolving discs on the plan described in detail on pp.182, 184, 195 and 243. They restored it as nearly as possible to its pristine state, and to them I am indebted for a photograph of it. The hour numerals and divisions are perforated and so the clock answers the purpose of a night clock of the kind referred to on p.216.

Fig. 441 shows a hanging clock in an ebonised case, by "A Fromanteel, London," of about the same date, and for which I am indebted to Mr Thomas Wyatt. The dial is of brass with a silvered band to contain the hour numerals, which are very small and formed each within a ring. The original hand is missing. There are three bells and five hammers, the hours and first,

Fig. 441.

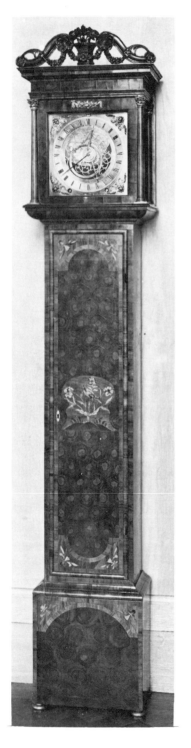

second, and third quarters being sounded. The movement is well made, with three trains, the back plate in one piece, the front arbors carried in three separate strips so that any of the trains may be removed separately. The pillars are square, and on one is engraved the name of the maker as quoted; the plates are fastened by hooks which fit into slots cut in the pillars. Below the moon are silvered rotating discs with figures on the edges to indicate the ages of the lunar and the calendar months. This was a long-case clock when I saw it, but examination showed that the lower part was a later addition. All that was original of the case is given in the engraving.

At the Guildhall Museum is a very well-made clock by Ahasuerus Fromanteel dating from about 1675. It has a bob pendulum; dial 8 in. square, with matted centre and cherub head corners. It is furnished with what is called the "bolt and shutter maintaining power." In this device a shutter which obstructs the winding hole has to be lifted before the key can be inserted, and this action causes a spring or a weighted lever to impel the wheels during the operation of winding, when the driving weight is inoperative.

Mercurius Politicus for 27th October 1658 contained the following advertisement which also appears in the *Commonwealth Mercury* of Thursday, 25th November 1658:—

"There is lately a way found out for making clocks that go exact and keep equaller time than any now made without this regulator, examined and proved before his Highness the Lord Proctor (Protector?), by such doctors whose knowledge and learning is without exception, and are not subject to alter by change of weather, as others are, and may be made to go a week, a month, or a year, with once winding up, as well as those that are wound up every day, and keep time as well, and is very excellent for all house clocks that go either with springs or weights; and also steeple clocks that are most subject to change of weather. Made by Ahasuerus Fromanteel, who made the first that were in England. You may have them at his house on the Bankside, in Mosses Alley, Southwark, and at the sign of the Mere Maid, in Lothbury, near Bartholomew Lane end, London."

Mosses Alley, or Moses Alley, was a passage leading from the northern end of Bankside, Southwark, to Maid Lane.

The Mermaid in Lothbury was for over a century a noted shop for clocks. In 1650 Thomas Loomes, who was associated with the eldest Fromanteel in his attacks on the government of the Clockmakers' Company, and to whom John Fromanteel was apprenticed, resided there, and, after the time of Loomes, it was occupied by John Fromanteel. Mr D. A. F. Wetherfield has a remarkably well-made long-case clock by him dating from 1676-80. It is

The only known example of an astrolabe clock by Thomas Tompion and perhaps the only known longcase astrolabe clock. The duration is for one month and the clock which belongs to the period before Tompion numbered his movements is ascribable to c.1676-77. The plated movement has the winding arbors geared so that the winding holes may be placed at the bottom of the dial plate, the centre of the dial being taken up by the astrolabe. There is an unusual form of the anchor escapement embracing five teeth and tending towards the form of the stirrup and the 'tic-tac'. Maintaining power is operated by a lever at the side without shutters for the winding holes.

The case is of olive-wood parquetry, with marquetry panels. The dial has a 24-hour chapter ring for meantime and hands for the sun and moon enabling their mean zodiacal position to be readily ascertained. The age and phase of the moon, the date and the times of high water at London Bridge are also indicated. The Fitzwilliam Museum, Cambridge.

shown in Fig. 442. The dial is 10 in. square with cherub corners, and in one line along the bottom is the inscription, *"Johannes Fromanteel, Londini fecit."* Around the hour circle every minute from 1 to 60 is numbered. The case is of walnut with small raised panels. The frame is large, having three trains, viz., going, striking, and ting-tang. The pendulum makes but forty-eight beats a minute and is therefore unusually long; regulation is effected by means of a large milled nut fixed above the pendulum cock, the spring rising and falling between chops as in many modern clocks. It has the bolt and shutter maintaining power referred to on p.238. The striking at the hour is peculiar, there being four bells of different notes, the shape of Chinese gongs, and four hammers which are on one arbor and strike a chord at each blow. The quarters are sounded on two bells.

There are two long-case clocks by John Fromanteel at the Dutch Church, Austin Friars, and one at the Philadelphia Library. Daniel O'Connell had a long-case clock by A. Fromanteel which was very similar to Fig. 442. Mrs Benwell has a long-case clock by "Fromanteel" dating from about 1720.

DR HOOKE

Fig. 442.

Robert Hooke was born in 1635 at Freshwater, Isle of Wight. After his father's death in 1648 he resided with Dr Busby, headmaster of Westminster School. He entered Christ Church College, Oxford, in 1653, and there his genius soon attracted the notice of Dr Wallis, whom he frequently assisted in his chemical operations. Dr Wallis introduced Hooke to the Hon. Robert Boyle, who engaged him as an assistant in his mechanical and philosophical works.

Hooke took part in and wrote upon all the scientific questions of his time. Sir Isaac Newton styled him "The Considerer." On the institution of the Royal Society he became one of its fellows, was afterwards entrusted with the care of its Repository, and made Professor of Mechanics to that body. About the same period he was elected Professor of Geometry in Gresham College.

I have been unable to obtain any portrait of Hooke, but will quote the following description of him from Aubrey's "Lives of Eminent Men": "He is of middling stature, somewhat crooked, pale-faced, and his face but little belowe, but his head is lardge; his eie is full and popping, and not quick; a grey eie. He has a delicate head of haire, browne, and of an excellent moiste curle. He is and ever was very temperate and moderate in dyet, &c. As he is of prodigious inventive head, so he is a person of great vertue and goodness."

He discovered that the resilience of a spring is proportional to the angle through which it has been wound, and propounded the whole theory in the sentence, *"Ut tensio sic vis,"* meaning that the force is proportionate to the tension. He proposed to patent his discovery in 1660, and, to quote his words, "Sir Robert Moray drew me up the form of a patent, the principal part whereof, viz., the description of the watch, is his own handwriting, which I have yet by me; the discouragement I met with in the progress of this affair made me desist for that time."

Derham describes the earliest of Hooke's essays in this direction as a "tender straight spring, one end whereof played backward and forward with the ballance." It is stated that several watches were made under Hooke's supervision at this period, and one of the first to which the balance-spring was applied he is said to have presented to Dr Wilkins, afterwards Bishop of Chester, about 1661.

A quarter repeating watch by George Graham London (p.228), number 570, with a cylinder escapement, white enamel dial, pierced gold hands, and gold pair cases. The inner case is pierced and engraved on the band and around the bell, the outer is repoussé *in a symmetrical frame and signed by Parbury. For the suggestion that it was Graham who invented the 'pulse' or 'deaf' piece there is no satisfactory substantiating evidence, although it is not in principle unlikely. The Trustees of the British Museum.*

It appears that Hooke then conceived it to be an advantage to have two balances coupled together, and had two double balance watches constructed. In the first, which had no balance-spring, the escape wheel was placed in the centre of the movement with its teeth in a horizontal plane. There were two verges standing vertically on opposite sides of the wheel and connected with each other by means of toothed wheels of equal size; each verge had one pallet and carried a balance at its upper end, one balance overlapping the other.

In the second watch the verge escapement was arranged in the ordinary way, the balance being mounted on a verge with two pallets; on the verge was also a toothed wheel which engaged with another of the same size mounted on a stud, and the pipe of this wheel carried the second balance; the toothed wheels being of small size, one balance was placed a little higher than the other and overlapped it. Each balance was controlled by a balance-spring.

However, Hooke turned his attention to other matters, and in January 1673 Huygens addressed a letter to Henry Oldenburg, secretary of the Royal Society, in which he described as his invention the application of a spring to control the balance in watches. This aroused the wrath of Hooke, who accused Oldenburg of having divulged the discovery in his correspondence with Huygens. Hooke enlisted the interest of Charles II., and in a lecture, entitled "Potentia Restitutiva," &c., said, "His Majesty was pleased to see the experiment that made out this theory tried at Whitehall, as also my spring watch."

In 1660, Hooke devised a pendulum timekeeper for ascertaining the longitude at sea. This was tried in 1662, and he subsequently proposed a compensation pendulum in the form of a rhomboid, the outline being of steel and the long horizontal diagonal of brass. This form, being wider than it was long, was considered to be impracticable. Troughton afterwards constructed a pendulum in which the rod was a series of small rhomboids arranged to compensate on Hooke's plan.

Hooke devised the first wheel-cutting engine about 1670. Prior to that time the operation of forming the teeth was tedious and imperfect. Blanks for watch and clock wheels were placed in the centre of a circular brass platform, having thereon concentric circles and radial lines corresponding to the various numbers of teeth in general use. An arm pivoted at the centre of the platform carried a hard point at its other extremity, by which the positions of the teeth were marked on the blanks. The spaces were then filed out. Hooke contrived a circular file and made the platform movable so that

A longcase month going astronomical regulator by George Graham, London, number 680, c.1740. The escapement is a dead-beat anchor, there is bolt and shutter maintaining power, and Graham's mercury compensated pendulum. Like many other clocks which had long working lives in observatories there have been numerous modifications to the clock which include the replacement of the escape wheel and pallets and the fitting of electrical contacts for hour and minute impulses. The clock was used in Cambridge University Observatories. National Maritime Museum, Greenwich.

each part of the circumference of the wheel could be brought within the action of the file or cutter.

Hooke also invented the anchor escapement for clocks about 1675. Among his conceptions for a marine timekeeper was one with two balances geared together, the idea being to avoid the effect of external motion. It is stated that this timekeeper had an escapement resembling the duplex.

His investigations covered a very wide field of science, but his restless disposition rarely allowed him to steadily pursue any subject to a conclusion. No sooner was he satisfied of the feasibility of any project, than he left it, thus allowing others to perfect his inventions. On the death of Oldenburg, in 1677 he was appointed secretary to the Royal Society, and, by an order of the Society, he was requested to give a full description of all the instruments which he had contrived, but ill health prevented him from performing it. During the last year of his life he was almost helpless. He died at Gresham College, 3rd March 1703, and was buried at St Helen's, Bishopsgate.

CHRISTIAN HUYGENS

This distinguished mathematician was born at The Hague in 1629. Early in life he devoted his attention to the principles on which timekeepers were constructed, and in 1657 presented to the States of Holland a clock controlled by a pendulum. He seems to have acquired the additional cognomen of Zulichem from the place of his birth, and is so referred to by Evelyn during a short visit he paid to England in 1661, as quoted in the account of Fromanteel. In 1665 his reputation induced Louis XIV. to invite him to Paris, in order to found a Royal Academy of Sciences there, and in 1673 was published his folio work, "Horologium Oscillatorium," &c., from which the appended drawings of his clock are taken.

The upper part of the pendulum is a double cord hanging between two cycloidal cheeks, to give a cycloidal path to the bob. Fig. 444 gives a better idea of this device, which was no doubt of advantage with the long arcs required by the verge escapement. Another feature of Huygens' clock is the maintaining power. P (Fig. 445) is the driving weight, supported by an endless cord, passing over the pulley D attached to the great wheel, and also over the pulley H, which is provided with ratchet teeth and pivoted to the inside of the clock case. The cord m is pulled down to wind the clock, and the ratchet wheel H then runs under its click. So that while winding, as in going, one-half of P minus one-half of p is driving the clock. The pulleys D and H are spiked to prevent slipping of the cord.

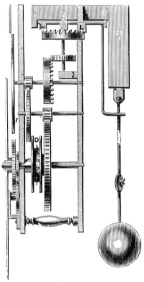

Fig. 443.

This ingenious maintaining power is to be found in many eighteenth century clocks. When applied to a clock with a striking train, the pulley with the ratchet is attached to the great wheel of the striking part, one weight thus serving to drive both trains. A chain is preferable to a cord, owing to the dust which accumulates in the clock through the wearing of the latter. The drawback to the arrangement is that it is not suitable for clocks going for more than thirty hours between windings. It is, however, worth knowing that a thirty-hour striking clock on this plan can be readily converted to an eight-day non-striker by simply disconnecting the striking work.

Huygens devoted much attention to the production of a timekeeper for ascertaining the longitude; and finding the pendulum too unstable at sea, he in 1674 constructed a marine timekeeper controlled by a balance and balance-spring. The balance, instead of being on the verge, was on a separate staff, and driven by a wheel and pinion, so as to vibrate through very long

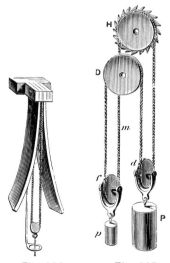

Fig. 444.   Fig. 445.

Fig. 446. — Clock-Watch by Nathaniel Barrow.

arcs; and this necessitated the use of a very long balance-spring. Huygens endeavoured to obtain a patent for the application of the balance-spring, but in this he was successfully opposed by the Abbé Hauteville, who alleged a prior use of springs for the purpose. The marine timekeeper was not a complete success, for Huygens found himself baffled by the error in changes of temperature. He returned to Holland in 1681, and died there in 1695.

An exceedingly well-made clock, exactly corresponding to Huygens' drawing, which I saw some years ago, bore the inscription, "Johanne Van Ceulin fecit, Hagae," and had a very handsome gilt skeleton dial, upheld by a figure of Time. This and many other watches and clocks of that period by Van Ceulin suggest the possibility of Huygens and Van Ceulin having been associated in Holland as were Barlow and Tompion in England.

NATHANIEL BARROW   A watch by this maker, with a short train and without a balance-spring, is shown in Fig. 326. Fig. 446 represents the exterior of a clock-watch with doubled pierced cases. A view of the movement will be given further on.

Probably to get room for the striking work a most peculiar arrangement of the going train is adopted; the winding square of the fusee arbor projects within the rim of the balance, which has three arms clustered together in the form of a *fleur-de-lis* or trident head, so that a vibration of over half a turn is possible before the balance arms bank against the fusee arbor.

KNIBB   Three or four members of this family are known among the seventeenth century clockmakers. Samuel Knibb was admitted to the freedom of the Clockmakers' Company in 1663; Joseph Knibb in 1670; Peter Knibb in 1677. In the Guildhall Museum is a verge watch with curiously wrought pillars, made about 1690, by "John Knibb at Oxon.," and among the Wetherfield collection are two long-case clocks, inscribed "John Knibb, London," one dating from about 1690, and the other a little later. Mr J. Drummond Robertson has a small-sized lantern timepiece with verge escapement by this maker.

Of these the most eminent maker was Joseph Knibb, mentioned as of Oxon., in the records of the Clockmakers' Company. He made a turret clock which was fixed over the state entrance in the quadrangle of Windsor Castle, which Captain Smyth (*Archaeologia*, vol. xxxiii.) speaks of as one of the earliest movements constructed with brass wheels. This statement may be correct if it refers to turret clocks only, but it would not apply to smaller timekeepers. This clock was inscribed "Joseph Knibb, Londini, 1677," and did duty till 1829, when a new one by B. L. Vulliamy replaced it. He issued a token, having on the obverse: "Ioseph Knibb, Clockmaker in Oxon.," and on the reverse, "I. K.," with a clock face and hand. In the Camden Society's "Secret Services of Charles II. and James II." are various records of payments on behalf of King Charles. In the account up to 3rd July 1682 is an item, paid "To Mr Knibb by his said Ma'tie's comand upon a bill for Clockwork, £141." Judging by the Windsor Castle clock, he was in London in 1677, and till nearly the end of the century he carried on business there. His work was of the highest class, judging from the specimens I have had the opportunity of examining. An alarm watch with pierced and engraved case of silver, dating from about 1690, in the South Kensington Museum, is signed "Jose Knibb, London." A short time ago Mr Thomas Peake had a square black case bracket clock by him, fitted with a curious striking part, of the locking-plate kind, but striking both hours and quarters from one pin-wheel, which had pins on both sides. The back plate was engraved to an ornamental design, and on it was the inscription, "Joseph Knibb, Londini, fecit."

Fig. 447.

A remarkable clock, formerly the property of the Duke of Sussex, but which now belongs to Mr Ernest Swanwick, is shown in Fig. 447. The case is of ebony, and measures 22 in. in height to the top of the knob. The particular feature which commands attention is the way in which the time is indicated. The upper portion of the dial is fixed and divided into four quarter-hours, the divisions being marked by Roman numerals. Each minute is indicated by a tooth at the edge, and five-minute intervals by round holes. The central part of the dial rotates, and carries at opposite points near its periphery two blue discs on which are gilded figures representing the hours. In the illustration the time shown is thirteen past two, and the two will move on till it disappears at the right hand behind a screen, when the figure three will appear at the left. The mechanism in connection with this device is illustrated in Fig. 352. In front of the centre part of the rotating dial is a fixed screen, on which stags and a landscape are painted. Below is the signature, "Joseph Knibb, Londini." The exposed annular space of the rotating dial is covered with a painting of cupids and clouds. On the plinth is a label inscribed in gold lettering, "From a model designed by Prince Rupert." Above the entablature of the case is a double-headed bird with outstretched wings and the motto, "DEUS MEUM QUE JUS." This clock is probably referred to in White's "Natural History of Selborne," in a letter to T. Pennant, speaking of the Royal Forest of Wolmer and Ayles Holt, which says: "The grantees that the author remembers are Brigadier-General Emanuel Scroope Howe and his lady Ruperta (who was a natural daughter of Prince Rupert by Margaret Hughes)." . . . "The lady of General Howe lived to an advanced age, long surviving her husband; and, at her death, left behind her many curious pieces of mechanism of her father's constructing, who was a distinguished mechanic and artist, as well as warrior, and among the rest a very complicated clock, lately in possession of Mr Elmer, the celebrated game painter, at Farnham, in the county of Surrey."

The miniature timepiece by Joseph Knibb shown in Fig. 448 belongs to Mr J. D. Robertson. It repeats the hour and quarters on two bells. The case is of black wood, and on the brass ornament at the left is represented the head of William III. This ornament is pivoted near the top, and is drawn aside to expose the keyhole. In the Wetherfield collection is a striking clock very similarly cased.

Messrs Desbois recently had a long-case clock made by Joseph Knibb when he was in London. It was formerly in the collection of the Duke of

A small bracket or table clock by George Graham London No. 689, c.1720. Ebony case with side frets of brass, caddy top with brass handle. There is a horizontal verge escapement and short pendulum, hour striking and quarter repeating mechanism. The subsidiary dials are for regulation, and strike/silent. There is a dummy pendulum aperture within the silvered chapter ring, while the applied spandrels are of silver. The Trustees of the British Museum.

244

Sussex, and therein described as having been the property of Charles II., when it was called a "drinking clock." * The dial was square, of brass well gilt, with a skeleton silvered ring to receive the Roman hour numerals and a subsidiary silvered ring for the seconds. The centre of the dial was coarsely matted, and every minute noted with Arabic figures. The corner pieces, boldly chased, were of the cherub-head pattern, and the hands finely carved. A herring-bone border was engraved at the edge of the square, and altogether the dial presented a handsome appearance.

But the distinctive feature of the clock was the peculiar striking work, which was on the locking-plate principle. There were two bells, a large and a small one, and two corresponding hammers; also two sets of lifting pins, one on each side of the pin wheel, one set actuating the large and the other the small hammer. And the pins were arranged so that at I. o'clock one stroke was given on the small bell, at II. two strokes, at III. three strokes, at IV. one on the small followed by one on the large, at V. one on the large, at VI. one on the large followed by one on the small, at VII. one on the large followed by two on the small bell, and so on. It will be noticed that so far each stroke on the small bell stands for the Roman unit, and each stroke on the large bell for the Roman V. Perhaps the procedure through the twelve hours will be best shown by different sized dots to represent the bells as follows:—

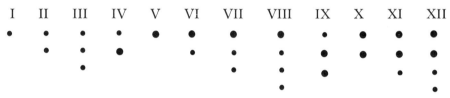

Among varieties of striking, this plan seems to have a distinct value, inasmuch as it materially economises the energy required for telling the round of hours, only thirty blows being required in place of the usual seventy-eight. This particular clock was arranged for a run of a month between successive windings.

When a few years ago it was proposed to alter the subdivision of the civil day by counting the hours continuously instead of duplicating them, whereby any possible confusion as to whether a particular hour meant A.M. or P.M. might be avoided, one of the difficulties presented to the minds of those who attached particular importance to a sound signal was the impracticability of counting so many strokes as would correspond to the hour as the day neared its close. But by adopting what perhaps may be called the Roman notation, as here shown to be practicable, even that reform may yet be approved of by the majority.

Viscount Ridley has a three-months long-case clock by Joseph Knibb, which is inscribed "Joseph Knibb, Londini, fecit," along the bottom of the dial, and has the striking arranged in the same way. The case is of ebony. The

Fig. 448.

---

* I confess I cannot understand this application of "Drinking Clock." August Demmin speaks of Drinking Clocks constructed at Nuremberg in the seventeenth century, which had extra outside wheels. At a banquet such a clock being put on the table commenced to slowly move along it, and the guest before whom the clock stopped was compelled to empty his flagon; but, though interesting, this does not help us in connection with Knibb's timekeeper.

Wetherfield collection includes two almost similar specimens. Mr T. W. Bourne owns a bracket clock, 12 in. in height, by Knibb.

In the *London Gazette*, July 9-12, 1688, "a striking watch, two gold cases engraven, a brass case over them, Joseph Knibb, maker, day of the month, pins to feel the hours," was advertised for, "information to be given to Mr Jos. Knibb, at the Dial, in Fleet Street." There are other references to him, of which the following may be of interest:-

"Lost, on the 26th inst., near the Ferry Place, Putney, a gold Pendulum Chain Minute-watch, made by Joseph Knibb, of London, in a shagreen case, studded, with a Gold Knob, and marked with 48 on the inside of the case. Whoever will give notice of it to Mr Joseph Knibb, watchmaker, in Fleet Street, shall have 2 guineas and charges; or if pawned or sold, their money again and a good gratuity" (*London Gazette*, April 30, May 4, 1691).

"Left in a coach or drop'd, the 12th inst., a Gold Out-Case of a striking watch, engraven. Whoever shall bring it to Joseph Knibb, clockmaker, at the Dyal, near Serjeants-Inn, in Fleet Street, shall receive 40s. reward" (*London Gazette*, January 11-14, 1691).

"At the Clock Dyal, in Suffolk Street, near Charing Cross, on Friday, the 23rd inst., will begin the sale of a great Parcel of very good Pendulum Clocks, some do go a year, some a quarter of a year, some a month, some a week, and some 30 hours; some are Table Clocks, some repeat themselves, and some, by pulling, repeat the hours and quarters; made and sold by Joseph Knibb, at his House at the Dyal, in Suffolk Street, aforementioned. There are also some watches to be then and there sold" (*London Gazette*, April 15-19, 1697).

I may mention that some time ago I saw a long-case clock dial, dating from about 1705, which was inscribed, "Joseph Knibb, of Hanslope." Hanslope is, I believe, a village near Stony Stratford, Bucks. In the Wetherfield collection is a long black case month clock signed "Joseph Knibb at Hanslop" which strikes the hours on two bells in accordance with the Roman numerals as described on p.245.

After an examination of many clocks by Joseph Knibb, I should be inclined to class him as a clockmaker with Tompion and Quare. Further on I will give some illustrations of his long-case clocks.

THOMAS HARRYS

Fig. 449.

ST DUNSTAN'S CLOCK. — Above the main entrance at the western end of the old church of St Dunstan's in the West, in Fleet Street, were erected in 1671 two gilt clock dials, placed back to back, and mounted in a handsome square case, with circular pediment, which projected well out over the footway, the tube containing the rod for actuating the hands being supported by a well-carved figure of Time. An alcove was built on the roof of the gateway, and within were large gaudily painted and gilt figures of Gog and Magog, which struck "ting-tang" quarters with clubs on two bells suspended above them. The clock and figures were designed and erected by Thomas Harrys, a clockmaker, then living at Water Lane, Blackfriars. Harrys submitted a statement of what he proposed to do, and after describing the "two figures of men with poleaxes to strike the quarters," continues, "I will do one thing more, which London shall not show the like; I will make two hands show the hours and minutes without the church, upon a double dial, which will be worth your observation, and to my credit." The figures of Gog and Magog proved to be a great attraction; they speedily became one of the sights of London, and their removal, in 1830, when the church was rebuilt, elicited many expressions of regret. Fig. 449, taken from an old print of the church in my possession, represents the clock as it was in 1737.

In 1830, when the old church was in course of demolition, the Marquis of Hertford bought for two hundred guineas the clock, the quarter figures, and three statues representing Kind Lud and his sons taken from the old Ludgate. The Marquis of Hertford was at that time building a residence at the north-west corner of Regent's Park. This he called St Dunstan's Lodge, and in the grounds thereof the clock and accessories are still to be seen from Regent's Park. The dials are now in a circular case; but the movement, though it has, of course, undergone repair from time to time, is still, I believe, substantially the one Harrys supplied over two centuries ago.

BRADLEY

ST PAUL'S CLOCK. — Langley Bradley was apprenticed to Joseph Wise in 1687, and admitted to the freedom of the Clockmakers' Company in 1694. Dr Derham, in acknowledging technical information obtained from Bradley for the first edition of the "Artificial Clockmaker," published in 1696, speaks of him as an ingenious workman of Whitechapel; but during the greater part of his career he resided at the "Minute Dyall" in Fenchurch Street. Watches by him with deep movements, very similar to Tompion's, will bear comparison with the works of that master. An exterior view of one is given in Fig. 450. In the Soane Museum is a calendar watch by him, which belonged to Sir Christopher Wren. It is a fine piece of work, and was probably made to the order of William III. for presentation to the architect of St Paul's. The dial resembles Fig. 395, and the pillars are pierced to form the royal monogram W. M., surmounted by a crown. Among other watches by him may be mentioned one in the British Museum and one in the Guildhall Museum. In the Wetherfield collection are a long marqueterie case three train chiming clock and a long walnut case clock. But Bradley seems to have devoted most attention to larger work, and is perhaps best known as the maker of the noted clock for St Paul's Cathedral, which did good service from 1708 till 1892, and was generally regarded as the standard timekeeper of the metropolis till the giant dials and Big Ben at Westminster took the popular favour. He made a clock for the Church of St Clements Dane, Strand, in 1721, and one for Cripplegate Church in 1722.

Fig. 450. — Watch by Langley Bradley, 1700.

The following particulars of the St Paul's clock, from notes I made shortly before it was taken down, will probably be of interest. The frame consisted of a cast-iron rectangular base plate, from which rose cast-iron columns supporting an entablature of the same metal. The going train occupied the centre of the space between the base and entablature, the wheels being arranged vertically; while the gun-metal bushes for the pivots were carried in wrought-iron straps bolted to the base plate and entablature. On one side of the going train was the quarter part, and on the other side the hour-striking part, similarly arranged. All the wheels were of gun-metal, the great wheels being 2 ft. 8 in. in diameter, 1 in. pitch, and 1¾ in. wide. For the original recoil escapement was substituted a half-dead one in 1805, but with this exception it may be said that the whole of Bradley's mechanism remained in good working order till the clock was taken down. The two-second pendulum had a wooden rod and a cast-iron bob weighing nearly 180 lbs. The striking work was on the rack principle. The mitre wheels for driving the dial works were commendably large, being 20 in. in diameter, and for supporting the dial end of the minute-hand arbor there were three friction wheels placed at equal distances apart round the outside of, and carried by the hour-hand tube. Slits were cut in the tube to allow a portion of the circumference of the friction wheels to enter, and the wheels were of such a size that they projected into the tube just sufficient to meet the minute-hand arbor. This ingenious contrivance is also applied to the Westminster clock, and is generally supposed to have been invented for it. Two sides of the St Paul's clock tower, one facing down Ludgate Hill, and the other looking towards the south side of the churchyard, were utilised for the dials of Bradley's timekeeper, black rings being painted on the stonework, on which the hour circles and the numerals were engraved and gilt. Each dial is a trifle over 17 ft. in diameter, and the central opening measures about 10 ft. 6 in., the hour numerals being about 2 ft. deep. Though but two sets of dial-work were used, the stonework of the four faces of the tower is alike, and on the eastern side, just visible from Cannon Street, although the dial was not painted, the hour numerals were cut in the stone; this suggests the inference that it was at one time intended to show the time there; it was probably found that the pediment over the southern entrance to the cathedral so obscured the view as to render the third dial comparatively useless. On the roof, just outside of this dial aperture, was a horizontal sun-dial, with a plate over 2 ft. in diameter, for the purpose of regulating the clock by the sun.

Bradley's bill appears in the Cathedral Accounts, December 1708, as follows:—

To Langley Bradley, Clockmaker, vizt:—

For a large Quarter clock, going 8 days, as by agreement dated 15 Novr 1706	£300	0 0
For 2 large Bellmetal Braces for the great bell, w^t 107^{li}, at 14^d per li.	6	4 10
For a large strong canvas bed stuffe with oakam and sewed wth strong thread line to receive the clock weight	2	5 0
	£308	9 10

A curious feature is the description of the clock as an eight-day one, whereas, for many years at least, it was but a thirty-hour one. Indeed, it seems doubtful if it ever went eight days between windings, for, by the arrangement of the train and barrel, the weight fell about 40 ft. for twenty-four hours' going.

From the clock room the upper part of the belfry is approached by a stone staircase formed in the wall of the tower itself, which is 5 ft. thick, composed of two stone shells, with a space of 15 in. between them. Here, 40 ft. from the clock floor, was hung the celebrated hour bell which, in addition to its primal duty of recording the hours, was tolled when the Sovereign, the Bishop of London, the Dean of St Paul's, or the Lord Mayor of London passed away.

The commissioners appear to have had just as much trouble with their hour bell as was afterwards experienced over the casting of Big Ben for the Houses of Parliament. In the year 1700, when the cathedral was approaching completion, they purchased, for 10d. a lb., from the churchwardens of St Margaret's, Westminster, the celebrated Great Tom, which formerly hung in a clock tower facing Westminster Hall, as related at p.40, and which appears to have been given to the churchwardens by William III. They then entered into a contract with William Whiteman to recast the bell, and when the work was done the bell was temporarily hoisted into the north-west tower of St Paul's and exhibited to the public, Whiteman being paid £509. 19s. for his labour. But lo! after sustaining many blows for the delectation of the ears of the citizens, Great Tom the Second exhibited a crack which rapidly developed, so that the bell was pronounced to be useless. The commissioners suggested that of course Whiteman would make good his work by recasting the bell. "Not so," rejoined Whiteman. "I delivered to you a sound bell for which I was paid, and since it has been in your possession it has been cracked." So, to make the best of a bad job, a very stringent agreement was entered into with another founder — Richard Phelps, to wit. The accident with the first hour bell accounts for the difference between the date of the finishing of the clock and the time when the Phelps hour bell was cast, around the waist of which is the inscription, "Richard Phelps made me, 1716." It is 6 ft. $9^{1}/_{2}$ in. in diameter at the mouth, and according to Phelps' account, dated 31st December 1716, weighs 99 cwt. 3 qrs. 7 lbs., of which 7 cwt. 1 qrs. 21 lbs. were new metal. For tolling it has a clapper weighing 180 lbs., and the total weight of the bell and fittings is, I believe, 5 tons 4 cwt. The hammer-head which struck the hours on the outside of the sound bow weighed 145 lbs. Just below the hour bell were two bells on which the "ting-tang" quarters were struck; the larger of these weighed 1 ton 4 cwt., and the smaller 12 cwt. 2 qrs. 9 lbs.

ELLICOTT
The first John Ellicott, watchmaker, whose parents came to London from Bodmin, in Cornwall, was apprenticed to John Waters in 1687, admitted to the freedom of the Clockmakers' Company in 1696, elected on the Court of Assistants in 1726, and served as warden from 1731 till his death in 1733. He resided in the parish of Allhallows, London Wall. But the most eminent watch and clockmaker of the family was his son John Ellicott, born in 1706, who established himself in business about 1728 at Sweeting's Alley, which was situated just where the statue of Rowland Hill now stands, near the Royal Exchange. After the fire which destroyed the old Royal Exchange in 1838, Sweeting's Alley was not rebuilt. He was elected a fellow of the Royal Society in 1738, being recommended for that honour by Sir Hans Sloane, Bart., Martin Ffolkes, John Senex, the celebrated globe maker, and John Hadley, the astronomer. At the meetings of the Royal Society he became acquainted with James Ferguson, who afterwards frequently visited Ellicott's private house at St John's, Hackney, where an observatory was fitted up, and various scientific experiments were made.

Ellicott was the inventor of a compensation pendulum in which the bob rests on the longer ends of two levers, of which the shorter ends are depressed by the superior expansion of a brass bar attached to the pendulum rod. In Fig. 451, a is the suspension spring; $s\,s\,s$ screws for uniting the steel rod to the brass bar, slotted holes in the latter allowing it to move freely in answer to changes of temperature; $f\,f$ the two levers pivoted to the steel rod; on the shorter ends rests the brass bar; the screws $g\,g$ pass through the pendulum bob C C, and rest on the longer ends of the levers. By turning the screws their bearing on the levers may be adjusted. This device has not proved to be of much practical value, although there is a clock to which it is attached still going at the London Institution, Finsbury Circus.

A well-proportioned long-mahogany-case clock by him, with dead-beat escapement, and a bracket repeating clock in a green lacquer case, are among the Wetherfield collection. In the same collection also is the bracket repeating clock shown in Chapter VIII., which is charming in its simplicity. The case is of mahogany.

Ellicott's productions were distinguished by excellent workmanship. He paid great attention to the cylinder escapement, and did much to bring it into use. In some of his later examples the cylinders were of ruby. His more costly watches were lavishly decorated, the cases in *repoussé*, and the dials enamelled on gold, some of these being really works of art. They are now rarely to be met with, for the iconoclastic dealer as a rule ruthlessly changes the dial for one of cheaper material. In reference to the prices Ellicott obtained, it may be mentioned that Horace Walpole, writing to Sir H. Mann at Florence, on 8th June 1759, with regard to a commission to purchase a watch, states that for one of Ellicott's the price was 150 guineas. In the British Museum is a silver repeater by him which belonged to Jeremy Bentham. Mr Talfourd Ely, M.A., in the *Archaeological Journal* for June 1895, gives an interesting description of a watch by John Ellicott. It is in gold cases, the outer one decorated in *repoussé*, and appears to have been made in 1751. A small gold watch by him with gold dial is in the Pierpont Morgan collection. The collection of the Czar of Russia in the Winter Palace at St Petersburg contains a good example of his manufacture. It is a large repeater in gold cases; the inner one bears the hall mark for 1760-61 and the outer one a *repoussé* decoration.

Ellicott was on the council of the Royal Society for three years, and read several papers before the Society. They included one on the "Influence which two Pendulum Clocks were observed to have on each other." The ball of each pendulum weighed above 23 lbs.; the cases were placed sideways to each other, so near that the pendulums when at rest were little more than 2 ft. asunder. In less than two hours after they were set going, one of them, called No. 1, always stopped. As it had always kept going with great freedom

Fig. 451.

Fig. 452. — JOHN ELLICOTT, 1706-1772.

The earliest example of an original anchor escapement known to survive is found in a turret clock not signed or dated but installed in Wadham College, Oxford by September, 1670, and ascribable to Joseph Knibb. There is a long standing tradition that Sir Christopher Wren presented the clock to the college in which case the question of his involvement in the development of the anchor escapement arises. For discussion of this see A.J. Turner, 'Sir Christopher Wren and the Wadham Clock', Antiquarian Horology VII, June 1971, pp.229-230. The clock has two trains side by side, seconds pendulum with wing nut regulation (a typical Knibb feature), and an original anchor escapement. For a detailed description of the clock see C.F.C. Beeson 'A History of the Wadham Clock' Antiquarian Horology, June 1957, pp.47-54. The Wadham clock predates the King's College clock by William Clement by at least a year, which has a later anchor. Ascription of the invention of the anchor escapement to William Clement is now extremely doubtful (Robert Hooke quite clearly had nothing to do with it), but ascription to Knibb still remains to be proved. Museum of the History of Science, Oxford.

before the other regulator, No. 2, was placed near it, Ellicott conceived its stopping must be owing to some influence the motion of one of the pendulums had upon the other; and upon watching them narrowly the motion of No. 2 was found to increase as No. 1 diminished. At the time No. 1 stopped, No. 2 described an arc of 5°, being nearly 2° more than it would have done if the other had not been near it, and more than it moved in a short time after the other pendulum came to rest. On this he stopped the pendulum of No. 2, and set No. 1 going, the pendulum describing as large an arc as the case would admit, viz., about 5°; he presently found the pendulum of No. 2 begin to move, and the motion to increase gradually, till in 17 minutes 40 seconds it described an arc of 2° 10', at which, the wheel discharging itself off the pallets, the regulator went, the arcs of the vibrations continued to increase till, as in the former experiment, the pendulum moved 5°, the motion of the pendulum of No. 1 gradually decreasing as the other

Fig. 453. — Long-Case Clock by John Ellicott with Equation of Time Dial below the Hood.

increased, and in 45 minutes it stopped. He then left the pendulum of No. 1 at rest, and set No. 2 going, making it also describe an arc of 5°; it continued to vibrate less and less till it described but about 3°, in which arc it continued to move; the pendulum of No. 1 seemed but little affected by the motion of No. 2. Ellicott's explanation was that, as the pendulums were very heavy, either of them set going communicated a slight motion to the case and in a lesser degree to whatever the case touched. Ellicott's experiment was useful as showing the necessity of fixing clocks with heavy pendulums to the wall of a building or other ponderous and unyielding structure.

In Fig. 453 is shown by favour of Mr E. Beaven the upper part of an exceedingly choice long-case clock by Ellicott. By means of two darkened annular segments, arranged to pass one over the other, the hours of day and night are indicated in the centre of the dial. Below the hood a secondary dial gives the equation of time. I remember seeing a sketch of a twelve-month timekeeper by Quare similarly equipped.

Ellicott designed several of our public clocks, amongst them that of the London Hospital, and was appointed clockmaker to the king. He died suddenly in 1772, having dropped from his chair and instantly expired. The accompanying likeness (Fig. 452) is from a fine portrait of him shortly before his decease by Dance, afterwards Sir Nathaniel Dance Holland. John Ellicott was succeeded by his eldest son, Edward, who had been in partnership with him since 1769. Edward Ellicott died at his residence in Great Queen Street, in 1791. The business was then carried on by his son Edward, who, after serving in the subordinate offices, was elected as master of the Clockmakers' Company in 1834. Though brought up as a watchmaker, he had but little liking for the business, and left the conduct of it in a great measure to others. From Edward Ellicott & Sons the title of the firm was altered to Ellicott & Taylor in 1811, and to Elicott & Smith in 1830. After the destruction of Sweeting's Alley, Ellicott & Smith removed to 27 Lombard Street, and remained there till 1842.

There was a third John Ellicott admitted to the freedom of the Clockmakers' Company by patrimony in 1792. He was the second son of the first Edward, but appears to have taken no part in the watch or clock making business. His grandson, Dr Ellicott, was the late Bishop of Gloucester and Bristol.

HENRY SULLY

This talented but unfortunate horologist was apprenticed to Charles Gretton, of Fleet Street, in 1697. On the completion of his apprenticeship he travelled over the Continent, visiting Holland and Austria. From Vienna he went to Paris with the Duke d'Aremberg, where he made the acquaintance of Julien Le Roy, Law the noted Scottish speculator, and others. Le Roy at once recognised the genius of the young enthusiast who was imbued with ideas for perfecting timekeepers, and encouraged him to continue his researches. In 1717 Sully published "Règle Artificielle du Temps." The following year, commissioned by Law, he journeyed to London and engaged sixty watch and clock makers, who, with their families, were located at Versailles, where a factory was started. After two years of unremitting toil Sully was displaced from the directorate, but a little later, under the protection of the Duke de Noailles, another factory was established at St Germain. This lasted but a year, when Sully returned to England, bringing his staff of workpeople with him. The same ill fortune

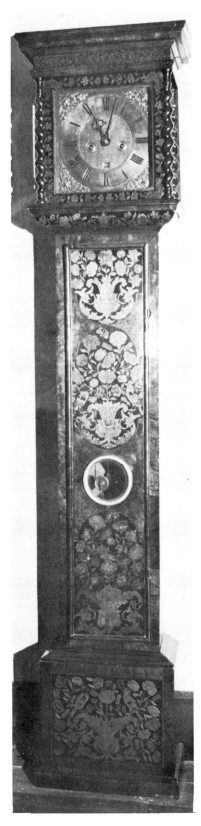

dogged his steps here, and in his extremity he returned to Paris, where for a time he sustained existence by repairing watches. In 1721, when a little more prosperous, he turned his attention to the production of a marine timekeeper, and in 1724 presented it to the Academy of Sciences. This instrument had a modification of Debaufre's escapement, which Sully devised for the purpose, and a vertical balance which was really a pendulum. It carried cycloidal metal pieces, around which the upper end of a slender wire was wound, the lower end being attached to a lever with an adjustable weight, with the idea of keeping the vibrations of the balance isochronous. The pivots of the balance, instead of being in holes, were supported on the edges of large rollers, to diminish the friction, a device adopted afterwards by Mudge. In 1726 Sully published "Abrégée d'une Horologe d'une Nouvelle Invention pour la Juste Mesure du Temps sur Mer." When subjected to the tossing of the ocean, his timekeeper failed to yield the results anticipated from its performance on land. Though mortified by his failure, he again set himself to the solution of the problem. He had already made a marine watch with two balances geared together, as designed by Dr Hooke, and now proceeded with a new timekeeper of different construction; but while engaged thereon he was seized with a serious illness, induced by over-application and worry, and succumbed to inflammation of the lungs in 1728.

At the church of St Sulpice, Paris, he had traced a meridian line on the pavement of the transept, and secured its permanence by inlaying a thin brass edge. He blocked up the south transept window except for a small hole in a metal plate at the upper part through which the rays of the sun cast a luminous disc about 10½ in. in diameter on the floor. The disc moves across the line which at noon bisects it. In this church he was buried, and a fine obelisk of white marble erected to his memory in the north transept, in a position that allowed the meridian line to be carried up the face of the monument. A laudatory inscription recounted his services to horology, but the greater part of it was cut out by the revolutionists of 1793, who possibly resented the suggestion that French watchmakers could be indebted to a foreigner.

In the Guidhall Museum is a timekeeper with Sully's curious vertical balance. It is in the form of a bracket clock with a walnut bell-top case, has a seconds hand above the centre of the dial, and shows the days of the month through a slit below the centre. It is inscribed "Henricus Sully, invenit et fecit (1724), Horloger to the Duke of Orleans."

A longcase marquetry clock by John Knibb, Hanslope, the village to which Knibb retired after his years in Oxford since he owned some property there. A small number of clocks from Hanslope are known to exist. The clock has a two train plated movement, anchor escapement with a pin count wheel. There are two hands, subsidiary seconds, applied cherub spandrels, and a pendulum aperture in the trunk. Museum of the History of Science, Oxford.

An ebony veneered bracket clock with bun feet by John Knibb of Oxford, c.1675-85. The clock has a two train plated movement with a tic-tac escapement which is a minor modification of the anchor in that one pallet is slightly larger than the other and only two or three teeth of the escape wheel are embraced. Invention of this escapement is generally ascribed to Joseph Knibb on the strength of two split-seconds observatory clocks made by him for St Andrews University in 1673. It never became very popular but was occasionally used by Tompion and Samuel Watson. Museum of the History of Science, Oxford.

JOHN HARRISON

Fig. 454.

John Harrison was born at Faulby or Wragby near Pontefract, Yorkshire, in 1693. He was the son of a carpenter, which business he followed for several years. In 1700 the family removed to Barrow, in Lincolnshire. At a very early age John Harrison showed a great predilection for mechanical pursuits, and particularly directed his attention to the improvement of clocks.

The offer, by Act of Parliament, of large sums for the production of a timekeeper sufficiently accurate to ascertain the longitude at sea, induced him to turn his attention to the subject. He devised a peculiar form of recoil escapement, and a pendulum in which the effects of heat and cold in lengthening and shortening the pendulum were neutralised by the use of two metals having different ratios of expansion. His escapement, generally called the "grass-hopper," is shown in Fig. 454. The pallets of ebony, or other hard wood, are jointed to a bell-crank lever carried by the crutch; though free to move at the joints they are kept sufficiently near to position by springs which are not shown in the drawing. The teeth of the escape wheel alternately push the left-hand and pull the right-hand pallet, this action giving the necessary impulse to the pendulum. The chief merit appears to be that as there is no rubbing between the pallets and the wheel teeth there would be no lubrication required at these contacts. However, the invention

Fig. 455.

Fig. 456. – JOHN HARRISON, 1693-1776.

was never adopted by others, and need not be further described. His pendulum, known as the *gridiron* form of compensation, shown in Fig. 455, is still the form of compensation adopted in many foreign regulators. It is composed of nine parallel rods, five of steel and four of brass, the total length of each kind being nearly as 100 to 60, that being the ratio of expansion of the two metals. Depending from the cross frame A are two rods of steel *a a*. The frame B, to which they are fixed at their lower extremities *b b*, carries also two brass rods *c c*, which at their upper ends *d d* are carried in the frame C, together with two other steel rods *e e*. Those at the lower extremities *f f* are fastened in the frame D, which also carries the brass rods *g g*. The frame F carries the upper ends of this last pair of brass rods at *h h*, and also the central steel rod to which the bob is attached.

One of his early efforts, with wheels and pinions of wood, which is in the possession of Mr Evan Roberts, has John Harrison's signature with the date 1713 on the face of the day of the month wheel. Another long-case clock by him is at the South Kensington Museum, and one made about 1730, fitted with the grasshopper escapement, which was for some years in the possession of Mr Thos. Nicholson, Barton-on-Humber, now belongs to his grandson, Mr W. W. Nicholson. In the Guildhall Museum may be seen a very similar relic.

In 1728 Harrison journeyed to London, taking with him his pendulum, his escapement, and drawings of his proposed timekeeper, hoping to obtain the approbation and aid of the Board of Longitude. Before being submitted to the notice of that body they were inspected by Graham, whose maturer judgment prompted him to advise Harrison to first make the timekeeper, and then ascertain, from its actual going, what claims it might have to further notice.

Harrison continued plodding on in the country repairing watches and clocks and making a variety of experiments till 1735; then, in his forty-second year, he came to London and took up his residence in Orange Street, Red Lion Square. He brought with him a timepiece he had invented and constructed. It was a cumbersome affair in a wooden frame, and had two balances. He obtained certificates of the excellence of this timekeeper from Halley, Graham, and others. On their recommendation he was allowed, in 1736, to proceed with it to Lisbon in a king's ship, and was enabled to correct the reckoning to within 1° 30′.

In consideration of this result, the Board of Longitude gave him £500 "to proceed with his improvements." It will be observed that the performance of his first timekeeper failed to attain the precision required by that Board; for had it determined the longitude to a degree, Harrison would have been entitled to £10,000 according to the provisions of the Act, as stated on p. 277. In 1739 he finished another timekeeper, and afterwards a third, which was smaller and appeared to the members of the Royal Society to be more simple and less likely to be deranged than either of the preceding ones. In 1749 he received the gold medal which was annually awarded by the Royal Society to the most useful discovery, but he was still not satisfied with his productions. The experience gained by prolonged trial led him to abandon the heavy framing and wheels which characterised his earlier essays and to devise and construct his celebrated "watch" which eventually won for him the coveted reward.

Fig. 457. — Harrison's celebrated Marine Timepiece.

He spent some time in improving and correcting his fourth nautical timekeeper, and then applied to the Commissioners of the Board of Longitude for a trial according to the Act of Parliament. This, after much delay, was granted, and his son William was in his stead allowed to take a voyage to Jamaica. William Harrison embarked in the "Deptford," at Portsmouth, on 18th November 1761. After eighteen days' navigation the vessel was supposed to be 13°,50′ west of Portsmouth by ordinary calculations, but by the watch was 15° 19′, and the timekeeper was at once condemned as useless. William Harrison, however, maintained that if Madeira were correctly marked on the chart, it would be seen on the following day; and in this he persisted so strongly, that the captain was induced to continue the same course, and as predicted the island was discovered the next day. In like manner William Harrison was enabled by the watch to announce all the islands in the order in which they would fall in with them. When he arrived at Port Royal, after a voyage of sixty-one days, the chronometer as we may now call it,* was found to be about nine seconds slow. On 28th January 1762 he set sail from Jamaica on board the "Merlin," and on his return to Portsmouth, after an absence of five months, the chronometer had kept time within about one minute five seconds, which gives an error of 18 miles. This was much within the limit of the 30 miles prescribed by the Act of 1713; yet, several objections being raised, William Harrison was obliged to undertake a second voyage, the proof from the first not being considered sufficiently decisive by the Board, although they advanced £5,000 on account of the reward.

* Mr R. B. Prosser says the term chronometer appears to have been introduced by Loulie of Amsterdam in 1698 as descriptive of the instrument now known as a metronome. John Arnold was the first to apply it to a precision timekeeper.

Accompanied by Dr Maskelyne as the representative of the Board, William Harrison embarked on the man-of-war "Tartar," on 28th March 1764, and arrived in Barbados on the 13th of May, when it was found the chronometer had gained forty-three seconds; he set out for the return journey on board the "New Elizabeth" on the 4th of June, and arrived at the Surrey Stairs on 18th July, when it was ascertained that after allowing for the estimated rate of one second a day gaining, there was an excess of fifty-four seconds for the whole period of 156 days. The result of this second voyage was so satisfactory, that the Board unanimously declared Harrison had really exceeded all expectations and demands of the Act of Parliament, and he was paid a further advance of £5,000, with the condition that he explained the construction of his timekeeper. A sub-committee, consisting of Maskelyne, John Mitchell, Ludlam, Bird, Mudge, Mathews, and Kendall, were appointed, and instructed to make themselves acquainted with the mechanism of the instrument. They reported themselves satisfied in 1765, but even then

A miniature alarm in the style of a lantern clock by John Knibb, Oxon, c.1690. Silvered chapter ring and alarm setting dial, horizontal verge escapement and original weights. The side frets have been left unfinished as not infrequently occurs in lantern clocks. Museum of the History of Science, Oxford.

A verge watch signed 'John Knibb at Oxford' of standard layout and design. The tortoise-shell outer case, however, is unusual being inlaid with silver, showing a huntsman blowing a horn and a hare pursued by a hound. In the centre is a Tudor rose surmounted by a crown. Few watches by John Knibb are known and whether he did more than order movements from London makers which were engraved with his name may be doubted. Museum of the History of Science, Oxford.

considerable delay occurred. Kendall was commissioned to make a duplicate of the chronometer, which appears to have taken three years to execute, for the date of Kendall's instrument is 1769, the year the final payment was made to Harrison.

Harrison's timekeeper is in the form of a large silver pair-case watch, with a centré seconds hand. The representation in Fig. 457 is from a photograph for which I am indebted to the Astronomer Royal. It has been stated that the piece hung in gymbals. This was not the case; it reposed on a soft cushion, and on its trial voyages was carefully tended by William Harrison, who avoided position errors as far as possible by shifting the timekeeper to suit the *lie* of the ship.

The plates are 3.8 in. and the balance 2.2 in. in diameter; the fusee makes six and a quarter turns. The escapement beats five times in a second. The pivot holes are jewelled with rubies.

One of the chief features is a bimetallic arm fixed at one end, and carrying at its free end two pins, to embrace the balance-spring near its outer point of attachment. "The thermometer kirb is composed of two thin plates of brass and steel riveted together in several places, which, by the greater expansion of brass than steel by heat, and contraction by cold, becomes convex on the brass side in hot weather, and convex on the steel side in cold weather; whence, one end being fixed, the other end obtains a motion corresponding

Above and right: silver-cased calendar watch by Langley Bradley, London, elaborately decorated and finished. The dial enables the owner to read the hour and minute of the day; the position of the sun and moon in the zodiac/calendar; the age, phase, and aspects of the moon from the aspectarium *and scales in the centre.*

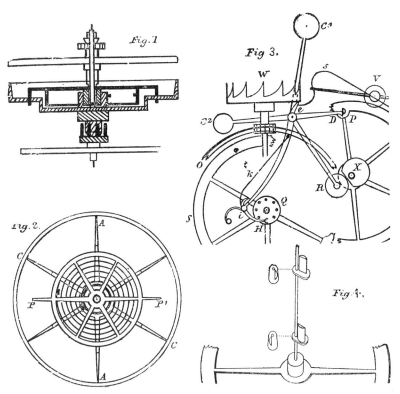

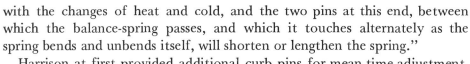

Fig. 458. — Harrison's Remontoire Escapement.

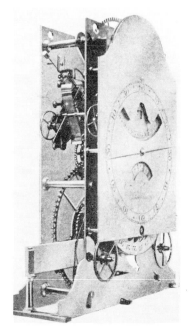

Fig. 459. — Late Clock by John Harrison, in possession of the Royal Astronomical Society.

with the changes of heat and cold, and the two pins at this end, between which the balance-spring passes, and which it touches alternately as the spring bends and unbends itself, will shorten or lengthen the spring."

Harrison at first provided additional curb pins for mean time adjustment, but had to abandon them; for it is clear, if they were placed behind the pins on the compensation curb, they would not act, and, if placed in front, the movement of the temperature pins would be ineffective.

It is, of course, easy to be wise after the event; but, on examining the remontoire and escapement of Harrison's chronometer in the presence of the simple detent escapement introduced shortly after, it seems marvellous that he should have spent so many years over such complicated and by comparison inefficient contrivances. Harrison's drawings are most difficult to understand, but I venture to reproduce some contributed to the *Horological Journal* by Mr H.M. Frodsham, which were made from Kendall's duplicate of Harrison's timekeeper at the Greenwich Observatory. [Fig. 458.]

Fig. 1 is a section through the fourth wheel. Fig. 2 a plan of the remontoire and contrate wheel. Fig. 3 a plan of the remontoire and escapement. The pinion at the top of Fig. 1 is driven by internal teeth on the third wheel of the train. The wheel immediately below the pinion in Fig. 1 is the fourth wheel, which drives a pinion x (Fig. 3). The dished wheel below the fourth wheel in Fig. 1 is the contrate wheel (c, Figs. 2 and 3). In the recess of the contrate wheel is contained the remontoire spring which is wound eight times in a minute. The wheel at the bottom of Fig. 1 is the seconds wheel. This and the contrate wheel move continuously, while the fourth wheel and the other part of the train are locked by the lever D catching the stop P on the wheel P x, except during the winding of the

remontoire. On the collet of the contrate wheel are eight pins, shown in Fig. 1, and at Q in Fig. 3. The eight pins in the contrate wheel in succession push the arm H (Fig. 3), and so unlock the train. The locking wheel P X drives a fly pinion and fly V to moderate the velocity with which the remontoire was wound. The seconds arbor is in the centre of the watch, and is driven by the seconds wheel below the contrate wheel. The projections P P' on the barrel of the remontoire are to prevent the remontoire running down.

Fig. 4 shows the pallets, which, instead of forming an angle of 95° or so, as is usual, are set parallel to each other, and in this way there is very little recoil, but increased tendency, to set. These acting surfaces of the pallets are diamonds set in brass collets.

During William Harrison's voyages, the rate of the watch could not of course be checked daily for want of some means of comparison, and so in May 1766 the Board of Longitude placed the instrument at the Greenwich Observatory in the hands of Dr Maskelyne, who had then been appointed Astronomer Royal, for the purpose of testing its daily rate. Dr Maskelyne was supposed to favour lunar observations as a solution of the longitude problem and William Harrison considered he was prejudiced against the watch; it was therefore put in a box having a glazed lid and two locks, the keys whereof were kept, one by Dr Maskelyne and the other by Captain Baillie, Governor of Greenwich Hospital. The trial lasted 298 days, during which the watch gained 1 hour 10 minutes 27.5 seconds. Its greatest gain in one day was 30 seconds, the temperature being 60° and the pendant vertical; its greatest loss in one day was 6.5 seconds, the thermometer being at freezing point, the piece lying dial up.

Harrison's watch and the three bulky timepieces which preceded it are all preserved in the Greenwich Observatory.

Besides the early clocks mentioned on p.255, one of very superior workmanship and much later date, in the possession of the Royal Astronomical Society, has been described in the *R.A.S. Notices* by Mr E. T. Cottingham. A view of the dial and movement appears in Fig. 459. The whole affair is a mass of ingenious complications departing, wherever possible, from the beaten track. Several of the contrivances embodied may be briefly summarised. The escapement is a variation of the "grasshopper." Cycloidal guides are provided for the pendulum, which vibrates through no less than 12° of arc. There is a double minute hand which goes round in two hours, being jumped forward at half-minute intervals by a remontoire which the escape wheel releases. The escape wheel has 120 teeth, and as it makes but one turn in four minutes a four-finger seconds indicator is provided. The seconds dial is sunk, and each of the fingers in succession comes into sight and points to the seconds figures. The bearings of the great wheel run on rollers pivoted into rings and the other bearings are supported on the edges

A month going regulator signed Ellicott London on the silvered dial, in a mahogany case with shaped and fluted hood, ogee-shaped door, and panel to the base. Plated movement with five pillars, jewelled dead-beat escapement with bolt and shutter maintaining power, six spoke wheels and worm gear regulation mounted above the movement operating on the dial in the arch. The clock is fitted with Ellicott's pendulum, spring suspended, with temperature compensation in the bob but not at the suspension point. Christie, Manson & Woods Ltd.

An 18th century attempt at a marine timepiece signed 'Henricus Sully Invenit & Fecit'. In appearance similar to a domestic mantel clock in a burr walnut case with circular dial and carrying handle, the clock has a plated movement, going barrel and Sully's own balance wheel and horizontal pendulum escapement which belongs to the frictional rest group of escapements. Sully (1680-1728), an Englishman, spent most of his working life in France whence he sent this clock to George Graham in 1724. It is not known if other examples of his work survive but he is well known for his published works Regle artifielle du Temps . . . (1737), and his Description abregee d'une Horloge d'une nouvelle Invention . . . (1726) which describes the clock shown here. Worshipful Company of Clockmakers.

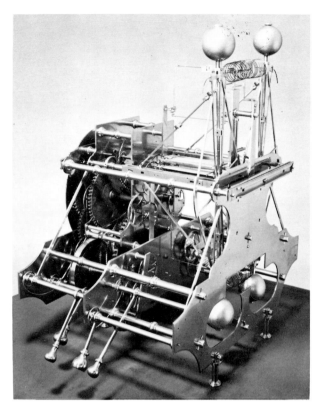

The first of the four timepieces constructed by John and James Harrison in their attempt to build a machine capable of keeping time accurately while at sea. Commonly known as 'H1', the instrument was completed and tried at sea in 1736. The National Maritime Museum, Greenwich.

of large friction rollers. Altogether the cost of this timekeeper must have been enormous.

On Harrison's tomb in the south-west corner of Hampstead Churchyard is the following inscription:—

"In memory of Mr John Harrison, late of Red Lion Square, London, inventor of the timekeeper for ascertaining the longitude at sea. He was born at Foulby, in the county of York, and was the son of a builder at that place, who brought him up to the same profession. Before he attained the age of twenty-one, he, without any instruction, employed himself in cleaning and repairing clocks and watches, and made a few of the former, chiefly of wood. At the age of twenty-five he employed his whole time in chronometrical improvements.

"He was the inventor of the gridiron pendulum and the method of preventing the effects of heat and cold upon timekeepers by two bars fixed together; he introduced the secondary spring to keep them going while winding up; and was the inventor of most (or all) the improvements in clocks and watches during his time. In the year 1735 his first timekeeper was sent to Lisbon, and in 1764 his then much-improved fourth timekeeper having been sent to Barbadoes, the Commissioners of Longitude certified that it had determined the longitude within one-third of half a degree of a great circle, having not erred more than forty seconds in time. After sixty years' close application to the above pursuits, he departed this life on the 24th day of March 1776, aged eighty-three. This tombstone was put up many years after his death."

In 1878 the tomb had become very dilapidated, the inscription being barely decipherable, and I then suggested to Mr W. H. Prosser that he should obtain subcriptions, and have it restored. This he proceeded to do; but on applying to the Clockmakers' Company, some members of the Court

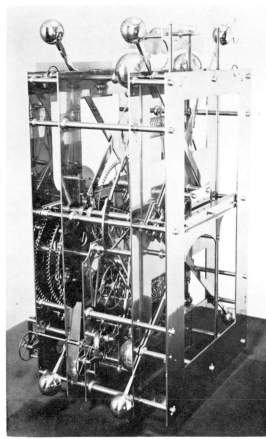

The second of the Harrison's longitude timepieces, H2, was completed in 1739. Detailed discussions of all the Harrison pieces may be found in R.T. Gould, The Marine Chronometer, *London, 1923; Humphrey Quill,* John Harrison, the Man who found Longitude, *London, 1966; William Laycock,* The Lost Science of John 'Longitude' Harrison, *Ashford, 1976. The National Maritime Museum, Greenwich.*

expressed a wish that the matter should be placed in the hands of the Company, and the restoration was accordingly made under the direction of the Court forthwith. The engraving in Fig. 456 is from one by P. L. Tassaert, after a portrait by T. King taken in 1768. Harrison's marine watch is at his right hand, and one of his earlier essays behind him.

PINCHBECK   Among the celebrated clock and watch makers of the eighteenth century must be reckoned Christopher Pinchbeck, known principally as the discoverer of an alloy of metals, called after him "Pinchbeck," and as an inventor of "Astronomico-Musical Clocks." In the "Dictionary of National Biography," R. B. P. suggests that he probably sprang from the small town of Pinchbeck in Lincolnshire. He resided at Clerkenwell in a turning out of St John's Lane called Albion Place, which, prior to 1822, when it was rebuilt, was known as St George's Court. From there he removed to Fleet Street, as is shown by the following advertisement which appeared in *Applebee's Weekly Journal* of 8th July 1721:—

"Notice is hereby given to Noblemen, Gentlemen, and Others, that Chr. Pinchbeck, Inventor and Maker of the famous Astronomico-Musical Clocks, is removed from St George's Court, St Jones's Lane, to the sign of the Astronomico-Musical Clock in Fleet Street near the Leg Tavern. He maketh and selleth Watches of all sorts and Clocks, as well for the exact Indication of Time only, as Astronomical, for showing the various Motions and Phenomena of planets and fixed stars, solving at sight several astronomical problems, besides all this a variety of Musical performances, and that to the greatest Nicety of Time and Tune with the usual graces; together with a wonderful imitation of several songs and Voices of an Aviary of Birds so natural that any who saw not the Instrument would be persuaded that it were in Reality what it only represents. He makes Musical Automata or Instruments of themselves to play exceeding well on the Flute, Flaggelet or Organ, Setts of Country dances, Minuets, Jiggs, and the Opera Tunes, or the most perfect imitation of the Aviary of Birds above mentioned, fit for the Diversion of those in places where a Musician is not at Hand. He makes also Organs performing of themselves Psalm Tunes with two, three, or more Voluntaries, very Convenient for Churches in remote Country Places where Organists cannot be had, or have sufficient Encouragement. And finally he mends Watches and Clocks in such sort that they will perform to an Exactness which possibly thro' a defect in finishing or other Accidents they formerly could not."

His reputation was world-wide, to judge from the appended extract from a letter of the period, quoted by W. J. Pinks:—

"Mr. P. has finished a fine musical clock, said to be a most exquisite piece of workmanship, and worth about £1,500, wch is to be sent over to ye King of France (Louis XIV.) and a fine organ to ye great Mogul, worth £300."

Pinchbeck exhibited his "astronomico-musical clocks," together with a variety of curious automata, at Bartholomew Fair, and the *Daily Journal* of 27th August 1729 announces that the Prince and Princess of Wales went to Bartholomew Fair to see his exhibition. Pinchbeck also attended Southwark Fair, and with Fawkes, a celebrated juggler and conjurer of that day, had a united "show." This may shock many who avail themselves of the fine arts of advertising in vogue to-day; but, however undignified it may have been, it cannot detract from his ability as a horologist.

Mr J. E. Hodgkin has a trade card, "Pinchbeck, senr., at Pinchbeck's Head in Fleet Street," a change of sign possibly induced by the popularity of Pinchbeck's name. Mr William Norman has a metal token; on the obverse, a bust of George II.; reverse, a bust in a frame, surrounded by representations of a walking-stick, snuff-box, signet ring, watch (or medal) attached to a double chain, and other articles, with the inscription, "Pinchbeck, senr., at Pinchbeck's Head in Fleet Street."

Pinchbeck gold was much used for watch cases and the like. It is an alloy of three parts of zinc to four of copper; but its composition was jealously guarded by the inventor, as may be gathered from the following extract from a letter quoted by W. J. Pinks:—

"Mr Xtopher Pinchbeck had a curious secret of new-invented metal wch so naturally resembles gold (as not to be distinguished by the most experienced eye), in colour, smell, and ductibility. Ye secret is communicated to his son."

Fig. 460. — CHRISTOPHER PINCHBECK, 1670-1732.

He died in 1732, at the age of sixty-two years, and was buried in St Dunstan's Church, Fleet Street. The annexed portrait [Fig. 460] is from an engraving by Faber after a painting by Isaac Whood.

Edward Pinchbeck, second son of Christopher, who was born in 1713, succeeded his father in the business, as is evident from a "Caution to the Public" which he inserted in the *Daily Post* of 9th July 1733.

"To prevent for the future the gross imposition that is daily put upon the publick by a great number of shopkeepers, hawkers, and pedlars, in and about this town, Notice is hereby given, that the ingenious Mr Edward Pinchbeck, at the Musical Clock, in Fleet Street, does not dispose of one grain of his curious metal, which so nearly resembles gold in colour, smell and ductility, to any person whatsoever; nor are the toys made of the said metal sold by any one person in England except himself." After recounting the various articles he makes from the alloy, the notice continues: "And in particular watches, plain and chased in so curious a manner as not to be distinguished by the nicest eye from real gold, and which are highly necessary for gentlemen and ladies when they travel, with several other fine pieces of workmanship of any sort made by the best hands. The said Mr Pinchbeck likewise makes astronomical and musical clocks; which new invented machines are so artfully contrived as to perform on several instruments great variety of musick composed by the most celebrated masters, with that exactitude, and in so beautiful a manner that scarce any hand can equal them. They likewise imitate the sweet harmony of birds to so great a perfection as not to be distinguished from nature itself. He also makes repeating and all other sorts of clocks and watches; particularly watches of a new invention, the mechanism of which is so simple, and the proportion so just, that come nearer truth than any others yet made."

Christopher Pinchbeck, eldest son of the first named Christopher, carried on a successful business as a clock and watch maker in Cockspur Street, being described as clockmaker to the king. In 1766 he is said to have bought from Ferdinand Berthoud, for George III., the first pocket watch made with a compensation curb. In 1781 he was elected as an honorary freeman of the Clockmakers' Company. He died at Cockspur Street in 1783, aged seventy-three, and was buried at St Martin's-in-the-Fields.

A Richard Pinchbeck, "toyman," who seems to have carried on business 1760-70, was probably a member of the same family.

PINCHBECK-NORTON

Fig. 461. — Square Four-Faced Clock by Eardley Norton, at Buckingham Palace.

THOMAS MUDGE.

In the *Gentleman's Magazine* of June 1765 it is stated that Pinchbeck and Norton had "just set up at the Queen's House a new complicated clock, having four dials, and amongst them it denoted clock and sun time, sunrise and setting for every day in the year in various places of the world, the Copernican motion of the planets, the ages and phases of the moon, high water at thirty-two different seaports, and the days of the week and the months of the year." Notwithstanding this announcement, it is very doubtful if Pinchbeck and Norton were ever in partnership. The probability is that each of them provided a clock, for there are still two astronomical clocks at Buckingham Palace, one by Christopher Pinchbeck the younger, and one by Eardley Norton. Each of these clocks chimes the quarters and has four enamel dials, one on each face of the square case. Pinchbeck's clock is the larger of the two, and has a handsome tortoiseshell case with silver spandrels at the corners of the dial. Norton's clock is shown in Fig. 461, for which I am indebted to Mr A. E. Rutherford. The dial on the left besides Greenwich mean time and solar time shows sunrise and sunset. A disc rotates once a day behind a rising and falling shutter. During the shortest days the shutter is at its greatest height and hides the sun from 3.53 P.M. till 8.5 A.M. After remaining stationary three days it falls gradually as required by the lengthening of the days. The right-hand dial is an orrery, having hands to represent the movement of Mercury, Venus, the Earth, Mars, Jupiter, and Saturn. The third dial is a calendar, and the fourth shows the age and phases of the moon, as well as the time of high and low tide at thirty-two places.

Thomas Mudge, born at Exeter in 1715, was the son of a clergyman, who kept a school at Bideford. Young Mudge showed so great a taste for mechanics, with a particular inclination for horology, that his father placed him as an apprentice with Graham. Here he made rapid progress in his art, and on the completion of his indentures took a leading position in the establishment. He was admitted to the freedom of the Clockmakers' Company in 1738, and called to the livery in 1766. At Graham's death, in 1751, Mudge succeeded to the business, as shown by the following from the

Started in 1741, 'H3' was not completed until 1760 partly perhaps because John Harrison's brother left London and returned to Barrow taking no further part in the project. The National Maritime Museum, Greenwich.

Daily Advertiser of 18th November 1751:— "Thomas Mudge, watchmaker, apprentice to the late Mr Graham, carries on the business in the same manner Mr Graham did, at the sign of the 'Dial and One Crown,' opposite the 'Bolt and Tun' in Fleet Street." Shortly after Mudge was established, Ferdinand the Sixth, of Spain, ordered an equation watch from a well-known English watchmaker, who, in consequence of the difficulties presented by this unusual construction, had recourse to Mudge. Ferdinand was a lover of mechanical work, and hearing of this circumstance, sent an order direct to Mudge to construct for him any piece of horology which he thought the most curious, and to charge for it whatever he chose. In response Mudge constructed a watch which showed true and apparent time, struck the hours, and repeated not only the hours and quarters, but the minutes also. The king set great store by this piece of workmanship, for which Mudge charged him 480 guineas. About 1755 he entered into partnership with William Dutton, another apprentice of Graham.

Mudge invented the lever escapement about 1765, but it appears only constructed two watches on this principle: one for Queen Charlotte, which performed admirably, the other for his patron and friend Count Bruhl, which, after several journeys, subjected to all the inconveniences of changes of position and quick travelling, kept time within a few seconds during several weeks. Mudge showed this escapement to Berthoud, when he was in

London in 1766, but he did not think so favourably of it as Margetts, Emery, and other English horologists did.

In 1765 he published "Thoughts on the Means of Improving Watches, particularly those for Use at Sea." From this time his attention was mainly directed to marine timekeepers, and in 1771, leaving the conduct of the Fleet Street business to Dutton, he quitted London, and went to reside at Plymouth, where he devoted himself to the construction of chronometers. The first one was sent to Greenwich Observatory in 1774, and afterwards to Baron Zach (who was astronomer to the Duke of Gotha), and lastly to Admiral Campbell, who took it a voyage to Newfoundland, when its performance was pronounced to be satisfactory. The Board of Longitude sent him £500, requesting him to continue his researches. Two other chronometers were sent to the Greenwich Observatory for trial in 1779.

Dr Maskelyne and Mudge could not agree. Maskelyne, who was Astronomer Royal, carried the Board of Longitude with him. It was asserted that chronometers by Arnold performed better than those of Mudge. Arnold had not submitted his chronometers for the Government reward, and therefore Mudge objected to the comparison. On the petition of Mudge, the House of Commons, in 1791, appointed as a committee to investigate the performance of his chronometers the Bishop of St David's, Mr Atwood, Mr De Luc, Mr Ramsden, Mr Edward Troughton, Mr Holmes, Mr Haley, and Mr Howells, the last three being watchmakers of repute. After much bickering, Mudge, in 1793, was paid £2,500, in addition to £500 he had already received as encouragement, although the Board of Longitude dissented from this course.

Mudge was often employed by George III. on delicate pieces of work, and on the death of George Lindesey, in 1776, was appointed watchmaker to the king. He was made free of the Clockmakers' Company in 1738, and admitted to the livery in 1766. The engraving in Fig. 462 is from a painting by Dance, executed for Count Bruhl in 1772. He died at his son's house in Walworth, on 14th November 1794.

Fig. 462. – THOMAS MUDGE, 1715-1794.

That an accomplished horologist and sound mechanic as Mudge seems to have been should, after his invention of the lever escapement, have persisted in the complication of a remontoire and vertical escapement for his marine timekeepers, must be ascribed to the perversity of genius.

The salient features of his chronometer are shown in the accompanying drawings. To obviate the difficulty of the compensating curb action interfering with the action of the regulating curb pins there are two balance-springs. The upper one for regulating has its stud c screwed to the balance-cock, the stud D of the lower spring, with which the pins of the compensation curb engage, being fixed to the upper plate of the chronometer. There are two *remontoire* springs, H and I, which are wound by the escape wheel G, and which alternately impel the balance through the pins a, b connected with the upper, and e, f with the lower one. The wheel and pallet actions will be understood from an examination of the lower figure, which is a plan. After the wheel tooth has given impulse to the pallet, and thereby wound the remontoire, it is locked on the projecting nib of the pallet till the balance in its excursion unlocks it, and allows the tooth on the opposite side of the wheel to impel the other pallet. The balance staff is cranked, and the pallets with the remontoires are pivoted partly in the

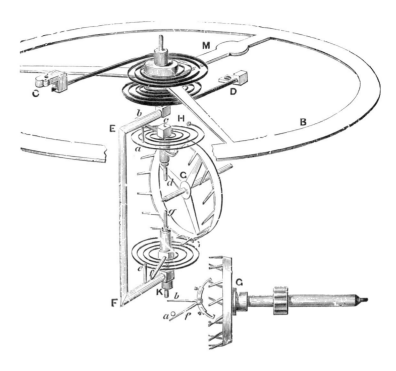

Fig. 463. — Mudge's Remontoire.

balance staff and partly in separate cocks, so that there are six pivots moving from the balance staff centre.

After Mudge's migration to Plymouth, the Fleet Street business seems to have reverted entirely to William Dutton, although the title of Mudge & Dutton was retained till 1794.

Thomas Mudge, junr., who was an attorney at 3 Old Square, Lincoln's Inn, engaged Messrs Howells, Pennington, Pendleton, and Coleman to produce chronometers on his father's plan; but they were too costly, and not successful. By 1799 the younger Mudge sold eleven at 150 guineas each, which did not pay him. Of others in course of manufacture some were finished by his coadjutors, and some by Messrs Barraud & Jamison. One of these instruments is in the Soane Museum, another at the Horological Institute, and another at the Guildhall Museum.

JOHN ARNOLD   This famous horologist was born in 1736, at Bodmin, in Cornwall, where he was apprenticed to his father, a watchmaker. While a youth he left home, and after a stay of some time in Holland he determined to try his fortune in London. At first he worked as a journeyman, but soon found an opportunity of establishing himself at Devereux Court, Fleet Street. One of his earliest acts here was to make an exceedingly small half-quarter repeating watch, which he had set in a ring, and presented to George III. in June 1764. When it is stated that the whole movement measured but little more than $1/3$ in. across, his ability as a fine workman and his marvellous sense of touch will be appreciated.* The escapement selected was a cylinder one, the cylinder, made of ruby and measuring 1/54 in. in diameter, being the first made of that material. The king accepted the repeater, and presented its maker with 500 guineas as an acknowledgment of his surpassing skill.

Arnold's achievement at once brought him into notice, and from that time his future success was assured.

It is said that the Empress of Russia offered Arnold 1,000 guineas for a duplicate of the repeater made for George III., but the offer was declined, not that Arnold doubted his ability to produce it, but because he desired the miniature timekeeper to remain unique.

Arnold now turned his attention seriously to the problem which was engaging the thoughts of leading horologists here and in France. John Harrison had already fulfilled the conditions laid down by the Board of Longitude, and thus practically secured the £20,000 offered by Parliament in 1714 for a timekeeper sufficiently exact to ascertain the longitude within certain limits. A subsequent Act of Parliament, however, devoted a further £10,000 as a stimulus to continued research and improvement. Mudge was already in the field, and seemed bent on adhering to the remontoire principle somewhat on Harrison's plan. But it was clear to other minds that a nearer approach to perfection might be obtained by a chronometer of altogether a different character to the one invented by Harrison.

One of Arnold's first essays was a chronometer which Captain Cook took with him in the "Resolution" on his second voyage, in 1772. Two other timekeepers of Arnold's were on board the "Adventure." Mr J. U. Poole, who has examined these early examples, two of which are the property of the Royal Society, states that they have plain circular balances with flat balance-springs acted on by a compensation curb; the escapements are a compound of the lever and the spring detent, and they beat half seconds, the workmanship being very rough compared with the finish exacted in the present day. It seems certain that a timekeeper of Larcum Kendall, which was also carried on the "Resolution," performed better than those of Arnold did.

Arnold was not to be daunted. He profited by experience, and devised the helical form of balance-spring, and a form of compensation balance. The spring, as shown in the sketch [Fig. 464], is very similar to the one now in most general use for marine chronometers, but the balance was rather a complicated affair. These components he patented in 1775 (Patent No. 1,113), and his specification described compensation to be effected by a

Fig. 464.

* According to the *Annual Register* for 1764, the whole of this repeater, composed of 120 parts, weighed but 5 dwts. 7¾ gr., the following being the weight of the principal items: The movement, complete, is 2 dwts. 2⅛ gr.; great wheel and fusee, 2¾ gr.; second wheel and pinion, ¾ gr.; barrel and mainspring, 3½ gr.; third wheel and pinion, 1/9 gr.; fourth wheel and pinion, 1/10 gr.; cylinder, wheel, and pinion, 1/16 gr.; balance-spring, cylinder, and collet, ⅔ gr.; the balance-spring, 1/300 gr.; the chain, ½ gr.; barrel and mainspring, 1¾ gr.; great wheel and ratchet, 1 gr.; second wheel and pinion, 1/7 gr.; third wheel and pinion, ⅛ gr.; fourth wheel and pinion, 1/9 gr.; fly wheel and pinion, 1/17 gr.; fly pinion, 1/20 gr.; hour hammer, ½ gr.; quarter hammer, ½ gr.; rack, chain, and pulley, 1⅓ gr.; quarter and half-quarter rack, ⅔ gr.; the quarter and half-quarter snail and cannon pinion, ⅔ gr.; the all-or-nothing piece, ½ gr.; two motion wheels, 1 gr.; steel dial-plate with gold figures, 3½ gr.; the hour snail and star, ½ and 1/16 gr.

brass and steel volute fixed at its inner end to the collet of the balance, and actuating weighted rods by means of a lever attached to its outer end. Some years later he adopted the simple circular bimetallic-rim balance practically as now used, except that he soldered the brass and steel together and formed the circular rim with pliers, whereas Earnshaw first turned a steel disc and then melted the brass on to its periphery, a plan which, according to Rees, was introduced by Brockbank.

In May, 1782 Arnold patented his improved detent escapement (Patent No. 1,328). This is practically the chronometer escapement of to-day, which was almost simultaneously invented by Thomas Earnshaw, except that in Arnold's escapement the escape wheel teeth, instead of being flat where they gave impulse, were epicycloidal curves, as shown in Fig. 465; but they required oiling, and were consequently abandoned. While Earnshaw's wheel is locked on the points of the teeth and the detent moves away from the centre of the wheel to unlock, Arnold's locked on the heel of the tooth and the detent moved towards the centre of the wheel to unlock, the sunk part of the body of the wheel allowing the locking stone to pass.

Arnold was now admitted to be a very successful chronometer maker, but he still continued his investigations, and made countless experiments with a view to improvements.

Some time after 1764 Arnold quitted Devereux Court for Adelphi Buildings, which is the address given in his patent specifications, and in an account of the going of a pocket chronometer, in 1781, it is stated to have been compared with the regulator at his house in the Adelphi. About 1785

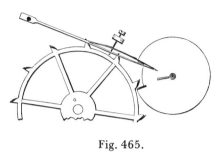

Fig. 465.

In 1753 Harrison's principal workman, John Jeffreys, made to Harrison's design a pocket watch which incorporated many features of his last marine timepiece 'H4' shown here. This watch completed by John and his son William in 1759 has Harrison's own form of verge escapement with diamond pallets, maintaining power, temperature compensation, and jewelled pivot holes. In the general use of these throughout a watch Harrison was something of a pioneer. National Maritime Museum, Greenwich.

he removed to 112 Cornhill, where he carried on business until his death, his son being admitted into partnership during the latter part of the time. Arnold & Son also had a chronometer manufactory at Chigwell in Essex.

In a book of "Certificates and Rates of Going," which he published in 1791, he gives the price of his large marine chronometers as from 60 to 80 guineas; pocket chronometers, in gold cases, 120 guineas, and in silver, 100 guineas; repeaters from 150 guineas for the best kind in gold, down to 25 guineas for the commonest, in silver cases.

The rival claims of Mudge, Arnold, and Earnshaw to the rewards offered for the best chronometer were submitted to a Select Committee of the House of Commons, assisted by a committee of experts, and eventually each was awarded £3,000; but a moiety of Arnold's portion was not paid till after his death, when it was received by his son. Arnold had not laid claim to the reward when depositing his chronometers at the Greenwich Observatory; but their good performance was made use of by Maskelyne as a reason why Judge's claim should not be recognised.

Fig. 466. – JOHN ARNOLD, 1736-1799.

Fig. 467. – JOHN ARNOLD, HIS WIFE AND SON.

Arnold told the committee he had then made upwards of 900 timekeepers, but never two alike, so long as he saw room for any possible improvements; adding, "I have twenty number ones."

According to Beillard, Arnold's son John Roger was apprenticed in Paris to Breguet. Some time ago, by favour of Mr Hurcomb, I examined a Tourbillon chronometer in an engine-turned silver case, with square edges, which appears to have been the original model for the celebrated Tourbillon of Breguet on a chronometer by Arnold. The foot of the balance-cock was especially wide, and bore the following inscription:— "Premier régulateur à tourbillon de Breguet réuni à un des premiers ouvrages d'Arnold. Hommages de Breguet à la mémoire révèrée d'Arnold offert à son fils. An 1808." The workmanship throughout was splendid, and the graceful tribute to Arnold's genius of course enhanced the value of the piece.

John Arnold was admitted as a member of the Clockmakers' Company in 1783, and chosen on the livery 1796. He died at Well Hall, near Eltham, Kent, in 1799. The portrait (Fig. 466) is from an engraving by Susan Ester Reid, after a painting by R. Davy.

At South Kensington is a painting showing John Arnold, his wife and son, together with a label stating that Arnold was assisted in his profession by his wife. A reproduction of this group is given in Fig. 467.

John Roger Arnold seemed to have inherited neither the horological ability nor the commercial aptitude of his father whom he succeeded. He was admitted to the Clockmakers' Company in 1796, and became master in 1817. In 1820 he removed from Cornhill to 27 Cecil Street, and from thence, in 1830, to 84 Strand, where he entered into a partnership agreement for ten years with E. J. Dent, and during this period the business flourished; but immediately the term expired Dent set up for himself at 82 Strand, carrying with him the confidence of most of the customers of the late firm. John R. Arnold continued at 84 Strand till 1843, when he died.

To Thomas Earnshaw, who was born at Ashton-under-Lyne in 1749, must be ascribed the merit of having devised the chronometer escapement and compensation balance precisely as they are now used.

The comparison of Arnold's and Earnshaw's escapement and balance just given in the sketch of the former's career may be referred to and need not be repeated.

That Earnshaw was a true horologist by intuition is evident. He is said to have been honest and straightforward, but somewhat rugged in his manner. There are, however, but few details of his life to be obtained. He was apprenticed to a watchmaker when fourteen years of age, and seems to have come to London immediately on completion of his indentures. After working for some time as a finisher of verge and cylinder watches, he taught himself watch jewelling and then cylinder- escapement making, using ruby cylinders and steel wheels. He married early in life, and the necessity of providing for a family out of his earnings seems to have hampered him considerably in carrying out his projects.

To improve the chronometer escapement he, in 1781, conceived the idea of substituting a spring detent for the pivoted form as applied by Le Roy and other French artists. After showing the new method to John Brockbank, for whom he worked, he took it to Thomas Wright of the Poultry, another of his customers, and agreed that when a watch with the device was finished, Wright should patent it. But the latter kept the watch for a year to observe its going, and did not obtain the patent till 1783. In the meantime John Arnold had lodged a patent specification, claiming the same thing as his invention. To the end of his life Earnshaw lost no opportunity of declaring in emphatic language his belief that John Brockbank had divulged his plan to Arnold. According to Earnshaw's account his own actions were always marked by trusting simplicity, though his confidence was continually betrayed. The patent cost Wright £100, and as all negotiations with Brockbank, Haley, Wm. Hughes, Best, and other leading watchmakers to purchase a share of it failed, watches with the new escapement were manufactured for various people on payment to Wright of a royalty of £1 each. The first dozen were not a success; the impulse roller being too small with relation to the escape wheel, they were liable to stop. Earnshaw

THOMAS EARNSHAW.

Fig. 468. — THOMAS EARNSHAW, 1749-1829.

Larcum Kendall's copy (K1) of John Harrison's fourth marine time-keeper. An apprentice of John Jeffreys who made Harrison's own pocket watch, Kendall (1721-1790) contracted with the Board of Longitude to produce an exact replica of H4 for £450. This he began in 1761, completing the task in 1769 and the machine performed extremely well being tried by Captain James Cook during his second voyage in H.M.S. Resolution. Cook praised the watch greatly. Subsequently Kendall made two further marine time-keepers in an attempt to simplify the mechanism and so reduce the costs of production. Neither of thse later machines were as successful as his first. Thereafter, with his remuneration from the attempt steadily diminishing, Kendall seems to have abandoned the enterprise. National Maritime Museum, Greenwich.

discovered the fault and with better proportions brought the new escapement into favour for pocket watches. The earlier ones were stamped [Wright's patent] in small characters, a form of marking which was dropped after a few years.

Dr Maskelyne, the Astronomer Royal, having tried one of his watches in 1789, advised Earnshaw to apply to the Board of Longitude for permission to submit timekeepers for official trial at Greenwich Observatory. Five of his watches were tested there in 1791, and then he obtained an order for two chronometers, and these were deposited at the Observatory on 1st January 1798.

In 1794 or 1795 Earnshaw succeeded to the business which had been carried on for some years by Wm. Hughes at 119 High Holborn, one door east of the turning then known as King Street but now called Southampton Row. The shop referred to was pulled down when the thoroughfare was widened in 1901.

The committee of investigation appointed to consider the claims of chronometer improvers awarded Earnshaw £500 in 1801 on account of his inventions, and in 1803 a further £2,500, making his total reward £3,000. Rightly or wrongly, he was of opinion that he was not well treated, and in 1808 issued "An Appeal to the Public," declaring he was entitled to more pre-eminent recognition. The engraving in Fig. 468 is copied from one by S. Bellin after a portrait by Sir M. A. Shee.

Earnshaw also made a number of clocks. For the first one, which was ordered by the Archbishop of Armagh, he was paid £150 and an additional £100 for going to Armagh to fix it.

He died at Chenies Street in 1829, but the business was carried on for some years by his son, first at the Holborn premises and afterwards at Fenchurch Street.

ASCERTAINING THE LONGITUDE AT SEA. DEVELOPMENT AND USE OF THE MARINE CHRONOMETER.

The discovery of America, in 1492 caused considerable attention to be paid to the question of finding the longitude at sea, for it was evident that if ocean navigation was to be carried on with anything like safety, some more certain means of ascertaining the position of a ship than was possible by dead reckoning would have to be provided.

Columbus had not an azimuth compass, nor a sextant, nor a chronometer, nor a patent log, and he, and his immediate successors, were several months making the voyage across the Atlantic, while the early voyagers took about three years to circumnavigate the globe. Even in the middle of the eighteenth century Commodore Anson, in his celebrated voyage round the world, had no safe guide. When he rounded Cape Horn he unexpectedly made the land on the western side, and found himself in consequence three hundred miles more to the east than he expected, and so his voyage was delayed. Then, again, he wanted to make the island of Juan Fernandez to recruit the crew. He got into the latitude of the island and thought he was to the west of it, but he was really to the east; he ran eastward and made the mainland of America, and turned round and had to sail westward again before he got to the island.

With a sextant the latitude may be readily ascertained by measuring the altitude above the horizon of certain of the heavenly bodies and reducing the observations by reference to tables.

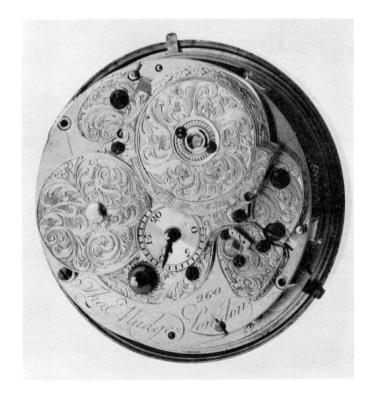

The watch made by Thomas Mudge for the King of Spain, 1755. Only the movement of this complicated piece survives. It has a white enamel dial and a centre seconds hand mounted between the hour and minutes hands. The cock is of the bridge type, probably for greater security, and there are two balance springs one having curb compensation the other a bimetallic regulator. There is a verge escapement and a one minute remontoir which supplies power to the train and obviates the need for maintaining power. Worshipful Company of Clockmakers.

An ebony veneered oak-cased 8-day striking and repeating bracket clock, typical in style of a good quality mid-18th century clock, signed 'Thomas Mudge, London'. Break arch case and dial with applied gilt brass mask spandrels, with strike/silent dial in the arch. The minutes hand is a modern replacement. Originally the clock, which has been drastically altered, seems to have had a silent escapement with lenticular pendulum and quarter repeating work similar to that of Graham. This similarity suggests that the clock was made during Mudge's earliest period of work. At a later date, the original escapement was replaced by a semi-dead-beat escapement, the fitting of which forced the repeating work to be removed.

Finding the longitude is not so simple a matter, owing to the rotation of the earth on its axis, and the apparent change of places of the stars. As early as 1530 Gemma Frisius suggested solar observations and a timekeeper as a possible solution of the problem. The captain of a ship can readily ascertain the instant of noon at any place by observation of the sun, and so it is clear that if he had an instrument that could be depended on to show him the time at Greenwich or any other starting-point, the calculation of his longitude would be an easy one. But the most important adjunct, an accurate timekeeper, was wanting.

In 1598 the matter had risen to such importance that the King of Spain offered a reward of one hundred thousand crowns for any invention which should gain that object. The rulers of one or two other maritime States followed his example, but all without effect.

Early in the seventeenth century John Baptist Morin proposed the preparation of tables with a view of making lunar observations available. Although Morin's suggestion was ridiculed at the time, it has become a perfectly practicable method. The moon is nearer the earth than the stars, and consequently appears to occupy a different position with regard to them when viewed from different points on the surface of the globe. And as the moon moves so swiftly from night to night through the sky, she shifts her position with respect to the stars very rapidly. If the sailor be provided with a book giving the distances of the moon from certain fixed stars for certain hours of say Greenwich time on every day of the year, he can, in any position in which he may be, by observing the position of the moon, secure a datum from which the longitude may be deduced. But even after the position of the moon with relation to these fixed stars had been ascertained, and the voluminous tables provided, somewhat tedious calculations are necessary to reduce the elements afforded by the observations obtained; besides which, if the lunar method alone is relied on, there is the disadvantage that the moon is not always visible. However, Morin's suggestion led to nothing at the time, and the greater simplicity of solar observations induced most investigators to consider the possibility of providing a correct timekeeper. The first attempts to supply the want seem to have been made by Huygens and Hooke.

Huygens' marine clock, constructed about 1660, suspended in gymbals and actuated by a spring, was controlled by a pendulum. It was tried at sea by a Scottish captain named Holmes with but moderate success. A marine pendulum clock constructed under the direction of Dr Hook, was tried by Lord Kincardine in 1662, only to demonstrate the futility of relying on the pendulum as a regulator when tossed about in a ship on the ocean.

In the course of a paper he read before the Royal Society in 1662, Dr Hooke said: "The Lord Kincardine did resolve to make some trial what might be done by carrying a pendulum clock to sea, for which end he contrived to make the watch to be moved by a spring instead of a weight, and then, making the case of the clock very heavy with lead, he suspended it underneath the deck of the ship by a ball and socket of brass, making the pendulum but short, namely, to vibrate half seconds; and that he might be the better enabled to judge of the effect of it, he caused two of the same kind of pendulum clocks to be made, and suspended them both pretty near the middle of the vessel underneath the decks. This done, having first adjusted them to go equal to one another, and pretty near to the true time, he caused them first to move parallel to one another, that is, in the plane of the length of the ship, and afterwards he turned one to move in a plane at right angles with the former; and in both cases it was found by trials made at sea (at which I was present) that they would vary from one another, though not very much." Dr Hooke concludes by saying that "they might be of very good use to the sea if some further contrivances about them were thought upon and put into practice."

In 1714 the British Parliament, on the recommendation of a commission, of which Sir Isaac Newton was a member, passed "an Act for providing public reward for such person or persons as shall discover the longitude at sea." This Act ordained "that any offered method or invention on this subject shall, in the first instance, be investigated by a specially selected body of practical men, who may then recommend it to the Royal Commissioners constituting the Board of Longitude." The award was fixed at £10,000 for a method or invention to define on a voyage from England to any of the West India Islands and back the longitude within one degree,

One of Thomas Mudge's three famous marine time-keepers signed on the backplate 'Tho Mudge 1777'. Among the most celebrated of all marine timekeepers, although they did not perform particularly well, they are remarkable examples of complexity and workmanship. Circular plated movement with bridge cock and Mudge's constant force escapement (a development of the verge) and jewelled pallets the whole being mounted in an independent assembly screwed to the back plate. All the pivots are jewelled. There is a three arm balance with two balance springs one above and one below the balance, meantime regulation being effected on the upper balance spring and temperature compensation on the lower. There is a fusee with Harrison's maintaining power. The dial plate is of gilt brass with enamelled chapter ring surrounded by decorative silver appliqué mounts. The whole machine is contained in a drum shaped box of brass with a green shagreen band. Christie, Manson & Wood Ltd.

£15,000 to define the longitude within two-thirds of a degree, and £20,000 to within half a degree.

The Paris Academy of Sciences in 1720 offered a prize for the best description of a suitable timekeeper. This was won by Massy, a Dutch clockmaker. In 1721 Sully produced a clock which he laid before the Academy in 1724. It had a vertical balance, which from the description seems to have been a pedulum with cycloidal guides. This timekeeper promised success till tested in the open sea, when its performance, like that of the preceding instruments, was found to be unsatisfactory. Sully, however, seemed to be on the high road to success, and he was engaged on another timekeeper just before his untimely decease.

In 1675 Greenwich Observatory was founded. Flamstead was instructed to rectify the tables of the motions of the heavens and the places of the fixed stars. He made a large star catalogue, and many observations on the moon and other bodies, and the results of his lunar observations were taken in hand by the philosophers of the time, Newton and others. The construction of lunar tables, and to predict the place of the moon with sufficient accuracy for the adoption of the lunar method of longitude, was a very serious task.

It was not until 1767 that Maskelyne, a succeeding Astronomer-Royal, founded the "Nautical Almanac," and gave therein, for the first time in any country, distances of the moon from certain fixed stars, that the lunar method came into use. In the early part of the nineteenth century the reliability of the chronometer was established, and since then the chronometer method had gradually superseded the "lunar." In the "Nautical Almanac" the lunar distances are still retained, and circumstances occasionally arise when the mariner is glad to have recourse to them.

Stimulated by the prospect of obtaining the reward offered by the British Parliament, John Harrison, after thirty years of unremitting labours and vicissitudes, recounted in the sketch of his life (see pp.254-264), fulfilled, in 1761, the conditions laid down by the Board of Longitude. Thoroughly as Harrison deserved the reward he so laboriously earned, it is curious to note that of all his inventions embodied in his timekeeper, the maintaining spring in the fusee is the only one that has survived.

Other Acts of Parliament relating to the subject were passed in 1741, 1753, and 1774. The last, repealing all former Acts, offered £5,000 for a timekeeper determining the longitude to or within one degree; £7,500 for determining the same to within 48 geographical miles; and £10,000 for a determination at or within half a degree. Further, to obtain the smallest portion of the reward, the error of the timekeeper was not to exceed more than four minutes in six months.

Mudge, the inventor of the lever escapement and an experienced horologist, with almost incredible infatuation, proceeded on the lines adopted by Harrison. Though he produced a superior instrument to Harrison's (see p.268), he allowed Arnold (p.269) and Earnshaw (p.273) to develop the marine chronometer of to-day.

The investigations of Berthoud and Pierre Le Roy were nearly contemporaneous with those of Mudge, Arnold, and Earnshaw. Each of the French masters designed a detached escapement, and while Berthoud used a gridiron arrangement of brass and steel to compensate for temperature

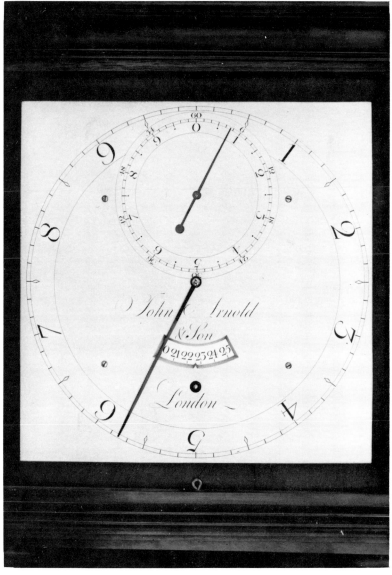

The regulator made in 1793 by John Arnold for Sir George Shuckburgh after the pattern of Tompion's degree clock. In the layout of the dial the only difference is that the subsidiary seconds dial has two sets of figures. The inner circle, like those of Tompion, indicates minutes and every ten seconds, the outer circle the actual beats of the pendulum up to sixty. The pendulum is a five bar grid-iron of steel and a compound of silver, brass, and zinc. Dead-beat escapement with jewelled pallets, and jewelled pallet and escape wheel arbors. Of five months duration, the clock has Harrison's maintaining power and stopwork on the barrel. The weight is unusual in being wide and flat with a slight taper. National Maritime Museum, Greenwich.

A large, highly finished, well-made watch, in plain gold pair cases, H.M. 1784, and signed 'Thomas Wright in the Poultry', number 2228. On the underside of the dial plate is scratched 'P & P Sept 18th 1784', the initials of the watch finisher Philip Pine. The watch however is of great interest being in all respects similar to the work of Thomas Earnshaw and almost certainly made for him by Wright with his spring detent escapement and temperature compensated balance. It may be noted that Earnshaw claimed to have developed his temperature compensation in this same year 1784. For a detailed description see Andrew Crisford in Antiquarian Horology *(June 1976) pp.785-788. Bobinet Ltd.*

errors, and fitted his timekeeper with two balances geared together, Le Roy experimented with a balance composed of two mercurial thermometers, the bulbs being furthest from the centre of motion and the ends turned inwards. No one could question the ability of Berthoud and P. Le Roy, but in executing their respective conceptions the Englishmen showed superior judgment. The French marine timekeepers were by comparison very unwieldy, which may perhaps be traced to the influence of M. Daniel Bernoulli, an eminent mathematician, who, says P. Le Roy, "wishes marine watches to be as large as good clocks are commonly made, that the pieces may be worked with greater exactness, and that their defects, if there are any, may be more easily perceived. This is nearly what I have practised in the new marine watch." However, the simplicity of construction and the compactness of Arnold and Earnshaw's chronometers have ensured the general adoption of their models.

VULLIAMY
This noted family of clockmakers was of Swiss origin. Justin Vulliamy emigrated from Switzerland and settled in London early in the eighteenth century. He became connected with Benjamin Gray, of Pall Mall, whose daughter he married, and with whom he subsequently entered into partnership. Watches of very fine quality, inscribed "Benj. Gray, Just.

Fig. 469. — Clock by Justin Vulliamy, Windsor Castle.

Fig. 470

Vulliamy," are occasionally to be met with. A choice example fetched £120. 15s. when the Hawkins collection was dispersed by auction in 1895. The case of gold was enamelled in colours with figures in a garden, birds and flowers; the outer case was of gold and crystal, and had a diamond thumbpiece to press back the locking spring. A fine watch by them, with the hall mark for 1757, formerly the property of Lieut. James Stockham, who commanded the "Thunderer" at the battle of Trafalgar, is in the Guildhall Museum. In the Wetherfield collection are two long-case clocks of their make, and two by Justin Vulliamy who carried on the business at Gray's death. Benjamin Gray was appointed as clockmaker to George II., and the family of Vulliamy held the office of clockmaker to the reigning sovereign till the death of Benjamin Lewis Vulliamy in 1854.

Benjamin Vulliamy, the son of Justin, was much favoured and consulted by George III. on mechanical subjects, especially in connection with Kew Observatory, which was a hobby of the king.

Benjamin Lewis Vulliamy, born in 1780, was noted for the exactness and excellent finish of his work, in both clocks and watches. The large clock at the old Post Office, St Martin's-le-Grand, and one at Christ Church, Oxford, are among the public timekeepers by him. He took an active interest in the Clockmakers' Company, of which he was five times master between 1821 and 1848. In 1849 the Court presented him with a piece of plate in recognition of his services to the Company. He wrote several pamphlets on trade subjects. One of them, on the construction of the dead-beat escapement for clocks, advocated the turning of the pallets for ensuring greater exactness.

Specimens of Vulliamy's handiwork abound at the royal palaces, and in many instances clocks originally by other makers now contain Vulliamy movements either wholly or in part. All those I have illustrated are at Windsor Castle.

On the mantelpiece of Queen Victoria's dining-room was a chiming clock by Justin Vulliamy, in a plain blackwood broken arch case as shown in Fig. 469. It has a white enamel dial, and was chosen by Her Majesty for the situation by reason of its particular legibility. The subsidiary dials in the upper corners are for guidance in actuating the rise and fall of the pendulum and strike-silent hands.

Fig. 471.

A pocket chronometer signed 'Robert Tomlin Watchmaker to the King London No. 1400'. The movement has Earnshaw's spring detent escapement, a plain steel balance and a bridge cock with diamond endstone. The movement which is well finished and executed is of the greatest interest since it is the only example of a watch marked 'Wright's patent' (p.274) so far found. The mark however is in a somewhat different form from that given by Britten. It is placed very discreetly on an inner plate and is not visible from the outside. The Trustees of the British Museum.

A clock by Vulliamy in an uncommon and well-executed case of white marble, with two boys of biscuit china and particularly realistic building materials, is shown in Fig. 470.

The Presence Chamber contains a sumptuous mantelpiece of white marble, a magnificent piece of sculpture by J. Bacon, R.A., executed in 1790, and incorporating the clock case as seen in Fig. 471.

The clock is by Vulliamy, the fine enamelled dial, slightly convex in form, measures about 10 in. across. Under the clock is the inscription by Cowper:—

QUAE LENTA ACCEDIT QUAM VELOX PRAETERIT HORA
UT CAPIAS PATIENS ESTO SED ESTO VIGIL‘,

which Hayley happily rendered:—

> "Slow comes the hour, its passing speed how great!
> Waiting to seize it — Vigilantly wait."

Fig. 472.

In the Grand Reception-room is a clock with a movement by Vulliamy and the peculiar case in the Chinese style shown in Fig. 472. This and the companion case which contains an aneroid barometer were made to the order of George IV. for the Pavilion at Brighton, and removed to Windsor on the accession of Queen Victoria.

A fine chiming clock by Vulliamy, with case in the Louis XIV. style, and dating from about 1820, which is in the Zuccerelli room at Windsor Castle, is shown in Fig. 473. The outline of the case is excellent, the surface of the black shell is inlaid with brass and decorated with bold but rather coarsely chased ormolu mounts.

On the landing by the Administration Offices of the Castle is the long-case clock by Vulliamy shown in Fig. 474. It is well made, with jewelled pallets, and is now used as a standard timekeeper. The dial is of enamel with gilt spandrels. The case though plain is of choice mahogany and has an effective appearance. A long-case clock by him with square silvered dial and case very similar to that in Fig. 474 is among the Wetherfield collection.

Over the state entrance in the Quadrangle of Windsor Castle was formerly a clock by Joseph Knibb, which B. L. Vulliamy replaced in 1829 by one, the dial and surroundings of which are shown in Fig. 475. Though plain, the dial and hands are certainly an example of the best style of that period.

Fig. 473. — Chiming Clock
by Vulliamy.

CHARLES CLAY

A pocket chronometer by Thomas Earnshaw number 580/3023 in a plain pair case H.M. 1801. The plain movement, in typical Earnshaw style, has his spring detent escapement, sugar tongs compensation, and a flat steel oversprung balance. Sotheby Parke Bernet & Co.

When the new Houses of Parliament were being built, the architect, Mr Barry, applied to Mr B. L. Vulliamy for information respecting the construction of the clock tower, and this circumstance, together with Vulliamy's influential position in the horological world, led people to think he would make the clock, as indeed it was intended by Barry and others that he should. But Vulliamy objected to the conditions laid down by Mr Denison, who was commissioned by the Government to draw up a specification in conjunction with the Astronomer Royal, and, backed by the Clockmakers' Company, declared the stipulations to be too onerous and unnecessary. Vulliamy submitted drawings of what he considered the clock should be like, and this design Denison ridiculed as being merely suited for a village clock of the old style, and quite unworthy of the national timekeeper. Denison's masterful attitude prevailed, and Vulliamy had to succumb, feeling, there is no doubt, the keenest mortification at being ousted from the proud position of leading clockmaker. It must be admitted that his talent lay rather in the perfection of details than in comprehensive departures from the beaten track. He died in January 1854. The appended portrait [Fig. 476] is from a miniature at the Horological Institute.

Justin Theodore Vulliamy, who was warden of the Clockmakers' Company from 1820 to 1822, appears to have had no other connection with the horological trades. He was, I believe, a brother of B. L. Vulliamy.

A remarkably handsome musical clock by Charles Clay, which stood for many years in a manor house in Suffolk, is shown in Fig. 477. It is 8 ft. 6 in. in height, the case being divided into two portions, the upper part of which is of Amboyna wood relieved with heavy brass mounts well finished. In the arch of the dial are shown the age of the moon, the day of the month, and the following list of tunes played by the clock:—

"(1) Mr Arcangelo Corelli's Twelfth Concerto, 1st Adagio, 2nd Allegro, 3rd Saraband, 4th Jigg.
"(2) The fugue in the overture of Ariadne."

On the hour circle is engraved the maker's name, "Charles Clay, London." The pedestal, which is of Spanish mahogany and Amboyna wood, contains

Clay's chiming machine with twenty-one bells. It is a fine piece of mechanism, driven by an ordinary chiming weight, though the barrel is fully 12 in. in diameter. Dampers are used to avoid vibration of the bells one with another, and by an ingenious contrivance the music starts immediately the clock finishes striking. The fly is attached to an endless screw, which ensures smooth running. This clock is apparently referred to in the following extract from the *Weekly Journal,* 8th May 1736:- "On Monday Mr Clay, the inventor of the machine watches in the Strand, had the honour of exhibiting to her Majesty at Kensington his surprising musical clock, which gave uncommon satisfaction to all the Royal Family present, at which time her Majesty, to encourage so great an artist, was pleased to order fifty guineas to be expended for numbers in the intended raffle, by which we hear Mr Clay intends to dispose of this said beautiful and most complete piece of machinery."

JAMES FERGUSON

James Ferguson was born at Keith, Banffshire, in 1710. He lived for some years at No. 4 Bolt Court, Fleet Street, where he died in 1776, and was buried in Marylebone churchyard. Among other conceptions of this celebrated astronomer and mechanician is a clock contrived with only three wheels and two pinions. It is shown in Fig. 478. The hours are engraved on a plate fitting friction tight on the great wheel arbor; the minute hand is attached to the centre wheel arbor, and a thin plate divided into 240 equal parts is fitted on the escape wheel arbor, and shows the seconds through a slit in the dial. The clock has a seconds pendulum. The number of teeth in the escape wheel is higher than is desirable, and the weight of the thin plate or ring in the escape wheel arbor is objectionable, though it might now be made of aluminium, vulcanite, or other very light material.

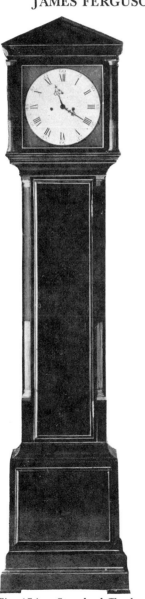

Fig. 474. — Standard Clock at Windsor Castle.

Fig. 475.

Ferguson also designed a curious and useful clock for showing the time of high and low water, the state of the tides at any time of the day, and the

Fig. 476. — BENJAMIN LEWIS
VULLIAMY, 1780-1854.

Fig. 477. — Musical Clock
by Charles Clay.

phases of the moon. The outer circle of the dial in the left-hand corner of Fig. 479 is divided into twice twelve hours, with halves and quarters, and the inner circle into 29.5 equal parts for showing the age of the moon, each day standing under the time of the moon coming to the meridian on that day. There are two hands on the end of the arbor coming through this dial, which go round in 29 days 12 hours 45 minutes, and these hands are set as far apart as the time of high water at the place the clock is to serve differs from the time the moon comes to the meridian; so that, by looking at this dial, one may see at what time the moon will be on the meridian and at what time it will be high water. On the dial in the right-hand corner all the different states of the tide are marked. The highest points on the shaded ellipse represent high, and the lowest, low water. The index travels round this dial in the time that the moon revolves from the meridian to the meridian again. In the arch above the dials a blue plate, to represent the sea, rises and falls as the tides do, and over this a ball, half black and half white, shows the phases of the moon.

The mechanism as it would appear at the back of the dial is shown in Fig. 480. A wheel of 30 fixed to the hour wheel on the centre arbor goes round once in twelve hours, and gears with a wheel of 60, on whose arbor a wheel of 57 drives wheel of 59, the arbor of which carries the hand for the right-hand dial. On this arbor is an elliptical cam which carries and lets down the tide plate twice in 24 hours 50.5 minutes. On the arbor of the wheel of 57 is a pinion of 16, driving a wheel of 70, on whose arbor is a pinion of 8 driving an idle wheel of 40. This idle wheel is merely to reverse the direction of the wheel of 54 with which it gears, and which carries the hands for the left-hand dial. The moon is driven from this last arbor by means of a pair of mitre wheels.

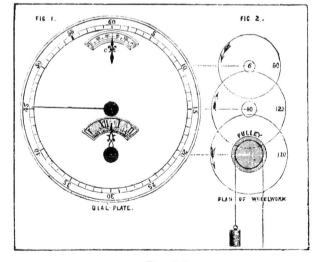

Fig. 478.

SMEATON — FRANKLIN

Two clocks by John Smeaton the eminent engineer are preserved at Trinity House, and he is said to have devised a clock having but three wheels and two pinions, the dial of which is shown in Fig. 481, though Rees attributed the design to Dr Franklin. Possibly Ferguson, Franklin, and Smeaton were all taken with the idea of a three-wheel movement, and each embodied it. The late R. J. Lecky had a clock on this plan made about 1820

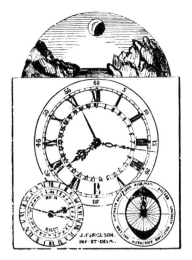

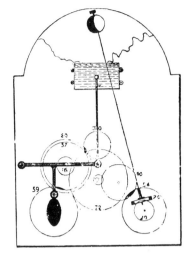

Fig. 479.　　　　　　　　　　　Fig. 480.

by Austen, of Dublin. It had a case of slate, the back, to which the pendulum was hung, being a single slab 1¼ in. thick. It was a thoroughly good clock and Mr Lecky converted it from a thirty-hour to an eight-day by providing a weight and counterpoise fitted as double sheaved blocks, the sheaves being contained in the body of the weights, and making the cord endless, on Huygens' principle illustrated in Fig. 445. Mr R. J. Lecky's son, Mr John Lecky, who now owns the clock, tells me it is still an excellent timekeeper.

Dr Herbert N. Evans has a bracket or table clock by Grant, with a similar

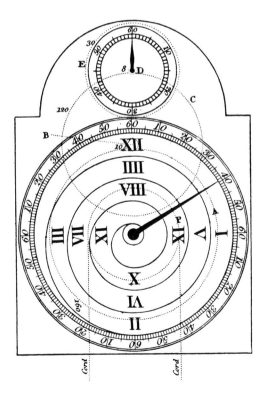

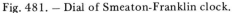

Fig. 481. — Dial of Smeaton-Franklin clock.　　　Fig. 482. — Clock by Grant.

A portrait of Dr Nevil Maskelyne (1732-1811). Educated at Trinity College, Cambridge, of which he became fellow in 1757, Maskelyne assisted James Bradley in astronomical observations as a young man and was then sent to St Helena to observe the transit of Venus in 1761. F.R.S. in 1758, he was appointed Astronomer Royal in 1765. At Greenwich he established the Nautical Almanac and with only one assistant made about 90,000 observations which were published between 1776 and 1811. It was to Maskelyne that the task of testing the various timepieces submitted for reward from the Board of Longitude fell and although he attracted some obloquy from disappointed applicants, he seems to have carried out the task fairly and impartially. National Maritime Museum, Greenwich.

One of the two known survivals of the work of George Margetts at Old Woodstock whence he derived. Only the dial of this clock has survived, and even that in an altered state since at some point an arch (since removed) was soldered onto the top. The dial is a striking illustration of how knowledge of a maker, or of one part of even a celebrated makers life, depends upon the chance survival of his work. In the case of Margetts it was only the recovery of this fragment which led to his identity being established. For details see A.J. Turner 'New Light on George Margetts', Antiquarian Horology, vii, 1971, pp.304-316. Museum of the History of Science, Oxford.

dial. It is shown in Fig. 482. Vulliamy made a bracket clock on the Smeaton-Franklin plan in which the pendulum, in order to beat seconds, was weighted above its point of suspension on the principle of the metronome.

JENKINS' ASTRONOMICAL
CLOCK

Henry Jenkins, who flourished from 1760 to 1780, first at 46 Cheapside, and afterwards at 68 Aldersgate Street, must be reckoned among the celebrated clockmakers of his time. Fig. 483 shows one of several astronomical clocks he contrived and produced. There are concentric second and minute hands, and among other motions are shown: equation of time, days of the month, age and phases of the moon, time of high water at many seaports, the apparent motion of the fixed stars, motions of the planets, &c.

The lunar and other motions, except the revolution of the planets, are nearly as in Enderlin's clock, and need not be recapitulated. From the earth's diurnal motion wheel, rotating once in twenty-four hours, is driven a worm which carries forward an annual wheel, and the representation of the fixed stars one tooth each day. From thence is a communication to the planetary system dial above, and the motions of the planets are obtained by six wheels fixed together on one stud and driving six other wheels whose sockets are

Fig. 483.

A twelve month time-keeper by George Margetts having a white enamel dial with subsidiary seconds. The very deep movement has Margett's characteristic steel baluster pillars and sideways winding. There is an extra long fusee for the year duration and a 19th century lever escapement. The whole is contained in a simple brass box. Sotheby Parke Bernet & Co.

A souscription *watch by Breguet signed 'Breguet' on the dial and 'Breguet 1590' on the backplate. Engine turned silver and gold dial and engine turned gold case with a* putto *figure* appliqué *on the back. The movement is of the bridge type with a ruby cylinder escapement, parachutes on the endstones of the balance arbor, and balance spring regulated by a sliding index. The certificate to the watch states that it was sold to Mr Recordon in June 1808. Almost certainly this is the Soho watch maker Louis Recordon who provided a London outlet for Breguet. Breguet's souscription watches, which were of relatively simple construction, were developed in order to provide a cheaper watch of good quality. The first example was entered in Breguet's books in 1794 and sold in 1796. Museum of the History of Science, Oxford.*

GEORGE MARGETTS

circles, and represent their respective orbits. On the stud are wheels of 108, 78, 84, 40, 8, 5, driving on sockets 26, 48, 84, 75, 95, 147.

By the originality of his conceptions embodied in exact and well-finished mechanism this chronometer and watch maker must be ranked with the masters. He was admitted as a member of the Clockmakers' Company in 1779 and carried on business at 21 King Street, Cheapside, till the end of the century, when he removed to No. 3 Cheapside. In Fig. 484 is shown a watch by him with a series of intricate superimposed dials and indicators. A small centre dial indicates mean time, and on this dial at the XII is the word Ports[h]; London at 7 minutes; Hull at 15 minutes; Yarmouth at 22 minutes; Dover at 29 minutes; Downs at 35 minutes; Plym[h] at 45 minutes, and Dublin at 55 minutes. An enamel ring outside this dial gives tidal hours. Through a hole in this ring is shown the age of the moon, and a hand attached to the ring indicates the part of the heavens the moon is in. A gold band below this carries a pointer indicating the position of the sun. The signs of the zodiac are painted on the lower large dial. Beyond the tropic of Cancer is figured the Sun's declination in correspondence with the days of the year; beyond that the degrees, 30°, of each sign of the zodiac; and nearer still to the edge of the dial the months and days of the year, so that, except that no provision is made for leap year, it is a correct calendar. The large dial makes one turn in a sidereal day; the sun hand, making one turn in a solar day, becomes the pointer indicating the date because it gets $1/365$th of the circle after the dial each day. A finger attached to a large gold band on the dial shows the declination of the sun throughout the year. The different pointers can be set independently of each other. Fitted round the smallest dial and extending to the large gold band is a curved frame of gold with arcs within it. It carries a pointer and may be moved round, but its purpose is not evident. An eccentric circle on the large dial represents the orbit of the earth, farthest from the sun in June, nearest in December. The watch is in pair cases, the inner one of brass, and the outer one of twenty-two carat gold bearing the London hall mark of 1783. I recently saw a watch of earlier date with a similar dial. Watches by him with complicated dial work are also in the British and Guildhall Museums.

As the cost of these watches must have been very great, one is inclined to think they were probably ordered for presentation by some wealthy corporation such as the East India Company. A ship's captain for instance would particularly appreciate such a piece of complicated horology. Some time ago I was shown a chromometer by him on the dial of which was inscribed "Margetts' eight-days timepiece, 202," and on the plate, "Geo. Margetts, London, Invt. et fecit, eight-day nautical chronometer." It was the size of a small two-day marine chronometer, the great wheel being planted near the top plate; it had a spring detent; an escape wheel of sixteen teeth, measuring ·470 of an inch in diameter, and an impulse roller one quarter the size of wheel. He made a regulator for the Archbishop of Armagh in 1790, and can be traced at 3 Cheapside till about 1806.

Fig. 484.

ABRAHAM LOUIS BREGUET

The intense and abiding interest taken in the works of this the predominant Continental horologist of his period, may be traced to the great variety of his conceptions and the exactness with which they were carried out. He seems to have had the faculty of surrounding himself with assistants who were good mechanicians and able to embody his ideas to the best advantage. Clocks, chronometers, and watches of his make all bore the stamp of originality in some particular. A defect in construction had only to be pointed out or the whim of a customer revealed, when Breguet was ready with the requirement. Of his more daring contrivances may be mentioned a "synchronizer" or clock for setting a watch right, a tourbillon or revolving carriage in which the escapement of a watch was placed so as to nullify the effect of change of position, which was one of the most perplexing problems of the adjuster, and a device for allowing the bearing surfaces to the balance staff pivots of a watch to yield, which he termed a "parachute," the object being to prevent damage to the pivots through shocks.

Beillard quotes a letter from Breguet to the "Citoyen" Minister of the Interior, asking for a patent for his escapement à Tourbillon, dated Paris le 18 Brumaire An IX.

Of Breguet's writing no extracts can be given, for he published nothing; his works form the best tribute to his memory. Of these a few are selected for illustration.

Fig. 485 is a view of a clock and watch forming the "Synchronizer" which is the property of His Majesty the King, and I am indebted for the illustration to Mr A. E. Rutherford. As already stated, the object of the invention is to set the watch right. Projecting above the case of the clock are two crescent-shaped clips to hold the watch. The clock may be regarded as a standard, and when the watch is placed in position, as shown, it is not only set to time at any desired hour, but if necessary the regulator of the watch is also shifted. Projecting from the top of the clock is a pin which enters a small hole in the case of the watch and so establishes connection between the special pieces added to the two. There is an extra train of wheels in the watch to set the minute hand to zero, and this train is discharged by a snail-shaped cam in the clock. With this general statement I must be content; the details are most complicated, and to attempt anything like a clear description within a reasonable space would be hopeless. In the Napier collection was a Synchronizer by Breguet similar in principle, but in which the clock was controlled by a pendulum instead of a balance.

In Fig. 486 are front and back views of a gold watch, No. 92, which was sold to the Duc de Praslin for 4,800 francs on the 11 Thermidor, An 13 (30th July 1805). It repeats the preceding hour, each period of ten minutes which has elapsed, and then the number of minutes beyond. On an

Fig. 485. — Breguet's Synchronizer. The mainspring barrels are in the base of the case, the winding being accomplished by means of a rack and lever underneath. Above the base may be seen the compensation balance, and rising from it part of a tall balance-spring, which is of gold.

A typical example of a minute repeating, gold cased, keyless wound chronograph by Breguet No. 5205. The watch has a lever escapement and a silver dial. It is shown resting upon its certificate which shows that it was sold to Mr Barry Ryan, 27 July 1948. Bobinet Ltd.

Fig. 486. — Watch with Perpetual Calendar and Equation of Time Register.

enamelled dial in front are a perpetual calendar and an equation of time register. It has an independent seconds hand. At the back of the watch is a gold engine-turned dial, showing the age of the moon, the amount the mainspring is wound, a regulator for time, and one also for the repeating train.

Front and back views of what is often spoken of as Breguet's *chef-d'oeuvre* are given in Fig. 487. It is a watch measuring 2⅝ in. across, which, as stated in Breguet's certificate, was ordered in 1783 by an officer of the Marie Antoinette Gardes, with the condition that it should contain all complications and improvements then known or possible, and that in its construction gold instead of brass should be used. No price was fixed, and its

Fig. 487. — Breguet's *"Chef-d'oeuvre"*. Perpetual or Self-Winding Watch with Gold Movement.

manufacture was begun in 1789, stopped during the Revolution of 1789, again started in 1795, and completed in 1802, costing altogether 30,000 francs. It is furnished with a lever escapement, compensation balances, gold balance-spring, and two parachutes. All the pivots, without exception, run in ruby or sapphire holes. All parts usually of brass are of gold. It repeats the hours, quarters, and minutes, has an independent seconds hand, perpetual calendar, equation of time register, and a thermometer. But perhaps the most ingenious feature of the mechanism is that there is no provision for a watch key, nor is any periodical operation needed to keep the watch going. So long as it is worn, recharging of the energy is automatically accomplished by a heavily-weighted but lightly-balanced arm or lever, to which ordinary movements of the wearer give sufficient up and down motion to wind the mainspring with which it is connected. Breguet is generally credited with the invention of this device, but of this I am not sure, for a patent granted in 1780 to Recordon may have been a prior disclosure of it. Back and front the movement is covered with rock crystal, and the dial also is of crystal, though another dial of white enamel with gold figures is provided. This extraordinary watch is the property of Mr Louis Desoutter, to whom I am indebted for the photographs of this and of the other Breguet watches here shown.

Fig. 488 gives front and back views of a watch by "Breguet et fils, No. 2,794," which was sold to Louis XVIII. in September 1821 for 7,000 francs. Here are really two movements side by side in one case, with separate numerals and hands for each. The object of its production was to demonstrate the effect on the timekeeping of a balance when another similar balance was set in motion near it. It was thought the errors of one would neutralise the errors of the other, and that they would vibrate in unison. There is a provision for lessening or increasing the distance the balances are apart. A counterpart of this watch was made for George III.

The watch of which a front view is given in Fig. 489 has a gold case and dial, repeats the hours and quarters, and is furnished with a calendar and a thermometer. It is numbered 1,806, and was sold to Prince Murat in 1807 for 4,000 francs.

In Fig. 490 is represented a silver watch having a chronometer escapement mounted in a tourbillon carriage. It is signed "Breguet et fils," and numbered 2,520. Its original cost was £96.

An exceedingly diminutive and thin double-cased watch is shown to its exact size, with the outer case detached, in Fig. 491. The cases and dial are of gold; it needs no key, but is wound from the pendant, has a lever escapement, and is numbered 5,102. It carries an especially interesting association, for it was sold to Queen Victoria on 17th July 1838. The price was 4,250 francs.

A clock by Breguet, held aloft by a kneeling figure of bronze gilt, is shown in Fig. 492. The clock has a chronometer escapement and silver dials front and back. On the back is a calendar, the indicators for which turn to the left, so that if viewed through a mirror the actions appear to be right handed. It is 19 in. in height.

The majority of Breguet's watches had very plain exteriors, the dials as a rule being either of silver or white enamel, while the cases were generally embellished with a delightful kind of fine engine turning which it was a

Fig. 488. — Watch with Synchronous Balances; two Movements in one Case.

pleasure to see and to handle; his less costly productions seemed to be purposely devoid of all enrichment. As an example, one of his *"souscription"* watches is here shown [Fig. 493]. It was made in 1821, bears the inscription "Breguet et Fils," and cost £26. The bezels and bow are of gold and the body and back of the case are silver. It winds at the centre of the dial and has an hour hand only, though this is of peculiar construction, for beyond the part which indicates the hour is a fine prolongation to reach the sub-divisions, which are each a twelfth of an hour, equal to five minutes. With practice one could doubtless estimate the time very closely in this way. It is said that the subscription watches obtained their title from the combination of Breguet and certain of his work-people to produce a reliable watch at a moderate price. Many of his watches had the signature *Breguet* scratched on the dial in script, the characters being so very tiny as to be indistinguishable without a magnifier. His early watches, it may be supposed,

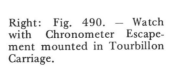

Left: Fig. 489. — Prince Murat's Repeating Watch.

Right: Fig. 490. — Watch with Chronometer Escapement mounted in Tourbillon Carriage.

Fig. 491. — Queen Victoria's Watch. Exact size.

were not so marked. I cannot ascertain when the practice began, but it doubtless continued during the "Reign of Terror." In some instances the number of the watch was on the pendant, but this again did not occur on all his watches.

Mr Lionel Faudel Phillips has a watch by Breguet in which the balance pivots are carried between friction rollers, a plan tried by Mudge in his marine chronometers.

Breguet was born at Neuchâtel, Switzerland, in 1747, his parents being of French origin. He settled in Paris in early manhood and quickly achieved success in business. Beillard relates that Marat, who also came from Switzerland, and Breguet were intimately acquainted, and one night when they met at a friend's house in the rue Greneta, the populace under the windows shouted, "Down with Marat!" The situation becoming serious, Breguet dressed Marat up as an old woman and they left the house arm in arm. Some time after, when the guillotine was set up *en permanence,* Marat, finding Breguet was in danger, gave him a pass to Switzerland.

Fig. 492.

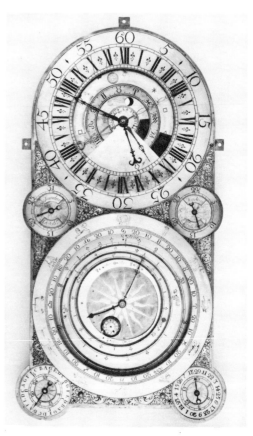

The remains of Henry Bridge's 'Microcosm', 1734 (pp. 299-300). The upper dial shows the hours and minutes, time of sunrise and sunset, sun's position in the zodiac and its relation to that of the moon, phase and position of the moon, moon's latitude. The lower dial represents the planets according to the Copernican system and the four subsidiary dials give the date, age of the moon, dominical letter, year in the solar cycle, golden number and epact.

The elaborate gearing necessary to represent the planetary positions accurately was originally driven by an anchor escapement with a long compensated pendulum. This has now been replaced by a dead-beat escapement perhaps of French origin in the late 18th or early 19th centuries. At the same time quarter and hour rack striking trains were added. Originally the elaborate casing around the clock contained moving pictures and an organ, but these have not survived. The Trustees of the British Museum.

EQUATION CLOCKS

Fig. 493. — Breguet's "Subscription Watch".

Fig. 494. — ABRAHAM LOUIS BREGUET, 1747-1823.

Breguet took a post chaise forthwith and reached Locle in safety. He afterwards returned to Paris and died there in 1823, being succeeded in business by his son, Louis Antoine, who retired in 1833, and was followed by his son Louis, a worthy grandson of Abraham L. Although as an horologist Louis was overshadowed by the greatness of his grandsire, he established a reputation among electricians, as well as among horologists, and timekeepers issued from the house of Breguet during his administration were of the highest possible quality.

To meet the perplexity caused by the fact that sun-dials recorded true solar time and clocks mean solar time, as explained on p.17, equation dials to indicate the difference each day were added in the latter part of the seventeenth century. Foremost among the inventors of equation work must be mentioned Joseph Williamson, whose paper in the *Philosophical Transactions* is referred to on p.232. As well as clocks to indicate the variation between solar and mean time, he appears to have arranged mechanism to raise or lower the pendulum of a clock as required, in order that the hands might indicate true solar time, as in the twelve-month timepiece at Hampton Court which bears Quare's name. Figs. 495 and 496 are drawings of an equation clock by Enderlin, which gives, in addition to true and mean solar time, a perpetual day of the month, the sun's place in the zodiac, his rising and setting, and the moon's age and phases.

Fig. 495 is the dial work, and Fig. 496 the dial itself. In Fig. 495 the wheel Q, of 24 teeth, takes its motion from the striking part. It impels the wheel R, of 32 teeth, with a vertical arbor, which has a bend and compound joint T. This arbor has an endless screw S, in the middle of the inclined half, turning wheel A, of 487 teeth, and also a pinion *a*, of 24 leaves, actuating a wheel V, of 32 teeth. This last wheel revolves in 24 hours, *a* in 18 hours, and with it the arbors R T S *a*. Q revolves in 13 hours 30 minutes, and A in 8,760 hours, or 365 days 6 hours, whence it is called the annual wheel. The wheel X, with 62 inclined teeth, and the wheel Z, with 90 teeth, revolve separately round one common centre 5, Z being in front. X is impelled by a tooth or pallet on the 24 hours arbor of the wheel V, and Z by an endless screw Y. This screw has a pinion 6, of 21 leaves, upon its upper end, and, impelled by the pinion *a*, turns Z in 59 days 1 hour 30 minutes, being the sum of two lunations. The wheel X is impelled one tooth every 24 hours, therefore an entire revolution would be performed in 62 days; but it does not in fact make more than one-half of a revolution when it jumps back.

On the point D, in Fig. 495, the rack E moves, its tail *c* resting on the circumference of the equation curve. At *o* is a box with a spring, which keeps the cord 15 always stretched. This cord surrounds a pulley on the plane of a concealed wheel N, under K, but not attached to it. This wheel acts into the rack which is always resting on the equation curve. The pinion I, of 30 teeth, revolving in 60 minutes and carrying the minute hand, turns the wheel K, of 60, which drives a pinion L, of 30, also in 60 minutes. To L is attached a wheel H, of 48 teeth, which turns a similar wheel F, and this again a third similar wheel G, the tube of which surrounds the arbor of I, and carries the equation hand with a little sun on it pointing to 30, in Fig. 496. The wheel N, below K, is pinned to a bar, which is not seen, but which carries the wheel H and pinion L; and as the teeth of the rack are acting in the wheel N, the concealed bar moves alternately towards I and 15 as the

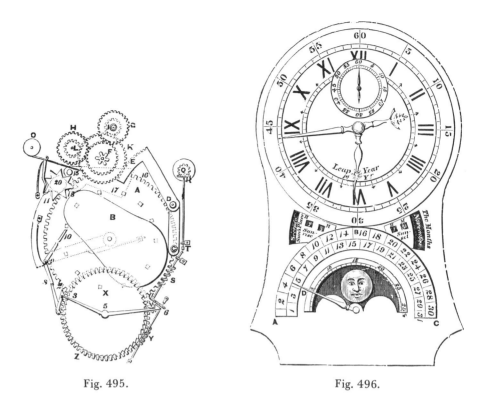

Fig. 495.   Fig. 496.

radius of the equation cam varies. This motion makes the pinion L sometimes advance and sometimes retrograde a few teeth, independently of the motion it receives from the rotation of K; and this additional motion is also communicated to the wheel H in consequence of its connection with L, and hence to both F and G, the latter bearing the equation hand.

Altogether this is an interesting example of the mechanism of early complicated clocks. The perpetual calendar work is now done with more simplicity, in cases where such devices are demanded, and the equation indicator of Tompion's Bath clock, of which a description is also given, is actuated in a more direct way, as may be seen from comparison.

GREEN'S LICHFIELD CLOCK

In the *Universal Magazine* for 1748 is illustrated a singular clock with a peculiar outer case, about 4 ft. high, built in three tiers, and shown in Fig. 497. The early history of the clock does not appear to be known, but at the date quoted it belonged to Mr Richard Green, of Lichfield.

The upper part represents a pavilion, whereon stands a brazen statue of Fame. Within the pavilion, in the centre, appears Pontius Pilate, having a basin of water before him, as washing his hands; and round him move continually three images, representing our Saviour as going to His crucifixion, the Virgin Mary, and Simon the Cyrenian bearing the cross. These three last-mentioned figures make one entire revolution every minute. The musical part of this clock executed eight different tunes, any one of which is played several times over every three hours, with also provision to play it occasionally.

The outward case of this horological machine occupies the left of the engraving. It represents a highly decorated church tower of Gothic architecture, with pinnacles, battlements, windows, mouldings, images, buttresses, &c., admirably painted and well carved. This perspective view of

Fig. 497. — Lichfield Clock.

Fig. 498. — Bridges' Clock.

the outward case is so contrived that no part of the inner structure but the dial appears to view, except the front of this case (which consists of an upper and lower door) is thrown open. The clock may be then taken out, appearing then as is shown on the right of the engraving, and placed on the table or elsewhere. The height of the outside case is 5 ft. 2 in.

HENRY BRIDGES

Henry Bridges, who lived at Waltham Abbey, and was brought up as an architect, seems to have obtained a greater reputation abroad than at home as the producer of clocks with motions representing the heavenly bodies. The specimen of his work delineated in the accompanying figure was publicly exhibited in 1741 at the Mitre, near Charing Cross, according to an advertisement in the *Daily Advertiser* for 23rd December of that year. It is a monumental clock 10 ft. high and 6 ft. broad at the base. Within the pediment at the top of the structure is a scene representing the Muses on Parnassus; this changes periodically to a forest with Orpheus and wild beasts, which in its turn gives place to a sylvan grove with birds.

On the upper large dial and the four small ones are indicated the seconds, minutes, and hours; the rising and setting of the sun; equation of time, the age phases of the moon, and signs of the zodiac. On the lower of the large dials is exhibited the Copernican system of time, consisting of seventeen bodies, the sun being in the centre and the planets moving round it. On a panel below are a landscape and the sea with representations of moving persons and vessels, and on a second panel men at work in a carpenter's yard. These automata were very popular, and quite suited to the taste of the period. Besides these, the edifice contained an organ, which was played at intervals. Altogether there were, it is stated, over a thousand wheels and pinions in the composition of the mechanism.

It is remarkable how little is to be gathered respecting Henry Bridges among English horological records. Dubois says he was clockmaker in the court of Charles I., and that the identical clock illustrated in Fig. 498 was made for the Duke of Buckingham. But this account cannot be accepted, for seconds and minute hands were not usual in the time of Charles I. In the Ashmolean Museum is a copy of the print from which Fig. 498 is taken and it is dated 1734. A portrait of Bridges appears on it, and the wig and dress are of the style in vogue at the beginning of the eighteenth century. In the *Daily Advertiser* announcement, already referred to, is the following note: "Mr Bridges being engaged in much Business at home would be willing to dispose of this Machine, either wholly, or in Partnership." In 1770, the clock was again exhibited, this time by one Edward Davis, who wrote a descriptive pamphlet concerning it.

LOVELACE'S EXETER CLOCK

It is stated that Jacob Lovelace, a native of Exeter, spent thirty-four years constructing the monumental clock shown in the accompanying engraving [Fig. 499]. A printed description of it says: "The mechanism is enclosed in

A typically ornate and extravagant spring driven mantel striking clock by James Cox, c.1765-70. The Ashmolean Museum, Oxford.

an elegant cabinet 10 ft. high, 5 ft. wide, and weighing half a ton, ornamented with Oriental figures and finely executed paintings, bordered by richly carved fretwork. The movements are: 1. A moving panorama descriptive of Day and Night. Day is represented by Apollo in his car drawn by four spirited coursers, accompanied by the twelve Hours; the Diana in her car drawn by stags, attended by the twelve Hours, represents Night. 2. Two gilt figures in Roman costume, who turn their heads and salute with their swords as the panorama revolves, and also move in the same manner while the bells are ringing. 3. A perpetual almanack, showing the day of the month on a semicircular plate, the index returning to the first day of every month on the close of each month, without alteration even in leap years, regulated only once in 130 years. 4. A circle, the index of which shows the day of the week, with its appropriate planet. 5. A perpetual almanack, showing the days of the month and the equation of time. 6. A circle showing the leap year, the index revolving only once in four years. 7. A timepiece that strikes the hours and chimes the quarters, on the face of which the whole of the twenty-four hours (twelve day and twelve night) are shown and regulated; within this circle the sun is seen in his course, with the time of rising and setting, by an horizon receding or advancing as the days lengthen or shorten, and under is seen the moon, showing her different quarters, phases, age, &c. 8. Two female figures on either side of the dial-plate, representing Fame and Terpsichore, who move in time when the organ plays. 9. A movement regulating the clock as a repeater, to strike or to be silent. 10. Saturn, the god of Time, who beats in movement when the organ plays. 11. A circle on the face shows the names of eight celebrated tunes played by the organ in the interior every four hours. 12. A belfry with six ringers, who ring a merry peal. The interior of this part of the cabinet is ornamented with beautiful paintings, representing some of the principal ancient buildings in the city of Exeter. 13. Connected with the organ is a bird organ, which plays when required. Beside the dial is the inscription, *Tempus rerum Imperator.*"

According to an advertisement in the *Exeter Flying Post,* 5th July 1821, this clock was about to be publicly exhibited; and in the same publication for 8th September 1834, it was announced that "Lovelace's celebrated clock," which for several years was in the collection of Mr James Burt, had the previous week been sold by auction for 680 guineas by the noted George Robins.

At the International Exhibition, 1851, it was a prominent feature in the Western Gallery. It then belonged to Mr Brutton, who had it put in order by Mr Frost, of Exeter, after it had been deranged for some years. In 1888 a suggestion in the Exeter Press that the clock should be purchased for the Imperial Institute, resulted in nothing, and it was afterwards acquired for the Liverpool Museum, where it remains.

There seems to be no reasonable doubt that Lovelace died at the age of sixty, in 1766. It has been suggested that his death occurred half a century earlier. There is nothing in the clock here shown to warrant such a conclusion, and he is known to have made long-case clocks of a style quite inconsistent with a period anterior to 1716.

Fig. 499. — Lovelace's Clock.

JAMES COX AND HIS PERPETUAL MOTION CLOCK

By favour of Mr George Ellis I am enabled to reproduce an engraving of a self-winding, or, as the inventor termed it, "a perpetual motion" clock, which belonged to the late W. F. B. Massey-Mainwaring. The energy for

Fig. 500. — Cox's Perpetual Motion.

Fig. 501.

keeping the mechanism in motion was obtained by changes in the pressure of the atmosphere. What at first sight seems to be a huge pendulum is an ornamental glass jar of mercury, suspended from chains. Into this is dipped a tube of mercury, also hung from chains, open at its lower end, and with a large bulb at its upper extremity. With increased atmospheric pressure a little of the mercury in the jar would be forced into the tube. The jar and tubes were balanced by weights, so that the tube being a little heavier by the addition of mercury, would fall a little, and in so doing would raise the weight; and with a fall in the pressure of the atmosphere, the mercury in the jar would be increased and the weight would be raised a little. There is no pendulum, but the escapement, which is at the back of the dial, is controlled by a straight bar balance. Wherever possible, the rubbing surfaces were jewelled with diamonds to reduce the friction. The clock, which is over 7 ft. in height, was constructed by James Cox, who resided for some time in Shoe Lane, and really devoted his life to the production of mechanical curiosities, very much in the style of those devised by Grollier de Servière. Cox obtained an Act of Parliament in 1773, authorising him to dispose of his museum by means of a lottery, and for some months his conceptions formed an exhibition at Spring Gardens, where half a guinea admission for each person was charged. It was stated in an advertisement that the perpetual motion would occupy the centre of the room. The following certificate was appended to the advertisement:—

SIR , — I have seen and examined the above described clock, which is kept constantly going by the rising and falling of the quicksilver, in a most extraordinary barometer; and there is no danger of its ever failing to go, for there is always such a quantity of moving power accumulated as would keep the clock going for a year, even if the barometer should be quite away from it. And, indeed, on examining the whole contrivance and construction, I must with truth say, that it is the most ingenious piece of mechanism I ever saw in my life.

"JAMES FERGUSON.

"Bolt Court, Fleet Street.
"Jan. 28th, 1774."

The awarding of the various prizes to subscribers of the lottery took place in June 1775. Mason, a rhymester of the time thus refers to one of his exhibits:—

> "Great Cox, at his mechanicall,
> Bids orient pearls from golden dragons fall;
> Each little dragonet, with brazen grin,
> Gapes for the precious prize, and gulps it in.
> Yet, when we peep behind the scene,
> One master wheel directs the whole machine;
> The selfsame pearls, in nice gradation, all
> Around one common centre, rise and fall."

Another of his "perpetual motion" clocks, which was really to be kept going by the opening and shutting of the door of the room in which it was contained, was for some years on view at the Polytechnic in Regent Street.

Apart from his mysterious mechanism, Cox was an accomplished horologist. I saw a large travelling watch by him, belonging to Mr William Johnson, in which everything was well proportioned and of the best execution. A chime clock of his make, in an ormolu case with allegorical figures surmounted by a lion holding the arms of England and a miniature of dancing bacchanals by Degault below the dial, fetched £861 at the Hamilton sale in 1882. The handsomely cased bracket chiming clock shown in Fig. 501 belongs to Colonel R. W. Peckitt. In the upper part of the dial is a semicircular band containing the list of tunes played, and below it the signature "James Cox, 1769."

HORSTMANN'S SELF-WINDING CLOCK

In a self-winding clock invented by the late Gustave Horstmann, of Bath, the expansion and contraction of a liquid are used to wind the clock. A strong metal vessel, A in the figure, is filled with an easily expanding fluid, such as benzoline, mineral naphtha, &c. Connected to this vessel by a strong tube with a very small bore are a cylinder and piston B and C. Owing to the fact that most expanding fluids are incapable of driving a piston, being too volatile and thin, the cylinder and tube are charged with a thicker and more lubricating fluid, such as glycerine. The vessel containing the expanding fluid is on a higher elevation than the piston and cylinder. This is done to prevent them mixing, as benzoline is lighter than glycerine, and, therefore, rises to the top. It is easy now to see how that when the temperature rises, the expanding liquid will force the piston upward, and, by means of a slight counterforce, the piston will fall on the temperature lowering.

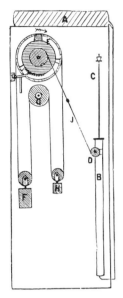

Fig. 502.

The piston terminates in a cross-bar, to each end of which is attached a steel ribbon like a wide watch mainspring. These two bands are brought down over pulleys at D, fixed on each side of the cylinder, and then carried direct to the winding mechanism E of the clock, which is all fixed on the back of the case and independent of the movement. The two bands join into one a little before they reach the winding. A large pulley E is fitted on a stud at the back of the case, and is driven by means of a ratchet and click. The pulley E has a flat groove, and is studded with short pins at equal distances apart, over which works a long steel ribbon perforated with oblong holes. This chain passes down through the weight pulley F, which also had a flat groove, but no pins, and is carried over the main wheel pulley G, which is supplied with pins, the same as the winding pulley. It then passes under the pulley of the counterweight H, and is then joined to its other end, thus forming an endless chain. As the piston falls a coiled spring causes the smaller pulley at the top of the case to turn independently of E, and to coil the band J on to itself, ready for the next rise of temperature.

FAN OR WINDMILL CLOCKS

Fans actuated by currents of air have been from time to time used as motors for actuating timekeepers. One, by Lepaute, is in the Louvre, Paris. Benjamin Hanks, of Litchfield County, Connecticut, patented one in 1783. In Dardenne's more recent patent the weight is wound up by the current of air in a chimney acting upon the blades of a fan, which is stopped by a self-acting brake as soon as the weight nears the top of its course.

Chapter VI

French Clocks and Cases in the French Style. Other Curious Timekeepers

BEYOND THE EXAMPLES which have already been given little need be said respecting French horology of the sixteenth and first half of the seventeenth century. Of the early French clockmakers, Julian Couldray (or Couldroy) is mentioned as having, in 1529, received from Francis I. xlix. livres iv. sols for two "monstres d'orloge" without weights. The same king, in 1531, caused to be paid to his "orlogeur" a sum of 50 écus (ducats) for taking in hand a "monstre d'orloge." The term "monstre d'orloge" seems to have been generally used to designate a chamber clock up to about the middle of the seventeenth century. Henry III. of France ordered Gilbert Martinot to make two "monstres," viz., a large round one to place in the apartment of the said "Seigneur" (the king), and another vertical clock with columns, which latter "hys majestie" had promised to the Bastard of Orleans, of both of which "hys majestie" had agreed the price.

After the introduction of the pendulum, the term horloge appears to have been dropped so far as clocks for domestic use were concerned, and the title of "pendule" substituted.

PARIS GUILD According to Savary, a corporate body of clockmakers was established about 1453, but the first statute of incorporation appears to have been granted by Francis I. in 1544, on the petition of Fleurent Valleran, Jean de Presles, Jean Pantin, Michel Potier, Anthoine Beauvais, Nicholas Moret, and Nicolas le Contandois. The enactment decreed that no one, of whatever station, if he has not been admitted as a master, should make, or cause to be made, clocks, alarms, watches, large or small, or any other machine for measuring time, within the said town, city, and precinct of Paris, on pain of forfeiture of the said works. There were provisions for the regulation of apprentices, and for the appointment of officers to enforce the powers conferred on the Corporation, very similar to the privileges accorded to the London Clockmakers in 1630. Upon the entry into Paris of Henri II., ten

"orlogeurs" formed part of the procession composing the crafts. The Paris Clockmakers had their statute varied in 1554 under Henri II., in 1572 under Charles IX., and in 1600 under Henri IV. In 1646, under Louis XIV., their laws were thoroughly revised, and it was ordained that apprenticeship should be for eight years, after which the apprentice could leave the employer, but subject only to the approval of his master, and that of the master of the Company. In 1691 was issued a regulation declaring that an apprentice was not qualified for membership, *i.e.*, for submitting a master work, until he had attained the age of at least 29 years. The number of members was limited to 72, of which only six could be admitted without qualifying. Special privileges were accorded to sons of members, a fact which perhaps accounts for so many successive generations of a particular family following the craft. Widows could continue the business of their husbands, and enjoyed the same privileges. Artisans who practised their trade in districts administered by the king, the lord of the manor, the Church, or the princes of the blood, claimed exemption from control of the Guild. The districts where this immunity existed were: the Cloistre Parvis of Notre Dame, the Court of the Church of Saint Benoit, the enclosures of Saint Denis de Chartres, Saint Jean de Latran, Saint Martin des Champs, Saint Germain de Prés; also the Rue de Lourcine (because subject to Saint Jacques de Latran), the Courts of the Temple and of the Trinity, and the Faubourg Saint Antoine. The work produced in these quarters was generally considered to be of an inferior order unless executed by a craftsman who had voluntarily joined the Corporation. To the privileged places enumerated have to be added those where work was carried out for the king or the State, such as the Galeries du Louvre. The Associated Clockmakers appear to have governed the trade till the Revolution of 1789, when all the guilds were abolished.

Alfred Franklin, in "La Vie Privée D'Autrefois," says the Martinots and Bidaults for a century and a half occupied lodgings in the Louvre, reserved by the king for distinguished artists. In 1712 Louis XIV. had for clockmakers Louis Henri Martinot, Augustus Francis Bidault, and Jérôme Martinot. They were engaged by the quarter, received 395 livres for salary, dined in the Castle, at the table of the Gentlemen of the Chamber, and had the right of entry to the king's presence along with the distinguished members of his household. Every morning, during the dressing of the king, the horologist on duty wound up and properly adjusted the watches which his Sovereign was about to wear.

Towards the end of the seventeenth century decorative art in France underwent a remarkable change, and cases of "Pendules d'appartement," or chamber clocks, were produced in harmony with the extravagant demand for

A good example of a typical French pedestal clock of c.1720. The clock itself is by Mynuel à Paris, and the case is attributed to André Charles Boulle (1642-1732) who gave his name to the technique of decorating furniture by inlays of gilt brass, silver, tin or pewter in complicated designs on a base of wood or tortoise-shell. The dial of the clock is relief engraved in the centre. has individual enamel plaques for the hour numerals, and each minute is separately numbered. Reproduced by permission of the Trustees of the Wallace Collection.

A further example of a French pedestal clock from their classic period. The case of this example is also attributed to Boulle himself, and the movement of the clock is by J. Thuret. Reproduced by permission of the Trustees of the Wallace Collection.

more sumptuous furniture of all kinds. Eminent artists and designers vied with each other in ministering to the pronounced taste for novelty of form and style. J. Berain, Jacques Caffieri, Boulle, and Marot were among the most noted of those engaged in horological coverings. As will be seen, some of the earlier designs were rather heavy and formal. The ornamentation consisted of masks, escutcheons, shields, and many other attributes of the style hitherto in vogue, the structure in many instances being surmounted by a representation of Father Time with his scythe, or Minerva helmeted and holding a lance, or warriors, ancient or mediaeval, and occasionally a cupid or nude female figure. Flatterers of Louis XIV. likened him to the sun, and it will be noticed that pendulums and other parts of many clocks produced during the latter part of his reign were decorated with the face of Phoebus. But in the closing days of Louis XIV. the comparatively stiff and sedate outlines gave place to freer and more coquettish forms, and the traditional masks, &c., to Rocaille or "Rococo" decoration.

Rocaille is, strictly speaking, a style of ornamentation which obtains its effects from the kingdom of shells, but the products of luxurious vegetation, such as palms and other leaves, were also put under contribution, blended and twisted to produce a fanciful confusion of curves and spirals. To make the eccentricity more marked, designers, borrowing an idea from the Chinese, perversely strove to obtain originality in their conceptions by the avoidance of symmetry, though it must be confessed that in some instances the judicious incorporation of well-posed figures and groups from the pictures of Watteau and other celebrated artists produced effects sufficiently beautiful to quite atone for the *outré* character of the surroundings.

Like many other fashions, the Rocaille style degenerated. It lost favour, and was done to death by the grotesque forms and unmeaning, contemptible decoration which characterises so many works executed during the latter part of the reign of Louis XV. Such mad travesty caused a reversion during the reign of Louis XVI. to simpler and more symmetrical designs.

BOULLE OR BUHL WORK

Charles André Boulle, who was born at Paris in 1642, became celebrated there as a chaser and inlayer. In 1672, Louis XIV. allotted to him rooms at the Louvre, and his effective inlay work of metal, usually brass and tortoiseshell or turtleshell, speedily became the favoured decoration for furniture of all kinds. He died in 1732. Boulle work for clock cases and pedestals continued popular in France throughout the eighteenth century, and in a lesser degree here, where the title became corrupted into "Buhl." In some instances the natural tint of the shell would appear. In others the shell would be painted on the back, red or black, according to the effect desired by the designer. Then by way of contrast the arrangement of the materials used was varied in different parts of the same object; for instance, if on the front the outline was of shell, with a design inlaid with metal, the sides or perhaps panels elsewhere would be decorated with the counterpart or "counter," that is, the outline would be metal and the inlay shell. "Counter" or metal outline, though often effective, is considered to be an inferior production.

Fig. 503.

Fig. 504.

Fig. 505.

Fig. 506.

The particularly handsome Louis XIV. clock and slender pedestal shown in Fig. 503 are in the Council Chamber at Windsor Castle. Together they stand over 7 ft. in height, and are decorated with red shell and white metal Boulle work, relieved with ormolu mounts sharply chased. The pendulum of the clock is 17 in. long, descending below the clock case into the pedestal. The upper panel of the latter is hinged to afford access for regulation. This and several other engravings of the clocks at Windsor Castle are reproduced from photographs taken for me by Mr J. H. Agar-Baugh.

A plainer but very effective pedestal, supporting a calendar clock as represented in Fig. 504, is in the corridor at Windsor Castle. The surface is Boulle work of black shell and brass.

Another choice example, in the Rubens room, appears as in Fig. 505. The front surface is brown shell inlaid with brass, the covering of the sides being

An attractive example of a clock absorbed into a piece of furniture. The clock signed Julien Le Roy, with a candelabra, surmounts a chest of drawers and cabinet of oak veneered with tulip wood mounted with plaques of apple green and white Sèvres porcelain, painted with flowers and fruit. The mounts are of gilt brass and there are chased and gilt figures of patinated bronze. Reproduced by permission of the Trustees of the Wallace Collection.

Fig. 507.   Fig. 508.   Fig. 509.

in counterpart. The clock case has sphinx corner supports of ormolu and a domed top surmounted by a figure of Time. At the base of the case the three Fates are represented. The hour numerals are on plaques of enamel. Through the glazed part of the front below the dial may be seen the pendulum and the inside of the back of the case, which is covered with inlay in counterpart. The style of this clock, apart from the pedestal, was long in favour with French manufacturers.

In the Wallace collection is a clock by Mynuel, with case and pedestal by Boulle of nearly the same period, and bearing a general resemblance to Fig. 505. They were purchased in 1863 for £6,000. The clock is supported on figures of fantastically costumed warriors with their accoutrements, and on its summit is a statuette of Cupid shooting. On the upper part of the pedestal is a medallion representing Hercules relieving Atlas of the burden of the Globe.

A clock and pedestal of the same dimensions, and nearly identical in design, is in the Bibliothèque de l'Arsenal at Paris. Another of the same type is in the collection at Waddesdon Manor. The splendid pedestal clock shown in Fig. 506 was at the Palais du Louvre, Paris.

Many of the best designs of the Louis XIV. period were by Daniel Marot, who was born in Paris in 1660. By the revocation of the Edict of Nantes he was driven to England, but in 1702 took up his abode in the Netherlands. Appended are some examples from a collection of his works published at

308

Fig. 510.

Amesterdam in 1712. In this book he was described as "Architecte de Guillaume III., Roy de la Grande Bretagne." Fig. 507 by him does not show the minutes; it has an hour hand for pointing to the day of the month on a circle outside of the hours. Fig. 508, also by Marot, has a minute indicator, and may be of a slightly later period. Fig. 509, though very much in the style of the Windsor Castle brass inlay clocks, is of more recent date.

Figs. 510, 511, and 512 are bracket or table clocks, by Marot. The superbly designed specimen shown in Fig. 510 is really perfect.

An interesting bracket clock, with complicated movements, in a case inlaid with white metal and brass Boulle work, dating from about 1690-1710, is shown in Fig. 513. At the top of the dial plate is engraved the motto, "Nec pluribus im par," the first two words preceding and the second two following a representation of the sun. At the foot of the dial plate is the inscription, "Henricus Martinot, motum adjunxit. Pouilly Inventor Feci Parisis." Henry Martinot was Chief Clockmaker to Louis XIV., having lodgings in the Louvre, and on the pedestals of the two columns, which are prominent features of the dial plate, is the doubled initial of the King, L.L., interlaced and reversed, surmounted by a crown. This treatment, coupled with the fleur-de-lys ornament formed by the Boulle work of the case, led to the conclusion that the clock was made for Louis XIV., possibly for presentation to some distinguished person. The dial circle, supported by a figure of Saturn, shows hours and minutes, besides which appear, through seven openings within the circle, sunrise, sunset, the length of the day, the length of the night, the month of the year, and certain events of the year as they occur.

Above the centre of the dial are eight tablets, and below the centre four more. These contain each the title of a month, with a number arranged in a peculiar way, thus: April 2; July 5; September 7; December 10; June 4;

Fig. 511. — Havard, "Dictionnaire de l'Ameublement."

Fig. 512. — Havard, "Dictionnaire de l'Ameublement."

Fig. 513. — Schloss Collection.

French clocks more than most are very obviously pieces of furniture valued as such rather than as mechanical contrivances. The cartel clock of gilt bronze (right) and figures of patinated bronze by M. Stollewercke, c.1746-76, is balanced by the matching barometer by M. Bourton (left) and would neatly have flanked a fireplace or mirror. Reproduced by permission of the Trustees of the Wallace Collection.

February 12; March 1; November 9. These are the eight upper ones, the four below, arranged in a cruciform frame, are August 6; May 3; January 11; and October 8. Underneath a fleur-de-lys, engraved over the words "Premiers jours du mois," points direct to the figure 8 of the month of October. On each side of the dial centre is engraved an oval border within which, showing through curved slits, are, on the left the age of the moon, and on the right the days of the month; the title of each day is engraved on the plate in each case, and on the right are also allegorical figures to represent the days.

The shafts of the columns already referred to are slit, and each has a pointer which travels from top to bottom during the space of one year. On the plate, beside the left-hand column, at equal distances are enumerated the months of the year, and on the corresponding space at the other side are the following twelve annual notes — Nombre d'or, Cicle solaire, Epacte, Indication romaine, Lettre dominical, Jours de cendres, Pasques, Rogations, Ascencion, Pentecoste, Festes Dieu, Premier Dimanche des Adüents. Below the figure of Saturn are two apertures, and an inscription underneath denotes the purpose to be to indicate the eclipse of the sun and moon.

Pouilly seems to have been a man especially ingenious in devising calendars and the like. He is referred to in the Paris Diectory for 1691 as "Le Sieur Pouilly, of Rue Dauphine, mathematical instrument maker and seller of a peculiar calendar." In 1692 is mentioned in connection with him an invention relating to the compass and an extraodinary microscope.

Another scientific instrument maker ("ingeniéur"), the Sieur Haye, collaborated with Martinot in the production of a movable sphere, which was presented to the king in 1701. Henry Martinot died at Fountainebleau in 1725 at the age of seventy-nine.

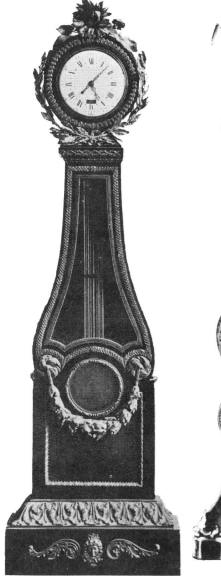

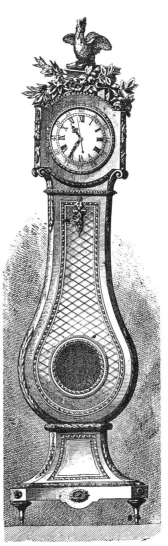

Fig. 514. — Timepiece by Lepaute.

Fig. 515. — Clock by Julien Le Roy.

Fig. 516.

Fig. 517.

Fig. 518.

In the corridor at Windsor Castle is the fine long-case clock by Julien Le Roy illustrated in Fig. 515. The dial has a brass centre with silvered border, and shows solar and mean time and the day of the month. The escapement is a modification of the Graham, each pallet being pivoted separately. On the dial is inscribed, "Inventé en 1736 par Julien Le Roy, de la Société des Arts."

The case is of kingwood inlaid with some lighter veneer to an angulated design and carries heavy ormolu well-chased mountings.

A companion case in the corridor contained a clock by Ferdinand Berthoud, but the movement has been reconstructed by Vulliamy and the dial altered.

In Fig. 514 is shown a superb twelve-month timepiece by Lepaute, which adorns the Zuccarelli room at Windsor Castle. The movement is exceedingly well made, and has a very light pin-wheel escapement furnished with pins on one side only. The pendulum beats seconds, and is compensated on Harrison's "gridiron" principle. The dial, of enamel, is very fine, and the lower edge of it bears in tiny characters the signature "G. Merler." Besides the hour and minute indicators, which still exist, there was originally a centre seconds hand and one for showing the equation of time. The month and day of the month appear through a slit in the lower part of the dial. There are no winding holes, the weight being raised on Huygens' plan, by pulling down the rope. The case is of ebony, relieved with exceptionally fine ormolu mountings. The Baroness Burdett Coutts had a similar timepiece, also by Lepaute.

Fig. 519.

Fig. 520.

Fig. 521.

Fig. 522.

Fig. 523.

Fig. 524.

Fig. 525.

Fig. 526.

Fig. 527.

Among French artists with wealthy patrons the formal square long-case so characteristic of English clocks, was never liked. As examples of their best style may be quoted the elegant regulator shown in Fig. 516, which is at the Conservatoire des Arts et Métiers, Paris, and the equally meritorious design on the same page, Fig. 517. Lepaute's clock shown in Fig. 514, and the more florid design which encloses Julien Le Roy's work as shown beside it, are also worthy of reference. In the series of bracket clocks, Fig. 518 to Fig. 527, arranged nearly in the order of date, every specimen contains, I think, some feature of excellence.

The word Cartel, probably from the Italian *Cartela,* a bracket, seems, during the seventeenth century, to have been applied to any ornament, frame, or other object fixed against a wall or ceiling and having a shape more or less rotund or oval with elongated or pointed ends. The intense desire for fresh forms in articles of furniture which permeated French society during the latter part of the reign of Louis XIV. led to the production of the "Pendule à Cartel" or "en cartel," a title subsequently contracted to simply "cartel." The cartel cases were made occasionally of wood, lead, or zinc, but more often of bronze, thickly gilt. As may be gathered from the examples I am able to illustrate, they were, as a rule, graceful in form and, when oxidation had toned down the somewhat obtrusive garishness of the gilding, of very pleasing appearance.

Small clocks of the same shape and of a size to be easily fastened on the inside of the bed curtain, were designated *Cartels de Chevet.* They were generally furnished with watch movements, the cases being of brass or of wood with Vernis Martin or other decoration, though large cartel clocks with pull strings for repeating were occasionally placed inside the bed against the hangings or wall, for the convenience of those French ladies who, in accordance with accepted custom during the earlier half of the eighteenth century, held receptions while reclining on their beds.

In Fig. 529 is shown a mural clock of Louis XIV. period by J. Thuret, Paris, which belonged to the Marquess of Hertford. The panels are filled with Boulle work which sets off and subdues the ormolu mountings. Figures 528 and 530 show two nearly contemporary designs.

Cartel timepieces were in especial favour throughout the time of Louis XV. A representation is given in Fig. 531 of a Rocaille cartel clock in the Caffieri style dating from about 1760. It is of medium size, measuring 2 ft. in length and 14 in. across the widest part. The movement is by Courtois, clockmaker to Louis XV., who had premises in the Rue Saint Jacques, facing the College du Plessis, and acquired a reputation for the excellence of his movements, both silent and musical. There is a pull string for repeating on two bells, it strikes the hours and half hours, also an alarm. The case of bronze gilded is boldly chased, and the modelling of the figures is exceedingly good. Pierrot and Pierrette appear to enjoy life among fantastical vegetation and scrolls, so popular during the epoch of Louis XV. The mandoline player at the top is well posed and of pleasing expression. Hardly so large and of perhaps ten years later date is another specimen, also of bronze, chased, and gilt, which is shown in Fig. 532. Below the dial is an aperture through which the vibrations of the pendulum may be seen, and the design includes a female figure and cupids, subjects brought into favour by Boucher and his school. The detail of the chasing is finer than was usual with

HANGING OR 'CARTEL' CLOCKS

Fig. 528.

Fig. 529.

Fig. 530.

Fig. 531.

Fig. 532.

Fig. 533.

Fig. 534.

an object to be exhibited on a wall at some distance from the eye. Dial and movement bear the signature of "Thiout l'aine, Paris." There are two bells and a pull string for repeating on them the hours and quarters at pleasure.

Fig. 533, a smaller striking clock of later date, indicates the decline of the more extravagant features observed in some of the Rocaille designs.

An excellent cartel clock of the Louis XVI. period, which belongs to the Hon. Gerald Ponsonby, is shown in Fig. 534.

I may mention that the movements of old cartel clocks are inserted into the case from the front. Ignorance of this has, I know, sometimes led to damage by attempts to force the movements out at the back.

MANTEL CLOCKS   Mantel clocks before the time of Louis XV. are exceptional. When not supported by a long case or a pedestal or a bracket, chamber clocks were hung to a nail on the wall. An early mantel clock, which is in the Octagon room at Windsor Castle, is shown in Fig. 535. The case is decorated with Boulle work and very fine ormolu mountings. A well-modelled Cupid surmounts the structure and below the dial is an equally effective reclining

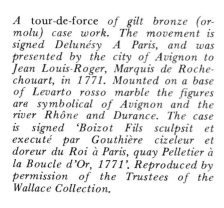

A tour-de-force *of gilt bronze (ormolu) case work. The movement is signed* Delunésy A Paris, *and was presented by the city of Avignon to Jean Louis-Roger, Marquis de Rochechouart, in 1771. Mounted on a base of Levarto rosso marble the figures are symbolical of Avignon and the river Rhône and Durance. The case is signed* 'Boizot Fils sculpsit et executé par Gouthière cizeleur et doreur du Roi à Paris, quay Pelletier à la Boucle d'Or, 1771'. *Reproduced by permission of the Trustees of the Wallace Collection.*

316

Fig. 535.

Fig. 536.

Fig. 537.

Fig. 538.

figure of Time holding a balance. Except the base, which is of later date, this splendid clock is of Louis XIV. period. Base and clock together are 3 ft. high.

The choice Louis XV. clock on a stand with Vernis-Martin and chased ormolu decoration as shown in Fig. 536 belongs to the Comte de Lambilly. A characteristic example of design in the Louis XV. style is the ormolu clock by "Gudin à Paris" at Windsor Castle, and shown in Fig. 537. The chasing is bold, though somewhat coarse. The pierced diaper work below the dial is backed with crimson silk with good effect.

Another excellent specimen of the Louis XV. style is the drawing-room clock represented in Fig. 538. The movement is by Etienne le Noir, a noted clockmaker of the time, while the chasing has been executed by Saint Germain, who also probably did the casting of the model. Saint Germain was one of the small number of founders and chasers of the period whose productions were characterised by remarkable excellence of finish and lightness. He was frequently employed by, or on behalf of, the king and the court. His productions bear his full name, punched in the metal. The crafts of founder and chaser were nearly always combined, forming an exception to the rule then prevailing as to regulation of trades by corporations or companies.

No better example of the Louis XVI. period could be selected than the chaste and elegant boudoir or ante-room clock shown in Fig. 539. It is of white polished marble, which age has tinted to a dark cream, with gilt mountings, the contrast harmonising perfectly. It dates from about 1780 and is by Robin, "horloger du Roy."

The splendid mantel clock shown in Fig. 540 in the Louis XVI. style is perhaps of a little later date, and well represents decorative art during the last few years of the reign of that monarch. The beautifully modelled cupids

Fig. 539.

Fig. 540.

Fig. 541.

Fig. 542.

representing sculpture (adjacent to the completed bust of Henri IV. of Navarre), music, dancing (or singing), and painting appear to be nestling in clouds around a celestial sphere in which the dial is placed. The base of the white marble with rounded ends contains a gilt frieze of trophies. It is 17½ in. in length and 18 in. high. The movement is inscribed ' L. J. Leguesse." The gilding and chasing are excellent, the minutest details of the bronze work being brought out in the style of a master artist. Here, as in the last example, the association of white marble and bronze produces a most pleasing effect. These two clocks are from the Schloss collection.

Fig. 543 shows a celebrated clock invented by Passement and constructed under his direction by Dauthiau, clockmaker to Louis XV. Passement is said to have been engaged for twenty years in calculating the various movements, and the construction of the machine occupied Dauthiau for twelve years. It was completed in 1749, and in 1750 presented to the king, who ordered a new case for it, after his own choice. This was made by Messrs Caffieri (father and son), and when finished in 1753, the clock was deposited at Versailles. It has a dead-beat escapement and a seconds compensated pendulum; indicates solar and mean time, has a seconds hand, strikes the hours and quarters, and has provision for repeating at pleasure the blows last sounded. The striking part is driven by a spring, and the remainder by a weight of 22 lbs., doubly suspended, which falls 8 in. in six weeks. Within a glass sphere over the clock are marked the age and phases of the moon, days of the week, month, and year correctly for a period of 10,000 years. Antide Janvier repaired the clock for the First Consul.

As a curiosity in design, the timekeeper by Lepine, shown in Fig. 544, is worthy of record. Hours and minutes are indicated on two bands rotating horizontally, and there is a long pendulum which terminates very effectively in a representation of the face of Phoebus.

Front and back views of a most effective mantel clock by Ferdinand

Fig. 543. — Astronomical Clock by Passement at Versailles. Havard, "Dictionnaire de l' Ameublement."

Berthoud are given in Figs. 545 and 546. The design as a whole is excellent; the primary object of a clock is to indicate the time, and this point, which seems to have been too often ignored, has here been properly kept in view, and the elegant supporters in no way detract from the due prominence of the dial which measures 9 in. across, the whole structure being 3 ft. 8 in. in height. The plinth is of white marble, with bas-reliefs of cupids struggling for vines; the Bacchantes are of dark-coloured bronze; the vase with overhanging leaves and grapes which surmounts the dial is gilded. Thus a charming combination of colour is obtained quite worthy of the modelling and chasing, which are admirable. The design altogether is a good example of the return to simpler and more reposeful forms suggested by Clodion and his school, in place of the overdone and discredited *Rocaille*. On the chased work is a punch mark corresponding to P. C., which may possibly be that of Pierre Cauvet, a celebrated modeller under Louis XVI., several of whose productions are in the collection of Garde Meuble at the Louvre.

Lyre-shaped exteriors were, it must be confessed, among the most elegant conceptions of the Louis XVI. period. From the example illustrated in Fig. 547, it will be seen that the upper part of the pendulum is formed to represent the strings of the instrument; the lower end, shaped as a ring, passes and repasses behind the dial with very pleasing effect. This clock, which is among the Jones collection at South Kensington Museum, is said to have belonged to Marie Antoinette. The case of Sèvres blue porcelain is 2 ft. in height, has ormolu mountings, and the ring of the pendulum being

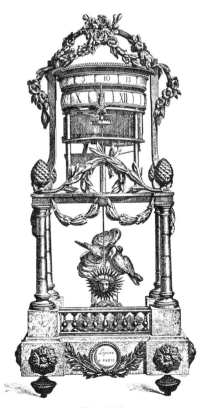

Fig. 544.

Fig. 545.

Fig. 546.

Fig. 547. — Lyre Clock, Sèvres.

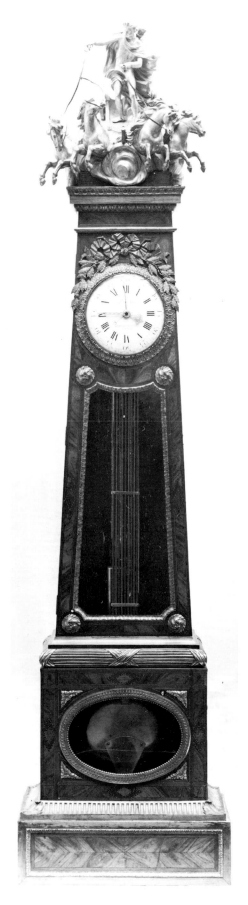

Left:
A remarkable seconds beating regulateur, with grid-iron pendulum and a calendar, signed '[J.J.] Lepaute de Belle Fontaine A Paris'. The case is of oak veneered with Kingwood, purple wood with chased and gilt bronze figures of Apollo in his chariot, and mounts. It is signed by N. Petit (1732-91). Reproduced by permission of the Trustees of the Wallace Collection.

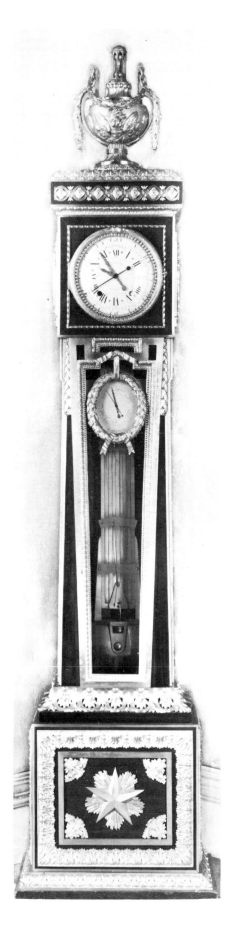

Right:
A long case regulateur with a barometer by Ferdinand Berthoud. The oak case is veneered with ebony and has chased and gilt bronze mounts and fittings. The movement has a dead-beat escapement, with Berthoud's own form of the grid-iron temperature compensated pendulum and there is a calendar volvelle in the dial. Reproduced by permission of the Trustees of the Wallace Collection.

Fig. 548.

Fig. 549.

Fig. 550.

Fig. 551.

Fig. 552.

Fig. 553.

studded with large pastes enhances its very handsome appearance. It bears the signature "Kinable." A somewhat similar clock realised £462 at the Hamilton sale in 1882.

The lyre clock shown in Fig. 548 is at Windsor Castle. The dial is quite modern and bears the inscription "Hanson, Windsor."

The blue Sèvres vase clock shown in Fig. 549, in the Louis XVI. style, affords another example of the fancies characterising the latter part of the eighteenth century.

The very pretty example of Louis XVI. style which is shown in Fig. 550 is by Vulliamy, and graces one of the drawing-rooms at Windsor Castle. On the ormolu slab above the dial is a drawing of the fusee and demonstration of its action.

Fig. 551 is another specimen by the same maker, and is also at Windsor Castle.

Fig. 554.

Fig. 555.

For the example shown in Fig. 552, dating from about 1790, I was indebted to the late Mr Robert Rolfe.

From about 1760 till well on in the nineteenth century, elegant mantel clocks of marble and bronze, in which the dial depended from a handsome entablature, were much favoured in France.

The two examples in Figs. 554 and 555, for which I am indebted to Messrs Jump & Sons, give a good idea of the best of them.

Fig. 554 is a clock by Engaz, of Paris, which shows the day of the week and the day of the month, on a dial bearing the signature of Dubisson.

Fig. 555 represents a somewhat similar design covering a clock by La Croix, Rue Denis, Paris.

Berthoud was apparently partial to this form, judging from the number to be seen with his name thereon.

The clock with white marble base and sphinx supporters for the dial, and shown in Fig. 556, by Solians, Paris, is at Windsor Castle.

In Chapter III. were given illustrations of early German timekeepers, in which figures of animals formed a most important part of the structure. A revival of this extraordinary conception seems to have found favour in France during the eighteenth century, when huge beasts were introduced as carriers for timekeepers.

The example illustrated in Fig. 557 is a clock by a noted Paris maker, Bailly l'aîné, dating from about 1769. It strikes the hour and half-hour in passing, and its dial, as in most French clocks of that period, stands out conspicuously. The occupants of the ponderous castle are evidently engaged in warfare. The elephant is of dark-coloured bronze, the remainder being chased and richly gilt, while the rajah, a coloured terra-cotta figure, seated inside the castle, complacently directs operations against the enemy. A small hole between his lips suggests the possibility of his having at one time a pipe

Fig. 556.

Fig. 557.

Fig. 558.

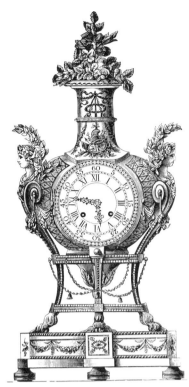

Fig. 559. — Porcelain Case with mounts by Gouthière.

in his mouth. In the Jones collection at South Kensington is an elephant with a clock on its back. It is signed by Caffieri, and illustrated in Fig. 558.

Clock cases of porcelain were made during the eighteenth century, chiefly at Dresden and Sèvres, though Berlin, Worcester, Derby, and Chelsea contributed to the demand. Some of them were very beautiful, especially French productions of Louis XV. period, which were decorated with figure subjects and scenery taken from pictures by Watteau, Lancret, and other artists. But comparatively few survive, for, apart from such accidents as lead to the destruction of china generally, the fixing of a clock movement to so brittle a material sufficiently tight to withstand the strain of winding is responsible for the fracture of a large proportion.

Among the Jones collection at South Kensington is a splendid clock in a case of Sèvres porcelain, formed like a vase, with mounts by Gouthière, which is believed to have been made for Marie Antoinette, and is shown in Fig. 559.* Charming it certainly is, and beyond criticism; still, if one might be permitted to complain, I would say it is too small, too condensed; it measures but about 12 in. in height.

The travelling or carriage clock belonging to the same royal lady, also in the Jones collection, of which a sketch appears in Fig. 560, has the dial, front, side, and back panels all of Sèvres porcelain, jewelled; it is between 10 and 11 in. high. The front panel bears the signature, "Robin Hʳ du Roy." Though undoubtedly of French make, the outline bears a singular resemblance to English productions of the period.

Fig. 560. — Carriage Clock of Marie Antoinette.

* The four illustrations of clocks in the Jones collection are from the Official Handbook, and are inserted by permission of the Controller of His Majesty's Stationery Office.

A vase containing a clock by L. Montjoye, fl.1748-89. The case is of green oeil de perdrix porcelain embellished with gold and with chased and gilt bronze mounts. Although relatively uncommon such magnificent table-pieces were popular in mid-18th century France. Reproduced by permission of the Trustees of the Wallace Collection.

Fig. 561.

Clocks at Windsor Castle.

Fig. 562.

Fig. 563.

The elegant lyre-shaped clock of Sèvres, illustrated in Fig. 547, is another excellent example. A clock by "Godon, Paris," in a vase-shaped case of Sèvres porcelain of Louis XVI. period, which was in Lord Strathallan's collection, realised two thousand guineas at Christie's in 1902. A quaint clock case of Chelsea china is to be seen at the British Museum.

From the middle to the end of the eighteenth century, the shops of leading horologists in Paris were, it is said, a great attraction to visitors. The earlier ones included Thiout l'aîné, at the sign of "La Pendule d'Equation," Quai Pelletier; Julien Le Roy, at Rue de Harley, where also was Berthoud; Pierre Regnault, père, Rue Vielle-du-Temple; Le Paute, aux galeries du Louvres, opposite the Rue Saint-Thomas; Lepine, and also Romilly, Place Dauphine; Leroux, Rue Guenegaud; Gosselin, Rue St Honoré. Later on were Carcel, at Pont Saint-Michel; Breguet, at Quai d'Horloge, 65; Caron, Rue Saint-Denis, 224; Lepaute jeune, Place du Palais-Royal; Lepine, Place des Victoires; Pierre Le Roy, Palais-Royal; and Wagner, at the sign of the Carillon, Bout-du-Monde, 2.

Louis XVI. had from a youth a liking for the mechanical parts of timekeepers, and Marie Antoinette possessed a large number of choice specimens, notably those illustrated in Figs. 559 and 560, but there are in existence clocks and watches purporting to have belonged to her, and having thereon M. A. interlaced, which were really made between about 1818 and 1830, when enthusiasm at the restoration of the French monarchy induced people to pay high prices for anything connected with the Court of Louis XVI. Watches apparently of Swiss manufacture, the cases decorated with gold of different tints (à quatre couleurs), as illustrated in Chapter IV., or with small oval plaques containing enamelled portraits of ladies, bordered with paste diamonds or pearls, and surrounded by engravings of bows and knots, are often seen, with a pedigree of former ownership which will not bear expert examination.

Undeterred by the failure of Sully's enterprise at Versailles in 1718, and the collapse of Voltaire's venture at Ferney sixty years afterwards, the French Government in 1786, on the strong recommendation of Berthoud, Gregson, Romilly, and Lepaute, established a clock manufactory at Paris, which, however, had but an ephemeral existence, for it succumbed to the stormy events of 1789. The episode is little known, and might escape record but for the splendid medal issued as a reward for meritorious pupils, the obverse of which is reproduced in Fig. 561. It was designed by Duvivier, engraver to the Paris Mint, and contains a representation of Father Time journeying round the periphery of a clock. The aphorism, "Le tems a pris un corps et marche sous nos yeux," is a quotation from Delille. In 1838 yet another attempt was made in the same direction, and a factory initiated at Versailles under the special protection of the king. This also proved to be an ill-starred venture, for it languished almost from its inception and collapsed in the course of three or four years.

With the return of Napoleon from Italy came a marked change in the French style of design. The soft harmonious conceits of Louis XVI. artists gave place to more severe and statuesque productions with heavy draperies, founded on ancient Roman models. Representative specimens at Windsor Castle are illustrated in Figs. 562 and 563. A good example having a characteristically long and deep base, is shown in Fig. 553. The case, 27 in.

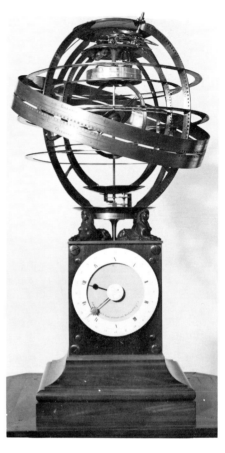

An astronomical clock combined with a Ptolemaic armillary sphere with a moon. On one dial the time is shown according to both the usual 24-hour system and the 10-hour system of the French republic. The phases of the moon and its position relative to the sun are also shown. On the second face are two concentric dials for mean and sidereal time. On top of the armillary are two cylindrical time recording rings which show the equation of time.

The clock which is signed 'An VII 1798-9 No 291 Janvier Inv. et Fecit. Breguet et Fils' has a dead-beat pin wheel escapement, runs for one month and has a grid-iron pendulum. In complication, accuracy, and execution it is a master-piece of its kind. Museum of the History of Science, Oxford.

Fig. 564. — Clock in Windsor Castle.

Fig. 565.

Fig. 566.

high, is of bronze, with finely executed chased work, gilded. It belongs to Mr A. House. The movement is signed "Le Roy & Fils, Hors du Rois, à Paris."

Fig. 564 shows a fine clock in the First Empire style, which is at Windsor Castle. It is by Jefferson, London, and dates from about 1810.

For a photograph of the little clock shown in Fig. 565, I am indebted to Messrs. Jump & Sons.

Portable table or bedroom clocks, cased in the form of a drum, and especially convenient to travellers, were in favour from the latter part of the eighteenth century till, debased and shorn of all enrichment, they degenerated both as ornaments and timekeepers. An example in the best style, with well-chased gilt fauns as supporters, and surmounted by an eagle holding a ring by which the clock could be lifted, is shown in Fig. 566. It strikes the hours and quarters, and the striking may be repeated at pleasure by pulling out the knob on the back of the eagle; it is also provided with an alarm.

Fig. 567.

Fig. 568.

Fig. 569. — Orrery Clock.

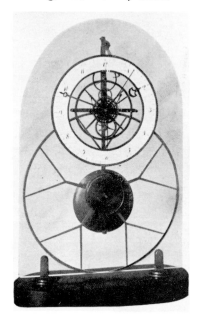

Fig. 570. — All parts mounted on a Glass Plate.

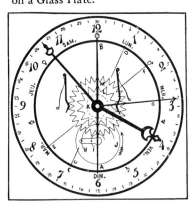

Fig. 571. — Dial of Glass Plate Clock.

Table clocks with horizontal dials were revived during the First Empire. A pretty specimen of gilt metal, in which the movement is enclosed by the base, is shown in Fig. 567. It dates from 1806-10 and has but one hand, which may be set by turning one of the little ornaments standing up from the lower part of the case. The band around the dial is pierced to a pretty design. It strikes the hours and quarters.

The handsome clock carrying an orrery actuated by the mechanism of the timekeeper which is shown in Fig. 569, belongs to Mr S. H. Hole. For the photograph of it I am indebted to Mr J. Bolton Smith. An orrery clock by Raingo, of a later date, in a plain case is at Windsor Castle, and in the Soane Museum is a similar piece by the same maker.

A fine example of French horological ingenuity, from the collection of Mr James Arthur, is depicted in Fig. 570. All the parts are attached to a sheet of plate glass, giving the structure the appearance of a clock floating in the air. The mainspring barrel is seen in front of and just a little higher than the pendulum bob, and on its arbor runs the truly great wheel. It goes for a month between windings, and shows the day of the week and day of the month.

An enlarged view of the ring dial, together with mechanism for operating the calendar which is given in Fig. 571, will repay examination. The hour and minute hands are easily distinguished, and of excellent form. There is a

An attractive demi-regulateur in a brass case glazed on four sides on a marble base. The dial is signed 'Lepine a Paris', has dead-beat escapement and a compensated pendulum. Of particular interest is the pulley wheel string arrangement to enable the weights to find sufficient drop in the small case. Sotheby Parke Bernet & Co.

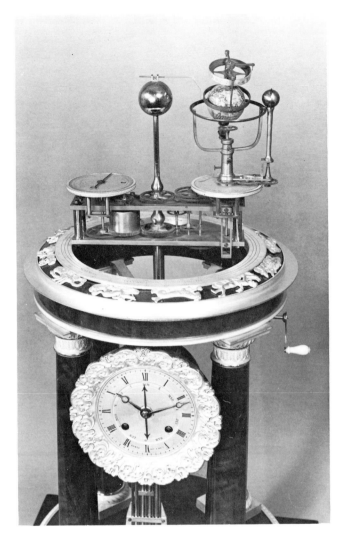

An orrery clock signed by Raingo Frères à Paris, c.1820. About ten clocks of this type are known to survive and although not identical are closely similar. The movement has a dead-beat escapement and a grid-iron pendulum, unlike some others it does not strike. It has a silvered dial with a concentric day of the week calendar, read against the double ended centre hand, which indicates the day at one end and a tutelary deity at the other. Set above the clock on a platform carried by four pillars is an orrery movement which may be driven either by the clock or, by loosening a set screw, manually by the crank handle at the side. Bobinet Ltd.

Fig. 572.

double-ended pointer marked A B which goes round in fourteen days. Each extremity of it alternately indicates the day of the week and the sign corresponding to that day. At present it is in position for Sunday (*Dimanche*) and the Sun. Next day the points will have shifted to C D, Monday (*Lundi*) and the Moon, the following day to E F, Tuesday (*Mardi*) and Mars, and so on throughout the two weeks, when the pointers will have returned to the position shown. The minute circle is utilised for the day-of-the-month hand G, every alternate minute mark being numbered for this purpose.

The pointer A B is connected with the star wheel L of fourteen teeth, the day-of-the-month hand G with the star wheel M of thirty teeth. The usual twelve-hour wheel K drives the twenty-four hour wheel J, carrying the crank H I and its two projecting pins, which in their course turn the star wheels one tooth per day.

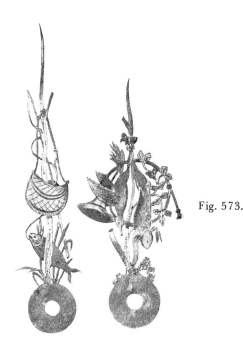

Fig. 573.

Fig. 574.

Fig. 575.

Fig. 576.

Fig. 577.

A more ingenious plan for day and month calendar work with so few extra parts it would be difficult to devise. It is clever by its simplicity. For months other than those of thirty days the hand G would, of course, have to be adjusted at the end of the month. A timepiece, doubtless by the same maker, but without the calendar, is in the Conservatoire National des Arts et Metiers, Paris.

Clocks with cases of a nondescript character, but abounding in ormolu or gilt metal ornament so popular at the latter part of the eighteenth and beginning of the nineteenth centuries, seem to have entirely died out of favour. At Windsor Castle is an early example with a winged boy on each side of the dial, and a celestial globe and mathematical instruments above it, as shown in Fig. 568.

Fig. 572 shows a remarkably well modelled figure of a harlequin, who is represented as drawing attention to the notes of the bird peeping from an alcove above the dial.

Clock hands do not as a rule lend themselves to decoration symbolical of a particular subject, but three pairs typical respectively of Sport, Agriculture, and Music, which appear to be worth reproduction, are shown in Figs. 573, 574, 575. They are French, and were, I believe, designed for presentation timekeepers.

It may be noted that up to the end of the eighteenth century movements of the French chamber clocks were rectangular even though the cases were circular, as in the example by Berthoud shown in Figs. 545, 546; the bell always surmounted the movement instead of being at the back of it, as the modern custom is, and the pendulum was suspended by means of a silken cord.

Adjuncts to a clock in the way of candelabra, tazzas or figures *en suite*, were not in use till nearly the end of the reign of Louis XVI.

By way of contrast to the French treatment the two cartel timepieces shown in Figs. 576 and 577 will be of interest. They are reproduced from

A directoire *French mantel regulator signed Henry N[ev]eu de Lepaute A Paris, c.1790-95, showing a typically severe line in the case but with a very well executed movement and dial. There are four hands for minutes, hours, centre seconds, and the concentric year calendar. At the centre of the dial is a moon phase aperture. The clock runs for three weeks, strikes on a bell, has a pin wheel escapement and grid-iron temperature compensated pendulum on a knife-edge suspension. The maker of the clock was Pierre Henry (1745-1806) who in 1761 entered the firm of his uncle Jean Baptiste Lepaute (1727-1802). On the retirement of Lepaute's partner (his brother the well known Jean André Lepaute) in 1774, Pierre Henry became a partner in the firm, probably adopting the form of signature shown on the clock after his uncle's retirement in 1789. Bobinet Ltd.*

The falling ball clock was not, as Britten implied, an 18th century novelty, but dates back at least to the 15th century. Full details for the construction of such a clock are, for example, given by the noted mathematician and instrument-maker, Jean Fusoris. The Trustees of the British Museum.

designs by Giovanni Battista Piranesi, which were published in 1761. Fig. 577 is modelled upon the form of an ancient Roman rudder, a conceit particularly to the taste of that age. It will be noticed that each of the dials is divided into six hours, in conformity with the counting of the hours in many parts of Italy at that time.

FALLING BALL TIMEKEEPERS

This remarkably clever and elegant piece of seventeenth century mysterious horology consists of a sphere of brass, to be suspended from a bracket, or the ceiling of a room. The upper and lower portions of the ball are gilt, while around a silvered band in the middle are marked two serials of Roman numerals from I. to XII., and subdivisions for the quarter-hours. The extremity of one of the wings of a cupid on the lower part of the ball points to the hour of the day or night. The construction may be gathered from the vertical and horizontal sections which are given in Fig. 578, borrowed from "Les Merveilles de l'Horlogerie." The suspending cord is coiled round a barrel, with which is connected a train of wheels terminating in an escapement and balance. While the top and bottom of the ball are rigidly connected, the middle is free to move, and is furnished with a ring of teeth projecting inside, through which the middle is rotated once in twenty-four hours, the weight of the ball acting as a driving force. The mechanism is wound by simply raising the ball with the hand, there being a weak spring in the barrel, which causes it to turn and coil the suspending cord on to itself.

At the British Museum are two of these falling ball timekeepers of 4 in. in diameter. One of them is inscribed "Jacob Behan, Vienna." In the National Museum, Cracow, is one signed "Davidt-Schröter-in Elbing." Schröter flourished about 1680-90. The Society of Antiquaries possesses a very fine

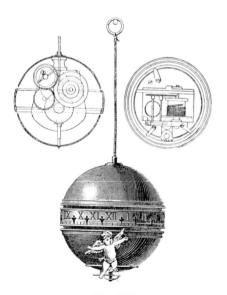

Fig. 578.

Fig. 579.

Fig. 580.

332

example, measuring 10 in. across, but of, I fancy, much later date. It was given to the Society by B. L. Vulliamy.

Figs. 579 and 580 represent two of many timekeepers designed and made by a truly remarkable mechanical genius, Nicolas Grollier, afterwards M. Grollier de Servière, who was born at Lyons in 1593, and passed his early manhood in the service of the French army. His later years he devoted to designing all sorts of mechanism, and, thus providing himself with ample occupation, he managed to reach the good old age of ninety-three years.

These two drawings are from a thick quarto book written by his grandson, and dedicated to Louis XIV. In the first example a small ball runs down inclined shoots, and by its momentum unlocks the train as it reaches the bottom. There are two balls, and as the first disappears from view the second one begins its descent. The balls are, in turn, carried up at the back by a kind of tape ladder with pockets, which passes over a pulley at the top, and another at the lower part of the case.

Left: a vase clock with projection facilities for reading the time at night. Mounted at one side of the vase is a double sided watch (i.e. having two dials). Opposite is a tube containing a lens. In the bottom of the urn is a lamp entirely enclosed but with a door in the side of the urn for access so that the light may be adjusted. Beneath it is a case to receive waste oil from the lamp. During the day the time is read from the outside dial in the normal manner. At night however the lamp is lit and the image of the interior dial which is made of concave polished steel or glass with the numerals reversed, is projected through the lens onto a wall.

This device was invented by Johan Schmidt, who took out a patent for it in 1808. In the same patent he also described a mystery clock (p.336-337) which could be made as an independent timepiece, or as an orrery clock, or used in association with the vase night clock. The basic form of the mystery clock is shown by Britten, who also mentions that illustrated here (right) by J. McNabb, Perth. It follows Schmidt's design but is an example of the clock in its orrery form, the watch globe being marked with the signs of the zodiac. The figure of Father Time which replaces Schmidt's dolphin may not be original. The movement is controlled by a verge escapement. *The Trustees of the British Museum.*

GLOBES, URNS AND VASES

Fig. 581. — The Jagellons Time-piece.

Fig. 582.

Fig. 583. — At Windsor Castle.

One of the most remarkable timepieces embodying the form of the earth is in the Bibliothèque des Jagellons, Cracow. For illustration and particulars of this I am indebted to Dr Tad Estreicher, professor of the University, Fribourg, Switzerland. The result of his research places the date of its construction at about 1510, the French astronomer, Louis Boulengier, being probably the inventor of it. The photograph is rather dim but the action will be understood with the following explanation. The outer part of the initial meridian is mounted on a stand and the inner is free for adjustment of the inclination of the earth. Fixed to it is a light cage giving the hours I. to XII. twice over on hourly meridians. Within is another frame of meridians with the ecliptic which, actuated by mechanism within the globe, makes one turn in twenty-four hours. A figure of the sun travels with the ecliptic, and denotes the time. The sun is carried by a curved wire emanating from a wheel near the south pole and, as it passes a fixed pin in the axis of the globe, it is, by the intervention of a pinion, each day put back on the ecliptic one 365th part of the circle. So that not only is mean solar time shown but the sidereal day, the height of the sun, and, as the months are named around the ecliptic, it forms a calendar as well. An interesting feature of this timekeeper is the globular representation of the earth, which has been pronounced by leading cartologists to be the earliest post-columbian globe, and the earliest to give any part of the new world. America, though, is put in quite a wrong place. A continent marked "AMERICA NOVITER REPERTA" corresponds fairly well with Australia, and is believed to be the first cartographical recognition of that place. In the "Atlas" timekeeper by Grollier de Servière (Fig. 580), the movement within the globe causes the central band, on which the hours are marked, to revolve, the arrow, of course, indicating the time. The upper and lower portions of the globe are stationary.

A taste for revolving band timekeepers, formed as globes, urns, and vases, revived in France during the eighteenth century. The exteriors of some of these were of very elegant design, as may be judged from the examples submitted.

Fig. 582 shows a particularly attractive one dating from about 1780, which is at the South Kensington Museum. The boys supporting the globe are of bronze. The moving band contains two sets of numerals painted blue on enamelled plaques; the lower set each fifteen minutes. The tongue of a snake forms a bar across each successive hour numeral, as an indicator, and reaching beyond it, points to the minutes also. By counting the hours I. to XII. twice over, the band as it travels in its course round the earth becomes a universal time-teller. At Nether Swell Manor is a somewhat similar structure standing on an ornamental base and surmounted by a pair of love-birds.

In the Throne room at Windsor Castle is a globe clock which has double revolving bands, Roman hour numerals being marked on one band, and on the other Arabic figures to represent the minutes. It is by Maniere, of Paris, and adorned with a well-executed group, as in Fig. 583. The ball, enamelled in royal blue, forms a properly conspicuous centre, on each side of which the statuettes are arranged. The hour is shown by the coincidence of a numeral with the brass vertical bar supporting the globe, while the Destroyer is posed to indicate the minute with his scythe.

Fig. 584.

The Wallace collection also includes more than one fine globe clock with hour and minute revolving bands.

Fig. 584 represents a vase clock, which is said to have belonged to Marie Antoinette. The movement was covered by a handsome carved marble pedestal, the urn being of porcelain with bronze mountings. A serpent coiled round the foot of the vase had its head erect to point to the hour on the double polygonal band.

Fig. 585 shows a larger urn or vase mounted on an elaborately carved square plinth; a somewhat similar clock by "Le Loutre, horloger du Roy, Paris," realised £903 at the Hamilton sale in 1882.

In Fig. 586 is reproduced a magnificent design by Falconet, wherein the Three Graces are portrayed, one of whom indicates the hour with her finger. The vase is supported by a column standing on a handsome plinth; the panels of the plinth show very choice carvings of groups of children at play. Etienne Maurice Falconet, whose production of this and some other clock cases stamps him as an artist of the front rank, was born in 1716 and died in 1791, and seems to have been more appreciated after his death than before. The Three Graces clock was sold in the early part of the nineteenth century for 1,500 francs, and in 1855 was purchased for 7,000 francs by Baron Double, whose collection was sold in 1881 when Comte de Camondo secured the Three Graces for 101,000 francs. His son, who is the present owner, has, it is said, refused an offer of over a million francs for the treasure, which, in accordance with the wish of his father, he will bequeath to the French nation.

Fig. 585.

Fig. 586.

Fig. 587. — Negress-head Clock at Buckingham Palace.

Among the eccentricities of French horology is one at Buckingham Palace in the form of the head of a negress, as shown in Fig. 587. Figures corresponding to the hours appear in proper order in one of the eyes of the negress, the minutes being denoted in the other eye in a similar way. By closing the eyelids the figures may be rendered invisible.

ROLLING CLOCK

This ingenious device appears to have been patented by that universal genius the Marquess of Worcester, in 1661 (No. 131). It was also made by Grollier de Servière probably about the same date. Maurice Wheeler published a description of it as his invention in Lowthorp's "Abridgment of the Philosophical Transactions in 1684." Its construction will be understood from the uncovered view of the front, Fig. 588. There is a train of wheels and an escapement as in a watch. The great wheel a carries the hand and also the weight b. The clock never requires winding. It is every morning simply placed at the top of the inclined plane, down which it gradually rolls during the day, the hand pointing to the hour marked on the dial, which of course covers the mechanism. The length of the plane had better be more than twice the circumference of the clock case c. Its inclination may be regulated by the screw g. The hand may be in the form of a figure of Time, as in Fig. 588, a serpent's head, or other grotesque design.

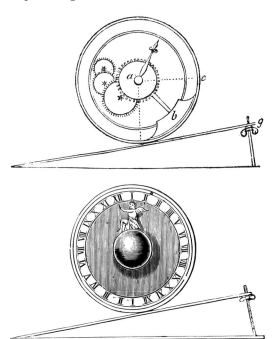

Fig. 588. — Rolling Clock. In the Upper View the Dial is removed to exhibit the actuating movement described above.

SCHMIDT'S MYSTERIOUS CLOCK

The weighted lever of the rolling clock, as shown in Fig. 588, has been utilised in another form of mysterious timekeeper, an exterior view of which is given in Fig. 589. It was patented in 1808 (No. 3,185) by John Schmidt, a watchmaker, living in St Mary Axe. He called it "The Mysterious Circulator, or Chronological Equilibrium." The ring is divided into hour and five-minute spaces. The watch movement, with the weighted lever, is contained in the box C, but it is now driven by a mainspring in the usual way. The hand is pivoted to the tail of the dolphin. D is a counterweight. The weighted lever revolves once in twelve hours; it would be nearest to the centre of motion of

Fig. 589.

Fig. 590.

the hand at twelve o'clock, and furthest from it at six o'clock; it is easy, therefore, to see that by this displacement of the centre of gravity the weighted lever would cause the hand to revolve and point to the time. It appears that Schmidt was a Dane, who was taken prisoner at Copenhagen, and brought to England. The clocks were sold by Rundell & Bridge, whose shop was in Ludgate Hill. Several distinguished persons are stated to have become purchasers. Some years ago I saw one which bore the name of McNab, Perth. It was then in the possession of Mr Robert Napier, but it now belongs to Mr Henry Levy.

This device has been several times re-invented, but never, I think, in so elegant a form as the original.

FAN-SHAPED CLOCKS M. Planchon has an engraving of the tutor to Charles, son of Phillippe II. of Spain, on which is shown a timekeeper, the dial being composed of a double fan of white and black slats which expanded and contracted to suit hours of varying length in day and night throughout the year. This dates from about 1570. Other forms of fan timekeepers have been constructed and should be mentioned as among horological curiosities. The illustration, Fig. 590, was published some time ago in *La Nature*. The fan, composed of thirteen very light slats, is pivoted to a backing covered with velvet, and at six o'clock in the morning and in the evening would be wide open as shown, and a serpent, fixed by its tail to the velvet, would point to the hour with its tongue. Immediately after six o'clock the fan suddenly closes, the serpent still pointing to six, but it would then be the figure on the right-hand side of the fan. On a continuation of the joint of the fan is a pinion actuated by a rack in connection with a snail-shaped cam, which causes the fan to gradually open as the hours progress, and then suddenly close.

SUSPENDED BIRD CAGE This, from the Schloss collection, is probably a combined French and Swiss production of about 1780. An enamelled dial with centre seconds hand projects below the bottom of the cage, the actuating mechanism being hidden in the plinth, which is adorned with oval enamels of scenery in the Swiss style. In niches at the corners are fine statuettes of Sèvres biscuit. At the completion of each hour the birds move, flutter, and trill a sort of duet, their actions and notes being remarkably natural. By means of rotating pieces of glass, a double-fall fountain appears to be playing in the centre. These motions can be caused to repeat at pleasure by pulling a string. The few somewhat similar clocks known to exist are highly prized by their owners. One not so decorative as the example here shown [Fig. 591] is in the King of Italy's summer palace at Monza.

MAGNETIC TIMEKEEPERS

Grollier de Servière devised a timekeeper resembling a shallow bowl with a wide rim, having marked thereon the twelve hour numerals, as in Fig. 592; the bowl being filled with water; the figure of a tortoise was placed on it and at once floated round till it pointed to the time, and then gradually crept to the figures in succession as the hours advanced. Underneath the rim of the bowl was a magnet of the horseshoe type, which was caused to revolve once in twelve hours; the tortoise was of cork and carried the "keeper" of the magnet. By the same agency he was enabled to cause a lizard to ascend a column and a mouse to creep along a cornice with the hours marked on the frieze below.

CONGREVE CLOCK

William Congreve, best known as an inventor of war rockets, was an ingenious mechanician, an officer in the Royal Artillery, and a member of Parliament. In succession to his father he in 1814 became a baronet and also Comptroller of the Royal Laboratory at Woolwich. In 1808 he patented a timekeeper in which a small metal ball rolled down grooves in an inclined plane, which was movable on its centre. The grooves were zigzag, forming a succession of V's, so that the ball, once started, traversed the whole surface of the plate by rolling down one groove and entering the next at the point of the V. On arriving at the lowest point of the inclined plane the ball with its acquired impetus unlocked the train, which thereupon reversed the inclination of the plane or table by the intervention of a crank and connecting rod, and the ball started on its journey in the other direction.

Fig. 591.

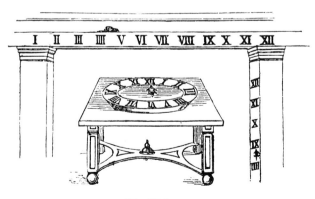

Fig. 592.

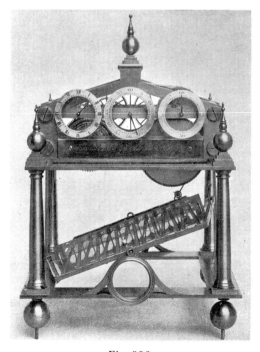

Fig. 593.

338

The ball should be of platinum or other dense material to ensure sufficient impact in unlocking. Congreve clocks, as they are called, go fairly well if made with exactness and kept free from dust, but in spite of their really attractive appearance but few of them appear to have been made. At the Rotunda, Woolwich, is one of these curiosities bearing the following inscription: "This first experiment of a new principle for the measurement of time, invented by William Congreve, Esq., is humbly presented to His Royal Highness the Prince of Wales, 1808." Mr R. Eden Dickson has one; another belongs to Mr W. W. Astor; I saw a fine specimen dating from about 1820, inscribed "John Bentley and James Beck, Royal Exchange." For the example in Fig. 593, which is signed "Henry Bell, Mount St.," I am indebted to Messrs Jump & Sons. The three dials indicate respectively hours, minutes, and seconds.

JAPANESE CLOCKS

四 4   七 7
五 5   八 8
六 6   九 9

Japanese Clocks are peculiar. Formerly the Japs divided the daylight and darkness each into a period of six hours, which therefore, except twice a year, would be of unequal duration. Here are representations of the six hour numerals which were used twice over and counted backwards. Mr James Arthur in "Time and its Measurement" tells us that animal equivalents were used to distinguish the two sets of hours, 9 at noon being *Horse*, and 9 at midnight *Rat*; the morning 8, *Ox*, the afternoon 8 *Sheep*; the morning 7, *Tiger*, the afternoon 7, *Monkey*; the morning 6 (sunrise), *Hare*, the afternoon 6 (sunset), *Cock*; the morning 5, *Dragon*, the afternoon 5, *Dog*; the morning 4, *Snake*, the afternoon 4, *Boar*. In the simplest forms of timekeepers the dial rotated, the hour being indicated by a fixed pointer. The hour numerals for noon and midnight remained stationary, the others were shifted on the dial at intervals as required by the season.

Fig. 594 shows a simple Japanese timepiece. There is no dial, but the progress of time is indicated by the downward motion of the driving weight. A pointer attached to the weight projects through a longitudinal slit running the length of the body of the case, and clasped on to the front are metal

A small Japanese clock in a fruitwood case with one hand and inro decoration. Sotheby Parke Bernet & Co.

A relatively small (170mm high) Japanese bracket clock, 19th century. Two train movement with a fusee for the going train, and a going barrel for the striking train. Verge escapement with balance wheel and locking plate strike on a bell. The dial plate, which is florally decorated, carries a revolving chapter ring and has a fixed hand. The movement is held between two platforms and has four scrolled pillars. The case is of shitan wood and the front and back panels are removable.

Fig. 594.

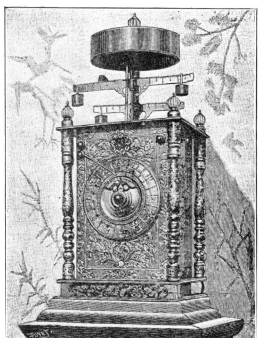

Fig. 595.

Fig. 596.

Fig. 597. — Japanese Table Clock.

hour marks which may be adjusted to different heights by the thumb and finger. There are thirteen of these marks, the last one being a repetition of the first. To the Rev. D. Holland Stubbs, who has a number of Japanese clocks, I am indebted for the illustration.

In a form of striking clock presumably used by the more wealthy classes, dials were provided and also two balances of the cross-bar kind, one of which controlled the motion by day and the other by night. At sunset, by means of a pin in the locking-plate of the striking train, one was automatically switched out of connection with the train, and the other substituted. Each arm of the balances had notches throughout its length, and the weights were shifted by hand at fortnightly periods as in the more primitive timekeepers. Half-hours as well as hours were sounded, the strokes on the bell being given in the following order: 9, 1, 8, 2, 7, 1, 6, 2, 5, 1, 4, 2. The hours are 9, 8, 7, 6, 5, 4, the halves, 1, 2, 1, 2, 1, 2. In this way, when the half-hour was struck the hearer knew to which one of any two hours it referred.

There is a cross-bar Japanese clock with dial at the Horological Institute, and one with the automatic alternating arrangement at the South Kensington Museum. Fig. 595 shows it very well. This and Fig. 596 are from *La Nature*, which two or three years ago contained an interesting article by Mons. Planchon on Japanese methods of timekeeping. No. 1 of Fig. 596 is of porcelain, and No. 2 decorated with Japanese lacquer. In the latter the small counterweights are masked with tassels.

For a view the exact size of the dial of a table clock I am indebted to Mr F. Lodder. The hand is stationary and the dial rotates. Attached to the shifting hour pieces are pins which let off the hour striking mechanism at the right moment whatever may be the position of the pieces.

Right: An example of a rack clock which somewhat unexpectedly appears to have been made in Japan. Plain oak case with carrying handle. The Trustees of the British Museum.

A month going mantel clock of oak veneered with ebony, with inlaid brass stringing and glazed sides. Brocot's visible dead-beat escapement very lightly and delicately made with carnelian pallets and embracing only thirteen teeth of the escape wheel rather than the more usual fifteen or sixteen. It has a very large and heavy temperature compensated pendulum with fine attachment adjustment and running in a guard at the bottom. White enamel dial, circular brass plated movement with going barrel, signed E. & E. Emanuel, the Hard Portsea, the retailers of the clock which was certainly made in France. An unusual feature is that in order that the dial need not be broken by a winding hole, the clock is wound from below the bottom front of the dial, the arbor being turned through the right angle by a bevelled gear.

A Japanese bracket clock on a plain stand, 19th century. Two train brass posted movement with two verge and foliot escapements to the going train. The sides, back, and dial plate are decoratively engraved. The chapter ring has a revolving pointer together with a brass disc and pointer to adjust the striking release. There are calendar apertures below. In the sides and back of the case are frets in the shape of birds, and the whole clock is driven by the brass weights which fall in the centre of the stand. Just under three feet in height, clocks like these may be considered the Japanese equivalents of the longcase clock.

MAILLARDET's
MAGNIFICENT
AUTOMATICAL EXHIBITION,
Great Room, Spring-Gardens,

Having been several Times honored with the presence of

Their Majesties,

And Patronized by SEVERAL of the NOBILITY,

IS NOW OPEN
FOR PUBLIC INSPECTION,

From 12 till 4 in the Morning, and from 7 till 10 at Night; And brilliantly Illuminated Every Evening.

I. AN elegant Figure of a YOUNG LADY, seated at an Organ, formed on a new Construction, which in Shape resembles a Piano-Forte, it plays with the most accurate precision, Sixteen Airs, every Note proceeding from the pressure of the Fingers, on the appropriated Keys; the Feet not only beat time and regulate the Piano and Forte Movements, but assist in playing several Notes in a new and improved manner; the Gracefulness of its gesture, and lively Motion of its Eyes, are heightened by the actual Appearance of respiration.

II. A ROPE DANCER, whose Agility surpasses every Feat that has hitherto been attempted, with the Advantage of perfect Security from Accident; its Movements are regulated by Music, to which it keeps Time with critical Punctuality.

III. A Figure of a CHILD, which with all the Movements of real Life, will execute (during the stay of the Visitor) Specimens of Writing and Drawing, equal to the most perfect productions of the first Masters in those Professions.

This Figure is likewise an adept in the Art of Engraving, and Specimens of his Abilities, are to be had at the Room.

IV. A CONJURER, who resolves every Question put to him with as strict an adherence to truth as any Astrologer in the World, whom he challenges, for a Trial of skill, with this advantage, that so far from employing any evil Agent, his Decisions proceed entirely from a combination of the Powers of Mechanism alone.

V. A GOLD BOX, from which a Bird suddenly darts, and in the Action of flying, warbles its native notes, and concludes with an Air; when finished it returns to the Box and shuts itself in.

VI. An exact Representation of that rare and beautiful Insect called ARANEA, which, by being placed on a Table, will traverse its Surface, self-moved, in a variety of Directions.

VII. The CURCULIO IMPERALIS, from the Brazils, which seen through a Glass, appears as if composed of precious Stones, in all their variety of Colours. Whoever Views this prodigy of Nature, must exclaim " Who can Form and who can *Paint* like her."

ADMISSION TWO SHILLINGS AND SIX-PENCE.

T. WOODFALL, PRINTER, DRURY-LANE.

A typical publicity announcement for an 18th century display of curious timepieces and automata.

Chapter VII

The Progression of English Domestic Clocks

THE MANUFACTURE OF chamber clocks for domestic use, as distinguished from the costly and highly decorated timekeepers made for public buildings or to gratify the tastes of the wealthy, seems to have commenced about 1600. These chamber clocks were of the pattern known as "lantern," "birdcage," or "bedpost." They were either hung against a wall or supported on a bracket, and wound by pulling down the opposite ends of the ropes to those from which the driving weights were hung. In some instances all the hours were struck in regular progression on the bell surmounting the structure, and sometimes the bell was only utilised as an alarm. In all cases the second train, for actuating the hammer, was placed behind the train for the watch, or going part. The framing was composed of four corner posts connecting top and bottom plates, the pivots of the trains being supported in vertical bars. In none of them was the train calculated for going more than thirty hours. At first the escapement with vertical verge and a balance as in De Vick's clock was used as the controlling medium, the verge being usually suspended from a string.

About 1658 the pendulum was introduced, and quickly superseded the balance. The escape wheel was then as a rule planted to work in a horizontal plane, the pendulum being attached to the verge, and swinging either between the two trains of wheels or behind, according to the fancy of the maker. The alternate appearance of the pendulum weight at each side of the case led to its being called a "bob" pendulum, and pendulums of this kind are still known as bob pendulums, in contradistinction to the longer variety which at a later period, and with the anchor escapement, vibrated in a much smaller arc.

The movement was enclosed at the back with a brass plate; at the front was the dial plate, also of brass, and superimposed thereon a silvered hour band with engraved numerals; at the sides were brass doors, and when the

Figs. 598, 599. — Clock by William Bowyer, about 1620. In the Side Views may be seen the Circular Balance used as a Controller.

Fig. 600. — "Great Chamber Clock", 1623.

pendulum was between the trains, a slit was cut in each door to allow the pendulum to "bob" in and out.

In the earliest of these clocks the dials were, as a rule, thickly gilt; the hour circles narrow and the numerals stumpy, the front one of the frets surrounding the bell at top, in many instances, had a shield for the crest or initials of the owner. The doors were often made of sun dial plates, as may be seen from the engraving on the insides of early specimens; doubtless the introduction of clocks played havoc with the demand for the older time recorder, and induced many sun-dial makers to turn their attention to the production of clocks. The maker's name was engraved along the base of the fret; or inscribed at the top or bottom of the centre of the dial, just within the hour ring; or placed out of sight under the alarm plate, the latter practice leading to the assumption that the clock was to be sold by some one other than the maker. It may be assumed that each of the leading craftsmen introduced alterations in style from time to time and designed fretwork and other ornament for his exclusive use; but it is pretty evident that such variations were speedily copied by the general run of makers, for most clocks of the same period bear a marked resemblance to each other; possibly much of the material was supplied from the same foundry and cast from the same patterns. About 1640 the hour bands were made wider, with longer numerals, and the fret with the crossed dolphins came into use.

Among those who subscribed to the fund for obtaining the Charter of Incorporation of the Clockmakers' Company in 1630 was William Bowyer, who then appears to have been a clockmaker of repute. It is stated in Overall's "History of the Clockmakers' Company," that in 1642 Bowyer presented to the Company a great chamber clock in consideration of his being thereafter exempted from all office and service as well as quaterage and other fees.

Mr J. Drummond Robertson possesses a lantern clock by Wm. Bowyer, which is shown in Figs. 598 and 599. It dates probably from about 1620. The hour circle is of a primitive character, there being no division strokes to

An example of a 'quaker' or ring and zig-zag dial signed by Richard Gilkes, mid- to late 18th century. Dials like this having the central area filled with bands of concentric rings, engraved on a ground of radiating zig-zags, are apparently unique to North Oxfordshire clockmakers who were also members of the Society of Friends. They are not standardized in design, and vary greatly in quality of execution which suggests that they may have been made individually by each clockmaker. Richard Gilkes of Adderbury (1715-1787) however may have originated this design and have manufactured them on a wider scale. See C.F.C. Beeson, Clockmaking in Oxfordshire 1400-1850, *Oxford, 1967, pp 100-102. Museum of the History of Science, Oxford.*

mark the half-hours and quaters. The trains of wheels run in opposite directions, and the original balance of circular form 4½ in. in diameter, is retained. The extreme height of the clock is 16½ in., and the width of the dial 5¾ in.

Fig. 600 shows another specimen of Bowyer's work. It is a "large Chamber clock," which measures 8½ in. across the dial, its total height being 16½ in. Around the centre of the dial is inscribed, "William Bowyer of London fecit 1623." This was doubtless formerly covered by an alarm disc. Along the bottom of the dial is engraved, "Samuel Lynaker of London." Now Samuel Linaker was named in the Charter of Incorporation of the Clockmakers' Company to be one of the assistants, as the members of the Committee of Management were termed, and it seems to be a fair inference that the clock was made by Bowyer for Linaker.

On the side door of the clock, which is visible in Fig. 600, a figure of Time is engraved; and on the other door a figure of Death, as shown to a reduced scale in the sketch, Fig. 601. In the right hand of the figure appears to be a torch, and depending therefrom is a streamer, on which are the words, "The sting of death is sinne." The left hand holds a sand glass, and underneath are the following lines:—

> "Man is a glase, Life
> Is as water weakly washed about,
> Sinns brought in death.
> Death breaks the glase,
> So runes this water out."

In larger characters is the admonition, "Memento Mory."

Very possibly the doors of such clocks were engraved to suit the tastes of purchasers. There are no particulars obtainable as to the early history of this example. I remember seeing another large lantern clock by the same maker which was inscribed, "William Boyear, in Ledenhall Streete, fecit." The movement of this clock was arranged in the usual manner, the striking train behind the going, and working in three upright bars. It required a great fall of the driving weights to go thirty hours, as each of the main wheels made

English lantern clock signed 'T. Dadswell Burwash', c.1740. An excellent example of the survival of traditional forms to a later date in rural areas. The crudely executed decoration on the face and frets is entirely derivative from earlier models although the silvered chapter ring is a feature of later date. Anchor escapement with locking wheel strike and an endless rope drive. The weight is not original to the clock and appears to have been removed from a steel yard. The ring counter weight however is typical.

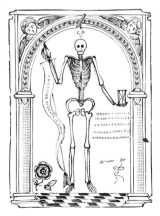

Fig. 601.

345

one rotation per hour. The original vertical escapement, as usual, had been removed; but from parts remaining it could be seen that it was identically the same as the drawings of De Vick's. The wheels and pinions, as one sometimes finds, were very little cut, and though evidently rounded by hand, seemed very nearly correct, and ran easily without chattering. The hour wheel was driven by a pinion of four, the end of the main wheel staff being filed up into four pins to serve the purpose.

Fig. 602.

Figs. 603, 604. — A large and a small Lantern Clock to the same scale, showing contrast in size.

Another interesting lantern clock of large size is shown in Fig. 602, the dial measuring 7⅛ in. across. The gallery fret above the dial is particularly well designed, and bears the inscription, "Thomas Knifton at the Cross Keys in Lothebury, Londini, Fecit. Thomas Knifton was well known among the early makers. On the upper part of the space within the hour ring is engraved, "This was given by William Adams, the founder of this Schoole, and is to be made use of for the benefit thereof, 1657." The reference is to a school in Newport, Shropshire, founded by William Adams and by him placed under the superintendence of the Haberdashers' Company, of which he was a member.

Clocks of this size were, I think, exceptional. Most that I have seen of the period varied from about 3 in. by 2½ in. to 5 in. square. Larger movements were more favoured at the end of the seventeenth century and beginning of the eighteenth century. After about 1660 the dial was, as a rule, increased in size with relation to the body of the clock so that it projected more on each side of the frame. This departure may be observed on the lantern clock by Tompion, which dated from about 1665, and is shown in Fig. 412.

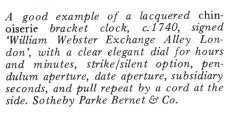

A good example of a lacquered chinoiserie bracket clock, c.1740, signed 'William Webster Exchange Alley London', with a clear elegant dial for hours and minutes, strike/silent option, pendulum aperture, date aperture, subsidiary seconds, and pull repeat by a cord at the side. Sotheby Parke Bernet & Co.

Left: Fig. 605. — Clock with Pendulum in Front of Dial. At the head of the pendulum is the figure of a Snipe which rocks to and fro.

Fig. 608. — Lantern Clock with Alarm as fixed to wall.

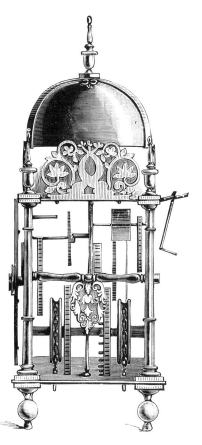

Far Left: Fig. 606.

Left: Fig. 607.

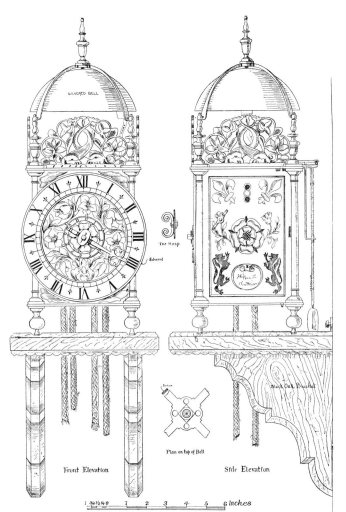

Front Elevation　　　　Side Elevation

Plan on top of Bell

1 ¾ ½ ¼ 0　1　2　3　4　5　6 Inches

*An entirely con-
ventional longcase
clock, signed in the dial
arch 'Wm Heard', late
18th century, with all
over silvered face and
hands of a later date. It
is of interest solely
because it is a miniature
clock, about 8in. high.
Christie, Manson &
Woods Ltd.*

Fig. 609.

Fig. 610. — Joseph Knibb, London. Alarm, Hour and Minute
Hands.

In Figs. 603 and 604 are shown to the same scale a fine specimen dating from about 1650 by Nicholas Coxeter and a smaller piece by Thomas Parker. These are both from the collection of Mr T. W. Bourne.

For the peculiar arrangement shown in Fig. 605 I am indebted to Mr W. H. Kendall. The pendulum is in front of the dial and on the top of it is perched a snipe which moves to and fro as the pendulum swings. The letters W. S., presumably the initials of the maker, are engraved on the clock, as is also the date, 1683.

Front and side views of a good specimen by Thomas Dyde, dating from about 1670, engraved by favour of Mr Shapland, are given in Figs. 606 and 607. A particular feature in this clock is the unusually elaborate pierced work attached to the hammer tail detent, which may be seen in Fig. 607.

Fig. 608 represents a little clock fixed to the wall. It is by Thomas Wheeler and belongs to Miss Mary F. Bragg. Fig. 609, taken from a drawing by Mr William Newton, shows well the usual arrangement on a bracket. The name, William Ruthven, on the door of the clock was probably that of the owner.

Lantern clocks, as a rule, were furnished with an hour indicator only. Fig. 610, from the Wetherfield collection, is an exceptional piece by "Joseph Knibb Oxon" dating from about 1670. It is 8½ in. high and 3½ in. across

Fig. 611. — Sheep's-head Clock.

the dial; has an alarm and both hour and minute hands. Among the few examples so fitted may be mentioned a much larger clock by David Mell, London, which dates from about 1660 and belongs to Mr Egerton Clarke. It is described in Chapter IX.

Many clocks made during the latter part of the reign of William III. and in the time of Queen Anne had the dials projecting beyond the frames from 2 to 3 in. on each side. These are generally known as sheep's-head clocks. However much the usefulness of the clock may have been increased by the superior legibility of its hour ring, it cannot be contended that the overhanging disc improved its general appearance. A good example by Robert Evens, Halstead, which belongs to Mr T. W. Bourne, is shown in Fig. 611.

With little variations in the style, these brass clocks seem to have been made from the time of Elizabeth until about the beginning of the reign of George III., the later specimens being principally of provincial manufacture, and with arched-top dials. They are still often to be met with in the country, enclosed in a wooden hood as a protection from dust, with pendulum and weights hanging below. Sometimes they are without any extra case, and, instead of being placed on a bracket, are simply attached to the wall by means of an iron loop and two prongs.

The "fret" at the top of the case may in many instances be somewhat of a guide in estimating the period of a lantern clock. Appended are examples, for several of which I am indebted to Mr Percy Webster.

The heraldic fret (Fig. 612) was in use at the earliest period up to 1630 or 1640. Frets of William Bowyer may be seen on Figs. 598 and 600. Another fret used by him and also by Thomas Loomes is shown in Fig. 614. The fret of Bowyer in Fig. 613 was used as well by Peter Closon, another early maker. The Thomas Pace fret (Fig. 615) may be taken to represent the period between 1630 to 1660. The crossed dolphins came into use about 1640, and were a favourite pattern from then as long as lantern clocks were made. An uncommon and unusually fine fret may be observed on the clock by Thomas Knifton, shown in Fig. 602. The fret on the clock by Thomas Parker (Fig. 604) will also bear examination. J. Michell of Chardstock, a village in Somersetshire, was an excellent maker of lantern clocks about 1700, and judging from the number of specimens still existing, he must have had a considerable connection. His frets were good and bore a distinctive character. The one shown in Fig. 617 is from a clock in the possession of

Fig. 612. — Heraldic.

Fig. 613. — William Bowyer.

Fig. 614. — William Bowyer; also Thomas Loomes.

Fig. 617. — Fret of J. Michell, Chardstock.

Fig. 615. — Thomas Pace at the Crown.

Fig. 618.

Fig. 616. — Dolphin fret, from Clock by Nicholas Coxeter.

Fig. 619. — Late period Fret used in the Eastern Counties.

Mr S. Good, Seaton, Devonshire. Michell was succeeded by the family of Drayton, of which several generations successively carried on the business till past initials preceding the date may be those of the owner or the maker. Frets similar to Fig. 619 are found upon later specimens, particularly those made in the Eastern counties.

HOOD CLOCKS

Fig. 620. — Joseph Knibb, London, about 1680.

Fig. 621. — Hindley, York, about 1710.

These have been referred to as a transition between the brass-cased lantern and the wooden long-case. Fig. 620 shows a diminutive thirty-hour hanging clock by Joseph Knibb, London, from the Wetherfield collection, and made about 1680. The carved bracket on which the movement rests and the hood are of walnut. The dial is 5 in. wide. A later and larger example signed "Hindley, York," in an oak case is shown in Fig. 621, by favour of Mr William Birchall. Captain Edward Lethbridge owns a clock by Thristle, of Williton, a village in Somerset, with a carved top hood of mahogany. The dial measures about 7 in. across, and has an arched top with a figure of Time and the motto "Tempus fugit." A long pendulum swings below the bracket. The date of its production would be about 1730. Mr W. T. Harkness has one by "Payne, Hadleigh," of the same period, also with a mahogany hood.

Hood clocks were popular in Holland for a long period. The best of these were made in Zaandam, but a larger number in Friesland. The earliest had but one hand, as in Fig. 622, which represents a Friesland clock, presented to the Bankfield Museum by Mr J. Whiteley Ward. There were usually two bells of different sizes. The completion of each hour was marked by strokes on the large bell, while the same number of strokes on the small bell denoted the succeeding half-hour. In the later clocks the intermediate quarters also were sounded, one blow on the small bell being given at the first quarter, and

Fig. 622. — Early Friesland Clock.

Fig. 623. — Zaandam Clock.

351

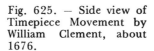

A month going tavern clock, with an octagonal dial, arched trunk door and ogee base. The base, trunk, and centre of the dial are lacquered with chinoiserie *designs on a black ground. The timepiece movement is five pillared with tapered plates and an anchor escapement.*

Mural clocks of this kind, with large easily read dials which are eminently suitable for use in public places, were particularly popular in inns and taverns. Examples may often still be seen in situ *for example in the George Inn, Southwark, or the Chequers at Oxford. That timepieces like this were produced in consequence of the 1797 tax on private clocks (pp. 396-397) is not only inherently improbable, but is demonstrably untrue from the number of such 'Act of Parliament' clocks surviving which are clearly of an earlier date than 1797. Christie, Manson & Woods Ltd.*

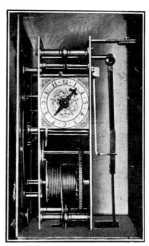

Fig. 625. — Side view of Timepiece Movement by William Clement, about 1676.

Fig. 624.

one blow on the large bell at the third quarter. Sometimes the pendulum was in front, and sometimes at the back of the bracket. In the latter case the bob would be of a fancy shape, such as that of a man on horseback, and be visible through an oval hole in the bracket. For Fig. 623 I am indebted to Mr Webster. Mr J. Drummond Robertson has a similar Zaandam clock in a case of ebony with the four posts of the movement of rosewood. The dial plate is covered with black velvet forming an effective background for the hour band and outer decorations which are all of brass. The front fret shows Faith, Hope, and Charity.

A much rarer style of Dutch clock, which strikes the quarters, and appears to date from about 1675, is shown in Fig. 624. The movement and case are entirely of iron, the sides and front being adorned with oil paintings, which are very effective. The main dial has an hour hand only and contains no minute marks, but fractions of an hour are indicated on a smaller dial below.

In Dutch movements, made at the beginning of the eighteenth century, a long while after the adoption of the pendulum, the crown wheel and verge were retained in a vertical position, and the pendulum was suspended above the movement at the back of the case, quite detached, and connected with the escapement only by means of a light wire crutch, working horizontally over the frame. Owing to this peculiarity, clocks of such a construction are often supposed to be much older than they really are, especially if, as occasionally happens, the pendulum gets removed or lost; for when this occurs, the remaining part of the movement almost identically resembles the drawings of De Vick's clock.

Another instance of the slow appreciation of improvement is the very gradual acknowledgment of the minute hand. Clocks with an hour hand only were produced by country makers till quite the end of the eighteenth century.

Lantern clocks were made long after the long case was introduced. Indeed, one occasionally sees an adaptation of the bedpost movement to the needs of the later construction, the two trains being placed side by side to allow of winding with a key from the front, but with six pillars instead of the more simple and convenient back and front plates.

It would be difficult to say exactly when the brass chamber clock with a wooden hood developed into the long-case variety now familiarly termed "Grandfather," but it was probably between 1660 and 1670. In the earliest the escapement was governed by a balance, or by a short pendulum. John Smith, in "Horological Dialogues," published in 1675, says: "If your pendulum clock be of the ordinary sort the trouble and manner of hanging it up is the same with the balance clock, viz., to drive an hook for it to hang on." But he also speaks of "setting up long swing pendulums after you have taken it from the coffin" and adds, "the same rule that is given for this serves for all other trunk-cases whatsoever."

In his "Horological Disquisitions," issued in 1694, Smith is much more precise and refers to the anchor escapement and improved pendulum "invented by that eminent and well-known artist, Mr William Clement." He gives a list of "Crown Wheel Pendulums," from 1 in. to 12 in. long, and then a list of "royal" pendulums, as in his enthusiastic approval he terms those of Clement, from 12 in. to 65 in. in length.

The long or "royal" pendulum, introduced about 1676, was pretty generally adopted by the leading makers for their best work within a few years from that date. The cases of the balance and short pendulum clocks were exceedingly narrow in the waist, only just sufficient width having originally been allowed for the rise and fall of the weights. In some instances a clock of this kind would be converted to the new style, and then a curious addition, in the form of a wing or projection was made on each side of the case to permit the swing of a "royal" pendulum. Sheraton seems to have suggested a revival of these wings in the case shown in Fig. 707.

But for a few exceptions that mark the rule, long-case clocks have the movement contained between two brass plates held together by horizontal pillars. This change came with the rearrangement of the trains side by side, to allow of winding with a key from the front of the dial.

It may be concluded that the earliest long-case clocks would go for but twenty-four or thirty hours between successive windings, and possibly at first they were wound by pulling down the driving cords. There is an early one by Tompion at the Guildhall Museum which has a lantern movement and is so arranged. But there is a very fine thirty-hour clock by the same maker in the Wetherfield collection, which winds through holes in the dial. The introduction of the "royal" pendulum and wheelwork for eight days' running seems to have been almost coincident. The evident success of

A provincial striking regulator by Edward Harrison of Warrington, late 18th century, with 12in. arched dial signed in the arch. Veneered oak case, conventional plated movement with four pillars, dead-beat anchor escapement and wood rod pendulum. At a later date, presumably in the mid-19th century, the dial has been silvered and decorated with flowing leaf designs. These are extremely fussy and distract attention from the hour and minute dials which are now difficult to read. Probably at the same time as this was done, an elaborately carved decoration was added to the case. Corinthian columns were added to the trunk, leaf decorations to the corners, and a mass of cross strap work with rosettes and formal leaf friezes. Although the carving of this decoration on the case is well done, the clock now has a somewhat incongruous appearance. Bobinet Ltd.

A typical example of a plain but elegant regency bracket clock with an enamelled dial, brass hands and an arched veneered oak case with brass fittings. The sides of the clock are fitted with fish scale fret decorations. The movement is of the usual layout with two trains, two fusees with chain held between the plates and with rounded shoulders to the back plate. Most clocks of this type were mass-produced by three or four London factories who added the retailer's name to the dial and back plate to order, or as in this case sold the clock plain. The makers of these clocks may sometimes be recognised by characteristic decorative features or from the punch marks. On this clock the cock, back plate, and the frieze are similar to the work of Thwaites & Reed. Since the bell, hammer, and pendulum are not of their characteristic style, however one would need the clinching evidence of Thwaites punched serial numbers or name elsewhere on the movement to be certain. For some details of this kind of production see G.T.E. Buggins & A.J. Turner, 'The Context of Production, Identification, and Dating of Clocks by A. & J. Thwaites', Antiquarian Horology. Bobinet Ltd.

eight-day movements induced clockmakers to calculate trains to go for a month, three months, and even a year, of which there are several examples by Tompion, Quare, and others.

In the striking part of the earliest eight-day clocks the locking-plate or count wheel was on the outside of the pillar-plate, instead of being attached to the great wheel. When the rack was introduced it was placed between the plates and lifted by a pin in the arbor; the superior method of an outside rack lifted by a gathering pallet seems to have come into use about 1700.

Mr D. A. F. Wetherfield has a month timepiece by William Clement, who is said to have been the first to apply the anchor escapement. It is in an oak veneered-walnut case, the case and dial being very similar to those of the Tompion clock shown in Fig. 672. There is no door to the hood, which has grooves to correspond with the back-board of the case; the hood thus slides upwards when taken off, or when the clock is to be wound. Preparatory to winding, the hood is raised until engaged by a spring, which holds it in the requisite position to admit of access to the winding-hole. A side view of the movement is given in Fig. 625. There are six pillars and catches pivoted on one of the plates shut into corresponding slots in the pillars, thus fastening the movement together. The escape wheel is solid, has twenty-four teeth, and is 1 in. in diameter; the pallets are about 7/8 in. across. The pendulum is 5 ft. 6 in. long, each vibration marking a second and a quarter, and the seconds circle has forty-eight divisions only instead of the usual sixty. Between the plates is a small brass dial with figures 1 to 12 engraved on it, and having a hand by turning which forwards or backwards the pendulum is lengthened or shortened. On the spindle to which the hand is attached is a worm which gears into a quadrant carrying an arm, and to this arm the pendulum is hung.

DIALS

In estimating the age of a clock many distinguishing features of the dial may be noted. From the first the hour circles were, with few exceptions, engraved on a separate silvered ring as in lantern clocks; the double circles within the numerals were retained, and in the space enclosed between them were radial strokes, dividing the hour into quarters, the half-hours being

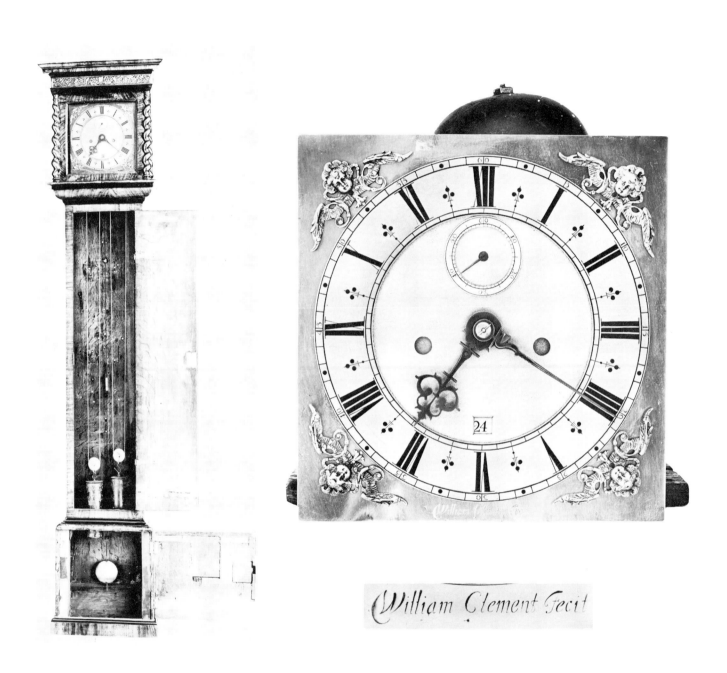

Eight-day striking movement, bolt and shutter maintaining power. Dial 10 in. wide, 10¹/8 in. high, inscribed "William Clement Fecit." 1¹/4 seconds pendulum. Case of oak veneered with marquetry panels of birds and flowers set in a walnut veneered background, c.1680-1685.

Fig. 626. — Andrew Prime, about 1670.

Fig. 627. — Thomas Tompion, Clock with Alarm, about 1670.

Fig. 628. — Dial of Long-case Clock by Thos. Tompion, 1676-1680.

Fig. 629. — J. Windmills, with name curved within minute marks.

Fig. 630. — Joseph Knibb, about 1685; 10-in. dial; month clock, striking on two bells.

Fig. 631. — Edward East, about 1690; month clock; 10-in. dial, very pretty hands.

Fig. 632. — Christopher Gould, about 1700; 12-in. dial.

Fig. 633. — Thomas Tompion, about 1705; 10½-in. dial.

Fig. 634.

denoted by longer strokes terminating in a *fleur-de-lys* or other ornament. The form of the hour hand differed but little from the indicators on lantern clocks. Fig. 626 shows the dial of a thirty-hour long-case clock by Andrew Prime, London, dating from about 1670, belonging to Mr C. J. Abbott, of Long Melford. Except for the difference in the name, the engraving on the thirty-hour Tompion clock at the Guildhall Museum is exactly similar. The dial of an early long-case alarm clock by Tompion which belongs to Mr T. W. Bourne is shown in Fig. 627.

It must not be assumed that of two long-case clocks, one with an hour hand only, and the other with a minute hand as well, that the one with the single index is necessarily of the earlier date, for though the minute hand was applied as early as 1670, clocks with an hour hand only were quite common throughout the eighteenth century. It is most probable that for some years the minute hand was only applied by the best makers and exclusively to clocks of a superior class; this assumption is justified by the fact that though many early one-hand clocks roughly made are met with, those with the minute hand are almost invariably well finished. The form of the hands is an excellent guide to the period. Fig. 628 shows the dial and hands of a very fine long-case clock by Tompion, belonging to Mr Wetherfield, and which may be safely placed as dating from between 1676 and 1680. The centre of the dial is matted, and this, though characteristic of the time, was not an invariable custom, for some makers adhered to the engraved centre as seen in lantern clocks of earlier times. The hands are good and well adapted to their office, the seconds indicator being a slender unbalanced finger. It was not till the time of Williamson about 1715 that double-ended seconds hands were applied. On dials of the William III. and Queen Anne periods, even when the centre was matted, there would be usually a "herringbone" or laurel leaf border along the edges, and engraving something in the form of birds and foliage surrounded the aperture showing the day of the month, as in the Quare dial in Fig. 646. This had a very good effect when burnished bright in contrast to the matting. Further relief was given by turning a number of bright rings around the winding holes. With the exception of those thirty-hour adaptations with lantern movements as in Fig. 626, the maker's name on the earliest of the seventeenth century clocks was, as a rule, inscribed in a straight line along the bottom of the dial, usually in Latin, thus: "Eduardus East, Londini, Fecit," and visible only when the hood was raised or removed, or the door of it opened. Later it was engraved within the minute circles between the numerals VII. and V. and the Latin form of inscription died out so far as the signature is concerned, though it was occasionally indulged in for such popular mottoes as *Tempus fugit, Vigilate et Orate, Tempus edax rerum,* &c. Fig. 629 shows the dial of a clock by Joseph Windmills, with the name curving round inside the minute marks. This clock belongs to Mr Wm. A. Jeffries, of Boston, Mass., U.S.A. A remarkably fine month clock by Tompion in a beautifully figured walnut case, dating from about 1705, which belongs to Mr J. Drummond Robertson, is shown in Fig. 680. To the top of the pinnacles it is 8 ft. 6 in. high. In this the name is inscribed in a straight line along the bottom of the dial, and the signature appears also on a label below the centre of the dial as in the Bath and Iscoyd Park clocks by Tompion, of a slightly later date, shown in Figs. 421 and 422. After about 1710 attached name-plates were

Another view of the Clement longcase clock on page 355.

Skeleton clocks in the form of well known buildings were not uncommon in the latter part of the 19th century. A particularly popular subject was Lichfield Cathedral, and other cathedrals are also known. The example shown here, the Scott Memorial, Edinburgh, is less common. Although not signed it was presumably made in Scotland, probably in Edinburgh. A well balanced and well made clock, the fusee movement has a lever escapement, with a large steel balance and ruby pallets. Bobinet Ltd.

occasionally used, but throughout the century most makers showed preference for the curved inscription between the numerals.

Speaking generally, it seems that up to the end of the seventeenth century long-case clocks were small in size; all had square dials measuring either 9½ in., 10 in., 10½ in., or 11 in. across. Square dials, 12 in. across, were later.

Fig. 634 represents a very early square engraved metal dial which is of particular interest, not only from its handsome appearance but from the fact that it discloses a peculiar plan of denoting the minutes. The short hand in the centre of the dial is the alarm index, which need not be referred to further. The hours and subdivisions representing quarter hours are engraved on the dial plate in the manner usual at the middle of the seventeenth century, and the hours and quarters are indicated by a pointer fixed to a plate of the form shown, and which revolves once in twelve hours. The revolving plate includes an outer ring connected with the centre by three arms, and projecting from the outer edge of this ring are twelve pointers placed equidistantly around the periphery. On the upper part of the fixed dial plate is a narrow band forming 30° or $\frac{1}{12}$ of the circumference. This band is divided into sixty equal parts, representing the minutes in an hour; and if at the beginning of an hour one of the pointers is just entering this arc, it is obvious it will in its course indicate the minutes which have elapsed since the completion of the previous hour. At the bottom of the dial is inscribed, "William Clay, King's Street, Westminster," and this William Clay was possibly the one recorded as the maker of a watch presented by Cromwell to Colonel Bagwell at the siege of Clonmel. This dial was sketched from a clock in the possession of Mr Percy Webster.

An arched top to the dial appears to have been first added early in the eighteenth century for the reception of an equation of time register, as shown in Tompion's clock in Fig. 422. It will be observed that the Hampton Court clock bearing Quare's name, and which was designed to show true solar time, has no arch to the dial, but a subsequent clock on the same plan by Joseph Williamson, has an arch containing a calendar for the year, as shown in Fig. 650. On another dial by Williamson, the day of the week is indicated, as seen in Fig. 651. Apart from its utility in this connection, the addition of the arched top was certainly a great improvement to the appearance of the dial, and from this time was generally retained for the better class of work even when not required as a field for the exhibition of any of the clock movements. In such cases the space was devoted to decoration, a favoured device being a domed plate on which was inscribed either the owner's or the maker's name, occasionally with a crest or motto, and generally flanked on each side by a dolphin or rococo ornament of the kind apparently introduced by Joseph Williamson, and shown on his dials, Figs. 650 and 651.

Calendar circles in the arch of the dial were very popular. The hands for these were generally worked as shown in Fig. 635. Gearing with the hour wheel is a wheel having twice its number of teeth, and turning therefore once in twenty-four hours. A three-armed lever is planted just above this wheel; the lower arm is slotted, and the wheel carries a pin which works in this slot, so that the lever vibrates to and fro once every twenty-four hours. The three upper circles in the drawing represent three star wheels. The one to the right

Two extremely fine skeleton clocks. That on the left is signed 'James Black Kircaldy, Chronometer' and strikes on a small bell. Simply made, it has a chronometer escapement with a conventional balance oversprung with a helical steel balance spring. The silvered chapter rings read to seconds. The example on the right is inscribed 'This clock was made by Thomas Black Clock Maker Kircaldy in 1891-1892 Brasswork moulded and cast by William D. Nelson Brass Founder Kircaldy'. This is a going barrel clock, by contrast with that by James Black which has a fusee, a lever escapement with compensated balance, jewelled pallets and a flat steel spring. The unusual inscription on the Thomas Black clock suggests that it was made for a special occasion, and both clocks are fine examples of their kind. Bobinet Ltd.

has seven teeth corresponding to the days of the week; the centre one has thirty-one teeth for the days of the month; and the left-hand one has twelve teeth for the months of the year. Every time the upper arms of the lever vibrate to the left, they move forward the day of the week and day of the month wheels each one tooth. The extremities of the levers are jointed, so as to yield on the return vibration, and are brought into position again by a weak spring, as shown. There is a pin in the day of the month wheel which, by pressing on a lever once every revolution, actuates the month of the year

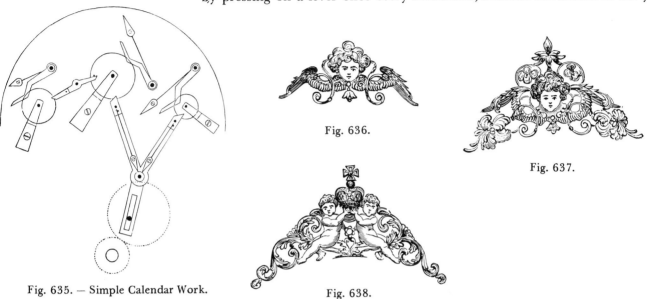

Fig. 636.

Fig. 637.

Fig. 635. — Simple Calendar Work.

Fig. 638.

wheel. This last lever is also jointed, and is pressed on by a spring, so as to return to its original position. Each of the star wheels has a click or jumper kept in contact by means of a spring. For months with less than thirty-one days the day of the month has to be shifted forward.

The spandrels or corners outside the circle of the dial form a tolerably reliable sign of the times. In some of the very earliest long-case clocks flowers were engraved there, as in William Clay's dial in Fig. 634. In Fig. 666 the corners are filled each with a line of verse, but more usually these spaces were occupied by raised gilt ornaments, of which the earliest were the cherubs' or angels' heads, Fig. 636. This pattern will be seen on the clock represented in the coat of arms granted to the Clockmakers' Company in 1671, and was largely used until the end of the century. It was succeeded by larger and more elaborate corners like Fig. 637. Then more ambitious designs came into use, notably two cupids or nude boys supporting a crown in the midst of ornamental scroll-work (Fig. 638); or a crown with crossed sceptres and foliage, as in Fig. 639. This is an unusually fine specimen taken from a clock of the Queen Anne period by W. Draper, a maker of whom I seem to have no precise particulars, though Mr William Norman has a metal token issued by W. Draper, watchmaker, which has on the obverse "Success to the Borough of Maldon" with the arms of the town, and on the reverse the arms of the Clockmakers' Company. Later in the eighteenth century different figures representing the four seasons were popular with some of the provincial makers, but they are seldom to be seen on clocks by London men. The naked boys were followed by various combinations of a rococo

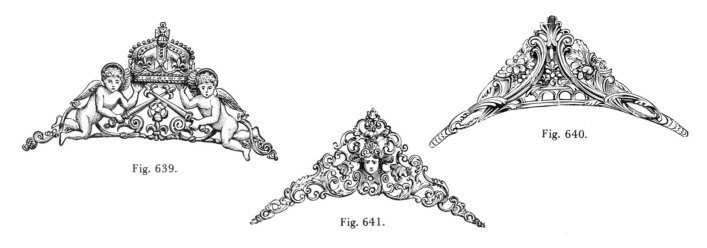

Fig. 639.

Fig. 641.

Fig. 640.

Fig. 642. — Edward East, about 1680. Eight-day clock; 10-in. dial; bolt and shutter maintaining power.

Fig. 643. — Joseph Knibb, about 1690. Month clock; 10-in. dial; unique corner pieces.

character, such as Fig. 640. One of the best and most popular of the designs used during the George III. period is shown in Fig. 641. Some of the corners and arch ornaments of this time were sadly degenerate in form and execution, being merely a mass of unmeaning curves reproduced in rough castings, not touched by the chasing tool or graver, but lacquered just as they left the sand. Many of the early dials and corners were water gilt. Occasionally, on clocks of a high class, silver corner-pieces pierced and engraved were substituted for the set patterns.

Among other useful purposes to which the arched space was applied, the "strike-silent" hand and the "rise-and-fall" register may be mentioned as two of the earliest. The titles of these are suggestive of their use. The strike-silent mechanism for stopping the striking of the clock at pleasure is older than the arch, and is to be seen on clocks having square dials. A particular form of strike-silent mechanism was incorporated in a patent granted to John Rowning, M.A., in 1732 (No. 535). Some dials made just after the accession of George I. contained instead of the words "strike-silent" the letters "S. N." engraved as a guide to the movement of a lever. The meaning of these letters, which stand respectively for "Schlag," "Nicht," has occasionally perplexed subsequent owners of such a clock, especially if, as was not unusual, the lever had disappeared.

The rise-and-fall hand was connected with the pendulum and served to regulate the time of its vibration by altering its effective length. An early example with this contrivance is the long-case clock by Jonathan Puller in the Wetherfield collection which is shown in Fig. 718.

For many years, but especially during the latter part of the eighteenth century, there was a great taste for moving figures placed in this part of the dial, such automata as see-saws, heaving ships, time on the wing, &c., being especially favoured. The Dutch seem to have greatly excelled at this kind of work. Occasionally an effective but somewhat ghastly attraction was arranged by placing in the arched space a painting of a human head; behind the head, instead of the tossing ship, which was worked to and fro by a wire from the pendulum, would be the eyes continually going to and fro.

Sometimes the seconds indicator was transferred from inside the hour ring to the space above.

The phases of the moon, usually accomplished by a disc turning once in two lunations, as shown in Enderlin's clock on pages 297 and 298, was also a favourite device for the arch of the dial.

A 19th century table clock, signed 'Hunt & Roskell London', effected in the style made popular by Thomas Cole. The triangular gilt metal case is engraved all over with leaf decoration. On one face is the hour and minute dial with blued steel fleur de lys *hands. On the second is a calendar of which the days of the month may be adjusted, while the third side contains a thermometer. The whole clock, which has a three quarter plate movement with lever escapement, compensated balance and contrate wheel drive from an eight-day going barrel, is mounted on three double cabriole-type legs with acanthus leaf decorations. Sotheby Parke Bernet & Co.*

In connection with the lunar record the time of high water at some particular place was popular in certain districts between 1730 and 1780. For people residing near a tidal river, and who desired to cross a ford, accessible only at low water, an indication of the tides would be especially useful. In many instances the figure of the moon had a slight pointed projection to

Fig. 644. — Joseph Knibb, about 1695. Month clock; 10-in. dial; skeleton hour ring; every minute numbered.

Fig. 645. — Thos. Tompion, about 1700. Month clock; 11-in. dial; bolt and shutter maintaining power.

Fig. 646. — Daniel Quare, about 1705. Month clock; 11-in. dial.

Fig. 647. — Jonathan Lowndes, about 1710. Eight-day clock; 12-in. dial.

show the age of the luminary. Around the top of the arched space, besides the usual figures for the moon's age would be a row of Roman numerals for the hours of high water, and perhaps a further arc with a register of the number of minutes past. Mr Charles J. Reynolds has a clock of this kind, with the inscription, "Charles Vaughan, Pontypool," outside the figures. Or there might be a fixed pointer above the arch; the numbers for the moon's

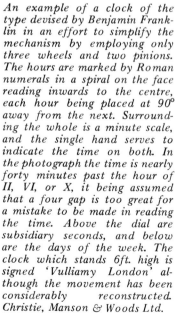

An example of a clock of the type devised by Benjamin Franklin in an effort to simplify the mechanism by employing only three wheels and two pinions. The hours are marked by Roman numerals in a spiral on the face reading inwards to the centre, each hour being placed at 90° away from the next. Surrounding the whole is a minute scale, and the single hand serves to indicate the time on both. In the photograph the time is nearly forty minutes past the hour of II, VI, or X, it being assumed that a four gap is too great for a mistake to be made in reading the time. Above the dial are subsidiary seconds, and below are the days of the week. The clock which stands 6ft. high is signed 'Vulliamy London' although the movement has been considerably reconstructed. Christie, Manson & Woods Ltd.

Fig. 648. — Richard Lyons, about 1690. 10-in. dial.

Fig. 649. — John Crampern, Newark, about 1775. Eccentric subject for engraving in centre space.

age and the tides would then occupy the edge of the moon's disc and travel with it. Mr George Liddell has a clock by Jacob Lovelace of Exeter, dating from about 1735, so arranged. The dial is shown in Fig. 652. Miss Mary F. Bragg owns a clock by Simpson, of Wigton, dating from about 1775, with half-hour marks instead of minute figures, as shown in Fig. 656. Another plan was to allow the phases of the moon to be seen through a hole in the arched part of the dial. Three sets of figures would be arranged round a whole circle, and two pointers, resembling an hour hand and a minute hand, would indicate the age of the moon and the hours and minutes of high water. A clock like this by Jno. Hunter, Bristol, is in the possession of Mr H. G. Townsend. Fig. 657 shows the dial of a clock by Thomas Moss of Frodsham, in which this arrangement occupies a space just above the centre of the dial. This clock belongs to Mr Wm. R. Moss. On a clock in the Wetherfield collection, by Isaac Nickals, of Wells, illustrated in Fig. 726, a tidal record in the arch may be observed.

Clocks with a globular rotating moon over the dial as used by Fromantil were popular in Yorkshire during the eighteenth century and were known locally as "Halifax clocks." Mr J. Whiteley Ward had a fine specimen, of which an illustration is given in Fig. 654. This clock was made by Thomas Ogden and formerly stood at the top of the stairs of the Old Assembly Room behind the Talbot Inn, Halifax.

The hands on eight-day clocks of the William III. period are most artistic, not only being elaborately pierced, but also carved and shaped on the surface. At my request Mr Wetherfield has favoured me with a series of dials reproduced in Figs. 628-30-1-2-42-3-4-5-6-7-50-51, from which may be noted the hands, marks between the hour numerals, and other distinguishing features ranging over about forty years from the Edward East specimen, Fig. 642, which is furnished with bolt and shutter maintaining power as described on page 238. The Tompion dial, Fig. 633, is from the collection of Mr T.W. Bourne, and the Richard Lyons, Fig. 648, is from a clock belonging to Mr Bernard Matthews. Later examples down to the end of the eighteenth century are shown on succeeding pages. Mr H. Cook has given me a print of a square dial by John Crampern, of Newark, dating from about 1760, with quaintly engraved centre. It is shown in Fig. 649.

Fig. 650. — Joseph Williamson, about 1715. Month clock; square of dial, 12 in. Inscription, *"Horae indicantur apparentes involutis aequationibus."* Calendar in the arch.

Fig. 651. — Joseph Williamson, about 1720. Eight-day clock; square of dial, 12 in. Lower hour numerals reversed. Day of the week indicated in the arch; an illustration for each day appears through an aperture.

Fig. 652. — Jacob Lovelace, Exeter, about 1735. Day of the month through hole in dial. Figures in the arch show age of the moon and time of high water in hours and minutes. Subsidiary pointers in the upper corners are for respectively "Strike-Silent" and pendulum regulation.

Fig. 653. — Dial of Clock by Andrew Padbury, with rotating centre to indicate time all over the world.

Fig. 654. — Rotating Moon Dial of "Halifax Clock" by Thos. Ogden, about 1750 (see p.364).

Fig. 655. — John Ellicott, about 1760.

Dials of brass, silvered all over, without a separate ring for the hour and minute circles, and in which the primitive practice of engraving instead of matting the central space was reverted to, were introduced about 1750. Many of these dials were characterised by really excellent engraving. Thomas Bewick, the celebrated engraver, who died in 1828 at the age of seventy-six, was apprenticed to Beilby, of Newcastle, and during his apprenticeship was frequently engaged in engraving clock dials. By favour of Mr Thos. Foster, I am able in Fig. 658 to show an excellent specimen, dating from about 1775,

Fig. 656. — Simpson, Wigton, about 1775. Has centre seconds and day of the month hands, and shows in the arch age and phases of the moon and time of high water, probably at Parton, near Whitehaven.

Fig. 657. — Thomas Moss, Frodsham, 1776. Shows day of the month, age and phases of the moon, and time of high water at Frodsham. Water scene and landscape painted in arch.

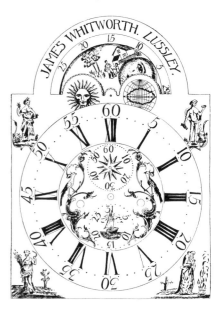

Fig. 658. — Finely Engraved Dial, about 1775. Figures at the corners to represent the four seasons.

Fig. 659. — Dial with Moving Figures, about 1780 (see pp.384 and 385).

Fig. 660. — Enamel centre, 1778 (see p.367).

Fig. 661. — "Johannes Duchesne, Amersterdam," about 1750.

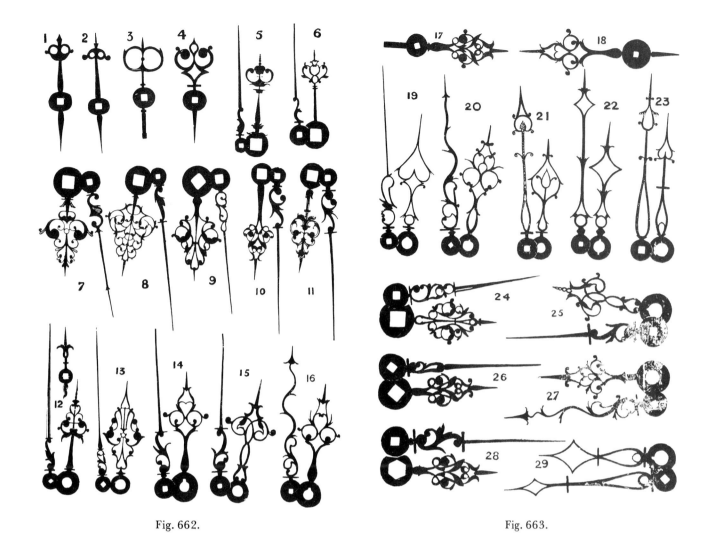

Fig. 662.

Fig. 663.

Fig. 661. continued (see opposite).

Inside the case is the following explanatory account of the remarkably effective painting: "Andromeda, chained to a rock by order of the Goddess Juno because her friends had said she was as beautiful as Juno. Hydra, the three-headed Sea Monster, was sent to devour her, which, being known to Perseus, the King's Son, he mounted Pegasus, the flying horse, and rescued and married her, and after living very happily together, she was at length placed among the stars."

by James Whitworth, of Lussley, a village near Newcastle. The figures at the corners to represent the seasons are engraved on the plate. The disc, which moves in the arch and contains two representations of the moon and rural scenes, is painted, and the moon in its course indicates its age by figures engraved on the fixed part of the arch.

Dials with enamelled centres were occasionally used for superior long-case clocks at the end of the eighteenth and beginning of the nineteenth century, but earlier ones are rare. In Fig. 660 is shown, by favour of Mr Wetherfield, the dial of a long-case clock dated 1778, by Richard Comber, of Lewes, a maker of good repute in Sussex for the excellent character of his work, which this example quite justifies. The hands will bear examination, the corner pieces and arch ornaments are of good design, well chased and water gilt; but the most remarkable feature is the position of the winding squares, which are below the enamelled disc, so that not only is the unsightliness of the holes got rid of, but one of the chief objections to enamel — the danger of chipping round the holes — is avoided. Wheels were added at the back of the movement to bring the winding squares down to the required position.

About 1780 silvered dials shorn of all decorative engraving were sometimes used, and at the same period dials of iron, tin, or wood painted over made their appearance. Speaking generally, the innovation must be

367

A well balanced decorative mantel clock signed 'James Tregent London no 2627' c.1790. Circular plated movement with cylinder escapement, diamond endstone, six spoked wheels and maintaining power. There is a bridge cock with pierced and engraved decoration. Enamel dial with separate dials for hours, minutes, seconds, and a central subsidiary quarter seconds dial. The clock is mounted in an ormolu case surmounted by a crest, supported on a garlanded ormolu urn on a square stepped ormolu and alabaster base. The whole clock is executed in the style of Matthew Boulton who produced many fine ormolu cases for clocks after original designs. Christie, Manson & Woods Ltd.

regarded as a degradation, although painted dials ornamented with nicely coloured representations of fruit and flowers after Dutch designs have a pretty effect. Some of the earlier Dutch dials of brass were adorned with pictures of considerable merit, of which an example is given in Fig. 661.

In Figs. 662 and 663 are shown some clock hands, nearly all from examples collected by Mr G. H. Newton, of Watford. Nos. 1, 2, 3, and 4 belonged to lantern clocks made between 1630 and 1680. No. 5 from a clock by Henry Jones, about 1670. Nos. 6 to 23 are from long-case, and 24 to 29 from bracket, clocks. No. 6 by John Tirry, York, about 1680; No. 7, J. Windmills, 1690; No. 8, John Smith, 1695; No. 9, Simon Lamb, Rochester, 1700; No. 10, Saml. Harris, 1710; No. 11, George Hewitt, Marlboro', 1720; No. 12 (hour, minute, and regulation hands), Geo. Graham, 1730; No. 13, Thos. Vernon, Ludlow, 1740; No. 14, Wm. Avenall, Alresford, 1750; No. 15, Thos. Andrews, Steyning, 1760; No. 16, Wm. Berridge, 1770. Nos. 17 and 18 are typical single hands from early eighteenth century long-case clocks. No. 19, S. Hoole, 1770; No. 20, Wm. Skeggs, 1780; No. 21, J. Lorimer, 1790; No. 22, Hugh Stockell, Newcastle, 1800; No. 23, another variety of about the same date; No. 24, J. Lowndes, 1690; No. 25, Asselin, 1720; No. 26, Wm. Kipling, 1710; No. 27, Joseph Emery, 1780; No. 28, Robert Newman, 1700; No. 29, Thos. Appleby, 1800. The best of these early hands were not only pierced but shaped or carved on the surface, if the file can be admitted as a carving tool.

For the examples of hour hands in Fig. 664, I am indebted to Mr T. W. Bourne, who traces progression from the plain arrow head No. 1. No. 2 is similar, but with curved sides. No. 3, really an ornate form of No. 2, was commonly used by the old makers of lantern clocks. If viewed from a distance it gives the same effect as the wavy arrow head. No. 4 marks the first real step in development; above the arrow head are two new limbs and a pointer. In No. 5 the curved limbs have grown and between the arrow head and pointer appears a solid enlargement which in No. 6 had been hollowed and rendered more ornamental. This part of the hand has in Nos. 6 and 8 been still further extended, the special features of each being combined in

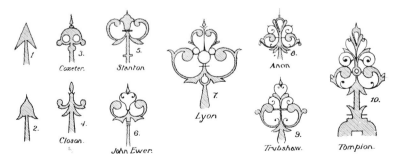

Fig. 664. — Showing gradual development of the Plain Arrow-head Hand.

No. 9. No. 10 may be called the final form. The arrow head has been retained throughout, the superstructure being the special object of extension and enrichment.

CASES As material for the cases, oak has been used from first to last, but rarely for high-class work. Walnut cases, both plain and inlaid, were largely made during the latter part of the seventeenth and beginning of the eighteenth centuries. The marqueterie work rarely extended to the sides of the case, which were plain as a rule, though occasionally panelled; the panels being filled with parquetry, that is, set with angular pieces of thick veneer. Oyster-shell veneer or inlay was another handsome style of ornament; the inlay consisted of roundish pieces of veneer cut from cross sections of small branches so as to exhibit the natural formation or ringed structure of the wood.

Ebony, rosewood, and hardwood of reddish colour called, I believe, kingwood, were occasionally used for cases, while laburnum, olive, yew, holly, sycamore, apple and pear as well as tulip wood, Amboyna and other fancy kinds were employed with good effect for inlaying. In some districts chestnut seems to have been utilised to a considerable extent for cases during the eighteenth century. Mahogany was not used till about 1716. The case of the Tompion one-year timepiece at the Admiralty, which is shown in Fig. 671, is distinctly later than Tompion's time, and it is related that the movement of a similar piece presented to the Royal Society in 1736 was discovered among lumber on the premises occupied by the Philosophical Society. At Child's Bank is a long-case clock by Richard Street dating from about 1710. It is in an oak case veneered with mahogany, but the veneer was, I am satisfied, not applied when the case was made; doubtless the rich appearance of mahogany led to its subsequent application.

The arched head to the long door of the case is not quite so old as the arched dial, but the introduction of curved door heads may be put, I think, at about 1725.

Numbers of cases covered with English copies of quaint-looking Japanese or Oriental lacquer-work were made between 1710 and 1750, and they have many admirers, but marqueterie and lacquer-work rapidly declined as mahogany became more known, and it must be confessed that some cases of mahogany in the Chippendale and Sheraton styles, inlaid with satinwood, &c., quite justify the admiration with which they are regarded. An exceptionally early lacquer case in the Wetherfield collection is shown in Fig. 716.

In a few of the early long pendulum clocks a bull's eye of greenish glass was let into the door of the case opposite the pendulum bob, magnifying and distorting the appearance of the bob as it swung to and fro, and for some years from about 1685 a round or oval hole with a flat glass was quite a usual feature.

The upper part of the case, or hood, which surrounded the dial, was at first made without any door. Most makers fitted the hood with grooves to the back as described on p.354. In other instances the hood had to be slid forward and entirely removed to obtain access to the dial. In the early cases the moulding under the hood was convex as distinguished from the concave moulding almost invariably used afterwards. Corkscrew pillars at the angles of the hood were much favoured during the William III. and Queen Anne

Fig. 665. — Brass Fret from Head of Long-case Clock, about 1700.

periods. The pillars supported an entablature which either terminated with a flat top or was surmounted by a pediment or some kind of ornament.

A domed or canopied structure was common, but there is no particular pattern which can be quoted as absolutely distinguishing the time. Some early hoods terminated in a pediment, simple and appropriate. The styles most in vogue may be gathered from illustrations of examples which I shall be able to give. In nearly all cases a frieze or other band was pierced to emit the sound of the bell; sometimes the fretwork was of wood and sometimes of brass. The brass fret strips, which were rather pretty, were often removed when the case subsequently underwent repair. One of them taken from a clock dating from 1700 is shown in Fig. 665.

The height of early cases seemed to be adapted in some measure to the places they were to occupy. The flat top of an entablature, as in Fig. 677, was suited for low rooms; where greater height allowed, the dome or double dome would doubtless be selected. For lofty apartments with other furniture of large size there would be gilded figures surmounting a high topped case, as in the example Fig. 723, or finials of gilded wood as shown in Fig. 724. To increase the height still further, the case occasionally would be stood on a

Fig. 666. — Primitive provincial style, 1681.

Fig. 667. — Clock at St Paul's Cathedral, 1698.

Fig. 668. — "George Ethrington, London," about 1695.

370

Fig. 669. — Tompion Clock at Windsor Castle.

Fig. 670. — Joshua Hutchin, about 1700.

Fig. 671. — Tompion One-year Timepiece at the Admiralty.

Fig. 672. — Thos. Tompion, 1676-1680 (see below).

Fig. 673. — Ed. East, 1680-1685.

Fig. 674. — Jos. Knibb, 1685-1690.

sub-base with carved panels as in Fig. 443. Now and then one may see an old clock in which, to suit the limited extent of low rooms, the top of the case has been shorn of all adornments.

Fig. 672 represents an eight-day Tompion clock dating from 1678-80, the dial of which, 9½ in. square, is shown separately in Fig. 628. The case is of oak veneered with walnut; at the corners of the hood are pillars with helical or "corkscrew" shafts, brass bases, and Corinthian capitals. Well-executed brass festoons of fruit and flowers adorn the hood over the dial and over the side lights, Mr Wetherfield, who owns this clock, has a timepiece by William Clement which is very similar in appearance.

By favour of Messrs Horne & Son, of Leyburn, I am able to give an engraving of a quaint thirty-hour long-case clock of provincial make which now belongs to Mr Thomas Bradley, Wensleydale. This case is of oak and panelled. The head is fixed on the trunk, and will not take off. Two slip doors at the sides of the head open to get to the works, and a sash door affords the same convenience for the dial. Both the case door and the sash door open from right to left. The initials E. F. M. with date, 1681, are carved on the case. The clock was made for Edward and Margaret Fawcett; the former was a clergyman, who lived at Hardraw, close to the Hardraw Waterfall. The works are of the lantern type, with a large bell and hammer

371

inside, and small dial as shown in Fig. 666. It was made by John Ogden, Bowbrigg(e). In Ogden's clocks of later date the name of the place was spelled Bowbridge, but the local name is Bowbrigge to-day. In each of the corner spaces outside of the hour circle is engraved one line of the following verse:—

"Behold this hand,
        Observe ye motions trip;
    Man's pretious hours
            Away like these do slip."

John Ogden was a member of the Society of Friends, and a friend of George Fox, who often visited Wensleydale.

MARQUETERIE (OR MARQUETRY)

The formation of designs by inlaying wood of different kinds is a very ancient art. The Italians particularly excelled at it in the fifteenth and sixteenth centuries. Early inlaying was done by cutting out from the solid wood which formed the groundwork such parts of a prearranged design as it was desired to have of a different colour and then inserting pieces of a suitable and different kind of wood. But in most of the marqueterie we see on clock cases the design is cut out of a groundwork of veneer which is filled in with other veneer and attached to the surface of the wood which forms the body of the case. This method is, I think, of French origin and dates from the middle of the seventeenth century, but it was first applied to clock cases about 1685, and remained in fashion, so far as clock cases are concerned, for about twenty-five years from that date.

Dutch marqueterie is effective, of a distinctly bolder or coarser character, and, as a rule, may be distinguished from what may be called English designs, which more favoured the Italian style. Arabesques, fine geometrical patterns, conventional flowers and foliage executed by inlaying wood, which, though of a different colour to the ground, was yet not in violent contrast to it, characterised the English, while Dutch artists, who accentuated more the difference between the groundwork and the inlay, indulged in quaint and fanciful designs in which grotesque masks and figures, as well as vases, birds, leaves, tulips and other flowers were portrayed by means of shading and the use of wood naturally of another colour or stained to the desired tint. It must not be assumed, though, that what is called Dutch marqueterie was necessarily executed in the Netherlands; there is no doubt that when William III. ascended the English throne his followers included Dutch inlayers who settled here and turned the public taste to their particular methods, which were followed by English workers.

At first the marqueterie was arranged on the front of the case in panels with semicircular ends, sometimes with a line border connecting the panels; afterwards the whole of the front surface might be covered with marqueterie, the door and base having set designs, enclosed in floral or other borders. In marqueterie work of the very highest class, it will be noticed that the whole of the inlay on any one surface forms a complete design; if birds or figures are introduced they are delineated as a whole and fall gracefully into the conception of the designer. More frequently a symmetrical pattern was taken and two pieces of veneer forming half of the pattern were laid one on the other and pierced together; the halves were then placed side by side and of course matched exactly. But however close the jointing of the halves, the line of junction down the centre may be discerned by close examination. Masks or cases containing leaves and flowers on stalks were commonly selected for such treatment and were displayed very effectively in this way. Sometimes the halving would extend to a portion of the design only, and advantage would be taken of the outlines of leaves or scrolls to join in the halved pieces very neatly.

In the South Kensington Museum are a clock by Mansell Bennett enclosed in a case decorated with marqueterie in panel, and an unusually fine example of English scroll marqueterie covering the case of a clock by Henry Poisson; on the staircase of the Soane Museum is a clock by William Threlkeld, the case of which is also adorned with marqueterie in the English style. The Wetherfield collection contains many choice examples.

Soho seems to have been a favoured district for marqueterie workers, though Tonbridge in Kent and St Ives and other smaller places in Cornwall are spoken of as being famous for marqueterie work in the eighteenth century.

After being neglected for fifty years or so marqueterie was to some extent revived as a decoration for clock cases. A sparing and tasteful display on a

Fig. 675. — Jonathan Lowndes, about 1695.

Fig. 676. — Dan. Quare, about 1705.

Fig. 677. — P. Garon, about 1705.

Fig. 678. — Thos. Tompion; Month Clock, about 1700.

Fig. 679. — Fromanteel & Clarke, about 1705.

Fig. 680. — Thos. Tompion, about 1705 (see p.357).

Fig. 682. — Danl. Delander; Year Equation Time-piece, about 1720.

Fig. 683. — Carved dark oak.

Fig. 684. — At Windsor Castle: Richard Vick, about 1740.

Fig. 685. — Philip Abbott; Red Lacquer Case, about 1750.

Fig. 681. — One-year Timepiece by Daniel Quare.

clock by Alexander Cumming dating from about 1790 is shown in Fig. 733. Chaste inlay in the Hepplewhite and Sheraton style, as in Fig. 735, is admirable. Sheraton's designs for clock cases are reproduced on p.379 [Figs. 707, 708].

A fine specimen, with English marqueterie in panels, which is in the Dean's Vestry, St Paul's Cathedral, is given in Fig. 667. The date of this can be well authenticated by the following extract which I have been allowed to make from the Cathedral accounts for the period from October 1697 to September 1698, when the clock was paid for:—

"ffor a pendulum Clock for the South East Vestrey that goes 8 dayes in a Wallnut Tree inlade Case £14 00 00."

There is now no maker's name on either the dial or movement, but the clock was doubtless the production of Langley Bradley, who was at that time the cathedral clockmaker.

The clock shown in Fig. 668 is the property of Mr Thomas Boynton, Bridlington Quay, and was made by George Ethrington, London, about 1695. The case is finely decorated with English marqueterie.

A very fine chiming clock by Tompion, with canopied head, which is at Windsor Castle, shown in Fig. 669. The upper part of the case is particularly good. The trusses supporting the hood, though somewhat unusual features, have an excellent effect.

Fig. 671 represents a Tompion one-year timepiece which is now at the Admiralty. The hours are marked twice from I. to XII. and at the top of the hood is the inscription, "Presented by Queen Anne." Dividing the hour numerals into two periods of twelve hours each provides a time-teller for the civil, as distinguished from the astronomical, solar day, but unless desired for some particular purpose such crowding of the hour numerals is objectionable. The case is certainly later than Queen Anne's time, as I have already said, and the dial looks more like Graham's production than Tompion's. It is quite likely that the timekeeper was ordered of Tompion and intended for Greenwich Observatory and that Graham's well-known desire to make as reliable a regulator as possible caused considerable delay in its construction, or the movement may have been lying by uncased. A very similar twelve-month timepiece bearing Tompion's name, and inscribed "Sir Jonas Moore caused this movement to be made with great care, Anno Domini 1676," was presented to the Royal Society in 1736.

An example of marqueterie arranged in geometrical patterns is shown in Fig. 670, which represents a clock by Joshua Hutchin belonging to Mr W. K. Bowen. The case, of walnut, is inlaid with stars, curved hexagons, &c., and a broad herring-bone border which runs around the door, up the sides, and across the top of the body; a banding inside this border is interspersed with bits of red wood at intervals of 3 in. The stars and hexagons are picked out with holly and set in selected pieces of yew.

The specimen shown in Fig. 673 by Edward East is from the Wetherfield collection and dates from 1680-1685. It has a dial 9½ in. square, goes eight days, and is in a walnut case with marqueterie panels showing flowers, birds, and butterflies; somewhat coarse but effective. The hood has a canopied top with brass side ornaments.

From the same collection, and of slightly later date is the fine eight-day clock with 10 in. square dial, by Joseph Knibb, shown in Fig. 674. The case of oak is covered with burr walnut oyster-shell veneer, the sides are panelled and inlaid down the front with large rosettes of dark and light wood mixed. There are gilt bases and capitals to the corkscrew pillars at the corners of the hood, and over the entablature is a finely carved ornament. There are two bells of Chinese gong shape and on the smaller of these the preceding hour is repeated at the half-hour.

An example of bird and flower marqueterie covering a clock by Jonathan Lowndes, shown in Fig. 675, is from the Wetherfield collection, as is also the splendid clock, Fig. 676, which is of later date. It has a dial 12 in. square; the name "Dan: Quare" being engraved between the hour numerals VII. and VI. and "London" between VI. and V. The case is decorated with marqueterie, birds and flowers arranged in panels with scroll borders around the door framing and the base; the pillars at the hood corners are also covered with marqueterie.

An eight-day chiming clock, giving ten changes in the hour, by Peter Garon, in a very fine arabesque marqueterie case, the property of Mr J. Drummond Robertson, is shown in Fig. 677.

The clock by Fromanteel & Clarke in a choice marqueterie case which is shown in Fig. 679 belongs to Mr William R. Moss. It strikes hours and half-hours, has an alarm, shows a day of the week and day of the month.

The Tompion clock, Fig. 678, is from the Wetherfield collection, as is also the twelve-month timepiece by Daniel Quare shown in Fig. 681, which is remarkable for the somewhat peculiar outline of the case and for its extremely beautiful marqueterie surface. Of the subsidiary discs in the upper corners of the dial plate the right-hand one is a twelve-month calendar and

Fig. 686. — Wm. Ball, Bicester; centre seconds, moon and calendar (see p.377).

Fig. 687. — Thomas Moss, Frodsham, 1776; enlarged view of Dial on p.336.

Fig. 688. — Higgs & Evans; extreme height, 5 ft. 5 in., about 1780.

Fig. 689. — Simpson, Southwell, about 1790.

that on the left is engraved *"Tempus aequale"* and *"Tempus apparens,"* and the main dial can be caused to show at pleasure either mean time or solar time according as the pointer is set.

A one-year equation timepiece by Daniel Delander, shown in Fig. 682, is also the property of Mr Wetherfield.

Dark oak cases carved in high relief do not seem to have been the fashion of any particular period, but the result rather of occasional efforts by enthusiastic artists in wood, and then in most instances they appear to have been made to enclose existing clocks in substitution for inferior or worn-out coverings. Mr Harry Clark owns a thirty-hour clock by Thomas Stripling, dating from about 1710. It is in a dark oak case. The bottom panel contains a well-carved scene showing the Lord Chancellor presenting the keys of office to Queen Elizabeth on her coronation. On the door panel is a carved representation of Oliver Cromwell. It is shown in Fig. 683.

ORIENTAL LACQUER   Cases coated with black, red, or green lacquer or with a coating of lacquer on black, red, or green ground, the surface being decorated in the Chinese or Japanese style more or less in relief and gilded, were much in favour from about 1710 to 1760. It is said that at first these cases were sent by ships engaged in the tea trade to China to be decorated, and that a delay of two years or so would occur before they reached England again. Then the Dutch engaged in the art, and afterwards the lacquering or japanning of cases was practised in England. While a few of the specimens now to be met with are worthy of admiration, the greater number attract merely by reason of the grotesque appearance of the ornament. Occasionally may be seen a clock, the door of which is ornamented with Oriental lacquer in relief, while the surface of the rest of the case is merely japanned with poor designs in stencil.

An unusually fine red lacquer case, covering a clock by Philip Abbott, in the Wetherfield collection, and dating from about 1750, is shown in Fig. 685. Another clock with lacquer decoration is shown in Fig. 686. It belongs to Mr George F. Glenny, and bears the inscription "Wm. Ball, Bisceter." It has a centre seconds hand, and just above the centre of the main dial is a subsidiary one showing the age and phases of the moon. The dials below give the day of the month, the title of the day; thus "St Monday," "St Tuesday," &c., and month of the year. It dates from about 1770.

CHIPPENDALE   Examples of what is generally accepted as an orthodox Chippendale case are represented in Figs. 687, 688 and 689. It is not easy to define exactly what constitutes a Chippendale case, nor why cases of this pattern should be ascribed to Chippendale. Thomas Chippendale was a noted upholsterer and cabinet-maker in St Martin's Lane. He published a splendid folio book of designs, of which three editions appeared between 1755 and 1763. Figs. 690, 691, 692, and 698 are copied from his work by favour of Mr B. T. Batsford. It must be confessed none of them bears a very close resemblance to the reputed Chippendale patterns. There are also representations of two other

Figs. 693, 694. — Chippendale Bracket Cases.

Fig. 690. — Chippendale, with "Fiddle" or "Kettle" Base.

Fig. 691. — Chippendale, with Enriched Front.

Fig. 692. — Chippendale, with Tapered Trunk.

Figs. 695, 696. — Chippendale Bracket Cases.

377

Fig. 697. — Perfect chippendale case Clock by John Holmes.

long-case clocks, the bracket-clock cases shown in Figs. 693, 694, 695, and 696, a cartel case, and two other small wall timepiece cases. The two long cases I have not reproduced are carved very much in the French style, as Figs. 507, 508, Chapter VI.

English clocks in cases following Chippendale's published designs are exceedingly rare. A bracket clock enclosed in a case similar to Fig. 693 bore the name of Jno. Archambo, who carried on business in Princes Street, Leicester Square, between 1720 and 1745. Among the Wetherfield collection is one superb example, which is shown in Fig. 697. It is a clock by John Holmes. The case is of mahogany, and the execution of every part scrupulously good. It dates from about 1770.

The characteristics of the cases now usually known as "Chippendale" are the pillars or pilasters rising at the front corners of the case, from the plinth to the entablature under the hood, and the corresponding pillars at the front corners of the hood. Generally the bases and caps are of metal, and the shafts fluted. The case is much higher than the dial, and the top of the pattern shown in Fig. 684, which is considered the more correct, or of the horn-top kind, in which the upper part terminates in two carved scrolls, curving inwards. It will be observed that the head above the dial in Fig. 684 is high, and most after the style of Chippendale's drawings. This clock was made by Richard Vick and is at Windsor Castle, and appears to be earlier than Chippendale's books. The horn-top style, which was very popular with provincial makers, is later. The horn or scroll-top case shown in Fig. 687 encloses a clock by Thomas Moss, of Frodsham, which belongs to Mr William R. Moss; the dial, to an enlarged scale, is shown in Fig. 657. This clock was made in 1776 or 1778. Fig. 689 represents a clock by Simpson, of Southwell, dating from about 1790, for which I am indebted to Mr H. Cook, of Newark. There are no pillars between the base and the hood, but the front corners of the waist are boldly chamfered.

It is a little curious that the handsome curved base of Figs. 690 and 698, though favoured by Dutch and French makers, was very rarely adopted by English. A clock by Joseph Rose, London, owned by Mr Charles Morson in America, affords an exceptional example of this "fiddle" or "kettle" shaped base, as it is indifferently called, applied to an English production.

A remarkably small and pretty Chippendale-case, quarter chiming clock, which belongs to Mr R. Lionel Foster, is shown in Fig. 688. Its total height is 5 ft. 5 in. The dial rings of enamel are good and clear, and above them is the signature "Higgs y Diego Evans," a form of signature used for the Spanish markets. For the photograph I am indebted to Mr J. Bolton Smith.

The clock by Andrew Padbury shown in Fig. 699 belongs to Mr C. J. Bentall. It is remarkably by reason of its dial, which is shown to an enlarged scale in Fig. 653.

Fig. 701 shows a clock by Nicholas Lambert, London, dating from about 1760. The case is of walnut with unusual arching at the bottom of the hood. For this and Fig. 703 I am indebted to Messrs W. Horne & Son. A clock by Henry Brownbill, Leeds, owned by Mr Cecil B. Morgan and shown in Fig. 702, has a painted dial. It dates from about 1780. Fig. 703 represents a clock by John Smith, Chester; the handsome case is of mahogany with what is called, I believe, a brickwork base.

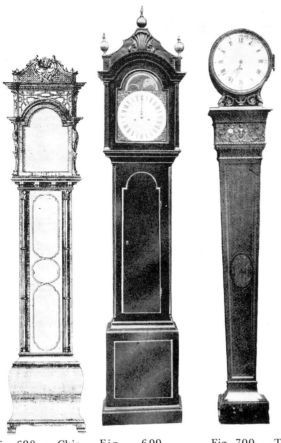

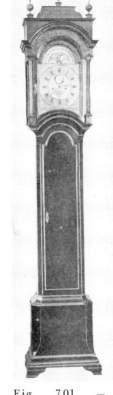

Fig. 698. — Chippendale, with "Fiddle" or "Kettle" Base.

Fig. 699. — Andrew Padbury, about 1760.

Fig. 700. — Timepiece by Ainsworth Thwaites at the India Office.

Fig. 701. — Nicholas Lambert, Case arched under dial.

Fig. 702. — Henry Brownbill; finely painted dial, about 1780.

Fig. 703. — John Smith, Chester, "Brickwork" base.

Fig. 704. — William Gib, Rotterdam.

Fig. 705. — Johannes Duchesne, Amsterdam.

Fig. 706. — T^s Thomasen, Amsterdam.

Fig. 707. — Sheraton design, with Side Wings.

Fig. 708. — Sheraton design suggesting Effective Inlay.

Fig. 709. — Clock by William Dutton, about 1780.

Dutch Examples, 1725-1750 (see p.380).

Examples of the best style of Dutch manufacture are reproduced in Figs. 704, 705, and 706. Sir James M. Moody has a long-case clock by Wm. Gib, Rotterdam. It chimes the quarters on eight bells and strikes the previous hour on a small bell at half-past. Representations of the moon are on cut crystal, gilt at the back. It is shown in Fig. 704. Fig. 706 shows a clock signed "T^s Thomasen Amsterdam," which belongs to Mr Francis H. Bigelow, of Cambridge, Massachusetts. Fig. 705, in a case of somewhat similar design, is a clock by Johannes Duchesne, Amsterdam, which is the property of Mr Lawrence Bentall. An especially attractive feature of it is a well-painted picture on the dial plate, which may be viewed with better effect in Fig. 661, where it appears to an enlarged scale.

SHERATON

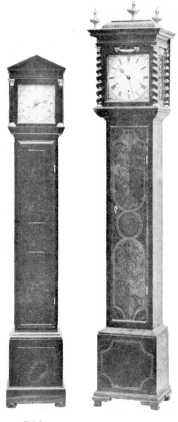

Thomas Sheraton was born at Stockton-on-Tees in 1751 and died in London in 1806. In 1791 was issued "The Cabinet-Makers' and Upholsterers' Drawing Book" by him, and in 1803 "The Cabinet Dictionary," of which another edition appeared in 1808. No mention is made of clock cases in the first edition of this work. From the later edition are copied Figs. 707 and 708. Though rarely made in this form with square dials, the ornate style and beautiful inlaid work associated with Sheraton have been very successfully applied by clock-case makers, and the popularity of Sheraton cases has never declined.

The handsome clock shown in Fig. 700 was made by Ainsworth Thwaites for the East India Company about 1770; the case is of figured wood, doubtless of Indian growth. A companion case, which originally held a dial to record the direction of the wind, seems to have mysteriously disappeared from the offices of the Company and to have been found on the Continent, where it was purchased by an official of the English Government, and the two now appropriately occupy positions in a room at the India Office, being symmetrically placed one on each side of the fireplace.

Fig. 709 represents a long-case clock of novel design by William Dutton, dating from about 1780, for which I am indebted to Mr Thomas Wyatt. The case, just upon 10 ft. in height, is of pine and mahogany painted light blue and white. The dial is of brass with a convex enamelled centre. The movement has a dead-beat escapement and a gridiron compensated pendulum. The lunar ball in the arch of the dial is rotated from the hour wheel arbor, on which is cut a screw to drive the intermediate lunar train. Below the moon is an oblong slit through which appears the day of the month.

In Figs. 710 to 733 are further examples from the Wetherfield collection showing some of the finest productions with variations in style and treatment, from the end of the seventeenth to the end of the eighteenth century. All will repay examination. Fig. 710, by Joseph Knibb, dates from about 1680; the dial is 8 in. square, with engraved corner decoration, the case of ebony being but 6 ft. 2 in. high, altogether a chaste and pleasing design. To the right of it is a larger and more ornate specimen of rather later date by the same maker, in a burr walnut case. It is a month clock, striking the hours on a large bell, and the quarters on a smaller one, in a peculiar way. One stroke is given for the first, and an additional one for each succeeding hour up to the sixth; then seven is given as one, and so on till the twelfth hour which is recorded by six strokes. Fig. 712 is a clock by Thomas Tompion dating from about 1690, and furnished with bolt

Fig. 710. — Joseph Knibb, Eight-day Quarter Clock, ebony case, 6 ft. 2 in. high; about 1680.

Fig. 711. — Joseph Knibb. Three-train Month Quarter Clock, walnut case; about 1685.

Fig. 712. — Thomas Tompion, Eight-day, walnut case, with carved superstructure; about 1690.

Fig. 713. — Daniel Parker, London; Month Clock, 1¼ seconds pendulum; door in base and glass therein; height 6 ft. 8 in. skeleton dial 10½ in. square; about 1690.

Fig. 714. — James Clowes; about 1695; 7 ft. 2 in. high, 10½-in. dial.

Fig. 715. — Christopher Gould, London; Eight-day, carved pediment surmounted by figure of Cupid, bolt and shutter maintaining power; height 7 ft. 2 in., dial 10½ in. square; about 1695.

Fig. 716. — Christopher Gould, London; lacquer decoration, each minute on dial numbered; height 7ft. 8in., dial 12 in. square; about 1700.

Fig. 717. — John Eagle, marqueterie, with grotesque pictures in-laid; height 7 ft. 3 in.; about 1700.

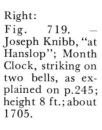

Left:
Fig. 718. — Jonathan Puller, Month Clock, chiming on six bells; 12-in. dial, height 8 ft. 1 in.; about 1700.

Right:
Fig. 719. — Joseph Knibb, "at Hanslop"; Month Clock, striking on two bells, as explained on p.245; height 8 ft.; about 1705.

Left:
Fig. 720. — Cornelius Herbert, Eight-day, marqueterie; 12-in. dial height 8 ft. 4 in.; about 1700.

Right:
Fig. 721. — Daniel Quare, Three-train Month Quarter Clock; burr walnut case; height 8 ft.; about 1705.

Fig. 722. — Christ-opher Gould, Eight-day, chim-ing on eight bells; 12-in. dial, height 8 ft.; about 1705.

Fig. 723. — From-anteel & Clarke, Quarters and Alarm Month Clock; 11-in. dial, height 7 ft. 9 in.; about 1710.

Fig. 724. — Charles Clay, Month Clock, with Perpetual Calendar; height 9 ft., 12-in. dial; about 1710.

and shutter maintaining power. The dial is 10 in. square, and the case, of burr walnut, is 7 ft. 3 in. high with a carved superstructure.

Fig. 713, a month clock by Daniel Parker, dating from about 1690, in a prettily arranged marqueterie case, has a skeleton dial 10½ in. square, and good hands. It is 6 ft. 8 in. high, with a long pendulum beating once in a second and a quarter; the bob extending below the trunk may be viewed through an oval hole in the regulating door at the base.

A remarkably fine surface of marqueterie over the front and sides of the case is the feature of Fig. 714, which represents a month clock by James Clowes. It dates from about 1695, is 7 ft. in height with a dial 11 in. square. On the same page and of even date is an example by Christopher Gould. The case has a carved head with a finial in the form of Cupid. Altogether it stands 7 ft. 2 in. in height; the dial is 10½ in. square, and maintaining power during winding is arranged on the bolt and shutter plan.

An unusually early specimen of Oriental lacquer decoration is shown in Fig. 716, another clock by Christopher Gould, dating from about 1700. It is 7 ft. 8 in. high; the dial, 12 in. square, has each minute numbered, and the hands are very fine. The other clocks on p. 381 are of about the same date. On the front of the case of Fig. 717 are grotesque pictures in marqueterie. This clock is by John Eagle; the height is 7 ft. 3 in., and the dial 11 in. square. Quite a different style of marqueterie adorns the case of Fig. 718, a clock by Jonathan Puller, chiming on six bells. The claw feet and finials are worthy of note. It stands 8 ft. 1 in. high, and the dial is 12 in. square, with subsidiary dials in the top corners for chime silent and regulation.

The dials and hands of three examples in Figs. 719, 720, and 721 are all good, though dissimilar. The first in an ebonised case is a month clock by "Joseph Knibb att Hanslop," and striking on the bells according to the Roman numerals, as explained on p. 245. The centre clock, in a marqueterie case, is by Cornelius Herbert. It is 8 ft. 4 in. high, and has a 12-in. dial.

Fig. 721 represents a month clock by Daniel Quare in a burr walnut case 8 ft. high. It has three trains, striking hours on a large bell, and quarters on a small one. The escutcheon over the keyhole of the door is amusing.

Three distinct styles of marqueterie may be observed in Figs. 722, 723, and 724. Fig. 722 is a three-train month clock, chiming on eight bells, by Christopher Gould. It is 8 ft. high, has a 12-in. dial, and dates from about 1705. A little later is the month quarter clock with alarm, by Fromanteel & Clarke, which is shown in Fig. 723. It is 7 ft. 9 in. high, and has an 11-in. dial. The trusses under the hood in Fig. 724, though not a very usual feature, are appropriate and in keeping with the rest of the handsome case, which is 9 ft. high. This clock is by Charles Clay. It has a 12-in. dial, and is furnished with a perpetual calendar.

Now we come to the arched dial period, and begin with three examples dating from about 1730. The extra large clock in Fig. 725, which is by Benjamin Gray, stood for 180 years in Sheffield Place, Sussex, being the property successively of the first Earl de la Warr and the three Earls of Sheffield until the death of the last. The bevelled corners of the trunk and base of the walnut case are effective. The dial is 14 in. wide, and shows the day of the month, the month of the year, and phases of the moon. It has a dead-beat escapement and maintaining power.

Left: Fig. 728. — George Lindsay, Eight-day Three-train, tune playing; 14-in. dial, mahogany case; height 8 ft.; about 1770.

Right: Fig. 729. — Thomas Colley, "Graham's Successor," mahogany case; dial 12 in. wide, height 8 ft. 10 in.; about 1770.

Fig. 725. — Benj. Gray; 10 ft. 3 in. high.

Fig. 726. — Isaac Nickals, Chiming Clock, Tidal Register in arch, lacquer decoration.

Fig. 727. — Wm. Hawkins, Eight-day, buff-lacquer decoration; 12-in. dial, height 9 ft. 9 in.; about 1740.

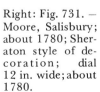

Left: Fig. 730. — Thomas Clare, Warrington; dial of Battersea enamel, 12 in. wide, height 7 ft. 7 in.; about 1775.

Right: Fig. 731. — Moore, Salisbury; about 1780; Sheraton style of decoration; dial 12 in. wide; about 1780.

Left: Fig. 732. — James Gray, Edinburgh; silvered dial, height 7 ft. 6 in.; about 1790.

Right: Fig. 733. — Alexander Cumming; height 8 ft.; about 1790.

Fig. 734. — At Windsor Castle, by Recordon, about 1800.

Fig. 735. — Clock with Moving Figures, about 1780.

Fig. 736. — Jas Lorimer, Musical Clock, about 1780.

Fig. 737. — Edward Staunton, London, Ebony Eight-day Bracket Quarter-Clock; three bells; height 17 in.; about 1680.

A quarter clock chiming on three bells with a dial 13 in. wide exhibiting the day of the week and month, and month of the year, phases of the moon and time of high water, is by Isaac Nickals, of Wells. It is shown in Fig. 726. The case, adorned with buff lacquer decoration, is 8 ft. 3 in. high.

Fig. 727, a clock by Wm. Hawkins, of Bury St Edmunds, has a dial 12 in. wide, giving the age and phases of the moon. This case stands 9 ft. 9 in. high and is also decorated with buff lacquer.

Fig. 728 shows a clock by George Lindsay in a mahogany case of unpretentious design, dating from about 1770. It stands 8 ft. high, and plays six tunes on twelve bells, has a dead-beat escapement with jewelled pallets, and a dial 14 in. wide.

Fig. 729 in a mahogany case of the conventional Chippendale style, standing 8 ft. 10 in. high, encloses an interesting clock signed "Thomas Colley, Graham's successor." It has a dead-beat escapement, and the dial is 12 in. wide.

The well-carved mahogany case shown in Fig. 730 may also be regarded as a typical Chippendale. It encloses a clock by Thomas Clare, of Warrington, having a dial 12 in. wide of Battersea enamel, a material but rarely adopted. It dates from about 1775, and stands 7 ft. 7 in. high.

A quarter clock by Moore, of Salisbury, in a mahogany Sheraton style of case is shown in Fig. 731. It has a painted dial 12 in. wide, and dates from about 1780. The height is 7 ft. 6 in.

Another case of mahogany in the Sheraton style is shown in Fig. 732. This clock is by James Gray, of Edinburgh, dating from about 1790. It has a silvered dial 13 in. wide, and stands 7 ft. 6 in. high.

Of about the same date is the clock by Alexander Cumming, the last of the series I have selected for illustration [Fig. 733]. The case of mahogany is 8 ft. high with tasteful marqueterie in panels. The dial is 12 in. wide.

In Fig. 735 is shown a remarkably fine musical clock with moving figures, the property of Mr E. E. Cook, of Walton-on-Thames. It was made by Pickett, of Marlboro', and dates from about 1780. The silvered dial is engraved with urns, and just inside the usual numeral circle and concentric therewith is a date circle to which an index from the centre points.

At 12, 3, 6, and 9 o'clock one of the following tunes is played:—

1. Marlbro' Jigg.
2. Jack's Jigg.
3. Ned's Hornpipe.
4. Batt's Hornpipe.
5. Ben's Delight.
6. Head's Whim.

These tunes are enumerated in the right-hand spandrel; the left-hand spandrel contains a chime-silent hand. In the arch of the dial is a curtain which rises when the clock chimes, and a male and female figure are discovered dancing. Below them is a river and a bridge; over the bridge people, carts, &c., pass, including a man carrying his wife to avoid the toll, which, tradition says, refers to a local bridge where a heavy toll was exacted. Below the bridge swans, boats, &c., pass to and fro on the water. In the lower part of the main dial is a moon calendar. In Fig. 659 the dial is shown to an enlarged scale.

A musical clock of unusually large size, which is the property of Mr R. Eden Dickson, is shown in Fig. 736. The case of mahogany is 8 ft. 5 in. high, and the dial measures 18½ in. by 22 in. The quarters are chimed on eight bells, and at every three hours, after the quarters are chimed and the hours struck, a tune is played. There are sixteen bells and twenty-four hammers; the music barrel is 14½ in. long and 3 in. in diameter. The subsidiary dials are "strike-silent" and "chime-silent," the name "James Lorimer, London," being on the plate between, while in the arch above is the following list of tunes:—

1. La Promenade.
2. Gavot.
3. Minuet.
4. Bagnigge Wells.
5. Duke of Gloucester's March.
6. Neu Alamand.
7. I do as I will with my Swain.
8. Lays of Paties Mill.
9. Flowers of Edinburgh.
10. Cuckoo's Nest.
11. Tweed Side.
12. Portsmouth Psalm.

The pendulum rod is of ebony, and above the bob on a small brass plate is engraved "John Marshall, London."

As examples of the plain early nineteenth century clocks of the best class with circular enamelled dials, and usually in cases of mahogany with finely figured surfaces, may be taken the one by Vulliamy illustrated in Fig. 471, and one by Recordon shown in Fig. 734. For a really perfect dial on this plan, one has to go to a comparatively obscure provincial maker (see Fig. 660).

The introduction of cheap American clocks was disastrous to the old English ones, and between 1850 and 1860 thousands of good serviceable

A good example of late 18th century provincial workmanship. 7ft. Scottish regulator signed 'Alex^r. Ferguson Cupar in Fife'. Brass dial with hour volvelle instead of a dial. Plain mahogany case in classical style with broken pediment. Conventional plated movement with dead-beat anchor escapement. Bobinet Ltd.

long-case timekeepers were sacrificed, the cases being chopped up for firewood and the substantial brass movements consigned to the melting pot.

Bracket or pedestal clocks, with enriched cases, as distinguished from the plain metal covering of the ordinary chamber clock, were in favour before the advent of the long-case variety.

Of the early types with metal cases, examples have already been given. Fig. 737 shows a large bracket clock by Edward Staunton which is in the Wetherfield collection, and dates from about 1680. Here, as in the long-case clock by John Fromanteel in Fig. 442, and the one by Joseph Knibb in Fig. 710, the case is surmounted by a pediment. During the latter part of the seventeenth and the beginning of the eighteenth century the square "squat" case of wood with a flat top and plain metal handle for lifting it by, as shown in Fig. 408, or with a perforated metal dome-shaped addition, chased and gilded, called basket-work, surmounted by an enriched handle, was very popular. The basket top is probably of Dutch origin. Engravings of this variety are given in Figs. 409 and 431. Most of them had a curved slit in the dial through which the motion of a mock pendulum could be seen.

Fig. 738, an early and choice example by Humfrey Adamson, London, is from the Wetherfield collection. For Fig. 739, a clock by John Harris, London, I am indebted to Mr William Newton. Mr J. Drummond Robertson owns the fine double basket top clock by Claudius Du Chesne, London, which appears in Fig. 740.

Sometimes, instead of the open-work metal basket, a basket-shaped curve of wood surmounted the case. The clock by Ben Collier, London, constructed in this way and shown in Fig. 741 belongs to Mr G. H. Jocelyn, Writtle, Essex. Three, selected from the Wetherfield collection, are reproduced in Figs. 742 to 744. One is by Joseph Knibb, London; one in a marqueterie case, quite an unusual style of decoration for such a piece, is by John Martin, London; and one by Thomas Tompion.

After the "basket" came the "bell" shaped case, so called from the hollow curved character of the top, as seen in Fig. 745. This is a very early example of that style, in the collection of Mr J. D. Robertson. It dates from about

Fig. 738. — Humfrey Adamson, red tortoiseshell case, about 1680.

Fig. 739.

Right: 741.

Left: Fig. 740.

Below: Fig. 743. — John Martin, London, Eight-day Striking and Repeating Clock; fine arabesque marqueterie, about 1700.

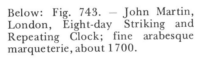

Fig. 742. — Joseph Knibb, London, repeats the last hour at the half hour on a smaller bell; about 1700; height 1 ft. 2 in.

Fig. 744. — Thos. Tompion, repeats quarters by pulling the knob and string on the right; about 1705.

387

1695, and is inscribed, "Stephen Asselin, London." The George Graham in Fig. 746 is from the Wetherfield collection. Mrs Francis J. Kidson owns a clock very similar to Fig. 746, signed "Tho Tompion & Edw Banger, London."

The "bell" top case continued in favour long after the introduction of the arched dial. Two views (Figs. 747 and 748) are appended of an early arch dial bracket clock by Jeremiah Hartley, of Norwich, from the Schloss collection. The case is of ebonised wood with brass mounts. In the spandrels

Fig. 745.

Right: Fig. 746. — George Graham, about 1715; ebony case with silver dial ornaments, height 13 in.

Fig. 747.

Fig. 748.

388

Fig. 749.

Fig. 750.

of the arch and at the sides is pierced diaper work backed by silk, to permit the sound of the bell to escape and yet prevent the ingress of dust. The clock shows days of the month, strikes the hours and quarters, and the strokes corresponding to the previous striking may be repeated at pleasure by pulling a string terminating in the knob which is seen at the right of the front view. In the arch of the dial is a rise and fall regulator which adjusts the length of the pendulum.

A later bell top case with fine claw feet, and surmounted by a plain brass handle instead of the side handles, is shown in Fig. 749.

Of the more ornate styles in vogue during the second quarter of the eighteenth century, the clock by Graham in Fig. 427 affords a good idea.

What perhaps may be termed a sporadic case of very elegant design is shown in Fig. 750, by favour of Mr William Horne, Leyburn, Yorkshire. The clock is undoubtedly the work of Edward East, and dates probably from about 1685, but the case is in many respects characteristic of the Sheraton style. It is of iron with brass mountings, finely chased and gilt, and measures 2 ft. 2 in. high and 12 in broad. On the dial of brass is engraved a peacock in full plume. On the back plate of the movement is engraved a basket of flowers, and underneath the inscription, "Eduardus East, London."

The handsome musical clock shown in Fig. 751 belongs to Mr Herbert A. Evans. The case is of mahogany with heavy brass handles and ornamentation at the corners, sides, and other parts; the face is a plain white dial, with a smaller dial at each corner, brass ornament filling the intervening spaces. It strikes the hours on a gong which can also be set to ring at any hour as an alarm, and has besides a chime of thirteen bells playing four tunes, any of which may be selected by moving a hand on one of the smaller dials. In the arch above the face is painted a landscape scene with three moving figures in the foreground; at each hour these figures respectively beat a drum, play a fiddle, and dance more or less in time to the music. By pulling one of three small knobs at the side of the clock the hour chimes or alarm can be repeated at will. Of the remaining three small dials one has a strike-silent hand, the second shows the date of the month, and the third one the age of the moon. The face of the clock is engraved with the maker's name, "Diego Evans, Bolsa Real, Londres," and this is also engraved on the back plate, which is finely chased with arabesques and flowers. James Evans was a well-known maker of good timekeepers for the Spanish markets, by himself and also in conjunction with Higgs. This clock had been many years in the possession of a Bolivian gentleman resident in the city of Potosi.

Clocks for Eastern countries, usually with Turkish numerals, were often in cases of special design in which a domed top was a distinguishing feature. A fine example, dating from about 1730, is given in Fig. 752. It is a musical clock by "George Clarke, Leaden Hall Street, London," from the Wetherfield collection. The movement is furnished with fourteen bells. In the upper part of the arched dial is engraved the following list of tunes, the playing of anyone selected being ensured by moving to it an indicator:—

Princess Amelia.	A Rigadoon.
A Turkey Tune.	A Minuet.
A Gallen of Craden.	Greeke Song.
A Greeke Song.	A Minuet.
A Rigadoon.	A March.
A March.	

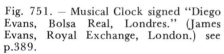

Fig. 751. — Musical Clock signed "Diego Evans, Bolsa Real, Londres." (James Evans, Royal Exchange, London.) see p.389.

Fig. 752. — Clock by George Clarke, about 1730. Turkish hour numerals.

Fig. 753. — Clock by Henry Borrell, about 1810. Turkish hour numerals.

Subsidiary dials on the left and right are respectively "Strike, Not Strike," and "Chime, Not Chime."

Another handsome domed clock, designed for the Eastern markets, having Turkish hour numerals, and nearly a century later, is shown in Fig. 753. For this illustration I am indebted to Messrs A. & H. Rowley. The dials are of enamel, and on the main one is the inscription, "Henry Borrell, Exchange, London." The upper central disc contains the following list of tunes: "St James' Minuet, Handel's Gavotte, A Hunting we will Go, Haymakers' Dance." George and John Prior were celebrated for clocks of this character, which are often taken to be older than they really are.

In Fig. 755 is shown the arrangement of the musical barrels in a very large clock by "William Webster, Exchange Alley," from the Eden Dickson collection. It is 26 in. high, the dial being 13½ in. by 9 in. There are twenty-four tunes engraved in three lines on the dial, and of these each cylinder plays eight.

The tunes are as follows:—

1st		2nd		3rd	
	Granadiers' March.		A young Virgin of 15.		Beautiful Phillis.
	A Minuet.			A English Sible.			Gle. Rainge all round.
	The Rumer.			Sweet is our Blessing.			O Nymph of Race Divine.
	The Spanish Jigg.			The Mouse trap.			Hunt ye Squirel.
	A Riggadoon.			A Minuet.			Bright Aurelia.
	Thomas, I cannot.			A Jigg.			St George's Minuet.
	Don't you tickle me.			An Ayre.			A Minuet.
	3 Generals' Health.			The Happy Clown.			Soldiers Rejoyce.

Fig. 754. — Musical Clock by Wm. Webster.

Fig. 755. — Showing arrangement of Barrel, &c., in a large Musical Clock by Wm. Webster.

Fig. 756. — Josiah Emery, Eight-day; pull repeating quarters on six bells.

The music is played every three hours at 12, 3, 6, and 9, the air being given twice each time. There are twelve bells and two hammers for each. The cylinders are each 10 in. long and $1\frac{1}{4}$ in. in diameter. Those not in use are kept in a drawer in the base of the case. The clock has also a full quarter movement, arranged to strike on six of the chime bells.

The charming diminutive clock by Josiah Emery, with bracket, shown in Fig. 756, is from the Wetherfield collection.

Towards the end of the eighteenth century the popularity of the "bell-top" case waned, and it was gradually supplanted by three set patterns, the "broken arch," the "balloon," and the "lancet."

The "broken arch" was not, as might be supposed, a circular pediment cut away in the middle, but an arched top not extending to the full width of the dial, the moulding surmounting the arch being continued from its springing along the front of the case in two short straight bands. This seems to have been taken from Chippendale's bracket cases, as in Figs. 693, 694, 695, 696, all of which have circular pediments of this kind, but the ornamental superstructure as suggested by Chippendale was not adopted. What is generally accepted as a "broken arch" case is shown in Fig. 757. It enclosed a clock dating from about 1790, by John Thwaites, an eminent maker who was several times master of the Clockmakers' Company.

A wide broken-arch mahogany case, containing a musical clock by Stephen Rimbault, is shown in Fig. 758. The clock plays six tunes on eleven bells. One air is "God Save the King"; the others are now obsolete and not easily recognised, but no doubt they were most popular about 1780, when the clock was made. A fine musical clock by Rimbault, which was formerly the property of Sir William Drake, is in the Ashmolean Museum, Oxford.

Stephen Rimbault carried on business in Great St Andrew's Street, St Giles, and was a maker of repute, particularly excelling in clocks, with mechanical figures dancing or working on the dials, and other complicated timekeepers. The artist Zoffany was for some time Rimbault's decorative assistant, and in him his master had a man of great ability and taste, who no

Fig. 757.

Fig. 758. — Chiming Clock by S. Rimbault.

Fig. 759. — James Cowan, Edinburgh, about 1770, Three-Train Bracket Clock, chiming on eight bells; Chippendale mahogany case, 2 ft. 3 in. high.

Fig. 760. — John Ellicott, about 1780.

Fig. 761. — Marriott, about 1780.

Fig. 762. — Jas. Tregent, about 1780.

Fig. 763. — Cade & Robinson, about 1800.

Fig. 764. — John Harris.

BACK PLATES

Fig. 765. — Thomas Tompion.

doubt helped to make his name. Zoffany painted a portrait of his master which pleased Rimbault so much that he introduced him to Wilson, the portrait painter. Zoffany was then employed by Wilson to fill in draperies, &c., at a salary of £40 a year, and while with him his ability was recognised by David Garrick, who put him into the channel of theatrical portraiture, where he made his name, becoming R.A. in 1798.

The following examples are from the Wetherfield collection:—

Fig. 759, by James Cowan, Edinburgh. Fig. 760, a repeating clock by John Ellicott, in a mahogany case 1 ft. 5 in. high. Fig. 761, by Marriott, London, is a quarter clock with one bell and two hammers. The dials are of enamel, the hours are marked 1 to 12 twice over, the case, of ebony with brass mounts, is 1 ft. 3 in. high. Fig. 762, by James Tregent, has enamel dials and an ebony case 1 ft. 3 in. high. Fig. 763, by Cade & Robinson, with enamel dial, is in a mahogany case 1 ft. 4 in. high.

Till towards the end of the eighteenth century bracket clocks had, as a rule, a glazed door at the back through which could be seen the back plate with ornamental engraving thereon. Six examples are given. John Harris, about 1690, from the clock shown in Fig. 739; Thomas Tompion, 1705, from the clock shown in Fig. 744; Peter Wise, 1710, from a clock belonging to Mr T. W. Bourne; Thomas Parker, about 1710, from a clock belong to Mr J. D. Robertson, having an ornamental pendulum cock similar to that on Sir Isaac Newton's clock in the Guildhall Museum; Joseph Knibb, about 1700; and John Ellicott, about 1770, which shows on the upper left-hand corner a repeating-barrel. When it was desired that the quarters should be repeated the mainspring in a barrel of this kind would be wound by pulling a cord outside the case; in unwinding, the force of the spring would be utilised to actuate the hammers. Figs. 765, 768, and 769 are from the Wetherfield collection.

Fig. 766. — Peter Wise.

Fig. 767. — Thomas Parker.

Fig. 768. — Joseph Knibb.

Fig. 769. — John Ellicott.

Fig. 770. — Joseph Thompson.   Fig. 771. — At Windsor Castle.   Fig. 772. — Sheraton Style, about 1790.

Ornamental engraving is rarely seen on nineteenth century productions. With the engraved plate disappeared, of course, the glazed door at the back of the case. The utilitarian spirit, which abolished these features as redundant, has, however, caused fine specimens which survive to be more highly prized. What can look meaner than the bare and often common wood at the back of many pretentious modern clocks if one of them happens to be in front of a mirror?

BALLOON   Fig. 770 gives an excellent representation of a balloon case inlaid after the Sheraton style, from the Wetherfield collection. The clock is signed "Jos Thompson London," and dates from about 1790. Fig. 771 shows a later and more ornate form of balloon clock at Windsor Castle. For the balloon clock and bracket shown in Fig. 772 I am indebted to Mr Webster. The graceful harmony of the curves constituting the case and bracket form a complete and pleasing design. The clock enclosed in this case was made by Robert Wood, of Moorfields. The round knob on top of the case served to regulate the time by shortening or lengthening the effective part of the pendulum. The clock by John Johnson on a bracket as in Fig. 773 is from the Wetherfield collection.

LANCET   The "lancet" case, in form the counterpart of a pointed Gothic arch, and named from its resemblance to the well-known cutting instrument used by surgeons, is shown in Fig. 774. This clock, dating from about 1820, was made by George Orpwood.

Of about the same date is a pretty little clock at Windsor Castle, which is shown in Fig. 775. It is English, with Boulle work decoration, after the French style.

Soon after its introduction, the pendulum was occasionally placed outside of the case in front of the dial, especially in small clocks like Fig. 605, but I saw a very fine bracket clock arranged in this way. It was by John Trubshaw, of London, and dated from about 1700. To put the pendulum outside is not a good plan, for it is clearly more liable to disturbance than when suspended inside the case. Captain Edward Lethbridge informed me that in the hall of Hinton Ampner House, near Alresford, is a timepiece, probably of German origin, in an oval case of embossed silver measuring about 20 in. by 12 in., mounted on a velvet block. The pendulum reaches from the top to the bottom of the case, and swings in the front on the outside of the dial. This also would probably be a very early eighteenth century production.

Fig. 773. — John Johnson, Ebony Brassmounted Eight-day Balloon Clock, Pin Wheel Escapement; height, including bracket, 27 in.; about 1800.

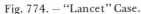

Fig. 774. — "Lancet" Case.

Fig. 775. — Small Clock at Windsor Castle.

A curious little timepiece, supported by a winged Mercury, shown in Fig 776, is fitted with a pendulum arranged to swing in front of the dial. Altogether it is 6 in. in height. Around the arch of the dial is engraved, "CITO PEREVNT ET IMPVTANTVR" (They pass quickly and are reckoned). On the dial are two labels bearing the words "Chasseur, London." The date of its production is uncertain.

In Figs. 777, 778 and 779 are front, side, and back views of an English travelling clock, dating from about 1710, which is interesting by its rarity, for it is a type, I think, but very seldom seen. From the bottom of the case to the top of the swivelled knob below the carrying ring measures 8 in. The movement is signed "Paulet, London." The gilt metal work of the case is finely pierced and carved, arabesques and faces being executed in a style not usual at this period on clock cases of English manufacture. The dial and back plates are covered with open lace work of hammered silver. Besides repeating the hours and quarters, the clock is provided with an alarm, and in a semicircle occupying the arch of the dial the day of the month is indicated. It belongs to the Schloss collection. A very similar clock by Paulet is to be seen at the South Kensington Museum.

TAXES RELATING TO CLOCKS AND WATCHES

Legislation has on more than one occasion affected the material used for watch cases. In 1719 a duty of sixpence an ounce was imposed on articles of silver, and this quickly led to an increased use of base metal cases. In 1758 an annual payment of forty shillings by dealers was substituted for the duty, and in 1759 the amount to be paid for a licence was raised to £5. But in

Fig. 777.   Fig. 778.   Fig. 779.

Fig. 776.

1784 the duty of sixpence per ounce was reimposed in addition to the dealer's licence. The effect was remarkable; the use of silver immediately declined, and for the next fourteen years large numbers of base metal cases were made. In 1797 a tax of eight shillings an ounce was levied on gold articles, which doubtless would have led to an increased use of silver-gilt and pinchbeck cases, but that Pitt, not content with taxing the cases, at the same time imposed a tax on all persons in respect of the possession and use of watches as well as clocks. The Act ordained that —

"For and upon every Clock or Timekeeper, by whatever name the same shall be called, which shall be used for the purpose of a clock and placed in or upon any dwelling house, or any office or building thereunto belonging, or any other Building whatever, whether private or publick, belonging to any person or persons, or Company of Persons, or any Body Corporate, or Politick, or Collegiate, or which shall be kept and used, by any Person or Persons in Great Britain, there shall be charged an Annual Duty of Five Shillings. For and upon every Gold Watch, or Watch enamelled on Gold, or Gold Timekeeper used for the Purpose of a Watch by whatever Name the same shall be called, which shall be kept, and worn, or used, by any Person or Persons in Great Britain, there shall be charged an Annual Duty of Ten Shillings. And for and upon every Silver or Metal Watch, or Silver or Metal Timekeeper used for the purpose of a Watch, or any other watch, or Timekeeper used for the like purpose, not before charged, of whatever materials the same shall be made, and by whatever name the same shall be called, which shall be kept and worn, or used, by any Person, there shall be charged an Annual Duty of Two Shillings and Sixpence."

It requires an effort to realise that such an impost prevailed but little over a century ago. Among other provisions of the Act was one declaring that every watch or clock maker or dealer in the cities of London and Westminster, the parishes of St Marylebone and St Pancras, the counties of Middlesex and Surrey shall pay an annual duty of two shillings and sixpence. In any other part of the country such a maker or dealer was let off by paying a shilling duty.

The produce was far from reaching the estimated yield, while the operation of the tax was such as nearly to ruin manufacturers. The demand for clocks and watches decreased to such an extent, that in less than a year the general manufacturers of these articles in the kingdom, and the various branches of trade connected therewith, had diminished by one-half, and thousands of persons were deprived of employment. It is not therefore surprising that the Act was repealed in April 1798.

A writer in *Notes and Queries* mentions that he met with a printed form of receipt for a half-year's taxes, due from a small farmer in Essex, in which occurred the item, "for clocks and watches, 5 . 7½ ." The receipt was dated 10th April 1798, the month in which the Act was repealed.

Although the imposition of this obnoxious tax paralysed the horological trades, it had the effect of creating one new kind of timekeeper; for tavern keepers, anticipating a scarcity of timekeepers among individuals, with one mind seem to have adopted a bold mural timepiece for the benefit of those who visited their public rooms. Mural timepieces with large dials were, of course, in use before 1797, and by favour of Sir George Birdwood I am enabled to represent in Fig. 780 a handsome one, which is now at the India Office. It was formerly at the entrance to the Special Assistants' Room at the House of the East India Company in Leadenhall Street, and dates from about 1725. Mr W. W. Hallam has a clock by Jasper Taylor in a similar case with lacquer decoration.

An "Act of Parliament" clock was altogether a plainer affair. It had usually a large dial of wood, painted black, with gilt figures, not covered by a glass, and a trunk long enough to allow of a seconds pendulum. In country inns and other places Act of Parliament clocks may still occasionally be seen.

Fig. 780. — Mural Timepiece, India Office.

Fig. 781. — "Act of Parliament" Clock.

The appended illustration (Fig. 781) of a specimen at Windsor Castle with a white dial is curious, inasmuch as the fourth hour is indicated by IV. instead of the almost universal IIII.

Watchmakers obtained from Parliament in 1798 some little recompense for the dire extremity to which they had been reduced, for from that time watch cases have been exempt from the plate duty. But watch manufacturers had nevertheless to continue the annual plate licence, although watch-case makers were absolved from the necessity of doing so.

In 1803 the licence underwent further alteration; for trading in gold over 2 dwts. and under 2 oz., or in silver over 5 dwts. and under 30 oz., an annual payment of £2 6s. was then demanded, and for trading in gold or silver articles above those weights an annual payment of £5 15s.

HOGARTH'S DIAL

I will append as a curiosity a strange dial [Fig. 782] published by William Hogarth in a paper called *The Masquerade Ticket,* which appears to have been put forth as a satire on the position accorded to Heidegger, "Master of the Revels," whose head is drawn on the upper part of the dial. The date, 1727, is indicated by figures in the corners. The sketch is reproduced from John Ireland's "Hogarth Illustrated."

Fig. 782.

Chapter VIII

Mechanism of Clocks and Watches

THE PENDULUM IT IS NOT certain who first used the pendulum as a controller for clocks. Galileo, the famous astronomer, in 1582 remarked the synchronous vibrations of the lamps suspended by long chains from the roof of the cathedral at Pisa, and it is said that when blind he dictated to his son Vincent a method of using the pendulum as a timekeeper, which the latter carried out in 1649. From the drawing of this contrivance it seems to have been merely a train of wheels and a rude escapement to keep a pendulum in motion, in order to determine the time by counting its vibrations. It is shown in Fig. 783, and a working model of it is to be seen at South Kensington Museum.

In the Vienna Treasury is a clock dating from the early part of the seventeenth century, and furnished with a pendulum which it is contended was invented by the maker of the clock, J. Burgi, of Prague, who was appointed as clockmaker to Rudolph II. in 1602.

Then it is stated that Richard Harris constructed a turret clock with a pendulum for the church of St Paul's, Covent Garden, which has since been burnt down. The authority for this statement rests chiefly on an engraved plate affixed in the vestry-room of the old church, with the following inscription on it:—

"The turret clock and bells of this church were made A.D. 1797, by Thomas Grignon, of Great Russell Street, Covent Garden, the son and successor of Thomas Grignon, who (A.D. 1740) brought to perfection what the celebrated Tompion and Graham never effected, viz., the horizontal principle in watches and the dead beat in clocks, which dead beat is a part of the mechanism of the turret clock. Thomas Grignon, senior, made the timepiece in the pediment at the east end of this parish church, destroyed by fire A.D. 1795. The clock fixed in the turret of the said church was the first long pendulum clock in Europe, invented and made by Richard Harris, of

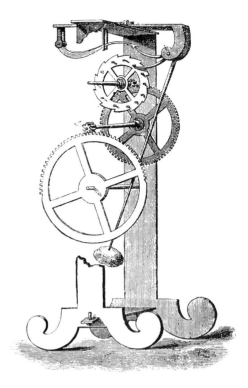

Fig. 783.

London, A.D. 1641, although the honour of the invention was assumed by Vincenzio Galilei, A.D. 1649, and also by Huygens in 1657. This plate is here affixed by Thomas Grignon, of this parish, the son of the above Thomas Grignon, as a true memorial of praise to those two skilful mechanicians, his father and Richard Harris, who, to the honour of England, embodied their ideas in substantial forms that are most useful to mankind."

It would be idle to treat this as conclusive evidence in favour of Harris; still it is entitled to consideration, for the elder Grignon alluded to was regarded as a man of integrity. He was a contemporary and friend of James Ferguson, and one of the first members of the Society of Arts, to which society he in 1759 presented a regulator, which is yet to be seen at the house of the Society in the Adelphi. Besides, that Galileo's observation would be followed by the application of a pendulum to a clock is only just what might have been expected. The weak part of the claim on behalf of Harris is that his application of a superior controller should have remained a solitary instance for twelve years or so, and have evoked no attention from scientists and others interested in the subject.

Huygens, it is certain, studied the action of the pendulum between 1650 and 1655, and demonstrated the fact that the path described as the centre of oscillation should be a cycloid for vibrations of varying extent to be passed through in the same time.

Dr Hooke also saw the advantage of the pendulum about the same time, and proceeded to apply it.

Fromanteel and others have also been named with confidence by their respective admirers as being entitled to the honour of introducing the pendulum; but indisputable proof of anyone's claim to originality in the matter there is none, and it is therefore useless to pursue this part of the subject further.

STRIKING WORK   Recording the completion of each hour by strokes on a bell has always been regarded as an important function of public timekeepers. In some of the early clocks, notably the first one at St Paul's Cathedral, the sound of the striking was the sole indicator of time provided, and in many later edifices, where the exhibition of dials was considered to be incongruous with the general design, timekeepers similarly restricted have been adopted and their convenience appreciated. The Church of St Vedast, Foster Lane, may be mentioned as an instance of a public building with a tower clock which struck but had no dial. Clocks striking the quarters as well as the hours are common enough, but Westminster Abbey furnishes a solitary instance of striking work for the quarters only. This is done, not by the turret clock with the well-known exterior dial, but by the timekeeper in the Poet's Corner, which is also peculiar in being probably the largest spring clock ever made, for the barrels and fusees are each over 7 in. in diameter.

Some of the early Dutch and German clocks were furnished with two bells, one larger than the other, mounted on the top of the case. The hour was struck on the larger bell; the first quarter noted by one stroke on the smaller bell; at the half-hour strokes corresponding in number to the previous hour were given on the smaller bell, and the third quarter was proclaimed by one stroke on the larger bell. This plan has the advantage of giving fuller information than modern methods. Where one stroke is given at the half-hour, as in modern French clocks, half-past twelve, one, and half-past one convey the same inexplicit signal.

Clocks by early English makers were occasionally made to indicate the half-hour by repeating on a smaller bell strokes corresponding to the hour last completed. Mr J. Drummond Robertson has a timekeeper by Joseph Knibb so fitted. On p. 382 is mentioned a clock in the Wetherfield collection by the same maker in which the quarters are sounded on a smaller bell in an ingenious way.

Another and most excellent arrangement for striking on two bells, as carried out by Joseph Knibb, is described on p. 245.

Unless altered very recently, the clock at the Church of St Clement Danes, in the Strand, strikes each hour twice. The strokes are given first on a large bell, weighing 24 cwt., and then repeated on the Sanctus — a bell in the spire which is said to date back to the fifteenth century, and to have been one of the bells used before the Reformation. On account of the roar of traffic along the road, the striking cannot be heard except at night, and when it is heard the effect is curious, for the repetition appears to the uninitiated to be the tardy striking of another clock in some adjacent tower.

Clocks are occasionally to be seen which strike the hours from one to six four times over during the twenty-four hours. In many parts of southern Italy the hours were regularly sounded in this way.

The Japanese had a decidedly ingenious method of sounding the hour and half-hour, which is described on p. 340.

Should the present method of splitting the day into two periods of twelve hours each be abandoned in favour of continuos counting of the hours from one to twenty-four, the striking would possibly be rearranged, and the plans just described give a choice for selection.

The earliest device for causing the hours to be struck automatically appears to be the locking-plate construction, as shown in De Vick's clock. A modification of this principle, to ensure greater exactness by using quicker moving parts to unlock the striking train, is still the most favoured for turret clocks. For house clocks the rack principle invented by Barlow is generally preferred, because in this the striking corresponds with the position of the hands on the dial, whereas with the locking-plate the hours are sounded successively without regard to the hands.

WATCH MOVEMENTS

Most of the early watches of pocket size were arranged to run for from twelve to sixteen hours between successive windings, the fusee making from ten to twelve turns. The train usually consisted of the great wheel which drove a pinion carrying the second wheel; the second wheel drove a pinion carrying the contrate wheel, and the last named drove the pinion carrying the escape wheel. The great wheel was fixed to its arbor, one end of which fitted loosely into a long hole in the larger end of the fusee, the other end was carried in a hole in that plate of the movement which is nearest the dial, and on the very extremity of this end was a pinion, usually of the lantern kind, gearing with a wheel whose pipe projected through the centre of the dial and carried the hand. Pinions having five leaves were, so far as my observation goes, almost invariably used for the train, and for the wheel teeth the following numbers: great wheel, 55; second, 45; contrate, 40; escape wheel, 15. A projection from the verge "banked" against the potence to prevent overrunning. There being a wheel and pinion less in the train than is usual now, the escape wheel ran the reverse way; its teeth and the verge therefore appear to be left-handed to the modern watchmaker.

Fig. 784. — English watch without screws, about 1600.

John Fitter, about 1665, made a watch with the extra wheel and pinion, the contrate wheel of which turned once in a minute, but there is no doubt the longer train was not generally viewed with favour till the balance-spring was introduced in 1675; very soon after that date it became universal, together with wheel-work arranged for a run of thirty hours.

Among earlier and exceptional departures from the three-wheel train may be mentioned an unnamed watch in the Guildhall Museum which has four low numbered wheels. The hand work consists of a three-leaved lantern on the great wheel arbor, driving a wheel of twenty-seven attached to the hand; the fusee being cut for twelve turns, the watch would run for fifteen hours only. This specimen dates apparently from about 1650.

Fig. 784 is a view of a very early English watch movement, certainly not later, I think, than 1600. There are no screws used in its construction, and the mainspring is adjusted by means of a ratchet and click. The train is of the numbers already given, the hand is driven by four pegs projecting from the great wheel arbor, acting with a hand-wheel of thirty-six teeth. The fusee makes barely eleven turns. Inscribed on the plate is the maker's name, "Simon Bartram." Either he or possibly his namesake and successor was appointed in the Charter of the Clockmakers' Company to be one of the "Assistants," as the members of the Committee of Management were termed.

Fig. 785. — English watch, about 1650.

The first noticeable departure from the primitive arrangement was the adoption of a tangent wheel and screw for the regulation of the mainspring, which was introduced about 1610, and is shown in Fig. 785. On the barrel arbor above the tangent wheel is a disc of silver with divisions figured as a guide in setting the mainspring up or down; this adjustment being evidently used to regulate in some measure the timekeeping of the watch.

Fig. 786.

Fig. 787.

BALANCE SPRINGS

Fig. 788. — Hog's Bristle as a balance controller.

An alternative attempt at regulation before the advent of the balance-spring was to fix on a movable plate two pins to intercept the arms of the balance at longer or shorter arcs, as illustrated in Figs. 78, 144 and 151.

A pendulum watch with a slit in the dial was illustrated in Fig. 357. This proved to be an inconvenient arrangement, but in the early part of the eighteenth century many watches were made with a cap over the balance as in Fig. 786. The arms of the balance were weighted, and a semicircular perforation in the cap allowed one weight to be visible, the motion of the weight as it vibrated resembling that of a pendulum. Pendulum watches having caps decorated with painting on enamel were very popular among Dutch makers. The watch illustrated is inscribed, "Flower, London," and dates from about 1740.

As a rule movements of watches were completed without reference to the proximate owner, but an exceptional construction is shown in Fig. 787. The watch dates from about 1700, and is by "Massy, London." Around an heraldic shield bearing the royal arms is the motto, "HONI SOIT QUY MAL Y PENSE," and below, "SEMPER EADEM." It is of Queen Anne period.

The movement of the watch by Mitzell, of which a front view appears in Fig. 357, is covered by a silver plate, on which the royal arms with supporters are chased; underneath is the motto, "Je Main Tiendrai."

The demand for verge watches continued till late in the nineteenth century, and they were made to my knowledge in Clerkenwell till 1882; the manufacture ceased then only because the verge finishers died out. The last specimens had lever cocks, because there was no one left to make the orthodox patterns.

The introduction of the balance-spring, which marks such an important epoch in the manufacture of watches, appears to be due principally to the investigations of Dr Robert Hooke, about 1660. There is no doubt that Huygens and others also experimented with various materials to find a satisfactory controller for a vibrating balance. Huygens' labours in this direction may, of course, have been spontaneous, but, as recounted on p. 240, Hooke asserted that a communication from him to the Secretary of the Royal Society induced Huygens to turn his attention to the subject.

The engraving (Fig. 788) represents a watch of German origin from the collection of Mr Willard H. Wheeler. It has a day of the month ring, and is generally of the construction usual soon after the middle of the seventeenth century. But the peculiar feature of the movement lies in the application of a straight hog's bristle to regulate the balance. There is no sign of any other spring having been attached, and the accessories of the bristle are quite in character with the rest of the work. There are two arms which embrace the bristle and practically determine its acting length, and by means of a screw these may be shifted to act over a considerable range.

Steel springs were, however, found to be the most suitable. The primitive straight ones would of course allow but a very small vibration of the balance, while the to-and-fro motion between pins where it made contact with the balance involved considerable friction. Of others, curved somewhat to the shape of a pothook, there are still examples, but eventually the more convenient and correct form was found to be a volute which had at first but one or two coils. The coils were increased to four or five as the advantage of

403

Fig. 789. — Tompion's Regulator.

a longer spring was understood, but the very long springs with which we are now familiar were not applied till the advent of the lever and other detached escapements which allowed the balance to have a larger arc of vibration.

To lengthen or shorten the acting length of the spring, Tompion appears to have used the circular slide with an index from the first. This arrangement, which remained in favour for a long period, is shown in Fig. 789. Below, and attached to a silver disc, graduated and figured as a guide to regulation, is a pinion which gears with teeth on the outer edge of the circular slide; from the inner edge projects an arm carrying two upright pins which embrace the spring. The projecting end of the pinion is square, so that it could be turned by means of a watch key.

In the Schloss collection is a clock-watch by Nathaniel Barrow, dating from about 1675, in which the outer end of the spring is continued in a straight line to the stud at the edge of the plate, and the regulation accomplished very much in the same way as the hog's bristle watch already delineated. Fig. 790 is a plan of this watch movement. The curved stud on the left is continued in a sort of zig-zag shape to hold one end of the regulating screw. The upper end of the nut points to an index engraved on the plate, and the lower extremity is notched to receive the spring.

Fig. 790. — Barrow's Regulator.

Fig. 791.

An early application of the balance-spring with quaintly worded instructions for regulating is shown in Fig. 791, which represents the movement of a large striking and alarm watch by Edward East.

A fine movement by Daniel Le Count, dating from 1680, and having a regulator on Barrow's principle, is shown in Fig. 792.

The chief drawback to Tompion's regulator is that owing to the backlash or freedom between the teeth of the pinion and slide, a slight reversal of the index has no effect on the curb pins. The simple regulator now generally employed consists of a lever, fitting friction-tight over a boss on the balance-cock; the shorter end of the lever carries the curb pins which embrace the balance-spring while the longer end through which it is moved serves also as an indicator of alterations in the position of the curb pins. This device was patented by Bosley in 1755.

Fig. 792.

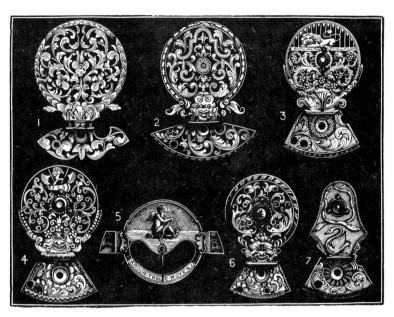

Fig. 795.

Fig. 793. — Watch by Baltazer Martinot, showing early French arrangement of Balance-spring Regulator.

WATCH COCKS

Fig. 794.

There is one point about the stud used in those of Tompion's watches I have seen which might well be revived. The hole in the stud for the reception of the spring was square. The modern system of pinning, by squeezing the flat side of a spring against the surface of a round hole, is altogether unmechanical and must distort the spring.

Fig. 793 represents the top plate of an alarm watch by the celebrated French maker, Baltazar Martinot. The balance is very large, planted nearly in the centre of the plate and covered by a handsomely engraved bridge. The pinion and teeth of the slide for regulation of the balance-spring are uncovered, and no index appears to have been provided.

A very similar watch by one of the Habrechts of Strasburg has the bridge covered with the picture of a woman smoking a pipe, as shown in Fig. 794. The painting is finely executed in enamel.

The first of the cocks or brackets used to support one end of the balance-staff were probably quite plain, but so prominent a feature of the movement speedily became an object of enrichment. Of the early pierced and engraved designs examples are given in Figs. 784, 785, 788, 790, 792, 416. These range from the end of the sixteenth century to 1680, and it will be observed that from its primal office of carrying the balance staff pivot the table of the cock was gradually spread to protect the balance from disturbance. In No. 1 of the subjoined Fig. 795, from a watch by "Jeremie Johnson, Royal Exchange," dating from about 1685, the edge of the table is of a plain circular form and coincident with the outside of the balance rim; the foot is very wide, but its outer edge is carved, and would not correspond with the outline of the plate, to which it would be screwed.

No. 2 is from a watch by Thomas Windmills, dating from about 1700. Here the outside of the foot followed the curve of the plate. The narrow neck at the junction of the table and the foot seen in this and in the preceding example appears to have been originally provided as a space for pinning the cock to a stud and to have survived the introduction of screw fastenings. The floral pierced work in No. 1 and No. 2 is very similar, but the basket or pot in the first is in the latter discarded for a mask, and from this period heads or masks seem to have been incorporated with most of the designs so long as the pierced cocks lasted. Curiously enough, the streamers at the sides of the basket, which look appropriate, are incongruously retained with the head; still, the streamers and masks were associated for thirty or forty years. About 1720, cocks with solid feet were made, though the pierced variety is met with till about 1770.

No. 3, with a jewelled centre and a representation of a lion in a cage, dates from about 1770, and No. 4, with the military emblems, from 1780.

With few exceptions, French and Dutch manufacturers used a bridge instead of a cock. No. 5, a pretty specimen, is from a pendulum watch made about 1740. Others are shown in Figs. 287, 370, and 793. In Figs. 287 and 794 are two finely enamelled.

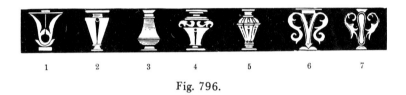

Fig. 796.

The beautiful pierced work was unable to withstand the utilitarian spirit of the nineteenth century, though it died hard. No. 6 is from a watch by James Wild, London, with the hall mark for 1788. The solid lever form of cock (No. 7) was taken from a verge watch with the hall mark of 1826. A few years ago a taste for watch cock necklaces, brooches, and bracelets arose, and thousands of interesting movements were destroyed in mad haste to supply material for an evanescent fancy.

WATCH PILLARS   Though the pillars which connect the two plates of a watch movement are now universally made of a plain cylindrical form, they have been formerly the subjects of considerable enrichment. In most of the early movements of a small size the pillars were round; the larger ones were usually square, and often engraved; but one of the first obvious departures from the utilitarian form in order to please the eye is shown in No. 1 of subjoined engraving [Fig. 796]. This is known as the tulip pillar, and seems to have been introduced in deference to what may be called the tulip mania, which followed the introduction of tulip bulbs into England and led artists to incorporate the flower with almost every kind of decoration. For about twenty-five years from 1676 many of the finest watches were made with tulip pillars. In some instances the vertical division shown in the engraving was omitted. The square Egyptian pillar, No. 2, was introduced about 1640, and continued in use for many years, the central slit being often wider than the examples, with a vertical division and decorations on the face; silver was the material favoured for the decorations and divisions. Occasionally in an extra wide division a head or bust would be inserted. The plainer square pillar, No. 3, had also a long life, for it is met with in watches nearly two hundred years old, and also in specimens produced in the early part of the nineteenth century. No. 4 is a form favoured by Dutch and some English makers from about 1730 to 1770, and is occasionally seen applied to much later productions. Pillars like No. 5, dating from the first half of the eighteenth century, are more often seen in French and German watches than in English, and are often of silver. No. 6 is taken from a watch by Ellicott, the case of which has the hall mark for 1746, and the elegant outline is quite in accord with the popular taste at that time. No. 7 is a little later, and is taken from a watch by John Markham, a well-known maker for the Dutch market. During the period devoted to fancy pillars, repeaters and clock-watches where room was an object did not usually conform to the popular taste in this particular, but were furnished with plain round pillars, having small bodies and collars formed at the top and bottom, to afford a more secure bearing on the plates.

ESCAPEMENTS

The verge, the earliest escapement, was explained on p. 47. About 1660 the Abbé Hauteville invented the "Virgule," illustrated in Fig. 797. Its action will be understood by those conversant with escapements. Dr Hooke invented the anchor escapement, which was applied to clocks by William Clement about 1676. Graham subsequently introduced the improvement known as "dead beat." Tompion devised a form of watch escapement shown in Fig. 417, and subsequently were introduced, among others, the cylinder and duplex. In accordance with my promise to avoid technicalities and modern construction, I do not propose to descant on these; they are dealt with fully in the "Watch and Clock Maker's Handbook." The best of all watch escapements, the lever, which Mudge invented and applied to a watch for Queen Charlotte, was analogous in its action to the present form of double roller escapement, except that the locking faces of the pallets were circular as in the dead-beat clock escapement of Graham. The impulse pin was divided, for the purpose of ensuring the safety action after the finger enters the crescent, and before the impulse pin is fairly in the notch, a result now attained very simply by having horns to the lever. Curiously enough, the advantages of Mudge's invention seem to have remained unrecognised for many years, except by a few of his watchmaking friends. George Margetts and Josiah Emery seem to have been impressed with it, and the latter made for Count Bruhl a watch furnished with a lever escapement on Mudge's plan, which performed so satisfactorily that Emery was induced to continue its use. In 1793 he told a committee of the House of Commons appointed to inquire into Mudge's claim to the Government reward, that he had made thirty-two or thirty-three such watches, and that his price for them was £150 each.

By favour of Mr George Burrell, I had the privilege a short time ago of inspecting a very fine watch which Emery made for the Duke of Portland. It had a lever escapement with straight locking faces to the pallets, angled so as to be drawn into the wheel by pressure, and a second roller for the safety action, practically similar to the arrangement in first-class timekeepers of to-day. The impulse pin was of steel, and pivoted in jewel holes, so that it rolled in and out of the notch. The watch, Mr Burrell said, was originally hung in gymbals in a wooden box. Mr J. J. Hedgethorne has a similar watch by Emery.

In the collection of the Clockmakers' Company at the Guildhall is an interesting watch by John Leroux, of Charing Cross, who was admitted an honorary freeman of the Company in 1781. This watch, by the hall mark in the case, was made in 1785, and the peculiar feature of it is the escapement, which is a lever, but the pallets are of unusual form and act with teeth

Fig. 797. — Virgule Escapement.

resembling those of the cylinder escape wheel, as shown in Fig. 798.

Peter Litherland in 1791 patented the rack lever escapement, in which the lever terminates in a segmental rack which gears with a pinion on the balance axis. Although this was an undetached escapement, and therefore wanting in the chief excellence of Mudge's conception, it met with considerable success, a large number being made at Liverpool, in the early part of the nineteenth century, chiefly for the American market.

About 1800, Edward Massey, a Staffordshire watchmaker, invented the crank roller, in which the impulse pin is projected beyond the periphery of the roller, something like the finger in the going barrel stopwork. Contact of the extremities of the lever with the edge of the roller formed the safety action. The final perfecting of the table roller variety is ascribed to George Savage, a Clerkenwell watch finisher, some years afterwards.

WATCH JEWELLING

In the early part of the eighteenth century was introduced the practice of using highly polished surfaces of hard stone for the bearings of the smaller quickly moving watch pivots and other rubbing contacts.

In 1704 a patent was granted to Nicholas Facio, Peter Debaufre, and Jacob Debaufre, for the application of jewels to the pivot holes of watches and clocks. Facio, the inventor, was a native of Basle, where he was born in 1664, coming to England in the early part of 1687. Here he seems to have busied himself with scientific pursuits, and towards the end of the century he was elected a Fellow of the Royal Society. His co-patentees were watchmakers, living in Church Street, Soho, and an advertisement in the *London Gazette* of 11th May 1704 announced that jewelled watches were to be seen at their shop, stating also that they made "free watches." A watch bearing the name of "Debauffre" is to be seen at the South Kensington Museum. Before the patent was many months old, the patentees applied to Parliament for a Bill to extend it; but this was opposed by the Clockmakers' Company, and on evidence produced by them a committee of the House of Commons recommended that the Bill be rejected. In reporting the successful result of their opposition, the master of the Clockmakers' Company acquainted the court that in the proofs brought against the Bill, there was an old watch produced, the maker's name Ignatius Huggeford (or Huggerford), that had a stone fixed in the cock and balance work, which was of great use to satisfy the committee.

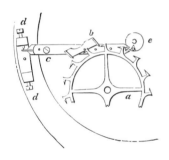

Fig. 798.

a. The wheel. *b.* The pallets. *c.* The lever. *d.d.* Banking screws. *e.* The detaining roller, below which on the same axis is another roller or disc with ruby pin, as usual, for receiving impulse from the lever fork.

But the best of the story has yet to be told. In recent years Huggeford's watch was taken down by Mr E. J. Thompson, a member of the court of the Company, and he reported that: "The movement is not in any sense jewelled, the verge holes being of brass. A piece of coloured glass or soft stone, fastened in a disc of silver and burnished into a sink in the steel cock, gives a fictitious appearance of jewelling."

About 1720 Facio settled at Worcester, where he died at the age of ninety, and was buried at St Nicholas' Church in that city in 1753.

COMPENSATION

Variation in the elasticity of the balance-spring when subjected to changes of temperature proved a fruitful source of trouble to horologists after the application of that most useful adjunct. Harrison's account of his "Thermometer Kirb" is given on p.258. Mudge strove to avoid the difficulty of regulation experienced by Harrison by using two balance-springs, as stated on p.268. Breguet invented a compensation curb on Harrison's principle, but shaped like a quadrant in order to get a greater length of laminae, and therefore more action. One end of the quadrant was fixed to the index and the other carried one of the curb pins, which by the movement of the laminae in changes of temperature was caused to recede from or approach the fixed curb pin, and thus to give more or less liberty to the spring. Various compensation balances from the time of Arnold are illustrated in "Watch Springing and Adjusting," and need not be repeated here.

EVOLUTION OF WINDING MECHANISM FOR WATCHES

One of the first references to winding without opening the case of a watch is to be found in an advertisement which appeared in the *London Gazette* for 10th-13th January 1686 where a watch by R. Bowen, London, is described as having one motion, and the spring being wound up without a key, and it opening contrary to all other watches. Then in Overall's "History of the Clockmakers' Company" it is stated that in 1712 John Hutchinson desired to patent a watch which, among other improvements, "has likewise a contrivance to wind up this or any other movement without an aperture in the case through which anything can pass to foul the movement." The Clockmakers' Company opposed the application, and a committee of the House of Commons examined witnesses, among others George Graham and Charles Goode. Mr Goode produced a movement made fourteen years before. Mr Hutchinson confessed Goode's movement was like his, and eventually withdrew his application.

The next in order is Pierre Augustin Caron, a clever watchmaker of Paris, who in 1752 made for Madame de Pompadour a very small watch, which gained for him a prize from the Academy of Sciences. This appears to have been wound either by turning the bezel or with a slide very similar to the winding slide now used for repeaters. A translation of his description is as follows: "It is in a ring, and is only four lignes across and two-thirds of a ligne in height between the plates. To render this ring more commodious, I have contrived, instead of a key, a circle round the dial carrying a little projecting hook. By drawing this hook with the nail two-thirds round the dial, the watch is re-wound and it goes for thirty hours." Caron was an accomplished musician as well as a playwriter, and is better known under the name of Beaumarchais, as the author of "Le Barbier de Seville" and "Le Mariage de Figaro."

In 1764 Frederick Kehlhoff, of London, patented a centre seconds and going barrel watch with a stackfreed remontoire. A watch on this plan by him was wound by turning the bow, the arbor of which terminated in a contrate wheel gearing with an intermediate wheel which engaged with a wheel on the barrel arbor; but nothing was said in his patent respecting the keyless work.

Lepine, who was associated with Voltaire in the establishment of a watch factory at Ferney, in Switzerland, devised a method of winding in which the button at the pendant was turned partly round, and then pushed in several times till the winding was completed. This was the first of a series of what is known as "pumping" keyless actions.

In 1792 Peter Litherland, who patented the rack lever, claimed (patent No. 1,889) "winding up watches, &c., by means of an external lever connected by mechanism by the barrel arbor."

Robert Leslie, in 1793, patented (No. 1,970) another pumping keyless arrangement. His claim says: "On the square on which the key should go is a ratch; the pendant, being alternately moved in and out, turns this ratch by

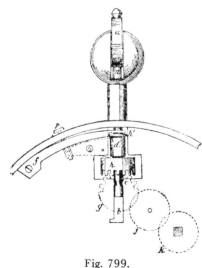

Fig. 799.

means of two clicks on either end of a fork fastened to the pendant."

A watch, dating from about 1790, signed "Jacquet Droz, London," which is shown in Fig. 315, is furnished with winding work of this kind.

J. A. Berrollas, in 1827 (No. 5,586), patented a somewhat similar contrivance, but used a chain coiled round the winding wheel. I wore for some years a duplex watch by Ganthony with this keyless work, and it answered well.

Edward Massey in 1814 (3,854), Francis J. Massey in 1841 (8,947), and Edward Massey again in 1841 (9,120), patented varieties of pumping keyless work.

Charles Oudin exhibited at Paris in 1806, an arrangement shown in Fig. 799: *k* is the barrel, *j* and *g* intermediate wheels gearing with the contrate pinion *h; a* is a disc at one extremity of the rod *n b*. The rod is supported by the cock *d*, and has two grooves, into one of which the spring *f* presses, according to the position of the rod. One of these grooves is seen at *c*, the other is hidden, owing to the position in which the parts are shown. When out of use the disc *a* forms part of the ball of the pendant. In order to wind, the rod *n b* is pulled up until the nib at the end of *b* comes in contact with the interior of the pinion *h*, where there is a catch; the spring *f* then falls into the groove *c*, and then the winding is accomplished by turning the ball at *a*. There was no provision for setting hands.

Thomas Prest, foreman to J. R. Arnold, at his Chigwell chronometer factory, patented in 1820 (No. 4,501) a very similar arrangement to the foregoing as far as the winding is concerned, but no provision was made for disconnecting the wheels from the pendant knob.

A. L. Breguet applied winding work to many of his watches, and an arrangement to connect with the motion work for setting hands by pulling out the bow.

Isaac Brown, in 1829 (5,851), patented a winding-rack attached to the bezel, the bezel being moved round to wind.

Adrien Phillipe, in 1843, invented the shifting sleeve keyless mechanism. Lecoultre and Audemars subsequently made alterations: the present construction of shifting sleeve mechanism is, however, similar in principle to the device of Phillipe.

Adolope Nicole, in 1844, patented (10,348) a fusee keyless work in which a knob on the pendant was pushed in to make connection with the fusee wheel, and pulled out to connect with the minute wheel.

The rocking bar mechanism for winding and setting hands was patented in 1855 (2,144) by Gustavus Hughenin.

SELF-WINDING WATCHES

Several methods have been devised for automatic winding, of which two examples are given.

Fig. 800 shows an arrangement by Lebet for winding a watch by the action of closing the hunting cover. There is a short gold arm projecting beyond the joint. This arm is connected by means of a double link to a lever, one end of which is pivoted to the plate. To the free end of this lever is jointed a scythe-shaped rack, which works into a wheel with ratchet-shaped teeth on the barrel arbor. A weak spring fastened to the lever serves to keep the rack in contact with the wheel teeth. Instead of the ordinary fly spring, there is a spring fixed to the plate and attached by means of a short chain to the lever. As this spring pulls the cover open, the teeth of the rack slip over

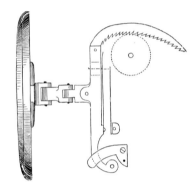

Fig. 800. — Self-winding Watch Mechanism to act on the closing of the Hunting Cover.

410

the teeth of the wheel on the barrel arbor. Each time the wearer closes the cover, the watch is partly wound. By closing the case eight or nine times, the winding is completed. The ordinary method of hooking in the mainspring

Fig. 801. — Self-winding or "Pedometer" Watch by Breguet.

would be clearly unsuitable with this winding work, because after the watch was fully wound the case could not be closed. Inside the barrel is a piece of mainspring a little more than a complete coil with the ends overlapping, and to this piece the mainspring hook is riveted. The adhesion of the loose turn of the mainspring against the side of the barrel is sufficient to drive the watch, but when the hunting cover is closed after the watch is wound, the extra strain causes the mainspring to slip round in the barrel.

The method of winding just described can be applied only to a hunting watch. Fig. 801 represents a watch by Breguet with what is known as a pedometer winding. Louis Recordon, in 1780, patented it (No. 1,249), and it has been several times re-invented. The motion of the wearer's body is utilised for winding. There is a weighted lever, pivoted at one end, and kept in its normal position against the upper of two banking pins by a long curved spring so weak that the ordinary motion of the wearer's body causes the lever to continually oscillate between the banking pins. Pivoted to the same centre as the weighted lever is a ratchet wheel with very fine teeth, and fixed to the lever is a pawl, which engages with the ratchet wheel. This pawl is made elastic, so as to yield to undue strain caused by the endeavour of the lever to vibrate after the watch is wound.

REPEATING WATCHES While the striking mechanism of clock-watches such as were produced by many of the early makers was founded on that used in De Vick's clock, repeating watches were similar in principle to the rack striking work for the house clocks invented by either Barlow or Quare. The number of hours or quarters struck depends on the position of the snails which revolve with the timekeeping mechanism. The hammers were actuated by a separate mainspring which was wound every time it was desired that the watch should repeat. This was done by pushing the pendant in. Connected to the inner end of the pendant was a chain coiled round a pulley attached to the mainspring barrel, and also a lever, which, by coming in contact with the snail, stopped the pendant; so that the mainspring was wound much or little according to the number of blows to be struck.

The chain was found to be the most unsatisfactory part of the mechanism, and at the beginning of the eighteenth century Matthew Stogden substituted a rack for it. Other alterations have since been made in the arrangement, one of the chief being the winding of the mainspring by means of a slide projecting from the band of the case. Barlow and Quare used a bell shaped to the inside of the case, such as had been used before their time for clock-watches; wire gongs, introduced by Julien Le Roy, are now used instead.

Graham introduced a "pulse piece," which upon being pressed kept the hammers off the bell, but allowed the time to be ascertained by counting the throbs or beats on the pulse piece.

Dumb repeaters, said to have been invented by Julien Le Roy, had neither bells nor gongs, the blows being struck on a solid block fixed in the band of the case.

In 1804 John Moseley Elliott patented (No. 2,759) an ingenious device for dispensing with the repeating train, as well as striking the hours and quarters and other subdivisions with one hammer. By turning a rod running through the pendant to the right, a pallet on the inner end of it moved round a lever till it came in contact with the hour snail, and while this was being done, each of the teeth of a ratchet wheel also mounted on the inner part of the pendant rod, engaged with the hammer stalk and caused it to strike on the bell. The number of blows struck depended, of course, on the position of the hour snail. By turning the pendant to the left, another lever was carried to the quarter snail, and the required number of quarters struck in like manner.

The time might in this arrangement be ascertained without a bell, by first turning the pendant rod as far as the snail allowed, and then reversing it and counting the number of clicks or obstructions caused by engagement with the ratchet. The Elder Grant made some dumb repeaters on this plan.

In Figs. 357, 358 and 371, are shown musical watches. They must be distinguished from repeaters or other watches which strike notes on gongs. They are provided with pins rising from a metal disc as shown in Fig. 802. The disc rotates and each pin in turn catches the free end of a steel spring of such a length and thickness as to yield the required note. The music may be let off by the striking-work at every hour or at pleasure by a pin which would project through the band of the case, or in both ways. A separate barrel is provided to drive the music disc and moving figures if any. The device is, I believe, of Swiss origin.

Fig. 802. — Mechanism of Musical Watch.

MUSICAL WATCHES

HALL MARKS

These marks are impressed on watch cases, jewellery, and plate after the quality of the metal has been ascertained by assay at certain official Assay Halls. The marking of jewellery is, with few exceptions, optional. The hall marking of all watch cases of gold or silver made in Great Britain and Ireland is compulsory. The cost is only the actual outlay incurred in assaying and stamping. The hall mark consists of several impressions in separate shields: there are the standard or quality mark; the mark of the particular office at which the article was assayed; some character by which the date of marking may be traced, and, if duty is chargeable, the head of the reigning sovereign.

412

The oldest and most important of the Assay Halls is that presided over by the Goldsmiths' Company of London, which is situated in Foster Lane, just at the back of the old General Post Office, St Martin's-le-Grand. The privilege of assaying and marking precious metals was conferred on the Company by statute in 1300. The Company received a charter of incorporation in 1327, and their powers have been confirmed subsequently by several Acts of Parliament.

Many early watch cases, especially silver ones of London make, are met with which have no hall mark, the powers of the Company not being so strictly enforced then as now, or the value of the official assay not being so generally recognised.

Repoussé cases, with other artistic wares of a similar character, are specially exempted from assay.

It was not till 1798 that a lower standard of gold than 22 carat was allowed, 18 carat was then recognised; in 1854 three further standards, 15, 12, and 9 carat, were introduced.

The standard mark of the London Hall is a lion passant for sterling silver. A lion passant was also the standard mark on 22-carat gold up to 1845.

For gold of 22 carats the standard mark is now a crown, and the figures 22. For 18-carat gold the standard mark is a crown and the figures 18.

For 15-carat gold	15 and 0.625	Pure gold being 24 carats, these decimals represent
" 12	" 12 " 0.5	the proportions of pure gold in the article
" 9	" 9 " 0.375	so marked.

The London Hall Mark prior to 1823 was a crowned leopard's head; from 1st January 1823 it was uncrowned; specimens of both styles are appended.

Date marks of the London Hall, given on p.415, are, with one or two exceptions, actual reproductions which I have made from watch cases. Specimens of the earliest marks are not to be obtained.

There was a duty on silver articles of sixpence an ounce from 1719 till 1758, but no special duty mark; in 1784 a similar duty was imposed, and then the head of the reigning sovereign was impressed to denote the payment of duty. The Act came into operation on 1st December 1784, and at first the head had a curious appearance, being incised, or incuse as it is called, instead of in relief as the other marks were. Cases with the London mark and the letter K, which corresponds to the period from May 1785 to May 1786, have the duty head incuse, after which the head appears in relief with London marks. The wardens of the Birmingham Assay Office have a pair of cases with the head incuse, and the Birmingham mark with the letter N, which would denote the period from July 1786 to July 1787. In 1804 the duty on silver was increased to 1s. 3d., and on gold to 16s. an ounce. In 1815 a further increase to 1s. 6d. and 17s. 6d. respectively was made, and the duty continued at these amounts till 1890, when it was finally abolished. Watch cases were exempted from duty in 1798.

The maker's mark before 1697 was some emblem selected by him; in that year it was ordered to be the two first letters of his surname; since 1739 it has been the initials of the maker's Christian and surnames.

On 25th March 1697 the quality of standard silver was raised from 11 oz. 2 dwts. to 11 oz. 10 dwts. of pure silver in 12 oz. of plate; a lion's head erased was then used as the standard mark, and a figure of Britannia as the hall mark; but on 1st June 1720 the old standard of 11 oz. 2 dwts., and the old marks of a lion passant and a leopard's head were reverted to, although the higher standard with the figure of Britannia is still occasionally used.

MARKS OF OTHER ASSAY OFFICES – CHESTER

Hall mark, a sword between three wheatsheaves. Prior to 1779 it was three demi-lions and a wheatsheaf on a shield. Standard mark for 18-carat gold, a crown and the figures 18. For silver, a lion passant. Before 1839 a leopard's head in addition. Chester date marks are given on p.416.

BIRMINGHAM

Hall mark, an anchor in a square frame for gold, and an anchor in a pointed shield for silver. Standard mark for 18-carat gold, a crown and the figures 18; for silver, a lion passant. Birmingham date marks are given on p.416.

SHEFFIELD — A York rose and a crown.
EXETER — A castle with three towers.
YORK — Five lions on a cross.
NEWCASTLE — Three castles.

NORWICH — A castle and lion passant. (The Norwich Assay Office is now closed.)
EDINBURGH — Edinburgh has a thistle for the standard mark, and a castle for the hall mark.

GLASGOW

Glasgow has a lion rampant for the standard, and a tree, a fish, and a bell for the hall mark.

DUBLIN

Dublin has a harp crowned as the standard mark for sterling silver and for 22-carat gold, with the figures 22 added in the latter case; for 20-carat gold, a plume of three feathers and 20; for 18-carat gold, a unicorn head and 18. The lower qualities of 15, 12, and 9 are marked with the same standard mark as is used at the London Hall. The hall mark for Dublin is a figure of Hibernia.

414

DATE MARK ON GOLD AND SILVER PLATE AND WATCH CASES MARKED AT GOLDSMITHS' HALL, LONDON.

The shields represented in the subjoined tables are those used for silver and for 22-carat gold. For lower qualities of gold the shield is invariably in the shape of a rectangle, with the corners taken off like the one surrounding the A in 1876.

NOTE. — The Date Mark is altered on the 30th of May in each year, lasting from the date indicated in the Table till the 30th of May in the following year.

Letter												
a	1678	*	1716	1736	1756	1776	1796	1816	1836	1856	1876	1896
b	1679	1697	1717	1737	1757	1777	1797	1817	1837	1857	1877	1897
c	1680	1698	1718	1738	1758	1778	1798	1818	1838	1858	1878	1898
d	1681	1699	1719	1739	1759	1779	1799	1819	1839	1859	1879	1899
e	1682	1700	1720	1740	1760	1780	1800	1820	1840	1860	1880	1900
f	1683	1701	1721	1741	1761	1781	1801	1821	1841	1861	1881	1901
g	1684	1702	1722	1742	1762	1782	1802	1822	1842	1862	1882	1902
h	1685	1703	1723	1743	1763	1783	1803	1823	1843	1863	1883	1903
i	1686	1704	1724	1744	1764	1784†	1804	1824	1844	1864	1884	1904
k	1687	1705	1725	1745	1765	1785	1805	1825	1845	1865	1885	1905
l	1688	1706	1726	1746	1766	1786	1806	1826	1846	1866	1886	1906
m	1689	1707	1727	1747	1767	1787	1807	1827	1847	1867	1887	1907
n	1690	1708	1728	1748	1768	1788	1808	1828	1848	1868	1888	1908
o	1691	1709	1729	1749	1769	1789	1809	1829	1849	1869	1889	1909
p	1692	1710	1730	1750	1770	1790	1810	1830	1850	1870	1890	1910
q	1693	1711	1731	1751	1771	1791	1811	1831	1851	1871	1891	1911
r	1694	1712	1732	1752	1772	1792	1812	1832	1852	1872	1892	1912
s	1695	1713	1733	1753	1773	1793	1813	1833	1853	1873	1893	1913
t	1696	1714	1734	1754	1774	1794	1814	1834	1854	1874	1894	1914
u (V)		1715	1735	1755	1775	1795	1815	1835	1855	1875	1895	1915

* This letter appears to have been used only from March to May 1697. From the 25th March 1697 to the 1st June 1720 the figure of Britannia and a lion's head erased was used instead of the crowned leopard's head and a lion passant, see page 413.
† Watch cases marked between December 1784 and May 1798 would bear an extra stamp representing the head of George III.; see page 413.

BIRMINGHAM ASSAY OFFICE DATE LETTERS.

NOTE.—The Date Mark is altered on the 1st July of each year, lasting from the Date indicated in the Table till the June following.

A - - 1773	a - - 1799	A - - 1825	A - - 1850	a - - 1875
B - - 1774	b - - 1800	B - - 1826	B - - 1851	b - - 1876
C - - 1775	c - - 1801	C - - 1827	C - - 1852	c - - 1877
D - - 1776	d - - 1802	D - - 1828	D - - 1853	d - - 1878
E - - 1777	e - - 1803	E - - 1829	E - - 1854	e - - 1879
F - - 1778	f - - 1804	F - - 1830	F - - 1855	f - - 1880
G - - 1779	g - - 1805	G - - 1831	G - - 1856	g - - 1881
H - - 1780	h - - 1806	H - - 1832	H - - 1857	h - - 1882
I - - 1781	i - - 1807	J - - 1833	I - - 1858	i - - 1883
J - - 1782	j - - 1808	K - - 1834	K - - 1859	k - - 1884
K - - 1783	k - - 1809	L - - 1835	L - - 1860	l - - 1885
L - - 1784	l - - 1810	M - - 1836	M - - 1861	m - - 1886
M - - 1785	m - - 1811	N - - 1837	N - - 1862	n - - 1887
N - - 1786	n - - 1812	O - - 1838	O - - 1863	o - - 1888
O - - 1787	o - - 1813	P - - 1839	P - - 1864	p - - 1889
P - - 1788	p - - 1814	Q - - 1840	Q - - 1865	q - - 1890
Q - - 1789	q - - 1815	R - - 1841	R - - 1866	r - - 1891
R - - 1790	r - - 1816	S - - 1842	S - - 1867	s - - 1892
S - - 1791	s - - 1817	T - - 1843	T - - 1868	t - - 1893
T - - 1792	t - - 1818	U - - 1844	U - - 1869	u - - 1894
U - - 1793	u - - 1819	V - - 1845	V - - 1870	v - - 1895
V - - 1794	v - - 1820	W - - 1846	W - - 1871	w - - 1896
W - - 1795	w - - 1821	X - - 1847	X - - 1872	x - - 1897
X - - 1796	x - - 1822	Y - - 1848	Y - - 1873	y - - 1898
Y - - 1797	y - - 1823	Z - - 1849	Z - - 1874	
Z - - 1798	z - - 1824			

CHESTER ASSAY OFFICE DATE LETTERS.

The Date Mark is altered on the 1st July, lasting from the Date indicated in the Table till the end of June in the following year.

A 1701	*A 1726	A 1752	a 1776	*A 1797	A 1818	A 1839	a 1864
B 1702	B 1727	B 1753	b 1777	B 1798	B 1819	B 1840	b 1865
C 1703	C 1728	C 1754	c 1778	C 1799	C 1820	C 1841	c 1866
D 1704	D 1729	D 1755	d 1779	D 1800	D 1821	D 1842	d 1867
E 1705	E 1730	E 1756	e 1780	E 1801	E 1822	E 1843	e 1868
F 1706	F 1731	F 1757	f 1781	F 1802	F 1823	F 1844	f 1869
G 1707	G 1732	G 1758	g 1782	G 1803	G 1824	G 1845	g 1870
H 1708	H 1733	H 1759	h 1783	H 1804	H 1825	H 1846	h 1871
I 1709	I 1734	I 1760	i 1784	I 1805	I 1826	J 1847	i 1872
K 1710	J 1735	J 1761	k 1785	K 1806	K 1827	K 1848	k 1873
L 1711	K 1736	K 1762	l 1786	L 1807	L 1828	L 1849	l 1874
M 1712	L 1737	L 1763	m 1787	M 1808	M 1829	M 1850	m 1875
N 1713	M 1738	M 1764	n 1788	N 1809	N 1830	N 1851	n 1876
O 1714	N 1739	N 1765	o 1789	O 1810	O 1831	O 1852	o 1877
P 1715	O 1740	O 1766	p 1790	P 1811	P 1832	P 1853	p 1878
Q 1716	P 1741	P 1767	q 1791	Q 1812	Q 1833	Q 1854	q 1879
R 1717	Q 1742	Q 1768	r 1792	R 1813	R 1834	R 1855	r 1880
S 1718	R 1743	R 1769	s 1793	S 1814	S 1835	S 1856	s 1881
T 1719	S 1744	S 1770	t 1794	T 1815	T 1836	T 1857	t 1882
U 1720	T 1745	T 1771	u 1795	U 1816	U 1837	U 1858	u 1883
V 1721	U 1746	U 1772	v 1796	V 1817	V 1838	V 1859	
W 1722	V 1747	V 1773				W 1860	
X 1723	W 1748	W 1774				X 1861	
Y 1724	X 1749	X 1775				Y 1862	
Z 1725	Y 1750					Z 1863	
	Z 1751						

* These are really Script capitals.

Chapter IX

Former Clocks and Watch Makers

THE DATES FOLLOWING the names in this alphabetical list signify the period when the person referred to was connected with the Clockmakers' Company, or known to be in business, or when some example of his work was made. It does not necessarily follow that he then either began or relinquished the trade. The letter f. after a date means that the person then became a freeman. Throughout the list C.C. stands for Clockmakers' Company, G.M. for Guildhall Museum, where the collection of the Clockmakers' Company is located, B.M. for British Museum, S.K.M. for South Kensington Museum, and h.m. for Hall Mark. Following the names or addresses of some of the makers is a slight description of specimens of their work which have been met with, or of some invention or distinguishing trait. Of the more important men, fuller descriptions are given in the body of the book, and reference is then made to the page where such particulars may be found.

On estimating the age of a timekeeper by a maker the only reference to whom is that he was admitted to the Clockmakers' Company, it may in the majority of cases be assumed that he was at the time of his admission a young man just out of his apprenticeship; but there are numerous exceptions. Many of those members who constituted the first roll of the Clockmakers' Company were of mature years at the time of the incorporation; and afterwards men who had made some mark or whom circumstances had brought into notice were then induced to join. Hon. freemen, elected after 1780, had all made their reputation before entry.

It is easy to understand that the roll of membership of the Company at no time represented the whole of the clockmakers and watchmakers within its sphere of action. Many who did not care to join would escape observation, and those who were free of other guilds at the incorporation made their apprentices free of the particular company to which they were attached.

Horological craftsmen belonging to other guilds, if they became associated with the Clockmakers' Company, were designated "brothers."

Although the addresses of the freemen at first are rarely given, it may be taken for granted that they were nearly all within a radius of ten miles, and among the later ones it will be found that very few of them resided at any great distance from the Metropolis.

Tracing the residence or business location of manufacturers is often more difficult than many would imagine. William Clement is referred to in scores of books as "an eminent London Clockmaker who first applied the Anchor Escapement to clocks," and was doubtless a leading member of his trade. He was master of the Clockmakers' Company, and presided when Graham took up the freedom on completion of his indentures, yet his name does not appear in any Directory of the period, and I am quite unable to discover where he resided or practised his craft. To mention another instance of a century later, Earnshaw, after he had enlisted the interest of Dr Maskelyne, Astronomer-Royal, who tried a watch of his at the Greenwich Observatory, was told by the doctor that he had lost an order for two watches because Maskelyne did not know where he lived!

On some of the early clocks and watches the name inscribed was that of the owner; but in 1777 an Act of Parliament required the name and place of abode of the maker to be engraved. Still it must not be concluded that in every instance the name engraved on a timekeeper indicates its maker or even that the inscription represents any corporeal existence. In 1682 the C.C. seized from workmen "using the art of clockmaking four unfinished movements two whereof have engraven thereon Ambrose Smith, Stamford and William Burges fecit, and another Jasper Harmar, all of which names are greatly suspected to be invented or fobbed." The practice of using apocryphal names has continued to the present day. Sometimes it was adopted by manufacturers of repute for watches of a lower quality than those of which they cared to own the paternity. Occasionally in such instances the letters composing the name of the manufacturers would be placed backwards. Many watches marked "Rentnow, London," are to be met with, and they doubtless emanated from the Wontners, well-known makers of a century ago. The mark "Yeriaf" on a watch in the Guildhall Museum is probably another example of this reversion. Some watches with fictitious names would be the production of workmen who occasionally made a watch for a private customer, and preferred to thus conceal their identity rather than brave the displeasure of their employers. Mr Evan Roberts has a watch marked "Notyap, London," which was possibly the production of Payton, a casemaker who in 1790 carried on business in Addle Street. But in most instances such pseudonyms appear to be really the trade marks of wholesale dealers, who in ordering watches would supply particulars of the name to be engraved. Many hundreds of watches for the Dutch market were marked "Tarts, London," or "Jno. Tarts, London." Yet I do not think anyone has been able to trace a manufacturer named Tarts. Between 1775 and 1825 the custom of having the name of the owner and not of the maker was often reverted to, usually with A.D. preceding the date figures, and occasionally also "aged 21," or "married," or "born." Watches by provincial makers sometimes had "London" engraved as the place of origin.

The more reprehensible act of adopting celebrated names appears also to have been of early origin. In Overall's "History of the Clockmakers' Company," it is stated that in 1704 the master of the C.C. reported "certain persons at Amsterdam were in the habit of putting the names of Tompion, Windmills, Quare, Cabrier, Lamb, and other well-known London makers on their works, and selling them as English." It is to be feared that some English makers were not free from suspicion of similar misdeeds both then and since.

Numbers on watch movements are very little, if any, guide to the extent of a maker's business. Till quite recent years the custom was for a new manufacturer to begin with a high number, the date, or two or three figures of the date, being often selected as a starting point. Letters following the name are seen on some nineteenth century watches. They represent a cryptogram whereby the initiated can obtain the date of manufacture.

Watches and clocks with Turkish numerals often bore more than one name. It appears that only the timekeepers of certain favoured manufacturers or dealers whose names were registered were admitted into Turkey, and on watches for the Byzantine markets made by others a registered name would be engraved, followed by the name of the actual producer. This, I presume, was usually done by arrangement with the "maker" who had the right of entry. On watches for Turkey the word "Pessendede," signifying warranted, sometimes followed the name or names. Occasionally the first, and perhaps the sole, name inscribed would be merely that of a registered agent. Persian and Turkish numerals are the same. A fairly clear example is given in Fig. 286.

The locality of the residences may not in all cases be readily recognised. A place called Swithen's Alley in early eighteenth century records, but more generally known as Sweeting's Alley, Cornhill, or Royal Exchange, evidently a favourite spot with the craft, was where the statue of Rowland Hill now stands. It was not rebuilt after the destruction of the Exchange by fire, in 1838. Bethlem, or Bethlehem, was in Moorfields, facing London Wall. In the early part of the eighteenth century the three Moor Fields extended from there over the space now occupied by Finsbury Circus and Finsbury Square to Windmill Hill Row, a continuation of which, called Hogg Lane, led into Norton Folgate. The whole of this thoroughfare is now known as Worship Street. Windmill Hill is now Wilson Street. The portion of the City Road by Bunhill Fields was then Royal Row. Love Lane now forms part of Southwark Street, and Maid Lane of Southwark Bridge Road. Rosemary Lane is now Royal Mint Street, Coppice Row is merged into Farringdon Road. Pickaxe Street was so much of Aldersgate as lies between the Barbican and Fann Street. Butcher Row, now pulled down, occupied the wide part of the Strand between the Church of St Clement Danes and Temple Bar. Brick Lane, St Luke's, is now Central Street, and Swan Alley is Great Sutton Street. Swallow Street is now incorporated with Regent Street, and Princes Street, Leicester Square, is merged into Wardour Street. Cateaton Street is now Gresham Street. One side of Wilderness Row remains; the row was widened and transformed into the thoroughfare which cut through St John's Square, and is called Clerkenwell Road. Union Street, Bishopsgate, or Spitalfields, is now Brushfield Street; the Bishopsgate Street end, with the larger part of Sun Street, was absorbed in building the terminus of the Great Eastern Railway, and the Post Office on the western side of St

Martin's-le-Grand occupies the site of Bull and Mouth Street. Wellington Street, St Luke's, is now Lever Street. King Street, Clerkenwell, is now Cyrus Street; King Street, Holborn, is Southampton Row, and Kingsgate Street, which was adjacent and parallel to it, has disappeared altogether. Grubb Street is now Milton Street. The Fleet Street end of what was Water Lane in Tompion's time is now Whitefriars Street.

It is stated that Prescott Street, Goodman's Fields, was the first London street in which the houses were numbered consecutively, and that this thoroughfare was so treated in 1708. Swinging signs were interdicted in 1762, though symbols on stiff brackets and mural carvings as signs for particular buildings were preferentially employed for some years after.

Hick's Hall is mentioned. This was the title given to the Sessions House, which at that time stood in the middle of St John Street, near Smithfield Market. It was afterwards rebuilt on Clerkenwell Green.

Taking into consideration the difficulty of obtaining precise information respecting the early names, added to the vagaries of seventeenth century orthography, I hope and believe the list is as nearly as possible correct, and tolerably complete, so far as London makers are concerned. Outside of the Metropolis I have not attempted to do more than record the facts which happened to be within my reach, and I venture to beg the favour of communications respecting corrections and additions.

Octavius Morgan's "List of Freemen of the Clockmakers' Company," published some years ago, has been of assistance, and particulars of some French makers have been obtained from Havard's "Dictionnaire d'Ameublement" and the "Book of Collections" by Alph. Maze-Sencier. The term "garde visiteur" attached to members of the Paris Guild appears to indicate a committee-man or inspector. Mr J. Whiteley Ward kindly placed at my disposal his extensive list of old makers, but he rarely ventured to hazard an approximate date. For several Edinburgh makers I am indebted to Mr John Smith's papers in the *Weekly Scotsman*. It will be noticed that in the seventeenth century records of the Edinburgh "Incorporation of Hammermen," the word "Knok" or "Knock" is used to designate a clock.

Some of the old art metal workers of Augsburg and Nuremberg affixed their signatures to clock cases of their production, a custom often followed by French clock case designers of more recent times. It should be remembered that such names, as a rule, have no reference to the movements. During the Reign of Terror in France timekeepers by the leading makers were mostly unsigned. As stated on p.295. Breguet watches are to be met with in which his name is scratched on the enamelled dial in well-formed script letters but so tiny as not to be distinguished except with the aid of a very strong magnifying glass. The silent period, as it may be termed, extended more or less for nine or ten years from 1789.

After 1842 the names are given only of those above mediocrity, or concerning whom some peculiarity is known, *and who have ceased to carry on business.* Many of those who are traced to 1842 probably continued for years afterwards, but the list is not intended as a guide to clock and watch makers of to-day. For many of the American names I am indebted to Mr John H. Buck, Curator at the Metropolitan Museum of Art, New York, who has compiled a list from various sources.

Aaron, Benjamin, 17 Bury St., St Mary Axe, 1840-42.

Abbis, J., 37 Bishopsgate St. Within, 1807.

Abbott. Richard, apprenticed in 1668 to Helkiah Bedford; C.C. **Philip,** London; C.C. 1703 (see p. 377). **Peter,** C.C. 1719. **Wm.,** Knaresboro', watch, three cases, about 1760. **Wm.,** Prescot, 1770. **John,** admitted C.C. 1788; charged with making an agreement to go to St Petersburg to work at clockmaking, and convicted at Hicks' Hall of the offence; known as a maker of long-case clocks, 1787-1800. **Thos.,** 41 Allen St., 1820-22. **Francis,** Manchester; 3 Smithy Door, 1825; afterwards at 50 Market St.; watch paper C.C. about 1840; wrote a book on the management of public clocks (n.d.), about 1838.

Abdy. William, livery Goldsmiths' Company, 5 Oat Lane, Noble St., 1768-1817. **Jno.,** London; watch, 1784.

Abeling, William, 7 Wynyatt St., Clerkenwell, 1817; 36 Spencer St., 1835-42.

Aberley, Joseph, apprenticed in 1664 to Isaac Sutton; C.C.

Abraham. Ebenezer, Olney; watch, 1773. **John,** 27 Steward St., Bishopsgate, 1820-23.

Abrahams. H., 21 Bevis Marks, 1800-20. **Godfrey,** 51 Prescot St., Goodman's Fields, 1835-42. **Samuel,** 23 Little Alie St., 1840-42. **A.,** 9 Great Prescot St., 1840-42. **Elijah,** 27 Hanway St., Oxford St., 1840-47.

Absolon, —, London; long-case clock, strike-silent, sunk seconds, scroll and foliage corners, about 1770.

Achard, George, et fils, Geneva; watch, about 1780 (see p. 154).

Acey, Peter, York, f., 1656.

Achurch, Wm., apprenticed in 1691 to Wm. Jaques, C.C.

Ackers, William, St Andrew's, Holborn; pair-case watch in S.K.M., early part of eighteenth century; his bankruptcy noted *Lond. Gaz.,* 28th Oct. 1706.

Acklam. John Philip, 423 Strand, 1816; 138 Strand, 1840. **T.,** 14 Birchin Lane, 1825-33.

Acton. Jno., Clerkenwell, C.C. 1677. **Abraham,** apprenticed in 1691 to Henry Montlow; C.C. 1700. **Chris.,** bracket clock, about 1725.

Adam, Melchior (? Melchior Adam), Paris; octagonal crystal-cased watch, Soltykoff collection, about 1585; **A.,** watch, Pierpont Morgan collection, signed "Melchoir Adam," balance-cock pinned on, about 1610.

Adams. Geo., apprenticed to Jos. Dudds, 1745; C.C. 1752; 60 Fleet St., 1770; table timepiece, Guildhall Museum, about 1795. **Jno.,** Halesowen, 1760. **John,** 1 Dove Court, Moorfields, 1770-72. **Stephen,** 3 St Anne's Lane, 1774; Stephen & Son, 1788. **C. & J.,** 10 King St., Cheapside, 1788. **John,** 31 Maiden Lane, Covent Garden, 1790-94. **Hy.,** Church St., Hackney; fine long-case clock, about 1800; watch, h.m., 1808; on a paper in the outer case the following :—

"To-morrow! yes, to-morrow! you'll repent
A train of years in vice and folly spent.
To-morrow comes—no penitential sorrow
Appears therein, for still it is to-morrow
At length to-morrow such a habit gains,
That you'll forget the time that Heaven ordains,
And you'll believe that day too soon will be
When more to-morrows you're denied to see."

Adams. Francis Bryant, succeeded Benj. Webb at 21 St John's Sq., Clerkenwell; master C.C. 1848; 1810-48. **F. B., & Son,** 21 St John's Sq., 1830-42. **Thos.,** partner

with Widenham in Lombard St.; afterwards at 84 Cannon St.; died at Catford, 1870. Of U.S.A.: **Nathan,** Boston, 1796-1825; **Wm.,** 1838.

Adamson. Humfry, maker of a clock for Whitehall Chapel, 1682; bracket clock about 1690; Wetherfield collection, see p. 543. **John,** admitted C.C. 1686; "A Gold Minute Watch, lately made by Mr Adamson, over against the Blue Boar in Holborn" (*Lond. Gaz.,* 3rd March 1686). —, Paris; clockmaker to the Royal Family, 1790.

Addis. William, Cannon St., afterwards at 3 Birchin Lane, son of Robert A., of Bristol; apprenticed to George Sims, 1738; admitted C.C. 1745; master 1764. **George Curson,** 3 Birchin Lane, afterwards 47 Lombard St.; livery C.C. 1787; 1780-98. **George,** 79 Cornhill, 1786-94.

Addison. Edmond, apprenticed in 1678 to Joseph Ashby, C.C. **Josh.,** London; watch, 1770. **Jno.,** York, f., 1789. **Josh.,** Lancaster, 1817; f., son of James Addison, London.

Adeane. Henry, apprenticed to Rich. Scrivener in 1663; C.C. 1675. **Henry,** C.C. 1705.

Adkins, Thos., Shoe Lane, 1735.

Adney, Richard, Bull and Mouth St., 1770-76.

Agar, —, York. Several generations. **Jno.,** f., 1707. **Francis,** 1708. **Seth,** f., 1743. **Jno.,** f., 1760; died 1808; Mr Thos. Boynton has a fine regulator by him. **Charles,** f., 1779, settled at Pontefract. **John,** f., 1782, settled at Malton. **Thos.,** London; watch, 1804. **Thos.,** Bury, 1814. **Thos.,** Chorley, Lancs., 1814.

Aicken, Geo., Cork; watch, 1780.

Ainsworth, Geo., Warrington, 1818.

Airey, Jno., Hexham, about 1770.

Airy, George Biddell, Astronomer-Royal, 1835-81; K.C.B., 1874; died 1892, aged 90; devoted much attention to the perfecting of timekeepers.

Aish, Simon, Sherborne; long-case lantern-movement clock, 10-inch dial, about 1690.

Aitken, John, 55 St John's St., Clerkenwell; received in 1824 a prize of twenty guineas from the Society of Arts for a clock train remontoire; 1800-26.

Aitkins, Robt., London; watch, 1780.

Akced, Jno., London; watch, 1795.

Akers, Jas., Derby; watch, 1802.

Alais, M., Blois; watch, about 1680.

Alasti, —, signature on case of sixteenth century watch, Pierpont Morgan collection.

Albert, Isaac, C.C. 1731.

Albrecht Michael George, gold repeating watch in the S.K.M., bearing the royal arms, outer case *repoussé,* about 1720.

Alcock, Thomas, petitioner for incorporation of C.C. 1630 (see p. 203).

Alden & Eldridge, Bristol, Conn., 1820.

Alder, J., London; bracket clock, crown wheel escapement, about 1700.

Alderhead, Jno., 114 Bishopsgate Within; livery Goldsmiths' Company 1775-94; card Ponsonby collection "at the Ring and Pearl, Bishopsgate St., near the Southsea House."

Alderman, Edwin, 22 Barbican, 1818-34; livery C.C. 1822.

Aldred. Leonard, C.C. 1671. **Jno.,** apprenticed in 1686 to Hy. Reeve, C.C. **Wm.,** 54 Wood St., 1793; watch-spring maker.

Aldridge. Daniel, apprenticed in 1806 to Hy. Young, C.C. **Edward,** striking

and pull quarter repeating bracket clock, about 1710. **Chas.,** Aldersgate, 1714, **John,** C.C. 1726. **James,** 11 Northumberland St., Strand, 1816-30.

Aldwin, Thos., London; watch, 1767.

Aldworth, Samuel, brother C.C. 1697. Mr C. E. Atkins has a lantern clock by him, inscribed "Saml. Aldworth, Oxon.," about 1700.

Aldy, Edwd., Lincoln, 1760.

Alexander. Robt., Edinburgh, 1709. **Isaac,** Nottingham; watch, about 1760 (see p. 169). **Wm.,** 10 Parliament St., 1828-40. **A., & Co.,** 25 Bedford St., Bedford Sq., 1840; Gray's Inn Passage, 1847.

Alexandre, Jacques, Paris; a priest who devoted much attention to clockmaking; published in 1734, "Traité Général des Horloges."

Aley, Thomas, 18 Park Side, Knightsbridge, 1840-42.

Alibert, F., Paris; watch, 1800.

Alker, Jno., Wigan, 1818.

Alkins (? Atkins), London, about 1730.

Alsope, see Allsop.

Allam. Andrew, Grubb St., apprenticed in 1656 to Nicholas Coxeter; C.C. 1664; maker of lantern clocks. **Michael,** London, 1723. **Robt.,** Fleet St., 1770-80. **William,** Fleet St., 1770-80. **& Stacy,** 175 Fleet St., 1783. **Wm.,** Bond St., bracket clock, about 1825.

Allams, Gabriel; repeating watch, silver cases, inner one pierced, outer one *repoussé,* with Minerva, &c., about 1760, Pierpont Morgan collection.

Allan. George, 9 New Bond St., hon. freeman C.C. 1781; 1760-83; maker of a watch found in a chimney at Newton St., Holborn, in 1895, and said to have belonged to Lord Lovat, who was beheaded in 1747; unfortunately for the legend, the hall mark corresponded to 1768. **Robert,** London; maker of repeating watches, 1780-90. **& Clements,** 119 New Bond St., 1785-94. **John,** 119 New Bond St., 1798-1800. **& Caithness,** 119 New Bond St., 1800-4.

Allaway, John, apprenticed to Bernard Rainsford; C.C. 1695.

Allcock. Jno., 30 St Martin's Lane; card, B.M., 1787. **William,** watch-hand maker, 36 Allen St., Clerkenwell, 1820.

Allen. Jas., brother C.C. 1635. **Elias,** brother C.C., master, 1636; died 1654. **Nathaniel,** apprenticed in 1650 to Wm. Bowyer, C.C. **Thos.,** apprenticed in 1663 to Robt. Whitwell, C.C. **John,** C.C. 1720. **John,** brother C.C. 1753. **P.,** Macclesfield, 1770. **John,** 42 Poultry, 1772-75. **George,** Fleet St.; liveryman C.C. 1776. **John,** watch-case maker, Barbican; convicted in the Mayor's Court for refusing to become a member of the C.C., although he was at the time free of the Goldsmiths' Company, 1785-89; Aldersgate St., 1794. **James,** 76 New Gravel Lane; an ingenious watchmaker to whom the Board of Longitude awarded £105 for engine dividing, 1790-1800. **George,** 14 Red Lion Passage, Holborn; watch paper C.C., 1812-42. **T.,** Preston, 1814. **Jno.,** London; watch, 1820. Of Boston, U.S.A.: **Jas.,** 1684.

Allenbach, Jacob, Philadelphia, 1825-40.

Allett, George, apprenticed in 1683 to Solomon Bouquet, but turned over to Thos. Tompion; C.C. 1691; bracket clock, ebony case, Wetherfield collection, about 1705.

Alling. Richard, admitted C.C. 1722. **James,** 22 Red Lion St., Whitechapel; "foreman to Mr Hatton, London Bridge"; watch paper C.C. 1838-42.

Allison. Wm., Liverpool, about 1765.

Gilbert, Sunderland, 1775. **Thos.**, London ; watch, 1790.

Allkins, Horncastle ; watch, 1785.

Allman, W., Prince's St., Storey's Gate, Westminster ; card, B.M., 1798.

Allory, —, Moorfields, 1774.

Allport, —, Birmingham ; bracket clock, about 1770.

Allsop, Joshua, Northamptonshire, brother C.C. 1689 ; handsome long Oriental lacquer-cased clock belonging to the Blecker family, New York ; long-case clock, richly inlaid, inscribed " Josh. Alsope, East Smithfield," about 1710.

Allvey, Hy., 5 Old St. Sq., about 1795.

Almond. William, Lothbury ; maker of a clock for Hall, Bishop of Exeter ; C.C. 1633. **Ralph**, apprenticed to Oswald Durant in 1637 ; C.C. 1646, master 1678. **John**, C.C. 1671.

Alrich (or Alrichs). Jonas, Wilmington, Del., born 1759, died 1802. **Jacob**, born 1775.

Alston & Lewis, 30 Bishopsgate St., 1820 ; Alston & Hallam, 1830-42.

Alvey, Samuel, apprenticed to Jas. Wood ; admitted C.C. 1757.

Alyers, Jas., Southwark ; watch, 1779.

Alysone, Jas., Dundee, 1663.

Amabric. Abraham, Geneva, 1760-80 ; barrel-shaped gold watch with *repoussé* ornament enamelled, Pierpont Morgan collection ; dial apparently later signed Amabric Frères. **Freres**, Geneva, 1793.

Amant, "maitre horloger, Paris" ; spoken of by Thiout in 1741 ; he invented the pin wheel escapement about 1749. **Peter**, Philadelphia, 1793.

Ambrose. Edward, apprentice of Elias Voland, 1634. **David**, C.C. 1669.

Ames, Richard, apprenticed in 1648 to Peter Closon ; C.C. 1653 ; died in 1682, after election as master ; clock by him with dolphin frets and bob pendulum working between going and striking. In 1684 Robert Browne was apprenticed to Katherine Ames. **William**, apprenticed to Richard in 1675 ; C.C. 1682.

Amey, Robt., London ; watch, 1780.

Ampe, Abraham ; watch, Napier collection, 1607.

Amyot. Peter, Norwich ; lantern clocks, about 1660. **& Bennett**, Brigg's Lane, Norwich ; in 1793 they issued a little book by J. Bennett on the management of a watch.

Amyott. Peter, Norwich ; watch, Nelthropp collection, about 1720. **Thos.**, London ; watches, h.m., 1751-71 ; one, Nelthropp collection, about 1770.

Anderson. Wm., apprenticed in 1646 to Simon Bartram. **Robt.**, apprenticed in 1691 to Thos. Tompion, C.C. **Richard**, C.C. ; Lancaster, 1767, f. ; also at London and Preston. **Alex.**, London ; watch, 1770. **Wm.**, Lancaster, about 1770. **J.**, London ; watch, 1775. **Geo.**, sued in 1777 by Cabrier for putting his name on five watches. **Richard**, Preston ; watch, 1778. **Wm.**, Lancaster, 1780. **Alex.**, Liverpool ; watch, 1786. **Hugh**, London ; watch, 1792. **R.**, London ; watch, 1812. **Edward C.**, Newington Butts ; a successful watchmaker who carried out the not unreasonable rule of making a charge for furnishing a repairing estimate if it involved taking a watch to pieces ; 1835-85.

Anderton. Jno., Little Wild St. ; repeating watch, about 1750. **Wm.**, London ; watch, h.m., 1767. **Jno.**, Huddersfield, 1833.

Andrew, J., 14 Queen St., Ratcliff Cross, 1820.

Andrews. Robert, apprenticed in 1661 to Benj. Hill ; C.C. 1709. **Isaac**, apprenticed in 1674 to Edm. Fowell, C.C. **Thos.**, apprenticed in 1686 to Joshua Hutchin ; C.C. 1705. **John**, Leadenhall St. ; admitted C.C. 1688. **Richard**, C.C. 1703 ; watch 1730. **James**, C.C. 1719. **William**, Bishopsgate St. ; C.C. 1719. **Benj.**, Bartholomew Lane, 1725. **Abraham**, Bank Coffee House, Threadneedle St., 1759. **Thos. Steyning**, 1760 (see p. 368). **Rich.**, 124 Leadenhall St., 1775. **Eliza**, 85 Cornhill, 1790-1800.

Angel, Richard, repairer of clock at Wigtoft, Boston, Lincolnshire, 1484.

Angus, Geo., Aberdeen ; long-case clock, about 1760.

Annat, Nicholas, apprenticed in 1673 to Henry Jones, C.C.

Anness, William, 102 Cheapside, 1798-1820 ; livery, C.C. 1802.

Annis, M., New York, 1786.

Annis, Jno., 13 Sparrow Corner, 1810-18.

Annott, Chas., apprenticed in 1673 to Jas. Ellis, C.C.

Ansell (or Anselme). Richard, apprenticed to Jeffery Baily ; C.C. 1680. **& Son**, watch-spring makers, 22 Whitecross Place, 1798-1820. **Hy.**, 17 Colchester Sq., Savage Gardens, 1830 ; 74 Leman St., 1838.

Anstey, Jno., apprenticed to George Nau in 1683.

Antes, Jno., London ; apprenticed to Wm. Addis ; pocket chronometer, G.M., h.m. 1787.

Anthony. — ; clockmaker to Henry VIII., 1529. **William**, 55 Red Lion St., St John's Sq., Clerkenwell. There was in the Dunn Gardner collection a magnificent long oval watch by him, in a gold case, bearing the hall-mark for 1796. It was rather a large size, back enamelled and decorated with diamonds and pearls ; but the peculiar feature was that the dial was also oval ; the hands were jointed, and automatically lengthened and shortened as they travelled across. This watch fetched £200 at Christie's in 1902. Another example is an 8-day watch of similar shape, duplex escapement, movement beautifully engraved, formerly in the Bentinck-Hawkins collection. He is reputed to have been one of the most expert watchmakers of his day, and such specimens of his work as remain quite bear out this belief. He carried on a successful business in Red Lion Street, St John's Square, and most of his watches bore the inscription " Wm. Anthony, St John's Square." At one time he was in good circumstances, and took an active part in founding the Watch and Clockmakers' Benevolent Institution in 1815, though he lived to be a recipient of its bounty. Apart from his art he did not exhibit particular sagacity. He engaged in litigation with Grimaldi & Johnson, which ended disastrously, and expended a large amount in the purchase of royal and other wardrobes of the time of Charles I. Of these he formed an exhibition at the Somerset Gallery, next door to Somerset House, and now 151 Strand. This also turned out an expensive failure. He had a considerable sum invested in good leasehold property on the Doughty estate. He died in Jerusalem Passage in 1844, and was then about eighty years of age. After his death the leases of this property were found in his safe. Curiously enough, the term for which he held had just about expired, but he had not troubled to collect any rents for at least twenty years previously, and it was concluded he had forgotten all about his possessions. Mr Wm. Bailey had a miniature painted when he was about fifty-five years of age.

Antis, Jno., Fulneck, near Leeds ; received in 1805 £21 from the Society of Arts for a clock escapement.

Antoine, —, Rue Galande, Paris, 1770.

Antram, Joseph, London ; apprenticed to Chas. Gretton ; C.C. 1706 ; long walnut-case clock, square dial, cherub corners, circles round winding holes, about 1700 ; watch, about 1720 ; " watch and clock maker to his Majesty."

Antt, G., 158 Strand, 1769-88.

Apiohn (Upjohn), Henry, apprenticed in 1649 to Robert Whitwell, C.C.

Appleby. Edward, London ; watch, about 1700. **Joshua**, Bread St. ; apprentice of Daniel Quare ; C.C. 1719, master 1745. **Thos.**, Charing Cross, 1800 (see p. 368). **P.**, London ; watch, 1825.

Applegarth, Thomas, apprenticed in 1664 to Hugh Cooper ; C.C. 1674.

Appleton. Jno., Liverpool, 1818. **Henry**, 50 Myddelton Sq., 1840-42 ; afterwards in partnership with Birchall in Southampton Row.

Appley, Edmund, Charing Cross ; apprenticed to Jeffery Bailey 1670 ; C.C. 1677 ; small repeating bracket clock, black case, basket top, about 1680.

Appleyard, R., London ; watch, about 1790.

Archambo, Jno., Prince's St., Leicester Fields ; bracket clock in case, similar to Chippendale's design, Fig. 693, p. 377) ; marqueterie case clock, arch dial ; *repoussé* case watch, hall-mark 1730, and another watch of a later date ; 1720-50.

Archer. Henry, subscribed £10 for incorporation of C.C. and was the first warden ; 1630-49. **John**, apprenticed in 1650 to Jas. Starnill ; admitted C.C. 1660. **Edward**, C.C. 1711. **Walter**, long-case clock, about 1715, at the Van Courtland Mansion, New York. **W.**, Stow, about 1715. **Samuel**, 15 Leather Lane, 1794 ; 33 Kirby St., Hatton Garden, 1810 ; a prominent man in the trade. In 1820 he was treasurer to the Watch and Clockmakers' Benevolent Institution. **Sam. Wm.**, Hackney, 1805-12. **Thomas**, 6 Long Lane, Smithfield, 1814-20. **Geo.**, Rochdale, 1818.

Argand l'Aine, Geneva, about 1740. **J. L.**, Place Dauphine, Paris, 1770 (see p. 154) ; repeating watch " Argand, Paris," about 1770, Pierpont Morgan collection.

Ariel. James, watch-movement maker, 10 Wilderness Row, 1815-20. **John**, 10 Percival St., 1822-39.

Aris. Samuel, Leicester Fields ; watch, 1750 ; Mr Evan Roberts ; long-case clock, about 1760. **Jno. & Co.**, Old Jewry, 1794.

Arlandi, John, chain-maker for watches, Red Rose St., Covent Garden, 1680 ; C.C. 1682.

Arlaud. Anthoine, cruciform watch, Pierpont Morgan collection, late sixteenth century. **Henry**, fine calendar watch, Schloss collection, about 1630, silver case, back inscribed " Richard Baille, at the Abbay." This watch was probably English work (see p. 189). Another specimen of a rather later date was inscribed " Arlaud, London." **Benjamin**, maker of a large silver repeating-watch in the B.M., about 1680.

Arlott, Thos., Sunderland, 1770.

Armand, J., Copenhagen ; born 1732, died 1809 ; a talented horologist.

Armingand, —, Paris ; watch, 1790.

Armitage. & Co. 88 Bishopsgate Within, 1798. **Thos.**, Manchester, 1815.

Armstrong. John, C.C. 1724. **Thos.**,

Manchester, 1818.

Arnold, Thomas, apprenticed in 1687 to Nat. Chamberlaine, jun. ; admitted C.C. 1703. **John,** Devereux Court, Fleet St., 1760 ; 112 Cornhill, 1780 (see p. 269). **Hy.,** 46 Lombard St., 1769-88. **Wm.,** London ; watch, 1790. **Edward,** London ; watch, 1790. **& Son,** 112 Cornhill, 1798. **John Roger,** Bank Buildings, 1802 ; 1804 ; 26 Cecil St., 1816-30. **John R., & Dent,** 84 Strand, 1830-40. **John · R.,** 84 Strand, 1842.

Arnolts, —, Hamburg, 1635 (see p. 136).

Arnott, Richard, 18 Red Cross St., Barbican, 1810-25.

Arnould, —, French clock, about 1720, inscribed " Arnould *pere.*"

Arthanel, Aron Louis, table clock, about 1640.

Arthaud, Louis, à Lyon ; silver alarm watch, nicely pierced case, Schloss collection, about 1650 (p. 168).

Arthur, William, apprenticed in 1669 to Nich. Coxeter ; C.C. 1676.

Arwen, Wm., Huddersfield, about 1770.

Ascough, see Ayscough.

Ash. —, subscribed £2 for incorporation of C.C. 1630. **Ralph,** C.C. 1648. **& Son,** 64 St James's St., 1822. **Joseph,** 146 Aldersgate St., 1822.

Ashbourne, Leonard, at the Sugar Loaf in Paternoster Row, next Cheapside ; inventor and maker of a clock lamp, 1731.

Ashbrooke. Thos., apprenticed to Cuthbert Lee in 1685 ; C.C. **Jno.,** apprenticed to Zach. Mountford in 1686 ; C.C.

Ashby, Joseph, apprenticed in 1663 to Matthew Crockford ; C.C. 1674 ; Edmond Addison was apprenticed to him in 1678.

Ashley. Jas., apprenticed in 1647 to Robert Smith, C.C. **Chas.,** London ; watch, 1767. **Jno.,** English watch, 1780. **J. P.,** 99 Baches Row, City Rd., 1800. **& Manser,** 34 Rosoman St., Clerkenwell, 1825-35, afterwards at 15 Garnault Place ; watch by them, h.m. 1823, cylinder escapement, brass escape wheel ; the teeth, instead of being in one horizontal plane, were on three different levels, touching on different parts of the cylinder, and so spreading the wear over a larger surface ; they were succeeded by E. F. Ashley ; he retired from business in 1898, and died in 1908. **Edward,** 9 John St., Pentonville, 1842.

Ashman & Son, 462 Strand, 1822.

Ashton. Miles, apprenticed in 1663 to Benj. Wolverstone, C.C. **Jno.,** apprenticed in 1672 to Jno. Savile, C.C. **Thos.,** apprenticed 1687 to Thos. Bradford, C.C. **—,** Tideswell, long-case clock, about 1710. **Thos.,** Macclesfield, 1760. **Saml.,** Bredbury, 1765. **Thos.,** Leek, 1790. **Jno.,** Leek, 1830. **—,** Philadelphia, 1797.

Ashurst. William, C.C. 1699. **James,** Chorley ; watch, 1777.

Ashwell, Nicholas, apprenticed in 1640 to Robt. Grinkin ; C.C. 1649.

Aske, Henry, apprenticed in 1669 to Edward Norris ; C.C. 1676 ; George Graham was apprenticed to him in 1688 ; 1676-96.

Askell, Elizabeth, apprenticed in 1734 to Elinor Mosely.

Askwith, Jno., York, f. 1740.

Aspinall, Hy., Liverpool, about 1770.

Aspinwall. Thomas, small oval watch (see p. 135), about 1605. **Samuel,** clockwatch in possession of Lord Torphichen, about 1655 ; clock-watch, similar period, Evan Roberts collection. **Josiah,** brother C.C. 1675. **John,** Liverpool ; long-case

clock, about 1750. **Robt.,** Liverpool, 1818.

Asprey, Wm., 4 Bruton St., 1820.

Asselin, Francis (French), C.C. 1687 ; bracket clock, case covered with tortoise-shell on a red ground, about 1690 ; another somewhat similar clock, inscribed "Stephen Asselin" (see p. 388). Mr W. T. Harkness has a 28-day long-case clock by Asselin, London, about 1700.

Astley, Ed., Liverpool, 1833.

Astwood, Joseph, apprenticed in 1659 to Ben. Bell, C.C.

Atchison, Robert, apprenticed to Robert Harding 1753 ; admitted C.C. 1760 ; 1760-1819.

Athaud, Louis, à Lyon ; mid-seventeenth century watch, S. K. M., silver case pierced and engraved.

Athern, Jno., Liverpool ; long-case clock, Mr E. H. Coleman ; above dial motto, "Time shows the way of life's decay," about 1780 (?)

Atherton. Thos., Liverpool ; watch, 1776. **T.,** London ; watch, 1780. **& Hewett** (tools), 49 Red Lion St., Clerkenwell, 1789-94.

Atis, Leonard, London ; lantern clock, about 1660.

Atkin. Robt., Liverpool, 1818. Also **Francis,** same date.

Atkins. Joseph, apprenticed to Robt. Fowler 1654 ; C.C. **Jonathan,** apprenticed in 1659 to Sam. Clay, C.C. **Francis,** 35 Clement's Lane ; born 1730 ; apprenticed to Joshua Hassell 1746 ; C.C. 1759, master, 1780, clerk, 1785 ; died 1809. **Samuel,** Palgrave Court, Temple Bar, 1752-65. **Samuel, & Son,** Palgrave Court, Temple Bar, 1759-63. **George,** son of Francis, born 1767 ; 35 Clement's Lane ; warden C.C. 1809, afterwards clerk ; died 1855. **Robert,** Palgrave Court, Temple Bar, 1769. **Robert,** 20 Salisbury St., Strand, 1770-88 ; Snow Hill, 1800. **Danl.,** London ; watch, h.m., 1776. **S.,** watch-case maker, 14 Bridgewater Sq., 1810. **W.,** 7 Upper Ashby St., Clerkenwell, 1820. **William,** 71 High St., Poplar, 1835-42. **W.,** 3 High St., Hoxton, 1835. **George, & Son,** 6 Cowper's Court, Cornhill, 1840-42. **Samuel Elliott,** son of George, whom he succeeded in business and as clerk of C.C., which office he resigned in 1878 ; chosen master in 1882 ; born 1807 ; died 1898.

Atkinson. James, C.C. 1667, assistant 1697. **Joseph,** Gateshead, 1770-90. Lancaster : **Thos.,** 1767 f. **Thos.,** 1785 f. **Wm.,** 1817 f. **Robert,** apprenticed to W. Bell, died 1900, aged 57, a clever mechanician. **Thos.,** 38 Piccadilly, 1814-17.

Atlee. Henry, apprenticed in 1662 to Charles Rogers ; C.C. 1671. **Roger,** apprenticed in 1664 to Job Betts, C.C.

Attbury, J., watch-movement maker, 15 York St., St Luke's, 1835.

Attemstetter, David, Augsburg ; a celebrated enameller, 1610.

Attwell. Thos., London ; clock, about 1750. **—,** near the Court House, Romford ; watch paper C.C., about 1790. **Robt.,** Brown's Lane, Spitalfields, 1810-18. **Wm.,** 11 Pitfield St., 1815-25.

Attwood, Geo., born 1746, died 1807 ; an eminent mathematician ; studied watch work, and reported to Parliament on Mudge's timekeeper, 1793.

Atwood. —, Lewes ; watch, 1774. **Richard,** 41 Poultry, 1800-10. **Geo.,** 17 Leonard St., Shoreditch, 1820.

Auber, Daniel, Whitefriars, 1750.

Aubert. Jean Jacques, Paris ; "horloger du Roy," 1737. **D. F.,** Geneva, 1820 ;

afterwards partner in London with C. J. Klaftenberger. **& Klaftenberger,** 157 Regent St., 1835-42.

Audebert, D., Amsterdam ; long-case clock, about 1720.

Audemars, Louis, La Vallée, Switzerland, 1811.

Audley, Jos., apprenticed to Thos. Tompion in 1683.

Augier, Jehan, Paris ; maker of large watches, about 1650.

Aukland, Wm., London ; watch, 1790.

Auld, see Reid & Auld.

Ault. Jos., Belper ; clock, about 1800. **Thomas,** 34 Prince's St., Leicester Sq., 1820-25.

Aussin, —, French cruciform watch, Wallace collection, about 1650.

Austen. John, Shoreditch ; C.C. 1711 ; maker of a bracket clock with square dial, pull-chime, black bell-top case, 1711-25. **—,** Cork ; about 1820 he made three-wheel clocks (see p. 287).

Austin. Isaac, Philadelphia, 1785-1805. **& Co.,** 176 Oxford St., 1820. **John,** 136 Oxford St., 1830-40.

Autray, Paris ; watch, 1750.

Aveline, Daniel, "7 Dials" ; died 1770, when warden C.C. ; 1760-70.

Avenall (or **Avenell**), a family well known as clockmakers in Hampshire for two centuries. **Ralph,** Farnham ; balance escapement clock, about 1640. **Edwd.,** apprenticed to Joseph Duke ; admitted C.C. 1706. **Jno.,** son of Edwd. ; admitted C.C. 1735. **Wm.** Avenall, Alresford, 1770 (see p. 368).

Avery. —, church clock, Kingston by Mere, Wilts., 1740. **Amos,** Cheapside, 1774. **Philip,** Red Cross Sq., 1790-94.

Axeborough, —, Otley, 1730.

Aylosse, Elizabeth, apprenticed in 1678 to Joane Wythe (widow) ; C.C.

Aylward, Jno., Guildford ; lantern clock, about 1695 ; another specimen, about 1710, said to be inscribed "John Aylward, Braintford."

Aymes, see Ames.

Aynsworth, J., Westminster ; maker of lantern clocks, 1645-80.

Ayres. Samuel, apprenticed in 1664 to Edwd. Norris, C.C. **Richard,** apprenticed in 1670 to Hy. Jones ; C.C. 1680. **Thos.,** 160 Fenchurch St., 1800-30. **& Bennett,** 160 Fenchurch St., 1815-20.

Ayscough, Ralph, livery Goldsmiths' Company ; St Paul's Churchyard, 1758 ; 18 Ludgate St., 1766-76.

Baccuet, —, watch enamelled, painting, "Roman Piety," on back, about 1690.

Bachan, Henry, London ; long-case clock, about 1770.

Bachelder, Ezra, Denvers, U.S.A., 1793-1840.

Bachoffner, Andrew, 112 Shoreditch, 1775.

Backhouse, Jas., Lancaster, 1726 f., died 1747.

Backler, Benj., London ; long-case clock, Mr R. Eden Dickson, about 1760. **Benj.,** Masham, 1823.

Backquett, Davyd, C.C. 1632.

Bacon. John, brother C.C. 1639. **—,** "Paid Mr Bacon, clockmaker, of Tewkesbury, for a clock and case, yᵉ summe of six pounds and five shillings," 1708. ("Diary of Thos. Newnham"). **Charles,** C.C. 1719. **Jno.,** London ; watch, 1810.

Bacott, Peter, London, about 1700.

Baddeley, Phineas, apprenticed to Evan Jones 1652 ; C.C. 1661 ; long-case clock, signed "Baddeley, Tong," about 1720; long-case clock, dead beat escapement, about 1750, signed "Jno. Baddeley, Tong."

Badger. Hy., apprenticed 1672 to Jno. Harris, C.C. **John,** apprenticed to Brounker Watts, C.C. 1720.

Badiley, Richard, London; long walnut-case clock, about 1730.

Badley, Thos., Boston, U.S.A., 1712.

Badollet. J. J., Geneva, 1770. **John,** 50 Greek St., 1842.

Baffert, à Paris; clock, Jones collection, S.K.M., about 1780.

Baggs, Samuel, 3 South St., Grosvenor Sq., 1820-35.

Bagley, Thomas, apprenticed to Richard Morgan 1650; C.C. 1664.

Bagnall. Benj., Boston, about 1700. **Benj.,** Charleston, U.S.A., 1740-60. (Or **Bagnell),** W. H., 42 Union St., Bishopsgate, 1835-49; 193 Bishopsgate Without, 1842.

Bagnell. William, C.C. 1719. **Wm.,** watch-spring maker, Greenhill's Rents, Smithfield, 1794.

Bagot, Jno., Lancaster, 1823 f.

Bagshaw. Edwd., apprenticed in 1681 to Thos. Wheeler; C.C. 1691. **William,** C.C. 1722. **Hy.,** London; watch, 1820.

Bagwell, Richard, 3 Queen St., Cheapside, 1790-94.

Bailey. Jeffery, "at ye Turn Style in Holburn"; C.C. 1648, master 1674; maker of lantern clocks. **Jeremiah,** C.C. 1724. **Ed.,** 13 Oxford St., 1730. **Jno.,** London; bracket clock, about 1730. **Jno.,** Hanover, U.S.A., 1770-1815. **Catherine,** watch-case maker, 22 Clerkenwell Green, 1790-94. **& Upjohn,** 12 Red Lion St., Clerkenwell, 1798. **Chas.,** London, about 1805. **Jno.,** London; watch in case of gilt metal decorated with machine engraving about 1780, S.K.M.; another watch, h.m., 1812. **W.,** 19 Radcliff Row, Clerkenwell, 1835.

Baillon. Albert, Paris; watch about 1695, Mr Evan Roberts. **Jean Baptiste,** Paris; horloger de la Reine Marie Leczinska 1751, later on horloger de la Reine Marie Antoinette; he did a large trade and was reputed to be the richest watchmaker in Europe; enamelled watch formerly in the Dunn Gardner collection, S.K.M., inscribed "J. B. Baillon, horlog. du Roy" (see p. 156). **Francis,** à Choudens, 1780.

Bailly l'Aine, Paris; an eminent maker 1750-75; clock on elephant's back, about 1760 (see p. 323). **Fils,** à Paris, about 1780; watch, "Bailly, Paris," 1790.

Bain, Alexander, Edinburgh; inventor of electric clocks, 1838-58.

Bains, Jno., Snaith, 1770.

Baird. John, 190 Strand, 1770-83. **W. & J.,** 4 Hatton Garden, 1810-30. **Geo.,** Carlisle, 1833.

Baitson, Thos., Beverley, 1822.

Baker. Richard, brother C.C. 1685; pull quarter repeating bracket clock, Wetherfield collection, square ebony case, brass basket top, about 1680; 8-day clock, ebony marqueterie case, square dial, cherub corners, no door to hood; also a similar clock in oak case, fine hands, 1685-1710. **Henry,** Maidstone; one hand lantern clock, about 1700. "A silver Minute Pendulum watch with a silver outcase and a coat-of-arms engraven on it (A Lyon Passant with three Cross Croslets, made by Richard Baker, London), lost in Dunghil Fields nigh Whitechapel Church" (*Lond. Gaz.*, March 3-6, 1689).

"A silver watch with a shagreen case,

with G. M. on it, and with Baker on the Dyal Plate" (*Lond. Gaz.*, April 15-18, 1685).

Baker. Richard, admitted C.C. 1726. **Francis,** Poultry, 1738. **Thos.,** Gosport; watch, about 1740. **—,** Hull, 1760. **Pointer,** London; repeating watch, h.m., 1772. **John,** 5 King St., Covent Garden; hon. freeman C.C. 1781; 1768-84. **Hy.,** hon. freeman C.C. 1781. **Edward,** 33 White Lion St., 1785-1805, afterwards at Angel Terrace, Pentonville; duplex watch, G.M., h.m., 1787. **Thos.,** Upper Stamford St., 1833. **W.,** 35 Long Acre, 1835-42; afterwards at 30 Cranbourne St.

Bakewell, —, lantern clock, about 1700, inscribed "Thomas Bakewell, on Tower Hill, fecit."

Balch. Of U.S.A.: **Daniel,** Newburyport, 1760-90. **Thos. H.,** died 1819. **Chas. H.,** 1787-1808. **Benj.,** Salem, 1837. **Jas.** (**& Lamson),** 1842.

Baldwein, of Marburg. In conjunction with H. Bucher, he made a clock similar to Fig. 38, 1563-68.

Baldwin. Chris., apprenticed 1656 to Jno. Freeman, C.C. **Thos.,** apprenticed 1672 to Jno. Benson; C.C. 1685. **Robt.,** apprenticed 1682 to Thos. Virgoe, C.C. **Jno.,** C.C. 1685. **Jno.,** apprenticed 1691 to Stephen Rayner, C.C., long-case clock, minute hand curved in the Dutch style, inscribed "J. F. Baldwin, Feversham, Kent," about 1740. **J.,** Andover, 1760. **Geo.,** Sadsburyville, 1808-32. **Anthony,** Lancaster, U.S.A., 1810-30. **T.,** 69 Curtain Rd., 1830-35. **Thomas,** 50 Brudenell Place, New North Road, 1840-42.

Baldwyn, Thomas, C.C. 1706.

Bale. Thomas, C.C. 1724. **Robert Brittel,** Poultry; dials bearing his name, 1813.

Balestree, J., 2 Queen St., Soho, 1811.

Baley, Thos., C.C. 1786.

Balfour, Gilbert, London; watch, 1760.

Ball. Victor, 1630-50. **John,** C.C. 1637; fine long lacquer-case calendar clock about 1760, signed "Wm. Ball, Biceter," Mr Geo. F. Glenny (see p. 377). **Jno.,** Newport Pagnell, 1760. **Edwd.,** 32 Ironmonger Row, 1794. **& Macaire,** watch-case makers, 32 Northampton Sq.; 26 Myddelton St., 1835.

Ballantyne, Wm., 6 Cable St., 1815-20; 2 White Lion St., Goodman's Fields, 1835; 1820-42.

Balliston, Thos., 5 Banner St., 1842.

Balmer, Thos., Liverpool, 1833.

Baltazar. Chas., Paris; about 1710. **Cadet** (the younger), Place Dauphine, Paris, 1769; "clockmaker to Mesdames filles de Louis XV." **Noel,** Paris; about 1770.

Balteau à Lyon; cruciform watch, Pierpont Morgan collection, about 1610.

Banbury, John, C.C. 1685.

Bancroft, Wm., Scarborough, 1822.

Band, Wm., London; watch, 1805.

Banfield, Jno., 116 Cheapside, 1814-17.

Banger, Edward, apprenticed to Joseph Ashby for Thomas Tompion 1687; C.C. 1695 (see p. 226).

Bangiloner, —, London; clock-watch, about 1660.

Banister. Thos., Norton; long-case clock, about 1765 (see also Hedge & Banister). **Joseph,** Colchester; patented a crutch for clocks in 1836 (No. 7,083). **Henry,** succeeded Jno. Grant the younger at 75 Fleet St., 1852, and remained there till 1860.

Bankes, William, apprenticed 1690 to Ben. Bell; C.C. 1698; on a large lantern

clock "Wm. Bankes in Sheffield," date about 1680.

Banks. S. & W., Leicester; chiming clock, about 1760. **J. C. & B.,** London; watch, 1802. **J.,** 68 Long Alley, Finsbury, 1830-35.

Bannerman, Gilbert, Banff, 1760.

Bannister. Anthony, C.C. 1715; watch with sun and moon indicator, signed "Anthony Bannister," on dial "Bannister, Liverpool," about 1705. **James,** 14 Clerkenwell Close, 1820-35; 32 Prince's St., Leicester Sq., 1810-42. **Thomas & James,** 39 Kirby St., Hatton Garden, 1825.

Banstein, John, Philadelphia, 1791.

Banting, William, C.C. 1646.

Barachin, Stephen (French), C.C. 1687.

Barbaull, see Widman, J.

Barber. Jonas, Ratcliffe Cross, brother C.C. 1682. **Jonas,** Winster, Windermere; died 1720; the Rev. F. C. Townson has a long-case clock, "J. Barber, Winster," about 1750; watch, "J. Barber, Winster," 1755. **Wm.,** 30 Cornhill, 1785-94. **Benjamin,** 21 Red Lion St., Clerkenwell, 1788-94. **Josh.,** 168 Borough, 1795-1817. **Hy.,** London; watch, h.m., 1805. **Thos.,** 75 Lamb's Conduit St., 1810-17. **Jas.,** York, f. 1814. **& Whitwell,** York, 1818. **Cattle & North,** 1830. **Abraham,** 56 Cheapside, 1835-42. **& North,** York, 1838.

Barberet, Jacques, Paris; octagonal watch, Garnier collection; cruciform watch, about 1620; splendidly enamelled watch, formerly in the Hawkins collection, about 1640 (see p. 149).

Barbier le Jeune, sur le Pont Marie, Paris, 1770.

Barbot, Paul, Great St., Seven Dials, 1768-69.

Barcelet, Mathieu, Paris, about 1570. M. Leroux has a square table clock, with dome over, by him.

Barclay. (? Barkley) **Samuel,** apprenticed to George Graham; C.C. 1722. **Hugh,** Edinburgh, 1727. **C.,** London; watch, 1815. **James,** 7 Jamaica Terrace, Commercial Rd., 1820; James Pyott succeeded him in 1873.

Barcole, John, admitted C.C. 1648.

Bareham, Samuel, 9 Chapel Street, Pentonville, 1842.

Barford. Thos., apprenticed 1655 to Thos. Daniell, C.C. **Henry,** London; watch, 1780.

Bargeau, Peter, London; long Oriental lacquer-case clock (*Tempus fugit*), 1740.

Baril. Lewis, Tokenhouse Yard, 1754-59. **Bercher,** 29 Prince's St., near Mansion House, 1763-72.

Barilon, —, Paris; watch, 1770.

Barin, John, livery C.C. 1776.

Barjon, John, C.C. 1776.

Barked, Edward, 2 St Martin's Churchyard, 1820.

Barker. William, C.C. 1632. **Wm.,** Wigan; about 1760. **B.,** New York, 1786. **Benj.,** 21 Red Lion St., 1788. **Thos.,** London; watches, 1792-1813. **R.** (tools), 4 Benjamin St., Clerkenwell, 1820-25. **James,** 38 Colet Place, Commercial Road, 1840-42.

Barkham, Geo., 1630-50; C.C.

"**Barkley & Colley, Graham's Successors**"; on a long-case clock, with ingenious mechanism for a perpetual diary, about 1760; see Colley.

Barling, —, Maidstone, 1835.

Barlow. (Booth) Edward, invented the rack striking work and cylinder escapement; born 1636, died 1716 (see p. 218). **—,** served as steward C.C. 1677. **Thos.,**

C.C. 1692. **W.**, Ashton, 1760. **Mat.**, Brumhill, Wilts., 1770. **Jas.**, Oldham, 1775. **Jno.**, Oldham; long-case clock, 1780. **Benj.**, Ashton, 1780; Oldham, long-case clock, about 1790. **J.**, London; watch, 1798. **J. H., & Co.**, 7 Vere St., 1812-20.

Barnard. **Nich.**, apprenticed 1662 to Thos. Claxton, C.C. **Jno.**, apprenticed 1675 to Francis Dinnis; C.C. 1682. **Ralph**, apprenticed 1678 to Jno. Cotsworth, C.C. **Phil.**, London; long japanned case clock, about 1745. **Wm.**, Newark, 1760-80. **Wm.**, London; watch, h.m., 1762. **Thos.**, 72 Strand, 1783-1823. **& Savory**, 1786-99. **& Kidder**, 72 Strand, 1809-12. **Jno.**, 36 Little Sutton St., 1817. **Jas.**, Peckham; bracket clock, about 1825. **Franz**, 57 Leman St., 1840-42.

Barnardiston, **Jno.**, London; long-case clock, 1760.

Barnes. **Ri.**, Worcester; oval watch, S.K.M., about 1600; also an oval watch, now in the Schloss collection; about 1610. **Geo.**, apprenticed 1693 to Josh. Allsop, C.C. **Jno.**, Badger Row, Red Lion St., 1770-94. **Thos.**, Lichfield county, U.S.A.; maker of American clocks, 1790.

Barnett. **John**, "at ye Peacock in Lothebury"; apprenticed 1675 to Jno. Ebsworth; C.C. 1682; long marqueterie case clock, ebonised dome top, 10-inch dial, Wetherfield collection. **J.**, "the corner of Shakespeare's walk, near Shadwell Church, Ratcliff Highway," card Hodgkin collection, about 1780. **G.**, 10 Staining Lane, Wood St., 1800. **J.**, 48 Shadwell High St., 1810-15. **J. W.**, watch-case maker, 43 Galway St., St Luke's, 1835. **Montague**, 16 Swan St., Minories, 1842.

Barnish. **Wm.**, Rochdale, died 1776. **Jno.**, a well-known maker of Toad Lane, Rochdale, who probably succeeded Wm., is traced till 1816.

Barnitt, Joseph, 23 London-Prentice St., Birmingham, 1768.

Barns. **Timothy** (**Thomas**), Lichfield, 1790. **& Co.**, 53 Duke St., Smithfield, 1800.

Barnsdale. **Thos.**, Bale, Norfolk, 1770. **John**, City Rd., 1840.

Baron, Edmd., apprenticed 1692 to Thos. Feilder, C.C.

Baroneau, Louys, Paris; clockmaker to the Queen 1760; fine enamel watch, about 1680.

Barr, Thos., Lewes; lantern clock, about 1700.

Barraclough, —, Haworth, 1780.

Barratt, P., Strand, 1785; 71 Swallow St., 1812; 83 New Bond St., 1830.

Barraud, Hy., presented a spoon to C.C. 1636; see Beraud. **Francis & Paul Jno.**, Wine Office Court, 1759-94; watch, h.m., 1756. **Paul Philip**, 86 Cornhill; master C.C. 1810, 1811; 1796-1813. **Fredk. Joseph**, Committee of C.C. 1813. **& Sons**, 85 Cornhill, 1813-36; 41 Cornhill, 1838. **& Lund**, 41 Cornhill, 1838-42.

Barret, —. In the churchwardens' book at Halifax Parish Church in 1720 is "Paid Wm. Barret for Clock work £0. 9s. 0d."

Barrett. **Simon**, apprenticed 1668 to Joseph Wells; C.C. 1678. **Robert**, C.C. 1687. **Thos.**, Lewes; known as a maker of lantern clocks; in 1690 he agreed to mend the town clock for twenty shillings, "Also hee to have four pounds yearley for ringing 'Gabriel' the Curfew Bell at four in the morning and eight at night." **Henry**, apprenticed to Chas. Gretton; admitted C.C. 1692. **Samuel**, C.C. 1701. **Thomas**, C.C. 1702. **Joseph**, Cheapside, 1738; clock-watch 4½ in. in diameter,

pair of metal gilt cases, the inner one pierced, the outer chased, about 1760, inscribed "Barrett, London." **William**, 50 Aldersgate St., 1783. **Henry William**, 24 Queen St., Bloomsbury, 1815; 25 Museum St., 1820; 18 Plumtree St., 1835-42. **John**, 47 New Compton St., 1820.

Barridge, Jno., apprenticed 1654 to Hugh Cooper, C.C.

Barrington, Vrian, apprenticed 1677 to Nat. Delander; C.C. 1684.

Barrister, Jas., 33 Fetter Lane, 1815-17.

Barron, —, London; watch, 1830.

Barrow. **Nathaniel**, apprenticed to Job Betts 1653; C.C. 1660, master 1689; in the Guildhall Museum are an astronomical watch and a repeater by him (see p. 242); "A large silver chain watch, having two motions, the hour of the day, and the day of the month, with a black case studded with silver, lined with red sattin, and a silver chain to it, made by *Nathaniel Barrow, in London*" (*Lond. Gaz.*, July 26-30, 1677). **John**, apprenticed 1671 to Francis Ireland; C.C. 1681, master 1714. **Samuel**, apprenticed to Jno. Barrow 1688; C.C. 1696; "at the Spring Clock in East Smithfield, near Hermitage Bridge," see Gatewood; 8-day long marqueterie case clock, "Samuel Barrow at the Hermitage," about 1705. **James**, see Brown, Andrew. **William**, admitted C.C. 1709; Hatton, 1773, highly esteems the work of a watchmaker named Barrow. **Wm.**, Lancashire; came to London before 1744; left London soon after 1746 (Ludlam).

Barry, Walter, Still Yard, Tower, 1788-94.

Bartholomew. **Jno.**, C.C. 1675. **Josiah**, 25 Red Lion St., Clerkenwell; watch, B.M. He was a witness before the select committee of the House of Commons to inquire into the causes of the depressed state of the watch trade in 1817; 1800-42.

Barthop, —, Isleworth; long-case clock, about 1780.

Bartlett. **Edward**, London; watch, 1818. **H. & G.**, watch-case makers, 3 King Sq., 1830-35. **Patten Sargent**, born 1834, died 1902; entered the employ of the watch company at Waltham, Mass., in 1855, where he designed several watch movements; was connected in 1864 with the inception of the National Watch Company, Chicago, afterwards the Elgin National Watch Company.

Bartlitt. **Geo.**, f., York, 1801; Malton, 1810. **Robt.**, Malton, 1823.

Barton. **Samuel**, brother C.C. 1641. **Jas.**, Prescott, about 1750. **Thomas**, Cheapside, 1750-78; Earnshaw challenged him to a contest of work in 1776. **Jos.**, Eccleston; long-case clock, about 1760. **T. & J.**, Market St. Lane, Manchester; watch, h.m., 1770. **John**, 64 Red Lion St., Clerkenwell, 1780-83. **Wm.**, London; large watch with Turkish numerals, Captain H. D. Terry, on dial "Markwick Markham, Wm. Carpenter," about 1780. **Thos.**, 7 Bermondsey Sq., 1799-1823; Thos. Mudge, jun., refers to Thos. Barton as "eminently skilled." **James**, 194 Strand, 1819-23.

Bartram. **Simon**, petitioner for incorporation of C.C. and one of the first assistants, master 1646 (p. 136). **William**, C.C. 1684. **& Austin**, 109, 103 Oxford St.; card B.M. 1808.

Bartrand, see Bertrand.

Barugh, William, C.C. 1715.

Barwick. **A.**, Great Alie St., 1788-93. **H. & B.**, 35 Wapping, 1794-96.

Barwise. **Nathanael**, London; clock-watch, 1710. **Lott**, Cockermouth, 1770. **John**, 29 St Martin's Lane, 1790; Weston & Jno., 1820-42; in 1841 John Barwise was associated with Alex. Bain in a patent for electric clocks, and in 1842-43 chairman of directors of the ill-fated British Watch Company. **& Sons**, 24 St Martin's Lane, 1819-23.

Basil, John, 76 St Paul's Churchyard, 1768.

Baskerville. **Thos.**, Bond St. Stables, 1730. **Richard**, London; clock in the sacristy of Bruges Cathedral, about 1750.

Bass, George, admitted C.C. 1722.

Bassereau, Gui., Palais Royale, Paris, 1780.

Basset. **Thos.**, apprenticed 1668 to Isaac Webb, C.C. **Jean, Jacques, Louis**, York, f., 1771. **Chas.**, 58 Upper East Smithfield, 1788-93; clock, Wm. Bassett, Mayfield, about 1790; Mr E. B. Faithfull. **Geo. Francis**, Philadelphia, 1797.

Bassold, Edwd., 55 King Sq., 1855 (afterwards Money & Bassold).

Bateman. —, seventeenth century oval watch belonging to the Rev. Chas. Beck, mentioned in vol. xxiii., *Archæological Journal*. Nathaniel Bateman said to have worked for Delander in 1730. **Nathaniel**, apprenticed to Nathaniel Delander; C.C. 1747. **Hy.**, 10 Bunhill Row, 1780-85. **P. & A.**, 10 Bunhill Row, 1798-1818. **H.**, Dublin, 1802-5. **Andrew**, 5 Great Tower St., 1804-20. **Teresa**, 5 Great Tower St., 1820-30. **Wm.**, 108 Bunhill Row, 1828-32.

Bates. **Thomas**, C.C. 1684. **Joseph**, White Alley, Holborn; admitted C.C. 1687. **T. P.**, Liverpool, 1780; issued a token "works, Duke St., Retail, Exchange St." **Ed.**, London; a good workman mentioned by Earnshaw, 1780-90. **John**, watch pinion maker, 40 Great Sutton St., 1820. **& Lowe**, London; clock, about 1835.

Bath. **Thomas**, 4 Cripplegate, 1740. **Jas.**, Cirencester; clock, about 1775.

Batten. **John**, brother C.C. 1668. **Edwd.**, apprenticed 1670 to Jno. Mark; C.C. 1677.

Battersbee, —, Manchester, 1770.

Batterson. **Robert**, C.C. 1693. **Henry**, C.C. 1701. **Jos.**, freeman of New York, 1708. **James**, New York, f., 1708-9; also at Boston, "lately arrived from London." **R.**, clock, long-case, lacquer decoration, about 1770.

Battie, Jas., Sheffield, 1770.

Battin, Thomas, apprenticed 1654 to Ed. Ward; C.C. 1661; a contrate second wheel of a "dyal" taken from him, and judged by C.C. to be bad, 1658.

Batting, —, Camomile St., 1842.

Battinson, Jno., Burnley, 1818.

Batty. **Anthony**, Wakefield, 1750. **Jno.**, Halifax; long-case clock, 1760. **Joseph**, Halifax, 1760-70. **Jno.**, Wakefield, 1770. **Jno.**, Moorfields, 1775. **Edwd.**, Lancaster, 1826; f.

Baudit, Peter, 4 St Martin's Lane, 1790-94.

Bauer, Carl, Amsterdam; cruciform watch, about 1650.

Baufay, B., & Son, 3 Bridgewater Sq., 1790-94.

Baugh, Valentine, Abingdon, U.S.A., 1820-30.

Baugham, John, Bridgewater Sq., about 1745.

Bauldwin, see Baldwin.

Baume & Lezard, Paris; clock, about 1830.

Baumgart, Charles, 37 Dean St., Soho,

1840-42, afterwards in Maddox St.

Baute & Moynier, Geneva ; watch, about 1823, dial gold *à quatre couleurs*, numerals of pearls, case with pearl decoration, Mr H. K. Heinz.

Bautte, J. F., Geneva, 1820-25 ; splendid watch by him, decorated with enamel, belonging to Dr Pasteur.

Bavis, Geo., C.C. 1687.

Bawdyson, Allaine, clockmaker to Edward VI., 1550.

Baxter. Wm., C.C. about 1640. **Charles**, C.C. 1681. **Matt.**, St Neots ; watch, 1723. **Pointer**, London, 1772. **Wm.**, London ; watch, 1790. **John**, watch-case maker, St Luke's, 1835. **Thos.** (Grimshaw & Baxter), 35 Goswell Rd. ; died 1897, aged 54.

Bayes. John, brother C.C. 1647, warden 1658 ; maker of a watch given by Charles I. to Mr Worsley on his removal to Hirst Castle, November 1647 ; another example, a lantern clock, inscribed "Johannes Bayes, Londini," date on fret 1643 ; watch, S.K.M. (see p. **141**). **Benjamin**, apprenticed to Jno. Bayes 1661 ; C.C. 1675.

Bayford, George, Upper Shadwell.

Bayle, Thomas, C.C. 1703.

Bayles, Chas., London ; bracket clock, about 1760.

Bayley. William, apprenticed 1654 to Ralph Ash ; C.C. 1663. **Edward**, C.C. 1658. " A silver watch with a silver studded case engraven Edwardus Bayley, London " (*Lond. Gaz.*, December 19-22, 1687). **Jno.**, Harrow, 1725. **Geo.**, London ; watch, 1750. **& Street**, Bridgwater ; long-case clock, Col. J. B. Keene, about 1750. **S.**, London ; watch, 1765. **John**, 106 Wood St., 1768-75. **Richard**, Ashford ; watch, 1780. **Thomas**, summoned to take up livery C.C. 1786. **& Upjohn**, Red Lion St., Clerkenwell, 1794. **Simeon C.**, Philadelphia, 1794. **Barnard, & Son**, 3 Bridgewater Sq., 1800-5. **Richard**, 12 Red Lion St., Clerkenwell, 1807.

Baylie, see Bailey.

Baylis, J., Tewkesbury ; lantern clock, about 1700.

Bayly. John, C.C. 1700. **Richard**, Ashford ; watch, 1770.

Bayne, Wm., Alston, 1833.

Bayse, Thomas, C.C. 1695.

Bazeley, Nathaniel, C.C. 1694.

Bazin, Paris, about 1700.

Beach, Thomas, Maiden Lane, Covent Garden, 1765-70.

Beadle, Wm., apprenticed 1667 to Wm. Raynes, C.C.

Beake, Jonathan, Savage Gardens, 1725.

Beal, Martin, 19 Gerrard St., Soho, 1842.

Beale. Jno., apprenticed 1658 to Nich. Coxeter, C.C. **Robert**, apprenticed 1677 to Bernard Rainsford, C.C. **Chas.**, London ; watch, 1767. **Wm.**, London ; watch, 1805. **Jas.**, 38 Regent St., 1820-25.

Beard. Wm., apprenticed 1667 to Jas. Ellis, C.C. **Chris.**, apprenticed to Jas. Atkinson 1670 ; C.C. **Duncan**, Appoquine-monk, U.S.A., 1755-97. **Wm.**, Drury Lane, 1812-17.

Beasley. Thos., C.C. 1683. **Nat.**, apprenticed 1686 to Hy. Hammond, C.C. **John**, C.C. 1719.

Beaton. Andrew, 22 Cannon Street Rd., St George's East, 1835. **& Campbell**, 110 High St., Whitechapel, 1840.

"**Beatson**, 32 Cornhill " ; M'Cabe's lowest grade full-plate watches, in silver cases, were so engraved.

Beauchamp, R., 147 Holborn Hill, 1819-23.

Beaumarchais, see Caron.

Beaumont. —, said to have made a clock at Caen in 1314 (see p. **43**). **Philip**, apprenticed 1689 to Wither Cheney, C.C.

Beauvais. Anthoine, Paris, 1544 (see p. **385**). **Simon**, admitted C.C. 1690 ; a celebrated maker ; among his productions is a double-case verge, with a rack and pinion motion work, the hour hand travelling round the dial in twelve hours, but the minute hand travelling only from IX. to III., in one hour, and, when arrived at the III., jumping back to the IX. The hand-setting is between III. and IIII., and the centre of the dial and motion work are hidden by a small painting on ivory. There is in the B.M. a similar watch of a later period by a German maker ; 1690-1730. **Paul**, London ; watch, about 1730.

Beavin, Hugh, 34 Marylebone St., Golden Sq., 1800-30.

Beavis, John, Peartree St., 1789.

Beck. Richard, "near ye French Church," C.C. 1653. **Nicholas**, apprenticed 1660 to Thos. Webb ; C.C. 1669. **Joseph**, C.C. 1701. **Christopher**, Bell Alley ; apprenticed to Francis Perigal ; admitted C.C. 1761, livery 1787. **James**, 5 Sweeting's Alley, Cornhill, 1815-23, see Bentley.

Becke, John, apprenticed to John White, but served Daniel Quare ; C.C. 1681.

Becket, Francis, Chester-le-Street, 1770.

Beckett. M., long-case clock, Mr T. F. Walker, about 1710. **Jno.**, 23 Greenhill's Rents, Smithfield, 1796-1803. **Sir E.**, see Denison.

Beckitt, Thos., Durham, 1770. **Mann**, Durham, 1780.

Beckman. Daniel, C.C. 1680. " A watch with a double case of Silver, with Minutes, Seconds and Hours, the name [Beckman] under the Crystal " (*Lond. Gaz.*, March 27-31, 1701). **John**, C.C. 1695. **Daniel**, C.C. 1726.

Beckford, Wm., London ; watch, about 1780.

Beckner, Abraham, Pope's Head Alley ; admitted as a brother C.C. 1652, warden and died 1665 ; known as a maker of oval watches ; 1650-65.

Beckwith, Wm., Rotherhithe St., 1794.

Beddel, see Biddle.

Bedell, Peter, Hull, 1822.

Bedford, Helkiah, in Fleet St. ; C.C. 1667 ; maker of lantern clocks ; to him in 1668 was apprenticed Richard Abbott. **Sam.**, apprenticed 1691 to Joseph Windmills, C.C. **Wm.**, London ; watch, Nelthropp collection, about 1790.

Beefield, —, London ; watch, 1760.

Beeforth, Jno., York, f., 1680.

Beeg, Christiana, C.C. 1698.

Beesley. Jno., Dean St., 1725. **Jas.**, Manchester ; long-case clock, about 1760 ; watch, 1770.

Begulay, Jno., Swanton, Norfolk ; church clock at Ludham, 1676.

Belk, William, Philadelphia, 1796.

Bell. Benjamin, apprenticed to Thos. Claxton 1649 ; C.C. 1660, master 1682 ; maker of a large verge watch weighing over 8 oz. 1660-83. " Taken way by 4 Highwaymen in Maiden-head Ticket, A plain silver chain watch made by Benjamin Bell, the case lined with Red Satten, on the back of the case a Perpetual Almanack and little spikes placed at every Hour " (*Lond. Gaz.*, July 7-10, 1690). **John**, New York, 1734.

" Lost on the 2nd inst., a gold watch

with one motion, having a gold chain and a steel hook ; made by Benjamin Bell. Whoever brings it to Mr Sweetapple, a Goldsmith in Lombard Street, shall have 2 guineas reward " (*Lond. Gaz.*, May 4-7, 1691).

" Lost a silver watch with a black case studded with Silver, made by Benjamin Bell, with an Onyx Stone in a gold Ring tied to the watch in which is engraven the Head of King Charles the First. Whoever brings the said watch and seal to Mr William Penrice, at the Black-Boy in Gracechurch Street, shall have 2 guineas reward " (*Lond. Gaz.*, December 3-7, 1691).

Bell. Joseph, C.C. 1691. **Thos.**, apprenticed 1691 to Sam. Mather, C.C. **John**, C.C. 1719 ; 30-hour long-case clock, " fecit 1751," Mr C. Atkinson. **Jno.**, New York, 1734. **Wm.**, Sunderland, 1740. **Joseph**, Shoe Lane, 1759. **Jno.**, Garstang, 1760. **Peter**, Garstang, 1770. **Jno.**, Doncaster, 1780. **James**, watch, h.m., 1792 ; 131 Mount St., Berkeley Sq., 1842. **Thos.**, London ; long-case clock, about 1800. **Wm.**, 2 Clement's Lane, 1812-18. **Jno.**, Leyburn, 1822. **John**, musical clock maker, 8 Elm St., Gray's Inn Lane, 1835-40. **Henry**, Mount St., 1850 (see p. **339**). **William**, Lancaster, apprenticed to his uncle William Hodgson, died 1910, aged 80. **John**, New York, 1734.

Bellamy, Adey, 10 Poultry, 1779-85.

Bellard. John, C.C. 1674. **François**, Paris ; horloger du Roy 1783.

Belle, T., French clock, about 1780.

Bellefontaine, A., 59 Brewer St., Summers Town, 1835.

Belliard, Chas., Pall Mall, 1769-94.

Bellin, see Mott & Bellin.

Belling, John, Bodmin, 1780, 1840.

Bellinge, Jas., Liverpool, 1770.

Bellinger. Richd., apprenticed 1676 to Edwd. East ; C.C. 1686. **Ch.**, apprenticed 1686 to Jno. Bellinger, C.C. **John**, C.C. 1725.

Bellinghurst, Henry, Aldersgate St. ; liveryman C.C. 1776 ; 1765-77.

Bellis, Jas., 9 Pall Mall, 1769-88.

Bellman, Daniel, Broughton, Lancs., 1818.

Bellune, Peter, 1630-50 ; C.C.

Belon, Pierre, Paris ; clockmaker to the dowager Queen 1649.

Belsey, John, Poland St., 1835.

Belson, Thos., 1630-50 ; C.C.

Benard, F., Paris ; oval watch with sun-dial inside cover, about 1600 (sun-dial signed " Chauvin ") ; Pierpont Morgan collection.

Benbrick, Jas., apprenticed 1671 to Helkiah Bedford, C.C.

Benbridge, Thos., apprenticed to Robt. Starr 1669 ; C.C. 1683.

Benfey, B., & Son, 3 Bridgewater Sq., 1794.

Benford, John, 1 Garnault Place, Clerkenwell, 1832-38.

Benjamin. Joel, 12 Bury St., St Mary Axe, 1820-35 ; J. Benjamin & Co., 1840. **M.**, Berner St., Commercial Rd., 1820 ; 77 Leman St., 1840-42. **A.**, Myrtle St., Hoxton, 1835.

Benn. Thos., apprenticed 1660 to Ben. Hill, C.C. **Jno.**, C.C., 1678. **Robert**, Fleet St. ; C.C. 1716. **Anthony**, 1750 ; died when master C.C. 1763.

Benner, Johannes, " Aug " ; table clock, about 1680.

Bennett. William, C.C., 1607. **Thomas**, apprenticed 1667 to Henry Harper ; movement of his condemned by C.C. 1677.

John, Fleet St. ; C.C. 1678. **Mansell,** Dial and 3 Crowns, Charing Cross ; C.C. 1685-99 ; fine marqueterie long-case clock, S.K.M., about 1695 ; Mr Robert Meldrum has a very similar specimen. **John,** Bristol ; C.C. 1712. **Richard,** C.C. 1715. **Samuel,** C.C. 1716. **Thomas,** apprenticed to Thos. Windmills ; C.C. 1720 ; fine long-case clock in the Wetherfield collection, on the inside of the door directions for winding, and at the foot thereof "Thos. Bennett, at the Dial in Exchange Alley, 1722." **William,** New St. Hill ; C.C. 1729. **J.,** Bugg Lane, Norwich, watch, 1786. **Thos.,** Norwich ; watch, 1795. **R.,** 159 Fleet St., 1817. **Joseph,** 60 Red Lion St., Holborn, 1830-38. **Wing, & Co.,** 60 Red Lion St., Holborn, 1840 ; "to H.R.H. the Duke of Sussex" ; watch paper C.C. **E.,** Stockwell St., Greenwich, 1840. **John,** 45 Seymour Place, 1842. **John,** did a large business in Cheapside ; Sheriff of London in 1872, when by virtue of his office he was knighted in commemoration of a Royal visit to the City ; died 1897, aged 81.

Benoit. J. E., watch, apparently English, about 1780. **A. H.,** Versailles ; born 1804, died 1895 ; many fine watches, signed " A. Benoit à Paris."

Bensley, J., maker of a watch for the Duke of Sussex, 1790-1820.

Benson. Jno., apprenticed 1652 to Jas. Starnell ; C.C. 1669 ; long-case clock dated 1709. **Samuel,** C.C. 1700 ; watch, 1730. **—,** Whitehaven ; long-case clock, about 1760. **& Higgs,** London ; bracket chiming clock, Sheraton case with lion-head handles, about 1790. **William,** watch and clock spring maker, 60 St John's St., 1818-23. **Robt.,** 16 Wilderness Row, 1818-40 ; auditor Watch and Clockmakers' Pension Society 1820.

Bent, Wm., Chadwell St., 1840-42.

Bentele (?Bentley), **Jacobus,** clock, Imperial collection, Vienna, 1735.

Bentley. John, Thirsk, 1770. **Sam.,** Kingsbridge ; watch, 1790. **& Beck,** 1815 (see p. 339). **John,** 5 Pope's Head Alley, 1820 ; Sweeting's Alley, 1823 ; "foreman to Jas. McCabe," watch paper C.C.

Benton, Wm., London ; watch, h.m., 1825.

Benwell, B., London ; watch, 1785.

Berain, J., Paris ; designer and chaser of clock cases, 1655-1711.

Berard, —, London ; watch, about 1730.

Beraud. Henri, Sedan, 1565. **—,** oval watch, about 1600, signed "A. Beraud à Bloys," Garnier collection. **Jas.,** 1632. **Hy.,** maker of a watch in the form of a shell, silver case enamelled, crystal over dial, about 1650 ; C.C., but date of election uncertain.

Berault, Jno., apprenticed 1691 to Thos. Jones, C.C.

Beresford, Thos., London ; watch, 1828.

Berg, F. L., Augsburg ; table clock, Nelthropp collection. 1719.

Bergier, S., Grenoble ; watch, Marfels collection, about 1550.

Bergstien, Lulam, 113 Great Titchfield St., 1840-42.

Berguer. John, 44 Great Russell St., Bloomsbury, 1810-20. **Frederick,** 201 High Holborn, 1810 ; 135 High Holborn, 1818-20. **Franz,** 17 Vere St., 1817. **Charles,** musical clock maker, 13 Richmond Buildings, Soho, 1825.

Berkenhead, John, 31 Gutter Lane, 1783-94.

Berkley, —, London ; watch, 1810.

Berlinson, Hy., Ripon, 1833.

Berman. J., & Co., wooden clock makers, 40 Norton Folgate, 1830-35. **& Co.,** 30 Park Terrace, Regent's Park Rd., 1830-42.

Bernard. Nicholas, Paris ; watch in case of rock crystal, primitive movement, balance-cock pinned on, about 1590, Pierpont Morgan collection ; two watches, bearing the same name, S.K.M., one about 1660 and the other about 1690. **E.,** Southampton ; clock about 1770.

Berninck, Jan, Amsterdam ; watch, B.M., a French enamelled inner case by G. Bouvier, outer *repoussé* case by H. Manley, about 1750.

Bernstein, H., Glasgow, 1830.

Berquez, Francis, 17 Vere St., 1822 ; 6 Thayer St., Manchester Sq., 1825-35.

Berquin, Urbain, Paris ; clock, 1680.

Berraud, see Barraud, also Beraud.

Berres, T., London ; watch, h.m., 1793.

Berridge. Jno., made a clock with compensated pendulum in 1738 to the order of Mr Fotheringham, a Quaker of Lincolnshire. **Wm.,** 69 Oxford Rd., 1770-94 (see p. 368). **Robert,** 2 John St., Oxford St., 1790-95. **William,** 4 Holles St., Cavendish Sq., 1800-20, see Bowra.

Berrington. Uriah, apprenticed to Nathaniel Delander ; C.C. 1684. **—,** Bolton ; watch, 1808. **Jas.,** St Helens, Lancs., 1818.

Berrisford, Edwd., apprenticed 1663 to Ben. Wolverstone, C.C.

Berrollas, Joseph Anthony, Denmark St., St Giles-in-the-Fields, 1800 ; Coppice Row, Clerkenwell, 1810 ; afterwards 51 Wellington St., Goswell Rd. ; an ingenious watchmaker. In 1808 he patented a repeater somewhat similar to Elliott's (p. 412). in 1810 a warning watch, in 1827 an alarm watch, also pumping keyless work (p. 410); 1800-30.

Berry. John, St Clement's Lane ; apprenticed 1674 to Richd. Pepys ; C.C. 1688, master 1723 ; maker of a long-case clock at Merchant Taylors' Hall, arch dial, brass figures holding trumpets on top of case ; 1688-1730. "Lost Nov. 14th, 1705, from a Gentlewoman's side between Honey Lane market and Great Eastcheap, A plain Gold Watch case. Whoever brings it to John Berry, watchmaker at the Dial in Clement's Lane, Lombard St., shall have 20s. reward for so doing" (*The Daily Courant,* 15th Nov. 1705). **Francis,** Hitchin ; lantern clocks, about 1700. **Samuel,** C.C. 1705. **John,** St Clement's Lane ; C.C. 1728. **Jas.,** Pontefract ; about 1740. **Jno.,** Manchester ; 1760. **Wm.,** London ; watch, 1815. **Frederick,** 2 Arcade, Hungerford Market, 1842.

Berthoud. Ferdinand, born in Switzerland 1727 ; went to Paris when nineteen and settled there ; died 1807 ; an eminent watchmaker, author of "Essai sur l'Horlogerie," "Traité des Horloges Marines," "Histoire de la Mesure du Temps," and other works containing a mass of useful information concerning the history, theory, and practice of the horological art, dealing with Harrison's, Sully's, and Le Roy's inventions, and, indeed, everything known in Berthoud's time (see p. 319). There are three clocks by him in the Wallace collection, one a splendid regulator in case of ebony with boldly chased mounts of gilt bronze ; around the dial is a serpent with the head and tail meeting —an emblem of eternity. This clock is said to have been taken from the Tuileries in 1793, having been whitewashed to hide its value. It and a commode were sold in Paris some

years ago to the Marquis of Hertford for 100,000 francs. **Louis,** Paris ; nephew of Ferdinand ; died 1813 ; watch, "Berthoud Freres à Paris," about 1800 ; Mr Evan Roberts.

Bertram, William, died in 1732, when master C.C.

Bertrand. Josephe, Paris (garde visiteur), 1769. **Robert,** 2 Stewart St., Spitalfields, 1790-94 ; Mr A. E. Owen has a long-case clock signed "Robert Bartrand, London," dating from about 1770. **L.,** Paris, 1810.

Berwick, Abner, Berwick, U.S.A., 1820.

Besse, Jeremy, 4 Richmond Buildings, Soho Sq., 1840-42.

Best. Robert, 5 White Lion Court, Birchin Lane ; a watch by him, S.K.M., hall mark 1769 ; 1765-88. **Thos.,** 3 Red Lion St., Clerkenwell ; between 1770 and 1794 he made a large number of watches for the Dutch market ; also known as a maker of musical clocks and watches. **T.,** at the Dial in Lewes ; card, B.M., 1780. **Thos.,** Newcastle ; watch, 1785. **Robert** (formerly foreman to Brockbank), 4 White Lion Court, Birchin Lane, 1790 ; 4 Sweeting's Alley, 1798 ; 1 Windsor Place, St Paul's, 1810-20. He attested the value of Earnshaw's improvements in 1804. **Richard,** 3 Fountain Court, Strand, 1830-42.

Bestwick. In 1672 Jas. Dearmar was apprenticed to Katherine Bestwick, widow, C.C. **Henry,** C.C. 1686.

Bethell. R., London ; watch, 1760. **Jno.,** Stowmarket ; clock, about 1800.

Beton, Jno., London ; watch, 1800.

Betson, J., London ; watch, 1797.

Betterton, —, London ; watch, about 1780.

Bettinson, Solomon, Newark, 1776-92.

Betts. Samuel, back of Exchange ; short train watch by him, about 1645 (see p. 218). He was an early member of the C.C., and in 1656 attested the genuineness of Jas. Lello's masterpiece. In the Wetherfield collection is a 30-hour bracket clock by him ; died before 1675 (see Marquet). "Lost on the 8th Inst. betwixt Enfield and Wormley, on the rode to Warre, a gold watch with a case and chain of gold, the Chrystall out, and the case lined with Pink-coloured Sattin, made by Mr Betts in Lumbard Street. Whoever shall discover and return or cause it to be returned to Mr Austin, Goldsmith at the Starre in Fenchurch St., shall have 40s. for his peynes" (*The Intelligencer,* 13th June 1664). **Job,** C.C. 1656. "Stolen from Cheyne Rowe, of Walthamstowe, in Essex, Esq., a gold watch with a gold chain made by Job Betts, with a silver Drinking Cup and other Plate. Whoever brings the said watch and chain or the watch only to Mr Johnson, Jeweller, at the 3 Flower-de-Luces in Cheapside, shall have 20s. reward, and charges, or if pawned or sold their money again with content" (*Lond. Gaz.,* August 11-15, 1692). **Samuel,** apprenticed to Samuel Davis for Job Betts 1675 ; C.C. 1682 ; calendar watch with revolving ring dials, to which a figure of Time points, in Dover Museum. In the G.M. is another specimen of his work : bracket clock, square dial, walnut case, Wetherfield collection, 1682-1700.

Bettwood, Jno., Rywick ; watch, 1725.

Beverley, Jas., apprenticed 1683 to Robt. Doore. ; C.C. ; bracket clock, about 1695 ; watch pendulum balance, about 1700, inscribed "Ja. Beverly, London."

Bevington, J., Bolton, Lancs., 1814.
Bewley, —, Whitecross St.; C.C. 1780.
Bezant, A. W., Hereford; watch, 1840.
Bezar, Stephen, brother C.C. 1648.
Bibberton, Thos., Silver St., 1774.
Bibley, Jno., Corporation Row, 1790-94.
Bickerstaff, Wm., Liverpool, 1770.
Bickerton, Benjamin, 14 Jewin St., 1795-1810. T. W., 14 Jewin St., 1816-20.
Bickley, Thomas, 195 Ratcliff Highway, 1790-94.
Bicknell. Francis, apprenticed to Job Betts 1653; C.C. 1665. Joseph, & Co., 119 New Bond St., 1807-13.
Bickton, Geo., London; watch, 1775.
Bidard, —, watch mentioned by Thiout, about 1730.
Bidault, Paris (see p. 386); a long succession of court clockmakers: Claude, 1628, he lodged at the Louvre 1642; Henri Auguste, succeeded his father at the Louvre 1652; Augustin François, 1693.
Biddle, Joseph, C.C. 1684.
Bidlake, Thomas, 31 Minories, 1765-94. James, 16 Sun St., 1798-1804; livery C.C. 1816; 48 Chiswell St., 1816-20. Thomas, 16 Sun St., Bishopsgate St., 1804-18; livery C.C. 1818. James, & Son, 48 Chiswell St., Finsbury, 1820-45.
Bidles, Thomas, London; maker of bracket clocks, about 1760.
Bidley, Wm., 24 Rahere St., Clerkenwell, 1840-42.
Biefield, Chas., London; watch, 1780.
Bieler à Bienne, calendar watch, about 1790.
Bigaud, Paris, about 1750.
Bigg, Ben., apprenticed 1678 to Robt. Cooke, C.C.
Biggs, Roger, 5 Crescent, Jewin St., 1800.
Bilbee, —, London; long-case 30-hour clock, one hand, about 1710.
Bilbie. A well-known Somerset family of clockmakers. The Hon. H. Hannen has a lantern clock by Thomas Bilbie dating from about 1660; the fret in front shows the royal arms, and the side frets are of the dolphin pattern. Among other specimens are a long-case clock by Edward Bilbie, Chewstoke, about 1700; one of later date by Thos. Bilbie, Chewstoke; an 8-day long-case clock by William Bilbie, of the same place.
The following is from an upright gravestone at Oxbridge:

"Bilbie, thy
Movements kept in play
For thirty years or more,
We say,
"Thy Balance or thy
Mainspring's broken,
And all thy movements
Cease to work.
" John Bilbie, of this parish, clockmaker, who died Sept. 13, 1767, aged 33 years."

Bilcliff (or Bycliff), York. Jno., f., 1617. Robt., f., 1627. Jno., f., 1639. Robt., f., 1653.
Bilger, Matthias, watch-spring maker, 4 New St., Covent Garden, 1790-94.
Billie, John, C.C. seized watches and movements by him 1687.
Billing, H. C. Cheapside, 1835.
Billinger, Jno., C.C. 1637.
Billinghurst. Wm., apprenticed to Thos. Fenn 1668; C.C. Anthony, apprenticed to Helkiah Bedford 1673; C.C. Wm., apprenticed 1694 to Sam Watson, C.C. Henry, 67 Aldersgate St.; livery C.C. 1766; 1760-71.
Billings, Jno., Bishopsgate, 1775.
Billington, —, Harborough, 1760.

Billon & Co., Philadelphia, 1797.
Billop, William, C.C. 1688.
Bindley, —, apprenticed 1674 to Rich. Pierce, C.C. William, 24 Rahere St., 1842.
Bingham. Thos., watch-chain maker, 3 Middle Row, Holborn, 1769-81. Wm., 27 Bucklersbury, 1842. & Bricerly, Philadelphia, 1778-99.
Bingley, Giles, apprenticed 1692 to Edwd. Eyston, C.C. John Bingley, watchmaker, advertised for in Lond. Gaz., 1st June, 1696.
Bings, Edward. "Whereas there was stolen from the House of Mr Thos. Dummer in Wellclose on Saturday night, between the hours of 9 and 11 o'clock, a Gold Pendulum Watch with a chain made by Mr Edward Bings. You are desired to stop them and give notice to Mr Thos. Beach, Goldsmith, at the Black-a-Moors Head in Cheapside, and you shall have 2 guineas Reward" (Daily Courant, 23rd Sept. 1706).
Binks. Thos., Birmingham, 1740. —, London; watch, G.M., about 1820.
Binley, J. W., Ironmonger Row, Old St., 1790.
Binns. —, Halifax; clock 1720. George, 137 Strand, 1832-38.
Birch. Thomas, apprenticed to Thos. Mills 1649; C.C. 1658; Mr John H. Baker has a lantern clock inscribed "Thomas Birch in the longe walke Neere Christ Church Londini fecit." Thos., apprenticed 1675 to Sam Clyatt; C.C. 1682. Richard, Bread St., Birmingham, 1776-87. William, succeeded Wm. Turner at 173 Fenchurch St., about 1840; died 1903, aged 88.
Birchall. & Son, Warrington, 1770. M., Derby, 1790. Wm., 5 St James's Walk, Clerkenwell, 1816; 5 Wellington St., 1834-42. Peter, a well-known chronometer maker. In partnership with Appleton, he succeeded Molyneux at Southampton Row; shortly after Appleton's death he disposed of the business to Wm. Cribb; lived subsequently at Islington; died 1885, aged 85.
Bird. Michael, apprenticed to Ed. Gilpin in 1648; brother C.C. 1682; bracket clock inscribed "Michael Bird, London." On a 30-hour clock, one hand, about 1650, was inscribed "Michael Bird, Oxon." Wm., apprenticed 1667 to Hy. Crump, C.C. Luke, apprenticed 1675 to Jas. Delander; C.C. 1682. Nat., C.C. 1693. Edwd., London, 1710. Thos., London; watch, h.m., 1753; 10 Salisbury St., Strand, 1816. Wm., London; watch, 1760. John, one of the examiners of Harrison's timekeeper, 1765. & Branstor, 30 Cheapside, 1775. Jacob, 7 Cornhill, 1783. Rich., watch-chain maker, Bartlett's Buildings, 1794. Samuel Joseph, watch-case maker (apprenticed to Jasper Swindells), Little Compton St.; C.C. 1813. John, & Son, 19 Bartlett's Buildings, Holborn, 1822-25. John, 11 St John's Sq., 1840-42.
Birdwhistell. Francis, C.C. 1687. Isaac, C.C. 1692; plain pair-case gold watch, small swivel bow to the inner case, larger bow on the outer one, high movement, very rich gold dial, nicely wrought square pillars, finely engraved and pierced balance cock, excellent work throughout; 1692-1705. Thomas, C.C. 1693. John, C.C. 1718.
Birge. Mallory & Co., Bristol, Conn., 1830. Peck & Co., 1830. John, Bristol, 1830-37.
Birkhead, Nicholas, removed from King's Head, Holborn, to White Hart, Knights-

bridge (Lond. Gaz., 29th May, 1st June 1693).
Birley, J., Sheffield; curious watch, one hand, "1638" on metal dial in place of name, probably made sixty or seventy years after that date.
Birney, Jno., Templepatrick, 1785.
Birt, Nathaniel, London; long-case clock, square dial, about 1710.
Bisbee, J., Brunswick, U.S.A., 1798-1825.
Bishop. Samuel, Portland St., 1769-94; hon. freeman of C.C. 1781. Thos., Wych St., 1774; watch, date on movement 1810. James Griffin, 97 Fetter Lane, 1816-24. William, 70 New Bond St., 1830.
Bisot, Jacques, Paris; clockmaker to the Duchesse d'Orleans 1681.
Bisse, English alarm clock in gilt metal case, about 1620, S.K.M., signed "Edward Bisse Fecit." The dial is provided with projecting pins for feeling the time at night. See Bysse.
Bissett, Jas. (late Gibson), 12 Sweeting's Alley, Royal Exchange, 1815-20.
Bittleston, John, 207 High Holborn, 1765-94; hon. freeman C.C. 1781. Example of his work—a very curious astronomical watch, with two elaborate enamel dials—one at the front, and one at the back—showing the hour and minute both sides, two centre seconds—one the usual long hand, the other having a small rotating enamel dial—day of the month, day of the week, the month, moon's age, the tide, and a regulator. case pinchbeck, with a border each side of fine old paste in imitation of rubies and diamonds.
Bittner, William, 26 Dean St., 1840-42.
Bixler. Christian, Easton, Pennsylvania, U.S.A.; clock, about 1750. Christian, Easton, 1785-1830; a famous 8-day clock manufacturer.
Blackborow, James, admitted C.C. 1711; died 1746, when warden.
Blackbourn, Saml., London; watch, about 1780.
Blackbourne, William, Paternoster Row, 1730.
Blackburn. William, summoned to take up livery C.C. 1786. Jno., watch-spring maker, 20 Aldersgate St., 1789-99; watch so named, 1790. Robt., Lancaster, 1817, f.
Blackhall, J., London; watch, 1800.
Blackie. Geo., Musselburgh; long-case dead-beat clock, about 1820, musical bead playing on fourteen bells added, Norman-Shaw collection. George, born in Scotland; settled in Clerkenwell as a duplex escapement maker and manufacturer; afterwards took Wilson & Gandar's shop at 431 Strand; died 1885, aged 74.
Blackmore, Jno., apprenticed 1689 to Ben. Bell, C.C.
Blacknell, Peter, London; bracket clock about 1705.
Blacksmith, Robt., London; watch, 1831.
Blackwell. Thos., C.C. 1654. J., 43 Plumber St., City Rd., 1820.
Blainville, —, Rouen; calendar watch, about 1795.
Blake. Jonathan, Fulham; watch, 1784. Wm., Whitecross St., 1789-90. Chas., 14 Bishopsgate Within, 1813.
Blakeborough, Henry, Burnley, 1818. Richard, Ripon, 1838.
Blanchard. Robt., within Temple Bar, 1675. Abraham, London; watch, 1730. Charles, London; long-case clock, about 1750; chiming quarter bracket clock, square black case, strike-silent, bronze,

handle on top, about 1760. **Wm.**, Hull, 1822.

Bland, Jas., 33 Norton Folgate, 1816-23.
Blandford, Hy. W., London ; watch, 1794.
Blay, William, 6 Princes St., Leicester Sq., 1825.
Blaylock, Jno., Carlisle, 1830-42.
Bligh, Thomas, watch-case maker, 37 Great Sutton St., 1820.
Bliss, Ambrose, C.C. 1653 ; signed a petition in 1656.
Blissett, Isaac, 70 Leadenhall St., 1823.
Block, Francis, apprenticed 1689 to Jno. Bellinger, C.C.
Blog, 129 Aldersgate St., 1825.
Bloud, Ch., à Dieppe, 1660.
Blundell. Jno., apprenticed 1678 to Geo. Nau ; C.C. **Richard**, threatened with prosecution by C.C. for exercising the art, not being admitted ; he promised to take up his freedom at the next quarter court, 1682. **William**, C.C. 1715. **Jos.**, Dublin ; bracket clock, about 1770. **Henry**, musical clock maker, 7 Red Lion St., 1830, see also Walker & Blundell. **Thos.**, Liverpool, 1833.
Blundy, Joseph, 21 St John St., Clerkenwell, 1781 ; Brookes Market, 1790.
Blunt, Morris, 1630-50 ; C.C.
Boad, Thos., apprenticed 1684 to Robt. Nemes ; C.C. 1692.
Boak, Samuel, Golden Spread Eagle, Without Aldgate, 1692.
Boardman, T., London ; watch, 1774. **Chauncey**, Bristol, Conn., 1815-38.
Bobinet. Abraham, cruciform watch in a case of crystal with a gilt and engraved cross, about 1630, probably French, Pierpont Morgan collection. **Chas.** (French), watch in circular crystal case, S.K.M., about 1650, also (Salting collection) a cruciform watch in crystal and silver case ; a circular watch by him in an agate case is in the Pierpont Morgan collection.
Bock, Johann, Frankfort ; oval calendar watch, about 1620 ; Pierpont Morgan collection ; clock, Vienna Treasury, about 1630 ; watch showing days of the month, about 1640.
Bockel, Mathys, Haarlem ; oval watch, S.K.M., 1610.
Bockels, —, Amsterdam ; in the Roskell collection was a handsome oval alarm watch by him, of large size, dating from about 1640 ; the inner case is of silver, and the outer one covered with fish skin ; on the dial is inscribed " Oliver Cromwell " ; the watch now belongs to Mr Evan Roberts.
Bockelts. Jan Janss, watch, Napier collection, 1620 (see pp. **118, 119**). —, watch, B.M., about 1640.
Bockett, Richd., London, 1712.
Bodd, Thos., London ; watch, 1715.
Boddell, Josiah, apprenticed to Daniel Delander ; admitted C.C. 1741.
Bode, William, Philadelphia, 1797.
Bodenham, Edward, apprenticed to Brounker Watts ; C.C. 1719.
Bodham, Steph., apprenticed 1680 to Ed. Enys ; C.C.
Bodily. Elizabeth, C.C. 1692. **N.**, 21 Butchers' Hall Lane, Newgate St., 1823.
Boekett, Jan Janse, Hague ; oval watch, about 1610, stolen from the Horological Institute in 1873.
Bogardus, Evarardus, New York, f., 1698.
Bohm, Marcus, Augsburg ; pendulum clock, about 1660 (see p. 98).
Boisson. Etinne, London ; watch, 1700. **M.**, London ; watch, 1745.
Boiteau, S., à L'Arcenal, Paris ; watch,

1695.
Bold. Jno., Warrington, 1770. **Wm.**, Liverpool, 1833.
Boley, Gustav, Esslingen, Wurtemberg ; noted maker of watch and clockmakers' tools ; died 1891, aged 56.
Bollard, Richard, London ; bracket clock, about 1770.
Bolt, Jno., London ; watch, 1820.
Bolton, —, Wigan, about 1760 ; Mr James Arthur has a finely made skeleton timepiece inscribed " Bolton, London," dating from about 1800.
Bompard, —, à Paris ; timepiece, G.M., about 1800.
Bonbruict à Blois, 1650.
Boncher, A., musical watch maker, 23 Frith St., Soho, 1835.
Bond. Tho., apprenticed 1685 to Wither Cheney, C.C. **G.**, London ; watch, 1800. —, Boston, U.S.A. It is claimed that in 1812, William Bond, the founder of this business, made the first marine chronometer produced wholly in the United States, and that, in default of a mainspring, he used a weight to drive it. Richard F. Bond in 1850 invented a remontoire, or spring governor, to be applied to a clock for ensuring continuous motion of an equatorial telescope.
Bone, Wm., Essex, about 1790.
Boney, Caleb, a well-known Cornish clockmaker ; died at Padstow 1827.
Bonfanti, Joseph, 305 Broadway, New York ; advertised in 1823 " German clocks, some plain with music and some with moving figures, and French clocks, some with music, and will play different tunes." All sorts of novelties could be purchased at Joseph Bonfanti's shop, and in 1824 he constantly endeavours to attract customers by verses proclaiming his wares, for example—

" Large elegant timepieces playing sweet tunes,
And cherry stones too that hold ten dozen spoons ;
And clocks that chime sweetly on nine little bells,
And boxes so neat ornamented with shells."

Bonna Frères, Geneva, 1780-1800.
Bonner. Charles, apprenticed to Nich. Cark 1650 ; C.C. 1658 ; watch, 1690, Mr Evan Roberts ; long-case marqueterie clock, Wetherfield collection, about 1710. **Jasper**, C.C. 1704. **Thos.**, Fair St., Southwark, 1790-94.
Bonnington. Wm., clock-case maker, 6 Red Lion St., Clerkenwell, 1793-99. **& Thorp**, clock-case makers, 22 Red Lion St., 1793-1816.
Bonny, —, London ; maker of a repeater centre-seconds watch for the Duke of Sussex ; 1790-1820.
Booker, Nugent, Dublin ; long-case clock, about 1750, Mr J. W. Gunnis.
Boole, Jonathan, apprenticed 1676 to Sarah Payne, C.C. **Thos.**, Reigate ; watch, 1758.
Boone, Edward, apprenticed to Robert Dent, and came by several appointments to Thos. Tompion ; admitted C.C. 1691.
Boot. Jno., long marqueterie case clock, inscribed " John Boot, Sutton, Ashfield," dating from about 1710, formerly belonging to Joseph Jefferson the distinguished actor, now owned by Mrs Thomas D. Goodell, New Haven, Conn., U.S.A. **John & William**, 1725. **John & James**, 1735 ; clock. **Jno.**, about 1740.
Booth. Josh., Manchester ; 30-hour long-case clock, about 1700. **W.**, long-case clock, about 1710. **Benj.**, Pontefract ; watch, 1738. **Jas. Bowker**, Manchester ; 1765. **Jno.**, Huddersfield, 1770. **Jno.**,

Manchester, 1775. **Ben.**, London ; watch, silver dial, red tortoiseshell case, *piqué*, inlaid landscape in silver, about 1780 ; Pierpont Morgan collection. **Jno.**, London ; watch, 1780. **Jas.**, 20 Little Tower Hill, 1788-92. **R.**, Church Hill, Woolwich, 1812-17. **Jno.**, Stalybridge, 1818. **Wm.**, Leeds, 1828.
Bor, J., Paris ; fine clock in a square brass case, minutes shown on a small circle below the hour dial, minute hand driven from fusee ; about 1590.
Bordier. Denis, watch, crystal case, about 1630 (see pp. **124, 136**). **A.**, Geneva ; watch, Schloss collection, case beautifully enamelled, about 1785 ; watch in octagonal case, " Leonard Bordier," S.K.M., 1800. **Frères**, Geneva ; 1820-30, see also Roux.
Borellas, J., 15 Spencer St., 1840.
Borelli, J., 8 Aldersgate St., 1790-95.
Borgin, Henry, Without Bishopsgate, issued a token bearing a dial and hands about 1677.
Borrel, A. P., Paris ; pupil and successor of A. Wagner ; born 1818, died 1887.
Borrell. Henry, 15 Wilderness Row, 1795-1840 ; watch in finely enamelled cases, Turkish numerals, on dial " Markwick Markham, Borrell, London," h.m. 1813 (see p. 160). **Maximilian, J.**, 19 Wilderness Row, 1830-42.
Borret, P., 5 Staining Lane, Wood St., 1805-16.
Borrett. Geo., Stowmarket ; watch, G.M., about 1750. **M. M.**, London, about 1790.
Borrough, Jno., Brampton, 1770.
Borwick, Jno., Bartholomew Hospital ; watch, 1785.
Bosch, Ulrich, C.C. 1652.
Bosen, —, Paris ; watch, 1806.
Bosley. Joseph, Leadenhall St. ; C.C. 1725 ; Clerkenwell Green, 1730. In 1755 he obtained a patent for using in watches pinions with more teeth than usual. This involved an extra wheel and pinion, and the balance wheel turned the contrary way. Also for (secondly) a slide index for watches, which has no wheel, but turns upon a brass socket and points to an arc of a circle, with the word " faster " at one end, and " slower " at the other. Patent unsuccessfully opposed by C.C. 1725-63. **Chas.**, Ratcliff Cross ; succeeded Wm. Kipling ; 1750-66 ; livery C.C. **Charles**, livery C.C. 1766. **Thos.**, London ; bracket clock, about 1780.
Bostock, Thos., Sandback, 1833.
Bottomley, Jno., Clayton, about 1750.
Bottrill, Ebenezer, Coventry, about 1740.
Botzmayr, Johann Simon, Dantzig ; clock-watch, about 1740.
Boucher, W., 4 Long Acre, 1820
Boucheret. Jacob, C.C. 1728. **Jno.**, London, 1750.
Bouchet, Jean Louis, Rue Saint Denis, Paris ; clockmaker to the King 1769.
Boudon, —, octagonal watch inscribed " J. Boudon à St Flour," about 1600 (see p. 130).
Boudry, Gustavus, 64 Frith St., Soho, 1826-42.
Boufler, see De Boufler.
Bouguet, see Bouquet.
Bouhier. Octagonal watches said to have been introduced by Bouhier à Lyon 1538.
Bouillard, Paul, " at the Eagle and Pearl in Great Suffolk St., near the Haymarket " ; card, Ponsonby collection, about 1775.
Boulanger, David, apprenticed 1691 to Wm. Bertram, C.C.

Boult. Joseph, C.C. 1709. **Michael**, Cheapside, 1738.

Boulter. **Noel**, long-case chiming clock, about 1790. **Samuel**, 12 Gloucester Place, Chelsea, 1840-42.

Boulton. **Job**, at the "Bolt and Tun," Lombard St., had a gold and a silver watch with other jewellery stolen in 1683. **Robt.**, Wigan, 1770. **T.**, watchcase maker, 49 Gray's Inn Lane, 1820. **John**, in St Oswald's Churchyard, Durham, is a headstone with the inscription :—

"To the Memory of John Boulton, Clock and Watchmaker, Durham, who ied Oct. 27th, 1821, aged 60 years.

"Ingenious artist! few thy skill surpast
In works of art, but death has beat at last.
Though conquer'd, yet thy Deeds will ever Shine,
Time can't destroy a genius large as thine."
"Monumental Inscriptions," by C. M. Carlton.

Boulu, "élève de Lepine, horloger de l'impératrice, à Paris," about 1805.

Bouquet. **David**, London ; C.C. 1632 ; died 1665 (the books of the C.C. in 1676 and for some years after refer to Dorcas Bouquet, who was probably the widow of David (see Knight, Thos., and Walkden, Thos.) ; maker of a watch in the B.M., fine case enamelled in relief and encrusted with jewels ; another and earlier example, an oval watch with covers back and front (see p. **144**) ; in the Dunn Gardner collection, was a watch in a finely enamelled case, the movement clearly signed "D. Bouguet, Londini," 1610-40. "Lost lately a steel watch, finely cut, and the work of it made by Bouquet, in a black shagreen case. Whoever hath found the same, if they bring it to Mr Michael Scrimpshire, Goldsmith, at the sign of the Golden Lyon in Fleet St., shall have 20s. reward" (*Lond. Gaz.*, Jan. 10, 1680).

"A Pocket Clock made some years since by Mr Boguett, of Black Fryars, Watchmaker, it hath two Silver Cases, the outmost plain, the other wrought ; two Brass Keys, one of the usual form, the other forked for turning the hand of the Alarum, tied to a Silver Chain ; it hath the day of the Month, Tides, age of the Moon, and some other motions ; it strikes every hour" (*Lond. Gaz.*, March 3-7, 1689).

"Lost the 15 instant, between Rosse and Linton in Herefordshire, a watch with an alarum in a Silver Case, with a Silver Chain, the case lined with Crimson Satten, being an old piece ; the name of the maker being exprest thus : *Daniel Bouquet, Londres*" (*Lond. Gaz.*, June 19-22, 1696). **Solomon**, C.C. 1650 ; a celebraied maker 1650-70. **Solomon**, C.C. 1683 ; in the B.M. is a watch of his with highly engraved gold cases, 1680-1700. **N.**, calendar watch, Schloss collection, about 1700.

Bouquett, **David**, apprenticed 1662 to Solomon Bouquett, C.C. ; watch made for a member of the family of Sir Hugh Brown of Newington Butts is in the Fitzwilliam Museum, Cambridge.

Bourchier, **W.**, 13 Broad St., Long Acre, 1835.

Bourdon, **Pierre**, master engraver of Paris ; did much to advance the art of engraving as applied to clocks and watches. He published an essay on the subject in 1703.

Bourelier, **John Francis**, Arundel St., Strand, 1769-83.

Bourghell, **J.**, New York, 1786.

Bourne, **Aaron**, Maiden Lane, Covent Garden, 1769.

Bourrit, **Daniel**, Geneva ; watch, 1775.

Boursault. **Helie**, Chatellerault, about 1680. **J.**, Paris ; watch, about 1690.

Boutell. **Sam.**, London ; watch, about 1690.

Boutevile & Norton, 175 Aldersgate St., 1810-19. **Wm. Hy.**, 1823.

Bouts, **David**, last representative of Parkinson and Bouts, Gracechurch St. ; died 1883, aged 61.

Bouvet, **Geo.**, Coleman St., 1730.

Bouvier. **G.**, a well-known French painter of watch cases in enamel, about 1740 (see p.**150**). **Jacques**, watch, about 1770. **Frères**, watch with performing automata (Swiss), 1780.

Boverick, —, "To be seen at Mr Boverick's, Watchmaker, at the dial, facing Old Round Court, near the New Exchange, in the Strand, at one shilling each person, the furniture of a dining-room in a cherry-stone, a landau with horses complete, so minute as to be drawn along by a flea ; 4-wheeled open chaise weighing one grain, so small, drawn by flea also ; a flea chained, 200 links, padlock and key all weighing one-third of a grain ; and steel sizzors so minute that six pairs could be wrapped in wing of fly, but cut large horse hair" (handbill 1745).

Bovet, —, Fleurier, began making watches for the Chinese market in 1830.

Bowden, **Jno.**, London ; long-case clock, about 1740.

Bowdon, **J.**, fine striking watch, about 1590, illustrated on p. 157.

Bowen. **Richard**, apprenticed to Robt. Smith 1650 ; C.C. 1657. A "Richard Bowen" was maker of a large silver watch with two cases, the outer one chased and engraved with a border of flowers and the figure of the king praying, and the words, "And what I sai to you I sai unto all, WATCH." It was said to have been given by Charles I. while at Carisbrooke to Colonel Hammond, 1647. **Francis**, apprenticed to John Bowyer ; brought his masterpiece on completion of his indentures, and was admitted C.C. 1654. Anchor escapement lantern clock inscribed "Francis Bowen in Leaden Hall streete Londini," in possession of Mr J. Drummond Robertson. **Richard**, apprenticed to Richard Bowen 1670 ; C.C. 1678. In 1677 Jno. Bowen was apprenticed to Mary Bowen. "Lost, a watch in black shagreen studded case, with a glass in it, having only one Motion and Time pointing to the Hour on the Dial Plate, the spring being wound up without a key, and it opening contrary to all other watches, 'R Bowen, Londini, fecit,' on the back plate" (*Lond. Gaz.*, Jan. 10-13, 1686). **Thos.**, apprenticed to Hy. Bridgen 1684. **John**, C.C. 1709 ; clock with tidal record, about 1730, signed "Bowen, Bristol." **Thomas**, 6 Charing Cross, 1797-1813 ; livery C.C. 1811. **John**, 143 Long Acre, 1807-10 ; 2 Tichborne St., Haymarket, 1812-42 (Bowen & Holt 1814-18). **D.**, Alfreton, Derbyshire, died 1877.

Bower. **Jno.**, London ; large lantern clock, dolphin frets, about 1690. **Peter**, Redlynch, 1760-80. **Michael**, Philadelphia, 1790-1800.

Bowers, **Wm.**, Chesterfield ; watch, 1807.

Bowles, **Jno.**, Poole, 1790.

Bowley. **Devereux**, 54 Lombard St. ; a well-known maker of repeating clocks ; born 1696, died 1773 ; apprenticed to Wm. Tomlinson ; C.C. 1718, master 1759 ; was a member of the Society of Friends, and bequeathed a large sum to their school in Clerkenwell, as well as £500 to the C.C. ; a clock belonging to Mr G. P. Osbaldeston bears the signature 'Devereux Bowly' ; the name is similarly spelt on the dial of another clock in the possession of Mr G. W. Toland, Washington, D.C. **Jno.**, London ; watch, 1760.

Bowman. **James**, apprenticed to Daniel Delander ; admitted C.C. 1743. **Jas.**, London ; watch, 1815. **Joseph**, Lancaster, U.S.A., 1821-44.

Bowness, **Geo.**, Lancaster, 1820.

Bowra, **John**, 4 Holles St., Oxford St., 1820-28 ; "successor to W. Berridge" ; watch paper C.C.

Bowtell. **Samuel**, C.C. 1681. **William**, C.C. 1703.

Bowvier, **Chas. F.**, Geneva, 1780.

Bowyer. **Wm.**, a good maker ; subscribed for incorporation of C.C. ; in 1642 he presented to the C.C. a great chamber clock, in consideration of his being thereafter exempted from all office and service, as well as quarterage and other fees (see p. 344) ; 1623-42. **Jno.**, possibly successor to Wm., see Bowen, F., & Bower.

Box. **John**, 17 Ludgate St., 1775-86. **William B.**, Clerkenwell ; died 1892, aged 76.

Boyce. **Thos.**, apprenticed 1687 ; C.C. **Jas.**, C.C. 1692 ; long marqueterie case clock, square matted dial, circles round winding holes, silvered ring, angel and crown corners, about 1720.

Boyer, **T.**, London ; lantern clocks, about 1690.

Boyle. **Richd.**, apprenticed 1652 to Jno. Bayes ; C.C. 1660. **William**, 11 Arundel St., Strand, 1840-42.

Boynton, **Jas.**, Howden, 1770.

Boys, **A.**, & **Duduict**, **Jaques**, makers of a large clock-watch, G.M., about 1700.

Bracebridge (& Pearce, Coppice Row, 1800). **Edward**, 8 Red Lion St., Clerkenwell, 1805-15 (Bracebridge & Sons, 1816-18). **J. & E. C.**, 8 Red Lion St., Clerkenwell, 1820-90 ; for a short time in 1865 they also had the shop 119 Bond St. **James**, treasurer to the Watch and Clockmakers' Benevolent Institution ; died 1892, aged 66.

Bracewell, **Huntley**, Scarborough, 1822.

Brackenrig, **Robert**, Edinburgh ; made an escapement similar to the duplex 1770.

Brackley, **George**, C.C. 1677.

Bradberry, —, Leyburn, 1805.

Braddock, —, Hayfield ; clock, about 1760.

Bradford. **Thomas**, C.C. 1680. **Thomas**, C.C. 1692 ; watch, about 1700, Norman Shaw collection. **Robert**, London ; Mr Eden Dickson has a small watch by him, with fine gold dial, about 1700. **Thomas**, Strand ; son of Robt. ; watch G.M. ; C.C. 1710-70. **J.**, Liverpool ; watch, 1816. **Hy.**, 89 Bethnal Green Rd., 1820.

Bradin (or **Braen**), **Caspar**, Westminster Churchyard ; C.C. 1715.

Bradl, **Anthony**, Augsburg, 1680 (see p.**192**).

Bradley. **Henry**, C.C. 1681. **Langley**, Whitechapel, afterwards in Fenchurch St. ; apprenticed to Joseph Wise 1687 ; admitted C.C. 1695, master in 1726 ; maker of the St Paul's and other turret clocks (see p. 247) ; long-case clock, Wetherfield collection. "Stolen out of Mr Bradley's Shop, the 'Minute Dyall' in Fanchurch St., on the 8th Inst., a Gold minute watch in an engraven case," &c. (*Flying Post*, 8th Oct. 1698). **Benjamin**, apprenticed to Langley Bradley ; admitted C.C. 1728. **L. & B.**, made a clock for Bancroft's School, Mile End, the date on the bell being 1734 ; the clock is now in Bancroft's new school at Woodford. **Thos.**, Ilkston, 1760. **Wm.**, London ; watch, h.m., 1784. **John H.**, 3 Great Russell St., Bloomsbury, 1842.

Bradshaw. Jno., apprenticed 1651 to Lancelot Meredith, C.C. **Jno.**, C.C. 1658. **Hy.**, apprenticed 1687 to Wm. Slough, C.C. ; Thos. Reynolds was apprenticed to him in 1699. **Edwd.**, Puddle Dock Hill ; C.C. 1725. **John**, C.C. 1731. **& Ryley**, Coventry, 1760. **Jno.**, York, f., 1762 ; at Manchester 1770. **Wm.**, Liverpool, watch, 1810.

Bræmar, Gerrett P., Amsterdam ; repeating watch, S.K.M., about 1735.

Braene, Caspar, London, 1729 ; C.C.

Brafield, William, C.C. 1678 ; fined 5s. by C.C. in 1688 for making a bad watchcase. **Thos.**, London ; long-case clock, about 1705.

Braithwaite, Geo., Lombard St., 1738. **& Jones**, Cockspur St. ; the Hon. Gerald Ponsonby has a fine repeater by them, about 1800.

Bramble. Joseph, 407 Oxford St., 1804-35 ; clock, enamel dial, Mr T. D. Chapman, " Joseph Bramble London," about 1805. **Wm. & Edwd.**, 407 Oxford St., 1840. **Eliza**, 9 Wells St., Oxford St., 1842.

Brambley, Joseph, 10 Maiden Lane, Wood St. ; in 1797 founder and citizen ; petitioned against being compelled to take up freedom in C.C. 1783-97.

Bramer, Paulus, Amsterdam ; watch, about 1700. **Garrit**, Amsterdam ; clock-watch, about 1750.

Brand. Basil, apprenticed 1660 to Jno. Matchett, C.C. **Alexander**, Edinburgh, 1727 ; though not apprenticed in Edinburgh, he was by favour admitted to the Incorporation of Hammermen, and in return presented a clock which is still in Magdalen Chapel, Cowgate, then the meeting-place of the Incorporation. **& Matthey**, Philadelphia, 1797. **C.** (see Brandt), musical watch maker to H.M., 22 Frith St., 1814-19.

Brandon, Benjamin, C.C. 1689.

Brandreth, Joseph, C.C. 1718 ; long-case clock, " Brandreth, Middlewich," about 1750.

Brandt, Chas., musical watch maker, 74 New Compton St., 1815 ; 82 Theobald's Rd., 1820 ; 145 Regent St., 1825 ; 22 Upper Belgrave Place, Pimlico, 1835.

Branston & Bird, 39 Cornhill, 1775 (Thos. Branston, livery Glovers' Company).

Brant, Richard, apprenticed to Sam Davis 1649 ; C.C. **Richd.**, apprenticed 1692 to Jno. Dickens ; C.C. 1700. **Brown & Lewis**, Philadelphia, 1795.

Brasbridge, Joseph, 98 Fleet St., 1794. **& Son**, 198 Fleet St., 1825.

Brasier, Amable, Philadelphia, 1811.

Brass, Thos., Guildford, 1725. **—**, London ; long-case clock, about 1750 ; Mr B. L. F. Potts has a bracket clock signed " Thomas Brass, London," about 1760. It formerly belonged to Jno. Thorpe, the antiquary.

Brasseur, —, Rue Bourg l'Abbé, Paris, 1770.

Bray. Robert, C.C. 1728. **Thomas**, St Margaret's Churchyard, 1798-1804 ; 8 Little Queen St., Westminster, 1807-25. **Wm.**, 171 Tottenham Court Rd., 1840.

Brayfield. William, apprenticed to Thos. Williamson 1671 ; C.C. 1678. " Drop'd the 21st December in Little Weld St. or thereabout, a middle siz'd Silver Minute Pendulum watch, going Thirty hours, with a chain, in a silver case, the name 'William Brayfield, London.' Whoever brings it to Remond Regard, Clockmaker, at the upper end of Russell St., near Drury Lane, shall have 40s. reward " (*Lond. Gaz.*, January 25-28, 1691). **Thos.**, apprenticed 1675 to Erasmus Micklewright ; C.C. 1682. **John**, C.C. 1716.

Brayley, Joseph, 6 Little Guildford St., Bernard St., Russell Sq., card, Hodgkin collection, about 1810.

Breakspear & Co., Oxford St., 1807.

Breames, Leonard, C.C. 1633.

Brear, Jas., Philadelphia, 1793-99.

Brearley, —, Spa Fields ; C.C. 1782. **Jas.**, Philadelphia, 1797-1811.

Brebant (or **Brebent**), **Peter**. Mr F. T. Proctor, Utica, N.Y., has a regulator by Peter Brebant, London, about 1710 ; repeating watch, Peter Brebent, London, about 1690.

Breese, Jas., 5 North Place, Gray's Inn Rd., 1842.

" **Breghtel, J. H. C.**, Hagae," signature on case of late seventeenth century clock, S.K.M., see Van den Bergh.

Breguet, Abraham Louis, born 1747, died 1823 ; a French watchmaker of rare attainments and inventive power ; Berthoud, who was Breguet's senior by two years, ends a brief notice of his brilliant contemporary thus : " Il n'a rien publié." Breguet lived sixteen years longer than Berthoud, but, although it must still be recorded " he published nothing " (see p. 291). **Louis Antoine**, son of the above ; retired 1833. **Louis**, son and successor of L. A. ; born 1804, died 1883, see Brown, Edwd.

Brentwood, Wm., London ; watch, 1775.

Brest, Edwd., Prescot, 1770.

Breton, Henry, keeper of the Westminster clock 1413.

Bretonneau, Auguste, Paris ; a watch by him belonging to Earl Amhurst, described in *Archæological Journal*, vol. xvii., enamelled, Holy Family on one side, St Catherine on the other, about 1680. In the Pierpont Morgan collection is a clock-watch by him of later date, with white enamel dial enclosing a gilt centre, silver case beautifully pierced with flowers and bird, a coat of arms on the back.

Brett, Jas., lantern clock, about 1695. **Thos.**, London ; bracket clock, about 1730.

Brewer. Edwd., apprenticed 1665 to Stafford Freeman, C.C. **John**, C.C. 1677. **Richard**, Norwich ; long-case clock, about 1720, Mr Sheldon Leicester. **Richd.**, Lancaster, 1783, f. **Wm.**, Philadelphia, 1785-91. **J.**, 25 New Surrey St., Blackfriars, 1810-15. **Wm.**, Blackburn, 1814-24. **Thos.**, Preston, 1818. **W.**, 149 Great Surrey St., Blackfriars, 1825.

Brewster & Ingraham, Bristol, Conn., 1827-39.

Brewton, Robt., apprenticed 1660 to Jno. Archer, C.C.

Breynton, Vaughan, C.C. 1693.

Brice, Wm., Sandwich ; watch, 1784.

Brickell, Edmund, London ; clock, red lacquer case, about 1730.

Brickenden, Nat., apprenticed 1651 to Robt Whitwell, C.C.

Bricker, Wm., Hosier Lane, 1730.

Brickle, William, 5 Church St., Mile End, 1842.

Bridgden, Henry, C.C. 1682.

Bridge, Wm., C.C. 1674. **Thos.**, Wigan, 1690-1720. **Thos.**, London ; long-case clock, marqueterie in panels, "Thos. Bridge Londini fecit," about 1695 ; another, arabesque marqueterie, about 1700, Wetherfield collection. **Richard**, London ; watch, 1748. **Edwd.**, London ; watch, 1802.

Bridgeman, Edwd., apprenticed 1655 to Jno. Matchett, Russell St., Covent Garden ; C.C. 1662.

Bridger, Samuel, admitted C.C. 1703.

Bridges. Henry, Waltham Abbey (see p. 299), 1730-41. **Thos.**, London ; long-case clock, bird and flower marqueterie in panels, about 1700. **Robt.**, London ; watch, 1784.

Bridgman, Richard, an excellent workman, some years with M'Cabe, then in Mount St., afterwards with Charles Frodsham & Co., then for a short time in the Haymarket ; died 1904, aged 62.

Briggs, John, " a cutter of glasses for watches " ; brother C.C. 1669 ; several generations of Briggs, clockmakers, in Gargrave and Skipton, Yorkshire.

Bright. Jno., 72 Long Acre, 1780-94. **John**, Sheffield, 1790. **Isaac**, Sheffield, 1810. **& Sons**, Sheffield, 1817-33. **Richd.**, 9 Foster Lane, 1815-26, see Upjohn.

Brille, Paris ; clock, about 1750.

Brimble & Rouckliffe, Bridgwater, 1770 ; clock by them belonging to Mr Edwin Ash ; their names are also on the weathercock of St Mary's Church, Bridgwater.

Brind, Walter, livery Goldsmiths' Company, 34 Foster Lane, 1773-88.

Brinkman, George, 12 Union St., Bishopsgate, 1815-40. **& Gollin**, 1842.

Briscoe, Stafford, at the " Three Kings and Golden Ball," Cheapside, 1738-59. **& Morrison**, 1768, see Morrison, Richd. **Sam.**, London ; watch, 1810.

Bristow, Jno., apprenticed 1653 to Richd. Craile, C.C. **Tim.**, apprenticed 1691 to Vrian Berrington, C.C. **Wm. G.**, 6 Hoxton Fields, 1790-1835 ; trunk dial, Guildhall, about 1800, inscribed " Bristow, London."

British Watch Company, 75 Dean St., Soho, formed in 1843, to manufacture watches with duplicating tools invented by P. F. Ingold. John Barwise was chairman of the directorate, and he with Thos. Earnshaw and Thos. Hewitt formed a committee of managers. John Frodsham & Son, Gracechurch St., were to be the London " agents." An excellent watch was designed, and several were made, but the " trade " successfully opposed the application to Parliament for an Act of Incorporation, and the enterprise came to a close. Ingold afterwards went to America ; and although he was not successful in forming a company there, it is said that some of the tools made for the British Watch Company formed the nucleus of the American factory system.

Brittaine. Boaz, apprenticed to Wm. Speakman 1670 ; C.C. 1679. **Stephen**, C.C. 1692.

Britten, S., watch-glass maker, 11 Charles St., Hatton Garden, 1835.

Britton. Stephen, C.C. 1728. **Sandys**, 48 Wynyatt St., 1835.

Broad. Thomas, C.C. 1682. **John**, Bodmin, 1790-1820. **Wm.**, 53 Leadenhall St., 1804-30. **R.**, 204 Bermondsey St., 1820.

Broadhead, Benjamin, C.C. 1709.

Broadley, Jas., 24 Wood St., 1772.

Broadwater, Hugh, C.C. 1692.

Broadwood, London ; watch, 1795.

Brock, James, foreman to Dent, afterwards at 18 George St., Portman Sq., died 1893, aged 67.

Brockbank. John, apprenticed to Joseph Hardin 1761 ; C.C. 1769, livery 1777 ; 7 Queen St., Cheapside, card, Hodgkin collection ; afterwards at 5 Cowper's Court, Cornhill. **John & Myles,** 6 Cowper's Court ; Myles was the son of Edward Brockbank, of Corners, in Cumberland, and was apprenticed to his brother John at 17 Old Jewry, 1769 ; C.C. 1776 ; they were eminent chronometer makers ; John died early in the nineteenth century, and Myles retired about 1808 ; they were succeeded by their nephews, John and Myles Brockbank, who for a few years carried on the business as John Brockbank & Company. **& Grove,** 6 Cowper's Court, 1812-14. **& Atkins,** 6 Cowper's Court, 1815-35. **Atkins, & Son,** 6 Cowper's Court, 1840-42.

Brocke, Samuel, oval watch, Whitcombe Greene collection, 1600-25.

Brockett, Richd., London ; bracket clock, about 1750.

Brockhurst, Thos., Coventry ; clock, about 1720.

Brocot, Achille, Paris ; a celebrated clockmaker ; born 1817, died 1878.

Brogden. Robert, York, f., 1713. **Joseph,** York, f., 1774. **James,** 148 Aldersgate St. ; liveryman C.C. 1765-94. **& Marriott,** 148 Aldersgate St., 1770-1804. **James,** 6 Bridgewater Sq., 1820-28. **& Garland,** 1830.

Bromley, Chas., Halifax, 1830 ; also **Wm.** ; also **Edwd.**

Bronson, Jno., London ; long-case and bracket clocks ; 1760-80.

Brook. Edmund, C.C. 1709. **Richard, & Son,** Poultry, 1795-1802 ; Richard Brook 1804-18 ; C.C. 1810.

Brooke. John, C.C. 1632. **George,** C.C. 1681. **William,** 192 Upper Thames St., 1783-94.

Brooker, Richard, C.C. 1694. **Nugent,** Dublin ; watch, 1770.

Brookes, Jno., apprenticed 1685 to Wm. Clement, C.C. **Edward,** C.C. 1690. **George,** London ; watch, 1700. **Josh.,** London ; watch, 1810. **Samuel,** watch-case maker, 5 Ashby St., Clerkenwell, 1835.

Brookhouse & Tunnicliffe, Derby ; watch, Mr H. Cook, on plate " Brookhouse's Improved Rolling Lever " ; the impulse pin was a pivoted roller such as Emery made, h.m., 1819.

Brooks. Jno., apprenticed 1693 to Mat. Crockford, jun., C.C. **William,** Church Row, Aldgate ; liveryman C.C. 1776 ; watch, 1790, " Wm. Brooks, Pentonville." **John,** 115 Bunhill Row ; liveryman C.C. 1786-88. **Thomas,** watch-case maker, 22 Golden Lane, 1790-94. **Robert,** London ; watch, 1795. **John,** 4 Bridgewater Sq., 1794-1813. **W.,** 14 Clerkenwell Green, 1825. **J. W.,** watch-spring maker, 5 Berkley Court, Clerkenwell, 1835. **Samuel Augustus,** watch jeweller, Clerkenwell, took an active part in trade affairs ; died 1901, aged 79.

Brooksted, Jno., apprenticed 1671 to Jno. White, C.C.

Broome, Thomas, admitted C.C. 1652.

Broomhall, Chas., 41 Stanhope St., 1794.

Bross, John, 106 Britannia St., City Road, 1820-35.

Brosy, Michael, London ; alarm watch, about 1640.

Brought, Hy., Workington, 1770.

Browmer, London ; watch, 1830.

Brown. James (Croydon), C.C. 1687. **Andrew,** Edinburgh ; apprentice to Humphrey Mylne, made a freeman of the Incorporation of Hammermen in 1675, his essay being, " Ane knock with a watch luminary globe upon the dial " ; died 1712. " James Barrow, aged about twenty, of a low stature, a little pock-marked, speaks the English accent, had on when he went away a short flaxen coll-cut wig, in an ordinary habit, run away from his master the nineteenth instant with a plain gold watch without a crystal (glass), with an enambled dial. The enambling on the figures is broken off. A silver pendulum watch, made by William Young, at Charing Cross, London, with a shagreen case ; the centre and balance wheels pierced. A plain silver watch and an oval brass watch and several other things. Whoever can secure the said youth, and give notice thereof to Captain Andrew Brown, watchmaker in Edinburgh, shall have two guineas reward " (*Edinburgh Gazette*, 1699). The title of " Captain " refers to Brown's position in the Trained Band which was organised to defend the city. **Thomas,** C.C. 1703. **Jno.,** Edinburgh, 1720. **Henton,** Borough, admitted C.C. 1726 ; master, 1753 ; livery, 1766 ; a maker of fine watches ; 58 Lombard St. in 1754. **Nathaniel,** Manchester, 1750. **Thos.,** Birmingham, 1760. **John Wm.,** 14 Cheapside, 1760-83. **Thos.,** 36 Bull Ring, Birmingham ; watch, silver cock, h.m., 1761. **John,** 76 St Paul's Chyd., 1769-83. **Geo.,** Beverley, 1770. **Jas.,** Matlock, 1770. **J.,** King St., Seven Dials ; an excellent cutter of clock-wheels on an engine designed by Hindley, 1770-1810. **Thos.,** Chester ; member of the Goldsmiths' Company, 1773. **John,** 118 Fleet St., 1775-82. **Nathaniel,** Whitefriars, liveryman C.C. 1776. **John,** 65 Charing Cross, 1783-1810. **Thos.,** 14 Cheapside, 1788-1800. **John,** 39 Grafton St., Soho, 1790-94. **Geo.,** mahogany broken-arch bracket clock signed " George Brown, Holbourn Hill," about 1790. **Richard,** watch-key and pendant maker, Greenhill's Rents, 1790-94. **—,** 119 Holborn, card B.M. 1798. **Wm.,** 40 Piccadilly, 1800-10. **—,** 65 Charing Cross ; watch, 1804. **James,** 56 George St., Portman Sq., 1810-42. **Geo.,** 8 Great Sutton St., 1820. **Isaac,** 32 Gloucester St., Clerkenwell, maker of bezel winding watches, patented 1829, No. 5851 ; 1820-35. **James,** 60 Rahere St., 1842. **Roger,** 25 Shepherd St., Mayfield, 1842. **Edwd.,** an accomplished horologist, head of the house of Breguet, died at Paris, 1895 ; aged 66. Of U.S.A. : **Garven,** Boston, 1789. **J. C.,** Bristol, 1827-37. **David,** Providence, 1834-50.

Brownbill, Liverpool : **Jas.,** 1760 ; **Jno.,** 1780. **Hy.,** Leeds, 1780 ; he issued tokens of good design in 1793. **& Son,** Leeds, 1810 (see p. 379).

Browne. Matthew, C.C. 1633. **John,** C.C. 1652 ; master 1681. **Thos.,** apprenticed 1653 to Richd. Beck ; C.C. 1676. **Richard,** C.C. 1675 ; at ye Green Dragon in Cheapside, on lantern clock, gallery frets, bob pendulum. " A watch having two motions, Richard Brown being engraved on it, in a studded case " (*Lond. Gaz.*, June 16-20, 1687). **Philip,** apprenticed 1680 to Nich. Beck ; C.C. 1688. **Robt.,** apprenticed 1684 to Katherine Ames, C.C. **Moses,** apprenticed 1687 to Robt. Nemes, C.C. **Chas.,** apprenticed 1692

to Thos. Brayfield, C.C. **Chas.,** London ; watch, 1820. **Richd.,** see Paterson.

Browning. Jas., apprenticed to Thos. Platt, 1650 ; C.C. **Isaac,** Penrith, 1770.

Brownless, —, Staindrop (Darlington) ; clock, about 1720.

Brownlie, Alexander, Edinburgh, 1710-25.

Brownson, Thos., London ; watch, 1799.

Bruce. James, C.C. 1721. **George,** London ; long-case clock, about 1740. **—,** Cranbourne St., Leicester Sq. ; watch, 1830.

Brugercia, C., musical snuff-box and clock maker, 13 Richmond Buildings, Dean St., 1820.

Brugger, John, Lynn, 1815 ; 252 High Holborn, 1830. **Beck, & Co.,** 15 Crown St., Finsbury, 1840-42. **L. A.,** wooden and musical clock maker, 79 High Holborn, 1840-42.

Brulefur, Jean, London ; clock in fine marqueterie case, S.K.M., about 1690.

Brumwell, Pall Mall, about 1760.

Brunette, Samuel, 13 Castle St., Bloomsbury, 1814 ; 34 Gloucester St., Queen's Sq., 1825.

Brunner, Gaspard, made a clock at Berne, 1557.

Brunsley, William, apprenticed to Thos. Carrington, but turned over to Thos. Gray ; admitted C.C. 1766. On reverse of a token " William Brunsley " ; at Lilly House, against Strand Bridge, his halfpenny, on obverse a clock dial and hands.

Brunwin, Henry, Whitecross St., 1770-85 ; watch, about 1780, stolen from Newington Free Library, engraved on the plate an eagle and a snail as a guide to regulation.

Bruton, J., dial enameller ; died 1863.

Bryan. Robt., apprenticed 1663 to Wm. Seabourne, C.C. **Sam.,** apprenticed 1685 to Jas. Hassenins, C.C. **Richard,** C.C. 1696. **Saml.,** 104 Golden Lane, 1755-94 ; japanned long-case clock, about 1760. **Henry,** Strand, 1768. **Jno.,** 3 Shadwell Dock, 1790-94.

Bryant. Geo., apprenticed 1657 to Wm. Smith, C.C. **& Son,** 47 Threadneedle St., 1781. **John,** Hertford ; maker of good clocks, 1790-1829.

Bryars, Saml., Chester, 1833.

Bryce, Clement, apprenticed 1689 to Vere Martin, C.C.

Bryer, John (apprenticed to E. J. Dent), 20 Northampton Sq., 1838, afterwards at Barbican ; died 1894.

Bryers, Arthur, Chester, 1814-18.

Bryson. Alexander, Edinburgh ; " Her Majesty's clockmaker for Scotland " ; died 1854 ; succeeded by Robert Bryson, his son, who died 1886. **Jno.,** Dalkeith ; apprenticed to Thos. Pringle, 1842.

Buchan, Henry, 37 Windmill St., 1830-42.

Buchanan. Arch., Dublin ; long-case clock, about 1760. **Jno.,** Ashton-under-Lyne, 1818.

Buck, Edward, exhibited his masterpiece, and was admitted C.C. 1632.

Buckenhill. Jno., apprenticed 1664 to Wm. Thorogood, C.C. 1672. **Edward,** C.C. 1687.

Bucket (? Bouquet) subscribed to Incorporation of C.C. 1630.

Buckhill, Jas., apprenticed 1768 to Robt. Fole, C.C.

Buckingham. Joseph, Black-moor's Head and Dial, Minories, 1690-1725 ; long-case clock with fine marqueterie case, about 1700, inscribed " Joseph Buckingham, London." " Stolen from Mr Richard

Parke, in Pey Alley, Fanchurch St., a gold watch made by Jos. Buckingham" (*Lond. Gaz.*, July 13-16, 1691). **Joseph,** junr., Minories, 1740-60.

Buckland, Jno., bracket clock, 1795.

Buckley. G., Hartshead ; clock, about 1760. Jno., Ashton-under-Lyne, 1818.

Bucklie, David, Bridgewater Sq., 1780-94 ; livery C.C. 1787.

Bucknall, Thos., Birkhampstead ; watch, 1740, Mr Evan Roberts.

Bucknell. W., 20 Kirby St., 1810. **Wm.,** 10 Parliament St., 1816-28 ; succeeded by **Wm. Alexander.**

Buckner. Philip, apprenticed 1658 to Nich. Coxeter ; C.C. 1667. **Richard,** C.C. 1710.

Bucksher, J., 37 Three Colts St., Lime-house, 1817.

Bucquet, Dan., 56 Cannon St., Ratcliff, 1812-20.

Budgen, —, Croydon, about 1740.

Buffet, Jno., Colchester ; watch, silver cock, 1735.

Bugden, —, 20 Brydges St., Covent Garden ; watch paper C.C., about 1800.

Buguon, Paris ; repeating watch, 1780.

Bukingham, see Buckingham.

Bulet, D., Geneva, about 1750.

Bull. Rainulph, keeper of the "great clock in His Majesty's Palace of Westminster" (see p. **199**) ; watch, probably by him, B.M., inscribed "Randolph Bull" and dated 1590. **Edmd.,** Fleet St. ; about 1610 (see p. **199**). **John,** subscribed to incorporation of C.C. 1630 ; admitted 1632. **Jno.,** apprenticed 1691 to Ben. Graves, C.C. **Jas.,** 124 Leadenhall St., 1813-18.

Bullby, John, C.C. 1632.

Bullimore, Hy., apprenticed 1687 to Jno. Fitter, C.C.

Bulline, Ben., London ; watch, h.m., 1763 ; long-case clock, about 1770.

Bullman, Thos., Swan Alley ; large marqueterie case clock, twisted pillars, square dial, about 1690.

Bullock. —, Widcombe, Bath ; **Zephaniah,** about 1740 ; **Thos.,** son of Z., 1765-95 ; **Wm.,** son of Thos., died 1846 ; succeeded by his nephew **Wm. Vokes,** who died 1870, aged 59. **Jas.,** Furnival's Inn Court, 1790-94. **Christopher,** London ; bracket clock, mahogany case, painted dial, about 1800.

Bulman, Jacob, Nuremburg ; clockmaker and master of the Locksmiths' Guild, 1780-98.

Bulstrod, Wm., apprenticed 1671 to Henry Hester, C.C.

Bult. Jas., London ; watch, silver case with landscape painted on the back, Schloss collection, about 1780. **James, & Co.,** 86 Cheapside, 1815-25.

Bultry, Dan., apprenticed 1655 to Ralph Greatorex ; C.C. 1663.

Bumstead, Robert, in Holborn ; C.C. 1707 ; fine pair-case *repoussé* repeater in leather case.

Bunce, Matthew, C.C. 1698.

Bunch, Nich., Bramshot ; 30-hour long-case clock, about 1730.

Bunnett, Wm., London ; watch, 1780.

Bunon, —, Rue Coquilliere, Paris, 1770.

Bunting. William, Pope's Head Alley, Cornhill ; admitted C.C. 1646 ; watch in the B.M., on the dial is inscribed "Ioanni Miltoni, 1631." **Joshua,** apprenticed to Wm. Bunting, 1648, C.C. **Josh.,** apprenticed in 1651 to Wm. Bunting for Thos. Wolverstone, C.C.

Bupert, Michel, Paris ; clockmaker to the Duke of Orleans 1641.

Burchall, Thos., Nantwich, 1760.

Burchett, John, C.C. 1731.

Burckhardt, J. C., 14 Northumberland St., Strand, 1816.

Burdon, Francis, 3 Hollen St., 1816.

Burgar, John W., 23 Banner St., 1842.

Burge, Caleb, apprenticed 1682 to Simon Barrett.

Burges. Henry, long-case clock, about 1690 ; Mr W. J. Clayton, South Australia. **Jno.,** London ; about 1720. **Chas.,** London ; watch, about 1740, Mr T. W. Bourne ; another, pendulum-balance under dial, 1750. **Thos.,** Gosport, 1750-60.

Burgess. Edwd., Londini ; long-case clock, about 1690. **Jno.,** Wigan, 1690-1740. **Elias,** London ; long marqueterie case clock, 11-inch dial, Wetherfield collection, about 1700. —, Old Bailey, 1774. —, 20 Cheapside ; card B.M., 1782 ; "from T. Wright, watchmaker to the King," watch paper, Ponsonby collection, about 1795. **Geo.,** 10 Bishopsgate St. Without, 1790 ; watch by him, 1768. **E.,** clock-case maker, 23 Percival St., 1835.

Bürgi, Jobst. (De Burgi or Burgius), Prague, born 1552, died 1632 ; a talented mechanician, who in 1602 was appointed clockmaker to Rudolph II. In the Vienna Treasury is a clock with a pendulum attributed to him. There are two oval dials of rock crystal framed with plates of smoky topaz. One dial shows the minutes and hours, and the other the days of the week, as well as the age and phases of the moon. Striking work for the hours is behind one dial, and quarter-hour striking mechanism behind the other. The case, in the form of an obelisk, is of agate, adorned by three circlets of garnets.

Burgis, John, subscribed to incorporation of C.C. 1630 ; 1632 ; oval calendar watch, in Dover Museum, about 1625 (see p. **135**). **Thomas,** apprenticed to Thomas Knifton, 1654. **Charles Edward,** apprenticed to James Clowes, 1678 ; long-case clock, bird and flower marqueterie in panels, "Edwd. Burgis," about 1690 ; bracket clock, black bell-top case, back plate nicely engraved and inscribed, "Edward Burgis, Londini, fecit" ; about 1720. **John,** London, 1680. **Elais,** London, C.C. 1681 ; long-case clock, about 1700, Wetherfield collection. **George,** London ; maker of a tall oak-case clock, 1720-40. **Wm.,** London ; watch, 1720.

Burke, —, 1630-50 ; C.C.

Burkeloe, Samuel, Philadelphia, 1797.

Burkham, —, London ; watch, 1720.

Burleigh, Ninyan, C.C. 1692 ; bracket quarter clock, ebony case, finely engraved back plate, inscribed, "Nin Burleigh, Durham," about 1730.

Burlingham, D. C., King's Lynn, died 1901, aged 78.

Burlinson, Hy., Ripon, 1830-40.

Burnap, Daniel, maker of brass clock movements at East Windsor, Connecticut, U.S.A., 1780-1800.

Burnet, Thomas, Bow, 1700.

Burnett, Richard, C.C. 1705. **Philip,** C.C. 1715. **Jno.,** London ; watch, 1755. **Chas.,** London ; watch, 1760. **Jno.,** Rosemary Lane, 1822.

Burns. Richard, Liverpool, 1770. **Jas.,** 76 Lisson Grove, 1804-42. **Hugh,** Philadelphia, Dty. 1811.

Burpull, John, Tooley St., 1720-50 ; a long-case clock dating from about 1735, appeared to be inscribed "John Burputh, Tooley St., near London Bridge," and Mr J. Terry has one signed John Burputt.

Burpur. "Lost Oct. 29, about 11 of the

clock, at the Queen's Head Ale House, a plain watch with a silver case made by one Burpur. Any person that shall see this watch offer'd to be sold or pawn'd are desired to send word to the Red Lyon behin'd the Royal Exchange, and they shall have a guinea reward" (*The Postman*, Nov. 1, 1705).

Burrill, Boys Err, Great Sutton St., 1805-20.

Burrows. Joseph, apprenticed to Wm. Addis ; C.C. 1777 ; livery 1803. **James,** 30 Goodge St., 1820-25. **E.,** 4 America Terrace, King's Rd., Chelsea, 1830-42.

Burton. Abraham, apprenticed in 1650 to Richd. Masterton, C.C. 1657 ; watch, 1700. **Jno.,** apprenticed 1672 to Richd. Warren, C.C. **Roger,** apprenticed 1678 to Ch. Bonner, C.C. **E.,** one-hand clock inscribed "E. Burton, Kirby Kendall," body of case very narrow with side wings, about 1690. **William,** London ; repeating watch, about 1740 ; known also as a maker of spring clocks about 1760. **Emanuel,** Kendal, 1760-90. **Jas.,** Whitehaven, 1770. **John,** Blue Anchor Alley, liveryman C.C. 1776. **W.,** Kendal, 1780. **Jas.,** Lincoln's Inn Gate, Carey St., 1806-20. **Hy.,** London ; watch, 1810.

Burwash. Wm., watch-case maker, 3 Red Lion St., Clerkenwell, 1782-1804. **Wm.,** 45 Red Lion St., Clerkenwell, 1790. **Thos.,** 91 Bishopsgate Without, 1825.

Busby, Nich., 1630-50 ; C.C.

Busch, Abraham, Hamburg ; watch, about 1710.

Buschman. Hans, Augsburg ; astronomical clock by him, Vienna Treasury, about 1600. **David,** Augsburg ; watch, Pierpont Morgan collection, about 1610 ; pretty floral balance-cock pinned on ; another watch, Vienna Treasury, about 1620 ; large alarm watch in pierced brass case, Schloss collection, inscribed, "David Buschman Augusta," about 1680 (see p. **192**) ; table clock, "David Buschman Augsburg," semi-circular dial with long light hand that jumps back, and three other dials ; Mr R. Norman Shaw. **Hanns,** clock, 1690 (see p. **102** **John** (German), C.C. 1692. **John Baptist,** C.C. 1725.

Bush, James, C.C. 1729. **James,** 104 High St., Shoreditch, 1804-42. **James,** 6 Hackney Rd., 1835.

Bushby, —, London ; watch, 1780.

Bushell. Timothy ; his son John was in 1681 apprenticed to Wm. Lavell of the Cutlers' Company. **Edward,** apprenticed 1687 to Wm. Bennett, C.C. **Samuel,** apprenticed 1690 to Wither Chesney, C.C. **Matthew,** Arley (Cheshire), 1740 ; on long-case clock, about 1750, "Mathew Bushell, Aston."

Bushman. Jno., watch, Nelthropp collection, tulip pillars, revolving hour circle, about 1670. **John Baptist,** livery C.C. 1786. —, Northwich, 1790. **Wm.,** Stratford, Essex, watch paper, C.C., about 1800. **Jno.,** Bolton, 1814.

Bushnells, Thos., at the Dial in East Smithfield, 1692.

Butler. John, C.C. 1724. **Jas.,** Bolton, Lancs. ; long-case clocks, about 1760-80.

Butter, Joshua, 36 New Bond St., 1804 ; 239 Oxford St., 1807.

Butterfield à Paris ; silver pocket sundial, about 1690. **Jno.,** Todmorden, 1770-1820. **Thos.,** London ; large-sized Parliament type of clock in japanned case, about 1790.

Butterworth. —, long-case clock, "John Butterworth fecit," about 1725. **Samuel,**

Rochdale, 1760.

Button & Putley, 204 Boro', 1788 ; card B.M.

Buz, Johannes, octagonal striking calendar watch, in brass case, German, about 1640.

Bye, Henry, clockmaker to the City of Paris, 1413.

Byford, William, 23 St Mary-at-Hill, 1820-35.

Bysse, Edward, curious watch, at the B.M., about 1620 ; prohibited from working by C.C. 1632, but afterwards joined the Company, see also Bisse.

Byworth, Thos., 28 King St., Snow Hill ; and 12 Bridge St., Lambeth, 1804-42.

Cabrier. Charles, Broad St., admitted C.C. 1697 ; clock, long marqueterie case ; "Carolus Cabrier, Londini, fecit," about 1690 ; in the B.M. is a very thick rounded repeater watch, period 1690, in the centre of the outer case is an enamel medallion, this is surrounded by a circle of *repoussé* work, outside of which the case is nicely pierced ; another example of his work is a silver verge watch, outside case embossed, 1690-1726. **Charles,** 79 Broad St., a celebrated maker ; C.C. 1726 ; master, 1757 ; Pig St., Threadneedle St., in 1759. **Charles,** C.C. by patrimony, 1756 ; in 1777 an action was tried in the King's Bench, Cabrier v. Anderson, the defendant having put on five watches the plaintiff's name, without his knowledge or consent : a verdict was given for the plaintiff with £100 damages. Specimens of Cabrier's work are in the Guildhall Museum ; one of them is a bell repeating verge watch movement, with nicely wrought and pierced pillars having broad bases and caps. The Czar of Russia's collection in the Winter Palace, St Petersburg, contains a prettily decorated repeating watch by him, h.m., 1752-53. It is suspended from a chatelaine which, like the watch, is ornamented with agate and sprays of diamonds. **Charles,** Stepney, C.C. 1692. **John,** son of Chas., C.C. 1730. **& Leeky,** 15 Basinghall St., 1781-1804. **Favey, & Exchequer,** 14 Wilderness Row, 1794. **Favey & Son,** 1798.

Cachard. —, "successeur de Charles Le Roy à Paris," about 1780. **Gaspar,** 13 Oxendon St., 1820, afterwards at Henrietta St., Covent Garden.

Cade. Simon, admitted C.C. 1688. **Geo.,** Market Weighton, 1820. **& Robinson,** 153 Leadenhall St., 1820-25 ; 8-day bracket clock, mahogany case, Wetherfield collection, see p. 392.

Cadgell, Thos., apprenticed 1682 to Wm. Elmes, C.C.

Caesar, Daniel, admitted C.C. 1703.

Caffieri, Philip, born at Rome 1634, died at Paris 1716 ; **Jacques,** Paris, 1678-1755 ; **Philip,** son of Jacques, 1714-74. Noted designers and makers of clock cases.

Caillate, A., Geneva, about 1725.

Caille, —, London, about 1770.

Cailliatte, Abraham, watch, about 1640, Pierpont Morgan collection.

Cainden, Wm., London ; long-case clock, about 1760.

Cairns. John, Providence, U.S.A., 1788. **Ralph,** Brampton, 1833.

Caithness, —, New Bond St. ; verge watch, about 1750, see Allan & Caithness.

Calbeck, Jno., apprenticed 1672 to Jas. Field, C.C.

Calcot, Tobias, admitted C.C. 1664.

Calderwood, Thomas, C.C. 1724.

Caldwell, —, Appleton ; clock, about 1770.

Callam. Alexander, 74 Lower East Smithfield, C.C. 1790-96. **Brothers,** Castle St., Long Acre ; celebrated makers of repeating mechanism, 1795-1825.

Calledon, —, London ; watch, 1795.

Calliber. John, C.C. 1703. **Thomas,** C.C. 1727.

Callwood, Jno., Liverpool, 1770.

Calvert, Nich., apprenticed 1655 to Robt. Grinkin, C.C.

Cam, William, C.C. 1686 ; lantern clock, inscription, "William Cam, Londini, fecit."

Cambridge, Samuel, C.C. 1697.

Camden. William, Plumtree Court, Shoe Lane ; C.C. 1708 ; Mr Alfred Bedford has a splendid long-case clock by him ; it is still a really excellent timekeeper, and is in a handsome mahogany inlaid case ; repeating watch in pierced cases B.M. ; watch reputed to have belonged to Charles XII. of Sweden, silver case, handsomely chased silver dial, silver balance-cock, the movement altogether a very fine one, 1708-35. **Geo.,** London ; watch, about 1820.

Cameel, C., Strasburg ; octagonal watch, S.K.M., about 1610.

Camerer. (Ropp, & Co., 2 Broad St., Bloomsbury, 1788.) **A., & Co.,** wooden clock makers, 2 Broad St., Bloomsbury, 1830-42. **M.,** wooden clock maker, 13 Brownlow St., Drury Lane, 1840.

Cameron, D., 318 Strand, 1820-25.

Camp, Hiram, New Haven, 1840-53.

Campart, Jno., Bishopsgate, 1774.

Campbell, John, 3 Crowns, Strand, 1691-1701. **Wm.,** Carlisle, 1765 ; Philadelphia, 1799. **Charles,** Philadelphia, 1797. **Alex.,** 393 Strand, 1800-05. **Colin,** Cherry Bank ; watch, 1810. **W. F.,** 60 Hatton Garden, 1825-35.

Campe, Tho., apprenticed 1672 to Corn. Harbottle, C.C.

Camper, James, 99 Bridge Rd., Lambeth, 1800-40.

Campey, Joseph, York, f., 1758.

Canby, Charles, Wilmington, 1815-50.

Canche, Jacques, London, brother C.C. 1692 ; silver alarm watch, in the B.M., plain silver cases, the outer one perforated.

Cann. John, brother C.C. 1649. **Judah,** apprenticed to Jno. Cann, 1650.

Cannans, John, London ; maker of clocks, about 1790.

Cannon, Joseph, London ; long Chippendale case clock, day of week, day of month, age of moon, high tide, dead beat escpt., centre seconds, about 1790.

Canson, see Cawson.

Capper. Sam., apprenticed 1674 to Wm. Bridge, C.C. **Michael,** Philadelphia, 1779.

Capstick, Thos., Knaresboro', 1745-85.

Capt, Henry, 56 Frith Street, 1840-42.

Card, Edmund, admitted C.C. 1679.

Cardwell, Thos. B., Liverpool ; died 1905, aged 68.

Carell, John, Philadelphia, 1791-93.

Carey. George, admitted C.C. 1679. **Jasper,** "in Gray's Inn" ; watch, about 1700. **Thomas,** admitted C.C. 1705. **James,** Brunswick, U.S.A., 1808-50. **George,** 3 Singleton St., 1842.

Carfoot, Chas., 32 Aldersgate St., 1814-25.

Carleton, Robt., apprenticed 1687 to Joseph Bates, C.C.

Carley, George, 18 Wilderness Row, 1842 ; afterwards at Ely Place ; died 1879.

Carlill, Jas. B., York, f., 1801.

Carlow, P., maker of a watch for the Duke of Sussex, 1780-1800.

Carmichael, Jno., Greenock, 1750.

Carncel, C., Strasburg, maker of octagonal pillar timepiece in S.K.M., about 1600.

Carolan, James, 69 Red Lion St., Holborn, 1816-25.

Caron. Andreas Charles, Paris ; horologer of Louis XV., 1720-60. **Peter Auguste,** Paris ; son of the foregoing, an eminent watchmaker ; he and Lepaute claimed the invention of an improved Virgule escapement, and in 1753 the Academy of Sciences decided the point in favour of Caron, who had by then made a watch for the king and a very small one for Madame de Pompadour, see p. 409 ; fine enamelled watch, see p. 155 ; he was an accomplished musician as well as a playwriter, and is better known, under the name of Beaumarchais, as the author of "Le Barbier de Seville," and "Le Mariage de Figaro," born in the Rue St Denis, 1732, died 1799.

Carovagius, —, Paris, 1550.

Carpenter. Thos., C.C. 1767. **Thos. & Richd.,** watch-case makers, 5 Islington Rd., 1776-1823. **William,** 10 St Martin's Court ; hon. freeman, C.C. 1781 ; 15 Frith St., 1793 ; 5 Haberdashers' Walk, Hoxton, 1817 ; 1770-1817. **& Son,** 4 Andrew St., Seven Dials, 1785-90. **Thomas,** 5 Islington Rd., summoned to take up livery C.C. 1786 (see T. & R. Carpenter). **F.,** 21 Percival St., 1830. **Wm.,** 4 Percival St., 1842.

Carr, Fred., 18 Bridge St., Westminster, 1822-25.

Carre, Daniel, calendar watch, Nelthropp collection, about 1690.

Carrington. James, posting office, 1730 ; warden, C.C. 1767. **Robert,** Noble St., 1730, 22 Old Bethlem, 1760 ; livery C.C. 1766. **Thos.,** St Paul's Churchyard, 1730, afterwards Bishopsgate St. ; liveryman C.C. 1766. **Richd.,** London ; clock, about 1760 ; watch, 1765. **Geo.,** livery C.C. 1786. **& Son,** 22 Old Bethlem, 1794.

Carruthers, Geo., Blewett's Buildings, Chancery Lane, 1789-94.

Carswell, Joseph, Hastings ; long-case clocks, about 1760. **J.,** London ; watch, 1770. **Wm.,** 58 Bishopsgate Within, 1822-25.

Carte, John, C.C. 1695 ; a large thick watch by him, inscribed "John Carte, in Garden Court, in the Middle Temple" ; double sets of hour and minute numerals in relief on silver dial ; hour hand rotates once in 24 hours, minute hand once in 12 hours. When Peter the Great was in England he sold him a great geographical clock which told the time at any part of the world. "John Carte, watch maker from Coventry, and lately lived at the Dial and Crown near Essex St. in the Strand, is now removed to the corner of Lombard St." (*Flying Post,* Oct. 1696).

Carter. Thomas, C.C. 1659. **Jno.,** apprenticed 1669 to Andrew Allum, C.C. ; **Francis,** apprenticed 1670 to Robt. Dingley, C.C. ; **Sam.,** apprenticed 1683 to Wm. Fuller, C.C. **Thos.,** apprenticed 1690 to Joanna May ; C.C. 1699. **Wm.,** Ampthill ; long-case clock, about 1710. **Wm.,** Cambridge ; watch, 1720, Mr Evan Roberts. **Wm.,** Cambridge ; watch, 1725. **Leon Augustus,** C.C. 1726. **John,** Bartholomew Close, C.C. 1728-72. **Wm.,** Ampthill ; curious short "Grandfather" clock, inlaid case, gives age of moon, high water at London Bridge, solar time, &c., about 1750. **William,** Bermondsey St., 1760 ;

207 Tooley St., 1794. **Jas.**, Hampstead ; fine chiming long-case clock, about 1770. **Hewes**, Cambridge, 1790. **J.**, 57 Church St., Mile End, 1804-20. **Wm.**, jun., 1805-26. **John**, son of Wm. Carter, Tooley St. ; apprenticed to Boys Err Burrill in 1819, 207 Tooley St., 1829-42 ; afterwards 61 Cornhill ; Lord Mayor, 1857 ; master C.C. 1856, 1859, 1864 ; died 1878. **Hy.**, Ripon, 1833. **William**, watch-case maker, 22 Galway St., St Luke's, 1835.

Cartier, Ja͏̀ques, maker of a watch said to have belonged to Oliver Cromwell, 1635 ; another watch, " Cartier, London," about 1680 ; watch, " Cartier, Geneva," about 1810.

Cartwright. Benj., 18 West Smithfield, 1669-72. **Thomas**, apprenticed to Christopher Gould, 1693. He lived "behind the Exchange" ; watch by him in gold *repoussé* case, Schloss collection, inscribed " Thos. Cartwright, watchmaker to the Prince," about 1715 ; another example in the Guildhall Museum is a watch with crystal cock, jewelled, 1700-30. **Geo.**, C.C. 1706-12. **Wm.**, C.C. 1713 ; long walnut case clock, about 1713, signed " Benjamin Cartwright junior, London," Mr Geo. F. Glenny. **N.**, Lombard St. ; watch with pierced silver pillars, in Guildhall Museum, about 1720. **Ann**, 45 New Bond St., 1783.

Carus à Paris ; clock-watch, S.K.M., Paris hall mark for 1733-4 ; silver gilt case pierced and chased, outer case of tortoiseshell.

Carver, Isaac, C.C. 1667. **Jacob**, Philadelphia, 1797.

Case. Erastus, Bristol, Conn., 1830-7. **Harvey**, 1830-7. **Dyer, Wadsworth, & Co.**, Augusta, U.S.A., 1835-6.

Cashmore, John, 11 Bevis Marks, 1852, afterwards at Eldon St., Finsbury.

Casinghurst, Christopher, apprenticed 1690 to Robt. Nemes, C.C.

Casper. (Ellis & Co., 29 Finsbury Place, 1804-42.) **Nathaniel**, 13 Bury St., St Mary Axe, 1804-42.

Cass, George, London ; long-case clock, Mr R. B. Prosser, about 1790.

Cassiway, Chas., apprenticed 1656 to Thos. Mills, C.C.

Castan, Stephen, & Co., Philadelphia, 1819.

Castang, Philip, London ; watch, Nelthropp collection, 1777.

Caster. Wm., apprenticed 1690 to Joshua Hutchin, C.C. **Wm.**, Ripon, 1765. **B.**, London ; watch, silver outer case embossed, about 1770.

Castlefranc, Peter, 40 Pall Mall, 1769-83.

Caston. Jno., Kirkham, 1765. **Wm.**, Kirkham, 1780.

Catchpool. Thos., 113 Strand, 1823. **Wm.**, Fenchurch St., 1830-35.

Cater. —, widow, Moorfields, 1671. **J.**, London ; about 1780.

Catherall, J., Chester, 1814.

Catherwood. Joseph, 10 Bunhill Row, 1775-1825. **Joseph & William**, 2 Newcastle Place, Clerkenwell, 1804-42. **G. & R.**, 35 Kirby St., Hatton Garden, 1809-30. **Robert**, 35 Kirby St., Hatton Garden, 1835.

Catley, Dan., C.C. 1731.

Catlin, Danl., Lynn ; bird cage clock, 4 in. by 3 in. ; bob pendulum, about 1652, Mr Albert Hartshorne ; watch, quite a century later, Mr Evan Roberts.

Caton, Robt., New St., 1730.

Cattell. William, Fleet St., C.C. 1672 ; lantern clock, inscribed " William Cattell, in Fleete Street, Londini," 1671-90. **Thomas**, C.C. 1688. " Lost in Chancery Lane, a silver Minute Pendulum Watch, with a green and silver ribbond to the key, the watch made by Cattle, London " (*Lond. Gaz.*, January 19-23, 1692). **Thos.**, apprenticed in 1691 to Thos. Cattell, C.C. **Wm.**, York, 1822.

Catterall, Jno., Liverpool, 1770.

Cattle, John, fecit 1633, inscription under alarm disc of a lantern clock. **Robt.**, York, f., 1807, Lord Mayor, 1841, died 1842 (see Barber & Cattle).

Cattlin, James, 58 Great Marylebone St., 1804-42.

Catton, Richd., Leadenhall St. ; duplex watch, h.m., 1818.

Caul & Dennis, 19 Plumtree St., 1816.

Causard, clock mounted on elephant, Mr James Arthur, dial very similar to that of Fig. 557 is signed " Causard Hor. du Roy suiv͏ͭ La Cour," date about 1760.

Cave, see Robinson & Cave.

Cavell, Nataniel, Ipswich ; clock, one hand, long-case of oak, about 1700, Mr H. Hogarth.

Cavendish, Richard, livery C.C. 1810.

Caveton & Clark, Fetter Lane, 1730 ; clock, about 1760.

Cawdrey, see Corderoy.

Cawdron, Geo., apprenticed 1675 to Jas Graves ; C.C. by patrimony, 1684.

Cawkutt, Thos., apprenticed 1693 Nat. Bird, C.C.

Cawley. Robert, Chester ; watch, 1719. **Sam.**, 115 Bermondsey St., 1842-8.

Cawne, Robt., apprenticed 1663 to Lionel Wythe ; C.C. 1675.

Cawson, Liverpool and Lancaster : **Jas.**, 1779, f. ; at Lancaster, **Edwd.**, 1790, f. ; **Wm.**, 1817, f. **Ellen**, Liverpool, 1833.

Caygill C., Askrigg, died 1792, aged 90.

Cayne, Andrew, Without Bishopsgate, 1696.

Cellier, Lyons, 1580-90.

Ceson, Londres ; on a watch with chain-repeating work, about 1710.

Cetti. Joseph, London ; watch, 1800. **& Co.**, London ; watch, 1830.

Cext, Catharine, apprenticed to James Hubert and his wife, 1730.

Chaband, Hy., 9 Plumtree St., Bloomsbury, 1816-25.

Chadd & Ragsdale, New Bond St., 1775.

Chadwell, Nat., London ; long-case clock, ting-tang quarters, moon in arch, Mr W. W. Pope.

Chadwick. John, Liverpool, 1770. **Jno.**, 36 Cornhill, 1783-1813 ; 138 Holborn Hill, 1817. **James**, 18 Great Bath St., Clerkenwell, 1804-42. **Joseph**, Boscowen, N.H., 1810-31. **Joshua**, 138 Holborn Hill, 1820-55. **Wm.**, London ; watch, 1825.

Chalfont, Walter, Barnsbury, an inventive watchmaker, 1850-86.

Chalk, James, 36 Bishopsgate St. Within, 1798.

Challoner William, Skinner St. ; liveryman C.C. 1776.

Chalmers, George, 1 Prince's St., Leicester Sq., 1783-88.

Chamberlain. Thomas, Chelmsford ; in the B.M. is a watch by him, about 1630 ; calendar and striking watch, S.K.M., with pierced case of silver-gilt, movement signed " T. Chamberlain fecit." **Dan.**, apprenticed 1660 to Thos. Chamberlain. **Jno.**, Hertford ; long-case clock, about 1780. **C.**, London ; watch, 1800.

Chamberlaine. Nathaniel, apprenticed 1650 to Ben. Hill ; C.C. 1685 ; master 1717. " These are to give notice that Nathaniel Chamberlin, Watchmaker (who hath lived several years at *Chelmsford*, in *Essex*), for the better accommodation of his friends and customers, hath, at the request of divers of them, taken a Chamber at *Mr John Rust's*, in *Angel Court*, in *Lombard Street*, where he doth intend, God willing, to attend the last Fortnight in every Term, for the mending his own Work, and accommodating all persons that shall have occasion for New " (*Lond. Gaz.*, January 22-25, 1676-77). **Nathaniel**, C.C. 1659. **Thomas**, apprenticed to Samuel Ross, and turned over to Henry Harper ; C.C. 1687. **John**, Bury ; C.C. 1687 ; watch with day of the month ring, B.M., about 1670 ; lantern clocks, about 1700. **Joseph**, Norwich. " A little Gold Watch made by Joseph Chamberlain, of Norwich, with a plain Dial Plate in a plain black Shagreen Case " (*Lond. Gaz.*, March 15-19, 1687). —, Mark Lane, 1717.

Chambers. Edwd., apprenticed 1670 to Evan Jones, C.C. **Jonathan**, London ; long black and gold case clock, 10-inch dial, about 1690, Wetherfield collection. **James**, 3 Squirrils, St Dunstan's Church, 1690. —, 56 Cornhill, 1823. **Wm.**, watch finisher, City Rd., 1830 ; afterwards in partnership with Prior, Ed., at 18 Powell St. East, King Sq.

Champion. Robert, lantern clock, " Robert Champion, of Wells, fecit 1630." **John**, brother C.C. 1641. **John**, C.C. 1651-76. **Denis**, Paris ; clockmaker to the Duke of Orleans, 1669. **Guillaume et Isidor**, Paris ; watch, in the possession of Mr Edward Watkins, Manchester, formerly the property of Love-Jones Parry, Carnarvonshire, about 1680. **John**, London ; a watch by him in S.K.M., outer case of shagreen, about 1770 ; watch, about the same date, pair cases, the outer one of agate, Chinese figures on dial, Pierpont Morgan collection ; another, enamelled case, Schloss collection, about 1780. **Charles**, Paris ; about 1770. **Aré**, Paris ; alarm watch, about 1820.

Chance. B., London ; maker of a watch in the B.M., about 1720. **W. & G.**, London ; watch, 1815.

Chancellor. Jno., 81 Bishopsgate Without, 1793. **& Son**, Sackville St., Dublin, well-known clockmakers, 1800-40 ; in 1811 Jno. Chancellor patented (No. 3,487) a musical clock.

Chancey, Jas., London ; watch, Nelthropp collection, 1741.

Chandlee, John, Wilmington, U.S.A., 1795-1810.

Chandler. George, lantern clock, about 1680. **B.**, Nottingham, 1770. **& Son**, London ; watch, 1775. **Timothy**, Concord, U.S.A., 1780-1840. **Robert**, Martin's Court, 1793 ; 8 Leicester Sq., 1815-25. **Abiel**, Concord, 1829-58.

Channell, Geo., London ; watch, 1795.

Chantler, —, London ; about 1750. Hatton speaks with admiration of his watches.

Chapeau, Peter, London, extra large repeating watch belonging to Mr Chas. Freeman ; cylinder escapement, three cases, inner pierced case silver, h.m., 1746, second case *repoussé* group portraying Æneas and Dido ; outer case fish skin.

Chapman. Thos., apprenticed 1648 to Ralph Ash, C.C. **Simon**, C.C. 1675. **Jno.**, apprenticed 1679 to Wm. Herbert, C.C. **Titus**, apprenticed 1683 to Thos. Williamson, C.C. **Peter**, C.C., St Anne's Lane, 1730. **Thos.**, Bath ; long case musical clock, about 1760. **B.**, London ; watch, 1765. **Jno.**, " opposite the Riding House in the Garrison, Sheerness," about 1780. **William**, 6 New Round Court, Strand, 1790-94. **J.**, clock-case maker, 6 Red Lion St., Clerkenwell, 1835.

Chappel. Robert, C.C. 1720 ; maker of small size sheep's-head arch-dial clocks, " Robert Chappel, London," on disc. **Thomas**, Little Tower St., 1753-63.

Chappuis, Jubilé, Geneva, 1800.

Charas, Charles Samson, C.C. 1692.

Charle, George, watch with Turkish numerals, h.m., 1794 ; 19 Wilderness Row, 1804-42.

Charlepose, —, London ; gold repeating watch, silver cap engraved with the arms of Queen Anne, outer case set with lapis lazuli, rubies, and diamonds, about 1705.

Charles, D., Brompton, Kent ; watch, 1798. **G.**, Paris ; clock, about 1840.

Charleston, Jno., apprenticed 1676 to Ed. Clough, C.C. ; watch, 1685 ; Mr Edwd. Sudell has another of a later date.

Charlson. P., London ; watch, h.m., 1764. **W.**, London ; watch, 1800.

Charlstrom, William, Percival St. ; livery C.C. 1810 ; 1800-38.

Charlton. John, one of the first assistants of the C.C. ; master, 1640. **Matjonah**, apprenticed to Geo. Graham ; admitted C.C. 1728. **Jno.**, Durham, 1770. **Jas.**, 13 Lisson St. North, 1842.

Charman, Peter, 64 Piccadilly, 1816-26.

Charnock, Jas., apprenticed 1693 to Thos. Wheeler, C.C.

Charrington, S., died while master C.C. 1768.

Chartier. —, Blois ; excelled as a watch-case enameller, 1650-70. **Francis**, 1 Angel Court, Throgmorton St., 1765-71.

Charwell, James, London ; repeating watch, S.K.M., outer case shagreen *piqué*, about 1740.

Chase, Timothy, Belfast, U.S.A., 1826-40.

Chassereau, Robt., 4 Beech St., Barbican, 1804-8.

Chasseur, —, London ; small timepiece with pendulum swinging in front, about 1700 (see p. 395).

Chatbourne, Jno., apprenticed 1677 to Jno. Bennett, C.C.

Chater. James, C.C., 1727. **James, & Son**, 3 Cherry Tree Court, Aldersgate, 1754-59. **Eliezer & James**, 3 Cherry Tree Court, 1760-86 ; in 1785 Jas. C. patented (No. 1,785) a watch guard. **Eliezer**, 10, Exchange Alley, Cornhill ; master C.C. 1772 ; livery, 1776. **Richd.**, 14 Cornhill, 1787-1812. **& Livermore**, 2 Exchange Alley, 1790 ; 10 Bartholomew Lane, 1794 ; 30 Tokenhouse Yard, 1800. **Wm.**, 134 Goswell St., 1804-42.

Chaters, J., watch motion manufacturer, 17 Gee St., Goswell St., 1835.

Chatfield, —. " Lost on Saturday last, between Frith St., Sohoe, and Lumbard St., a Silver Minute Pendulum Watch in a tortoise shell case with a black ribon, engraved on the Dyal Plate (Chatfield, Londini). Whoever brings it to Mr Clerkson at the King's Head, near the Pump in Chancery Lane, shall have 20s." (*Lond. Gaz.*, April 4, 1695).

Chatham, Wm., London ; watch, 1782.

Chatier, Isaac, 1 Angel Court, Throgmorton St., 1768-88.

Chaudron, S., & Co., Philadelphia, 1811.

Chaulter. Hatton, writing in 1773, esteems his work.

Chaund, John, London ; long-case clock, about 1760.

Chaunes, —, Paris ; watch, 1620 ; small watch, " Chaunes le jeune," about 1650 (see p. 136).

Chauvell, James D., Old Broad St. ; C.C. 1699 ; clock-watch, 1705 ; also a repeating watch in S.K.M., about 1720 ; watch, 1714, signed " James Chauvel, London."

Chauvin, see Benard.

Chawner, Thos., 34 Ludgate Hill, 1783-88.

Cheasbrough, Aaron, long-case clock, about 1705 ; Rev. W. B. Atherton.

Cheeny, J., clockmaker at East Hartford, Connecticut, U.S.A., 1790.

Cheeseman, Daniel. C.C. 1699.

Cheesman, R., Horsmunden ; lantern clock, about 1700.

Cheetham, —, Leeds ; long Sheraton case clock, about 1790.

Cheltenham, Michael, C.C. 1712.

Cheneviere. Urban, Geneva, 1760. **& Deonna**, Geneva, about 1800.

Cheney. Withers, apprenticed 1646 to Elias Allen ; admitted C.C. 1657 ; elected master 1695, but excused on making a contribution to the poor-box. **Benjamin & Timothy**, East Hartford, Conn., 1745-81. **Benjamin**, Manchester, U.S.A., 1770-80.

Cheriton, Geo., apprenticed 1685 to Jno. Buckenhill, C.C.

Cherril, Edwd., 6 Newcastle Place, 1814. **E., & Son**, 1825-30.

Chesnon, Solomon, Blois ; maker of a very diminutive watch in the B.M., with outer leather case, about 1640 ; another watch by him described in vol. xi., *Archæological Journal*, had no hands ; the hours indicated by an escutcheon engraved on a circular plate, which revolved within the hour circle. " Lost on Sunday, the eighth of this instant March, about 12 o'clock, between St Paul's and St Dunstan's Church, a French gold watch enameled with Flowers in a Case studded with gold studs made by Solomon Chesnon at Blois, tyed with a Pink-coloured Ribbon. Whoever shall bring the same watch to Major Pinkney's shop at the Three Squirrels over against the West End of St Dunstan's Church in Fleet Street shall have fourty shillings" (*Lond. Gaz.*, March 12, 1673).

Chesson, Thos., Ludgate Hill, 1754-59.

Chester. George, from London, opens a shop at the sign of the Dial, on the New Dock (advt., New York), 1757. **Wm.**, 55 Shoreditch, 1840-44.

Chettle, W., 35 Commercial Road, Lambeth, 1830-38.

Chetwood, John, apprenticed 1692 to Jno. Pilcher, C.C.

Cheuillard, —, Blois ; watch, Marfels collection, about 1620.

Chevalier. (& Co., Geneva ; watch, about 1750). **& Co.**, Paris ; many watches, 1760-90.

Chevallier, aux Tuileries, Paris ; clock-maker to Louis XV. ; fine long-case clock, somewhat similar to Fig. 515, about 1760. **& Cochet**, Paris, 1790-1805.

Chilcott. Richard, C.C. 1690 ; long-case clock, about 1700, inscribed, " Richard Chillcott, London." **John**, C.C. 1721.

Child. Richard, Fleet St., C.C. 1632 ; warden, 1640-43 ; in 1638 the Blacksmiths' Company sued " Child, the clockmaker," for breach of his oath. **Henry**, brother, C.C. 1642 ; died, while master, 1664 ; Mr Eden Dickson has a three train " ting tang " lantern clock by him, inscribed, " Henricus Childe, Londini." **Ralph**, C.C. 1661. **Henry**, apprenticed 1670 to Nich. Russell, Tower Royal, Budge Row, 1677-93. " Lost the 28 instant at Aldermary Church, or between that and the Tower Royal, a plain Gold Pendulum Watch, in a new Fashion Gold Grav'd case, name, Henry Child. It had a Tulip Hand, long freised hours, in the middle of the dial plate engraven with two Birds and Flowers ; it was in a Gold Pinned Case " (*Lond. Gaz.*, May 25-29, 1693). **Jno.**, apprenticed to Thos. Taylor, C.C. 1769.

Chilton, Thos., London ; lantern clock, with arch dial added about 1700.

Chinn, T. W., Huddersfield ; three train bracket chiming clock, arch dial, walnut case, about 1720, Wetherfield collection.

Chipp, Robt., apprenticed 1679 to Robt. Seignior, C.C.

Chippendale, Gilbert, Halifax, 1781.

Chismon, Timothy, summoned to take up livery C.C. 1786 ; master, 1803.

Chophard, Saul, Artillery Lane, apprenticed to David Hubert ; admitted C.C. 1730.

Christian, Jno., Aylsham ; clock, about 1750.

Christie. Wm., 22 Chancery Lane, 1804-42. **Hy.**, 3 Duke St., Manchester Sq., 1842.

Christin, —, Paris, 1770.

Christmas, Jas., apprenticed 1682 to Thos. Birch, C.C.

Church. Jno. Thos., 19 Oakley St., 1835. **Lorenzo**, Hartford, U.S.A., 1846. **Duane, H.**, Mechanical Superintendent and Master Watchmaker at the Waltham Watch Factory, died 1905. " Of superior ability as a practical watchmaker, he possessed to a marked degree the inventive faculty, which in his last years found opportunity for exercise in the designing of automatic machines for the production of the various parts of Waltham watches. In this line of work Mr Church ventured into original fields in which he evinced the boldness of his convictions, and in which his successes were many and his failures relatively few," is the testimony of Mr E. A. Marsh who was closely associated with him for some years.

Churchill, Chas., London ; centre-seconds watch, h.m., 1787.

Churchman, Michael, C.C. 1694.

Clagget, Thomas, Newport, U.S.A., 1730-49 ; also **Wm.**, same date.

Clapham, Geo., Brigg, 1770.

Clarburg, Jno., made a clock for York Minster in 1370.

Clare. S., Hatton (near Warrington), 1770. **Peter**, Manchester, 1780-1805, a Quaker and watchmaker ; in an account of the village of Hatton, Chester, where he resided, the following reference to him is made :—

> There's the cottage of Peter,
> That cunning old fox,
> Who kept the sun right
> By the time of his clocks.

He appears to have been derided for asserting that the sun was wrong and his clocks right, though of course if mean time was desired he would have been doubtless correct in his assertion. **Peter**, son of the foregoing ; born in Manchester in 1781, was a prominent figure there till he died in 1851. **Thos.**, Warrington ; long-case clock, Battersea enamel dial,

Wetherfield collection, about 1790. **Henry T.**, 15 Meredith St., 1804-42.

Clark. Mary, apprenticed 1674 to Hy. Fevon and Christian his wife, C.C. **Elizabeth**, apprenticed to the same, 1676. **Stanford**, London, C.C. 1696; watch, 1710. **Thomas**, C.C. 1720. **Wm.**, Kendall; clock, 1720. **Wm.**, 26 Abingdon St., 1730; Bishopsgate St., 1754-74; Paternoster Row, 1775. **—**, Lancaster: **Cornelius**, 1733, f.; **Thos.**, 1767, f. **Jas.**, Morpeth, 1750. **Cure**, watch, 1750. **Wm.**, York, f., 1758. **Anthony**, Serjeants' Inn, Fleet St., 1763. **Edw.**, 56 Cornhill, 1768-75. **Thos.**, Ulverstone, 1770. **Edwd.**, 17 Middle Moorfields, 1772. **Robert**, clock and watch-spring maker, Providence Row, 1775-99; watch, Robert, London, 1780. **David**, watch-case maker, 58 Featherstone St., 1789-94. **Francis**, 10 Jewin St., 1789-94. **Jno.**, 73 Mark Lane, 1794-1823. **Wm.**, 6 King St., Clerkenwell, 1800. **Thos.**, 9 Goswell St., 1830-40. **George**, 24 Bartholomew Terrace, St Luke's, 1842. Of U.S.A:—**Benjamin S.**, Wilmington, 1737-50. **Benjamin, Edward, Ephraim**, Philadelphia, Dty., 1797. **Benjamin & Ellis**, Philadelphia, 1811. **Jesse, W. & C.**, Philadelphia, 1811. **Daniel**, Waterbury, 1815-20. **Sylvester**, Salem Bridge, 1830.

Clarke. John, Bristol; watch, B.M., in an outer case of leather *piqué*, 1630-40. **George**, Whitechapel; C.C. 1632. **William**, C.C. 1654. **Humphrey**, Hertford, C.C. 1668; lantern clock by him about 1700. **Andrew**, apprenticed 1682 to Chris. Gould, C.C. **Sam.**, apprenticed 1687 to Jno. Martin, C.C. **Wm.**, apprenticed 1688 to Thos. Clifton, C.C.; on the mantelpiece of the *Punch* Dining Hall at Bouverie St. is a small bracket clock inscribed "Wm. Clarke, Whitechaple," dating from about 1700. **Jno.**, C.C. 1691. **John**, Stanford, C.C. 1696. **& Dunster**, London; repeating watch, about 1705, Mr E. Wehrle; repeating watch in silver cases, pierced, engraved, and *repoussé*, early eighteenth century, S.K.M. **Thomas**, admitted C.C. 1709. **Richard**, Cornhill, C.C. 1720; calendar watch by him, dials back and front, 1745; Richard Clarke & Sons, Cheapside, 1815. **Geo.**, Leadenhall St., 1725-40; the Earl of Macartney, our first Ambassador to China, mentioned as a prominent object in the palace of the Chinese Emperor at Pekin, a musical clock inscribed "George Clarke, Clock and Watch Maker in Leadenhall Street, London"; it was in a case ornamented with crystal and coloured stones and played twelve old English tunes, "Black Joke," "Lillibullero," and other airs of the *Beggars' Opera*. There is a fine table clock by him in the Wetherfield collection. **Edward**, 9 Holborn, 1768. **Jas.**, Paternoster Row, 1768. **William**, George Yard, Whitechapel, 1769-72. **John Basul**, St John's Lane, liveryman C.C. 1776. **Jas.**, 52 Rahere St., 1778-1840. **Wm.**, 87 Gt. Sutton St., 1804-20. **Robt.**, York, f., 1807; settled at Hull. **Jos.**, Tuxford; watch, 1812. **—**, Richmond, Yorks., 1814. **Hy.**, warden C.C. 1822-26. **William, & Sons**, 8 Goswell St., 1830-42. **Job Guy**, 15 King William St., London Bridge, 1851-8; Sir Edward Clarke, K.C., is his son, and when a lad was his assistant. **William** (Clarke & Sons, Goswell Rd.), died 1875, aged 75. **Abraham**, (Clarke & Sons, Goswell Rd.), died 1890, aged 79. **Daniel** (Clarke & Sons, Goswell Rd.), trustee of the Horological Institute, master C.C. 1892, died 1897, aged 78.

Clarkson. Jno., apprenticed 1649 to Jno. Nicasius; C.C. 1657. **H.**, Stockport, 1770.

Claxton, Thomas, C.C. 1646; signed petition against oppression of the Company in 1656; master, 1670.

Clay. William, brother C.C.; maker of a watch Cromwell presented to Col. Bagwell at the siege of Clonmel; also of a clock, inscribed "William Clay, King's Street, Westminster" (see p. 359); watch of later date, G.M., 1645-80. **Thomas**, Chelmsford; lantern clocks, about 1650. **Samuel**, apprenticed to Jeremy Gregory, 1680; C.C. 1687. **Charles**, Stockton, Yorkshire, petitioned Parliament for a patent in respect of a repeating and musical watch or clock, his invention; Mr Quare produced a watch to answer the same end as Mr Clay's; the Attorney-General reported in favour of Mr Clay: the C.C., however, opposed Mr Clay, and after a tough fight, extending from Feb. 1716 to the latter part of 1717, the patent was not granted. He seems to have lived subsequently in the Strand (see p. 284). **Charles**, Fenchurch St.; watch in crystal case, S.K.M., 1740; another example with chased outer case, about 1750. **Wm.**, London; about 1750. **B.**, London; watch, h.m., 1770.

Claypot, Dennis, York, f., 1697.

Clayton. Thomas, admitted C.C. 1646; assistant, 1671. **Jno.**, Prescot, about 1745. **Ralph**, Marple, 1750. **Jno.**, Marple, 1765. **Jno.**, Blackburn, 1770. **Chas.**, London; watches, 1805-20.

Cleare, Wm., apprenticed 1688 to Hy. Jones, C.C.

Cleeke, Henry, C.C. 1655.

Cleeve, William, brother C.C. 1654.

Clegg, —, London; long-case clock, about 1790.

Cleghorn, Saml., 65 Shoe Lane, 1790.

Clement. Edward, C.C. 1671; the inscription "Edward Clement, Exon," on a lantern clock may apply to him. **William**, brother C.C. 1677; he applied to clocks the anchor escapement invented by Dr Hooke, probably about 1676; this allowed of the use of a long pendulum with a lesser angle of vibration than was possible with the verge escapement; instead of hanging the pendulum from a cord or a shackle he used a spring to suspend it from; this proved to be a much better attachment and one which has continued in favour. He was master of the C.C. in 1694. Mr Wetherfield has a long-case timepiece by him inscribed "Gulielmus Clement, Londini, fecit," the construction of which is very similar to that of the clock by Jno. Fromantil described on p. 237. In 1684 William Clement, presumably his son, was apprenticed to him. **& Son**, Tring, 1773; watch, "Clement, Tring," 1798.

Clements. Robt., C.C. 1686. **Moses**, Broadway, New York, 1747. **Thos.**, London; maker of bracket clocks, about 1760. **Jno.**, London; watch, 1820; 214 Oxford St., 1840.

Clemson, Richd., apprenticed 1661 to Thos. Claxton; C.C. 1673.

Clench, —, Dublin; watch, 1797.

Clent, Geo., apprenticed 1684 to Jno. Barnett, C.C.

Clerk, Jno., Bristol, 1687.

Clerke. Danl., Amsterdam, about 1720. **Jno.**, Brentwood, about 1780. **George**, 3 Cherry Tree Court, Aldersgate St.; summoned to take up livery C.C. 1786; 1780-

1820. **Geo.**, Cherry Tree Court, son of the foregoing; livery C.C. 1810-42. **Nathaniel**, London; watch, h.m., 1811. **F. W.**, Cornhill; died 1885, aged 65.

Clewes, see Clowes.

Clidesdale, —, Bell Yd., Temple Bar; C.C. 1780.

Cliff, Wm., apprenticed 1670 to Sam. Davis, C.C.

Clift, Thos., Hull; long black lacquer case clock, about 1730.

Clifton. Thomas, brother C C. 1651. **Thomas**, apprenticed to Chas. Gretton; C.C. 1687. **John**, 14 Fazakerley St., Liverpool, 1785-90.

Clinch, George, London; long japanned case clock, about 1740.

Clinsworth, G., Warrington; bracket clock, about 1790 (he was really a bell-founder).

Cliverdon, Thomas, Holborn; C.C. 1722.

Clodion, Michel Claude, born at Nancy 1728, died at Paris 1814, celebrated artist and designer of clock cases.

Clopton, Wm., apprenticed 1655 to Onesiphorus Helden, C.C.

Closon, Peter, at Holborn Bridge; subscribed to incorporation of C.C. 1630; three years senior warden, 1636-38; lantern clock with balance escapement, inscription on fret, "Peter Closon at London, fecit" (see p. 349). On another example is "Peter Closon, at Holborne Bridge." Sir Theodore Fry has a lantern clock inscribed "Peter Closon, neare Holborn Bridge, fecit."

Clothier, Jas., 121 Pall Mall, 1842.

Clough. Edward, Fetter Lane; a watch of his make, with an outer case of leather *piqué*, in the B.M., is inscribed, "Mayor Johne Miller, his watche," 1630-40. "Stolen a silver watch in a black case, studded about the edges, and one studded flower at the back of it, having a minute motion and the figures of the hours and minutes twice over the plate, made by Edward Clough, near Gray's Inn Gate, in Holborn" (*Lond. Gaz.*, October 6-9, 1690). **Samuel**, Boston, U.S.A., 1701.

Clowes. Jas., brother C.C. 1670; long-case clock, about 1690. **John**, C.C. 1672; elected a warden, 1713, but unable to serve through ill-health; small square bracket-clock, bob pendulum, locking plate, cherub corners, inscribed, "J. Clowes, Londini, fecit": long-case clock inscribed, "Jon. Clows, Russell St., Convent Garden." **B.**, Liverpool; watch, 1795. **O. B.**, Liverpool; watch, 1805. **Robt.**, London; watch, 1812.

Cluer. Obadiah, apprenticed 1682 to Hy. Evans; C.C. 1709; long-case clock signed, "Obed. Cluer," a man-of-war above the dial rocks with the swing of the pendulum; underneath are the words, "The Royal Ann." **John**, 22 Skinner St., Clerkenwell, 1835.

Cluter, William, C.C. 1709.

Clutton & Co., 48 Rupert St., 1825.

Clyatt. Samuel, C.C. 1672, Bell Alley, Coleman St. **Abraham**, C.C. 1680. **John**, C.C. 1708. **William**, C.C. 1709. **Samuel**, C.C. 1711.

Coastfield, Jno., apprenticed 1682 to Robt. Starr, C.C.

Coats. Archibald, Wigan; about 1780. **Thos.**, London; watch, 1780.

Coates. W. & J., Cirencester; watch, 1786. **Jas. & R.**, Wigan; watch, 1794.

Cobb. Wm., York, f., 1659. **John**, apprenticed to Andrew Yeatman; C.C. 1703.

Cobham. Jno., Barbican; C.C. 1725; pendulum watch, 1750. **Stockley,** C.C., Red Lion St., Clerkenwell, 1730.

Cochard, Geo., 10 Henrietta St., Covent Garden, 1822-25.

Cochin. D., a celebrated *repoussé* chaser of watch cases, 1740-70. **D.,** Paris; watch, 1790.

Cochran. Saml., 291 Wapping, 1760-94. Mr Edward C. Cockey, New York, has a pair-cased watch by him, h.m., 1768. **W.,** 266 Regent St., 1825.

Cock. Jno., London; long-case square dial clock, chiming on six bells, about 1700. **Chas.,** Bow Lane; apprenticed to Thomas Reynolds; C.C. 1736. **Chas.,** Macclesfield, 1760.

Cockeram, Jno., Downham; Halifax clock, lacquer decoration, about 1750.

Cockerton, Jonas, 1751-78.

Cockford, Matthew, C.C. 1693.

Cockshutt, Edmund, Liverpool, 1770.

Cocky, Cockey, Cokey, Cockney. Several generations of Somerset clockmakers; clock, Wm. Cokey, Wincanton, about 1700; astronomical clock, dating from about 1780, by Edward Cockney, Warminster, formerly belonging to Lord Carrington, sold at Stevens' in 1900 for £235.

Codevelle, —, Rue de Bussy, Paris, 1770.

Codling, W., Sutton; clock, about 1795.

Cogdon, Thomas, Budge Row, chronometer maker, apprenticed to Jno. MacLennan, died 1885, aged 67

Coggs, John, against St Clement's Church, 1690-1700.

Cogniat, —, Paris; watch, 1720.

Cohen. Sam Jacob, 3 Castle St., Whitechapel, 1815. **A. S.,** 9 Newcastle St., Whitechapel, 1820.

Coignet, —, began in 1665 and in 1667 finished the clock of the Pont Neuf, Paris, since known as "l'horloge de la Samaritaine."

Coke, Wm., apprenticed 1673 to Wm. Glazier; C.C. 1681.

Coker, Ebenezer, Clerkenwell Close, 1754-69.

Colambell, Anthony, Aldersgate St., liveryman C.C. 1776.

Colbert, J. G. I., Grafton St., 1825.

Cole. Daniel, apprenticed to Geo. Graham; C.C. 1726. **John,** C.C. 1729; long-case clocks, 1729-60. **Thos.,** Lombard St., 1754-63. Ipswich: **Richard Stinton,** 1780; **Richard,** 1830. **Wm.,** Gutter Lane, 1780-1805; pedometer by him, B.M. **I. B.,** 54 Barbican, 1785. **James Ferguson,** Hans Place, Chelsea; then Park St., Grosvenor Sq.; then 9 Motcombe St., Belgrave Sq.; born 1799, died at Tower House, Bexley Heath, 1880; an able watchmaker and expert springer; he devoted much attention to the lever escapement, of which he devised several forms, and was for some time a vice-president of the Horological Institute. **Thomas,** 11 Upper King St., Bloomsbury, an excellent maker of spring clocks; brother of J. F. Cole; died 1864.

Colehed, Richd., Liverpool, 1800.

Coleman. —, clock, signed, "F. Francis Coleman, Ipswich, fecit, 1665." **Fr.,** Ipswich; watch, 1720. **Geo.,** London; bracket clock, about 1780. **John,** 115 Newgate St.; hon. freeman of C.C. 1781; 1768-83. **William,** Arthur St., 1790; 14 Strand, 1794-99. **Sampson,** London; watch, 1795. **Thomas,** 6 Westmoreland St., St Mary-le-bone, maker of bracket clock, Chippendale style of case, 1810-42; livery C.C. 1813.

Coles, M. A., 25 Red Lion St., 1790.

Coley, S., London; watch finely enamelled royal blue, Schloss collection, 1795.

Colladon. —, Geneva; watch, silver bridge, about 1765. **& Sons,** watch, painting on dial, about 1785.

Collard, Leonard, apprenticed 1675 to Jno. Delander.

Colles, Christopher, long-case clock, about 1700.

Collett, John, Royal Hospital Row, Chelsea; mahogany long-case clock, about 1780; watch, h.m., 1799.

Colley. Joseph, apprenticed to James Harrison; C.C. 1752. **Thos.,** Fleet St., 1765-85; an exceedingly fine long-case clock, Wetherfield collection, inscribed "Graham's successor Thos. Colley London" (see p. 386); see also Barkley & Colley.

Colliber, Jno., apprenticed 1690 to Wm. Slough, C.C.

Collier. Benjamin, a noted maker; C.C. 1693; Lord Chesham has a gold double-case repeater made by him; 1693-1730, see Collyer; also p. 386. **Robt.,** C.C., Gutter Lane, 1730. **David,** Gatley; clock, about 1760. **Thos.,** Chapel-en-le-Frith, 1760. **Sam.,** Eccles; clock, about 1770. **John,** Red Lion St., Clerkenwell, 1770-85. **Peter,** Manchester, 1784. **Archibald,** 9 New Bond St., 1790-1830. **Chas.,** 159 Sloane St., 1822.

Collingridge. Edmund, 27 Wilderness Row; livery C.C. 1810; 1793-1830. **Thos.,** 136 Aldersgate St., 1838-42.

Collingwood. Samuel James, 8 Long Alley, livery C.C. 1786; 1766-94. **Robt.,** Rochdale, 1816. **Henry,** Rochdale, 1833.

Collins. Robt., apprenticed 1646 to Ahasuerus Fromantil, C.C. **Peter,** apprenticed 1679 to Jas. Atkinson; C.C. 1687. **John,** C.C. 1701; at the "White Horse and Black Boy," Great Old Bailey, in 1705, see Shelton, John. **Clement,** C.C. 1705. **John,** C.C. 1727; repeating watch, silver case pierced, silver dial with raised figures, about 1730. **Thos.,** Wattisfield, born 1750, died 1829. **Richard,** Margate, 1798. **Wm.,** London; watch, 1810. **R.,** 52 Strand, 1813. **Jas.,** 66 Long Acre, 1822.

Collinson, Jas., London; watch, 1770.

Collis. Chas., London; watch, 1720. **Richd.,** Romford, 1802-7.

Collomby. Jacob, London; watch said to have belonged to Oliver Cromwell, Mr Ambrose Phelps. **Henri,** Hüningen (Upper Alsace), 1680-1730; watch in enamelled case, S.K.M., signed "H. Collomby à Huninguen." **Jaques,** watch, Pierpont Morgan collection, silver cases, outer one chased, about 1700. **Abraham,** Geneva; watch, 1745, Mr Paul Ditisheim; another with calendar, Messrs Lambert; another specimen suspended from a long and handsomely enamelled chatelaine, outer case enamelled and studded with diamonds about the same date; at the S.K.M. is a calendar watch, about 1750, signed "Abr. Collomby, London."

Collum, A., 74 Lower East Smithfield, 1800.

Collyer, Benj., London; long green lacquer case clock, arch dial, about 1725, Wetherfield collection.

Colman, —, Ipswich; watch, one hand, about 1685, Mr Evan Roberts.

Colson (? Colston), Richd., apprenticed 1637 to Jas. Vantrollier; C.C. 1646.

Colston. Jno., C.C. 1653. **Richard,** free of C.C. by patrimony, 1682; curious 24-day clock at Battle Abbey, Sussex; other examples of his work are a fine watch, Evan Roberts' collection, with pierced contrate wheel, and a watch (inscribed "Colston London"), with sun and moon pointers (see p. 182); long burr walnut case clock, 12-inch dial, Wetherfield collection; watch, about 1720, Pierpont Morgan collection.

Colyer, see Collyer.

Combault à Paris, watch, about 1780.

Comber, Richard, Lewes, died 1824, aged 82; chiming clock, 1778 (see p. 500); clock, Victoria Hospital, Lewes, about 1790. Mr S. Tanner, Lewes, says: "I have never met with a bad or imperfect specimen; his work will endure for many generations."

Combes, Simon, watch, 1780.

Combret, Pierre, Lyons; calendar watch (see p. 119), 1613; watch in shell-shaped case, S.K.M., about the same period; cruciform watch, about 1620, Pierpont Morgan collection.

Combs, Joseph, C.C. 1720.

Comfort, William, brother C.C. 1647; signed a petition in 1756.

Comley, Thos., London; watch, G.M., about 1780.

Commander, Sam., St James' St., Clerkenwell, 1845.

Compigné, —, bracket clock, about 1710, inscribed "Compigne, Winton"; watch, "Dav. Compigne, Winton," about 1750; good long-case clocks by him are to be met with in Hampshire.

Comport, Ebenezer, Temple Bar; C.C. 1728.

Compton. Walter, Vere St., 1692. **Adam,** C.C. 1716.

Comtesse, Louis, watch-case maker, succeeded Peterman & Debois at Soho, 1810; afterwards at East St., Lamb's Conduit St., see Stram.

Conant, Elias, Bridgewater, U.S.A., 1776-1812; Lynn, 1812-15.

Conden, Robert, 51 Clerkenwell Close, 1780-85.

Conduitt, Sam., apprenticed 1671 to Robt. Halsted, C.C.

Condy, Thos., apprenticed 1684 to Cornelius Jenkins; C.C. 1692.

Congreve, William, Garden Court, Temple, and at Woolwich; inventor of curious clocks (see p. 338).

Connell, William, 22 Myddelton St., 1839; a clever watchmaker who succeeded Ganthony, at 83 Cheapside, in 1845; died 1862; his son, Wm. Geo., died 1902.

Connelly, Wm., 93 Piccadilly, 1825.

Connoley, M., Dublin; watch, 1790.

Conrad & Reiger, German octagonal timepiece in S.K.M., about 1590.

Constable, W. & G., Bunhill Row, 1804; 27 Finsbury St., 1807.

Constantin (or Constatine). Philip, London; bracket clock, about 1710; long-case clock, about 1730. —, Geneva; heart-shaped watch, S.K.M., about 1740.

Constantine, Pet., 33 Park St., Grosvenor Sq.; card B.M., 1802.

Contandois, see Le Contandois.

Contard & Co., Paris; 15-day watch, 1831.

Cony, John, brother C.C. 1641.

Conyers. Richard, C.C. 1689. **Thos.,** London; watch, about 1715, Major R. H. Raymond Smythies.

Cook. Wm., London; long-case clock, about 1700. **Edwd.,** 210 Borough, 1763-72. **John,** 22 Cheapside, 1768; 24 Wood St., 1772-75. **Joshua,** Blue Anchor Alley, 1793. **Zenas,** Waterbury, 1815-20. **J.,** watch-cap maker, 5 Robert St., Hoxton, 1835.

Cooke. Lewis, f., of York, 1614; petitioner for incorporation of C.C. 1630-32.

John, apprenticed to Isaac Law, 1641; C.C. 1649; hexagonal watch in case of rock crystal set in enamelled gold, Wallace collection, about 1660. **John**, apprenticed to Wm. Dobb, 1655; C.C. 1662; fine long-case clock, marqueterie case, about 1680. **Robert**, C.C. 1667. **William**, C.C. 1681. **Edwd.**, apprenticed 1687 to Wm. Kenning. **Thomas**, C.C. 1699; long-case clock, "Thos. Cook, London," about 1720. **William**, C.C. 1708. **John**, C.C. 1712. **Joseph**, C.C. 1715. **& Gurney**, Foster Lane, 1754-59. **John**, 22 Cheapside; livery Goldsmiths' Company, 1765-77. **Robert**, 7 Star Alley, Fenchurch St., 1804-10. **G. E.**, 5 Jewin St., 1822.

Cooley, Hy., London; long Sheraton case clock, about 1805.

Coombes. Wm., apprenticed 1689 to Isaac Lowndes, C.C. **Fisher**, admitted C.C. 1728. **Jas.**, 10 Mitchell St., St Luke's, 1815; 3 Clerkenwell Green, 1825.

Cooper. Hugh, C.C. 1653. **Stephen**, apprenticed 1675 to Thos. Morgan, C.C. **Jas.**, apprenticed 1693 to Wm. Boad, C.C. **Jno.**, Cardiff; watch, pendulum balance showing through dial, minute hand only, blued steel rotating hour disc showing through curved slit in the lower half of the dial, silver medallion over top plate, with finely chased female head and military trophies, about 1700. **Edwd.**, London; watch, silver dial, raised figures, about 1730, conversion to rack lever and very large balance, about 1805. **Geo.**, London; mahogany long-case clock, about 1760. **Jos.**, Whitchurch, 1765. **Benj.**, Brownlow St., 1775. **& Son**, Derby; watch, 1780. **Edward**, clock-case maker, 91 Sutton St., 1789-94. **Thos.**, Newport; watch, 1796. **Thomas**, 1 King St., Little Tower Hill, 1800. **Wm.**, 8 Old Bailey, 1804. **William**, 44 Red Lion St., 1816; 12 Gee St., 1820-42. **E.**, Wynyatt St., 1820. **Thomas Frederick**, Duncan Place, City Road, and afterwards at 6 Calthorpe St.; a well-known watch manufacturer, who made chiefly for the American market. His son told me the American reputation was obtained through the good going of a watch by Cooper, which was used as a Greenwich time standard on a ship when the chronometer had accidentally failed, 1820-62.

Coote, Thos., Dublin; bracket clock in pear-wood case, about 1750.

Cooth, Jno., London; watch, 1720.

Cope. Peter, brother C.C. 1638. **Chas. Jno.**, 38 Berners St., 1800-30; he was a man of some note, and attested the value of Earnshaw's improvements in 1804.

Copeland, Alexander, 113 Leadenhall St., 1800-15; livery C.C. 1810.

Copestake, Hy., 8 New Bridge St., 1793.

Coppet, Reg. A., watch; on plate over balance, "Geo. Virtue his watch. From Berne,—1750."

Copping. Richd., about 1640; C.C. **Geo.**, apprenticed to Richard, 1654.

Coppinge, —, long-case clock, "Richard Coppinge, at St Edmund's Bury in Suffolke," about 1720.

Copplestone, Wm., apprenticed 1683 to Wm. Robinson, C.C.

Corbet, Nathaniel, maker of a silver watch with studded case, frosted dial plate (*Lond. Gaz.*, Sept. 21-25, 1693).

Corbett. —, Hadleigh; watch, G.M., about 1780. **J.**, 42 Clerkenwell Close, 1825. **T.**, 22 Goswell Terrace, 1835.

Corbigny, —, French watch, 1700.

Corbitt. Ben., apprenticed 1682 to Thos. Snelling, C.C. —, 10 Short's Bdgs., 1835.

Corderoy. Thos., apprenticed 1663 to Nicholas Coxeter; C.C. 1670. **Phil.**, apprenticed 1672 to Robt. Seignior; C.C. 1679. **Walter**, apprenticed 1692 to Thos. Taylor.

Cording. Jno., 232 Strand, 1812-30. **Josh.**, 21 Holborn Hill, 1817-25. **Chas.**, 118 Minories, 1822-25. **Thomas**, 38 Aldgate, 1822-30.

Cordingley, Thos., Leeds, 1829.

Cordon, Richard, C.C. 1729.

Cordrey, see Corderoy.

Cordwell, Robt., C.C. 1646.

Corghey, John, Fleet St., 1754-59.

Corker. D., 18 Langley Place, Commercial Rd., 1820-42. **Nath.**, 48 Sth. Moulton St., 1842.

Corless, Richd., Stockport; about 1750.

Cormier. In 1481 a sum of four livres tournois was paid to Pierre Cormier, locksmith, for making a clock case and doing sundry other work for Louis XI. for his Château at Plessis-du-Parc.

Cornelius, Jacob, London; small diamond-shaped spring timepiece, catgut line, about 1620; C.C., but date of election uncertain.

Cornish. Wm., apprenticed 1659 to Robt Hanslapp, C.C. **Michael**, C.C. 1661.

Cornwallis, William, London; watch, silver case, enamelled dial, with Hope and a ship, about 1800.

Cornwell. Danl., London; small silver watch, Mr A. E. Clarke, about 1750. **Hy.**, London; watch, 1790; another, 1800.

Corp, Wm., 84 Aldersgate St., 1835.

Corrall, Fra., Lutterworth, 1740.

Corrie, —, Langholme; long-case clock, about 1770.

Corson. Joseph, Maryport, Cumberland, 1832. **Thos.**, 119 High St., Wapping, 1835-42.

Cortauld. Samuel, Cornhill, opposite Royal Exchange, 1759-63. **P., & Cowles**, 21 Cornhill, 1768-75.

Cosbey, Robert, at ye Diall, Rood Lane, C.C. 1653-79.

Cosens, Nicholas, hour glass maker, York, f., 1638.

Cosman, Philip, Amsterdam; watch, about 1790.

Cosse, James, Cornhill; watch, 1720.

Cosson, S., St George's East, 1835.

Costa. Timepiece of gold, signed, "Inventé et executé par Jh. Costa Amateur d'Horlogerie à Marseille," Turkish numerals, Wallace collection, about 1790.

Costem, Adam, Kirkham; long-case clock, about 1760; on another clock, about 1770, "Adam Costen, Kirkham."

Coster. Robert, C.C. 1655. **William**, admitted C.C. 1660.

Costontin, Vincent, Dieppe; watch, Schloss collection, about 1660.

Coteau, —, Paris; his signature on many good clock dials, Louis XVI. period.

Cother, William, brother C.C. 1668.

Cotsworth, Jno., C.C. 1669; **Edwd.** Crouch was apprenticed to him in 1691; long-case month clock, about 1730, signed "John Cotsworth, London."

Cottel, John; lantern clock, inscribed, "John Cottel, fecit 1653."

Cotter, Ebenezer, 13 Goldsmith Ct., Wood St., 1775.

Cotterel. William, C.C. 1694. **John**, C.C. 1721.

Cotterell, Thos., 163 Oxford St., 1830.

Cotton. John, London, C.C. 1695; watch, sun and moon hours (see **p. 182**), about 1710. **John, & Son**, watch, about

1715. **John**, admitted C.C. 1718; he worked for Pepys in 1730. **Wm.**, London; watch, 1740. **Francis**, 90 Shoreditch, 1822. **R. & T.**, watch-spring makers, 17 President St. East, 1835.

Cottonbelt, John, Wild St., C.C. 1729.

Couche, Charles, C.C. 1727.

Couchon à Paris; fine Boulle clock, Wallace collection, about 1690.

Couldray, Julian, Paris, 1529 (see p. **304**; **William**, clockmaker to Henry II., 1550.

Coulin Frères, Geneva; watch, 1780.

Coulon. Charles, Panton St., watch, 1762; Prince's St., Leicester Fields, 1765-68. —, Geneva, 1780.

Coulson. Charles, Soho, 1769. **Robert**, Whiskin St., 1800-38; livery C.C. 1810. **Saml.**, 16 North Audley St., 1825.

Coulton. Richd., apprenticed 1641 to Morris Blunt, C.C. **Francis**, C.C. 1690. **Wm.**, York, f., 1701; long-case clock, about 1740. **Jno.**, York, 1780.

Coupé. Jacques, Paris; clockmaker to the King, 1680; watch, enamelled case and dial, about 1670, name-plate engraved "James Coupé, London"; underneath on the plate of the watch was inscribed "Marc Grangier." **Edward**, Paris; clockmaker to the King, 1683.

Courter, Wm., Ruthin, 1780.

Courtois, —, Rue Saint-Jacques, Paris; clockmaker to Louis XV. 1750-72 (see p. **314**.

Courvoisier à Paris; fine ormolu wall clock, belonging to the Hon. Gerald Ponsonby, about 1780 (see p. **316**); many watches bear this signature; others signed "Courvoisier Frères"; see also Robert and Courvoisier. **Fredk. Alex.**, Chaux de Fonds, born 1799, died 1854.

Cousens. Thos., pendant maker, Bunhill Row, 1793. **R. W.**, 6 York St. East, Commercial Rd., 1835.

Cousins, Wm., 13 Finsbury Place, 1814-18, see Cozens. **& Whitside**, 20 Davies St., 1842; 14 Pont St., 1850.

Couta, G., 12 Blenheim St., Oxford St., 1822-25.

Coutois, Jha., London; watch, Pierpont Morgan collection, about 1780.

Covell, Richd., apprenticed 1671 to Chris. Maynard, C.C.

Coventon, Joshua, clock-case maker, 60 Red Lion St., Clerkenwell, 1835.

Coventry. Carr, apprenticed 1649 to Sam. Davis; C.C. 1657. **R.**, 21 Queen St., Clerkenwell, 1830. **J.**, 8 Paragon Place, New Kent Rd., 1835.

Coverdall, Dan., apprenticed 1683 to Thos. Rudkin, C.C.

Cowan, James, Edinburgh; apprenticed to Archibald Straiton 1744; on completion of his indentures he went for a short time to Paris, and worked under Julien Le Roy; watch, Schloss collection, engraved Jas. Cowan, Edinburgh, gold *repoussé* case, about 1765; bracket clock, about 1770, Wetherfield collection (see p. **392**); died 1781, see Reid, Thos.

Coward. William, apprenticed to John Fromanteel; C.C. 1681. **& Co.**, Cornhill; centre seconds watch, 1780. **& Jefferys**, 149 Fleet St., 1783. **Wm.**, Lancaster, 797-1830.

Cowderoy, R. F., fine watch, Hawkins collection, about 1750.

Cowdery, Geo., 6 King St., Holborn, 1817.

Cowell, John, 97 Royal Exchange, 1763-1800.

Cowen, H., 3 Sidney's Alley, Leicester Sq., 1800.

Cowie, Jno., 8 Aldermanbury Postern, 1814-18.

Cowles, Geo., & Co., 30 Cornhill, 1780-90.

Cowley, Robt., Chester; member of the Goldsmiths' Company, 1773.

Cowling, Richd., London; watch, 1820. **Edwd.**, Richmond, Yorks., 1823.

Cowpe. James, C.C. 1654. **Edward**, brother C.C. 1687.

Cowper, —, London; watch, 1800.

Cowta, Geo., 12 Blenheim St., Oxford St., 1817.

Cox, Thomas, C.C. 1708. **Jason**, Long Acre, 1745-60. **James**, 103 Shoe Lane, a clever mechanician, who opened at Spring Gardens a museum of quaint clocks, singing birds, and costly mechanical toys. There were fifty-six pieces in the collection, and the charge for admission was half-a-guinea each person; a regulation providing for the presence of but few visitors at one time was, needless to say, quite unnecessary; in the B.M. is a large centre seconds elaborate watch by him, suited for the Oriental market, 1760-88 (see p. 301). **Wm.**, 70 Cox Court, Little Britain, 1763-72. **Samuel**, Long Acre, 1770. **& Watson**, 23 Aldersgate St., 1780-85. **Jas., & Son**, 1789-1800. **Robt. N.**, Pickering, Yorks., 1822-40. **Nathaniel**, 140 Goswell Road, 1835-42.

Coxall, Samuel, "from London, late apprentice and now successor to Mr Thos. Kefford, at the Dial in Fore St., Royston," advertisement inside long-case clock, about 1750.

Coxeter. Nicholas, apprenticed to Jno. Pennock, 1638; C.C. 1646; master, 1671, 1677; a celebrated maker; lantern clock, inscription, "Nicholas Coxeter, neare Gold Smiths' Hall Londini fect," Mr T. W. Bourne (see p. 348); clock, Wetherfield collection, small narrow long-case with olive and laburnum veneer with stars inlaid. **Wm.**, apprenticed to Nich. Coxeter 1647; C.C. 1654. **John**, master C.C. 1661-63. **Thos.**, C.C. 1673.

Cozens, William, 3 Wilderness Row, 1804-10; 13 Finsbury Place, 1822-25; a prominent man in the trade; trustee to the W. and C. Benevolent Inst. in 1820; died 1842. **William, & Son**, 10 Bunhill Row, 1822-42. **J.**, 10 Bunhill Row, 1835-42; afterwards Cozens, Matthews, & Thorpe.

Crabb, Jas., Sarum, 1780-95.

Cradock, E., 13 Charlotte Terrace, Lambeth, 1835.

Cragg. Richard, C.C. 1660. **Sam.**, apprenticed 1690 to Jno. Northcott, C.C. **Jas.**, Lancaster, 1779, f. **John**, 10 President St. East, 1835; 8 Northampton Sq., 1840-62.

Craig, Chas., Dublin; cylinder repeating watch, 1780.

Craighead & Webb, Royal Exchange, 1848-54.

Craigingle, John, 90 Park St., Grosvenor Sq., 1839-42.

Cramber, R. P., London; watch, 1810.

Crampern. Wm., Newark, died 1770. **John**, Newark; long-case clock, about 1775 (see p. 364).

Cranage (or Cronage), Thos., Liverpool, 1818, also **Joseph**.

Cranbrook, Geo., London; watch, 1770.

Crane, Thos., apprenticed 1682 to Thos. Hollis, C.C.

Cranfield, Henry, C.C. 1706.

Cranmer, Chas., London; watch, 1800.

Cratzer, Nicholas, clockmaker to Henry VIII., 1538 (see p. 195).

Craven, Thomas, brother C.C. 1688.

Crawford. Alex., Scarboro', 1770. **Alex.**, jun., Scarboro', 1822.

Crawley. Thomas, C.C. 1660. **William**, apprenticed to James Harrison; admitted C.C. 1756. **J.**, London; watch, 1785.

Crawshaw. Wm., Washborough (near Barnsley), 30-hour clock, about 1720. **Jas.**, Rotherham, about 1740. **Thos.**, Rotherham, 1770. **Thos.**, Retford, died about 1814. **Andrew**, Rotherham, 1810-42.

Crayle. Richard, member of the Blacksmiths' Company, petitioner for incorporation of C.C. (see p. 202), 1610-55. **William**, Fleet St.; afterwards at the Black Boy in the Strand; watch by him, B.M., about 1660. "Lost a plain gold watch made by William Crealy, in a black shagreen case with gilt pins. If any can give notice to one of the King's Trumpeters next doore to the Kirk House near Charing Cross, they shall upon delivery thereof have five pounds for their peyns" (*The Intelligencer*, Jan. 11, 1663). "Lost on the 13 inst., a Gold Watch enamelled, the outside case seal-skin studded with gold; in the backside of it was the history of St Paul's Conversion, with small character *Saul Saul quid me persequoris?* And on the Dial part was the stoning of Stephen, with Lanskip round about; and in the inside of the back, a Damask Rose exactly enamelled, the Key fastened with a black Ribon. Whoever gives notice of it to Mr William Crayle, a watchmaker at the Black Boy in the Strand, near the Savoy, shall have 3*l*. reward" (*Lond. Gaz.*, July 13-17, 1676). "Lost on Wednesday, the 2nd Inst., at night, in Kings St., near Southampton Fields, a Gold Watch with a Pink coloured Sattin Ribon to it, the case studded with a Heart darted and the watch made by Mr Crayle in the Strand, and St George and the Dragon engraven on the Dyal Plate. Whoever brings it to Mr Norman Nelson, Stationer, at Grays Inn Gate, shall have 40s. reward" (*Lond. Gaz.*, 3rd June 1680). "Lost on the 22 inst., between St Andrews Church in Holborn and the further end of Grays Inn Road, a gold watch with the outer case studded, with Mr William Craile's name engraved on the bottom plate of the said watch. Whoever gives notice of the said watch to Mr John Wheatley, at the 3 Cups in Hatton Street, shall have two guineas reward" (*Lond. Gaz.*, March 20-24, 1690).

Crayton, Wm., London; watch, 1770.

Creak, William, Cornhill and Bunhill Row; watch, G.M., 1740-68.

Creaser, Thos., York, f., 1815-22.

Creed. Thomas, brother C.C. 1668. **Thomas**, brother C.C. 1674. **Robt.**, apprenticed 1689 to Thos. Tompion; C.C. 1699.

Creede, John, C.C. 1727.

Creeke, Henry; a suit by C.C. for using clockmakers' trade contrary to the statute, compromised by Creeke promising to present to C.C. a new house clock and alarm, and 20s., 1654.

Crespe, François, Geneva; "Essai sur les Montres à repetition," 1804.

Cressener, A. M., Red Lion Sq.; long inlaid case clock, about 1725.

Cressent, Charles, Paris; maker of clock cases (1720-60), two examples, Wallace collection.

Cressner, Robert, London; maker of

lantern bracket clocks, 1690-1730.

Creswell, Joseph, corner of Adelphi, Strand, 1775.

Creuzé. Francis Creuzé, a Huguenot, settled in London, carried on business in the parish of St Peter le Poor; resided at Clapton; died in 1758, aged 64, and was buried in the old Churchyard at Hackney. His sons, **Francis** and **John**, carried on business at Broad St., City. Francis, born 1726, died 1809, and was buried at Leyton, Essex. John, born 1737, died 1823, at Stoke-next-Guildford. For most of these particulars I am indebted to Mr Herbert H. Sturmer.

Crewe, James, an able horologist, many years in London, where he died in 1908.

Cribb, William, 58 Theobald's Rd., 1816-22; 17 Southampton Row, 1829; a chronometer maker who succeeded Birchall & Appleton, formerly Molyneux, died 1876.

Cripple, Wm., C.C. 1702.

Cripps. John, St Thomas Apostle, 1758-63. **John & Francillon**, 43 Friday St., 1769; 24 Norfolk St., Strand, 1793.

Crisp. Nicholas, Bow Churchyard, 1754-59. **John**, 22 Old Jewry, 1783. **Wm.**, Wrentham, 1790. **William Baker**, Clerkenwell; apprenticed to John Bryer, Northampton Sq., became a chronometer maker of repute, lived for some time at 174 St John's Street Rd.; died at the Clockmakers' Asylum, New Southgate, 1895, aged 70.

Cristoff, —, fine travelling watch, signed "Jo. Cristoff, Kerizer."

Critchley, Wm., Liverpool, 1818.

Crocker. James, C.C. 1716. **Wm.**, 34 Great Alie St., 1842.

Crockford, Matthew, C.C. 1659; lantern clock, engraved on the fret "At the Royall Exchang."

Croft. John, C.C. 1665. **John**, watch-case maker, 51 Wynyatt St., Clerkenwell, 1835.

Crofts, Richard, at the Bear in Foster Lane, right against Goldsmiths' Hall. "A gold watch by Goulon à Paris, the inside a landscape, a studded case, lost near St Martin's, to be taken to him if found" (*Lond. Gaz.*, March 25-29, 1675).

Crolee. Jam., London; clock, about 1730. **Natt.**, London; watch, 1775.

Crolet à Paris; late seventeenth century watch in engraved brass case, S.K.M.

Crome, Robt., apprenticed 1644 to Sampson Shelton, C.C.

Cronier à Paris, about 1790; watch, G.M.; clock, Wallace collection; bracket clock, Mr Alfred Spencer.

Crooke. Sampson, apprenticed 1661 to Sam. Horne; C.C. 1668. **Isaac**, apprenticed 1675 to Nicholas Russell. **Peter**, C.C. 1724. **Benj.**, Church St., Hackney, 1802-8.

Crosbey, —, long-case clock, about 1690, inscribed "Robert Crosbey, In King Street near the Sqr."

Crosby, Joseph, Bridlington, 1838-41.

Crosmier (? Cronier), —, Paris, 1790.

Cross. Jas., apprenticed 1687 to Jno. Browne, C.C. **Jno.**, Liverpool, 1770. **James**, Fetter Lane, liveryman C.C. 1776. **Edward**, Blewitt's Buildings, Fetter Lane, 1780-94. **John**, 131 Old St., 1804; 35 Cursitor St., 1823. **John Berryhill**, Jewin St., and 10 Charterhouse Sq., 1822-45; 23 Moorgate St., 1850-52; livery C.C. 1834.

Crossley. James, London; maker of lantern clocks, about 1710. **Richd.**, 14 Giltspur St., 1800-25. **Jas.**, King's Ct.,

Bunhill Row, 1814-18. **Humphrey**, also **Henry**, Manchester, 1818.

Crosthwaite, Jno., Dublin ; a good maker mentioned by Earnshaw, 1760-95.

Crouch. George, C.C. 1668. **Edward**, apprenticed 1682 to Jno. Cotsworth ; C.C. 1691 ; master, 1719 ; in 1697 his address was " Under St Dunstan's Church in Fleet St.," see Westoby. **Robert**, C.C. 1722. **John**, Knightsbridge, 1761.

Croucher, Joseph (associated with J. G. Ulrich), 27 Cornhill, 1825 ; livery C.C. 1828 ; Swithin's Lane, 1838.

Croudhill, Thomas, 19 Bedford St., Bedford Row, 1790-94.

Crow. Nat., apprenticed 1654 to Wm. Petty ; C.C. 1661. **George**, Wilmington, U.S.A., 1740-70. **John**, 1770-98. **Thos.**, 1770-1824.

Crowford, G., London ; watch, 1768.

Crowther. Wm., London ; watch, 1805. **Wm.**, Halifax, 1830.

Crucifex. Robert, Sweeting's Alley ; brother C.C. 1689 ; bracket clock, about 1700, Mr A. W. H. Hornsby-Drake ; long-case clock, about 1725. **John**, brother C.C. 1712 ; maker of sheep's-head brass clock, with arch dial, bought in Holland, and of a similar one at Stirling Castle.

Cruickshanks, Robert, 17 Old Jewry, 1772-75.

Crump. Henry, admitted C.C. 1667. **Thos.**, Liverpool, 1770.

Cruttenden, Thomas, apprenticed to John Fromanteel ; C.C. 1677 ; f. of York, 1680 ; died 1698.

Cryton, Wm., see Crayton.

Csacher, C., Prague ; watch, 1750.

Cubley, Thos., 54 Crawford St., 1820 ; Homer St., New Rd., Marylebone, 1830.

Cuendel, Samuel, 52 Red Lion St., Clerkenwell, 1815.

Cuff. James, London ; C.C. 1699 ; Mr Charles Winter has a fine marqueterie long-case clock by him, dating from about 1700-05. **John**, C.C. 1718. **Wm.**, Shepton Mallet ; long-case clock, Bishop's Palace, Wells, about 1720 ; his name is also on the sun-dial in the palace grounds. **Broadhurst**, 204 Regent St., 1823. **Jno.**, 138 New Bond St., and 106 Regent St., 1823. **Jas.**, 70 St Paul's Churchyard, 1823.

Cufford, Francis, C.C. 1718.

Culliford, J., Bristol, 1680.

Cullum, A., Lower East Smithfield, 1789-94.

Cumming. Alexander, born at Edinburgh, about 1732, died at Pentonville, 1814 ; a celebrated chronometer and clockmaker, who first suggested curved teeth for the cylinder escape wheel ; author of an excellent treatise on clockwork, which was published in 1766 ; elected hon. freeman of the C.C. in 1781 ; he resided at 12 Clifford St. till 1794, then he kept a shop in Fleet St., which after his death was occupied by his nephew, John Grant ; among the fine and curious clocks at Buckingham Palace is one by Alexander Cumming, made for George III., which registers the height of the barometer every day throughout the year ; he had £2,000 for the clock, and £200 a year for looking after it ; in the Wetherfield collection are a bracket clock, and a long mahogany case clock with marqueterie decoration (shown on p. 383), by him, dating from about 1790 ; some time ago I saw a watch inscribed Cumming & Grant, London ; it had no case but dated from about 1805. **W. M.**, Bond St., 1756-64. **Alex.**, Inveraray ; watch, 1775. **John**, " at the Dial," 202 Oxford St., 1816-42,

see Panchaud & Cumming.

Cummings. T., London ; watch, 1802. **G.**, London ; watch, 1805. **William**, Roxbury, U.S.A., 1820-30. **Charles**, 148 Leadenhall St., 1842, a maker of chronometers and fine watches ; a watch by him contained an ingenious form of fusee stop which seems to have been invented, though, before his time ; a little finger projecting from the smaller end of the fusee was pressed by the chain into the way of a stop on the plate.

Cuningham. Hugh, Dublin, 1770. **—**, London ; silver watch, enamelled dial with Arabic numerals, about 1790.

Cuper. Watch, about 1590, " signed Pierre Cuper à Blois," Garnier collection (see also p. 130). **Josias** (French), Blacksmiths' Company and C.C. 1627-34. **Loys**, C.C. 1632. **James Boyd**, clock, about 1700.

Current, Jno., London ; watch, 1770.

Curryer, Thos., watch-glass maker, 134 Whitecross St., 1835.

Curson, George, livery C.C. 1756.

Curteen, see Monkhouse.

Curtis. John, C.C. 1671. **Solomon**, Philadelphia, 1793. **Jas.**, London ; watch, 1810.

Curtiss, Wm., Exeter ; watch, 1805.

Curzon, Chas., Tottenham ; an excellent lever escapement maker ; some time teacher at the Horological Institute, died 1903, aged 79.

Cusin. Charles, born at Autun, in Burgundy, settled in Geneva, where it is said he introduced watch manufacturing, about 1587 (see p. 77) ; cruciform watch, about 1600, signed " J. Cusin," Pierpont Morgan collection. **Noel**, Autun, about 1630. **A.**, clock-watch, Pierpont Morgan collection, signed " A. Cusin à Corbigny," about 1700.

Custer, J. D., Norristown, Pa. ; watch marked " Feb. 4, 1843, Patented."

Cutbush. Jno., Maidstone ; long-case clock at Welbeck Abbey, dating probably from about 1700 ; at the top of the door of the case is an index hand pointing to the following, arranged in short lines to suit the width of the door down which the words are cut in relief : " Master, Behold me Here I stand, To tell ye hour at thy command, What is thy will 'tis my delight, To serve thee well by daye and night, Master be wise and learn from me, To serve thy God as I serve thee." **Edwd.**, Maidstone ; long-case clock, about 1705.

Cuthbert. Amariah, C.C. 1694. **J.**, 27 Piccadilly, 1790-94.

Cutler, Geo., apprenticed 1692 to W. Jacques, C.C.

Cutlove, John, Harleston, Norfolk ; long-case clock, moving ship, about 1760.

Cutmore, Jno., watch, h.m., 1819 ; 6 St Ann's Lane, 1846-58.

Cutting, Christopher, C.C. 1694.

Dadswell, John, Burwash, 1700-20 ; maker of lantern clocks ; Mr H. Stanley Cooke has a converted lantern in wooden case about 6 ft. high.

Daft, Thomas, New York, 1786.

Daglish, Joseph, Alnwick, 1770.

Daillé, fine ormolu three-part clock, Wallace collection, signed " Daillé horloger de Madame La Dauphine," about 1750.

Daking, Richd., Halested ; watch, 1780.

Dalby, John, 105 New Bond St., 1783-1804.

Dale, Roger, Baynes Row, 1774.

Dalemaige, Jehan, Paris ; clockmaker to the Duchess of Orleans, 1401.

Dalgleish, J., Edinburgh ; long-case clock, about 1750.

Dallas, James, maker of a pocket chronometer for the Duke of Sussex, 1800-20.

Dallington, William, London ; maker of a watch, silver case and dial, day of the month circle, about 1680.

Dalton. Jac., London ; watch, 1720. **James**, watch movement maker, Red Lion St., 1790 ; 12 Bunhill Row, 1810 ; 27 Percival St., 1815-20. **Jno.**, 27 Percival St., 1816-22. **Jno.**, York, f., 1830.

Damant, Saml., Ipswich ; watch, 1800.

Dammant, Barn., Colchester ; long-case clock, about 1700 ; watch, 1715 ; lantern clock, square dial, about 1725.

Dana, Payton & Nathaniel, Providence, U.S.A., 1800.

Dancer, see Tolkien.

Dane. Thos., 133 Oxford St., 1790-1817 ; Regent St., N., 1823. **Robert**, 72 Long Acre, 1807.

Danell, Joseph, 214 Oxford St., 1822-30.

Daniel à Paris ; watch, about 1650. **Stephen**, brother C.C. 1698. **Robert**, C.C. 1708. **Thomas**, 20 Foster Lane, 1783.

Daniell. William, C.C. 1632. **Hy.**, apprenticed 1646 to Hy. Kent, C.C. **Edward**, brother C.C. 1647. **Isaac**, C.C. 1648 ; warden 1674 ; did not become master. **Thos.**, C.C. 1656. **Thos.**, Kirkham, 1770.

Daniels, London ; watch, 1820.

Dannes, Robert, Clerkenwell, liveryman C.C. 1776 ; 1766-80.

Darby. Jas., London ; watch, 1770. **John**, 51 Gee St., 1820-42.

Darbyshire, —, Wakefield ; centre seconds watch, 1785.

Dare & Peacock, 103 Minories, 1770-72.

Dargent, James, C.C. 1700-05.

Dariford, —, maker of fine *repoussé* gold pair-case watch, gold dial, with calendar, about 1735.

Darle, Thomas, London, about 1769.

Darling. Robert, Fenchurch St. ; Sheriff of London, and knighted in 1766 ; on the court of C.C. 1766. **& Wood**, York, 1810. **Wm.**, f. of York, 1829.

Darlow, Thos., apprenticed 1685 to Geo. Deane ; C.C. 1692.

Darno, D., London ; watch, about 1750.

Darrell. Francis, apprenticed 1693 to Thos. Speakman, C.C. **Joseph**, 214 Oxford St., 1812-15.

Darrow, Elijah, Bristol, Conn., 1822-30.

Darvell (or **Darwell**), **Robert**, apprenticed to John Ellicott, C.C. 1708. **Edwd.**, 64 Watling St., 1775-94.

Darvil, Geo., London ; watch, G.M., 1766.

Darwin, E., London ; watch, 1770.

Dashper, Frederick, 10 Pierpoint Row, Islington, 1820-46. To him was apprenticed Egbert Storer.

Dasypodius, Conrad, born 1531 ; supervised second Strasburg clock, 1571 (see p. 54) ; died 1601.

Dauthiau, Paris ; clockmaker to the King of France, 1735-56.

Davenport. Wm., apprenticed 1669 to Robt. Smith, C.C. **Jas.**, London ; watch, 1780. **Sam.**, 15 Lime St., 1788. **Jas.**, Macclesfield ; watch, 1790.

Daverill, Jno., C.C. 1636.

David, Louis, 1550-60 (see p. 84).

Davidson. C., London ; watch, h.m., 1802. **J.**, 12 Red Lion St., Clerkenwell, 1814-17. **Adam**, 21 Norton St., Fitzroy Sq., 1835 ; 44 Goswell St., 1842.

Davie, Joseph, 201 High Holborn, 1830-42.

Davies. William ; Mr E. J. Nally, of

Chicago, has a sun-dial inscribed " William Davies, Clerkenwell, 1670." **Jenkin**, London, long-case clock, 1770. **Timothy**, Clifford St., Broad St., 1783 ; 15 New Bond St., 1793. **Wm.**, Chester ; watch, 1784. **Robert**, 85 Gracechurch St., 1788-94. **John**, 153 Leadenhall St., 1788. **Richard**, 85 New Bond St., 1790-1800. **T. & H.**, 39 Brewer St., Golden Sq., 1800. **James Callard**, College Place, Camden Rd. ; in 1840 he patented (No. 8,515) a one year clock.

Davis. Samuel, at yᵉ Golden Ball in Lothbury, C.C. 1647-82. **Tobias**, C.C. 1653. **John**, brother C.C. 1653. **Sam.**, junr., C.C. 1673. **Thomas**, C.C. 1674. **Benjamin**, C.C. 1678 ; fine long marqueterie case clock, Mr Miller Christy. **John**, Windsor ; walnut long-case clock with pendulum beating 1¼ sec., about 1678, the front of the base formed a door to get at the pendulum for regulation, and contained a bull's eye of glass through which the bob could be seen ; clock in the Curfew Tower, Windsor Castle, made by him in 1689. **Andrew**, apprenticed 1679 to Robt. Nemes, C.C. ; fine marqueterie long-case clock, Wetherfield collection, about 1720. **Wm.**, Boston, 1683. **Jeffry**, C.C. 1690. **John**, apprenticed to Daniel Quare, admitted C.C. 1697. **William**, C.C. 1699. **George**, C.C. 1720. **Thomas**, C.C. 1726 ; watch, Newington Free Library, 1740. **I.**, probably the son of John Davis, of Windsor, made the clock at Colnbrook Church, Bucks., 1746. **Wm.**, Lancaster, 1761, f. **John**, Lamb's Conduit St., 1769. **& Bennett**, London ; watch, 1795. **John**, New Holland, 1802-05. **Wm.**, 124 Newgate St., 1810-23. **Saml.**, Pittsburgh, Dty., 1815. **David**, 28 Bury St., St Mary Axe, 1830-42. **& Plumley**, 9 Red Lion St., Clerkenwell, 1830. **A. & C.**, 118 Houndsditch, 1835.

Davison. William, C.C. 1686. **Jno.**, London, 1786. **C.**, London ; watch, 1820.

Davy, Robt., Hoveton ; clock, about 1770 ; watch, about the same date, signed " Robt. Davy, Aldeburgh."

Daw, Josh., 39 Cheapside, 1822.

Dawes, Wm., 131 Upper St., Islington, 1835-42.

Dawkes, John, admitted C.C. 1707.

Dawson. Thomas, petitioner for incorporation of C.C. 1630 ; transferred from the Imbroderers' Co. to C.C. 1636. **Wm.**, apprenticed 1659 to Ben Wolverston, C.C. **Robert**, of Alford, C.C. 1678. **Jno.**, C.C. 1688 ; long-case clock, bird and flower marqueterie in panels, 11-in. dial, domed hood, about 1700. **John**, Holborn Bridge, 1763. **Wm.**, London ; watch, 1778 ; another 1805.

Day. Isaac, C.C. 1678. **Thomas**, C.C. 1691. **Edmund**, C.C. 1692 ; long marqueterie case month clock, Wetherfield collection, about 1700 ; bracket clock showing day of the month, and in an oak case veneered with tortoiseshell ; 1692-1720. **Jacob**, apprenticed 1693 to Isaac Day, C.C. **Jno.**, Wakefield, 1770. **Richd.**, 14 Drury Lane, 1780-94.

Deacle, Joana, apprenticed 1672 to Eliza, widow of Thos. Webb, C.C.

Deacon. Joseph, 27 Rosoman St., 1814-18. **Thos.**, Pentonville, 1830. **F.**, St Michael's Alley, 1835. **J. C.**, 18 Guildford St., Borough, 1835-42.

Dealtry, Thomas, 85 Cornhill, 1783.

Dean. George, engraver, admitted to C.C. 1671 ; in 1677 he presented to the Court, through Mr Henry Jones, a plate

with the coat of arms. **Deodadus**, 80 Minories, 1793-1804. **Thos.**, Old Jewry, 1810 ; 1 Swithin's Lane, 1820-42.

Deard, J., Corner of Dover St., Piccadilly, 1775.

Dearmar. Jno., apprenticed 1672 to Katherine Bestwick, widow, C.C. 1680. **Abraham**, apprenticed 1692 to Thos. East, C.C.

Death, Isaac, Maldon ; watch, 1790.

Deaves, Richard, Whitechurch ; long-case clock, about 1770.

De Baghyn, Adrian, Amsterdam, 1710-50 ; watch, silver dial with pierced centre, silver cases, the outer one *repoussé*, said to have belonged to the first Duke of Marlborough.

De Baufre, —, watch, (Garnier collection, signed " De Baufre, Paris," about 1650.

Debaufre. Peter, Church St., Soho ; admitted C.C. 1689. The Debaufres were an exceedingly clever French family of horologists, probably driven over here by the revocation of the Edict of Nantes. Peter and Jacob were associated with Facio in the patent he obtained in 1704 for watch jewelling. Peter Debaufre also invented a dead-beat or " club-footed " verge escapement, in which there were two escape wheels, having between them a truncated cone formed of diamond, and cut away at the side to form an impulse plane acted on by the wheels alternately. Sir Isaac Newton had a watch so made, and spoke favourably of its performance. Sully modified it by using two pallets and one wheel. Under the title of the club-footed verge, each kind was used for watches by Garratt, of Ormskirk, and also by Houghton, of the same place. More recently the two-wheel form has been revived for French carriage clocks ; alarm watch, about 1710, inscribed " ' Pie' De Baufre, Inglese, Roma," 1686-1720. **James**, Church St., Soho, admitted C.C. 1712 ; gold watch, S.K.M., h.m., 1723 ; another example, large silver watch with day of the month circle ; 1712-50.

De Beaulieu. M. Eugene Wehrle has a fine striking alarm and calendar watch, signed " C. De Beaulieu a Basl," about 1640.

De Belle, Paris ; watch, about 1780.

Debelle. —, Paris, 1790.

Debenham, —, Melford ; lantern clock, about 1690.

Debois, see Desbois, also Dubois.

De Bon, Jacque, Paris ; clockmaker to the Duke of Orleans, 1776.

De Boufler, Andrew, London, completed his apprenticeship 1769.

Debry, Theodore, a famous French chaser of watch cases, 1590-1630.

De Caux, Lucas, Norwich ; pendulum watch, 1700.

Decele, Sam., Norwich ; lantern clock, about 1710, Mr Hy. Brittain.

De Charmes. David, admitted C.C. 1692 ; plain silver pair-case repeater, rich cock and pillars, " Des Charmes, London," inscribed on enamel dial, 1692-1740. **Simon**, (French), Warwick St., Charing Cross ; came here through the revocation of the Edict of Nantes ; built Grove Hall, Hammersmith, in 1730 ; his son David lived there ; admitted as a brother C.C. 1691 ; 1688-1730. " Lost between Convent Garden and Leicester Fields, on Wednesday, Nov. 14th, a silver Watch with a silver Chain, a steel Chain Diamond Cut, &c. Whoever brings the said Watch to

Mr S. de Charmes, Watchmaker, at his House the Sign of the Clock, the corner of Warwick St., Charing Cross, shall have 2 guineas Reward " (*The Daily Courant*, Nov. 16, 1705). **J.**, bracket clock, 1740. A David De Charmes was buried in Fulham churchyard in 1783.

Décheoly à Caen, 1730-40 ; example at S.K.M.

De Choudens, watchmakers in France and Switzerland from the end of the seventeenth to the end of the eighteenth century ; see p. 150, and also Esquivillon.

Decka. John, apprenticed to Wm. Addis ; C.C. 1757 ; maker of an 8-day long-case clock mahogany case, inlaid with marqueterie ; 1757-90. **& Marsh**, Broad St., Ratcliff Highway, 1790-1800.

De Clareburg, see Clarburg.

Decle, J. H., père, Paris ; (garde visiteur, 1769).

De Cologny, Geneva ; about 1770.

Decoviguy, —, Paris ; watch, 1710.

De Crüe, Geneva ; about 1775.

Dee, William, Blackfriars ; C.C. 1729.

De Féalins, Jehan, clock for Rouen, 1389 (see p. 43).

De Fontaine, L., 18 Wilsted St., Somers Town, 1835.

Deforges, —, à Dijon ; watch, 1700.

Defour Fob et Cie. ; fine gold repeater, probably French, about 1780.

Degan, Mathew ; watch, Vienna Treasury, oval brass case, about 1630.

De Handis, see Handis.

De Heck, Gerhart ; engraved a watch said to have belonged to James I. (see p. 203).

De Jersey, Westminster ; maker of long-case clocks, about 1810.

De Kabors à Geneva ; clock-watch, about 1725.

Delabere, London ; watch, Mr George Carr Glyn, about 1730.

De la Chana, Dan., C.C. 1687.

De la Chaussée, fils, Rue Galande, Paris, 1770.

De Lacor, J. N., Geneva ; watch, about 1790.

De la Corbiere à Nismes, 1790.

Delacroix, —, Paris ; died 1862.

De la Fonds, watch-spring maker, 44 Salisbury Court, Fleet St., 1790.

De la Fons. John, Pinner's Court, Old Broad St., 1790-94. **James**, Royal Exchange, and 66 Threadneedle St., 1790-95. **John**, 66 Threadneedle St., 1800 ; corner of Bartholomew Lane, 1810 ; 25 St Swithin's Lane, 1815 ; received 30 guineas from the Society of Arts in 1801 for a remontoire ; in 1805 he patented (No. 2,893) a marine alarm chronometer.

Delafosse, Samuel (French), brother C.C. 1692.

De la Garde. Spherical striking watch, signed " Jacques De la Garde, Bloys, 1551," Garnier collection. **A.**, Paris, 1630. **Gustavus**, 17 Lowther Arcade, 1840-42.

Delaine, —, " South Work " ; clock, about 1720.

De Lance, Jas., Frome, 1720-35 ; Mr F. J. Butts has an early long-case 30-hour one-hand clock by him ; it plays a tune at twelve, four, and eight.

Delande, Pierre, à Paris ; octagonal watch, about 1600, Pierpont Morgan collection.

Delander. R., oval watch, about 1610 (see p. 135). **Nathaniel**, brother C.C. 1668 ; assistant, 1689. **John**, case maker, admitted C.C. 1675 ; Salisbury Court, 1730. " Lost on Monday, August 2, between Fleet Street and the Old Bailey, a gold watch box not finished, in a brass case. Whoever gives notice of it to Mr John Delander, watch-case maker, over against St Clement's Church, shall have 10s. reward" (*Lond. Gaz.*, August 5-9, 1675). **Daniel**, apprenticed 1692 to Chas. Halstead ; C.C. 1699. According to the *Spectator*, D. Delander in 1712 moved from Devereux Court to a house between the two Temple Gates ; he had been servant to Mr Tompion. Mr Wetherfield has a gilt framed hanging 8-day timepiece and a fine thirteen month clock with equation work by him (see p. 374) ; at Child's Bank in Fleet Street is a long trunk mural timepiece in a japanned case by him ; other examples of his work are a silver-gilt clock-watch and a watch in silver pair cases, notable as being an early application of a jewel to the centre of the balance-cock, both in the Pierpont Morgan collection. "Lost some time since a large jewel watch, the box and case in one, it winds up on the dial plate and has a steel plate inlaid with gold to make it go faster and slower made by Dan Quare ; whoever brings it to Dan Delander, watchmaker within Temple Bar, shall have 10*l.* reward and no question asked, where all sorts of repeating jewel watches and other are made and sold" (*Lond. Gaz.*, October 5-9, 1714). 1699-1721. **John**, Salisbury Court ; apprenticed to Nathaniel ; C.C. 1705. **Nathaniel**, Fleet St., near Temple Bar, son of Daniel Delander, C.C. 1721 ; master, 1747. **John**, apprenticed to Richard Conyers, C.C. 1744.

De Landre, Peter, brother C.C. 1641.

Delandre, James, brother C.C. 1668.

Delaplaine, Jas. K., f., New York, 1786.

De la Porte, C. H., Delft, 1720.

De la Salle. Thomas, Brookers Row, Moorfields, 1780 ; 42 St Catherine's, Tower Hill, 1800-18. **Jas. Thos.**, 18 Cannon St., 1810-42 ; livery C.C. 1826 ; succeeded by his nephew, **Wm. Christie**.

Delaunay à Paris ; large bracket clock, inlaid with tortoiseshell and brass, about 1760.

Delaunce, James, brother C.C. 1650.

De Laundre, see De Landre.

Delauney, Peter, 68 New Bond St., 1822-25.

Delaversperre, Wm., brother C.C. 1650.

Delaville, Jas., apprenticed 1662 to Evan Jones, C.C.

De Lespinasse, Paris ; very fine pair of obelisks, veneered with lapis lazuli, Wallace collection ; on one a clock, over the dial a female figure holding a fan through a diminutive hole in which the light passes and at noon crosses a vertical meridian line, after the style of Fig. 2 ; on the companion obelisk is mounted a barometer.

Delisle & Moricand, watch so signed, about 1760, Mr Willard H. Wheeler.

Dellesser, Ellis, Liverpool, 1818.

Dellung, Paul, apprenticed 1659 to Paul Lovell, C.C.

Delolme. Nicholas, London, 1770-96. **Henry**, 48 Rathbone Place ; a good watchmaker who also imported Swiss watches and materials ; died 1890, aged 87.

De Lorme, Paris, 1720-40 ; alarm watch, Evans Roberts collection, with inscription, "From Admiral Lord Nelson to Post Captain Jonas Rose," silver pillars.

Delunésy ; finely decorated clock, Wallace collection, about 1770. — à Paris ; clock presented by the muni-

cipality of Lyons to the Duc de Mortemar, governor of that city, gilt case finely chased by Gouthière and dated 1771, now in the Wallace collection.

Del Valle, Vincent, Gibraltar ; watch, 1780.

Demaza, George, 95 Strand, 1825.

Demelais, —, London ; watch, Dutch style, 1750.

De Moylym, John, keeper of the Dulwich College clock in 1553.

Dempster. Anthony, York, 1822. **Mark Anthony**, York, f., 1829-34.

Demster, Roger, London, about 1790.

Denham, Geo., London ; watch, Hawkins collection, about 1785.

Denier, M., Paris ; vase-form clock with revolving band and held up by two boys, Legion of Honour, 1844.

Denison, Edmund Beckett, born 1816 ; elected President of the British Horological Institute, 1868 ; succeeded his father as a baronet, taking the title of Sir Edmund Beckett in 1874 ; called to the House of Lords under the title of Baron Grimthorpe, 1886 ; died 1905 : designer of the Westminster clock, see Dent, E. J. & Dent, F.

Denizave, —, London ; watch, 1802.

Denman, Geo., 24 Greek St., Soho, 1820 ; 39 Newgate St., 1823. **John F.**, 13 Cannon Street Rd., Commercial Rd., 1842.

Denn, Basil, Tooley St., 1776.

Denne, John, 28 Lamb's Conduit St., 1820-23.

Dennett, Jas., St Helens, Lancs., 1818.

Denning, J., 32 Ludgate Hill, 1840.

Dennis. Thos., apprenticed 1672 to Jas. Wightman, C.C. **Francis**, brother C.C. 1673. **Peter**, C.C. 1712. **D.**, 54 New Bond St., 1816.

Dennison, Aaron L., born at Brunswick, Maine, 1812, died at Birmingham, 1895 ; a pioneer of American watch-making ; in 1853 he started a factory at Roxbury ; in 1854 removed to Waltham ; subsequently settled in England and devised machinery for making watch-cases at Birmingham, see Howard, Ed.

Dent. William, C.C. 1674. **Robert**, London, C.C. 1681 ; watch, 1710. Canon Greenwell has a long-case clock marked on dial "Dent London, 1746." **Edmd.**, case maker, C.C. 1730. **Edward John**, born 1790, died 1853 ; was apprenticed to a tallow chandler, but disliking that business, induced Richard Rippon, in whose house he lived, to instruct him in making repairing mechanism ; he worked as a finisher of repeating watches till 1830, when he joined J. R. Arnold in partnership, at 84 Strand ; during the ten years they were together the business was greatly extended, chiefly through the energy and ability of Dent, who, after the partnership expired, established himself at 82 Strand, afterwards removing to No. 61 ; he also took Desgrange's shop at 33 Cockspur St., and another inside the Royal Exchange near the entrance to "Lloyds" ; he married the widow of Richard Rippon, whose sons, Frederick and Richard, took the name of Dent ; he turned his attention to the compensation of chronometers, and secured the confidence of Professor Airy, the Astronomer - Royal. When the Royal Exchange was rebuilt, Dent, on Airy's recommendation, was selected to provide the large clock ; for this work Dent equipped a suitable workshop in the Savoy and made an excellent clock, which was fixed in the tower of the Exchange in 1844. In the same year Vulliamy was com-

missioned to prepare a plan for the great clock of the Houses of Parliament. Dent asked to be allowed to compete for the making of the clock, but objected to having anything to do with Vulliamy's plans ; he said he would be willing to follow instructions of the Astronomer-Royal, as he had done with the Exchange clock. The Commissioners applied to Airy, and on his advice plans and estimates were obtained from Vulliamy, Dent, and Whitehurst of Derby. In May 1847 Airy reported and recommended Dent for the work. In 1851 Lord Seymour, Chief Commissioner, asked Edmund Beckett Denison, a barrister who had taken an interest in horology, to act as referee with the Astronomer-Royal, and in February 1852 a contract was signed with Dent to make the clock, he to do everything ordered by the referees who described in a general way what was required. Airy went abroad for a time about March 1852, giving Denison power to act for him. E. J. Dent died in March 1853. The businesses in the Strand and Royal Exchange were taken over by Frederick Dent, and the one in Cockspur St. by Richard. **& Son**, watch-glass makers, 50 Northampton St., Clerkenwell, 1835. (Rippon), **Richard**, stepson of E. J. Dent, 33 Cockspur St. ; died 1855. (Rippon), **Frederick**, stepson of E. J. Dent, 61 Strand ; died 1860. The initial proceedings in connection with the Westminster clock have been related under the head of Dent, E. J. Frederick had but little liking for clock work, and as the Astronomer-Royal in November 1853 resigned the office of joint referee, which he had held in conjunction with E. B. Denison, the superintendence of the making of the Westminster clock movement was left entirely to Denison. Dent's contract did not include the dials and hands, which were designed by the architect, Mr (afterwards Sir Charles) Barry, nor the provision or fixing of the bells. The clock was set going in May 1859. On the frame of the movement is the inscription, "*This clock was made in the year of our Lord 1854 by Frederick Dent of the Strand and Royal Exchange, clockmaker to the Queen, from the design of Edmund Beckett Denison, Q.C. Fixed here 1859.*" Vulliamy had many influential friends, and what with their opposition at every stage and the incidental difficulties of the work, any less determined man than Denison would have thrown up the matter in disgust. He prepared a specification for the bell founders in February 1855. The first hour bell weighing nearly 16 tons, cast in August 1856, became cracked and useless ; the second bell weighing 13 tons 11 cwt. was tried with the four quarter bells in June 1858, but shortly after the clock was started a fissure was noticed, and in October 1859 the striking was stopped. Then for a short time the hour was struck on the largest of the quarter bells, but afterwards the hour bell was turned round so as to present a different surface to the hammer, and has ever since performed its office satisfactorily. The first set of hands, with their counterpoises, weighed 2¼ tons and proved to be too heavy for the clock to drive. The hour indicators were retained, but the minute hands rejected in favour of lighter ones made of copper and tubular, and so the clock was not really finished till 1860. All's well that ends well, and the splendid timekeeper at Westminster, of which the nation may be proud, remains as an appropriate tribute to the ability and dogged perseverance of E. B. Denison (Lord Grimthorpe). Some particulars of the mechanism are given in the "Watch and Clock Makers' Handbook." The hour bell was named "Big Ben" in honour of Sir Benjamin Hall (Lord Llanover), who as Commissioner of Works in 1856, gave the order for it to be cast.

Denton. Robert, Oxford; long-case clock, about 1750, Mr H. Clark. **Joseph,** Hull; long-case clock, about 1760, Mr Thos. Boynton. **Wm.,** Oxford; watch, 1764. **Isaac,** London; about 1790. **Wm.,** Poultry, 1816-20.

Depree, Elie, C.C. 1634.

De Presles, Jean, Paris, 1544 (see p. 304).

Derby. Aron, apprenticed 1687 to Wm. Garfoot, C.C. **Charles,** Salem, U.S.A., 1846-50.

Derham, William, born 1657, died, and buried in Upminster, in 1735; a clergyman and Canon of Windsor, author of "The Artificial Clock-maker," published in 1696; second edition in 1700; third in 1714; fourth and last in 1734. He appears to have been acquainted with and assisted by Hooke, Tompion, and Langley Bradley.

Dermere, Abraham, C.C. 1703.

Derne, Louis, Nancy; watch, B.M., about 1640.

Deroche (or Deroches), Fras., Geneva; watch, Wallace collection, about 1720; enamelled watch, about 1750; watch signed "Frs de Roches & Fils," about 1760; another "Derocher Geneva," 1775.

De Rouvroy, Jean. In 1446 he acquired the title of clocksmith and orloger of the town of Amiens.

Derwood, W. M., London; watch, h.m., 1780; another, 1805.

De Salle à Caen; watch, about 1720.

Desarts, —, et Cie., Geneva; watch, 1780.

Desassars, Abraham, C.C. 1682.

Desbois. Several generations of this family have carried on business in the neighbourhood of Holborn. **& Wheeler,** 9 Gray's Inn Passage; a watch by them is in the Guildhall Museum; 1803-35. **Daniel,** apprenticed to John Johnson, whom he succeeded at 9 Gray's Inn Passage; died 1848, aged 75. **Daniel,** 9 Gray's Inn Passage, and afterwards 79 High Holborn; died 1885, aged 76.

Desborough, Christopher, C.C. 1665.

Desbrow. Elizabeth, apprenticed 1676 to Hy. Jevon and Christian his wife; C.C. **Robert,** C.C. 1704.

Des Granges, Peter, successor to Recordon, 33 Cockspur St., 1816-42, see Dent.

Deshais, Matthew, London; bracket clocks, 1690-1710.

Desmarais, Peter, St Martin's Court, 1794.

Desmee à Paris; watch, enamelled dial, Schloss collection, about 1750.

Desmore, T., 11 Clerkenwell Green, 1830.

Destaches, Jno., C.C. 1660.

De St Leu, Daniel, a good maker; was watchmaker to George III. In 1753 his establishment in Cloak Lane was called "The Golden Head"; later it was 17 Cloak Lane. A fine large watch of his make sold in 1895 from the Bentinck-Hawkins collection; in the Hilton Price collection is a clock-watch by him, made for Eastern markets; it strikes hours and quarters, is in a pinchbeck case, with outer case of imitation tortoiseshell; bracket clock, chiming on eight bells, inscribed "To Her

Majesty." He afterwards removed to 38 Cornhill, and was succeeded about 1790 by Rivers & Son.

Destouche à Middelbourg; watch, about 1800.

Dethau, Matthew, London; about 1720.

Devall, Jno., apprenticed 1670 to Andrew Pryme; C.C. 1677.

Devere, Frederick, 7 Angel Court, Throgmorton St., 1769-75.

Deverell. Jno., London; watch, 1780. **John,** Boston, 1789.

De Vick, Henry. About 1364 he made for Charles V. of France the first turret clock of which we have reliable record (see p. 45).

De Villeneuve, —, Rue de l'Arbre Sec, Paris, 1770.

Devis. William, Fleet St., 1750-65. **John,** Gloucester St., Bloomsbury, 1764, afterwards 76 Lamb's Conduit St.; hon. freeman C.C. 1764-83.

Dewe, Jno., Gravel Lane, Southwark; C.C. 1730.

De Welke, Christian, one of the signatories to the petition of incorporation of C.C. In the eighteenth century an oval watch by him was found in a field near Kettering; 1620-30.

Dewey, William, Dutch clockmaker, 59 Broadwall, Blackfriars, 1835.

Dewin, —, watch-case maker, 17 Red Lion St., Clerkenwell, 1835.

Dexter, M., London; watch movement, G.M., about 1790.

Deykin, —, long-case clock, signed "Tho. Deykin, in Worcester, fecit," beautiful inlaid case, birds and flowers, about 1700; 30-hour long-case square dial clock, inscribed "Henry Deykin, Worcester," about 1710.

Dichous à Paris; clock, about 1785.

Dickens, John, C.C. 1688.

Dickenson, Rich., London; watch, 1710. **F. C.,** 1 Upper Ashby St., 1840.

Dickerson, Danl., Yarmouth, about 1750.

Dickie. Andrew, Edinburgh; repeating watch in S.K.M., h.m., 1735. **Andrew,** London; long-case clock, 1765.

Dickinson. Rd., Liverpool; watch, 1715. **Robert,** York, f., 1810-16. **Thos.,** Lancaster, f., 1817-20.

Dieu, R., à Paris; oval watch, no screws, about 1590; another, later, Newington Free Library.

Digby, —, London; repeating watch, 1760.

Dighton, Wm., apprenticed 1687 to Sam. Rosse, C.C.

Dike, Nathaniel, C.C. 1663.

Dillington, —, London; watch, Mr Geo. Carr Glyn, about 1750.

Dingley. Robert, George Yard, Lombard St.; apprenticed 1661 to Lionel Wythe; C.C. 1668; Mr G. Ericsson, of Stockholm, has a beautifully inlaid long-cased clock by him, about 1700; another specimen of his work is a gold watch, hour-hand only, case with *appliqué* gold flowers, enamelled. **Robert,** Bishopsgate St., corner of Great St Helen's, 1728-40.

Dingwall & Bailliam, 9 St James's St., 1813.

Dinizard, —, Paris, 1790.

Dinnis, Francis, engraver; C.C. 1666.

Dinnott, Robt., London; watch, 1795.

Dissmore, Richd., York, 1818.

Distin, Jno., Totness, 1750.

Ditchfield, Richd., C.C. 1677.

Divernois, —, Rue Dauphine, Paris, 1770.

Dixon. Wm., apprenticed 1686 to Dan. Beckman, C.C. **Wm.,** 26 Smith St., Clerk-

enwell, 1835; 32 King's Sq., 1840-42.

Dobb, William, brother C.C. 1646.

Dobbings, Wm., Leeds, 1830.

Dobell, Ebenezer, Hastings; patented electric clocks in 1853 (No. 2,036).

Dobree. Elisha, London; watch, h.m., 1761. **John,** 3 Charing Cross, 1815; 69 Charlotte St., Oxford St., 1823.

Dobson. William, brother C.C. 1670; large lantern clock, about 1680, inscribed "William Dobson, in High Holbourne, Londini, fecit." **Arl.,** London; watch with finely enamelled case in the B.M.; another example is an oval watch at S.K.M., inscribed, "This watch was a present from ye King to the Countess of Monteith, 1675." **Thos.,** Red Lion St., Holborn; C.C. 1730. **Arlander,** London; pull repeating bracket clock, about 1740; watch, 1765 (see p. 154). **Charles,** Coldbath Fields; livery C.C. 1776. **Frank,** Gt. Driffield, 1822. **Geo.,** Leeds, 1829.

Dockwray & Norman, 16 Princes St., Leicester Sq., 1815-19.

Dod, Richard, London; long-case clocks, 1695-1720.

Dodd. G., wrote a paper on clockmaking in British manufactures, 1845. **G. P., & Son,** Cornhill; chime clock, about 1855.

Doddington, Jno., apprenticed 1685 to Ben. Wright, C.C.

Dodson, Jno., apprenticed 1655 to Isaac Law, C.C.

Dodsworth, John, brother C.C. 1648.

Doke, Richard, Prescot; eminent as a chronometer wheel-cutter; died 1906, aged 83.

Dolley, Thos., master C.C. 1808.

Donac, —, London; inscription on a watch, gold cases, outer one *repoussé*, h.m., 1807.

Donaldson, Geo., 121 Pall Mall, 1842.

Dondi. John, maker of a clock with wheels and balance, 1334. **Joseph,** son of the foregoing, 1350-60.

Donisthorpe, Geo., 85 High St., Birmingham, 1770-1810. Ludlam speaks of him as "the best maker of church clocks I know."

Donne. Anthony, Red Lion St., Holborn; C.C. 1730. **Robert,** Lamb's Conduit St., 1763-94. **Griffith,** Denton St., Somers Town; apprenticed to John Moore & Son, afterwards at Dent's; died 1884, aged 70.

Doolittle, Isaac, New Haven, 1785-1810.

Doore, Robt., C.C. 1671.

Dorer, Robt., Paris; about 1760.

Dorigny, Robert, clockmaker to the Duke of Orleans, 1397.

Dormer, P., London; watch, 1800.

Dorrell. Francis, Honeysuckle Court, Grub St.; known as a maker of long-case clocks; C.C. 1702. **Francis,** C.C. 1755. **William,** Bridgwater Sq., summoned to the livery C.C. 1786; restored Cripplegate Church clock, and made it to strike the hours on the tenor bell, in 1797.

Dorsett, Wm., London; watch, 1790.

Dossett, Gregory, C.C. 1662.

Doud, James. Mr T. W. Greene has an oval metal watch by James Doud, dating from about 1600.

Doughty. Tobias, C.C. 1696. **Jno.,** York, f., 1772. **Thos.,** Charles St., Somers Town; invented a compensation pendulum, 1811. **Wm. P.,** 10 Great Ormond St., 1816-20.

Douglas. J., London; watch, 1745. **Robt.,** Bolton, 1775. **Walter,** Dollar; long-case clock, four season corners to dial, about 1790. **Alex.,** 18 Cross St., Hatton Garden, 1810-18. **Jno.,** 52 Red Lion St., 1816. **Sam.,** Liverpool, 1818; also **Robt.,**

same date.

Douglass, John, New Haven, 1800-20.

Dove. Arthur, apprenticed to Wm. Clay; C.C. 1659. **Henry**, C.C. 1667. **Arthur**, "Gold Watch taken by Highwaymen with a gold Chain and a gold studded case made by Arthur Dove, of St Martin's," &c. (*Lond. Gaz.*, Sept. 8, 1681).

Dovey, Richard, 6 Craven Buildings, Drury Lane, 1765-70.

Dow. Roger, Vere St., 1780-85. **Robert**, Clerkenwell Close, 1790; 72 Long Lane, 1810-35. **James**, watch-case maker, 15 St James's Buildings, Clerkenwell, 1820. **William**, watch-case maker, 54 Percival St., 1835. **Robert**, 96 Upper St., Islington, 1842.

Downes. Chris., C.C. 1632. **Jere.**, apprenticed 1688 to Jas. Jackson, C.C. **Jno.**, Shoe Lane; C.C. 1725. **Joe**, London; watch, h.m., 1774. **Valentine**, Louth, 1790. **Robt.**, Clerkenwell Close, 1793. **Robt.**, Long Acre, 1798-1818. **Joseph**, Coventry, 1817.

Downie, Will., Edinburgh, 1770.

Downing. Jno., Liverpool, 1770. **George**, watch-chain maker, Covent Garden, 1790.

Downinge, Humfrey, apprenticed to Mr Grinkin, free of Barber Surgeons; Blacksmiths' Company in 1637 applied to have him disfranchised.

Downs. Benj., Mansfield, 1790. **Anson**, Bristol, Conn., 1830; also **Ephraim**.

Dowse, Gabriel, apprenticed 1649 to Wm. Godbed, C.C.

Dowsett, Jeremiah, C.C. 1708.

Dowson. —, Bath; watch, 1760. **John**, 77 Holborn Bridge, and Field Court, Gray's Inn; watch, skeleton movement, h.m., 1764; a later specimen, G.M. **& Peene**, Gray's Inn, 1800.

Doyle, James, watch-glass maker, Queen's Sq., Bartholomew Close, 1790.

Drabble, J., London; bracket clocks, 1710-20.

Drake. John, Fleet St.; action by Blacksmiths' Company to disfranchise him 1633; C.C. fined him £10 for binding his apprentice to the Blacksmiths' Company 16—; signed a petition to C.C. in 1656; Lady Fellows had a round silver watch of his make, with plain outer case, silver dial, and steel hand, now in the B.M.; 1630-59. **J.**, London; watch, 1760.

Drakeford, Edwd., Congleton, 1818; also **Jno.**, same place and date.

Draper. Simon, apprenticed 1688 to Sam. Drosade, C.C. **John**, C.C. 1703; Mr T. D. Chapman has a long-case clock by Jno. Draper, Maldon, about 1720. **James**, C.C. 1712. **William**, Maldon; lantern clock, about 1760 (see p. 361).

Draycott, Francis, C.C. 1678.

Drayton, —, Chardstock, eighteenth century (see p. 351).

Drescher, Jno., Hull, 1822.

Drew. John, C.C. 1684; long-case clock, about 1695, inscribed "John Drew, Johnson Court in Fleet St." **Edward**, C.C. 1692.

Drills, Jno., London, 1780.

Drosade, Samuel, C.C. 1675; watch by him, B.M., about 1680; another, with sun and moon hour indicators, about 1690.

Droshute, John, C.C. 1632.

Drown, C. L., Newburyport, U.S.A. 1848.

Droz. Pierre Jacquet, born at Chaux de Fonds 1721, died at Bienne 1790; a clever mechanician; he made a curious clock for the King of Spain; his sons, Henri Louis

(born 1752) and Daniel, also good watchmakers in Chaux de Fonds; Humbert Droz settled in Philadelphia in the latter part of the eighteenth century (see·p. 167). **Henry Louis**, son of Pierre Jacquet; born 1752, died 1791; excelled, if possible, his father as an ingenious mechanician; he journeyed to England, France, and Spain; was condemned to death at Madrid by the Inquisition as a necromancer, and saved by the Bishop of Toledo. **& Leschot**, clock, about 1795, signed "Pierre Droz & Leschot." **Humbert**, Philadelphia, 1797.

Humbert A. L., Philadelphia, 1811. **& Sons**, 1811. **Charles A.**, 1819.

Drozte, Jeune, Rouen; watch, 1799.

Drummond. Francis, apprenticed 1676 to Sam Davis the elder; C.C. **Thos.**, Liverpool, 1818.

Drury. James, C.C. 1694, master 1728, clerk 1731; died 1740. **John**, Red Lion St., Clerkenwell; C.C. 1720. **Dru.**, 32 Strand, 1770-85; card, Ponsonby collection, "Dru; Drury, Goldsmith to Her Majesty, in the Strand, successor to Nath. Jeffreys." There seems to have been an earlier D. Drury. Mr J. Hall has a clock, long-case inlaid in front, oyster shell veneers on sides, spiral pillars to hood, which has no door, dial signed "D. Drury, London," dating from about 1705. **Wm.**, 32 Strand, 1800-25. **James**, Banbury, Oxon., 1800. **J. F.**, 19 Clerkenwell Green, 1810.

Dryden, G., 30 Little Guilford St., 1835.

Dryer, Sam., London; single-cased watch by him, about 1674, belonging to Mr Geo. Carr Glyn; another specimen, silver dial, about 1690.

Drysdale, Wm., Philadelphia, 1819-51.

Dubant à Grenoble; watch, about 1690.

Dubbar, Hugh, apprenticed 1648 to Jno. Freeman, C.C.

Dubie, J., Paris; Court goldsmith who resided in the Louvre, excelled in fine enamelled watch-cases, 1640 50 (see p. 130).

Dubois (or **Debois**). **Jacob**, apprenticed to David Hubert; C.C. 1730. **G.**, small pillar clock, Wallace collection, signed "Gm. Dubois, in Paris," about 1770. **Et Fils**, watch, with modification of Debaufre's escapement, bought in Hanover by George IV., G.M., about 1770; watch, Wallace collection, about 1785. **Frederic Wm.**, Neuchatel; born 1811, died 1869. **Pierre**, Paris; wrote "Histoire de l'Horlogerie" 1849, "La Tribune Chronometrique" 1852, and description of the Soltykoff collection 1858.

Duboule, Jean Baptiste, lion-shaped watch, about 1600 (see p. 121); watch in nut-shaped case, Wallace collection, about 1620.

Dubuisson, —, Paris, his signature on many good clock dials, period Louis XVI.

Duc, —, alarm watch, Garnier collection, signed "Dominique Duc à Loche," about 1570.

Ducastel, Isaac, admitted C.C. 1703.

Duchemin, Dr, horloger, Rouen, 1570.

Duchen. In the B.M. is a watch by him, in a chased case by D. Cochin, 1730.

Duchêne, Ls. & Fils, Geneva; watch in gold egg-shaped case, S.K.M., about 1785.

Duchesne, Claude, in Long Acre (of Paris); C.C. 1693; square full-repeating bracket clock, inscription on back plate, "Claudius du Chesne, in Long Aker"; long-case clock in lacquer case, Agence de

Commerce Etranger Ltd.; John Wesley's long-cased clock by him, arch dial, age of the moon, walnut case, is still preserved in the Wesley Museum, City Rd. In the Green Vaulted Chambers of the Treasury at Dresden is a pair of long-cased clocks in walnut cases signed "Claudius du Chesne, Londini, fecit"; they stand about 12 ft. high; the dials show the phases of the moon, the months, and days of the month, which are written in French; both clocks chime and play tunes before striking the hour; on the dial of one is a list in Dutch of the tunes played, and the repertory of the other consists of "Aire Polonaise No. 1," "Aire Polonaise No. 2," "Aire Italien," and "The King enjoys his own." Fine bracket clock; 1690-1720. **Johannes**, Amsterdam; fine clock, about 1750, Mr Lawrence Bentall (see pp. 366, 379).

Ducimen, Jacop, Amsterdam; large oval watch, Pierpont Morgan collection, about 1625.

Duck, H., London, about 1720.

Ducker, H., 3 South Place, Kennington Lane, 1835-42.

Ducommun, A. L., Philadelphia, 1797.

Duddell, Thos., 106 Holborn Hill, 1817-23.

Dudds, Joseph, Coleman St., 1730; Geo. Adams apprenticed to him in 1745; livery C.C. 1766. In the Czar of Russia's collection at the Winter Palace, St Petersburg, is a watch by him. It has a case of faceted crystal and is suspended from a chatelaine.

Dudley, Benjamin, Newport, U.S.A., 1840.

Dudson, Simon, Tower St.; C.C. 1654.

Duduict, Jacques, Blois, 1560-90 (see p. 75).

Duet, Pierre, Paris; fine enamelled watch, Pierpont Morgan collection, about 1740.

Dufalga, Ppe., Geneva; watch, about 1775.

Duff, James, 24 Castle St., Houndsditch, 1840-42.

Duffett, Jno., Bristol; long-case tidal clock, "High Water at Bristol Key," about 1780.

Duffield, Edward, Philadelphia, 1741-80.

Dufour. Abraham, watch, leather case, ornamented with silver, Schloss collection, about 1630. Mr Willard H. Wheeler has a curious and well-made watch dating from about 1710 signed "Isac Dufour." The collection of the Czar of Russia in the Winter Palace, St Petersburg, contains a repeating watch signed "Dufour London"; the outer case is cut out of a solid piece of lapis-lazuli carved with scrolls in the Louis XV. style, and set with a large spray of very fine diamonds; it is suspended from a chatelaine with decoration of the same character; in the Evan Roberts collection is an alarm watch of about 1798 by "Dufour, Geneva." **—**, Paris; curious watch by him, B.M., enamelled portrait over the dial, about 1730. **& Ceret**, associated with Voltaire at Ferney 1770, see Lepine. **—**, Geneva; alarm watch, about 1800.

Dugard, Thos., 34 Red Lion St., Clerkenwell, 1812-19. **& Simpson**, 1830.

Dugdale, Richd., 12 Broad St., 1800-5; 39 Great Marlborough St., 1817.

Duhamel, Pierre, Blois. In the Hawkins collection was a small watch by him with enamelled dial in plain gold case, black shagreen outer case studded with gold, and with gold plate engraved with the monogram of Mary, Queen of Scots; a cruciform watch by him, about 1590, Ecole d'Horlogerie, Geneva.

Du Hamel à Paris ; mid-seventeenth century watch in enamelled gold case, S.K.M. (see p.145). **Isaac**, long-case clock, Canon Greenwell ; watch, G.M., about 1785.

Duke. John, Fleet St. ; watch, B.M. (see p. 141), 1650. **Nat.**, apprenticed 1656 to Thos Wheeler ; C.C. 1663. **Joseph**, apprenticed 1666 to Jas. Markwick ; C.C. 1682. **Joseph**, C.C. 1728. **George**, 8 St John's St., Clerkenwell, 1835-42.

Dulin, W. T., 10 Cornhill, 1816-30.

Dumbell. Josh., Prescot, 1816, see Dunbill. **Thos.**, Rochdale, 1818. **Joseph**, Rochdale, 1833.

Dumont Frères, Besançon ; watch, silver cock, one hand, Schloss collection, 1735.

Dumvile, Nat., Stockport, 1820-33.

Dunbar Geo., London ; watch, 1770. **Butler**, Bristol, Conn., 1830.

Dunbill, Josh., Prescot ; watch, Evan Roberts collection, h.m., 1820.

Duncan. Geo., London ; watch 1737. **Jas.**, watch, h.m., 1775, Mr William Ranken ; 98 Chancery Lane, 1800-10 ; 44 St James's St., 1815-25 ; 33 Old Bond St., 1825-30. **Robt.**, London ; watch, 1790 ; fine lancet-case clock, "Duncan London," Dr W. J. Dunwoody, about 1800.

Duncarton, Robt., London ; watch, 1765.

Duncombe, Richard, master C.C. 1798.

Dundas, Jas., Edinburgh ; apprenticed to Andrew Brown in 1710.

Dunheim, Andrew, New York, 1775.

Dunkerly, Samuel, 1770.

Dunkley, Benj., London ; long-case clock, japanned case with rococo figure subjects painted on door and plinth ; plays seven tunes ; on each side of the usual date a wedge-shaped opening showing month and day of week ; moon in arch, about 1760. **John**, 88 Bethnal Green Rd., 1825-35. **Thos.**, 25 Galway St., St Luke's, 1840-42.

Dunlop, Andrew, C.C. 1701 ; known as a maker of watches and long-case clocks ; turret clock, Hawley House, Blackwater, Hants, dated on movement 1716. **Conyers**, Spring Gardens, Charing Cross ; C.C. 1733, master 1758.

Dunn. Henry, C.C. 1677. **Benj.**, apprenticed 1691 to Thos. Gibbs, C.C. **Anthony**, C.C. 1719. **Jno.**, Hull, 1822. **William**, Islington Green, 1835. **Chas.**, apprenticed to Richard Hislop, carried on business in Upper Gloucester St., Clerkenwell, died 1907, aged 88.

Dunster, Roger. In the Hawkins collection was a repeating watch by him in delicately pierced and chased gold case ; hands and thumbpiece set with diamonds ; gold outer case chased with allegorical figures ; pierced border chased with scrolls, about 1700. M. Ern. Roux has a clock-watch and repeating movement by him ; on the plate and the cock is engraved *Omnia metitur tempus sed metior ipsum*, see Clarke & Dunster.

Dunston, Paul, apprenticed 1687 to Simon Chapman C.C.

Duntnell, Danl., 131 Oxford St., 1783.

Du Peron, C., à Lyon ; oval watch, brass case with rock-crystal cover, Pierpont Morgan collection, about 1600.

Dupin, Paul, London ; fine repeating watch in gold pair cases, Schloss collection (p. 162), about 1710 ; also bracket clock in red shell case, about 1720 ; repeating watch, Guildhall Museum, three cases, inner case engraved and pierced, enclosed in a richly chased one by Moser,

outer case of leather *piqué*, h.m., 1739 ; in the B.M. is a repeating watch by him inscribed " Dr Samuel Johnson 1767."

Duplock, Chas., 129 Borough, 1790-1815. **& Wiggins**, 1816-30.

Dupons, Edwd., London ; watch, 1785.

Dupont à Castres ; watch, B.M., about 1650. **Peter**, London ; long-case clock in raised ornament Oriental lacquer case at the Armoury Museum, Government House, Malta, about 1725 ; another clock inscribed " Peter Dupont, St John's, London." **J. P.**, Rotterdam, about 1750. **Paul**, 27 Ivy Lane, Newgate St. ; watch, G.M., case finely worked in *repoussé* by Moser, 1759-72 ; clock, "Dupont late Emerys," not later than 1780. **Chas.**, Cockspur St., 1798-1800.

Duppa. Chas., apprenticed 1646 to Wm. Clay, C.C. **James**, 15 Aldgate Within, 1765-70.

Dupree, Elias, a Dutchman, who worked for Edwd. East in 1635 ; he had then been in London about twenty years.

Dupuy. Odran, Philadelphia, 1735. **Jno.**, 1770.

Durade, Abel ; watch, bridge over balance with enamelled portrait, Dutch style, about 1770, Pierpont Morgan collection.

Durand, —, octagonal watch, Garnier collection, signed " P. Durand à Rouen " ; watch, P. Durand, London, 1790.

Durant. Oswald, petitioner for incorporation of C.C. ; admitted as brother in 1632 ; warden in 1645 ; did not become master ; Ralph Almond apprenticed to him in 1637 ; 1630-45. **J. L.**, a watch in B.M., finely enamelled case, about 1690.

Durdent, Andrew, C.C. 1662.

Durfalga, Paris, 1790.

Durley, T., 33 Northampton St., 1835.

Durn, —, Paris ; watch, 1690.

Durrant. Richd., 36 Museum St., 1820-42. **Thomas**, near the Broadway, Hammersmith, 1840.

Durtnall, Daniel, 131 Oxford St., 1780-1805.

Durward, Jno. ; watch paper dated 1816, " John Durward, 6 Leith Street, New Edinburgh."

Duseigneur, Pierre, Geneva, about 1750.

Dutens. Geo., London ; small watch in case of blood-stone, diamond push piece, silver cock over balance, about 1750. **Peter**, Leicester Sq., 1759-65.

Dutertre, Jean Baptiste, Paris, 1750-80 ; inventor of an escapement with two balances. Mr H. W. Wilson has a clock by Jean Baptiste Dutertre very similar to that shown in Fig. 526, but on a bracket more resembling the one in Fig. 525 ; there were others of the family ; a vase-shaped clock by Dutertre in Louis XVI. style fetched £441 at the Hamilton sale in 1882. Repeating watch, " Dutertre Paris," about 1750, Pierpont Morgan collection.

Du Thuillay, —, Hull ; watch in large medallion frame, S.K.M., frame signed " J. S. Meyer, Zerbst, 1788."

Dutton. William, apprentice of Graham, and afterwards partner with Mudge, 148 Fleet St. ; C.C. 1746, liveryman 1766 ; 1746-94. **Guy**, quarter clock, Shandon collection, about 1760. **Jno.**, Liverpool, 1770. **Matthew & Thomas**, 148 Fleet St. ; Matthew Dutton, son of and apprenticed to William Dutton ; admitted C.C. 1779, assistant 1793, livery 1785, master 1800 ; Thomas Dutton, also apprenticed to William, admitted C.C. 1791, livery 1796 ; long mahogany-case clock inscribed " Matthew and Thomas Dutton," about

1795, Wetherfield collection ; **& Son**, 1810-18. **Jno.**, Liverpool, 1818. **Matthew**, 148 Fleet St., 1819-42 ; he retired to Church St., Stoke Newington, and died about 1843.

Duval. John, C.C. 1677. **Francis & John**, Warnford Court, Throgmorton St., 1755-65. à Paris ; fine clock, about 1810.

Dwerrihouse, Thos., Garston ; watch, h.m., 1774.

Dwerryhouse. John, 23 Charles St., Berkeley Sq., 1770-1805 ; hon. freeman C.C. 1781. **& Carter**, 30 Charles St., Berkeley Sq., 1809-18 ; 27 Davies St., 1823 ; bracket clock, Wetherfield collection, about 1810 ; bracket clock, Dwerryhouse, Carter, and Son, Berkeley Sq., about 1820, Mr T. S. Wheater. **Ogston, & Co.**, 27 Davies St., Berkeley Sq., 1835-42. **& Bell**, 131 Mount St., 1840.

Dyde, Thomas, London ; lantern clocks, about 1670. He was free of the C.C., but date of election uncertain (see p. 348).

Dyer. Joseph, Addle St., 1735-40. **& Newman**, 9 Lombard St., 1768-72.

Dyke, —, Exchange Alley, 1685.

Dymond, John, watch-case maker, Windmill Court, Smithfield, 1790.

Dyson, John, admitted C.C. 1694. **Humphrey**, Manchester, 1818. **& Brookhouse**, Sheffield, 1833.

Eaden, Richd., London ; watch, 1800.

Eady, Wm., 14 West St., Smithfield, 1800-18.

Eagle. John, C.C. 1690 ; long-case clock, about 1700, Wetherfield collection. **Nath.**, London ; metal-case watch, outer case tortoiseshell, about 1776.

Eagleton, Christopher, apprenticed to Charles Halstead 1683. In the Guildhall Museum is a watch by him, silver case, silver dial, outer case tortoiseshell *piqué* ; 1690-1710.

Eames & Barnard, 9 Ave Maria Lane, 1816.

Earle, Thos., admitted C.C. 1720.

Earles. — (or **Eryles**), subscribed to incorporation of C.C. 1630. **Jno.**, London, 1700-15.

Earnshaw. Thomas, Ashton-over-Lyne ; Mr T. R. Howarth has a 30-hour one-hand clock by him, about 1730. **Lawrence**, a clever watchmaker ; born at Mottram, near Longendale, Cheshire, where he died in 1767, aged about 60 years ; a monument was erected to his memory by public subscription in 1868. **Edwd.**, Stockport ; an ingenious clock and watch maker, his shop was said to be a " regular Noah's Ark of mechanical nicknacs " ; he was a friend of Jas. Ferguson, 1740-70. **Thomas**, 119 High Holborn, born 1749, died 1829 (see p. 273). **Thomas, junr.**, 87 Fenchurch St., 1825-42.

East. Jeremy, admitted as a brother C.C. 1640 ; maker of a small hexagonal watch, balance-cock pinned on, plate inscribed " Jeremie East, Londini," crystal case, about 1600 (see p. 130).; also a small oval watch, plain silver dial, one hand, about 1610. **Edward**, Pall Mall, 1632 ; Fleet St. later ; one of the first assistants of C.C. ; a very eminent maker (see p. 214) ; 1610-73. **Jere.**, apprenticed 1653 to Jas. Seabourne, C.C. **Thomas**, C.C. 1677. **Peter**, C.C. 1692. **Edward**, apprenticed to R. Lyon and turned over to Saml. Clyatt ; admitted C.C. 1696. **Edward, junr.**, apprenticed to Thomas East ; admitted C.C. 1710. **Jordon**, son of Edward East ; C.C. 1720. **Edwd.**, case-maker, Addle St., C.C.

1730. **Edward,** apprenticed to Joseph Pomroy; freeman C.C. 1743.

Easterley, John, New Holland, 1825-40.

Eastland, Thomas, London; maker of repeating watches, about 1750.

Eastley, —, 73 High Holborn, card, Hodgkins collection, about 1810.

Eastman. Of U.S.A.: **Robert,** Brunswick, 1805-08. **& Cary,** Brunswick, 1808. **Abel B.,** Haverhill, 1816-21.

Eastwick, Adrian, 102 Aldersgate St., 1770-85.

Eastwood, Wm., Burnley, 1748-70.

Eaton, J., London; watch, 1790.

Eave, John, 8 Oxford St., 1790.

Eayre. Thos., Kettering; Ludlam in 1758 wrote, "He was for 40 years the first in his profession, chiefly church clocks and bell foundry; he died greatly regretted, 1757." **Josh.,** St Neots; watch, 1770.

Ebben, Wm., 37 Islington Green, 1816-42.

Eberman, John, Lancaster, U.S.A. 1780-1820.

Ebsworth. John, a good clockmaker. On many full-sized lantern clocks with dolphin frets (originally with balances) is inscribed the address, "At ye Cross Keys in Lothebury." He probably succeeded Knifton at the Cross Keys, and afterwards removed, for on another clock is the address, "New Cheap Side"; apprenticed 1657 to Richard Ames; C.C. 1665, master 1697. Lantern clock 1665, Agence de Commerce Etranger, Ltd. "Lost, a small silver watch made by J. Ebsworth, in a tortoiseshell flowered case, and notice being given so as they may be recovered to Mr John Ebsworth, watchmaker, at the sign of the Cross Keys in Lothbury, two guineas reward" (*Post Boy*, May 2, 1699). **Christopher,** C.C. 1670.

Ecles, Hy., apprenticed 1654 to Tobias Davis, C.C.

Eclipse, Jno., London; watch, 1798.

Eden. William, admitted C.C. 1726. **Ralph,** Liverpool, 1770.

Edgecombe, Thos., St Stephen's, 1780.

Edington. —, 24 N. Audley St., 1815. **Jno.,** 10 Portland St., 1816. **& Son,** 1830.

Edkins, James, 2 High St., Kensington, 1830-42.

Edley, Wm., London; watch, 1748.

Edlin. John, apprenticed to Robert Webster; admitted C.C. 1687. **George,** 6 Aldgate Within, livery C.C. 1800-13.

Edlyne, Edgar, Nevill Alley, Fetter Lane; C.C. 1710-30; verge bracket clock, engraved back.

Edmonds. Eliza, apprenticed 1679 to Hy. Fevon and Christian his wife, C.C. **Chas.,** apprenticed to Thos. Taylor; C.C. 1772. **& West,** 14 Strand, 1797-1810. **D.,** Liverpool; watch, 1810. **Jno.,** 14 Strand, 1820-30.

Edmondson. Jno., apprenticed 1660 to Hugh Cooper, C.C. **Jno.,** Liverpool, 1770.

Edmunds, Wm., London; watch, painted outer case, Schloss collection, about 1785.

Edson, Jonah, Bridgewater, U.S.A., 1815-30.

Edwards. Joseph, apprenticed 1655 to Jno. Nicasius, C.C. **Thos.,** apprenticed 1680 to Robt. Player, C.C. **Nich.,** apprenticed 1687 to Robt. Dingley, C.C. **Isaac,** C.C. 1719. **Thos.,** Epping, 1720. **T.,** London; watch, h.m., 1766. **Adam,** London; watch, about 1768. **Jno.,** Norwich, 1770. **William,** 4 Holborn; livery Blacksmiths' Company; 1775-83; 109 Cheapside, 1790-94. **Wm. Jno.** Coleman

St., 1783. **D.,** Liverpool, 1790. **James,** 180 Fleet St., 1790-94. **Wm.,** 26 New Bond St., 1800. **Jas.,** Commercial Rd., 1814-35. **Jas.,** 93 Wood St., Cheapside, 1820-25. **Robt.,** Great Sutton St., 1820-25. **Benj.,** 17 Shoreditch, 1830-42. **W.,** & Son, 2 Theberton St., Islington, 1835-42. **A.,** watch-cap maker, 14 Great Sutton St., 1835. **Jas.,** 43 Cornhill, 1841-49.

Effington, John, admitted C.C. 1702.

Egersley, Jas., apprenticed 1660 to Wm. Godbed, C.C.

Egleton, Christopher, apprenticed to Charles Halstead in 1683, admitted C.C. 1695.

Ehrhardt, Wm., a clever horologist; founded a watch factory on advanced principles at Birmingham; born 1831, died 1897.

Eiffe, James Sweetman, born 1800, died 1880; a clever chronometer maker, who for some time carried on business at 48 Lombard St.; in the Wetherfield collection is an astronomical regulator by him; he invented a compensation balance very similar to that patented by Molyneux, see Fletcher, Jno.

Eisele, W. A., Brussels; oval watch, Pierpont Morgan collection, about 1760.

Eisen, Heinrich, Nuremberg, 1510.

Elchinger, Hans Conrad, Amsterdam; watch, the dial engraved with representation of a pedlar crossing a brook, 1620.

Eldridge, John, admitted C.C. 1677; long-case clock inscribed "John Eldridge, Alresford," about 1730.

Eley, James, 11 Fenchurch St., 1770-85.

Elfes. Thos., apprenticed 1671 to Geo. Hambleton, C.C. **Benjamin,** C.C. 1674.

Eliason, Daniel, 18 Leman St., Goodman Fields, 1785-90.

Elisha, Caleb, ·Duke St., St James's; bracket clock, about 1810, Mr William A. Atkinson; 3 Marylebone St., Golden Sq., 1820; 175 Piccadilly, 1835; 8 New Bond St., 1842.

Elkins. Chas., apprenticed 1677 to Dan. Le Count, C.C. **William,** apprenticed to John Ellicott; C.C. 1710; assistant 1730; large bracket clock at the India Office, "Windmills and Elkins," about 1725.

Ellam, Thos., Runcorn, 1833.

Elled, —, London, 1780.

Ellerton, Robt., Lancaster, 1721, f.

Elley, Jas., 52 Rathbone Place, 1816.

Ellicott. John, C.C. 1696; apprenticed to John Waters, 1687, All Hallows, London Wall, 1696-1733. **John,** 17 Sweeting's Alley, Cornhill, an eminent maker (see p. 249); born 1706, died 1772. **John, & Sons,** 17 Sweeting's Rents, 1769-88. **& Taylor,** Sweeting's Alley, Cornhill, 1811-30. **& Smith,** 17 Sweeting's Alley, Cornhill, 1830; 27 Lombard St., 1839-42. **Edward, & Sons,** Edward Ellicott, master C.C. 1834; 17 Sweeting's Alley, Cornhill, 1783-1810.

Elliot, Wm., Whitby, 1770.

Elliott. Jno., apprenticed 1681 to Jno. Goode, C.C. **Henry,** brother C.C. 1688. **Thos.,** Greenwich; long-case clock, about 1740. **Josh.,** Berkhampstead; musical clock, about 1750. **Jas.,** Oxford St., 1780-1800. **Wm.,** London; watch, h.m., 1787. **John Moseley,** Aylesbury St., Clerkenwell; patented a repeater in 1804 (No. 2,759) (see p. 412). **& Son,** 119 Oxford St., 1805. **J. J.,** clockmaker, Clerkenwell; died 1904, aged 55.

Ellis. Jacob, York, f., 1636. **James,** C.C. 1667. **Richard,** Westminster, apprenticed 1673 to Geo. Deane; C.C. 1683; bracket quarter clock, about 1730. **Thomas,**

C.C. 1682. **Paul,** brother C.C. 1682. **John,** Little Old Bailey, C.C. 1726. **& Collins,** 52 Strand, 1804. **Henry,** Exeter, 1810. **David,** 2 John St., Oxford Rd., 1817. **T.,** London; watch, 1838. **Michael,** 18 Bevis Marks, 1842.

Ellison. Caleb, apprenticed 1691 to Sam. Vernon, C.C. **Thos.,** York, f., 1826.

Elliston, Robert, Orange St., 1770; 12 Charles St., Covent Garden, 1790-1820. His son, Robt. Wm. Elliston, the celebrated actor, was born at Orange St., 7th April 1774.

Ellwood. Martin, brother C.C. 1687; a watch by him in the Guildhall Museum, silver dial, curious tortoiseshell case inlaid with silver, 1680-1700. **John,** C.C. 1702; long marqueterie case clock, square dial, 1702-25.

Elmes. William, brother C.C. 1667. **Joseph,** apprenticed 1673 to Wm. Elmes, C.C. **Richard,** apprenticed to Edward Banger, admitted C.C. 1708; worked for Webster in 1730.

Elsgood, Wm., Norwich; clock, about 1770.

Elson, David, brother C.C. 1646.

Elsworth, David, Windsor, U.S.A., 1780-1800.

Elton. John, C.C. 1675. **Thos.,** C.C. 1677.

Ely, James, 8 Soho Sq., 1825.

Eman, Jno., apprenticed 1669 to Isaac Daniell, C.C.

Emanuel. Joel, Bevis Marks, 1812-17. **Lewis, & Son,** 36 Swan St., Minories, 1820-42. **Brothers,** 1 Bevis Marks, 1830.

Embree, Effingham, New York, Dec. 785.

Emerson; lantern clock, signed "Richd. Emerson, fecit," about 1690.

Emery, Josiah, an eminent Swiss watchmaker, who settled here and carried on business at 33 Cockspur St., Charing Cross. Mr Hedgethorne has a watch by him made about 1780, lever escapement with draw on the locking faces of the pallets; hon. freeman C.C. 1781 (see p. 407); an 8-day watch by him with extra wheel in the train, about 1780; another example is a watch in the Guildhall Museum, ruby cylinder, helical balance-spring, compensation curb; a bracket clock by him in an ebony case, dating from about 1790, is in the Wetherfield collection; 1770-1805 (succeeded by Recordon).

Enderlin, —, Bale; maker of equation clocks (see p. 297), 1715-60.

Enen, Wm., apprenticed 1687 to Thos. Wise, C.C.

Engall, Abraham, brother C.C. 1648.

Engaz, —, Paris; handsome clock, about 1790 (see p. 322).

England, Jno., apprenticed 1692 to Thos. Taylor, C.C.

Englois, Geo., apprenticed 1648 to Ed. Ward, C.C.

Enon, Chas., apprenticed 1666 to Jere. East, C.C.

Entwisle, Laurence, apprenticed 1638 to Thos. Pace, C.C.

Enys. Edward, C.C. 1658. **Edmund,** C.C. 1684.

Erb, Albrecht, cross shaped watch, case enamelled white, with bevelled cover of rock crystal, date doubtful.

Erbury, Henry, C.C. 1650.

Erhardt, J. C., watch, B.M., about 1700.

Ericke, Robert, Maiden Lane, C.C. 1719. **William,** C.C. 1730; watch by him with extra wheel in the train, the minute hand travelling once round the dial in two hours.

Errington, F., Savile Row, Walworth, 1835.

Ervin, see Irvine.

Eryles, see Earles.

Esplin, —, Wigan, 1790.

Esquivillon. Several watches, ranging from 1750 to 1790. Esquivillon & De Choudens ; melon shaped gold enamelled **watch** ; watch with gold outer case set round with pastes, portrait in enamel of a lady on the back, also set in paste ; these two examples are in the Pierpont Morgan collection, and date from about 1765. Esquivillon Frères & De Choudans, Paris ; watch, *repoussé* outer case, about 1775. "Esquivillon et Cie.," watch, probably Swiss, enamelled case, about 1790.

Essen, —, Paris, 1790.

Essex. Joseph, Boston, U.S.A., 1712. **Robt.**, 223 Strand, 1823.

Ester (Esther), Henry (French) ; a watch resembling a pelican, S.K.M. ; another (B.M.) in the shape of a tulip ; another example of his work is a watch in the Vienna Treasury, the case is circular, worked à jour representing foliage and enamelled in different colours, on the dial of enamelled gold are the signs of the zodiac, 1630-60.

Esterbrook, —, Theobald's Rd., 1830-70.

Eston, Edward, C.C. 1708.

Etherington. George, Fleet St., C.C. 1684 ; master, 1709 ; Mr F. Hockliffe has a choice bracket pendulum clock of his make, and Mr J. Francis Mallett owns a somewhat similar specimen ; a long-case clock by him belonging to Mr Thos. Boynton is illustrated on p. 374. " A Gold Minute Watch with a green Shagreen case, with gold studs, made by George Etherington " (*Lond. Gaz.*, Dec. 25, 1689). "George Etherington, Watchmaker, is Removed from the Dial in Fleet St. to the Dial over against the New Church in the Strand, London, where all sorts of Jewel Watches and others are made and sold" (*Lond. Gaz.*, October 5-9, 1714). Of York : **Thos.**, f., 1684 ; **Thos.**, f., 1727 ; **Thos.**, f., 1740 ; **Wm.**, f., 1788.

Ettry, Abram, Vlissingen ; bracket clock, about 1740, Mr J. H. Davidson.

Etty, Marmaduke, C.C. 1716.

Eustace, Richd., apprenticed 1687 to Withers Cheney, C.C.

Evans. Thomas, apprenticed to Samuel Davis, C.C. 1673. **Henry**, apprenticed to Thomas Bagley for Thomas Trippett, C.C. 1682. **Geo.**, apprenticed 1692 to Geo. Rant, C.C. **Thomas**, apprenticed to Jane Barker, widow of Richard Barker, C.C. 1718. **Thomas**, apprenticed to George Cartwright, Royal Exchange ; C.C. 1720 ; watch, 1749. **Robert**, Halstead ; 30-hour clock, one hand, about 1740. **Thomas**, New York, 1766. **Thomas**, apprenticed to William Haward, and turned over to Josiah Alderson, C.C. 1769. **Jno.**, Shrewsbury, 1770. **David**, Baltimore, 1770-73. **James, & Son**, 7 Sweeting's Alley, 1770-1800 ; Evans, Thomas, of Swithin Alley, son of James Evans, C.C. 1788 ; James, son of Thomas, was admitted in 1811 ; many timekeepers of good quality bear the names of some member of this family, which had a considerable connection in Spain and the Spanish markets ; clocks dating from the latter part of the eighteenth century, signed " Diego Evans, London," or " Diego Evans, Bolsa Real, Londres " (James Evans, Royal Exchange, London), are to be met with ; Higgs & Evans, both of Swithin, or "Sweeting's" Alley, seem to have been associated in partnership from about 1780, or 1785, although the name of Evans appears independently after that date, see Higgs & Evans. **William**, 23 Aldgate Without, 1775. **Pryce**, Shrewsbury ; watch, 1789. **David**, see Higgs & Evans. **Dymoke**, C.C. 1800 ; **James**, C.C. 1816 ; **Samuel**, C.C. 1822. **W.**, Dublin ; watch, 1802. **William Fredk.**, Handsworth, Birmingham, succeeded John Houghton ; died 1899, aged 81. **John**, apprenticed to Gartner, carried on business in Mount St., Grosvenor Sq., died 1905, aged 67 ; clock by him with double three-legged gravity escapement, Wetherfield collection.

Eve, John, 19 New North St., Red Lion Sq., 1842.

Evens, Robert, Halstead ; lantern clock, about 1710.

Everell, John, " by ye new church in ye Strand " ; maker of a verge watch, square pillars, outer case of tortoiseshell, 1730-60.

Everett, Jno., London ; watch, 1770.

Evers, Peter, Chester ; 1814-18. **Chas.**, Coventry, 1818.

Evill. Two or three generations of clockmakers in Bath. James Evill, about 1750. William Evill, Union St., about 1800.

Ewbank, Geo., Ellam, 1770.

Ewer, Jno., apprenticed 1687 to Luke Bird ; maker of long-case and bracket chime clocks, see Eyre.

Ewett, Robt., C.C. 1636.

Exchagnet, Louis, Wilderness Row, 1790.

Exelby. James, St John's Lane ; C.C. 1718 ; a good watchmaker, quoted by Hätton, known also as a maker of long-case clocks ; 1718-50. **George**, watch jeweller, 6 Red Lion St., Clerkenwell, 1790-94.

Eyre. Richd., apprenticed 1637 to Oswald Durant, C.C. **John**, C.C. 1703.

Eyston, Edward, C.C. 1659.

Ezekiel, —, Exon. ; watch, h.m., 1794.

Faber, Joseph, apprenticed 1678 to Edwd. Whitfield, C.C.

Fabre, G., Paris, 1620.

Facio, Nicholas, born at Basle, 1664, died in Worcester, 1753 ; introduced watch jewelling (patent No. 371, May 1704) (see p. 408).

Fage, Edward, admitted C.C. 1667.

Fagg, John, Queen St., Margate ; watch, h.m., 1781 ; lever alarm watch, 1821.

Fairclough. Thos., C.C. 1660. **Richard**, Liverpool, 1770. **Edwd.**, Liverpool ; watch, about 1795, with the pedometer self-winding device patented by Recordon in 1790, Mr Edwd. H. Bulley. **Sam.**, Halifax, 1830.

Fairer, Joseph, Bishopsgate, 1850 ; he seems to have been but a short time in business, but his name was on several clocks for public companies.

Fairey. John, 22 Ratcliff Highway, 1810-42. **Richard**, 150 Tooley St., 1814-42. **Richard, junr.**, 68 High St., Borough, 1835.

Fairfax, Wm., apprenticed 1685 to Jno. Warner, C.C.

Fales, James, New Bedford, 1810-20. **G. S.**, 1827.

Falke, —, Leipzig ; watch, about 1780.

Falkner. Edwd., apprenticed 1692 to Cornelius Herbert, C.C. ; quarter clock, Mr Eden Dickson, about 1740. **Wm. W.**, shagreen case maker, Shoe Lane, 1793. **John**, 153 Newman St., Oxford St., 1824-28.

Falks, Robert, C.C. 1720-25.

Fallow. Matthew, Liverpool, 1814. **Matthew, & Co.**, Manchester, 1820 ; also **J. Fallow & Co.**, same date.

Farewell, John, apprenticed to Isaac Nicholls, and turned over to Charles Gretton, C.C. 1697.

Farmer. Leonard, received £37 in 1617 for a clock and chimes and "twoe dyalls, and for a barrel and pricking thereof," from the churchwardens of St Margaret's, Westminster. **Thomas**, C.C. 1647. **Thomas**, C.C. 1653 ; in the St Margaret's, Westminster, churchwardens' accounts for 1658 appears "Item to Mr Farmer for making of the new diall on the westward of the church, as by his bill appeareth, 14l. 10s. " ; also, "Item to Mr Farmer for a new diall at the west end of the church on the churchyard side, 7l. " ; 1653-60. **Jno.**, C.C. 1657. **Jas.**, apprenticed 1661 to Ralph Almond, C.C. **Richard**, C.C. 1683. **Thomas**, brother C.C. 1689. **Thos.**, Stockton, 1770. **William**, 20 Hanover St., 1800. **G. W.**, 32 Tavistock St., 1822-30.

Farnborough, Richd., apprenticed 1685 to Wm. Newton, C.C.

Farquhar, W., Tower Hill, 1830 ; 6 Upper East Smithfield, 1835-42.

Farquharson, Geo., 66 Strand, 1775 ; 421 Strand, 1780 ; 8 Exchange Alley, 1793.

Farr, John C., Philadelphia, 1831.

Farran, Robt., watch-chain maker, 9 Moorfields, 1780-83.

Farrar. Jonathan, long-case clock, about 1720. **Joshua**, Brighouse, 1750. **Charles**, Pomfret, 1790.

Farrend, V., 48 Cheapside, 1825.

Farrer. Samuel, York, f., 1625. **William**, Pontefract ; 1-day long-case clocks, about 1730. **Abraham, junr.**, Pontefract, 1760 ; **Benj.**, also **Jno.**, 1790 ; and **Joshua**, 1800-1834. **Thos.**, London ; long-case clock, about 1770.

Farrett, Richard, C.C. 1670.

Fatio, L. U., Geneva, died 1887.

Fatton, Frederick Louis, New Broad St. ; independent centre seconds watch marked " Fatton, eléve de Breguet patent, London, No. 16 " ; in 1822 he patented an astronomical clock and watch (No. 4,645) ; many fine travelling clocks and good watches in the Breguet style of about the same period signed " Fatton, Paris."

Faulkner. Edward, master C.C. 1734 ; 1710-35. **William**, 1770-88 ; livery C.C. 1787.

Faux, John, Worship St., Moorfields, 1780-85.

Favey. Francis, 12 Wilderness Row. 1785-90. **& Son**, 5 Corporation Row, 1804.

Favre. Henrique, Londres ; watch, the Hon. Phinney Baxter, Portland, Maine, U.S.A. ; bracket clock, about 1730. **Henry**, London ; watch, the Edward Devotion House, Brookline ; bracket clock, about 1730. **—**, London ; watch, about 1750. **John James**, Philadelphia, 1797. **Henry** 27 Pall Mall, 1800-18.

Fawcett. Wm., apprenticed 1638 to David Bouquett, C.C. **William**, Liverpool ; long-case clock, about 1730. **Jno.**, apprenticed to J. Bartholomew, Clerkenwell ; settled in Richmond, Yorks. ; a good maker ; died 1869, aged 88.

Fayrer, Thos., Lancaster, 1744, f. **Jas.**, clockmaker and wheel cutter, 35 White Lion St., Pentonville, 1810 ; in 1819 he was at 40 White Lion St., and was awarded by the Society of Arts the silver Isis medal for a sidereal regulator with a three-wheel train. I recently saw a fine regulator by him inscribed "Invt. and fecit"; he had a son a clockmaker.

Fazakerley, Thos., "at the Dial and Crown in St John's St., near Hick's Hall, London"; card, Hodgkin collection, about 1780.

Fazy. Jean, gold enamelled watch, S.K.M. (French), about 1750, see Terrot. **John**, 7 Red Lion Court, Fleet St., 1780-85.

Fealins, see De Fealins.

Fearn, John Geo., 114 Strand, 1800; 73 Strand, 1813; 18 Cornhill, 1814; 22 Regent St., 1840; among the effects of Charles Kean sold at his decease wa a gold duplex watch, gold dial with raised polished numerals, serpent hands, hall mark 1816, movement inscribed "J. G. Fearn, 73 Strand."

Fearnley, Peter, Wigan, 1780-1816.

Fearon, Daniel, Fetter Lane, liveryman C.C. 1776.

Febuce, see Le Febuce.

Fehmel, Andreas, table clock, about 1680 (see p. **102**).

Feilder, Thomas, C.C. 1689; master 1715; 1689-1716.

Fell. William, C.C. 1705. **John**, C.C. 1727. **Abraham**, Ulverston, 1740-70; he made a new style for the church sun-dial in 1763. **Jas.**, Lancaster, 1767, f.

Felmore, E., London; watch, 1778.

Felter, Thomas, C.C. 1709.

Felton, George, Bridgnorth; long-case clock, about 1780, Mr W. P. W. Phillimore.

Fenn. Thos., apprenticed 1647 to Thos. Claxton; C.C. 1657. **Robert**, Westminster, C.C. 1687; long marqueterie case clock, Wetherfield collection, about 1690. **Daniel & Samuel**, 105 Newgate St.; D. Fenn master C.C. 1766; 1760-87. **Samuel, & Sons**, 105 Newgate St.; S. Fenn master C.C. 1793; 1806-15. **Joseph**, 105 Newgate St.; master C.C. 1842 and 1863; 1830 till 1868, when the shop, which projected by the railings of Christ's Hospital, was pulled down to widen the thoroughfare.

Fennell, Richd., C.C. 1679; bracket clock, arch dial, bell-top shape with handle; also a long mahogany case clock inscribed "R. Fennell, Kensington."

Fenney, ——, Liverpool; clock, about 1770.

Fenton. John, apprenticed to Thos. Taylor; C.C. 1662. **Jas.**, York, f., 1740. **Wm.**, Newcastle, 1780. **Wm.**, London; watch, h.m., 1784. **Jno.**, Congleton, 1833. **Sam.**, 4 Gower Place, Euston Sq., 1840.

Ferguson. James, born 1710, died, and buried in Marylebone churchyard, 1776; astronomer and mechanician (see p. **285**). **Wm.**, Alnwick; long-case clock, about 1770.

Ferment. John, C.C. 1679; Wood mentions a square pedestal watch by Ferment, 1670-90. **Paul**, London; watch, about 1745.

Fernal, Jno., Wrexham, 1770.

Feron. ——, Rue Dauphine, Paris, 1770. **Jno.**, Lewes; watch, 1780.

Ferrers, Jno., London; long-case clock, about 1700.

Ferrey, Jas., London; clock, about 1770, Mr W. Popkin.

Ferrier. Antoine, Paris; lodged at the Louvre 1607. **William**, son of Antoine, whom he succeeded in 1622. **Thornton**, Hull, 1822.

Ferris. Benjamin, C. & W., Philadel-

phia, 1811. **Tiba**, Wilmington, U.S.A., 1812-50.

Ferron. John, London; C.C. 1692 (see p. 166). **Lewis**, London; long marqueterie case clock, pull chime quarters, angel and crown corners, about 1720. **Abraham**, St Anne's Churchyard, C.C. 1730.

Fessler, John, Frederickstown, U.S.A., 1782-1840.

Fétil, Pierre, born at Nantes 1753, died at Orleans, 1814.

Fetter, Nicholas, C.C. 1632.

Fetters. Henry, East Smithfield; free Blacksmiths', 1630; C.C. 1653. **Richd.**, C.C. about 1640.

Fever, Hy., Pall Mall; watch, about 1750, see Favre.

Fevon, Hy., C.C. 1674.

Fiacre, Clement, Paris; watch, 1700.

Fidgett, William, C.C. 1789; Dockhead, Bermondsey; and 3 Bell Court, Fenchurch St., 1780-1825.

Fidler, ——, made an orrery for Dr Pearson 1805.

Fidley, Geo., see Findley.

Fieffé, Jean Jacque, père, Rue de la Vieille Draperie, Paris (garde visiteur), 1769.

Field. Jas., C.C. 1672. **Wm.**, London; C.C. 1733; watch, 1750. **T. W.**, Aylesbury; watch, 1790. **Thos.**, Bath; watch, 1795. **Daniel**, 21 Red Lion St., Clerkenwell, 1798. **Geo.**, London; watch, 1800. **James**, Hertford; long-case clocks, about 1800.

Fielder, Thomas, apprenticed 1678 to Withers Cheney; C.C. 1687.

Fieldhouse, ——, Leinster; clock, about 1740.

Fierville, ——, Caen; watch, 1770.

Filber, John, Lancaster, U.S.A., 1810-25.

Filon, ——, Paris, 1790.

Finch. John, C.C. 1675, master 1706. "A gold minute pendulum watch, with a chain and a large gold engraved case, made by John Finch, of London, about £20 value, was put to be mended to a watchmaker in Bristol who is since gone" (*Lond. Gaz.*, June 16-19, 1706). **Thomas**, brother C.C. 1676-1706, possibly a cousin of T. Tompion (see p. 226). **Jacob**, apprenticed 1686 to Isaac Carver, C.C. **William**, Kingston; C.C. 1691; maker of long-case clocks, 1691-1720. **Robert**, C.C. 1691. **Simon**, C.C. 1706. **Wm.**, Halifax; watch, 1759.

Finchett, Arnold, Cheapside; a water clock by him in B.M., 1735 (see p. 28).

Findbow, Chas., London; long-case clock, about 1780.

Findley. J., 5 Duke St., 1820. **Geo.**, 43 Ratcliff Highway, 1835-42.

Fine, Oronce, Paris; professor of mathematics and designer of clocks; born 1494, died 1555 (see p. 65).

Finelly, ——, Aix; watch in the form of a pectoral cross, about 1560.

Finer. Jno., apprenticed 1688 to Hy. Merryman, C.C. **John**, 5 Hatton Garden, 1791-1800. **Thomas & Nowland**, 5 Hatton Garden, 1800-5; 48 High Holborn, 1808-23. **Horatio**, 48 High Holborn, 1840-42.

Finlow, Zach., London, 1780.

Finney. Thos., Liverpool; curious watch, 1735, Mr Evan Roberts. **Josh.**, Liverpool; long-case clock, about 1750, Mr Duncan D. Dexter, Boston, U.S.A.; clock-watch, about 1760. Picton, in his "Memorials of Liverpool," says, "Mr Joseph Finney, a clock and watch maker in Thomas St., designed an octagonal chapel about 1763."

Finnie, Henry, admitted C.C. 1728.

Fish. Henry, 4 Sweeting's Alley, Royal Exchange; black bell-top case bracket clock, inscription on arch "Henry Fish, Royall Exchange," probably son of Henry Poisson; 1730-75. **John**, apprenticed to his mother, Mary, wife of William Fish; C.C. 1766. **C. H.**, 13 Mill St., Hanover Sq., 1830-35.

Fisher. Chas., apprenticed 1679 to Thos. Player, C.C. **Rebeckah**, apprenticed to George Taylor and Lucy, his wife, 1715. **Ebenezer**, C.C. 1725. **Jno.**, Preston; long-case clock, about 1750, with the inscription "Dum Spectus Frigis." **Dan.**, Bunhill Row, 1769-72. **Joseph**, 2 Leicester Sq.; livery Cutlers' Company, 1773-1815. **Hy.**, Preston, 1775. **Daniel, & Son**, 9 Worship St., Finsbury, 1790-1804. **Isaac**, 3 Cockspur St., 1804-23. **——**, 97 Portland Place, Edgware Rd.; bracket clock, about 1810.

Fishwater, John, C.C. 1726.

Fitree, Samuel, Whitecross St., 1790.

Fitter. John, Battersea, C.C. 1685; splendid watch by him, 1665 (see p. **180**); Wood mentions a gold enamelled watch by Fitter, 1660-1700. **Thomazon**, 37 St John's Sq., Clerkenwell, 1759-83; watch, h.m., 1759, Mr Edwin P. Baker.

Fitton. Thos., apprenticed 1638 to Thos. Laud, C.C. **Chas.**, apprenticed 1667 to Sam. Horne; C.C. 1674. **Dan.**, apprenticed 1675 to Jno. Bartholomew, C.C.

Fitzjames, Thos., apprenticed 1648 to Jno. Walters, C.C.

Fix, Joseph, Reading, U.S.A., 1820-40.

Flack, G., 9 Princess St., Drury Lane, 1820.

Fladgate. (& Wilder, Conduit St., Hanover Sq., 1765.) **John**, Conduit St., Hanover Sq.; hon. freeman C.C. 1781. In the B.M. is a small clock by him, brass dial with arch cherub corners. Mr Thos. Boynton has a bracket clock in ebonised case by him; 1760-83, see Simpson, H.

Flaig, Robert, & Co., wooden clockmakers, 39 Kingsland Road, 1840.

Flameyer, B., London; small watch, silver pair cases, outer one curiously engraved, h.m., 1765.

Flashman, George, 18 Fleet St., 1790-1815 (succeeded by Jno. Tunnell).

Fleetwood. John, Dorrington St., Clerkenwell; born 1748, died 1812. **Robert**, Featherstone Buildings, Holborn, 1760; 13 Abchurch Lane, 1776; liveryman Goldsmiths' Company, died 1789; Robt. Fleetwood & Co. till 1792.

Fleming. Andrew, C.C. 1725. **Curtis**, opposite Shadwell Church; livery C.C. 1774. **David**, 36 Shadwell High St., 1817.

Flemming, Wm., 105 Whitechapel, 1815-19.

Fletcher. Daniel, brother C.C. 1646; in 1653 Richd. Roberts was apprenticed to Eliza Fletcher. **Widdon**, Ant. Freeman was apprenticed to him in 1653; C.C. **Jno.**, apprenticed 1654 to Jno. Saville, C.C. **Thomas**, in St Martin's; admitted C.C. 1676; threatened with prosecution by C.C. for undue taking of apprentices 1682. **Bazil**, apprenticed 1692 to Thos. Wise, C.C. **Edward**, C.C. 1697. **Jno.**, Barnsley, 1750. **Jno.**, Ripponden, 1760. **Jno.**, Holbeck; clock, about 1760. **William**, Leeds, 1770. **Geo.**, Dewsbury, 1770. **Cecilia**, Rotherham, 1780. **Tobias**, Barnsley, 1790. **Robt.**, Chester, 1814-34. **Jas.**, Rotherham, 1818. **Thos.**, Leeds, 1829. **M.**, 25 Charlotte St., Fitzroy Sq., 1835. **Charles**, 29 Marylebone St., Piccadilly, 1840-42. **John**, a Lancashire pinion maker, who started in London as a chronometer escapement maker, and afterwards manufactured unsprung marine chronometers for the trade at 14 Chapel St., Liverpool Rd. During a period of depression in the chronometer trade Fletcher bought the business of Dwerrihouse in Davies St., Berkeley Sq., which he carried on for a year or two. But as a West End shopkeeper he was quite out of his element, and on looking out for a more congenial sphere of action he learnt that Eiffe, who had made for himself a name as a chronometer maker in Lombard St., was anxious to retire ; and Fletcher made arrangements to take over Eiffe's shop. In Lombard St. Fletcher was most successful. He learnt springing from William Cribb, and settled down as a chronometer maker, springing and adjusting his own work. When the lease of the premises in Lombard St. expired, he bought the business of Cummins at 148 Leadenhall St., and having by this time also established a reputation of his own, he did a very flourishing business there for many years. As age crept on him he gave up the more active superintendence of his business, which declined ; and after removing from 148, which was pulled down, to 99 Leadenhall St., and again to Billiter St., he finally retired about 1880, and died in 1882, aged 80.

Fleureau, Esaye, London ; in the Wetherfield collection is a long-case clock by him, dating from about 1710. It embodies a fine specimen of arabesque marqueterie, which is continued on the moulding supporting the hood, over the base and round the sides of the case.

Fleutry, —, Paris, 1788.

Flexney, Hy., apprenticed 1657 to Gower Langford, C.C.

Fling, Daniel, Philadelphia, 1811.

Flockhart, Andrew, 5 King St., Covent Garden, 1814-35.

Floden, William, 20 Skinner St., and Coburg St., Clerkenwell, 1835.

Flood, Humphrey, received £220 for a clock "covered with gold and set with rubies and diamonds, delivered to his Majesty's use" (James I.), 1607-17.

Flook. J., Strand, London ; bracket clocks, about 1750. **Jno.**, Bristol, 1770.

Floward, Wm., London ; watch, 1790.

Flower. Geo., apprenticed 1670 to Jas. Atkinson ; C.C. 1682 ; watch, about 1700 (see p. 165). **Jno.**, Fenchurch St. ; C.C. 1725-30. **Thomas**, C.C. 1730 ; pendulum watch, Schloss collection, fine dial, about 1740. **Henry**, Philadelphia, 1753. **& Mainwaring**, London ; watch, 1818.

Flowers, Edward, Rolls Buildings, Fetter Lane ; watch, beautiful outer case, set with pearls, h.m., 1783 ; 1769-84.

Floyd, Wm., apprenticed 1660 to Richd. Lyons, C.C.

Fly, Joseph, London ; calendar watch, Schloss collection, about 1770 ; another, about 1780.

Foden, —, Congleton ; clock, about 1770.

Fogg. Hugh, near Exeter Change, Strand, 1765-70. **Chas. W.**, Waltham, Mass. ; died 1893, aged 76. He patented a safety pinion formed with an internal screw for attachment to the centre arbor of a watch, so that it could twist to recoil from a shock induced by the breaking of the mainspring.

Foilman, John, watch-glass maker,

George St., St Martin's Lane, 1790.

Foissey, Jules, Boulogne ; died 1892, aged 57.

Fol, —, Paris, 1770-87 ; watchmaker to the King of Poland ; maker of 8-day watches. His son was clockmaker to Louis XVI.

Fole, Robert, C.C. 1667.

Folkard, Jas., 124 Great Surrey St., 1823.

Follett, Richd., apprenticed 1653 to Thos. Wolverstone, C.C.

Fontac, —, London ; watch, 1796.

Fontane, John & Moses, London ; half-quarter silver repeating watch, about 1790.

Foote, William, admitted C.C. 1726.

Forbes. Wm., London ; watch, 1805 ; Hide Market, Leadenhall, 1838. **John**, 122 Leadenhall St., 1835-40.

Ford. Hy., apprenticed 1647 to David Parry, C.C. **Robt.**, apprenticed 1652 to Richd. Record, C.C. **Thomas**, C.C. 1724. **Jno.**, Arundel, 1750. **William**, C.C. 1770. —, 31 Gracechurch St., 1820. **& Simmons**, 16 King St., Seven Dials, 1842.

Forde, Jno., Oxon., 1750.

Fordham. Thomas, C.C. 1687. **Joseph**, Bocking, 1700 ; fine long-case clock by Thos. Fordham, Braintree, Essex, about 1730.

Foreman. Francis, St Paul's Gate ; petitioner to Charles I. for incorporation of C.C. and one of the first assistants ; lantern clock, about 1620 ; 1620-49. **Michael**, livery C.C. 1810.

Forester, J., Union St., Bishopsgate ; card, Hodgkin collection, about 1810.

Forfaict, N., Paris ; maker of an octagonal watch presented to John Knox by Mary, Queen of Scots, which is now in the B.M. ; oval watch, about 1590, Pierpont Morgan collection.

Forfard, Augustin, Sedan ; oval watch, about 1650.

Forfax, Isaac, Sedan ; oval watch, Schloss collection, about 1605.

Forgat, —. "A round brass clock, the Box well gilt and pearced all over, in a leather Case, the name *Forgat*" (*Lond. Gaz.*, March 29, April 1, 1680).

Formant, Philip, C.C. 1687.

Forrest. Matt., apprenticed 1672 to Jno. Lowe, C.C. **Joseph**, C.C. 1692. **John**, 12 Hanover St., 1850 ; afterwards 29 Myddelton St. ; died 1871 ; most of his customers were chapmen in Scotland, where his watches obtained some repute ; several years after his death the use of his trade mark, a tree, led to litigation.

Forster. John, apprenticed 1680 to D. Quare ; C.C. 1689. **William**, brother C.C. 1681. **Clement**, C.C. 1682. **Jacob**, apprenticed 1690 to Jno. F., C.C. **John**, C.C. 1726. **John**, Carlisle, 1810.

Forsyth, James, Albion Buildings, Bartholomew Close, 1790-1800.

Forte, John, C.C. 1672.

Fortfart, Isaac, Sedan, 1585.

Fortier, see Stollewerck.

Fortin, Auguste, père, Rue de la Harpe, Paris ; garde visiteur 1769. **Michel**, same date.

Foss (? Fox), **Thomas**, 131 Strand ; maker of 8-bell chime clock, brass dial, with strike-silent, silvered circles at top ; 1780-95.

Foster. Joseph, Exchange Alley ; C.C. 1691. **Thos.**, apprenticed 1693 to Nat. Smith, C.C. **S.**, Birchin Lane ; watch, bloodstone and gold case, Hawkins collec-

tion, about 1780. **Isaac**, 1 Bartlett Passage, 1788. **J. Benj.**, 22 Cursitor St., 1817. **Nathaniel**, Newburyport, 1818-28.

Fothergaile, Jas., apprenticed 1661 to Ralph Almond, C.C.

Fotter, Wm., C.C. 1660.

Fouch, Wm., Goswell St., 1775.

Foucher, B., Blois, 1630 ; the Comte de Lambilly has a watch signed "Blaise Foucher A Blois" (see p. 147).

Foulcon, Benj., London ; about 1780.

Fould, Humphrey, apprenticed 1646 to John Willowe, C.C.

Foulkes, David, apprenticed 1671 to Peter Southworth, C.C.

Fowell. Edmund, C.C. 1670. **J. & N.**, Boston, U.S.A., 1800-10.

Fowkes, Gabriel, Dartford ; long Oriental lacquer case clock, with picture in centre of door, arch dial, engraved silver centre, flower and scroll corners, about 1750 ; bracket clock, about 1780.

Fowlds, Andrew, 9 St John's Sq., 1790-94.

Fowle, East Grinstead. **Thos.**, about 1700. Several generations after till 1842.

Fowler. Robt., C.C. about 1650. **D.**, London ; lantern clock, about 1690. **Abraham**, Amersham, about 1760. **Wm.**, London ; watch, 1780. **Thos.**, London ; watch, 1782. F. of York : **Robert**, 1810, settled at Leeds ; **Geo.**, 1819, afterwards at Doncaster. **Robt.**, Leeds, 1829.

Fowles, Allen, Kilmarnock ; said to have made a watch for Robert Burns in 1771.

Fowls, And., London ; watch, about 1780, case decorated with pearls.

Fox, Charles, C.C. 1662 ; lantern clock, belonging to Mr Meggat, U.S.A., inscribed "Charles Fox, at the Fox, Lothbury, Londini, fecit," about 1670 ; Mr Meggat has also a stumpy bracket clock by him. There must, I think, have been a second Charles Fox ; I saw a long-case clock dating from about 1730 inscribed "Charles Fox, London." **Mordecai**, C.C. 1689. **Isaac**, 39 Minories, 1772 ; 7 Great Prescot St., 1782-94. **& Son**, 7 Magdalen Buildings, Prescot St., 1788. **Thomas**, 131 Strand, 1790, see Foss. **Hudson**, Beverley, 1822.

Foy. At Deene Park is a Louis XIV. chiming clock in Boulle work case which belonged to the Duke of Sussex, and was acquired by the late Earl of Cardigan ; it is marked "T. Foy, La Roux a Paris." **Jas.**, Taunton, about 1770. **Henry Jno.**, London ; clock, about 1790.

Frail, Thos., 92 Edgware Rd., 1814-18.

Fraincomme, —, London ; watch, 1778.

Framborough, Edward, admitted C.C. 1689.

Frame. —, Warrington ; long-case clock, about 1770. **Geo.**, Gateshead, 1833.

Francillon, Ernest, Longines, Switzerland, did much to advance the duplicating system of watchmaking ; died 1900.

Francis. Balmer, St Bartholomew's ; C.C. 1731. **Basil & Alexander**, Baltimore, 1766. **William**, 15 King St., Clerkenwell ; livery C.C. 1810.

Franciycifs, Joh., Dresden ; clock-watch, about 1740.

Franck, Thos., crystal-cased watch, about 1580 (see p. 123).

Francom, Chas., Bath ; watch, 1807.

Franklin. Joseph, apprenticed 1679 to Hy. Harper, C.C. ; tall oak double-dome case clock at Innholders' Hall, signed on convex disc in arch of dial "Josephus, Franklin, London," about 1720. **Thos.**, apprenticed 1692 to Ben. Merriman, C.C. **William**, C.C. 1712. **William**, C.C. 1731.

William, watch shagreen-case maker, Shoe Lane, 1790; livery C.C. 1810.

Fraser, John, apprenticed 1681 to Edwd. Eyston, C.C.

Frazer, —, Bond St., 1788.

Frearson, John, C.C. 1689.

Free. Jno., Oxon.; watch, about 1700. **A.**, Blackburn; long-case clock, 1770.

Freebody, Jno., apprenticed 1671 to Jno. Sweeby, C.C.

Freeman. John, C.C. 1646, assistant 1671; died 1680. **Anthony**, apprenticed 1653 to Widdon Fletcher, C.C. **Stafford**, apprenticed 1656 to Wm. North; C.C. 1663. **Thomas**, C.C. 1698. **James**, C.C. 1719. **Jas.**, St Botolph, Bishopsgate; apprenticed to John Watford, and turned over to Francis Robinson; C.C. 1736; in 1769 he patented a stop watch (No. 946). **Nathaniel**, 26 Upper King St., Bloomsbury, 1840-42.

Freestone, Thos., Bury, 1765.

Freethy, Jno., apprenticed 1672 to Chas. Rogers, C.C.

French. Thos., Norwich, 1770. **John**, 21 Tavistock St., 1783-88; Mile End, 1800. **James Moore**, 15 Sweeting's Alley, 1808-38; 18 Cornhill, 1839-42; livery C.C. 1810, see also Mitchell & French. **James**, 17 Castle St., Holborn, and 21 Tavistock St., 1810. **Wm.**, 9 Royal Exchange, 1850.

Frencham, James, C.C. 1698.

Freshfield. Jas., watch-case coverer, 19 Smithfield. **James**, junr., C.C. by redemption 1774; letter as to non-payment of quarterage, 1796; centre seconds watch, about 1800. **James William**, son of the foregoing, C.C. 1801.

Frippett, John, C.C. 1665-70.

Frisby, Jno., 5 Duke St., Grosvenor Sq., 1816-25.

Frisquet, Peter, 30 Lothbury, 1768-75.

Frodsham. William, Kingsgate St., Red Lion Sq.; born 1728; hon. freeman C.C. 1781; Earnshaw claimed to have taught him watch jewelling; he attested the value of Earnshaw's improvements in 1804; died 1807. For some years from 1790 the business was carried on in conjunction with his eldest son, William, under the title of William Frodsham & Son; the younger William predeceased his father, and the elder William bequeathed the business in Kingsgate St. to his grandson, John Frodsham. **William James**, F.R.S., born 1778; grandson of the first-named William; eldest son of William and Alice Frodsham (Alice being the granddaughter of John Harrison, famous as the inventor of the marine timepiece); he entered into partnership with William Parkinson, and commenced business in 1801 in Change Alley; admitted C.C. 1802, master 1836 and 1837; died 1850, bequeathing £1,000 to the C.C., to be known as the Parkinson and Frodsham Charity; he had brought up four sons to the trade: **Henry**, who settled in Liverpool; **George**, who succeeded him; **John**; and **Charles. John**, born 1785; he entered into partnership with one Baker in 1809, and, under the style of Frodsham & Baker, continued the business at Kingsgate St. till about 1823, and afterwards at 31 Gracechurch St.; elected to the livery of the C.C. in 1830; died in 1849; he had two sons associated with him in the business: **Henry John**, who died 1848, and **George Edward**, who succeeded him. **Charles**, son and apprentice of W. J. Frodsham, born 1810, died 1871; a skilful and successful watchmaker, 7 Finsbury Pavement, 1842; afterwards succeeded J. R. Arnold at 84 Strand; he conducted many experiments with a view of elucidating the principles underlying the action of the compensation balance and the balance-spring, and wrote several papers on technical subjects; he was for some time a vice-president of the Horological Institute; admitted C.C. 1845, master 1855-62. **George**, Change Alley, 1850-73.

Froissard, —, Geneva, about 1800 (see p. 191).

Fromanteel. Ahasuerus, East Smithfield; Blacksmiths' Company 1630; C.C. 1632 (see p. 236).; 1630-50. **Ahasuerus**, Moses Alley, Bankside; C.C. 1655. **Dan.**, apprenticed 1661 to A. F., sen., C.C. **Ahasuerus**, Ye Mermaid at Lothbury and Moses Alley, Bankside; apprenticed to Simon Bartram; C.C. 1663-75; Daniel O'Connell had a clock by A. Fromanteel dating from about 1675, which is now in the possession of Mr Walter Conan, Dublin; it has a verge escapement, and is in a long-case of oak veneered with ebony; the hour band is of silver. **John**, Ye Mermaid at Lothbury; apprenticed to Thomas Loomes; 1663-80 (see p. 237). one of John Fromanteel's long-case clocks at the Dutch Church, Austin Friars, is dated 1679. **Ahasuerus**, apprenticed 1679 to Jno. F., C.C. **Abraham**, son and apprentice of Ahasuerus Fromanteel; C.C. 1680; refused to serve as steward 1701. **& Clarke**, London; watches, from about 1680; long marqueterie case month clock, domed hood with gilt figures on top, 12-in. dial, strikes the quarters, about 1710; a somewhat similar specimen, in the possession of Mr Wm. R. Moss, is shown in Fig. 679; it strikes hours and half hours on different bells, has an alarm and shows day of the week and of the month; Mr Walter H. Durfee, Rhode Island, U.S.A., has a long-case clock by Fromanteel & Clarke with the additional signature "A. Fromanteel" along the bottom edge of the dial.

Frost, —, Exeter; put Lovelace's clock in order in 1849 (see p. 301).

Frowde, Jno., apprenticed 1646 to Hy. Wansey; C.C. 1658.

Fry, Edward, 13 Park Side, Knightsbridge, 1835.

Fryer. William, f., of York, 1809; settled at Pocklington. **John**, f., of York, 1812; then at Pocklington. **Moses**, York, 1822. **William James**, 50 Cheapside, 1842.

Fryett, S., 130 Whitecross St., 1823.

Fueter, —, Berne, about 1740.

Fulkener, Edward, C.C. 1675.

Fuller. William, C.C. 1675. **Samuel**, 64 Red Lion St., Clerkenwell, 1800-40; gave evidence in 1817 before a committee of the House of Commons on the distress among watchmakers in Clerkenwell. **Crispin**, Monkwell St., 1817.

Fulwell, Hy., apprenticed 1649 to Hy. Child, C.C.

Furet. Clock, Wallace collection, about 1740, signed "Furet l'aîné à Paris."

Furnace, Geo., Dublin; watch, 1781.

Furness. Joseph, Uppingham, 1784. **—**, Monkwearmouth, 1802. **John**, 9 Cross St., Hatton Garden, 1830.

Furnesse. Thomas, near Three Compasses, Gravel Lane, 1701. **Joseph**, Monkwearmouth, 1770.

Furnifull, Richard, C.C. 1722.

Furnis, Thomas, 25 Crawford St., 1840-42.

Furstensteller, Benedict, Friburg; hexagonal alarm table clock, brass case, silver dial plate, Hilton Price collection, about 1650.

Gabrier, Charles, London; this name on clocks and watches 1705-20 may possibly be fictitious, see Cabrier.

Gadsby, —, Leicester, 1770.

Gadsdon, Wm., London; long-case clock, about 1750.

Gagnebin, Dan., Chaux de Fonds, about 1750.

Gaill, Mattheis, large German watch, S.K.M., about 1670.

Gailliard, N., oval watch, about 1590, Pierpont Morgan collection.

Galbraith, Patrick, Philadelphia; 1797-1811.

Gale. James, 64 Cannon St., 1783-89. **John**, 5 Red Lion Court, Spitalfields, 1790-1829; Lamb St., 1800-42.

Galemin. Watch, Pierpont Morgan collection, signed "J. Galemin Autin," about 1620.

Gallhans, Gabriel; watch, Pierpont Morgan collection, about 1740.

Gallimore, Joseph, Manchester, 1775.

Gallott, Isaac, apprenticed in 1655 to Thos. Weekes, C.C.

Galloway. Christopher, clock in a gateway of the Kremlin, Moscow, 1626. **Jno.**, apprenticed in 1683 to Wm. Foster, C.C. **Walter**, Kilbirnie, 1780. The Galloways were well known in Leeds: **Jas., J. & T. S., Matthew**; all above 1830.

Galt, Samuel, Williamsburg, U.S.A., 1751.

Gamble. Thomas, C.C. 1657. **Henry**, Bramley, 1770.

Gammage, T., musical clockmaker, 6 Bridgwater Sq., 1823; 8 Wood St., Goswell Rd., 1835. Mr B. G. Wattson has a "Universal" clock by him, which was shown at the 1851 Exhibition.

Gammon. Jno., London; lantern clock inscribed "John Gammon, Londini, fecit," about 1670; silver watch, about 1680, Mr J. Drummond Robertson. **Jno.**, Lambeth; watch, 1725; another, 1760.

Gamod, G., Paris; watch, about 1660; another watch signed "G. Gamos, Paris."

Gamp, P. J., wood clockmaker, 28 Hatton Wall, 1835.

Gandy, —, Cockermouth; long-case clock, inscribed "LIDDL Wm. and Mary, 1768."

Ganeral, Aug., 7 Baker St., Clerkenwell, 1835.

Gannery, —, chronometer maker, died 1851.

Ganter, J., 39 Marshall St., London Rd., 1835.

Ganthony. Richard, 27 Cannon St., 1803; 49 Lombard St., 1807; 83 Cheapside, 1825; master C.C. 1828-9. **Richard Pinfold** (son of the above), 83 Cheapside; died while master C.C. 1845, see Connell.

Gany, Thomas, C.C. 1699.

Garbett, Jere., apprenticed to Conyers Dunlop, turned over to Arthur Downes; admitted C.C. 1768.

Garbrand, Jno., apprenticed 1654 to Thos. Loomes, C.C.

Garde, Jas., London; bracket timepiece, square black case, minute circle within hour circle, about 1700.

Garden. William, C.C. 1712. **Philip**, St Paul's Churchyard, 1759.

Gardener. John, C.C. 1682. **Joseph**, Lancaster, 1767, f. **Henry**, 36 Norton Folgate, 1794-1804.

Gardiner. John, Croydon; C.C. 1687. **Henry**, Rolls Buildings, Fetter Lane, 1759-60.

Gardner. Thomas, C.C. 1689 ; Mr Walter Hosmer, Wethersfield, Conn., has a long-case clock by him ; another in the Wetherfield collection, a three-train chiming clock, arch dial, burr walnut case, about 1710. **William Obadiah,** C.C. 1711. **William,** Sandwich ; walnut long-case clock, about 1760. **T.,** London ; watch, 1762. **Joseph,** Lancaster, 1767, f. **Thos.,** London ; bracket clock, plain mahogany case, about 1790. **Jno.,** Hull, 1822. **W. K.,** Bridlington, 1822. **Edwd.,** Lancaster, 1841, f.

Garfoot, William, C.C. 1680.

Garland, John, Barbican ; liveryman C.C. 1776 ; 1766-98.

Garle, Richd., apprenticed in 1682 to Joseph Windmills, C.C.

Garne, T., London ; bracket clock, about 1680.

Garnegy, Chas., 55 King St., Soho, 1817.

Garner, Thos., London ; watch, 1770.

Garnet, W., London ; watch, 1766.

Garnett. Jno. Anthony, apprenticed in 1672 to Chas. Gretton, C.C. ; he settled in France. **Wm.,** London, about 1680.

Garnham, Abel, 1 Lincoln's Inn Fields, 1816.

Garnier. Watch, about 1700, " F. Garnier à Paris." **Jean Paul,** Paris ; born at Epinal, France, 1801 ; settled in Paris 1820 ; died 1870.

Garon, Peter, London ; C.C. 1694 ; watch, B.M., with day of the month circle ; curious watch with one hand (see p. **180**) ; Mr J. Drummond Robertson has a long-case chiming clock with ten changes in the hour by him (see p. **373**) ; his bankruptcy noted (*Lond. Gaz.,* Oct. 31, 1706).

Garrandol, —, French hexagonal watch, crystal case, Wallace collection, signed " Garrandol à Verdun," about 1640.

Garrard. R. S., & Co., London ; watch, case set with rubies, 1780. **Robt.,** 31 Panton St., Haymarket, 1815-18, see Wickes, Wm. **R. J. & S.,** 31 Panton St., 1822-42.

Garrat, Hugh, Ormskirk ; maker of watches with Debaufre's dead-beat escapement, 1775-1800.

Garraway, C., Queen St., Westminster, 1820.

Garret. Ferdinando, English watch in the form of a Tudor rose, about 1600 (see p. **200**). **Hugh,** see Garrat.

Garrett. Charles, C.C. 1690. **Charles,** admitted C.C. 1720. **William,** 188 Wapping, 1804-15. **Philip,** Philadelphia, 1819.

Garron, see Garon.

Garrot, Jno., Warrington, 1770.

Garth, John, Aylesbury St., Clerkenwell, 1750-55.

Garthwaite, Jno., Colne, Lancs., 1818.

Gartly, Jno., Aberdeen, 1810.

Gartner, C. M. E., Ashby St., Clerkenwell ; in 1856 he, in conjunction with W. S. Mitchell, patented a form of winding for fusee watches and a regulating lever actuated by a screw.

Gascoigne. Wm., Newark ; maker of lantern clocks, born 1659, died 1740 ; Owin Gascoigne, Newark ; long marqueterie case clock, about 1705 ; another, rather later, " Owen " Gascoigne. **Richd.,** apprenticed in 1676 to Sam. Gascoigne, C.C. **Samuel,** C.C. 1676. " Lost, between Ludgate and Lothbury, on the 8th instant, a pendulum watch in a Tortoise-shell Case, with a steel Chain and 2 Swiffles ; made by Samuel Gascoigne " (*Lond. Gaz.,* July 14-18, 1692).

Gaskell, Thos., Knutsford, 1760.

Gaskin, Jno., Dublin ; watch, 1780.

Gass, David, & Co., 42 Oxford St., 1810-23.

Gate. Archer, apprenticed in 1674 to Jas. Ellis, C.C. **Thos.,** Carlisle, 1770.

Gates, Francis, London ; watch, 1795.

Gatewood. " Lost on 26 July 1705 a silver minute Pendulum Watch on the upper plate Gatewood and on the Dyal Plate, Gatewood, London. Whoever has taken it ups if they will bring it to Sam. Barrow, Clockmaker at the Sign of the Spring Clock in East Smithfield near Hermitage Bridge shall have 20s. reward " (*The Postman,* July 31, 1705).

Gatford, Wm., Uxbridge ; watch, 1759.

Gathercole, John, London ; maker of a bracket clock, silvered arch dial, about 1780.

Gatty, Thos., Bodmin, 1790-1820.

Gatward (? Gatewood), **Thos.,** apprenticed in 1693 to Dan Rose, C.C.

Gaudron, P., Paris ; clock and watch maker of repute, 1690-1730 ; spoken of as an authority by Thiout and by Lepaute ; a handsome clock by him is illustrated on p. **312** ; watch by him, Mr Henry Carr Glyn ; watch, leather case *piqué* with gold, wind in centre of dial, about 1720, Mr Evan Roberts.

Gaudy, J. A., Geneva, about 1780.

Gaunt. Joseph, apprenticed to James Wood, and turned over to Francis Rooker, and afterwards to Samuel Allvey, admitted C.C. 1761. **John,** 2 Bridgewater Gardens, 1825-42.

Gauthier, Pierre, Paris ; enamelled watch, Pierpont Morgan collection, about 1710.

Gautier, J. A., first director of the Geneva Observatory, died 1881.

Gautschy, Jas., London ; watch, apparently Swiss, about 1785.

Gavelle. James (alien), C.C. 1683 ; clock with square dial, boy and crown corners, " James Gavelle, Londini, fecit," on circle ; 1683-1700. **Jno.,** Morefields ; long-case clock, about 1705. —, Paris ; clock, 1820.

Gay, see Guy.

Gaze, James, Primrose St., Bishopsgate, 1782. **Samuel B.,** son and successor of James, a well-known clockmaker, 26 Princes St., Spitalfields, 1814-59. **Peter,** Liverpool Rd., son of Samuel B., died 1892, aged 73 ; he and his brother were among the best clockmakers of the period.

Gazuet, Jerome, admitted C.C. 1682 ; lantern clock, about 1700, Mr E. Wehrle, Brussels ; long-case clock, at Belem, Lisbon, signed " J. Gazuet, St John's, London," about 1710.

Gee, see Guy.

Gefael, U., 28 Langley Place, Commercial Rd., 1835-42.

Gegenreiner, F. Z., Augsburg, about 1720.

Geldarte, Jno., York, f., 1674.

Gell, York : **Jno.,** f., 1634 ; **Jno.,** f., 1663.

Gells, Thomas, admitted C.C. 1720.

Gent. Joseph, Walsall, 1818. **Ralph,** London ; made watches for the Turkish market, 1842.

George. Andrew, apprenticed in 1649 to Peter Delaundre, C.C. **Richard,** C.C. 1681.

Gerard, J. B., Quai des Grands Augustins, Paris (garde visiteur), 1769.

Gernon, Bernard, apprenticed to Solomon Wagson, of Bristol ; admitted C.C. 1659.

Geronst, Alex., Coventry St., London ; bracket clock, about 1730, seen at The Hague.

Gerrard, John, London ; bracket clock, about 1725 ; verge watch, h.m., 1740.

Gervas, Thos., Epworth ; clock, about 1770.

Gewoll, Gregory, senr., London, 1730.

Gib. William, Rotterdam ; two pendulum watches, G.M., about 1710 ; watch, silver cock, Nelthropp collection, about 1725 ; fine long-case chiming clock, Sir James M. Moody (see p. **379**). **B.,** Rotterdam ; watch, Nelthropp collection, about 1720.

Gibbard, Thomas, Quakers' Buildings, 1780-85.

Gibbons. Edward, New St., C.C. 1730. **Benjamin,** C.C. 1750 ; died 1769. **Joshua,** 45 White St., Borough, 1810-18. **John,** 6 King St., Clerkenwell, 1810-23 ; 64 Hatton Garden, 1836-42 ; livery C.C. 1811.

Gibbs. Walter, admitted C.C. 1648. **Thomas,** apprenticed 1672 to Hy. Hester ; admitted C.C. 1681 ; master 1711. **Joshua,** apprenticed in 1689 to Thos. Gibbs, C.C. **William,** Morefields, C.C. 1707-30 ; pair-case verge watch, *repoussé* case, about 1720. **Jas.,** Whitefriars, C.C. 1725. **Stephen,** Milford Lane, C.C. 1728 ; watch, 1750. **Richd.,** London, 1760 ; long-case clock, said to be signed " Pick Gibbs," is probably by him, and signed " Rich. Gibbs." **Jno.,** 11 Castle St., Aldersgate, 1815-19. **Thomas,** 11 Nichol Sq., Aldersgate St., 1825. **Geo.,** 38 Banner St., 1835-42.

Gibson. Benj., apprenticed 1654 to Richd. Masterton, C.C. **James,** brother C.C. 1669. —, Newcastle, about 1750. **Mary,** at the Dial and Crown, Newgate St., dealer in all sorts of clock and watch makers' tools and materials, and for near twenty years the first in the business ; having acquired a good fortune with a fair character, she retired from business in 1757 (Ludlam). **Jno.,** Beith ; curious geographical clock, 1761. **John** (? Jas.), Whalebone Court, Lothbury, 1761-1813. **Wm.,** Barnard Castle, 1770. **John,** Jedburgh ; long-case clock, about 1770. **Edward,** livery C.C. 1787 ; master 1802 ; 1780-1803. **& Faust,** 5 Charlotte St., Rathbone Place, 1800. **Jno.,** Royal Exchange, C.C. 1800-10 ; succeeded by Jas. Bissett. **C.,** 71 Bishopsgate Within, 1830.

Gideon, Robert, admitted C.C. 1691.

Giffin, Thos., London, 1820.

Gifford, Thomas, apprenticed to Robert Seignior, and turned over to Robert Webster, admitted C.C. 1692.

Gil, Wm., Rotterdam ; watches, 1770-90 ; watch, about 1780, signed " Gil l'aîné," see Gill, also Gilb.

Gilbard, Thos., watch-case maker, Clerkenwell Green, 1793.

Gilbert. Thos., apprenticed 1656 to Robt. Coster, C.C. **Austin,** C.C. 1661. **Richd.,** apprenticed in 1664 to Thos. Hancorne, C.C. **Joseph,** apprenticed in 1682 to Thos. Fenn, C.C. **William,** C.C. 1695. **Charles,** C.C. 1700. à Paris ; watch, about 1780. **Philip,** 20 Cockspur St., 1807 ; 5 St James's Sq., 1820, see Green.

Gilbertson, Jno., Ripon, 1770.

Gildchrist (or **Gilchrist**). **Archibald,** C.C. 1729. **Sterling,** Lombard St., 1755-65.

Gilkes. Richd., apprenticed in 1678 to Wm. Hancorne ; C.C. 1686. **Geo.,** apprenticed in 1693 to Richd. Watts, C.C. **Jno.,** Shipston, on plate of watch, Mary Gilkes on dial, hall mark 1766.

Gill. Wm., Maidstone ; lantern clock, about 1700, Dr Wm. A. Day. **John,** C.C. 1707. **John,** Gracechurch St., 1753-65. **Daniel,** Rye, 1790. **Wm.,** Rotterdam ; watch, 1794.

Gille, —, Paris, 1769.

Gillespy, —, Dublin ; watch, 1796.

Gillett. Cha. Edw., Manchester ; 30-

hour one-hand clock, about 1740. **Edwd., & Son**, Manchester, 1775. **& Healy**, Manchester, 1800. **Chas. Ed.**, Manchester, died 1819, aged 74.

Gillier, C., Berne ; maker of an oval watch, about 1650.

Gillies, Robt., Beith, 1780.

Gillmore ; lantern clock, inscribed "Jno. Gillmore, Battel," about 1700.

Gilpin, Edmund, petitioner for incorporation of C.C. ; a watch by him mentioned in *Archæological Journal*, vol. xxii. ; oval watch, about 1620, Whitcombe Greene collection.

Gimblet, Jno., junr., **& Vale**, 106 Snow Hill, Birmingham, 1770.

Gingner, Anthony (French), admitted as a brother C.C. 1687.

Ginn, William, freeman C.C. 1699.

Giox, —, Paris ; enamelled watch, 1780.

Girard. Marc, Blois ; oval watch, Soltykoff collection, about 1590 ; watch signed " M. Girard, Bloy," in case of rock crystal, about 1580, Pierpont Morgan collection. **Marc**, Paris ; oval, chased watch-case of silver-gilt and rock crystal, Shandon collection, about 1600. **J.**, London ; watch, 1700.

Girardier l'aîné, Geneva, 1780-1805.

Giraud, Christophe, Geneva, 1814.

Girod. Gasper ; an astronomical watch by him in B.M., about 1610. **James** (French) ; watch, about 1660, signed " Jacques Girod à Copet," admitted C.C. 1692 ; bracket clock, about 1700, inscribed " James Girod, London." **Benj.**, London ; repeating watch, 1775.

Giroust. Alexander, Coventry St., 1760 ; clock, Mr Eden Dickson. **à Paris** ; fine clock, about 1790.

Giteau, Eve de Breguet, Paris ; watch, 1790.

Gitter, Jno., apprenticed in 1683 to Nat. Pyne, C.C.

Gladstone, Thomas, C.C. 1703.

Glaesner & Preud'homme, Lyon ; repeating watch, about 1780, M. Th. de Saussure.

Glanville, Richard, Strand, 1775.

Glase, Thos., Bridgnorth ; watch, 1790.

Glasgo, Phil., & Son, Dublin ; pull repeating bracket clock, about 1720, Mr D. T. Halsey.

Glass, Alexander, 306 High Holborn, 1783.

Glassup, Thos., London ; bracket clock, about 1755 ; another, about 1780.

Glazebrook, Jno., Mansfield, 1780.

Glazier, William, C.C. 1666 ; to him Simon Lamb was apprenticed in 1669.

Gleave, Matthew ; watch by him, G.M., 1700.

Gleeter, —, London ; watch, about 1740.

Glenc, Joseph, Prag ; watch about 1710.

Glenny, Joseph, watch-case maker, 20 Red Lion St., Clerkenwell ; livery C.C. 1810.

Glossop, Robt., London ; watch, 1815.

Glover. Samuel, C.C. 1694. **Daniel**, C.C. 1699. **Thos.**, New St., C.C. 1700. **Richard**, C.C. 1703. **Boyer**, Leadenhall St., C.C. 1740 ; died while serving as senior warden, 1768. **Ralph**, Hyde Park Corner ; watch, about 1770. **Wm.**, Worcester, 1770. —, watch-spring maker, 81 Aldersgate St., 1800-5. —, Pimlico, 1810. **J.**, 9 May's Buildings, St Martin's Lane, 1835. **Jno.**, chronometer maker ; apprenticed to J. R. Arnold, 1835-80.

Gluck, Adam ; watch by him in B.M. in a case of bloodstone, 1650-60.

Glyd, Jas., Westminster ; watch, h.m., 1771.

Glynn, Richard, C.C. 1705.

Gobert. Peter (French), admitted C.C. 1687. **Matt.**, London ; watch, 1760.

Gobrecht, Christian, Baltimore, 1820.

Godbed. William, apprenticed 1638 to Thos. Reeve, admitted C.C. 1646 ; watch, Whitcomb Greene collection, inscribed " Guliemus Godbed, Lumbert Street, Londini," octagonal case ; another at the B.M.; signed a petition to C.C. 1656. **Matt.**, apprenticed in 1657 to Hy. Kent, C.C.

Godbere, Saml., " late Mr Stamp, 85 Cheapside," card Ponsonby collection.

Goddard. Reymond. John, Hounsditch (from Paris), described as a Papist who resided with and worked for Isaac Sunes in Hounsditch, 1615-18. **Thos.**, apprenticed 1638 to Richd. Child, C.C. **Isaac**, apprenticed 1675 to Thos. Grimes ; C.C. 1684 ; long-case clock, Museum, Brunswick, inscribed " Isaac Goddard, Londini." **Thos.**, apprenticed 1685 to Jno. Stanley, C.C. **Ben.**, apprenticed 1691 to Isaac Goddard ; C.C. 1701 ; long-case clock by him in the Mosque of Achmet, Constantinople. **Stephen**, C.C. 1727 ; long-case clock, about 1740. **Nicholas**, Newark ; maker of lantern clocks ; died 1741. **Francis**, 49 Oxford St., 1792 ; 8 Rathbone Place, 1794-1825. **T.**, 28 Pitfield St., 1814 ; 20 New Gloucester St., Hoxton, 1835. Of U.S.A.: **Luther**, Shrewsbury, Mass.; between 1809 and 1817 he manufactured watches.

Godfrey. Jno., apprenticed in 1682 to Jas. Hatchman, C.C. **Henry**, C.C. 1685. " A pretty large-sized Pendulum-watch in a Tortoiseshell Case ; it shews the Hours and Minutes with a Sun and Moon Dial Plate, made by Henry Godfrey, London" (*Lond. Gaz.*, Oct. 7-10, 1700). **Wm.**, Winterton, 1773 ; succeeded by his son Wm., see Tate, Thos. **George**, 22 Charterhouse St., 1835. **& Storer**, 19 Princes St., 1860.

Godlyman, Peter, Hurley ; clock, brass dial 5½ in. square, lantern movement, about 1700.

Godon, —, Paris, 1780-90 ; appointed horloger to the Court of Spain in 1786 ; splendid clock in vase-shaped case of Sèvres porcelain, painted with birds in a medallion, and mounted with handles formed as caryatid figures, dating from about 1785, which was in Lord Strathallan's collection, fetched 2,000 guineas at Christie's in 1902.

Godwin. John, 161 Strand, see Goodwin. **Jas.**, 304 High Holborn, 1801-42.

Goff, Thos., 8 Rosoman St., 1793.

Gold. Christopher, London ; watch, B.M., gold *repoussé* case, about 1760. **Rich.**, London ; watch, h.m., 1772. **John**, 118 Fleet St., 1806-19.

Golding, J., 55 Cornhill, 1775.

Goldney, Thos., 4 St James's St., 1815-25.

Goldsborough, Geo., Scarborough, 1775.

Goldsmith. John, C.C. 1681. **Thos.**, apprenticed in 1683 to Wm. Brafield ; C.C. 1692. **William**, C.C. 1719. **John**, C.C. 1720.

Goldsworthy, E., Chelsea, 1820.

Golledge, Richard, Stratford, 1835.

Gom, David, Lyons ; maker of a watch cased in jacinths, about 1650.

Gomps, —, hexagonal watch, silver case, signed " Gomps à Armstrand, 1586."

Gondoux, Jno., London ; watch, 1780.

Gooch. (& Harper, 12 Red Lion St., Clerkenwell, 1810-13). **Jno.**, 25 Banner St., 1814-18. **Albert**, 13 Red Lion St.,

Clerkenwell, 1816-25. **Wm.**, Bunhill Row, 1825. **H.**, 25 Coppice Row, Clerkenwell, 1830.

Good. John, author of " The Art of Shadows ; or, Universal Dialling," 2nd ed., London, 1711 ; C.C. 1678. **John**, 305 High Holborn, 1780-94.

Goodall. Geo., Micklefield ; long-case clock, square dial, about 1720. **Jas.**, London ; watch, 1779. **Chas.**, 26 Bridges St., Covent Garden, 1793-1818.

Goodchild, John, C.C. 1726.

Goode, Charles, brother C.C. 1686 ; bracket quarter clock and also very fine long marqueterie case clock, about 1690, Wetherfield collection.

Goodfellow. Wm., 378 Oxford St., 1793. **William**, Philadelphia, 1797.

Goodfriend, John, London ; bracket clock, about 1750.

Goodhall, Geo., Aberford, 1775.

Goodhugh. R. & B., 2 Welbeck St., Cavendish Sq., 1825-35. **William**, 126 Regent St., 1825. **Richard**, 32 Edward St., Portman Sq., from 2 Welbeck St., Cavendish Sq., 1840-42.

Gooding, Henry, Boston, 1810-30.

Goodlad, Richard, admitted as a brother C.C. 1689.

Goodlin, Peter, admitted C.C. 1637.

Goodman. Geo., London, 1771 ; fine repeating watch, Pierpont Morgan collection ; watch in case of red agate, about 1780, Pierpont Morgan collection ; another watch, about 1785. **H. N.**, London ; watch, 1820. **J., & Son**, 1 New Chappel Place, Kentish Town, 1840-42.

Goodrich. Wm., apprenticed in 1689 to Amos Winch, C.C. **Simon**, received a reward from the Society of Arts in 1799 for an improved escapement.

Goodwin. Wm., apprenticed in 1675 to Jno. Harris, C.C. ; lantern clock, about 1700, inscribed " Wm. Goodwin, Stowmarket" ; watch, about 1720, with the following on a paper in the outer case :—

" Content thy selfe withe thyne estat,
    And sende no poore wight from thy gate ;
For why, this councell I thee give,
    To learne to dye, and dye to lyve."

Thos., London ; watch, about 1760. **John**, 70 Strand, 1770-1800. **James**, watch and clock enameller, 37 Red Lion St., Clerkenwell, 1810 - 40. **Hy.**, Newark, 1821-42.

Goodyear. John, Shoe Lane ; C.C. 1722. **Joseph**, Shoe Lane ; C.C. 1732.

Gordon. John, Black Spread Eagle, Ludgate St. ; C.C. 1698 ; bracket clock, black case, arch dial inscribed " John Gordon, London," on oval silvered plate, 1698-1712. **Robert**, Edinburgh ; an eminent maker ; admitted freeman of the Incorporation of Hammermen in 1703, afterwards " boxmaster" or treasurer ; was also captain of the trained band for protecting the city ; a chiming clock by him in the Bank of Scotland, another in the possession of Mr L. W. Auchterlonie, Amhurst Park, Stamford Hill ; 1703-29. **Thos.**, Edinburgh, 1703, f.; long-case clock, arabesque marqueterie, about 1710. **Patrick**, Edinburgh, 1705-15. **Thomas**, " from London "; opposite the Merchants' Coffee House, New York, 1759. **Alex.**, Dublin ; watch, about 1780. **Jas.**, Beith, 1780. **William**, 15 Cross St., Islington, 1794-1805. **& Fletcher**, Dublin ; watch, 1795. **Alex.**, 336 Strand, 1815-19. **Jas.**, London ; watch, 1842. **Theodore**, Great James St., Bedford Row ; born at Barbados ; apprenticed in Aberdeen ; horizontal and duplex escapement maker, also assistant of B. L. Vulliamy, sometime editor of the *Horological Journal*; died 1870, aged 81.

Gore, Wm., Dublin; watch, 1770.

Goret, Jean, Rue Courture Ste. Catherine, Paris; garde visiteur, 1769.

Gorham, James, High St., Kensington, 1815-42.

Gorsuch. Thos., Salop; watch, 1720. **Thos.**, watch pillar maker, 199 St John St., 1792.

Gosler, Thos., 51 Fore St., 1815-19.

Gosling. Richard, apprenticed in 1649 to Thomas Claxton, C.C. **Richard, & Son**, 55 Cornhill, 1765-75. **Robert**, 160 Fenchurch St., 1770-85. **Joseph**, 55 Cornhill, 1775-85. **Wm.**, watch-case maker, 4 Corporation Row, 1793. **Thos.**, watch-case maker, 3 Staining Lane, 1793.

Gosse. Jno., apprenticed in 1662 to Richard Scrivener, C.C. **Jeremiah**, C.C. 1667.

Gosselin, J. Ph., Rue St Honoré, Paris; clock, about 1760; garde visiteur, 1769.

Gossoin. In 1667 he constructed the clock at Val de Grâce, for which he received 3,000 livres.

Gostage, Sam., Birkenhead, 1833.

Goubert, James, admitted C.C. 1890.

Gough. Wm., Devizes; watch 1720, in each of the pillars a niche containing a silver statue. **Wm.**, London; watch, 1745, also curious touch watch, G.M., about 1760; in this a push piece at the pendant drove a rod against a snail pivoted to the plate, and turned by a pin in the cannon pinion.

Gougy, Pierre Frederick, Tavistock St., Westminster; bracket clock at Windsor Castle, about 1830; patented in 1839 (No. 8,308) a supplementary second hand, so adjusted by mechanism that it may be stopped while the other second hand is going, and on being set free will recover its original position, and rotate as before along with the other.

Goujon. Jean, Paris; cruciform watches, about 1590. **Stephen**, Seven Dials; C.C. 1725. **Peter**, London; watch, 1735. **Samuel**, 42 Newgate St.; master C.C. 1760; 1752-94.

Gould. Christopher, C.C. 1682; in the Wetherfield collection are long-case clocks by him: one with bolt and shutter maintaining power, 10½-in. dial, in marqueterie case with finely carved pediment, about 1685; another, exceedingly small, repeats the quarters on five bells, dial 7⅝ square, burr walnut case with domed hood, about 1690; watch, Pierpont Morgan collection, about 1700. "Supposed to be drop'd in a Hackney coach on the 4th inst., a gold watch in a black shagreen case, made by C. Gold, the word 'Friendship' graved on the Movement" (*Lond. Gaz.*, March 18-21, 1694). Mr Jno. T. Trotter had a long-case clock by him of later date. **Abel**, C.C. 1683. "Lost on the 28th inst., a gold watch with two movements, having a black filagreen case studded like shells, made by Abel Gould" (*Lond. Gaz.*, March 26-30, 1691). **Thos.**, London; watch, 1780. **Chester**, Red Lion St., Clerkenwell; he patented in 1803 (No. 2,706) a nautical time glass, 1780-1803.

Goullons. à Paris; watch by him in Guildhall Museum, short train, escape wheel of 17, handsome enamelled case, 1⅓ in. in diameter, and ½ in. thick, about 1660, see Crofts. à Marseille; fine enamelled watch, about 1670 (see p. **150**).

Gourlay, Alex., London; watch, 1785

Gout. Ralph, 6 Norman St., Old St., 1770-1800; 122 Birchin Lane, 1815; he patented in 1799 (No. 2,351) apparatus for recording the paces made by man or horse, also an application of the invention for recording the revolutions made by the wheels of a carriage; Mr Thos. Boynton has a bracket clock by him, mahogany case, silvered dial, engraved with festoons, &c., quarters chimed on eight bells, see Recordon. **David Ralph**, 122 Bunhill Row, 1830-42.

Gouthière, —, Paris; celebrated chaser and gilder of clock cases; from 1740 (see p. **323**).

Gow, Wm., London; watch, h.m., 1787.

Gowerth, John, Oxford, 1701.

Gowland. Clement, Sunderland, 1775. **Thos.**, 15 Bishopsgate Without, 1834; 5 Leadenhall St., 1838-42. **James**, 11 Leathersellers' Buildings, London Wall, 1835; London Wall, 1860; died 1880; in 1837 he patented (No. 7,456) a device for communicating motion to a balance through the balance spring.

Grace. Wm., Cronton; sun and moon watches, about 1695. **Thos.**, London; bracket clock, about 1720, Major W. G. Thorold.

Gradelle, —, London; watch, Schloss collection, about 1740.

Graet, Philip, Lintz; fine travelling watch, about 1695 (see p. **192**).

Grafton. John (*alias* **Solomons**); in 1831, on the passing of an Act of Common Council permitting the admission of Jews to the freedom, C.C. withdrew opposition to his election. **J. & E.**, 42 Coleman St., 1834; 81 Fleet St., 1838-42; afterwards Edward Grafton, who published a small historical review of horology. **Henry**, 18 Barbican, 1840.

Graham. George, "honest George Graham," a most eminent clock and watch maker (see p. **227**); C.C. 1695, master 1722; died 1751, aged 77. **William**, at the Dial in Lombard St.; a good maker; fine repeating watch, Mrs H. Sidebottom, S.K.M., 1724; long-case clock, Wm. Graham, London, about 1730. **D.**, London; watch, 1798. **James**, 85 Piccadilly, 1800-5. **Jas.**, London; watch, 1825. **Frank**, Newcastle-on-Tyne, died 1855.

Grainger, Richard, apprenticed in 1685 to Francis Munden, C.C. —, Holborn Hill; watch, 1830.

Gramot, G., Paris; watch in enamelled case, Pierpont Morgan collection.

Gran, —, Fleet St.; watch, h.m., 1776.

Grand, John, 3 Cockspur St., 1780-1800, see Fisher, Isaac.

Grandeau, —, oval watch, about 1590, signed "Grandeau à Paris," Garnier collection.

Grandin, Jno., 2 Macclesfield St., Soho, 1815-19.

Grandjean, David Henry, Locle, died, 1845. **Henry**, Locle, born 1803, died 1879.

Granger, Richard, C.C. 1695.

Grangier (French), about 1650 (see p. **145**).

Grant. Wm., London; watch, 1740. **Richard**, London; bracket clock, 1760. **John**, 75 Fleet St.; apprenticed to Alexander Cumming, whose nephew he was; hon. freeman C.C. 1781, warden 1810, when he died; several specimens of his work are in the Guildhall Museum. **John**, 75 Fleet St., son of the preceding, and an equally celebrated maker; C.C. 1817, master five times 1838-67; he left Fleet St. in 1852, and for some years carried on a pawnbroking business in London Wall which had been bequeathed to him; he died 1882, aged 85; he was succeeded in Fleet St. by Henry Banister. **Chas.**, London; watch, 1800. **Joseph**, Chester, 1814-18. **Jesse**, 16 Woodstock St., 1830. **Henry**, 9 Finch Lane, 1835. **William**, 36 Haymarket, 1835. **& Terry**, 35 Prince's St., 1840.

Grantham, J., London, 1750-70.

Grape. Richard, apprenticed in 1685 to Jno. Wheeler, C.C. **John**, London; watch, G.M., 1737.

Gratrex, Edward, Birmingham; long-case clock, about 1750.

Graupner, J. G., clock, Green Vaulted Chambers, Dresden, about 1700.

Grave. Joseph, apprenticed in 1687 to Joseph Williamson, C.C. **Geo.**, 271 Whitechapel Rd., 1815-42.

Gravell. (**& Tolkein**, successors of Eardley Norton), 49 St John St., 1790-1820; in 1817 they made a new clock for Winchester Town Hall, the cost of which was borne by the Powlett family. **William, & Son**, 49 St John St., 1820; later and till 1850 at 29 Charterhouse Sq.; W. Gravell, master C.C. 1840; well-known watchmakers; on the outer cases of their watches were papers with the equation of time printed round the edge (see p. **169**); they were succeeded by Robert Rolfe.

Graves. Jas., C.C. 1675. **Benjamin**, C.C. 1676, master 1705, clerk 1719; died 1731; Wm. Neighbour apprenticed to him 1678. **Wm.**, York, f., 1730. **Hy.**, 25 Goswell Terrace, 1835.

Gray. Timothy, brother C.C. 1633. **Jno.**, apprenticed in 1680 to Jno. Westoby, C.C.; long-case clock, "John Gray in Johnson's Court, Londini, fecit," about 1705. **William**, apprenticed in 1691 to Peter Lodowick, C.C.; watch, about 1730, belonging to M. Chas. Sivan, is inscribed "Wm. Gray, Bond St., London." **Benjamin**, Pall Mall; clockmaker to George II. (see p. **281**); in the G.M. is a gold repeating watch by him, which was made for Sir Peter Somes in 1732; extra large long-case clock, with dead-beat escapement, about 1730, Wetherfield collection, 1720-60. **& Vulliamy**, Pall Mall (see p. **281**), 1746-60. **Jas.**, London; watch, 1756. **Jos.**, Durham, watch, 1777. **Jno.**, 68 Leadenhall St.; apprenticed to Thos. Hardy; C.C. 1769; watch by him, G.M., 1769-1817. **& Constable**, Sackville St.; makers of a thin verge watch decorated with enamel and jewels, G.M., about 1780. **Thomas**, 25 Strand, 1780; 42 Sackville St., 1793. **James**, Edinburgh; long mahogany case clock, Sheraton style, about 1790, Wetherfield collection. **Adam**, 17 Berkeley St., Clerkenwell, 1788-1812. **Robert & William**, 13 New Bond St., 1793; William, 1800-28. **T. J. & G.**, 25 Strand, 1800-5. **G. & W.**, 114 Fleet St., 1830.

Graye, —, subscribed £2. 10s. for incorporation of C.C. 1630.

Grayham. Timothy, Workington, 1770. **Chas.**, London; watch, 1810.

Grayhurst. B., London; watch, 1778. **P. & M.**, 65 Strand, 1785-1800. **& Harvey**, 65 Strand, 1810-30. **Harvey, Denton, & Co.**, 64 Strand and 128 Regent St., 1835-40.

Grayson, Wm., Henley-on-Thames, 1826.

Greatorex. Ralph, C.C. 1653. **Henry**, C.C. 1711; in the *Postman*, 1710, is an advertisement for a silver pendulum watch, lost in White Conduit Fields, for which

Mr Greatorex at Bushby's Folly offers a guinea reward, 1710-11.

Greaves. **Samuel,** London; marqueterie long case clock, square dial, about 1720. **Wm.,** Newcastle, 1760. **Robert,** Macclesfield, 1770. **S.,** Mansfield, 1770. **Thos.,** 92 High St., Birmingham, 1770. **Wm.,** York, died 1796.

Grebaunal. **Jerome,** watch, B.M., about 1600. **Robert,** Rouen; fine octagonal watch, G.M., about 1620.

Grebauvel, Hierosme, Lyons; oval watch, Soltykoff collection, about 1595.

Grebay. **Phillipe,** à Londres; watch, about 1610. **Phillipe,** Paris; alarm watch, S.K.M., about 1670.

Greblin, see Gribelin.

Green. **Geo.,** apprenticed in 1661 to Matt. Crockford, C.C. **James,** Morefields; C.C. 1664; lantern clock with handsomely chased dial. **Edwd.,** apprenticed in 1682 to Thos. Davis, C.C. **Nat.,** apprenticed in 1688 to Dan Beckman, C.C. **Jno.,** London; sheepshead lantern clock, about 1700. **Joseph,** C.C. 1723; long-case clock signed "Jos. Green, North Shields," about 1730. **Jno.,** St Martin's Court, 1750-70. **Joseph,** North Shields; bracket clock, about 1750, Mr E. C. Cheston. **James,** 5 Fenchurch St.; calendar watch, pinchbeck, set with garnets, Hilton Price collection; Ludlam, in 1755, refers to him as a watchmaker and seller of tools; master C.C. 1784; 8 Philpot Lane, 1794. **Richd.,** Richmond, Yorks., 1760. **George Smith,** "an eccentric watchmaker of Oxford, with a turn for literature," died 1762. **Margaret,** St Martin's Court, Leicester Sq., 1765-71. **& Aldridge,** 62 St Martin's Le Grand, 1765-85; Henry Green, livery Clothworkers' Company. **Robt.,** Lancaster, 1767, f. **Joseph,** North Shields, 1770. **Geo.,** Leicester, 1775. **Samuel,** 112 Bunhill Row, 1788-1800. **Edwd.,** 10 King's Stairs, Rotherhithe; watch for the Turkish market, Schloss collection, about 1790. **& Bentley,** makers of a very complicated long-case musical and astronomical clock, about 1790. **Joseph,** tools, 129 Whitecross St., 1793. **& Ward,** 1 Ludgate St., 1793. **John,** Philadelphia, 1794. **Robt.,** London; watch, 1798. **Ward, & Green,** 1 Ludgate St., 1800; 20 Cockspur St., Pall Mall, 1817-38. **Abraham,** London; watch, 1804. **Wm.,** Grantham; watch, 1830. **J., & Son,** 94 Hatton Garden, 1830. **Thos.,** 30 Rahere St., 1835; 9 Lower Ashby St., Northampton Sq., 1842. **Henry,** 10 Quebec St., 1835-42. **Robt.,** 20 Cockspur St., 1842.

Greenaway. **Richard,** Whitecross St.; C.C. 1718. **Wm.,** Cripplegate; C.C. 1730. **John,** 54 Bath St., St Luke's, 1842. **John,** 4 St John's Sq., 1842.

Greene. **James,** apprenticed to Henry Jones; C.C. 1685. **John,** C.C. 1711.

Greenhill. **Nat.,** apprenticed in 1674 to Edwd. Clough, C.C. **Charles,** watch-key maker, 12 Great Sutton St., 1842.

Greenough, N. C., Newburyport, U.S.A., 1848.

Greensill. **Joseph,** 36 Strand, 1775-1800. **Edwd.,** 34 Strand, 1793.

Greenwood, G., 12 Hanway St., 1817.

Gregg. **Francis,** apprenticed to John Clowes 1691; in the Wetherfield collection is a long-case clock with a remarkably fine dial having a revolving equation of time calendar showing through an aperture below the centre; above the centre is the inscription "Fran. Gregg, Covent Garden." "Francis Gregg, watchmaker, is removed

from the Dial in Russel Street, Covent Garden, to the Dial in St James St. over against the Palace Gates" (Lond. Gaz., October 11-23, 1714). In the G.M. is a repeating watch by him with silver cap, 1698-1715. **Rd.,** London, about 1730 (see p. 153). **Wm.,** London; watch, 1796.

Gregoire, P., à Blois; striking watch, about 1620.

Gregory. **Jeremie,** at yᵉ Royal Exchange; early oval watch by him, similar to the one illustrated on p. 163, Stamford Institution; C.C. 1652, master 1665, 1676; died 1685; a good maker of lantern clocks and watches (see p. 137); in Mercurius Publicus, 7th May 1663, is advertised a gold watch lost. "Give notice to Mr Gregory, watch maker, near the Castle Tavern in Cornhill." In the Lond. Gaz., Oct. 13, 1678, he advertises for Nester Holmes, aged 18, a runaway apprentice. "A silver watch with a String, made by Jeremiah Gregory, showing the days of the month, the Box engraven with the King's Picture in the bottom" (Lond. Gaz., March 29, 1680). Mr John H. Baker has a lantern clock, inscribed "Jeremie Gregorie at the Royal Exchange." **Thomas,** C.C. by redemption 1671. **Robert,** C.C. 1678. **Jeremiah,** C.C. 1694. **Jno.,** Upton Magna, 1760. **Jas.,** Ormskirk; watch, Debaufre escapement, Guildhall Museum, about 1765.

Gregson. **Philip,** apprenticed in 1663 to Ahasuerus Fromanteel, junr., C.C. **Pierre,** Paris, horloger du Roy; watch, case finely enamelled, medallion with figure painting in centre, surrounded by a border of royal blue, 1780-90 (p. 157). **John,** watchmaker to the Prince of Wales, 36 Bruton St., Hanover Sq., 1794-1800. **& Jefferson,** 36 Bruton St., 1800-5. **Jno.,** Lancaster, 1818.

Grendon, Henry, at ye Exchange; admitted C.C. 1640; watch, S.K.M., about 1610 (see p. 126); another watch inscribed "Henry Grendon at Exchange, Fecit," not later than 1630, Pierpont Morgan collection.

Grennell, Richard, maker of a fine long case clock, about 1750.

Gretton. **Chas.,** The Ship, Fleet St.; apprenticed to Lionel Wythe in 1662; C.C. 1672, master 1701; an eminent maker; to him was apprenticed in 1697 the celebrated Henry Sully; in the Wetherfield collection are a lantern clock, a bracket clock repeating the quarters on six bells, and three long-case clocks by Chas. Gretton. "Lost the 24th Instant, a Gold Pendulum watch in a gold Fillegreen case, with a plain shagreen case over it, the name Charles Gretton, London, with a round Pendulum Spring, a steel chain, and Tulip Pillars, the Dial Plate straight, and a small long Hand to show the Hour. Whoever gives notice of it to Mr Charles Gretton, Watch Maker in Fleet Street, shall have two guineas reward" (Lond. Gaz., March 26, 1683). "Lost or taken away the 13th Instant at night out of a Gentleman's Pocket, a gold watch, with a gold chain to it, the case studded with gold, of Mr Gretton's making, watchmaker living in Fleet St. over against Sergeants Inn Gate. Whoever brings the aforesaid watch to Mr Fowles, goldsmith, at the Black Lyon in Fleet Street, shall have five guineas reward" (Lond. Gaz., Jan. 18, 1685-6). "Taken away the 2nd Instant at night by two Highwaymen, a large silver watch by Charles Gretton, London. If the said

watch be offered to be sold, Pawned, &c., you are desired to stop the watch and Party, and give notice to Mr Charles Gretton at the Ship in Fleet Street, and you shall have a guinea reward" (Lond. Gaz., Sept. 20, 1697). **William,** of Black Fryers; maker of a lantern clock, balance escapement, dolphin frets, about 1665.

Greville, Jno., apprenticed in 1675 to Jere. Gregory, C.C.

Grey. **Joseph,** Durham, 1765. **John,** 68 Leadenhall St., 1823-30.

Gribelin. **Abraham,** Blois; in the B.M. is a watch by him, dated 1600; another, S.K.M., 1614; afterwards at Paris; clockmaker to the King 1631 (see p. 154). **Nicholas,** Paris; square watch, about 1600, Pierpont Morgan collection; very small oval watch in crystal case, with enamelled gold mounting, Garnier collection, early seventeenth century. **Simon,** C.C. 1686. **N.,** Paris; watch by him, B.M., case finely enamelled by Muisard, about 1700; late seventeenth century French watch, in brass case, signed "Gribelin à Paris," S.K.M.

Grice. **Thomas,** C.C. 1675. **Wm.,** apprenticed in 1687 to Mordecai Fox, C.C. **Job,** Lancaster, 1797-1830.

Gridin (or **Gredin**), Paris; watch, Pierpont Morgan collection, about 1750.

Griell, Sam., apprenticed in 1648 to Peter Bellune, C.C.

Griffin. **John,** Noble St.; C.C. 1720. **& Adams,** 76 Strand, 1800-23. **Francis,** 25 Gloucester St., Clerkenwell, 1830-42. **G.,** 30 King St., Clerkenwell, 1835.

Griffis, Paul, Birmingham; watch, 1782.

Griffith. **Jas.,** C.C. 1667. **Robt.,** London; C.C. 1706; watch, 1725. **Wm.,** Shoe Lane; C.C. 1720. **Richard,** London; long-case clock, 1790. **R.,** Denbigh; watch, 1830. **J. W.,** 15 Wentworth Place, Mile End Rd., 1840-42.

Griffiths. **Edward,** River St., Islington; livery C.C. 1810. **Nehemiah,** Chester, 1833. **& Son,** 1 Ireland Row, Mile End Rd., 1835.

Grigg, Jno., apprenticed in 1684 to Edwd. Hunt, C.C.

Griggs, Richd., C.C. about 1660.

Grignion. **Daniel & Thomas,** fine repeating watch with beautifully enamelled case, about 1730; another watch in the Dunn Gardner collection bears the hall mark for 1748; a clock in the possession of Mr Eden Dickson is inscribed "Dan. and Tho. Grignion from the late Mr Quare." "Thos. and Danl. Grignion, finisher to the late Mr Danl. Quare, at the King's Arms and Dial in Russel Street, Covent Garden," card Hodgkin collection. **& Son,** Russell St., Covent Garden, 1775; spring clock with peculiar dead beat escapement, G.M. (see p. 399); **Thomas,** 7 Great Russell St., Covent Garden (see p. 400); a watch by him with a repoussé case in S.K.M.; small travelling clock dated 1780, Major R. H. Raymond Smythies; died 1784, aged 71. **Thos.,** 7 Great Russell St., Covent Garden, 1800-25.

Griliat, — In 1729 had a project for stamping dial plates for watches, discouraged by C.C. as being detrimental to engravers.

Grimadell. —, Holbeach, 1760. **Peter,** Stamford, 1770.

Grimalde. **Peter,** 431 Strand, a celebrated chronometer maker, 1800-10. **& Johnson,** 431 Strand, 1815-25; see Anthony, Wm.

Grimes. Edwd., apprenticed 1640 to Elias Allen, C.C. **Thomas**, C.C. 1671. **William**, C.C. 1682; long-case clock, Dutch marqueterie, about 1700.

Grimley, William, C.C. 1694.

Grimshaw. Jno., Liverpool, 1814. **James**, 146 Goswell St.; died 1846, aged 43. **William, senr.**, 130 Goswell St.; died 1851, aged 80. **William**, eldest son of W. Grimshaw, senr., Goswell Rd.; died 1853, aged 54. **Frederick**, Goswell Rd. (Grimshaw & Baxter); died 1893, aged 77.

Grimstead, Thomas, St Paul's Churchyard, 1753-63.

Grindley, William, 32 Crown St., Moorfield, 1820.

Grindon, W., 7 Tabernacle Walk, 1820-30; watch paper with the following lines:—

" Canst thou recover thy consumèd flesh
From the well-feasted worms, or put on fresh?
Canst thou redeem thy ashes from the dead,
Or free thy carcase from its sheet of lead?
Canst thou awaken thy earth's closed eyes,
Or yet unlock thy monument and rise?
All this thou mayst perform with as much ease
As to repent, ye mortals, when ye please."

Grinkin. Robert, C.C. 1632, master 1648, 1654; died 1660 (p. 201). **Edwd.**, petition C.C. 1656.

Gritting, Jno., London; long-case clock, about 1750.

Grizell, John, C.C. 1687.

Gro, Wm., Rotterdam; watch, about 1770.

Grocot, Thos., Liverpool; a watch by him with Manx crest on cock, 1780.

Grohe, James (succeeded Haley), 7 Wigmore St., 1834-42.

Grollier de Servière, Nicholas, born at Lyons in 1593; maker of many curious clocks and automata (see p. 333); died, aged 93.

Gros, —, Paris, 1780.

Grose. Richard, C.C. 1632. **Anthony**, C.C. 1658.

Grosrey, Calestin, 74 Newgate St., 1838-42.

Gross, Philip, 12 Panton St., 1817.

Grossmann, Moritz, Glashütte, Saxony; winner of the prize offered in 1863 by the British Horological Institute for the best essay on the lever escapement. A very capable horologist; born 1826, died 1885.

Grosvenor & Jones, 85 Wardour St., 1815.

Grotz, Isaac, Easton, U.S.A., 1810-35.

Grounds, Jonathan, London; watch, Nelthropp collection, about 1690.

Grounet, S., Amiens, 1650.

Grout, William, C.C. 1660.

Grove. Thomas, C.C. 1715. **George**, 95 Wood St., Cheapside; C.C. 1715. **Wm.**, watch, 1781. **Richard**, 93 Wood St.; livery C.C. 1786; 1770-1817. **W. R.**, partner with Myles Brockbank; C.C. 1811-15.

Grover & Co., 10 Greek St., 1817.

Groves. George, 105 Bishopsgate St., 1790-95. **Wm.**, Leeds, 1829.

Gruber. Hans, Nuremberg; clockmaker and master of the Locksmiths' Guild in 1552; died 1597. **Michel**, Nuremberg, 1600.

Gruet, —, a Swiss, inventor of fusee chain, 1664.

Grundy, J., Whalley, 1760.

Gruse in Wien; watch so signed, about 1840.

Guardsell, —, London; long-case clock, about 1770.

Guay, see Le Guay.

Gudgeon, Jno., Bury; watch, 1794.

Gudin, Jacques Jerome, Quai des Orfèvres, Paris, 1769; clock by him at Windsor Castle, about 1770 (p. 316).

Guepin, Jno., apprenticed 1687 to David Minuel, C.C.

Gueriman, G., London; watch, about 1720, Mr Horace L. Wheeler, Boston, Mass.

Guerint, Francis, Geneva; said to have invented engine turning, about 1780.

Guest. Georgius, 30-hour long-case clock, about 1690. **Geo.**, Aston, 1760. **Jno.**, 64 Fleet Market, 1816.

Guex, Paris; watch, 1790.

Guibet l'Aîné à Paris; clock, Jones collection, S.K.M., about 1790.

Guidon & Co., Paris, 1795.

Guiguer, —, London; watch, about 1750; another about the same date signed "Guiguer, Amsterdam."

Guillaume. E. T. & George, 16 Myddelton Sq., 1836-45. **E. & C.**, 16 Myddelton Sq., 1846-65. **Louis Alex.**, 24 Spencer St.; died 1873, aged 59.

Guillemot, —, London; about 1810.

Gullock, Philip, 31 Minories, 1790-95.

Gunston, John, London; bracket clock, about 1750.

Gunter. Hildesley, apprenticed in 1693 to Jno. Eagle, C.C. **R.**, Queen St., May Fair, 1790-95.

Gurden, Benjamin, & Son, 144 Wood St., 1775; **Benj.**, 1794.

Gurney, Ezekiel, apprenticed in 1692 to Edwd. Speakman, C.C.

Gutch, John, C.C. 1673.

Gutheridge, William, C.C. 1728.

Guthrie, —, Glasgow; clock, about 1770.

Gutteridge, John, 54 Coppice Row, 1835.

Guy. Samuel, apprenticed in 1692 to Jno. Andrews, C.C.; fine long-case clock, decorated with Oriental lacquer work, about 1730; another by him belongs now to Mr Wm. Craig, Detroit, U.S.A. **Henry**, C.C. 1702. **Charles**, C.C. 1714. **Jno.**, Liverpool, 1770. **Edwd.**, 49 Rahere St.; 1830; 19 Powell St., King's Sq., 1842.

Guye, Auguste, a pioneer of machine watchmaking in England; born at St Olivier, Switzerland, 1835; settled in London 1856, where he died in 1893.

Guyerd, —, Paris; watch, 1812.

Gwillim, Eli, brother C.C. 1647.

Gwinnell, J., 34 London Rd., 1812-15.

Gyott. Abraham, C.C. 1648. **Abraham**, apprenticed in 1648 to Abraham Gyott, C.C.

Haas-Privat, I., Geneva; died 1881.

Habel; watch, gold case in the form of a mandoline, enamelled white and blue, signed "Joh. Georg. Habel à Güngs," about 1790; Pierpont Morgan collection.

Habert. James, C.C. 1682. **David**, Strand; C.C. 1730.

Habrecht. In 1571 the mechanical construction of the Strasburg clock was entrusted to **Isaac Habrecht**, a clockmaker of Schauffhouse, Switzerland, and his younger brother **Josias** (see p. 54); before this work was begun Josias migrated to Cologne, having been summoned by the Elector to make a clock for the castle of Kayerswerth. Of other clocks constructed by Isaac an example is given on p. 67. He died in 1620, aged 76. **Michael Isaac Habrecht** restored the Strasburg clock in 1669, and **Jacques S.** made a further restoration in 1732. Skull watch by **Daniel Habrecht**, about 1630 (see p. 112).

Hack, Grace, apprenticed in 1692 to Jas. Jenkins, C.C.

Hackett, Simon, Royal Exchange; C.C. 1632; master 1646-60; watch with movement 1 in. in diameter, pierced square pillars; dial of metal with a raised hour-band; outside of it an engraved border with the figure of a cherub over the XII.; inside the hour-circle a view of Old London Bridge, tolerably well engraved. Case ornamented in high relief, and enclosed in an outer case of shagreen; movement exceedingly rough, and on the top plate, partly hidden by the balance-cock, an inscription, "Simon Hackett, of the Royall Exchannge, fecit," the form of the letters being as fanciful as the spelling; in the S.K.M. are an alarm watch by him, in a pierced and engraved silver case, and one in an enamelled case; watch, about 1635, in enamelled case, Pierpont Morgan collection.

Hackings, John, successor to Henry Haines. Ludlam in 1759 wrote, "has worked for me constantly since midsummer, 1753; all my best tools were made by him; whatever has been done by him may be depended on."

Hackney, Thos., London; chime clock, 8 bells, inch dial, marked centre, about 1740.

Haddack, Wm., 14 New Bridge St., Bath, 1798-1800. **& Lansdown**, 1832; afterwards George Lansdown.

Haden, Thos., clock, about 1720.

Hadley, Humfrey; received in 1708 £16 from the churchwardens of Aston, near Birmingham, for a new clock.

Hadwen, —, Kendal; clock, about 1710. In each corner of the dial was engraved one line of the following verse, "Winged Time, Will not stay, Fleeting hours, Glide away."

Haehnel, C. H., London; repeating watch, decorated with portraits of Joseph II. and his family; Pierpont Morgan collection, about 1780; there is no hall mark in the case.

Hager & Wolffenbutel; watch by them, about 1730, mentioned by Thiout.

Hagger, James, Grove Hall Lane, square bracket-clock, Japanese case, cherub corners to dial, pull repeater, style about 1700.

Hague, Jas., London; watch, 1760.

Hahn, Mathais, Stuggart; designer of clocks; born 1739.

Haines. Francis, admitted C.C. 1706. **Hy.**, "an excellent workman"; worked for Ludlam from 1747 to 1753, when he was succeeded by John Hackings. **Jno.**, 49 Northampton St., Clerkenwell, 1835.

Hair. George B., 129 High St., Borough, 1835-42. **Wm.**, Birmingham; clock movement, S.K.M., dated 1809, in Italian case, dated 1592.

Hairl, Jno., Horselydown, 1817.

Halaicher, Mathais, Augsburg; watch, about 1650.

Hale & Broadhurst, 81 Cheapside, 1800-5.

Haley. Sam., apprenticed in 1657 to Jno. Hillersden, C.C. **Thos.**, Norwich, 1750. **Thos.**, London, 1781. **Charles**, 7 Wigmore St.; a celebrated maker, hon. freeman C.C. 1781; patentee of a remontoire escapement for chronometers (1796, No. 2,132). He was one of the experts appointed by the select committee of the House of Commons to report on Mudge's chronometers in 1793; 1770-1800. **& Milner**, 7 Wigmore St., 1800-15. **& Son**, 7 Wigmore St., 1832, see Grohe.

Halford, Robt., 3 Old Orchard St., St Luke's, 1823.

Halifax, Sam. Joseph, London; watch, silver cock and name-plate, 1775; watch, "Halifax London," Fitzwilliam Museum, Cambridge.

Halked, Thomas, C.C. 1702.

Halksworth, William, 58 Fleet St., 1840-42.

Hall. Ralph, C.C. 1638. **Christopher,** apprenticed in 1646 to Simon Bartram; C.C. 1655. **Peter,** C.C. 1648. **Jno. Baptist,** apprenticed in 1669 to Edward Clough, C.C.; long-case clock, square dial, inscribed "John Hall, London," about 1700. **Thos.,** apprenticed in 1675 to Geo. Hambleton, C.C.; timepiece, "Thos. Hall, London," about 1700. **Wm.,** apprenticed in 1680 to Cornelius Herbert, C.C.; long-case clock, about 1720, inscribed "Wm. Hall, Woodborrow." **Joseph,** apprenticed in 1684 to Edwd. Norris, C.C.; long-case clock, inscribed "Jos. Hall, London," dating from about 1700. **Edwd.,** C.C. 1710. **Thos.,** Runcorn; watch, 1763. **Jno.,** Beverley, 1770. **Martin,** Yarmouth, 1780. **John,** Philadelphia, 1811. **Wm.,** 39 Gee St., 1814-19. **Wm.,** 93 High St., Marylebone, 1815-19. **Charles,** 162 Fleet St., 1817; 118 Chancery Lane, 1820. **Chas.,** 84½ Edgware Rd., 1840.

Hallam, E., 15 Bateman's Row, Shoreditch, 1835.

Halleway, —, London; clock-watch, about 1685.

Halley, Wm., apprenticed in 1663 to Thos. Battin, C.C.

Hallier, London, about 1800.

Hallifax. John, Fleet St.; maker of chime clocks; his bankruptcy noted *Lond. Gaz.,* June 14-17, 1740; Mr Eden Dickson has a fine specimen of his work, a musical clock with automatic figures. **John,** Barnsley; on his tombstone in St Mary's Churchyard, Barnsley, is the following: "In memory of Mr John Hallifax of this town, whose abilities and virtue few in these times have attained. His art and industry were such that his numerous inventions will be a lasting monument of his merit. He departed this life Sept. 25, 1750." A fine long-case by him is at Wentworth House, the seat of Earl Fitzwilliam. His second son, Thomas, came to London, and carried on business as a goldsmith, became a partner in the Bank of Glyn & Hallifax (afterwards Glyn, Mills & Co.), was Lord Mayor of London in 1776, knighted in 1778, sat in Parliament as member for Aylesbury in 1784, and died in 1789.

Halliwell, Wm., Chorley, 1765. —, York, 1814.

Halloway, Wm., Blackburn, 1776.

Hallows, Jonathan, Liverpool, 1818.

Hallsman, Wm., London; watch, 1790.

Hallus, *alias* **Linus Franciscus,** author of "Explicato Horologii in Horto Regis," London, An. 1659 (see p. 24).

Hally, Thos., London; bracket clock, about 1660; watch 1675.

Halsey. Geo., C.C. 1687. **Jno.,** Norwich, 1725.

Halstead. Richard, C.C. 1669. **Charles,** C.C. 1677. **John,** C.C. 1698; long-case clock, arabesque marqueterie. **William,** C.C. 1715.

Halsted, Robert, Fleet St.; bad watch movement seized by C.C. 1662; admitted C.C. 1668; master 1699.

Ham. Jno., apprenticed in 1673 to Geo. Stevens, C.C. **John,** 47 Skinner St., Snow Hill, 1820; 126 Newgate St., 1835-42,

livery C.C. 1821.

Hambleton, George, C.C. 1669.

Hamden, Jno., apprenticed in 1638 to Jno. Charlton, C.C.

Hames, Jno., 9 Chandos St., 1835.

Hamilton. Geo., apprenticed in 1690 to Nathaniel Delander, C.C. **Richard,** C.C. 1712. **Jas.,** London; watch, 1800.

Hamlen, George, Augusta, Me., 1795-1820.

Hamlet, Thos., 1 and 2 Prince's St., Soho; in partnership with Francis Lambert, 1800; subsequently carried on business by himself; maker of a gold horizontal watch for the Duke of Sussex; 1795-1832.

Hamley, junr., Newcastle St., Strand; bracket clocks, about 1790. **J. O.,** 1 Warwick Place, Bedford Row, 1800-10; 24 Red Lion St., Holborn, 1816-40. **J. O., & Son,** 284 Holborn, 1810-16. **O. Jas.,** 23 Duke St., St James's Sq., 1815-18.

Hamlin, Richard, London; bad watch of his seized by C.C. 1676.

Hamlyn, Thos., apprenticed in 1638 to J. Bisse, C.C.

Hammers, Jno., London; long-case clock, ab 1715.

Hammersley, Jno., Clerkenwell; afterwards at Ventnor, at Walham Green, and at St Albans; a clever watchmaker; died 1901, aged 82.

Hammon, J., 9 Northampton Sq., Clerkenwell, 1840-60.

Hammond. Hy., C.C. 1680. **Anthony,** apprenticed in 1681 to Jno. North, C.C. **& Co.,** 45 St Martin's-le-Grand, 1768. **Thos. C.,** York, f., 1825.

Hampson. Warrington; lantern clock, about 1700; long-case clock, "Robert Hampson, Warrington," about 1730. Wrexham; long-case clock, about 1720, Mr Henry Grogan. **& Thelwall,** Manchester, 1812-23. **Robert,** Manchester, 1823-30.

Hampton. Joseph; long-case clock, about 1700, Mr J. H. Fleming. **Rd.,** London; watch, 1782. **W., & Sons,** 77 Theobald's Rd., 1842.

Hanbury, Jno., apprenticed 1664 to Hy. Jones, C.C.

Hancock. Yeovil; long-case clock, about 1800. **Anthony,** Otley, 1822. **Thomas,** 17 Bond St., 1830-35.

Hancorne. Thomas, C.C. 1658; elected warden 1683, but excused on paying a fine. **Jas.,** apprenticed in 1675 to Philip Buckner, C.C. **William,** C.C. 1676.

Handcock. —, Yeovil, 1773. **Edwd.,** 23 Queen St., Clerkenwell, 1842.

Hande, Thomas; in the B.M. is an oval tulip-shaped watch by Thos. Hande, about 1700.

Handiside, Geo., London; repeating bracket clock, about 1720.

Handley. (**& Moore,** apprentices of Jno. Thwaites, 39 Clerkenwell Close, 1798; a specimen of their work B.M.; G. Handley died 1824), see Moore, Jno., & Sons. **Jno.,** Runcorn, 1833.

Hands, Tim., London; watch, Guildhall Museum, about 1750; another, 1765.

Handscomb, E., Woburn, 1780.

Hanet. S., London; long-case clock, Mr J. Drummond Robertson, about 1725. **John & George,** Porter St., Leicester Fields, 1768; a specimen of their work B.M.

Hanks, Benjamin, Litchfield, Conn., U.S.A., patentee of self-winding clock with air vanes, 1783.

Hannet, Samuel Stephen, London; long-case clocks, about 1780.

Hannington, Wm., London; watch, 1800.

Hansard, William, watch-spring maker, 6 King's Head Court, Holborn, 1790.

Hanslapp. William, C.C. 1603. **Robert;** apprenticed to Edward East; C.C. 1653.

Hanson. Geo., apprenticed in 1688 to Jno. Clowes, C.C. **George,** Windsor; watch,1791. **Wm.,** Windsor, 1820. **Charles,** Huddersfield, 1833. **Charles,** 160 High Holborn, formerly of Huddersfield; in 1845 he patented a detent escapement (No. 10,876); 1839-45.

Hanush, —, maker of a clock for Prague Town Hall, about 1497.

Hanwell, Zachariah, C.C. 1694; fine marqueterie long-case clock, straight pillars, square dial, cherub corners, "Z. Hanwell, Londini," on circle, Mr J. Drummond Robertson.

Happack, London; repeating watch, about 1760.

Harben, Thos., Lewes, 1740-70; long-case clock, inscribed "In the Cliff, Lewis." One-hand clock of rather earlier date, Mr Jno. Stringer, Johannesburg.

Harbert, see Herbert.

Harbottle, Cornelius, C.C. 1667.

Harbud, Jeremiah, watch-movement maker, 2 Green Terrace, 1810-38; livery C.C. 1812.

Harcourte, —, maker or repairer of clocks, near Westminster Abbey, 1469 (see p. 60).

Harden, Chas., 120 Fleet St., 1816-25.

Hardie & Christie, Manchester, 1818.

Hardin, Jos., St John's Lane, 1730, afterwards at Old Jewry; livery C.C. 1766.

Harding. John, C.C. 1685. **Francis,** C.C. 1687; clock, about 1700, inscribed "Francis Harding, Portsmouth." **John,** C.C. 1721. **Robert,** London, 1753. **Thomas, & Co.,** 43 Minories, 1760-1800. **Wm.,** London; watch for the Dutch market, finely embossed outer case, 1769. **Jno.,** Portsmouth, 1780; long-case clock with rotating hour dial as in figure on p. 346. **Jno.,** Abingdon; watch, 1782. **Sam.,** 131 Oxford St., 1816-23. **& Co.,** 26 Great Winchester St., 1817. **Henry,** 1 Holles St., Cavendish Sq., 1840.

Hardstaff, Zach., apprenticed in 1655 to Jno. Samon, C.C.

Hardwidge, Wm., 52 Wapping, 1823.

Hardy. John, Smithfield, 1730, afterwards 8 Bridgewater Sq.; livery C.C. 1766. **Edwd.,** Hull, 1770. **Jno.,** Morpeth, 1775. **Robt.,** C.C. 1776; watch G.M., h.m., 1803. **Thomas,** watch-case maker, 14 Roseman St., Clerkenwell, 1780-1820. **Joseph,** 26 Clement's Lane, Lombard St., 1800. **Richd.,** Newark, 1805. **William,** 28 Coppice Row, Coldbath Sq., Clerkenwell; a chronometer and clock maker of repute; he devised a compensation balance and an escapement for clocks for which he in 1820 received from the Society of Arts the gold medal and fifty guineas, 1800-30.

Hare, Alexander, 17 Grenville St., Hatton Garden; hon. freeman C.C. 1781; maker of a finely enamelled watch, h.m., 1782; a verge metal watch by him in the Guildhall Museum; 1770-1815.

Harford; lantern clock inscribed "John Harford in Bath, 1658."

Hargraves (or **Hargreaves**). **Wm.,** Settle, 1710-30. **Thomas,** Settle, 1770.

Hargroves, Wm., apprenticed 1688 to Isaac Carver, C.C.

Harker, George, master C.C. 1852.

Harland. Hy., apprenticed in 1647 to W. Godbed and put to Peter de Laundre; C.C. 1654. **Theodore,** Norwich, Conn.,

U.S.A., 1750-90? ; to him was apprenticed Ely Terry in 1786.

Harley, Wm., Salop ; fine clock, 1760.

Harlock, James, 7 Horseferry Rd., Westminster, 1842.

Harlow, Samuel, Ashbourne, Derby, in 1789 patented (No. 1,708) the Breguet or tipsy watch-key, in which the upper and lower portions are connected by means of a ratchet clutch kept in gear by a spring, so that the upper part will turn the lower part in the proper direction for winding, but if the upper part is turned in the opposite direction, the ratchet clutch slips without moving or straining the lower part of the key. In 1813 he published "The Clockmakers' Guide to Practical Clockwork." He there described himself as clockmaker and brassfounder, Summer Hill, Birmingham, but mentions that his book may be obtained at his house in Ashbourne and also of Walker & Sons, 49 Red Lion St., Clerkenwell.

Harman, Jno., apprenticed in 1681 to Thos. Jenkins, C.C. **John**, "watchmaker and astrologer," of Bloomsbury, 1753. **George**, High Wycomb, maker of the chimes of Cripplegate Church, 1792.

Harmar, Jas., London ; watch, 1690.

Harmer, Jasper, near Smithfield Bars, cited by C.C. for exercising the art of clockmaker without having served seven years, 1685.

Harns, Geo., Old Jewry, 1808-10.

Harold, Richard, C.C. 1690.

Harper. Henry, Cornhill, apprenticed 1657 to Humphrey Pierce ; C.C. 1664, assistant 1682 ; watch by him in silver case, Schloss collection, said to have belonged to Cromwell's daughter Bridget ; the arms of the Protector incorporated with the royal arms are engraved on the case ; in 1688 at the Mayor's Court some watch or pocket clock chains of steel belonging to him, and seized by C.C., were declared to be insufficient, and broken ; he was the maker of a long-case month clock, presented to the Ironmongers' Company by John Woolfe, about 1689 ; a very similar clock at the Balls Hut Inn, Walberton, was sold by auction in 1910 ; a gold watch by him mentioned in *Lond. Gaz.*, Jan. 11, 1691 ; in the Guildhall Museum is a watch movement signed "Harper, London" ; it has tulip pillars, and dates from about 1680 (see also p. 153). **Thomas**, son of John Harper, of St Giles-in-the-Fields ; apprenticed to Theophilus Davys, C.C. 1760 ; long-case clock, about 1770. **Thomas**, apprenticed to Henry Taylor, C.C. 1771. **& Son**, Salop ; clock, about 1775. **Thos.**, 207 Fleet St., 1800-30. **John**, 1 Pear Tree St., Goswell St., 1810 ; 16 St John St., 1815 ; 78 Goswell Rd., 1825.

Harplett, Cornelius, apprenticed in 1659 to David Mell, C.C.

Harrache, Thos., Pall Mall, 1765-75.

Harris. John, one of the first assistants C.C. 1631 ; master 1641. **Richard**, said to have been the maker of a pendulum clock for St Paul's Church, Covent Garden, in 1641 (see p. 399). **Jacob**, apprenticed in 1646 to David Bouquett, C.C. **John**, Holborn Bridge ; C.C. 1659 ; master 1688 (see p. 386). **Geo.**, apprenticed 1668 to Thos. Long ; C.C. 1674. **John**, C.C. 1677. **Thomas**, in ye Strand ; good lantern clock, inscribed "Thomas Harris, in ye Strand," about 1680. **Ebenezer**, apprenticed in 1682 to Ben. Bell, C.C. **Anthony**, C.C. 1683 ; lantern clocks by him ; also a fine long Orien-

tal lacquer case clock, goes seven weeks ; formerly at Ruchbrooke Hall, Suffolk. **John**, C.C. 1690 ; long-case clock, Wetherfield collection, about 1700. **Richd.**, apprenticed in 1693 to Thos. Brafield, C.C. **Charles**, apprenticed to Robert Webster, C.C. 1695. **Christopher**, Lombard St., admitted C.C. 1695-1720. **Jeffrey**, "ting tang" pull repeating bracket clock, inscribed "Jeffrey Harris, London," about 1700. **Francis Wm.**, C.C. 1702. **Samuel**, C.C. 1708 (see p. 368). **Geo.**, Fritwell, 1710-30. **Henry**, Barbican, C.C. 1711 ; watch, silver dial, 1711-20. **Joseph**, at the Dial and Cup, just above ye Upper Court House, Maidstone, about 1770 ; card, Hodgkin collection. **Thos.**, St Sepulchre's ; in 1770 he patented (No. 965) a rotating dial. **Wm.**, Chippenham, clock, about 1770. **William**, Temple Bar, liveryman C.C. 1776. **Saml.**, London, C.C. 1787 ; long-case clock, about 1790. **Richard**, 27 Old Jewry, 1790-1810. **E.**, Warrington ; watch, 1790. **John**, apprenticed to Robert Poole, 27 Old Jewry, C.C. 1795-1808. **William**, 27 Goswell St., apprenticed to Joseph Robinson, C.C. 1796 ; master 1830 32. **Saml.**, C.C. 1802. **L.**, Brown Lane, Spitalfields, 1810. **Henry**, 6 Curtain Rd., 1815-25. **Geo. Harris**, same address. **Jas.**, 8 Parliament St., 1820. **Clement**, 76 Cornhill, 1822-42, C.C. 1816 ; livery 1825 ; chronometer, Guildhall Museum, signed "Harris, late Hatton and Harris." **John**, 22 Gloucester St., Clerkenwell, 1835. **Wm.** ; watch-case maker, 21 Red Lion St., Clerkenwell, 1835. **John James**, 11 Upper East Smithfield, 1840-42.

Harrison. George, apprenticed 1689 to Johana May, widow ; turned over to Thomas Tompion, C.C. 1698. **Anthony**, Birchin Lane, apprenticed in 1693 to Joana May, widow ; C.C. 1701 ; in 1721 appeared an advertisement respecting a small gold watch made by Anthony Harrison, and lost between Leadenhall and "Spittel-fields" markets ; the finder was offered nine guineas reward, and no questions asked, if the watch were restored to Mr John Chadwell, goldsmith, Castle Alley, Birchin Lane, 1701-20. **John**, born 1693 ; died in Red Lion Sq., and buried in Hampstead churchyard in 1776 (see p. 254). **William**, C.C. 1699. **James**, Barrow ; brother of the preceding ; long-case clock by him in the G.M., 1720-50. **Jas.**, Grub St., C.C. 1730. **Thos.**, Liverpool, 1776. **Edwd.**, Warrington, 1776. **James**, apprenticed to James Freeman, C.C. 1776. **Wm.**, 48 Fetter Lane, 1780-94. **James**, Waterbury, Conn., U.S.A., founder of the Connecticut wooden clock industry, 1790-1830. **Edwd.**, Warrington ; centre seconds watch, 1795. **Thos.**, 68 Fetter Lane, 1795-1804. **Thos.**, Regent St. ; watch, with hare and snail indicator, 1810. **James**, Barton-on-Humber and Hull ; a grandson of John Harrison and a clockmaker of some celebrity, made a fine clock for Christ Church, Hull ; a clock by him in Filey Church had a detached escapement, an invention for which the Society of Arts awarded him a silver medal and £10, 1810-30. **Francis**, 91 Broad St., Ratcliff, 1835-41.

Harrocks. Lancaster : **Joshua**, 1748, f. ; made a church clock in 1759 ; **Jno.**, 1783, f.

Harrys (Harris), Thomas, Water Lane ; maker of the celebrated clock with figures on the front of Old St Dunstan's Church, Fleet St. (see p. 246), 1671.

Harshell, D., 12 Bevis Marks, 1830.

Hart. Noe, C.C. 1695. **John**, C.C. 1720.

Henry, C.C. 1720. **S. & M.**, 52 Prescot St., Goodman's Fields, 1804-18. **Jacob**, Hull, 1822. **& Harvey**, 5 King's St., Finsbury, 1825. **Andrew B.**, London ; watch, 1830. **Napthali, & Son**, 5 King's St., 1835-42. **& Son**, 77 Cornhill, 1839-47 ; two watches supplied to the Sultan of Turkey in 1844, cost £2,000 ; they were pair-case repeaters 5 in. in diameter ; duplex escapements. **Orrin**, Bristol, Conn., 1840. **Maurice**, 6 Haydon Sq., 1842.

Hartford, Jno. ; C.C. 1632.

Hartley. —, New St., Shoe Lane ; cited by the C.C. for trading in watches and clocks without having served seven years in the trade, 1680. **Jeremy**, Norwich ; fine bracket clock, about 1715 (see p. 388) ; Mr W. H. Helm has a long-case clock by him of rather earlier date ; he voted at the Parliamentary election in 1710. **Thos.**, Snaith, 1770. **Jno.**, George Court, Red Lion St., 1790-94.

Hartman, John George ; watchmaker to the University of Halle, 1756.

Hartnup, John, superintendent of Liverpool Observatory, Birkenhead, from 1843 to 1885. He invented a compensation balance with an oblique laminated rim, and tabulated the errors arising from the change of temperature in ordinary chronometers.

Hartung, Chas., 61 St Martin's Lane, 1840.

Hartwell, Francis, apprenticed in 1678 to Dan. Stevens, C.C.

Harvey. Jno., apprenticed in 1691 to Philip Corderoy, C.C. **Samuel**, C.C. 1696. **Alexander**, C.C. 1726 ; in 1730 he worked for Clark, Leadenhall St. **John**, 16 Fenchurch St., 1798-1800 ; 3 Falcon St., 1815 ; 1798-1818. **Thos.**, York, f., 1808. **—**, Richmond, Yorks. ; watch, 1814. **& Co.**, 2 King's St., Finsbury, 1830. **George**, 110 High St., Whitechapel, 1830 ; 22 Cannon St. Rd., 1840 ; 142 Ratcliff Highway, 1842 ; 1830-42.

Harward, Robert, C.C. 1730.

Harwood. Jas., Churchwarden's book, Halifax Parish Church, "1714 paid James Harwood for clock mending £1 12s. 6d." ; again, "1721, paid James Harwood for mending the clock, 10s." **Laurence**, "Acorn," Belle Sauvage Yard ; died 1716.

Hasius, see Hassenius.

Haskins, William, 79 Quadrant, Regent St., 1830.

Haslam. Watch signed "John Haslam, Cheshire," 1810.

Hasleden, Charles, 20 Waterloo St., 1840.

Haslewood, Roger, 53 Salisbury Court, 1772.

Hasluck, Jacob, St John St., London ; watch, with sun and moon hour indicator, about 1695, Pierpont Morgan collection.

Hassell, Joshua, Carter Lane, C.C. 1730, see Atkins, F.

Hassenius, James (alien), admitted C.C. 1682. Mr W. B. Redfern has a long-case clock inscribed "J. Hasius, Amsterdam," possibly by him.

Hastings, David, Alnwick, 1770.

Haswell. Alex., 10 Clifford St., New Bond St., 1780-94. **Archibald**, 13 Skinner St., Clerkenwell, 1835 ; 8 Woodbridge St., Clerkenwell, 1840-42. **Robert**, 12 Upper Ashby St., 1842, afterwards at 49 Spencer St., Clerkenwell ; died 1874, aged 58.

Hatch, John, admitted C.C. 1693.

Hatchman, James, C.C. 1680.

Hatfield, David, Bosworth ; watch, h.m., 1737.

Hathornthwaite, Lancaster: **Peter**, 1703; **Jno.**, 1744, f., long-case clock, "Peter Hathornthwaite, Kirby Lonsdale," about 1750.

Hatton. Jno., C.C. about 1650. **Peter**, Stafford, 1735. **Thomas**, Lombard St.; watchmaker, and author of "Introduction to the Mechanical Part of Clock and Watch Work," published 1773; 1760-74; watch, "Thos. Hatton, Preston," 1776. **Sam.**, Rose St., Soho, 1775. **Joseph Yorke**, 40 Tooley St.; apprenticed to Newman Peachey, and turned over to John Chancellor; C.C. 1796; livery 1810; St Magnus, London Bridge, 1830; many watches inscribed "Yorke Hatton, Thames St." **James**, 4 St Michael's Alley; apprenticed to Geo. Margetts; C.C. 1799; livery 1810; 1799-1812. **Christopher**, apprenticed to George Margetts, and turned over to James Hatton; C.C. 1815. **& Harris**, 4 St Michael's Alley, Cornhill, 1816-20, see Harris, Clement. **Geo. C.**, Lancaster, 1826, f. **Wm.**, Horselydown, London, 1830. **J.**, 15 Store St., 1835.

Hauchar, J. D., Paris, élève de Breguet; watch; about 1830.

Hauck, Antoine, Bamb; repeating watch, Mr Alfred A. de Pass, about 1690.

Haughton. Wm., C.C.; in 1703 he worked for Heardman. **Geo.**, London, about 1760; long-case chiming clock, Hotel de Madrid, Seville.

Hautefeuille, John (The Abbé), Paris; born 1647, died 1724. He is said to have invented, about 1722, the rack lever escapement, which was patented in England by Peter Litherland in 1791. Huygens, endeavouring to obtain a French patent for the balance-spring, was successfully opposed by the Abbé, who claimed to be the prior inventor of it.

Havelland & Stephens, 32 Aldgate High St., 1794.

Haven. Thos., C.C. 1652. **Robt.**, C.C. 1657.

Hawes, John, 31 New Bond St., 1775.

Hawkes, Susan, apprenticed in 1683 to Sam. Davis and Mary, his wife, C.C.

Hawkesbee, Benjamin, C.C. 1709.

Hawkesworth, John, C.C. 1709.

Hawkins. Pretty lantern clock, about 1650, inscribed "Ambrose Hawkins Je Wells, ffecit." **Marke**, Bury St Edmund's, 1670. **Wm.**, apprenticed in 1676 to Francis Dinnis; C.C. 1684; fine lacquer long-case clock, about 1740, signed "Wm. Hawkins, St Edmund's Bury," about 1730, Wetherfield collection. **Richd.**, apprenticed in 1677 to Wm. Fuller, C.C. **Geo.**, apprenticed in 1688 to Ben. Wright, C.C. **Mark**, Bury St Edmund's, 1710. **James**, C.C. 1730. **Wm.**, Bury St Edmund's, 1735. **Thomas**, C.C., 6 Castle Alley, Cornhill, 1777-1816.

Hawksey, Enoch, Nantwich; watch, 1787.

Hawley. Thomas, & Co., 75 Strand; "watchmaker to His Majesty," 1795-1828. **—**, 120 Fleet St., card Hodgkin collection, about 1830. **John**, 56 Frith St., Soho, 1842. **—**, High Holborn, 1860-62.

Hawthorne, Ferguson, & Co., London; watch, 1808.

Hawton, Sam., apprenticed in 1690 to Jno. Wise, junr., C.C.

Hawxhurst, Nathaniel, New York, 1786.

Hay. Alexander, Edinburgh; 1718. **Peter**, 20 Davis St., Berkeley Sq., 1805-40. **Geo.**, York, f., 1808. **Elizabeth**, York, 1822.

Hayden. John, Deptford; long-case clock, about 1710. **William**, C.C., Noble St.; 1717.

Haydon, William, Croydon, C.C. 1687.

Hayes. Walter, C.C. 1654; master 1680. **Jno.**, apprenticed in 1676 to Jas. Wolverstone, C.C. **Edmond**, C.C. 1682. **Wm.**, apprenticed in 1686 to Daniel Le Count, C.C. **Jas.**, apprenticed in 1693 to Harris, C.C. **Wm.**, Warrington; watch, 1782.

Hayford, Henry, 2 Star Alley, Fenchurch St., 1842.

Hayle, —, watch, Whitcombe Greene collection, in fritillary shaped case of silver, beautifully engraved, movement inscribed "Thomas Hayle (or possibly Hople) in Popeshead Alley," about 1650.

Hayley, William, 30 Great Marylebone St., 1788-93.

Haynes. John, C.C. 1676. **Wm.**, apprenticed in 1680 to Thos. Williamson, C.C. **F.**, London; pendulum watch, about 1708, see Haines, Francis. **& Kentish**, 18 Cornhill, 1804-18.

Hays. Michael Solomon, New York, f. 1769.

Hayter, Wm., apprenticed in 1685 to Jno. Parker, C.C.

Hayton, F., London; watch, 1760.

Hayward. William, Union Ct., Holborn; C.C. 1720. **Robert**, Bermondsey, 1815-35. **John**, 22 Bush Lane, Cannon St., 1820. **J.**, 2 Summers Court, Bishopsgate Without, 1835-42.

Haywood, Peter, Crediton, Devon. In 1766 he patented (No. 836) a calendar ring.

Head, Thomas Cartwright, apprenticed to Christopher Gould in 1693.

Headworth, P., 46 St John's St., 1815-42.

Heady, George, apprenticed to Dan. Quare 1675; admitted C.C. 1682.

Healey. Jno., Manchester, 1818; also **Thos.**, same date.

Heap, Richard, 5 King St., Covent Garden, 1800-4; 39 Maiden Lane, 1815-25.

Heaph, Jno., Stockport, 1770.

Heardman. Jacob, Plum-tree Court; C.C. 1720. **Joseph**, Plum-tree Court; C.C. 1730-35.

Hearn. Joseph, apprenticed in 1690 to Cornelius Jenkins, C.C. **Hen.**, London; watch, 1775.

Heath. Ben., apprenticed in 1661 to Chas. Rogers, C.C. **J.**, London; watch, h.m., 1770.

Heathcote, Timothy, C.C. 1698.

Hebert. Anthony, "Moorefields, nere London," 1670; Mr Benj. G. Wattson has a long-case clock so inscribed which strikes the hours twice; bracket clock, about 1690, inscribed, "Anthony Hebert in Porter Street." Anthony Hebert, 7 Dials; C.C. 1725. **J.**, Brightelmston, about 1716. **Jno.**, Isleworth, 1770.

Hebden. Francis, Halifax, 1830; also **Jas.**

Hebrat, Jean, Brussels, 1640 (see p. 147).

Hebting. F., wooden clockmaker, 19 Moor St., Soho, 1835.

Heck, see De Heck.

Heckel, Francesco, à Fridberg, 1730.

Heckle, A., Liverpool, 1818.

Heckstetter, Joseph, C.C. 1694.

Hedge. Nathaniel, Colchester; lantern clocks, about 1740; also a fine long-case clock, about 1780. **& Banister**, Colchester, known as makers of long-case and other clocks, about 1800; watch by them, 1808.

Hedger. W., London; watch, 1790. **George**, 48 Great Sutton St., 1822-35; 10 St John's Row, St Luke's, 1842.

Hedges, John, 4 St James's Walk, Clerkenwell, 1800.

Heeley & Burt, Deptford; long-case clock, 1780.

Heerman, John (Dutch), C.C. 1691.

Heffer, W., 2 George St., Grosvenor Sq., 1835.

Heidmark, P., London; watch, 1780.

Heilig. Jacob, Philadelphia, 1770-1824. **John**, Germantown, 1824-30.

Heitzman, F., & Co., 40 Norton Folgate, 1840.

Heizman, Matthew, 1 Charles St., Soho Sq., 1840.

Helden. Onesiphorus, C.C. 1632; warden, 1648; did not become master. **Cornelius**, apprenticed in 1686 to Dan. Delander, C.C.

Hele, Peter, Nuremberg, invented the mainspring, 1500 (see p. 71); died 1540.

Heliger, J., Zug; crystal case watch, about 1590.

Hellam, James, apprenticed to Daniell Steevens, and turned over to Evan Jones, and afterwards to Henry Jones; C.C. 1690.

Hellier, Wm., London; watch, 1740.

Helliwell. —, Warrington; clock, about 1770. **Wm.**, Leeds, 1829.

Helme. —, London, 1700. **Thos.**, Ormskirk; repaired town clock, 1770.

Helsby, Jas. G., also **Jno.**, Liverpool, 1833.

Helye, F. Baptiste, Paris; clock, about 1780.

Heming. Ed., Bicester, about 1705; clock, Mr Samuel E. Groves, inscribed "Ed. Heming, Bisiter." **Thomas**, Piccadilly, 1763; 131 New Bond St., 1769-75. **Artis**, Shadwell, liveryman C.C. 1776. **& Crawner**, New Bond St., 1780-90. **Geo.**, 151 New Bond St., 1793.

Hemingway, Jno., Manchester, 1818.

Hemlett, J., London; watch, 1810.

Hemmen, Edward, London; watch, about 1710; another, h.m., 1760.

Hemming. Chas., apprenticed in 1678 to Jas. Wolverstone, C.C. **Hen.**, London; watch, 1780.

Henche, Uldrich. Payment to him of £100 for a clock "in manner of a branch," made by him and set up at Whitehall, 1605.

Henderson. R., Scarborough; long-case clock, about 1705, Sir Theodore Fry. **Robt.**, Edinburgh; watch, S.K.M., about 1750. **Thos.**, Hull, 1770. **Robert**, St Martin's Court, 1772; 18 Bridgewater Sq., 1800-5; Gen. J. Watts de Peyster, New York, has a chiming bracket clock by him; names of tunes engraved in the arch of the dial, "March from Scipio, Sukey Bids Me, Miss Fox's Minuet." **John**, 13 Broad St., Exchange, 1775; 21 Cornhill, 1783-1800. **R. T.**, St Martin's Court, 1800. **E.**, "Treatise on Horology," London, 1836.

Hendrick, Jno. & Peter, Liverpool, 1818.

Hendricks, Aaron, Devonshire St., 1760-68.

Hendrie, Ja., Wigton, 1770.

Heney, Richard, apprenticed in 1646 to Isaac Law, C.C.

Hening (? Heming), Josh., long-case clock, about 1780.

Henkels, H., Amsterdam, watch, 1780.

Henley. J., London; watch, 1810. **Thos.**, London; watch, 1829.

Hennett & Son, 16 Foster Lane, 1772.

Hennington, Wm., London; watch, 1795.

Hennon, William, C.C. 1674.

Henriot à Geneva; watch in case of

tinted gold, S.K.M., about 1785.

Henry. Autin, à Paris ; clock-watch, about 1740. **Peter**, London ; watch, 1780. **W. & S.**, 44 Taylor's Buildings, Islington, 1804. **S.**, 59 Lower Brook St., 1810. **S.**, 70 Leman St., 1830. **Stephen**, 3 Berkeley Sq., 1835-40.

Henshaw. Walter, C.C. 1667 ; master, 1695. **John**, C.C. 1696.

Hepton. Thos., Northallerton, 1770. **Frederick**, Philadelphia, 1785. **Jno.**, 1823-40. **Wm.**, 1840.

Herant Brothers & Son, Berlin ; enamelled watch, S.K.M., about 1680.

Herbault, L. Fr., Rue St Honoré, Paris ; garde visiteur, 1769.

Herbert. Wm., apprenticed 1663 to Hy. Child ; C.C. 1671 ; watch without a balance-spring, about 1675. **Edward**, C.C. 1664. **Cornelius**, London Bridge, 1670-1720. **Jno.**, apprenticed in 1672 to Nich. Payne ; C.C. 1682. **Thomas**, Whitehall, C.C. 1676 ; red tortoiseshell bracket clock, about 1690, Wetherfield collection. **Morgan**, clock-watch, 1690. **Cornelius**, London Bridge, apprenticed to the above C. H., 1690 ; C.C. 1700 ; master 1727 ; in the vestry of St Lawrence Jewry is a long-case clock by him, dated 1721, and among the church papers is a receipt as follows : " Received from the church for the clock the sum of eight pounds. Cornelius Herbert " ; a fine marqueterie long-case clock by him in the Wetherfield collection is shown on p. 381. **Evan**, C.C. 1691. **Edward**, Old Bailey, C.C. 1710-30. **Henry**, C.C. 1713. **Cornelius**, apprenticed to his father, Cornelius ; C.C. 1735. **Jas.**, London ; repeating watch, 1740.

Herman. Peter, Leeds, 1830. **Ignaz**, 13 Compton St., Clerkenwell, 1840.

Herne, Edwd., apprenticed in 1680 to Cornelius Jenkins, C.C.

Heron. Isaac, New York, 1769-80, f., 1769. **Isaac**, New York, watch by him belonging to Philip Livingston, signer of American Declaration of Independence in 1776, now in the museum of the " Sons of the Revolution," New York. **Wm.**, Newtown Ards, 1784.

Herring. Joseph, free C.C. by redemption, 1770. **(Herren), Joshua**, 38 Cornhill, known as a maker of bracket clocks, 1753-75. **Richd.**, Newark, 1805-20.

Hertford, see Hartford.

Hertham, T. S., London ; watch, 1795.

Hervé, fine clock, Wallace collection, signed " Hervé à Paris," about 1740.

Herwick, Nicholas, Cheapside, 1580.

Heselwood, Jno., York, f., 1835.

Hesk, William, Horseferry Rd., Westminster, 1835.

Hess, L. Zurich, watch, about 1760.

Hessen à Paris ; enamel watch, about 1775.

Hessichti Dionistus, book-shaped watch, 1627 (see p. 120).

Hester. Henry, C.C. 1670. **Henry, junr.**, C.C. 1687. " Lost in Whitehall, on Sunday the 26th past, a Gold Watch with a plain Outside Case, made by — Hester, of West minster, with a ribbon tied to it of Changeable Purple and Gold, and upon that two Seals, the one an Onyx with a Head cut in it, set with small Diamonds ; and the other Seal a Stone set with rubies. Whoever brings the said Watch, &c., to Mr Snagg, Goldsmith, in Lombard St., shall have 5 guineas reward " (*Lond. Gaz.*, July 30, Aug. 3, 1691).

Hettich, C., Lynn, 1825.

Heuss, George, Nuremberg, 1509-60.

He made a clock with automatic figures.

Heward, Jno., apprenticed in 1686 to Jno. Miller, C.C.

Hewison, Chas., London ; watch, 1800.

Hewitt. Geo., Marlboro', 1720-30 (see p. 368). **Benjamin**, C.C. 1724. **Alexander**, London, C.C. 1725 ; watch, about 1730. **Jas.**, Sunderland, 1760. **Thomas**, 12 Upper Ashby St., and 10 King St., Tower Hill ; a chronometer maker who devised different forms of compensation balances ; was a director of the British Watch Company ; born 1799, died 1867. **Sam.**, 60 St Martin's Lane, 1836.

Hewkley, John, C.C. 1732.

Hewlett, Bristol ; long-case clocks : **Isaac**, about 1750 ; **Isaac and Joshua**, about 1780 ; **Andrew**, a little later.

Hewlitt, G., Foxley, 1780.

Hewson, Jno., apprenticed in 1683 to Jno. Sellars, C.C.

Heydon, Saml., London ; watch, 1757.

Heyer, F. M., Amsterdam ; watch, about 1775.

Heywood, William, 12 King St., Covent Garden, 1807-10 ; 35 Goodge St., 1815-42.

Heyworth, John, 218 Tottenham Court Rd., 1823.

Hibbert, John, 7 Jewry St., Aldgate, 1840.

Hiccox, Jno., apprenticed in 1650 to Nicholas Ashwell ; admitted C.C. 1657, repeating watch, inscribed " Jno. Hiccox, London," about 1710.

Hick, Matthew, York, f., 1812 ; died 1834.

Hickling, John, 122 St John's St., Clerkenwell, 1835-42.

Hickman. Joseph, 20 Bridgewater Sq., 1779. **Wm.**, 89 Borough, 1816-25. **Edwd.**, High St., Oxford, 1818-20.

Hicks. Thomas, C.C. 1664. " Lost Sep. 21, betwixt Ingerstone and Rumford, a watch with a silver-pinned Case, showing the day of the month, the hour of the day, made by *Thomas Hicks, Londini*, with a blue taffety ribon fastened to the key thereof. Whoever will give notice thereof to Mr Christopher Maynard, watchmaker at the Royal Exchange, London, shall have 40s. reward " (*Lond. Gaz.*, Sept. 23-27, 1675). **Thomas**, C.C. 1666. **John**, C.C. 1694. **Samuel**, London ; about 1780. **Jas.**, 112 Whitechapel, 1804-15. **Chas.**, 112 Whitechapel, 1810-15.

Hickson, Thomas, C.C. 1690.

Higgins. Banger, apprenticed to Edward Banger, and turned over to William Wilde ; C.C. 1724. **Thos.**, London ; long-case clock, about 1760.

Higginson. Henry, C.C. 1662. **Samuel**, C.C. 1697. Hatton speaks of the splendid polish of the work of Higginson Brothers, watch finishers. **Geo.**, East India House, C.C. 1730. **Richard**, Fazakerley ; watch, 1743. **John**, 27 Strand, 1780 ; 38 Southampton St., Strand, 1798-1815. **—**, Kirby St., 1782.

Higgnett, Jno., London ; watch, 1725.

Higgs. John, apprenticed to Robert Robinson, C.C. 1661. **Jno.**, C.C. 1688. **Robert**, apprenticed to Richard Blundell, C.C. 1714 ; Mr R. W. Llewellyn has a small bracket clock by him, finely engraved back plate, two bells, coming hour struck on smaller one, pull for repeating hour at pleasure. **Thomas**, C.C. 1716. **Robert & Peter**, 7 Sweeting's Alley, 1740-69 ; Peter Higgs was apprenticed to Robert, C.C. 1740, and became master in 1767. **Robert**, London ; long-case clock, about 1750, Mr W. L. Unkill, Mexico city ; half-quarter repeating watch, 1785. **& Evans**, 7 Sweeting's Alley, 1780-1822 ; a verge

watch movement by them, with curious pillars, in the Guildhall Museum ; clocks inscribed, " Higgs y Diego Evans," for Spanish markets (see pp. 376, 389).

Highfield, Josiah, 55 Rosoman St., 1790-94.

Highmore. Lancaster, apprenticed in 1685 to Jno. Fitter, C.C. **Edwd.**, C.C. 1687. **Jacob**, 52 Aldersgate St., 1790-94.

Higon, Pierre, Place du Palais-Royal, Paris ; garde visiteur, 1769.

Hildeburn, Samuel, Philadelphia, 1811. **& Woodworth**, Philadelphia, 1819.

Hill. John, petitioner for incorporation of C.C. 1630. **Benjamin**, C.C. 1641 ; master 1657 ; in the B.M. are specimens of his work, one a small circular watch in a blue steel case, with exceedingly handsome covering of filigree gold ; another plainer with outer case of shagreen ; in the S.K.M. is a watch by him in a case of rock crystal ; he died 1670. " Lost a gold watch made by Benjamin Hill in a black case studded with gold, with a double chain, and the key on a single chain with a knob of steel upon it. Whoever gives notice of it to Mr Ambrose Mead, at the Bird-in-Hand, Fleet St., shall be rewarded " (*The Newes*, April 27, 1665). **Francis**, C.C. 1679. **Thomas**, Fleet St., 1680-90 ; his name was engraved, in conjunction with that of Henry Harper, on a long-case clock in possession of the Ironmongers' Company ; on the clock is the further inscription, " The gift of John Woolfe, member of the Company." " Thos. Hill, over against Chancery Lane, Fleet St." card, Ponsonby collection. He was a liveryman of the Ironmongers' Company. **Wm.**, apprenticed in 1682 to Sam Clyatt, C.C. **Edward**, C.C. 1698. **Jno.**, King St., Covent Garden ; long-case clock, about 1700. **John**, Seven Dials ; C.C. 1705-30. **Wm.**, Walsingham, long-case clock, about 1713, Mr Geo. F. Glenny. **John**, Fleet St., C.C. 1731-70. **Geo.**, Lambourn, about 1770. **Sam.**, Sheffield, maker of good clocks, 1770-1814. **Jno.**, Prescot, 1775. **Thomas**, Aldersgate St., 1777-86 ; Thomas Hill was the maker of a gold verge watch, embossed case, said to have belonged to Captain Cook. **Matt.**, London ; watch, about 1790. **Chas.**, 3 Charing Cross, 1793-95. **Jas.**, 5 Ball Alley, Lombard St., 1793-1810. **Sampson C.**, 9 Ball Alley, Lombard St. ; card Hodgkin collection, about 1815. **Leonard**, 61 Fleet St., 1817-23. **John**, 15 James St., Covent Garden, 1820. **D.**, Reading, U.S.A., 1820-40. **Sam.**, 13 Hooper St., Clerkenwell, 1842.

Hillcoat, William, 33 Queen St., Cheapside, 1790-94.

Hillersden, Jno., C.C. 1656.

Hillery, Jno., apprenticed in 1681 to Richard Farrett, C.C.

Hilliard, G., 35 Queen St., Cheapside, 1820.

Hillier. William, C.C. 1679. **James**, watch-glass maker, 12 Church St., Spitalfields, 1790-1810.

Hillings, Bernard, C.C. 1652.

Hillman, Wm., Plymouth Dock, 1770.

Hillrich, Johann, Pestteine ; regulator, Buda-Pesth Museum, about 1800.

Hills. Fleet St., 1774. **Ralph**, Sunderland, about 1775 ; he was apprenticed to David Paterson, who was apprenticed to Jno. Ogden. **Amariah**, New York, 1845.

Hilson, Thos., apprenticed in 1674 to Jno. Mark, C.C.

Hilton, John, apprenticed to Wm. Moraley but turned over to Thos. Tompion, admitted C.C. 1698. **Emanuel**, Portsmouth ; long-case clock, about 1790. **Jno.**, Halifax, 1830. —, London ; watch, 1840.

Himele, Jas., New York, 1786.

Hind, Paris, watch jeweller, 26 Spa Rd., 1790-94.

Hinde. Thos., Bolsover, died 1836. **Benjamin**, musical clockmaker, 20 Banner St., Clerkenwell, 1835-40.

Hindley. —, hanging clock, about 1710, signed "Hindley, York," oak case, Mr Wm. Birchall (see p. 351). **John**, a man of good repute, 1730-65 ; he made a clock for York Cathedral in 1752. **Henry**, York, f., 1731, died 1770 ; a clever clock and watch maker ; watch by him in S.K.M., London, h.m., 1766 ; made a clock for York Minster in 1750 ; also several others with pendulums 56 ft. long ; is credited with having invented the screw cutting lathe about 1740 ; about the same date he devised an improved wheel-cutting engine, see Brown, J. **Joseph**, York, f., 1754 ; made a clock for Holy Trinity Church, Hull, in 1772.

Hine. Thos., Fleet St., 1760-74. **John**, 68 Red Lion St., Clerkenwell, 1790-94.

Hinks, Wm., Southampton ; lantern clock, Mr W. W. Tamplin, about 1700.

Hinksman, —; Madeley ; clock, about 1770.

Hinmers, Robert, Edinburgh ; watch, about 1800.

Hinton, J., 91 Boro', 1815-20 ; 20 Tabernacle Row, Finsbury, 1835.

Hiorne. John, Bartholomew Close ; C.C. 1707, master 1744. **Jas.**, Snow Hill, C.C. 1730.

Hirsch, Ad., for forty-three years Director of the Neuchatel Observatory, died 1901.

Hirst, Bury St Edmunds : **Isaac**, 1740 ; **John**, 1760. **Sam.**, Leeds, 1770-95. **Sam., & Son**, Leeds, 1830.

Hiscocks, T., 9 Princes St., Drury Lane, 1835. **Zachariah**, 7 Little Russell St., Covent Garden, 1840-42.

Hislop. Richard, Rosoman St., Clerkenwell, 1775-1803. **Richard**, son of the above, 53 Rosoman St., 1804-29. **William**, younger son of the first-named Richard, 15 Rosoman St., 1820 ; 96 St John St. Rd., 1835-72 ; was some time hon. sec. and an active member of the governing body of the Horological Institute ; died in 1876.

Hitchen, John, Queen St., C.C. 1720 ; watch, 1740.

Hitchins, Joseph, Brown's Buildings, St Mary Axe, 1779-94.

Hitchman, Nicholas, apprenticed in 1677 to Richard Ames, C.C.

Hoadley, Calvin, associated with Eli Terry, at Plymouth, Connecticut, in the production of American clocks during the early part of the nineteenth century.

Hobart, Gabriel, York, f., 1750.

Hobbins, —, Freckenham, Worcester, 1820.

Hobbs. James, Lambeth, 1830. **Jas.**, 142 Great Tower St., 1830.

Hobler, Paul, Porter St., Newport Market ; hon. freeman C.C. 1781 ; 1770-90. **Fras.**, Porter St., Newport Market, 1793.

Hobson. John, petitioner for incorporation of C.C. 1630. **James**, 21 James St., Oxford St., 1835.

Hochicorn, Isaac, C.C. 1728.

Hochnadel. Small repeating bracket clock, about 1700, inscribed, "Pietro Hochnadel, Venezzia," Mr Louis Prevost Whitaker, Washington.

Hock, C., wooden clockmaker, 40 Charles St., Hatton Garden, 1840.

Hocker. John, Reading ; apprenticed to

John Martin, and turned over to Edward Josslin ; C.C. 1729 ; lantern clock, about 1730. **Jos.**, Basingstoke ; 30-hour clock, about 1740.

Hockson, Jno., London ; watch, 1700.

Hoddle. John, Reading ; maker of lantern clocks, 1688. **Jno.**, Pye Corner, C.C. 1705-30.

Hodge, H., London ; watch, 1795.

Hodges. Nathaniel, "in Wine Office Courte, Fleete Street" ; C.C. 1681 ; bracket clock, small square dial, ebony case with brass basket top, about 1685, Wetherfield collection ; another specimen, about 1700. **William**, C.C. 1719. **Jono**, 227 High Holborn, card B.M., 1780. **James**, London ; long mahogany inlaid Sheraton style, case clock, Wetherfield collection, about 1800. **Fredk.**, Dublin ; rack lever watch, about 1806. **J.**, Kingsland Rd., 1835.

Hodgkin. Sarah, C.C. 1699. **Robert**, 8-day square dial clock, fine movement, inscribed, "Rob. Hodgkin, Londini," about 1705.

Hodgkins, Robt., London ; bracket clock, about 1750.

Hodgson. York : **Marcus**, f., 1676 ; watch inscribed, "Mark Hodgson, Eboraci," 1710. **Jno.**, Skipton, 1720. **Wm.**, Philadelphia, 1785. Lancaster : **Hy.**, 1816, f. ; **Wm.**, 1820, f., long-case clock, about 1840, with name "G. Hodgson," Mr Taylor Heape.

Hodierne, Jno., apprenticed in 1638 to Platt, C.C.

Hodsoll. William, 31 Primrose St., Bishopsgate, 1800-8. **William**, 29 Ratcliff Row, City Rd., 1842.

Hodson, Jno., apprenticed in 1666 to Thos. Rotherham, C.C. At Bolton : **Geo.**, 1765 ; **Wm.**, 1780.

Hoffmann, octagonal watch, Marfels collection, signed "Melchior Hoffmann Augspurg," about 1600.

Hoffner, Hy., Philadelphia, 1791.

Hogan. J., watch movement maker, 6 Badgers Yard, St John St., 1808-20. **& Smith**, 15 Key St., Clerkenwell, 1835.

Höheer, Johan Christoph, clock, green vaulted chambers, Dresden, about 1680.

Hohwii, Andreas, born in Schleswig 1803, apprenticed to his father, Thomas Hohwii ; for four years to 1839 he worked in Paris for the house of Breguet ; settled in Amsterdam, where he died in 1885 ; a celebrated maker of chronometers and astronomical clocks.

Holborn, Robt., Sheffield, 1770.

Holborough, Thos., Ipswich, 1715.

Holbrook, Hy., Liverpool, 1770.

Holdcroft, Hy., apprenticed in 1678 to Chas. Halstead, C.C.

Holder, Henry, London ; watch, brass inner, enamelled outer case, 1760.

Holds, Chas., Silver Dials, St Bartholomew Close, 1793.

Holdway, George, 305 Strand, 1779.

Hole. Henry, 11 Lisle St., Leicester Sq., 1810 ; 12 Kingsgate St., 1817-23. **F. W.**, Weymouth Terrace, City Rd., patented a mainspring in 1852 (No. 40).

Holeyard, Samuel, C.C. 1705.

Holgate, —, Wigan, 1770.

Holland, George, petitioner for incorporation of C.C. 1630-55. **Thomas**, C.C. 1632 ; master 1656. **Henry**, probably apprenticed in 1657 to Walter Gibbs, C.C. ; the Hon. H. Hannen has a bracket clock by him—it strikes the hours but has only one barrel ; black case. **Thomas**, C.C. 1658. **Lewis**, apprenticed in 1691 to Thos. Birch, C.C. **Lewis**, C.C. 1699. **Robert**,

London ; bracket clock, about 1740. **Gabriel**, Coventry ; bracket clock, about 1750. **John**, 5 Bishopsgate Without, livery Goldsmiths' Company, 1765-77. **James**, Bury (Lancs.), 1770. **Reuben**, London ; bracket clock, about 1780. **Wm.**, Chester, 1814-18. **Thos.**, 167 Fleet St., 1815-18.

Hollidaie, Edwd., freeman of C.C. and signed petition in its favour, 1656.

Hollier, Jonathan, Skinner St., liveryman C.C. 1776, see Houlliere.

Hollinshead, Jacob, Salem, 1771.

Hollis, Thos., apprenticed in 1649 to Jas. Seabourne : C.C. 1656.

Hollisone, Alex., Liverpool ; watch, 1795.

Holliwell, Wm., Liverpool ; clock, about 1750.

Holloway, Robert, C.C. 1632. **Edward**, C.C. 1650. —, brass clock, signed "William Holloway, at Stroud," 1669. **Richard**, apprenticed in 1675 to Cornelius Herbert, C.C. **William**, Cullum St., C.C. 1697. **Thos.**, Winton, 1740.

Hollyar, Sam., apprenticed in 1693 to Jno. Barrow, C.C. ; clock, about 1710.

Holm, Jno., Lancaster, 1783.

Holman, see Kemp and Holman.

Holmden, John, musical clockmaker, 18 St James' Walk, 1806 ; 50 King St., Goswell Rd., 1840 ; livery C.C. 1807.

Holme, John, Cockermouth, freeman of Lancaster, 1783. **Lawrence**, Liverpool, about 1820.

Holmes. Nestor, apprenticed in 1674 to Jere. Gregory, C.C ; he ran away from his apprenticeship (see p. 455). **Thos.**, apprenticed in 1686 to Peter Miller ; C.C. **John**, apprenticed to Peter Miller ; C.C. 1697. **John**, C.C. 1697. **Thos.**, Cheadle, 1735. **Saml.**, Liverpool ; watch, 1758. **Edward**, 9 Foster Lane, Cheapside ; 1773-94. **Wm.**, 12 Clerkenwell Green, 1783. **John**, 156 Strand, near Somerset House ; he seems to have been one among the leading mechanicians, and when the turret clock at Greenwich Hospital was destroyed by fire in 1779 was given the order for a new one, in connection with the design of which he sought the advice of Smeaton and Ludlam ; a gold watch by him is in the Fitzwilliam Museum, Cambridge ; it belonged to William Pitt, and bears the Pitt crest, a heron holding an anchor in the right claw ; the Wetherfield collection contains two long mahogany case clocks of his manufacture, one a particularly choice example of Chippendale dating from about 1770, which is illustrated on p. 378. and another about twenty years later ; he was one of the experts appointed by the select committee of the House of Commons in 1791 to report on Mudge's timekeepers. George Yonge succeeded him in 1798. **Wm.**, 156 Strand, 1810-12. **Matthew Steel**, 10 Shoemaker's Row, Blackfriars, 1820-42 ; livery C.C. 1825. **Richd. Hy.**, Hull, 1822.

Holoway, Jo., Newbery ; watch, with sun and moon hour indicators 1680 (see p. 182).

Holroyd, Jno., Wakefield, 1775-1814. **T.**, Huddersfield, 1810-14. **Richard**, Chester, 1833.

Holt, Lancaster : **Thos.**, 1747, f. ; **Wm.**, 1767, f. **Matthew**, Wigan, 1775. **Richard**, Newark, 1804-42. **T.**, Wakefield, 1814. **John**, Rochdale, 1818 ; also **Valentine**, 1818-21. **Matthew**, Coventry, 1818.

Holtham, Geo., London ; watch, 1720.

Holtzman, Johannis, in Wienns ; in the Schloss collection is a watch invented by him about 1775, in which the dial is raised much above the movement, the hands being driven through a tube (p. **191**).

Hone, Rt., London ; watch, 1750.

Honeybone, Thomas, Old Brentford, 1830-40.

Honeychurch, Saml., Cheapside ; long-case clock, about 1770.

Honison, J., Wilderness Row, and 5 Charlton Place, Islington, 1835.

Hood, Jas., London ; watch, 1805.

Hooke. Robert, born 1635, died 1703 ; invented the balance-spring for watches and the anchor escapement for clocks (see p. **239**). **A.**, silver-gilt watch, Fellows collection at the B.M., inscribed, "A. Hooke, 1661." **John**, C.C. 1698.

Hooker. Thos., London ; long-case clock, about 1780. **Jas.**, 22 Five Fields Row, Chelsea ; card B.M. 1791.

Hoole, S., London, 1770 (see p. **268**).

Hooper. Jno., Winton ; clock, about 1760. **Henry**, 39 Cheapside, 1792.

Hope. Wm., watch, h.m., 1767. **Edward**, Bridge St., Strand, 1775 ; 97 Oxford St., 1783-85. **Peter**, Liverpool ; pair case watch, h.m., 1795, Mr Evan Roberts. **Chas.**, London, 1820. **Geo.**, London ; watch, 1825.

Hopetown, Wm., London ; watch, 1822.

Hopgood, T. B., 202 Bishopsgate Without, 1807-23 ; afterwards Hopgood & Salmon.

Hopkins. John, C.C. 1641. **Thos.**, Maiden Lane ; C.C. 1730. **John**, Fleet St., 1753-56. **Edwd.**, 48 King St., Soho, 1817 ; Mr W. H. Naish has a long-case timepiece, corner figures representing seasons, signed "Edwd. Hopkins, Bradford," about 1800. **Asa**, Northfield, U.S.A., 1820. **A. B.**, 32 Aldgate, 1823.

Hople, see Hayle.

Hopper, Jas., Stockport, 1770.

Hopperton. Long-case clock, "Emmanuel Hopperton, Leeds," about 1760. **Saml.**, Leeds, 1770.

Hornblower. William, C.C. 1713 ; long-case clock, Japanese decoration, arch dial, style about 1740. **William H.** (possibly a son of William), was beadle of C.C. 1779. **Wm.**, 9 Powell St., King's Sq., 1842.

Hornby. Geo., Liverpool, 1765. **Gerard**, Liverpool, 1780. **Jno.**, Liverpool, 1790. **Richd.**, Pool Lane, Liverpool, 1810-30. **Hy.**, Liverpool, 1818. —, London ; watch, 1825.

Horne. Samuel, C.C. 1654 ; master 1672-73. **George Henry**, C.C. 1718. **Henry**, London Bridge, master C.C. 1730-68. **William**, 114 Ratcliffe Highway, 1830-42.

Hornsby. Robert, apprenticed to William Harris, admitted C.C. 1788. **Gerrard**, Liverpool, 1817.

Hornsey, Thos. E., York, f., 1826.

Horseman, Stephen, was apprenticed to Daniel Quare 1702, admitted C.C. 1709 ; Quare prior to his death, seems to have taken Horseman into partnership, judging from examples with their joint names, including repeating and clock-watches, and a 30-day clock, 1724-40.

Horsfall, Wm., Bradford, Yorks., 1830.

Horsley. Cornelius, York, f., 1656, **Ben.**, apprenticed in 1693 to William Watson, C.C.

Horsnaile, Geo., Warfield ; one-hand clock, about 1730.

Horstmann, Gustave, inventor of perpetual clock (see p. **303**) ; died at Bath, 1893, aged 66.

Hoskins. & Bird, 11 St John's Sq., Clerkenwell, 1822-30. **Jonah**, 6 Hatton Garden, 1840. **George**, 75 Old Broad St., 1842.

Hotham, Hy., apprenticed in 1665 to Jno. Pennock ; C.C. 1673.

Houblin l'aîné, Rue Montague, St Genevieve, Paris ; garde visiteur, 1769.

Houdin, Robert, Paris, 1820-30.

Hough. Jno., Knutsford, 1740. **Jno.**, Warrington ; clock, about 1760.

Houghman, Charles, Aldersgate St. : C.C. 1770-80.

Houghton. Richard, C.C. 1690. **Jas.**, Macclesfield ; clock, about 1770. **Thos.**, Chorley, 1780-1840. **James**, 198 Tooley St., 1790-94. **James**, Ormskirk, assistant of William Garrat, and afterwards maker of watches with Debaufre's dead-beat escapement, with two escape wheels as modified by Sully, known in Lancashire as the club-footed verge, 1800-20. **John**, Handsworth, Birmingham ; a well-known clockmaker, died 1863, see Evans, W. F. **Wm.**, Lever St., died 1890, aged 75.

Houlhere, —, "Jona Houlhere at the sign of the spring clock in Broad St., London," watch paper, Ponsonby collection, about 1760, see Hollier.

Houllgatt, —, oval watch, S.K.M., inscribed, "W. Houllgatt, att Ipswich," about 1640.

Houriet, Jacques Frederic, Locle ; born 1743, died 1830 ; clever horologist and maker of spherical balance-springs.

House, J., Gray's Inn Lane ; pair-case silver verge, showing day and night by means of a revolving plate, serving as hour hand, minutes shown in the usual way, period 1700. **Matt.**, Cork Lane ; C.C. 1730. **Robert**, 32 Upper Moorfields, 1790.

Housman, Jacob, Lancaster, 1732, f.

Houson, Jas., York, f., 1832.

Houston, S., Dublin ; watch, 1799.

How. William, C.C. 1667 ; elected assistant but excused, 1697. **Thos.**, apprenticed in 1670 to Isaac Romien, but turned over to Nat. Delander ; C.C. 1677. **Benjamin**, C.C. 1691. **& Masterman**, White Hart Court, Gracechurch St., 1750-60.

Howard. John, C.C. 1694. **Richard**, apprenticed to Daniel Delaunder ; C.C. 1718 ; long-case clock, arch dial, Mr D. Foale, inscribed, "Richard Howard, New Brentford." **Wm.**, repaired the clock at Exeter Cathedral, 1760 (see p. **51**). **Edwd.**, 5 Kirby St., Hatton Garden, 1775-1804. **Wm.**, London ; watch, h.m., 1777. **Thomas**, Philadelphia, 1789-91. **John Jarvis**, 68 Aldersgate St., 1790-94. **H. & M.**, London ; watch, steel index disc, 1792. **Edward**, died 1904, aged 90 ; apprenticed to Aaron Willard, Boston, U.S.A.; joined, in 1847, David P. Davis, who had been a fellow-apprentice ; Howard & Davis made clocks and scales at Roxbury. Met A. L. Dennison in 1849 and became associated with him ; a factory was built at Waltham, and, in 1854, watches produced there marked, "Dennison Howard & Davis"; Waltham factory disposed of to Royal E. Robbins in 1857 ; in 1861 Howard returned to Roxbury and started the Howard Clock & Watch Company ; in 1863 the title was altered to the Howard Watch & Clock Company ; from this he retired in 1882.

Howarth, Ja., Blackburn, 1770.

Howden, Francis, Edinburgh, 1842.

Howe. Samuel, C.C. 1712. **Ephraim**, apprenticed to Graham, C.C. 1729. **Jno.**, Alresford, 1800. **Jubal**, Boston, U.S.A., 1833. **Samuel**, 173 High Holborn, 1840.

Howell. Dan., C.C. 1637. **Benjamin**, C.C. 1699. **Joseph**, Golden Sq., C.C. 1721.

John, Bull's Head Court, Newgate St., C.C. 1724-30. **Stephen**, London ; watch, 1770. **Wm.**, Bristol ; Sir Theodore Fry has a long-case clock by him, dating from about 1770, which shows "High Water at Bristol Key." **Geo.**, London ; watch, 1785.

Howells. William, Kennington, apprenticed to Thos. Sheafe ; C.C. 1780 ; one of the experts appointed by the select committee of the House of Commons to examine Mudge's timekeepers (see p. **268**). **William Henry**, apprenticed to William Howells ; admitted C.C. 1820.

Howes. Jno., C.C. 1672. **Thos.**, London ; clock, Mr W. H. Wilding, about 1680. **Wm.**, Temple Bar, C.C. 1730. **Jos.**, Fleet St., 1760-75. **S.**, Downham ; clock, about 1770.

Howlbrook, see Holbrook.

Howlett. Stephen, apprenticed in 1657 to Peter Bellune, C.C. **John**, London, known as a maker of good watches, about 1750 ; a specimen in a gold repoussé case, Schloss collection, about 1770. **Jno.**, son of the above, migrated from London to Bath ; his son afterwards carried on business at Calne.

Hows, Thos., The Sun, Pope's Head Alley ; admitted C.C. 1632 ; known as a maker of watches, 1630-40.

Howse. John, Croydon, C.C. 1687. **Joseph**, 1698, see Howes. **John**, admitted C.C. 1706. **William**, 13 Fleet St., C.C. 1731 ; master 1777 ; 1731-80. **Charles**, 5 Great Tower St.; watch, 1768 ; master C.C. 1787 ; 1768-94.

Howson, John, admitted C.C. 1699.

Hoyle. Hy., C.C. 1677. **Wm.**, Bolton-le-Moors, 1818.

Huaud (or **Huaut**) ; this Swiss family, noted as painters in enamel for watch cases, from about 1660-1750 (see p. **149**).

Hubbard. John, C.C. 1722. **Joseph**, watch gold hand maker, St John's Sq., 1790. **E.**, musical clockmaker, 33 Gibson St., Waterloo Rd., 1840.

Hubberd, C., watch-case maker, 9 Peerless Row, City Rd., 1835.

Hubert. Timothee, oval watch, signed "Timothée Hubert à Rouen," in crystal case, about 1600, Pierpont Morgan collection ; melon-shaped watch, Ashmolean Museum, silver case, richly chased dial, about 1650. **Noel**, Rouen ; oval watch, S.K.M., about 1620. **Jean**, Rouen ; oval silver watch, about 1650 ; Buhl case bracket clock, about 1670 ; verge escapement, brass dial arched, silvered circle inscribed "Jean Hubert" ; below is a figure of Time with scythe, under which is the inscription, "Solem Audet Dicere Falsum" ; in the Pierpont Morgan collection is a watch, signed "Jean Hubert, Rouen, au Grd. Monarque" ; it has Turkish numerals, and dates from about 1680 ; watch, Evan Roberts collection, about 1795, inscribed, "P. Hubert l'aîné a Toulouse." **Estienne**, Rouen ; maker of a watch said to have belonged to Mary, Queen of Scots ; in 1657 John Smith was fined 10s. for putting the name of Estinne Hubert on a watch ; alarm watch in pierced and engraved silver case with inscription, "Estinne Hubert à Rouen," S.K.M., about 1610 ; watch, Pierpont Morgan collection, of about the same date. "Lost upon New-years-day, above stairs in Whitehall, a gold watch with a plain shapen case ; the watch was made at Rouen, maker's name Hubert. Whoever brings it to her Royal Highness the Princess of Denmark's porter at the Cockpit, shall have two guineas reward" (*Lond. Gaz.*, Jan. 2, 1689). **Estinne l'aîné**, Amsterdam ; repeating watch, about 1690. **David**, Strand ; admitted C.C. 1714, master 1743 ; repeating watch, silver case engraved and pierced, enamel dial, Roman hour numerals, Arabic figures outside for minutes, the plate covered with engraving, and inscribed "Dav. Hubert, London" ; Mr Evan Roberts has a repeating watch by him which sounds the minutes, and is therefore an early specimen of the kind ; another specimen of his work is a bracket clock repeating the quarters on six bells by pulling a cord, which winds up the quarter repeating train, brass arched dial, strike-silent, day of the month, verge escapement ; 1714-48. **Oliver**, his son ; C.C. 1749. **James** ; Charlotte Hubert was apprenticed to him and Elizabeth his wife in 1725 ; and in 1730 Catherine Cext was also apprenticed to them. **Pascal le jeune**, Rouen ; enamel watch ; 1749 (see p. 153).

Hubner, —, Vienna ; gold watch, Fitz-william Museum, eighteenth century (?).

Huchason, Richard, C.C. 1702.

Hudleston. Chas., apprenticed in 1673 to Hy. Harper, C.C. Letter from L. Hudleston, at Mr Keats, surgeon in Parliament St., 20th Oct. 1773, relating to a watch made by him for Miss Walter, Bury Hill, near Dorking ; the price of the watch was 80 guineas, including enamelling, gold hands, and shagreen cases :—

"As to the inside I can speak with more confidence, as there is not a single article but what is in part or altogether the work of my own hands ; and this is one reason why I cannot dispatch a watch as expeditiously as others who trust to the work of other men's hands without making use of their own. To alter its going the silver plate in the inside should be moved by the little end of the key, bringing a higher figure towards the index in the cap to make it go faster and *vice versa*. Moving the plate from one division to another will alter the watch's going about 2 minutes per day" ("MSS. of the Earl of Verulam").

Hudson. Jno., apprenticed in 1684 to Chas. Halstead, C.C. **John**, St Martin's Churchyard, 1780-85. **Jno.**, Nottingham ; watch, 1780. **T.**, Cheapside, near the Hen Cross, Nottingham, about 1790. **William**, Griffin St., Shadwell, 1835.

Hues. Pierry (Peter), C.C. 1632. **Thos.**, apprenticed 1662 to Jno. Pennock, C.C.

Huges, Jno., Maidstone ; lantern clock, about 1710.

Huggeford. Ignatius, brother C.C. 1671 ; a watch by him played a prominent part in respect of the petition of Facio and Debaufre for extension of their watch jewel patent (see p. **408**), 1671-1705. **Peter**, apprenticed to Ignatius Huggeford 1686, C.C.

Huggins, J., Macclesfield, 1810-15.

Hughes. Morris, apprenticed in 1691 to Hy. Hammond, C.C. **John**, C.C. 1703 ; long-case clock, about 1710, signed "John Hughs, London," see Hughes. **Thomas**, Broad St. Buildings ; C.C. 1712-35. **Thomas**, 25 Broad St. Buildings, master C.C. 1765 ; first liveryman 1776 ; 1750-83. **S.**, Gracechurch St., 1774. **William**, 119 High Holborn, hon. freeman C.C. 1781 ; centre seconds watch by him in the Guildhall Museum ; four of Earnshaw's watches with his name thereon were deposited for trial at Greenwich Observatory in 1791 ; small enamelled watch, Schloss collection, about 1790 (see p. **158**) ; Mr Henry Levy has a fine travelling watch by him from the Summer Palace, Pekin ; it is in pair-cases 7 in. in diameter, chimes on six

bells and sets in motion mechanical figures, 1766-94. He was succeeded by Thos. Earnshaw. **John**, 92 Minories, 1800. **H.**, Caernarvon ; watch, 1806. **David**, 30 Frith St., 1835-42.

Huguenail, Charles T., Philadelphia, 1799.

Huguenin. Charles F., Philadelphia, 1797. **Aimé**, Liverpool, 1820. **A.**, 67 Great Russell St., 1830-42.

Hulbert, William, Castle Green, Bristol, 1708.

Hulier, Wm., apprenticed in 1669 to Thos. Creed ; C.C. 1679.

Hull. Philip, apprenticed in 1693 to Wm. Young, C.C. **Hy.**, apprenticed to Geo. Graham, C.C. 1738 ; a cylinder escapement maker, who worked for Ellicott and other celebrated manufacturers. **Jno.**, York, 1822.

Hulme, Peter, Preston, 1814. **Jas.**, 11 Bow St., 1817.

Hulst, Jacob, admitted C.C. 1645.

Hulton, John, admitted C.C. 1724.

Humber, Thos., London ; long-case clock, about 1790.

Hume, Benj., apprenticed in 1691 to Jno. Barnett, C.C. **Chas.**, London ; watch, 1830.

Humfrey, Nicholas, apprenticed in 1689 to Thos. Wheeler, C.C.

Humfreys, Wm., apprenticed in 1692 to Nat. Higginson, C.C.

Humphrey, W. H., 17 Great Surrey St., 1830-35.

Humphreys, Samuel, Fore St., C.C. 1728. **Wm.**, watch, about 1760.

Humphries, J., London ; mantel clock, about 1750.

Humphrys, William, C.C. 1699.

Hunot, Sam., 28 Rathbone Place, 1842.

Hunsdon, Edwd., Chelmsford, 1750.

Hunt, Robt., apprenticed in 1661 to Lawrence Sindrey, C.C. **John**, C.C. 1671. **Edward**, apprenticed to Thos. Williamson ; C.C. 1684 ; watch movement with tulip pillars, in the Guildhall Museum. "Lost the 17 past, out of Mrs Man's Lodgings in Sohoe, a gold minute pendulum watch, with a gold-studded case, the inward box marked E.H. and a coronet, made by Edw. Hunt" (*Lond. Gaz.*, September 15, 1692). — , long-case clock, square dial, cherub corners, inscribed, "Rich : Hunt, Bristoll," about 1700. **James**, C.C. 1708. **William**, Ludgate St., 1753-56. **Jas.**, 5 King St., Cheapside, 1772. **Thos.**, 151 Tottenham Court Rd., 1835. **Wm.**, Stafford St., Bond St., 1835. **Saml.**, Buttesland St., Hoxton, 1842. **Hiram**, Robbinston, Maine, U.S.A. ; was said to have been the original "Sam Slick" of Haliburton ; he died at an advanced age in 1886.

Hunter. Thomas, 43 Lombard St., 1754 ; 156 Fenchurch St., 1763 ; liveryman C.C. 1768 ; 1754-94. **Jno.**, Bristol, about 1760 (see p. **364**). **William**, 51 Lombard St., livery Goldsmiths' Company, 1766-94. **Jno.**, Bridlington, 1770. **Thos.**, Liverpool, 1780. **Thomas, junr.**, 156 Fenchurch St., 1781-1800. **Thomas**, 54 Goswell Road, 1788-94. **Wm.**, 156 Fenchurch St., 1804. **& Son**, 156 Fenchurch St., 1810-17. **J.**, Clapham ; watch, 1815. **Jno.**, Bridlington, 1822. **& Edwards**, 43 Cornhill, 1840-42.

Huon, Jacques, Paris ; splendidly enamelled watch, S.K.M., about 1650.

Hurley, Isaac, Red Lion St., Clerkenwell ; C.C. 1730-80.

Hurst. Isaac, C.C. 1677. **Arthur**, Ashford ; lantern clock, about 1690. **Stephen**, Liverpool ; watch, 1807. **W.**,

(? **M.**), 9 Lambeth Walk, 1835-42.

Hurt. Noe, apprenticed in 1686 to Joseph Biddle, C.C. **Henry**, Ludgate Hill ; C.C. 1730-56.

Hurtin & Burgi, Bound Brook, U.S.A., May 1766.

Husband, Thomas, Hull, 1760-86 ; long-case clock, Mrs Maria Duane Bleecker Cox, New York.

Hussam, Chas., apprenticed in 1672 to Jas. Wolverston, C.C.

Hussey, Joseph, admitted C.C. 1685.

Hutchin. Joshua, C.C. 1682 ; in the B.M. is a watch by him, handsome silver dial with a semicircular slit above the centre, through which appears blue sky, the sun in the day and the moon at night pointing to the hour ; Mr W. K. Bowen has a long-case clock by him, case of walnut with fine geometrical marqueterie (see p. **371**) ; 1670-1705. **James**, C.C. 1697. **Joseph**, C.C. 1703. **John**, C.C. 1703.

Hutchins, Abel (also **Levi**), Concord, U.S.A., 1785-1818.

Hutchinson. Wm., apprenticed in 1688 to Geo. Ethrington, C.C. **Anthony**, Leeds ; clock, about 1700. **Richard**, C.C. 1702-36. —, Worksop, clock, 1710-20. **John**, petitioned Parliament to grant a longer period than usually covered by a patent for his improved watch, which would be wound without an aperture in the case ; successfully opposed by C.C., Mr Charles Goode producing to the Committee of the House of Commons a watch made fourteen years previously, which Mr Hutchinson confessed was made as his ; 1712. —, Retford ; clock, 1710. **Edwd.**, London ; watch, Nelthropp collection, about 1750. **Jno.**, Burnley, 1780-1818. **Jno.**, London ; watch, 1825.

Hutton. Richd., apprenticed in 1691 to Thos. Brafield, C.C. **Jos.**, London ; watch, 1750. **Thos.**, London ; mentioned by Earnshaw, 1776. **Patrick**, 83 Cannon St., 1790. **John**, chronometer maker, Commercial Rd., E., 1830 ; Mark Lane, 1830-68.

Hux. Thos., London ; watch, 1825. **John**, 41 Percival St., 1840-42. **R. R.**, Spencer St., Clerkenwell, a well-known maker ; died 1869.

Huygens, Christian, born 1629, died 1695 (see p. 241).

Hyams. Woolf, Portsea ; watch, 1815. **Joshua**, 32 Leman St., Goodman's Fields, 1840-42.

Hyatt, Jno., Chester, 1818.

Hyde. Jno., apprenticed in 1637 to Simon Hackett, C.C. **Thos.**, apprenticed in 1691 to Hy. Harper, C.C. **Thomas**, 33 Gutter Lane, 1773-94. **James**, 38 Gutter Lane, 1783.

Hyett, Nicholas, apprenticed in 1648 to Richd. Morgan, and put to Robt. Rothwood, C.C.

Hyland, Jno., London ; watch, 1770.

Hyman. Watch, signed "S. Hyman, Dock," 1811.

Hynam. Robt., horloger *de la Cour*, St Petersburg ; quarter clock, about 1750 ; he probably went from London, for he was on the livery of the Joiners' Company till 1776, when his address was given as "Russia." In the Czar of Russia's collection, at the Winter Palace, St Petersburg, is a small watch by him entirely covered with brilliants ; it is suspended from a chatelaine of seven chains set with diamonds which also carries a watch key, a small seal of agate, and an enamelled acorn. **Robert**, 4 Clement's Lane; Hatton says, "the much improving Mr Hynam makes his watches without collars to his pendants"; liveryman C.C. 1769-90.

Hyon à Paris, on a watch, S.K.M., about 1740.

Ibel, **Thomas**, watch-spring maker, Featherstone St., 1790.

Idelot. Fine Boulle work clock and bracket, inscribed "Idelot à Paris," about 1710.

Ilbury, **Wm.**, Goswell St., 1780; afterwards at Duncan Terrace, died 1851; a well-known manufacturer of fine enamelled and other watches for the Chinese market. Mr Willard H. Wheeler has a watch dating from about 1800, signed "Ilbury, Paris," the case is finely decorated with pearls.

Iles, **Thomas**, London; long-case clock, Mr D. A. F. Wetherfield, about 1790.

Imhof, **Nicholas**, 24 Curtain Rd., 1848.

Imison. **Jno.**, Manchester; clock, about 1770. —, London; watch, h.m., 1786.

Immisch, **Moritz**, clever horologist and electrician; died 1903.

Ingerham, **Thos.**, apprenticed in 1686 to Alex. Warfield, C.C.

Ingersoll, **Daniel G.**, Boston, U.S.A., 1800-1810.

Inglish. **Jas.**, 36 Watling St., 1790. **David**, Manchester, 1818. **Adam**, wooden clockmaker, 39 St John's Sq., 1840.

Ingold, **Pierre Frederick**, born at Bienne 1787, a clever mechanician, who devised machinery for duplicating parts of watches. He visited Paris about 1817, and worked for Breguet; started business for himself in Paris 1830; came to London 1840. In 1842 and 1843 he took out various patents for protecting the tools to be used by the British Watch Company; visited New York in 1845; afterwards returned to Switzerland and devoted himself to the manufacture of the "Ingold Fraise," a serrated cylindrical cutter for shaping wheel teeth; he died 1878.

Ingram. **Thomas**, C.C. 1695. **William**, C.C. 1730. **John**, Spalding, 1770. **William**, 40 Goswell St., 1842.

Inkpen, **John**, Horsham; long-case clocks, about 1770.

Inman, **Jas.**, Colne, Lancs., 1818; Stockport, 1833; and at Burnley.

Innes, **R.**, London; watch, 1760.

Innocent, **Robt.**, 16 Gwynn's Place, Hackney Rd., 1835.

Inwood, **S.**, London; watch, green leather case *piqué*, about 1700; another watch exhibited at the Guelph Exhibition by Mr Geo. Carr Glyn.

Ireland, **Henry**, Lothbury; C.C. 1654; maker of lantern clocks, 1650-75. **Francis**, C.C. 1668. **Ant.**, Mile End; long-case clock, about 1770. **John**, 21 Maiden Lane, 1779.

Ironside & Belchier, Lombard St., 1737-40.

Irvin, **Jean**, 32 Kirby St., Hatton Garden, 1825.

Irvine, **J.**, watch movement maker, 23 Rahere St., 1835.

Irving, **Alexander**, C.C. 1695; long-case clock, about 1700, signed "Alexander Irving, Londini, fecit"; another, inscribed "Alex. Ervin, London."

Isaac. **Sutton**, apprenticed in 1655 to Jno. Samon, C.C. 1662. **Daniel**, assistant C.C. 1670; 1660-70.

Isaacs. **Levy**, 57 Mansell St., 1769-83.

Lewis, 23 Houndsditch, 1830-42.

Israel, **John**, 180 Whitechapel, 1783.

Ive. Francis, C.C. 1634. **G. H.**, 10 Finsbury Place, 1825; also at 17 Cornhill, 1826-42.

Ivery, **John**, repairer of the clock of St Margaret's, Westminster, 1548.

Ives. Zacharia, C.C. 1682; 30-hour clock, hour hand only, inscribed "Zac. Ives, fecit for Thos. Sclater, Gentl." **Jno.**, apprenticed in 1693 to Jno. Benson, C.C. **Francis**, C.C. 1709. **Joseph**, Bristol, Conn., 1811-25. **Lawson**, 1827-36.

Ivison, **Jno.**, Carlisle, 1810.

Ivory. Jas., Dundee, 1760-90. **Thos.**, son of Jas., 1795-1810.

Izod, **William**, admitted C.C. 1649.

Jaccard. J., 60 Red Lion St., Clerkenwell, 1820-22. **David**, 26 Percival St., 1840-42. **Ami**, son of David, suicide 1909, aged 69.

Jackman, **Joseph**, large verge watch movement in the G.M., inscribed "Jos. Jakeman, on London Bridge," about 1690.

Jackson. Richard, C.C. 1632. **Joseph**, C.C. 1646. **Sampson**, apprenticed in 1656 to Joseph Jackson, C.C. **Edward**, C.C. 1669. **Edward**, Newington, Surrey, apprenticed in 1672 to Robert Wilkins; C.C. 1680. **John**, C.C. 1682. **David**, apprenticed in 1684 to Luke Bird, C.C. **Thomas**, C.C. 1688. **James**, C.C. 1689. **Martin**, C.C. 1697, master 1721; maker of a bell-top ebony case, pull-repeater clock, brass arch dial, 1697-1721. **Matthew**, C.C. 1730. **William**, Old Broad St., afterwards Tower St., 1730-76; bracket clock by him in walnut case, about 1750, Wetherfield collection; known also as a maker of long-case clocks; liveryman C.C. 1776. **John**, 37 Basinghall St., 1759-74. **Thos.**, Preston, 1760. **John**, 2 Bridgewater Sq., livery C.C. 1776, master 1796; 1760-1800. **Randal**, 8 Chapel Row, Spa Fields, 1780. **Henry**, 29 St Martin's Lane, 1790-94. **Thomas**, 52 Upper East Smithfield, 1790; 53 Red Lion St., Clerkenwell, 1810. **Isaac**, Wylam, Northumberland, born 1796, died 1862; a good mechanician; clock by him with three-legged gravity escapement, at Stephenson's factory, Newcastle. Lancaster: **Wm.**, 1801; **Wm. W.**, 1817. **Wm.**, Frodsham, f., of Lancaster, 1801. **Joseph**, **H.**, Philadelphia, 1802-10. **Isaac**, 145 St John's St., 1804. **Geo.**, 82 Charlotte St., Rathbone Place, 1815-25. **Wm. W.**, Frodsham, 1817, f., of Lancaster. **Edwd.**, York, 1818. **Jno.**, Lancaster, 1820. **Wm.**, 31 Cowcross St., 1820. **John**, junr., Bridgewater Sq.; master C.C. 1822; 1800-30. **John**, watch-case maker, 10 Norman St., St Luke's, 1835. **William**, 6 Brunswick Place, Brompton, 1835-42. **Henry & Son**, 66 Red Lion St., Clerkenwell, 1835-42, afterwards W. H. & S. Jackson; Samuel Jackson for many years identified himself with the work of the Horological Institute, filling in succession the offices of Treasurer and Vice-President; died at Tonbridge 1904, aged 81. **William**, 29 Exeter St., Sloane St., 1835. **John**, 72 Hackney Rd., 1842.

Jacob. Benjamin, C.C. 1706. **Benjamin**, C.C. 1718. **Dennis**, Cockspur St., 1775-1800. **Dan.**, 57 Margaret St., 1817.

Jacobs. Jean, Harlem; octagonal watch, dated 1560. **Conrad**, Leewarden; watch, about 1610. **Judah**, Whitecross St., 1769; 1 Little Mitre Court, Fenchurch St., 1771; Mr Thos. Boynton has a bracket clock by him, brass and silvered dial, mahogany case.

E., 86 York St., Westminster, 1820; 25 Bevis Marks, 1825-35. **A.**, Bowery, N.Y., 1833-36. **Edward**, 29 Earl St., Westminster, 1835.

Jacques, see Jaques.

Jadwin, **Robt.**, apprenticed in 1647 to Wm. North, C.C.

Jaggar, **Edward**, Fleet St.; C.C. 1702-30.

Jakeman, —, see Jackman.

James. John, apprenticed to Thomas Loomes; C.C. 1661. **Francis**, C.C. 1662. **Joseph**, C.C. 1689; long-case clock, one hand, about 1700, signed "Benj: James, Shaston" (Shaftesbury). **Monaghan**, apprenticed in 1692 to Chas. Goode, C.C. **J.**, London; long-case clock, 1770. **W.**, Bath; watch, 1796. **Robert**, 23 White St., Borough, 1835.

Jamison, **George**, 33 Charing Cross, 1800-5; in conjunction with Howells & Barraud he completed chronometers on Mudge's plan; he also attested the value of Earnshaw's improvements in 1804; afterwards he carried on business at High St., Portsmouth. **Wm.**, Dublin; watch, 1809.

Jammett, —, admitted C.C. 1704.

Janaway. Wm., apprenticed in 1675 to Jno. Saville, C.C. **Jno.**, 114 Cheapside, 1815.

Janvier, **Antide**, born 1751 at St Claude in the Jura, settled in Besançon, and became an authority on horological construction; migrated to Paris and repaired Passemant's clock for the first Consul. His "Essai sur les Horloges" was published at Paris in 1811; died 1835.

Japy, **Frederic**, Beaucourt, France; born 1749, died 1812; in 1799 he patented a series of machines for producing parts of watches by unskilled labour; this appears to be the first attempt to manufacture watches on the factory system.

Jaques. William, apprenticed in 1679 to Jno. Wright, and turned over to Nathaniel Delander; C.C. 1687; master 1716. **Wm.**, Achurch apprenticed to him in 1691. **William**, C.C. 1724. **Aug.**, 4 President St., 1842; small watch, gold case enamelled, "G. Jaques London," h.m., 1843.

Jaquet; watch, inscribed "Jaquet, London," silver dial and cock, brass cases, inner one beautifully engraved and pierced, Pierpont Morgan collection, about 1705; another watch of later date, inscribed "Peter Jaquet, London."

Jardin, **John**, Bartholomew Close, one of the witnesses to the will of Christopher Pinchbeck the younger in 1780; admitted hon. freeman C.C. 1781; maker of a repeating watch in shagreen case, style 1745; 1745-81.

Jarman. John, C.C. 1728. **John B.**, 25 Strand, 1815-23. **& Co.**, 33 St James' St., 1825.

Jarossay, —, Paris, 1788.

Jarratt, **Wm.**, London, about 1760; long-case clock, belonged to Mrs Inchbald.

Jarratt. Richd., C.C. 1632. **Richard**, C.C. 1670; master 1685; watch, Schloss collection, about 1665 (see p. 174). **& Sons**, watch-case engravers, Albemarle St., St John's Sq., 1780-94. **Barnard**, City Rd., livery C.C. 1786-1820. **John Wm.**, livery C.C. 1786-1816.

Jarvis. Simon, apprenticed in 1670 to Richd. Ames, C.C. **Joseph**, apprenticed in 1670 to Bart. Powell, C.C. **Saml.**, Birmingham, 1710. **George**, C.C. 1728. **John**, Aldersgate St., 1775-94.

Jeanin, A., 28 Cranbourne St., 1842.

Jeeves; fine Chippendale long-case clock, Gillespie's School, Edinburgh, inscribed "Anthony Jeeves, musical clock maker from Oxford," about 1770; the name "Daniel Davidson" in arch of dial.

Jefferies, John, C.C. 1639.

Jefferson. Samuel, 35 Bruton St., 1805-42 (see p. 327). & Son, 38 Fetter Lane, 1815. Reed & Walton, 38 Fetter Lane, 1820-25. Jno., Gt. Driffield, 1822. Matthew, 236 High St., Shadwell, 1835-42.

Jeffery. William Knight, C.C. 1712. Thomas, & Jones, Cockspur St., Charing Cross, 1769-94.

Jefferys. Nathaniel, 22 Queen St., Mayfair, 1768-1804. Nathaniel, Strand, 1771, see Drury Dru. Thomas, Cockspur St., 1771. Nathaniel, junr., 70 Piccadilly, 1780-94. Geo., Chatham; long-case clock, 1790. Henry, 96 Fleet St., 1793; 49 Salisbury Sq., 1798-1804. G., 86 New Bond St., 1800. & Gilbert, Cockspur St., 1800. & Ham, 49 Salisbury Sq., Fleet St., 1810-15; 46 Skinner St., 1825.

Jeffreys, John, Holborn, C.C. 1726; to him was apprenticed Larcum Kendall in 1735.

Jeffrys & Jones; thin watch, Evan Roberts collection, about 1795.

Jeffs. John, apprenticed to Jeffery Bayly, and turned over to John Walter; admitted C.C. 1697. Benjamin, C.C. 1702.

Jelf, William, C.C. 1717.

Jenkins. Thomas, C.C. 1678. Cornelius, C.C. 1678. James, C.C. 1692; fine month clock, arch dial, by him, about 1710. Henry, 68 Aldersgate St., maker of curious astronomical and other clocks, 1756-83 (see p. 289). —, Cheapside, 1774; long-case clock, mahogany Chippendale case, about 1780. F., 7 Tyler St., Regent St., 1835.

Jenkinson, J., Sandwith, watch, 1770.

Jennens, J. C., London; chiming bracket clock, about 1790, seen at The Hague.

Jennings. Emanuel, apprenticed 1682 to Jno. Colston, C.C. Robert, C.C. 1703. Thomas, C.C. 1721. Charles, C.C. 1725.

Jernegan, Edward, Great Russell St., 1737-40; Featherstone Buildings, 1750-59.

Jerome, Chauncey, pupil of Eli Terry, maker of American clocks, born at Canaan, Litchfield Co., 1793; with his brother, Noble Jerome, he began business at Bristol, Conn.; in 1842 he shipped clocks to England, which the Customs authorities seized and paid for, believing they were undervalued. Shortly afterwards he started the Jerome Manufacturing Co. at New Haven, Conn.

Jerrard, Henry, Hinton; clock, about 1770.

Jersey, Francis; bracket clock, about 1760.

Jervis. Francis, apprenticed in 1656 to Ralph Greatorex, C.C. Jno., Stockport, 1833.

Jessop, Josias, 38 Southampton St., Covent Garden, 1781-90, see Wilson, W.

Jeubi, Josias, Paris; watch, about 1630.

Jevon. Henry, C.C. 1673. May, C.C. 1706.

Jeyes, Sam., apprenticed in 1670 to Philip Smith, C.C.

Job. W., London; watch, 1795. Robert, 25 Charlton St., Somers Town, 1835; 7 Park Terrace, Camden Town, 1842. Fredk., 25 Sherrard St., Golden Sq., 1835; 17 Tichborne St., Haymarket, 1842.

Jodin, Pierre, born at Geneva 1715, died 1761; author of "Les Echappemens à repos à ceux échappemens à recul," published in 1754.

Johann; clock at Mainz, about 1820, signed "Nicolas Alexius Johann à Mayance." A., author of "Traité Générale d'Horlogerie," born 1822, died 1882.

John, Hans, Konigsberg; maker of a curious watch, B.M., having attached a small wheel-lock pistol, supposed to have been used as an alarm, about 1650.

Johnson. Roger, petitioner for incorporation of C.C. 1630. George, C.C. 1649. Jery, Exchange Alley; apprenticed in 1660 to Abraham Beckner, admitted C.C. 1668; in the B.M. is a small watch of his make in an irregular octagonal-shaped case with a faceted crystal over the dial, about 1650. Wm., f., of York, 1665-1713. Jeremiah, Exchange Alley, C.C. 1668-90; bracket clock, strike-silent, full quarter, about 1700. John, C.C. 1678. John, 3 Flower de Luces, Cheapside; C.C. 1680, see Betts, Job. Michael, Barnard Castle; C.C. 1687; watch, about 1720. Benj., London; long case clock, about 1690. William, apprenticed to Dan. Quare [in 1690; C.C. 1702; bracket clock, bell-top ebony case, with handle, brass dial, bob pendulum, style 1725, strike-silent. Cornelius, C.C. 1694. Robert, Edinburgh, apprenticed to Andrew Brown in 1696; watch, signed "R. Johnson, Wooltown," 1720. Thomas, C.C. 1700; Mr R. Eden Dickson has a fine inlaid long-case clock, inscribed "Tho. Johnson Ratcliff Cross," about 1705. John, C.C. 1701. John, Fleet Lane, 1701. Isaac, C.C. 1705; watch by him, 1720. James, apprenticed to James Delaunder; C.C. 1706. Thomas, Richmond; C.C. 1713; watch, S.K.M., about 1745. Isaac, C.C. 1723. Thomas, 9 Gray's Inn Passage, about 1730. Charles Jacock, apprenticed to Robert Higgs; C.C. 1750. Roland, Liverpool, 1766. Jno. & Thos., also James, Prescot, 1770. Richard, Ripon, 1770. Jno., Walton; clock, about 1770. Wm., Flixon; clock, about 1770. John, 9 Gray's Inn Passage, 1770-99; balloon bracket clock, round enamelled dial, case and bracket of ebony with brass mountings, about 1790, Wetherfield collection (see p. 395). Christopher, Knaresbourgh, 1775. Peter, Mitcham; watch, 1790. James, New Rd., St George's East, 1790-94. Jno., Elm St., Gray's Inn Lane, 1790-1835. Joseph, Liverpool, 1796-1830. J. F., Dublin; watch, 1812. Richd., 18 Francis St., Bedford Sq., 1815-20. C., 7 Sweeting's Alley, 1820-23. J. & W., 19 Cross St., Hatton Garden, 1825. Leond., 19 Bartletts Buildings, 1825. William, 50 Strand, 1825-42; diminutive bracket clock, about 1825. & Co., London; repeating watch, 1830. James, 18 Paddington St., 1835-42. —, High Wycombe; long-case clock, about 1840. Edward Daniel, 9 Wilmington Sq.; a leading watch manufacturer, formerly with James Stoddart; retired from business 1879; died at Highbury, 1889, aged 73.

Johnston & Brecians, London; watch, h.m., 1816. G., 7 Queen St., Northampton Sq., 1835. Jno., Glasgow; patented a pedometer watch in 1840 (No. 8,645).

Jole. Robt., C.C. 1667. Thos., apprenticed 1680 to Robt. Fole, C.C.

Jolly. J., watchmaker to the Paris Town Hall in 1550; worked also for Catherine de Medicis; a watch by J. Jolly, Paul Garnier collection (see p. 125); skull watch (Soltykoff collection) by Jacques Jolly, about 1580; two watches by Joshua Jolly, Vienna Treasury, splendidly enamelled cases and dials, about 1670; at Deene Park is a magnificent Louis XIV. bracket clock, inscribed "I Jolly a Paris"; it belonged to the Duke of Sussex and was purchased at the sale of his effects by the late Earl of Cardigan. Dan., apprenticed in 1637 to Jno. Droshute, C.C. Joseph, 11 Dean St., Fetter Lane, 1790-94.

Joly. Jacques, London; in the B.M. is a watch by him, 1620-30; watch, signed "Geo Joly à Mondont"; on dial, "Joly le Cadet," about 1765.

Jon, J., London; lantern clock, arch dial, about 1730.

Jonas, Saml., Exon; watch, 1783.

Jones. Evan, C.C. 1648; signed petition 1656, assistant 1671. Marmaduke, apprenticed in 1652 to Evan Jones, C.C. Henry, Inner Temple Gate; apprenticed in 1654 to Edward East; C.C. 1663; master 1691; an eminent maker (see p. 217). "Lost on 29th instant in Lincolns Inn fields, one silver striking watch with the day of the month in a steel case studded and garnished with silver made by Mr Jones in the Inner Temple Lane, watchmaker. Whoever can give notice hereof and bring the said watch to Mr Humphry Davis at the Duke's Head in Lincolns Inn Fields or to Mr Jones aforesaid shall have 40s. reward" (Lond. Gaz., 27 Jan. 1675-6). Chas., apprenticed in 1663 to Walter Gibbs, C.C. William, C.C. 1663. Henry, apprenticed in 1668 to Chas. Bonner, C.C. Dan., apprenticed in 1672 to Edwd. Wilson, C.C. Benj., apprenticed in 1676 to Richd. Halstead, C.C. Thomas Wm., C.C. 1679; very small watch by him, Schloss collection, gold dial, raised figures, outer case leather piqué; another with splendid pillars, balance-spring stud underneath plate; watch, "Thos. Jones, London," about 1680. Wm., apprenticed in 1682 to Henry Jones, C.C. Edwd., apprenticed in 1686 to Wm. Bartram, C.C. Jas., apprenticed in 1687 to Philip Thacke, C.C. Jonathan, apprenticed to Robert Smith, and turned over to Nathaniel De Launder; C.C. 1687. David, C.C. 1687. Sam., apprenticed in 1688 to Edmund Massey, C.C. Henry, apprenticed in 1690 to Hy. Jones, his father; C.C. 1698. Henry, C.C. 1697-8. Richd., London; long-case clock, about 1700. Valentine, C.C. 1704. John, C.C. 1716. John, master C.C. 1762; 1748-63. Saml., Bath; watch, 1769. Jno., London; repeating watch, 1775. Jenkin, 61 St James's St., 1775-83. Owen, Little George St., Minories; livery C.C. 1786; 1780-94. William, 27 Barbican; livery C.C. 1786; 31 Little Moorfields, 1810; 1780-1810. David; watch-pendant maker, 69 Bunhill Row, 1790-94. James, 65 Banner St., 1795-1810. Robert, 49 Little Bartholomew Close, 1800. Wm., White Cross St., 1810-15. Jno., Chester, 1814-28. & Grant, 123 New Bond St., 1815-18. Robert, Ruthin; watch, 1819. Sam., 78 Cheapside, 1820-25. John, 338 Strand, 1821; succeeded by his son, John Jones, a man of high attainments and a successful manufacturer; vice-president of the British Horological Institute; he retired from business in 1885; and died at Send Green, near Woking, 1910, aged 94. & Forester, Hull, 1822. F., 62 Cornhill, 1825. W., 132 Holborn Hill, 1825. John & Timothy, 20 Red Lion St., Clerkenwell, 1825-30. Timothy, 18 Ludgate St., 1826-40.

Jonston Robt., Cumber; clock, about 1770.

Jordan. Jas., Chatham, 1710. Jno., Bristol; watch, silver cock, about 1720; long-case clock, about 1730. Timothy, 40

Snow Hill ; maker of a tall mahogany-case clock, brass dial, period 1780 ; 1769-80. **Aaron,** London, 1790.

Joselin (or **Josslin**), **Edwd.,** apprenticed in 1690 to Jas. Wolverston, C.C; John Hocker served him as apprentice in 1728.

Josephson, —, London ; many watches, Dutch style, 1760-90.

Joslyn, James, New Haven, 1798-1820.

Jouard, L., Paris ; garde visiteur, 1769.

Jourdain. William, apprenticed in 1646 to Robt. Smith, C.C; timepiece with crown wheel escapement, short pendulum with pear-shaped bob, and 8-in. silvered dial ; through a short circular slit in the upper part of the dial is shown a small silvered star, which vibrates with the pendulum, about 1680 ; clock by him, German oak case, dial Dutch style, in the Central Hotel, Kassel ; watch, about 1690. **A.,** 6 Wheeler St., Spitalfields, 1790-94. **R.,** 29 Marshall St., Golden Sq. ; 1835.

Jovat, —, London ; calendar watch, about 1700.

Joyce. George, C.C. 1692. **Jno.,** Ellesmere, 1698. **Stephen,** Moor St., Soho, 1769. **Samuel, & Co.,** 38 Lombard St., 1790-1842. **James,** Whitchurch, a well-known clockmaker, died 1883, aged 62.

Joyne. Jno., apprenticed in 1660 to Jno. Smith, C.C. 1687. **Jno.,** St Germain, Paris ; watch, B.M., square case, crystal cover, 1690-1710.

Judson, Thomas ; sent a letter to C.C. relative to watches seized, 1790.

Juhan, A., Dortdrecht ; watch, 1776.

Juler, Jno., N. Walsham, 1770.

Julian, Gregory, C.C. 1664.

Jullion. John, Brentford, 1730. **& Son,** New Brentford, 1771 ; watch, " J. Julien, Brentford," 1792. **Francis,** London ; long-case clock, about 1780.

Julliott, Solomon, London ; verge watch by him in the Guildhall Museum, date on mainspring, 1738.

Jump. Richard Thos. ; inventor of the proportionate gauge called a sector, which is used chiefly for wheels and pinions ; joined B. L. Vulliamy in 1812. **Joseph,** son of R. T., apprenticed in 1827 to B. L. Vulliamy, with whom he remained till Vulliamy died in 1854 ; afterwards at Bond St. and Pall Mall ; died 1899.

Jung, Herman, a clever Swiss horologist who settled in Clerkenwell ; assassinated 1901.

Jürgensen. Jœrgen, Copenhagen ; died 1811. **Urban,** Copenhagen, son of the foregoing ; born 1776, died 1830 ; an eminent maker ; author of " The Higher Horological Art " and " Principes de la Mesure du Temps " ; Jürgensen was associated with the leading men of his day ; he experimented with compensation balances made of brass and platinum, and strongly advocated the use of gold springs for marine chronometers ; he made many excellent chronometers for the Danish navy, and very successful metallic thermometers. **Louis Urban,** Copenhagen, eldest son and successor of Urban ; born 1806, died 1867. **Jules Frederik,** another son of Urban, was born in 1808 at Locle during a short sojurn of his parents there in 1808 ; on attaining manhood he returned to Locle where he founded a business ; his watches were highly esteemed in America ; he died in 1877. **F. U.,** son of Jules F., published in 1887 a biography of Ingold.

Just. Leonard, St John's Sq., 1790-1825 ; maker of watches for the Chinese market. **Leonard,** Myddelton Sq., 1830-

42. **George,** 22 Anderson's Buildings, City Rd., 1830-42 ; he made watches with movements wholly of steel, except the jewels and the bushes for the larger pivot holes, which were of gold ; they were chiefly for the Chinese market ; the pinion leaves wore into ruts quicker than if working with brass wheels.

Justis & Comp, Well Yard, St Bartholomew's Hospital, 1769.

K. Watch ; tambourine case of brass, stackfreed, foliot balance, signed " A. K." about 1570, Pierpont Morgan collection ; octagonal watch, about the same date, marked " M. K."

Kaiser, Kleyser, & Co., wooden clockmakers, 4 Broad St., 1840.

Kaltenback & Fuller, 77 Blackman St., 1834-42.

Kammerer, Joseph, wooden clockmaker, 51 King St., Borough, 1840.

Kangiesser, S., 24 Southampton St., Strand, 1816-25.

Kanns, John, C.C. 1712.

Kater, Captain Henry, F.R.S., conducted experiments for determining the length of the seconds pendulum in the latitude of London, 1817.

Kay, Jno., London ; long-case chime clock, about 1750.

Keal, Wm., London ; watch, 1799.

Keandler, Chas., Jermyn St., 1793.

Keat. Joseph (? Kent), 19 Cock Hill, Ratcliff, 1810. **Edward,** 69 Banner St., St Luke's, 1830-40. **Mrs Mary Anne,** 19 Broad St., 1840. **Sophia,** 60 Banner St., 1842.

Keate, Robt., Wallingford, 1780.

Keates, Wm., 135 Fleet St., 1783-1800.

Keating, A., 114 Strand, 1796-1815.

Keddon (or **Kedden), Daniel,** Little Britain, C.C. 1717 ; fine japanned long-case clock, about 1730 ; watch, about 1740.

Keef, Thomas, 22 Rosoman St., Clerkenwell, 1835.

Keeling, George, musical clockmaker, Webber St., Blackfriars Rd., 1840.

Keely, W. ; gilder, Orange Court, Clement's Lane, 1790-94.

Keeys, Jeremiah, London ; watch, 1800.

Kefford, Thomas, Royston ; lantern clock, about 1710 ; long Oriental lacquer case clock, about 1730, see Coxall.

Kehlhoff, Frederick, St George-the-Martyr, Southwark ; patented in 1764 (No. 819) a centre-seconds going-barrel watch, with stackfreed and remontoire'.

Kelham, Mathias, near Vintners' Hall, C.C. 1730.

Kell, Jno., C.C., about 1650.

Kellet, Thos., fined by C.C. for defective watch, 1635.

Kellett, —, Bredbury ; long-case clock, about 1770, Mr T. R. Howarth ; at top of the arch is the motto, " Time feasts on all terrestrial things."

Kelley, Allan, Sandwich, U.S.A., 1810-30.

Kello, Simon, apprenticed to John Higgs and turned over to Jos. Jackman ; C.C. 1723.

Kells, Edwd., Shepley, 1770.

Kelly, Richard, Devereux Court, Strand ; long Chippendale case clock, about 1790.

Kelme, —, London ; small timepiece on a horse, in the Massey-Mainwaring collection, 1670.

Kelton, Simon, C.C. 1723.

Kember, Jos. Shaw ; watch, 1776.

Kemble. William, New York, 1786. **J. T.,** Knightsbridge, 1817.

Kemp. Charles, apprenticed to Pretty-

man Sergeant, and turned over to Charles Gretton ; C.C. 1688 ; Thos. Tompion, junr.; apprenticed to him in 1694. **Richard,** C.C. 1701. —, Lewes ; watch, 1760. **& Holman,** Lewes ; watch, 1782. **William,** livery C.C. 1786. **Joseph,** Curtain Rd., 1790.

Kemps. Anthony, 1650. **Matthew,** son of Anthony ; C.C. 1670.

Kendall. Larcum, born at Charlbury, Oxford, 1721 ; apprenticed in London to John Jeffreys, 1735 ; 20 Wood St., Cheapside, 1750 ; Furnival's Inn Court, 1765, when he was one of the judges appointed to report on Harrison's timekeeper ; in 1766 he agreed to make a duplicate for the Commissioners of Longitude, undertaking to faithfully reproduce the various parts without being held responsible for the performance ; the price was to be £450, and he stipulated that one-half should be paid in advance ; the date on this instrument is 1769 ; but it was in January 1770 that he addressed a letter to the Committee desiring them to inspect it. Kendall afterwards made a much simpler instrument than Harrison's, without the remontoire action, and with an ordinary seconds hand ; the date on this is 1771 ; it was presented to the United Service Institution by Rear-Admiral Sir Thomas Herbert, K.C.B., in 1854, when this inscription was engraved on it by Messrs Lambert : " This Timekeeper belonged to Captain Cook, R.N., and was taken by him to the Pacific, 1776. It was again taken to the Pacific by Captain Bligh in the ' Bounty,' 1787. It was taken by the mutineers to Pitcairn Island, and was sold, 1808, by Adams to a citizen of the United States, who sold it at Chili, where it was purchased by Sir Thomas Herbert." There is a fine watch with a remontoire escapement by him in the Guildhall Museum. He died in 1795. —, 17 St John's Sq., 1790-94.

Kendrick. John, C.C. 1719. **John,** C.C. 1726. **Wm.,** 36 Lombard St., 1772.

Keney, Vincent, received £19. 16s. 8d. from Henry VIII. for " xj clocks and dialls," 1530.

Kenfield, Richd., Winton ; fine long-case clock, about 1740.

Kennedy. Thos., Wigan ; watch, 1759. **Patrick,** Philadelphia, 1797. **Jas.,** London ; fine duplex watch, Mr Thos. Fisher, 1813.

Keney, William, threatened with prosecution by C.C. for exercising the art, not being admitted, 1682.

Kenning. Wm., C.C. 1684. **Edwin,** London ; lantern clock, about 1705.

Kennon, Wm., apprenticed in 1656 to Job Betts ; C.C. 1674.

Kent. Henry, Westminster ; C.C. 1646. **Wm.,** apprenticed in 1681 to Sam. Marchant, C.C. **Jas.,** Manchester, 1759. **Jno.,** Manchester, 1770. —, Monmouth ; watch, 1799. **Joseph,** 19 Cock Hill, Ratcliff, 1806-17. **Jno.,** 19 Broad St., Ratcliff, 1817-35.

Kentish. John, Pope's Head Alley, 1758-61. **John, & Haynes,** 18 Cornhill, 1769-88 ; watch, skeleton movement, about 1800, signed " John Kentish, junr."

Kenton, Joseph, admitted C.C. 1686.

Kerby, Thomas F., London ; clocks, about 1760. **Fras.,** St Helier ; long-case clock, about 1810, Mr C. Davis.

Kerner & Paff, 245 Water St., New York, 1796 ; " Musical clocks with figures, and cuckoo clocks " (advt. New York).

Kershaw, George, Tyler's Court, Carnaby Market, 1780-94,

Kersill, William, 21 Aldersgate St., 1775.

Kessborer, Johan, Ulm (South Germany); watch in engraved silver case, second half of seventeenth century, S.K.M.

Kessels, Heinrik Johannes, Altona; a celebrated maker of astronomical clocks; died 1849.

Kettle, G., London; watch, 1795.

Kettlewell, Jno., Ripon, 1833.

Kewell, Thos., apprenticed in 1685 to Richd. Colston, C.C.

Key, Jno., Warrington, 1770.

Keyes, Markham, apprenticed in 1653 to Jere. Gregory, C.C.

Keymes, Joseph, apprenticed in 1673 to Dan. Stevens, C.C.

Keys, David, Craven St., Strand, a well-known manufacturer of watches, died 1887, aged 74.

Keyte, Rd., Whitney, 1770.

Keyzor, Louis, 16 Tottenham Court Rd., 1835-40.

Kiblich, Matthew, Presburg; watch by him, Vienna Treasury, oval white enamel case ornamented with flowers, bezel encrusted with brilliants and emeralds, about 1716.

Kidd. Jno., apprenticed in 1656 to Job Betts, C.C. **Gilbert,** Malton, 1760-80.

Kidder, John, 6 Strand, 1816-23.

Kidson, Wm., York, f., 1614.

Killingworth Jno., 200 Brick Lane, Spitalfields, 1815-18.

Kilminster, Henry, C.C. 1677.

Kimbell, Thomas, 214 Tottenham Court Rd., 1842.

Kinable, —, lyre clock (see p. 319).

King. Thomas, C.C. 1669; marqueterie long-case square dial clock, 1669-90. **Jonathan,** C.C. 1689. **Nehimiah,** lantern clock, Mr C. H. Read, dated 1693. **William,** in "Birching Lane, watchmaker," admitted a freeman of the Cutlers' Company in 1707. **Peter,** Long Acre, C.C. 1715; Mr Norman Shaw has a long-case clock by him in a fine marqueterie case. **William John,** Monkwell St., C.C. 1720; in the B.M. is a watch by him with *repoussé* case, 1730; another example, a repeating watch, 1745. **Henry,** Lincoln's Inn, C.C. 1720; watch, gold *repoussé* case, Schloss collection, h.m., 1786. **John,** C.C. 1729. **Isaac,** Moorfields, 1730. **John,** Gough Sq., 1758-61. **Thomas,** Alnwick, 1773. **Thomas & Benjamin,** 82 Upper East Smithfield, 1802-25. **W.,** 34 High Holborn, 1822-30. **Thomas,** 130 Minories, 1835-42.

Kingman, James, 104 Leadenhall St., livery Goldsmiths' Co. 1774-83.

Kingsmill, George, C.C. 1667.

Kingsnorth, Jno., apprenticed in 1688 to Thos. Stubbs, C.C.

Kinnear, Charles, 33 Frith St., 1833.

Kinning, John, C.C. 1701; watch, encased in glass, B.M., 1700-30.

Kipling, William, Broad St., near Ratcliff Cross; oak long-case clock, square dial, about 1710; watch with sun and moon hour indicators, Whitcombe Greene collection, about 1720; another watch, h.m., 1730; another example, bracket clock, brass arched dial, strike-silent, day of month, elaborately inlaid case of hard wood, prolongation of pendulum seen through arc slot in dial; brought from the Emperor's Summer Palace at Peking, 1860; had then crown escapement, and was a "pull repeater" with eight very sweet bells; engraved back plate, 1705-37. Mr Edward Campbell has a clock by him with Turkish numerals and corner pieces

on the dial in the form of a crescent. "Wm. and John Kipling, London," on clocks about 1750, see Bosley, Charles.

Kippis, Geo., apprenticed in 1687 to Chris. Gould, C.C.

Kirby. Robert, C.C. 1722. **Charles,** London; watch, 1795.

Kirk. John, C.C. 1677. **Joseph,** Nottingham; long-case clock, about 1750. **Wm.,** Stockport, 1760. **Wm.,** Manchester, 1770.

Kirke, Charles, Bristol, Conn., 1840.

Kirnier & Kleyser, 14 Oxford St.; card B.M. 1791.

Kirton. John, apprenticed to Daniel Quare; C.C. 1705. **R.,** enameller, Red Lion St., 1790.

Kissar, Samuel, C.C. 1712.

Kitchen (or **Kitching**). **Jno.,** Nantwich, 1775. **& Lloyd,** Nantwich; long-case clock, about 1790. **B.,** 32 Compton St., 1842.

Kitching, Joshua, 14 Dover St., Piccadilly, 1816-23.

Klaftenberger, C. J., 157 Regent St., a skilful watchmaker, some time vice-president of the Horological Institute; died 1874, aged 79.

Kley. Mr R. Norman Shaw has a musical clock which plays every hour, dating from about 1750, and inscribed "John Kley, London." It was brought from Amsterdam.

Kleyser. Jno., wooden clockmaker, 191 High Holborn, 1790-94. **George, & Co.,** wooden clockmakers, 3 Little Tower Hill, 1790-94. **& Kaltenback,** wooden casemakers, 196 High St., Borough, 1810-25. **T. & J.,** 191 High Holborn, 1810-30. **& Fritschler,** 405 Oxford St., 1835-42. **John,** wooden case-maker, 66 Borough High St., 1840.

Kline, Philadelphia: **Jno.,** 1820; **B.,** 1841.

Kloch, P., Amsterdam; enamelled watch, about 1700.

Kneeshaw, Robt., Stokesley, 1822.

Kneller, Johann Michael, watch, B.M., square brass case with silver filigree overlay, 1630-40.

Knibb. Samuel, C.C. on redemption 1663. **Joseph,** Oxon., C.C. 1670 (see p. 242). **Peter,** C.C. 1677. **John,** Oxon., verge watch movement, with curiously wrought pillars, G.M., style 1690; long-case clock, about 1695; in the Wetherfield collection is a bracket repeating timepiece by him. **Ed.,** apprenticed in 1693 to Joseph Knibb, C.C.

Knifton, Thomas, at Yᵉ Cross Keys, in Lothebury, 1640-57. Fine lantern clock by him (see p. 346). Another specimen is in the possession of Mr A. Stanley Cooke. He was probably succeeded by John Ebsworth.

Knight. Michael, apprenticed to Lionel Wythe and turned over to Thos. Tompion; C.C. 1681; fine long-case clock, bird and flower marqueterie, about 1690. **Richard,** C.C. 1682. **Charles,** Flower-de-luce, Great Russell St.; C.C. 1685-97. **Thos.,** apprenticed in 1686 to Dorcas Bouquett. **Henry,** C.C. 1723. **Wm.,** West Marden, about 1750. **—,** Thaxted, 1760. **John,** 6 Carpenters' Buildings, London Wall, 1768. **—,** Dunmow, 1780. **Benjamin,** New St., Dockhead, 1790. **—,** West Marden, about 1790. **Valentine,** gold dial maker and engine turner, Newcastle Place; first president of the British Horological Institute; born 1793, died 1867. **Jno.,** Portsea; watch, 1837.

Knollys, Francis, apprenticed in 1669

to Jno. Harris, C.C.

Knott, Robt., apprenticed in 1682 to Clement Forster, C.C.

Knottesford. William, apprenticed to Hy. Child; C.C. 1663; master 1693; bracket clock, about 1680, with seconds dial and maintaining power; walnut case with spiral ebony columns as seen on hoods of long-case clocks; circular silver watch, B.M., also a repeater in S.K.M., h.m., 1684, and a large clock-watch, G.M. **Jno.,** apprenticed in 1680 to Wm. Knottesford, C.C.; month chiming clock in fine marqueterie long case, Wetherfield collection, about 1700, inscribed "John Knotsford, London."

Knowles. Joseph, Epsom; watch, 1760. **James,** 2 Hospital Row, Chelsea, 1835-40.

Knox. John, Belfast, 1729-83; **John,** nephew of the preceding, to whom he was apprenticed, started business in Larne, and on the death of his uncle succeeded him in High St., Belfast; engraved a portrait of Washington for a watch paper; retired 1816, see Neill, R. **Alex.,** Berwick, 1770. **Wm.,** Paisley, 1780.

Köberle, Wilhelmus, Eijstet (Eichstadt, South Germany); early clock-watch in case of gilt brass, pierced and engraved, S.K.M.

Koch, Johann, Cöllen; alarm calendar watch, about 1630, Miss M. Humphreys.

Kock, Pieter, Haerlem; watch, 1776. **Peter,** Harlem; watch, 1780.

Koppaun, Christof, German square table clock, S.K.M., signed and dated 1582.

Koster, Dirk, Amsterdam; watch with sun and moon indicators, G.M., about 1695.

Kotte, Jacob, antique watch, Shandon collection, about 1630.

Kover, —, handsome watch, gold *repoussé* case, about 1720.

Kratzer, see Cratzer.

Krauth, F. T., Gt. Hampton St., Birmingham, died 1909, aged 62.

Kreitt-Mayer, Johann, about 1645; watch ascribed to Bruce (see p. 145).

Kreizer, Conrad, watch in the form of a cross, Vienna Treasury, case of crystal, dial of silver, dial of gold, with instruments of the Passion engraved thereon, about 1600; octagonal watch by him, S.K.M., about 1610; octagonal watch, about 1600.

Krenckel, Peter, Eüchstet (or Füchstet); alarm table clock belonging to Major W. J. Myers, S.K.M., about 1700.

Kroese, J. P., Amsterdam; watch, fine enamel painting of Cleopatra; about 1770.

Kullberg, Victor, born at Gothland, Sweden, 1824. In 1851 he came to London, where he died in 1890. One of the most brilliant and successful horologists of the nineteenth century. Inventor of a compensation balance with flat rim.

Kyezor, Louis, 46ᴀ Edgware Rd., 16 Tottenham Court Rd., and 3 Great Turnstile, 1842.

Kyffin, Edward, apprenticed in 1682 to Jno. Brown, C.C.

Kynvyn, Jonas, maker of a clock belonging to the Earl of Essex, 1593.

Laborne, Christopher, Gt. Driffield, died 1831.

Labru, —, London; hexagonal table clock, about 1680.

Lacey. Paul, Bristol, 1780. **Chas.,** 12 Ludgate St., 1783.

Lacon, Peter, London; watch, 1785.

Lacour, Daniel, New St., Covent Garden, 1825.

La Croix. —, Rue Denis, Paris; handsome clock, about 1790 (see p. 322). —, Geneva; watch, 1814.

Ladd. Sam., C.C. 1709. **J.**, 35 Cornhill, 1823.

Ladoneau, Jean, Paris; clockmaker to Louis XIV., 1680.

Lafons, see De Lafons.

Lafosse, Wm., 32 Old Broad St., 1738-94.

Lagoe, Jno., apprenticed in 1671 to Richd. Halsted, C.C.

Laidlaw, Thomas, 16 Salisbury Sq., 1770-94; hon. freeman C.C. 1781.

L'Ainge, —, 82 Cheapside, 1842.

Lainy. David, watch in the Guildhall Museum, about 1670. **John**, C.C. 1720.

Laisne, Sibelin, Neuchatel, about 1750.

Lake. Bryan, C.C. 1674. **Thos.**, Taunton, 1770.

Lamb (or **Lambe**). Several generations beginning with Thomas Lambe, 1630; in 1704 it was reported to the C.C. that among other well-known makers the name of Lamb had been engraved on watches by persons in Amsterdam, which watches were sold as of English make. **Abraham**, apprenticed in 1651 to Wm. Petit, C.C. **Simon**, apprenticed 1669 to Wm. Glazier, C.C.; long-case clock, about 1700, inscribed "Simon Lamb, Rochester" (see p. 368). **Luke**, apprenticed in 1683 to Johnson Weekes, C.C. **Jno.**, Henrietta St., C.C. 1714. **Benj.**, 21 St John's Sq., 1769-79. **& Webb**, 21 St John's Sq., Clerkenwell, 1780-95. **Thos.**, Union St., Spitalfields, 1790. **Jno.**, 13 Red Lion St., Clerkenwell, 1822-52. **Sarah**, 2 Lower Queen's Row, Pentonville, 1842.

Lambden, Richd., apprenticed in 1685 to Joseph Hussey, C.C.

Lambe. Thomas, C.C. 1632. **Edward**, C.C. 1675; long-case clock, about 1690. **John**, 29 Fetter Lane, 1774-1800.

Lambell, Samuel, Northampton, 1750.

Lambert. Pierre, Abbeville; watch, about 1680. **Jno.**, London; Mr Herbert Southam has a long-case square dial clock by him, the movement dated 1703. **Wm.**, Cannon St.; C.C. 1730. **Nicholas**, London, 1750-70; long-case clock (see p. 378); chiming clock by him on the mantelpiece of the vestry of Lady Huntingdon's Chapel, Bath, with the inscription, "This clock is the property of the Church at the Vineyards, Bath, given by the Countess of Huntingdon for the use of the minister for the time being." **Jas.**, London; watch, 1760. **John**, 2 Tichborne St., 1775-1810. —, Besançon; French enamelled watch, about 1780. **Francis**, partner with Hamlet in 1800; afterwards started business at 12 Coventry St., and subsequently entered into partnership with Rawlings at the same address. **Henry**, 93 Piccadilly, 1840. **Henry**, 119 Cheapside, 1842.

Lamione, A., Philadelphia, 1811.

Lampe, John, Henrietta St., admitted C.C. 1713; Chippendale long-case clock, large hood and gallery round the top, inscription on disc, "John Lampe, London"; 1713-65.

Lamplough, Jno., Bridlington, 1822.

Lamport, —, Bow St., Bloomsbury; watch, h.m., 1810.

Lamson, Charles, Salem, 1850, see Balch.

Lamude, Peter, apprenticed in 1684 to Nat. Delander, C.C. **Jno.**, Chard, about 1740. **Reu.**, Chard; watch, 1760.

Lancaster. Richd., apprenticed in 1677 to Thos. Hollis, C.C. **Nicholas**, apprenticed in 1679 to Stafford Freeman, C.C.

Richard, apprenticed in 1684 to Hy. Merriman, C.C. **Francis**, London; a good workman, 1790-1800.

Landlen, Thos., 16 Salisbury Court, 1794.

Landre. Pierre, Blois; skull watch, Pierpont Morgan collection, about 1630. **L.**, Brussels, about 1650. **P.**, Brussels, 1700.

Lane. Jno., apprenticed in 1679 to Sam. Vernon, C.C. **W.**, Calstone; long-case chiming clock, about 1750. **Henry**, Bristol; long-case clock, tidal time in arch, and above, "High Water at Bristol Key," about 1780. **Geo.**, 185 High Holborn, 1893.

Langcroft, Richard, C.C. 1718.

L'Ange, A., 51 Cornhill, 1835.

Lange, Adolf Ferdinand, born and apprenticed at Dresden; afterwards worked for Winnerl, Paris; an excellent and progressive watchmaker; settled at Glashutte, Saxony; died 1875, aged 60. **Christian**, 99 Strand, 1870-86.

Langford. Gowen, C.C. 1652. **Ellis**, apprenticed in 1663 to Gowen Langford; C.C. 1672. **Wm.**, Ludlow, 1770. **Thos.**, hon. freeman, C.C. 1781; long-case clock, "Langford, Southampton," about 1780; White Horse Hotel, Romsey; broken arch bracket clock, enamel dial, about 1795.

Langhorne, Thomas, Threadneedle St., liveryman C.C. 1776.

Langley. Thomas, C.C. 1664. **Cornelius**, C.C. 1706.

Langstaff, Thos., Middlesboro', 1843.

Langton, Jas., Founders' Ct., Lothbury, 1776.

Langwith. Jas., York, f., 1722. **Sam.**, York, 1770.

Lansdown, Bath, see Haddack.

Lanson, J., Bradford: long-case clock, about 1750.

Lants, Niklas, Innsbruck, 1550.

Larard. Thos., Hull, 1814-40. **Jas.**, 7 New Bridge St., 1830-42.

Larcay, L., Paris; an eminent horologist, 1725-35; he is spoken of by Thiout as Larsé.

Large. Jonathan, London; long-case clocks, about 1790. **Augustus**, 51 Cornhill, 1840.

Larmett, Abraham, C.C., about 1650.

Laroch, John, 18 High St., Bloomsbury, 1815-25.

Lasarus, Abraham, Gun Yard, 1760-65.

Lashbrook, Jno., apprenticed in 1655 to Wm. Pettitt, C.C. **Thos.**, apprenticed in 1693 to Richd. Conyers, C.C. **Henry**, C.C. 1715.

Lasoffe, William, 52 Old Broad St., 1765-70.

Lassel. Toxteth Park, Liverpool; long-case clock, "Lassel, Park," about 1735. **William**, several long-case clocks, 1740-70. **Thurstan**, long-case clock, about 1775.

Lasseter, William, Arundel; maker of long-case clocks, about 1770.

Last, W. R., Yarmouth; watch, 1810.

Latham. Hy., apprenticed in 1655 to Humfrey Downing, C.C. **John**, C.C. 1700; watch with gold *repoussé* case, S.K.M., 1720; in the Church of the Cappucino, Cadiz, is a long-case clock by him; Mr Beck, the Plough Inn, Cadsdean, Princes Risborough, Bucks, has another in a mahogany case, inscribed "John Latham, London." **Wm.**, Macclesfield, 1775. **T.**, London; watch, 1795. **Jas.**, Preston, 1814.

Latimer, Jas., Philadelphia, 1819.

Latour, René, admitted C.C. 1730.

Laud, Thos. In 1638 Thos. Fitton was apprenticed to him; C.C.

Launay, David F., watchmaker, 9 Warren St., New York, 1801, "has a high finished clock which decorated the library of the late King of France, made by Charles Berthand, of the Royal Academy; its original price 5,000 livres; to be sold for 500 dollars."

Laundy, Jno., apprenticed in 1692 to Thos. Walford, C.C.

Lauriere, J., 62 St James's St., 1822-30.

Lautier, Bath, see Vigne.

Laver, Benjamin, 4 Bruton St., Berkeley Sq., 1790-1800.

Lavespeare, Wm., C.C., about 1650.

Law. Isaac, forbidden to work by C.C. in 1632, afterwards made free of the Company. **Silvester**, apprenticed in 1689 to Richard Baker, C.C. **Timothy**, apprenticed in 1690 to Wm. Carr, C.C. **Jere.**, Rochdale, 1780. **Thomas**, 27 Thomas St., Southwark, 1790-94. **Anthony**, 68 Borough High St., 1840-42.

Lawell, Paul, C.C. 1653.

Lawley, Bernhard, 253 Borough High St., 1840-42.

Lawrence. Hy., apprenticed in 1691 to Richd. Colston, C.C. Lancaster: **Jno.**, 1761, f.; **Wm.**, 1785, f. Bristol: **Henry**, 1770; **Wm.**, 1780; —, Bath, 1763; **w.**, Thame, 1765. **Thos.**, London; watch, 1772. **James**, 13 Bolingbroke Row, Walworth Rd., 1835. **G.**, 74 Paradise St., Rotherhithe, 1835-42. **& Son**, 171 Tooley St., 1835.

Lawrie, —, Carlisle; clock, about 1770.

Lawriere, Jno., 13 St James's St., Pall Mall, 1815-19.

Lawson. Sam., Keighley, 1740. **Jno.**, Bradford, 1750. **Jno.**, London; watch, 1763. **Thos.**, Keighley, 1765. **Wm.**, Newton-le-Willows, 1770. **Ramsey**, Wigan, 1770. **Wm.**, Keighley, 1780; long-case clock bearing the inscription :—

"So glide the hours, So wears the day.
These moments measure life away."

John Edwd., 58 Bishopsgate Within, 1800-25; livery C.C. 1812. **W.**, Keighley, 1810-14. **Jno.**, Warrington, 1818.

Lawton, Thos., London; watch, 1820.

Laxton. Thomas, C.C. 1642. **Thomas**, C.C. 1653.

Laybourn, Christopher, Driffield, 1770.

Layfield, Robt., Lancaster, 1785, f.

Layton. John, C.C. 1653. **Francis**, C.C. 1726. **Thomas**, Dean St., liveryman C.C. 1776; 82 Wardour St., 1794-1823.

Lazare, —, a Servian; made a clock for Moscow, 1404.

Lazarus. H., 112 Upper East Smithfield, 1815. **J.**, 15 Carter St., Houndsditch, 1825; 39 Minories, 1830. **J.**, 13 Oakley St., Lambeth, 1835. **H. L.**, 3 Bury St., St Mary Axe, 1835. **E.**, **& Son**, 3 Bury St., St Mary Axe, 1840-42.

Lazenby. R., Knightsbridge; on a small clock, with sunk seconds and day of the month circles, about 1770. **Wm.**, Paradise Row, Chelsea; card B.M., 1784.

Lea, Thomas, Old Jewry, livery C.C. 1766; master, 1782; 1760-83.

Leach. Thos., Lombard St., 1753-60. **Caleb**, Plymouth, U.S.A., 1776-90. **Benj.**, Winchester; watch, 1790; long-case clocks by him are much esteemed in Hampshire; in 1803 he submitted an estimate of seven guineas to repair the Winchester Town Hall clock, and substitute a long pendulum for the short one then existing, which would · necessitate a new wheel and pinion. **Jno.**, Kirkham, 1816. **Chas.**, 59 King William St., London Bridge, 1820-30.

Leadbeater. Peter, Congleton, 1818-34. Chas., Wigan, 1820. Thos., Sandbach, 1833.

Leadbetter, William, Cross Keys Court, Little Britain, 1785-94.

Leah. Samuel Henry, 29 Bath St., City Rd., 1823-42. Sam. Hy., junr., Mare St., Hackney, 1835; 79 Shoreditch, 1842.

Leake. Faith, apprenticed to John White, but served Daniel Quare; C.C. 1685. George, apprenticed to John Wright, C.C. 1693.

Leathwaite, Geo., Ulverstone, 1770.

Leavenworth, Mark, also Wm., Waterbury, Conn., 1810-30.

Leaver. Nat., apprenticed in 1679 to John Wright, senr., C.C.; bracket clock, about 1730, inscribed "Leaver, London." Wm., 45 Great Sutton St., 1822-30.

Le Blond; watch, signed "Le Blond," in rock crystal case, about 1600. Robt., Artillery Lane, Stewart St.; livery Blacksmiths' Company, 1770; watch, 1770; bracket clock, 1790.

Le Bon, Alex., Paris; maker of equation clocks, 1727-30; clock, Jones collection, S.K.M., about 1770, inscribed "Le Bon à Paris."

Lechaud, J.; one of the first makers of lever escapements in Geneva, died 1882.

Leckie, Andrew, watch, 1780.

Le Clerk, Daniel, Paris; watch, Pierpont Morgan collection, about 1630.

Lecomte (Lecount), Daniel, brother C.C. 1676. "Taken from Mr Robert Murrel, on the 5th inst., by Foot Pads, near Newington, a Pendulum Watch made by Daniel Lecount" (Lond. Gaz., Aug. 4-8, 1692). The Hon. H. Hannen has a clock by him with long case, finely inlaid; clock-watch, Turkish numerals, silver-gilt pierced case, Pierpont Morgan collection. James, C.C. 1687. "Stolen a silver watch, made by Mr Le Count" (Lond. Gaz., Feb. 15-18, 1691). J. R., 60 Dean St., Soho, 1763-83.

Le Contandois, Nicolas, Paris, 1554 (see p. 304).

Lecoultre. Antoine, La Valée, Switzerland, 1825. H. A., talented Swiss horologist; devised an improved form of shifting-sleeve keyless mechanism, died 1881.

Lecount, Peter, livery C.C. 1810; 36 Pitfield St., 1823.

Ledart, Richard, in Strasburg; watch, about 1620.

Ledeur, —, London; hexagonal table clock, about 1600; small octagonal watch, rock crystal case, signed "R. Ledeur," Pierpont Morgan collection.

Ledieu, Jas., Soho, 1817.

Ledru, Wm., London, 1795.

Lee. Ezekial, apprenticed 1668 to Jeffrey Baily, C.C., lantern clock, about 1700. Cuthbert, C.C. 1676; long-case month clock, about 1710, signed "Cuthbert Lee, Jewen St." Underwood, apprenticed in 1688 to Edwd. Staunton, C.C. Christopher, apprenticed in 1691 to Wm. Young, C.C. Samuel, C.C. 1694; long-case clock, arch dial, burr walnut case with black carved mouldings, Wetherfield collection, about 1720. Roger, Leicester; watch by him, about 1700, Leicester Museum. John, C.C. 1719. Thomas, apprenticed to Francis Robinson, C.C. 1730. George, Lombard St., 1737-40. John, 31 Noble St., Forster Lane, 1800-4. Isaac, 10 Devonshire Buildings, Great Dover St., 1840-42.

Leeds, W. H., 20 Wilderness Row, 1817.

Leekey. Gabriel, 15 Basinghall St., 1755-78. Gabriel, probably son of the foregoing, C.C. 1778-1815, see also Cabrier.

Leeming. Edwd., livery C.C. 1787. Edward, watch-case maker, 8 Little Britain, 1790-94.

Lees. Jonathan, Bury, 1770. Thomas, Bury, 1790-1816. Wm., Haslingdon, 1816. Sam., Ashton under-Lyne, 1818. Jno., Middleton, 1818. Thomas, Drury Lane, 1821-32. Thos., Chorley, 1851. J. Henry, Chorley, 1861.

Leeson, William, Coleshill, Birmingham; well known as a maker of turret clocks throughout the midland counties; died 1886, aged 77.

Le Faucheur, Alexandre, Paris; horologer to Louis XV. in 1746; his son Jean Ignace succeeded him in 1773. In December 1905 a clock by Alex. le Faucheur fetched 1,150 guineas at Christie's.

Le Febuce, Charles (French), admitted C.C. 1687.

Le Febure, E., Rouen; watch, about 1660.

Lefebury. Dan., apprenticed in 1686 to Dan Lecompte, C.C. Chas., C.C. 1687.

Lefebvre, Th., Rue St Louis, Paris; garde visiteur, 1769.

Lefferts (Chas.) & Hall, Philadelphia, 1819.

Leffin, Thomas, C.C. 1720.

Lefosse, Wm., 52 Old Broad St., 1769-72.

Leg, Jno., London; a good workman, taught by Earnshaw, 1780.

Le Gaigneur, Jean, master clockmaker in Paris. Received in 1639 the sum of 1,500 francs for a clock for the Château de Saint-Germain-en-Laye.

Legeips, John, London; in the B.M. a very large repeating watch with silver case decorated in repoussé, 1720-30.

Legg, John, C.C. 1724; watch, signed "John Legg, Blechingly," 1787.

Le Grand. James, C.C. 1641. Francis, C.C. 1647. Simon, Paris; clockmaker to the King, 1657.

Legrand, James, junr., C.C. 1664.

Legrande, —, Rouen, 1552.

Le Gros, P. J., 1 Upper Crown St., Westminster; bracket clock, about 1800. In 1817 Philip Gross carried on business at 12 Panton St., Haymarket.

Le Guay. Fine Boulle clock with bracket inscribed "Guillaume Le Guay, à Paris, au Louvres," about 1750.

Leguesse, L. J. (see p. 318).

Lehr, Sebastian; clockmaker to the city of Nuremberg; died 1556.

Le Huray, Nich., Philadelphia, 1819.

Leicester, Jas., Drury Lane; pull repeating clock with visible pendulum, about 1710. Black lacquer long-case clock, inscribed "Ye Strand, London."

Leif, G. T., Sheffield, 1821.

Leigh. Thomas, C.C. 1730. Wm., 71 Oxford St., 1792. & Phillips, 40 Mansell St., 1840.

Leighton, —, Warrington; clock, about 1770.

Leignes, Charles Peter, Northumberland St., Strand, 1790-94.

Lejeune, —, Paris; enamelled watch, about 1780.

Lello, James, apprenticed in 1647 to Thos. Alcock; C.C. in 1656, on producing his masterpiece with his name, its genuineness being attested by Samuel Betts.

Le Loutre; "horloger du Roy, Paris," 1754-80 (see p. 335).

Lemaindre, Nicholas, Blois, large alarm watch in pierced and engraved brass gilt case, S.K.M., 1620-30.

Lemaire à Blois; hexagonal watch, rock

crystal case, Wallace collection, about 1610.

Le Maire, London; watches, Nelthropp collection, about 1700.

Lemaitre, Paul, watch tool maker, 28 Grafton St., 1790-1810.

Leman, Thos., London; watch, 1738.

Lemand, —, Blois, about 1580.

Lemann, Johan, Wien; clock, about 1800.

Le Mazurier, —, Rue de la Comedie-Française, Paris; garde visiteur, 1769.

Lemmon. Edwd., London; watch, 1790. Hy., 19 Grenville St., Hatton Garden, 1835; 6 Upper North Place, Gray's Inn, 1842.

Le Montjoye, Paris; clock, Wallace collection, about 1770.

Lemude, Reuben, long-case clock, about 1715.

Lenham, Wm., London; watches, 1815-25.

Lenker, Elias, Nuremberg, celebrated silver clock case maker, died 1591 (see p. 88).

Lenoir à Rennes, watch winding from the centre of the dial, G.M., about 1700.

Le Noir, Baptiste, Paris; alarm watch, brass case, pierced and chased, about 1760, Pierpont Morgan collection. Marie Toussaint, fils, cadets place du pont St Michel, Paris; garde visiteur in 1769. Eight watch and clockmakers of that name at about the same period, Etienne Le Noir being the most celebrated (see p. 317).

Lens, William, C.C. 1711.

Lenwood, Sam., apprenticed in 1655 to Thos. Claxton, C.C.

Leon, George Isaac, 56 Great Prescot St., 1842.

Lepaute. Jean André, born at Montmedi, 1709, attained considerable eminence as a clockmaker in Paris; was appointed "horloger du Roy." He improved the pin-wheel escapement of Amant by putting pins on both sides of the wheel. Lepaute constructed several fine turret clocks and clocks for the Louvre at Paris, wound by means of an air current and fan, a method re-invented recently. He made many curious timepieces (equation, one wheel clocks, &c.), and was the author of an excellent "Traité d'Horlogerie" (Paris, 1760), revised and augmented, says Moinet, by the celebrated Lalande. In the second edition of this work appears Lalande's treatise on "perfect pitching." In the Jones collection at S.K.M. is a fine clock in case of Vincennes porcelain and ormolu with the date letter for 1754 and signed "Lepaute de Belle fontaine à Paris." Twelve-month timepiece by him at Windsor Castle (see p. 312); there are four clocks by him in the Wallace collection. Jean Baptiste, brother and pupil of J. A.; continued his business and was in turn succeeded by his sons.

Lepine. —, "There is lately arriv'd in this city, Monsieur de l'Epine, Engineer and Machinist of the late King of France, who has brought over with him a piece of ingenuity, which is an Opera by Machines, that had been seen by his Majesty, by their Royal Highnesses the Princesses, likewise by a great number of persons of quality of this kingdom, with their general applause and satisfaction. And being to make but a short stay here, he invites the curious to come and see the said machine, giving no other explication of the same, only that there are symphonies, musick-master, whistler, drawing of the curtain, changes of scenes, thunder and lightnings, &c., and what surprises the more, is, that all is performed without any body's touching it. To be seen from Ten in the morning to Ten at night, at the Mews Chocolate House near Charing Cross, up one pair of stairs. Price Half a Crown" (*Daily Post*, Feb. 1720). This is of interest, because the Lepine referred to was probably the father of John Antoine, a watchmaker of remarkable attainments who is referred to below. **Jean Antoine**, was born at Gex, in France, in 1720, and is said to have been apprenticed to one Decrose of Grand Sacconex, Switzerland; at the age of 24 he went to Paris and worked for the elder Caron; afterwards he established a reputation, and became watchmaker to Louis XV.; about 1770 he introduced bars for carrying the upper pivots of a watch train instead of a top plate, rearranged the movement, dispensed with the fusee, used the cylinder escapement, and a mainspring barrel arbor supported at one end only. Forty or fifty watchmakers having been exiled from Geneva, Voltaire engaged Lepine to establish a watch factory at Ferney, about a league from Geneva. Voltaire for a time ensured its success by persuading political friends to buy the watches, but after a few years the artisans returned to Geneva and Lepine to Paris, where he died in 1814. The business was continued by his grand-nephew. In 1902, a clock by Lepine in an altar shaped case of ormolu, with figures by Falconet, and dating from about 1760, fetched 450 guineas at Christie's (see p. **318**). —, High St., Canterbury; watch, 1805.

Leplastrier. John, 138 Upper Shadwell, 1790; 125 Minories, 1815. **Louis**, 142 High St., Shadwell, 1804-15. **& Son**, 142 High St., Shadwell, 1820-28. **Isaac**, 17 King William St., Strand, 1828; 21 Holles St., Cavendish Sq., 1840-42; livery C.C. 1829. **& Son**, 20 Ludgate Hill, 1835. **& Young**, London; good bracket clock, oak case, about 1840; Mr Kimpton. **Louis**, 50 Alfred St., City Rd., 1842.

Leptrope, —, London; long-case clock, about 1740.

Le Queux, see Pierre.

Lerolles, fine ormolu cased clock signed "Lerolles Freres," about 1760, sold for £336 at Christie's in 1902; on another clock in the possession of Mr Hy. Townsend is a representation of Amphitrite in Neptune's chariot, accompanied by her son blowing his concha to still the ocean.

Leroux. Alexander, C.C. 1706. **Jno.**, London; watch, 1710. —, Rue Guenegaud, Paris; maker of repeating watches, 1770-89. **Jno.**, 8 Charing Cross; hon. freeman, C.C. 1781; there is a fine watch by him in the Guildhall Museum (see p. **156**); 1750-1800, see Rigby, Jas.

Le Roy. "Lost a Gold Watch, made in Paris, not so broad as a shilling, in a case of black leather with gold nails, on the 11th instant, about 11 at night, betwixt King Street, Westminster and Convent Garding. Whoever gives notice to Mr Le Roy at the sign of the Pearle of Venice, in St James Street, Convent Garding, shall have three pounds for his pains" (*Mercurius Publicus*, 8th Jan. 1662). This is interesting as showing that one of the French family of Le Roy resided here before the time of the distinguished Parisian member, Julien. **Julien**, Paris; a scientific watchmaker, born 1686, died 1759; he devised a form of repeating

mechanism much used in French watches, and substituted springs for the bell in use before (see p. **312**); two fine watches by him, Wallace collection, and one in the Pierpont Morgan collection. **Pierre**, eldest son and successor of Julien Le Roy, born 1717, died 1785, the most eminent of French horologists; among his conceptions was a form of duplex escapement and an escapement on which the present chronometer escapement is founded; in 1766 he exhibited a chronometer having a compensation balance composed of mercurial thermometer tubes, a plan afterwards adopted by Loseby.

Leroy. Chas., Paris; 1765, succeeded by Cachard; clock, about 1808, signed "Leroy & Fils" (see p. **327**). **Theodore Marie**, Paris, chronometer maker, died 1899, aged 72.

Lesage, Augustus, Cockspur St., 1775; St James's, Haymarket, 1788.

Le Schegs, Abraham, Amsterdam, 1730 (see p. **155**).

Leschot. Jean Frederick, apprenticed in Geneva to P. J. Droz in 1784. **Georges Auguste**, (Geneva); son of Jean F., born 1800, died 1884; in 1840 he designed a series of machines for watchmaking on the factory system; it is claimed that he was the first to make lever escapements with draw on the pallets, but in this he was certainly anticipated by Emery (p. **407**).

Lescot, Pierre, Paris; cruciform watches, about 1588.

Leslie. Jas., 6 Maiden Lane, Covent Garden, 1784-88, seconds and calendar watch, Schloss collection, about 1786; 5 Parliament St., 1790-94; 35 Oxford St.; card B.M., 1799. **Robt.**, Philadelphia, 1788-91. **Robert**, Merlin Place, Clerkenwell; patentee of pumping keyless work (No. 1,920); 1793. **& Price**, Philadelphia, 1799.

Lesser, T., Paris; enamelled watch, S.K.M., about 1770.

Lessware, —, Dublin; large trunk-dial timepiece, about 1800.

Lester. Thomas, C.C. 1697. —, Lombard St., 1774. **Robert**, Philadelphia, 1791-98.

Lestourgeon. David, brother C.C. 1698; watch, sun and moon hour indicator, Schloss collection, dated 1696 (see p. **182**); another watch with finely pierced cock and pillars; curious pendulum watch, Pierpont Morgan collection; on the movement is a medallion portrait of William III. and the date 1702; inlaid long-case clock, flat top, about 1715; a specimen of his work is also in the G.M.; 1690-1731. **David**, C.C. 1721-51. **Thomas**, 49 High Holborn; maker of long-case clocks, 1760-75.

L'Estrange, David, C.C. 1697.

Letwitch, William, 42 Lombard St., 1769-72.

Leudl, Johan; maker of a skull watch, about 1630 (see p. **111**).

Leumas, J. & L., London; watch, 1828.

Leutier, Pierre, Paris; timekeeper mounted on the back of a finely moulded bull of Dresden china, about 1750.

Levasseur, Firmin, Frith St., Soho, 1825-56.

Levens, John, Shoemakers' Row, Blackfriars, 1790-94.

Lever, Ben., 3 Bruton St., 1792.

Levin. Moses, 7 Cook's Court, Carey St., 1790-94. **Lewin**, 63 Prescot St., 1804; 51 Mansell St., 1815; 123 Leadenhall St., 1830.

Levitt. Jno., apprenticed in 1681 to Robert Williamson, C.C. —, sometime

partner with Tobias, whose nephew he was. **Levy. Michael**, Hull, 1770. **Hyam**, 121 Whitechapel High St., 1775-85. **Joseph**, New Round Court, Strand, 1780-85. **Lyon**, 121 Whitechapel High St., 1780-85. **M. & C.**, 19 Maiden Lane, Covent Garden, 1790. **Philip**, 30 Jewry St., Aldgate, 1798-1803. **Jonas**, 18 Somerset St., 1800; 135 Whitechapel, 1810; 38 Minories, 1820. **J.**, Coventry St., Haymarket, 1815. **B.**, High St., Whitechapel, 1820. **J., & Son**, 49 Tooley St., 1820. **& Co.**, 408 Strand, 1825. **A.**, 17 Camomile St., 1825-35. **S.**, 19 Crutched Friars, 1830. **Jonas**, 13 Bevis Marks, admitted free of the C.C. by redemption, being the first Jew, 1831; 1820-42. **A.**, 183 Ratcliff Highway, 1835. **Abraham**, 36 Trinity Sq., Tower Hill, 1840-42. **& Moss**, 1 Liverpool Buildings, Bishopsgate, 1842.

Levyson, Montague, 125 Pall Mall, 1840.

Lewin, William, C.C. 1731.

Lewis. E., London; small watch, about 1590, Mr F. A. Poynder. **John**, C.C. 1705. **Ambrose**, C.C. 1725. **T.**, London; watch, 1776. **Joseph**, 38 Foster Lane, 1783. **& Alston**, 30 Bishopsgate Within, 1815-25. **Henry**, London; watch, 1830.

Ley. William, C.C. 1711. **Jno. K.**, London; about 1760.

Leyden, see Stubbs & Co.

Leyland, Thos., Prescot, 1816.

L'Hospital, J., 13 Oxenden St., Haymarket, 1842.

Liddel, Chas., Stockton, 1770.

Liddell, Joseph, Old Swinford, Worcester, 1760.

Liddiard, Thomas, 54 St Paul's Churchyard, 1775-83.

Liddle, Jno., Morpeth, 1770. **Adam**, Newry; long-case clock, about 1830, Mr J. W. Gunnis.

Lief, Geo., Sheffield, 1814.

Lietuyt, John, from Delft; 1368 (see p. **43**).

Lieutaud, Honoré, Marseille; watch, about 1750 (see p. **153**).

Light. John, C.C. 1648. **Ben.**, apprenticed in 1687 to Geo. Cawdren, C.C. **Jno.**, Lit. Old Baily, C.C. 1730.

Lightfoot, Peter, a monk, maker of the Glastonbury and Wimborne clocks (see p. **41**), 1335.

Like, George, 29 Butcher's Row, 1785-94.

Lillie, Charles, corner of Beaufort Buildings, Strand; "a seller of watches, &c.," 1710.

Lilly, —, Smithfield Bars, 1775.

Limeburner, John, Philadelphia, 1791.

Limmard, —, 54 St Paul's Churchyard, 1796.

Limoniere, Stephen, C.C. 1712.

Limpard, John; a watch by him in the B.M., about 1620 (see p. **136**).

Linaker, Samuel; oval watch, Pierpont Morgan collection, about 1610. Samuel Linnaker was named in the Charter of the Clockmakers' Company to be one of the assistants (see p. **209**).

Lincoln, —, London; bracket clock, about 1790.

Lind. Nich., 4 Norman St., Old St., 1780-95; watch, silver cock. **John**, Philadelphia, 1791-99. **William**, apprenticed to William Harris, admitted C.C. 1796.

Lindd, Hy., Farnham; lantern clock, about 1700.

Lindemann, G. H., director of the Horological School at Glashütte, died 1885.

Lindesey (or **Lindsay**), **George**, watchmaker to George III.; a verge movement by him in the Guildhall Museum; died

1776. A splendid mahogany long-case three-train tune-playing clock in the Wetherfield collection, signed "Geo. Lindsay ser^t to the Prince of Wales London" (see p. 383). Fine long-case clock with dead-beat escapement, about 1770.

Lindley, —, 10 St Martin's Court, Old St., 1810.

Lindsey. Wm., London; watch, G.M., about 1780. **John,** 69 Banner St., 1825.

Lindstrom, London; bracket clock, strikes the hours with but one barrel, about 1800.

Linford. Thomas, London; watch, 1626. **Hy.,** apprenticed in 1691 to Edwd. Orton, C.C.

Lingford, Jno., Nottingham; watch, 1798.

Linley, Thos., Leather Lane, C.C. 1732.

Linnet, John, 9 Cursitor St., 1815-25.

Linney, John; watch-case maker and liner, Featherstone St., 1790.

Lipp. Nicholas, Basle; maker of a remarkable clock at Lyons, 1598. **Peter,** Pool Terrace, St Luke's; a noted finisher of repeating watches; died 1848, aged 79.

Lippyus, see Lipp.

Lipscomb, Benj., London; maker of long-case clocks, about 1760.

Lipsy, Dan., 136 Old St., 1817.

Liptrop, Peter; a well-known wheel-cutter; born in Prescot, 1793; died in London, 1879.

Liptrot, Wm., London; watch, Mr H. Hogarth, about 1780.

Lister. Thos., Luddenden, Yorkshire, born 1718, died 1779. **John,** Noble St., C.C. 1730. **Thos.,** Halifax, son of the above Thos., born 1745, died 1814; a good maker; in 1774 he contracted to make for £60, Halifax Church clock; in 1801 he made to the order of Dr Birkbeck, for the Anderson College, Glasgow, an orrery which had been designed by Joseph Priestley, of Bradford; in 1802 he made for Illingworth Church a clock having a pendulum 30 ft. long, vibrating twenty times a minute. On a paper pasted inside one of his long-case clocks was the following :—

> "Lo! Here I stand by you, upright,
> To give you a warning, day and night;
> For ev'ry tick that I do give,
> Cuts short the Time you have to live.
> Therefore, a warning take by me,
> To serve thy God as I serve thee;
> Each day and night be on thy guard,
> And thou shalt have a just reward."

William; long-case clock, about 1750, inscribed "Wm. Lister, Midgley," bearing the motto, "No Time for Sin"; long-case clock of slightly later date, signed "Wm. Lister, Keighley"; another, about 1770, signed "Wm. Lister, Halifax." **Sam,** Bolton, 1770. —, Lombard St., 1770. **Joseph,** Halifax; died 1805.

Litherland, Peter, Liverpool; patentee of the rack lever escapement (No. 1,830), Oct. 1791; and in 1792 (No. 1,889) of (1) a watch to beat once a second, and (2) a compensation curb, and (3) mechanism to wind watches by means of an external lever. Under the title of Peter Litherland & Co., he carried on a successful business for some years. A watch so named belonged to Col. Benjamin Tallmadge, an intimate friend of Washington, and is now in the museum of "Sons of the Revolution," New York. Early in the nineteenth century his patent lever watches were made in large numbers by Litherland, Whiteside, & Co., first at Ranelagh St.,

and afterwards at Church St. In 1816 the firm became Litherland, Davies, & Co. Of other members of the family were **John** and then **Richard** Litherland at Brownlow Hill. Richard in 1817 patented (No. 4,103) a modification of the chronometer escapement and also a compensation curb.

Little, Joseph, 179 Strand, 1800.

Littlemore, Whitestone, apprenticed to Thos. Gibbs, but turned over to Thos. Tompion; admitted C.C. 1698.

Littleton, Jas., London; repeating watch, 1773.

Littlewort. George, 34 Cannon St.; maker of watches for the use of the guards of the Royal Mail coaches, 1816-32. **Geo.,** Rahere St., 1834.

Livermore, Edward, 30 Tokenhouse Yard, Lothbury, and 3 Cross St., Islington, 1798-1810.

Livesey. —, Bolton, Lancashire; lantern clock, about 1700. **Jno.,** Bolton; long-case clock, about 1730.

Livingstone, J., London; watch, 1785.

Livy, see Levy.

Lloyd. William, Pye Corner; C.C. 1668. **Edwd.,** C.C. 1670. **Joseph,** C.C. 1673. **Lewis,** apprenticed C.C. 1673. **Nat.,** apprenticed C.C. 1673. **David,** C.C. 1677. **Richard,** C.C. 1681. **Charles,** apprenticed to Thos. Tompion, C.C. 1691. **James,** C.C. 1700. **James,** Sheep Pens, Smithfield; C.C. 1722. **Philip,** Bristol; long-case clock, about 1770. —, 128 Minories, 1785; card B.M. **& Northleigh,** London, 1785. —, at the "Dial," 21 Aldersgate St.; card B.M., 1790. **John,** 21 Aldgate Within, 1790-94. **J.,** Brecon; watch, 1802. **Joseph,** Wigan, 1816. **Wm.,** 6 Britannia Row, Hoxton, 1842.

Lochard. Robert, apprenticed in 1647 to Jno. Matchell; C.C. 1655. **John,** C.C. 1655; thick round silver watch, gut to fusee, engraved dial, serrated trident hand, inscribed "John Lochard, fecit," 1655-70.

Lockin, Wm., apprenticed in 1687 to Isaac Goddard, C.C.

Lockwood. Robt., apprenticed in 1647 to Edward Taylor, C.C. **Benj.,** Swaffham, Norfolk; long-case clock, about 1740; watch, 1765.

Loddington, Isaac, "The Dial," Tavistock St., Covent Garden. Anna Maria Shaw was apprenticed to him and to Elizabeth his wife, 1733; 1719-34.

Lode, —, London; pocket chronometer, about 1802.

Lodge, Thos., London; "Ordered that the Master should give directions to the Clerk to deliver the clock to Mr Thomas Lodge to be cleaned" (*Minutes of the Cutlers' Company*, 1st October 1713); maker also of a long-case clock, about 1730.

Lodowick, Peter, admitted C.C. 1689.

Loftuss, Thos., Wisbeach; lantern clock, about 1720.

Logan, Jno., Waltham, Mass.; good maker of balance-springs; died 1893, aged 49.

Logg, M., Vienna; about 1725 (see p. 182).

Loggen, Johannes, Amsterdam; fine calendar watch, Schloss collection, sun and moon hour indicators, as illustrated on p. 226, about 1680.

Lomas. Jas., Blackburn, 1770. **Jno.,** Sheffield, 1814.

Lomax, Sam., Blackburn, 1780.

London, Jno., Bristol; lantern clock, about 1690.

Long. Thomas, C.C. 1653. **John,** C.C. 1677. **Jno.,** Nottingham; clock-watch, about 1692. **John,** C.C. 1698. **Henry,** 200

High Holborn, 1770-80. **Thomas,** hon. freeman C.C. 1781; 1760-81. **& Drew,** enamellers, 5 Red Lion St., Clerkenwell, 1794-1810. **Theodore,** Gateshead, 1833.

Longland. Francis, apprenticed in 1671 to Bert. Powell, C.C. **John,** brother C.C. 1677; Mr Chas. M. Newcomen has a long-case clock by him, William III. period, inscribed "Johannis Longland, Londini, fecit;" case, oak with walnut veneer. **Thomas,** London; 30-hour long-case clock, about 1725.

Loomes, Thomas, at ye Mermayd in Lothebury, apprenticed to Jno. Selwood, brother C.C. 1649; a celebrated maker. Example, a small lantern clock (frets, Fig. 614), inscription, "Thomas Loomes, at ye Mermayd in Lothebury, fecit, 1674"; 1630-74.

Loor, Thos., Amsterdam; watch, 1715.

Lord. Richard, C.C. 1632. **Joseph,** apprenticed in 1684 to Jonathan Puller, C.C. **& Godard,** Rutland, U.S.A., 1797-1830.

Lorimer. Isaac, London; long-case clock, about 1740. **Jas.,** London; musical long-case clock, about 1780 (see p. 385). **David,** 17 Shoreditch, 1805-18; afterwards Lorimer & Edwards. **William,** 24 Crown St., Finsbury, 1830; 93 Wood St., Cheapside, 1835-40.

Losada, Jose R., a Spaniard who in his younger days was attached to the Court at Madrid, came to London and in 1835 set up as a watch and clock maker close to Euston Road; afterwards at Regent St., near the Polytechnic; then at 105 Regent St. He did a large business in really first-class timekeepers, chiefly with Spain and South America; after his death his nephew, Riego, continued at 105 Regent St., till about 1890.

Loseby, Edward Thomas, apprenticed to Rotherhams, of Coventry, afterwards at Gerrard St., Islington; inventor of a compensation balance, which acted by the expansion and contraction of mercury in a curved glass tube fixed at each end of the laminated rim, which was shorter than usual (Patent 1,011, Dec. 1852); he was successful at the Greenwich chronometer trials, but feeling aggrieved at what he considered to be inadequate appreciation on the part of the Admiralty, he retired in dudgeon to Leicester; for the Market Hall at Coventry he made a remarkably fine clock, which may be called the standard timekeeper of the place.

Lossier, —, London; watch, 1770.

Louarth, Jasper, C.C. 1641.

Loubet, Felix, au St Esprit; French table clock in gilt brass case, engraved with the four seasons after Etienne Delaune, second half of the sixteenth century, S.K.M.

Louchet, Boulogne; watch, 1815.

Loudan, Wm., 149 Great Surrey St., 1822; 228 Blackfriars Rd., 1840-42.

Lough. Thos., apprenticed in 1680 to Geo. Tomlinson, C.C. **Robert,** Penrith, 1770.

Loughton, William, C.C. 1683.

Lounde (Lowndes), Jonathan, in Pall Mall, C.C. 1680; steward, 1696; a celebrated maker. Square black basket-top bracket clock, Wetherfield collection, about 1685; walnut inlaid long-case clock, about 1695; bracket clock belonging to the Long Island Historical Society of New York, about 1700; fine long panelled marqueterie case, domed hood clock, 11-inch dial, Wetherfield collection, about 1700; another, 12-inch dial, about 1710.

"Lost in St James Chappel on Sunday

the 17 February a gold pendulum minute watch, going with a chain the maker Lowndes in Pall Mall London : it hath two gold cases, the out case graved with a cypher and an earl coronet over it : Whoever can bring the said watch to Jonathan Lowndes at the Dial in Pall Mall shall have 3 guineas for ther trouble" (*Lond. Gaz.,* 18th February 1683-4).

"Lost on the 19 past, from a gentlewoman's side, a gold pendulum watch, 2 gold cases, the outer case engraved ; made by J. Lowndes, in Pall Mall, London. Whoever brings it to Mr Lowndes, at the Dyal, in Pall Mall, shall have three guineas reward ; or, if bought, their money again with content" (*Lond. Gaz.,* Oct. 1-5, 1691).

"Lost on the 10 instant, in a Hackney Coach, between Covent Garden and Jermyn St., a Gold Pendulum Watch, the maker's name Lowndes, the Chrystal crack'd ; with 2 Steel Seals tyed to it, the Coat of Arms, 10 Crosses and a Baron's Coronet, and a small Famble [*sic*], made up of 2 little Diamonds and 4 or 5 Rubies. Whoever brings them to Sir Francis Child, Goldsmith, within Temple Bar, shall have 2 guineas reward" (*Lond. Gaz.,* Nov. 16-19, 1691).

Loundes. Charles, Pall Mall ; apprenticed in 1674 to Thos. Player ; C.C. 1682 ; maker of a long-case clock belonging to the Bishop of Chester ; also of a striking and repeating basket-top bracket clock. **Isaac,** Pall Mall Court, C.C. 1682 ; long clock, Wetherfield collection, panelled marqueterie case with domed hood, 12-inch dial, about 1705 ; long-case month clock, about 1710. **Wm.,** apprenticed in 1690 to Chas. Loundes, C.C.

Love. Jas., 23 Aldgate, 1770-90 ; enamelled watch, S.K.M. **Christopher,** 6 Old Bond St., 1816-25.

Lovelace, Jacob, Exeter ; died 1766, aged 60 ; maker of a famous clock (see p. 379). Mr Geo. Liddell has a long-case clock by him (see p. 300).

Loveland, —, London ; watch, 1770.

Loveles, W., 14 Charles St., Hoxton, 1796.

Lovell. Paul, subscribed to incorporation of C.C. in 1630 ; in 1654 Mr Paul Lovell the elder did deliver to the renter warden one silver bowl in full of all demands due to the Company. **Paul,** apprenticed to Paul Lovell in 1646 ; C.C. 1653. **Nathan,** apprenticed in 1655 to Jno. Samon, C.C.

Lovett. Jonathan, apprenticed in 1692 to Hy. Pigott, C.C. **William,** C.C. 1702 ; watch, about 1710.

Low, Jno., C.C. 1692.

Lowden, Jas., Edinburgh ; watch, about 1760. **Thos.,** London ; watch, 1768.

Lowe. Edwd., London ; watch, 1793. **Jno.,** 19 Lower Smith St., Northampton Sq., 1802-18. **Thos.,** Dartford ; watch, hare and snail indicator, 1818. **Edwd.,** Chester, 1833. **Geo. & Son,** Chester, 1833. **Jno.,** Chester, 1840-42.

Lowens, David, Philadelphia, 1785.

Lowrie, J. C., London ; watch, about 1800.

Lowry, Morgan, Holborn, 1700 ; Leeds, 1760 ; long-case twelve-month clock, about 1730, Mr John Walker. Morgan Lowry was sergeant-at-mace for the borough of Leeds till 1755.

Lowther, Thomas, clock-case maker, 58 Red Lion St., Clerkenwell, 1822-30.

Loyd, see Lloyd.

Lozano, Thos., London ; watch, 1700 ; bracket clocks, 1700-15.

Lucas. William, C.C. 1669 ; watch, apparently English, S.K.M., about 1690, inscribed "Lucas, Amsterdam," in a finely enamelled case, signed "Huaud l'aisne pinxit a Geneue." **Edward,** C.C. 1727. **Henry,** C.C. 1731. **Wm.,** London ; fine chiming clock, inlaid mahogany case, about 1800, Mr Samuel W. Scoble. **John,** Pear Tree St., 1800-10.

Lucie, John, C.C. 1663.

Ludford, Ralph, apprenticed in 1655 to Wm. Almond, C.C.

Ludlam, William, Professor of Mathematics at Cambridge, generally regarded as an authority on horology ; one of the judges of Harrison's chronometer, 1765. He corresponded with John Holmes in 1779.

Ludlow, Samuel, C.C. 1706.

Ludwig, John, Philadelphia, 1791.

Lueb, Michael, apprenticed in 1655 to Isaac Daniel, C.C.

Lugg, Jasper, "of Glocester, fecit" ; miniature lantern clock, with pendulum shaped like an anchor, Mr J. D. Robertson, about 1690.

Luitprand, a monk of Chartres, who at the end of the eighth century resuscitated the art of glass blowing, is said to have also invented the sand glass (see **p.32**).

Luke, William, shagreen and morocco case-maker, 147 Aldersgate St., 1810.

Lukins, Isaac, Philadelphia, 1790-1828.

Lullin, Paul, watch without hands (see **p.158**). French or Swiss, about 1690.

Lum, Joseph, Spitalfields, 1700.

Lumb. Jos., London, 1760. **John,** 16 Southampton Buildings, 1790-94.

Lumbley, G., junr., watch, 1760.

Lumley, Geo., Bury ; watch, 1780.

Lumpkin, Thomas, C.C. 1694 ; maker of a walnut marqueterie long-case clock, centre engraved ; over day of month circle G. R. and three crowns ; 1694-1715.

Lumsden, Jas., Aberdeen, 1770.

Lund. John Richard, Hatton Garden, and afterwards 41 Cornhill ; apprenticed to John Pennington, senr., for some time partner in the well-known firm of Barraud & Lund ; died 1868, aged 63. **John Alexander** (Barraud & Lund), died 1902, aged 66.

Lunod, H., Geneva, 1799.

Luntley, Thos., apprenticed in 1684 to Wm. Dobson, C.C.

Lupton. Wm., York, f., 1645 ; died 1680. **Wm.,** York, f., 1681. **Geo.,** Altrincham, 1780. **Jno.,** Altrincham, 1825. **& Gillam,** 23 St Martin's Lane, 1825. **Clifford,** some time with Barraud, afterwards at 3 Newman's Court, Cornhill ; died 1910, aged 85.

Lushbrook, —, admitted C.C. 1701.

Luttman, William, C.C. 1720.

Lutwiche. Wm., Fenchurch St., livery Embroiderers' Company, 1775. **Thos. Wm.,** Forgate St., Worcester, card B.M., 1794.

Lutz, Jean Celanis, Geneva, born 1800 ; introduced superior balance-springs at a low price, 1847 ; died 1863.

Lyddiatt, Thos., London ; watch with sun and moon hour indicator, Mr Drummond Robertson, about 1695.

Lyman, —, London ; watch, 1810.

Lynaker, Samuel, one of the first assistants of the C.C. 1630-49.

Lynam. Philip, apprenticed in 1682 to Jno. Harris, C.C. **& Bull,** "at the Golden Salmon, 36 New Bond St.," card Ponsonby collection, about 1785. **& Warwick,** 76 Strand, 1793.

Lynch, Robert, admitted C.C. 1670.

Lyndon, G., 30 Gerrard St., Soho, 1825-30.

Lyne, William, C.C. 1703.

Lyon. Matthew, Lanark, 1770. **Thos. Geo.,** St Martin's-le-Grand, 1793. **Craven,** Bridlington, 1822. **Lewis,** 64 Gray's Inn Lane, 1840.

Lyons, Richard, apprenticed in 1649 to Wm. Almond ; C.C. 1656 ; master 1683 ; calendar watch by him, Shandon collection, 1670-84. Fine long-case clock, about 1690, belonging to Mr Bernhard Matthews ; case of figured walnut veneered on oak, 6 ft. 8 in. high ; hood slides up and had a contrivance to keep it in position above the winding holes ; the door of the case as it is shut pushes forward a spoon-shaped piece of iron which keeps the hood from being raised ; twisted columns at corners of hood, bases and caps carved in Corinthian style with acanthus foliage ; dial 10 in. square (see p. 364).

Lysney, Sebastian, clockmaker to Edward VI., 1548.

Mabb, Wm., apprenticed C.C. 1688.

Maberley, John, Red Lion St., Clerkenwell ; master C.C. 1738. The springs of Harrison's chronometer were made by Maberley in 1755.

Mabille, Chas., Paris ; fine repeating watch, about 1785.

Macaire. F., London, 1732 ; handsome alarm watch by him, belonging to M. G. Mirabaud. **Antoine,** Paris ; watch, silver *repoussé* case, 1770 ; watch, about 1775.

McCabe. This house was much esteemed for fine watches and clocks, especially in India. James McCabe was from a watch and clock making family in Belfast. He came to London at the latter part of the eighteenth century, and was at 11 Bell's Buildings, Fleet St., in 1778 ; 34 King St., Cheapside, in 1783 ; 8 King St., Cheapside, in 1788 ; 97 Cornhill Royal Exchange in 1804. He was hon. freeman C.C. 1781 ; livery 1786 ; warden 1811, when he died, and was succeeded by his son James, who was apprenticed to Reid & Auld, and admitted to the C.C. in 1822. The business was carried on as McCabe & Son, 99 Cornhill, till 1820 ; McCabe & Strahan, 1825-26 ; J. McCabe, 97 Cornhill, till 1838, when the Royal Exchange was destroyed by fire ; then J. McCabe, 32 Cornhill. **Robert Jeremy McCabe,** nephew of James, who succeeded his uncle at 32 Cornhill, retired in 1883, when he closed the shop, declining all offers to purchase the business. He died in 1902, aged 67. McCabe's best watches were engraved "James McCabe," the second grade "McCabe," and the lowest quality "Beatson." **—,** Lurgan ; clock, about 1770. **Wm.,** Newry ; watch, 1798.

McCarthy, Jas., 47 Holborn, 1798.

Macdonald. Joseph, Liverpool, 1770 ; **John,** Inverness ; watch, about 1780, Mr J. D. Robertson.

MacDowall. Jas., Philadelphia, 1797-1825. **Chas. & Joseph,** "Helix lever and horological machine manufacturers," Vicar Lane, Leeds, 1830. **Charles,** Church St., Kensington, 1836 ; 8 Victoria Rd., Pimlico, 1839 ; 2 Mall, Kensington, 1840 ; Jermyn St., 1858 ; a clever horologist, born in Wakefield ; patented the single-pin escapement, 1851 ; made a 30-day skeleton clock, with Hooke's helix gearing ; died 1872, aged 82. **Joseph Eden,** 257 High St., Southwark, patented an escapement in 1838.

McDuff, Jas., 47 Bury St., 1835.

Mace. Barthelmy, à Blois ; enamel watch, about 1660 (see p. 179). **Lawrence,** Drapers' Court, Aldermanbury, C.C. 1730 ;

to him was apprenticed Wm. Plumley, 1749.

Macfarlane. John, Boston, U.S.A., 1800-10. **Peter**, London; watch, 1801.

Macgregor, J., 14 Charterhouse St., 1830.

Macham, Samuel, London; long-case clock, about 1710; repeating bracket clock, about 1720.

Mackarsie, G., 14 Great Queen St., 1820.

Mackarthy, James, 47 Holborn, 1790.

Mackdonald, Peter, New Compton St., 1790-94.

MacKenny, G., 8 Lower Ashby St., 1840-42.

Mackie. James, Banner St., Bunhill Row, 1810-35. **Geo. & Son**, 54 City Rd., 1822-25. **James**, 4 White Rose Court, Coleman St., 1830-42. **James & George**, 31 City Road, 1835-42.

McLachlan. Jno., C.C. 1791. **Hugh**, son of Jno., 17 Upper East Smithfield, 1810-42; E. J. Thompson was apprenticed to him in 1829.

Maclennan. Kenneth, May's Buildings, St Martin's Lane, 1778-1825; in 1801 he made a planetarium for the Royal Institution. **R. & W.**, 9 Great May's Buildings, St Martin's Lane, 1815-25. **John**, a watch and chronometer maker of the front rank, who worked for McCabes; born at Dingwall, died in London, 1886, aged 72.

McMaster, Wm. Jno., 26 Bartlett's Buildings, 1814-19.

McNab, —, Perth, about 1816 (see p. 337).

McPhail, C., 14 Regent's St., Pall Mall, 1830.

Macpherson, Normand, London; long-case musical clock, about 1790.

Macure, Thomas, musical clock maker, 7 Great New St., Gough Sq., 1788.

Macy, Benjamin, C.C. 1712.

Madden, Thos., apprenticed in 1647 to Wm. Rogers, C.C.

Maddock. Thos., Leek; long-case clock, about 1725. **Randle**, Leek; long-case clocks, about 1760. **L.**, London; watch, 1787.

Maddox, Edwd., London; centre-seconds watch, h.m., 1769.

Madelainy, —, Paris; curious watch, about 1690, formerly in the Dunn-Gardner collection, sold at Christie's in 1902; the movement, suspended on a gymbal ring and controlled by a short pendulum, was inserted in a spherical case rather less than 2 in. in diameter.

Madell, Charles, 1 Waterloo Place, Clerkenwell Close, 1835.

Maffid, P., Monmouth; watch, 1798.

Maggs, William, claimed to be successor to D. Quare, 1724-30.

Maginie, Samuel, Duke's Row, Pimlico, and 9 Prince's St., Westminster, 1835.

Magito, —, Rue Saint Dominique, Paris, 1770.

Magniac, Francis, St John's Sq., Clerkenwell, manufacturer of complicated clocks and automata, 1770-1814; made for the Emperor of China two musical clocks with figures of soldiers, musicians, birds, and beasts put into motion by the mechanism; was Colonel in command of the Clerkenwell Volunteers, who were organised in 1797 and disbanded in 1814.

Magnin, J. S., London; watch, 1760.

Magnus, N., 7 James Court, St Martin's Lane, 1823.

Magson, John, Essex St.; in the Hawkins collection was a repeating watch by him, in pierced and finely engraved gold case, second case chased with classical figures and scrolls, in outer case of shagreen, about 1700; long-case clock, about 1720, signed "John Magston, Essex St., London."

Maillett, Hy., 16 Bartlett's Buildings, 1790-94.

Mainglair à Geneva; watch, about 1795.

Mainwaring, Thos., apprenticed in 1686 to Jeffrey Staines, C.C.

Mairet, Sylvain, born 1805, died 1895; a clever Swiss watchmaker; lived in London 1831-34, manufacturing chiefly for B. L. Vulliamy; returned to Switzerland and settled in Locle; inventor of keyless mechanism for watches with two barrels; his son, Charles, who settled in London, died 1908.

Maisonneuve, Benjamin, Craven St., Strand, 1769-72.

Major, Nat., apprenticed in 1686 to Thos. Player, C.C.

Makepiece, Robt., 6 Serle St., Lincoln's Inn, 1775-88; afterwards Makepiece & Walford.

Malden, Samuel, Rainham, Essex, maker of lantern clocks, about 1725.

Malet, — , Paris, 1780.

Malleson, Thos., 62 Cornhill, 1769-83.

Mallet, L., Paris, "Horloger duc d'Orleans"; repeating watch, about 1790.

Mallett. Stephen, apprenticed in 1689 to John Trubshaw, C.C. —, a Devonshire family of clockmakers; long marqueterie case clock by **Peter Mallett**, about 1705. **John Mallett**, Barnstable, 1842.

Mallingley, Robt., 135 Goswell Rd., 1790-93.

Malpas, J., 91 Wood St., 1753-75.

Maltby. Henry, York, f., 1812. **H. D.**, York, 1814-22.

Man, Jonathan, Retford, 1770.

Manasiere, —, Smithfield, 1774-82.

Manby, Edwd., London; watch, 1828. **Jno.**, Skipton, 1833.

Manchester, John, C.C. 1700.

Mangaar, J. A., Maiden Lane, Covent Garden; very fine duplex centre seconds watch, 1834.

Mangeant, —, Rue du Pourtour-Saint-Gervais, Paris, 1770.

Mangie, Edwd., York, f., 1659.

Maniére, Paris; Louis XVI. clock by him sold at Christie's in 1905 for £1,260.

Maniglier, John, 4 Frith St., Soho, 1840-42.

Maning, Richard, Ipswich, U.S.A., 1748-60.

Manley. Dan, apprenticed in 1650 to Ed. Gilpin; C.C. 1660. —, Norwich; lantern clock, about 1680. **Daniel**, watch by him, Lond. Gaz., Sept. 21-25, 1693. **H.**, repoussé watch cases, 1695-1730; fine specimen S.K.M., signed "H. Manly, Fec."

Mann. Joseph, apprenticed in 1687 to Thos. Davis, C.C. **Theo.**, apprenticed in 1693 to Jas. Boyce, C.C. **Jno.**, Kentish Town; long-case clock, about 1770. **Percivial**, Lincoln's Inn Fields, 1780; Charlotte St., Oxford St., 1790-94. **Josh.**, London; watch, 1782. **& Muddell**, 114 Leadenhall St., 1830.

Manning & Edmonds, Strand; watch, 1780.

Manross, Elisha, Bristol, Conn., 1827-40.

Mansell, William, watch-case maker; 1800, Rosoman St., Clerkenwell; fined £15 by C.C. in 1813 for refusing to take up the livery; 26 Spencer St., 1826.

Manser, Robert, Clerkenwell, 1780, afterwards Ashley & Manser.

Mansfield, Jno., London; clock, about 1750.

Mansir, R., watch-case maker, Northampton Sq., 1835.

Mantir, G., 71 Snow Hill, 1830.

Mants, —, London; watch, 1760.

Manwaring, Thomas, C.C. 1694.

March. "Lost from a gentleman about the 14th Instant, but he knows not how, a silver minute Pendulum Watch, the name William March. Anyone that will bring it to Mr Hanne, Goldsmith, at the Bunch of Grapes in the Strand, near York Buildings, shall have a guinea reward" (Daily Courant, Feb. 19, 1705).

Marchand, —, Geneva; about 1725. **Fils à Paris**; watch, about 1790.

Marchant. Richd., apprenticed in 1664 to Jere. Gregory, C.C. **Samuel**, C.C. 1689; warden, 1704; did not serve as master. —, Prince's St., Leicester Fields, nephew of — Archambo, 1750. **Andrew**, London; watch, 1760. **William**, 255 High Holborn, 1775-83. **M.**, 350 Oxford St., 1823. **R.**, 20 Mortimer St., 1823.

Marche, —, Rouen; watch, 1730.

Marchet, Richard, Fulwood Rents, Holborn, 1790-94.

Marder, Henry & William, 20 Artillery Place, Finsbury, 1842.

Marduit, Isaac, C.C. 1724.

Maré, J. Louis, Geneva; enamelled watch, Marfels collection, about 1790.

Margan & Sherban, 6 Strand, 1793.

Margary, Thos., 4 Walbrook, 1790.

Margetts, George, 21 King St., Cheapside, 1785; 3 Cheapside, 1804; a celebrated maker, C.C. 1779, livery 1799 (see p. 290).

Margot. Green, Pall Mall, 1700. **D.**, 19 Arlington St., Clerkenwell, 1835.

Margotin à Paris; bracket clock with Boulle decoration, about 1770.

Marie, David, St Martin's-in-the-Fields. In 1762 he patented (No. 771) a form of going barrel.

Marinot, see Martinot.

Mariston, Robt., apprenticed in 1649 to O. Helden, C.C.

Mark, Jno., C.C. 1667.

Markham. Markwick, behind the Royal Exchange. From the number of watches and clocks bearing his name and having Turkish hour numerals, it may be assumed that he did a large business with the Turkish market; there are two watches by him in S.K.M., two in the G.M. In the Pierpont Morgan collection are several examples; in the Czar of Russia's collection at the Winter Palace, St Petersburg, is a large repeater watch in a pierced gold case with repoussé decoration; it is attached to a chatelaine. I have seen scores of watches dating from the end of the eighteenth century, and inscribed Markwick Markham together with the name of another maker added, e.g., "Markwick Markham, Perigal"; "Markwick Markham, Recordon"; this may possibly have been done by arrangement with Markham's representatives after his death, and seems to show that he left a good reputation, 1720-60. **Robert**, behind the Exchange, 1736-40. **John**, London; maker of watches for the Dutch market, 1760-85.

Marks. Saml., Cowbridge, clock, about 1770. **Lewis**, 127 Jermyn St., 1830-35; 59 Prince's St., Leicester Sq., 1840-42.

Markwick. James, Royal Exchange; apprenticed to Edmund Gilpin; C.C. 1666-98; in the Wetherfield collection is a bracket clock signed "Jacobus Markwick London," dating from about 1680, see Marquet.

"Dropt the 3rd instant between the Cross Keys in Holborn, and the Temple

Gate, a Gold Pendulum Minute watch made by Jacobus Markwick, London. Whoever brings it to Mr Wilkinson at the Black Boy against St Dunstan's Church, in Fleet Street, shall have 3*l.* reward" (*Lond. Gaz.*, July 6-9, 1691). **James**, C.C. 1692; master 1720; several watches by him in the B.M.; one, in very large silver cases, is inscribed, "Made for F.B., M.D.," another, a clock-watch of a slightly later period; long marqueterie case clock, "Marwick Londini," about 1695, Mr Robert Meldrum.

Marlack, White C., New York, f., 1769; afterwards **Wm.**

Marquet. Jacob, Augsburg, 1567 (see p. 89). **—**, (Markwick?). "That divers Watches and Pocket Clocks which were Mr Samuel *Betts*, deceased, are to be sold at his late shop, now the shop of Mr Marquet, watchmaker, on the backside of the Royal Exchange" (*Lond. Gaz.*, Feb. 28, March 2, 1675).

Marr. Jas., C.C.; about 1650. **Frères à Geneva**; watch, about 1795.

Marriott. John, C.C. 1715. **W.**, 10 Fetter Lane, about 1760. **John**, musical clockmaker, 10 Fleet Lane, 1780; 175 Fleet St., 1790; master C.C. 1799; bracket clock, ebony case with brass mountings, enamel dial, about 1780, Wetherfield collection (see p. 392). **J.**, 148 Aldersgate St., 1806-10. **Wm. & J.**, 27 Fenchurch St., 1823-30.

Marris, Chas., Hull, 1822.

Marsden. John, C.C. 1698; master, 1731. **Josh.**, Gainsboro'; long-case clock with motto, "The Moon Do's Best Appear," "When ye Air is most Clear," about 1760. **Samuel**, 4 Leathersellers' Buildings, 1820. **Thos.**, Hensingham, 1833. **Samuel**, 23 Great Winchester St., 1835-42.

Marsh. Jno., apprenticed in 1676 to Thos. Parker, C.C. **Jonathan**, London; apprenticed in 1691 to Richard Symonds, C.C.; long-case clock, about 1720. **Anthony**, at yᵉ dial opposite Bank of England; C.C. 1724. **Jacob**, 78 Lombard St., 1754-68. **Richd.**, Ipswich, 1770. **James & Samuel**, 79 Broad St., Ratcliffe, 1790-1810. **Sam.**, 79 Broad St., Ratcliffe, 1793-1818. **Wm. B.**, London; handsome long-case clock, about 1800. **Thos.**, King St., Clerkenwell; in 1811 he patented (No. 3,488) an escapement. **Jas.**, watch-movement maker, 22 Tysoe St., Clerkenwell, 1835. **Jno.**, watch-case maker, 35 Clerkenwell Green, 1835. **Edward & John**, 61 Whiskin St., 1840. **H.**, 20 Town St., Piccadilly, 1840-42. **Richard**, Diss, 1846.

Marshall. Benjamin, C.C. 1680. **Matthew**, C.C. 1689. **John**, Rainbow Coffee House, Cornhill, apprenticed to Sam. Rouk, but turned over to D. Quare; C.C. 1689; long panelled marqueterie case clock, hood with spiral pillars, 12-in. dial, about 1705, Wetherfield collection. "Lost out of a gentleman's pocket on the 2nd inst., a silver minute watch in a studded shagreen case. John Marshall, watchmaker, at the Rainbow Coffee House in Cornhill, near Birchin Lane" (*Lond. Gaz.*, March 12, 1693-4). **Chris.**, appointed in 1701 to uphold the clock and chimes of Halifax Church in succession to Sam. Ogden. **Samuel**, New St.; C.C. 1718. **John**, Newark; maker of long-case calendar clocks, cast dial plates, about 1730. **Geo.**, New St.; C.C. 1734. **Richd.**, 1751. **Francis**, Durham, 1770. **Wm.**, Newark; died 1770. **Jno.**, London; probably about 1780 (see p. 498). **Thos.**, Lincoln; watch, 1790. **Wm.**, 3 Corporation Lane, 1816; 6 Percival St.,

1830-35. **Hy.**, 3 Fore St., Limehouse, 1817. **E.**, 61 Cannon St., 1825-30.

Marster, W. J., 26 Bartlett's Buildings, Holborn, 1825.

Marston. Jno., his movement seized by C.C. 1661. **William**, C.C. 1669. **John**, 4 Oxenden St., Haymarket, 1842.

Marten, Hy. & Wm., 20 Bunhill Row, 1840.

Martin. Edwd., apprenticed in 1662 to Jno. Nicasius, C.C.; pair case watch, Dutch style, Fitzwilliam Museum, Cambridge. **Zacharie**, clockmaker to Louis XIV., 1674. **John**, White Gate Alley, admitted C.C. 1679; threatened in 1682 with prosecution by C.C. for undue taking of apprentices. **Abraham**, engraver, C.C. 1682. **Francis**, apprenticed 1683 to Jno. Wells, C.C. **Jno.**, apprenticed, C.C. 1684; bracket clock repeating quarters on six bells, marqueterie case with domed top, Wetherfield collection, about 1700. **Jeremiah**, apprenticed to Wm. Dent and turned over to Thos. Tompion; C.C. 1687. **Thomas**, Royal Exchange; apprenticed in 1692 to Jere. Martin; C.C. 1699; diminutive bracket clock, about 1705. **Richard**, Northampton; maker of lantern clocks, about 1695. **William**, Bristol; lantern and bracket clocks, 1700-30. **Benjamin**, "Newton Head, Fleet St., a friend of Jas. Ferguson"; maker of a curious table clock; born at Chichester 1704, died 1782. **William**, C.C 1709. **William**, apprenticed to John Uffington; C.C. 1751. **Jonathan**, London; watch, *repoussé* case, hall mark, 1759. **John**, 16 Brownlow St., Bedford Row, 1763-69. **T. G.**, Dublin, 1771. **Thomas**, son of Thomas Martin, citizen and poulter, being by trade a clockmaker, C.C. 1771; a good maker; mentioned by Earnshaw, 27 Cornhill, 1778-81; St Michael's Alley, 1788-94; pocket chronometer, G.M., h.m., 1780. **Jno.**, Spalding, 1773; long Sheraton case clock, signed "Jos. Martin, Kippen," about 1790. **Edmund**, London; long-case clock, about 1790. **Edmund**, 44 Queen St., Cheapside, apprenticed to William Howells, C.C. 1795. **John**, Eton Bridge, 1809; long-case clock, about 1820, Mr Gerald Watts. **J. F.**, 26 High St., Marylebone, 1810. **William**, 75 King St., Westminster, 1810-40. **& Saul**, 9 Bow, 1817. **G.**, 13 Church Lane, Whitechapel, 1835. **H.**, Bunhill Row, 1835. **James**, 26 Hanway St., 1835. **M.**, 18 Aylesbury St., Clerkenwell, 1835. **& Mosse**, 8 Charing Cross, 1835.

Martineau. Joseph, St Martin's Court, 1750-70; bracket clock, engraved "Josh. Martineau, senior"; maker also of gold *repoussé* watches; repeating watch, Pierpont Morgan collection, about 1760. **Joseph**, 65 Red Lion St., Clerkenwell, 1790-94.

Martinique à Paris; clock in vase-shaped case of white statuary with side figures of nymphs of chased ormolu, dating from about 1790, sold for 350 guineas at Christie's in 1901.

Martinot. Gilbert, Paris; clockmaker to Henry III., 1572 (see p. 304), first of a long succession of Court clockmakers: **Denis** succeeded in 1611; **Zacharie** in 1637; **Gille** in 1662; **Jean** in 1686; **Louis Henry** in 1688; **Henri**, nephew of Jean and son of Gille, succeeded his father at the Louvre in 1670 (see p. 309); **Jerome** in 1695; **Jacques** in 1718; **Jean** in 1727; **Claude** in 1729. **Barnaby**, Farringdon Within, 1618. Alfred Franklin says one of the Paris Martinots, who had become a Protestant, was successful in a London business after

the revocation of the Edict of Nantes, but I have never met with any timekeepers by him. **Balthazar**, Paris; horologer to Louis XIII., 1637 (see p. 133). "A four-square Gold Watch, made at Paris by Monsieur Martinot. Whoever can give notice of it to Mr East, watchmaker, at Charing Cross, or else to the porter of Madam Gwinn's House in Pall Mall, shall have 20s. reward" (*Lond. Gaz.*, June 4-7, 1677). **B.**, Rouen; specimen at B.M., about 1680. **M.**, Avignon; a watch by him, G.M., about 1700; presented an armilary sphere to the King of France in 1701. **Baltazar**, Paris; watch, 1714; Boulle work clock, Jones collection, S.K.M., about 1725. **Jerome**, Paris; "horloger du Roy"; fine astronomical and calendar clock by him in the Paris Observatory, described by Thiout in 1741; clock, in case of ormolu, supported by a bronze elephant, Jones collection, S.K.M., about 1760; the case is inscribed "fecit par Caffieri" (p. 305).

Mascarone, Gio. Batt., padlock-shaped watch, about 1635 (see p. 120).

Masey, Thomas, mended St Mary's clock, Oxon., 1550.

Mason. Richard, C.C. 1632. **Robt.**, apprenticed in 1658 to Peter Bellune, C.C. **Jno.**, Bristol; made a clock for the church of Alderly to the order of Sir Matthew Hale, 1673. **William**, C.C. 1688. Several generations of Mason in Yorkshire: **Timothy**, Gainsborough, 1695; then **John**, Doncaster; long lacquer case clock by him, about 1740; then **John** at Bawtry; **Thomas** at Bawtry; **Timothy** at Chesterfield, watch, h.m., 1795; then **John**, apprenticed to Timothy at Chesterfield, began business at Rotherham in 1801. **Samuel**, C.C. 1712. **John**, C.C. 1712; lantern clock, square dial, cherub corners, bob pendulum, 1712-20. **Henry**, C.C. 1715. **John**, C.C. 1718; long-case clocks, 1718 30. **William**, near East Lane, Rotherhithe Wall, 1760-69; Dockhead, Southwark, 1781-83. **—**, Bedford; watch, 1763. **Wm.**, Bexley; watch, 1768. **& Hudson**, Strand, 1772. **J. Ladson**, London; watch, 1780. **Robert**, 11 Strand; in 1790 he sent a letter to the Clockmakers' Co. respecting watches seized on his premises. **John**, 3 Helmet Row, 1816-20; 1 Jubilee St., Mile End, 1840.

Masquerier. & Perigal, Coventry St., 1775. **Lewis**, 12 Coventry St., 1780-85. **Wm.**, Gerrard St., Soho, 1790-94.

Masse, James, Broad St., 1753-60.

Masset, Peter, long marqueterie case clock, about 1700 (? Mallett, Peter).

Massey. Edmund, C.C. 1682. **Paul**, Coventry St.; long-case clock, revolving months, date dial, about 1760, see also Massy, Paul. Mr A. W. H. Hornsby-Drake has a long-case clock, dated 1725, inscribed "Jᵒⁿ Massey, Dundalke." **Benj.**, 116 Leadenhall St., 1810-26. **John**, 89 Strand, and 40 Bridge Rd., Lambeth, 1810-35. **C.**, 40 Bridge Rd., Lambeth, 1823-35. **F. & E.**, King William St., City; peculiar watch to show tenths of a second, h.m., 1835. **Thomas**, 4 Birchin Lane, and 32 Wilmington Sq., 1835-42. **Edmund**, 89 Strand, probably the son of John, of the same address, 1835-42; a watch by him, Evan Roberts collection, centre seconds, beating full seconds, the balance nearly as large as the plate, makes 3,600 vibrations an hour; it has a lever escapement, the pallets anchor shaped as in a clock. **Edward John**, 78 Cornhill, and 3 Tysoe St., Spa Fields, 1835-42; in 1838, when he patented a chronometer escapement (No. 7,678), he is described as of Liverpool. **Francis**

Joseph, 17 Chadwell St., 1840-42. Edward, 28 King St., Clerkenwell ; a Staffordshire watchmaker, who migrated from Burslem to Coventry, from thence to Prescot, and afterwards settled in London ; inventor of a form of lever escapement called the crank roller, and forms of keyless winding for watches (see p. 410) ; he died in 1852, aged 82, and was buried at St John's, Duncan Terrace, Islington.

Massingham, J., Fakenham ; bracket repeating clock, about 1770, Mr H. Langley.

Masson. R. Aime, London ; watch, Evan Roberts collection, about 1700. Denis, Paris ; clock, Jones collection, S.K.M., about 1760.

Massy. Nicholas, a French refugee, brother C.C. 1682 ; in the Pierpont Morgan collection is a small watch, signed "Nicholas Massy à Blois," balance-cock pinned on, gold case with outer case of leather piqué with gold, about 1660 ; in the same collection is a silver alarm watch, signed "Massy, London" ; this dates from about 1690 ; no minute hand, pair cases, pierced, the outer one, of particularly fine design and workmanship, has on the back a cypher, C.B., reversed. "Lost the 17 instant, between the Haymarket and Temple Bar, a new Silver Pendulum Watch made by Nich. Massy, with a tortoise-shell studded case, the studs wrought, and the case lined with red sattin ; and 2 seals" (Lond. Gaz., Nov. 24-28, 1692) ; 1690-1712. Henry, son of Nicholas ; C.C. 1692 ; Charles St., near St James's Sq., 1707 ; thick round silver watch, silver dial, showing day of the month, elaborately pierced movement. Nicholas, son of the foregoing Nicholas, Cranbourne St., near Leicester Fields ; C.C. 1693 ; striking watch, Schloss collection, royal arms and motto Semper Eadem on the movement (see p. 403) ; a watch movement by him, with an index on top of the cock, is in the Guildhall Museum. Jacob, Leicester Fields ; C.C. 1715 ; maker of a black arch bracket clock, 1715-25. Paul, Coventry St. ; long Oriental lacquer case musical clock, tunes as engraved on the dial, "Grannadears' March," "The Happy Clown" ; shows also days of the week and month, and signs of the zodiac, about 1740. & Windham, 4 Birchin Lane, 1830-35.

Master, W. J., 26 Bartlett's Buildings, 1823.

Masterman, J., White Hart Court, Gracechurch St., 1769-73 ; Masterman & Springhall, 1793.

Masters. William, C.C. 1701. Jno., London ; watch, single case, about 1735. Jno., Bristol, about 1780. James, 52 Strand ; card B.M. 1803 ; livery C.C. 1810 ; after much negotiation he was in 1812 transferred to the Goldsmiths' Company on payment of £30 to C.C.

Masterson. Richard ; early watch signed "Ri Masterson at the dyall at Mooregate," balance-cock pinned on, about 1610, Pierpont Morgan collection ; afterwards at the Royal Exchange ; subscribed to the incorporation of C.C. in 1630 ; C.C. 1633 ; master 1642 ; died 1653 ; in the G.M. is an oval watch by him, cockle-shell case, plain silver dial, hour-hand only, catgut ; a somewhat similar watch by him, Whitcombe Greene collection. Jno., apprenticed in 1648 to Richd. Masterson, C.C.

Maston. Richd., apprenticed in 1649 to Wm. North, C.C. Thos., Bawtry, 1775. D., London ; watches, 1795-1820.

Matchett. John, Covent Garden, C.C. 1648 ; signed a petition against the company's oppression, 1656 ; assistant, 1670 ; suspended, as well known to be a Popish recusant, 1678. "Lost on the 11th inst. about Lincoln's-Inn-Fields or Covent Garden, a silver watch ingraven with several Figures, made by John Machett, a studded case with silver Pins" (Lond. Gaz., June 12-15, 1676). "Lost on Thursday the 3rd instant, between eight and nine in the evening, in the Pall Mall, a gold watch with a silver-gilt chain, and a little cabinet key linked to it, made by John Matchet in Convent Garden. Whoever brings it to Mr Mawson, Goldsmith, at the Golden Hind in Fleet Street over against St Dunstan's Church, shall have five pounds reward" (Lond. Gaz., June 1680). Geo., apprenticed in 1651 to Wm. Petty, C.C.

Matham, Robt., 66 Newgate St., 1783.

Mather. Samuel, C.C. 1691. D., watch with skeleton movement, about 1820.

Mathew, Francis, C.C. 1656.

Mathews. William, 27 Fleet St., apprenticed to Charles Tolley, and turned over to John Smith ; C.C. 1731 ; assistant and livery, 1766 ; one of the examiners of Harrison's timekeeper in 1765 ; watch, 1800, signed "Matthews, Leighton Buzzard." W. & C.S., 128 Minories, 1817. & Thorpe, 10 Artillery Place, 1840-42.

Mathey, Lewis, Philadelphia, 1797.

Mathieu, —, Paris ; Horloger du Roy, 1830-42.

Mathison, —, London, 1750.

Matlack, W. C., f. of New York, 1769.

Matthew, John, C.C. 1731 ; long oak-case clock, with day of the month circle, about 1740.

Matthews. Thos., London ; figure of Time working backward and forward ; motto, "Tempus Fugit," dated 1702, J., Leighton ; long-case clock, about 1810, Mr Wm. Norman. John, 36 Goswell Rd., 1840.

Mattison, Thos., 62 Cornhill, 1793.

Mattocks, John, St Bride's Lane ; livery C.C. 1786.

Maubert, Peter, apprenticed in 1679 to David Meggret, C.C.

Maude. Benjamin, 53 St Martin's-le-Grand, 1770-94. Edward, 14 St Paul's Churchyard, 1793-98.

Maudsley, G., Wakefield, 1770.

Maughan, Jos. H., Gateshead, 1833.

Maurer, Johann, in Fiessta. In the B.M. is a small skull-watch by him, 1650-60.

Mauris, signature on chased watch case, about 1760.

Mavor, Jno., apprenticed in 1637 to Jas. Allen, C.C.

Maweis (possibly Mauris), —, chased watch case, about 1770-80, see Potter Harry, and Smidt.

Mawkes. T., Belper ; long-case clock, about 1710. J., Derby ; watch, 1794.

Mawley. Robt., London ; Mr Donald Armour has an all-brass bracket timepiece with alarm by this maker, dating from about 1695, case plain except the sides which are decorated with a Cupid's head with radiating bars ; bracket clock, about 1725. H., watch, 1705.

Mawman, Geo., Beverley, 1822.

May. William, C.C. 1679. Edwd., Henley ; long-case clock, lantern movement, about 1680. John (Dutch), C.C. 1692 ; watch, about 1710 ; Pierpont Morgan collection. John, Witney ; long-case clock, about 1700. Edwd., Witney ; long-case clock, about 1725, no minute divisions on outer circle. Geo., C.C. 1754. "A large

quantity of gold and silver watches, with a time piece, and some other curious things of value, were found in the gully hole at Holbourn bridge, by the workmen, in cleaning it. These things had been taken some days before from the house of Mr May, watchm'ker, in Bridgewater square ; and were returned on the payment of 10 guineas, prom'd by advzt. for the recovy. of them" (Gent.'s Mag., Aug. 24, 1765). David, Prescot, 1770. & Son, Dublin, 1798. Samuel, 51 Myddelton St., Clerkenwell ; an expert watch and chronometer springer ; died 1871, aged 58.

Mayers, Jno., Richmond, 1770.

Mayes, John, 8 Lower Charles St., Goswell Rd., 1842.

Mayhew. Hen., Parham ; lantern clock, say, 1690. Wm., Woodbridge, long-case clock, about 1730.

Mayland, Thomas, C.C. 1698.

Maynard. —, Long Melford ; he made the church clock there about 1650 ; lantern clock, Mr W. B. Redfern. Christopher, Royal Exchange, apprenticed to Hackett, C.C. 1667, see Hicks. Geo., apprenticed in 1692 to Chris. Maynard, C.C.; f. of New York, 1702. Geo., Metford ; watch, 1767. Chas., St Martin's-le-Grand, 1774.

Mayne, —, 111 Union St., Stonehouse ; watch paper, about 1790.

Mayo. Wm., apprenticed in 1676 to Robt. Cawne, C.C. Thomas, Hereford, 1760. Joseph, Craven St., Strand, 1769-72. —, Coventry, about 1780-90.

Mayr. At Buckingham Palace is an astrological clock dating from 1680, signed "Jacob Mayr Junger, Augsburg," square case covered with turtle-shell, adorned with silver scrolls and bands ; four dials.

Mayrium, Johann Georg, Munich ; spherical clock, about 1690.

Maysmore, Wm., Wrexham, about 1720.

Mayson, Jonn, C.C. 1704.

Mazzel, Cor., Bolney ; watch, 1740.

Mead. R., Lancaster, 1760. Benjamin, Casline, Me., 1800-10. Wm., 1 Corporation Lane, 1835.

Meade, Garrett, C.C. 1703.

Meades, Thomas, C.C. 1687.

Meadows, Wm., London ; watch, 1760.

Meak, John, musical clock and watch maker, 7 Worship St., 1825.

Meanley, —, London ; pair-case verge watch, with an engraving on the back representing the Queen of Sheba before Solomon ; about 1770.

Mears. Isaac, apprenticed in 1661 to Robt. Whitwell, C.C. Josias, Dublin ; long-case clock, about 1760, Sir Theodore Fry. Jno., watch engraver, 48 Cloth Fair, 1790-94. Jno., York, 1822.

Measure, A., 420 Strand, 1815-20.

Mebert, Isaac, C.C., about 1660.

Medcalf, Wm., Liverpool, 1770.

Medhurst, Richard, Croydon, C.C. 1687.

Meeberry, Elizabeth, apprenticed in 1680 to Edwd. Norris and his wife, C.C.

Meek. Jno., musical clock and watch maker, 7 Worship St., 1812-18.

Meeks, Edward, junr., 114 Maiden Lane, New York, 1796 ; "has eight-day clocks and chiming time pieces" (advt.).

Meigh, Moses, C.C. 1712.

Melchior, see Adam.

Mell. David, C.C. 1655. Cornelius, Harplett was apprenticed to him through the C.C. in 1659 ; Mr Egerton Clarke has a fine lantern clock, inscribed "David Mell in Crutched Fryers, Londini," about 1660 ; it has a minute hand, and the first fourteen minutes of each quarter hour are marked on the minute band in Arabic figures, the quarters being distinguished by Roman numerals, IIII. at the hour, I. at 15 minutes, II. at 30, and III. at 45 minutes past the hour; beneath the hour bell are three smaller ones; in John Aubrey's "Miscellanies" is mentioned "Mr Davys Mell (the famous Violinist and Clock-maker)."

Mellin, Gui, Blackfriars, maker of an oval watch in the B.M., glass over the dial, 1600-20.

Melly, Frères, Paris; watch, 1780.

Melrose, James, 34 Nicholson St., Edinburgh; watch paper endorsed "July 9, 1827, Captain Smith."

Melville. John, hon. freeman C.C. 1781. **& Stoddart,** 61 Red Lion St., Clerkenwell, 1804-10. **Jas.,** watch-case maker, 13 Spencer St., 1816. **Robert,** 40 King St., Clerkenwell, 1835.

Memeis, Robt., Margaret St., Wilmington Sq.; clock, about 1820.

Mendham, —, received a silver medal from the Society of Arts in 1807 for a remontoire.

Mends, James, Philadelphia, 1795, afterwards **Benj.**

Menessie, Elisha, Aldersgate St., 1790-95.

Meniall, James (French), threatened with prosecution by C.C. for exercising the art, not being admitted, paid costs, and was admitted forthwith, 1682.

Menzies. J., Philadelphia, 1811-1816. **John,** 4 Charles St., Northampton Sq., 1840-42.

Mercator. Evelyn's "Diary," 28th Aug. 1666: "To the Royal Society where one Mercator, an excellent mathematician, produced his rare clock and new motions to perform the equations, and Mr Rooke" (evidently should be Hooke) "his new pendulum" (see p. 240).

Mercer. Edwd., apprenticed in 1690 to Cuthbert Lee, C.C. **John,** Hythe, maker of long-case clocks, 1720. **Brothers,** Coventry, about 1770-90. **John,** Manchester, about 1800. **Jno.,** Liverpool, 1818. **Thos.,** born at St Helens, Lancashire, 1822, died 1900; a leading chronometer maker; he learnt springing from Jno. Fletcher, carried on business for some time in Clerkenwell and afterwards at St Albans; was for many years treasurer of the British Horological Institute.

Merchant, Samuel, admitted C.C. 1677; assistant, 1698.

Mercier. Louis, Geneva, about 1690. **—,** London; watch, 1725.

Meredith. Lancelot, C.C. 1637; signed a petition against the tyranny of the Company, 1656. **John,** C.C. 1664. **Jno.,** Carlisle, about 1740. **Jno.,** London; watch, gold box, h.m., 1758, outer case *repoussé*. **Wm.,** Chepstow; fine long-case clock, about 1775, Mr W. W. Trotman.

Merigeot, John, livery C.C. 1766.

Merison, Jas., Anderston; clock, inscribed "Dial made for Robt. Liddal."

Meriton, Samuel, livery Turners' Company, 18 Foster Lane, Cheapside, 1763-1800.

Merlin, Joseph, mechanical genius; born 1735 at Huys, near Liège. Arrived in England in 1760. Soon after this became principal mechanic at Cox's Museum, which he left in 1773; was an expert designer of engines, mathematical instruments, and a watch and clock maker. He constructed a curious dial or regulator which was wound by the room door opening; died 1803.

Mermillon Freres et Cie., Swiss watch, 1780.

Merny, Charles, Spitalfields, liveryman C.C. 1776.

Merrell, Jno., London; watch, enamelled case, 1790.

Merrick, Joseph, 28 Paul St., Finsbury, 1835-42.

Merrill. Charles, livery C.C. 1810. **H.,** Hill St., Richmond, 1840.

Merriman. & Dunbar, Bristol, Conn., 1810. **Titus,** 1830.

Merrin, Henry, 100 High St., Shadwell, 1840-42.

Merry. Charles, London; long-case clock, about 1740; livery C.C. 1766; master, 1768. **F.,** Philadelphia, 1799.

Merryman. Henry, C.C. 1674. **Benjamin,** C.C. 1682; clock-watch mounted as a sedan-chair timekeeper, Captain R. Feilden; watch, tulip pillars, about 1695, inscribed "Benj. Merriman, London." **Thos.,** apprenticed in 1692 to Ben. Merryman, C.C.

Merton & Co., Liverpool; watch, 1792.

Merttins, George, Cornhill; goldsmith and watchmaker, succeeded to the business of his father; C.C. 1688; master, 1713; knighted, 1713; Lord Mayor, 1724; died 1727.

Mesniel, James (French), C.C. 1682.

Mesnier, Claude, Paris; clockmaker to the Duke d'Anjou, 1655.

Mestager, Henry, C.C. 1712.

Mesure, Anthony, 8 Craven Buildings, Drury Lane, 1810; 420 Strand, 1814-23.

Metcalf. Edwd., apprenticed in 1684 to Richd. Blundell, C.C. **George Marmaduke,** Round Court, St Martin's-le-Grand, admitted C.C. 1781; livery, 1786; 122 Newgate St., 1794-1825. **Josh.,** 146 Oxford St., 1816-42.

Metcalfe. Mark, Askrigg; died 1776, aged 89. **& Nicholl,** Halifax, 1780.

Methem, Robt., 66 Newgate St., 1775.

Meuron, —, Paris; watches, 1770-90. **& Co.,** Paris, about 1798.

Meybom, F., Paris, 1650.

Meye, Diet, Bâle; watch, about 1750.

Meyer. Jaques, Basle; about 1760. **—,** Paris; watch, 1780.

Meyers, John, Frederickstown, Md., 1793-1825.

Meylan. F. & A., Geneva; watch, 1820.

Micabius, John. C.C. ordered him to be sued for failing to pay a promised contribution towards incorporation, 1632.

Michael, D., & Sons, Swansea; watch, 1801.

Michand, P., Paris; about 1755.

Michant, Daniel, 28 Greek St., 1794.

Michard. Repeating watch, signed "Vve Michard, Paris," about 1750, Pierpont Morgan collection.

Michel, Jacques, Paris; lantern clock, about 1650, Mr John H. Baker.

Michelin, Saml., à Langres; splendid travelling watch, about 1680 (see p. 192).

Michell. Jo., Chardstock; lantern clocks, about 1700 (see p. 349). **Jam.,** London; long-case clock, marqueterie flowers in vase, about 1710. **Geo.,** Bristol, Conn., 1827-37.

Michells, 63 St Mary Axe, 1830.

Micklewright. Erasmus, C.C. 1673. **—,** C.C. 1708.

Middlecoats, Wm., Newington, Surrey; bracket clock, about 1730.

Middleditch, John, 156 High St., Shadwell, 1835-42.

Middlemiss, Robt., Hull, 1822.

Middleton. Timothy, apprenticed in 1680 to Robt. Dingley; C.C. 1687. **William T.,** 10 Grenada Terrace, Commercial Rd., 1835-42.

Midgley, Richd., Halifax, 1720-40; many long-case clocks.

Midnall, John, in Fleet St., one of the first assistants C.C.; maker of a small oval watch said to have belonged to Oliver Cromwell, B.M. (see p. 140); small oval watch, Pierpont Morgan collection; pretty balance-cock pinned on, about 1620; another watch by him of rather later date in silver cases, outer case engraved with flowers.

Midwinter, Jno., London; watch, h.m., 1763.

Miege à Geneve; watch, G.M., about 1750.

Milborne, John, admitted C.C. 1698.

Miles. —, Stroud; clock, lantern movement, square brass dial, about 1700, Mr W. Birchall. **—,** Lowley; chiming clock incorporated with mahogany bureau, about 1750, Mr G. A. W. Tuckley. **& Morgan,** 32 Ludgate St., 1790-94. **Septimus,** 32 Ludgate St., 1794; livery C.C. 1810; 8 Little Carter Lane, Doctors' Commons, 1825-42. **G.,** Guildford St., Boro', 1830.

Milfield, D., London; watch, 1790.

Mill, David, see Mell.

Millard, D., à Paris; alarm watch with enamelled dial, pierced and engraved silver case, late seventeenth century, S.K.M.

Millenet, Daniel; clock-watch with alarm, about 1630.

Miller. John, C.C. 1674; lantern clock, dolphin frets, inscribed "John Miller, Showe Lane," belonging to Mr Edward Sudell; Fromanteel in 1665 speaks of one Miller as taking many apprentices. **Peter,** C.C. 1681. **Ralph,** C.C. 1697. **Joseph,** C.C. 1728; Jas. Wood apprenticed to him in 1738. **Aaron,** Elizabethtown, New Jersey, U.S.A., 1747. **Wm. Jas.,** Ludgate St., 1760. **—,** Lurgan, Ireland; maker of a curious clock in which the hour was uttered by a human figure, as appears from the journal of the Rev. John Wesley, in a clear articulate voice, 1762. **Thos.,** London; maker of a pair-case watch, outer case tortoiseshell, painted dial, h.m., 1764; another, Dutch style, 1780. **Geo.,** Gateshead, 1770. **Fred.,** 38 Greek St.; card B.M. 1797. **Abraham,** Easton, U.S.A., 1810-30. **Chas.,** Aldgate Within, 1816-25. **Robt.,** Tottenham, 1820; 2 George St., Commercial Rd., 1835; 4 Upton Place, 1842. **F., & Co.,** 10 Broad St., Bloomsbury, 1835-40. **Jas.,** 262 High St., Poplar, 1842.

Milleret. —, Extra small watch, gold case, enamelled with a rose.

Millet, William, C.C. 1714.

Millett, Edward, C.C. 1680.

Millig, Michael, Southwark, 1734.

Millington. Thomas, 31 Gutter Lane, Cheapside, 1760-69; watch, brass cases, outer one *repoussé* and gilt. **& Lancashire,** London; watch, 1768; watch, signed "Millington Salop," 1780. **Thomas,** 33 Wapping, 1790.

Million, William, Blackfriars, C.C. 1671.

Millot. "Horloger du Roy, rue du Bac, Paris," 1764-72; fine urn timekeeper, about 1680; the movement was by Dwerryhouse, London.

Mills. Thomas, in Shoe Lane, C.C. 1652; maker of lantern clock with dolphin frets; another example, inscribed "Tho. Mills, Soe Lane, Londini," 1648-60. **Jere,** apprenticed in 1676 to Jno. Miller, C.C. **Richard,** Edinburgh; apprenticed to Humphrey Mylne; made a freeman of the Incorporation, 1678; his essay being, "Ane clock watch and luminary, with the further addition of a lock and key"; declined the office of "box-master" or treasurer in 1703; died 1705; lantern clock, signed "Humphrey Mills. Edinburgh, 1685," Mr Robert Meldrum. "Stolen out of a house near the West Port on the 19th, a gold watch with a steel chain and a shagreen case. Whoever can bring the said watch to Richard Mills, watchmaker in Edinburgh, shall have two guineas reward" (*Edinburgh Gazette*, 1695). **Ralph,** apprenticed to Charles Gretton, and turned over to Cuthbert Lee; C.C. 1697. **George,** long-case clock, "George Mills, de Sunderland, fecit," about 1710. **Thomas,** London; watch, h.m., 1762. **Robert,** 141 Ratcliff Highway, 1790-94. **Wm.,** same address, 1809-18. **Thomas, & Son,** 26 Red Lion St., Clerkenwell, 1812-18 91 Bishopsgate Without, 1823. **George** 141 Goswell St., 1825. **Hy.,** 171 Oxford St., 1845.

Milner. Thomas, London; long-case clocks, some inscribed "Thomas Millner," 1740-70. **Henry,** 7 Vere St., Oxford St., 1815.

Milnes, Geo., Huddersfield, 1833.

Milton, —, 29 Mary-le-bone St., Golden Sq.; card B.M., 1802.

Milward, Geo., 2 Little Brook St., 1806-15.

Mimess, R., Woolwich, 1816.

Minchener, Saml., London; long-case clock, about 1810.

Minchin, J., Moreton-in-Marsh, 1799-1821, afterwards at Stow-on-the-Wold.

Minchinale, William, C.C. 1701.

Minshull, Wm., apprenticed in 1666 to Nicholas Reeves, C.C.

Minten, Jno., London; watch, 1760.

Minuel, David, admitted C.C. 1683.

Miroir, a large pull-repeating travelling clock-watch in silver case, outer case of leather with silver mountings, dating from about 1740, signed "Miroir, London"; a very similar watch of apparently rather earlier date, inscribed "J. Miroir, Augspurg," was formerly in the Shandon collection; another travelling watch dating from about 1760, inscribed "J. Miroir, London."

Miroli, Denis, Geneva; about '20.

Mison, Jere, apprenticed C.C. 1688.

Misplace, R., Searle St., Lincoln's Inn Fields, 1775-88.

Mitchell. Myles, C.C. 1640. **Joseph,** apprenticed in 1674 to Nat Delander, C.C. **John,** St James's St., apprenticed to Jno. Earles, C.C. 1712. **Samuel,** St James's St.; repeating watch, about 1745; another, h.m., 1776. **Robert,** livery C.C. 1766. **& Viet,** 6 Cornhill, 1768. **Hy.,** f. of New York, 1787. **William,** Richmond; watch, 1804. **Jno.,** 6 Cornhill, 1817. **T. & W.,** Glasgow; watch, 1820. **Chas.,** 84 Tower Hill; watch, 1822. **& French,** 5 Clerkenwell Close, 1825. **& Son,** Glasgow, 1830.

Mitchelson. Jas., Thogmorton St., 1753-56. **Alexander,** 45 Michael's Alley, Cornhill, 1769-72. **Walter,** 3 Helmet Row, 1780-1800.

Mitford, John, apprenticed to Sir George Mertins, of Cornhill, whose daughter he married in 1714, when he was nineteen years old. £200 stock of the Exchange Assurance Association standing in his name, which, with interest, had accumulated to £6,600 in 1883, was then ordered by Mr Justice Williams to be paid to his nearest relatives.

Mitten, Francis, Chichester; 30-hour long-case clock, about 1750.

Mitzell, —, London; pendulum watch, Schloss collection, about 1700 (see p. 187).

Moginie, Samuel, 1 Prince Row, Pimlico, 1820-42 (succeeded Glover).

Moilliet. Dan., Geneva; watch, 1780. **A., & Co.,** Geneva; watch, 1790.

Moinau, Auguste, Philpott Terrace, Edgware Rd.; patented in 1840 (No. 8,501) a system of detached weights for clocks.

Moinet, Louis, born at Bourges 1768; died 1853. Author of "Nouveau Traité Général Astronomique et Civil d'Horlogerie Theorique et Pratique"; Paris, 1843.

Mole, James, Birmingham; long-case clock, about 1760, Sir James M. Moody.

Molee, P., 44 Great Sutton St., 1835.

Molens, Charles, C.C. 1709.

Molineux. Thos., Rochdale, 1770. **Wm.,** Rochdale, 1818.

Molleson, Thos., 62 Cornhill, 1788-1810.

Molyneux. R., & Sons (Robt. & Henry), 30 Southampton Row, Russell Sq., 1835-42; they were succeeded by Birchall & Appleton; Robert Molyneux, junr., went to America and settled there. **Robert,** a chronometer maker who carried on business at 44 Devonshire St., Queen's Sq., and afterwards in King St., Holborn; inventor of a compensation balance with auxiliary (Patent No. 8,418), March 1840. **& Cope,** London; clock, about 1840.

Moncas, Jno., Liverpool, 1818. **John,** 75 Myddelton St., Spa-fields, 1835.

Moncrief, Jno., apprenticed in 1688 to Jno. Bellard, C.C.

Monday, Joseph, C.C. 1654.

Money, Henry, 49 King Sq., 1855 (afterwards Money & Bassold).

Monk. Small sheep's-head clock, signed "William Monk Barwick St John," about 1730. **Edwd.,** 171 Fleet St., 1793, see Monks.

Monkes, Geo., Prescot, 1770.

Monkhouse. Thomas, Duke St., fecit, anno 1759; inscription on the barrel of a fine 8-day long-case clock with high numbered train, end pieces, and all the repeating work pivoted with cocks; on the dial the name Curteen, 1759. **Jas.,** Carlisle, 1768. **John,** London; on dial of clock by Vullin, B.M., about 1770. **& Son,** Carlisle, 1785-1810.

Monks, Chas., Prescot, 1812; also **Geo.,** same date.

Monnée, —, Vienna; tulip-shaped watch, Pierpont Morgan collection, about 1770.

Monnier, John, 38 Southampton St., Strand, 1812-28, see Wilson, W.

Monro. George, Edinburgh; watch, Evan Roberts collection, about 1730. **Benjamin,** 13 Moor St., Soho Sq., 1830-42.

Montagu. Jno., apprenticed in 1641 to Jno. Midnall, C.C. **T.,** London, about 1760; a watch by him, pinchbeck inner and shagreen outer case, exhibited at the Guelph Exhibition by Mr Geo. Carr Glyn.

Montgomery, Robt., New York, 1786.

Montlow. Henry, apprenticed in 1678 to Richard Browne, C.C. 1685; Abraham Acton apprenticed to him in 1691; fine long-case clock, about 1695, inscribed "Henricus Montlow, Londini—fecit"; another long-case clock, named "Mowtlow." **Conon,** apprenticed 1691 to Richd. Harold, C.C. **Henry,** apprenticed to John Delander; C.C. 1715.

Moody. David, C.C. 1649; gave a silver dish in 1651. **Charles,** 45 Rupert St., Piccadilly, 1815-25.

Moolinger, Henry, Philadelphia, 1794.

Moon. Thos., London; a "¾ wall clock" by him offered in the *Collectors' Circular*. **& Co.,** 4 Holborn Bars, 1790. **Christopher,** 4 Lower Holborn, 1810; watch, Schloss collection. **William,** 4 Lower Holborn, 1815-42; livery C.C. 1820.

Mooran, Andrew, London; maker of

clocks, about 1760, see Moran.

Moore. Robt., apprenticed in 1662 to Sam. Davis, C.C. **Edwd.,** London; lantern clock, 1680. **Joseph,** C.C. 1690. **Wm.,** apprenticed in 1693 to Ben Johnson, C.C.; C.C. 1701; fine long-case clock with large seconds circle in the arch of the dial, about 1715. **Daniel,** C.C. 1697. **Thos.,** Ipswich; the Wetherfield collection contains a striking and repeating bracket clock by him in an ebonised case, dating from about 1720; there are six bells on which the pull-repeating quarters are sounded; Mr W. W. Pope has a particularly attractive long-case musical and calendar clock by him; it chimes the quarters on four bells and plays one of seven tunes every hour, in the arch of the dial is an orchestra of eight moving figures; Mr R. Allen, Bridlington Quay, has a long-case clock by him; at Long Melford Church is a fine long trunk dial by him, the case with lacquer decoration. "Whereas Thos. Moore, clock and watchmaker in Ipswich, have for many years observ'd the misfortunes which

very frequently happen to pocket-watches of all sorts—viz., by sometimes coming into unskilful hands, &c., and often into the hands of servants (in absence of the owners thereof) they, endeavouring to wind up the watch, have turned the wrong way, and by so doing, they have broke the work (and the like often happens when Juice of Grape Predominate). Therefore this to give notice. That the above Thos. Moore have now made up several curious Silver and Gold Watches (and will continue to do so) so curiously contriv'd, that let the watch be wound up which way they please, either to right or left, they cannot fail of winding up the watch, with more safety than if wound but one and the common way, and are to be sold at very reasonable price. Any person or persons may have the freedom to seeing any of the said watches at his house in Ipswich aforesaid" (Ipswich Newspaper, 1729). At the Horological Institute is a fusee of one of Moore's watches, which was sent from Syracuse, New York, by Mr Geo. R. Wilkins; the great wheel and larger end of fusee are shown in the accompanying cut, and the action will be understood by those conversant with watch work; the device was described by Thiout in 1741, some years after Moore's advertisement appeared. Mr R. Eden Dickson has a clock by "Moore Melford" which he bought at the sale of the effects of Edward Fitzgerald to whom it was given by his friend W. M. Thackeray. **T.,** London; watch, 1763. **John,** 118 Fleet St., 1769-75. **Robt.,** Stoney St.; long-case clock, about 1770. **F.,** 37 Gracechurch St., 1770-75. **Francis,** Ferry Bridge; long-case clock, about 1775. **Wm.,** 55 Paternoster Row, 1775-88; 5 Ludgate St., 1793; watch, about 1790, silver case with crystal back showing the movement, Pierpont Morgan collection. —, Salisbury; long-case clock, Wetherfield collection, about 1780. **Peter,** 15 Sweeting's Alley, 1780-1806; verge watch by him, square pillars, in the Guildhall Museum. **& Gearing,** 55 Paternoster Row, 1783. **& Edwards**, 4 Holborn, 1793. **Patrick**, 15 Sweeting's Alley, 1806-10. **& Starkey**, 89 St Martin's Lane, 1823. **E. T.**, 37 Clement's Lane, 1823 ; 8 Prospect Pl., Kingsland, 1835. **Jno.**, formerly partner with Handley,· Clerkenwell Close, then Jno. Moore & Sons ; 1824-42. **George**, third son of Jno. Moore (Handley & Moore), 23 Percival St., 1838 ; afterwards succeeded F. B. Adams & Sons at 21 St John's Sq. ; died 1894, aged 80.

Moorhouse, —, Knaresborough, about 1825.

Moraley. **Wm.**, apprenticed in 1680 to Hy. Child ; turned over to Philip Corderoy, and afterwards to Thos. Tompion ; C.C. 1688. **Wm.**, London, 1828.

Moran, Andrew, Earl St., St Giles. This name appears on the disc at the top of an arch-dial 8-day case clock at the Crown, Harlesden, where it is stated to have been since 1740.

Morcombe, Jno., made the town clock for Hartland, Devonshire, in 1622-23 ; "new made" it 1657-58 ; the latter entry from the accounts refers, it is suggested, to a conversion from balance to pendulum.

More. **B.**, London ; watch, 1760. **Charles**, 19 Holywell Row, Shoreditch, 1840-42.

Morecand & Co., Paris, 1800.

Morehouse, W., London ; watch, 1807.

Morel, P., Geneva ; watch, 1780.

Moreland. **Thos.**, Chester ; watch, 1726. **John**, apprenticed to John Pike, C.C. 1738. **Thos.**, Chester, 1810-42.

Morell, Jas., apprenticed in 1676 to Michael Rose, C.C.

Moret, Nicholas, Paris, 1544 (see p. 304).

Morey, S., London ; lantern clock, 1700.

Morgan. **Richard**, petitioner to Charles I. for incorporation of C.C., and one of the first assistants, 1629-49. **Robert**, C.C. 1637. **Jude**, C.C. 1654. **Thomas**, C.C. 1658. **Hy.**, C.C. 1677. **William**, Southwark, 1696. **John**, C.C. 1703 ; long-case clock, inscribed "John Morgan, Chancery Lane, London." A Minute of the Court of the Cutlers' Company of the 30th October 1710 runs as follows :—"A peticon was read of Anthy Russell praying to have liberty to prosecute one John Morgan (a watchmaker for fitting up joyneing and selling Swords altho' he served noe apprenticeship to that trade) in the name of this Corporacōn, and that the Charter and By Laws of this Company might be produced before Councell or otherwise as the nature of his case should require." **Thos.**, Baltimore, Md., 1774. **Thos.**, Philadelphia, 1779-93. **& Miles**, 32 Ludgate St., 1790. **Wm.**, London ; watch, 1810. **Theodore**, Salem, 1837-42 ; then **Luther**.

Moricand ; French watch, 1780.

Morice. **Geo.**, apprenticed in 1653 to Thos. Eyston, C.C. **David, & Son**, 15 Fenchurch St., 1804-23 ; 86 Cornhill, 1826-36 ; Mr J. Drummond Robertson has a gold watch, h.m., 1816, "D. & W. Morice, Fenchurch St." ; another watch, 1823, "Fenchurch St. and Cornhill."

Moriffet, R. & C., 22 Denmark St., Soho, 1783.

Morizot à Paris ; watch, about 1824.

Morland. **Jno.**, Smithfield, C.C. 1734. **Wm.**, Red Cross St., 1780-85. **—**, 17 Red Cross St., 1790-94.

Morley, Wm., apprenticed in 1691 to Jno. Willoughby, C.C. **Robt.**, York, f., 1732. **Robert**, Hursley church clock, 1808.

Morliere, born at Orleans ; excelled as a watch-case enameller at Blois, about 1650.

Mornand, I., Paris ; thick alarm watch, hour numerals on enamel plaques, single case covered with leather *piqué*, about 1690 (see p. 176).

Morpeth, Thos., Hexham, 1770.

Morrel, Benj., Boscowen, U.S.A., 1816-45.

Morrell, Jno., Whitby, 1822-33.

Morreton, —, London ; watch, about 1775.

Morris. **Edwd.**, C.C. 1672 ; assistant 1677. **Henry**, 82 Fleet St., 1733-75. **T.**, 68 Bell Dock, Wapping, 1794. **John**, C.C. 1799.

Morriset & Lukin, 22 Denmark St., St Giles, 1793.

Morrison. **Richd.**, 15 Cheapside, 1769-83. "Richard Morrison at his old shop [No. 15] the Three Kings and Golden Ball opposite Foster Lane, in Cheapside, successor to Mr Stafford Briscoe," card Ponsonby collection. **William N.**, 33 Ludgate Hill, 1840. **John**, 27 Packington St. ; a well-known clockmaker ; died 1893, aged 77.

Morritt & Lee, 93 High Holborn, 1816.

Morse, Richard, 8 Charing Cross, 1835-42 (succeeded Rigby).

Morson. **(& Stephenson**, 98 Fleet St., 1760-72.) **Richard**, 12 Ludgate St., 1775.

Mort, Richd., apprenticed C.C. 1693.

Mortimor, Chas., London ; watch, 1824.

Mortimore, —, Dartmouth ; watch, 1825.

Morton. **Samuel**, 210 Borough, 1775. **& Milroy**, 1800.

Mosbrucker à Saverne, about 1750.

Mose, Jas., Litchfield ; long-case clock, about 1760.

Moseley. **William**, C.C. 1680. **Lewis**, Liverpool, 1770. **Charles S.**, born at Westfield, Mass., 1838 ; a clever mechanician, devised the early machines of the American Watch Company of which he was master mechanic in 1859 ; in 1864 he joined the Elgin Watch Company of which he became superintendent.

Mosely. **Elinor** ; Elizabeth Askell was bound apprentice to her in 1734 ; C.C. 1726-34. **Martin**, 28 Goulston Sq., 1804 ; 6 Bevis Marks, 1815-35. **Robert, & Son**, 113 Fetter Lane, 1822-42. **Moses**, 26 Bury St., 1830-42. **Ephraim**, 48 Leadenhall St., 1838-42. **Robert E.**, Newburyport, U.S.A., 1848.

Moser, George Michael, born at Schaffhausen in 1705 ; came to England, and in 1768 was appointed keeper of the Royal Academy ; died 1783 ; fine *repoussé* work by him on watch-cases ; he was also of repute as an enameller.

Moses. **Selegman**, London ; long-case clock, about 1775. **Ephraim**, 135 Whitechapel, 1790.

Moss. **Thos.**, Frodsham ; long-case clock, about 1740 ; Mr Wm. R. Moss has a bell-top bracket clock by him in mahogany case which strikes on three bells and repeats the quarters ; also a long-case clock made in 1776 or 1778 showing days of the month, age and phases of the moon, and time of high water (see p. 364). **Thomas**, 24 Ludgate St., 1775 ; livery C.C. 1786 ; died 1827. **John**, 106 Holborn Hill, 1825. **B.**, Tabernacle Walk, 1835.

Motley. **Richard**, Wapping ; C.C. 1682 ; long Oriental lacquer case clock, strike-silent, about 1720 ; long-case clock, ship worked by pendulum, mahogany case ; on trade bill inside the case "Richard Motley at the Hand & Buckle near King Edward Stairs, Wapping."

Mott. **(Or Moth)**, **Thos.**, apprenticed in 1648 to Jere. Gregory ; C.C. 1656. **Hy.**,

apprenticed in 1655 to Jno. Palfrey, C.C.; watch, about 1665, inscribed "Henricus Mott in Drury Lane." **& Bellin**, 91 Bishopsgate Without, 1815. **William**, 91 Bishopsgate Without, 1830 ; 55 Cheapside, 1835.

Motteux, Samuel, C.C. 1697.

Mottram, John, Warden Court, Clerkenwell Close, 1780-94 ; large musical clock by him in splendid case designed apparently for some Eastern potentate.

Mottu Brothers, 11 Richmond Buildings, Soho Sq., 1840-42.

Moule. **Jno.**, apprenticed in 1679 to Richd. Jarrett, C.C. **Jas.**, London ; long-case clock, about 1785.

Mouline, A., & Co., 29 Percy St., Tottenham Court Rd., 1842.

Moulinie & Co., Geneva ; watch, 1820.

Moulton. **Henry**, C.C. 1685. **Saml.**, 210 Borough, 1788-1800.

Mount, William, C.C. 1692.

Mountford, Zachariah, St Albans ; admitted C.C. 1684 ; "Mountford for mending my masters watch 0 2 0" (*MSS., Earl of Verulam*, 1696) ; long-case clock, about 1700. **John**, London ; long-case arabesque marqueterie clock, about 1705.

Mountlow, see Montlow.

Mousley, Arthur, apprenticed 1671 to Jere. Johnson, C.C.

Mowbray, Wm., Doncaster, 1770.

Mowlton. **Conan**, C.C. 1700. **Henry**, C.C. 1715.

Mowtlow, see Montlow.

Moxon, Josh., Bradford ; watch, 1780. **J.**, skeleton clock at Buckingham Palace, about 1820, inscribed "Invented by William Congreve Esq., J. Moxon fecit."

Moy, Matt., apprenticed in 1661 to Ben Hill, C.C.

Moynier, Geneva ; watch, 1790. **Et Fils**, Geneva ; watch, 1830.

Moysant, —, Blois ; watch, case finely painted in enamel (see p. 112).

Moyse, —, Blois ; maker of a skull watch (see p. 111), 1587.

Moyser, Thos., apprenticed in 1653 to Wm. Godbed, C.C.

Moze, Henry, Shadd Thames ; clock, about 1740 ; watch, 1760.

Muckarsie, George James, 47 High Holborn, 1794 ; livery C.C. 1824.

Muddle, Thos., Rotherfield ; lantern clocks, 1700-10.

Mudge. **Thomas**, Fleet St. ; a celebrated maker ; born 1715, died 1794 (see p. 266). **& Dutton**, 148 Fleet St., 1759-90 ; Reid mentions an equation clock they made for General Clerk, and which, together with a spring clock having the striking work described on p. 245, was entailed on the house of Pennycuick ; in the Wetherfield collection is a striking and repeating bracket clock by them dating from about 1780 ; the Rev. A. F. Sutton has a watch inscribed "Mudge & Dutton," and bearing the hall mark for 1759 ; I am uncertain when the partnership was dissolved, but T. Mudge, junr., refers to Dutton in 1790 as Mudge's late partner, see Dutton. **Jno.**, London ; long-case clock, about 1800, Wetherfield collection ; regulator, about 1830. **Geo.**, 430 Edgware Rd., 1855.

Mugnier, horloger du Roy, Paris ; artistic watches, Breguet style, about 1820.

Mulford. **Wm.**, apprenticed in 1682 to Jno. Norcott, C.C. **John**, Cursitor's Alley ; died while warden C.C. 1748.

Mulgrave, Geo., London ; watch, 1800.

Muller. **Andreas** ; clock, Soltykoff collection, about 1570. **Johan Conrad** ; clock, about 1705. **& Thum**, 40 King St., Soho, 1842.

Mulliken, Samuel, Newburyport, U.S.A., 1740-56; then Jonathan, then Saml., at Salem.

Mullineux, Thos., apprenticed in 1693 to Edwd. Boone, C.C.

Muncaster. Lancaster: Thos., 1797-1830; Wm., 1806, f.; Jno., 1806, f. Jno., Ulverstone, 1818. Jno., Whitehaven, 1833.

Munday. Thos., apprenticed in 1688 to Jno. Benson; C.C. 1692. Wm., C.C.; in 1734 he worked for Marshall.

Munden, Francis, C.C. 1653.

Munkerson, David, Edinburgh, apprenticed to Paul Romieu the younger and admitted a free "knockmaker" in 1712, his essay being a watch movement.

Munroe & Whitney, Concord, Mass., 1805-25.

Murphy. John, Northampton, 1775. P., Dublin; watch, 1797.

Murray. Wm., Edinburgh, 1712. T., London; watch, Schloss collection, about 1780. James, a celebrated chronometer and watchmaker who carried on business at Cornhill from about 1814; livery C.C. 1817; one Strahan seems to have been in partnership with him at 19 Sweeting's Alley, from about 1816 till about 1825. James Weddell, in his "Voyage towards the South Pole in 1822-4," stated: "Of chronometers I had one of eight days, No. 820, made by Jas. Murry; one of two days by Murry and Strachan, No. 403; one of twenty-four hours, also made by Murry; and they all performed sufficiently well to recommend the makers for their very improved mechanism in this important art." After the Royal Exchange was destroyed by fire in 1838 James Murray carried on a successful business at 30 Cornhill; he was succeeded by his two sons, James and John. James afterwards went to India and established a successful business in Calcutta; he died in 1892; John Murray, at 30 Cornhill, was joined in partnership by one Mitchell, and continued there with him for some years.

Musgrave, Jno., Keswick, 1833.

Musket, Jno., Prescot, 1770.

Mussard, Daniel (Genevese), C.C. 1686; watch in the Hamilton collection, bought by Lord Moray at the auction sale in 1882, for £154. 10s.; portraits of the Stuart family were enamelled thereon; 1670-90.

Musson, —, Paris, 1782-95.

Muston. & Gath, Bristol, 1790. Geo., Red Lion St., Clerkenwell, 1835-42.

Mut, Gerard, Frankfort; watch, Vienna Treasury, with train wheels quadrangular and pentagonal, about 1670.

Myddleton, see Middleton.

Myers. John, f. of York, 1778; in London at 255 Borough till 1804; long-case clock by him, S.K.M. John, 255 High Holborn, 1790. Hy., 164 Ratcliff Highway, 1804. Moses, 152 Regent St., 1830. Abraham, 79 Leman St., 1840-42.

Mylne, Humphrey, Edinburgh, admitted as a locksmith and knockmaker 1647; made a clock for Magdalen Chapel, Cowgate, the meeting-place of the Incorporation of Hammermen, in 1666, died about 1690. G. E., foreman for Yonge; afterwards at 9 Upper Chadwell St., maker of high-class watches, sometime hon. secretary to the Horological Institute; died 1868, aged 53.

Mynuel, —, Paris; clock, S.K.M., 1700; another, Wallace collection (see p. 308).

Myrmecides, —, Paris, about 1530; thought by Dubois to be the inventor of cruciform watches.

Myson, Jeremiah, C.C. 1698.

Nadauld. Wm., 129 Houndsditch, 1804-20. W. R., White Hart Court, Lombard St., 1819-33.

Naish, Jas., London; clock, about 1770.

Naizon, Francis, 42 Poultry, 1780-85.

Napton, Wm., apprenticed in 1686 to Edwd. Engs, senr., C.C.

Nardin, Ulysse, Neuchatel; born 1823, died 1876.

Nash. Wm., oval watch, metal case, Mr Edwd. Parr, about 1605 (p. 136). Wm., apprenticed in 1663 to Thos. Birch, C.C. Jno., C.C. 1667. Thomas, C.C. 1717; clock, "Tho. Nash, Salop," about 1770. Samuel, 11 Broadway, Blackfriars, 1790-94.

Nathan. Henry, Ratcliff Highway; C.C. 1673; maker of long-case clocks, 1673-1700. Phineas, 9 Magdalen Row, 1840-42.

Nau. Richard, C.C. 1661. George, C.C. 1675.

Naudey, Francis, 59 Dean St., Soho, 1842.

Naylor, J., Mr J. B. Cooksen, Meldon Park, Morpeth, has a remarkably interesting astronomical clock by "Ion Naylor, near Namptwich, Cheshire," about 1725; another astronomical clock by him is at the Cluny Museum, Paris. Charles, Liverpool, about 1770.

Neale. Thos., apprenticed in 1655 to Joseph Quash, C.C. John, Leadenhall St., 1743-59; in 1744 he obtained a patent for a "Quadrantal planetarian."

Neat, J., 40 Duke St., Manchester Sq., 1817.

Neate, Wm., 3 Sweeting's Alley, 1817.

Needham. Jno., apprenticed in 1691 to Richd. Parsons, C.C. Benjamin, C.C. 1709. Jas., Fleet Lane, C.C. 1734. Robt., 56 Piccadilly, 1793. Charles, 55 Piccadilly, 1825.

Negus, Willy, C.C.; to him was apprenticed in 1815 Samuel Evans. The Negus's who established a leading position in New York during the nineteenth century, possibly sprang from the Willy Negus here mentioned, whose business in London I am unable to trace.

Neighbour, William, C.C. 1685, apprenticed to Ahasuerus Fromanteel, junr., and turned over to Benjamin Graves.

Neild, James, 4 St James's St., 1755-94. J., 4 Upper Thames St., 1788.

Neill, Robert, High St., Belfast; succeeded John Knox in 1816.

Neiser, Augustine, Philadelphia, 1739-80.

Nelmes, Robert, 21 Whiskin St., 1827; 38 Upper King St., Bloomsbury, 1842.

Nelson. James, apprenticed to Oswald Durant, 1638; admitted C.C. 1645; maker of an astronomical watch in Guildhall Museum. John, apprenticed to Daniel Stevens and turned over to Daniel Quare; C.C. 1697. Robert, C.C. 1697. Wm., Liverpool, 1775. H., London, watch, 1799. John, 15 Hayfield Place, Mile End, 1842. Thomas, London, chronometer maker, died 1882.

Nelthropp, The Rev. Henry Leonard, an authority on antique timekeepers, who gave his collection to the Clockmakers' Company, of which he was master in 1893 and 1894; died 1901, aged 81.

Nemes. Robt., apprenticed to Bart. Powell 1669; C.C. 1667. John, Queen St., C.C. 1724.

Nerry, Jno., London; a watch by him, Guildhall Museum, about 1730.

Netherwood, Job, apprenticed in 1686 to Clem Forster, C.C.

Netter, Robt., apprenticed in 1681 to Jno. Winn, C.C.

Neué, Hen., Strand, about 1740.

Neuens, Peter, 32 Bread St., 1840-42.

Neuren, D. (also spelt Neveren and Neweren), London; maker of verge watches, 1760-90.

Neuwers, Michael, made a clock for the Earl of Shrewsbury (see p. 61), 1599, see Nouwen.

Neve, John, "in ye Strand"; basket top bracket clock, about 1680.

Nevill, Geo., apprenticed in 1653 to Wm. Comfort, C.C.

Neville, J., London; watch, about 1704.

Newad, W., London; watch, 1760.

Newbald, James, f., York, 1830.

Newbrough, Jeremiah, Grayes Inn, maker of long-case clocks, 1700-10.

Newby. Wm., Kendal, 1770. Jas., Kendal, 1785. John, 3 Judd St., 1825.

Newcomb, Joseph, livery C.C. 1810.

Newell. Jno., apprenticed in 1681 to Robt. Doore, C.C. Thomas, Sheffield, U.S.A., 1809-20. William, livery C.C. 1810.

Newland, Ab., London; watches, 1813-25.

Newlove, Jno., York, f., 1823-30.

Newman. Nat., apprenticed in 1694 to Hy. Merryman, C.C.; Broad St. in 1734. Robert, London; clock, 1700 (see p. 368). Richd., Lynn; watch, shagreen case, Mr A. E. Clarke, about 1750. John, 49 Lombard St., 1775-83. Joseph, 30 Great Alie St., 1790. John, 17 Piccadilly, 1804-25; livery C.C. 1810. Wm., 109 Golden Sq., 1840-42.

Newnham, Nathaniel, C.C. 1703.

Newsam. Jno., York, f., 1568-98 (see p. 197). Bartholomew, Strand; appointed, in 1572, clockmaker to Queen Elizabeth, in succession to Nicholas Urseau (see p. 196, also p. 108).

Newsham. Wm., Clerkenwell Close, 1765-93. Richard, Liverpool; calendar watch, 1791.

Newsom, Thos., London; watch, 1828.

Newson, Jno., Basinghall; C.C. 1734.

Newstead, Chris., York, f., 1797.

Newton. Herbert, apprenticed in 1663 to Thos. Wheeler, C.C. George, London; about 1680. William, East Smithfield, C.C. 1685. Thomas, Fenchurch St., 1753-56. John, 76 Lamb's Conduit St., 1788-1810. Jno., 10 Great Ormond St., 1788-1815. Alexander, Levi, & Co., 4 Bury St., St Mary Axe, 1839-42.

Nicasius, John, C.C. 1632; several times fined for abuse and disrespect, and in 1679 was suspended from being assistant; master 1653-55. Octagonal watch, G.M., inscribed "Nicasius, London."

Nichol, Isaac, C.C. 1681.

Nicholas. —, lantern clock, inscribed "David Nicholas, fecit," about 1680. Benj., apprenticed in 1682 to Thos. Taylor (Holborn), C.C. W., 158 Tooley St., 1825. Samuel, & Son, 158 Tooley St., 1835-40.

Nicholls. Roger, C.C. 1667. Thomas, C.C. 1707. George, New York, f., 1728-50. John, clock-case maker, 6 Red Lion St., Clerkenwell, 1804-10. & Harris, Canterbury, 1815.

Nichols, Thomas, apprenticed to Edward East; C.C. 1720.

Nicholson. Richd., C.C.; worked for Dudds in 1734. Jno., Durham 1770. J., Whitehaven, 1775. John, 53 Cornhill, 1816-30.

Nickals, Isaac, Wells; splendid long-case chiming clock, with lacquer decoration, phases of the moon and time of high water in arch, about 1740, Wetherfield collection.

Nickisson, S., Lower Ashby St., 1815-40 ; 33 Northampton Sq., 1842.

Nicole. John, keeper of the great clock within the Palace of Westminster in 1371, his wages being sixpence a day. **Adolphe**, Dean St., Soho ; a remarkably clever horologist ; in 1844 he patented keyless work (No. 10,348) (see p. **410**) ; the patent included a chronograph with heart-shaped cam ; in 1862 he patented an improved chronograph with castle-ratchet (No. 1,461).

Nicolet. Jacob Louis, settled in St Imier 1770 ; made nearly all the parts of his watches, and when he had completed three, rode on horseback to Chaux de Fonds to sell them. **Joseph Marce**, Philadelphia, 1797.

Nicoll. Wm., 117 Great Portland St., 1790-1835. **John**, 117 Great Portland St., 1814-42.

Nielsen, Emil, Soho Sq., died 1899.

Nightingale. Jno., apprenticed C.C. 1655. **Wm.**, Red Lion St. ; liveryman C.C. 1776-94.

Niloe, Hans (Dutch) ; maker of a musical clock for James I. In August 1609 Sir Julius Cæsar writes to the Clerks of the Signet to the effect that Niloe is pressing for the £300 due to him for the clock.

Nixon, Thos., oval watch, G.M., about 1605.

Noades, J., Strand, 1775.

Noakes. Jas., watch movement maker, 34 Charterhouse St., 1776-94 ; livery C.C. 1776. (& Nylder, 129 Houndsditch, 1790-94.) **Jas.**, 126 Houndsditch, 1800 ; 24 Bishopsgate St. Within, 1810-18.

Noble. John, London ; 30-hour long-case clock, about 1690. **Phineas**, apprenticed in 1693 to Edwd. Whitfield, C.C. **Jas.**, Lancaster, 1733, f. **Wm.**, London Bridge ; long-case clocks, about 1760. **Wm.**, 2 Cow Cross St., 1804. **& Harrison**, 35 Fetter Lane, 1816-25. **C.**, 211 Strand, 1830.

Nobson, John, apprenticed to Daniel Quare ; C.C. 1697.

Nodes. John, Strand, 1770-75. **William**, 126 New Bond St ; in 1790 he wrote to C.C. respecting watches seized on his premises ; 1783-94.

Noel. Aymé, maker of a watch, B.M., crystal case, dial and outer case of silver, about 1620. **Saml.**, London ; watch, Schloss collection, about 1800.

Noir, Paris ; watch, about 1770.

Noisy, —, Paris, clockmaker to Louis XV., 1750.

Nokes, see Noakes.

Nolda, J. A., London ; watch, about 1740, Mr E. Wehrle.

Nollorth, Chas., Yarmouth, 1775.

Nolson, Jno., apprenticed in 1689 to Jno. Pilcher, C.C.

Noon. Jno., apprenticed in 1655 to Francis Munden, C.C. **—**, seller of lamp clocks at the White Hart, in the Poultry, 1731. **W.**, Ashby-de-la-Zouch ; good long-case clocks, from about 1800 ; Mr W. B. Hextall has one bought in 1828, high mahogany case, painted dial.

Norcell, Jno., London ; clock-watch, 1681.

Norcott, John, C.C. 1681. " Lost on my Lord Mayor's Day, a middle-size Gold Pendulum and Minute Watch, with an engraven Out-Case, having a scarlet French Ribon flower'd with Gold and black, the Inner-Case scraped on the backside with a Touch-stone ; the name John Norcott. Whoever brings it to Shuttleworth's Coffee House at Charing Cross, shall have 5 Guineas Reward " (1691).

Norgate, John, C.C. 1712.

Norman. Chas., London ; watch, 1820. **Samuel**, 50 and 51 Prince's St., Leicester Sq., 1825.

Norris. Edward, at the Cross Keys in Bethlem ; apprenticed in 1650 to Wm. Selwood ; C.C. 1658 ; master 1686 ; full-size lantern clock, balance escapement, dolphin frets, inscribed " Edward Norris, at the Cross Keys in Bethlem, Londini." **Joseph**, C.C. 1670. **Charles**, C.C. 1687. **Dav.**, London ; long-case clock, about 1750. **Chas.**, 18 Gracechurch St., 1763-94. **Patrick**, Liverpool, 1765. **Wm.**, Birmingham, 1770. **Wm.**, Liverpool, 1785. **Chas.**, junr., 22 Cheapside, 1795.

Norry, N., Gisors ; small clock-watch, about 1620.

North. —, f. of York, 1623. **William**, admitted C.C. 1639 ; maker of an oval watch ; silver case, B.M. (see p. **202**), 1620-64. **John**, C.C. 1650. **John**, Silver St., C.C. 1720. **Richard**, Driffield, 1770. **Richd.**, 44 Lombard St., 1772-1800. **Wm.**, White Hart Yard, Drury Lane, 1790. **Wm.**, York, f., 1816. **Fredk.**, 2 Old Compton St., 1816. **Thos.**, same address, 1820.

Northam. J., 46 Greek St., 1817. **G.**, musical clockmaker, Tabernacle Sq., Finsbury, 1825. **& Son**, 49 Greek St., Soho, 1825.

Northcote. Jno., C.C. 1681. **Samuel**, son of a Plymouth watchmaker, and elder brother of James Northcote the artist, was sent to London to Mudge to be instructed in watchmaking in 1766 ; a watch by him inscribed " Samuel Northcote, Plymouth," about 1780.

Northen, Richd., Hull, 1780-1822.

Northey. J., Bethlem Court ; watch, 1784. **John**, 181 Brick Lane, Spitalfields, 1790-94. **J.**, Spitalfields ; watch, 1794.

Northgraves, Denton, Hull, 1822.

Norton. Thomas, C.C. 1720. **Samuel**, Fish St. Hill ; liveryman C.C. 1776 ; 1770-80. **Eardley**, 49 St John St., Clerkenwell, a well-known maker of musical and astronomical clocks and watches, 1760-94 ; in 1771 he patented (No. 987) " a clock which strikes the hours and parts upon a principle entirely new ; and a watch which repeats the hours and parts, so concisely contrived and disposed as to admit of being conveniently contained not only in a watch, but also in its appendage, such as a key, seal, or trinket." In Buckingham Palace is an astronomical clock with four dials he made for George III. (see p. **266**) ; a splendid four-train, repeating, and musical clock which is in the possession of Mr J. E. Whiting, Andover, Mass., U.S.A., was formerly the property of Mr Edward Savage, Mr Whiting's grandfather ; it is 28 in. high, chimes the quarters on eight bells, and plays on sixteen bells of eleven tunes every three hours ; Mr W. L. Unkill, Mexico City, has a fine clock by him, and other Eardley Norton clocks have been seen recently in Russia ; Dr Tad. Estreicher has a repeating watch by him in gold cases—it formerly belonged to Ambrose Grabowski, a distinguished Polish archæologist ; watch, about 1785, inscribed " Eardley & D. Norton " ; they were succeeded by Gravell & Tolkein. **—**, Market Row, Yarmouth, 1788. **Graham**, clock, about 1790. **Thomas**, Philadelphia, 1811. **W. D.**, London ; watch, about 1820. **B.**, watch-case maker, 59 Banner St., 1835.

Notron, Yeldaye, London ; bracket clock, about 1780, so named, seen at the Hague ; the name is a curious jumble of " Eardley Norton," a well-known maker of the period.

Notyap, see Payton.

Nourisson, Guillaume, reconstructed the Lyons clock in 1660 (see p. **67**).

Nourse, Thomas, 22 Beach Lane ; apprenticed to Edward Avenell ; C.C. 1740 ; livery 1766.

Noury, Pierre, Paris ; clockmaker to Louis XIV., 1650.

Nouwen, Michael, London ; 1590-1613 (see p. **200**).

Noyes, Leonard W., Nashua, U.S.A., 1830-40.

Nuer, Jean, " A. Saintes " ; oval watch, about 1600 ; Mr Max. Rosenheim (see p. **136**).

Nurse, John, C.C. 1718.

Nutsford, Wm., Whitehaven, 1833.

Oakes. Richard, shagreen case maker, 86 Snow Hill, 1775. **John**, 4 Grub St., 1775-80. **Jno.**, Oldham, 1818-32. **Wm.**, Oldham, 1833.

Oakey, Jno., apprenticed in 1685 to Wm. Dent, C.C.

Oakley, Wm., 39 High St., St Giles, 1804-20.

Ofard, —, enamelled watch, " Ofard a Gex," about 1675 (see p. **151**).

Ogden. Thomas, C.C. 1659. **Jno.**, Bow Brigg, Yorkshire ; long-case clock, 1681 (see p. **372**). Mr J. Whiteley Ward had a lantern clock crown wheel escapement, bob pendulum, by **Sam. Ogden**, a son of Isaac Ogden, of Sowerby ; he was born in 1669 and baptized at Halifax Parish Church ; there are numerous entries in the accounts of Halifax Parish Church between 1693 and 1700 of payments to him in respect of the clock ; he probably died in 1701, for in that year Chris. Marshall was appointed to succeed him in upholding the clock and chime for 20s. per annum. There was a **James Ogden** at Water Green in Soyland, who died in 1715. Two brothers, **Samuel** and **Thomas Ogden**, each carried on business at Ripponden ; they were nephews of John Ogden and Quakers ; experiencing trouble with the Church party at Ripponden they shifted, Samuel to Newcastle and Thomas to Halifax, where he carried on business in Crown St. ; Mr J. Whiteley Ward had also a long-case clock by Thos. Ogden, Halifax (see p. **365**) ; in the Church-wardens' accounts at the Parish Church, Halifax, is the following : " 1725 Tho. Ogden for mending the chimes, 3s." ; he died in 1769, and by his will he left his engines, tools, implements of his trade as watchmaker, and stock to John Knight, " he paying for the gold cases prepared for an eight days watch of his own making." **John Ogden**, son of John Ogden, of Bowbridge Hall, was born 1704 and lived at Sunderland ; Mr Robt. Brown has a clock by Jane Ogden, widow of John Ogden, of Sunderland. **Ben.**, Darlington, about 1740.

Ogston & Bell, Davies St. ; patented a watch with two barrels in 1826 (No. 5,314), see also Dwerryhouse.

O'Hara, Charles, Philadelphia, 1799.

Okeham, Edward, admitted C.C. 1632.

Okes, Thos., Oldham, 1818.

Okeshot, Robt., apprenticed in 1664 to Ralph Greatorex, C.C.

Oldham, Joseph, Liverpool, 1818.

Oliver, Sam., London ; watch, 1725. **—**, Cambridge, 1780-95. **Thomas**, 17 Fleet

St., 1780 ; 2 Brook St., Hanover Sq., 1790-1800. **Griffith**, Philadelphia, 1785-93. **Jas.**, watch-case maker ; died 1892, aged 76.

Olley & Clark, Poplar, 1817.

Ollivant. & Morton, Manchester, 1818. **T. & J.**, Market St., Manchester, 1832.

Oltramare, Estinne ; large watch in enamelled case, about 1610, Pierpont Morgan collection.

Oosterwyk, Abram, Middleburgh ; month long clock, Wetherfield collection, repeating on small bell at the half-hour the time struck at the previous hour, 12 in. dial, fine marqueterie case, with domed hood, about 1710.

Oram. Morris, apprenticed in 1684 to Richard George, C.C. **Geo.**, 13 Whiskin St., 1842.

Orange, —, Versailles ; watch, about 1780.

Ordson, William. In the Guildhall Museum is a verge watch by him, square pillars, enamel dial, the hours represented by letters forming the name " James Newman*," about 1720.

Orel, Thos., London ; watch, 1770.

Orford, Robt., 71 Oxford St., 1795-1810.

Orme. Jno., Lancaster, 1712, f. **Thos.**, Oldham, 1818.

Ormond, David, Westminster ; long-case clock, square dial, about 1710.

Orpwood. Wm., Ipswich ; clock, about 1790, Mr J. O. Payne. **Richard**, 7 Worship St., Finsbury, about 1800. **Geo.**, 58 Bishopsgate Within, 1810-42 (see p. 394).

Orr. Thomas, Philadelphia, 1811. **Peter**, 17 Myddleton Sq., 1840 ; he afterwards established a business at Madras.

Orrell, Jno., Preston, 1818.

Ortelli, A., Oxford ; watch, about 1790.

Orton. Edward, C.C. 1687. **Jno.**, Manchester, ·1818. **William F.**, 5 York Rd., 1835. **Preston, & Co.**, Farmington, U.S.A., 1836.

Osborn, William, C.C. 1700.

Osborne, Birmingham ; on clocks, 1800-42.

Osmond. Hy., apprenticed in 1681 to Sam Gascoigne, C.C. **Jas.**, apprenticed in 1681 to Jas. Clowes, C.C.

Osmont, Jean B., 41 Strand, 1840 ; 6 Victoria Rd., Pimlico, 1842.

Otley. Thomas, 55 Piccadilly, 1823. **Jonathan**, Keswick, 1833.

Oudin, Charles, Rue Vivienne, Paris, pupil·of Breguet ; maker of fine watches, and inventor of a form of keyless work (see p. 410).

Oughtred. Benjamin, C.C. 1639. **William**, author of several books on mathematics, including "Clavis Mathematicæ," Oxford, 1677 ; Derham speaks of him with admiration.

Outhwaite, Thos & Co., Liverpool, 1818.

Overbury. Hy., apprenticed in 1687 to Thos. Overbury, C.C. ; pendulum watch, Nelthropp collection, signed " Henry Overbury, Rotterdam," about 1705 ; repeating watch, 1718, signed " Henry Overbury, Overschie." **Thomas**, brother C.C. 1688.

Overton, P., London ; watch, 1835.

Overzee. Gerard, Isleworth (naturalised), brother C.C. 1678 ; maker of lantern and other clocks, 1670-90. **Timothy**, apprenticed in 1693 to Thos. Whitehead, C.C.

Ovingham, —, watch, Mr R. T. Mole, London, h.m., 1819.

Owen. Ben, London, completed his apprenticeship 1694 ; maker of long-case clocks, 1694-1740. **William**, Cheapside, 1737-40. **Watkin**, Llanrwst, 1770. **John**, Llanrwst ; clock, about 1780. **Joseph**, 10

Helmet Row, 1800 ; 243 St Margaret's Hill, 1810. **Griffith**, Philadelphia, 1811 ; then **Jno. Richd.**, London ; watch, 1830.

Owston, Michael, Scarboro', 1822.

Oyens, Peter, London ; long-case clock, about 1730. Mr William Norman has a token issued by Oyens, No. 60 Fore St., Dock.

Oyster, Daniel, Reading, U.S.A., 1820-40.

Pace. Thomas, at the Crown in Fleet St. ; maker of several small-sized lantern clocks, originally with balances (frets, Fig. 615), 1630-60. **Thomas**, 128 Whitechapel ; a well-known maker of bracket and long-case clocks, 1788-1840 ; watch by him, 1800. **Jno.**, 19 Cock Hill, Ratcliffe, 1790-94. **John**, Bury St Edmunds ; patented in 1833 (No. 6,506) a night timepiece. **Edmund**, 21 Thavies Inn, 1840-42. **Chas.**, 128 Whitechapel High St., 1842. **Henry**, 11 Green Terrace, Clerkenwell, 1842 ; 35 King St., Cheapside, 1848-58.

Pacificus, Archdeacon, Verona ; one of those to whom the invention of wheel and weight clocks is ascribed. Claim disputed by Dithmar ; 850.

Pack, Richard, C.C. 1712.

Packer. Wm., Buckingham ; watch, 1795. **Wm.**, 376 Oxford St., 1840.

Padbury, Dorset and Hampshire : **Andrew**, 1730-75 ; **Thos.**, 1800 ; **Jno.**, 1825 ; **Jas.**, Bishops Waltham, died 1898, aged 82. Mr C. J. Bentall has an early long mahogany case clock by Andrew Padbury ; the centre of the dial rotates with the hour hand showing time at different places throughout the world (see p 365).

Pagars, Dan, 44 St Martin's Lane, 1793.

Page. Joseph, apprenticed to Jeffery Bailey ; C.C. 1683. **Luke**, apprenticed in 1683 to Ben Marshall, C.C. **Henry**, Jewin St., C.C. 1713. **Thos.**, Norwich ; watch, about 1750. **Jno.**, Ipswich ; long-case month timepiece, about 1750 ; bracket clock, crown wheel escapement, having the acting parts of catgut, about 1770. **John**, 129 Strand, 1775-90 ; 8 Hind Court, Fleet St., 1794. **Wm.**, 17 Liquorpond St., 1815-18.

Paget, Ambrose, C.C. 1728.

Pagnes, William, Butcher's Row, East Smithfield ; lantern clocks, about 1690.

Paillard. Baptiste ; watch, 1760. **C. A.**, Geneva ; inventor of palladium alloy nonmagnetic balances and springs ; died 1896.

Pain. Benj., apprenticed 1672 to Wm. Watmore, C.C. **William**, C.C. 1729 ; 8-day clock, brass dial, "William Pain, Darlington." **David**, London ; watch, gold-chased case, about 1735 ; bracket chime clock, about 1740. **Thomas**, long-case clocks, about 1760. **Wm.**, Trowbridge ; long-case clock, about 1790.

Paine. Edmond, London ; watch, 1711. **John P.**, 39 High St., St Giles's ; received in 1826 a silver medal from the Society of Arts for a method of illuminating dials, 1826-40. **& Balleston**, 5 Banner St., 1840.

Pairas, Charles, Blois ; two octagonal watches by him, S.K.M., about 1605 ; on one in the Salting collection the name is spelt Perras.

Palethorp, Wm., Liverpool, 1833.

Palfrey, John, C.C. 1654.

Palin, Wm., Nantwich, 1833.

Pallier, —, locksmith, of Valence ; in 1451 contracted with the town of Montelimart for a public clock.

Palliser, Jno., Thirsk, 1822.

Pallisone, Jno., London ; watch, 1792.

Palmer. Jno., apprenticed in 1647 to Hy. Ireland, C.C. **Jno.**, apprenticed 1692

to Alex. Warfield, C.C. **Hy.**, apprenticed 1693 to Josiah Ridley, C.C. **Thos.**, Sheffield, 1740. **Robert**, liveryman C.C. 1776. **Thomas**, Fetter Lane, liveryman C.C. 1776. **William**, Shoe Lane, liveryman C.C. 1776. **Thomas**, 132 Lower Holborn, 1783-1810. **Samuel Richd.**, gold watch-case maker, 2 Red Lion St., 1790-1810. **John**, Philadelphia, 1795. **Thos.**, Sheffield, 1800. **Joseph**, 112 Whitechapel, 1814-18. **John**, 58 Great Marylebone St., 1825-35. **B.**, 21 King St., Covent Garden, 1830. **Robert**, 24 White Hart Place, Kennington, 1832-42. **Hy.**, 25 Buttesland St., 1842.

Pamer, Edward, London ; watch, 1802 ; another, 1826.

Pamphillon, William, C.C. 1725.

Panchard, Abel, Oxford St., 1765-80.

Panchaud, David, 202 Oxford St., 1790-1825 ; livery C.C. 1802. **& Cumming**, 202 Oxford St., 1806-10.

Panck, Ralph, apprenticed C.C. 1677.

Panier, Jossué, Paris ; clock, S.K.M., 1725 ; also a watch of earlier date, signed " Iosve Panier à Paris."

Pannell. Robt., apprenticed in 1653 to Paul Lowell, senr., C.C. **Joshua**, Northallerton, 1770.

Panther, B., London ; watch, 1785.

Pantin. Jean, Paris, 1544 (see p. 385). **Nich.**, apprenticed in 1651 to Downing, C.C. **Robt.**, apprenticed in 1674 to Wm. Robinson, C.C. **Lewis**, 45 Fleet St., 1770-75 ; 62 St Martin's-le-Grand, 1800.

Papavoine, Isaac (French), Duke's Court ; admitted C.C. 1687 ; maker of long-case clocks, 1680-1710. Mr R. W. Llewellyn has a fine bracket clock by him, basket top, claw feet ; long-case clock, Wetherfield collection.

Papon, Leonard ; watch, B.M., about 1620.

Papworth, John, C.C. 1688.

Paradise. John, C.C. 1716. **John**, 13 Newcastle St., Strand, 1823.

Parbury. This name is on a very fine *repoussé* gold watch case in the Mainwaring collection ; in the Dunn-Gardner collection was a watch by Jno. Latham, h.m., 1719, enclosed in a choice *repoussé* case signed Parbury.

Pare, Thos., London ; clock, long marqueterie case, Mr Norman Shaw, about 1700.

Paria, S. ; clock, about 1780.

Paris. M., Rennes ; watch, B.M., about 1620. **John**, watch engraver, 7 Dean St., Fetter Lane, 1790-94.

Parish, Simon, C.C. 1723.

Park. Nicholas, C.C. 1641. **Jno.**, apprenticed in 1659 to Jno. Bayes, C.C. **Seth**, Park Town, Pa., 1790. **James**, Preston, 1818.

Parke, Solomon, Philadelphia, 1791-1811.

Parker. Thomas, "in St Ann's Lane, neere Aldersgate, fecit," inscribed on a lantern clock ; apprenticed to Wm. Almond in 1658 ; C.C. 1669. **Cuthbert**, apprenticed in 1659 to Wm. Petty, C.C. **John**, C.C. 1674 ; John Pinson was his apprentice in 1677. **John**, Cateaton St. ; C.C. 1678. **Daniel**, "in Fleete St., London" ; marqueterie long-case month clock, 1¼ seconds pendulum, about 1690, Wetherfield collection. **Robert**, apprenticed to J. Markwick ; admitted C.C. 1698. **John**, apprenticed to James Delander, C.C. 1706. **Thos.**, Dublin ; watch, 1709 ; Mr J. D. Robertson has a fine bracket clock by him, about 1710. **Edward**, about 1710. **& Wakelin**, Panton St., 1760-75. **John**, 55 St Paul's Church-yard, 1769-75 ; Parker & Son, 1794. **Jas.**, Cambridge ; watch, 1770. **Thos.**, Warrington; watch, 1786. **Thos.**, 37 Berners St.; watch, h.m., 1786; 1786-1817. **Thos.**, 15 Wilderness Row, 1788. **John**, High St., Marylebone, 1793; 2 Rathbone Place, 1804. **Thomas**, Philadelphia, 1797-1811. **& Birketts**, 16 Prince's St., 1804. **Geo.**, Ulverstone, 1818. **James**, 17 King St., Clerkenwell, 1835.

Parkes. (**& King**; watch, about 1750). **Jno.**, Old Change, 1800.

Parkhouse, Roger, Richmond, Yorks., 1730.

Parkhurst, Michael, apprenticed in 1683 to Jno. Bellard, C.C.

Parkinson. Robt., C.C. 1637. At Lancaster: **Wm.**, 1708, f.; **Robt.**, 1732, f.; **Wm.**, 1789, f. Clock, "Parkinson, Richmond," about 1730. At Settle: **Edwd.**, 1775. **Francis**, London; watch, 1788. **Wm.**, & **Frodsham**, 4 Change Alley, 1801-42; Wm. Parkinson and W. J. Frodsham, both admitted C.C. 1802. At Bury: **Thos.**, 1814. **James**, 4 Cross St., Goswell Rd., 1820. **Henry**, 50 Great Sutton St., 1835; 65 Red Lion St., Clerkenwell, 1842. **James**, 70 Red Lion St., Clerkenwell, 1842. **& Bouts**, Gracechurch St., 1857, see Bouts.

Parkwick, Jas., assistant C.C. 1698.

Parmier, John Peter, Philadelphia, 1793.

Parnell, Thomas, High St., Bow, 1815-42.

Parquot, P., London; watch, 1706.

Parr. Jno., apprenticed in 1692 to Jno. Herbert, C.C. **Thos.**, 27 Cheapside, 1735-75. **William**, 20 Strand; watches by him from 1790-1808; in 1804 he published a "Treatise on Pocket Watches." **Edward**, apprenticed to Jas. Plumbly, 16 New Cavendish St., 1824.

Parratt. Hy., apprenticed 1678 to Jno. Finch, C.C. **Jno.**, apprenticed 1691 to Chas. Knight, C.C. **Sam**, Bridge Row, C.C. 1730.

Parrault, Thos., apprenticed in 1667 to Ed. Whitfield, C.C.

Parry. David, at Fleet Bridge; very small silver watch, Ashmolean Museum, about 1630; brother C.C. 1646; Hy. Ford was apprenticed to him through the C.C. in 1647. **Francis**, apprenticed in 1646 to Thos. Land, C.C. **Jonathan**, apprenticed in 1659 to Richd. Lyons, C.C. **John**, Philadelphia, 1797-1811.

Parsons. Richard, apprenticed in 1682 to Isaac Day; admitted C.C. 1690; known as a maker of bracket and other clocks at 54 Goswell St., 1690-1730. **John**, admitted C.C. 1696. **John**, 8 St Martin's Court, 1775. **Geo.**, Goswell St.; watch, h.m., 1778. **& Horne**, Castle St., Holborn, 1825.

Parten, William, C.C. 1720.

Parter. William, C.C. 1692. **Francis**, C.C. 1730.

Partington. J., High St., Marylebone, 1790. **William**, 53 Paddington St., 1815-42. **C. F.**, author of "Clock and Watchmakers' Complete Guide," 1826.

Partridge. Wm., C.C. 1640; gave a silver spoon to the Company prior to 1652. **Walter**, London; long-case clock, Hampton Court, about 1700. **Joseph**, Bartholomew Close, 1760-63. **C.**, 13 Wentworth Pl., Mile End Rd., 1840-42.

Pascal, Claude, à la Haye, on a splendidly decorated watch, about 1650.

Pascall, Jas., 18 Wilderness Row, 1820; treasurer W. and C. Pension Socy., 1857; died 1863.

Pashler. Jno., London, 1755; long-case clock, about 1760. **Edwd.**, Bishopsgate St., 1774; large ebonised case, bracket clock, tunes at the hour; Psalm 104;

March in Rinaldo; air, Duke of Cumberland's Minuet; March in Scipio; "Britons, Strike Home." In addition to the tunes plays "runs" at the 1st, 2nd, and 3rd quarter; dial figures in Turkish characters; "strike and silent," "chime and silent," engraved back plate, brass arched dial, ten bells and striking-bell; had formerly crown escapement; bought at the Bazaar at Constantinople in 1881.

Pasquier, —, horloger du Roy In 1773 made a hunting watch for 1,200 livres for the Comte d'Artois as a wedding present. This Prince, brother of Louis XVI., became Charles X., see also Pierre.

Passanine, Hy., apprenticed C.C. 1646.

Passement, Admiral, designer of equation and astronomical clocks, 1720-50 (see p. 318).

Passevant, Wm., 10 Red Lion Passage, 1793.

Pasteur, Jacques, Geneva, about 1780.

Patching, Elisha, C.C. 1728.

Paterson, David, Sunderland, 1825-40; he was apprenticed to John Ogden; Canon Greenwell has a bracket clock with "D Patirson Sunderland" on dial, and "Richard Browne London" on back.

Patmore, Peter, Ludgate Hill, C.C. 1813.

Patrick. Edwd., London; long-case clocks, 1690-1710. **John**, C.C. 1712. **Thos.**, Market Weighton, 1775. **Miles**, Greenwich; cylinder watch, 1790.

Patron, J., Geneva, 1760-80; watch, globular gold enamelled case, Pierpont Morgan collection.

Patry, Alex., Geneva; watch, 1790.

Pattee, Thomas, Mile End Rd., livery C.C. 1810.

Pattison. Robert, apprenticed in 1676 to Thos. Tompion; C.C. 1688. **George**, 16 King St., Seven Dials, 1835.

Patton, Abraham, Philadelphia, 1799; also **David**, then **Patton & Jones**.

Pattru, —, watch, B.M., about 1620.

Paty, Wm., London; watch movement, G.M., about 1760.

Paul. Nowell, alien, threatened with prosecution for working as clockmaker within the liberties of C.C. 1668. **Thomas**, apprenticed to John Fromanteel; C.C. 1670.

Paule. Philip, 15 Cleveland St., Fitzroy Sq., 1810-23. **George**, 15 Cleveland St., 1830-35.

Paulet, Jno., C.C.; watch, S.K.M., 1703; another of about the same date, marked "I. Paulet Without Temple Bar"; long arabesque marqueterie case clock, Wetherfield collection, about 1705; travelling clock, about 1710, illustrated on p. 516; repeating watch, 1728; in 1730 he worked for Ellicott.

Paulin, Lewis, 45 Fleet St., 1772.

Paulus, Pieter, Amsterdam; enamelled watch, "Roman Piety," by Huaud, about 1710.

Paxton, Jno., St Neots; long-case musical clock, ten tunes; movement said to be by Mudge, about 1770; watch, "Jno. Puxton, St Neots," h.m., 1790, probably by him.

Pay. C., London; repeating watch, 1730. **Jas.**, London; watch, 1750.

Payn, John, Southwold, a smith, received 6s. 8d. for a new clock from the churchwardens of Walberswick, Suffolk, 1451.

Payne. Nicholas, apprenticed in 1641 to Wm. Daniel; C.C. 1648; was assistant C.C. in 1671; in 1676 Jonathan Boole was apprenticed to Sarah Payne. **Geo.**, apprenticed 1687 to Jere Johnson, C.C. —, Hadleigh, about 1720. **Richd.**, Carthusian

St., C.C. 1730; watch, 1765. **Lawrence**, New York, 1732-55, f., 1732. **H. & John**, 44 Cheapside, 1753-75. **Southern**, Bridgewater Sq., livery C.C. 1766; master 1778. **J.**, 17 Foster Lane, 1794; 18 St Ann's Lane, Aldersgate, 1800-25. **Robt.**, Waltham, 1813. **Wm.**, 62 South Moulton St., 1816; 39 High St., Bloomsbury, 1825; 163 New Bond St., 1830-50; in 1849 he patented (No. 12,516) musical clocks.

Payton, Wm., watch-case maker, 3 Addle St., Wood St., 1790-94; a watch inscribed "Notyap, London," probably by him.

Peachey. William, New St.: C.C. 1727. **Newman**, 12 Dean St., livery C.C. 1766; 1760-78.

Peacock. George, 65 Threadneedle St., 1769-75. **Geo.**, 4 Sweeting's Alley, 1778-81. **Wm.**, York, f., 1789 1832. **Samuel**, 30 Old Exchange, 1793. —, Richmond, 1814.

Peake, Thos., Soho, died 1905, aged 83.

Pearce. Adam, C.C. 1664. **Jno.**, Newgate St., 1753-60; Pearce & Newton, 1760-63. **William**, livery C.C. 1787, master 1804. **J.**, Stratford-on-Avon; watch, h.m., 1825. **John**, 101 Great Peter St., Westminster, 1835-40.

Pearkes, F., 15 St Martin's Court, 1823.

Pearne, Wm., 11 Leicester Sq., 1793.

Pearsall & Embree, New York, 1781-86.

Pearse, John, Newgate St., 1753-60.

Pearson. Thos., Berwick, 1765. **Mary**, 31 Fleet St., 1772-75. **Wm.**, Blackburn, 1775. **Sam.**, Halifax, 1790. **The Rev. W., LL.D., F.R.S.**, East Sheen, 1811; South Kilworth, Leicestershire, 1821; author of the splendid treatise on horology which appeared in Rees' "Cyclopædia," published in 1791 and revised in 1819; died 1847, aged 80. **& Price**, 11 Great Sutton St., 1830.

Peatling, Thomas, C.C. 1682.

Peck. George, C.C. 1725. **Wm.**, Keysoe; long-case clock, fine Oriental lacquer decoration, about 1750. **Edson C.**, Derby, U.S.A., 1827.

Peckett, John, C.C. 1691.

Peckham, Henry, Bermondsey; patented in 1798 (No. 2,280) the application of a compass to a watch.

Peckover, Richard, Change Alley, Cornhill; maker of long-case clocks and repeating watches. He probably succeeded Quare & Horseman, 1737-56; watch, with Turkish numerals, Pierpont Morgan collection, movement signed "R. Peckover, London," "Markwick Markham Perigal London," on dial, about 1750.

Peers. Jno., apprenticed 1676 to Rob Cosby, C.C. Chester: a noted family of clockmakers from about 1745-1840. **Benj.**, long-case clock, about 1790.

Peffinhaus. Oval watch, signed "Wilhel Peffinhauss," Pierpont Morgan collection, about 1620.

Peiras. Oval watch, 1590, Garnier collection, signed "Pasquier Peiras, Blois"; another also in the Garnier collection, about the same date, signed "Charles Peiras, Bloys."

Peirson. Wm., Kirby Moorside, 1770. **Worthy**, 92 Whitechapel High St., 1840.

Pelleter, Solomon, 14 Broad St., 1775.

Pelletier, Paris; clock, about 1810.

Pemberton (Samuel), Son, & Mitchell, Birmingham, 1818.

Penard, Isaac, skull watch, about 1630 (see p. 111).

Pendleton, —, worked for Mudge, junr., 1795.

Penfold. Joshua, C.C. 1695. **Miles**, 115 Newgate St., 1769-75.

Penkethman, Thomas, C.C. 1692.

Penlington, Thos., Sheffield, 1770-1814.

Penn, Richd., London; watch, 1780.

Pennington. Christopher, Kendal; watch, 1780. Robert, chronometer maker, Camberwell; invented an improved form of sector, 1780-1816. John, also Joseph, Liverpool, 1818. Robert, & Son, 11 Portland Row, Camberwell, 1832-42; John Pennington, the son referred to, afterwards succeeded Grohe, at Wigmore St.

Pennock, John, Lothbury, C.C. 1638, master 1660; gave a fine house clock of his own make to the Company in 1652; on a lantern clock by him, dating from about 1640, is the address "Within Bishopsgate"; another lantern clock by him with dial, engraved "at Petty France Gate in yᵉ Moorfields."

Penny, Richard, London; watches, 1695-1715. "Deliver'd to a carter in Whitechapel to be carried to Mr Pearson's, at the Warren by Sir Henry Hicks, an old bob clock with John Webster's name on it, which clock was not brought thither. If any persons give notice of this clock to R. Penny of Whitechappel clock maker so as it may be had again shall receive 5s. as a reward" (The Post Man, Aug. 28, 1705).

Penton, Charles, Upper Moorfields, 1760-75.

Penty, Wm., York, f., 1831.

Pepin, —, Rue de la Coutellerie, Paris, 1770.

Pepper. Sam, apprenticed in 1655 to Thos. Mills, C.C. Jno., apprenticed 1684 to Geo. Ethrington, C.C. Jas., Biggleswade, 1770. Thomas, 5 George St., St Martin's, livery C.C. 1787; 1776-94.

Peppin, Sam., 22 Greville St., Hatton Garden, 1517.

Pepys. John, apprenticed in 1672 to Jno. Harris, C.C. 1680, master 1707; watch by him, B.M.; long-case month clock, 11-in. dial, burr elm case, Wetherfield collection, about 1705; other examples are occasionally met with, 1680-1708. Richard, C.C. 1674. Peter, apprenticed 1680 to Richard Pepys, C.C. John, junr., Fleet St., C.C. 1715, master 1739. "Lost on Saturday night last a gold repeating watch in chased case with an enamel dial plate, the maker's name John Pepys, London, No. 3,470. Whoever brings the same to Mr John Pepys, at the 'Crown and Sceptre,' in Fleet St., shall have twenty guineas reward and no questions" (Public Advertiser, April 10, 1744). William, C.C. 1723.

Perchard. Matthew, Cannon St., 1753-59. Peter, 15 Abchurch Lane, 1760-72.

Percival. Jno., Woolwich; clock, 1790. N., 36 Old Bond St., 1798-1800. Thos., 36 Old Bond St., 1804. M., Woolwich, 1817.

Perdra, Wm., London; watch, 1805.

Peres, Mark, C.C. 1680; large lantern clock with two bells, about 1700, inscribed "Marcos Pères," London.

Perier, H., London; watch, about 1730, see Perrier.

Perigal. Francis, 9 Threadneedle St., Royal Exchange, the first of a family of able horologists; excellent watches and clocks of their make are to be met with; C.C. 1741; master 1756. Francis, C.C. 1756; master 1775. Francis, junr., Royal Exchange; apprenticed to his father 1778; C.C. 1786; livery 1787, see Francis Perigal & Son, below. Francis, watchmaker to the king, 37 New Bond St.; hon. f. C.C. 1781; watch, S.K.M., signed "Francis Perigal, Bond St., watchmaker to His Majesty," h.m., 1786; 1770-94. John, 12

Coventry St., Haymarket; hon. f. C.C. 1781; 1770-1800. Francis, & Son, 9 Royal Exchange (Francis S. Perigal, junr., master C.C. 1806), 1790-1808. & Browne, 11 Coventry St., Piccadilly, 1794-1800. Jno., 55 Prince's Street, Soho, 1810. & Duterrau, "Watchmakers to His Majesty," 62 New Bond St., 1810-40. Thos., London; watch, 1812.

Perin, Chas. Henry, George Yard, Lombard St.; patented winding work in 1842 (No. 9,438).

Perinot, Abraham, known as a maker of long-case clocks, about 1780.

Perins, John, 193 Strand, 1750-94.

Perkin, R., 55 Tooley St., 1790.

Perkins. Jno., apprenticed in 1661 to Sam Horne, C.C. Eylum, of "Rederiffe, the end of Love Lane"; apprenticed in 1670 to Jas. Atkinson; in 1682 he was threatened with prosecution by C.C. for exercising the art, not being admitted; he promised to take up his freedom at the next quarterly court. James, C.C. 1730. & Spencer, 44 Snow Hill, 1765-75. Thomas, Philadelphia, 1778-99. Vineyard, 53 Dorset St., Salisbury Sq., 1793. Thomas, Pittsburgh, U.S.A., 1815.

Pernell, —, London; 30-hour long-case clock, about 1730.

Peron, see Du Peron.

Perrache, —, "Fournisseur du Roy," Paris. In 1752 made a clock with a balance-spring going a fortnight.

Perras, see Pairas.

Perrault, —, contrived a clock driven by water and controlled by a pendulum, 1699.

Perregaux. Edouard, Neuchatel, born 1819, died 1878. Girard, Chaux de Fonds; pocket chronometer with spherical balance-spring, about 1825.

Perrelet. Abram Louis, Neuchatel, born 1729, died 1826. Louis Frederic, grandson of Abram Louis, born at Locle in 1781, migrated to Paris and worked for Breguet; died 1854.

Perrenoud, F., 192 Brick Lane, Whitechapel, 1810.

Perret, Theodore, "Gentil Horologer de sa Majeste le Roy de Prusse, au Locle"; balloon clock, about 1750.

Perrier. Peter, apprenticed to Jas. Lello in 1660, C.C.; silver watch, the back plate covered with representation of Crucifixion, about 1680. H., 2 Giltspur St., 1830-42.

Perrin, C., Paris, 1780.

Perring, H., 179 Great Surrey St., 1830.

Perringham, Francis, back of Exchange, 1790.

Perron. Richd., 7 Worship St., 1790-94. —, Geneva; in 1798 he introduced a lever escapement with round pins as pallets.

Perry. Richd., apprenticed in 1656 to Sam Davis, C.C. Henry, C.C. 1691. Thos., Dock St., New York, 1749. "Thomas Perry, watchmaker from London, makes and cleans all sorts of clocks and watches. He will import, if bespoke good warranted clocks at £14 they paying freight and insurance, and clocks without cases for £10" (Advt., New York, 1756). New York: Thomas, f. 1750; Marvin, f. 1769. Mervin; advertisement, New York paper, 1776, "Mervin Perry repeating and plain watchmaker from London where he has improved himself under the most eminent and capital artists in those branches, has opened shop in Hanover Square at the sign of the Dial. He mends and repairs musical, repeating, quarterly, chime, silent pull and common weight clocks." Thos., London; watch, about 1790. John, 40 Oxford St., 1835-42.

Persigny, Pierre, Paris; circular box-

shaped watch of white metal, separate dials for hours and minutes, about 1680, Pierpont Morgan collection.

Petch, Jno. T., Huddersfield, 1833.

Peterkin, John, 25 Cleveland St., 1810-40.

Peterman & Debois, watch-case makers, Bateman's Buildings, Soho Sq., 1800-10, see Comtesse.

Peters, Edwd., Sheffield, 1770-1814.

Petit. Guillaume, petitioner for incorporation of C.C. 1630; Abraham Lamb was apprenticed to him in 1651; gave a silver bowl to the Company in 1656. Jacob, clock in china case, dated 1827.

Peto, —, prohibited from working by C.C. 1632. —, London; spoken of by Earnshaw as a capital workman, 1780-1800.

Petri, J. H., Heydelbergh; watch, about 1700.

Petter, Christopher, C.C. 1730.

Pettit. —, 54 Bethnal Green Rd., 1835. Isaac, 22 Fieldgate St., Whitechapel, 1835. William, 7 New Rutland St., 1840. Eliza, 22 Fielding St., Whitechapel, 1840-42.

Petty. William, C.C. 1646. —, Richmond, Yorks., 1812.

Pewtress, Thomas, Gracechurch St., 1753-56.

Peyton, Richard, Gloucester; in the composing room of the Gloucester Journal is a long-case clock by him, which belonged to Robert Raikes, who founded the journal in 1722 and died in 1757.

Pfaff, Jeremas, Augsburg; fine table clock by him, which is provided with an alarm, and repeats the hours and quarters. There are, besides the barrel and fusee for the going part, four barrels, four hammers, and three bells, the largest bell serving for the hour and for the alarm. The cocks and hammers are beautifully engraved, and the work throughout is excellent. The dial ring is about 5 in. diameter, having within it the alarm disc. The case is square, measuring 7 in. across and 3 in. in height, besides the feet. In each of the four sides of the case is a glass panel. It dates probably from the end of the seventeenth century; clock inscribed "Jereme Pfaff, Augsburg," about 1680, Mr R. Norman Shaw (see also p. 100).

Phelippson, J., London; watch, h.m., 1735.

Phelisot, —, Dijon; crystal case watch, about 1560.

Phelps, Richard, founder of the great bell for Bradley's St Paul's clock (see p. 249), 1716.

Philcox, George, 24 Great Dover St., Borough, 1835; 22 Southwark Sq., 1842. He spent his life in endeavouring to improve timekeepers by various inventions in connection with escapements and compensation; died in Watchmakers' Asylum, New Southgate, 1878.

Philibert, —, French clock, about 1785.

Philip. —, Brighton, about 1760. Robert, musical clockmaker, 6 New Court, St John St., 1779-88 (Robert Philip on some watches).

Phillesson, Isaac, London; quarter chime bracket clock, about 1740, see Rimbault.

Phillipe, Adrien, a leading Swiss horologist, partner in the firm of Patek, Phillipe, & Co., Geneva; inventor of shifting sleeve keyless work; died 1894, aged 79.

Phillips. Sam, apprenticed 1671 to Nat. Chamberlain, C.C. Joseph, f. of New York, 1713-35. —, Birkenhead; long-case clock, about 1770. Saml., Oswestry, 1780. W.,

Ludlow; watch, 1782. **Philip**, 10 St John's Sq., C.C. 1790-1800. **John**, Coldbath Fields, 1817; 91 Goswell St., 1835. **Joel**, 35 Norton Folgate, 1820. **P.**, 19 Crown St., Finsbury, 1830; 3 Steward St., Spitalfields, 1840-42. **Abraham**, 33 City Rd., 1835. **Joseph**, 55 Belvedere Place, Boro' Rd., 1835. **James & Charles**, 25 Coppice Row, Clerkenwell, 1835-40. **Brothers**, 31 Cockspur St., 1839-40. **P.**, 15 Bury St., 1840-42. **& Phillips**, 12 Queen Square, 1855.

Phillipson, Thos., London; watch, 1815.

Phipps, James, 40 Gutter Lane, 1783.

Phithian & Garnet, Lancashire; toolmakers about 1720, quoted by Hatton.

Phylander, Sylvanus, pair-case silver calendar watch, h.m., 1772.

Pichon, —, Cherbourg; watch, 1790.

Pickering, Jno., apprenticed 1686 to Richd. Knight, C.C.

Pickett. William, 32 Ludgate Hill, 1768-72; succeeded Thead & Pickett. **& Rundell**, 32 Ludgate Hill, 1775-83; afterwards Rundell & Bridge. —, Marlboro'; fine clock, long Sheraton style of case, plays a dance tune every three hours, when a curtain rises in the arch of the dial, a couple appear dancing, while other figures pass in procession, about 1780, Mr E. E. Cook (see p. 366).

Pickford, Jno., Liverpool, 1833.

Pickman, Wm., 57 Dean St., Soho, 1816-25; 6 Albany St., 1835.

Pide, David; watch, 1740.

Pidgeon, Thos., apprentice in 1660 to Jno. Bayes, C.C.

Pierce. Humphrey, apprenticed in 1646 to Robt. Smith; C.C. 1653. **Richd.**, apprenticed in 1646 to Thos. Reeve; C.C. 1657. In 1678 Jno. Papworth was apprenticed to Sarah Pierce. **Adam**, apprenticed to Edward East; C.C. 1664.

In Berkeley churchyard is the following quaint epitaph:—

Here lyeth Thomas Pierce, whom no man taught,
Yet, he in iron. brasse, and silver wrought;
He jacks and clocks and watches (with art) made,
And mended too, when others work did fade.
Of Berkeley five times Maior this artist was,
And yet this Maior, this artist, was but grasse!
When his own watch was down on the last day,
He that made watches had not made a key
To winde it up; but useless it must lie
Until he rise again, no more to die.

Thomas Pierce, five times Mayor of this Towne, died Feb. 25, 1665, aged 77. **Jno.**, apprenticed in 1680 to Geo. Tipping, C.C.

Pierre, Le Queux; clockmaker to the Duke of Orleans, 1396. **Pasquier**, C.C. 1648.

Pierret. Mathew, Philadelphia, 1795. **Victor A.**, Paris; noted maker of complicated watches; born 1806, died 1893.

Pigg, Robt., apprenticed in 1674 to Jno. White, C.C.

Pigott, Henry, C.C. 1687.

Piguet, see Piquet.

Pike & Green, 48 Bunhill Row, 1806; Bartholomew Sq., 1820-30.

Pilkington. R. J., London; bracket clock, about 1760. **J.**, Woolwich, 1815.

Pilling, Jno., Boothfield, 1800.

Pillon, —, Paris; watch, about 1720.

Pilon, Germain, Paris; cruciform watches, about 1590.

Pilson, Abraham, Plymouth; watch, about 1700.

Pinard, Paul, 2 New St., Covent Garden, 1775.

Pinchbeck. Christopher, Clerkenwell and Fleet St.; a clever maker of musical clocks and of watches; inventor of pinchbeck alloy (see p. 264); 1690-1732.

Edward, Fleet St.; son and successor of the above (see p. 265); 1732-66. **Christopher**, son of the above-named Christopher, Cockspur St.; died 1783, aged 73 (see p. 266).

Pinckney, W. "There was a watch found some time past near the Temple Gates, which was made in London by a Frenchman. If any person lay claim unto it, so as to describe the same, they may have it at Mr W. Pinckney's, a goldsmith, near the Inner Temple" (*Lond. Gaz.*, March 2-6, 1675).

Pindar, Joseph, apprenticed in 1692 to Geo. Halsey, C.C.

Pine, Philip, 20 Aldgate, 1779-82; card, B.M.

Pinfold, Thomas, Banbury, 1760, see Penfold.

Pingo, Jno., apprenticed to Rob Thompson, C.C. 1684.

Pinhorne, —, Portsea; quarter clock, about 1800.

Pink, J., London; watch, h.m., 1767.

Pinkart, Jno., apprenticed in 1663 to Joseph Quash, C.C.

Pinkerton, Jas., 20 Percival St., 1836, afterwards Pinkerton & Miller.

Pinon, —, Horloger du Roy and des Princes, 1765-70. Here is a curious memorandum from an account for work done for the Comte d'Artois (subsequently Charles X.): "For repairing a movement of a clock in the Prince's apartment, renew, in fine bronze, the female figure on the clock case which the Prince amused himself in scratching with a knife from one end to the other with the object of cleaning it, renewing the cock and other accessories; total, livres, 2,068."

Pinson, Jno., apprentice of Jno. Parker, London, 1677.

Piolaine & Co., 67 Great Russell St., 1815-25.

Pipes, John, London; maker of long-case clocks, about 1750.

Pipps, Jno., London; watch, about 1790.

Piquet à Rennes; watch, B.M., 1700. **& Meylan**, Geneva, about 1810.

Pistor. Edward, 116 Leadenhall St. and 105 Strand, 1764-90; Mr Beaven, Enfield, had a clock of an earlier date engraved "Edwd. Pistor, Prescott St., Goodman's Fields." **Edwd. & Jno.**, 116 Leadenhall St.; watch, musical clock, and organ makers, 1793-98.

Pitcher. Job, apprenticed in 1662 to Thos. Claxton, C.C. **Jno.**, C.C. 1689.

Pitkin, Henry, Hartford, Connecticut, U.S.A. Watches by him and his brother James F., engraved with the American flag, were made in 1838.

Pitman, John, admitted C.C. 1714; watch, "J. Pitman Dublin," about 1750.

Piton, James, Shad Hill, C.C. 1710.

Pitson, Chas., London; watch, 1700.

Pitt. David, Hampstead; watch, 1780; watch, "D. Pitt & Sons, London," Mr H. Hogarth. **Thyar**, 24 Great Bush Lane, livery C.C. 1787; watch clock playing every three hours; 1770-94. **William**, livery C.C. 1787. **Caleb**, 292 Oxford St., 1790; 43 Duke St., 1800-30. **John**, 37 Crown St., Finsbury, 1830-42. **Chas.**, 152 Sloane St., 1835-40. **W. G.**, 25 Thyar St., Manchester Sq., 1840-42. **J.**, Kingsland Rd., 1842.

Pittit, Jno., Bethnal Green Rd., 1817.

Pittney, Thos., Featherstone St., 1769-72.

Pitts, Sam, apprenticed in 1689 to Robt. Fenn, C.C.

Plairas, Solomon, Blois, 1620-40 (see p. 147).

Plaire, see Player.

Planck, Anthony, Fleet St., 1760-72.

Plankh, Nicholas, Augsburg; clock by him, Vienna Treasury, about 1580.

Planner. Thomas, apprenticed 1694 to Ben Collier, C.C. 1701; 1730. **Thomas**, C.C. 1730; the Planners were known as makers of long-case clocks; 1730-45.

Plant, Edward, admitted C.C. 1664.

Plantart. French circular table clock, late sixteenth century, stamped ABB and N. Plantart on a scroll (see p. 84); a similar piece at S.K.M. M. Leroux has, by the same maker, a clock with removable alarm, as shown on p. 99.

Plaskett. Reuben, Raven St., Whitechapel; died 1845, aged 80. **Jas.**, West India Dock Rd.; died 1860.

Plate, Richard, 58 Carey St., Lincoln's Inn, 1835.

Platt. Thos., C.C. 1637. **Edward**, 33½ Wilderness Row, Clerkenwell, 1835.

Plattes, Robt., York, f., 1590.

Player. Simon, apprenticed in 1671 to Wm. Speakman, C.C. **Thomas**, C.C. 1672. "A silver watch in the form of 5 crowns, a Flower-de-Lis under each crown, with a Knot, in the middle the name *Thomas Plaire, Londini;* the hours engraven in a six-square, with a chain and 5 wheels" (*Lond. Gaz.*, March 29, April 1, 1680). **Lionel**, apprenticed in 1680 to Sam. Drosade, C.C. **Robert**, C.C. 1700; walnut long-case clock, arch dial, 1700-40. **H. J.**, 2 North Place, Gray's Inn Lane, 1820-40.

Pleuvier (or **Plovier**), Isaac, a Dutch clockmaker who settled in London in 1641; C.C. 1652; died 1665; a dispute respecting his goods referred to in the Calendar of State Papers, Domestic Series, 1670.

Pley; Geo., apprenticed 1691 to Chas. Loomes, C.C.

Pleydell, Jno., London; apprenticed in 1666 to Thos. Bagley, C.C.; long marqueterie case clock, square dial, about 1720.

Plowman, Thos., Lancaster, 1814.

Pluett, Anthony, C.C. 1697.

Plumbly, Jas., 16 New Cavendish St., 1820; Plumbly & Tupman, 1824; Plumbly & Parr, 1840-42.

Plumley. Edwd., apprenticed in 1682 to Ed. Millett, C.C. **Jno.**, apprenticed in 1686 to Thos. Taylor, C.C. **William**, 43 Ludgate Hill; apprenticed to Lawrence Mace; C.C. 1756; master 1779. **Wm.**, 43 Ludgate Hill, son of the preceding; C.C. 1780; livery 1797; master 1831; 1780-1825; retired to Shepton Mallet. **Chas.**, 231 Strand, 1835-42.

Plummer. Joseph, apprenticed in 1669 to Chris. Maynard, C.C. **G.**, London; watch, 1780. **Wm.**, 45 Gutter Lane, 1793.

Plumper, Thos., London; watch, 1760.

Plunkeld, Richard, 8 Fieldgate St., Whitechapel, 1820.

Pocock, Jno.: clock chiming on eight bells, long mahogany case, 12-in. dial, hours marked 1 to 12 twice over; rotating centre with moon indicating time of high water, days of week in corner of dial, phases and age of moon in arch, about 1750.

Poestdorffer, Johann, Dresden; fine octagonal watch in crystal case, foliot balance, about 1550, Green Vaults, Dresden.

Pohlmann, Peter, Leadenhall St.; maker of long-case clocks, 1760-75.

Poidevin, F., 16 Brewer St., 1830.

Poisson, Henry, London; long-case marqueterie scroll-work clock, S.K.M., period Queen Anne; also silver watch of a slightly later date; 1695-1720, see Fish.

Poite, Jaques, Blois; watch case enamelled by him, Vienna Treasury, about 1720.

Polack, Benj., Sheffield, 1814.

Pollard, —, Crediton, about 1760.

Polliscott, Thos., apprenticed in 1684 to Jno. Brown, C.C.

Pomeroy, Joseph, Whitehorse Alley, Moorfields, C.C. 1728 ; horn-covered paircase verge watch, about 1738.

Poncy, J. P. I., Well St. ; patented in 1840 (No. 8,602) a clock with two springs.

Poney, Abraham, 82 Wells St., Oxford St., 1840-42.

Ponson, Richd., London ; watch, 1810.

Pontem, Jas., London, 1780.

Pool, J. C., St Anne's Lane ; made a clock for the Mayor of Kendal as a gift to that town. On the dial was the motto, "Time runneth. Your work is before you," 1654.

Poole. Geo., C.C. 1654. Jno., near Norfolk St., Strand, C.C. ; arch top bracket clock, about 1712. Robert, Aldersgate St. ; livery C.C. 1766 ; master 1781 ; 1760-81. & Bickerlo, 88 Bartholomew Close, 1769-75. George, 88 Bartholomew Close, 1783-85. John, 36 Charles St., City Rd., 1822 ; 7 Brunswick Terrace, Commercial Rd., 1835-40. John, born 1818, died 1867 ; 7 Brunswick Terrace, Commercial Rd., in 1842, afterwards in Fenchurch St. ; a clever chronometer maker, and inventor of an auxiliary compensation.

Pools, Edmonde, admitted C.C. 1722.

Pope. Nich., apprenticed 1678 to Gerard Overzee, C.C. Thos., Wharton's Court, Holborn, 1793.

Poppe, Jno. Hy., Göttingen, 1797.

Popplewell, Jno., Bridlington, 1770.

Portal. & Coyle, Ludgate Hill, 1760-63. Abraham, & Gearing, 34 Ludgate Hill, 1769-75.

Porter. Sebastian, apprenticed in 1680 to Jef. Bailey, C.C. Matt., apprenticed 1682 to Thos. Taylor, Strand ; C.C. 1682. Robt., apprenticed in 1687 to Jno. Cotsworth, C.C. Chas., 227 Bermondsey St., 1835-40.

Porteus, Robt., Manchester, 1818.

Porthouse. Wm., Penrith ; clock in carved long case, on dial a tablet inscribed "Thos. & Ann Harrison, 1749." Wm., Barnard Castle, 1760. Geo., Penrith, 1790-1810 ; Mr Francis B. Fairley has a long mahogany case clock with dial inscribed "Matt. & Catherine Fairless 1771." "Wm. Porthouse, Penrith." The Matt. Fairless referred to was a colliery proprietor ; he was murdered for the money with which he was going to pay the men at the pit. Thomas, High St., Poplar, 1815-30 ; 10 Northampton Sq., Clerkenwell, 1840 ; treasurer, W. and C. Bene. Inst., died 1860 ; the business was carried on for a short time at 16 Northampton Sq., under the title of Porthouse & Son.

Portsmouth, Jno., apprenticed in 1660 to Isaac Puzzy, C.C.

Post, William, 42 Fish St. Hill ; watch, 1760 ; long-case clock, "William Post, London Bridge" ; liveryman C.C. 1776.

Potier, Michel, Paris, 1544 (see p. 304).

Potter. George, watchmaker, and Mayor of Coventry, 1727. Christopher, Shoe Lane, C.C. 1730. Harry, 5 Well St., Aldersgate ; master C.C. 1795, and again in 1812, when he died before the expiration of his year of office ; 1775-1812 ; a watch by him, exhibited at the Guelph Exhibition by Mr Geo. Carr Glyn, had an outer case embossed by Maweis. Ephraim, Concord, U.S.A., 1775-90. Thos., Gainsboro', 1795. James, livery C.C. 1810.

Pottinger, Jno., 6 Bell's Buildings, Salisbury Sq., 1793.

Potts. Jno., Partrington, 1775. Joshua, York, f., 1810-33, maker of musical clocks. Jno., Redcar, 1823. Wm., Leeds, 1840.

Pouchoulin, J. L., Geneva, 1750.

Pouilly, —, Rue Dauphine, Paris, 1690 (see pp. 309, 311).

Poulson, Thos., London ; watch, 1815.

Poulton, R., 2 Mayfield Place, High St., Kennington, 1840-42.

Pound, Jno., apprenticed 1673 to Joseph Wincoek, C.C.

Pouzait, Moise, Geneva ; a clever watchmaker ; made centre seconds watches ; did much to popularise the lever escapement and executed a large model of it in 1786 ; watch, virgule escapement, signed "Pouzait & Godemar Frères," about 1780.

Pow, see Poy.

Powell. Jno., apprenticed in 1665 to Isaac Daniel, C.C. Bartholomew, C.C. 1668. Robert, Chelsea, C.C. 1710. H., 56 St Paul's Churchyard, 1793. James, 7 Prince's St., Leicester Sq., 1828-35.

Power, Thos., lantern clock inscribed "Tho Power de Wellingborou Hoc Fabricavit," about 1700 ; also a basket top bracket clock, inscribed "Thos. Power, Wellingbrow."

Powers, Thos., St Albans, 1798.

Powis, Robt., 36 Rosoman St., 1806-23.

Powley, —, Asby, Westmorland, 1730. Robt., Appleby, 1770.

Pownall, Nat., apprenticed in 1649 to Wm. Izod, C.C.

Poy. Godfrie, a choice, small pull-repeating and alarm clock by him, said to have been made for George II. when Prince of Wales. Gilt case with military emblems over the arched top surmounted by a handle ; silvered dial, in the arch strike-silent plate marked "Schlaat, Nit schla" ; engraved back plate ; bell at the bottom of the movement. Also maker of a very fine quarter repeater, inner case pierced and repoussé, h.m., 1729, outer case shagreen ; another of his productions is a black, pull-chime bracket clock ; in the collection of the Czar of Russia at the Winter Palace, St Petersburg, is repeating watch by him, the outer case set with emeralds and diamonds ; it is attached to a chatelaine which is also decorated with precious stones ; 1718-50. Godfrey, 78 Mortimer St., 1775-95.

Pozzi, A., Wooton Bassett ; watch, 1840.

Praefelt, John, Philadelphia, 1797.

Pratt. Of Askrigg, 1790. He was apprenticed to C. Caygill, and had two sons, Jas. and Wm., who were in partnership till 1830. Wm. continued till 1841. Smith, & Hardy, 82 Cheapside, 1793. Chas., 30 Camden St., Islington, 1830-35.

Preddy, Wm., Taunton ; in 1849 he patented (No. 12,656) a sliding plug for watch-keys.

Preist, Wm., corner of Lad Lane, Wood St., 1763.

Prentis. Daniel, 25 Charterhouse Lane, 1788-96. & Son, 25 Charterhouse Lane, 1804-7. John, same address, 1817.

Presbury & Son, 9 New St., Covent Garden, 1804.

Presciot, Peter, New Rents, St Martin's-le-Grand, 1790-94.

Prest, —, Fleet St., see Priest. Thomas, Chigwell, Essex ; patentee of keyless action for watches (No. 4,501), 1820 ; he was foreman to J. R. Arnold (see p. 591) ; died 1855.

Prestbury, Chas., 9 New St., Covent Garden, 1793.

Prestige, Bartholomew, C.C. 1703.

Preston. Tobias, apprenticed in 1640 to Christopher Vernon, C.C. Edward, C.C. 1721. Wm., Lancaster, 1818.

Prestwood, Joseph, C.C. 1703 ; maker of long-case clocks, 1703-20.

Preudhomme, L. B., Paris, 1780, see Glaesner.

Prevost. Ni., London ; year clock, about 1710 ; watch, 1730. L. N., London ; watch, 1750. Adolphe, 20 King St., Soho, 1840-42.

Price. Jno., apprenticed in 1678 to R. Nemes, C.C. Chas., apprenticed 1680 to Geo. Stevens, C.C. George, St Martin's Churchyard, 1788 ; 89 Oxford St., 1793-1806. J., Deptford ; watch, 1796. Isaac, Philadelphia, 1797. W., 17 Maiden Lane, Wood St., 1825. R., Hoxton, 1842.

Prickett, G. J. B., a noted maker of gold and silver dials, 5 Corporation Row ; died 1898, aged 71.

Priddith, John, C.C. 1639.

Prideaux, Edmund, 31 Hatton Garden, 1780-94.

Pridgrin. Wm., York, f., 1778. W., Hull ; watch, 1797.

Pridham, William, Great Alie St., Goodman's Fields, 1760-63.

Priest. Thos., St John's Lane ; C.C. 1729. Jno., Aldersgate, C.C. 1730. John, apprenticed to George Graham, C.C. 1746. —, Fleet St., 1765-75. W. & James, 30 White Cross St., 1768-72. —, Bugg Lane, Norwich ; watch, 1796. Jno., Liverpool, 1833.

Priestman. Joseph, apprenticed to Henry Jones, C.C. 1703. M., 19 Prince's St., Leicester Sq., 1817.

Prigg. Matt., London ; watch, 1750. John, Bethlehem ; livery C.C. 1776. & Ansell, clock and watch spring maker, Middle Moore Fields, 1781-94.

Priggin. Jno., apprenticed in 1646 to Elias Allen, C.C. Wm., Hull. Mr Thos. Boynton has a mahogany long-case clock by him about 1770, brass and silvered dial, 13 in. in diameter, shows the phases of the moon, time of high water, and days of the month.

Prime. Andrew, C.C. 1647, lantern clock, S.K.M. (see p. 357). Abraham, apprenticed in 1665 to Andrew Prime, C.C. 1672.

Prince. Thos., apprenticed in 1674 to Jno. Bellard, C.C. Richard, C.C. 1680. —, Hammersmith ; watch, 1835.

Pringle. Adam, Edinburgh, 1800. Thos., Dalkeith, 1810-43.

Print, Richard, C.C. 1698.

Prior. John, Nessfield, near Skipton-in-Craven, Yorkshire, born 1747 ; received the following rewards from the Society of Arts : 1798, 30 guineas for detached escapement ; 1803, 30 guineas for improved striking work ; 1805, silver medal and 20 guineas for an alarm ; 1811, silver medal and 10 guineas for striking work ; 1817, silver Isis medal and 2 guineas for striking work ; 1820, large silver medal and 20 guineas for striking work. George, 31 Prescot St., Goodman's Fields, 1765-88 ; Rosomond's Row, 1794 ; 5 George Yard, Lombard St., 1798-1810. Wm., 82 Minories, 1793. George, son of John, of Otley and Leeds ; in 1809 he received from the Society of Arts a silver medal and 25 guineas for a clock escapement, and in 1811, 20 guineas for a remontoire escapement ; in 1818 he patented (No. 4,214) a remontoire ; in the Yorkshire Directory for 1822 he is described as of Woodhouse Lane, Leeds, but he afterwards removed to City Rd., London, and became reputed as a maker of watches

485

for the Turkish market. **Edward**, also a maker for the Turkish market contemporaneously with the last-named George, carried on business in Clerkenwell at first alone, and afterwards in partnership with Wm. Chambers; a long-case clock by Edward Prior is in the Mosque of Achmet, Constantinople; watch, "Edward Prior, London," Turkish numerals, about 1800, Hilton Price collection. Leeds: **Hy.**, 1818. **Geo.**, 1840. **I. W.**, Newington Causeway, 1830.

Pritchard, Phil., junr., C.C. about 1650. **Geo.**, Madelywood; watch, 1802.

Pritchford, Zachariah, apprenticed 1674 to Ed. Eyston, C.C.

Procter, Wm., apprenticed to John Brockbank; admitted C.C. 1797; livery 1810.

Proctor. William, New York, f., 1737-60; then **Cardan**.

Prosser. Edwd., apprenticed in 1655 to Robert Lochard, C.C. **William**, Strand, 1769-72. **John**, 61 Piccadilly, 1822-30.

Pryme, see Prime.

Pryor, Robert, 254 Tottenham Court Rd., 1835-40.

Puckridge. J., 73 Snow Hill, 1716-40. **Charles**, Goldsmiths' St., Shoe Lane, 1788-94. **John**, 72 Snow Hill, 1790-1818; livery C.C. 1814. **Alfred**, 7 Orange St., Bloomsbury, 1840-42.

Pugh. Ellis, Cockspur St., 1775-94. **Benj.**, watch gilder, 34 Jewin St., 1790-94. **—**, London; watch, about 1780.

Puiguer, —, London; watch, about 1780.

Pullan, Ben, Bradford, 1710-35.

Pullen. Jas., apprenticed C.C. 1669. **David**, Coleman St., C.C. 1730.

Puller, Jonathan, apprenticed 1676 to Nich. Coxeter; C.C. 1683, assistant 1705; long clock, 11 in. dial, marqueterie case with domed hood, about 1700, Wetherfield collection.

"Whereas an old Silver Watch in a black studded case made by one Puller, was taken away from a gentleman on Bagshot Heath, on Monday, April 29. This is to desire them by any hand to send it to Thomas Newman at The Naked Boy in West Smithfield, and no questions shall be asked, but a Reward of 2 guineas shall be given to the Person that brings it" (*Postman*, 11th May 1706).

"A large House-Clock supposed to be stolen 16 or 18 months since is now in the hands of Jonathan Puller Clockmaker in Red Lion Court in Fleet St." (*Lond. Gaz.*, July 24-28, 1690).

Punchard, Wm., apprenticed 1676 to R. Seignior, C.C.

Purnell, J., 106 Up. Seymour St., 1842.

Purrier, Richard, C.C. 1705.

Purse. William, 336 Strand, 1804. **George**, 487 Strand, 1804-25. **& Catchpole**, 120 Regent St., 1835.

Purton, Francis, 2 Carey St., 1793.

Purvis, Alexander, 4 North Audley St., 1825-42.

Putland, G. & J., 287 High Holborn, 1793.

Putley, Francis, 40 Newington Causeway, 1806-42; livery C.C. 1812.

Puxton, see Paxton.

Puzy, Isaac, London; apprenticed in 1651 to Jno. Freeman; C.C. 1658; 12-hour lantern clock, about 1665, inscribed "Isaac Puzzy."

Pybus, William, 66 Threadneedle St., 1789-94.

Pyke. John, watch motion maker, Bedford Row, C.C. 1720. **Stephen**, London; long-case clock, about 1750. **George**, son of Jno., C.C. 1753. **Jno.**, Newgate St.; "clock and watch maker to the Prince of

Wales," 1755; centre seconds watch, about 1770. **Jno.**, High St., Eltham, 1820-42; an excellent maker, formerly Arnold's foreman.

Pyne, Nathaniel, C.C. 1677; Mr Norman Shaw has a long marqueterie case month clock by him.

Pyott, see Barclay, Jas.

Quaife, Thos., Battle, Sussex. In 1853 he patented (No. 1,140) forming watch cases by pressure.

Quare. Daniel, St Martin's-le-Grand; afterwards at the King's Arms, Exchange Alley; born 1649; brother C.C. 1671; master 1708; died 1724; a celebrated maker, inventor of the repeating watch (see p. 236). **& Horseman**, at the King's Arms, Exchange Alley; in the Czar of Russia's collection is a gold repeating watch by them; the outer case is enriched with one large square and four pear-shaped topazes, interspersed with several scrolls of diamonds and twelve large single diamonds. It is suspended from a chatelaine ornamented in the same style; 1700-30, see Peckover.

Quarman, Saml., Temple Cloud; long-case clocks, also watch with day of the month hand, silver cases, the outer one *repoussé*, h.m., 1768; he died 1772; long-case clock showing "High water at Bristol Key," about 1775, signed "Geo. Quarman, Temple Cloud."

Quarrel, Richd., apprenticed 1691 to Phil. Corderoy, C.C.

Quari (or Quarie), London. Table clock in engraved brass case, about 1700, S.K.M., inscribed "De Jean Quari, London."

Quartermaine, Joseph, Aylesbury; watch, tortoiseshell case, Mr A. E. Clarke, about 1750.

Quash, Joseph, apprenticed 1637 to Geo. Smith, C.C. 1646; watch, about 1650, signed "Josephus Quash Londini," silver engraved case, S.K.M.

Quelch. John; C.C. 1646; maker of lantern clocks. **Richard**, Oxford; octagonal watch, Whitcombe Greene collection, about 1650. **Jerem.**, London; long-case clock, 1735; watch, 1754.

Quenonault, Chas., London; watch, 1760.

Quentin, Gilles, Paris; clockmaker to Louis XIV., 1657.

Quested, Thos., Wye; long-case clock, about 1800.

Quick, Thos., London; watch, 1780.

Quillan, —, Airvalt; French lantern clock, about 1650.

Quillet, Paris; made the Bastille clock, for which, including three bells with flat tops, he received £3,767 in 1762; he had charge of the clock till his death; his widow in 1776 attended to some repairs.

Quilliam, Liverpool, see Townley.

Quimby. William, Belfast, Me., 1821-50. **Phineas Parkhurst**, Belfast, Me., 1830-50.

Quin, T. D., 18A Great Titchfield St., 1840.

Quinton, Stephen, London; maker of long-case clocks, about 1750.

R., Cruciform watch, stackfreed movement, signed "A. R.," Pierpont Morgan collection. Watch marked "N. R.," about 1620, Pierpont Morgan collection.

Racine, Chas. Fredk., Chaux de Fonds; celebrated enameller and dial painter, died 1832; watch, Pierpont Morgan collection, modern movement, signed "Racine, Berlin."

Radcliffe, Charles, Liverpool, 1680.

Radford. Henry, C.C. 1721. **Thos.**, Leeds; 1770. **Jas.**, 75 Gray's Inn Lane, 1793.

Rafe, Thos.; lantern clock, Mr Albert Hartshorne, 1661.

Rafford, F., London; watch, 1780.

Ragsdale, George, 25 New Bond St., 1769-83.

Raiment, Thomas, C.C. 1719.

Rainaldi. Giovannia P.; maker of the first clock in the square of St Mark, Venice, 1495. **Carl**, son of the foregoing; assisted his father.

Rainbow, Wm., London; long-case clock, about 1770.

Raines (Raynes), William, Butcher Row, East Smithfield; C.C. 1660; maker of lantern clocks.

Raingo, M., Paris; orrery clock, Windsor Castle, 1823; a similar one in the Soane Museum (see p. 328).

Rainier, John, livery C.C. 1787.

Rainsford. Bernard, apprenticed 1657 to Ed. Clough; C.C. 1677. **Francis**, Charing Cross; apprenticed to Robt. Gregory, 1680; C.C. 1689. **Francis**, apprenticed to Brounker Watts; C.C. 1708. **Jno.**, New St. Sq., C.C.; Mr Thos. Boynton has a clock by him, brass and silvered dial, engraved laurel border, chimes quarters on six bells, shows days of the month, about 1725; another fine long-case clock by him at the Duke of York Tavern, Potters Bar, about 1750; in the Wetherfield collection is a regulator by him.

Raitt, Alexander, London; maker of long-case clocks, with striking racks between the plates; 1685-1710.

Raker, P., 95 Bishopsgate St., 1775.

Rallart, —, Paris; watch, 1630.

Ram, Hewett, apprenticed 1691 to Thos. Hickman, C.C.

Rambley, Wm., 407 Oxford St., 1775-94.

Rambrant, Jas., London; watch, 1805.

Ramsay. David, near Temple Bar, watchmaker to James I.; first master of the C.C. (see p. 203); 1600-50. **John**, oval watch, Pierpont Morgan collection, signed "John Ramsay, Londres," about 1620; tangent wheel and screw adjustment, balance-cock pinned on.

Ramsbottom, Jno., Hall Green; clock, about 1770.

Ramsden. Thomas, C.C. 1648. **Jno.**, apprenticed 1654 to Thos. Loomes, C.C. **J.**, Hall Green; clock, about 1785.

Ramsey. Jno., C.C. 1637. **—**, Islington, 1800-8.

Rand, Wm., London; repeating watch, 1760.

Randall. Hy., apprenticed 1660 to Wm. Dobb. **Richd.**, apprenticed 1665 to Francis Bicknell, C.C. **Morris**, apprenticed 1680 to Jno. Dearmar, C.C. **Timothy**, apprenticed 1683 to Francis Hill, C.C. **John**, Wine Office Court, Fleet St., 1790-94.

Raneage, Isaac, C.C. 1635.

Ranna, —, Vienna; small watch in lyre-shaped enamelled case, about 1790.

Ransom. T., London; watch, about 1790. **M.**, London; watch, 1802. **George**, 18 King St., Soho, 1825.

Rant. Geo., C.C. 1687. **Jonathan**, C.C. 1687; bracket quarter repeating timepiece, arched dial, with calendar, ebony case, Wetherfield collection, about 1710.

Ranzonet, The Sieur, Nancy; said to have made a musical watch in 1770.

Raphard, —, London; watch, gold case, Schloss collection, 1760 (see p. 153).

Rapier, Jno., "in Wisbech, fecit," clock, about 1700.

Rapson, Thos., 4 Montague St., Portman Sq., 1814-18.

Ratcliffe, J., 45 Clerkenwell Close, 1835.

Ratherain, C., 25 Cursitor St., 1825.

Raulet, Samuel, Monmouth, U.S.A., 1800.

Raven. Crispin, London; long solid walnut case clock, about 1780. **Wm.,** Sheffield, 1832.

Rawford, James, 75 Gray's Inn Lane, 1770-90; livery C.C. 1787.

Rawlings. George, 88 Whitechapel, 1790. **Charles,** Brook St., Holborn; C.C. 1818, livery 1826; died 1864.

Rawlins. Henry, C.C. 1706. **James,** livery C.C. 1787. **Geo.,** 85 Whitechapel, 1793.

Rawson, Jno., Penrith, 1770.

Raxhall, Chris., apprenticed 1657 to Jas. Seabourne, C.C.

Ray. Daniel, Sudbury; long-case clock, about 1730. **& Montague,** 22 Denmark St., Soho, 1804-19. **Samuel,** 35 Great Castle St., Oxford St., 1820-30. **Henry,** 3 Commercial Place, City Rd., 1835; 22 Great Russell St., 1840.

Rayley, Jno., London; watch, 1830.

Rayment. Richd., St Edmunds Bury; a good maker of lantern clocks, about 1700; Sir Ernest Clarke had one by him, and Dr L. Brunton another; a later specimen, with arched dial, signed "Richd. Rayment, Bury"; long-case clock, about 1705, Mr A. G. Cockburn. **Thos.,** apprenticed to Thos. Taylor; C.C. 1719; watch, *repoussé* gold case, Schloss collection, about 1768; another, painted tortoiseshell case, Mr R. T. Mole, about 1765. **Wm.,** Stowmarket, 1750. **Thos.,** Stamford, 1760; clock, long-case with Oriental lacquer, Mr Thomas Sandall.

Raymond, Jno., Leadenhall St., 1774.

Raymonde. Water clock, dated 1581, and marked "Raymonde, Chester."

Rayner. Step.; Jno. Baldwin was apprenticed to him in 1691; watch, S.K.M., about 1730. **John,** London; C.C. 1697; watch, h.m., 1727.

Raynesford, see Rainsford.

Read. Thos., Manchester, 1770. **Geo.,** 10 Rotherhithe St., 1815-25. **George,** Old Sq., Lincoln's Inn, 1820. **Wm.,** Newcastle Pl., Clerkenwell, 1820. **William,** 84 Jermyn St., Piccadilly, 1825.

Reader. Wm., Hull; long-case clock, about 1760, Mr W. Metcalfe. **J.,** London, 1825.

Recordon, Louis, Greek St., Soho, 1780; afterwards succeeded Emery at 33 Cockspur St., Charing Cross. In 1780 he patented (No. 1,249) a pedometer winding for watches (see p. 411); 1778-1810, see Desgranges.

Red, Cr., London; watch, 1783.

Redier, Antoine, Paris; born 1717, died 1792.

Redrupp, Eli, Chesham, 1780.

Redstall, Francis, Overtons; long-case clock, Mr James Carter, about 1700.

Reead, Thos., C.C. 1632.

Reed, Alexander, admitted C.C. 1706; clock-watch, Schloss collection, about 1710.

Reeve. Thomas, in Pope's Head Alley, C.C. 1632; assistant 1655. **Robert,** York, f., 1660. **Thos.,** Harlestone, 1660. **Henry,** C.C. 1682. **Joseph,** Yarmouth, 1700. **John,** C.C. 1712. **Gowar,** The Fleet, C.C. 1730. **Jarvis,** C.C. 1731. **Sam,** Stonham, 1770. **Wm.,** 24 Ludgate St., 1830; 13 Vigo St., Regent St., 1835.

Reeves. Richard, 208 High St., Shoreditch, 1820-42. **Wm.,** 37 Newington Causeway, 1825-42.

Regard, Reymond, clockmaker at the upper end of Russell St., near Drury Lane; admitted C.C. 1677; mentioned in *Lond. Gaz.,* Jan. 25-28, 1691.

Regnauld (or **Regnault**). —, Chalons, France; devised a compensated pendulum, 1733; Thiout mentions a repeating clock by him. **Pierre,** père, Rue Vielle-du-Temple, Paris; garde visiteur in 1769; clock and bells of the Bastille placed in his custody, 1789.

Regnier, "Maitre," Paris, 1605; octagonal watch, Garnier collection, late sixteenth century, case of crystal, movement signed "J. Regnier, Paris."

Regeynolds, Geo., York, f., 1641; died 1680.

Rehle, —, Freiburg; table clock, 1690.

"**Reicardledert** in Strasburg"; oval alarm watch, about 1595.

Reicheneder, Leopold, Burckhausen; brass box-shaped circular watch, two dials, numerals up to twenty-four, engraved with views of a town; on back is engraved the Wisdom of Solomon, about 1550; Pierpont Morgan collection.

Reid. Thomas, born 1746, died ·1831; a celebrated Edinburgh clockmaker, apprenticed to Jas. Cowan, whom he succeeded in 1781; watch, "Thos. Reid & Co., Edinburgh, 1800"; from 1806 he was in partnership with **Wm. Auld** till 1823, when he retired from business; Thos. Reid was author of "Treatise on Clock and Watchmaking," published in 1826, the major part of which was taken from an article by him in Brewster's "Edinburgh Cyclopaedia," published in 1819; hon. f., C.C. 1825. **Adam,** Clerkenwell and Woolwich; inventor of an adjustment for Graham's pendulum, 1779-1835. Henderson, in his "Life of Ferguson," speaks of **Andrew** Reid, a clever watchmaker, who died at Brixton in 1835, aged 85. **F., & Sons,** Glasgow, 1786; Reid & Todd, 1825-42. **Wm.,** 32 Rosoman St., Clerkenwell, 1790 1820; fine pocket chronometer, Arnold escapement, h.m., 1795. **J.,** Ball Alley, Lombard St., 1800-16. **& Auld,** Edinburgh, 1806-23; E. J. Thompson gave to the Horological Institute a fine regulator, inscribed "Reid & Auld, 1818." **Jno.,** Edinburgh; long-case clock, about 1820.

Reidl, Joseph, Vienna; watch, 1770.

Reilly. John, Dublin, 1778. **John,** Philadelphia, 1785-97. **J. C.,** 12 Middle Row, Holborn, 1815-25.

Reinhold, large octagonal watch, rock crystal case, Pierpont Morgan collection, signed "Johan Georg Reinhold," about 1600; see Roll.

Reith, James, repeating watch, about 1700, in pierced and engraved gold case, signed "James Reith Versailles," S.K.M.; admitted C.C. 1705; long-case clock, about 1715, Mr J. Terry.

Relph, E., 182 Tooley St., 1835.

Remmerdell, Thos., Wigan; watch, 1776.

Renching, Edmd., apprenticed 1659 to Robt. Robinson, C.C.

Rener, Michael E., Kronstat; table clock, about 1590.

Rennie, Jas., Carlisle, 1833.

Renshaw, Thomas, Ship Alley, Wellclose Sq., 1825.

Rentnow, see Wontner.

Renton, Jas., York, 1838.

Rentzsch, Sigismund, 2 St George St., St James's Sq.; a clever mechanician and excellent workman; he devised and made a peculiar chronometer escapement; his regulator had original features, among them a pendulum, with the mercury divided in several small tubes; he patented in 1813 an automatic timekeeper somewhat similar to Horstmann's (see p. 303); 1813-42.

Restell, Thos., Tooting. In 1848 he patented (No. 12,154) escapement; Strand in 1852, when he patented another escapement (No. 324).

Rettord, Jno., London; watch, 1798.

Revel, —, Palais-Royal, Paris, 1770.

Revell. Sam, apprenticed 1664 to Thos. Loomes, C.C. **Jno.,** Eye, 1775.

Rewalling, Thomas, C.C. 1715; watch, about 1720, signed "Thos. Rewalling, London."

Rex, Thomas, 96 Broad St., Ratcliff, 1842.

Rey, —, enamelled watch, about 1785, signed "Jn. Ant. Rey & Fils."

Reyner. Stephen, at ye Dial, Bishopsgate Within, admitted C.C. 1691. **Thos.,** Oxon.; bracket clock, about 1740.

Reynolds. Alban, apprenticed 1670 to Jno. Wise, C.C. **Joseph,** C.C. 1691. **Thomas,** apprenticed to H. Bradshaw; C.C. 1706; small bracket chiming clock, two trains only, arch dial, with strike-silent hand, inscribed "Thomas Reynolds, St Martin's-le-Grand," about 1740. **Thos.,** son and late apprentice of the preceding T. R., 2 St Martin's-le-Grand, admitted C.C. 1736; watch, G.M., about 1770. **Thos.,** Warwick; watch, silver cock, silver name-plate, steel index disc, about 1730. **Jno.,** blacksmith, Hagbourn, Berks; made a clock and chimes for Brampton Church, for which he was paid £34; 1732. **Jacob,** Shaston; long-case clock, about 1750. **Jas.,** Holborn Hill; livery C.C. 1766. **Thos.,** Oxon., about 1770. **Francis,** Kensington, 1776. **Thos., & Son,** 1 Sparrow Corner, Minories, 1783-94. **G.,** 10 Gough Sq., 1830. **T.,** 25 Coppice Row, Clerkenwell, 1835.

Rhetorick, Walter, apprenticed 1651 to David Moody, C.C.

Rice, Stephen, 20 Pall Mall, 1793.

Rich. Jno., London; watch on chatelaine, Pierpont Morgan collection, about 1750; repeating watch, 1775. **John,** Bristol, Conn., 1820.

Richard. Daniel John, born at La Sagne 1665, died at Locle 1741; is said to have introduced watchmaking into Neuchatel in 1781; his five sons devoted themselves to the new industry. **Peter,** C.C. 1679. **Francois,** Hambourg, watch, S.K.M., about 1780. **Louis Jean,** Neuchatel, born 1812, died 1875. —, silver watch, signed "Auguste Richard sur la Port à Rouen," has John Mattin round the dial instead of figures, about 1820; Pierpont Morgan collection.

Richards. Luke, C.C. 1648. **Richd.,** free of C.C. by redemption, 1652. **Jno.,** apprenticed in 1654 to Wm. Pettitt, C.C. **Hugh,** Bread St.; apprenticed 1691 to Hy. Bradley, master C.C. 1735. **Henry,** London, C.C. 1699; watch, 1725. **Thomas,** 114 Strand, 1770-72. **Jno.,** London; C.C. 1770; several watches, 1780-96. **William,** Albemarle St., Clerkenwell; liveryman C.C. 1776. **B.,** London; watch, 1790. **William,** 43 Brick Lane, Old St., 1794. **Thomas,** 17 Bridgewater Sq., Barbican, 1804; 96 Shoreditch, 1830. **& Morrell,** 240 Pearl St., New York, 1809. **S. & J.,** 1817. **Theophilus, & Co.,** centre seconds watch, about 1820. **W.,** 49 Oxford St., 1830.

Richardson. Wm., apprenticed 1647 to Jas. Starnell, C.C. **Richard,** C.C. 1675; "a good wheel cutter" (Hatton). **Francis,** Philadelphia, 1736 **James,** Bradford; clock, "Jas. Richardson. — Bradforth," about 1760. **Richard,** Liverpool, 1776.

Richard, Hexham, 1780. **James**, Luton, 1780; Pentonville, 1800; master C.C. 1788. **Thos.**, Weaverham; long-case clock, about 1780, with the following inscription round arch of dial, "That man is yet unborn who duly weighs an hour." **John**, Racquet Court, 1798-1811; liveryman C.C. 1810.

Richmond. **Joseph**, York, f., 1810. **Robt.**, Lancaster, 1817, f.

Rickman, **W.**, 35 Great Pulteney St., 1820.

Ricord. **Richard**, C.C. 1649. **Jno.**, C.C. 1657.

Riddlesdon. **Samuel**, C.C. 1766. **Jno.**, watch-spring maker, Red Cross Sq., 1790-94.

Rider. **Thos.**, apprenticed 1691 to John Johnson, C.C. **Job**, Belfast; advertisement 1791: "Job Rider, from London and Dublin, and last from Hillsborough has commenced business at 'The Reflecting Telescope' Shambles Street, where he makes clocks and watches of all kinds to the common manner, with Harrison's and other modern improvements. His turret and steeple clocks are in an entirely new construction"; made a self-winding barometric clock somewhat on the plan of Cox described on p. **301**; he removed to High St., Belfast, and retired from the clock and watch business in 1807; a clock by him is in the possession of Sir W. Q. Ewart. **John**, Camberwell Green, 1835. **—**, Poole; at the Dean sale of Chippendale furniture at Christie's, 15th June 1909, a long-case clock about 9 ft. high by him fetched 460 guineas.

Ridereau, **—**, established at Place Maubert, Paris, in 1769; presented the Academy of Science with a clock striking hours, quarters, and repeating all with the same striking train.

Ridgdale, N.; oval watch, S.K.M., about 1610.

Ridley. **Josiah**, C.C. 1685; the late Mr Frederick Morris had a fine long marqueterie case chiming clock by him, dating from about 1700. **Joseph**, received a reward of 20 guineas from the Society of Arts, for a sector and depthing tool, 1788. **Thos.**, 14 Waterloo Rd., and Enfield, 1830-42.

Riego, **Miguel**, 284 Regent St., 1868.

Riesle, **E.**; wooden and musical clockmaker, 2 Garden Row, London Rd., 1840.

Rigaud, **—**, London; watch by him, about 1740, belonging to Mr Geo. Carr Glyn.

Rigby. **Joshua**, 5 Berkeley St., Clerkenwell, hon. freeman C.C. 1781; spoken of by Hatton and by Earnshaw; maker of a repeater watch for the Duke of Sussex; 1765-1800. **E.**, **& Son**, 6 Berkeley St., Clerkenwell, 1795-1800. **James**, 35 Rosoman St., Clerkenwell, 1804. **James**, 8 Charing Cross, 1806-30 (succeeded Leroux, see Morse, Richd.). **Thos.**, 29 Alfred Place, Goswell Rd., 1816-18. **Joshua**, 8 King St., Goswell Rd., 1820. **Jas.**, Liverpool, 1830.

Rigmaiden, **—**, Dublin, about 1760.

Riley. **John**, Gillingham, Halifax, 1804. **G.**, Halifax, 1809, see Ryley.

Rimbault. This family of clockmakers flourished from about 1700 till nearly the end of the century. A clock signed "Stephen Rimbault, London," belonging to Senor Espéz of Galicia and attributed to the seventeenth century, was mentioned in *Notes and Queries* for 1st October 1910; I saw a bracket clock not later than 1730 signed "Rimbault junr."; on the movement of a clock by "Phillesson," was scratched "Rimbault fecit 1744." **Stephen**, 7 Great

St Andrew St., 1760-81 (see p. **391**). **Paul**, 9 Denmark St., St Giles's, 1779-85.

Rimer, **Wm.**, Liverpool; watch, 1769.

Ring, **Joseph**, C.C. 1693.

Ripley, **Jno.**, York, f., 1471.

Rippin, **William**, Holbeach, Lincolnshire; worked at his trade as watch and clock repairer for thirty years after he lost his sight; vouched for by his daughter and many other persons; he died in 1857.

Rippon, **Richard**, 46 King St., Seven Dials, 1816; afterwards of Cooks' Court, Long Acre; a well-known maker of English repeating work for watches. E. J. Dent married his widow; fine watch movement by him, G.M.

Risbridger (or **Ribridger**). **William**, Dorking; lantern and 30-hour long-case clocks, about 1700. **John**, Brentford; long-case clock, square dial, one hand, with date "1740" scratched on back of dial and also "1777 cleaned." **John**, New Brentford, 1800-20.

Risdon, **Francis**, London; watch, about 1780.

Rishton, **James**, Rochdale, 1821.

Ritchie. **George**, Philadelphia, 1785-93. **Jas.**, Leith St., Edinburgh, 1809-42. **David**, Clerkenwell; devised a compensation pendulum in 1812. **Fredk. Jas.**, born 1825, died 1906; succeeded his father at Leith St., Edinburgh; he was a capable horologist who perfected a system of electrically driven clocks described in detail in the "Watch and Clock Makers' Handbook."

Rithe, **Jno.**, apprenticed in 1654 to R. Scrivener, C.C.

Ritherdon. **Geo.**, Aldgate, 1753-83. **Robert**, 3 Aldgate Within, 1758-1800.

Rittenhouse. **David**, Philadelphia, 1751-97. **Dan.**, Philadelphia, astronomical clock, 1767.

Rivaz, **Pierre de**, Paris; a celebrated horologist. In 1748 he made a marine timepiece which had a temperature compensating device attached to the balance. He converted clocks going a fortnight only into twelve months without winding, and claimed that by adding another wheel his clocks could be made to show the true time, exactly following the sun, even in his inequalities.

Rivers. **David**, 3 Bridgwater Sq., 1753-75. **David**, 3 Sweeting's Alley, livery C.C. 1766; master 1773; 1760-83; watch, David Rivers & Son, h.m., 1782. **Jno.**, 1 Holborn Bars, 1783. **& Son** (successors to D. St Leu), 38 Cornhill, 1790-1812; Wm. Rivers, master C.C. 1794. **William**, 33 Cornhill, 1818-20.

Riviere, **Samuel Newton**, 63 New Bond St., 1790-1804.

Rix, **—**, London; watch, 1750; clock, about 1760, inscribed "I. Rix, London."

Robarts, **B.**, London; watch, 1783.

Robb, **Wm.**, Montrose, 1780.

Robbin, **Fabian**, London; walnut marqueterie long-case month clock, square dial, bull's-eye in front of pendulum bob, 1690-1700, see Robins, Fabian.

Robbins. **J.**, 24 Percival St., 1842. **Royal Elisha**, purchased in 1857 the Boston Watch Company of Waltham, Mass., which he steered to prosperity and greatness as the American Watch Company; died 1902, aged 78.

Roberson, **Jas.**, London, 1760.

Robert. **—**, Chaux de Fonds; quarter repeating work described by Thiout in 1741. **& Courvoisier**, Geneva, 1790-1800. **Henri**, Paris, chronometer maker, 1830-65.

Roberts. **Richard**, apprenticed 1653 to

Eliza Fletcher, C.C. **Hugh**, apprenticed 1657 to David Bouquett; C.C. 1664; in the B.M. is a large astronomical watch by him. **Wm.**, apprenticed 1692 to Mordecai Fox, C.C. **Timothy**, Otley, 1770. **Samuel**, C.C. 1776; watch, G.M., h.m., 1778. **Gideon**, Bristol, Conn., 1780-1804; then **Jno.**; then **Jacob**. **Gideon**, Bristol, Conn., U.S.A., maker of American clocks, 1790. **Jno.**, St James's Market, 1790. **Josiah**, 88 Bishopsgate St., 1793. **J. B.**, London; watch, 1795. **J.**, Dudley; watch, about 1800, around bezel, "Keep me clean and use me well, then I to you the time will tell." **Wm.**, St James's Market, 1806; 5 St Alban's Place, Pall Mall, 1820-30. **C.**, London; watch, 1820. **George**, 27 Marchmont St., Brunswick Sq., 1820. **Jas.**, 87 Union St., Boro', 1842.

Robertson, **Benj.**, 14 Jewin St., 1783.

Robin, **Robert**, Paris; born 1742; died 1799; clockmaker to Louis XV.; two excellent examples of his work are in the Jones collection at S.K.M., and one in the Wallace collection; a calendar clock by him in case of chased ormolu with figures of boys allegorical of Sculpture and Architecture surmounted by a vase fetched £661 at the Hamilton sale in 1882 (see also p. **317**).

Robins. **Fabian**, London; walnut marqueterie long-case month clock, square dial, glass in front of pendulum bob, about 1695, Mr James Arthur. **John**, 67 Aldersgate St., 1783-94. **Wm.**, 13 Fleet St., 1783; master C.C. 1813. **John**, 13 Clerkenwell Green, 1800-4; 65 Charing Cross, 1817. **John**, 13 Frith St., 1823-30.

Robinson. **Geo.**, apprenticed 1631 to Simon Hackett, C.C. **Robert**, C.C. 1652; lantern clock, inscribed "Robert Robinson in Red Cross St of London," about 1655, dial 3 in. in diameter of silver, days of the month engraved outside the hour band with indicator on rotating ring; another lantern-clock, marked "Robert Robinson at the Style in Lothbury, London," about 1670. **William**, C.C. 1667. **Dan.**, apprenticed 1681 to Wm. Arthur, C.C. **Jno.**, apprenticed 1681 to Wm. Robinson. **Thomas**, C.C. 1703. **Francis**, "in the Temple"; apprenticed to Henry Jones, C.C. 1707; master 1725; repeating watch with silver case in the G.M., inscribed "Servant to His Royal Highness"; another example, a small square case clock, square dial with cherub corners, 1707-26. **Ruhamer**, Gracechurch St., 1713. **William**, apprenticed to Daniel Delander; C.C. 1720. **James**, at the Dial in Grace's Alley, Well Close Sq.; maker of long-case clocks and watches, 1730-70, afterwards Samuel Robinson. **Philip**, Fleet St., 1737-40. **& Cave**, "232 Strand, near Temple Barr," card Ponsonby collection, about 1770. **M.**, repeating watch, gold *repoussé* case, Schloss collection, 1780. **Owen**, an escapement maker who worked for Arnold, mentioned by Reid as the maker of a double chronometer escapement, 1780-1810. **Thos.**, London; watch, 1780. **Jno.**, Lancaster, 1783, f. **Anthony**, 232 Strand, 1783. **Richard**, watch-chain maker, 4 Goldsmith Row, 1790. **Matthew**, watch movement maker, 8 Charterhouse St., 1790-94. **Geo.**, London, 1806; clock so inscribed in the lighthouse at St Agnes, Scilly Islands. **Thos.**, London; apprenticed to Paul Barraud; C.C. 1812; watch, 1825. **Wm.**, Leyburn, 1822-40. **John**, Winterton; an ingenious clockmaker; he succeeded to the business of Thomas Tate, and in 1834 made a clock for Winterton Church; the dead-beat escapement had round pins as pallets hinged to allow movement equal to half the diameter of a pin. **Richard**, watch movement maker, 27 Ray St., Clerkenwell, 1835.

Robotham, Fras., High St., Hampstead, 1836-40.

Robson. Wm., Curtain Rd., 1780-94. **William**, musical clockmaker, 48 Red Cross St., 1797-1810 ; master C.C. 1809.

Roby, James, 2 Prince's St., Leicester Sq., 1793-1800.

Rochat, Jules, 82 Frith St., Soho, 1840-42.

Rochford, M. F., 212 Piccadilly, 1804-25. **F.**, 49 Jermyn St., 1830.

Rodanet, J. H., Paris ; chronometer maker ; died 1884, aged 78.

Rodet, —, London ; quarter repeating watch in gold case beautifully pierced with birds and scrolls ; outer case pierced and ornamented in *repoussé* with medallions, escallop shells, and flowers, about 1740, Pierpont Morgan collection ; another watch of Dutch character similarly inscribed, about 1750 ; watch, "Isa Rodet, London," about 1770, Mr E. Wehrle.

Rodgers. Benj., London, 1720. **J.**, 39 St Paul's Churchyard ; rack-lever watch, 1818.

Roe, Joshua, apprenticed 1687 to Edmd. Appley, C.C.

Roger, —, repaired the clock at Exeter Cathedral, 1424 (see p. 50).

Rogers. William, C.C. 1641 ; Nicasius Russell was apprenticed to him in 1653. **Chas.**, apprenticed 1649 to Wm. Almond ; C.C. 1657. **Wm.**, apprenticed 1682 to Thos. Taylor, Holborn. **John**, C.C. 1731. **B.**, London ; watch, 1735. **Isaac**, White Hart Court, Gracechurch St., a maker of good watches ; a specimen in gold *repoussé* outer case is in the B.M. ; did a good trade in foreign markets ; bracket clock with painted case, Persian flower pattern, brass arched dial, Turkish figures ; engraved back plate and formerly crown escapement ; tunes at the hour ; had dancing figures, a ship or other mechanism, showing through dial, the pulleys for this alone remain ; bought in the bazaar, Constantinople, 1881 ; 1750-94 ; large travelling watch, dated 1759, Pierpont Morgan collection. **S.**, Fenchurch St., 1774-82. **William**, Broad St. Buildings, liveryman C.C. 1776. **Isaac**, 4 White Hart Court, Gracechurch St.; C.C. 1776 ; master 1824 ; succeeded to his father's business 1776 ; removed to 24 Little Bell Alley, Colman St., in 1802 ; died 1839. **Jno.**, Hackney ; watch, 1780. **Samuel**, Plymouth, U.S.A., 1790-1804. **Thomas**, 63 Charing Cross, liveryman C.C. 1810. **Wm.**, same address, 1817. **John**, 22 Wilmington Sq. ; made watches for the American market ; born 1817 ; died 1868. **C.**, 59 Charlton St., Somers Town, 1820.

Rogerson, Henry, London, about 1780.

Roget, —, London ; watch, about 1740 ; another, 1755.

Rohr, John A., Philadelphia, 1811.

Roizin, —, Rue de Charonne, Paris, 1770.

Rolf, Joseph, & Son, 17 Foster Lane, 1769-88.

Rolfe, Robert, 29 St John's Sq., Clerkenwell, 1835 ; succeeded Gravell & Son in 1850. **Robert**, his son, died 1901, aged 65.

Roll, George, Augsburg. In 1588 he made a clockwork globe, which Rudolph II. bought for 1,000 florins ; at the S.K.M. is a striking clock in a celestial sphere of gilt brass on four feet ; the sphere is inscribed, "Elaborabat Georgivs Roll et Johannes Reinhold in Avgvsta Anno Domini 1584."

Rollison, Dolly, Halton ; died 1752, aged 36 ; long-case clock, inscribed "Dollif Rolisson, Halton," Dr Wm. A. Day ; long-case clock, signed "Dolf Rollinson, Halton, Essex," Sir James M. Moody.

Roman, Bordier, & Co., watch, about 1825, see Roux.

Rombach, J., 103 Regent St., 1835-42.

Rome, Wm., 6 Shepperton Place, North Rd., 1842.

Romer. Flack, C.C. 1661. **Thos.**, 20 George St., Adelphi, 1817.

Romeux, Lewis de, C.C. 1706.

Romieu, L., Rouen ; watch in silver case, outer case of leather *piqué* with silver, centre of dial enamelled green, hours on white ring of enamel, about 1630, Pierpont Morgan collection. — à Rouen ; enamelled watch, about 1660 (see p. 150).

Romilly. John, born in Geneva 1714. A clever watchmaker who migrated to Paris and set up business in the Place Dauphine, where he was very successful ; he advocated 8-day watches and made several, also watches with cylinder escapements and very large balances to vibrate seconds, as well as equation watches (see p. 369) ; is said to have produced a self-winding watch, possibly on the plan patented in England by Recordon in 1780, and of which Breguet made several (see p. 293) ; a fine watch by him with enamelled case forms part of the Pierpont Morgan collection ; at South Kensington Museum is a watch signed "I. Romilly à Paris," dating from about 1760 ; the case is inlaid with tinted gold ; died 1796, aged 82. **Peter**, 17 Frith St., Soho, 1769-94 ; long-case chiming clock, inscribed "Romilly, London," about 1770.

Romley, Chris., apprenticed to Wm. Addis ; C.C. 1755. Ludlam quotes both Chris. and Rob. Romley.

Romney, Joseph, admitted C.C. 1664.

Ront, Wm., Endfield ; watch, 1765.

Roof, Daniel, C.C. 1676.

Rooke, John, 26 Berkeley Sq., 1765-94 ; hon. f. C.C. 1781.

Rooker. Richd., apprenticed 1685 to Jno. Clowes ; C.C. 1694. **Richard**, Chelsea, C.C. 1728 ; large silver watch, silver chased dial, having an aperture in which a pendulum swings, about 1740.

Rookes, Barlow, admitted C.C. 1667.

Rooksby. John, York, f., 1647. **—**, A small timepiece with repeating work, dial brass gilt, beautifully engraved, inscribed "J. Rooksby in Yorke," about 1690.

"Stolen on the 23rd instant, out of Mr Jeffreys' House in Yorke, a gold pendulum watch with minutes and seconds, made by Mr Rooksby, of Hull, with a gold studded case. Notice to be given to Mr Hill, Goldsmith, in the Strand" (*Lond. Gaz.*, Nov. 26-30, 1691).

Roque, —, Passage du Saumon, Paris, 1770.

Rose. Michael, C.C. 1676 ; 8-day chiming clock in long case, with scroll marqueterie decoration, signed "Rose & Son," about 1720. **John**, Bishopsgate, C.C. 1730. **William**, London ; watch in painted tortoiseshell case, Mr A. E. Clarke, about 1750. **Joseph**, London, about 1750 ; Mr Charles Morson (U.S.A.) has a musical clock by him in a long case, the plinth of which is kettle shape. **Joseph, & Son**, 19 Foster Lane, 1765-68. **—**, junr., St Ann's Lane, 1774. **Joseph, Son, & Payne**, 17 Foster Lane, 1771-94. **Daniel**, Reading, U.S.A., 1820-40. **John**, 96 Fleet Market, 1830.

Roselet, —, Geneva ; watch, 1809.

Rosier, John, Geneva ; watch, 1815.

Roskell, Robert, the elder, Liverpool, many rack lever and cylinder watches by him ; he was also a collector of curious horological specimens, 1800-30.

Ross. Thos., Hull, 1770. **Jno.**, Tain, 1775. **Wm.**, Cork ; watch, handsome *repoussé* case, h.m., 1793. **& Peckham**, 41 Bedford St., Covent Garden, 1810.

Rosse, Samuel, C.C. 1672.

Rossi, W., 5 Blackman St., 1830.

Rotherham. Thomas, apprenticed to Simon Hackett 1654 ; C.C. 1662. **R. H.**, Coventry ; died 1864, aged 74. **John**, Coventry, died 1905, aged 67, see also Vale.

Rotherodd, Benjamin, silver rose-shaped watch in the Bernal collection, seventeenth century work.

Rothwood. Robert, C.C. 1632. **Robert**, C.C. 1648.

Rouckleiffe, Jno., Bridgwater ; maker of brass clocks, 1770, see Brimble.

Roumieu. Paul, Edinburgh, probably from Rouen ; submitted his essay, made in his own chamber and vouched for by George Mill and Andrew Brown, and was admitted to the incorporation of Hammermen 1677 ; died 1693 ; watch, about 1680, formerly in the Hawkins collection, now in Nelthropp collection, G.M. **Paul**, Edinburgh, son of the foregoing, admitted 1682, his essay masters being Richard Mill and Jno. Sympson ; died 1710. "Stolen this day in the Parliament House, out of a gentleman's pocket, a silver pendulum watch with a minute hand and a green shagreen case, some of the studs broken off. Whoever can give notice of the said watch to Mr Romieu, watchmaker, shall be thankfully rewarded" (*Edinburgh Gaz.*, 1699). **Adam**, C.C. 1695. **John**, C.C. 1720. **Adam**, C.C. 1726.

Roumyeu, James, C.C. 1692.

Rountree, Robt., f., York, 1828.

Rousby, Jno., York, f., 1683.

Rouse Robert, apprenticed 1682 to Chas. Baxter, C.C.

Rousseau. David, sixteenth century cruciform watch, Garnier collection. **Jean**, a clever watchmaker ; a crystal cased watch in the form of a cross by him in the Fellows collection, about 1590. **Jean**, son of the above, born 1609, died 1684 ; silver watch, S.K.M., engraved with figures of the seasons and with flowers (see p. 189). **—**, the father of Jean Jacques Rousseau was a watchmaker of Geneva in the early part of the eighteenth century.

Roussel, —, Master Horologer of Paris, mentioned by Thiout in 1741.

Routh, Saml., C.C. ; to him Jno. Marshall was apprenticed in 1682 ; clock by him, about 1720.

Routledge, Geo., Lydford, Devon, died 1801 ; curious epitaph in Lydford churchyard as follows :—

Here lies in a horizontal position the outside case of
GEORGE ROUTLEDGE, Watchmaker.
Integrity was the mainspring and prudence
the regulator of all the actions of his life ;
humane, generous and liberal,
His hand never stopped till he had relieved
distress.
So nicely regulated were his movements that
he never went wrong, except when set going
by people who did not know his key.
Even then he was easily set right again.
He had the art of disposing of his time so well,
that his hours glided away, his pulse
stopped beating.
He ran down November 14, 1801, aged 57,
In hopes of being taken in hand by his Maker,
Thoroughly cleaned, repaired, wound up, and
set going in the world to come, when
time shall be no more.

Roux, Bordier, & Roman, Geneva, about 1810.

Rowden, John, London ; apprenticed to Dinnis 1683 ; C.C. 1691 ; watch, silver dial, with raised figures, square pillars, about 1700.

Rowe. Thomas, C.C. 1699. **Benjamin,** C.C. 1708. **John,** St Paul's Churchyard, liveryman C.C. 1770-82.

Rowland. Jno., Manchester, 1765. **& Co.,** 8 Coventry St., 1825.

Rowlands. Walter, Berwick, 1775. **Christopher,** 132 Long Acre, 1815 ; 9 Coventry St., 1835 ; 33 Leadenhall St., 1840. **William,** Smith St., Clerkenwell, watch-case maker, apprenticed to T. & R. Carpenter ; treasurer and a liberal supporter of the Clock and Watchmakers' Asylum ; livery C.C. 1820 ; master 1860 ; died 1868, aged 77. **William, & Son,** 92 Quadrant, 1823. **R.,** watch-case maker, 35 Meredith St., Clerkenwell, 1835.

Rowley. Eliza, apprenticed 1694 to Andrew Yeatman and Mary his wife, C.C. —, associated with Graham in constructing an orrery, 1716. **Francis,** removed from Birmingham 1792 to Turnmill St., Clerkenwell ; died 1824, aged 70. His son **Francis,** Faulkner's Alley, died 1837, aged 49, the business being carried on by his widow Elizabeth ; she died in 1870, aged 88. **Arthur & Henry,** Red Lion St., Clerkenwell, afterwards at Gray's Inn Rd., and then Theobald's Rd. ; Arthur died 1900, aged 85 ; Henry died 1902, aged 75. **Hy.,** Liverpool, 1833.

Rowning, "Once a bad clockmaker in Cambridge" (Ludlam, 1758) ; John Rowning, M.A., in 1732 patented a clock (see p. **362**), and reference is made in the "Dictionary of National Biography" to a brother a watchmaker. In *East Anglian Notes and Queries* are mentioned, as early clockmakers, J. Rowning, Newmarket ; Stephen Rowning, Thetford, and Rowning of Brandon ; these all probably lived about the middle of the eighteenth century.

Roy. David, C.C. 1682. **William,** 30 Bell Yard, Lincoln's Inn, 1804.

Roycroft, Thomas, admitted C.C. 1699.

Royd, Stephen Joseph, C.C. ; to him was apprenticed Dymoke Evans in 1800.

Royer, William, 40 Gee St., Goswell Rd., 1820.

Roylands, William, watch movement maker, 29 Chiswell St., 1790-94.

Royle, Jos., Chorley, 1780.

Roze, A. C., a French horologist, died 1862, aged 50.

Rubins, Richard, Grantham, 1780.

Rubottom, Wm., Liverpool, 1770.

Rudkin, Thomas, C.C. 1683.

Rudrupp, Jno., Amersham ; maker of lantern clocks, about 1710.

Ruegger, —, Geneva, 1800.

Ruel, Samuel, Rotterdam ; calendar watch, Schloss collection ; nicely pierced work on movement, "The Triumph of Venus," h.m., 1788 (p. 190).

Rugend, —, Auch ; tulip watch, Solty-koff collection, about 1570 (see p. 125).

Rugendas, Nicholas, Augsburg, 1605-30 (see p. 116).

Rugg & Thaine, 15 Cheapside ; enamelled watch by them, Dunn Gardner collection ; this, with a chatelaine partly of gold, fetched £100 in 1902 at Christie's ; 1769-94.

Rugless. Sam., 37 Ratcliff Highway, 1815-25. **T.,** 3 Cannon St., St George's East, 1842.

Rule. Jas., Portsmouth ; watch, 1779. **Jas.,** York, f., 1797.

Rumford, Jno., Bishops Auckland, 1776.

Rundell. Edwd., Norton St Phillip's ; fine musical clock, about 1710. **Philip,** Ludgate Hill, livery Drapers' Company, 1770. **& Bridge,** 32 Ludgate Hill, 1788-1824 ; watch, marked "Rundell, Bridge, & Rundell, 1830" ; Rundell & Bridge succeeded Picket & Rundell ; they were silversmiths to the Crown, and their shop one of the attractions of London ; the business was purchased by Francis Lambert, and transferred to Coventry St.

Rush, Samuel, 16 Ludgate Hill, and Porter St., Leicester Fields, 1759-90.

Russel. Thomas, watch-case maker, 18 Barbican, 1775. **Charles,** 18 Barbican, 1790.

Russell. Nicholas, apprenticed to William Rogers in 1653 ; C.C. 1663 ; master 1692 ; died 1700. "A plain hour watch goes but 24 hours, the name on it is Nicolus Russell, Londini, fecit" (*Lond. Gaz.*, Dec. 22-27, 1697). **Jno.,** C.C. about 1660. **Cornelius,** apprenticed 1686 to Ab. Clyatt, C.C. **Thomas,** at the Clock Case in Barbican ; liveryman C.C. 1776. **Charles & Thomas,** 18 Barbican, 1787-1815. **Thos.,** Lancaster, 1797, f., 1832. **A. C.,** London ; watch, Schloss collection, about 1800. **Benj.,** Thirsk, 1822. **T.,** 50 Great Sutton St., 1842.

Rust. Wm., Lincoln, 1775. **Wm.,** Hull, 1780. **& Shipham,** 1822.

Rutherford, Michael, Hawick, 1803.

Rutland. Jonathan, 110 Oxford St., 1793-1804. **James,** 83 Oxford St., 1822-30.

Rutter, Jno., St James's Walk, 1793.

Rycroft, Thos. ; a watch by him is mentioned in the *Lond. Gaz.*, Sept. 21-25, 1693.

Ryder. Thomas, C.C. 1698. **Thomas,** C.C. 1712. **Josh.,** London ; watch, h.m., 1761.

Ryland, Jno., London ; watch, 1780.

Ryler, William, C.C. 1712.

Ryley. Laurence, apprenticed C.C. 1662. **Geo.,** apprenticed C.C. 1683. **Thomas,** C.C. 1704. **Erasmus,** Wood's Close, C.C. 1730. **Jno.,** Coventry, 1812-18.

Rymer, Hy., 6 George St., Adelphi, 1817.

Rypplay, Jno., York, f., 1471.

S. H., see Schnier.

Saber, Edwd., Cannon St., 1783.

Saberty, J., London ; watch, 1765.

Sacheverell, Benasir, apprenticed 1680 to W. Thoroughgood ; turned over to Tompion ; admitted C.C. 1687.

Sadd, Thomas, East Windsor, U.S.A., 1750.

Sadleir, Samuel, Hackney, warden C.C., 1723.

Sadler. Sam., apprenticed 1687 to Sam. Vernon, C.C. ; long marqueterie case clock, about 1700. **Robert,** London ; long-case clock, about 1740. **Thos.,** Norwich ; long-case clock, about 1770. **Stephen,** 134 Bishopsgate Without, 1830.

Saer, Joseph, admitted C.C. 1687 ; maker of a square-dial brass 8-day clock, two hands, inscription, "Joseph Saer, in Penpool Lane, London," 1686-1700.

Saffory, John, 13 Tokenhouse Yard, 1760-70.

Sagar. Edmund, Middleham, 1750. **Robt.,** Blackburn, 1818.

Sage, Matthew, Oxon. ; watch, about 1760.

Sainsbury. Robert, Chippenham, 1775. **Richard,** Bridgwater ; long-case clock, about 1780. **J.** (tools), 2 Cowcross St., 1806-23. **Richard,** 9 Wingrove Place, Clerkenwell, 1840-42.

St Andrew, G., London ; watch, 1790.

St George, Jno., apprenticed 1674 to Barlow Rookes, C.C.

St Leu, see De St Leu.

Salisbury, Wm., London ; watch, 1730.

Salmon. Jno., Bristol ; bracket clock, repeating on eight bells, ebony case, Mr J. Drummond Robertson, about 1700. **Henry,** Coventry St., Piccadilly, 1769-82. **Robert,** 49 Strand, 1790-94. **C. E.,** 151 Bishopsgate Without, 1823.

Saltby, Thos., Grantham, 1770.

Salter. Edward, 20 Cannon St., 1788-94. **John,** 35 Strand, 1804 ; 73 Strand, 1825-30.

Saltmarsh, Samuel, 74 Middleton St., Clerkenwell, 1840.

Sambrook, John, C.C. 1680.

Samley, —, Gutter Lane, 1775.

Samon, John, C.C. 1654.

Sampson. Umfrevil, apprenticed to Chas. Cabrier, C.C. 1735. **Robert,** Westminster ; invented a two-part chime clock, described in *Transactions of the Society of Arts,* vol. iv., 1786 ; card, B.M., "Robert Sampson, 2 Petty France, Westminster, 1788." **Wm.,** London, about 1800.

Samson, London, on many watches, Dutch style, 1760-96. **Samuel,** Westminster ; watch, B.M., about 1780 ; also a silver *repoussé* pair-case watch, apparently for the Dutch market, h.m., 1800 ; other examples are a long-case musical clock, inscribed "Samson, maker to His Majesty" ; and a musical and mechanical bracket clock ; 1778-1805. **J.,** 11 Denmark St., Soho ; watch with engraving of the Crucifixion in white metal fastened above the balance on a semicircular metal ground, decorated with rubies, emeralds, and topazes, 1800-5. **& Grandin,** Denmark St., Soho, 1810.

Samuel. Humphrey, Panton St., Haymarket, 1790. **& Hill,** 3 Charing Cross, 1793. **Moses, Louis, & Co.,** Solomon, all of Liverpool, about 1818. **David,** York, f., 1820. **Abraham,** 11 Little Alie St., Goodman's Fields, 1820-25. **J.,** 142 High St., Shadwell, 1835. **Abraham, & Son,** 11 Little Alie St., Goodman's Fields, 1840-42.

Samwell, Jno. ; lantern clock, 1665.

Sande, Thos. ; watch, B.M., 1620.

Sanders. Daniel, C.C. 1632. **Alex.,** apprenticed 1665 to Hugh Roberts, C.C. **Chas.,** apprenticed 1672 to Isaac Carver, C.C. **Nath.,** Manchester, 1770. **George,** 57 Sion Gardens, Aldermanbury, 1790-94. **Jas.,** 46 St John St., 1790-94. **John,** 3 Holborn Hill, 1810-15. **George,** 8 Gee St., Goswell Rd., 1820.

Sanderson. Jno., Wigton ; Mr Charles Hunt has a long-case clock by him, dating from about 1690, with these lines in the centre of the dial :—

"Days, hours and years goes ower a pace,
So happy are they that mind God's grace,
That when their days are ower and glass is run,
They may receive the sentence of Well Done."

On the dial of another clock, dating from about 1715, was engraved the following couplet :—

"Remember Man that die thou must.
And after that the judgment just."

He removed to Carlisle about 1730. **Jno.,** Newcastle, eldest son of the foregoing, 1750. **Robert,** Strand, C.C. 1703 ; afterwards Sanderson & Son ; Hatton in 1773 speaks of the late Mr Sanderson as an improver of calendar work, and the son as clever ; 1703-50 ; silver alarm watch, "Robert Sanderson, London," h.m., 1769, Pierpont Morgan collection. **George,** Exeter, patentee of tools for duplicating parts of watches (1761, No. 763) ; also a lunar and calendar watch-key (1762, No. 777). **Hy.**, 301 Strand, 1778-81. **Thos.**, 105 Bishopsgate Within, 1815. **Samuel**, 63 Mark Lane, 1840-42.

Sandford, William, 15 Conduit St., 1800-25.

Sandiford, Jas., Manchester, 1780.

Sandoz. Jacques, Geneva; fine travelling repeating watch, about 1750. **J. G.**, Paris; born 1836, died 1891.

Sands. Jno., apprenticed 1668 to Isaac Puzzy, C.C. **Stephen**, New York, 1786, **Jno.**, St Dunstan's Alley, 1790,

Sandys. Wm., apprenticed 1662 to Robert Grinkin, C.C. **Jas.**, 137 St John's St., 1800.

Sanford, Eaton, Plymouth, U.S.A., 1760-76.

Saplin. P., 42 Whitcomb St., Haymarket, 1835-42. **T.**, 17 East Rd., Hoxton, 1842.

Sarbitt, John, 11 St Martin's Court, 1804.

Sargeant. Jacob, Hartford, U.S.A., 1828. **B.**, 43 Garden Row, London Rd., 1835. **H.**, 10 Wells St., Oxford St., 1835.

Sargent. Robert, C.C. 1720. **Benjamin**, 133 Fleet St., 1769-88. **Josh.**, 106 Jermyn St., 1794-1818.

Sarl, John, 18 Cornhill, 1842 (afterwards Jno. Sarl & Sons).

Sarrabel, T., Tours, 1670.

Sarton, Hebert, Liege; watch, about 1800.

Satchabell, Thomas, 9 Bridgewater Sq., 1804.

Sather, Thos., London; bracket clock, 1730.

Sattell, C., watch-case maker, 36 Clerkenwell Green, 1795-1800.

Saude, Pierre, Paris; clockmaker to the King, 1658.

Saunders. Robt., apprenticed 1675 to Robt. Halstead, C.C. **John**, C.C. 1721. **John**, C.C. 1730. **Joshua**, Cripplegate Buildings, 1765-70. **D.**, Parkside, Knightsbridge, 1800-40. **Thos.**, 258 Whitechapel, 1817.

Saunier, Claudius, born at Macon, France, 1816. When a young man he worked for Patek, Phillipe, & Co., Geneva; author of "Traité d'Horlogerie Moderne, Paris, 1870"; founded in 1859 *Revue Chronometique*, which he edited till his death in 1896.

Saurin, —, 1720.

Sauvage, Paris, on French clock, about 1790.

Savage. Abraham, apprenticed 1648 to Hy. Child, C.C. **Thos.**, apprenticed 1659 to Joseph Quash, C.C. **Thomas**, London; 1677. "Stolen out of the house of John Shorren, Esq., Norfolk Street, a gold watch made by Thomas Savage, of London" (*Lond. Gaz.*, Sept. 10-14, 1691). **de Salop**, fecit '98 signature on 30-hour square dial long-case clock. **T.**, Clifton, Cumberland; long-case clock, about 1740, Mr Jno. J. De Lacy. **& Vincent**, 60 Red Lion St., 1802-15. **Thos.**, livery C.C. 1804. **George**, a watchmaker who, in the early part of this century, did much to perfect the lever escapement; he lived at Huddersfield, where in 1808 he patented a remontoire; afterwards at 5 St James's St., Clerkenwell; in 1822 he received the large Silver Medal from the Society of Arts for a detached escapement for watches, which was a combination of the lever and the chronometer; he in his old age emigrated to Canada, and founded a flourishing retail business in Montreal, where he died. **Thos.**, 3 Red Lion St., 1816-40. **W.**, 8 Chapel St., Bedford Row, 1820-25. **Samuel**, 8 Red Lion St., Clerkenwell, 1825. **D.**, 7 Queen St., Northampton Sq., 1835. **Thos.**, 21 Sidney St., Goswell Rd., 1842.

Saville. John, C.C. 1656; assistant 1675; died 1679; maker of a watch reputed to have belonged to William of Orange, dated 1656, silver box, outer case of tortoiseshell decorated with silver, 1656-79. **John**, C.C. 1678; there was a brass lantern clock of his production at Blackburn in 1887. **Wm.**, apprenticed 1686 to Jas. Wolverstone, C.C.; Mr J. W. Gunnis has a long-case clock marked "Wm. Saville, Dublin," an eighteenth century production.

Savory. Andrew, apprenticed 1668 to Thos. Parker; C.C. 1676; maker of lantern and bracket clocks. **Joseph**, 48 Cheapside, 1788. **Farrand, & Co.**, 48 Cheapside, 1793-1800. **Joseph, & Co.**, 1820. **A.**, 54 Cheapside, 1825. **Thos. Cox**, 47 Cornhill, 1834-64. **Adey B., & Son**, 11 and 12 Cornhill, 1865; afterwards "Goldsmiths' Alliance"; Joseph and H. R. Savory, managing directors; closed in 1893.

Sawen & Dyer, Boston, Mass., 1800-20.

Sawyer. Paul, C.C. 1718. **Jno.**, Leeds, 1770. **John**, 1 Poultry, 1804.

Saxbey, Christopher, apprenticed to Charles Cabrier, C.C. 1749.

Saxon, Jas., Liverpool; long-case clock, about 1795.

Saxton & Lukens, Philadelphia, 1828-40.

Say. Nehemiah, C.C. 1654. **Richard**, apprenticed 1688 to Jno. Johnson.

Sayer, Matt., Oxon.; watch, 1757.

Sayller, Jno., oval watch by him, Vienna Treasury, about 1650.

Sayre. John, New York, 1800. **& Richards**, New York, 1805.

Scafe, William, "at yᵉ sign of the clock in King Street, near Guild Hall"; C.C. by redemption, 1721; master in 1749. The Hon. B. Fairfax, writing to his nephew in 1727, said, "One William Scaife, a watchmaker, born at Bushey, near Denton (co. York) served his time to his father, a blacksmith, but now the most celebrated workman, perhaps, in London and Europe."

Scale. Henry; of him was bought Huggerford's watch with false jewelling used as evidence against Facio (see p. **408**); 1705. **G.**, musical clockmaker, 15 Wellington St., Goswell St., 1840.

Scales, Edwd., 33 Strand, 1775-80.

Scantlebury, W., 17 Golden Lane, 1780-92.

Scardeville, Jno., apprenticed 1663 to Gregory Dossett, C.C.

Schalck, Johann, Engel, Prague; cruciform watch, Soltykoff collection, about 1580.

Schardees, Tho., London; watch, about 1715, Nelthropp collection.

Scheirer, Johan, hexagonal clock, about 1620, Schloss collection (see p. **96**).

Schelhorn, Andreas, Schneeberg, Saxony; clock, Green Vaulted Chambers, Dresden, 1570.

Scherer, George F., 227 Regent St., 1835-40.

Scherwerer, —, York, about 1835.

Scheurlin. Jacob, Dresden, 1614; "Electoral Saxonian Court clockmaker." **Abraham**, Augsburg, born 1616, died 1694; apprenticed to Martin Zoller; table clock, about 1650.

Schilsky, Joseph, 90 Houndsditch, 1840-45.

Schlesinger, C. W., Liverpool, 1833.

Schlotheim, Hans, Augsburg; celebrated "Tower o' Babel" clock by him in the Green Vaulted Chamber, Dresden, 1602 (see p. **86**).

Schlott, Hanns. In the B.M. is a clock in the form of a ship by him, said to have been made for the Emperor Rudolph II.; 1578-81.

Schmidt. Carl, oval clock-watch, strikes 1 to 6, brass case, Pierpont Morgan collection, about 1600. **Ulrich**, watch, about 1610; finely enamelled case, Pierpont Morgan collection; another watch, signed "Jo. Ul. Sch.," about the same date. **Nicolaus**, clock with automata, signed "Nicolaus Schmidt der junger"; ebony case with the Augsburg work mark, about 1620 (see p. **101**). **Johannes**, Amsterdam; clock, about 1700. **J.**, Hamburg; table clock, about 1710. **John**, St Mary Axe; patentee of mysterious clock (1808, No. 3,185) (see p. **336**).

Schneider, octagonal pedestal gilt-metal clock, signed "Johannes Schneider Augustæ," about 1620.

Schnier, Hans, sixteenth century book-shaped watch, Pierpont Morgan collection, signed "H. S." (Mr F. Hilton Price, to whom it formerly belonged, concluded it was by Hans Schnier, of Speyer, 1583).

Schofield. Major, Rochdale; born 1707, died 1783. **Edmund**, son of Major; born 1730, died 1792. **William**, Barnish, 1776. **John**, Barnish; in 1789 a new clock with chimes for the parish church ordered of him, to cost £193; he was living in 1821. **Jno.**, 29 Bell Yard, London, 1793. **Wm.**, 35 Cheyne Walk, Chelsea; long-case clocks, 1815-25. **William**, 2 Clerkenwell Close, 1830-32.

Scholer, Johann, Bavaria; table clock, about 1570, Mr H. K. Heinz.

Scholfield. John, long-case clock, lantern movement, about 1690, Mr F. Johnson; Mr Richard Heape, Rochdale, has a long-case "Halifax" clock, signed "Johannes Scholfield," dating from about 1720. **James**, London; long-case clock, about 1770. **Major**, Manchester, 1775.

Schouffelberger, H. A., director of the Horological School at Chaux-de-Fonds, and author of technical works; died 1879.

Schretger, —, Augsburg, 1660.

Schriner, Martin, Lancaster, U.S.A., 1790-1830.

Schröter, Davidt, 1680-90 (p. **332**).

Schuler, M. & J., 16 Commercial Pl., London Rd., 1835-42.

Schultz, —, Augsburg; Latin cross watch, Schloss collection, about 1570.

Schuster, Paul, Nuremberg, 1591 (see p. **88**).

Schute, Jasper, C.C. 1648.

Schwilgue, Jean B., born 1776, died 1856; restored Strasburg clock, 1838 (see p. **56**).

Science, John, C.C. 1724.

Scolding, John, 7 Great Prescot St., 1794-1810.

Scotchford, Thomas Charles, London; a good maker of lever pallets, 1830-76.

Scott. Simon, apprenticed 1647 to Wm. Comfort, C.C. **Edwd.**, apprenticed 1650 to Wm. Rogers, C.C. **Joseph**, apprenticed 1674 to Cornelius Herbert, C.C. **Daniel**, C.C. 1697. **Joshua**; the Minutes of the Cutlers' Company for 1705 record that "Joshua Scott of the parish of St Boltoph without Aldgate, watchmaker, his son Caleb bound to Ephraim How, cutler," &c. **Geo.**, "Cannon Gate"; long-case clock, about 1740. **James**, apprenticed to John Jackson, 1752; C.C. 1766; in 1809 James Scott, watchmaker, of Grafton St., Dublin, communicated to *Nicholson's Journal* a paper on the application of platinum to balance-springs; in 1820 he took out patents for obtaining motive power. —, Gracechurch St., 1770-82. **John**, 40 Gloucester St., Red Lion Sq.; bracket clock, Wetherfield collection, about 1775; honorary freeman, C.C. 1781; 1770-94. **Wm.**, Beith, 1780. **Thos.**, Gainsboro', 1790. **Wm.**, 39 Dartmouth St., 1790-94. **& Thorpe**, Strand; watch, 1796. **Thos.**, 65 Charing Cross, 1810-20. **Robert**, 20 Bell Yard, Temple Bar, 1815-40. **A.**, **& Co.**, 64 West Smithfield, 1828-32. **Wm.**, 40 Skinner St., Clerkenwell, 1830-42. **Jesse**, 45 King Sq., 1835-42. **Wing, & Co.**, 59 and 60 Red Lion St., Holborn, 1840-42.

Scrivener, Richd., C.C. 1639; Henry Adeane was apprenticed to him in 1668; long-case clock, about 1710, signed "Richard Scrivener, London."

Scurr, Richd., Thirsk, 1822; died 1887; long-case clock, Mr Hy. Limbear.

Sea, Frederick, 18 Bartholomew Close, 1820-30.

Seabourne. James, apprenticed to Richd. Seabourne, 1642; C.C. 1649. **Wm.**, apprenticed 1651 to Sam. Horne; C.C. 1659.

Seager, Jno., Liverpool, 1817.

Seagrave. Matthew, C.C. 1730. **Robert**, 35 Gutter Lane, 1790.

Sealey, Wm., Egremont, 1833.

Seaman, London, watch; Dutch style, about 1765.

Seamer. (Or **Seymour**), York: **Wm.**, f., 1627; **Peter**, f., 1636; **Abel**, f., 1649; also **Joseph**, same date.

Seamore, W., Minories; watch, about 1750, Mr Geo. Carr Glyn.

Searle, George, 15 Wellington St., 1830-40.

Seatoun, G., 29 Gutter Lane, Cheapside, card, Ponsonby collection, about 1795.

Seddon. James, in St James's, C.C. 1662. **Nathaniel**, in St James's, C.C. 1691; watch, Schloss collection. **Humphrey**, Southwark, about 1730. **D.**, Frodsham, 1785.

Sedgwick, Sam, apprenticed 1692 to Thos. Beasley, C.C.

Sedley, Thos., London; watch, 1710.

Sedwell, Edward, apprenticed to Thomas Loomes; C.C. 1664.

Sefton, Edward, Tadcaster; long-case clock, 1775.

Segner, Geo., C.C. 1689.

Seheult, J., à Paris; watch, about 1650.

Seigneuret, clock, S.K.M., about 1750 in hanging case of gilt and blued bronze; signed on face, "Seigneuret H'ger de M'gneur le Com' D'Artois."

Seignior, Robert, C.C. 1667; an eminent maker; received, in 1682, £20 for a clock set up in the Treasury Chambers; month long clock, 10-in. dial, locking-plate striking; laburnum and olive wood case, domed hood with metal fret and spiral pillars, Wetherfield collection, about 1685; bracket clock in case of red tortoiseshell and ebony, same collection, about 1690.

"Lost at Somer Hill a gold chain watch in a new fashioned case round hours, the chrystal and Pendant Ring broken off, made by Robert Signior, on the outside of the shagreen shell a cipher of 2 L.L.'s. There was tyed to the watch 2 seals, one a small gold seal with a Coat of Arms, the other enameled set with Cornelian, and thereon engraved the Figure of Plenty. Whoever can give notice thereof so that it be recovered by the owner, or to Mr Hoare, Goldsmith at the Golden Bottle in Cheapside, or to Mr Robert Signior in Exchange Alley, shall have five pounds reward, and if bought the money that shall be paid with content" (*Lond. Gaz.*, 9 Dec. 1678).

"A silver Pendulum watch, with a Tortoise-shell case inlaid with silver, made by Mr Seignior, Exchange Alley" (*Lond. Gaz.*, Dec. 16-19, 1695), see also Senior.

Selby. Thos., C.C; he worked for Chater in 1730. **Thos.**, Knaresboro', 1765.

Sellars, John, C.C. 1667; warden 1692; excused from serving as master in 1696, on account of ill-health.

Sellers. William, apprenticed 1681 to Jno. Clowes; C.C. 1691; Long Acre, 1740. **Wm.**, London; watch, 1713.

Selwood. William, ye Mermaid, in Lothbury, C.C. 1633; maker of lantern clocks, 1620-36. **John**, C.C. 1641.

Senebier, —, cruciform watch, S.K.M., about 1595; watch, G.M., signed "A. Senebier à Geneve," about 1630.

Seney, G., "orloger du Roy, à Rouen," crystal case watch in the form of a fleur-de-lys, S.K.M., about 1640.

Senior (Seignior?), a watch by him mentioned *Lond. Gaz.*, Aug. 1690.

Sens, William, admitted C.C. 1711.

Sergeant. Prettyman, apprenticed 1664 to Hy. Child; C.C. 1671. **Robt.**, Foster Lane, C.C. 1730. **Benjamin**, 133 Fleet St., 1754-68. **Nathaniel**, London; watch, h.m., 1762; Nathaniel Sergeant, who was admitted to the C.C. in 1763 and who served as master in 1783, was possibly his son, but he does not appear to have practised the craft.

Sermand, —, tulip watch, Nelthropp collection, about 1680, signed "F. Sermand"; a similar specimen of about the same date, signed "J. Sermand," Pierpont Morgan collection; watch, Marfels collection, outer case *piqué* with gold pins, about 1675, signed "J. Sermand, Geneva."

Sermon, Joseph, apprenticed C.C. 1675.

Serré, —, London; repeating watch in finely enamelled case, about 1750, Czar of Russia's collection.

Servant, H., 68 Salisbury Court, 1775.

Servier, see Grollier.

Seugnet, E., London; long-case clock, about 1750.

Seur, Chas., London, 1700.

Severberg, Christian, New York, 1755-75.

Sewell, Geo., 47 Blackman St., 1790-94. **G.**, Bury, Lancs., 1814.

Sexty, R., 71 Carlisle St., Lambeth, 1830-40.

Seydell, Ferd., London; repeating watch, 1775.

Seyffert, Frederick W., St John St., Clerkenwell, patented in 1818 (No. 8,317) a repeating motion.

Seymore, John, Cherry Tree Court, C.C. 1711. **Jno.**, Wantage; long-case clock, 1712. **John**, son of John Seymore; C.C. 1744; watch, G.M., about 1760. **William**, Minories; mahogany case bracket clock, handle on top, brass dial, style 1750; watch, h.m., 1780.

Shakeshaft, Joseph, Preston; also **Laurence and William**, all 1800-24.

Shalcross, Josiah, maker of cylinder escapements with ruby cylinders, and of duplex escapements; for many years in the employ of McCabes; born 1800, died 1866.

Shaller, Nicholas, apprenticed 1672 to Jas. Grimes, C.C.

Sharp. Jno., apprenticed 1647 to Hy. Child, C.C. **Thos.**, apprenticed 1667 to Robt. Whitwell, C.C. **Thos.**, Stratford-on-Avon; about 1750; the sexton's clock by him spoken of by Washington Irving in his "Sketch Book" is at the Red Horse, Stratford-on-Avon. **& Williams**, 6 Strand,

1790. **J.**, 20 Little Tower St., 1794-1808. **John**, 30 Fish St. Hill, 1806-25. **T.**, 9 Postern Row, Tower Hill, 1816. **George**, 1822-25. **& Son**, 30 Fish St. Hill (John Sharp, master C.C. 1833 and 1835); 1826-40; watch, h.m., 1823; "Sharp & Son, London Bridge"; bracket clock, "Sharpe & Son, London Bridge," about 1830, Mr Edmonds Massey.

Sharpe. William, C.C. 1681. **Wm.**, 75 Holborn Bridge, 1793.

Sharples, Jas., Liverpool, 1817.

Sharpnell, see Shrapnell.

Shaw. John, "near the Bars in Holborn"; apprenticed to Thos. Taylor of Holborn in 1672; C.C. 1682; master in 1712; splendid marqueterie case clock as above; another fine specimen bore the signature "John Shaw at the Dyall in Holborne"; 1682-1714. **Edward**, apprenticed 1689 to Clem. Forster, C.C. Lancaster: **Thos.**, 1726, f.; **Robt.**, 1789, f. **Anna Maria**, apprenticed to Isaac Loddington and his wife, 1733. **William**, 22 Wood St., Cheapside, 1760-72. **Jas.**, Kember; watch, h.m., 1777. **Jno.**, Liverpool; watch, h.m., 1786. **Wm. J.**, Sheffield; died 1909, aged 56.

Shayler. Richard, Ball Alley, Lombard St., 1753-56. **William**, 44 Lombard St., 1755-75.

Sheafe. William, 16 Bell Alley, Coleman St., 1770-94; watch with "E. Mason, Greenwich," on dial. **Thos.**; to him was apprenticed Wm. Howells, 1773.

Shearer, James, 23 Devonshire St., Queen Sq. The Duke of Sussex had a skeleton-movement astronomical clock by him; 1825-42.

Shearman, Robert, Wilmington, Del., 1760-70; Philadelphia, Pa., 1799.

Shearwood, Jas., London; watch, 1767.

Shedel, Jas., London; small bracket clock, about 1750.

Sheily, Samuel, 61 St Paul's Churchyard, 1775.

Sheldrick, Edward, 48 Cheapside, 1798-1803.

Shelley, Jno., lantern clock, 1636.

Shelly. Joseph, C.C. 1717. **& King**, 149 Shoreditch, 1772-75.

Shelton. Samson, member of the Blacksmiths' Company; active in obtaining the charter of the C.C., of which he was one of the first wardens in 1631; died 1649, leaving £50 to the C.C.; fine clock-watch by him, B.M.; 1623-49. **Jno.**, apprenticed 1662 to Thos. Mills, C.C. "Whereas there was a Silver Minute Pendulum Watch dropt on my Lord Mayor's day between the hours of 9 and 10 at night, the name John Shelton, London. If the person who took it up will bring it or send it to John Collins, Watchmaker, 'The White Horse and Black Boy,' in the Great Old Bailey he shall receive full satisfaction even to the whole value if desired" (*The Post-Man*, Nov. 1, 1705). **John**, Shoe Lane, C.C. 1720; livery 1766; in a letter to the Royal Society from Jas. Short in 1752, Jno. Shelton is referred to as "the principal person employed by Mr Graham in making astronomical clocks"; he published a description of the dead-beat escapement in the *Gentleman's Magazine* for September 1754. Nevil Maskelyne in 1761 tested a clock of his make.

Shephard, Jno., Whitehaven, 1770.

Shepheard, Thos., London; C.C. 1632; maker of an oval watch, about 1620.

Shepherd. Jno., apprenticed 1674 to Robt. Storr, C.C. **Thos.**, apprenticed 1689 to Jno. Barnard, C.C. **Henry**, 4 Pope's

Head Alley, Cornhill, 1760-75. **Thos.**, Liverpool, 1770. **Thos.**, Wootton-under-Edge, 1792. **Wm.**, 199 Strand, 1815-25. **Charles**, 53 Leadenhall St. ; in 1849 he patented (No. 12,567) an application of electricity for impelling clocks, and afterwards supplied an electric clock for driving the large dial just outside the gateway of the Greenwich Observatory.

Shepley. John, Stockport ; died 1749 ; long oak case clock, Mr Benj. Heape ; long oak case chiming clock, Mr Rt. G. Heape ; on another long-case clock, "John Shepley, Glossop and Stockport" ; clock, about 1760. **William**, 1780. **Edwd.**, Manchester, 1780.

Sheppard, Samuel, 1 Hanover St., Hanover Sq., 1830.

Shepperd. Thomas, see Shepheard. **Sarah**, 199 Strand, 1830. **Charles**, 7 Chadwell St., 1840-42.

Sheraton, Thomas (see p. 380), 1803.

Sherbird, J., Turk's St., Bethnal Green, 1820.

Sherborne, Thos., 6 Strand, 1793-1800.

Shere, Henry, & Arnold, 46 Lombard St., 1753-68.

Sherwin, —, London ; watch, about 1705.

Sherwood. William, apprenticed to James Delander, 1686 ; C.C. 1695. **Jno.**, apprenticed 1690 to Hy. Jones, C.C. **William**, C.C. 1720 ; master in 1740. **John**, apprenticed to John Jeffs, and turned over to George Graham, C.C. 1721. **James**, Yarm, 1816. **Thos.**, Yarm, 1823. **Thos.**, Leeds, 1830.

Shick, William, 43 Brick Lane, Old St., 1820.

Shield, Thos., apprenticed 1691 to Jno. Harris, C.C.

Shields, John, 19 Bridge St., Lambeth, 1835.

Shindler, Thomas, Canterbury ; maker of long-case clocks, about 1720.

Shipley, John, Hyde, Cheshire ; very fine marquetry long-case clock, about 1705.

Shirley. Jas., apprenticed 1679 to Jas. Delander, C.C. **John**, C.C. 1720 ; in 1724 paid £20 to be transferred to the Vintners' Company.

Shirt. Wm., 25 Coleman St., Bunhill Row, and 10 City Rd., 1815-35 ; a capable man ; he published a "train card" for watchmakers.

Shole, Sim., Deptford, 1825.

Shorrock, Thurston, Preston, 1770.

Short. Joshua, C.C. 1665. **James**, Surrey St., Strand, 1740-70 ; a maker of repute who sent to the Royal Society in 1752 an interesting letter on compensated pendulums ; Harrison's son, before starting on his voyage to Barbados, in 1764, set his chronometer by Short's regulator.

Shorter. In 1798, Edward Shorter, clockmaker, Giltspur St., was associated with Wm. Anthony, of Clerkenwell, in a patent for carriages, &c. **E.**, 4 Bridge Rd., Southwark, 1830.

Showell. Hy., apprenticed 1660 to Lionel Wythe, C.C. **Jas.**, apprenticed 1691 to David Minuel, C.C.

Shrapnell, James, 36 Ludgate St., 1761-70 ; 60 Charing Cross, 1775 ; afterwards Jas. Shrapnell & Son.

Shrubb, Thos., apprenticed 1689 to Phil. Browne.

Shuckburg, Charles, C.C. 1719.

Shurwood, Thos., Yarm, 1775.

Shute, Geo., London ; bird and flower marqueterie long-case clock, about 1705.

Shuttleworth. Henry, C.C. 1669. **Fras.**, Sarum, 1760. **Francis**, 23 Duke St.,

Piccadilly, 1806-10.

Shwerer. Joseph, Hull, 1822. **Matthew**, also at Hull, 1822.

Sibbald, William, 4 Cannon St. Rd., 1815-35.

Sidey, Benjamin, Cow Lane, Moorfields, C.C. 1730 ; master 1761 and 1789 ; known as a good watchmaker, and active in matters affecting the interests of the trade. —, junr., London ; watch, 1798.

Sidley. John, C.C. 1701. **Benjamin**, Watling St. ; C.C. 1710.

Sidwell, see Sedwell.

Silke, Jno., Elmsted ; lantern clock, Mr F. A. Field, about 1670.

Sillito, Chas., Uttoxeter, 1760.

Sills. J., Manchester ; watch, 1809. **J.**, Manchester ; watch, 1811. **William**, a marine chronometer finisher of surpassing merit ; born 1812 ; died 1884 ; he worked for Robert & Henry Molyneux and other eminent makers.

Silver. Jon., London ; watch, 1645. **Joseph**, 28 Hatton Garden, 1793. **Fredk.**, livery C.C. 1810. **J. & J.**, 28 Hatton Garden, 1825-30.

Silvester, John, apprenticed to Thomas Bates, and turned over to Henry Jones ; C.C. 1693.

Simcock, Thos., Warrington, 1818.

Simcox. Josiah, apprenticed 1675 to Hy. Adeane, C.C. **William**, C.C. 1682. **Samuel**, C.C. 1708.

Simistere, Richard, Birmingham ; long-case clock, about 1765, Mr Francis H. Bigelow.

Simkin, Ben., 16 High St., Boro', 1788-93.

Simkins, Jno., apprenticed 1694 to Thos. Taylor.

Simmonds, Thos., London ; clock, about 1730.

Simmons. John, Fleet St., 1753-56. **Ebenezer**, 1 Pavement, Moorfields, 1816 ; 26 Coleman St., 1825-76. **Geo.**, 49 King's Sq., 1840-42. **Morrice**, 40 Great Prescot St., 1842.

Simms, Isaac ; watch, B.M., about 1600.

Simonds. Thomas, Fleet St., C.C. 1661 ; lantern clock, balance escapement ; 1661-70. **J. L.**, 19 Holborn Hill, 1820-30.

Simons. John, watch-case coverer, Sutton St., 1790-93. **G.**, 49 King's Sq., 1840-42.

Simpkin, Benj., 6 Tooley St., 1800.

Simpkins. Thomas, C.C. 1710. **Benjamin**, 35 Frith St., 1800.

Simpkinson, Roger, 41 Fleet St., 1758-75.

Simpson. William, C.C. 1700. **John**, C.C. 1723. **& Ward**, Fleet St., 1737-40. **Stephen**, Greta Bridge ; long-case clock, with "Peter & Mary Winder" in the centre of the dial, about 1770. **Benj.**, Halifax, 1776. **William Ellison**, hon. f. C.C. 1781 ; Miss Mary F. Bragg has a fine long-case repeating clock signed "Simpson Wigton," dating from about 1775 ; hands from the centre of the dial indicate seconds, minutes, hours, and day of the month ; in the arch above are shown the age and phases of the moon and time of high water, probably at Parton near Whitehaven (see p. 366). **Robt.**, Halifax, 1785. **Hector** ; card, B.M., "H. Simpson, Old Bond St., foreman to the late Mr Fladgate," 1785 ; 127 Pall Mall, 1788-94. —, Southwell, 1790 (see p. 378). **Archibald**, 10 Prince's St., Leicester Sq., 1790-94. **Richd.**, watch-case maker, 19 Albion Bdgs., Clerkenwell Close, 1790-95. **R.**, 481 Strand, 1805-15. **Daniel**, Workington, 1810. **Anthony**, Cockermouth, 1810. **John**, 6 Middle Row, Holborn, 1815-40. **Robert**, 55 Park St., Dorset Sq., 1835-40 ; 15 New St.,

1842. **Thos.**, Oxford St., 1835-42. **Robert**, junr., 11 Great Castle St., Regent St., 1840.

Sims. Wm., apprenticed 1693 to Thos. Bradford. **Geo.**, 1738, see Addis, W. **Geo.**, Canterbury, 1745-91. **Henry**, Canterbury, maker of long-case clocks, 1758-80. **Geo.**, Rochester, 1760. **Geo.**, Prescot, 1770. **John**, 64 Lombard St., 1773-78. **& Son**, London ; watch, 1830.

Sinclair, Chas., 69 Old St., 1835-42.

Sinclare, —, Dublin, 1782.

Sinderby, Francis H., 14 Devereux Court, Strand, 1790 ; livery C.C. 1810 ; 18 Bull and Mouth St., 1816-42.

Sindrey, Lawrence, C.C. 1661.

Singleton, John, Lancaster, 1806, f.

Skeggs. Wm., London ; long-case clock, about 1780 (see p. 368). **L.**, 355 Rotherhithe St., 1788-1810. **Wm.**, 355 Rotherhithe St., 1816-40.

Skelton, C., Malton, 1823, see Shelton.

Skepper, Thos., apprenticed 1675 to Thos. Taylor, Strand.

Skerry, W., Dartmouth St., Westminster, 1835-42.

Skinner. Matthew, apprenticed to Francis Hill ; C.C. 1713 ; master 1746 ; watch, G.M., about 1750. **Benj.**, Islington ; bracket clock, Mr R. S. Weir, about 1770. **Chas.**, 23 Pool Terrace, City Rd., 1840.

Skipworth, Francis, apprenticed 1670 to Robt. Lynch, C.C.

Skirrow. Jas., Wigan, 1780. **Jas.**, Lancaster, 1783, f. —, 1818.

Skittlethorpe, Richard, Southwark Rd., lantern clock, about 1690.

Slack. Joseph, C.C. 1723. —, Ipstones ; long-case clock, about 1790.

Slade, J. L., London ; watch, 1790.

Slater, W., 13 Ship Alley, Wellclose Sq., 1835.

Slipper, Jere., Maiden Lane ; C.C. 1726.

Slough, William, C.C. 1687.

Sly, Robert, C.C. 1720.

Small, Wm., apprenticed 1684 to Richd. Farmer, C.C. ; pendulum watch, Nelthropp collection, about 1705.

Smalle, Lewis, received payments for "keping the clocke" of Lambeth parish church, 1585-1605.

Smalley. Thomas, C.C. 1687 ; maker of a clock at Battle Abbey, Sussex ; 1687-1700. **John**, Lancaster, 1721, f.

Smallpage. Jas., Sandbach, 1790. **Josh.**, Leeds, 1829. **Jno.**, Malton, 1840.

Smallwood, Ed., Dublin, 1780.

Smart. John, C.C. 1682. **Orpheus**, 1750. **Benjamin**, 35 Frith St., 1800-18. **Thomas**, 4 Little Ryder St., St James's, 1816-30. **Saml.**, 198 South Audley St., 1835. **Alex.**, 70 South Audley St., 1835-40.

Smeaton. John, York, f., 1646 ; in the B.M. is a rather large silver watch by him, silver dial, outer case of leather *piqué*, about 1650. **Tobias**, apprenticed 1664 to Hy. Harland, C.C. **Jno.** ; at Trinity House is a clock bearing the name of Jno. Smeaton, the celebrated engineer, the initials "J. S." being on the hour socket. There is also preserved at Trinity House a long-case clock, on a brass plate affixed to the door of which is inscribed, "This timepiece was placed in the old Eddystone Lighthouse by John Smeaton, C.E., F.R.S., on the 8th October 1759" ; in Smeaton's book on the building of the Eddystone Lighthouse, the following reference is made to it : "This timepiece by a simple contrivance being made to strike a blow every half-hour, would thereby warn the keepers to snuff the candles." Mr T. P. Cooper says Smeaton and Hindley of York were lifelong friends (see **p. 286**);

he corresponded with John Holmes in 1779, and with Thos. Reid in 1786.

Smeed, George, 17 Chapel St., Edgware Rd., 1835-42.

Smint, calendar watch, inscribed "Smint, London," silver dial with gilt rosettes between the figures ; outer case embossed by " Mavris," about 1775, Pierpont Morgan collection.

Smison, Thos., Hartford ; watch, 1796.

Smith. John, petitioner for incorporation of C.C., and one of the first assistants, 1630-49. **Robert**, watch, Pierpont Morgan collection, about 1630, inscribed " Robert Smith at Popeshead Alley " ; C.C. 1648 ; warden in 1650, and died during his year of office. **George**, C.C. 1632. **Walter**, C.C. 1641. **Nat.**, apprenticed 1647 to Wm. Bunting, C.C. 1654. **Wm.**, C.C. 1654. **John**, C.C. 1656 ; in 1657 Jno. Smith was fined 10s. by C.C. for putting the name Estine Hubert on a watch. **David**, C.C. 1662. **Ruth**, apprenticed 1674 to Thos. Birch and Jane his wife, C.C. **John**, C.C. 1674, clockmaker and author of " Horological Dialogues, by J. S., clockmaker, in three parts, showing the nature, use and right managing of clocks and watches ; with an appendix containing Mr Oughtred's method for calculating of numbers " ; 120 pp. 12mo, London ; published at " The Three Roses," in Ludgate St., 1675 ; this was probably the first book in English on watch and clock making. J. S. quite appreciated the pendulum as a controller ; he remarks, " As to their regularity I shall say only thus much, that those clocks who have their motion regulated by a pendulum are more excellent than those regulated by a balance, and those that are regulated by a long pendulum are far more excellent than those that are regulated by a short one." Rules are given for calculating the length of a pendulum, and a three-second pendulum is mentioned which " will be 28 ft. 8 in. from the term of suspension to the centre of the bob." In 1694 he published " Horological Disquisitions " (see p. 353), of which a second edition was issued in 1708 ; his observations covered a wide field ; he discoursed on the Baroscope or quicksilver weather glass, on painting, and on the plentiful use of cold water as a preservative of health. He was a Unitarian and plunged into theological discussion ; the Rev. Francis Gregory answered him and advised him to go back to the noise of his hammers and the use of his pincers. St Augustine, in the city of London, is given as his residence ; but Hatton says he was originally a Lancashire tool maker, and his " engines " the best in use ; he died prior to 1730, at which date it was advertised that his books could be obtained of Mary Smith, at the Fan and Flower de Luce, over against Somerset House in the Strand, and nowhere else. **Robert**, C.C. 1695 ; on the disc of a long walnut-case clock appeared the inscription, " Robert Smith, Dunstable " ; 1680-1700. **Gabriel**, long-case clock, signed " Gabriel Smith, Bartholmey," about 1695, Mr Robert Meldrum. **Joseph**, C.C. 1700. **Thomas**, Gray's Inn ; admitted C.C. 1700 ; in the Wetherfield collection is a long-case clock by him dating from about 1710, with very fine scroll marqueterie over the whole surface of the case. **Morris**, C.C. 1702. **Henry**, C.C. 1703 ; probably successor to Thomas ; Mr W. C. Woollard has a pull repeating clock in mahogany case, about 1720, inscribed " Henry Smith, Gray's Inn." **John**, C.C.

1703 ; maker of the turret clock at Westminster Abbey, 1730 ; the movement of this clock was replaced by a modern one in 1860. **Maurice**, Royal Exchange, 1705-32. **Tudor**, C.C. 1717. **Thomas**, C.C. 1718. **Obadiah**, C.C. 1725. **Dan.**, Dorking ; sheep's-head clock, dial 11½ in. square, long pendulum, about 1730, Mr R. Norman Shaw. **Geo.**, Artillery Ground, C.C. 1730. **Edward**, Bury ; lantern clock, about 1730. **Joseph**, Bristol ; long-case clock, about 1730. **Joseph**, Chester ; bracket clock, about 1740. **James**, Stow-on-the-Wold ; clock, about 1740. **Joseph**, apprenticed to Daniel Delander, C.C. 1742. **Susanna**, apprenticed to Hannah, wife of Jas. Wilson, 1747. **Jno.**, York, f., 1750 ; in 1754 he made a new clock for St Martin's Church, projecting into Coney St., being paid £30 for this work. **Jas.**, Chiswell St., 1758-60. **William**, Cheapside, livery Blacksmiths' Company, 1759 ; 32 Cornhill, 1769-80. **James**, 115 Fleet St., 1760-80. **Wm.**, Lancaster, 1767, f. **John**, son of Benjamin Smith, C.C. 1768. **Jas.**, & Son, 118 Bunhill Row, 1769-94. **Geo.**, 110 Wood St., 1770-76. **Abraham**, wooden clockmaker, Manchester, 1770. **Gabriel**, Chester, 1773. **John**, Pittenweem ; 8-day musical clock, described by the namesake of the maker ; the case of mahogany is 7 ft. high, with fluted columns on each side of the body ; the upper part of the head is ornamented with carving, fretwork, birds' eyes, and a golden bird with expanded wings, standing in the middle of the head ; there are three dial-plates and a chime of sixteen bells ; the work is divided into five parts, each of which has its own weight ; the first is the going part ; the second drives a small musical barrel, which plays a chime at the first, second, and third quarters, and plays once over a tune before striking the hour ; the third part strikes the hours, and the fourth drives a large musical barrel containing eight Scotch tunes, one of which is played every three hours ; the last part changes the tune ; the clock plays all the eight in the twenty-four hours ; the front dial plate measures about 15 in., and has an arch which shows the hour, minute, and seconds, with the day of the month, and day of the week ; when Sunday comes these words cast up, " Remember Sunday " ; at twelve o'clock on Saturday night the clock stops playing till twelve strikes on Sunday night ; when the clock begins to play there is a procession of moving figures representing the City Guard of Edinburgh ; the maker of this clock exhibited it at a coffee-house in Edinburgh in 1774, and tried to dispose of it by lottery. Lord Provost M'Grady, of Dundee, has another musical clock by the same maker ; it plays any one of the following tunes : " Flowers of the Forest," " Willie was a Wanton Wag," " Maggie Lauder," " Logan Water," " East Neuk of Fife," " The Lass of Pattie's Mill " ; the titles of the tunes are marked on the dial, and there is an indicator which may be turned to the tune desired. **Jno.**, Thirsk, 1775. **Danl.**, Aldermanbury, 1775. **Philip**, C.C. 1776. **Jas.**, White Horse Court, Bishopsgate, 1776-90 ; all sorts of clocks and watches made, mended, and sold by James Smith in White Horse Court, Whitecross St., watch paper, Ponsonby collection, about 1770 ; Bishopsgate, 1776-90. **James** (clockmaker to George III.), Jermyn St., 1776-94 ; hon. f. C.C. 1781. **John**, 143 Houndsditch ;

livery C.C. 1776-90. **J.**, 40 Duke St., Manchester Sq., 1780. **& Sharp**, 14 Bartholomew Close, 1780-85. **Richd.**, Cloak Lane, 1780-85. **Joseph**, 49 Lombard St., 1783-90. **Geo.**, 4 Huggin Lane, 1783-90. **Jno.**, Chester, 1785. **Sam.**, Walford, watch, 1787. **& Wareham**, Davies St., Berkeley Sq., 1790. **Jabez**, 16 Fenchurch St., 1790. **Chas.**, 118 Bunhill Row, 1790-1823. **Jas.**, 98 Oxford St., 1790-1815. **Walter**, 98 Bishopsgate St., 1795. **Wm.**, 170 Wapping, 1800-4. **Wm.**, 3 Bridgwater Sq., 1803-10. **Jno.**, Wrexham ; watch, 1807. **H. D.**, London ; watch, with hare and snail on plate as a guide to regulation, 1808. **Samuel**, Coventry ; patented (1812, No. 3,620) a vertical escape wheel with five teeth ; several watches were made on this plan ; 7 Clerkenwell Close, 1819-22. **& Asprey**, 4 Bruton St., 1817. **George**, Charlotte Terrace, New Cut, 1820. **T. W.**, 27 Fenchurch St., 1820-30. **Thomas**, 17 John St., Oxford St., 1820-35. **Horatio**, York, f., 1822-32. **William**, 35 Poultry, 1823. **G.**, 11 St Martin's Churchyard, 1823-30. **John**, 27 Cornhill, 1825. **H.**, watch-movement maker, 12 Berkeley St., Clerkenwell, 1825-35. **& Co.**, Piccadilly, 1825. **J.**, 256 Borough, 1825-30. **B.**, 12 Duke St., Lincoln's Inn Fields, 1830. **J.**, & Son, St John's Sq., Clerkenwell, 1835-42. **John**, 70 Charlotte St., Fitzroy Sq., 1842. **Joseph**, 18 Bride Lane, 1842.

Smithfield, **W.**, Romford, about 1760.

Smithyes. **Wm.**, Holborn ; long-case clock, about 1740. **Jno.**, London ; bracket clock, about 1750.

Smitton, Peter, 12 Crown St., Russell Sq., 1820-35.

Smod, —, Geisheim ; watch (see p. 403).

Smorthwaite, Colchester ; lantern clock, about 1680, Mr J. H. Davidson.

Smoult. Thos., Lancaster, 1708, f., Mayor of Lancaster in 1739. **Jas.**, 1739, f., died 1768.

Smyth. Joshua, " Steyning in Sussex " ; maker of lantern clocks, 1690. **Wm.**, Woodbridge ; long-case clock, about 1800, Mr J. Hall.

Smythies. Jas., apprenticed 1679 to Geo. Hamilton, C.C. **Jno.**, London ; bracket clock, about 1750.

Snatt, Jno., Ashford. Mr Hy. Fitzwalters, Salem, Mass., has a brass clock by him dating from about 1700.

Sneeberger, Michael, Prague ; pupil of Burgi, 1605-20.

Snell. George, C.C. 1688-1700 ; maker of long-case clocks. **Albion**, Holborn ; clock, about 1850.

Snelling. Thomas, C.C. 1680. **James**, Poultry, C.C. 1712 ; master in 1736 ; watch, B.M. ; another, Dunn Gardner collection, fetched £75 at Christie's in 1902, S.K.M. **Henry**, Ball Alley, Lombard St., 1769-75.

Snidal, Jas., Sheffield, 1770-1814 ; his second quality watches were signed " Dalsni."

Snoswell, William, 24 Farringdon St., 1835-42.

Snow. Jno., London ; in the coffee-room of Simpson's " Old Choppe House " in the Poultry is a lantern clock inscribed " Jno. Snow Aᵒ dmi 1630." **Daniel**, lantern clock, 1664. **John**, Sarum. " A watch the hours in the form of Diamonds, the Out-case holes with bizels for the sound of the Bell " (Lond. Gaz., April 1, 1680). **Jno.**, Frome, about 1760. **Wm.**, about 1780. **Thos.**, Otley, 1780. **Z.**, Bury, 1814.

Richd., Pateley Bridge, 1837. **Thos.**, Knaresboro', 1837.

Soar, Jas., 5 Paradise St., Finsbury, 1842.

Socteryk, Daniel, Dortrecht; the Comte de Lambilly has a watch by him with outer case chased by Cochin.

Soffleur, Thos., London, 1680.

Soltians, Paris; clock, Windsor Castle, about 1790 (see p. 322).

Sollinger, Jacob, Vienna, 1760; afterwards at Paris; complicated clock with dancing figures, &c.

Solomon. Hy., Coventry St., 1775. **S. C.**, 13 St Mary Axe, 1794-1804. **Edwd.**, Margate; watch, 1799. **Moses**, King St., 1810; Bevis Marks, 1820; Great Alie St., 1830. **Henry**, 46 Duke St., Aldgate, 1835. **Henry, & Co.**, 31 Houndsditch, 1840-42. **P.**, 26 Mansell St., 1840-42. **J.**, 24 Great Prescot St., 1842.

Somersall. Mandeville, Fore St.; C.C., lantern clock, about 1685. **John**, Cripplegate Church, C.C. 1708. **George**, Leadenhall St., 1750; Finsbury, Moorfields, 1779 **Richard**, Finsbury Pl., Moorfields, 1776-1804; livery C.C. 1786.

Somilier, Jno., apprenticed 1649 to Luke Richards, C.C.

Sommerson, G., Minories; lantern clock with Turkish numerals, about 1710.

Somner, Jno., apprenticed 1663 to Wm. Raines, C.C.

Sones, Thos., watch-case maker, 6 Lillypot Alley, 1790-94.

Sonnereau à Rochelle; French octagonal watch, about 1640, S.K.M.

Soret. Pierre, watch in enamelled case, about 1620 (see p. 145). **Abraham**, Dublin; about 1750. **Isaac, et Fils**, Geneva; watch, 1765. **Jean Robert**, Geneva; watch with representations of hammermen striking on bells, G.M., about 1780.

Soubeyran à Geneva; watch, 1760.

South. Joseph, C.C. 1709. **Henry**, Rotherham, 1710.

Southan. Saml., 28 Red Lion St., 1790-94. **Geo.**, London; rack lever watch, about 1810.

Southcote, Josiah, apprenticed C.C. 1681.

Southern, Jno., apprenticed C.C. 1681.

Southwarth, John, C.C. 1689.

Southwood, Sam., apprenticed 1662 to Chas. Fox, C.C.

Southwork, Thos., apprenticed 1677 to Barlow Brookes, C.C.

Southworth, Peter, C.C. 1664.

Souza, Samuel, Philadelphia, 1819.

Sowerby. Jas., London; long-case clock, lacquer decoration, about 1760, Mr Wm. Bolton. **Jno.**, 100 Brick Lane, 1817; 79 Chiswell St., 1830. **Thos.**, 124 Long Acre, 1830.

Sowter, John, admitted C.C. 1683.

Spaldin, Wm., Liverpool; watch, 1784.

Sparck, Peter, Philadelphia, 1797.

Sparkes, Nicholas, presented C.C. with a piece of plate in lieu of serving as steward, 1659.

Sparks. Thos., London; apprenticed 1689 to Jno. Drew; watch, 1732. **Angel**, Plymouth, about 1760.

Sparrow. Thos., 113 Leadenhall St., 1790-94. **Jno.**, 15 Leicester St., Leicester Sq., 1815-18.

Spaulding, Edward, Providence, U.S.A., 1788.

Speakman. William, apprenticed 1654; C.C. 1661; master 1701. **Thomas**, C.C. 1685; Mr J. Hall has a long-case clock by him dating from about 1710. **Edward**, C.C. 1691. **Jno.**, apprenticed 1692 to Wm.

Speakman. Richd., apprenticed 1692 to E. Micklewright. **John**, junr., C.C. 1706.

Spear, Jacob, musical clockmaker, 39 Myddelton St., 1835.

Speedwell, London; bracket clock, red lacquer case, about 1760.

Speight, James, Tong, 1785.

Spence. John, London; in the B.M. is a silver watch by him, silver dial, matted ground with Roman hour numerals engraved on polished lozenge-shaped plaques, day of the month shown on outer circle, glass over dial: 1650-70. **—**, Dublin; watch, 1750.

Spencer. Thomas, Strand, threatened with prosecution by C.C. for undue taking of apprentices, 1682; C.C. 1685; long-case clock, with fine Dutch marqueterie, 10-in. dial, inscription at bottom, "Thos. Spencer, Londini, fecit," about 1695, Mr E. E. Cook. **Richard**, Dublin, watch, 1725, Mr Evan Roberts. **Arthur**, C.C. 1732. **Jno.**, Colne, 1770. **& Perkins**, 44 Snow Hill, 1775-94. **W.**, London; watch, 1785. **Eli.**, Bolton-le-Moors, 1818. **J.**, 20 Red Lion St., Clerkenwell, 1820-30. **Thos.**, Manchester, 1820. **& Wooster & Co.**, Salem Bridge, 1828-37.

Spendlove, Jno., Thetford, 1775.

Spiegalhalter, G., musical clockmaker, 6 Mount Place, Whitechapel, 1835-42.

Spilsbury, Jas., London; watch, 1758.

Spink, Marshall, 1 and 2 Gracechurch St., 1772; afterwards Spink & Son, 1772-1842.

Spittal, Jas., Whitehaven, 1833.

Spittle, Richard, admitted C.C. 1699; tall walnut long-case clock, brass dial with arch riveted on, containing Father Time on wing, with the words, "Tempus fugit," 1699-1720.

Spitz, Gaspar, Schwartz; clock, square case, filigree covers over the dials, Vienna Treasury, about 1590.

Spratnell, Sam., Cockspur St., 1793.

Sprigg, Hy., apprenticed 1637 to Simon Bartram, C.C.

Springer, Sam., clock, about 1810.

Springfield, T. O., Norwich; long marqueterie case clock, about 1770.

Springhall, see Masterman.

Sprogell, John, Philadelphia, 1791.

Spur, Geo., Aylesburn; lantern clock, about 1710.

Spurgin, Jere., Colchester, 1770.

Spurrier, John, admitted C.C. 1684.

Spyer, J., & Solomon, 26 Prescot St., 1793-1804; 20 Leman St., 1825.

Stacey. John, C.C. 1683. **William**, Fleet St.; bell-top mahogany case bracket clock, about 1750; livery C.C. 1766.

Stach, Heinrich, Hanover; watch, 1800.

Stacy, Thos., Farnsfield, Notts., 1759.

Stafford. John, C.C. 1708. **T.**, Chelsea, 1810-20.

Stainsburg, Robert, Chippenham. "A silver watch with a black Fish-Skin case, studded with silver, Robert Stainsburg, Chippenham, engraven on the Dial Plate" (*Lond. Gaz.*, Aug. 29, Sept. 1, 1698).

Stainton, Matthew, 1 Aldermanbury, 1772.

Stallard, Philip, 3 New Sq., Shoe Lane, 1793.

Stamford, Richd., apprenticed 1652 to Peter Willerme, C.C.

Stamp, Jas., 86 Cheapside; livery Goldsmiths' Company, 1775, see Sutton & Son, also Godbehere.

Stamper, Francis, at "ye Golden Ball in Lumbarde Streete," a good maker; C.C.

1682; in 1687 ordered by the C.C. to be prosecuted for refusing to admit to his workroom master and wardens when they were upon a search, but he submitted himself to the court, and was fined 20s.; maker of a clock with square dial on a lantern movement; watch by him, S.K.M.; 1682-1700. **John**, 148 Fleet St., 1772.

Stanbury, Henry, C.C. 1709; maker of a 30-hour long-case clock, 1709-20.

Stancliffe, Jno., Askrigg, 1775-90. He was apprenticed to C. Caygill. Long-case clock by him with the inscription, "Time stayeth not."

Standish, William, apprenticed to Jeffery Baily; C.C. 1688.

Standring. Jas., Rochdale, 1770-92. **Jere.**, Bolton, 1790.

Stanes, Jeffery, C.C. 1686.

Stanford, Wm., South Walsham, 1780.

Stanger, Hugh, 46 Old St. Rd., 1835-40.

Stanley, John, C.C. 1732. Mr A. H. Turnbull has a long-case clock signed "J. Stanly, Nth Shields."

Stanton. (Or Staunton) Edward, Leadenhall St.; apprenticed 1655 to Francis Bowen; C.C. 1662; master 1696; bracket clock, three trains, ebony case, Wetherfield collection (see p. 384)); Mr T. W. Bourne owns a long-case clock by him. "A new Gold Clock-Watch graved with a cypher, on the back Edward Staunton, maker" (*Lond. Gaz.*, Nov. 16-19, 1696). **Sam.**, apprenticed 1692 to Thos. Fletcher, C.C. **John**, C.C. 1692. **Joseph**, C.C. 1692. **Samuel**, London; maker of lantern clocks; C.C. 1714. **Job**, New York, 1810.

Staples. Richd., apprenticed 1684 to Henry Jones, C.C. **Jas.**, Oldham; watch, 1780. **Jas.**, 7 Rosoman St., Clerkenwell, 1788-94.

Stapleton. Thomas, C.C. 1694; watch, about 1700. **W.**, London; watch, silver dial, about 1730. **Stephen**, Sutton; watch, 1750; another, rather earlier, "Stephen Staplets, Sutton."

Staptoe, William, Charing Cross, admitted C.C. 1703; 1703-1710, see Stepto.

Starey, John, 4 Sweeting's Alley, Cornhill; 1770-94; C.C. 1785; livery 1787; long-case clock, Mr W. C. Woollard.

Starkey, Joseph, C.C. 1706.

Starnill, Jas., C.C. about 1660.

Starr, Robt., C.C. 1667.

Startridge, Roger, Gravesend; clock, about 1750.

Statter, Richd. D., wrote a pamphlet on the advantage of a decimal division of the hour; watch on this plan, G.M., is inscribed "Richd. Dover Statter and Thos. Statter, Liverpool, No. 1," h.m., 1862.

Stauffer. Robert, Son, & Co., 43 Skinner St., Snow Hill, 1830-42. **Julius**, 43 Skinner St., 1830-42.

Staunton, see Stanton.

Stayne, Thomas, C.C. 1654.

Stead. Thos., apprenticed 1668 to Jno. Webb; C.C. 1678. **Jno.**, Fetter Lane, C.C. 1730. **Jno.**, apprenticed to David Hubert; C.C. 1747.

Steadman & Varden, London; balloon clock, about 1780.

Steath, Thos., apprenticed 1683 to Jno. Wheeler, C.C.

Steber, J. N., Dover; watch, 1789.

Stedman, J., Red Lion St., 1790.

Steele. Wm., Milecross; watch, 1819. **F.**, 71 Oxford St., 1825-33.

Steers, Jno., 9 Pall Mall, 1793.

Stegar, John, C.C. 1699.

Steibel (or Stebbell), Christopher, Augsburg; striking clock with minute hand, also square clock with cupola by him, Vienna Treasury, 1635-60.

Steil, Jno., Edinburgh; watch, h.m., 1752.

Stein, Abraham, Philadelphia, 1797.

Steinmann, Daniel, 29 North Audley St., 1840-42.

Stem, Richard, London; watch, 1760.

Stennett, Robt., Bath; watch, 1790.

Stephens. Francis, C.C. 1632. **Edwd.**, apprenticed 1693 to Jonathan Jones. **Thos.**, apprenticed 1693 to Jno. Marshall. **Joseph**, Whitechapel, C.C. 1721; master 1752. **Philip**, Minories, C.C. 1730. **Joseph**, 32 Aldgate; master C.C. 1776. **Thomas**, 93 Strand, 1823.

Stephenson. Benjamin, 5 Ludgate Hill, 1774-77. **William**, 27 Lombard St., 1793, see Stevenson & Farrow. **Geo.**, London; watch, 1797. **Thos. Sam.**, Hoxton; livery C.C. 1810. **D. W.**, 27 Lombard St., 1820-30. **Jno.**, Leeds, 1830.

Stepto, Wm., St Giles'; arabesque marqueterie long-case clock, about 1705.

Sterck, William, Portugal St., Lincoln's Inn, 1760-68; 16 Poland St., 1793.

Sterk, William, Cockspur St., 1772-90.

Sterling, Josh., London; watch, 1791.

Stern, Francis, Charleston, U.S.A., 1840.

Steuart, James, 8 Green St., Leicester Sq., 1790.

Stevens. Daniel, C.C. 1661. **Giles**, apprenticed 1671 to Robt. Wilkins, C.C. **George**, C.C. 1673. **Samuel**, Grub St., C.C. 1680; threatened in 1682 with prosecution by C.C. for undue taking of apprentices. **John**, apprenticed 1684 to Jno. Wynne; C.C. 1691; lantern clock, about 1710, signed "John Stevens, Colchester." **Ralph**, apprenticed 1687 to Richd. Warren. **Thomas**, C.C. 1700. **Nathaniel**, C.C. 1702. **Samuel**, C.C. 1706; square-dial lantern clock, cherub corners, inscribed "Sam Stevens, Londini, fecit," on circle; 1706-18. **Richard**, C.C. 1715. **Joseph**, 32 Aldgate Without; master C.C. 1752 and 1756; 1745-94. **Samuel**, "20 Princes St., nere Spittlefields Church," card, Ponsonby collection, about 1780; 26 Whitechapel, 1790-93. **W.**, Cirencester, 1795. **W.**, 31 Ironmonger Lane, Old St., 1835. **Ezek.**, 49 King Terrace, New North Rd., 1840-42. **William**, junr., 11 Ironmonger St., 1840-42. **William**, 14 Bartholomew Sq., St Luke's, 1840-42. **D.**, Gloster St., Hoxton, 1842. **Edwd.**, 24 King Sq., 1860-85.

Stevenson. —, Penrith, 1730. **—**, Dublin; centre seconds clock-watch, about 1760. **John**, Stafford, 1770. **Adam**, livery C.C. 1786. **& Farrow**, 27 Lombard St., 1810-24. **J.**, Bethnal Green Rd., 1835.

Stever & Bryant, Whigville, U.S.A., 1830.

Steward. Jno., 99 Wood St., 1793. **Henry**, York, f., 1816, died 1870.

Stewart, Joseph, 61 Red Lion St., 1842.

Stiebel, B., 5 Chandos St., 1823.

Stiff, Wm., apprenticed 1676 to Simon Chapman, C.C.

Stileman, Jno., C.C. 1640.

Stiles. John, C.C. 1704. **Nathaniel**, Wood St., C.C. 1725, master 1751; 1725-70. **Richard**, probably son of the above; master C.C. 1790; 1770-90. **William**, 28 Tottenham Court Rd., 1835.

Still, Francis, C.C. 1699.

Stillard, George, London; watch, 1815.

Stillas, John, Philadelphia, 1785-93.

Stilletto, Sam., apprenticed to Jno. Spurrier, 1686, C.C.

Stillman. William, Burlington, U.S.A., 1789-95.

Stimner, Richd., Roe Buck Court, Chiswell St., 1780.

Stimson. —, London; bracket clock, engraved plate, knife suspension, about 1710. **H.**, Sleaford, Lincolnshire, 1780.

Stirling, John, 38 Abchurch Lane, 1788.

Stirrup, Thomas, published "Hoometer; or, Complete Dialist," in 1652.

Stookes, J., London; watch, Dutch style, Schloss collection, about 1765; another, about 1780.

Stock, Jabez, Whitechapel; long black narrow-case clock, with Japanese decoration down the front, and a small circular glass in the door, about 1700; in the panel the following:—

> "I labour here with all my might,
> To tell the time by day and night;
> In thy devotion copy me,
> And serve thy God as I serve thee."

Stockar, Henry, London; marqueterie long-case clock, about 1700, Mr Alfred Marks; Mr Geo. E. H. Abbot, Groton, Mass., U.S.A., has a long-case clock by him, dating from about 1725. It formerly belonged to Edward Holyoke, President of Harvard College, who died in 1769.

Stockell, Hugh, Newcastle; watch, 1765, signed "Hugh Stokell, Newcastle," 1765-1800 (see p. 368).

Stockton, Francis, Yarm, 1820-27.

Stockwell, Hy., Bell's Buildings, 1793.

Stoddart. Robert, 61 Red Lion St., Clerkenwell, 1815-42. **James**, 13 Red Lion St., 1825-42; died at Hastings, 1886, aged 80. **J.**, 7 Charles St., Northampton Sq., 1835-40.

Stogden (Stockten), Matthew, worked for Graham; invented improved repeating motion about 1712 (see p. 412); admitted C.C. 1717; died in abject poverty, at an advanced age, in 1770.

Stokel, John, New York, 1820-43.

Stokes. Henry, Turnmill St., Clerkenwell; bequeathed his best clock to Robert Stokes, 1586. **Sam.**, London; long-case clock, about 1695. **Jno.**, Bawdley, 1760.

Stollewerck à Paris; clock in ormolu case, Jones collection, S.K.M., about 1740; two clocks, Wallace collection; a handsome regulator, signed "Alexandre Fortier invenit, Stollewerck fecit à Paris," finely chased gilt mounts, about 1740; also a cartel clock, signed "Stollewerck à Paris," about 1770; a clock by Stollewerck in ormolu case chased with masks and festoons and surmounted by a vase, fetched £68 at the Hamilton sale in 1882.

Stone. Andrew, C.C. 1699. **William**, C.C. 1700. **Roger**, C.C. 1710. **Richd.**, Thame; watch, h.m., 1771. **Francis**, Bristol, 1790. **Chas.**, Liverpool; watch, 1798. **Samuel**, 8 London Rd., 1820. **David**, Hull, 1822. **J.**, Aylesbury, 1822-30.

Stonehouse. Richard, Whitby, 1715-65; 30-hour long-case clock, Dr Wm. A. Day. **Robt. & Jno.**, Leeds, 1829.

Stones. Simon, Sheffield; made a clock for Marston Church in 1654. **Thomas**, Lothbury, C.C. 1692, master 1730; small striking and alarm long-case clock, dial 6 in. square, about 1695, Mr Hubert Bates; watch, 1735.

Stopforth, Edwd., apprenticed 1691 to Hy. Merriman.

Stoppes, Aylmer, London; long-case clock, about 1740; on another clock, oak long case, the inscription, "Elias Aylr Stopes, London."

Storer. Robert, born 1721; started business at 11 Berkeley Court, Clerkenwell, about 1743. **Robert** and James Storer, his sons, at the same address, 1768; James retired; Robt. Storer & Son, 1788; Robert Storer, the elder partner, who was grandson of the first-named Robert, retired to Olney, Bucks., in 1820, and died in 1832, aged 86; Robert & Walter Storer, 1822. **Walter**, who was great-grandson of the first-named Robert, retired about 1840, closing a business carried on at the same address for nearly a century, and died at Olney in 1865, aged 65. **Egbert**, cousin of Walter Storer, an excellent watchmaker, was apprenticed to Henry Dashper, and resided for some time at 46 Myddelton Sq.; he went to Switzerland in 1871, returned to London in 1892; died 1897, aged 86.

Storey. James, C.C. 1703, see Story, Jas. **Charles**, Sidney Alley, Leicester Fields, 1758-60; 1 Poultry, 1743. **J.**, 176 Regent St., 1830.

Storie, W., 8 Warwick St., Charing Cross; card, Hodgkin collection, about 1810.

Storr. (& Gibbs, London; watch, 1745). **Marmaduke**, 20 Lombard St., 1760-74. **Jonathan**, York, 1765-80. **William**, Jermyn St., 1765; 44 St James's St., 1779-94; hon. f. C.C. 1781. **& Mortimer**, 13 New Bond St., 1830-42.

Storrs, Joshua, Cheapside, 1835-42.

Story. Jas., London; long-case clock, scroll marqueterie case, about 1710. **Samuel**; clock, long red lacquer case, similar to Fig. 641, Rev. J. W. R. Brocklebank. **William**, Red Lion St., Clerkenwell, 1760-72. **Hy.**, 7 Charterhouse Lane, 1820.

Stothard, Benj., South Cave, Yorks., 1822.

Stowell, John, Medford, Mass., 1815-25; Boston, 1825-36.

Stracey, John, 34 Prince's St., Lothbury, 1790.

Strachan. Andrew, a Scotsman; to avoid prosecution for practising his art in the city of London he bound himself apprentice to Thomas Warden; the Chamberlain ordered the indenture to be cancelled, as Strachan was between thirty and forty years old, 1691; long-case clock, A. Strachan, Newcastle, about 1730. **Archibald**, Newcastle; watch, about 1775; clock, Arch. Strachan, Tanfield, about 1790. **A. & J.**, 125 Long Acre, 1830. See M'Cabe, and also Murray.

Strahan, Jno., London; long-case clock, about 1780.

Straiton. Archibald (or Straton), Edinburgh, about 1780. **Alexander**, a clever watchmaker; apprenticed to Reid & Auld, St Martin's Lane, 1820; 146 Leadenhall St., 1825; 15 Little Knightrider St., 1842; died 1873, aged 83.

Stram, Alfred, Ashby St., Clerkenwell; born in Switzerland; died 1893, aged 80. An excellent watch-case maker, who succeeded Comtesse.

Strange, Thos., Kingston; watch, 1799.

Stratford. George, C.C. 1704. **Jas.**, London; enamelled watch, about 1790.

Stratton. Richard, C.C. 1720. **Joseph**, Church St., Hackney, 1810-35. **Jno.**, 133 Bunhill Row, 1816-25. Of U.S.A.: **N. P.**, born 1836, apprenticed to J. F. Pitkin, associated with Hy. Pitkin at East Hartford; afterwards joined the American Watch Company, and presided over its first London office in 1874 until 1888.

Strebell, Christopher; watch, Vienna Treasury, oval case, of brass gilt, about 1625.

Strech, Peter, Philadelphia, 1750-80.

Street. Long-case month clock by

"John Street, Londres," which he presented about 1685 to his friend Abraham Martin, an engraver ; Martin was made free of the C.C. in 1682. **Geo.**, apprenticed to Roger Nicholls, 1687, C.C. **Richard**, Shoe Lane ; C.C. 1687, warden 1715 ; maker of a clock costing £50, which was presented by Sir Isaac Newton to Dr Bentley, Master of Trinity College, Cambridge, in 1708 ; long clock, 12-in. dial, walnut case, Wetherfield collection, about 1710 ; Mr John Lowe had a clock by him in which the hour band was shaped like a heart, the tip of the hand being caused to move in a corresponding path ; watch, 1784, signed, "Richard Street, Kepples, Surrey."

Streeter, Gilbert L., Salem, 1846.

Streller, Jacob, Nuremberg ; clock, Green Vaulted Chambers, Dresden, about 1700.

Strelly, Francis, C.C. 1665.

Stretch. Sam., Birmingham ; watch, h.m., 1712. **Jas.**, Birmingham ; watch, S.K.M., about 1740. **Benj.**, Bristol ; quarter repeating watch, about 1750. **Samuel**, High St., Birmingham, 1770.

Stretche, —, Leke (Leek) ; lantern clock, about 1670.

Stretton, Sarah, C.C. 1710.

Stribling, Benjamin, Stowmarket ; lantern clocks, about 1700.

Strigel. William F., St James's St., 1760-75. **George Philip**, Stafford Row, near Buckingham Court, 1760-88 ; hon. f. C.C. 1781.

Strigell, Johan, Christoph, Kreilsheim ; handless watch (as Fig. 350), silver pair cases, Schloss collection, about 1700.

Strigner, —. In the B.M. is a watch by him in an outer case of carnelian. It was made for James II., and by him given to his daughter Catherine, Countess of Anglesey and Duchess of Buckingham, about 1687.

Stringer, Josiah, Stockport, 1742-50.

Stringfellow, Jno., London ; C.C. 1691 ; lantern clock, about 1698.

Stripling, Thos., Barwell, about 1700 ; Mr Harry Clark has a long-case clock by him (see p. 376). **Thos.**, Litchfield ; watch, 1816.

Strixner, —, London ; watch, Evan Roberts collection, about 1745.

Strong, T., London ; watch, 1823.

Strongfellow, see Stringfellow.

Stroud. Robt., London ; watch, 1822. **Elizabeth**, 5 Henry St., Pentonville, 1835-40.

Struggle, Christopher, apprentice 1671 to Isaac Puzzy, C.C.

Strutt, J. D., London ; watch, 1790.

Stuart, Bernard (Scotsman) ; born 1706, died 1755 ; clock, Imperial collection, Vienna, 1735.

Stubb, Thos., London ; long-case clock, about 1690.

Stubbs. Gabriel, C.C. 1675 ; "a small clockmaker" (watchmaker) and a celebrated member of the Company ; 1675-77. **Thos.**, C.C. 1685. **& Co.**, London ; on watch movement, about 1760 ; on dial, Leyden, London. **Joseph**, 241 Holborn, 1793. **J.**, Prince's St., Leicester Sq., 1830 ; 28 Panton St., Haymarket, 1830 ; gold chronometer half-quarter repeater, gold dial, raised numerals, 1819.

Studley, David, Hanover, U.S.A., 1806-35.

Stuk, William, Cockspur St., 1781.

Stumbels, B., London ; watch, about 1760.

Style. Nathaniel, Wood St. ; C.C. 1725 ; master 1751 ; livery 1766 ; long-case clock,

about 1750, signed "Nathaniel Styles, London." **Richard**, 3 Carey Lane, Foster Lane ; livery C.C. 1766 ; master 1790 ; 1764-96.

Sudbury, John, C.C. 1686.

Sudell, Jno., apprenticed 1683 to Ben Bell, C.C.

Sudlow, Benj., Yarmouth ; watch, about 1780 ; monogram, "J.D.C.," on balance-cock.

Suggate, Geo., Halesworth ; lantern and 30-hour long-case clocks, about 1700 ; watch, same name and address, 1781.

Sully, Henry, apprenticed to Charles Gretton, C.C. 1704 ; an eminent man who settled in France ; died 1728 (see p. 252).

Sulman, see Hopgood.

Sumer, Jno., C.C. 1634.

Summer. William, C.C. 1662. **Francis**, 26 Greek St., Soho, 1790-94.

Summerhayes, Robert, Ilminster, afterwards at Taunton ; died 1857.

Summers, Chas., London ; watch, Schloss collection, case beautifully enamelled, about 1785.

Supple, John, Vigo Lane, Piccadilly, 1783.

Sutherland. D., Leith ; clock, belonging to Mr Wm. Collie, Manitoba, with moving figures representing Adam and Eve in the Garden of Eden, apparently about 1775. **Thos.**, 2 Vigo Lane, 1793.

Sutor, Wm., Edinburgh, 1712.

Sutton. Jno., apprenticed 1661 to Ed. Norris, C.C. **Isaac**, C.C. 1662 ; to him in 1664 was apprenticed Joseph Aberley. **Thos.**, Maidstone, 1760. **Wm.**, Liverpool, 1770. **Wm. & Co.**, 85 Cheapside, 1790-93 ; card, Ponsonby collection, "successors to Mr Stamp." **Robert**, Whitehaven, 1840.

Swain, —, London ; watch, 1832.

Swale, Jaques (alien), threatened with prosecution for working as clockmaker in liberties of C.C. 1668.

Swan. Edwd., apprenticed 1650 to Ralph Ash, C.C. **Wm.**, apprenticed 1692 to Thos. Tompion ; C.C. 1703. **Robt.**, Bridlington, 1770. **Benjamin**, Haverhill, Mass., 1810-40.

Swannell & Co., Staples Inn, Holborn, 1790-94.

Swannick, G., 38 Banner St., 1820.

Swanson. Robert, C.C. 1730.

Swearer & Sons, wooden clockmakers, 7 Upper East Smithfield, 1820. **J.**, 30 Park Terrace, Regent's Park, 1840-42.

Sweeby, John, C.C. 1671 ; fine long inlaid-case clock, about 1700.

Sweman, —, London ; watch, probably Dutch, about 1730. **William**, 5 Banner St., 1790.

Swetman, Thos., London ; watch, about 1740 ; another, engraved "Sweteman, London," repoussé case with enamelled centre, Schloss collection, about 1760.

Swift. M., 68 Red Lion St., Clerkenwell, 1793. **Thomas**, Essex St., Islington, lever pallet maker, 1825-67.

Swinburn, Jno., Bishops Auckland, 1775 ; Sunderland, 1785.

Swindells, Jasper, watch - case maker, Salmon and Ball Court, Bunhill Row, 1800-13.

Swindels, —, Macclesfield ; clock, about 1800.

Swinden, Francis Charles, born in Brentford, settled in Birmingham ; at Bath St., 1824 ; 91 New St., 1825 ; afterwards at Temple St.

Swingler, Jas., Holbeach ; watch, 1802.

Swinton, George, water clock, 1661.

Sword & Sons, Cornhill, 1838.

Sydenham. H. & J., 126 New Bond St.,

1800-4. **J.**, 126 Bond St., 1816-23.

Syderman, Philip, Philadelphia, 1785.

Sykes. W., Holbeck, 1790. **Geo.**, Malton, 1823.

Sylvester, John, C.C. 1693.

Symes, Robt., London ; long-case clock, about 1800.

Symms, Isaac, Aldgate, about 1600 ; watch, Pierpont Morgan collection, signed "Isaac Symmes at Aldgette," about 1620.

Symonds. Richd., apprenticed 1668 to Fras. Strelly ; C.C. 1691. **Thomas**, 57 Cheapside, 1770-75 ; 20 Fleet St., 1755-88. **Joseph, & Co.**, Liverpool, 1780.

Symons, Moses, Hull, 1822.

Taber, Thos., 29 Compton St., Clerkenwell, 1825.

Tackley, C., London ; watch, 1826.

Taf, John James, Philadelphia, 1794.

Tailour, Edward, clockmaker, admitted to Blacksmiths' Company, 1629.

Talbot, Thomas, lantern clock, about 1675, Mr Arthur R. Hinks.

Tallans, Gabriel, about 1720.

Tallibart, Louis, 48 Rathbone Pl., 1842.

Tallis, Aaron. C.C. 1722.

Tallon, —, Paris ; watch, 1720.

Tanner. Joseph, C.C. 1682. **—**, clock engraver and varnisher, Fleet Market, 1790-94.

Tansiey, Thos., Birmingham, 1818.

Tantum. Bracket clock, about 1700, inscribed "Dan. Tantum, in Derby, fecit."

Tapp. Geo., apprenticed 1691 to Sam. Bowtell, C.C. **Francis**, 85 Strand, 1775-85.

Tappy, Abraham, watch, 1778, "Abe Tappy, Totveeren" ; bracket timepiece, small movement in large mahogany case, about 1790.

Taquet, —, watch, 1790.

Tarbuck. Robt., apprenticed 1686 to Thos. Stubbs, C.C. **John**, St Mary's Gate, Manchester, died 1739.

Tarles, Jno., C.C. 1690.

Tarleton. Jere., apprenticed 1690 to Walter Henshaw, C.C. **Richd.**, Liverpool, 1760. **Wm.**, Liverpool, 1770-95 ; he made good watches and did much to advance the reputation of Liverpool as a manufacturing centre.

Tarman, J. B., 34 Regent St., Piccadilly, 1825.

Tarts, J., London ; watches for the Dutch market, 1755-90.

Tate. Ruth, East Sheen ; oak long-case clock, about 1790. **Thos.**, Winterton ; succeeded Wm. Godfrey ; died 1821.

Tatum, Jno., 53 Dorset St., Salisbury Sq., 1817.

Tavan, Antoine, born at Aost, France, 1742, died at Geneva, 1836. An excellent watchmaker who wrote an analysis of various escapements.

Tavernier. Jean Pierre, Paris ; died 1793. **Louis**, eldest son of J. P. ; born 1754, died 1840. **Etienne**, second son of J. P. ; an eminent watchmaker, born 1756, died 1839 ; in 1772 he, from the Rue de Bussy, advertised watches in rings, bracelets, tops of canes, and other small articles ; his keys were particularly admired ; he constructed one to show the days of the week, the days of the month, the age and phases of the moon ; adjusting the key to wind the watch actuated the mechanism concealed in the middle part of the key ; this was a device for which a patent had been obtained in England by George Sanderson in 1762.

Tawney, Pepe, watch, about 1700.

Tayler, Thos., lantern clock, see Taylor.

Taylor. A well-known name among London watchmakers from 1640 till past the middle of the nineteenth century ; the two Thomas Taylors, who were active members of the C.C. during the seventeenth century, are distinguished as "of Holborn" and "of the Strand"; in 1676 Thomas Taylor, of Essex House Gate, is mentioned. **Edwd.,** apprenticed 1637 to Wm. Almond, C.C. **Thomas,** Strand ; apprenticed 1638 to Simon Hackett ; C.C. 1646, master 1668 ; watch, Pierpont Morgan collection, signed "Thos. Taylor, Londini," balance-cock pinned on, not later than 1650. **Geo.,** apprenticed 1648 to Ben. Hill, C.C. **Richard,** C.C. 1655. **Thos.,** Holborn ; C.C. about 1660. **Abraham,** C.C. 1668. **Thomas,** Holborn, at the end of Fetter Lane, apprenticed 1678 to Thos. Taylor, Holborn ; C.C. 1685, master 1710 ; fine pair-case *repoussé* repeating watch, gold dial. "Lost between Pickadilly and St James Street, a gold watch made fast in a gold studded case, with high pins at each hour ; made by Mr Taylor, at the Upper End of Fetter Lane, in Holborn. Whoever brings it to Mr Harrison, Goldsmith, etc., the Three Flower-de-Luces, in the Strand, shall have a guinea reward" (*Lond. Gaz.*, Feb. 9-12, 1692). **William,** apprenticed to John Wright and turned over to Isaac Webb ; C.C. 1682. **Jasper,** in Gray's Inn, apprenticed 1685 to Thos. Taylor ; C.C. 1694 ; pair-case copper verge watch, outside case of leather, with many small rivets, lockspring projecting through the dial, inscription, "Jasper Taylor, in Holbourn" (see p. **167**). **John,** C.C. 1687 ; two clocks by him seen at Moscow ; one in large mahogany case, silvered dial, verge escapement, chimed on eight bells and played a tune. **Jon.,** Ormskirk ; long-case clock, about 1690. **Rob.,** apprenticed 1693 to Jas. Hatchman, C.C. **John,** C.C. 1702. **George,** C.C. 1703 ; to him and his wife Lucy, Rebecca Fisher was apprenticed in 1715. **Geo.,** Liverpool, about 1720. **Charles,** C.C. 1723. **Richard,** C.C. 1724. **Jasper,** of Barnard's Inn, admitted C.C. 1729 ; took an active part in the affairs of the Company ; was master in 1754, and clerk from 1760 to 1770, when he died, leaving £10 to C.C. for the poor. **James,** Ashton-under-Lyne ; in 1754 he took out a patent for spinning ; in 1769 one for raising weights ; died 1813, aged 89. **Henry,** London ; watch, 1760. **Jno.,** Petworth ; watch, 1762. **Jno.,** Lancaster, 1772, f. **Samuel,** Maiden Lane, Wood St., 1774 ; livery Goldsmiths' Company ; afterwards at 10 Ball Alley, Lombard St. ; master C.C. 1807 ; 1774-1810. **Wm.,** Whitehaven, 1775. **Benj.,** Ball Alley, Cornhill, 1793 ; 45 Lombard St., 1798-1800. **& Son,** Bristol ; watch, 1797. **Samuel,** Philadelphia, 1799. **& Samuel,** London ; watch, about 1800. **John S.,** 8 Wilderness Row, 1809-40. **Edward,** livery C.C. 1810 ; in the B.M. is a curious watch of his, with symbolical figures and texts of Scripture in the enamel on the dial and case, 1800-30. **Wm.,** Dumfries, 1817. **J. & S.,** Liverpool, 1818. **Edward,** 25 Leadenhall St., 1822-25. **Kennard, & Co.,** 3 Crescent, Jewin St., 1822-30. **Joseph.** 2 Bouverie St., 1825. **Jas.,** 3 Corporation Lane, 1835. **Robert,** 47 William St., Regent St., 1835. **Charles,** 62 John St., Fitzroy Sq., 1840. **David,** 27 Northampton Sq., 1842 ; between 1850 and 1864 he did a large trade with the American market. **Andrew,** a watchmaker of exceptional ability, born in Clerkenwell ; patented a tourbillon carriage for watch escapements in 1902 ; died 1910, aged 51.

Teams, John, 25 Red Cross Sq., 1790-94.

Tearson, Stephen, Ipswich ; watch, about 1700.

Tebbatt, Benoni (or **Benomi**), Little Old Bailey ; apprenticed to Robt. Doore, 1676 ; C.C. 1683. C.C. in 1688 seized at his shop a gold watch-case, both for that it was of coarse and unwarrantable gold, and also so extremely thin that it was insufficient in strength. William Brafield who made the case, admitted his fault, and was fined 5s., the case being broken up.

Telforth, Isaac, London ; watch, 1765.

Tempest, Hy., apprenticed 1638 to Robt. Grinkin, C.C.

Temple, Thomas, C.C. 1720. **J.,** London ; watch, 1780 ; another, 1800.

Templer, Charles, C.C. 1673.

Tenant, Leonard, paid £37 for a new clock and chimes for St Margaret's Church, Westminster, 1617.

Tennant, Thomas, C.C. 1668.

Terold, Henry, Ipswich ; round silver watch-case with interlacing bands, silver dial, Fellows collection, about 1640.

Terrey, Jas., London ; long-case clock, about 1770.

Terrier. James, C.C. 1694. **Thomas,** C.C. 1694. **—,** Paris ; clock-watch, Pierpont Morgan collection ; numerals on porcelain enamel plaques ; single brass case covered with leather *piqué*, 1700. **Mary,** C.C. 1713.

Terrot. Philippe, Geneva ; 1740-50 ; watch in silver case, shaped like a cockle shell, G.M. **& Thuillier,** Geneva, 1760-76. **Ph., & Fazy,** Geneva ; watch, 1770 ; watch, "Ph. Terrot, Geneva," 1780.

Terroux l'aîné, Geneva, 1770-85.

Terry, Hy., apprenticed 1688 to Richd. Farmer, C.C. **John,** York, f., 1713 ; died 1783 ; in 1716 he made a turret clock for York castle, **—,** Thoralby, 1730. **Jno.,** York, f., 1759 ; watch, 1770. **Wm.,** Bedale ; long-case clock, about 1770. **Garnet,** 54 Paternoster Row, 1785-93 ; clock-watch, silver embossed case, Schloss collection, probably by him, though apparently of rather an earlier date. **Eli,** Plymouth, Litchfield County, Connecticut, U.S.A. ; said to be the Sam Slick of Haliburton ; patented an equation clock in 1797, and in 1816 patented the well-known type of cheap American shelf or mantel clock which became popular all over the world ; he died in 1853. **—,** Richmond, Yorks., 1820-50. **Leonard,** York, f., 1822. **Wm.,** Hull, 1822. **Wm.,** Richmond, Yorks., 1822. **Isaac,** 15 King St., Clerkenwell, 1835 ; 35 Prince's St., Leicester Sq., 1842.

Terweer, Hy. ; watch, Dutch style, about 1750.

Tesseyman, Geo., Northallerton, 1822-40.

Teulings, C., 15 Charing Cross, 1793.

Tew, Thos., apprentice ; C.C. 1674.

Thacke. Robt., apprenticed 1681 to Jno. Benson, C.C. **Philip,** C.C. 1685 ; marqueterie long-case clock, square dial, about 1770.

Thackray, Robert, York, f., 1832.

Thatcher, Geo., Cranbrook ; watch, about 1760.

Thead & Pickett, Ludgate Hill, 1758-65, see Pickett & Rundell.

Theodricke, Hy., apprenticed to Jno. Curtis 1679, C.C.

Therasby (or **Thoresby**), Peter, York, f., 1666.

Thierry, —, Caen ; watch, 1690.

Thillier, I. P., London ; watch, 1745.

Thioust, Nicolas ; calendar clock, about 1730.

Thiout. Antoine, l'aîné ; born 1692, died 1767 ; Quai Lepelletier, Paris ; inventor of many ingenious forms of repeating work, curious clocks, &c., described in his "Traité d'Horlogerie," Paris, 1741 ; clockmaker to the Duke of Orleans, 1752 ; garde visiteur in 1769 (see p. **325**). **le Jeune,** Paris ; bracket clock, about 1780.

Thitchener. W., 36 High St., Shadwell, 1835-40. **J.,** 14 Maiden Lane, Covent Garden, 1835. **Thomas,** 18 High Row, Knightsbridge, 1840-42.

Thomaque, Abraham, C.C. 1675. **Isaac,** silver repeating watch, about 1729.

Thomas. Dan., apprenticed to Jno. Browne, 1675 ; C.C. 1682. **Hugh,** apprenticed 1686 to Richd. Ellis, C.C. **Francis,** Dublin ; watch, 1750. **M., & Sons,** Carnarvon ; long-case clock, about 1780. **Samuel,** Keynsham, 1785. **Thomas John,** 55 St James's St. ; verge watch movement, G.M. ; another example, watch with cylinder escapement, 1790-1804. **& Evans,** Staining Lane, 1793. **Richard,** 98 Strand, 1793-1804 ; 17 Bridgwater Sq., 1817. **Jno.,** 153 New Bond St., 1810. **Seth,** Plymouth, Conn. ; he learnt clockmaking of Eli Terry, whose business he (in conjunction with Silas Hoadley, another of Terry's workmen) acquired in 1810 ; died 1859. **F. L. & J. W.,** 153 New Bond St., 1821-30. **Thomas,** 314 Borough, 1825. **& Son,** 3 Strand, 1825-30 ; Wm. Thomas, of 3 Strand, retired to Brompton, and died 1869, bequeathing £200 to the Watch and Clockmakers' Benevolent Institution. **John,** New Rd., St George's East, 1835.

Thomasen, Ts., Amsterdam ; fine long-case clock, about 1760, Mr Francis H. Bigelow.

Thomegay, Mark, Moorfields, 1760-8.

Thomlinson, Geo., apprenticed 1669 to Thos. Bayley ; C.C. 1678 ; lantern clock, about 1680, inscribed "Geo. Thomlinson, in George Yard, in Lumbard Street, fecit."

Thompson. John, C.C. 1662. **Rowland,** apprenticed 1674 to Kath. Bestwick, widow. **Geo.,** apprenticed 1676 to L. Sindrey, C.C. **Robert,** C.C. 1681. **Jno.,** York, f., 1692. **Isaac,** C.C. 1699. **William,** apprenticed to Thos. Tompion ; C.C. 1703 ; watch, 1725 ; in the Nelthropp collection is a watch, "William Thompson, Chester," date mark, 1703. **John,** C.C. 1720 ; large silver watch, 1759, inscribed, "J. Thompson, London," in an outer case of fine English chasing, Pierpont Morgan collection. **Hy.,** Bartholomew Close, C.C. 1730. **Troughton,** C.C. 1731. **Thos.,** Lancaster, 1747, f. **C.,** London, about 1760 ; pair-cased watch by him, outer case enamelled blue ; exhibited at the Guelph Exhibition by Mr Geo. Carr Glyn. **John,** 10 Red Lion St., Clerkenwell, 1765-94. **Ann, & Son,** Red Lion St., Clerkenwell, 1790-94. **James,** Bride Lane, Fleet St., 1790-94. **Jos.,** London ; pretty balloon timepiece, Sheraton style, about 1790 (see p. **395**). **W.,** Skinner St., Clerkenwell, 1790. **Joseph,** Atherstone ; clock, about 1800. **Edward John,** born 1815 ; apprenticed to Hugh McLachlan, 1829 ; Wellington St., St Luke's, 1842 ; 5 Percival St., 1848 ; Goswell Rd., 1871 ; Aldersgate St., 1878 ; died 1896 ; he was a trustee of the Horological Institute, and twice master of the Clockmakers' Company. **Thomas, & Storrs,** 16 Staining Lane, 1817. **Ebenezer,** 32 Exeter St., Sloane St., 1830-40 ; afterwards at 181 Sloane St. ; died 1866. **John,** 19 Red Lion St., Clerkenwell, 1835 ; died, 1847. **Hy.,** London ; watch, 1838. **William,** 5 Great Tower St., 1844-02.

Thomson. Philip, & Son, 11 Exeter Court, Strand, 1769. **James,** Pittsburgh, U.S.A., 1815. **Adam,** 25 New Bond St. ; a

498

very able man ; published "Time and Timekeepers" in 1843 ; 1830-60 ; afterwards Thomson & Profaze.

Thorelet, Jonas, London ; watch in plain silver case, dial with gold centre and large figures on white enamel ring, about 1720. Pierpont Morgan collection ; long-case clock, about 1740.

Thorn, Thomas, 23 Wood St., Cheapside, 1758-69.

Thorndike, Sam., Ipswich ; watch, 1740.

Thorne. Sim., Tiverton, 1740. **Simon.** London ; fine bracket clock, pull repeater on eight bells, about 1750. **Robert**, 12 Wood St., Cheapside, 1760-68 ; repeating watch in gold repoussé case, with outer case of shagreen piqué, Pierpont Morgan collection. **John**, 56 Whitechapel, 1790-1818 ; John, & Son, 56 Whitechapel, 1820. **Wm.**, London ; clock, about 1800. **James**, Limekiln Hill, Limehouse, 1835-42. **John**, 49 Rahere St., 1842.

Thornham, Geo., Hull, 1822.

Thornhill, Bryan, apprenticed 1683 to Thos. Bradford.

Thornton. Henry, C.C. 1699 ; long-case clock, playing six tunes, seen in Moscow ; Mr E. Alfred Jones mentions two large chiming clocks bearing his name, one in the Winter Palace at St Petersburg, and the other in the Troitsa Monastery near Moscow. The collection of the Czar of Russia contains two watches by him ; one, a repeater, has cases of gold, the inner bears the hall mark for 1729-30, and the outer repoussé decoration representing St Christophorus carrying the infant Jesus ; it is suspended from a chatelaine. The other watch, also in gold cases and furnished with a chatelaine, is of about the same period. **John**, C.C. 1731. **William**, York, f., 1747. **Jas.**, London ; watch, B.M., h.m., 1771. **Thos.**, London ; watch, 1796. **Andrew.** Philadelphia, 1811.

Thorogood. John, C.C. 1660. **Wm.**, C.C. 1660. **James**, apprenticed to Jno., 1660. **Edwd.**, C.C. 1668. **Etinne**, 9 Burrows Buildings, Blackfriars Bridge. **Stefano**, same address ; card, B.M., about 1770 ; watch, "Thoroughgood, S., London," about 1772. **Richard**, 175 Fenchurch St. 1783-90.

Thorowgood, Luke, apprenticed to Thos. Hunter ; C.C. 1768, London ; long-case clock, about 1770.

Thorpe, Jno., C.C. 1657.

Threlkeld. William, "in ye Strand," 1700. "A silver watch with an engraved Case and a Cipher, G. K., in the middle, the Dial Plate having Flower-de-luces at the half-hours, the Maker's name, W. Threlkeld, London" (Lond. Gaz., May 12-15, 1701). In the Soane Museum is a clock by him in a long case decorated with fine English marqueterie in panel, about 1710. **Ralph**, London ; bracket clock, about 1740 ; seen at The Hague.

Threlkell. —, C.C. about 1632. **R.**, London ; watch, 1730.

Thristle. —, Williton ; hood-case clock, about 1730 (see p. 351).

Thuret. Isaac, Paris ; lodged at the Louvre, 1686. **Jacques**, son of Isaac, obtained the reversion of his father's privileges in 1694 ; Boulle clock, S.K.M., about 1700 ; another with reclining figure of Time below the dial, Wallace collection (see p. 314).

Thwaites. Ainsworth, Rosoman St., Clerkenwell ; made the Horse Guards clock, 1756 ; 1740-80. **Jas.**, Ratcliff Highway ; 1768-90. **John**, 4 Rosoman St., Clerkenwell ; master C.C. three times,

1815, 1819, 1820 ; presented to the C.C. Sully's timekeeper ; 1780-1816. **& Reed**, 4 Rosoman St., Clerkenwell, 1817-42.

Thylet, London, 1705 ; watch and chatelaine which had belonged to Queen Anne fetched £150 at Christie's in 1904.

Tickle. Jno., junr., Crediton ; 30-hour clock, lantern movement, about 1730. **Wm.**, Newcastle, 1765-85.

Tidbury & Son, 206 Oxford St., 1822-25.

Tiese, J., London ; oval watch, 1620.

Tillbrooke, Jno., Bury ; watch, 1785.

Tills, Richd., London, 1760.

Tilly, Joseph, C.C. 1703 ; walnut long-case clock, square dial, 1703-20.

Timner, Richd., London ; watch, 1805.

Tingley, Thos., apprenticed 1686 to Wm. Glazier, C.C.

Tinham ; long-case clock, bird and flower marqueterie in panels, about 1690, inscribed "Samuel Tinham, Sarum fecit" ; another, about 1725, with the inscription, "Saml. Tinham in New Sarum."

Tinson, Thos., 1 Charing Cross, 1793.

Tipping, George, C.C. 1674.

Tirry, Jno., York, about 1680 (see p. 368).

Titherton, Jno., London ; long-case clock, about 1700.

Tobias. Morris, 68 Bell Dock Yard, Wapping, 1798-1800. **Morris, & Co.**, 68 Bell Dock Yard, Wapping, 1804 ; in 1812 Morris Tobias patented (No. 3,584) a binnacle timepiece, to show the time by "bells," as watches are kept on board ship ; rack lever watches, "Tobias & Co., Liverpool and London," 1808-25. **& Levitt**, 31 Minories, 1816-42.

Todd. Robt., apprenticed 1654 to Dan. Quare, C.C. **Jno.**, York, f., 1665. **Samuel**, York, f., 1686. **Ben.**, Aldersgate St., C.C. 1730. **Jas.**, Bradford ; clock, about 1760.

Tolby, Charles, C.C. 1720.

Tolkien. & Dancer, 145 St John St., 1807. **George**, same address, 1810.

Toller Bros., London ; watch, 1760.

Tolley, Charles, C.C. 1683.

Tollison, John, C.C. 1714.

Tolson, Ralph, apprenticed 1693 to Cuth. Lee, C.C. ; watch, about 1700, signed "Ralph Tolson, London."

Tomes, Jas., apprenticed to Jno. Saville, 1676, C.C.

Tomkins, William, 11 Winchester St., 1768-72.

Tomlin, Edwd., 69 Threadneedle St., 1770-98 ; bracket clock, mahogany case, round enamelled dial, marked "Tomlin, Royal Exchange."

Tomlins, Nich., apprenticed 1639 to Ed. Stevens ; C.C. 1646.

Tomlinson. Thomas, C.C. 1647. **William**, brother, C.C. 1699 ; master in 1733 ; chiming bracket clock in ebony case, about 1710, Wetherfield collection ; watch by him in S.K.M., h.m., 1719 ; inside a fine 8-day Oriental lacquer clock-case by him were directions to set up and keep a pendulum clock, and underneath, "The said clocks with all other sorts and all sorts of watches are made by William Tomlinson at the Dial and Three Crowns in Birchin Lane, near the Royal Exchange, London, now in White Hart Court, Gracechurch St." ; he retired to Stoke Newington ; Mr Geo. E. H. Abbot, Groton, Mass., U.S.A., has a watch by him which belonged to Edwd. Holyoke, president of Harvard College ; the outer silver case was made into a drinking cup for Mr Abbot's father.

Tomlyns, Nicholas, C.C. 1647.

Tompion. Thomas, "father of English watchmaking." Fleet St., born 1638, died

1713 (see p. 175 ; also p. 218). **Thomas**, junr., apprenticed to Charles Kemp, 1694 ; admitted C.C. 1702 (see p. 226). **& Graham**, watch movement, G.M., about 1705. **T.**, **& Banger, E.**, on clocks and watches (see p. 224) ; Mrs Francis J. Kidson has a fine bracket clock, signed "Tho Tompion & Edw Banger London," dating from about 1715 (see p. 388).

Tompkinson, Humphry, Maiden Lane, Covent Garden, 1768-75.

Tompson, J., 9 Hooper Court, Clerkenwell, 1842.

Toms, T. E., 7 Swan St., Minories, 1820.

Tomson, Sn., London ; pair-case watch, Mr H. F. Geyer, about 1770.

Tooke, —, Lynn ; watch, 1790.

Tootele, Wm., Chorley, 1770.

Topham, J., 9 Basing Lane, 1788-1800.

Topping, Jno., London ; apprenticed 1691 to Wm. Grimes, C.C.

Torado, Francis, Gray's Inn ; brother C.C. 1633 ; oval watch in G.M. His widow became a pensioner of C.C. in 1690.

Torin. James Lewis, 30 Throgmorton St., 1738-80. **Daniel**, Hoxton Sq., 1766.

Torkler, Peter, 9 Red Lion St., Clerkenwell, 1782-90.

Tornique, J., London ; silver alarm watch by him, about 1670, exhibited at the Guelph Exhibition by Mr Geo. Carr Glyn.

Tortorre, Jas., London, 1770.

Tory, Sarah, apprenticed 1660 to Richd. Bowen and Mary his wife, C.C.

Tothaker, William, C.C. 1703.

Touch, Chas., St Albans ; watch, 1744.

Toulmin. Samuel, London ; watch, about 1745 ; Wm. Curteen apprenticed to him in 1759. **Samuel**, 27 Strand, 1765-83 ; centre-seconds watch, beating full seconds, cylinder escapement, in the G.M.

Toutin. Jean, Château Surr ; celebrated enamel painter (see p. 147). **Henry**, Blois (brother of Jean) (see p. 147).

Tovey. Wm., apprenticed 1655 to Simon Dudson, C.C. **Wm.**, watch and clock spring maker, 64 Red Lion St., Clerkenwell, 1798 ; 53 Upper Moorfields, 1804.

Towell, Nich., apprenticed 1668 to Sam Davis, C.C.

Tower, Reuben, Plymouth, U.S.A., 1813-20.

Towne, Joseph, Horncastle ; watch, silver dial, about 1700.

Townley. Lantern clock, signed "William Townley Bourton," with heraldic fret engraved "B.R.F. 1724." **Thos., & Son**, Liverpool, 1818. **Jno.**, Liverpool, 1833 ; also **Thos.** ; also **Townley & Quilliam**.

Townsend. Jno., forbidden to work by C.C. 1632. **Samuel**, C.C. 1702 (Townson (?)). **Joseph**, Helmdon, 1710. **Elizabeth & John**, 61 St Paul's Churchyard, 1760-69. **Rt.**, Greenock, 1770-90 ; he was paid £2 for keeping the town clock in 1785 ; long-case clock, Mr E. R. De Long, Boston, Mass. **William**, 74 Fleet St., 1773 ; 99 Guildford Place, Spafield, 1842. **Elizabeth**, 119 Fetter Lane, 1804. **Charles**, Philadelphia, 1811. **R.**, London ; watch, 1815.

Towson, Jno. Thos., Devonport ; received Vulcan medal and £10 from Society of Arts for chronometer banking, 1826.

Trabet. —, London ; watch, apparently Dutch, about 1750.

Tracy. Richd., apprenticed 1660 to Nich. Coxeter, C.C. **Steven**, Rotterdam, 1683 (see p. 150). **Step.**, London ; striking watch, Marfels collection, about 1700.

Trail. Edwin, 68 Old Broad St., 1835-40. **Edwin**, Edgware Rd., 1835-42.

Tramieri, J., à Turin ; watch in case of

rock crystal formed as an escalop shell, about 1600, Pierpont Morgan collection.

Trap, Richard, London; watch, 1762.

Trattle, Joseph, Newport; clock, about 1780.

Traver, Jno.; watch, h.m.. 1748.

Travers. Adam, Liverpool, 1775; 9 Red Lion St., Clerkenwell, 1783-94. **Wm.,** Red Lion St., Clerkenwell, 1788-1810. **Mathew,** watch-case maker, 12 Great Sutton St., 1810.

Travis. Geo., Rotherham, 1770. **J.,** Thorne, 1780. **Wm.,** Leek, born 1781, apprenticed to Joseph Wild, Macclesfield; died 1875.

Tregent, James, 35 Strand, 1775; 29 Cranbourne St., Leicester Sq., 1780; hon. f. C.C. 1781; watchmaker to the Prince of Wales; was intimate with Garrick, Sheridan, and other notabilities of the theatre. Kelly refers to him as "Mr Tregent the celebrated French watch-maker" and relates how Sheridan, by attributing his proverbial unpunctuality to the lack of a timekeeper, obtained from Harris, proprietor of Covent Garden Theatre, a watch of Tregent's make. The Duke of Sussex paid him £400 for a re-peater and alarm travelling watch. A bracket clock in the Wetherfield collection is shown on p. **392**). Mr Thos. Boynton has a long-case clock by him, about 1770, silvered dial engraved with festoons, &c., day of the month, strike-silent; bracket clock with Battersea enamel face, Schreiber collection, S.K.M., signed on face "James Tregent, Leicester Square, London," 1770-1804.

Trelegon. James, Strand, 1775. **& Ockley,** 54 New Bond St., 1793.

Trembley. J. L., Geneva, about 1710. **David,** Geneva, about 1750.

Trenholme, Wm., C.C. 1728; in 1735 he worked for Bayley.

Trent, Wm., London; watch, 1770.

"**Trevan, Marseille**"; watch, 1780.

Trevor, Thos., apprenticed 1654 to Peter Delandre, C.C.

Trewinnard. Joshua & James, 16 Rotherhithe Wall, 1790-1842. **Joshua,** 40 Strand, 1807-10. **Edward,** Grange Rd., Bermondsey, 1825. **James,** 32 London Rd., 1835. **Joseph,** 23 Grange Rd., 1835. **George,** Kingsland Place, 1835.

Tribe, John, Petworth, died 1728; hanging clock by him repeats hours and quarters, Sir James M. Moody.

Trigg, Thomas, C.C. 1701.

Triggs, Thomas, C.C. 1708.

Trim, John, London; maker of house clocks, 1790-1800.

Tringham. J., London; watch, 1790. **Geo.,** 15 Golden Lane, 1828-42.

Tripp, Job, Bridge St., 1772.

Trippett. Thos., apprenticed 1654 to Geo. Poole, C.C. **Jno.,** Kingston, C.C. 1668. **Robert,** C.C. 1700; long-case clock, about 1705, Rev. W. B. Atherton. **William,** C.C. 1706.

Triquet, Jas., 35 Strand, 1768-72.

Tritschler & Co., wooden and musical clockmakers, 191 High Holborn, 1835-40.

Troth, James, Pittsburgh, U.S.A., 1815.

Trott, Andrew C., Boston, U.S.A., 1800-10.

Troughton. Bryan, 35 Fenchurch St., livery Clothworkers' Company, 1760-75. **Nathaniel,** 25 Rood Lane, 1768. **Joseph,** London, f. of Lancaster, 1779. **Edward,** Fleet St.; invented a wheel-cutting engine in 1780, and a compensated pendulum in 1790; died 1835, aged 81.

Troup. W., London; bracket clock, about 1760. **Jas.,** 233 Tooley St., 1822. **Jno.,** 120 Cheapside, 1835, afterwards at Hatton Garden; died 1901, aged 92.

Trout, —, watch in silver-gilt case, inscribed "Trout, Westminster," about 1790, Hilton Price collection.

Trowe. Jno., apprenticed 1685 to Wm. Speakman, C.C. **Gilbert,** C.C. 1722.

Trubshaw, John, apprenticed to Robt. Halsted 1679; admitted C.C. 1686; bracket clock chiming on six bells, about 1700; a gilt metal-cased repeating watch by him, S.K.M., about 1710.

Tuck, J. & L., 8 Haymarket, 1800-30.

Tuckey. Thos., C.C. 1646. **Edwd.,** apprenticed 1681 to Robt. Ayres, C.C. **Giles,** London; repeating watch, 1776.

Tudman, James, The Crown, Lombard St., 1697-1710; long marqueterie case clock, about 1700, Sir James M. Moody.

Tuite, William, 41 Great Queen St., 1761-75.

Tunnell, Jno., successor to Geo. Flash-man, 18 Fleet St., 1816-30; livery C.C. 1826; watch duplex escapement compensation balance, h.m., 1821, Mr H. Cook.

Tunstal, Stephen, Skipton; long-case clock, about 1725, Dr Wm. A. Day.

Tupling, B., 191 Strand, 1820.

Tupman, Geo., Vigo St., 1790; 6 Charles St., Grosvenor Sq., 1806-30; 6A Old Bond St., 1842; there a succeeding generation of the Tupmans, **George** and **James,** carried on business for many years; they were noted for good work, and contrary to the usual practice, attended to the winding of customers' clocks and other outdoor require-ments themselves, leaving the shop to the care of assistants. George Clifton Tupman, the last of the two brothers, a handsome man of very engaging manners, retired to Ashford, Middlesex, where, having entered his ninetieth year, he died in 1903.

Turges. Jas., apprenticed 1660 to Ahasuerus Fromanteel. **Josiah,** 23 Smith-field, 1768-72.

Turlis, Jas., Windsor; silver watch by him, shagreen outer case, exhibited at the Guelph Exhibition by Mr Geo. Carr Glyn.

Turmeau & Kettlewell, 23 Villiers St., 1793.

Turnbull. Francis, apprenticed 1692 to Sam Marchant, C.C.; watch, 1740. **Thos.,** Whitby, 1818. **Wm.,** Whitby, 1823.

Turner. Hy., apprenticed 1694 to Richd. Westwood, C.C. **Joseph,** C.C. 1717. **Thos.,** London; fine long-case clocks, about 1745. **William,** Church St., Spitalfields, 1760-72. **Wm.,** 18 Cornhill, 1775; Fenchurch St., 1825-40, see Birch. **John,** 10 London Wall, 1788-94. **J. & Charles,** 58 and 59 New Bond St., 1830.

Turnham, Rd., London; watch, 1785.

Turpin, Benj., 62 Banner St., 1835-40; his widow Susanah afterwards carried on the business for some years and then his two sons, **John** and **Henry,** trading as "Turpin Brothers," manufactured full plate watches; some marked "Railway Timekeeper" were exported to America. The business lapsed about 1885.

Turton. & Walbancke, 8 Fore St., 1793. **Nath.,** Manchester 1818.

Turvee, Jarrett, C.C. 1688.

Tussingham, Jno., apprenticed 1682 to Richd. Prince, C.C.

Tutst, Edward, 10 Fenchurch St.; livery C.C. 1766; master 1786; bracket clock, enamel dial, case very similar to Elliott's bracket clock shown on p. 561, Wetherfield collection; 1760-94.

Tuttell, Thomas, C.C. 1695; pocket sun-dial and "Perpetuall Almanacke," about 1700.

Twell, Geo., apprenticed 1685 to Wm. Hawkins, C.C.

Twells, Wm., High St., Birmingham, 1770.

Twhing, James, C.C. 1688.

Twycross. Stephen, Gough Sq., 1793. **Stephen, & Son,** 8 Haymarket, 1800-4; 13 Newcastle St., 1817.

Twyford. Josiah, Manchester, 1765. **Robert,** 40 Strand, hon. f. C.C. 1781; 1770-82. **Wm.,** Manchester, 1775. **John,** Bank Top, Manchester, died 1789. **Robert, & Co.,** 9 Finch Lane, Cornhill, 1790; 10 Salisbury St., Strand, 1800-10. **Josiah,** 35 Deansgate, Manchester, 1794. **William,** 88 Bank Top, Manchester, 1794. **R.,** 20 Salisbury St., Strand, 1815-19. **Josiah,** Manchester, 1818.

Tyas. W. T., Thavies Inn, Holborn, 1820-35. **J. A.,** watch-case maker, 77 Rahere St., 1835.

Tyler. Jno., apprenticed 1667 to Jno. Matchett, C.C. **George,** Pope's Head Alley; apprenticed to Robt. Dingley, 1691, C.C.; bracket clock in Japanese tortoiseshell case, about 1715; bracket clock in walnut case, pull repeating quarters on six bells, about 1720, Wetherfield collection; clock-watch, 1735. **Richd.,** Wallingford, about 1740. **Jas. Hy.,** Northampton St., 1835. **C.,** 15 Holywell St., Strand; watch paper, Ponsonby collection, with portrait of the Queen, and around it "Victoria the First, Queen of England," about 1840.

Tymms. Jno., apprenticed 1666 to Nich. Tomlins, C.C. **A.,** 6 Kennington Lane, 1820. **M.,** 5 Kennington Lane, 1820.

Tyrer. Thomas, Red Lion St., Clerken-well, patented in 1782 (No. 1,311) the duplex escapement. His specification says, "Horizontal seapement for a watch to act with two wheels." **Jas. Hy.,** 32 North-ampton St., Clerkenwell, 1806-30. **Jas.,** 65 Red Lion St., 1842.

Tyson, Hy., Egremont, 1833.

Udall. Thos., 8 Flower-du-luce Court, 1793. **J.,** 5 Great New St., Shoe Lane, 1819-22.

Uffington, Jno., 53 Bunhill Row, 1793.

Ullmeyer, Christoph., Augsburg; clock, Green Vaulted Chambers, Dresden, about 1570.

Ulph, Thos., Stalham, 1840.

Ulrich, John Gottleib, of many addresses; 26 Nicholas Lane, in 1835; he devised and patented several methods of compensating chronometers, 1830-74.

Underhill; Cave, admitted C.C. 1655.

Underwood. Wm., London; clock, about 1720. **John,** 36 Noble St., Cheapside, 1754-75. **John, & Sons,** Foster Lane, 1758-63. **Robt.,** 3 Falcon St., 1769-1810. **Cæsar,** 3 Panton St., 1798-1800; 9 Ranelagh St., Pimlico, 1820.

Uneman, John & William, Dutch clock-makers in England (see p. 43). 1368.

Unwin. Wm., Newark, 1776-1804, after-wards Unwin & Holt. **Edward,** 30 Upper Lisson St., Paddington, 1820.

Upjohn. Richd., Exon.; long-case clock, about 1730. **Wm.,** Exon.; watch, silver dial, raised figures, h.m., 1741. **James,** Threadneedle St., 1760-63; Lombard St., 1779; watch in gold and enamelled cases, S.K.M., h.m., 1778. **James, & Wirgman,** 18 Red Lion St., Clerkenwell, 1769-81; **Jas., & Co.,** 1794. **Peter,** Bideford; watch, 1780. **Peter,** 11 Red Lion St., 1783-1835. **Francis,** 1 Bridgewater Sq., livery C.C. 1786; suggested distinctive marks on foreign watches, 1780-87. —, Brentford ; watch, 1810. **W. J.**, 11 St John's Sq., 1815-20. **J. & T.**, 5 Chandos St., Covent Garden, 1835. **& Bright**, 5 King William St., Strand, well-known makers for some years from 1840.

Upton. Nat., apprenticed 1674 to Jno. Nash, C.C. **Rich.**, London ; watch, about 1755.

Urick, Valentine, Reading, U.S.A., 1760.

Urseau. Nicholas, entry of a payment to him as a clockmaker in 1553, and on New Year's Day, 1556, he presented a clock to Queen Elizabeth. **Nicholas**, probably a son of the preceding, clockmaker to Queen Elizabeth, 1572-90.

Usher, Joseph (Usher & Cole), a clever horologist ; died 1903, aged 71.

Usherwood, William, 19 Strand, 1830.

Uytemveer, C., Rotterdam ; watch, about 1705.

Vaillant à Paris ; clock, at Nether Swell Manor, about 1780.

Vale. Samuel, Coventry, 1747. **Howlett, & Carr**, Coventry, 1754-90 ; watch, "Vale & Howlett, London," 1782. **Wm.**, 6 Colmore Row, Birmingham, 1770 ; see also Gimblet. **Wm.**, 12 Bunhill Row ; a good maker, mentioned by Earnshaw, 1776-94. **& Kenyon**, about 1780. **& Rotherham**, Coventry (R. K. Rotherham apprenticed to Vale, Howlett, & Carr), 1790-1840. **William**, musical clockmaker, 32 Paul St., Finsbury, 1816-40.

Valentine. Bart., London ; watch, 1800. **Chas. D. F.**, livery C.C. 1810.

Valeran, —, hexagonal table clock, Wallace collection, stamped on the bottom " E. Valeran, Paris," with the Royal Crown of France and fleur-de-lys, about 1600. " **Valére**, Paris " ; watch, 1789.

Vallance, Thos., 5 Wilderness Row, 1820.

Valleran, Fleurent, Paris, 1544 (see p. **304**).

Vallete, Sd., **& Fils**, Geneva ; watch, about 1785.

Vallier, Jean, Lyons ; in the Pierpont Morgan collection is a triangular watch, on one side portrait of Charles V. and on another the arms of Besançon, with the date 1564 ; fine astronomical watch, uncased, by him, B.M., about 1610 ; watch, Vienna Treasury, case in the form of a star, mounted in brass and silver, covered on both sides with rock crystal, about 1605.

Vallin, —. In the Pierpont Morgan collection is a very small oval watch, signed " I. Vallin," which seems to be late sixteenth century work. On the back is a representation of St George and the Dragon in raised enamel work, and around the band of the case the inscription " Honi soit que mal y pense " ; this gem was formerly in the Spitzer collection, and at the dispersal by auction fetched £860. Brass clock, B.M., signed " N. Vallin, 1600 " ; with arms of Viscount Montagu, who died 1629 ; probably from Courdray House, Sussex ; modern enamel dial, named " John Monkhouse, London " (see also p. **96**).

Van Aleurs, H., Amsterdam ; watch, about 1775.

Van Blade, Laurens, Hague ; watch, about 1780.

Vanbroff, Jas., watch, Soltykoff collection, about 1605 (see p. **124**).

Van Ceule, J., le jeune, Hague ; repeating watch, Pierpont Morgan collection, about 1750.

Van Ceulen. John, Hague ; clock on Huygens' plan (see p. **242**). about 1660 ; clock-watch, Schloss collection, about 1700 (see p. **177**). a watch with large balance and primitive arrangement of spring, in the Pierpont Morgan collection, dating from about 1680 ; bears the signature, " Jo. Gannes Van Ceulen fecit Hagae." **Phillippus**, Hague ; watch, B.M., the case enamelled by J. L. Durant, about 1690.

Vanden Bergh, A., large late seventeenth century Dutch clock, in silver filigree case, S.K.M. ; movement signed " Adriaen Vanden Bergh fecit, Hague " ; case signed " J. H. C. Breghtel."

Vandenburg, J., 8 Owen's Row, 1830.

Vanderwood, —, long-case clock, about 1780, inscribed " Wm. Vanderwood, London."

Vanenhove, —, Amsterdam ; enamel watch, about 1730.

Vanham, Leonard, Addle St., 1737-40.

Vanlone, Matt., brother C.C. 1692.

Van Meiors, Otto, Amsterdam, 1780.

Vans. Pat., apprenticed 1672 to Joseph Knibb, C.C. **Chas.**, apprenticed 1682 to Edwd. Norris, C.C.

Vanscolina. Jere., apprenticed to Wm. Ericke ; turned over to Francis Atkins ; C.C. 1776. **Richard**, 70 Charlotte Ter., New Cut, 1842.

Vantrollier, James, one of the first assistants C.C. 1630 ; watch of an earlier date, Nelthropp collection.

Van Voost ; watch, about 1730, inscribed " Hendrick Van Voost in de Rye."

Vardon, Samuel & Thomas, 29 Frith St., Soho, 1783-94.

Varley, Wm., 1763.

Varnish, Jno., Rochdale, 1770.

Vaslet, Andrew, C.C. 1717.

Vaucanson, —, born at Grenoble, 1709 ; constructor of automatic movements.

Vaucher. Frères, Swiss watch, 1780 ; another watch, inscribed " Presented by Napoleon I. to Thalma," now at the museum of the " Sons of the Revolution," New York. **Fritz**, 27 Gerrard St., Soho, 1842.

Vauchez, —, Paris, 1790 (see p. **156**).

Vaughan. Robt., apprenticed 1655 to Jno. Broome, C.C. **Geo.**, Pontypool ; clock, about 1760 (see p. **363**). **Geo.**, Greville St., Hatton Garden, 1816-28.

Vauguion, Daniel, Spring Gardens, 1790-93.

Vauquer, Robt., Blois ; a celebrated painter in enamel of watch cases ; died 1670.

Vautier, —, calendar watch, Garnier collection, about 1600, signed " Loys Vautier, Blois."

Vautrollier, see Vantrollier.

Vautyer, —, Blois ; handsome octagonal watch, B.M., case decorated with filigree work and jewels, 1620.

Vecue, Thomas, C.C. 1632.

Veigneur, —, Geneva ; watch, 1775.

Venault, —, Paris ; watch, 1790.

Verback, Wm., apprenticed C.C. 1681.

Vere, John Henry, 48 Lombard St., 1769.

Vergo, —; Thiout credits him with the invention of a fusee to wind both ways, see Moore, Thos.

Verité, —, Paris, 1820-30.

Vermculen, A., Amsterdam, about 1750.

Vermeule, Nicholas, Rotterdam ; pendulum watch, about 1714 ; another watch, about 1732, signed " Nicolas Vermeule Amsterdam."

Verneuil. Jne., Paris ; clock, about 1780. —, Dijon, about 1800.

Vernon. Christopher, in "ye Great Turnstyle, Holborne " ; C.C. 1638 ; lantern clocks, about 1650. **Samuel**, C.C. 1649, master 1679. —, C.C. 1685. **Thos.**, watch, *repoussé* case, about 1710 ; bracket clock, about 1740 (see p. **368**).; bracket clock, inscribed " Vernon, London," about 1725, plays four tunes on twelve bells, curious motive force consisting of heavy straight springs outside of back plate. **Thos.**, Ludlow, 1780. **& Eden**, Liverpool ; watch, 1789.

Verow, Jno., Hinckley ; watch, with curiously shaped fluted pillars, about 1795.

Vesey, Chris., apprenticed 1692 to Jno. Sowter, C.C.

Vesper. J., Fore St., Limehouse, 1820. **T. & W.**, 4 Grosvenor Pl., Commercial Rd., 1835-42.

Vevers, Richard, 2 Cateaton St., 1825-30.

Veyrin, —, Paris, 1775-92.

Vial, Charles, 1685. " Silver pendulum watch made by Charles Vial, with a tortoise-shell case inlaid " (*Lond. Gaz.*, Jan. 17-20, 1697).

Vicary, Geo., apprenticed 1682 to Thos. Brafield, C.C.

Vick. Richard, in the Strand ; C.C. 1702, master 1729 ; repeating watch, inscribed " Richard Vick, watchmaker to his late Majesty " ; another, about 1740 or 1750. **Thos.**, London ; about 1780.

Vickerman, Thos., " Maiden Lane, opposite Goldsmiths' Hall, Cheapside," card, Ponsonby collection, about 1760.

Vidal, A., St Giroud ; fine repeating watch, about 1800, Lt.-Col. L. D. Mackinnon.

Viel. Richd., apprenticed 1651 to Dan Fletcher, C.C. **Chas.**, apprenticed 1678 to Richd. Jarrett ; C.C. 1686. **George**, 29 King St., Soho, 1842.

Viet. Mr Alfred Wood has an early seventeenth century striking and alarm watch, inscribed " Jean Viet, Aorlean " ; there are two sets of figures, and between the X and the II of the outer set are the words " Solem audet dicere falsum." **Paul**, Blois ; fine watch by him, B.M., about 1635, case beautifully painted in enamel by Henry Toutin. **Claude**, C.C. 1698 ; his daughter Marianne was bound apprentice to him in 1715 ; gold watch, inscribed " C. Viet, London, watchmaker to Her Majesty,' h.m., 1729, outer case engraved, see also Mitchell & Viet.

Vievar, Geo., apprenticed 1693 to Dan Lecount, C.C.

Vieyres, Anthony, 40 Pall Mall, 1840-43 ; he was one of the directors of the ill-starred British Watch Company.

Viger, —, musical clock, Wallace collection, signed " Viger à Paris," about 1740.

Vigne. James, 2 Strand, 1770-94 ; hon. f. C.C. 1781. **Peter**, Green St., Bath, 1798-1800. **& Lautier**, 19 Union St., 1809. **Benj. Lautier**, Bridge St., 1819-50 ; his widow carried on the business for a short time at 4 Orange Grove till 1852, when it was taken over by George Wadham, a sound horologist ; he removed to Bridge St., and afterwards to Milson St., having secured a leading position in the city ; Mr J. Stopford Taylor tells me of a pocket chronometer by Vigne & Lautier, bought in Bombay, where he also purchased a fine clock in lancet case by B. Lautier.

Vigniaux, P., Toulouse, 1788.

Vilbar, —, Paris ; horloger de la Reine, 1787.

Villiscun, Stephen, Church Alley, Basinghall St., 1780-85.

Vincent. **Wm.**, York, 1770. **Chas.**, London ; watch, 1820. **John**, 157 Drury Lane, 1840-42.

Vinco, Dan, apprenticed 1691 to Richd. Baker, C.C.

Vine. Jas., 2 Charing Cross, 1790-94. **James**, 5 Staining Lane, 1825.

Viner. Charles Edward, 151 New Bond St. and Royal Exchange, 1776-1820 ; card, B.M. ; 19 Sackville St., 1840-42 ; livery C.C. 1819. **Charles Edward, & Hopkins**, 8 Sweeting's Alley, 1829 ; also 235 Regent St., 1829-42 ; Mr Thos. Boynton has a fine regulator by "Viner, 235 Regent St., London," which winds at the side without opening the door, about 1835.

Vines. James, C.C. 1708. **Joseph**, Newbury, Berks ; curious astronomical clock, 1836.

Vipont, Jno., apprenticed 1682 to Hy. Morgan, C.C.

Virgoe, Thomas, C.C. 1682.

Visbach, —, spring clock, G.M., inscribed "Pieter Visbach, fecit Hague met privilege," about 1700.

Visconti, G., clock at Pavia, about 1410.

Vise, see Vyse.

Vitrolle, —, fine bracket clock, signed "Vitrolle à Paris," about 1650.

Vizier, Barnaby, Dublin, 1790.

Voight. Henry, Philadelphia, 1775-93 ; then **Sebastin** ; then **Thos**.

Voght (or Vogt), Auty, 26 Upper Cleveland St., 1830-35.

Vogt. (& Co.), 35 Wigmore St., 1830). **Chas. & Fredk.**, 35 Wigmore St., 1836-42.

Voisin, A., l'aîné, Rue Hyacinthe, Paris ; garde visiteur in 1769. **Le jeune**, Rue Dauphine, Paris, 1769.

Vokins, Jno., Newtown ; long-case clock, centre seconds, dead beat, about 1800.

Voland, Elias, C.C. 1632 ; Edward Ambrose apprenticed to him in 1634.

Volk, P., 38 Goodge St., 1835-40.

Vossière, Thomas, C.C. 1698.

Votter, Peter, Vienna ; watch, 1764, Mr H. K. Heinz.

Voughan. Edward, C.C. 1715. **Daniel**, Charing Cross, 1775. **George**, 11 Granville St., Hatton Garden, 1820.

Voyce. Gamaliel, apprenticed 1687 to Sarah Payne ; C.C. 1694 ; arch-top ebony bracket clock, pull quarters, original rise and fall, about 1710. **Richd.**, apprenticed 1693 to Geo. Ethrington, C.C.

Vrythoff, Jas., Berns, Hague ; enamel watch, about 1740 (see p. **152**).

Vrytroft, L., Hague ; clock, about 1790.

Vuicar, J. B., Zug ; small round watch, silver dial, about 1610.

Vuille. Alexander, Baltimore, 1766. **Brothers**, 2 Easton St., Spitalfields, 1840-42.

Vulliamy. Justin, carried on business at Pall Mall, in partnership with Benjamin Gray, whose daughter he married ; 1730-75. **Benjamin**, Pall Mall, son of Justin, and father of Benjamin Lewis ; hon. f. C.C. 1781 ; 1775-1820. **Benjamin Lewis**, 68 Pall Mall, an eminent maker (see p. **282**). 1810-54. **& Son**, 76 Pall Mall, 1793-1820.

Vuolf, J. C. ; skull watch in the B.M., 1600.

Vyse. Wisbech : Wm., 1730 ; **Jno.**, 1760.

Wade. Henry, apprenticed to William Webster, and turned over to John Rainsford ; C.C. 1728. **Jos.**, Clerkenwell Close, 1793.

Waddy, Jno., London, 1730.

Wady. Jno., London ; bracket clock in japanned case, about 1740. **James**, New-

port, U.S.A., 1750-55.

Wagdon, Stephen, C.C. 1724.

Waggitt. Michael, Richmond, Yorks., 1753. **Charles**, York, f., 1818. **Michael**, York, 1822.

Wagner. Johan Heinrich, à Pirna ; square table clock, about 1650. **E. M.**, Berne ; the Hon. Gerald Ponsonby has a watch by him, pendulum vibrating under dial, very fine painting on enamel over balance-cock, about 1760. **J.**, born 1800, settled in Paris 1821 ; died 1875.

Wagstaff. Edwd., apprenticed 1650 to Edward East, C.C. **Thomas**, 33 Gracechurch St., 1766-94 ; long plain mahogany case clock in the Kasan Cathedral, St Petersburg ; bracket clock playing four tunes at the hour, black wood case ; in the Pierpont Morgan collection is a repeating watch in silver pierced cases, the thumb piece or opener of the outer case being a diamond ; there are a number of long-case clocks by him in America, generally in the possession of Quakers and their descendants ; I learn from Dr Walter Mendelson of New York that Wagstaff was a Quaker, and members of the Society of Friends, when visiting London, were accustomed to lodge at Wagstaff's house and on their return frequently took one of his clocks with them ; watch, h.m., 1770, Evan Roberts collection, with cap and two-train wheels of silver. **James**, 10 Brown's Lane, Spitalfields, 1835-42.

Waight, Wm., Birmingham ; watch, 1792.

Wain, Wm., Burslem, 1803.

Waine, —, Queen St., 1774.

Wainwright. John, C.C. 1679. **Jno.**, Manchester, 1765.

Wait, Jno., & Son, Gun Dock, Wapping, 1765-72.

Waithman, Anthony, Leeds, 1830.

Wakefield. Wm., Lancaster, 1782, f. ; **Timothy**, 1811, f. **Robt.**, Tanfield, Durham, 1820. **John**, 3 South St., Berkeley St., 1835-42. **T.**, 5 Smith St., Northampton Sq., 1835.

Wakelin & Taylor, Panton St., 1788-94. **& Garrard**, Panton St., 1800-5.

Waker (Walker?), Peter, C.C. 1663.

Waklin, —, lantern clock, about 1700.

Waldegrave, Thos., apprenticed 1654 to Thos. Belson, C.C.

Waldoe, John, C.C. 1677.

Waldron, John, 38 Cornhill, 1760-82 ; watch, gold case, *repoussé*, about 1770.

Waldvogel, Anthony, 82 Ratcliff Highway, 1835-40.

Wale, Andrew, apprenticed 1664 to Rich. Ricord, C.C.

Walford. Thos., C.C. 1690. **John**, C.C. 1717. **J. G.**, Banbury, 1830.

Walkden, Thomas, apprenticed 1682 to Dorcas Bouquet, C.C. 1694.

Walker. Jas., C.C. 1632 ; lantern clock, inscribed "James Walker in Lowthbery, fecit." **Peter**, apprenticed 1681 to Andrew Savory, C.C. ; lacquered long-case clock, about 1730. **George**, C.C. 1683. **Jonadab**, C.C. 1687. **John**, Fleet St., and afterwards at the White Horse and Bell, near Cheapside Conduit ; C.C. 1717 ; inventor of a lamp clock, 1710-30. **Jonah**, apprenticed to Langley Bradley ; C.C. 1734. **Jno.**, Newcastle-on-Tyne, 1770. In the Czar of Russia's collection at the Winter Palace, St Petersburg, are two watches signed "Sam Walker London" in cases of greyish-brown agate with plain gold mounts ; they both appear to date from about 1760 and are suspended from chatelaines. **Ezekiel**,

Lynn, 1770-1804 ; wrote an article in *Nicholson's Journal* on longitude and the use of chronometers. **Jno.**, watch-case maker, York, f., 1772. **Allen**, London ; watch, Schloss collection, handsome *repoussé à jour* outer case, 1783. **Joseph**, 1 Warwick Court, Holborn, 1790-94. **Wm.**, 38 Fetter Lane, 1790-94. **John**, Newcastle-on-Tyne, 1795. **Robert**, Montrose ; watch, 1795. **R.**, London ; watch, 1800. **Jos.**, Nantwich, 1800. **Wm.**, Loughborough ; watch, 1804. **D., & Son**, 49 Red Lion St., Clerkenwell, 1806-16 ; 46 Clerkenwell Close, 1820, see Harlow. **Chas.**, Coventry, 1815. **Thomas**, 17 Castle St., Oxford St., 1815 ; **Thos., & Son**, same address, 1820-30. **John**, 29 Gloucester St., Queen's Sq., 1816. **J.**, musical watchmaker, 7 Nassau St., Soho, 1820. **Robert**, York, f., 1820. **Geo.**, Hull, 1822. **E.**, watch-case maker, 46 Whiskin St., 1835. **& Blundell**, 4 Red Lion St., Clerkenwell, 1835-42. **Edwd.**, 55 Red Lion St., 1839-42. **Jno.**, 48 Princes St., Leicester Sq., 1840 ; afterwards at 68 Cornhill ; died 1880. **William**, Standish St., Liverpool, patented (1841, No. 8,997) a wheel for lever escapement, in which the spaces between the teeth were portions of circles, so as to dispense with the necessity of banking pins.

Wall. Jno., apprenticed 1676 to Thos. Davis, C.C. **B.**, Richmond, 1800. **& Westlake**, Chatham ; watch, 1805. **Jno., & Co.**, Coventry, 1810. **Wm.**, Wandsworth ; patented an escapement in 1817 (No. 4,097). **& Alney**, New Bedford, Mass., 1820-23.

Wallace. Blackett, Brampton, 1760. **Michael**, Chester-le-Street, 1770. **Hy.**, Royal Exchange, 1775. **Thos.**, Brampton, 1780-1810.

Wallen, Wm., Henley ; watch, 1725.

Waller. Richard, watch, the time shown on a semicircular dial by the sun at day and the moon at night, said to have belonged to William of Orange ; another, showing regulator on dial, about 1740. **J.**, 17 Shoreditch, 1790.

Walley, Sam., Manchester, 1770.

Wallington, Sam., apprenticed 1689 to Jno. Shaw, C.C.

Wallis. William, C.C. 1715. **Peter**, Fleet St., 1737-40. **Henry**, Red Lion St., 1765-68. **Jacob**, London ; clock, about 1780. **Jno.**, 14 Skinner St., Bishopsgate, 1825-40.

Wallitt, Richard, C.C. 1693.

Walloon, H., London ; watch, 1812.

Walmsley, Alex., London, f. of Lancaster, 1779.

Walsh, Arthur Paul, a celebrated watch and chronometer maker and springer ; apprenticed to T. F. Cooper ; carried on business as a tool dealer, at Frith St., Soho, in partnership with Robert Oliphant, and afterwards settled in George St., Euston Rd. ; born 1815, died 1893.

Walter, Nicholas, oval watch in the B.M., about 1620 ; subscribed to incorporation of C.C. 1630.

Walters. Jno., apprenticed 1638 to Thos. Howse ; C.C. 1645 **John**, London ; bracket clock, about 1750, strikes once at the hour, plays a tune every three hours, Mr J. Major.

Walthall, Jno., apprenticed 1684 to Wm. Coward, C.C.

Walton, J., London ; watch, 1807. **Christopher**, 24 Ludgate St., 1823-35.

Wanfield, Edmd., apprenticed 1655 to Nich. Coxeter, C.C.

Wanford, Jno., apprenticed 1686 to Ed.

Whitfield, C.C.

Wansey, Hy., apprenticed 1662 to Jno. Hiccock, C.C.

Warburton. William, C.C. 1693. **Jno.**, Liverpool, 1818.

Ward. Thos., C.C. 1632. **Edwd.**, C.C. 1638. **Anthony**, Truro; long-case clock, about 1700. **Anthony**, New York, f., 1724-50; then **John. John**, New St., C.C. 1731. **Edward**, C.C. 1731. **Joseph**, f. of New York, 1735. **Robert**, 19. Abchurch Lane, Cannon St., 1762-85. **W. John**, Barbican; livery C.C. 1766; a tiny pair case gold watch, diameter of a sixpence, nearly a ball, inscribed "W. J. Ward, London," about 1780. **Richard**, Winchester; long-case clock, about 1770. **Benjamin**, London Rd., Southwark; fine bracket clock, about 1770. **Henry**, Blandford, a well-known clockmaker, from about 1775 to 1820; in 1814 the Society of Arts awarded him a silver medal and five guineas for equation work for clocks. **Benjamin**, London Rd., Southwark, 1780; 45 Upper Moorfields, 1790-1808. **Richard**, Liverpool, 1780. **Richard**, 18 Tower St., 1790-94. **John**, 39 Greek St., 1790-94. **Robert**, musical clockmaker, 20 Plumtree St., Bloomsbury, 1790. **Jas.**, Birmingham; watch, 1790. **John**, 9 Fore St., master C.C. 1797. **Nathan**, Fryebury (Maine?), 1801. **Isaac**, Philadelphia, 1811; then **Jehu. Rich.**, 27 Banner St., 1826-42. **Henry**, York, f., 1830. **Richard**, Salem Bridge, 1832-40. **Edwd.**, Grimsby; on his tomb in Grimsby Parish Churchyard is the following:—

Sacred to the memory of Edward Ward, who died
12th December, 1847, aged 54 years.

" Here lies one who strove to equal time,
A task too hard, power too sublime;
Time stop't his motion, o'er threw his balance-
wheel,
Wore off his pivots, though made of hardened
steel;
Broke all his springs, the verge of life decayed,
And now he is as though he'd ne'er been made;
Not for the want of oiling, that he tried,
If that had done, he ne'er had died."

Warden. Wm., apprenticed 1666 to Thos. Loomes, C.C. **Thomas**, 1691, see Strachan. **Robt.**, London; watch, 1790.

Wardlow, Hy., Liverpool, 1833.

Ware, Robert, C.C. 1701.

Wareham, John, 18 Davies St., Berkeley Sq., 1816-23.

Wareing, Jas., Liverpool, 1818.

Warfield, Alexander, C.C. 1692.

Warmingham, Andrew, Manchester, 1775.

Warne. Nich., apprenticed 1680 to Hy. Adeane, C.C. **Robt.**, apprenticed 1693 to Sam Stevens, C.C. **James**, 7 Queen St., Cheapside, 1760-85; repeating watch, Pierpont Morgan collection.

Warner. Wm., C.C., about 1675. **John**, Golden Anchor, near Temple Bar, C.C. 1682-92. **John**, Temple Bar; apprenticed to Wm. Warner 1689; C.C. 1696. **Jno.**, Draycott; made the church clock at Chipping Campden (Gloucestershire), for £8, 1695. **Thos.**, Chipping Campden; descendant of the foregoing, substituted a dead-beat escapement, about 1820. **John**, 8 Trinity Row, Islington, 1835.

Warnes, Robert, 2 Leicester Sq., 1822-25.

Warre, W. H., Skinner St., Snow Hill; free of C.C. by redemption 1857; assistant 1863; died 1866, leaving £100 to the Company.

Warren. Thos., apprenticed 1667 to Ben Bell, C.C. **Richard**, C.C. 1668. **Jno.**, apprenticed 1693 to Richd. Medhurst, C.C. **—**, Canterbury, 1820-40.

Warrington, John, Philadelphia, 1811.

Warswick, Thos., Lancaster, 1775.

Warwick. Jas., apprenticed 1656 to Ed. Gilpin, C.C. **Wm.**, 88 London Wall, 1793. **Jas.**, Newcastle Place; watch, h.m., 1829.

Washborn, John, 30-hour clock, about 1710, Mr W. P. W. Phillimore. Several generations of Washborns clocknakers of Gloucester; long-case clock by Nat. Washbourne, Gloucester, about 1750.

Washbourn. Thomas, Queen Sq., Bartholomew Close, 1750-60. **Geo.**, Gloucester; watch, 1770.

Washington, Mark, apprenticed 1687 to Rich. Brown, C.C.

Wasse, Thos., apprenticed C.C. 1682.

Wassell, J., 9 Picket St., Strand, 1830.

Wastnesse, Francis. apprenticed 1671 to Jno. Trippett, C.C.

Waterfall, W. & J., Coventry, 1814.

Waterman, Wm., apprenticed 1682 to Amos Winch, C.C.

Waters. John, C.C. 1646; to him in 1687 was apprenticed the elder Jno. Ellicott. **John**, C.C. 1683. **Jonathan**, apprenticed 1686 to Ed. Hine, C.C. **Thomas**, C.C. 1731. **John**, 4 Cornhill, 1775.

Watford, Jno., C.C. In 1729 Jas. Freeman was apprenticed to him.

Watkin, Owen, Llanrwst; watch, 1791.

Watkins. Joseph, 21 Great Warner St., Coldbath Fields, 1800-19; he attested the value of Earnshaw's improvements in 1804. **John**, 9 Giltspur St., Smithfield; received £33 from Society of Arts for improvement in the spring detent escapement, 1804; livery C.C. 1820; Great Sutton St., 1838. **—**, 126 Drury Lane, 1820.

Watson. Thos., apprenticed 1662 to Jno. Hillersden. **Robt.**, apprenticed 1689 to Jno. Warner, C.C. **William**, C.C. 1691; long-case clock, chiming quarter and half hours, about 1720; name-plate inscribed " William Watson, Angel Alley in Leadenhall Street." **Samuel**, Coventry, admitted C.C. 1692; inventor and maker of a curious piece of clockwork; in 1682 is mentioned a payment of £215 for a clock he sold to his late Majesty, Charles I.; the clock " showes the rising and setting of the sun and many other motions " (*Lond. Gaz.*, Sept. 4-8, 1690). Very small bracket clock in black case, about 1710, inscribed " Samuel Watson, London." " Lost the 15th Instant on Cheshunt Common, a gold watch in a black Shagreen case with Gold Studs, tyed with a black Taffaty Ribon to a Steel Hooke, Engraven on the Inside Samuel Watson. Whoever gives notice of the same to Mr Howell at the Penny Post Office in St Martin's Lane, Westminster, shall have a Guinea Reward " (*Lond. Gaz.*, Oct. 18, 1687). Under the head of Celestial Motions, Derham speaks of an elaborate and curious piece by Mr Watson; in the Wetherfield collection is an 8-day bracket quarter clock, chiming on three bells, by Samuel Watson, London, dating from about 1700. **Walter**, C.C. 1720; Hatton, in 1773, mentions the astronomical or complicated work of Mr Watson as being rare. **John**, Michael's Alley, Cornhill, apprenticed to John Hacker; C.C. 1744-85. **Henry**, Blackburn, 1760. **Thos.**, Blackburn, 1770. **Jno.**, Kirby Moorside, 1770. **Jno.**, Pocklington, 1770. **Wm.**, Blackburn, 1780. **Wm.**, Glasgow, 1785. **Thomas**, 23 Aldersgate St., 1785-94. **James**, 24 Arundel St., Strand, 1788-1805. **Wm.**, 190 Strand, 1793-1805. **Wm.**, York, f., 1815. **W.**, 67 Red Lion St., Clerkenwell, 1820. **Edward**, 6 King St., Cheapside, 1820-42; livery C.C. 1820. **Christopher**,

York, f., 182?. **Francis**, Beverley, 1822. **& Bell**, York, 1833. **Wm.**, 25 North Audley St., 1842.

Wattes, John, C.C. 1664.

Watts. Richard, C.C. 1680. " Lost the 22nd Inst. out of a Gentleman's Pocket, a Silver Pendulum Watch, with the name Rich. Watts. Whoever brings it to Charles Ferrers at the Chirurgeons Arms in Queen Street, London, shall have 20s. Reward " (*Lond. Gaz.*, Aug. 30, 1688). **Thos.**, apprenticed 1681 to Ed. Stanton, C.C. **Brounker**, apprenticed to Joseph Knibb, 1684; C.C. 1693; a repeating watch by him in the Guildhall Museum, engraved cap, gold dial, well engraved and pierced inner case; Mr Eden Dickson has a month clock by him; Mr Thos. Boynton has an 8-day long-case clock of his make; watch, h.m., 1720, Mr William Ranken; the Rev. A. F. Sutton has a long-case clock, signed " Brounker Watts & Co.," about 1720. " Lost, on the 21st instant, in Gutter Lane, Cheapside, a Silver Watch with Tortoiseshell Out-case, with a Lion Rampant and 3 oaken leaves for the coat, engraven on the Backside, made by Bro. Watts; the movements are the hours, minutes, and seconds. Whoever brings it to the sign of the Goldsmiths' Hall in Gutter Lane, or to Bro. Watts in Fleet Street, shall have a Guinea reward " (*Lond. Gaz.*, April 27-30, 1696). **Walter**, apprenticed 1688 to Chas. Halstead, C.C. **John**, C.C. 1712. **James**, C.C. 1720. **Thos.**, Lavenham; long-case clock, about 1730. **Thos.**, St Edmunds Bury, 1760. **Robert**, Stamford, 1760. **Chas.**, Frome, 1770. **William**, 8 Cripplegate Buildings, 1770; 8 Fore St., 1775. **Wm.**, Wotton-under-Edge; watch, 1779.

Waugh, Wm., Liverpool, 1818.

Wawen, Gervas, apprenticed 1689 to Richd. Conyers, C.C.

Way. Jno., apprenticed 1659 to Thos. Taylor, C.C. **Jas.**, apprenticed 1681 to Dan Lecount, C.C.

Wayland, Henry, Stratford, Essex; apprenticed to Wm. Bushman, 1820.

Waylett. Jas., 7 Mark Lane, 1793. **John**, 9 Ball Alley, Lombard St., 1795-1810.

Waynd, Richard, York, f., 1667.

Weadon, William, C.C. 1695.

Weakman, William, C.C. 1661.

Weare, Robt., Argyle St., Birkenhead. In 1846 he patented (No. 11,776) electric timekeepers.

Weatherhead, Leonard, Kirby Lonsdale; died 1774.

Weatherhilt, S., Liverpool; watch, about 1760.

Weatherley. Thos., Berwick, 1775. **& Roberts**, 9 Poultry, 1800-5. **& Son**, 9 Poultry, 1810-23.

Weatherly, David, Philadelphia, 1811.

Weatherston, Jno., Newcastle-on-Tyne, 1770.

Weaver. Cuthbert, C.C. 1682. **Simon**, apprenticed 1684 to Jas. Wightman, C.C. **Geo.**, Fetter Lane; C.C. 1730.

Webb. Isaac, apprenticed 1650 to Richard Masterton; C.C. 1660. **Thos.**; in 1672 Joana Deacle was apprenticed to Eliza, widow of Thos. Webb, C.C. **Edward**, Chewstoke; lantern clock, dated 1681; Mr G. M. Bick has a long-case clock, " Edward Webb Chewstoke 1688," lantern movement, plays three tunes on eight bells, surmounting them is one larger bell. **Matt.**, Chewstoke; lantern clock, 1688. **Dan**, apprenticed 1692 to Peter Southworth, C.C. **Francis**, Watlington, Oxon.; hood clock, about 1710, Mr W.

Walden ; long-case clock, about 1730. **Charles**, Cheapside, 1737-40. **Peter**, 28 Throgmorton St., 1753-68. **Benjamin**, "maker to His Majesty," 21 St John Sq., 1778-90 ; hon. f. C.C. 1787 ; 3 Red Lion St., 1806-10 ; watch, with compass in dial, inscribed "By the King's Patent" ; this appears to have been patented by Hy. Peckham in 1798. **Wm.**, London ; watch, about 1780. **Arthur**, 86 Portland St., 1780-94. **Robert**, 14 Berkeley St., St John Sq., 1815-19. **Edward**, 245 Tottenham Court Rd., 1816-20. **Wm., & Co.**, 19 Wilderness Row, 1816-20. **J.**, Seward St., 1820. **William**, 2 Northampton Ter., City Rd., 1840 : afterwards at Pullen's Row, Islington ; a noted watch and chronometer maker ; died 1887, aged 78.

Webber, W., Woolwich, 1817.

Webster. Many generations of this family have carried on business in the city of London from 1675. **Robert**, brother C.C. 1675 ; watch, G.M. ; in 1688 Sarah Webster was apprenticed to Robt. Webster, her father, C.C. **John**, apprenticed 1676 to Thos. Tompion ; C.C. 1695, see Penny, R. **Thos.**, Dundee ; "Cnocksmith," 1689. **George**, C.C. 1703. **Henry**, C.C. 1709. **Thomas**, C.C. 1709. **William** ; from the books of the C.C. he appears to have been apprenticed to Jno. Barnett and to have been free in 1710, though the following extract from the *Lond. Gaz.*, from Nov. 24-28, 1713, seems to refer to him : "On the 20th Instant, Mr Tompion, noted for making of all Sorts of the best Clocks and Watches, departed this Life : This is to certify all Persons of whatever Quality or Distinction that William Webster, at the Dial and Three Crowns in Exchange Alley, London, served his apprenticeship, and served as a Journeyman a considerable Time with the said Mr Tompion, and by his Industry and Care is fully acquainted with his secrets in the said Art." William Webster was warden C.C. 1734, and died in office, 1735. **Robt.**, C.C. 1721. **William**, 26 Change Alley ; C.C. 1734 ; master 1755 ; livery 1766. **William**, son of and apprenticed to William Webster, C.C. 1763 ; in the Pierpont Morgan collection are two watches by William Webster, one a clock-watch and the other, of later date, a repeater ; they are both in finely pierced gold cases. **Samuel**, livery C.C. 1766. **Robt.**, Whitby, Yorks. ; in 1772 he patented (No. 1,021) a repeater. **Richard**, son of William Webster ; C.C. 1779 ; livery 1787. **& Son**, 11 Change Alley, 1781-1800. **Richard**, 26 Change Alley, 1784-1840 ; livery C.C. 1810. **Jno.**, Whitby, 1822. **Charles**, 19 Broad St., Long Acre, 1835 ; 24 Red Lion St., Holborn, 1842. **Richard**, Birchin Lane, 1842 ; 43 Cornhill, 1850, and afterwards at No. 5 Queen Victoria St., which he built in 1872, when the thoroughfare was formed ; died in 1882, aged 62 ; an accomplished horologist. **Ambrose**, Waltham, Mass., U.S.A., a clever mechanician, engaged in producing machines for watch construction ; died 1894, aged 65.

Weedon, Wm., apprenticed 1686 to Nat. Barrow ; C.C. 1695.

Weekes, Thomas, C.C. 1654 ; fined by C.C. in 1657 for abuse to Warden Coxeter.

Weeks. Johnson, C.C. 1683. **Charles**, C.C. 1713. **—**, Coventry St., London ; English clock movement, dead beat escapement, in French Empire case, about 1810. **John**, clock-case maker, Great Sutton St., 1810-23.

Wehrle, —, Cambridge ; watch, 1835.

Weight, Henry, Gloucester, 1810-42.

Welborne, William, Leather Lane, Holborn ; in 1813 fined £15 by C.C. for refusing to take up the livery, 1800-13.

Welch, E. N., founder of E. N. Welch Clock Co., Forestville, New England, U.S.A. ; died 1887, aged 78.

Welcome, John, C.C. 1705.

Welder. Richard, St Anne's, Westminster, livery Turners' Company 1774. **Thos.**, 40 Foster Lane, 1780-85.

Weldon. Saml., London ; watch, Nelthropp collection, date letter, 1774.

Welke, see De Welke.

Welldon, W., silver *repoussé* and tortoiseshell watch, 1744 ; Hilton Price collection. **W.**, Pierpont Morgan collection, bridge over balance, Dutch style, about 1790.

Welle, Robt., 30 Red Lion Sq., 1825.

Weller. (& Magson, long narrow marqueterie case clock, about 1705.) **John**, C.C. 1713 ; the Prince of Wales exhibited at the Guelph Exhibition a clock-watch by him ; on the back three plumes, "Ich Dien" and also "Pro Principe Semper."

Wellington. John, C.C. 1726. **Jas.**, London ; watch, 1778.

Wells. Joseph, C.C. 1667. **Isaac**, C.C. 1668. **John**, C.C. 1682 ; long-case clock, arabesque marqueterie, about 1700. **Wm.**, C.C. 1689. **Jonathan**, 1700. **Neddy**, Shipley ; fine long-case clock, Mr J. Whiteley Ward, about 1700. **Matthew**, Russell Court, Covent Garden, 1755-60. **John**, 4 Cheapside, 1758-68.

Welsh, Robt., Dalkeith, about 1790.

Wenday, Anne, apprenticed in 1685 to Hy. Jevon and Christian his wife, C.C.

Wenham. John, Dereham ; watch, 1763. **D.**, Dereham ; long-case clock, about 1770.

Wentle, Jas., 147 Aldersgate St., 1793.

Wentworth, Wombwell, apprenticed 1656 to Hy. Harland. **Wm.**, Sarum ; long-case clock, about 1740.

West. Thomas, London ; completed his apprenticeship in 1694 ; long-case clock, Wetherfield collection, about 1700 ; large metal pair-case watch, elaborate dial and movement, inscribed "Thomas West, London," about 1710 ; long-case clock, about the same date, with the signature, "Thos, Westt, London" ; long marqueterie case clock, about 1700, Sir James M. Moody. **William**, C.C. 1697. **Samuel**, Royal Exchange, livery C.C. 1766 ; 8-day bracket clock, verge escapement, in black wood case, with brass mounts and brass dial silvered, has a landscape painted at the top, with two men in the foreground playing tennis, the ball being represented by a small brass button, attached by a wire to the staff of the verge, and working backwards and forwards in a slot cut in the dial ; 1750-67. **Thos.**, Reading ; watch, 1780. **Thos.**, 3 Ludgate St., 1820-42.

Westaway, John, 1 Gower St., 1840.

Westbrook, William, London ; long-case clocks, about 1700 and 1730.

Westcott. John, C.C. 1703. **Jno.**, London ; long-case clock, about 1750.

Westerman, Richd., Leeds, 1828 ; he retired in 1850.

Westfield, Robt., St James's St., Clerkenwell ; patented in 1813 (No. 3,732) a cylinder wheel with teeth of unequal height.

Westlake, John, 33 High St., Boro., 1820 ; 41 Castle St., Boro., 1835-42.

Westmore, Robt., Lancaster, 1761. **Thos.**, 1779, f. **Robt.**, 1785, f.

Westoby, John, C.C. 1677. "Lost out of a Gentleman's Pocket on the 12th Inst., between the Rose Tavern without Temple

Bar and West Smithfield, a silver Minute Pendulum Watch in tortoise-shell case, inlaid with this figure in the bottom, viz. : A man driving a Hog into a House, the name of the watch, Westobe, London. It had a narrow Ribband flowered with silver and gold to hand the key by, when lost. Whoever brings it to Edw. Crouch, Watchmaker, under St Dunstan's Church, in Fleet Street, shall have a guinea Reward " (*Post Boy*, 13th April 1697).

Weston. Abram, Lewes ; long-case clock, Mr J. Terry, about 1690. **& Willis**, enamellers, 23 Greenhill's Rents, Smithfield, 1810. **Wm.**, Newark, 1810 ; afterwards **James** ; then **James and John**.

Westwood. Richard, C.C. 1691 ; maker of lantern clocks. **Robert**, Prince's St., Leicester Sq. ; in 1829 he patented (No. 5,850) an 8-day watch with large barrel extending over the train.

Wethered, Geo., apprenticed 1677 to Hy. Wynne, C.C.

Wetherell. Thos., apprenticed 1664 to Jno. Clarkson, C.C. **& Janaway**, 114 Cheapside, 1785-94. **Nathan**, Philadelphia, 1830-40.

Weylett, Jos., 7 Mark Lane, 1790-94.

Whaley. Barnaby, apprenticed 1675 to Jno. Fitter, C.C. **J.**, 14 Mount St., Lambeth, 1840-42.

Whalley, Sam., Manchester, 1770-86.

Wham, —, 13 Knightsbridge, 1820.

Whaplett, Thos. ; prior to 1686 he presented a tankard to C.C. ; Wharton Rd., London ; watch, 1785.

Wharton, Jno., apprenticed 1687 to Thos. Speakman, C.C.

Wheatley. John, apprenticed to Jeffery Bailey, C.C. 1668. **William**, C.C. 1698. **John**, 18 Bull and Mouth St., 1820-25.

Wheaton, Caleb, Providence, U.S.A., 1785-1822.

Wheatstone, Sir Charles, an eminent electrician, inventor of a system of synchronous clocks driven by magneto-electric currents ; died 1875, aged 73.

Wheeler. Thomas, apprenticed to Nich. Coxeter, 1647 ; C.C. 1655 ; master 1684 ; lantern clock, dolphin frets, altered balance escapement, inscribed "Thomas Wheeler, near the French Church in Londini" ; another lantern clock by him is owned by Miss Mary F. Bragg (see p. **348**). died 1694. **John**, C.C. 1680. **Vincent**, apprenticed 1683 to Ed. Holliday, C.C. **Thos.**, London ; in the Wetherfield collection is a marqueterie long-case clock by him with peculiar high dome, surmounted by carved gilt ornaments, dating from about 1700 ; 114 Oxford St., 1793.

Wheels, Sam., London ; calender watch, 1790.

Whellan, Thos., "in Bishops Gate Street, Londini" ; lantern clock, about 1680.

Wheller. Maurice, invented a rolling clock, 1684. **John**, 17 Shoreditch, 1787-94.

Wheynard, Edwd., London ; watch, 1784.

Whichcote. Samuel, Crane Court, Fleet St. ; C.C. 1724 ; master in 1748. **Samuel**, 175 Fleet St. ; master C.C. 1764 ; livery 1766.

Whinfield, Philip, apprenticed 1651 to Sam Davis, C.C.

Whipham. Thos., 61 Fleet St., 1775. **& North**, 1793.

Whipp, Thos., Rochdale ; long-case clocks, 1820-42.

Whipple, G. M., superintendent of the Kew Observatory, Richmond ; initiated a system of watch rating in 1884 ; died 1893, aged 50.

Whitaker. S., 12 Long Lane, 1830. **Wm.**, 8 High St., Camberwell, 1835-42.

Whitby, Robt., Chester, 1814-18.

Whitchurch. Samuel, Kingswood; long-case chiming clock, phases of moon and high water at Bristol in arch, about 1760, presented to King Haakon of Norway by the Corporation of London. **Saml.**, Bristol, 1760-80.

White. Edward, apprenticed 1647 to Jno. White, C.C. **John**, brother C.C. 1647. **John**, apprenticed to Thomas Loomes and turned over to Thomas Bagley, C.C. 1670. **Thomas**, C.C. 1683; watch, gold *repoussé* case, outer case of shagreen, Schloss collection, 1743. **Cæsar**, C.C. 1692. **Joseph**, C.C. 1713. **Amos**, Fetter Lane; C.C. 1730. **Sebastian**, Philadelphia, 1795. **John**; watch, 1829; 3 Northampton Ter., City Rd., 1838-42. **Wm.**, 306 Oxford St., 1830.

Whitear & Raves, 30 Fleet St., 1790-94.

Whiteaves, Richard, 30 Fleet St., 1804-40; livery C.C. 1812.

Whitebread, William, High Holborn, C.C. 1728.

Whitehead. Richard, C.C. 1671. **Simon**, apprenticed 1677 to Richard Whitehead, C.C. **Chas.**, apprenticed 1693 to Whitehead, C.C. **Robt.**, 3 St James's St., Clerkenwell, 1810-15.

Whitehear, Richard, C.C., 1648; seems to have settled at Reading; lantern clock, dolphin frets, inscribed "Richard Whitheare, Reading, fecit."

Whitehurst. John, Derby, and afterwards of Bolt Court, Fleet St., F.R.S.; a well-known maker of turret and other clocks, inventor of tell-tale clocks; born at Congleton 1713, died in London 1788; his descendants continued the business at Derby; clock in "The Chauntry," Newark, inscribed, "Made 1807, and fixed here 1808, by Mr John Whitehurst, senior, of Derby." **& Son**, Derby; rack-lever watch, about 1805; Whitehurst of Derby was one of three clockmakers invited to tender for the Westminster clock in 1846.

Whiteley, Thos., Ripponden, 1833.

Whiterow, Jno., 20 Bridge St., Covent Garden, 1840.

Whitewick & Moss, 24 Ludgate Hill, 1790-94.

Whitfield. Edwd., C.C. 1663. **J.**, London, about 1749; watch by him belonging to Mr Geo. Carr Glyn, Guelph Exhibition.

Whitford. Thomas, 1 Smithfield Bars, 1790-1800; Whitford & Son, 1810-23. **George**, 1 Smithfield Bars, 1830-42.

Whitham, Jonathan, Sheffield, 1770.

Whiting, Riley, Winchester and Winsted, U.S.A., 1798-1820.

Whitlach, Jno., admitted C.C. 1637; presented a cup to the Company prior to 1652.

Whitman, Ezra, Bridgewater, U.S.A., 1790-1840.

Whitmore, Wm., Northampton; watch, 1811.

Whittaker. James; long-case clock, about 1700. **Edward**, C.C. 1711. **William**, f. of New York, 1731-55.

Whittey, John, 42 Wynyatt St., 1842.

Whittingham, William, cited by C.C., he not having served seven years, 1688.

Whittle, Thomas, apprenticed to Henry Harper, C.C. 1683. "Lost in Lincoln's Inn Fields, on the 15th Instant, betwixt 5 and 6 o'clock, a Pendulum Watch in a black seal skin case, studded with silver, a cipher on the back and lined with Red Sattin, made by Angil White. Whoever brings it to Mr Wilson's, at the Fleece Tavern, in Fleet Street, shall have a

guinea Reward " (*Lon. Gaz.*, Oct. 22, 1688).

Whitton, Chas., apprenticed 1690 to Jno. Higgs, C.C. 1698.

Whitway, Saml., Cheapside, 1735-40.

Whitwell. Robert, apprenticed to Robt. Grinkin, 1641; C.C. 1648; in 1651 he presented one cup and three spoons to the Company; early minute-hand watch by him, Mr Charles Shapland (see p. **180**). **Wm.**, apprenticed to Robt. Whitwell, C.C. In 1678, at Cutlers' Hall, **Hugh** Whitwell, son of Robert, late citizen and clockmaker, was bound apprentice to Edmond Whitwell, member of the Cutlers' Company.

Whood, Isaac, apprenticed 1680 to Thos. Fenn, C.C.

Wibrandt, Jacob, Leuwarden; small watch, about 1630 (see p. **136**).

Wich, Gabriel, Nantwich, 1780.

Wichell, Samuel, St James's St.; marqueterie long-case clock, about 1710; another long-case clock bears the address, "Pickadilly."

Wickes. Wm., Threadneedle St., 1680; Geo. Wickes, his son, removed to Leadenhall St., and from thence, in 1720, to the King's Arms, Panton St.; for continuation of this business see Wickes & Netherton, Parker & Wakelin, Wakelin & Taylor, Wakelin & Garrard, and Garrard, Robt. **John**, 27 Cannon St., livery C.C. 1786; 8 Clement's Lane, 1804. **John Haughton**, 8 Clement's Lane, 1806; livery C.C. 1810; J. H. Haughton & Son, same address, 1810-35. **W. G.**, 114 Leadenhall St., 1823. **W.**, 8 Skinner St., Clerkenwell, 1835.

Wicks. (& Netherton, Panton St., 1753-60.) **William**, London; long-case clocks, about 1800. **& Bishop**, 170 New Bond St., 1820-25. **Wm.**, watch-case maker, 34 Percival St., 1820. **Thos.**, 34 Union St., Kingsland Rd., 1835. **W. G.**, 120 Long Lane, 1836. **Alfred**, 8 Clement's Lane, 1842.

Wicksteed, Edward, 9 Fore St., 1768; 114 Bunhill Row, 1795.

Widdowson, Joseph, 100 Fleet St., 1830.

Widenham. Richard, 6 East St., Clerkenwell, 1830; 13 Lombard St., 1835. **& Adams**, 13 Lombard St., 1840-42.

Widman, Jacob, Augsburg, 1680; Mr Norman Shaw has a clock inscribed "Jacob Widman, Augustanus," an English dial engraved "William Barbauld, London," has been added.

Wiedeman. In the Horological Museum, Copenhagen, is a curious watch signed "Theodor Wiedeman, Wienna." It has three balances geared together, and dates probably from about 1700.

Wieland. Fredk., Walworth, 1835-42. **Chas.**, 12 Workworth Pl., Commercial Rd., 1835-42. **R. & W.**, 7 Lower Rd., Islington, 1835-42.

Wiggin, Robt., Colne, Lancs., 1818.

Wiggins, Thos., 129 High St., Borough, 1835.

Wigginton. Jno., apprenticed 1663 to Bernard Gernon. **Wm.**, 11 St James's Walk, 1806-20.

Wight, Jas., 12 Union St., Southwark, 1816-20.

Wightman. Jas., apprenticed in 1663 to Ed. Eyston; C.C. 1670. **Jno.**, apprenticed 1688 to Jno. Jones, C.C. **Thos.**, apprenticed 1692 to Hy. Hester, junr.; watch, about 1700; gold watch, h.m., 1745, Mrs G. F. Thompson, Ottawa. **William**, C.C. 1696; the Rev. Lewis Gilbertson has a long-case clock by him, very similar to

Fig. 622, and dating from about 1700. **Thomas**, 95 St Martin's Lane, 1798-1818.

Wightwick & Moss, 24 Ludgate St., 1775-1804 (John Wightwick, hon. freeman C.C. 1781).

Wignall (or Wignell), Jno., also **F.**, Ormskirk; long-case clocks, 1760-85.

Wigram, Thos., 67 St James's St., 1804.

Wilbur, Job, Newport, U.S.A., 1815-40.

Wilcocks, T., 2 Red Lion St., Clerkenwell, 1817.

Wild. Jas., Frith St., Soho, 1790. **Joseph**, Macclesfield; William Travis was apprenticed to him about 1794. **E.** (tools), 2 St John's Sq., 1798-1810.

Wilde. Wm., C.C. 1717-24. **Michael**, Wakefield, 1775. **Josh.**, Macclesfield, 1782. **Saml.**, Islington; maker of lever escapements, a remarkably good workman and sound horologist, 1800-42; his son afterwards with A. P. Walsh. **J.**, Preston, 1814.

Wilder. Richard, Richmond Buildings, Soho; C.C. 1776; watch, h.m., 1785. **Jno.**, C.C. 1790. **Ezra**, Hingham, U.S.A., 1800.

Wilders, —, London; many watches, Dutch style, 1760-80.

Wildman. Watkinson, Cheapside, 1753-63. **Samuel**, 63 Cheapside, 1760-88. **Chas.**, 6 Great Newport St., 1800.

Wilkes, Jno., London; watch, 1740.

Wilks, Wm., Wolverton, near Stratford-on-Avon. In 1779 he was paid £20 for "erecting and setting up a church clock" for the parish of Clarendon.

Wilkins. Robt., C.C. 1670. **Jno.**, apprenticed 1693 to Jno. Howse, C.C. **Wm.**, Devizes, about 1730. **Robt.**, London; watch, 1750. **John**, Bath, 1770. **Ralph**, Stamford, 1775. **& Son**, Long Acre, 1805. **George**, 36 Frith St., Soho, 1810-25; card, B.M. **Samuel**, 4 Norman St., St Luke's, 1835.

Wilkinson. Edward, apprenticed C.C. 1655. **Jno.**, Leeds; long-case clock, about 1695. **William**, C.C. 1718. **Willm.**, Leeds; long-case clock in the possession of Mr Alfred Sykes, Huddersfield; dial, 16½ in. broad; centre seconds hand; in the arch on a convex disc, "Time stayeth not." On the dial:

"Hark how the fleeting moments pass,
How swift they haste away.
O, reader, here as in a glass,
Behold thy life decay."

—, Wigton, about 1740. **Thos.**, London; fine musical long-case clock, about 1760, plays at the hour either Lady Coventry's Minuet, or the 101st Psalm. **J.**, London; watch, 1765. **Thos.**, York, f., died 1776. **Wm.**, Congleton, 1780. **T.**, 32 Piccadilly; 8 Cornhill, 1793; 1825-30. **James**, 18 Castle St., 1830; 19 Farringdon St., 1835.

Willard, —, Boston, U.S.A. Several generations beginning with **Benjamin** about 1770. In the *Boston Gazette* for 22nd Feb. 1773, was announced, "Benjamin Willard, at his shop in Roxbury Street, pursues different branches of clock and watch work, has for sale musical clocks playing different tunes, a new tune every day of the week and on Sunday a psalm tune. These tunes perform every hour without any obstruction to the motion or going of the clock, and new invention for pricking barrels to perform the music, and his clocks are made much cheaper than any yet known. All the branches of the business likewise carried on at his shop in Grafton." He was followed early in the nineteenth century by Aaron, who had a shop in Boston, and by Simon. "Willard" or "Banjo" clocks, well known in the neighbourhood of Boston, are of the hanging variety, and have below the dial a long trunk, narrow for the greater part of its length, and a square panelled enlargement near the bottom, which is in some instances painted with figures or a landscape, in others having inserted a circular glass through which the motion of the pendulum bob could be seen. Many of these bore the name, "Willard, Jr."

Willcocks, Richard, 46 Red Lion St., Clerkenwell, 1785-1800.

Willen, Johan, London; watch, 1720.

Willerton, Skull, & Green, 21 New Bond St., 1783-94.

Willett, Jas., London; watch, silver cock, 1727; long Oriental lacquer case clock, about 1730.

Williami, Justin, London; clock-watch, Mr Norman Shaw, about 1670.

Williams. Joseph (Ireland), C.C. 1685. **Thos.**, apprenticed 1689 to Isaac Day, C.C. **Jno.**, Leeds; long-case clock, about 1700. **Jno.**, 11 Old Bond St., 1769. **P.**, Lombard St., 1770. **David**, "Endfield," 1774. **Thos.**, Haverfordwest; watch, 1780. **Jas.**, 35 Goodge St., 1794. **John**, 168 Shoreditch, 1800-4. **R.**, Liverpool; watch, 1810. **David**, Newport, U.S.A., 1810. **Geo.**, 7 Bridgwater Sq., 1817. **John**, watch-case maker, 56 Great Sutton St., 1820. **John**, 4 Amen Corner, 1821; 70 St Paul's Churchyard, 1831. **E.**, 1 Albany, Saville Row, 1825. **S.**, 16 St John's Row, St Luke's, 1840; Baldwin St., 1842. **Chas.**, 223 Oxford St., 1842. **J. G.**, Denbigh; watch, 1842.

Williamson. Robert, St Bartholomew Lane; apprenticed 1658 to Jas. Letts; C.C. 1666, master 1698; watch with a shagreen case in the B.M.; another in case of white agate, about 1740, Pierpont Morgan collection. **William**, C.C. 1664. **Thomas**, C.C. 1668. "Lost on the 19th day of August, from Mr Will. Clinch's house at Epsom, a silver Minute Pendulum Watch with a scollop-shell case studded with silver, made by Thomas Williamson, London, with a silk string and a silver seal with a Coat of Arms. Whoever brings it to Mr Robert Dingly, watchmaker in George Yard, Lombard Street, shall have 2 guineas Reward" (*Lond. Gaz.*, Sept. 5-8, 1692). **John**, C.C. 1682; late seventeenth century alarm watch, signed "John Williamson in Leeds," S.K.M., silver case pierced and engraved. **Edward**, apprenticed to Jonathan Puller for seven years ending 1694; long marqueterie case clock, about 1710; Mr W. L. Unkill, Mexico City, has a long-case clock, about 1700, by Dave Williamson. **Joseph**, a first-rate horologist, inventor and maker of equation clocks; outside of the craft his reputation here was not commensurate with his merits; he held the appointment of watchmaker of the cabinet of Charles II. of Spain, for whom he made a 400-day long-case equation clock; Mr Edward Hawes has a long-case clock by him with dial very similar to the one in the Wetherfield collection which is illustrated by Fig. 650; master of C.C. 1724, and died in office, 1725 (see pp. **232, 357**). **Timothy**, 196 Fleet St., 1769-75; 90 Great Russell St., 1788; large watch, silver-gilt case, taken from Pekin, Mr H. K. Heinz. **J.**, London; watch, 1790.

Williamston. Ralph, C.C. 1706; watch, "R. Williamston, London," S.K.M., h.m., 1749. **Christopher**, 24 Cornhill, 1840-42.

Williarme, Pierre, admitted C.C. 1648. A correspondent of *Notes and Queries* has

a MS. return of strangers dwelling within Aldersgate Ward, October 1635, which states that Peter Williarme, watchmaker, resided in the parish of St Botolph, and had then been in England twelve years, being a native of Geneva.

Willin, Wm., Percival St., 1800-11; livery C.C. 1810.

Willing, —, London; calendar watch, one hand, nicely engraved dial, Schloss collection, about 1720.

Willis. Ambrose, apprenticed 1687 to Thos. Baldwin, C.C. **Mary**, 81 Bishopsgate St. Without, 1822-5. **Jno.**, enameller, 23 Greenhill's Rents, 1823; afterwards Percival St. **Thos. J.**, son of Jno., an excellent dial enameller; died 1893, aged 57.

Willmot. Thomas, C.C. 1715. **John**, 86 St Margaret's Hill, 1762-75.

Willoughby. Benjamin, High Cross, apprenticed 1676 to Robt. Dingley, C.C. **John**, C.C. 1686. **Benj.**, Bristol; watch, about 1730; another, about 1765.

Willowe, John, Fleet St. One of the first wardens C.C., master 1635; watch, B.M., in a fancy case of escallop shape, 1620-40.

Wills. Jno., apprenticed 1682 to Wm. Hillier, C.C. **Joseph**, long-case clock, about 1740, Mr G. W. Price, Salem, New Jersey, U.S.A.

Willshire. James, Glasshouse Yard, Goswell St., 1769; Mr J. L. Raymond, New York, has a long-case clock by him. **James**, 19 High Holborn, 1781.

Willson. Thomas, C.C. 1659, assistant 1685. **George**, C.C. 1692. **William**, C.C. 1693. **John**, King's Head Court, Holborn; C.C. 1714. **Jas.**, London; watch, 1768. **G. V.**, 5 St Alban's Place, St James's, 1835-40.

Wilmer, Thos., London, about 1760.

Wilmot. Thos., apprenticed 1653 to Thos. Loomes,. C.C. **Isaac**, apprenticed 1662 to Jno. Bayes, C.C. **Stephen**, London, apprenticed 1667 to Ed. Staunton; C.C. 1674; 30-hour long-case clock, square dial, about 1720. **George**, apprenticed to Jeffery Baily and turned over to John White; C.C. 1670. **Jno.**, apprenticed 1676 to G. Stubbs, C.C. **Richard**, 1 Wilmington Sq., 1842, see also Willmot.

Wilmshurst. T., Deal; watch, Schloss collection, 1746. **& Son**, Brighthelmstone (now Brighton); watch, 1765. **Stephen**, Basingstoke, 1770.

Wilson. Richard, York, f., 1586. **William**, his son, f., 1611. **Thos.**, apprenticed 1651 to Simon Hackett, C.C. **Nat.**, apprenticed 1658 to Edward East, C.C. **Edwd.**, apprenticed 1663 to Richard Nau; C.C. 1670. (Or **Willson**) **Joshua**, London; apprenticed 1688 to Wm. Fuller, C.C.; lantern clock, finely engraved dial, about 1700; long clock, 11-in. dial, fine marqueterie case, about 1705, Wetherfield collection; watch, h.m., 1707. **Jno.**, Edinburgh, apprenticed to Andrew Brown in 1711. **James**, against St Lawrence Church; C.C. 1723; Susannah Smith was apprenticed to his wife Hannah Wilson in 1747. **George**, C.C. 1730. **Jno.**; clock in America, dating from about 1740, marked "John Wilson from London." **James**, Hawick, born 1748, died 1821. **John**, Corn Market, Belfast, 1750, afterwards at Linen Hall St., Belfast. **Nich.**, Kendal, 1765. **James**, 4 King St., Westminster, 1770-94; hon. f. 1781. **Jno.**, London; watch, 1772. **Jno.**, Ulverstone, 1775. **Titus**, Lancaster, 1779, f. **Alexander**, 132 Drury Lane, hon. f. C.C. 1781; maker of a verge watch, pair of brass cases, with

outside case of tortoiseshell, on which are representations of ferns, 1770-94. **Jas.**, Askrigg; died 1786. **Will.**, Kendal, 1790. **Thos.**, London; watch, 1791. **Thos.**, Spalding; clock, about 1800. **Jno.**, Dublin; watch, 1804. **James**, 27 Threadneedle St., 1804; 53 Lombard St., 1810. **G.**, 17 Craven Buildings, Drury Lane, 1820. **W.**, 38 Southampton St., Strand, 1829-42; afterwards Wilson & Gandar, see Jessop. **Jno.**, Peterborough; in 1835 he put a new escapement to the Minster clock. **& Gandar**, 431 Strand, 1855-65, see Blackie.

Wilter, John; watch, G.M., silver dial, silver *repoussé* case, signed Cochin; another example, a silver *repoussé* pair-case watch, Dutch style; another, a calendar watch in the Schloss collection, has a painting of the Queen of the Poppies on the back of the case; watch, Mr Evan Roberts, 1769; 1760-84.

Wilton. Clay, C.C. 1697; watch by him with embossed case by Cochin, exhibited at the Guelph Exhibition by Mr Geo. Carr Glyn. **John**, London; watch, silver inner case, outer one green shagreen with *piqué* ornament, about 1767, Hilton Price collection.

Wiltshire & Sons, 136 Cornhill, 1822-30.

Wimble, Nemih, Maidstone, about 1760.

Wimper, David, Hammersmith; long-case clock, about 1740.

Winch, Amos, C.C. 1677.

Winckles, Jno., London; watch, 1782.

Winder, of Lancaster: **Thos.**, 1795, f.: **Stephen**, 1823, f.; **Thos.**, 1825, f.; **Wm.**, 1830, f.

Windess, Lancaster: **Thos.**, 1795; **Stephen**, 1823; **Thos.**, 1825; **Wm.**, 1830.

Windham, Jas., 22 Birchin Lane, 1840.

Windmills. Joseph, St Martin's-le-Grand, afterwards in Mark Lane; well known as a good maker of clocks and watches; C.C. 1671, master 1702 · Mr Albert Hartshorne has a fine lantern clock of his make; Mr Norman Shaw has a clock by him with very good engraved brass dial, on the upper part of which is inscribed "Thomas Pardey, 1697"; another production is a bracket clock, inscribed "Joseph Windmills, at Mark Lane End, next Tower Streete, Londini, Fecit"; among the Wetherfield collection is a long-case clock, 10-in. dial, bolt and shutter maintaining power, inlaid laburnum and olive wood case, sliding hood, with spiral pillars, about 1690; another with an 11-in. dial, marqueterie case, about 1700; in the B.M. is a handsome watch by him, silver dial, in which is a semicircular opening above the centre; through it appears a representation of blue sky, with the sun pointing to the hour by day, and the moon by night; tortoiseshell case; there is a similar watch by Joshua Hutchin. "Gold watch lost, made by Mr Windmills, in Mark Lane. Give notice as above, or to Mr Rudge, over against the Swan Tavern, in King's Street, Westminster" (*Lond. Gaz.*, April 25th, 1687). **Thomas**, apprenticed to Joseph Windmills, 1686; C.C. 1695, master 1719; a repeating watch by him in the G.M. **J. & T.**, Great Tower St. (Thomas Windmills, master C.C. 1718); many excellent long-case clocks by them are to be met with; 1710-40. **& Wightman**, London; long-case clock, about 1720. **& Bennett**, long-case clock, about 1725. **& Elkins**, London; bracket clock, about 1725.

Windon, Daniel, C.C. 1718.

Windsor, James, 99 Paul St., Finsbury, 1835-42.

Winerow, William, C.C. 1718.

Wing, Mark, 27 Goswell St., 1816-42.

Wingate. Paine, Boston, U.S.A., 1789; Newburyport, 1803. Frederick, Augusta, U.S.A., 1800.

Wingrove, Jno., St John's Sq., C.C. 1730; watch, about 1745, inscribed "Sarah Wingrove, London."

Winkley, Jno., Canterbury, about 1760.

Winne, Hy., see Wynne.

Winnerl, Joseph Thaddeus, born in Styria, 1799; settled in Paris 1829; a celebrated chronometer maker; died 1886.

Winnock. Joshua, apprenticed to Ahasuerus Fromanteel the Elder; C.C. 1672. Daniel, C.C. 1707.

Winrowe, Wm., London; watch, 1760.

Winsmore, John, C.C. 1712.

Winson, Thos., London; watch, 1782.

Winstanley. Jere., apprenticed 1687 to Jno. Wheeler, C.C.; long-case clock, about 1750, inscribed "Winstanley, Holy Well, North Wales." Edward, Liverpool, 1770. Peter, Huyton; watch, silver balance-cock, about 1775, Mr E. A. Laurence. E., London; watch, with minute circle inside hour circle, about 1780. Alex., Wigan, about 1780. Robt., Ormskirk, 1818. Edwd., Wigan, 1820.

Winstendley, Thos., Modely; watch, h.m., 1774.

Wint. Dan., apprenticed 1693 to J. Clowes, C.C. —, Smithfield, 1774.

Winter. Sam., apprenticed 1683 to Ed. Stanton, C.C. Wm., apprenticed 1686 to Robt. Dingley, C.C. Robt., 59 Cannon St., Ratcliffe, 1817.

Winterhalder, —, London; watch, 1810.

Winterhalter, J., 47 St Andrew St., 1840.

Wintle. David, London; clock, about 1680. Thos., 9 Poultry, 1760-68.

Wintworth, Thos., Sarum; lantern clocks, 1700-40.

Wirgman, Peter, 79 St James's St., 1775-94. C. & G., 31 Castle St., Holborn, 1804. Thomas, 68 St James's St., 1823. G., Hewitt's Court, Strand, 1825. C., 5 George St., 1830.

Wirrall, Copley, C.C. 1648.

Wise (or Wyse); several generations among the early makers. Jno., apprenticed 1638 to Peter Closon; C.C. 1646. John, C.C. 1669; clock, inscribed "John Wise Londini, fecit," given to Zion College in 1672. Richard, C.C. 1679. John, C.C. 1683; on 1st Nov. 1693, "John Wise dwelling neere the popes head in Moore-fields citizen and clockmaker of London," became a joint surety for Richard Wise, Renter to the Cutlers' Company for 1693-4. Luke, Reading, 1686; watch, about 1720, stolen from Newington Free Library. Thomas, London; C.C. 1686; long-case clock in the Vestry of Westminster Abbey, square dial, rings round winding holes. Joseph, C.C. 1687; in the same year was apprenticed to him the celebrated Langley Bradley. Peter, son of John, admitted C.C. 1693, master 1725; Mr T. W. Bourne owns a bracket clock by him (see p. 393). 1693-1726. Luke, C.C. 1694. Robert, C.C. 1694. John, C.C. 1710. Mark, C.C. 1719. Matthew, London; watch, 1740; Daventry, 1780. Featherstone, Hull, 1822.

Wiseman, John, C.C. 1647.

Wiss. Frères, Geneva, about 1775. & Menu, Geneva, 1790.

Wiswall. Thos., 20 Ely Pl., 1800. & Co., 52 Red Lion St., 1810.

With, Thos., London; fine bracket clock, date of the month hand, Sheraton case, about 1790.

Wither. Jas., apprenticed 1637 to R. Child, C.C. Richd., apprenticed 1681 to

Andrew Prime, C.C. John, C.C. 1699; maker of long-case clocks.

Withers. Wm., London; long-case clock at the Church of the Cappucins, Cadiz, about 1760. Wm., Bristol; lever watch in French case, about 1820.

Witherspoon, Alex., Tranent, Scotland; invented a clock escapement, 1835.

Witness, Francis, apprenticed 1650 to Job Betts, C.C.

Witson, H., London; watch, 1825.

Witte, Samuel, C.C. 1660.

Wittingham, Wm., London; watch, about 1700. Chas., London; watch, 1820.

Wittit, James, London; watch, G.M., about 1750.

Woerd, Charles V., born 1821, died 1888; a clever mechanician who did much to advance the art of machine watchmaking by designing automatic tools for the Waltham Watch Co., of which he was mechanical superintendent from 1875 to 1882.

Wogdon, Stephen, Greenwich; small arch-dial clock, about 1730.

Wolf, J., Wienne; maker of a book-shaped watch, 1627.

Wolfe. Jno., Noble St., C.C. 1730. Joseph, Mitre Court, near Aldgate, 1762-72.

Wolfgang, Johann, Pollinger, Fridtberg; repeating watch, S.K.M., about 1730.

Wolkstein, David, Augsburg; associated with Dasypodius in the superintendence of the second Strasburg clock in 1570. He is said to have invented the Carillon.

Woller, Matt., Coventry, 1816.

Wolverstone. Benjamin, apprenticed to Richd. Richardson in 1647; C.C. 1656; alarm watch, silver dial, one hand, in the G.M. Thomas, C.C. 1650. Jas., C.C. 1670.

Womersley; long-case clock, square dial, rings round winding holes, signed "Geo. Womersley," about 1720.

Wontner, John, Minories; a well-known maker, 1770-1812; livery C.C. 1810. John, & Son, 125 Minories, 1804-12, see also Rentnow.

Wooborn, Geo., London; watch, 1798.

Wood. Richd., apprenticed 1651 to Jno. Cooke, C.C. G., Exon.; lantern clock, about 1660. Jas., apprenticed 1668 to Ed. Gilpin, C.C. Robert, C.C. 1670. Thomas, C.C. 1691. John, C.C. 1701. Henry, C.C. 1720. Thomas, Barbican, C.C. 1727. Dan., London; watch, 1745. James, apprenticed to Joseph Miller, C.C. 1745; Samuel Alvey apprenticed to him in 1750; watch, G.M., about 1780. Peter, long-case clock, about 1750. Joseph, Scarboro'; long-case clock, about 1760, Mr Logan. David, Newburyport, U.S.A., 1765-90. John, Philadelphia, 1770-93. "Clocks, watches, gold & silver work made, mended, and sold at the sign of the Dial, the corner of Front & Chestnut Streets." F., Scarboro', 1770-90. John, 32 Minories, 1775. Robert, Horse Shoe Alley, Moorfields, 1785-1810; fine bracket clock, about 1790 (see p. 372). Josiah, New Bedford, 1797-1810. Benj., London; watch, 1800. Robert, 4 Hartley Pl., Kent Rd., 1820-35. Thomas Jas., 86 Charlotte St., Rathbone Pl., 1822-30. Hy. Sam., Canterbury, 1835. Thos. Jas., Long Lane; died 1890. Joseph J., Richmond; died 1909, aged 80.

Woodall. Thos., apprenticed to G. C. Addis; C.C. 1796. T. J., 3 Birchin Lane, 1804-10. F., 1817.

Woodfine, Rt., Liverpool; watch, 1809.

Woodford, Jonathan, apprenticed 1684 to Jno. Ebsworth, C.C.; watch, 1736.

Woodhill, Jabez, 63 St Paul's Churchyard, 1830.

Woodington, Wm., apprenticed 1638 to Ed. Gilpin, C.C.

Woodman. Jno., London, about 1800. Mary, 29 Paradise Row, Chelsea, 1835. Phillip & John, succeeded Rowlands as watch-case makers in Smith St., Clerkenwell, did much to support trade charities; Phillip was for some years treasurer of the Clock and Watchmakers' Asylum; John died in 1903, and Phillip in 1908.

Woodruff & Son, 43 Kirby St., Hatton Garden, 1822-30.

Woods. Thomas, C.C. 1713. Jno., Liverpool, 1770. C. R., 21 White Lion St., 1842.

Woodward. Jno., apprenticed 1656 to Ben. Hill, C.C. Thos., apprenticed 1671 to Jno. Frowde, C.C. J., 8 New Inn Yard, 1835. Thos., 24 Curtain Rd., 1835.

Woolard, John, 14 Bridge Rd., Lambeth, 1810-18.

Wooley, Thos., 41 Hutton St., 1793.

Woolhead, Maj., London; watch, 1780.

Woolley, —, Tenterden; Act of Parliament clock, about 1797.

Woolridge, Stephen, apprenticed 1652 to Jere. Gregory, C.C.

Woolverton. Jas., C.C. 1677. James, C.C. 1690.

Wopshot, Thos., London; watch, 1773.

Worboys. Arthur, 4 Wine Office Court, Fleet St., 1769-85. Jno., 30 Ludgate Hill, 1780-94.

Worke, Jno., London; many watches, Dutch style, 1760-85.

Workman, Ben., portable sun-dial, B.M., about 1700.

Worlidge, Nat., apprenticed 1661 to Ed. Norris, C.C.

Wormesley, —, Macclesfield, 1814.

Worrall. John, 71 Goswell Rd., 1836-42.

Worrell, Jno., London; long-case clock, about 1760.

Worsfold. Jno., Dorking; long-case clock, about 1720. Jno., Hampton-Wick; watch, 1773.

Worsley. Thos., 22 Cheapside, 1783-1805. Thos., Liverpool; watch by him said to have been presented to Robert Burns by his brother ploughmen of Ayr in 1785. John, London; watch, 1802.

Worswick, Thos., Lancaster, 1753, f.

Worthington. Edwd., apprenticed 1655 to Jas. Cowpe, C.C. John, C.C. 1721; watch, 1740.

Wortley, Humphrey, apprenticed 1653 to Ab. Gyott, C.C.

Wotton, Thomas, Fleet St., maker of lantern clocks, 1690-94.

Wragg, Houblon, C.C. 1724, known as a maker of long-case clocks.

Wranch (? Wrench), Jno., Chester; lantern clock, about 1700.

Wren, John, 96 Bishopsgate Without, 1780-85.

Wrench. Edwd., watch, about 1690. John, Chester; died 1716; Mr Edward Sudell has a lantern clock engraved "John Wrench in Chester," dating from about 1680. John, Chester; died 1751; long inlaid case clock by him, about 1730. W., Chester; long-case clock, about 1760. Charles, "near the Turnpike, Shoreditch," card, Ponsonby collection, about 1780; 57 Bishopsgate St. Within, 1790; 25 Camomile St., 1798; 29 Paternoster Row, 1810-15.

Wright. John, oval watch, B.M., inscribed "Wm. Heade, the owner," representation of the Crucifixion engraved inside, about 1620; part of a circular watch movement, dating from about 1640, and engraved "Johannes Wright in Covent Garden," is in the Guildhall Museum. **Robt.**, C.C. 1634. **John**, C.C. 1661. **Joseph**, C.C. 1671. **Benjamin**, Bell Alley, Coleman St., apprenticed to Abraham Prime, 1678; C.C. 1685. **Edmd.**, apprenticed 1682 to Joseph Knibb, C.C. **Wm.**, London; apprenticed 1684 to Hy. Brigden, C.C.; long clock, 11-in. dial, panelled marqueterie case, with spiral pillars to hood, about 1695, Wetherfield collection; at Goldsmiths' Hall is a long-case clock by him. **Richd.**, C.C. 1696. **John**, C.C. 1700. **John**, New York, 1712-35; f., 1713. **John**, C.C. 1715. **Thomas**, Duke St., St Martin's Lane, 1765-75. **& Sellon**, watch, 1769. **Thomas**, 6 Poultry; admitted C.C. 1770; "maker to the King" on a bracket clock; he was a Quaker and a leading watchmaker; in 1783 he patented (No. 1,354) a form of detent escapement and compensation balance (see Earnshaw, p. **273**); 1770-94. **Edwd.**, London; watch, 1775. **Chas.**, 9 Avemary Lane, 1780; 76 Strand, 1788; 94 Watling St., 1790. **Jno.**, hon. f. C.C. 1781. **T.**, watch-glass maker, Red Lion St., Clerkenwell, 1798; 127 Bunhill Row, 1805-20. **Charles Cushing**, New York; after 1812 settled in Utica. **S.**, 141 Ratcliff Highway, 1820. **Jas.**, 181 Union St., Borough, 1820-35. **Elizabeth**, 141 Ratcliff Highway, 1825. **Thos.**, 22 Lisle St., Leicester Sq., 1835-42. **William**, 212 Tooley St., 1840-42. **John**, Pentonville, 1842.

Wrightman, Thomas, admitted C.C. 1701.

Wrightson, Thomas, master C.C. 1737; 1724-38.

Wrightwick, Jno., long-case clock, about 1770 (? Wightwick).

Writs, W., Amsterdam; watch, 1767.

Wutky, —, clock-watch, signed "Johann Wutky in Breslau," about 1660, Pierpont Morgan collection.

Wyatt. Anthony, 367 Oxford St., 1800-18. **Hy.**, 46 South Audley St., 1840-42.

Wych. Jno., apprenticed 1677 to Jno. Fitter, C.C. **David**, next door to the Cross Keys Tavern, Strand; C.C. 1694.

Wycherley, John, born in 1817, at Prescot, Lancashire, where he founded the machine-made watch movement industry; died at Southport, 1891.

Wyeth. John, brother C.C. 1655. **Lionel**, see Wythe.

Wyke. Arthur, apprenticed 1691 to Thos. Wood, C.C. **Jno.**, Liverpool; long-case clock, about 1760. **Jno. Prescot**, 1780; good maker of tools for watch and clock makers; afterwards at Liverpool, with Green. **& Green**, Wyke's Court, Dale St., Liverpool; makers of watches and clocks and parts thereof and watchmakers' tools; published a quarto illustrated catalogue

of tools, about 1810. **R.**, 2 Evelyn's Buildings, Oxford St., 1825.

Wyld, John, Nottingham; clock, about 1720.

Wylde, Jno., London; watch, 1810.

Wylder & Hall, 16 Sun St., Bishopsgate St., 1794.

Wymark, Mark, 5 Percival St., 1816-42.

Wynn. W. M., 135 Fleet St., 1804. **William**, at Farnham in 1817, when he was awarded the Isis gold medal and twenty guineas by the Society of Arts for a timekeeper and compensation pendulum; in 1822 he was at 19 Dean St., Soho, and received a prize of twenty guineas from the Society for an improved method of lifting the hammers in striking clocks; maker of an exceedingly fine clock for Boston (Lincolnshire) Church, no dials, hours and quarters on bells; is said to have died in Clerkenwell workhouse; 1810-35.

Wynne. Robt., apprenticed 1641 to Jas. Vantrollier, C.C. **Henry**, apprenticed to Ralph Greatorex, 1654; C.C. 1662, master in 1690. **Jno.**, apprenticed 1670 to Wm. Watmore, C.C.

Wyse, see Wise.

Wythe. Lionel, C.C. 1646; a good maker; to him was apprenticed Charles Gretton, in 1662. **Richd.**, apprenticed 1682 to Jno. Johnson, C.C.

Yarde, Thomas; watch, B.M., about 1580.

Yardley, James, Bishop's Stortford; long-case clock, arch dial, date on back of day of month circle, 1763.

Yate, Wm.; oval watch, about 1605.

Yates. Samuel, C.C. 1648. **Wm.**, C.C. about 1660. **Michael**, apprenticed 1664 to Isaac Plovier, C.C. **Samuel**, C.C. 1685. **George**, Malden; watch, G.M., h.m., 1746. **Richd.**, London; clock, 1760. **Henry**, Liverpool, 1770, opposite the church, Wandsworth, 1800. **& Hess**, Liverpool, 1833. **Thomas**, Preston; in 1846 he patented (No. 11,443) having fewer teeth in the escape wheel, so that a watch balance would vibrate only twice a second.

Yeadon, Wm., Stourbridge, 1830.

Yeates, Thos., Penrith, 1832.

Yeatman, Andrew, apprenticed in 1684 to Jas. Woolverton; C.C. 1692; silver watch, in the G.M., about 1700.

Yelah, Jno., Wrexham, 1780.

Yelverton, Wm., 115 Portland St., 1780-94.

Yeomans. Ralph, C.C. 1722. **Joseph**, Cockermouth; died 1905, aged 65.

Yeriaf, see Fairey.

Yewdall, Jno., Bradford; watch, 1803.

Yoakley, Thos., London; watch, 1760.

Yonge. Robert, Bennet St., Westminster; C.C. 1730. **George**, 131 Strand, 1798; Yonge succeeded the celebrated Holmes (the shop was pulled down to make the entrance to Waterloo bridge in 1824). **George, & Son**, 156 Strand, 1823. **Geo. & Walter**, same address, 1830-42. **Walter**, 171 Strand, 1850-54.

Yorke. Thomas, Turnagain Lane; C.C. 1716. **Joseph W.**, Turnagain Lane; C.C. 1735. **John**, 8 Nelson St., City Rd., 1840.

Youell, Robt., apprenticed 1689 to Michael Knight, C.C.

Young. William, Charing Cross; C.C. 1661, assistant 1695; maker of a long oak case clock, square dial, day of month circle, see Brown, Andrew. **Richd.**, apprenticed 1669 to Ed. Fage, C.C. **Henry**, near the Wine House in the Strand; C.C. 1672. "A Gold Watch made by Mr H. Young, that went with a chain, the Hour of the day and day of the Month. Having a studded Shagrine case, and the square in the inner case where the ring is riveted" (*Lond. Gaz.*, April 26-29, 1680). **Henry**, 89 Fleet St., 1679-1700. **Francis**, apprenticed 1680 to Hy. Young, C.C. **William**, Charing Cross, C.C. 1682; small walnut and ebony long-case clock, solid hood, spiral pillars, square dial, cherub corners, about 1700. **Thomas**, C.C. 1699. **Richd.**, London; watch, 1775. **John**, 44 Great Russell St., Bloomsbury, 1778-1807; livery C.C. 1781; very small bracket clock by him, round enamelled dial fitted in square brass plate. **Saml.**, Perth; watch, 1781. **James**, 32 Aldersgate St., 1783; livery C.C. 1786. **Hy.**, 18 Ludgate St., 1783-88. **Wm.**, Bath; watch, 1790. **Chas.**, London; centre seconds, duplex watch, free balance-spring, stud screwed to plate, about 1805; marine chronometer, G.M., about 1815; pocket chronometer, about 1817. **J.**, 40 Old Gravel Lane, 1820. **Wm.**, 15 Butcherhall Lane, 1825. **William**, Harrogate, 1827; long-case clock with the old sulphur well painted on the dial, Miss Violet Young; in 1838 he made a clock for Low Harrogate Church at a cost of £120; he died in 1876. **Jas.**, 34 Rosoman St., 1835.

Zacharie le jeune, clever horologer in Lyons, 1769.

Zachary, John, apprenticed to William Simcox, and turned over to Daniel Quare; admitted C.C. 1694.

Zahm, G. M., Lancaster, Pa., 1843.

Zech, Jacob, Prague; invented the fusee in 1525; died 1540 (see p. **79, 81**).

Zinzanth, Hy., apprenticed 1656 to Jno. Coulson, C.C.

Zoller (or Zollner), Martin, Augsburg; clock by him, Vienna Treasury, about 1590; Abraham Scheurlin apprenticed to him, 1633.

Zucker, Jno., Tiverton, 1710.

Index

NOTE. — If particulars of a maker are required, refer first to the Alphabetical List, which begins on page 421.

In compiling the index, the same policy has been pursued as in the rest of the book, i.e. Britten's original index with the new page numbers has been reproduced, with references to new material in italics. It would arguably have been better to have compiled a new index, but the Britten index is so delightfully characteristic of the book; there is even an entry for "King, his majesty the", but best of all, "Clock, the" with one page reference.

Occasionally we have deleted an entry where we have been unable to trace the reference, and in some of the longer entries, have taken the liberty of quoting the first reference and then using et passim *for the rest.*

512